# Dictionary
# of the Literature
# of the Iberian
# Peninsula

# Dictionary of the Literature of the Iberian Peninsula

## A–K

EDITED BY
Germán Bleiberg, Maureen Ihrie,
and Janet Pérez

**GREENWOOD PRESS**
Westport, Connecticut · London

Publisher's Note: This reference work was initiated with the distinguished scholar Germán Bleiberg, but due to his ill health (and subsequent death), Maureen Ihrie took over its editorial direction, later bringing in a colleague, Janet Pérez. As publisher of this volume, we wish to acknowledge our profound appreciation of the extraordinary effort Dr. Ihrie put into this project. Without her dedication, this project would never have seen print.

**Library of Congress Cataloging-in-Publication Data**

Dictionary of the literature of the Iberian peninsula / edited by
  Germán Bleiberg, Maureen Ihrie, and Janet Pérez.
     p.  cm.
  Includes bibliographical references.
    1. Spain—Literatures—Dictionaries.  2. Spain—Literatures—Bio-
bibliography—Dictionaries.  3. Portugal—Literatures—
Dictionaries.  4. Portugal—Literatures—Bio-bibliography—
Dictionaries.  I. Bleiberg, Germán.  II. Ihrie, Maureen.
III. Pérez, Janet.
PN849.S6D54   1993
860'.03—dc20        90–2755
ISBN 0–313–21302–X (set : alk. paper)
ISBN 0–313–28731–7 (v. 1 : lib. bdg. : alk. paper)
ISBN 0–313–28732–5 (v. 2 : alk. paper)

British Library Cataloguing in Publication Data is available.

Copyright © 1993 by Germán Bleiberg and Maureen Ihrie

Library of Congress Catalog Card Number: 90–2755
ISBN: 0–313–21302–X (set)
ISBN: 0–313–28731–7 (vol. 1)
ISBN: 0–313–28732–5 (vol. 2)

First published in 1993

Greenwood Press, 88 Post Road West, Westport, CT 06881
An imprint of Greenwood Publishing Group, Inc.

Printed in the United States of America

The paper used in this book complies with the
Permanent Paper Standard issued by the National
Information Standards Organization (Z39.48–1984).

10 9 8 7 6 5 4 3 2 1

The editors would like to dedicate the dictionary to the memory of Germán Bleiberg, whose life and work enriched us all so very much.

# Contents

# Contributors

Samuel Amell
*Ohio State U*

Joseph R. Arboleda
*Lafayette College*

Samuel G. Armistead
*U of California, Davis*

Pamela Bacarisse
*U of Pittsburgh*

Emilie Bergmann
*U of California, Berkeley*

Maryellen Bieder
*Indiana U*

Frieda H. Blackwell
*Howard Payne U*

Germán Bleiberg
*(deceased) SUNY Albany*

Peter Bly
*Queen's U*

Carole Bradford
*Bowling Green State U*

Mary Lee Bretz
*Rutgers U*

James F. Brown
*Isidore Newman School*

Donald C. Buck
*Auburn U*

Israel Burshatin
*Haverford College*

Rosario Cambria
*Baldwin-Wallace College*

Anthony J. Cárdenas
*U of New Mexico*

Manuela Renata Valente de Carvalho
*Vanderbilt U*

C. Maurice Cherry
*Furman U*

Victoria Codina-Espurz
*U of Pittsburgh*

Deborah Compte
*Trenton State College*

Porter Conerly
*(no affiliation)*

Joanna Courteau
*Iowa State U*

Betty Jean Craige
*U of Georgia*

Sydney Cravens
*Texas Tech U*

Anne Cruz
*U of California, Irvine*

Eugene Del Vecchio
*U of Maine*

Angelo DiSalvo
*Indiana State U*

Brian Dutton
*U of Wisconsin*

Cristina Enríquez
*U of Minnesota*

Frances Bell Exum
*Winthrop College*

William Ferguson
*Clark U*

Elisa Fernández Cambria
*Cleveland State U*

Dario Fernández-Morera
*Northwestern U*

Joseph A. Feustle
*U of Toledo*

Peter Fothergill-Payne
*U of Calgary*

E. Inman Fox
*Northwestern U*

Natércia Fraga
*(No affiliation)*

David Frier
*U of Glasgow*

Carolyn Galerstein
*U of Texas at Dallas (recently deceased)*

Salvador García Castañeda
*Ohio State U*

David Thatcher Gies
*U of Virginia*

Joan Gilabert
*U of Arizona*

Judith Ginsberg
*(no affiliation)*

Richard Glenn
*U of Alabama*

Alan A. González
*North Carolina State U (emeritus)*

Luis F. González-Cruz
*Pennsylvania State U*

Luis T. González-del-Valle
*U of Colorado*

James Ray Green
*Boston U*

Patricia Grieve
*Columbia U*

Reginetta Haboucha
*Herbert H. Lehman College*

Martha T. Halsey
*Pennsylvania State U*

Russell G. Hamilton
*Vanderbilt U*

Andrea Warren Hamos
*Assumption College*

David K. Herzberger
*U of Connecticut*

Elizabeth T. Howe
*Tufts U*

James Iffland
*Boston U*

Maureen Ihrie
*Kansas State U*

Estelle Irizarry
*Georgetown U*

Salvador Jiménez Fajardo
*SUNY Binghamton*

Roberta Johnson
*U of Kansas*

Harold G. Jones
*Syracuse U*

Margaret E. W. Jones
*U of Kentucky*

Theodore L. Kassier
*U of Alaska, Anchorage*

Charles King
*U of Colorado*

Edmund L. King
*Princeton U (emeritus)*

Willard F. King
*Bryn Mawr College*

Kathleen L. Kirk
*(no affiliation)*

Robert Kirsner
*U of Miami*

Kathleen Kish
*U of North Carolina*

Dennis Klein
*U of South Dakota*

Robert R. Krueger
*U of Northern Iowa*

Joy Buckles Landeira
*(no affiliation)*

Ricardo Landeira
*U of Colorado*

Catherine Larson
*Indiana U*

Robert E. Lewis
*Simon's Rock of Bard College*

Margarita Lezcano
*Eckerd College*

Gabriel Lovett
*Wellesley College (emeritus)*

Drosoula Lytra
*City College CUNY*

G. Grant MacCurdy
*California State U*

Ann L. MacKenzie
*Liverpool University*

Linda Maier
*Wake Forest U*

Howard Mancing
*Purdue U*

Robert Manteiga
*U of Rhode Island*

Kathleen March
*U of Maine*

Fernando J. B. Martiñho
*(no affiliation)*

Luis Martul Tobío
*(no affiliation)*

Carmen Chaves McClendon
*U of Georgia*

Douglas McKay
*U of Colorado at Colorado Springs*

Kathleen McNerney
*West Virginia U*

Isabel McSpadden
*Texas Tech U*

Hector Medina
*Rhode Island College*

Maria Rosa Menocal
*Yale U*

Martha Miller
*U of North Carolina at Charlotte*

Stephen Miller
*Texas A. and M. U*

Harold K. Moon
*Brigham Young U*

Eunice D. Myers
*Wichita State U*

Eric Naylor
*U of the South*

Esther Nelson
*California State U at Northridge*

Colbert Nepaulsingh
*SUNY Albany*

Geraldine Nichols
*U of Florida*

D. J. O'Connor
*U of New Orleans, Lakefront*

Patricia W. O'Connor
*U of Cincinnati*

Fernando Operé
*U of Virginia*

Nelson Orringer
*U of Connecticut*

José Ortega
*U of Wisconsin, Parkside*

Marie-Sol Ortolá
*U of Connecticut*

María Teresa Pajares
*U of Georgia*

Gilbert Paolini
*Tulane U*

Carlos J. Pereira
*(no affiliation)*

Genaro J. Pérez
*U of Texas at Permian Basin*

Janet Pérez
*Texas Tech U*

Daniel Pires
*U of East Asia*

Peter L. Podol
*Lock Haven U*

Phoebe Porter Medina
*U of New Hampshire*

Kay Pritchett
*U of Arkansas*

Helen H. Reed
*Syracuse U*

Elizabeth Rhodes
*Boston College*

Laura Rivkin-Golden
*U of Colorado, Boulder*

Nicholas Round
*U of Glasgow*

Anna Sánchez Rue
*(no affiliation)*

Pilar Sáenz
*George Washington U*

María A. Salgado
*U of North Carolina*

Jana Sandarg
*Augusta College*

Robert Sandarg
*Paine College*

Veronica Sauter
*(no affiliation)*

Raymond Sayers
*Queens College CUNY*

Stacey Schlau
*West Chester U*

Kessel Schwartz
*U of Miami*

Sara Schyfter
*SUNY Albany*

Isabel Segura
*(no affiliation)*

Dennis P. Seniff
*Michigan State U (deceased)*

Leopoldo Serrão
*(no affiliation)*

Nina Shecktor
*Kutztown U*

George Shipley
*U of Washington*

Jaime H. da Silva
*U de Puerto Rico*

Lucy Sponsler
*U of New Orleans*

María Stycos
*Cornell U*

Catherine Swietlicki
*U of Wisconsin, Madison*

Robert ter Horst
*U of Rochester*

Currie K. Thompson
*Gettysburg College*

Leslie P. Turano
*Girton College*

John Turner
*Bowdoin College*

Noël M. Valis
*Johns Hopkins U*

John E. Varey
*Editor, Tamesis Books Ltd.*

Louise O. Vasvari
*SUNY Stony Brook*

Gloria Feiman Waldman
*York College, CUNY*

Merry Wheaton
*(no affiliation)*

John Wilcox
*U of Illinois, Urbana-Champaign*

Victoria Wolff Unruh
*U of Kansas*

Frederick G. Williams
*U of California, Santa Barbara*

Phyllis Zatlin
*Rutgers U*

Marielena Zelaya Kolker
*(no affiliation)*

# *Preface*

The goal of this reference work, which was begun in the late 1970s, is to acquaint a wider audience with the rich history of literary achievements in the Iberian Peninsula. It is a sad fact that the contributions of Iberian-born writers continue to be largely unknown territory for most European and American readers. The *Dictionary of the Literature of the Iberian Peninsula* is intended to ease access to such writers and movements. We have defined literature in a broad sense, to include historical, religious, cultural, and philosophical writings as well as prose, poetry, and drama. Entries on selected literary movements, styles, and literatures have been included, as have a limited number of definitions pertinent to literary or cultural terms.

The point of departure for the present work and a guide in determining format was the classic *Diccionario de literatura española* by Germán Bleiberg and Julián Marías. Many changes were made in coverage, however, particularly the exclusion of Spanish-American writers and foreign-born Hispanists of this century. Major emphases in new entries are writers in other languages of the peninsula (in addition to Spanish) and updated coverage to better represent authors of the second half of the twentieth century, including many who have become recognized as important only in the last two decades. While all major entries have been reworked, and many entries are entirely new, others, especially those on lesser figures, are based largely on former editions of the Bleiberg and Marías *Diccionario*.

The present *Dictionary* generally includes literature from the tenth century to the mid–1980s. With a very few exceptions, it is limited to writers born in the Iberian Peninsula. Unlike similar reference works, this one includes representatives from all major peninsular literatures: Catalan, Galician, Portuguese, and Spanish. Where contributors have been available for the lesser vernacular languages, we have included their entries, but systematic coverage of these languages has not been possible. Some literatures are covered less comprehensively than we would have wished, but what is included constitutes a solid advance in presenting otherwise generally underrepresented literatures—Portuguese, Catalan, and Gallego—in an English-oriented work. The *Dictionary* also devotes more attention to writings by traditionally neglected or forgotten female authors, especially those of the twentieth century. Consistent, broad-based coverage has been our general goal, but by no means is this dictionary to be considered comprehensive or all-inclusive. Ultimately, constrictions of time and space and a shortage of willing contributors became determining factors in delimiting content. Many entries originally commissioned were not done by those who had agreed to do them, with the result that some had to be done very late and hastily by the editors to prevent exclusion. And, as one might expect, there are inevitable sins of omission and commission on our part.

The *Dictionary* has been compiled to appeal to users ranging from English-speaking nonspecialists to scholars of Iberian literature. To address needs of the former group, virtually all literary titles have been followed in the text with either a published translation or a literal rendering of the original, and an effort has been made to list existing English translations of works in the Bibliography. To ensure the *Dictionary*'s value to specialists, virtually all major entries have been composed by noted scholars and are complemented by bibliographies of primary texts and selected critical studies, as well as the earlier-mentioned translations. The citations are as complete as possible. Because the limitations imposed by the formats of all dictionaries and reference works necessarily exclude anything other than selected bibliography, we have emphasized items on the basis of accessibility and representativeness wherever choices were made.

More than 140 experts contributed their labor and expertise to this work, and we are proud of the caliber of scholars who joined together to compile it. Although many individuals made numerous and significant contributions to the Spanish section of the *Dictionary*, they compose a group too large to mention individually. We do wish to mention those authors who contributed to literatures not covered in the original *Diccionario*: Joan Gilabert, for many Catalan entries, Peter Fothergill-Payne, for coverage of Portuguese literature, Kathleen McNerney, for contributions of Catalan and Galician female writers, and Kathleen March, for many Galician entries. Gratitude is also due to Sara Schyfter for her assistance in launching the project. We thank all of the contributors for their help, and many others who eased our work by suggesting likely contributors, editing the manuscript, typing, and so forth. We would also like to thank various institutions for their support: Union College granted a summer stipend to help support research of minor entries; Lafayette College awarded funds for typing, research assistance for one semester, and much interlibrary loan and photocopying support; the Graduate School of Texas Tech University subvened substantial duplication and mailing expenses; Kansas State University granted funds to process the copyedited manuscript and to prepare the *Dictionary*'s index. We also thank Greenwood Press for its patient commitment to this task.

## GENERAL FORMAT OF ENTRIES

1. Biographical entries first give the person's name, in inverted order with the last name capitalized, followed by any pseudonym, dates and places of birth

and death—or active period—and then a short phrase identifying the person and/or field of activity. If the author is better known under a pseudonym, the pseudonym will come before the real name in the entry. Important "less-preferred" names, pseudonym or real, will be cross-referenced to the main entry. Punctuation is consistent with the following example:

> **CLARÍN,** pseudonym of Leopoldo Alas (1852, Zamora–1909, Oviedo), critic and novelist.

Although diacritical marks are not customarily placed on capitalized letters, they are here indicated in names and words at the beginning of each entry in order to assist in pronunciation.

2. If the entry is the title of a work or name of an institution, it is followed by a translation to English, pertinent dates as appropriate, and a brief explanation. For example:

> *MISERIA DE OMNE, Libro de* (Book of Man's Misery), anonymous mid- to late-fourteenth-c. narrative poem.

or

> *MESTER DE CLERECÍA* (Craft of Clerks or Clerics), a medieval form of verse.

3. Within the main text of each entry, titles authored by the subject of the entry are followed by a translation to English placed within parentheses. Where possible, publication, or sometimes composition, dates are indicated immediately *before* the translation to English. If a published English translation of a work has been found, that title is given, underlined, and followed by the date of publication. If no published translation has been located, a literal rendering of the original is given without italics (or, in the case of poems, without quotations). Titles of journals, newspapers, and so forth, in an entry are not generally translated, unless they are pertinent to the subject. The entry of a translated work appears as follows:

> *SU ÚNICO HIJO* (1891; *His Only Son*, 1980).

An untranslated work is listed according to the following example:

> *LA PALABRA EN LA REALIDAD* (1963; The Word in Reality).

When titles are names of people, places, or characters, they generally are not translated unless a published translation exists. Quotes are translated.

4. Most entries conclude with a three-part bibliography. Section A lists main primary texts or additional titles not discussed in the body of the entry. Section B contains translations to English of any primary texts. Section C indicates

pertinent critical studies in any language but emphasizing English where available. Sections A and B are arranged alphabetically by titles and followed by editor, translator, and so forth. Section C is arranged alphabetically by author. Where extensive bibliography exists, we have had to be selective for reasons of space. We have attempted to make citations complete, but here, too, explanation is in order. The long period of time (more than a decade) required for completion of this task has meant that some entries done early in the process are not entirely up to the moment bibliographically. Although on-line computer searches on each entry might theoretically have remedied some of this, the editors had no funds available for this endeavor. The time elapsed since original submission of certain entries has also meant in the cases of some contemporary writers that significant recent events (major awards, death of author, etc.) may not be indicated. For obvious reasons, we could not rectify all such problems.

5. The English alphabetical order has been followed; thus, CH and LL are not treated as separate letters but are interfiled appropriately.

6. Regarding the names of religious figures, custom exercises a strong role in determining whether a writer such as San Juan de la Cruz, Sta. Teresa de Jesús, or Fray Luis de León is indexed by his or her first or last name. In general, we have followed Spanish usage and employed cross-referencing to guide readers.

7. Cross-referencing has been indicated with asterisks. If a person, topic, or such, that appears as a main entry elsewhere in the *Dictionary* is mentioned in an article, at the first incidence of the term an asterisk is placed immediately before the part of the name or title under which it is entered. If there are other complementary subjects or titles not mentioned in the text of a particular entry, they will be listed at the end of the entry's text. For example:

*CABALLERO DEL CISNE, Leyenda del* (Legend of the Knight of the Swan), a tale which first appeared in Germany and then in other countries. . . . The legend, closely allied with the French epic, appeared in Spain in the pseudo-history *La gran *conquista del Ultramar* (c. 1300; The Great Conquest of the Holy Land).

In a few cases plural forms of an entry have been asterisked, although the entry is entered in its singular form.

8. Entry authorship is indicated at the conclusion of each article. When no author is indicated, the responsibility is that of the editors.

# *Abbreviations*

---

| | |
|---|---|
| abr. | abridged, abridgment |
| anon. | anonymous |
| bibliog. | bibliography, bibliographic |
| bio. | biography |
| c. | century, circa |
| cf. | *confer*, compare |
| ch. | chapter(s) |
| comp. | compiled, compiler |
| cont. | continued |
| d. | deceased |
| e.g. | *exempli gratia*, for example |
| ed. | editor, edited by, edition |
| et al. | *et alii*, and others |
| facs. | facsimile |
| ff. | following |
| fl. | flourished |
| i.e. | *id est*, that is |
| il. | illustrated, illustrated by |
| intro. | introduction |
| l., ll. | line, lines |
| lges. | languages |
| lit. | literature |
| ms., mss. | manuscript, manuscripts |
| n. | note(s) |
| n.d. | no date |
| n.p. | no place of publication, no publisher, no pages |

| P | Press |
| pref. | preface |
| prol. | prologue |
| pseud. | pseudonym |
| pub. | publication, published |
| repub. | republished |
| rev. | revised, revised by, revision |
| rpt. | reprint |
| sel. | selected by, selection |
| ss. | following |
| st. | stanza |
| supp. | supplement |
| tr. | translated by |
| U | University |
| UNESCO | United Nations Educational, Scientific and Cultural Organization |
| UP | University Press |
| vol(s). | volume(s) |

## JOURNALS, PUBLISHERS, AND SERIES

| BAE | Biblioteca de Autores Españoles |
| *BBMP* | *Boletín de la Biblioteca Menéndez Pelayo* |
| *BH* | *Bulletin Hispanique* |
| *BHS* | *Bulletin of Hispanic Studies* |
| *BRAE* | *Boletín de la Real Academia Española* |
| *BRAH* | *Boletín de la Real Academia de Historia* |
| *BSS* | *Bulletin of Spanish Studies* |
| *CH* | *Cuadernos Hispanoamericanos* |
| CSIC | Consejo Superior de Investigaciones Científicas |
| *DA* | *Dissertation Abstracts* |
| *DAI* | *Dissertation Abstracts International* |
| EDHASA | Editora y Distribuidora Hispano Americana, S.A. |
| *HR* | *Hispanic Review* |
| HSMS | Hispanic Seminar of Medieval Studies |
| *JHP* | *Journal of Hispanic Philology* |
| *JSS:TC* | *Journal of Spanish Studies: Twentieth Century* |
| *KRQ* | *Kentucky Romance Quarterly* |
| *MLN* | *Modern Language Notes* |

| | |
|---|---|
| *MLR* | *Modern Language Review* |
| *MLS* | *Modern Language Studies* |
| NBAE | Nueva Biblioteca de Autores Españoles |
| *NRFH* | *Nueva Revista de Filología Hispánica* |
| PUF | Presses Universitaires de France |
| RABM | Revista de Archivos, Bibliotecas y Museos |
| RAE | Real Academia Española |
| RAH | Real Academia de la Historia |
| *RCEH* | *Revista Canadiense de Estudios Hispánicos* |
| *REH* | *Revista de Estudios Hispánicos* |
| *RFE* | *Revista de Filología Española* |
| *RFH* | *Revista de Filología Hispánica* |
| *RH* | *Revue Hispanique* |
| *RHM* | *Revista Hispánica Moderna* |
| *RN* | *Romance Notes* |
| RO | Revista de Occidente |
| *RPH* | *Romance Philology* |
| *RR* | *Romance Review* |
| SBE | Sociedad de Bibliófilos Españoles |
| SUNY | State University of New York |
| *TLS* | *Times Literary Supplement* |
| TWAS | Twayne's World Authors Series |
| UNAM | Universidad Nacional Autónoma de México |
| UCLA | University of California, Los Angeles |
| UNCSRLL | University of North Carolina Series in Romance Languages and Literatures |
| *YFS* | *Yale French Studies* |

# A

A., **Ruben,** pseudonym of Alfredo Andresen Leitão (1920, Lisbon–1975, London), Portuguese man of letters and historian. A graduate in history and philosophy of the U of Coimbra, he taught in Portugal and abroad. His studies in history and literature are highly regarded in academic circles, and there is increasing appreciation of his novels, short stories, and autobiographical notebooks, *Páginas* (Pages). Given that most of his writing appeared under the censorship imposed by the regime that governed Portugal between 1927 and 1974, there is an enigmatic and allegorical cast allied to a flexible crispness and sharp sense of irony. His early novel *Caranguejo* (1954; The Crab) and play *Júlia* (1963) are more traditional, and the real new departure in his writing dates from the appearance of his short story collection *Côres* (1960; Colors) in which the colors of the title constitute a code establishing character types and situations. His storytelling combines the real and the surreal in such a way that the easily recognizable (and often typically Portuguese) setting is overlaid with a science fiction–like surreality. Such is the case of his better known works *A Torre de Barbela* (1964; The Tower of Barbela), *O Outro que era Eu* (1966; The Stranger That Was Me), and *Silêncio para 4* (1973; Silence for 4). A short, equally surreal novel, *Kaos,* was published posthumously in 1981 by Imprensa Nacional. Both his autobiographical notebooks *Páginas* (1949—6 volumes to date) and his three volumes of autobiography *O Mundo à Minha procura* (1964–68; The World As It Sought Me Out) at times partake of this quality of his fiction.

BIBLIOGRAPHY

Primary Texts

*A Torre de Barbela*. 3rd ed. Lisbon: Pereira, n.d.
*Caranguejo*. Coimbra: Coimbra, 1954.
*Côres*. Lisbon: Atica, 1960.
*Júlia*. Lisbon: Livraria Portugal, 1963.
*O Mundo à Minha procura*. Lisbon: Livraria Portugal, 1964–68.
*O Outro que era Eu*. Lisbon: Livraria Portugal, 1966.

*Páginas.* Coimbra and Lisbon: 6 vols. to date, 1949–70. Vols. 1–4, Coimbra: Coimbra; Vols. 5–6, Lisbon: Pereira.

*Silêncio para 4.* Lisbon: Moraes, 1973.

Criticism

França, J. A. "Lembrança de Ruben A." *Colóquio/Letras* 29 (1976): 5–8.

*Ruben A.—In Memoriam Ruben Andresen Leitão.* Eds. A. O'Neill et al. 3 vols. Lisbon: Imprensa Nacional, 1981. 1: 27–56 contains the most complete bibliography available of his works and of works on him.

Peter Fothergill-Payne

*A LO DIVINO* (in the religious way), literary term denoting works of religious or pious nature, in contraposition to *a lo humano* (of a profane nature); it also may refer to a work which recasts a secular model in the religious sphere. A popular practice in the *Siglo de Oro (Golden Age), examples of recastings include Father Bartolomé *Ponce's *Clara Diana a lo divino* (1599; Illustrious Diane in the Religious Way), based on Jorge de *Montemayor's *Diana*, and the reworking of *Boscán and *Garcilaso de la Vega's poetry by Sebastián de *Córdoba, titled *Obras de Boscán y Garcilaso trasladadas a materias cristianas y religiosas* (1575; The Works of Boscán and Garcilaso Transposed to Christian and Religious Matters).

BIBLIOGRAPHY

Primary Texts

Córdoba, S. de. *Obras de Boscán y Garcilaso trasladadas a materias cristianas y religiosas.* Ed. G. R. Gale. Ann Arbor: U of Michigan, 1971.

Ponce, B. *Clara Diana a lo divino.* N.p.: n.p., 1599.

Criticism

Wardropper, B. W. *Historia de la poesía lírica a lo divino en la cristiandad occidental.* Madrid: RO, 1958.

Maureen Ihrie

*ABAD DE MONTEMAYOR, Gesta del* (Deeds of the Abbot of Montemayor), epic poem. This *cantar de gesta* became popular the first half of the fourteenth c. and later figured in several novels of the *Siglo de Oro (Golden Age). *Menéndez Pidal attributed it to a Leonese author, possibly from Astorga. The most complete extant version is that of Valladolid (1562).

The plot revolves around an abandoned child, Don García, cared for and educated by the Abbot Don Juan. Don García subsequently betrays his adoptive father, converts to Islam, and changes his name to Don Zulema. Allied with the Moors, he storms the town of Montemayor and profanes the church of Santiago. Confronted with an overwhelming battle, the abbot decides to kill all women, children and elderly before engaging in a deadly, sacrificial battle with the infidels. Unexpectedly, the Christians triumph, and when they return to Montemayor, they find the women, children, and elderly miraculously alive again.

BIBLIOGRAPHY

Primary Text

*La leyenda del Abad don Juan de Montemayor.* Ed., study R. Menéndez Pidal. Dresden: Gesellschaft für Romanische Literatur, 1903.

Criticism

Menéndez Pidal, R. *Poesía árabe y poesía europea.* 4th ed. Madrid: Espasa-Calpe, 1955.

**ABARBANEL.** *See* Hebreo, León

**ABARCA DE BOLEA, Ana Francisca** (1623 or 1624, Casbas–late 1600s?), nun, religious author. She entered the Cistercian Order at age three, rising to become abbess for four years, beginning in 1672. She wrote poems, letters, saints' lives, and one *pastoral novel *a lo divino* titled *Vigilia y octavario de San Ivan Baptista* (Vigil and Octave Celebration of St. John the Baptist). *See also* Hagiography.

BIBLIOGRAPHY

Primary Text

*Vigilia y octavario de San Ivan Baptista.* Zaragoza: Pascual Bueno, 1679.

**ABATI, Joaquín** (1865, Madrid–1936, Madrid), lawyer and composer of many comic plays and librettos for *zarzuelas. Best known of his many works are *Los perros de presa* (The Bulldogs), *Genio y figura* (Temperament and Countenance), and *El gran tacaño* (The Great Cheapskate). Abati also composed the music for some of his librettos, such as *Las venecianas* (The Venetian Women).

BIBLIOGRAPHY

Primary Text

*Las venecianas.* Madrid: Sociedad Anónima Casa Dotesio, 1900?

**ABBAT, Per,** popular medieval name. The name ''Per Abbat'' is found in many medieval Spanish documents, but it is famous because it also appears in the *explicit* (ending) of the *Cantar de mio Cid*: ''Per Abbat le escrivió en el mes de mayo'' (1. 3732; ''Per Abbat wrote it in the month of May''). No contemporary documentation has been found for ''escrevir'' meaning ''to compose,'' and consequently it cannot be established beyond a doubt that Per Abbat was the author and not merely the scribe of the work. Nevertheless, Colin Smith, using falsified documents published by *Menéndez Pidal in *La España del Cid (The Cid and His Spain)*, has argued persuasively that a Pedro Abad who was connected with the monastery of Santa Eugenia de Cordobilla before 1223 did know enough about the Cid to have been either the author or at least the reviser of the *Cantar*. In support of Smith's claims, it should be noted that this Pedro Abad, like the author of the ''Afrenta de Corpes'' (''Insult at Corpes'') was very familiar with the martyrological tradition to which the beating of the Cid's daughters belongs (as doña Sol reminds us: "mártires seremos nós," 1. 2728; "we will be martyrs"). Certain details in the "Afrenta de Corpes" episode recall the *Peristerphanon* of Prudentius and, even more, the famous accounts of Cordovan martyrs by St. Eulogius and Paul Albar of Cordova. Santa Eugenia was one of the Cordovan Martyrs, and since Pedro Abad explains how relics were collected from all over the world (including Oviedo, where the relics and, presumably, the writings of Eulogius of Cordova were transferred) for the monastery named after her, it is quite likely that he was acquainted with the literature about Cordovan martyrs which seems to have been used in the composition of the "Afrenta de Corpes."

BIBLIOGRAPHY

Criticism

Menéndez Pidal, Ramón. *La España del Cid*. 5th ed. Madrid: Espasa-Calpe, 1956. 2; 840–46; tr. Sunderland H. *The Cid and His Spain*. 1934. London: Cass, 1971.
Smith, Colin. "Per Abbat and the *Poema de mío Cid*." *Medium Aevum* 42 (1973): 1–17.
Walsh, John K. "Religious Motifs in the Early Spanish Epic." *RHM* 36 (1970–71): 165–72.

Colbert Nepaulsingh

*ABENCERRAJE Y LA HERMOSA JARIFA* (Abencerraje and Beautiful Jarifa, 1964), a sentimental *novella*. This sixteenth-c. story has an unusual happy ending and a different setting—the frontier between the Moors and Christians in Spain. It appeared in print in the *Inventario* (Inventory) of Antonio de *Villegas which, although published in 1565, received license for publication in 1551. Differing versions of the *novella* are also found in the 1561 Valladolid edition of Jorge de *Montemayor's *Diana* (wherein it was included by the printer Francisco Fernández de Córdoba), in the 1561 Cuenca edition of the *Diana*, in a ms. belonging to the National Library, and in a book printed in Toledo in 1561. All five versions have been edited and discussed by Francisco López Estrada.

The novella tells how Abindarráez, el Abencerraje, on his way to consummate his love for a childhood sweetheart, Jarifa, is ambushed by a scouting party of Christians led by Rodrigo de Narváez, mayor of Antequera and Alora. Abindarráez, although outnumbered, fights valiantly; he is finally overcome by Rodrigo himself and taken prisoner by him. On the way to prison, the sorrowful Abindarráez is persuaded by Rodrigo to tell his story. Rodrigo is so moved by it that he grants his prisoner three days leave to consummate his marriage on condition that he then return to prison. Abindarráez keeps his promise but returns with Jarifa, who insists on joining him in captivity. Rodrigo not only grants them liberty, but intercedes in their behalf with the King of Granada, who in turn persuades Jarifa's father to accept a marriage to which he otherwise would have reacted violently. The novella continues the old tradition of the impeccably virtuous, noble Moor which reaches back in Spanish literature as far as Abengalvón in the *Cantar de mio Cid*. It also varies with sublime artistry themes like falconry as a metaphor for seduction, the fortune of lovers, the prison of love, the epistolary intermediary of love, and arms and letters, all found in works like *La *Celestina* (*Celestina*), Diego de *San Pedro's *Cárcel de Amor* (Prison of Love), Juan *Rodríguez de la Cámara's *Siervo Libre de Amor* (Voluntary Servant of Love), etc. Fortune first makes Abindarráez a prisoner of war, when he is captured by Rodrigo; then a prisoner of love, when he consummates marriage with Jarifa; and finally a prisoner of letters, when epistolary exchanges of great and subtle diplomacy between enemies (Rodrigo, the Moorish King of Granada, and Abindarráez) decide the final fortune of the lovers.

*Cervantes remembered this novella when he composed the first chapters of the *Quijote*. Apart from Don Quijote's comparison of himself with Abindarráez (I,5), and apart from the omnipresence of the themes of arms and letters, love, and Moorish captivity throughout the *Quijote*, a case can also be made for the *Novela del curioso impertinente* (*Novel of the Impertinent and Curious One*) as an obverse variant of the story of Rodrigo de Narváez and the wife of the gentleman who praised him excessively. The tale's influence outside of Spain must also be noted, especially in France, in such works as Pierre Davity's *Travaux sans travail* (1599), Florian's *Gonzalve de Cordove ou Grenade reconquise* (1723), and Chateaubriand's *Les aventures du dernier Abencérage* (1826).

BIBLIOGRAPHY

Primary Text

*El Abencerraje y la hermosa Jarifa, cuatro textos y su estudio*. Ed., study F. López Estrada. Madrid: RABM, 1957.

English Translation

*Antonio de Villegas. El Abencerraje*. Ed. F. López Estrada and tr., intro. J. E. Keller. Chapel Hill: U of North Carolina P, 1964. Spanish and English.

Criticism

Carrasco-Urgoiti, M. S. *The Moorish Novel:* El Abencerraje *and Pérez de Hita*. TWAS 375. Boston: Twayne, 1976.

López Estrada, F. "*El Abencerraje* de Toledo, 1561." In *Anales de la Universidad Hispalense* 19 (1959): 1–60.

Colbert Nepaulsingh

**ABRABANEL.** *See* Hebreo, León

**ABRIL, Manuel** (1884, Madrid–1946, Madrid), poet, dramatist, critic of art and drama. Abril's literary activities spanned several genres and media. His poetic works include *Canciones del corazón y de la vida* (1904; Songs of the Heart and Life) and *Hacia la luz lejana* (1914; Toward the Distant Light), and two of his most successful dramas were *Un caso raro de veras* (n.d.; A Truly Strange Incident) and *La princesa que se chupaba el dedo* (1918; The Princess Who Sucked Her Thumb). His children's stories, read on the radio before the

Civil War, were enormously popular. His critical essays appeared in publications such as *La Ilustración Española y Americana*, *Revista Musical* and *Cruz y Raya*, in the sections titled ''Criba'' (The Screen) and ''Cristal de Tiempo'' (The Window of Time). Abril also translated several works of Edgar Allan Poe, and of Alfred Musset and other French authors, into Spanish.

BIBLIOGRAPHY

Primary Texts

*De la naturaleza al espíritu; ensayo crítico de pintura contemporánea desde Sorolla a Picasso*. Madrid: Espasa-Calpe, 1935.

*Hacia la luz lejana*. Madrid: n.p., 1914.

*La princesa que se chupaba el dedo*. Madrid: Renacimiento, 1918.

**ABRIL, Pedro Simón** (1530?, Alcaraz–1595?, Zaragoza), translator, humanist. Professor of Latin and Spanish at the U of Zaragoza for over 25 years, Abril wrote two grammars in Spanish: one for Latin and one for Greek. He was the first to follow *Nebrija's recommendation, in *Introductiones latinae*, that books destined for language instruction be in Spanish. Abril defends this position in his *Apuntamientos de cómo se deben reformar las doctrinas y la manera de enseñallas* (1589; Notes on How to Reform Scholarly Knowledge, and How to Teach). Abril also furthered the humanist movement in Spain in his role as prolific translator of Aristotle, Aesop, Plato, Euripides, Aristophanes and Cicero. *See also* Humanism; Renaissance.

BIBLIOGRAPHY

Primary Texts

*Apuntamientos de cómo se deben reformar las doctrinas y la manera de enseñallas*. BAE 65.

*La gramática griega escrita en lengua castellana*. Madrid: Madrigal, 1586, 1587.

**ABULBACA DE RONDA** (13th c., ?–?), Andalusian Arabic poet. He is best known for his elegy mourning the loss of Valencia, Murcia, Cordova and Seville, which were conquered by James I and Ferdinand III the Saint. In it, Abulbaca seeks help for the Spanish Moors as he bemoans the passage of time and life. The elegy was translated into Spanish by Juan *Valera.

BIBLIOGRAPHY

Primary Text

*Elegía de Abul beka de Ronda, a la pérdida de Córdoba, Sevilla y Valencia*. Tr. Juan Valera. In *Juan Valera, Obras Completas*. Madrid: Alemana, 1905. Vol. 18, p. 233 and ss.

**ACADEMIA** (Academy), intellectual and cultural clubs. The original Academy was a garden near Athens where Plato (427?–347 B.C.) taught. The term later was extended to mean his philosophy and its followers. Today it refers to meetings of scholars and artists, or to those institutions responsible for monitoring language (Real Academia Española de la Lengua [See Academia Española]), the arts (Academia de Bellas Artes), the sciences (Academia de Medicina), history (Academia de la Historia), or political sciences (Academia de Ciencias Morales y Políticas).

## The Spanish Academies of the Golden Age

The Jesuits introduced major reforms in Spanish education through their emphasis on the imitation of classical modes of rhetoric and literature, particularly poetry. They made fashionable the ability to write poetry in both Latin and Spanish. They also formalized the organization of academies, promoting literary competitions and discussions there with the aim of fostering students' agility and elegance of expression, and their interest in literary, poetic, and philological issues. Literary contests (*torneos literarios* or *justas poéticas*) became quite popular—*Cervantes alludes to them in the *Quijote* (II,18). Participants in these contests included Lope de *Vega, Cervantes, *Calderón, *Tirso, *Pérez Montalbán, and others.

At the end of the sixteenth and beginning of the seventeenth c., private academies appeared, the most famous being the Academia de los Nocturnos (Academy of the Night Revelers). Patterned after the Jesuit model, this academy was governed by a board whose duty it was to choose a topic for each meeting, preside over the meetings, and read all poetry submitted. Meetings were held every Wednesday at dusk, in the home of don Bernardo Catalán de Valeriola, in Valencia. They began with a lecture, which then served as the basis for the evening's discussion, and ended with the formal recitation of the week's poetry, chosen by the secretary. The members, or academicians, wrote under various pseudonyms, all associated with images of night and darkness. Guillén de *Castro (alias *Secreto*, Secret), López Maldonado (*Sincero*, Sincere), and *Rey de Artieda (*Centinela*, Sentinel) were among the most famous members. The Academia de los Nocturnos was active from 1591 to 1594. In 1616, it was revived by Guillén de Castro under the name of Montañeses del Parnaso (Scalers of Mt. Parnassus).

Although many other academies were active in the late sixteenth and early seventeenth c., there is little direct information about them. Around 1586, Madrid had an active academy called La Imitatoria (Imitation), and in 1600 in Granada, another is known to have existed under the leadership of Pedro Vanegas; in 1610, Lope de Vega, *Mira de Amescua, *Villamediana and the *Argensola brothers were members of the Academia del Conde de Saldaña (Academy of Count Saldana); and from 1617 to 1622, Tirso de Molina participated in a Madrid academy led by Sebastián Francisco de *Medrano. The Argensola brothers were active in two other academies: Academia de los Anhelantes (Academy of Yearners) and the Academia de los Ociosos (Academy of the Idlers). Of all these, only the Nocturnos have left a record of their proceedings: 805 poems and 85 fragments are included in the *Cancionero de los Nocturnos* (Songbook of the Night Revelers). Nevertheless, the Nocturnos were more of an informal gathering of literary friends than a rigorous academy.

## Academies after the Golden Age

In 1713, don Juan Manuel Fernández Pacheco, Marquis of Villena, founded the Real Academia Española de la Lengua (Spanish Academy of Language), of enormous importance to this day. The Academia de la Historia (Academy of History), established in 1735 under the name of Academia Universal (Universal Academy), has also furthered the study of literature through its investigation of archives and libraries. Seville and Barcelona each had an Academia de Buenas Letras (Academy of Literature); that of Seville was founded in 1752, and that of Barcelona, in 1729. Both pursued investigation of local and regional history. Along with these public academies, several private ones existed, including the Academia del Buen Gusto (Academy of Good Taste), led by the Countess of Lemos and Marquise of Sarria from 1749 to 1751; the Tertulia de la Fonda de San Sebastián (Gathering of the Inn of San Sebastian); the Academia de Letras Humanas (Academy of Humanities); and the Academia del Mirto (Academy of the Myrtle)—which was of importance to the Romantic period. The Academia del Buen Gusto played a significant role in popularizing French neoclassical ideas, having Ignacio *Luzán as one of its most prestigious and influential members.

BIBLIOGRAPHY

Primary Text

*Cancionero de los Nocturnos*. Ed. Martí Grajales. 4 vols. Valencia: Vives y Mora, 1905–12.

Criticism

Hazañas y la Rúa, Joaquín. *Noticia de las Academias literarias, artísticas y científicas de los siglos XVII y XVIII*. Seville: Torres y Daza, 1888.
King, Willard F. "The Academies and Seventeenth-Century Spanish Literature." *PMLA* 75 (1960): 367–76.
———. *Prosa novelística y Academias Literarias en el siglo XVII*. Madrid: RAE, 1963.
Sánchez, José. *Academias literarias del Siglo de Oro*. Madrid: Gredos, 1961.

Sarah Schyfter

**ACADEMIA ESPAÑOLA** (Spanish Academy), first official academy established in Spain, formally known as the Real Academia Española de la Lengua (Royal Spanish Academy of Language). Its founder and first president was don Juan Manuel Fernández Pacheco, Marquis of Villena and Duke of Escalona, and Major General under Philip V. The first meeting was celebrated on June 6, 1713, and on October 3, 1714, it received official sanction from Philip V, as well as various important privileges including the authority to publish books and to appoint its own members. A year later, in 1715, the Academy's emblem was chosen: a torch afire with the inscription "limpia, fija y da esplendor" ("to purify, to legislate and to give splendor").

Meetings of the new Academy first took place in its founder's palace. After several different locations, the Academy was finally housed, in 1894, in its present site. The original regulations of the Academy limited the number of statutory members to twenty-four. Later revisions have allowed for twelve more members, as well as twenty-four associates outside of Madrid. In 1926, regional academies were established, but then banned in 1930. In 1978, Carmen *Conde became the first woman to be elected. Membership in the Academy is a distinct honor.

The first task the Academy set for itself was the publication of a dictionary. The *Diccionario de Autoridades* (Dictionary of Authorities), dedicated to Philip V (who paid for its publication), is based on the language usage of one hundred literary authorities, hence its name. Published in six volumes from 1726 to 1739, the *Diccionario* comprises a lexical compendium to this day unequaled in the Spanish language. In 1963, it was reprinted in Madrid by Gredos, in three volumes.

In 1780, the Academy published its one-volume *Diccionario usual* (Common Dictionary), a work that has repeatedly been reissued to this day. The *Ortografía* (1741; Orthography) established much-needed orthographical rules and put an end to the confusion of phonetic versus etymological spelling. The *Gramática* (1771; Grammar) was also of great importance. The following derivative works have also been published by the Academy: *Prontuario de Ortografía* (1887; Orthography Handbook); *Compendio de la Gramática* (1880; Synopsis of Grammar); *Epítome de Gramática* (1938; Summary of Grammar); *Diccionario manual e ilustrado* (1927; Illustrated Hand Dictionary); *Diccionario Histórico* (1960–63; Historical Dictionary), edited by Casares and LaPesa; and *Esbozo de una nueva gramática* (1973; Outline for a New Grammar).

Among the most important publications of the Real Academia are its editions of classical texts. Some of its most distinguished publications include the 1780 edition of the *Quijote*; Valmar's edition of the *Cantigas* (Canticles); the 1917 facsimile *Obras completas* (Complete Works) of *Cervantes; the *Obras dramáticas* (Dramatic Works) of Lope de *Vega; a series containing the famous prologues of Marcelino *Menéndez y Pelayo; the distinguished series *Biblioteca selecta de clásicos españoles* (Selected Library of Spanish Classics). In 1914, the prestigious quarterly *Boletín de la Real Academia Española* (Bulletin of the Royal Spanish Academy) first appeared.

The speeches (*discursos leídos*) given by members upon their acceptance into the Academy are also of tremendous intellectual significance. Particularly memorable are those of *Campoamor, *Castelar, *Valera, Menéndez y Pelayo, *Pérez Galdós, *Pereda, *Menéndez Pidal, *Baroja, and Dámaso *Alonso.

BIBLIOGRAPHY

Primary Text

*Memorias de la Real Academia Española.* 13 vols. Madrid: RAE, 1870–1926.

Germán Bleiberg

**ACADEMY.** *See* Academia

**ACEBAL, Francisco** (1866, Gijón–1933, ?), short story writer, novelist, editor. His novel *Huella de almas* (1901; *Face to Face,* 1906) and his short story collection, *De mi rincón* (1901; From My Corner), were quite popular at the turn of the century. Of particular interest is the influential magazine *La Lectura* which he founded; from it evolved the very important series Clásicos Castellanos, which continues to this day.

BIBLIOGRAPHY

Primary Texts

*De mi rincón.* Salamanca: n.p., 1902.
*Huella de almas.* Madrid: La Lectura, 1901.

English Translation

*Face to Face, and Dolorosa. Two Novels of Modern Spain.* Pref. M. Hume. London: Constable; New York: Dutton, 1906.


**ACEVEDO, Alonso de** (1550?, Vera de Plasencia–1620?, ?), poet, prebendary of Plasencia. Precise data regarding Acevedo is unknown. In 1615 he published an epic poem, *La creación del mundo* (The Creation of the World), and several other poems appear in a collection published in Italy, *Poesías diversas* (1612; Various Poems). He also appears in *Cervantes's *Viaje del Parnaso*, speaking Italian.

BIBLIOGRAPHY

Primary Texts

*La creación del mundo.* BAE 24.
*Poesías diversas.* Rome: n.p., 1612.
*Poetas placentinos contemporáneos de Lope de Vega.* Ed. D. Bejarano Escobar. Cáceres: n.p., 1901.


**ACEVEDO, Luis de** (1562, Medina del Campo–1600, Salamanca), Augustinian monk, religious writer. He wrote *hagiographies and a classic Marian devotional work composed of meditations on the various events in the life of the Virgin Mary or on her feast days in the liturgical year. Titled *Marial* (1600; Marial), it contains moral treatises (*discursos morales*) for each of the feast days dedicated to the Virgin, beginning with the Immaculate Conception (December 8). Acevedo's lives of saints and holy men—the *Vida del Santo Fr. Tomás de Villanueva* (Life of St. Thomas of Villanova) and *Vida del venerable P. Fray Luis de Montoya* (Life of the Venerable Fray Luis de Montoya)—remain in ms. form.

BIBLIOGRAPHY

Primary Text

*Marial; Discursos morales en las fiestas de la Reina del Cielo Nuestra Señora.* Valladolid: n.p., 1600.

Criticism

Herrera, Tomás de. "Fr. Luis de Acevedo." In *Historia del convento de San Agustín de Salamanca*. Salamanca: n.p., 1652. 351.

Angelo DiSalvo

**ACOSTA, José de** (1540, Medina del Campo–1600, Salamanca), priest, historical and religious writer. A member of the Jesuit order from an early age, Father Acosta journeyed to Peru in 1571, and spent the next six years handling a variety of responsibilities in the New World. He wrote several religious works but is most remembered for the *Historia natural y moral de las Indias* (Seville, 1590; *Natural and Moral History of the Indies*, 1604). His clear, detailed documentation of the geography, history, culture, politics, religious beliefs and practices of the Indians he met are invaluable to later scholars. Father Acosta also wrote an adventure story about a cleric in the Indies, titled *Peregrinación del hermano Bartolomé Lorenzo* (1586?; Pilgrimage of Brother Bartholomew Lorenzo). In 1588 he became the first Jesuit professor of theology at the U in Salamanca.

BIBLIOGRAPHY

Primary Texts

*De procuranda Indorum salute*. Ed., tr. to Spanish, notes, F. Mateos. Madrid: n.p., 1952.
*Historia natural y moral de las Indias*. Ed. E. O'Gorman. 2nd ed. Mexico: Fondo de cultura económica, 1962.
*Obras*. Ed. F. Mateos. BAE 73 (1954). Includes study.
*Peregrinación del hermano Bartolomé Lorenzo*. Ed. C. Fernández-Duro. *BRAH* 35 (1899): 226–57.

English Translation

*The natural and moral history of the Indies, by Father Joseph de Acosta*. Ed., intro., C. Markham. London: Hakluyt, 1880. Rpt. of 1604 tr. by E.G.

Maureen Ihrie

**ACQUARONI, José Luis** (1919, Madrid–1983, Madrid), short story writer and novelist. Best known for his brief fiction, including the short novels *El cuchillo de la madrugada* (Knife at the Dawning), *Suceso en la playa de Évora* (Happening on the Beach at Evora [Portugal]), and *La corrida de toros* (The Bullfight), he is the author of numerous short stories published in magazines and periodicals and in this genre has won a number of prizes, including Insula and Ateneo. Some of his short stories have been collected in *Nuevas de este lugar* (News from These Parts), and he has written at least one long novel, *El turbión* (1967; The Downpour).

BIBLIOGRAPHY

Primary Texts

*A la hora del crepúsculo.* Barcelona: Plaza y Janés, 1983.
*Andalucía, más que nacionalidad.* Barcelona: Noguer, 1980.
*Copa de sombra.* Madrid: Cupsa, 1977.

**ACUÑA, Hernando de** (1520, Valladolid–1580, Granada), Petrarchan poet and soldier. After a distinguished military career in Africa and Italy, he returned to Granada and became a mentor to several young poets. His widow, dona Juana de Zúñiga, published his work in Madrid. Titled *Varias poesías* (1591; Various Poems), it is a collection of songs, sonnets, madrigals and translations. His best known poems include the *Fábula de Narciso* (Fable of Narcissus), *Contienda de Ayax Telamonio y de Ulises sobre las armas de Aquiles* (Dispute of Ajax Telemon and Ulysses over Achilles's Weapons) and his versification of the *Caballero determinado* (1591; The Resolved Knight), which was based on a prose translation, by Charles V, of Olivier de La Marche's *Le Chevalier délibéré.* *See also* Italian literary influences.

BIBLIOGRAPHY

Primary Text

*Varias poesías.* Ed. Elena Catena de Vindel. Madrid: CSIC, 1954.

English Translation

"Soneto al Rey Nuestro Señor." In *Renaissance and Baroque Poetry of Spain.* Tr., intro, ed. E. L. Rivers. New York: Dell, 1966.

Criticism

Alonso Cortés, N. *Don Hernando de Acuña, noticias biográficas.* Valladolid: Sever Cuesta, 1975.
Holzinger, W. "Acuña's Sonnet 'Al Rey Nuestro Señor' and the Tradition of European Millenial Prophecy." *Philological Quarterly* 55 (1976): 149–65.

Veronica Sauter

**ACUÑA Y VILLANUEVA DE LA IGLESIA, Rosario de,** pseud. Remigio Andrés Delafón (1851, Madrid–1923, Gijón, Asturias), Spanish playwright, essayist, and story writer.

A controversial sensation during her lifetime because of her liberal and progressive subject matter, she was considered a bold freethinker because of treating civil marriage, religious fanaticism, illegitimacy, delinquency, prison reform, atheism and other similarly polemical topics. She also dealt with a number of patriotic themes, for example, in *Amor a la patria* (1877; Love of the Fatherland), a one-act tragedy in verse which celebrates the heroism of the people of Zaragoza during the 1808 Spanish War of Independence against Napoleon. It is especially noteworthy that she emphasizes the patriotism of women. Acuña also treated the conflict between love, familial duty and patriotism in *La voz de la patria* (1893; The Voice of the Fatherland), in which an Aragonese mother and her son's pregnant fiancée join forces in an unsuccessful attempt to prevent his re-enlisting in military service.

Acuña authored studies on Spanish rural life, including *El hijo de los pueblos rurales* (1882; The Child of Rural Villages) and *Influencia de la vida del campo en la familia* (1882; Influence of Country Life upon the Family), and showed her concern for social deviants in *El crimen de la calle de Fuencarral; odia el delito y compadece al delincuente* (1880?; The Crime of Fuencarral Street; Hate the Crime and Pity the Criminal) and *Consecuencias de la degeneración femenina* (1888; Consequences of Feminine Degeneracy). She tried her hand at poetry in *Ecos del alma* (1876; Echoes of the Soul), *Morirse a tiempo* (1880; Dying at the Right Time) and *Sentir y pensar* (1884; Feeling and Thinking), comic verse.

*Rienzi el tribuno* (1876; Rienzi the Tribune) is a verse tragedy in two acts and an epilogue, a historical drama which is Acuña's best-known work. Fourteenth-century Roman tribune Nicolás de Rienzi's efforts to unify Rome by putting an end to blood feuds among the nobles seem initially to succeed, but eventually end with the hero's beheading by a mob, while his virtuous wife Maria stabs herself to death to escape dishonor at the hands of the sinister Colonna. *El padre Juan* (1891; Father Juan), a three-act prose drama, treats religious fanaticism via the conflict between conservative orthodoxy and freethinking as personified in the hypocritical Padre Juan and an atheistic man of science (who is ultimately revealed as the priest's illegitimate son). The ending strays perilously close to melodrama when the rabble-rousing Padre provokes the villagers to acts which lead to the son's murder.

BIBLIOGRAPHY

Primary Texts

*La casa de las muñecas*. Madrid: Ramón Angulo, 1888.
*Cosas mías*. Tortosa: Monclús, 1917?
*La siesta, colección de artículos*. Madrid: G. Estrada, 1882.
*Tiempo perdido, cuentos y bocetos*. Madrid: Minuesa de los Ríos, 1881.
*Tribunales de venganza, drama trágico-histórico . . . en verso*. Madrid: Rodríguez, 1880.

Criticism

Álvarez Lázaro, P. *Masonería y librepensamiento en la España de la Restauración*. Madrid: Universidad Pontificea Comillas, 1985. 179–88.
Castañón, L. "Aportación a la biografía de Rosario Acuña." *Boletín del Instituto de Estudios Asturianos* 117 (1986): 151–71.
Suárez Solís, S. "Una obra de teatro olvidada: 'Rienzi el Tribuno' de Rosario de Acuña." *Magister* (Oviedo) 1 (1983): 203–10.

Cristina Enríquez

**ADORANTES, Academia de los** (Academy of the Adoring Ones), a Valencian literary gathering. This club, founded by Carlos *Boyl, met every Monday night to discuss amorous themes. It was dissolved in 1600. *See also* Academia.

**AFÁN DE RIBERA, Fulgencio** (fl. 1729, ?–?), writer. He is best known for his satirical *costumbrista* sketches in *Virtud al uso y mística a la moda* (1734; Present Day Virtue and Fashionable Mysticism). The work is a collection of letters and documents which attack false humility, virtue and religion—it holds enormous cultural interest for its minute account of early eighteenth-c. life. *See also* Romanticism.

BIBLIOGRAPHY

Primary Text

*Virtud al uso y mística a la moda.* BAE 33.


**ÁGREDA, María de Jesús de** (1602, Agreda–1665, Agreda), Franciscan mystic nun. Prioress and abbess of her convent, she was much given to visions and raptures. Her book, *Mística ciudad de Dios* (1670; *City of God*, 1949), is an imaginative, detailed account of the daily life of the Holy Family. Of equal interest is her correspondence over the course of twenty-two years with Philip IV, who visited her in 1643. The king writes to her of state affairs, and she answers him in simple yet patriotic terms. The letters remained unpublished until 1885, when they were edited by F. Silvela. *See also* Mysticism.

BIBLIOGRAPHY

Primary Texts

*Correspondencia con Felipe IV.* Ed. G. Torrente Ballester. 2 vols. Madrid: Fe, 1942.
*Mística ciudad de Dios.* Ed. Ozcoidi. 5 vols. Barcelona: Gili, 1911–1914.

English Translation

*City of God.* Tr. F. Marison (pseud. of Rev. G. J. Blatter). 3rd ed. Santa Fe, NM: Catholic Information Service, 1949.

Criticism

Sánchez de Toca, J. *Felipe IV y Sor María de Jesús de Agreda.* 2nd ed. Barcelona: Minerva, 1924.

Maureen Ihrie


**AGUADO, Emiliano** (1907, Cebolla, Toledo–?), essayist and literary and theatrical critic. He flourished in the early Franco era, cultivating preferentially biblical and classical themes. His books include *Del siglo XVIII a nuestros días* (1941; From the 18th Century to Our Days); *Leyendo el Génesis* (1942; Reading the Book of Genesis); *El arte como revelación* (1943; Art as Revelation); and *En los caminos de la noche* (1944; In the Roadways of Night). His volume, *Theater*, which includes three tragedies, was awarded the National Literary Prize. Among additional works are *Job estaba solo* (1963; Job Was Alone) and *Meditación de los Salmos* (1964; Meditation on the Psalms). *See also* Essay.

BIBLIOGRAPHY

Primary Texts

*Del siglo XVIII a nuestros días.* 2nd ed. Madrid: Escorial, 1942.
*Job estaba solo.* Madrid: Nacional, 1963.
*Ortega y Gasset.* Madrid: EPESA, 1970.
*La república, último disfraz de la Restauración.* Madrid: Nacional, 1972.

**AGUADO, Pedro de** (?, Valdemore, Madrid–after 1589, ?), Franciscan missionary. Aguado spent many years in the New World, and set down his observations in two histories: *Historia de Santa Marta y del Nuevo Reino de Granada* (n.d.; History of St. Marta and the New Kingdom of Granada) and *Historia de Venezuela* (1581; History of Venezuela). The latter was not published until 1913. Both works provide valuable firsthand information about the people and events of the conquest and colonization of the New World.

BIBLIOGRAPHY

Primary Texts

*Historia de Santa Marta y del Nuevo Reino de Granada.* Ed. J. Becker. Madrid: RAH, 1916–17.
*Historia de Venezuela.* Ed. J. Becker. Madrid: RAH, 1918–19.

**AGUAYO, Alberto de** (fl. late 15th-early 16th c., ?–?), translator. First prior of the convent Santa Cruz of Granada (1492), Aguayo translated Boethius's famed *De consolatione philosophiae* (The Consolation of Philosophy) into Spanish in 1518.

BIBLIOGRAPHY

Primary Text

*La consolación de la filosofía.* Ed. Luis P. Getino. Buenos Aires: Espasa-Calpe Argentina, 1943.

**AGUILAR, Gaspar de** (1561, Valencia–1623, Valencia), poet, playwright. Secretary to the Duke of Gandia, Aguilar suffered financial and legal difficulties throughout his life. A charter member of the Academia de los Nocturnos (*Academia), he used the name *Sombra* (Shadow). His poetic works, of secondary merit, include *La expulsión de los moros de España* (1610; The Expulsion of the Moors from Spain) and *Relación de las fiestas nupciales que la ciudad de Valencia hizo al casamiento de Felipe III* (1599; Account of the Wedding Festivities Held by the City of Valencia on the Marriage of Philip III). Aguilar's dramatic works are of three types: religious, such as *Vida y muerte de San Luis Beltrán* (Life and Death of St. Luis Beltran); ''de costumbre,'' popular, topical works such as *La fuerza del interés* (The Strength of Money) or *La venganza honrosa* (Honorable Vengeance); and ''de ruido'' (noisy), plays which require many mechanical devices for elaborate stage effects, as in *Los amantes de*

*Cartago* (The Lovers of Carthage) and *La gitana melancólica* (The Melancholy Gypsy). *Cervantes praised Aguilar's *El mercader amante* (*The Merchant Lover*, 1965). Aguilar was a respected member of the Valencian dramatists considered precursors to Lope de *Vega.

BIBLIOGRAPHY

Primary Text

*Fiestas nupciales*. Ed. Martí Grajales. Valencia: n.p., 1910.
*Poetas dramáticos valencianos*. Ed. E. Juliá Martínez. 2 vols. Madrid: RAE, 1929.
*Rimas*. Ed. F. de A. Carreres. Valencia: n.p., 1951.
"Rimas inéditas de ingenios españoles." Ed. Mele. *BH* 3 (1901): 328–47.

English Translation

*The Merchant Lover*. Tr. G. Ticknor. In *History of Spanish Literature*. New York: Gordian, 1965. Excerpt.

Criticism

Weiger, J. C. *The Valencian Dramatists of Spain's Golden Age*. TWAS 371. Boston: Twayne, 1976.

Maureen Ihrie

**AGUIRRE, Francisca** (1930, ?– ), poet. Largely autodidactic, Aguirre is eclectic and often intimate, in spite of her beginnings with the "Social Poets" of the 1950s and early 1960s. The acknowledged influence of Luis *Rosales combines with the emotional traumas of the Civil War which she experienced as a child to produce a poetry in which existential notes blend with autobiographical echoes to express a persistent sense of solitude, anguish and longing. Childhood, history, and the need for others, for companionship and solidarity, are persistent themes, as are the need for understanding, for rational lucidity as well as for the light of faith.

Important collections include *Itaca* (1972; Ithaca), which utilizes the Homeric myth of Ulysses as a point of departure for Penelope's reflections on marital fidelity, betrayal and desolation. *La otra música* (1977; The Other Music) employs as a unifying metaphor the analogy between music and poetry whereby both are expressions of torrential emotions. *Los trescientos escalones* (1977; Three Hundred Stair-Steps) is written from the perspective of the mature woman who examines her roots, her painful childhood and struggles for clarity, with the theme of memory sometimes recalling Antonio *Machado Ruiz.

BIBLIOGRAPHY

Primary Texts

*Itaca*. Madrid: Cultura Hispánica, 1972.
*La otra música*. Madrid: Cultura Hispánica, 1977.

*Los trescientos escalones.* San Sebastián: Caja de Ahorros, Provincia de Guipúzcoa, 1977.

Janet Pérez

**AGUSTÍ, Ignacio** (1913, Llisá del Vall–1974, Barcelona), Spanish novelist, journalist, essayist and poet. Agustí, of an upper-middle-class family, was educated through the *bachillerato* (bachelor's degree) in private schools run by the Jesuits, and received a law degree from the U of Barcelona in 1934. He exercised this profession only until the outbreak of the Civil War (1936–39), after which he devoted himself to journalism, serving as an international correspondent for *La Vanguardia* (Barcelona) during World War II. He founded the weekly news magazine *Destino*, and was its director 1944–58. Writing both in his native vernacular (Catalan) and Castilian, Agustí produced solid novels of the "testimonial" variety, historical chronicles of his time. Although he had a reputation for innovativeness, he was actually a rather traditional realist in the vein of Benito *Pérez Galdós, Charles Dickens, and the Catalans Narcís *Oller and Víctor *Català. *Los surcos* (1942; The Furrows), his first attempt at the novel, is in the lyric mode, a prelude to his extended cycle, "La ceniza fue árbol" (The Ashes Were Once a Tree). This pentalogy appeared over a period of some thirty years, from 1944 to near the end of his life, and includes *Mariona Rebull* (1944), *El Viudo Ríus* (1945; Widower Rius), *Desiderio* (1957), *19 de julio* (1966; July 19th) and *Guerra civil* (1972; Civil War). Unquestionably his major literary achievement, this cycle spans the years from 1865 to the outbreak of the Civil War, portraying the transition of Barcelona from a peaceful provincial capital to the industrial and commercial center of Spain, torn by class strife and labor disputes. Agustí studies the lives of two families, the industrial Ríus clan and the merchant Rebulls, united by marriage, and their struggle to defend their inheritance and privileged position.

Considered moderately important as a poet in Catalan, Agustí was included by Félix Ros in his *Antología poética de la lengua catalana puesta en versos castellanos* (1965; Anthology of Catalan Poetry in Castilian Verse), and his first publication was a collection of Catalan lyrics, *El veler* (1932; The Sailboat). He tried his hand at the theater (*La coronela*, 1932; The Colonel's Lady) and produced several other plays during the 1930s.

BIBLIOGRAPHY

Primary Texts

*Desiderio* (1957). 6th ed. Barcelona: Destino, 1967. ("La ceniza fue árbol" 3)
*Diecinueve de julio, novela.* (1965). 4th ed. Barcelona: Planeta, 1965. ("La ceniza fue árbol" 4)
*Guerra civil.* Barcelona: Planeta, 1972. ("La ceniza fue árbol" 5)
*Mariona Rebull* (1943). Barcelona: Argos, 1962. ("La ceniza fue árbol" 1)
*El vuido Ríus.* Barcelona: Destino, 1947. ("La ceniza fue árbol" 2)

Criticism

Miranda, W. *Ignacio Agustí, el autor y su obra: Interpretación y realismo de guerra civil*. Washington, DC: UP of America, 1982.

Nora, E. G. de. *La novela española contemporánea*. vol. 3. Madrid: Gredos, 1967. 130–39.

Valbuena Prat, A. *Historia de la literatura española*. vol. 4. Barcelona: Gili, 1968. 10.

Janet Pérez

**AHRIMÁN.** Pseudonym of José Martínez Ruiz. *See* Azorín

**AIRÓ, Clemente** (1918, Madrid–1975, Bogota, Colombia), novelist. Best known outside Colombia as the founder of Editorial Iqueima and *Espiral*, a literary magazine, Airó was also a novelist whose main theme was his adoptive country, where he arrived at age 22. He had served as a volunteer in the Spanish Republican Army and upon its defeat he went into exile in France. Once in Colombia, toward the end of 1940, he studied in the Facultad de Filosofía y Letras; from then on he fully participated in the intellectual life of the community. He was a journalist, a critic, a university professor and a founding member of the Association of Writers and Artists of Colombia. His published books include *Viento de Romance* (1947; Wind of Ballads), short stories; *Sombras al sol* (1951; Shadows in the Sunlight), novel; *Yugo de niebla* (1948; Yoke of Fog), novel; *Cardos como flores* (1967; Nettles as Flowers), short stories; *El campo y el fuego* (1972; The Field and the Fire), novel; and *Donde no canta el gallo* (1974; Where the Cock Does Not Crow), short stories. He left unpublished an early novel about the Spanish Civil War, *Alambre de púas* (Barbed Wire), and two recent ones, *Todo nunca es todo* (1973; All Is Never All) and *Puente colgante* (1974; Suspended Bridge). Airó found inspiration in the lives of the urban middle class and its fringes, whose problems and style he knew well and chronicled with mastery. The omnipresence of Bogota is also a distinctive trait of his narrative. Although he often probed individual lives, his work is permeated by social and political awareness: poverty, repression and even the rural violence of the fifties are never very far away from the ostensibly personal affairs he depicts. He bears witness to a society where the illustrious names of the oligarchy merge with upwardly striving *mestizos* and foreigners to form a new power alliance; he also explores the dynamics of that new class as it pushes the poor and the rural population into a further decline, often in the name of commercial and industrial progress. Airó is particularly acute in his observation of personal relationships wielded as weapons. Marriage is foremost among them: his stories show how it is used by men and women, both young and old, and by their relatives, to destroy one another and to gain economic and political advantage. An original and perceptive aspect of Airó's writings is his admiration and respect for Colombian women; he sees them as hard workers where their men often are not. The women are talented in disciplines ranging from business to music, capable and reliable under the most adverse circumstances. Airó has only one novel dealing with the plight of the peasants. In it he abandons his lucid and realistic prose and experiments with a poetic, stylized technique. *El campo y el fuego* might have been the beginning of a new narrative manner for Airó, had he not died, suddenly, in 1975.

BIBLIOGRAPHY

Criticism

Irizarry, Estelle. "Novela colombiana: dos voces de novelista en Clemente Airó." *Espiral* 134 (March 1975): 13–28.
Zelaya Kolker, Marielena. *Visiones americanas de los transterrados españoles de 1939.* Madrid: Instituto de Cooperación Iberoamericana, 1985.

Marielena Zelaya Kolker

**ALARCÓN, Juan Ruiz de.** *See* Ruiz de Alarcón

**ALARCÓN, Luis de** (16th c., ?–?, Alcalá de Henares), religious writer. This Augustinian monk wrote an ascetical-mystical work called *Camino del cielo* (1547, Alcalá; The Way to Heaven) in which he guides the reader on how to search for and find God. It has ascetical characteristics in that it demonstrates the way one is to shun the evil in the world and to avoid its vanity as Alarcón sees it. García López describes the book as a mystical work because of its spiritual content, and further adds that its literary style makes the *Camino del cielo* one of the best books of its kind at that time in Spain. Palau y Dulcet adds that it details the harmful books that the reader should avoid altogether along with the many good books available. The original edition is held by the National Library in Madrid (R–21.713). *See also* Ascetical Literature; Mysticism.

BIBLIOGRAPHY

Primary Text

*Camino del cielo en que se demuestra cómo se busca y halla Dios.* Alcalá: Juan de Brocar, 1547.

Criticism

García López, Juan Catalina. *Ensayo de una tipografía complutense.* Madrid: Tello, 1889. 77, No. 216.

Angelo DiSalvo

**ALARCÓN, Pedro Antonio de** (1833, Guadix, Granada–1891, Madrid), politician, prose author. The fourth of ten children, he began studying law at the U of Granada (1847), but for financial reasons switched to theological studies at the local seminary (1848). This, too, he abandoned, as the pull of literature finally took over. Alarcón's early years were marked by intense involvement in politics, and great journalistic activity, as he composed many sketches and short stories which appeared in leading periodicals of the day. In 1852 he co-founded and began editing a weekly magazine, *El eco de occidente* (The Echo of the West). Early in 1853, he traveled to Madrid, hoping to establish himself as a writer there. Funds soon ran low, and he returned to Granada (1854), becoming an active member of the political-literary group *La cuerda granadina* (The Granada Chain). The same year, he founded an anti-clerical paper, *La redención* (Redemption), and returned to Madrid. Alarcón's first novel, *El final de Norma* (Norma's End), appeared in 1855. It was a juvenile, melodramatic love story that he revised twenty-three years later (1878). Alarcón's first solid literary success was the *Diario de un testigo de la Guerra de Africa* (1860; Diary of an Eyewitness to the African War)—a two-volume collection of articles about the conflict with Morocco which he penned for the Spanish press. Now financially secure, he traveled to Paris, Geneva, and Italy. This experience inspired a travel account, *De Madrid a Nápoles* (1861; From Madrid to Naples).

The next nine years, roughly 1861–70, were consumed by Alarcón's intense political involvement. He produced one volume of short stories, *Novelas* (1866; Novels), and little else. He also married in 1865, and subsequently fathered eight children.

From 1870 to 1884, Alarcón returned to literature, publishing several collections of earlier writings: *Poesías serias y humorísticas* (1870; Serious and Humorous Poetry); *Cosas que fueron* (1871; Things That Were); a three-volume edition of his short stories, appearing 1881–82, with the titles *Cuentos amatorios* (Love Stories), *Historietas nacionales* (National Anecdotes), and *Narraciones inverosímiles* (Improbable Narrations); and *Viajes por España* (1883; Travels through Spain) and *La Alpujarra* (1874; The Alpujarra), both travel accounts. Alarcón's novels also date from these years. In 1874 came the publication of his finest work and primary reason for his enduring fame, *El sombrero de tres picos* (*The Three-Cornered Hat*, 1958). A fast-paced tale of foiled seduction, starring a village magistrate, a miller and the miller's wife, its enthusiastic critical and popular reception in Spain was complemented by translations to seven languages within the next ten years. It subsequently inspired three operas, several dramatic renditions, and a ballet by Manuel de Falla. A year later, *El escándalo* (*The Scandal*, 1945) met with a good public reception, but critics generally objected to its strong Catholic message. *El niño de la bola* (1880; *The Infant with the Globe*, 1959), a tragic tale of ill-fated love, like *Los *Amantes de Teruel*, again met with popular success and critical hostility. *La pródiga* (1882; The Prodigal Woman), again, was rejected by the critics, and the love story *El capitán Veneno* (1881; Captain Poison) was ignored by them. The rather unabated negative reactions persuaded Alarcón, who was sensitive to critical opinion, to renounce writing. He lived the rest of his life quietly, dying at age 58.

In general terms, Alarcón's early writing is romantic and melodramatic, often to excess. Later compositions are often conservative and didactic, although *Romanticism and *costumbrismo* resurface throughout his writing. Although only *El sombrero de tres picos* was critically acclaimed, his other novels contributed significantly to the reemergence of the novel in nineteenth-c. Spain. The quality of his short stories varies, but even those which are flawed show him to be a talented narrator worthy of memory for this part of his opus. He possessed an excellent sense of the comic. His best short stories include "La Comendadora" ("The Nun"), "Moros y cristianos" ("Moors and Christians"), and "El libro talonario" ("The Stub Book").

BIBLIOGRAPHY

Primary Texts

*"La Comendadora" y otros cuentos.* Ed., prol. L. de los Ríos. Madrid: Cátedra, 1975.
*Dos ángeles caídos y otros escritos olvidados.* Ed. A. Aguilar y Tejera. Madrid: Latina, 1924.
*El escándalo.* Ed., prol. L. Izquierdo. Estella: Salvat, 1971.
*Novelas completas.* Madrid: Aguilar, 1974.
*Obras completas.* Madrid: Fax, 1943, 1954, 1968.
*La Pródiga.* Ed., intro. A. Navarro González. Madrid: Nacional, 1975.
*El sombrero de tres picos.* Ed., intro. V. Gaos. Clásicos Castellanos 200. Madrid: Espasa-Calpe, 1975.
*Verdades de paño pardo y otros escritos olvidados.* Ed. A. Aguilar y Tejera. Madrid: Iberoamericana, 1928.

English Translations

*The Infant with the Globe.* Tr. R. Graves. New York: Yoseloff, 1959.
*The Scandal.* Tr. Ph. H. Riley and H. J. Tunney. New York: Knopf, 1945.
*The Three-Cornered Hat.* Tr. H. de Onís. Great Neck, NY: Barron's, 1958.
*Tales from the Spanish.* Sel. J. I. Rodale. Allentown, PA: Story Classics, 1948.

Criticism

DeCoster, C. C. *Pedro Antonio de Alarcón.* TWAS 549. Boston: Twayne, 1979.
Gaos, V. "Técnica y estilo en *El sombrero de tres picos.*" In *Temas y problemas de la literatura española.* Madrid: Guadarrama, 1971. 179–201.
Montesinos, J. F. *Pedro Antonio de Alarcón.* Madrid: Castalia, 1977.
Ocano, A. *Alarcón.* Madrid: EPESA, 1970.
Pardo Canalis, E. *Pedro Antonio de Alarcón.* Madrid: Compañía Bibliográfica Española, 1965.
Pérez Gutiérrez, F. *El problema religioso en la generación de 1868.* Madrid: Taurus, 1975.

**ALAS, Leopoldo.** *See* Clarín

*ALBA* (Dawn), a love poem. These poetic compositions of the Provençal troubadors are characterized by their reference to dawn, or sunrise, which inevitably separates the lovers. In Spain, the *albas* are not exclusively love poetry; they often praise the day and the morning. *See also* Gallic Portuguese Poetry.

**ÁLBAR DE CÓRDOBA, Paul.** *See* Córdoba, Paulus Álvaro de

**ALBARUS, Paulus.** *See* Córdoba, Paulus Álvaro de

**ALBERCA LORENTE, Luisa** (1920, Alcázar de San Juan– ), novelist, scriptwriter, dramatist and writer of stories for children. A prolific broadcast journalist, Alberca is a facile writer who prefers to treat the materials of which soap operas are made, themes such as love, tangled family relationships, madness, religious conflicts, money, sex, betrayal, hate, ambition, defeat and reunion, usually with some consideration of values and mores and the generation gap. Alberca's enormous appeal for the Spanish public is due to her able exploitation of the *novela rosa* formula, popular romances or pulp novels of little sociological or historical value, but with the traditional conflicts between good and evil, youth and age, hope and despair. Many of her works are collaborations with Guillermo Sautier Casaseca, including *Lo que nunca somos* (1952; That Which We Never Are), *La segunda esposa* (1956; The Second Wife), *En nombre del hijo* (1957; In the Name of the Son), *La Dama de Verde* (1958; Lady in Green), *Amor en París* (1959; Love in Paris), *Historia de una mujer; Rosa María* (1964; Tale of a Woman, Rosa Maria), and its sequel, *Historia de un hombre; Rosa María* (1964; Tale of a Man, Rosa Maria).

*Lo que no muere* (1953; What Doesn't Die) is a collection of ten novelettes which were originally radio serials, treating such themes as the separation and opposition of siblings, traditional patriotic values versus communism, sacrifice and ethics versus cynicism and evil, and the ultimate triumph of true love against incredible odds. Among Alberca's best works is a children's book dedicated to her daughters, *Los mensajeros del diablo* (1958; The Devil's Messengers), with each narrative dedicated to one of the seven capital sins. The confrontation between good and evil is treated with humor and restraint with delightful results.

The typical girl-meets-boy romance with a super-abundance of coincidence and such devices of melodrama as the mistaken identity and hero or heroine of mysterious origins leading to the final "happily ever after" marriage appear in *Dina* (1965) and its sequel, *La Isla de Adriana* (1965; Adriana's Isle), while more complex and problematic family relationships (including abuse, the conflict between feminine self-realization and motherhood, and the struggle for survival) are depicted in *Palabras en la tierra* (1958; Words in the Dirt), *Patricia Rilton* (1950) and *La última dicha* (1956; Ultimate Happiness).

BIBLIOGRAPHY

Primary Texts

*Al regresar de las sombras*. Madrid: Cid, 1963.
*El camino solitario*. Madrid: Cid, 1966.
*Cera fundida*. Barcelona: Bruguera, 1962.
*Extraño poder*. Madrid: Cid, 1959.

                                                                    Janet Pérez

**ALBERT, Catarina.** *See* Català, Víctor

**ALBERTI, Rafael** (1902, Puerto de Santa María– ), poet, playwright, and painter. Alberti's childhood years were spent in Puerto de Santa María, a small picturesque fishing village near Cádiz. As a child Alberti revealed an interest in painting, and when in 1917 his family moved to Madrid he spent countless hours in the Prado Museum, making friends within the artistic circles. In 1922 a few of his works were displayed in an exhibition at the Atheneum (*Ateneo*) in Madrid. His style, intuitively yet unmistakably Cubist, classifies him as one of Spain's first Cubist painters. For no obvious reason other than his poor health— Alberti suffered from tuberculosis—he suddenly abandoned painting. His friendship with Juan Ramón *Jiménez and the *Generation of 1927 changed the course of Alberti's life, and he began writing poetry, winning the National Literary Prize in 1925 for his book *Marinero en tierra* (Landlocked Sailor). During the Spanish Civil War, Alberti took an active political stance in defense of the Republic, and later became a member of the Communist party. His self-imposed exile took him first to Paris and later to Buenos Aires, where he resided until 1963. The next fifteen years were spent in Italy, until Franco's death in 1975, and the resulting changes in Spain's political system finally prompted the poet's return to his beloved "patria" (homeland). In 1983 he was awarded the very prestigious Cervantes Prize for Literature.

**Poetic Works**

Prewar publications include *Marinero en tierra* (1924; Landlocked Sailor); *La amante* (1925; The Lover); *El alba del alhelí* (1925–26; The Dawn of the Gillyflower); *Cal y canto* (1926–27; Passion and Form); *Sobre los ángeles* (1927–28; Concerning the Angels, 1967); *Yo era un tonto y lo que he visto me ha hecho dos tontos* (1929; I Was a Fool and What I Have Seen Has Made Me Twice a Fool); *Sermones y moradas* (1929–30; Sermons and Sojourns); the civil elegy *Con los zapatos puestos tengo que morir* (1930; I Must Die with My Shoes On), which marks a transition to Alberti's political and Civil War poetry; *Consignas* (1933; Watchword); *Un fantasma recorre Europa* (1933; A Ghost Travels across Europe); *13 bandas y 48 estrellas* (1935; Thirteen Bars and Forty-eight Stars); *El poeta en la calle* (1931–35; The Poet in the Street), *De un momento a otro* (1934–39; From One Moment to the Next); *Vida bilingüe de un refugiado español en Francia* (1939–40; The Bilingual Life of a Spanish Refugee in France); and some less significant works not included in Alberti's Complete Works, like *El burro explosivo* (1934–35; The Explosive Donkey), *Romances de la guerra de España* (1936; Ballads of the Spanish War), and *Cantata de los héroes y la fraternidad de los pueblos* (1938; Song of Heroes and of Fraternity among Peoples). Collections of poetry written in exile include *Entre el clavel y la espada* (1941; Between the Carnation and the Sword), *Pleamar* (1944; Highwater), *A la pintura* (1945–52; To Painting), *Signos del día* (1945–46; Signs of the Day), *Coplas de Juan Panadero* (1949–53; Songs of Juan Panadero), *Retornos de lo vivo lejano* (1948–56; Memories of a Vivid Past), *Buenos Aires en tinta china* (1950; Buenos Aires in India Ink), *Poemas diversos* (1945–59; Various Poems), *Poemas de Punta del Este* (1945–56; Poems from Punta del Este), *Baladas y canciones del Paraná* (1953–54; Songs and Ballads of the Paraná), *Ora marítima* (1953; Now, the Sea), *La primavera de los pueblos* (1955–57; Springtime for a People), *Poemas escénicos* (1962; Scenic Poems), *Escrito en el aire* (1964; Written on the Wind), *Abierto a todas horas* (1964; Open at All Hours), *Poemas de amor* (1967; Poems of Love), *Roma, peligro para caminantes* (1968; Rome,

Danger to the Traveler), *Los ocho nombres de Picasso* (1970; The Eight Names of Picasso), *Canciones del alto valle del Aniene* (1972; Songs of the Upper Valley of the Aniene), *El matador, poemas escénicos 1961–1965* (1979; The Matador, Scenic Poems 1961–1965), *Versos sueltos de cada día* (1982; Scattered Daily Verses). In addition to these collections, Alberti has written an elegy on the death of the bullfighter Ignacio Sánchez Mejías, *Verte y no verte* (1934; To See You and Not to See You), numerous poems composed prior to *Marinero en tierra* (Landlocked Sailor) and first published in 1969, and less significant works done in collaboration with his wife María Teresa *León like *Sonríe China* (China Smiles) and *Doinas y baladas populares rumanas* (Popular Romanian Songs and Ballads).

## Plays

*La pájara pinta* (1924; The Speckled Bird), *El hombre deshabitado* (1930; The Uninhabited Man), *Fermín Galán* (1931), *De un momento a otro* (1938–39; From One Moment to the Next), *El trébol florido* (1940; The Flowering Clover), *La Gallarda* (1944; The Graceful Woman), *El adefesio* (1944; The Ridiculously Attired Gentleman), *Noche de guerra en el Museo del Prado* (1956; A Night of War in the Prado Museum), *La Lozana andaluza* (1964; The Haughty Andalusian Woman), and several short plays of the type Alberti called "urgent theater" which were written at the time of the Spanish Civil War and which include *Bazar de la Providencia* (The Bazaar of Providence), *Farsa de los Reyes Magos* (Farce of the Three Kings), *Los salvadores de España* (The Saviors of Spain), *Radio Sevilla* (Radio Seville), and *Cantata de los héroes y de la fraternidad de los pueblos* (Song of Heroes and of Fraternity among Peoples).

## Prose

Alberti's two significant prose works are his autobiography *La arboleda perdida* (*The Lost Grove*, 1976), which was published by Seix Barral in a revised and updated edition in 1975, and *Imagen primera de . . .* (1945; A First Look at . . . ). In addition to these, Robert Marrast has published a collection of Alberti's prose works entitled *Rafael Alberti: proses retrouvées (1924–1942)* (Rafael Alberti: Discovered Prose Writings [1924–1942]).

## Poetry

Ricardo Gullón writes that to read the works of Rafael Alberti from 1924 to 1962 is to study the evolution of contemporary poetry in full. Indeed, Alberti is one of the more prolific and versatile poets of the Generation of 1927. Throughout his work Alberti consciously strives to incorporate new forms and ideas brought about by the changing times. His first three collections, *Marinero en tierra*, *La amante*, and *El alba del alhelí*, all deeply rooted in the popular tradition, give way to a more stylized, baroque type of poetry in *Cal y canto*, incorporating innovations of the Ultraist movement. *Sobre los ángeles* is somewhat surrealistic in nature. The political situation of the 1930s affected Alberti very deeply and his poetry suddenly became rather "engagée." Two of the more successful postwar collections are *Pleamar* and *Retornos de lo vivo lejano*.

Additional sources of inspiration for the poet have been the bullfight and the poet's most cherished hobby, painting (*A la pintura* [To Painting]).

Through his poetry Alberti reveals that he is cognizant of and responsive to shapes, forms and, above all, color. Repetitive images call into play the four principal elements of nature, fire, earth, air and water, which provide the framework for much of Alberti's poetry. These elements are often represented as inseparable dualities, the most common of which is "mar-tierra" (earth/sea), the inspiration for his first three collections. In *Marinero en tierra* the poet makes a conscious attempt at seeing things through the eyes of a child, unable to distinguish the limits which separate the opposing worlds of land and sea. Hence, commonplace reality suffers dramatic transformations; Puerto de Santa María, where the poet was born and raised, becomes a kind of mythical paradise or world of fantasy. The everyday activities of the small fishing village are seen superimposed on an undersea environment and vice versa.

The popular element is more pronounced in Alberti's two subsequent works. Through the poems of *La amante*, the poet brings his love, the sea, to the landlocked people of Castile. *El alba del alhelí* is a veritable "cante hondo andaluz" (a collection of songs and ballads which expresses the popular customs, myths, and beliefs that are a part of Andalusia's cultural heritage). The poems are expressions of the land, its traditions, its joys and its sorrows, drawn from popular poetry of the traditional type: the *Kharja*, romances (see Romancero), *cantigas*, *villancicos*, and *serranillas*. The great majority are dedicated to the tragic side of the Andalusian culture or what the Andalusians themselves refer to as *la pena negra* (dark sorrow).

With *Cal y canto* (Passion and Form) there is a noticeable change in the direction of Alberti's work, due in part to the rediscovery of *Góngora and growing interest in the literature and art of the Vanguard movement rapidly spreading its influence across Europe. Alberti manages, with a relative degree of success, to combine Baroque forms and techniques artistically with Ultraist or Futurist images.

An emotional crisis was responsible for the more serious and subjective poetry of *Sobre los ángeles*, considered by many the poet's best work. *Sobre los ángeles* is a book of contrasts. Reality is broken down in terms of good and evil, light and dark, and up and down. Through the use of antithetical images the poet symbolically depicts a war raging within his subconscious mind. Air and fire replace earth and water as the principal elements of this oneiric landscape.

Alberti's political poetry has not been carefully examined or impartially judged. While some political poems are overly allegorical and suffer from a lack of internal rhyme, they present unique stylistic, rhetorical and metrical innovations, along with many new creative and expressive images. Alberti's finest and most creative political expression can be found in the collection *Entre el clavel y la espada*, in particular in "Toro en el mar" (A Bull on the Sea), where Spain is symbolically presented as a bull wounded and in agony.

Rafael Alberti's elegy on the death of Ignacio Sánchez Mejías, *Verte y no* *verte* (To See You and Not to See You)—unlike *García Lorca's more famous and highly subjective poem—bears little resemblance to the typical elegy. Instead of simply eulogizing the bullfighter, the poet depicts an eternal struggle between the forces of light (the bullfighter) and darkness (the bull). Ironically, the principal character of the drama is not the bullfighter, but the bull.

Of the poetry written in exile, the two collections which clearly stand out are *Retornos de lo vivo lejano*, the poet's recollections of some of the special moments in his life, and *A la pintura*, his personal tribute to an art form which, from the time he began writing, had a significant effect on his poetry.

### Theater

It is difficult to separate Alberti's theater from his poetry; the thematic and stylistic parallels are astounding. His first dramatic effort, *La pájara pinta*, in the "guiñolesque" tradition, is remarkably similar to his early poetic works. *El hombre deshabitado*, written shortly after *Sobre los ángeles*, repeats many of its surrealistic images. Alberti's Civil War plays often bear the same titles as the poetry and repeat the themes of some collections of poetry written at that time. The play *Noche de guerra en el Museo del Prado* emerged as a direct consequence of his book *A la pintura*. While recognized primarily as a poet, Alberti rivals most 20th-c. dramatists. Since Franco's death, his plays have been performed by numerous theater groups.

Most of Alberti's play's are historical or political and, despite what some critics have claimed, are clearly propagandistic, especially those dubbed "urgent theater," including such works as *Farsa de los Reyes Magos*, *Los salvadores de España*, and *Radio Sevilla*. Alberti's best political play, *Noche de guerra en el Museo del Prado*, shows influence of Bertolt Brecht both in the staging of the play—a play within a play—and in its intent. The action set against the Nationalist bombardment of Madrid during the Spanish Civil War features militia men and citizens attempting to save the paintings. Characters from Goya's paintings come to life and join their contemporary comrades in their timeless struggle against tyranny and injustice. Another historical play, *La Lozana andaluza*, is based on the 1528 book by Francisco *Delicado.

Rafael Alberti is one of those rare individuals who has been able to adapt well to the changing times, remaining always in the vanguard of literature and art.

BIBLIOGRAPHY

Primary Texts

*Antología*. 6th ed. Buenos Aires: Losada, 1972.
*La arboleda perdida*. Barcelona: Seix Barral, 1975.
*Imagen primera de.* . . . Madrid: Turner, 1975.
*El matador (poemas escénicos 1961–1965)*. Barcelona: Seix Barral, 1979.
*Los ocho nombres de Picasso*. Barcelona: Kairós, 1978.
*Obras completas*. Madrid: Aguilar, 1972.
*Poesías completas*. Buenos Aires: Losada, 1961.

*Relatos y prosa.* Barcelona: R.M., 1977.
*Roma, peligro para caminantes.* Barcelona: Seix Barral, 1976.
*Teatro.* 3rd ed. *El hombre deshabitado, El trébol florido, El adefesio, La Gallarda.*
Buenos Aires: Losada, 1959.
*Teatro. La Lozana andaluza, De un momento a otro, Noche de guerra en el Museo del Prado.* Buenos Aires: Losada, 1964.
*Versos sueltos de cada día.* Barcelona: Seix Barral, 1982.

English Translations

*Concerning the Angels.* Ed. and tr. Geoffrey Connel. Chicago: Swallow, 1967.
*The Lost Grove.* Ed. and tr. Gabriel Berns. Berkeley: U of California P, 1976.
*Mapper of Mists. Poems and Translations.* Ed. and tr. Tom Gatten. Stony Brook, NY: Wambli, 1974.
*The Owl's Insomnia.* Tr. Mark Strand. New York: Atheneum, 1973.
*Selected Poems.* Ed. and tr. Ben Belitt. Berkeley: U of California P, 1966.

Criticism

Jiménez Fajardo, Salvador. *Multiple Spaces: The Poetry of Rafael Alberti.* London: Tamesis, 1985.
Manteiga, Robert. *The Poetry of Rafael Alberti: A Visual Approach.* London: Tamesis, 1979.
Morris, Cyril Brian. *Rafael Alberti's 'Sobre los ángeles': Four Major Themes.* Hull: U of Hull P, 1966.
———. *A Generation of Spanish Poets (1920–1936).* Cambridge: Cambridge UP, 1969.
Nantell, Judith. *Alberti's Poetry of the Thirties.* Athens: U of Georgia P, 1986.
Popkin, Louise. *The Theater of Rafael Alberti.* London: Tamesis, 1975.
Salinas de Marichal, Solita. *El mundo poético de Rafael Alberti.* Madrid: Gredos, 1968.
Tejada, José Luis. *Rafael Alberti, entre la tradición y la vanguardia.* Madrid: Gredos, 1977.

Robert Manteiga

**ALBÓ I CORRONS, Núria** (1930, La Garriga– ), teacher, writer, and mayor of La Garriga. As a writer, she started out with poetry and more recently has prolifically written prose. *Desencís* (1980; Disillusion) has a political background—municipal and parliamentary elections. Her contradictory characters are tender, intelligent, and sometimes lucid, but at the same time conformist and passive. This novel won the Premi Vila d' Arenys. *See also* Catalan Literature.

BIBLIOGRAPHY

Primary Texts

*Agapi Mou.* Barcelona: Pòrtic, 1980.
*Desencís.* Barcelona: La Magrana, 1980.
*Díptic* (with Maria Angels Anglada). Barcelona: Balmes, 1972.
*L'encenedor verd.* Barcelona: Vosgos, 1980.
*Fes-te repicar.* Barcelona: Destino, 1970, 1979.

*La mà pel front.* Barcelona: Pedreira, 1962.
*Tranquil, Jordi, tranquil.* Barcelona: Pòrtic, 1984.

Kathleen McNerney

**ALBORADA** (Dawn), a type of poem. *Alboradas*, which often had musical accompaniment, were sung or recited in the morning. Similar to the Provençal *albas*, they are very popular in Galician folklore, which is rich in poetry to the early morning. *See also* Gallic Portuguese Poetry.

**ALBORNOZ, Aurora de** (1926, Luarca, Asturias– ), poet and critic. An expatriate who has resided in Puerto Rico since 1944, Albornoz has been for many years a professor of Spanish literature at the U of Puerto Rico. Important poetry collections include *Brazo de niebla* (1955; Arm of Mist), *Poemas para alcanzar un segundo* (1961; Poems to Catch an Instant) and *En busca de esos niños en hilera* (1967; In Search of Those Threads of Children). Existential solitude, the problems of poetic creation and self-expression, childhood memories, the passage of time and longing for lost youth, the Spanish Civil War and death are among her most frequently repeated themes. *Por la primavera blanca (fabulaciones)* (1962; During the White Springtime [tales]) is a collection of ten vignettes in prose with many lyric qualities, evoking the emotions awakened by recollections. Two important critical studies date from 1961, *Poesías de guerra de Antonio Machado* (Antonio Machado's War Poems) and *La prehistoria de Antonio Machado* (Prehistory of Antonio Machado).

BIBLIOGRAPHY

Primary Texts

*Brazo de niebla.* San Juan, PR: Coayuco, 1955.
*En busca de esos niños en hilera.* Santander: Isla de los ratones, 1967.
*Hacia la realidad creada.* Barcelona: Península, 1979.
*Palabras reunidas (1969–1977).* Madrid: Ayuso, 1983.
*Poemas para alcanzar un segundo.* Madrid: Rialp, 1961.
*Por la primavera blanca (fabulaciones).* Madrid: Insula, 1962.

Janet Pérez

**ALCALÁ, Xavier** (1947, Miguelturra, Ciudad Real– ), Galician writer of novels and short stories. An information engineer by profession, Alcalá has written essays and poetry in addition to the prose of a fictional sort. He was involved in the beginnings of the *nova canción galega* (new Galician music) through the writing of lyrics. He has also translated *Treasure Island* into Galician and has worked in group to produce school texts for the Galician language. *See also* Galician Literature.

BIBLIOGRAPHY

Primary Texts

*Fábula.* 4th ed. Vigo: Galaxia, 1986.
*A fundición.* No city: n.p., 1978.

*A ínsua.* No city: n.p., 1978. (novel)
*O Larvisión.* No city: n.p., 1981.
*O Larvisión e outros relatos.* No city: n.p., 1984.
*A nosa cinza.* Vigo: Galaxia, 1987.
*Nos pagos de Huinca Loo.* No city: n.p., 1982. (novel) Version in "Argentinian":
    *Cristiano muerto.* No city: n.p., 1983.
*Tertúlia.* No city: n.p., 1985.
*Voltar.* Vigo: Galaxia, 1972.

                                                      Kathleen March


**ALCALÁ GALIANO, Antonio** (1789, Cadiz–1865, Madrid), important liberal
crusader in politics and literature. Alcalá Galiano belongs to that generation of
Spanish intellectuals that fought the obscurantism of Ferdinand VII. In exile for
his political beliefs, he fled to England in 1823, remained there until 1834, and
occupied the first chair in Spanish literature at the U of London. His books on
literature and political science date from this period: *Historia de la literatura
española, francesa, inglesa e italiana en el siglo XVIII* (1845; History of Spanish,
French, English and Italian Literatures in the Eighteenth Century) and *Lecciones
de Derecho, político y constitucional* (1843; Lessons on Political and Constitutional Law). While in England he was influenced by the thinking of Montesquieu and the English utilitarians; his literary perspective was molded by the
English Romanticism then in vogue. He championed the liberalism and aesthetics
of Hugo, Scott, and particularly Byron, to Spanish intellectuals who wished to
return to the Christian idealism of *Siglo de Oro (Golden Age) literature. Together
with Joaquín de *Mora, he participated in the controversy with Johann Nikelaus
*Böhl de Faber which opened the discussion of *Romanticism in Spain. His
prologue to *Rivas's *El moro expósito* is an eloquent attempt to present Romanticism as a modern phenomenon associated with liberalism and with contemporary politics and philosophical issues. His statement that Romantic poetry
arises out of an inner turmoil within the poet was an important step towards the
understanding of that movement.

Other books by Alcalá Galiano include his posthumously published memoirs,
*Recuerdos de un anciano* (1878; Recollections of an Old Man) and *Memorias*
(1886; Memoirs); both are interesting accounts of the period. Besides his poetry,
*Poesías* (nd.; Poems), he also translated and amplified the *Historia de España*
by Dunham—the last volumes (5–8) are totally by him and constitute an excellent
study of eighteenth- and early nineteenth-c. Spanish history.

BIBLIOGRAPHY

Primary Texts

*Conferencias y ensayos.* Madrid: n.p., 1919.
*Discursos leídos de ingreso.* Madrid: RAE, 1864.
*Literatura española Siglo XIX.* Ed. Vicente Lloréns. Madrid: Alianza, 1969.
*Obras escogidas.* Ed. Jorge Campos. BAE 83 & 84.
*Recuerdos de un anciano.* Buenos Aires: Espasa-Calpe, 1951.

English Translation

*An Introductory Lecture in the University of London, Nov. 15, 1828.* 2nd ed. London: Taylor, 1829.

Criticism

Díez del Corral, Luis. *El liberalismo doctrinario.* Madrid: Instituto de Estudios Políticos, 1945.
García Barrón, Carlos. *La obra crítica y literaria de don Antonio Alcalá Galiano.* Madrid: Gredos, 1970.
Marías, Julián. "Antonio Alcalá Galiano." In *Meditaciones sobre la sociedad española.* Madrid: Alianza, 1966.
Ximénez de Sandoval, F. *Alcalá Galiano: El hombre que no llegó.* Madrid: Espasa-Calpe, 1948.

**ALCALÁ Y HERRERA, Alonso** (1599, Lisbon–1682, Alcalá), poet and short story writer. Noted for his baroque excess and artifice, his five novelettes, contained in *Varios effetos de amor* (1641; Various Effects of Love), are each written with a different missing vowel. His poetry appears in his *Jardín ana-gramático de divinas flores lusitanas, españolas y latinas* (1654; Anagramatic Garden of Divine Lusitanian, Spanish and Latin Flowers). The precedent for writing without the use of a particular vowel is found in the *picaresque novel, *La vida de *Estebanillo González.*

BIBLIOGRAPHY

Primary Texts

*Jardín anagramático.* . . . Lisbon: Craesbeeckiana, 1654.
*Varios effetos de amor en cinco novelas exemplares.* Lisbon: M. da Sylva, 1641.

**ALCALÁ YÁÑEZ Y RIVERA, Jerónimo de** (1563, Segovia–1632, Segovia), physician and writer. He studied medicine in Segovia and later practiced in Valencia. Alcalá composed minor devotional literature such as *Los milagros de Nuestra Señora de la Fuencisla* (1615; Miracles of Our Lady of Fuencisla), and *Verdades para la vida cristiana* (1632; Truths for the Life of a Christian). He is best known for a *picaresque novel, *Alonso, mozo de muchos amos* (*The Life and Adventures of Alonso the Chattering Lay Brother and Servant of Many Masters,* 1844–45). The first part of *Alonso* appeared in Madrid in 1624, when its author was 61; part two followed in 1626, in Valencia. Unlike most picaresque narratives, this good-humored tale is in dialogue form; it suffers, however, from a lack of focus and absence of evolution in the hero.

BIBLIOGRAPHY

Primary Texts

*Alonso, mozo de muchos amos.* Crit. ed. by J. H. Utley. Diss. U of Illinois, 1938.
*El donado hablador Alonso.* BAE 33.

English Translation

*The Life and Adventures of Alonso the Chattering Lay Brother and Servant of Many Masters.* New York: Christy, 1844–45.

**ALCÁNTARA, San Pedro de.** *See* Pedro de Alcántara, San

**ALCÁZAR, Baltasar del** (1530, Seville–1606, Seville), poet, soldier and administrator. His light, humorous verse belongs to the classical tradition of jocund poetry in imitation of Martial and Horace. He praises good food, worldly comforts and love's delights in works such as *La cena jocosa (En Jaén donde resido* (n.d.; The Festive Meal [In Jaén Where I Live]), *A dos corcovados* (n.d.; To Two Hunchbacks), *Tres cosas me tienen preso, A Constanza, A Magdalena, A una dama* (n.d.; Three Things Hold Me Captive, to Constance, to Magdalene, to a Lady).

BIBLIOGRAPHY

Primary Text

*Poesías.* Ed. Rodríguez Marín. Madrid: RAE, 1910.

**ALCOCER, Pedro de** (fl. 1555, Toledo– ), historian. He is author of the richly documented *Historia de la imperial ciudad de Toledo* (1554; History of the Imperial City of Toledo) and the *Relación de las cosas que pasaron en estos reinos desde que murió doña Isabel hasta que acabaron las Comunidades* (Report of What Happened in These Kingdoms from the Death of Isabel Up To the End of the Peoples' Uprisings). The latter was not published for over four hundred years.

BIBLIOGRAPHY

Primary Texts

*Hystoria, o descripción . . . de Toledo.* Toledo: Ferrer, 1554.
*Relación . . . las Comunidades.* Ed. A. Martín Gamero. Seville: Tarascó, 1872.

**ALCOVER I MASPONS, Joan** (1824, Palma de Mallorca–1926, Palma de Mallorca), Catalan poet, biographer and essayist. The son of a prominent magistrate, he was trained as a lawyer and devoted many years to the practice of this profession, beginning to write in Catalan around the turn of the c. His name is linked with that of Miguel *Costa i Llobera as a major representative of the Catalan Renaissance in Mallorca, and the two contributed poems (later set to music) which are the equivalent of the "national anthems" of Mallorca (Alcover's is "La Balanguera" [The Spinning Girl]). An important element of Alcover's poetic inspiration is bereavement: he married young, fathering five children, of whom four died, as did his first wife. His deeply felt grief is expressed in finely crafted *Elegies* as well as a few other poems in his collected *Poesies* (1921). Touches of instinctive Parnassianism appear in his poems, although his prose writing resembles later aspects of European Modernism. Alcover also drew inspiration from the Bible, from nature, from landscapes, and from popular figures. Three collections of poems in Castilian were published before Alcover began to write the compositions in Catalan for which he is most remembered: the former include *Poesías* (1887; 2nd ed. 1892; Poems), *Poemas y armonías* (1894; Poems and Harmonies), and *Meteoros* (1901; Meteors); the latter are *Cap al tard* (1909; Close to Twilight) and *Poemes biblics* (1918; Biblical Poems), the fruit of a more serene old age. *See also* Catalan Literature.

BIBLIOGRAPHY

Primary Text

*Obres Completes.* Barcelona: n.p., 1951.

Janet Pérez

**ALDANA, Francisco de** (1537, Alcántara–1578, Morocco), soldier and poet. Aldana's poetry, at times strikingly original, was collected and published by his brother Cosme, first in Milan (1589) and then in Madrid (1591). *Pastoral love sonnets and heroic poems exalting Spain's destiny and empire abound. His religious, meditative verse, such as the *Epístola a Arias Montano* (Epistle to *Arias Montano), is heavily neo-Platonic and contemplative. His contemporaries greatly admired him; *Cervantes called him "el Divino" (the Divine One) and equated him to *Garcilaso de la Vega, Fernando de *Herrera and Francisco de *Figueroa. *Quevedo intended to re-edit his works, and Lope de *Vega spoke of him in *El laurel de Apolo.* Aldana perished in battle. *See also* Ascetical Literature; Platonism.

BIBLIOGRAPHY

Primary Texts

*Obras completas.* Ed. M. Moragón Maestre. Madrid: CSIC, 1953.
*Poesías.* Ed. E. L. Rivers. Clásicos Castellanos 143. Madrid: Espasa-Calpe, 1957.

Criticism

Moñino, A. R. "Francisco de Aldana (1537–1578)." *Castilla* (Valladolid) 2.3 & 4 (1943): 57–137.
Rivers, E. L. *Francisco de Aldana, el divino capitán.* Badajoz: Instituto de Servicios Culturales, 1955.

**ALDECOA, José Ignacio** (1925, Vitoria/Alava–1969, Madrid), novelist and short story writer. Involved in literature since childhood, Aldecoa entered the U of Salamanca in 1942, changing to that of Madrid in 1945, where he became involved in the *postista* movement in poetry. *Todavía la vida* (1947; Yet Life), his first volume of verse, was followed by several short stories and *Libro de las algas* (1949; Book of Algae), his last poetry collection. In 1952 he married Josefina Rodríguez (later a writer), and began to write commercially. His first recognized novel, *El fulgor y la sangre* (1954; Glare and Blood), is part of an unfinished trilogy, together with its sequel, *Con el viento solano* (1956; With the Desert Wind). A corporal of the Guardia Civil (Spanish police force) is killed by a gypsy delinquent, providing the basic situations for the two novels (and presumably the unpublished third part). The first novel studies reactions to the news by wives of the civil guards, who do not know which of their men is the victim, while the second novel presents the consequences from the perspective of the murderer: flight, rejection by his own people fearful of the law, desperation and ultimate capture. In the interim between these novels appeared two story collections, *Espera de tercera clase* (1955; Third-Class Waiting Room) and *Vísperas del silencio* (1955; Vespers before the Silence), both of which incorporate previously published tales as well as new material. *Gran Sol* (1957; Great Sole), Aldecoa's third novel, portrays life on a Cantabrian fishing vessel during a regular trip to the cod fishing area, "Great Sole," off the Banks of Newfoundland. Written in Objectivist (impassive, neo-Realist) fashion, *Gran Sol* (together with *El Jarama* of *Sánchez-Ferlosio) is a technical high point of Objectivism in Spain, with its masterful re-creation of the monotony, boredom and triviality of everyday conversation and shipboard routine in the lives of the men confined to their narrow quarters. Aldecoa's enduring love of the sea and his knowledge of its people appear again in *Parte de una historia* (1967; Part of a Story), his last novel. These two were planned as parts of another trilogy, truncated by Aldecoa's death from a heart ailment at age 44.

Aldecoa's greatest achievement is his short stories, masterfully crafted brief fiction which already achieved recognition during his lifetime. Since his death, his fame has grown considerably. *El corazón y otros frutos amargos* (1959; The Heart and Other Bitter Fruits), *Caballo de pica* (1961; The Picador's Horse) and *Arqueología* (1961; Archaeology) show some influence of Objectivism, while a far more sardonic and burlesque attitude is evinced in *Los Pájaros de Baden-Baden* (1965; The Birds of Baden-Baden), which portrays the parasitic life of tourists and the bourgeoisie in the Balearic Islands. In *Santa Olaja de acero y otras historias* (1968; Saint Olaja Made of Steel and Other Stories), Aldecoa returns to his portraits of lower-class subjects. His stories, masterpieces of condensed narrative and artistic elaboration, most often portray the sufferings of humble people, although there is a growing tendency in the later collections to parody the *dolce vita* of the wealthy. *Cuaderno de godo* (1961; Gothic Notebook) and *El país vasco* (1962; The Basque Country) are travel books on the Canaries and Aldecoa's native Basque region, respectively. *Neutral Corner* (1962; only the title is in English) is a half-narrative, half-documentary, attesting to the writer's strong interest in prizefighting. A superb stylist, Aldecoa achieved heights of excellence with his short fiction rivaled only by the works of Francisco *Ayala.

BIBLIOGRAPHY

Primary Texts

*Cuentos completos*. Ed. A. Bleiberg. 2 vols. Madrid: Alianza, 1973.
*La tierra de nadie y otros relatos*. Barcelona: Salvat, 1970.

English Translation

"Poor Men's Calling." *Arena* 23 (1965): 3–9.

Criticism

Borau, P. *El existencialismo en la novela de Ignacio Aldecoa*. Zaragoza: Talleres Gráficos, 1974.
Carlisle, C. R. *Ecos del viento, silencios del mar: la novelística de Ignacio Aldecoa*. Madrid: Playor, 1976.
Fiddian, R. *Ignacio Aldecoa*. TWAS 529. Boston: Twayne, 1979.
García Viño, M. *Ignacio Aldecoa*. Madrid: EPESA, 1972.
Landeira, R., and C. Mellizo, eds. *Ignacio Aldecoa: A Collection of Critical Essays*. Laramie: U of Wyoming P, 1977.
Lasagabáster, J. M. *La novela de Ignacio Aldecoa: De la mímesis al símbolo*. Madrid: Sociedad General Española de Librería, 1978.
Lytra, D. *Soledad y convivencia en la obra de Aldecoa*. Madrid: Fundación Universitaria Española, 1979.
————, ed. *Aproximación crítica a Ignacio Aldecoa*. Madrid: Espasa-Calpe, 1984.

Janet Pérez

**ALDERETE, Bernardo José de** (1565, Malaga–1641?, Cordoba), antiquary, theologian, linguist. In 1614 he became canon of the Cathedral of Córdoba. In a cultivated prose he wrote *Varias antigüedades de España, Africa y otras provincias* (1614; Some Antiquities of Spain, Africa and Other Provinces) and *Del origen y principio de la lengua castellana o romance que hoy se usa en España* (1606; On the Origin and Beginning of the Castilian or Romance Language Used Today in Spain). The latter has been a valuable source for subsequent philologists.

BIBLIOGRAPHY

Primary Texts

*Varias antigüedades de España. . . .* Antwerp: Hasrey, 1614.
*Vocablos godos. . . .* In *Orígenes de la lengua española*. Ed. G. Mayáns y Siscar. Prol. E. Hartzenbusch. Madrid: Suárez, 1873.

**ALEIXANDRE, Vicente** (1898, Seville–1984, Madrid), poet. Aleixandre lived in Málaga and later Madrid. He taught mercantile law. A grave illness forced his retirement, and thereafter he dedicated himself almost exclusively to writing poetry. Aleixandre was a member of the Spanish Royal Academy (*Academia Española), and in 1977 he won the Nobel Prize for Literature.

In his first work, *Ambito* (1928; Ambit), we see the poet, victimized by his biologically limited libidinal energy and repressed existence, yearning for light and love. Although these poems exude, at times, a traditional almost classic ambience, they prefigure, through an elusive imagery and constant chiaroscuro, what some have seen as Aleixandre's surrealistic vision of cosmic love, as he attempts to fuse with his beloved universe.

*Pasión de la tierra* (1935; Passion of the Earth) reflects a creative chaos, irrational and jarring metaphors, and Freudian and surrealistic elements based on subconscious associations and dream sequences, which in turn express telluric and human elements, both creative and destructive. The poet opposes these human and elemental primitive forces in an attempt to overcome loneliness. He strives to escape erotic limits, and, as in his previous volume, the opaque labyrinth of night in order to search passionately for light and love.

*Espadas como labios* (1932; Swords Like Lips) juxtaposes love and death yet again and allows us a glimpse of an irrational and erotic pantheism in which they become interchangeable.

*La destrucción o el amor* (1935; *Destruction or Love*, 1977) depicts unleashed cosmic forces in a mysterious universe where nature is both destroyed and engendered, and death becomes the final transfiguration of love. Aleixandre establishes a cosmic hierarchy in which the inanimate triumphs over the living, for man finds himself hemmed in by the limits of life and the reality of nature. Some see in this volume a kind of mystic pantheism; others a spiritualization of the physical; but the amorous unity engenders an internal logic of its own. Filled with light and darkness, this collection, beyond its violence and anger, shows us that love is an all-consuming force and man's best hope for identification with the natural world.

*Mundo a solas* (1950; World Alone) de-emphasizes man's presence as a component of its virginal and elemental world of light and purity. Dealing with erotic and physical pleasure as well as with psychological death, its difficult symbols remind us of the enigmas which beset us all in our search for fulfillment through love, a salvation offered by nature which we are incapable of achieving because of telluric destructive impulses.

*Sombra del paraíso* (1944; Shadow of Paradise), a masterpiece of chiaroscuro and metaphorical experimentation, portrays a purified prehuman world of beauty, serenity, innocence, and love, though only through a half-glimpsed and shadowy recall. Filled with ecstatic states, this poetic creation nonetheless reveals the human ego outmatched by elemental forces, unable to regain a lost happiness and the visionary landscape of a Paradise filled with an amatory symbolism and luminescence. Yet, as the poet explores the metaphysical content of this shadow world, he tries to recapture an unconscious knowledge and to achieve a spiritual resurrection.

His next three collections, beginning with *Nacimiento último* (1953; Final Birth), which closes his cosmic cycle, explore the human world, and Aleixandre first examines the idea of birth into death as an aspect of human destiny. In *Historia del corazón* (1954; History of the Heart), Aleixandre emphasizes the historical aspects of existence and the joys and sorrows of human love in a temporal rather than cosmic universe. *En un vasto dominio* (1962; In a Vast Dominion) finally unites the human and the cosmic, establishing unity and order through love. Humanity becomes a part of the material world, a double reality involving space and time in a constantly fluctuating cosmos.

*Poemas de la consumación* (1968; Poems of Consummation) involves epistemological preoccupations for the aging poet who faces an approaching death. Aleixandre muses on the nature of knowledge and its interpretation, contrasting doubt and hope, youth and old age, sterility and innocence, life and death. He offers no final solutions, for, in the final analysis, life and not wisdom holds the answers.

In his final collection of poetry, *Diálogos del conocimiento* (1974; Dialogues of Knowledge), the poet introduces a number of speakers who, in their mono-logues, reinforce the contrast between sensual and reflective man. Aleixandre constantly juxtaposes intuitive, existential, cynical, idealistic and transcendental views in his search for truth and for ultimate knowledge in a universe of rupture and continuity.

Aleixandre's poetry comprises a single body of vast proportions, whatever the emphasis of his individual volumes. In his cosmic vision, embracing human and universal imperatives, he attempts to synthesize the disparate elements of a series of oppositions which reflect the dichotomy between feeling and commu-nication, the conscious and the unconscious, the Apollonian and the Dionysian, youth and old age, good and evil, light and darkness, despair and hope, negation and affirmation. In his voyage through time toward death in an ambivalent universe of heterogeneous limits, the poet discovers, nonetheless, that *thanatos* and *eros* are identical and that man's sublimation of his erotic impulse identifies him as a cosmic being who seeks communion and a metaphysical union with nature. But, whatever the metaphysical interpretation, the poet, a physical and psychological entity, confronts his own impotence, aging, and death.

In his cosmic comparisons and contrasts Aleixandre, through a dizzying series of irrational sequences and strange metaphors, affords us a glimpse of invariable truths by combining the instinctive poetic vision of innocence with the experi-enced one of adult knowledge.

BIBLIOGRAPHY

Primary Texts

*Ambito*. Málaga: Litoral, 1928.
*Diálogos del conocimiento*. Barcelona: Plaza y Janés, 1974.
*En un vasto dominio*. Madrid: RO, 1962.
*Historia del corazón*. Madrid: Espasa-Calpe, 1954.
*La destrucción o el amor*. Madrid: Signo, 1935.
*Los encuentros*. Madrid: Guadarrama, 1958.
*Mundo a solas*. Madrid: Clan, 1950.
*Nacimiento último*. Madrid: Insula, 1953.
*Pasión de la tierra*. Mexico: Fábula, 1935.
*Poemas de la consumación*. Barcelona: Plaza y Janés, 1968.
*Retratos con nombre*. Barcelona: El Bardo, 1965.
*Sombra del paraíso*. Madrid: Adán, 1944.

English Translations

*The Crackling Sun*. Tr. L. Bourne. Madrid: Sociedad General Española de Librería, 1981.
*Destruction or Love*. Tr. S. Kessler. Santa Cruz, CA: Green Horse, 1977.

*A Longing for the Light. Selected Poems of Vicente Aleixandre*. Ed. L. Hyde. New York: Harper and Row, 1979.

"Poems by Vicente Aleixandre." Tr. B. Belitt, A. Brilliant, D. A. Yates, M. Rukeyser, W. Barnstone. *Mundus Artium II* (Summer 1969): 6–59.

*Twenty Poems*. Tr. L. Hyde and R. Bly. Madison, MN: Seventies, 1977.

Criticism

Bousoño, C. *La poesía de Vicente Aleixandre*. Madrid: Gredos, 1977.

Cabrera, V., and H. Boyar, ed. *Critical Views on Vicente Aleixandre's Poetry*. Lincoln, NE: Society of Spanish and Spanish-American Studies, 1979.

Daydi-Tolson, S., ed. *Vicente Aleixandre. A Critical Appraisal*. Ypsilanti, MI: Bilingual, 1981.

Jiménez, J. O. *Vicente Aleixandre*. Madrid: Júcar, 1981.

Luis, L. de. *Vida y obra de Vicente Aleixandre*. Madrid: EPESA, 1970.

Puccini, D. *La palabra poética de Vicente Aleixandre*. Barcelona: Ariel, 1979.

Schwartz, K. *Vicente Aleixandre*. TWAS 85. New York: Twayne, 1970.

Kessel Schwartz

*ALEJANDRINO* (alexandrine), a type of poetry. *Alejandrinos* are verses of fourteen syllables divided into two hemistiches of seven syllables each. It forms the basis for the medieval *cuaderna vía* used by *Berceo, the *Arcipreste de Hita, and Pero *López de Ayala. Also known as the *mester de clerecía or *nueva maestría*, it probably entered Spain through the influence of the French clergy. In French prosody, however, the verse has only twelve syllables. The origin of the name is due to its presence in medieval poetry about Alexander the Great. The Romantics revived its use in the nineteenth c., and Rubén Darío recast it in this c. into a new rhythmical pattern, accentuating the third and sixth syllable of each hemistich in his famous *Sonatina*.

*ALELUYAS* (alleluias), a form of poetry. This two-line, octosyllabic verse in consonant rhyme is used in popular poetry or in the explanatory notes placed under religious pictures and drawings, to explain these to the masses.

**ALEMÁN, Mateo** (1547, Seville–1616?, Mexico), author of the *picaresque novel, *Guzmán de Alfarache (The Rogue or the life of Guzmán de Alfarache*, 1924). Son of the physician to the royal prison in Seville, Alemán studied medicine at Salamanca and Alcalá de Henares, and law at Seville. His frequent changes in career, his disastrous years as a civil servant and his poor judgment in commercial ventures resulted in constant debts and time spent in the royal prisons in Madrid and Seville. He married in 1571 in order to escape a debt. In 1582, hoping to improve his fortunes, he attempted to emigrate to the New World, but was denied permission because of his Jewish origins. In 1593 Alemán was appointed judge to investigate the inhumane working conditions of the galley slaves in the royal quicksilver mines at Almadén, administered by the German banking family of Fugger. Alemán's findings were ignored by the authorities, but probably influenced his novel. In spite of the success of the first part of

*Guzmán de Alfarache*, published in 1599 and appearing in 26 editions (some of them pirated), Alemán was imprisoned for his debts in 1602. In the same year, a Valencian lawyer, Juan Martí, published an apocryphal second part of the *Guzmán* under the pseudonym Mateo Luján de Sayavedra. Alemán's *La vida de San Antonio de Padua* (The life of Saint Anthony of Padua), written to fulfill a vow, was published in 1604, immediately followed by his second part of the life of Guzmán de Alfarache, subtitled *Atalaya de la vida humana* (Watchtower of Human Life). In 1607 Alemán obtained permission to emigrate to Mexico, probably through bribery, and left with his mistress, Francisca de Calderón, two children and a niece. His last published work was a biography of his patron, the Archbishop of Mexico, Fray García Guerra. The last document concerning Alemán's life indicates that he was still living in Mexico in 1615.

Alemán, like his contemporary *Cervantes, wrote his masterpiece relatively late in life, but unlike *Don Quijote*, *Guzmán de Alfarache* was its author's first serious literary effort, and its profound pessimism contrasts with Cervantes's humor and skepticism. Alemán's bitter distrust of humanity is reflected in his novel and in the emblem he chose, a spider and a serpent with the motto, "Ab insidiis non est prudentia" (There is no defense against treachery). An astute reader of *Lazarillo de Tormes*, Alemán saw the possibilities of the ironic structures of that work, and the social and aesthetic implications of narration by a lower-class protagonist in a serious work of fiction. It was, however, the printers who made the crucial connection between the two works by adding the word "pícaro" to the title of the first part, and printing the *Lazarillo* and *Guzmán* together. The structural symmetries of the *Lazarillo* are transformed into Guzmán's repetitions of the pattern of rising and falling, sin and repentance, acceptance and rejection of and by society. Américo *Castro's studies of the novel and its historical context show how, as a *converso in a society obsessed by purity of lineage, the protagonist's inability to escape his origins has social as well as theological significance. Guzmán narrates the family history that makes him a social outcast, his departure from home and initiation into the hypocrisy and corruption of the world as he serves various masters from Seville to Italy, from the lowliest to a cardinal in Rome. From his "watchtower," Guzmán simultaneously confesses his own moral fallibility and satirizes his society. He is always the "half-outsider" as Claudio Guillén defines the pícaro, using deceit to gain an advantage, while that same deceit causes him to lose each foothold toward security and respectability. He forfeits his position with the cardinal by committing a petty theft, and he abandons his religious vocation to marry a woman symbolically named Gracia (Grace), whom he later prostitutes. The second part ends with Guzmán serving a penal term rowing on the galleys. The older, and presumably wiser, Guzmán narrates the misadventures of Guzmanillo (Little Guzmán), interspersing the adventures with *consejos* (moralizing) and *exempla*. The novel includes interpolated narratives: the Moorish tale of Ozmín y Daraja and tales of love, jealousy, vengeance, and the wages of discord (drawn from Italian *novelle*) such as those of Dorido and Clorinia, Bonifacio and Dorotea, and Don Luis de Castro. The author's prologue reminds the reader that the sententious digressions and the exemplary anecdotes and novellas are as essential to the unity and interpretation of the work as the pícaro's adventures. Eighteenth- and nineteenth-c. translators and editors mistakenly omitted or bracketed the digressions, but twentieth-c. critics have sought to restore the unity of the Guzmán through analysis of its complex rhetorical and conceptual structure.

The first person narration of the pícaro's life in *Guzmán de Alfarache* has contributed to the controversies over its interpretation. Since the narrator-protagonist claims to have repented of his sinful life at the end of the second part of the novel, presenting his betrayal of a group of mutinous fellow galley slaves as a sign of his rejection of wrongdoing, it would seem that the narrator has acquired a morally superior point of view. Taking seriously the narrator's claim to have repented and applying the model of Augustinian confession to picaresque narrative, Enrique Moreno Báez and A. A. Parker interpret the work as representative of Counter-Reformation theology, demonstrating the doctrines of free will and divine grace and the possibility of salvation for the sinful protagonist no matter how often he fails to repent. Joan Arias, Benito Brancaforte, Américo Castro, Edmond Cros, Carroll Johnson, Fernando Lázaro Carreter, and Francisco Rico point out the profound linguistic, rhetorical, structural, psycho-logical and thematic ambivalence of the work, calling into question the final "conversion" of the protagonist-narrator, and the supposed moral authority of the narrator-protagonist. The promise of a third part leaves the ending of the novel open, implying more of the same deceitful way of life.

## BIBLIOGRAPHY

### Primary Texts

*Guzmán de Alfarache*. Ed. Benito Brancaforte. 2 vols. Madrid: Cátedra, 1979.

*Odas de Horacio, traduzidas por Mateo Alemán* [Madrid, 1598?]. Ed. R. Foulché-Delbosc. *RH* 42 (1918): 482–85.

*Ortografía castellana*. Mexico: Ieronimo Balli, 1609. (Ed. José Rojas Garcidueñas, intro. Tomás Navarro. Mexico: Colegio de México, 1950.)

*Primera Parte de Guzmán de Alfarache*. Madrid: Várez de Castro, 1599.

Prologue to Alonso de Barros. *Proverbios morales*. Madrid: Sánchez, 1598.

*San Antonio de Padua*. Seville: Clemente Hidalgo, 1604.

*Segunda parte de la vida de Guzmán de Alfarache, atalaya de la vida umana por Mateo Alemán su verdadero Autor*. Lisbon: Pedro Crasbeeck, 1604.

*Sucesos de d. Frai Garcia G[u]er[r]a arçobispo de Mejico, a cuyo cargo estuvo el govierno de la Nueva España*. Mexico: Viuda de Pedro Balli, 1613. (Ed. Alice J. Bushee, *RH* 25 [1911]: 359–457.)

### English Translation

*The Rogue or the life of Guzman de Alfarache*. Tr. James Mabbe. 2 vols. London: Edward Blount, 1622–23. (Ed. James Fitzmaurice Kelly. 4 vols. London: Nut, 1924.)

### Criticism

Arias, Joan. *Guzmán de Alfarache: The Unrepentant Narrator*. Prol. J. H. Silverman. London: Tamesis, 1977.

Castro, Américo. *Cervantes y los casticismos españoles*. Barcelona: Alfaguara, 1966.
Cros, Edmond. *Mateo Alemán: Introducción a su vida y a su obra*. Salamanca: Anaya, 1971.
———. *Protée et les gueux. Recherches sur les origines et la nature du récit picaresque dans Guzmán de Alfarache*. Paris: Didier, 1967.
Guillén, Claudio. "Genre and Countergenre: The Discovery of the Picaresque." In *Literature as System. Essays Toward the Theory of Literary History*. Princeton: Princeton UP, 1971.
Johnson, Carroll B. *Inside Guzmán de Alfarache*. Berkeley and Los Angeles: U of California P, 1978.
McGrady, Donald. *Mateo Alemán*. TWAS 48. New York: Twayne, 1968.
Moreno Báez, Enrique. *Lección y sentido del Guzmán de Alfarache*. Madrid: CSIC, 1948.
Parker, Alexander A. *Literature and the Delinquent*. Edinburgh: Edinburgh UP, 1967.
Rico, Francisco. Introduction to *La novela picaresca española*. Barcelona: Planeta, 1967.
———. *The Spanish Picaresque Novel and the Point of View*. Tr. Charles Davis, with Harry Sieber. Cambridge: Cambridge UP, 1984.

Emilie Bergmann

**ALEMÁN SÁINZ, Francisco** (1919, Murcia– ), biographer, novelist and short story writer. His biographies include *Saavedra Fajardo y otras vidas de Murcia* (1949; Saavedra Fajardo and Other Lives from Murcia) and *Gálvez, Tornel, Maestro (tres vidas del siglo XIX)* (1950; Gálvez, Tornel, Maestro [Three Nineteenth-Century Lives]). His novel *El sereno loco* (The Crazy Nightwatchman) received the Gabriel Miró prize. His short stories are collected in *La vaca y el sarcófago* (1952; The Cow and the Sarcophagus), *Cuando llegue el verano* (1953; When Summer Arrives), and *Patio de luces y otros relatos* (1957; Illuminated Patio and other Tales).

BIBLIOGRAPHY

Primary Texts

*Cuando llegue el verano.* . . . Murcia: Patronato de cultura . . . , 1953.
*Gálvez, Tornel.* . . . Murcia: Nogués, 1950.
*Patio de luces y otros relatos.* Murcia: Patronato de cultura . . . , 1957.
*Regreso al futuro.* Murcia: Nogués, 1969.
*Saavedra Fajardo.* . . . Murcia: La verdad, 1949.
*La vaca y el sarcófago. 12 cuentos.* Murcia: n.p., 1952.

Sara Schyfter

**ALEXANDRE, Libro de** (Book of Alexander), a long narrative written in the *mester de clerecía*, between 1178 and 1250. It has come down to us in two mss., called P and O respectively, and three fragments. Neither of the two mss. appears to be the original one. Ms. O is the older copy; it was written around the end of the thirteenth and the beginning of the fourteenth c., and contains 2,510 stanzas of *cuaderna vía* and two letters. This ms. O, so-called because it once belonged to the Duke of Osuna, was also known to the Marquis of *Santillana and is described by Mario Schiff in his book. Ms. P was written in a fifteenth-c. hand and contains 2,639 stanzas of *cuaderna vía*. Although it is a later copy, P is usually considered to be the more reliable version. P and O complement each other so as to make an intelligible whole. A most reassuring way of reading the *Libro de Alexandre* is in the excellent paleographic edition by R. S. Willis, Jr., which has ms. P on one side of the page and ms. O on the opposite side, with the fragments at the bottom, so that one can usually be rewarded instantly by having a suspicious reading corrected by another version.

The *Libro de Alexandre* was composed between 1178, the earliest date of composition of one of the main sources, and 1250, which is the approximate date of composition of the *Poema de *Fernán González*, whose author made use of the *Libro de Alexandre*. The Alexandre in the title refers to the legendary Alexander the Great who was a pupil of Aristotle, and who during a short lifetime (356–323 B.C.) conquered most of the known world. There was, within one hundred years of Alexander's death, a great proliferation of literature, both historical and fictional, concerning the Macedonian king, and many of these early accounts have survived. The earliest known romance about Alexander was written sometime around 200 B.C. in Greek, by an Egyptian living at Alexandria. This romance was soon translated into thirty languages, and because it was often wrongly attributed to Callisthenes (nephew of Aristotle) it has come to be called the pseudo-Callisthenes. Two important translations into Latin were made of the pseudo-Callisthenes, one in the fourth c. A.D. by Julius Valerius called *Res Gestae Alexandri Macedonis*, and the other by the archpriest Leo of Naples in the tenth c. A.D. called the *Historia de Proeliis*. In addition to these popular romances there exist several historical accounts of the life of Alexander the Great, by Arrian (based on a biography by Ptolemy, who was one of Alexander's generals), by Plutarch, Diodorus, Quintus Curtius, and Justinus. Toward the end of the twelfth c. A.D. Gautier de Châtillon, using the historical account by Quintus Curtius as his main source, wrote an epic poem in Latin about the life of Alexander which he called the *Alexandreis*. It was this poem by Gautier which served as the principal source for the *Libro de Alexandre*. I say "principal source" precisely because it was by no means the only work referred to by the author of the *Libro de Alexandre*. The method employed by our author was to give an account of the greatest things that he had read and heard, or to put it in his own words: "el uno que leyemos, el otro que oyemos / de las mayores cosas Recabdo vos daremos." Source studies indicate that he was acquainted not only with Gautier de Châtillon's work but also with the *Historia de Proeliis,* with Quintius Curtius, Flavius Josephus, the *Pindarus Thebanus,* Isidore of Seville, and others. Thus, with the Spanish *Libro de Alexandre* we are faced with an accumulation of some fifteen hundred years of tradition concerning the life and legend of Alexander the Great. The *Libro de Alexandre* begins with a short introduction of six stanzas and then proceeds in strict chronological order from an account of the birth and infancy to the death of Alexander, ending with a brief conclusion in seven stanzas. There are many digressions for descriptions, authorial intrusions, and incidental demonstrations of contemporary erudition, but these are all effected so as not to disrupt the smooth, chronological flow of narration, and in such a way that the figure of the authorship of the work is a very vexing one. Claims have been made for the authorship of Gonzalo de *Berceo and Juan Lorenzo de Astorga, but the problem remains unresolved.

BIBLIOGRAPHY

Primary Text

*Libro de Alexandre.* Ed. R. S. Willis. Princeton: Princeton UP, 1934.

Criticism

Michael, Ian. *The Treatment of Classical Material in the* Libro de Alexandre. Manchester: Manchester UP, 1970.
Sas, Louis F. *Vocabulario del* Libro de Alexandre. Madrid: Academia Española, 1976.
Schiff, M. *La Bibliothèque du Marquis de Santillane.* Paris: E. Bouillon, 1905.

Colbert Nepaulsingh


**ALFARO, José María** (1905, Burgos– ). A career diplomat who represented Spain as ambassador to Argentina during the Franco era, Alfaro is known primarily as a journalist and poet. A long-time collaborator of the major Madrid daily, *El Sol*, he was also director of the literary review *Escorial* in the early post-war years. His poems appeared for the most part in little magazines. Alfaro is credited with a novel entitled *Leoncio Pancorbo* (1942).

BIBLIOGRAPHY

Primary Text

*Leoncio Pancorbo.* Madrid: Nacional, 1942.


**ALFARO, María** (1900, Gijón– ), poet, novelist, critic and essayist. Beginning as a literary critic for *El Sol*, Madrid's major daily in the pre-war era, Alfaro later lived in Paris where she directed a literary segment for Radio Mundial (World Radio). Travel in the United States sharpened her English, and she has translated novels of Mark Twain to Spanish, as well as some of Corneille's plays from the French. Her works of poetry include *Poemas del recuerdo* (1951; Poems of Memory) and *Poemas líricos: selección, versión y prólogo* (1945; Lyric Poems: Selection, Version and Prologue). Alfaro has also published *Memorias de una muerte* (n.d.; Memoirs of a Death) and *Teatro mundial* (1961; World Theater).

BIBLIOGRAPHY

Primary Texts

*Memorias de una muerte.* Spain: n.p., n.d.
*Poemas líricos.* Madrid: Hispánica, 1945.

*Poemas del recuerdo.* Madrid: Méndez, 1951.
*Teatro mundial.* Madrid: Aguilar, 1961.

Janet Pérez

**ALFONSO, Pero** (1062, Huesca–1110, ?), *converso* writer. Rabbi Moses Sefardi was baptized in 1106, and then took Petrus Alfonsi as a name. He is the author of *Disciplina clericalis* (Instruction on Life for the Educated), an important collection of Persian and Arabic tales that initiates the Spanish fascination with oriental narrative. The work has survived in more than sixty mss., clear demonstration of its enormous popularity. It contains thirty-three stories, many of a licentious nature, recounted in an unsophisticated Latin. Storytellers and moralists throughout Europe utilized the collection; in Spain, it was a source for works such as *Calila e Digna, Sendebar,* and the writing of *Juan Manuel. See also* Hispano-Judaic Literature.

BIBLIOGRAPHY

Primary Text

*Pedro Alfonso* Disciplina Clericalis. Ed., tr. to Spanish by A. González Palencia. Madrid/ Granada: CSIC, 1948.

English Translation

*The* Disciplina Clericalis *of Petrus Alfonsi.* Ed. & tr. E. Hermes. Eng. tr. by P. R. Quarrie. Berkeley: U of California P, 1977.

Criticism

Schwarzbaum, H. "International Folklore Motifs in Petrus Alfonsi's *Disciplina clericalis." Sefarad* 21 (1961): 267–99; 22 (1962): 17–59 and 321–44; 23 (1963): 54–73.

Maureen Ihrie

**ALFONSO ONCENO, Poema o crónica rimada de** (Poem or Chronicle in Verse of Alphonse the Eleventh), historical poem. Written in 1348, and numbering almost 10,000 lines, this last manifestation of *mester de juglaría* was probably translated by Ruy Yáñez (long considered the author) from the original Galician. The poem gives a historically accurate account of the reign of *Alphonse XI.

BIBLIOGRAPHY

Primary Texts

*Poema o crónica rimada de Alfonso onceno.* BAE 57.
*Poema o crónica rimada de Alfonso onceno.* Ed. Yo ten Cate. RFE Anejo 65. Madrid: CSIC, 1956.

Criticism

Catalán y Menéndez Pidal, Diego. *Poema de Alfonso XI; Fuentes, dialecto, estilo.* Madrid: Gredos, 1953.

**ALFONSO X, EL SABIO.** *See* Alphonse X, the Learned

**ALFONSO XI.** *See* Alphonse XI

*ALIXANDRE, Recontamiento del rey* (Narration of King Alexander), narrative based on the deeds of Alexander the Great. An example of *aljamía, the work was first published in 1888 by Guillén Robles. Greek and Persian legends provide much material for this rendition.

BIBLIOGRAPHY
  Primary Text
Guillén Robles, F. *Leyendas de José, hijo de Jacob, y de Alejandro Magno. . . .* Zaragoza:
    Hospicio provinciano, 1888.

**ALJAMÍA** (Arabic for ''indistinct,'' also used to describe foreign speech). Aljamiada literature refers to early Spanish literature in the Castilian language, but written with the Hebrew or Arabic alphabet, prevalent in the fourteenth to sixteenth centuries (e.g., *Poema de *Yuçuf; Recontamiento del rey *Alixandre). S. M. Stern's investigations of the *Kharjas* have traced aljamiada writing back to the tenth c. The phenomenon evolved because over the years Jews and Moors very often would adopt Castilian as their native tongue but continue to use Hebrew or Arabic script when writing.

**ALMADA NEGREIROS, José Sobral de** (1893, São Tomé–1970, Lisbon), artist, poet, dramatist, essayist. José Sobral de Almada Negreiros was born April 7, 1893, on the former Portuguese island of São Tomé, near the African continent. His father was a Portuguese government official and poet of Jewish ancestry, and his mother a well-to-do Eurafrican educated in Lisbon. He was sent to Lisbon when he was only two, prompting many biographers to assert that he was born in the capital. He attended the Jesuit College of Campolide for ten years, then the Lyceum at Coimbra and later the Escola Internacional da Rua da Emenda, Lisbon. He married fellow artist Sara Afonso.

An all-around man of arts and letters, he was a poet, novelist, short story writer, essayist, and dramatist, as well as a dancer, choreographer, illustrator, muralist and artist, working in many media, including stained glass and tapestries.

One of the most prominent members of Portugal's first generation of Modernists, he actively participated with his noted colleagues, Fernando *Pessoa and *Sá-Carneiro, as editor and contributor (with poems, essays and drawings) in numerous journals and newspapers, among them *Orpheu, Portugal Futurista* and *Contemporânea.* He also wrote some of the most thought-provoking poems (e.g., ''Mima-Fataxa'' and ''Cena do Ódio'') and manifestos (e.g., ''Manifesto Anti-Dantas,'' ''Ultimatum Futurista,'' ''Direção Única'') associated with the vanguard movement, urging his countrymen to renew themselves individually so that collectively there could be a new Portugal (''É preciso criar a pátria portuguêsa do século XX'').

Always active, and always writing, Almada Negreiros was a regular contributor to journals and magazines, but his literary production, although significant, is not extensive even if it is varied. A few of his poems were published separately as reprints, thus having their own separate identity as pamphlets or booklets. However, he prepared only two volumes for publication: *A Invenção do Dia Claro*, 1921—a book classified as poetry but made up almost entirely of narrative vignettes, some of which are properly regarded as prose poems—and his only novel, *Nome de Guerra* (which explores the masks a beautiful prostitute hides behind in order to endure her existence), written in 1925 but not published until 1938.

The task of collecting his scattered and unpublished literary production began just prior to his death in 1970. The first volume of his complete works appeared in 1970 and contains three short stories and one novelette, all of which appeared in print by 1921, and most as early as 1915. The second in the complete works series was his novel. Volume 3 contains theater: nine plays, written between 1924 and 1965. The fourth contains poetry. Of the thirty-four titles which appear, twenty-two were previously unpublished. Some selections when they first appeared in print were called prose by the author. Perhaps the distinction is not important, for Almada Negreiros often spoke against there being a clear line of demarcation between prose and poetry, or between literature and painting. The final volumes in his complete works contain essays, manifestos and criticism.

Almada's major contribution, however, is to art. He began his artistic career as a humorous illustrator and had his first exhibition when he was only eighteen. It was Fernando Pessoa who brought him recognition first, in a review published in *Á Aguia*, entitled "As caricaturas de Almada Negreiros."

The artistic period immediately preceding the advent of the first Modernist generation is characterized by the Realist, Naturalist and Symbolist schools. The major artists were Columbano (1857–1929) and Malhoa (1855–1933), but their imitators were academy painters of far less talent. Almada Negreiros and the Modernists attacked the formal schools, scandalizing the literary and artistic circles, and society in general, with their new ideas.

Almada Negreiros produced nearly all his literary works between 1911 and 1932. This was his combative period. His artistic production was also influenced by Futurism, Sensationism, Simultaneity (with influence from Picasso and Cubism). His recurring themes are Harlequin and Pierrot. His greatest desire was to renew Portugal and find the essence of truth: of Portugal, of reality. He was also obsessed with finding the key to the medieval paintings by Nuno Gonçalves. He published scandalous manifestos and, like his Modernist contemporaries, enjoyed shocking people. He studied in Paris from 1919 to 1920 and in Madrid from 1927 to 1932. His major works from this period included "Portrait of a Family" (1927), and the decorative panels in the Cinema San Carlos (Madrid, 1929).

When Almada returned from Spain, he was a mature, confident artist. Not leaving behind his Futurist ideas, he was successful in new media (stained glass and frescoes) on a large scale, incorporating historical and cultural themes into new forms. His works of art were conceived on a grand scale and focus on Portuguese culture. The major works of the period between 1933 and 1949 include the windows of Our Lady of Fátima Church (1938), the murals at the Diário de Notícias building, the post office, and the Lisbon Port-of-Entry, where the medieval ballad "A Nau Catarineta" is portrayed.

The final two decades of his life saw Almada turn to abstract and geometric designs for murals and tapestries. He continued to search for the key to culture. He explored Greek mystery religions, Masonry and numerology. After forty-four years of study, he announced the key to Nuno Gonçalves's paintings. His major works include "Fernando Pessoa" (1954), the murals at the administration building of the U of Lisbon (1961), and the mural entitled "Começar" (1969), found at the Gulbenkian Foundation.

Whether in his painting or in his writing, Almada Negreiros had a kind of intuitive sense of Portugal's cultural heritage and identity. With characteristic humor, he asserted that the Portuguese were the living descendants of the Greeks of old, that Homer was therefore Portuguese. He never forgot his early identification with the common man, and both his prose and poetry are characterized by colloquial or popular language, written in a short, telegraphic, linear style. Whether inciting his countrymen to renew themselves and enter into the modern era (which he accomplished with jibes, ironies, satires and humor), or probing the mysteries of ancient cultures and peoples, Almada was consistently original, frequently surprising, and always fresh. His ability to visualize the world as a plastic entity, decipherable by means of geometric measurements, gave him a positive outlook on life and a confidence which permitted him to approach anything, no matter how powerful, no matter how sacred, no matter how dangerous to himself. His daring, coupled with his considerable gifts, both artistic and intellectual, places him not only at the forefront of contemporary Portuguese cultural figures, but as one of the world's preeminent modern men.

## BIBLIOGRAPHY

### Primary Texts

*Contos e novelas.* Vol. 1 of *Obras Completas.* Lisbon: Estampa, 1970.
*Ensaios I.* Vol 5 of *Obras Completas.* Lisbon: Estampa, 1971.
*Poesia.* Vol. 4 of *Obras Completas.* Lisbon: Estampa, 1971.
*Romance, Nome de Guerra.* Vol. 2 of *Obras Completas.* Lisbon: Estampa, 1971.
*Teatro.* Vol. 3 of *Obras Completas.* Lisbon: Estampa, 1971.

### Criticism

Ambrósio, António. *Almada Negreiros Africano.* Lisbon: Estampa, 1979.
França, J. A. *Almada Negreiros.* Lisbon: Coleção de Arte Contemporânea, 1963.
―――. *A Arte em Portugal no Século XX.* Lisbon: Livraria Bertrand, 1974.

*Líricas Portuguesas.* 3rd series, vol. 1, ed. Jorge de Sena. Lisbon: Portugália, 1972.
Vasconcelos, Florido de. *História da Arte em Portugal.* Lisbon: Verbo, 1972.

Frederick G. Williams

**ALMAGRO SAN MARTÍN, Melchor** (1882, Granada–1947, Madrid), diplomat, author. He composed an interesting account of literary life in Madrid, the *Biografía del 1900* (1943; Biography of the Year 1900), based on his diary notes of that year. He is also remembered for historical writings and a small collection of modernist short stories, *Sombras de vida* (1903; Shadows of Life), with a prologue by *Valle-Inclán. See also Modernism.

BIBLIOGRAPHY

Primary Texts

*Biografía del 1900.* 2nd ed. Madrid: RO, 1944.
*Sombras de vida.* Intro. P. Gimferrer. Prol. Valle-Inclán. Granada: Diputación provincial de Granada, 1986. Facs. of 1943 ed.

Sara Schyfter

**ALOMAR, Gabriel** (1873, Palma de Mallorca–1940 or 1941, ?), political activist, poet, essayist. He wrote in both Spanish and Catalan and is author of *La columna de foc* (1904; Column of Fire), poetry; *El futurisme* (1905; Futurism), a speech given at the *Ateneo of Barcelona; *El frente espiritual* (1918; The Spiritual Front); *La pena de mort* (1912; The Death Penalty), to name a few of his writings. During the Republic, he served as Spanish ambassador to Rome and then later to Cairo. *See also* Catalan Literature.

BIBLIOGRAPHY

*La columna de foc.* Prol. S. Rusiñol. 2nd ed. Palma de Mallorca: Moll, 1973.
*El frente espiritual.* Tortosa: Monclús, 1918.
*El futurisme i altres assaigs.* Barcelona: Edicions 62, 1970.
*La pena de mort.* Intro. A. Serra. Palma de Mallorca: Mascaró Pasarius, 1972.

Sara Schyfter

**ALONSO, Amado** (1896, Lerín, Navarre–1952, Cambridge, MA). A former disciple of *Menéndez Pidal in the Madrid Centro de Estudios Históricos (Center for Historical Studies), Alonso devoted his life completely to teaching and to linguistic investigation. As director of the Institute for Philology at the U of Buenos Aires, he formed generations of future teachers and philologists for Argentina and other countries throughout the Americas. He organized and directed the study series Hispanoamerican Library of Dialectology, the Library of Philosophy and Theory of the Language, and various other similar series. In 1939, he founded the *Revista de Filología Hispánica*, one of the most important journals in its field and (a half-century later) a premier journal of Hispanism. When he moved to Mexico, it became the *Nueva Revista de Filología Hispánica*, also a distinguished scholarly journal.

Alonso published studies of phonetics and dialectology in various journals and reviews as well as the collections he founded. His own original contributions, as well as his translations of Vossler, Bally and other theoreticians, are the basis for scientific studies of stylistics in Spanish. Among his more important books are *El problema de la lengua en América* (1935; The Language Problem in America); *Poesía y estilo de Pablo Neruda* (1940; Poetry and Style in Pablo Neruda); *Castellano, español, idioma nacional* (1942; Castilian, Spanish, National Language); and *Problemas de dialectología hispanoamericana* (n.d.; Problems in Hispanoamerican Dialectology). His works of literary criticism include essays on Jorge *Guillén, Rubén Darío, Ramón del *Valle-Inclán and other contemporary writers. Alonso's scholarly contributions were recognized by the U of Chicago, which awarded him the title of Doctor *honoris causa*. From 1946 until his death, he was a professor at Harvard U.

BIBLIOGRAPHY

Primary Texts

*Castellano, español, idioma nacional*. 2nd ed. Buenos Aires: Losada, 1949.
*El problema de la lengua en América*. Madrid: Espasa-Calpe, 1935.
*Problemas de dialectología*. Buenos Aires: n.p., 1930.
"The Stylistic Interpretation of Literary Texts." *MLN* 57 (1942): 489–96.

Criticism

The *Revista de Filología Española*, 1 and 2 (1952), contains several articles which appeared at Alonso's death.

**ALONSO, Dámaso** (1898, Madrid–1990, Madrid), essayist, philologist, literary historian and poet. Another disciple of the great critical theorist *Menéndez Pidal in the Center for Historical Studies in Madrid, Alonso later became his mentor's collaborator. The holder of chairs in the Universities of Madrid and Valencia until his retirement in 1968, he also taught and lectured in several American and European universities. For many years, Alonso had been the senior member and director of the Royal Spanish Academy of the Language (*Academia Española) and was also a member of the Royal Academy of History. His scholarly achievements have been recognized by honorary doctorates from the Universities of Bourdeaux, Hamburg, Rome and Massachusetts.

Many of Alonso's works concern the Baroque poet *Góngora, on whom he is the primary authority. His critical edition of the latter's masterpiece, *Soledades* (1927; Solitudes), is a key work for understanding Góngora, as is his masterful study, *La lengua poética de Góngora* (1935; The Poetic Language of Góngora). Another major essay on the same figure is his study *Góngora y el "Polifemo"* (1960; Góngora and the "Polyphemus"). He has made major contributions toward a definitive biography of Góngora, as well as many other critical studies.

Alonso is ubiquitous in modern poetics and criticism, with works on *La poesía de San Juan de la Cruz* (1942; The Poetry of St. John of the Cross); *Ensayos sobre la poesía española* (1944; Essays on Spanish Poetry), one of his masterpieces; *Vida y obra de Medrano* (1948; The Life and Works of Medrano); and *Poesía española* (1950; Spanish Poetry), a major contribution to stylistic methodology. Other significant essays on poetics include *Seis calas en la expresión literaria española* in collaboration with Carlos *Bousoño (1951; Six Stages in Spanish Literary Expression); *Poetas españoles contemporáneos* (1952; Contemporary Spanish Poets); and *Primavera temprana de la Literatura Europea* (1961; Early Springtime of European Literature). In addition, Alonso wrote critical editions of Erasmus, Gil *Vicente and many others, as well as several volumes of collected articles and studies.

Alonso's original poetry comprises various collections: *Poemas puros: Poemillas de la ciudad* (1921; Pure Poems: Little Poems of the City); *Oscura noticia* (1944; Dark News); *Hijos de la ira* (1944; Children of Wrath), his most significant title; and *Hombre y Dios* (1955; Man and God), which brought together all of his lyrics to that date. *Hijos de la ira*, with the biblical allusion of the title, is a work of mixed religious and existential inspiration, full of anguished doubt, bitter despair, and penitence, addressing God in tones ranging from anger to impassioned love and desperate disillusionment (a characteristic found in much post-war protest poetry in Spain: unable to address their complaints to the dictator, the poets addressed them to God). Some poems are autobiographical, others have strong undertones of social criticism and denunciation of inequities and injustice. Most of Alonso's poems are written in unrhymed, irregular metrics, strongly cadenced. The aesthetic refinement and cult of the metaphor which characterize much of the poetry of the *Generation of 1927 appear in many of Alonso's poems, although others are humorous or ironic, with some verging upon the surrealistic, oneiric and hallucinatory.

BIBLIOGRAPHY

Primary Text

*Poemas escogidos* (Selected Poems). Madrid: Gredos, 1969.

Criticism

Canals, S. Olives, and S. S. Taylor, eds. *Who's Who in Spain*. Barcelona: Intercontinental, 1963.
Debicki, Andrew P. *Dámaso Alonso*. TWAS 126. New York: Twayne, 1970.
———. "Dámaso Alonso's Views on Poetry." *HR* 34 (1966): 111–20.
Flys, M. J. *La poesía existencial de Dámaso Alonso*. Madrid: Gredos, 1968.
Ley, C. D. *Spanish Poetry since 1939*. Washington, DC: Catholic UP, 1962. 45–49.

Janet Pérez

**ALONSO, Luis Ricardo** (1929, Parres, Asturias– ), lawyer, journalist, novelist. Alonso resided for many years in Cuba, becoming ambassador of the Castro regime in London, Norway and Peru before breaking with the revolutionary government. A political refugee in the United States, he became a professor of Spanish, and produced a number of politically oriented novels, including *El candidato* (1970; *The Candidate*, 1972) the diary of a man who intends to assassinate a U.S. presidential candidate; *Los dioses ajenos* (1971; Alien Gods), a view of Cuban exiles in the United States, presented in counterpoint with their past in the Cuba of Batista; and *El palacio y la furia* (1976; The Palace and the Fury), set in Havana under the Batista regime, with a young priest as protagonist, collaborating with clandestine revolutionary elements to plan an assault on the presidential palace.

BIBLIOGRAPHY

Primary Texts

*El candidato*. Barcelona: Destino, 1970.
*Los dioses ajenos*. Barcelona: Destino, 1971.
*El palacio y la furia*. Barcelona: Destino, 1976.

English Translation

*The Candidate*. Tr. T. de Gámez. New York: Pocket Books, 1972.

**ALONSO DE SORIA** (c. 1520, Garcimuñoz, Cuenca–c. 1600, Garcimuñoz), ascetical writer. An Augustinian monk, he wrote an important "libro de caballería *a lo divino" (spiritual romance of chivalry) titled *Historia y milicia cristiana del cavallero Peregrino* (1601; History and Christian Campaign of the Pilgrim Knight). Inspired by a medieval Hispano-Arabic philosophical novel of Abubeker (Tofail), Alonso de Soria's narrative describes the protagonist's struggle to attain the state of Christian perfection. The work is divided into five books comprising both prose and verse. Book 1 relates the abandonment of the child in a desert and tells how he is raised by the animals. The author describes how innate reason (*luz natural*) guides the child in the practice of the Christian virtues. However, as a young man he is forced to flounder within the Abode of Disenchantment. Books 2 and 3 are ascetical treatises in which Soria presents the fortresses of the church: the theological and cardinal virtues, the sacraments and religious mysteries. He describes how these are pitted against the vices of the world. In Book 4 the Pilgrim, already knighted, enters into the Abode of Oblivion followed soon after by his death and resurrection whence he journeys onto the Battlefields of Truth; at that point the Pilgrim Knight begins to see clearly what he previously had only believed. Book 5 recounts the victory and crowning of the Knight, after which he arrives at the summit of the Sacred Mount and peers into the Celestial City. This religious work had a direct influence on *Gracián y Morales's *Criticón* and possibly on the *Quijote*. *See also* Ascetical Literature; Caballerías, Libros de.

BIBLIOGRAPHY

Primary Text

*Historia y milicia cristiana del cavallero Peregrino, conquistador del cielo, metaphora y symbolo de qualquier Sancto que peleando contra los vicios gano la victoria.* Cuenca: n.p., 1601. (The Hispanic Society of America holds the original edition.)

Angelo DiSalvo

**ALONSO GAMO, José María** (1913, Torija, Guadalajara– ), poet and critic. A lawyer and diplomat who has published several literary and historical studies, Alonso Gamo is also known for his poetic works, which include *Paisajes del* *alma en guerra* (1943; Landscapes of the Soul at War), *Tus rosas frente al espejo* (1952; Your Roses Before the Mirror), *Paisajes del alma en paz* (1976; Landscapes of the Soul at Peace), and a book of poems on the life and work of Spanish painter Francisco Zurbarán. His critical examination of the poetry and poetics of George Santayana, *Un español en el mundo* (1966; A Spaniard in the World), received the Fastenrath Prize. He has also published a study of three Argentine poets, Marechal, Molinari and Bernárdez as well as translations of the travel memoirs of two sixteenth-c. Italian ambassadors to the Spanish court, Francesco Guicciardini and Andrea *Navaggiero.

BIBLIOGRAPHY

Primary Texts

*Paisajes del alma en guerra*. Buenos Aires: Emecé, 1945.
*Paisajes del alma en paz*. Madrid: Oriens, 1976.
*Tus rosas frente al espejo*. Valencia: Talleres de tipografía moderna, 1952.
*Un español en el mundo*. Madrid: Cultura Hispánica, 1966.

Victoria Wolff Unruh

**ALONSO I MANANT, Cecilia,** also known as Cecília A. Màntua (1905, Barcelona–1974, ?), playwright. The Institut de Teatre has most of her work.

BIBLIOGRAPHY

Primary Texts

*La cançó de la florista*. Barcelona: Nereida, 1958.
*La cinglera de la mort*. Barcelona: Nereida, 1955.
*Història d'un mirall*. Barcelona: Millà, 1966.
*Maria Cural, la pessebrista*. Barcelona: Millà, 1961.
*La Pepa Maca*. Barcelona: Millà, 1960.
*Princesa de Barcelona*. Barcelona: Nereida, 1959.

Kathleen McNerney

**ALONSO MILLÁN, Juan José** (1936, Madrid– ), Spanish playwright. Alonso Millán, a writer of comedies which were originally compared with those of *Mihura and *Jardiel Poncela, actually possesses a somewhat more facile and less searching humor, together with an exceptional inventiveness, a capacity for stringing together endless chains of absurd, outlandish, and ridiculous situations with an equally foolish dialogue. His first two plays, *Operación A* and *Las señoras, primero* (Ladies First), were produced in 1959. Several others followed in rapid succession: *La felicidad no lleva impuesto de lujo* (1961; Happiness Has No Excise Tax), *La señora que no dijo sí* (1962; The Lady Who Didn't Say Yes), *El cianuro . . . ¿solo o con leche?* (Your Cyanide—Plain or with Milk?), *El agujero* (The Hole), and *El ex presidente* were all produced in 1963. Other titles include *Carmelo* (1964), *El crimen al alcance de la clase media* (Crime within the Reach of the Middle Class) and *Mayores con reparos* (For Adults Only, With Caution), both in 1965, and *Pecados conyugales* (1966; Conjugal

Sins). The vision of humanity presented is somewhat hard to believe, conventional and trivialized, following well-worn formulas and avoiding any semblance of engagement, criticism or serious themes. *See also* Contemporary Spanish Theater.

BIBLIOGRAPHY

Primary Texts

*Damas, señoras, mujeres*. Madrid: Machado, 1988.
*Revistas del corazón*. Madrid: Machado, 1986.
*Tratamiento de choque*. Madrid: Machado, 1987.

**ALONSO MONTERO, Xesús** (1926, Vigo– ), Galician critic, philologist and literary scholar. The son of rural tavern-keepers, he obtained a degree in Romance philology from the U of Madrid. Alonso Montero has taught language and literature at the university and secondary levels during most of a life devoted primarily to the study, defense and preservation of Galician culture. As a proponent of Galician autonomy and an independent leftist, he was active politically during the Franco regime, and experienced political fines, discrimination, "exile" from Galicia to Andalusia, and loss of his passport, partly because of his attending a Peace Congress in the Soviet Union in 1962. In the post-Franco transition to democracy, he was a leftist candidate for Congress from Lugo (where he had served pedagogically for sixteen years). Devoted above all to Galician nationalism, he has striven to maintain and propagate knowledge of Galicia's language and literature in nearly twenty books (including two or three prohibited by the censors under Franco). His linguistic treatises include *La palabra en la realidad* (1963; The Word in Reality), *O que compre saber da lingua galega* (1969; What One Must Know of the Galician Language), *O galego na escola* (1970; Teaching Galician in the Schools), *Constitución del gallego en lengua literaria. Datos de una problemática cultural y sociológica* (1970; Making Galician a Literary Language. Data Concerning a Cultural and Sociological Problem), *Informe—dramático—sobre la lengua gallega* (1973; Dramatic Report on the Galician Language), and a number of specialized dialectical studies of socio-cultural subgroups, as well as historical studies. Alonso Montero's studies of Galician literature include *Cen anos de Literatura galega* (1964; 100 Years of Galician Literature), *Realismo y conciencia crítica en la literatura gallega* (1968; Realism and the Critical Conscience in Galician Literature), *Rosalía de Castro* (1973), *Pedro Petouto (Traballos e cavilaciós dun mestre subversivo)* (1974; Works and Speculations of a Subversive Master), *Castelao* (1975), and *Manuel Curros Enríquez* (1977). In addition, he published a number of socio-political works: *Encuesta mundial sobre la lengua y la cultura gallegas y otras áreas conflictivas: Puerto Rico, Cataluña . . .* (1974; World Survey on the Language and Culture of Galicia and Other Areas of Conflict: Puerto Rico, Catalonia . . .), *Lingua, literatura e sociedade en Galicia* (1977; Language, Literature and Society in Galicia), *Politica e cultura en Galicia* (1978; *Politics and Culture in Galicia*, 1977) and the anthology, *Trinta anos de poesía crítica* *en Galicia (1936–1965): a protesta de trinta poetas* (banned in 1967; Thirty Years of Critical Poetry in Galicia [1936–1965]: The Protests of Thirty Poets). In addition, he has published many other anthologies and numerous translations, either from Galician to Castilian or vice versa, and bilingual editions of Galician texts, as well as scholarly and annotated editions, articles, prologues and essays. *See also* Galician Literature.

Janet Pérez

**ALÓS, Concha** (1922, Valencia– ), novelist and short story writer. Born of a working-class family, Alós underwent hunger and privation during the Civil War and the imprisonment of her father. After her mother's death, she had to work, and became a schoolteacher for some ten years in the villages of Majorca (reflected in her fiction). After moving to Barcelona in 1960, she began to write, and won the well-endowed Planeta Prize with her third novel, *Las hogueras* (1964; Bonfires), which contrasts the parasitic lifestyle of a wealthy foreign couple in a Majorcan village with the poverty and frustration of local peasants. Most of the early fiction of Alós is Social Realism, concerned with inequities and injustice in society, usually with a feminist bent. *Los enanos* (1963; The Dwarfs) describes life in a run-down boardinghouse in a Spanish metropolis (probably Barcelona), combining an existentialist anguish with a Darwinian view of human life. In neo-Naturalist fashion, humanity is seen as helpless before powerful forces. *Los cien pájaros* (1963; The Hundred Birds) portrays the socio-sexual awakening of Cristina, a working-class girl in a provincial capital, employing a first-person narrative viewpoint to present the seduction and exploitation of the governess by the playboy married brother of her pupil.

*El caballo rojo* (1966; The Red Horse Inn) depicts the refugee experience of the Alós family during the Civil War in the guise of a group of Republicans who temporarily meet in the ''Caballo Rojo'' where one of their number works as a waiter. The second novel in which Alós deals rather directly with the civil conflict is *La madama* (1970; The Madam), a work set at the war's beginning, portraying a formerly wealthy family whose members barely manage to survive under the stress of strife. In *El rey de gatos (Narraciones antropófagas)* (1972; King of Cats, Cannibalistic Tales), Alós presents nine short stories with a wide variety of themes, held together by their closeness to the world of fantasy or madness always just out of touch beyond the limits of daily reality. Fantasy reappears in *Argeo ha muerto, supongo* (1983; Argeo's Dead, I Suppose), a narrative in autobiographical form which develops the theme of childhood as a lost paradise and explores the loss of illusion and of first love.

BIBLIOGRAPHY

Primary Texts

*El asesino de los sueños*. Barcelona: Plaza y Janés, 1986.
*Os habla Electra*. Barcelona: Plaza y Janés, 1975.

Criticism

Ordóñez, Elizabeth J. "The Barcelona Group: The Fiction of Alós, Moix and Tusquets."
    *Letras Femeninas* 6.1 (Spring 1980): 38–49.
Rodríguez, Fermín. "La mujer en la sociedad española en la novelística de Concha
    Alós." Diss. U of Arizona, 1973.

Janet Pérez

**ALPERI, Víctor** (1930, Mieres, Asturias– ), literary critic, journalist, novelist
and short story writer. Alperi obtained his doctorate in law at the U of Oviedo,
but also studied philosophy and literature. Very devoted to his native region, he
has usually resided away from the metropolitan literary centers. *Como el viento*
(1958; Like the Wind) was his first novel, followed by his first book of non-
fiction, *Ruta y leyendas de Oviedo* (Roads and Legends of Oviedo), in the same
year. Three novels were written in collaboration with Juan Molla: *Sueño de
sombra* (1959; Dream of Shadows), treating life in the mines of Asturias; *Agua
india* (1960; Indian Waters), on the *indiano*, or adventurer, who strikes it rich
in South America; and *Cristo habló en la montaña* (1961; Christ Spoke upon
the Mount). *Dentro del río* (1963; Within the River) portrays Asturias torn by
the transition to modernity, and *Una historia de guerra* (1972; War Story) traces
the life of an elderly woman with special emphasis upon her experience in
wartime Madrid during Spain's civil strife.

BIBLIOGRAPHY

Primary Texts

*Agua india.* Madrid: Cultura clásica y moderna, 1960.
*Cristo habló en la montaña.* Barcelona: Destino, 1962.
*Dentro del río.* Barcelona: Plaza y Janés, 1963.

Janet Pérez

**ALPHONSE X THE LEARNED, OR WISE,** Alfonso X el Sabio (November
23, 1221, Toledo–April 24, 1284, Seville; reign June 1, 1252), scholar-patron
and king of Spain. He was the son of Ferdinand III, later *el Santo* (the Saint),
and of Beatriz, a Swabian princess. Although we know little of his infancy and
youth, we are relatively certain that he grew up in the village of Orense in
Galicia, an influence which may have manifested itself in one of Alphonse's
most personal compilations, the *Cantigas de Santa Maria* (13th c.; Canticles of
Holy Mary) and his *Cantigas de escarnho e mal dizer* (13th c.; *Ribald Poems
of Invective*, 1970), both written in Galician. His excellent education prepared
him for practical matters as head of state, and under the watchful eye of his
grandmother, Queen Berenguela, Alphonse also developed a love for learning
that allowed him not only to appreciate what he commissioned to be written,
but also to serve as an active patron and collaborator in many of the compilations
written at his behest. In both affairs of state and in intellectual matters, Alphonse's
direction is characterized more by energetic idealism than by successful pragmatism. His personal and political life was beset by vicissitudes not uncommon

for a Spanish king of the Middle Ages (see Edad Media, Literatura de la)—
rebellion by his Moorish subjects as well as by his discontented nobles, death
of his eldest son, Fernando de la Cerda, and a problem of succession that racked
his kingdom and alienated his second eldest, Sancho el Bravo (the Fierce).

In letters he was most successful. His brilliant literary legacy is often divided
into five general categories: legal, historical, scientific, poetic (religious), and
recreational. There can be little doubt that for this legacy Alphonse gathered in
his court some of the best minds of his age to aid him in his intellectual pursuits.
Although it is impossible to name all of his collaborators, we can obtain some
idea of their identification by examining his chancery documents and the prologues to his various works.

### Legal treatises

Alphonse sponsored four legal treatises during his reign: the *Espéculo* (May 5,
1255: Mirror); the *Fuero real* (Aug. 25, 1255: Royal Municipal Law); the *Siete
partidas* (June 23, 1256, to Aug. 28, 1265, with subsequent revisions; *Seven Divisions*, 1931); and the *Setenario* (after 1272?; Sevenfold Law). The *Espéculo*,
often considered an earlier draft of part of the *Siete partidas*, is comprised of five
extant parts, although evidence points towards seven originally planned. It is the
first of several attempts toward a more centralized, uniform law of the land. The
*Fuero real* appears to be a less ambitious, more practical thrust toward uniform
law. Deriving from local statutes, it was much more palatable to Spanish nobles
and was in fact given to several cities and townships in Castile. Perhaps most ambitious in that it is based more than any of the others on Roman Canonical Law, the
*Siete partidas* was likely inspired by Alphonse's quest for Holy Roman Emperorship,
a failed enterprise. The *Siete partidas* comprises branches of canon and civil law, and
as a law of laws, it also portrays the ideal state. It is important even today, because
Spanish custom does not abrogate old law codes superseded by new ones. Instead,
the old code provides governing precedence for cases not accommodated by new
codes. Thus, even today, both in Spain and the New World, cases occasionally arise
which revert to Alphonse's *Siete partidas* for solution.

Jerry R. Craddock has cogently and tantalizingly argued that the *Setenario*,
a potpourri of philosophy, theology, and some astrology, and once thought to
be Alphonse's earliest treatise (begun by his father with Alphonse's collaboration)
may in fact be Alphonse's last legal endeavor. Although several outstanding
lawyers populated the kingdon of Alphonse's day (Jacome Ruiz, Maestro Fernando Martínez, Bishop of Zamora, Maestro Roldán, and others) their connection
to Alphonse and his law awaits determination.

### Historical treatises

The two great pieces of historical prose issuing from Alphonse's royal scriptorium are the *Estoria de Espanna* (c. 1270; History of Spain), also known as
the *Primera crónica general* (First General Chronicle), and the *Grande e general
estoria* (c. 1280; Great and General History). E. S. Procter (1951) proposes that
the *Estoria de Espanna* was begun early in Alphonse's reign with the first part,

the portion up to the Moslem invasion of Spain, completed before Alphonse's death. Scholars are generally certain that nearly 400 chapters of this work were completed before Alphonse began his second great historical venture, the *Grande e general estoria*. One of the immediate effects of this second venture, it seems, was that the *Estoria de Espanna* was never finished as Alphonse planned. His plan was to bring the first work up to the time of his father, Ferdinand III. It begins with Moses and works its way up to the reign of his father, but breaks off within Ferdinand's reign. Between these two extremes, Alphonse treats pre-Roman Spain, Roman Spain and Visigothic Spain. Sources for the *Estoria de Espanna* and the *General estoria* are many. Among those for the former we find Arabic sources, classical (Suetonius, Orosius, Ovid, and Lucan) and medieval Latin authors such as St. Isidore, Vincent of Beauvais, and especially Lucas of *Tuy and Rodrigo of Toledo (whose history serves as the framework for Alphonse's *Estoria de Espanna*). A source of special significance for students of literature is Alphonse's use of epic poetry, which he incorporated into the text. Among these we find texts for *La *condesa traidora* (The Traitorous Countess), *Romance del *infante García* (Tale of the Nobleman Garcia), the *Siete *Infantes de Lara* (The Seven Young Nobles of Lara), the *Cantar del Rey don Sancho el Fuerte* (The Epic of King Sancho the Strong [see Sancho II de Castilla]), and perhaps most famous of all, the *Cantar de mio Cid* (The Song of the Cid).

The *Grande e general estoria,* like any universal history, begins with the creation of the world. Indubitably grandiose in design, the account is incomplete, going only as far as the parents of the Blessed Virgin Mary, Joachim and Anne. Following standard practices in other universal histories, we find the Augustinian concept of the six ages of the world as well as the Eusebius-Jerome formula for the synchronization of pagan and Christian sources. As Alphonse himself indicates, the Bible, specifically the Old Testament, serves as the trunk and other sources, specifically pagan (classical) accounts, function as branches. This work, begun about 1272, had just as many sources as, if not more than, the *Estoria de Espanna*. Besides the already-mentioned Bible, there is Josephus's *Antiquities of the Jews,* Peter Comestor's *Historia Scholastica,* the *Libro de *Alexandre* (Book of Alexander), and other classical stories in Spanish version. Alphonse's collaborators even managed to include the *Roman de Thèbes* (Story of Thebes), a French source. Perhaps nowhere better do we find an example of what is often referred to as the great, medieval synthesis. Historians associated with the court of Alphonse are Juan Gil de Zamora, Bernardo de Brihuega, and Jofre de Loaisa. But what their role may have been in these compilations is not known.

### Scientific treatises

Unlike the works in the above categories, the prologues of Alphonse's scientific treatises name at least fourteen scholars who collaborated on them. The works in this category far outnumber those in the others. In all (depending on how they are divided) there are ten, and all but one, the *Tablas alfonsíes* (1483, [in Latin]; Alfonsine Tables), survive in the same royal scriptorium ms. prepared for the Learned King by his very scribes. The Tables, which treat the stars, astronomy, instruments and the calendar, following Ptolemy's system, were translated into Latin, and revised for the locale in which they were to be used. They enjoyed tremendous popularity throughout Europe. Some say that the Alfonsine Tables far surpass the quality of the Toledan Tables and thereby replaced them. Others disagree with the claim for superiority of the Alphonsine Tables, but none can deny their ubiquity.

The earliest scientific treatise, if we can trust the dates contained in its prologue, is one today known as the *Lapidario* (1250; Lapidary). It was finished "two years after the noble King, Don Ferdinand, conquered Seville," or in 1250, prior to Alphonse's accession to the throne. The date of this text is still debated. Its content is generally astrological, dealing with the magical properties of stones under astrological influences. Other astrological treatises are his *Libro conplido en los iudizios de las estrellas* (1254; Definitive Book on the Judgment of the Stars) and the *Libro de las cruzes* (1259; Book of the Crosses). Both concern judicial astrology. Another text of magical and astrological character is the *Picatrix*. It probably dates from the 1250s and as it survives today is incomplete in the beginning. The *Picatrix* was also translated into Latin, *Liber Picatrix* (Book of Buqatris?), and it is from the Latin that the Spanish derives its present appellation. Alphonse's anthology on the construction and use of known astronomical instruments is his *Libro del saber de astrología* (1276–79; Book of the Knowledge of Astronomy), formerly and erroneously known as *Libros del saber de astronomía*. Astronomy and astrology, it must be remembered, were not dichotomized in the Middle Ages as they are today. If they were distinguished, it was only as are the two sides of the same coin. In his own usage of these terms, Alphonse for the most part does not distinguish one from the other. If he must, more often than not "astronomy" and "astrology" mean the opposites of what they denote today. The *Libro de las formas e de las ymagenes* (1276–77; Book of Forms and Images) is a sibling anthology to the *Libro del saber*. The former is primarily astrological and survives only in fragment form, and the latter, as has been noted above, is primarily astronomical since its main concern is instruments. Both incorporate texts originally compiled in the 1250s. The final three scientific treatises—the *Canones de Albateni* (13th c.; Canons of Albateni), the *Tablas de Zarquiel* (13th c.; Tables of Azarquiel), and the *Quadrante sennero* (13th c.; Single-Piece Quadrant)—are all contained in the Paris, Arsenal codex 8322. It is uncertain whether these three actually form a compendium as do the books of the *Libro del saber*. These three texts are the least well-known of the scientific treatises.

### Poetic works

This category consists of the *Cantigas de escarnho e mal dizer* and the *Cantigas de Santa Maria*. Of supreme importance, they come to us in four distinct codices representing "at least two, if not three, distinct editions of the collection" (Procter, 1951). The basic format for the 427 (Deyermond, 1971: 93) poems is that every tenth is a *cantiga de loor* (song of praise) with the intervening nine being *cantigas de miragre* (songs of miracles). The *loores* are the most personal of the collection and many of the *miragres* deal with narratives standardly found in Marian literature of the period. Others are distinctly Spanish in origin, and some relate personal favors granted to Alphonse by the Virgin—notably *Cantiga* 209 in which Alphonse is cured of an illness only when a volume of the *Cantigas*, actually illustrated in the accompanying miniatures, is brought to him. Although the majority of these poems appear to have been compiled by Alphonse's collaborators (one of whom we know is Airas Nunes), there are several which seem to be penned by Alphonse himself. Several great themes bring the various miracles into one cohesive unit: Alphonse's personal quest for salvation; his poetic ineffability before the Virgin; his forsaking worldly *donas* to be her troubadour exclusively. In all instances, Alphonse appears to be promoting public piety and devotion to the Virgin. Although most of his codices are elaborately illustrated, none is so lavishly as the *Cantigas*. The art has been studied from an archaeological point of view by Guerrero Lovillo and also by Domínguez Bordona among others. If there is still much work to be done with the art found in the *Cantigas*, there appears to be even more with the music. Julián Ribera y Tarragó and Higinio Anglés have founded the two basic schools of thought concerning the music of the *Cantigas*. Ribera espouses Arabic origins and Anglés espouses European sources for the *Cantigas*. The latter point of view seems to be the more favored.

### Recreational category

The only text in this category is the *Libro de açedrex & dados & tablas* (c. 1283; Book of Chess, Dice and Backgammon) as the text appears to be titled. We are privy even here to Alphonse's serious bent. These games are essentially for the recreation of the soul so that the individual will be more able to carry on his everyday affairs. The text, of Arabic origin, is very richly illuminated—perhaps vying with the *Cantigas* mss. in beauty.

To conclude, there are other minor texts—not necessarily royal scriptorium—associated with Alphonse which have received lesser or greater scholarly attention. These can be found in the bibliographic sources listed below.

It is difficult to determine just exactly what Alphonse's impact on later Spanish culture was. There can be no doubt that he did have an influence, but we are only beginning to reconstruct an accurate picture of it.

BIBLIOGRAPHY

Primary Texts

*Alfonso X, o Sábio. Cantigas de Santa Maria.* Ed. W. Mettmann. 4 vols. Coimbra: Acta Universitatis Conimbrigensis, 1959–72. Rpt. in 2 vols. Vigo: Xerais, 1981.

*Alfonso el Sabio. General estoria, primera parte.* Ed. A. G. Solalinde. Madrid: J. Molina, 1930.

*Alfonso el Sabio. General estoria, segunda parte.* Ed. A. G. Solalinde, L. A. Kasten, and V. R. B. Oelschläger. 2 vols. Madrid: CSIC, 1957 and 1961.

*Alfonso el Sabio: "Lapidario" and "Libro de las formas & ymagenes."* Ed. R. C. Diman and L. W. Winget. Madison, WI: HSMS, 1980.

*Alfonso el Sabio: Libro de las cruzes.* Ed. L. Kasten and L. B. Kiddle. Madrid: CSIC, 1961.

*Alfonso el Sabio. Libros de açedrex, dados e tablas (Das Schachzabelbuch König Alfons*

*des Weisens mit 51 Miniaturen auf Tafeln)*. Ed. and tr. A. Steiger. Románica
Helvetica 10. Zürich-Erlenbach: Eugen Rentsch; Geneva: Droz, 1941.

*Aly Aben Ragel. El Libro conplido en los iudizios de las estrellas: traducción hecha en
la corte de Alfonso el Sabio*. Ed. G. Hilty. Madrid: RAE, 1954.

"An Astrological Manuscript of Alfonso X." Ed. George O. S. Darby. Diss. Harvard
1932. [*Picatrix*]

*Los canones de Albateni*. Ed., intro., notes G. Bossong. *Zeitschrift für Romanische
Philologie* 165. Tübingen: Niemeyer, 1978.

*Cantigas d'escarnho e de mal dizer dos cancioneiros medievais galegos portugueses*.
Ed. M. R. Lapa. Colección Filolóxica. Vigo: Galaxia, 1965. 2nd ed., rev. and
expanded, 1970.

*Concordances and Texts of the Royal Scriptorium Manuscripts of Alfonso X, el Sabio*.
Ed. L. Kasten and J. Nitti. Microfiche publication. Madison, WI: HSMS, 1978.
Includes *Canones de Albateni, Estoria de Espanna* I and II, *General estoria* I
and IV, *Lapidario, Libro complido en los judizios de las estrellas, Libro de las
cruzes, Libro de las formas e ymagenes, Libro de las leyes, Libro del quadrante
sennero, Libros de ajedrez, dados e tablas, Libro del saber de astronomia, Picatrix, Tablas de Zarquiel*.

*Estudios sobre Azarquiel*. By M. M. Millás Vallicrosa. Madrid: CSIC, 1950. Contains
*Tablas de Zarquiel*.

*Lapidario. Según el manuscrito escurialense H.I.15*. Ed. S. Rodríguez M. Montalvo.
Madrid: Gredos, 1981.

"Una nueva obra astronómica alfonsí: el tratado del cuadrante 'sennero.' " Ed. J. M.
Millás Vallicrosa. *Al-Andalús* 21 (1956): 59–92.

*Opúsculos legales del Rey Don Alfonso el Sabio*. Vol. 1, *El espéculo o espejo de todos
los derechos*. Vol. 2, *El fuero real, Las leyes de los adelantados mayores, Las
nuevas y el ordenamiento de las tafurerias, Las leyes del estilo*. Madrid: Imprenta
Real, 1836.

"A Paleographic Edition of the Alfonsine Collection of Prose Miracles of the Virgin."
Ed. J. R. Chatham. In *Oelschläger Festschrift*. Ed. D. H. Darst et al. Estudios
de Hispanófila 36. Chapel Hill: Hispanófila, 1976. 73–111.

*Primera crónica general de España*. Ed. R. Menéndez Pidal. 2 vols. 1906; 3rd ed.
Madrid: Gredos, 1978.

*Setenario*. Ed. K. H. Vanderford. Buenos Aires: Instituto de Filología, 1945. Rpt. Barcelona: Crítica, 1984.

*Las siete partidas del Rey Don Alfonso el Sabio*. Vol. 1, *Partida primera*. Vol. 2, *Partida
segunda y tercera*. Vol. 3, *Partida quarta, quinta, sexta, y séptima*. Madrid:
Imprenta Real, 1807.

"A Study and Edition of the Royal Scriptorium Manuscript of *El libro del saber de
astrologiia* by Alfonso X, el Sabio." Ed., study A. J. Cárdenas. Diss. Wisconsin
1974. (Editio princeps by Rico y Sinobas, Manuel, ed. *Libros del saber de
astronomía del Rey. D. Alfonso X de Castilla*. 5 vols. Madrid: Eusebio Aguado,
1863–67.)

*Tabulae Astronomicae*. Venice: Erhardus Ratdolf, 1483.

English Translation

*Las Siete Partidas*. Tr. S. Parsons Scott. Chicago: Commerce Clearing House, 1931.

Criticism

Anglés, H. "La música de las *Cantigas* del Rey Alfonso el Sabio." *Arbor* 1 (1944):
327–48.

————. *La música de las "Cantigas de Santa Maria" del Rey Alfonso el Sabio*. Facs., Transcription, and Critical Study. 3 vols. Barcelona: Diputación Provincial de Barcelona, Biblioteca Central, 1943–64.

Ayerbe-Chaux, Reinaldo. "El uso de la 'exempla' en la *Estoria de España* de Alfonso X." *La Corónica* 7.1 (1978): 28–33.

Cárdenas, A. J. "Toward an Understanding of the Astronomy of Alfonso X, el Sabio." *Indiana Social Studies Quarterly* 31.3 (Winter 1978–79): 81–90.

————. "Alfonso X and the *Studium Generale*." *Indiana Social Studies Quarterly* 33.1 (Spring 1980): 65–75.

Chisman, Ana McG. "Rhyme and Word Order in *Las Cantigas de Santa Maria*." *KRQ* 23 (1976): 393–407.

Craddock, J. R. *The Legislative Works of Alfonso X, el Sabio*. London: Grant and Cutler, 1986.

Cummins, J. J. "The Practical Implications of Alfonso el Sabio's Peculiar Use of the *Zéjel*." *BHS* 47 (1970): 1–9.

Deyermond, A. D. *A Literary History of Spain: The Middle Ages*. London: Benn; New York: Barnes & Noble, 1971. 87–96.

Domínguez Bordona, Jesús. *La miniatura española*. Florence: Pantheon, 1930. 2: 38–42, especially.

Eisenberg, D. "The *General Estoria*: Sources and Source Treatment." *Zeitschrift für Romanische Philologie* 89 (1973): 206–27.

Guerrero Lovillo, J. *Las Cantigas. Estudio arqueológico de sus miniaturas*. Madrid: CSIC, 1949.

Hartman, S. L. "Alfonso el Sabio and the Varieties of Verb Grammar." *Hispania* 57 (1974): 48–55.

Harvey, L. P. "The Alfonsine School of Translators: Translations from Arabic into Castilian Produced under the Patronage of Alfonso the Wise of Castile (1221–1252–1284)." *Journal of the Royal Asiatic Society* (1977): 109–17.

Impey, O. T. "Ovid, Alfonso X, and Juan Rodríguez del Padrón: Two Castilian Translations of the Heroides and the Beginnings of Spanish Sentimental Prose." *BHS* 57 (1980): 283–97.

Keller, J. E. *Alfonso X el Sabio*. TWAS 12. Boston: Twayne, 1967. Includes anthological translations.

————. "The Depiction of Exotic Animals in *cantiga* XXIX of the *Cantigas de Santa Maria*." In *Studies in Honor of Tatiana Fotitch*. Ed. J. Solá-Solé, A. Crisafulli, and S. A. Schulz. Washington, DC: Catholic U of Amer. and Consortium P, 1972. 247–53.

————. *Pious Brief Narrative in Medieval Castilian and Galician Verse: From Berceo to Alfonso X*. Studies in Romance Languages 21. Lexington: U of Kentucky P, 1978.

Kiddle, L. B. "A Source of the *General Estoria*: The French Prose Redaction of the *Roman de Thèbes*." *HR* 4 (1936): 264–71.

Longland, J. R. "A Preliminary Bibliography of Medieval Galician-Portuguese Poetry in English Translation." In *Studies in Honor of Lloyd A. Kasten*. Madison, WI: HSMS, 1975. 135–53.

MacDonald, R. A. "Alfonso the Learned and Succession: A Father's Dilemma." *Speculum* 40 (1965): 647–53.

Mettman, W. "Airas Nunes, Mitautor der *Cantigas de Santa Maria*." *Ibero-romania* 3 (1971): 8–10.

Procter, E. S. *Alfonso X of Castile: Patron of Literature and Learning*. Oxford: Clarendon, 1951. Rpt. Westport, CT: Greenwood Press, 1980.

———. "The Scientific Works of the Court of Alfonso X of Castille [*sic*]: The King and His Collaborators." *MLS* 40 (1945): 12–29.

Ribera y Tarregó, Julián. *Music in Ancient Arabia and Spain*. Tr. and abr. by E. Hague and M. Leffingwell. Palo Alto, CA: Stanford UP, 1929; rpt. New York: Da Capo Music Reprint Series, 1970.

Snow, J. T. "The Central Rôle of the Troubador *Persona* of Alfonso X in the *Cantigas de Santa Maria*." *BHS* 56 (1979): 305–16.

———. "A Chapter in Alfonso X's Personal Narrative: The *Puerto de Santa Maria Poems* in the *Cantigas de Santa Maria*." *La Corónica* 8.1 (1979): 10–21.

———. "Poetic Self-Awareness in Alfonso X's *cantiga* 110." *KRQ* 26 (1979): 421–32.

———. *The Poetry of Alonso X, el Sabio. A Critical Bibliography*. Research Bibliographies and Checklists 19. London: Grant and Cutler, 1977.

Trend, J. B. "Alfonso el Sabio and the Game of Chess." *Revue Hispanique* 81.1 (1933): 393–403.

Van Kleffens, E. N. *Hispanic Law until the End of the Middle Ages*. Edinburgh: Edinburgh UP, 1968.

Anthony J. Cárdenas

**ALPHONSE XI,** King of Castile and León, Alonso XI (1311, Salamanca–1350, Gibraltar), monarch, lawgiver, huntsman, poet. Alphonse was only a year old when he came to the throne; his reign is one of the most significant of medieval Castile. Contained in the *Canzionere portoghese della Biblioteca Vaticana* (Portuguese Songbook of the Vatican Library) is the first troubadoresque lyric in Castilian, which is attributed to Alphonse. It is a composition of fresh and delicate beauty, as can be seen in its first verses:

> En un tiempo cogí flores
> del muy noble paraíso,
> cuitado de mis amores
> e d'el su fremoso riso.

(Once I gathered flowers / from very noble Paradise, / longing for my love / and her sweet laughter.)

An even better-known work of his is the *Libro de la montería* (Book of Hunting) that was prepared c. 1345–50. In the oldest extant codex, Escorial Y.II.19, the text is divided into three books. The first of these describes methods of big-game hunting (*caza mayor*) on horseback and on foot, which also allowed nobles to stay prepared for war during times of peace— one of the great benefits that the pastime afforded. The second part of Book 2 derives largely from a veterinary treatise found in the *Libro de las animalias que caçan* (Book of Hunting Animals) that Alphonse's great-grandfather, King *Alphonse the Learned (reign 1252–84), had translated from the Arabic *Kitāb al-Ŷawārih* (Book of Falcons) of Moamyn the Huntsman of Baghdad (d. 860 A.D.). The *Montería's* third book details more than 9,000 places of the hunt throughout Spain. This scientific treatise is interspersed with brief venatory narratives and numerous allusions to literary figures such as Juan Ruiz, *Arcipreste de Hita, the *Cid, Per *Abbat, Merlin, Roland's sword Durendal, etc. It is the most famous hunting text of Medieval and *Renaissance Spain. *See also* Edad Media, Literatura de la.

BIBLIOGRAPHY

Primary Text

*"Libro de la montería": Based on Escorial MS Y.II.19.* Ed. D. P. Seniff. Madison, WI: HSMS, 1983.

Criticism

Funes, L. R. "La distinción entre texto y manuscrito: Observaciones sobre crítica textual a propósito de una reciente edición del *Libro de la montería* de Alfonso XI." *Incipit* 3 (1983): 25–51.
Seniff, D. P. "Alfonso X and the Literary Histories of Ticknor and Amador de los Ríos." *KRQ* 33 (1986): 355–64.
———. "Falconry, Venery and Fishing in the *Cantigas de Santa María*." *Studies on the "Cantigas de Santa María": Art, Music and Poetry.* Ed. S. G. Armistead et al. Madison, WI: HSMS, 1987. 459–74.

Dennis P. Seniff

**ALTAMIRA, Rafael** (1866, Alicante–1951, Mexico), historian, man of letters. Before going into exile at the end of the Civil War, Altamira was a professor at the famous Institución Libre de Enseñanza, associated with the foremost intellectuals of the *Generations of 1898 and 1927, and also held chairs at the Universities of Oviedo and Madrid. Although he wrote some works of fiction, such as his short story collection *Cuentos de amor y tristeza* (1897?; Tales of Love and Sorrow) and the novel *Reposo* (1903; Rest), he was known above all for his historiography. Altamira produced several highly reputed works in which he studied the relationship between culture and historiography, including his masterpiece, *Historia de España y la civilización española* (1900–1930; *A History of Spain from the Beginnings...*, 1966), as well as his *Psicología del pueblo español* (1902; Psychology of the Spanish People) and *Historia del derecho español* (1903; History of Spanish Law). He enjoyed an international reputation and was in demand as a lecturer in several countries.

BIBLIOGRAPHY

Primary Texts

*Historia de España.* 4th ed. Barcelona: Gili, 1928.
*Historia del derecho español.* Madrid: Suárez, 1903.
*Psicología del pueblo español.* 2nd ed. Barcelona: Minerva, 1917.
*Reposo.* Barcelona: Henrich, 1903.

English Translations

*A History of Spain from the Beginnings to the Present Day.* Tr. M. Lee. Princeton: Van
   Nostrand, 1966.
*A History of Spanish Civilization.* Tr. P. Volkov. London: Constable, 1930.

Janet Pérez


**ALTOLAGUIRRE, Manuel** (1905, Málaga–1959, Burgos), poet, editor,
printer, filmmaker, anthologizer, translator. Altolaguirre's range of creative
achievements has been overshadowed by his monumental contribution, as a
printer and publisher, to disseminating the work of several major twentieth-c.
Hispanic poets. In 1924 he and Emilio *Prados opened a print shop, and in 1926
they founded the literary magazine *Litoral*, enterprises which led to the publication of works by *García Lorca, Miguel *Hernández, Rafael *Alberti and Luis
*Cernuda. In 1935 Altolaguirre published Pablo Neruda's literary magazine,
*Caballo verde para la poesía*, and the same year he published the bilingual
(Spanish and English) *1616* in London, a poetry magazine whose title alludes
to the year that *Cervantes and Shakespeare died.
   As a member of the *Generation of 1927, Altolaguirre shared that group's
early interest in *Góngora and the experimental metaphor. His later writing,
however, shows a greater interest in and influence of Juan Ramón *Jiménez and
Antonio *Machado, as well as of the Spanish classical writers, a preference
already evident in his biography of *Garcilaso de la Vega (1933) and in his
collaboration with José *Bergamín on the play *El triunfo de las germanías* (written
1937 but evidently never published; The Triumph of the Thieves), based on a
Cervantes play.
   Altolaguirre saw poetry as a source of knowledge of himself and the world
and as a link between the individual and the universal; his poetic themes include
time, loneliness, love and death. His *Poesías completas* (1960; Complete Poems)
includes selections from his most important previous volumes: *Las islas invitadas*
(1926; The Invited Isles), *Soledades juntas* (1931; Joined Solitudes) and *Fin de
un amor* (1949; End of a Love).
   Altolaguirre also wrote and produced films, including *Subida al cielo* (translated as ''Life and Afterlife''), which was directed by Luis Buñuel and won the
Cannes Critics Prize in 1952, and *El Cantar de los cantares* (1959; The Song of
Songs), based on the version of *Siglo de Oro (Golden Age) poet Luis de *León.
His extensive translation work includes Shelley's *Adonais*; he also edited a well-
known anthology of Spanish romantic poetry. Altolaguirre died in a car accident.

BIBLIOGRAPHY

Primary Texts

*Fin de un amor.* Prol. M. Smerdou Altolaguirre. Madrid: Trece de Nieve, 1974.
*Las islas invitadas.* Intro. M. Smerdou Altolaguirre. Madrid: Castalia, 1972.
*Obras completas.* Ed. J. Valender. 2 vols. Madrid: Istmo, 1986- .
*Poesías completas.* Mexico: Fondo de Cultura Económica, 1960.

English Translations

Selected poems. In *The Oxford Book of Spanish Verse*. Ed. J. B. Trend. Oxford: Oxford UP, 1965. 437–38, 508.

Selections from *Las islas invitadas* and *Soledades*. In *Contemporary Spanish Poetry*. Ed. E. L. Turnbull. Baltimore: Johns Hopkins UP, 1945. 377–401.

Criticism

Cano, J. L. *La poesía de la generación del 27*. Madrid: Guadarrama, 1957. 273–82.

Crispin, J. *Quest for Wholeness: The Personality and Works of Manuel Altolaguirre*. Valencia/Chapel Hill: Albatrós Hispanófila, 1983. Includes thorough inventory of Altolaguirre's publications and writing, a critical bibliography, and English translation of 15 poems.

Hernández de Trelles, C. *Manuel Altolaguirre: vida y literatura*. Río Piedras: U of Puerto Rico, 1974.

Morris, C. B. *A Generation of Spanish Poets 1920–1925*. Cambridge: Cambridge UP, 1969.

Victoria Wolff Unruh

**ALUMBRADOS** (Illuminists; c. 1525-c. 1559), a group of religious radicals of sixteenth-c. Spain which originated in Castile. They were also called *Iluminados* or *Dejados*. Their religious practices were judged heretical because of the *mysticism they practiced, which involved complete abandonment (*dejamiento*, *dejación*, or *dejadez*) to God. The Illuminists perceived themselves impervious to sin; as a consequence rumors of alleged promiscuity at their gatherings circulated. They also evaded all liturgical ceremonies and deemed the sacraments unnecessary for salvation. Illuminists centered around the cities of Toledo, Llerena, Guadalajara, Jaén, and Seville. One of the principal centers of the movement was at the home of the Marquis of Villena at Escalona. Scholars believe that Illuminism became prevalent among some *conversos and that it was an offshoot of Erasmian teachings. Many prominent Illuminists were tried by the *Inquisition, which was instrumental in obliterating them. *See also* Erasmism.

BIBLIOGRAPHY

Criticism

Asín Palacios, M. ''Shadiles y alumbrados.'' *Congreso de Espiritualidad de Salamanca* 2 (1956): 69.

Boehmer, E. *Bibliotheca Wiffeniana. Spanish Reformers of Two Centuries from 1520*. vol. 1. Strasbourg: Trübner, 1874.

Carreter Parrando, J. M. *Movimiento alumbrado y Renacimiento español. Proceso inquisitorial contra Luis de Beteta*. Madrid: Calatrava, 1980.

Longhurst, J. E. ''The Alumbrados of Toledo: Juan del Castillo and the Lucernas.'' *Archiv für Reformationsgeschichte* 45.2 (1954): 233–53.

Márquez, A. *Los alumbrados: orígenes y filosofía 1525–1559)*. Madrid: Taurus, 1972.

Angelo DiSalvo

**ÁLVAR LÓPEZ, Manuel** (1923, Benicarló, Castellón– ), literary critic. The holder of a chair of historical grammar of the Spanish language in Granada, he is known especially for his studies of the Judeo-Spanish *endechas* (early poetic form). Among his linguistic investigations, the following titles are noteworthy: *Atlas lingüístico y etnográfico de Andalucía* (1960, vol. 1; Linguistic and Ethnographic Atlas of Andalusia) and *Textos hispánicos dialectales* (1961, 2 vols.; Texts on Hispanic Dialects). He has taught in the United States and has published several works of literary criticism, including *Granada y el Romancero* (1956; Granada and the Ballad Collections), *La poesía de Delmira Agustini* (1959; The Poetry of Delmira Agustini), and *Unidad y evolución en la lírica de Unamuno* (1960; Unity and Evolution in the Lyrics of Unamuno).

BIBLIOGRAPHY

Primary Texts

*Atlas lingüístico y etnográfico de Andalucía.* 3 vols. Granada: CSIC, 1961.

*Atlas lingüístico y etnográfico de las Islas Canarias.* 3 vols. Madrid: La Muralla, 1975.

*Cantos de boda judeo-españoles.* Madrid: Instituto Arias Montano, 1971.

*Endechas judeo-españolas.* Granada: Universidad, 1953.

**ALVARADO, Francisco** (1756, Marchena–1814, Seville), minor philosopher and critic. He entered the Dominican order at age 16. His prose was published posthumously in eleven volumes under the pseudonym "El filósofo Rancio" (The Overripe Philosopher). *Azorín admired him, as did the historian Narciso Alonso Cortés, with reservations.

BIBLIOGRAPHY

Primary Texts

*Cartas Críticas.* 6 vols. Barcelona: Peninsular, 1881.

*Obras escogidas.* Madrid: Administración de 'La Ciencia tomista,' 1912.

**ÁLVAREZ, Miguel de los Santos** (1818, Valladolid–1892, Madrid), poet and short story writer. As a Foreign Service officer he served in Rio de Janeiro (1842) and in Mexico as a plenipotentiary minister (1856); in 1868 he became a state counselor. In his youth Alvarez was a close friend of José de *Espronceda, who quoted from Alvarez's works in his *El estudiante de Salamanca* and *Canto a Teresa*. After Espronceda's death, Alvarez published the only known fragments of the eighth canto of Espronceda's *El Diablo Mundo*. Álvarez wrote lyric poetry and began an ambitious poem titled *María* (1840), but his short stories and the short novel *La protección de un sastre* (1840; A Tailor's Protection) are of greatest interest. They were subsequently collected under the name *Tentativas literarias* (1864; Literary Attempts). He was one of the first to write about Spanish contemporary customs and thus can be considered a precursor of Realism. His tales employ detailed observation of reality and a macabre, humoristic view of life.

BIBLIOGRAPHY

Primary Texts

*La protección de un sastre.* Madrid: Sánchiz, 1840.

*Tentativas literarias.* 3rd ed. Madrid: Rivadeneyra, 1921.

*Tentativas literarias*. 5th ed. Biblioteca Universal, vols. 119, 120, and 122. Madrid:
    Hernando, 1927.

Criticism

Baquero Goyanes, M. *El cuento español en el siglo XIX*. Madrid: CSIC, 1949.
García Castañeda, S. *Miguel de los Santos Alvarez (1818–1892) Romanticismo y Poesía*.
    N.p.: n.p., 1979.
Genover, Ignacio de. "Un poeta difunto muerto ya en vida." *La Ilustración Ibérica* 540–
    44 (1893): n.p.
Palau, Melchor de. "Acontecimientos literarios. Miguel de los Santos Alvarez." *Revista
    Contemporánea* 88 (1892): 529–37.
Valera, Juan. *Crítica literaria. Notas biográficas y críticas*, and *La poesía lírica y épica en la
    España del siglo XIX*. In his *Obras Completas*. Vol. 1. Madrid: Aguilar, 1942.

                                                              Salvador García Castañeda

**ÁLVAREZ, Valentín Andrés** (1892, Grado, Asturias–197?, ?), economist,
dramatist. Alvarez was nominally a professor of economics, although he dabbled
in several literary genres, producing a book of poetry, *Reflejos* (1921; Reflections), and a novel, *Sentimental Dancing* (title only in English). At his best as
a writer of farces and light comedies, he is remembered for *Tararí* (1929),
considered his best work, and *Pim pam pum* (1946).

BIBLIOGRAPHY

Primary Texts

"Memorias de medio siglo." In *Estudios en homenaje al profesor Valentín Andrés
    Alvarez*. Ed. J. L. García Delgado and J. Segura. Madrid: Tecnos, 1978. Also
    in *RO* 2.5–6 (1976): 83–88.
*Tararí. Pim pam pum. Sentimental Dancing*. Prol. V. A. Alvarez. Madrid: Aguilar, 1948.

**ÁLVAREZ DE CIENFUEGOS, Nicasio** (1764, Madrid–1809, Orthez,
France), pre-romantic poet, dramatist, editor. At age 16, he began classes at the
U of Salamanca, and met his mentor, poet *Meléndez Valdéz. He studied law,
graduating in 1785. As he attended Meléndez's *tertulia, his love for poetry was
born, and also his knowledge of French thinkers such as Rousseau, and their
social attitudes and concerns. In 1787 he returned to Madrid and two years later
was appointed attorney for the Reales Consejos (Royal Council). At this time
he also met and became a fast friend of *Quintana—also of a liberal political
bent. Cienfuegos's only volume of poetry which appeared in his life was published in 1798, titled *Poesías* (Poems).

    Despite his liberal leanings, he also was named editor of the official paper *La
Gaceta*. In his final years, as he struggled with bouts of pulmonary tuberculosis,
Cienfuegos witnessed the social and political upheaval in Spain which culminated
in the 1808 invasion by Napoleon. As editor for the *Gaceta*, he courageously
denounced this act; as a consequence he was taken hostage and removed to
France, where he died.

    Cienfuegos's verse was pre-romantic, as such it concentrated on such themes as loneliness, death, and alienation, with a pessimistic outlook. His poems also give voice to fervent humanitarian desires and liberal social concerns.

BIBLIOGRAPHY

Primary Text

*Poesías.* Ed., intro., J. L. Cano. Madrid: Castalia, 1969.

**ÁLVAREZ DE TOLEDO, Gabriel** (1662, Seville–1714, ?), poet. Descendant of an illustrious Portuguese family, he was librarian and secretary to the king, and one of the founding members of the Spanish Academy (see Academia Española). He was also a polyglot, able to translate Greek and Latin, and to speak several European languages. Though most of his poetry is religious, he is also remembered for a burlesque piece titled *La burromaquia* (The Art of Burro Fighting), extant today in an incomplete form. His *Historia de la iglesia y del mundo* (History of the Church, and the World) attempts to tell the history of the world from Creation; it provoked impassioned discussion, so characteristic of the eighteenth c.

BIBLIOGRAPHY

Primary Texts

*Historia de la iglesia, y del mundo.* . . . Madrid: Rodríguez y Escobar, 1713.
*Poesías.* BAE 61.

**ÁLVAREZ DE TOLEDO, Hernando** (c. 1550?, Seville–?, ?), soldier and poet. He traveled to the New World with Alonso de Sotomayor, and fought against the Araucan Indians in Chile. His poem *Purén indómito* (Indomitable Puren Indian) chronicles the war which broke out in 1598 between the Chileans and the Araucan Indians. Written in *octavas reales*, it is a less-inspired imitation of *Ercilla's masterpiece, *La Araucana*.

BIBLIOGRAPHY

Primary Text

*Purén indómito.* Ed. D. Barros Arana. Leipzig: Franck, 1862.

**ÁLVAREZ DE TOLEDO, (Luisa) Isabel,** Duchess of Medina Sidonia (1930, ?), novelist and essayist. A social activist whose work focuses on human-itarian issues and economic exploitation, Alvarez de Toledo writes of the affluent primarily to criticize and denounce. Jailed in 1969 for her defense of the villagers of Palomares after the hydrogen bomb incident, she wrote of her experience in a series of memoirs published in the periodical press, expanded and translated to English as *My Prison* (1972). In addition to autobiographical content, the mem-oirs include her observations on the prison system, treatment of prisoners, and criminal justice. *La huelga* (1967; *The Strike*, 1971) is a thesis novel written to show the unjust and brutal treatment of Andalusian workers by the ''Establish-ment,'' including the clergy. In *La base* (1971; The Base), the author portrays the effects upon a fictional family and town of the establishment of a joint U.S.–Spanish air base in the vicinity, the resulting loss of autonomy, increase in corruption, and decline in self-esteem. *La cacería* (1977; The Hunt) uses the annual outing of a group of Madrid aristocrats on a hunting expedition in an Andalusian village as a background for the denunciation of the decadence of the elite and an exposé of social injustice in the closing years of the Franco era.

BIBLIOGRAPHY

Primary Texts

*La base*. Paris: Grasset, 1971.
*La cacería*. Barcelona/Buenos Aires/Mexico: Grijalba, 1977.
*La huelga*. Paris: Librarie du Globe, 1967.

English Translations

*My Prison*. Tr. H. Briffault. New York: Harper and Row, 1972.
*The Strike. A Novel of Contemporary Spain*. Tr. W. Rose. New York: Grove, 1971.

Janet Pérez

**ÁLVAREZ DE VILLASANDINO, Alfonso** (fl. 1370, ?–1425, ?), the most prolific and best known poet of the last quarter of the fourteenth c. and first quarter of the fifteenth. His earliest poems can be dated around 1370, and his latest around 1425. The Marqués de *Santillana described him in his *Prohemio e Carta* as a "grand decidor; del qual se podría deçir aquello que en loor de Ovidio un grand estoriador describe; conviene a saber que todos sus motes e palabras eran metro. Fiço tantas canciones e deçires, que sería bien luengo e difuso nuestro proçeso, si por extenso, aun solamente los prinçipios de ellas a recontar se oviessen. E asy por esto, como por ser tanto conosçidas e esparçidas a todas partes las sus obras, passaremos a Miçer Françisco Imperial, el cual yo non llamaría deçidor o trovador, mas poeta" (fine versifier, of whom one could say what a great historian wrote in praise of Ovid; all his sayings and words were in verse. He composed so many poems and songs that our task would be quite long and drawn-out if we were even to recount the beginnings of all of them. For this reason, and because his works are so well known and circulated, we will turn to Master Francisco Imperial, whom I would not call a versifier or troubadour, but rather a poet). The passage is worth quoting at length because it might not be accidental that Santillana passes from Villasandino to *Imperial: Juan Alfonso de *Baena did the same thing in his *Cancionero de *Baena*, which opens with some two hundred poems by Villasandino before passing on to those of Imperial. Clearly, in the minds of contemporary literary observers, Villasandino represented one style of poetry, that of the popular "trovador," and Imperial quite another, that of the elite allegorical mode. Baena, however, did not agree with Santillana about Imperial's superiority: for Baena, Villasandino "fue esmalte e lus e espejo e corona e monarca de todas los poetas e trobadores que hasta oy fueron en toda España" (was the luster and light, mirror, crown and monarch of all poets and troubadors in Spain to this day). Villasandino seemed to have lived by his pen; he composed a series of poems in praise of Seville for which he was handsomely paid (Baena nos. 28–31), and he wrote a poem to Pero *López de Ayala that tells posterity that the Chancellor had promised him some clothes (Baena no. 102). Some of Villasandino's *cantigas* were written in Galician, another indication, along with Ayala's preference for *cuaderna vía, that literary traditions died slowly in Castile.

BIBLIOGRAPHY

Primary Text

*Cancionero de Juan Alfonso de Baena*. Ed. J. M. Azáceta. 3 vols. Madrid: CSIC, 1966.

Colbert Nepaulsingh

**ÁLVAREZ FERNÁNDEZ, Pedro** (1910, Madrid– ), novelist. A professional bureaucrat who rose to a high position in Franco's Dirección General de Seguridad, Alvarez also authored several novels, including *La espera* (The Wait), which deals with the Spanish securities exchange and world of high finance; *La paradójica vida de Zarraustre* (1946; The Paradoxical Life of Zarraustre), a humorous, episodic work in the *picaresque tradition; *Los Pimentel* (The Pimentel Family), *Mi hermano Emilio* (My Brother Emilio), and *Indecisión* (several of these undated, but all prior to 1954). *Alguien pasa de puntillas* (1956; Someone Tiptoes By) reflects the air of mystery which might be expected of a writer with a background in law enforcement and investigation. Perhaps his most significant novel is *Quince noches en vela* (1959; A Fortnight without Sleep), whose protagonist, Vadillo, is a victim of the society in which he was formed, a reflection of the Spanish class struggle, but also a delinquent guilty of violent crimes.

BIBLIOGRAPHY

Primary Texts

*Alguien pasa de puntillas*. Madrid: Marype, 1956.
*La espera*. 2nd ed. Madrid: Cultura clásica y moderna, 1963.
*La paradójica vida de Zarraustre*. Madrid: Marype, 1946.
*Quince noches en vela*. Madrid: Cultura clásica y moderna, 1959.

**ÁLVAREZ GATO, Juan** (1433 or 1440?, Madrid–1496 or 1509?, ?), poet. Of the *Cancionero tradition, Álvarez Gato is best known for his love songs, *villancicos, satires and religious poetry; sensitivity and charm often grace his verse. Some scholars also attribute to him the *Breve suma de la santa vida del reverendísimo e bienaventurado don fray Fernando de Talavera* (n.d.; Brief Summary of the Saintly Life of the Most Reverend and Blessed Friar Ferdinand of Talavera).

BIBLIOGRAPHY

Primary Text

*Obras completas de Juan Alvarez Gato*. Ed. J. Artiles Rodríguez. NBAE 4.

Criticism

Márquez Villanueva, F. *Investigaciones sobre Juan Álvarez Gato*. Madrid: RAE, 1960.

**ÁLVAREZ QUINTERO, Serafín** (1871, Utrera [Sevilla]–1938, Madrid) and Joaquín (1873, Utrera [Sevilla]–1944, Madrid), dramatists. These two "Quintero brothers," whose lifelong theatrical collaboration began in their teens and extended to other activities as well, were highly regarded and successful playwrights whose achievements were recognized by membership in the Royal Spanish Academy of the Language (*Academia Española). Nevertheless, their dramaturgy was thoroughly traditional and conservative, belonging to the picturesque, regionalistic current of Andalusian folklore, local color and *costumbrismo* typical of much of the 19th c. Although their dramatic forms were far from innovative, the Quinteros were able technicians of the theatrical art, and are noted for their lively, witty dialogue, the skillful placing and handling of situations, and their graceful mastery of Andalusian dialect. Despite popular elements, their language is refined and polished, their jokes tasteful and never vulgar. *Pérez de Ayala, a prestigious and demanding critic of the epoch, considered their theater to be of the highest order.

They moved to Madrid in 1889, working as civil servants while becoming established in the literary world. Their first theatrical success came with *El ojito derecho* (1897; The Right Eye), and their careers were assured by the successful *zarzuela, La buena sombra* (1898; Good Luck Charm). Many other triumphs followed, with their total output of theatrical works of various kinds eventually reaching a total of 228, often averaging half a dozen new pieces annually. They also cultivated the colorful *sainete form, with its single act filled by regional types and dialect, following the tradition of the 16th-c. *pasos (one-act curtain raisers) of Lope de *Rueda, the *entremeses of *Cervantes and the 18th-c. master of *sainetes*, Ramón de la *Cruz. Typical of their brief works are *La reja* (1897; The Iron Window-Grate), *El patio* (1900; The Patio), and *Mañana de sol* (1905; *A Sunny Morning*, 1950), which glosses one of the best-known poems of *Campoamor concerning long-separated lovers who meet again in old age. The Quintero brothers also wrote the librettos for many *zarzuelas*, including *La reina mora* (1903; The Moorish Queen), for which the music was composed by the well-known maestro Serrano.

Among the most characteristic and best known of their longer theatrical pieces are *Los Galeotes* (1900; The Galley Slaves); *Las flores* (1900; The Flowers); *El genio alegre* (1906; The Happy Spirit); *Amores y amoríos* (1908; Loves and Love Affairs); and from the same year, *Las de Caín* (The Cain Girls), a title involving a pun on the tribulations of the father of five marriageable daughters (this work involves an atypical setting in Madrid). Other notable successes include *Doña Clarines* (1909; tr. to Eng., 1930) which portrays the risks of over-truthfulness; *Malvaloca* (1912; *Malvaloca* [Wild Mallow], 1916), and from the same year, *Puebla de las mujeres* (*The Women Have Their Way*, 1928). Other notable titles are *Cancionera* (1924; Song-Book), *La boda de Quinita Flores*

(1925; Quinita Flores's Wedding) and *Mariquilla Terremoto* (1930; Earthquake Maria). During their lifetime, they were among the most successful Spanish playwrights, and with more than 100 of their works translated into a variety of foreign languages, they were also well known abroad. However, their portraits of Andalusia are idealized and sentimental rather than realistic, and tend to fall short in serious social concerns, psychology and even characterization which would be believable for contemporary audiences. Since their deaths, their work has been increasingly relegated to literary attics, considered formulaic, escapist or lacking in substance. *See also* Romanticism.

BIBLIOGRAPHY

Primary Texts

*Teatro completo.* 46 vols. Madrid: Espasa-Calpe, 1923–44.

*Teatro selecto.* Ed. J. M. Alonso. Madrid: Escelicer, 1971.

English Translations

"Doña Clarines." In *Twentieth-Century Plays.* Ed. F. W. Chandler and R. A. Cordell. New York: n.p., 1934.

*Four Comedies by Serafín and Joaquín Alvarez Quintero.* Tr. H. and H. Granville Barker. New York: French, 1932.

*Four Plays.* Boston: Little, Brown, 1928. "The Women Have Their Way," "One Hundred Years Old," "Fortunato," "The Lady from Alfaqueque."

"Grief." Tr. A. L. Utt. *Poet Lore* 43.3 (1930): 391–402.

*Malvaloca.* Tr. J. S. Fassett. Intro. J. G. Underhill. Garden City, NY: Doubleday, 1916.

"A Sunny Morning." Tr. L. X. Floyd. In *Modern One-Act Plays.* Ed. F. J. Griffith. New York: n.p., 1950.

For translations of individual stories, excerpts, consult Rudder, Robert S. *The Literature of Spain in English Translation.* New York: Ungar, 1975. 511–13.

Criticism

Díaz Hierro, D. *Huelva y los hermanos Alvarez Quintero.* Huelva: Girón, 1972.

Janet Pérez

*AMADÍS DE GAULA* (*Amadis of Gaul*), sixteenth-c. romance of chivalry. The earliest conserved edition of this best known of all the Spanish novels of chivalry was printed in 1508 in a version reworked around 1492 by Garci Ordóñez de *Montalvo, who claimed that he rewrote the first three books and added the fourth. A version existed as early as the fourteenth century, and the discovery of a fragment dated about 1420 confirms that Montalvo tightened the style and probably changed some elements of the plot. The possibility that the *Amadís* is based on a French or Portuguese original is now discounted, although it is clearly allied to the Breton cycle and particularly to the *Lancelot*.

Amadís, son of unwed but secretly trothed parents, is placed in a chest and set adrift. Recovered by a nobleman, he is raised at the Scottish court where he falls in love with Oriana, daughter of the English king. Throughout his life he is faithful to Oriana, and from this relationship derives a strength which makes him superior to all other knights. He receives knighthood from his father, King

Perión de Gaula, although both are unaware that they are related, and soon defeats King Abiés of Ireland, his father's arch enemy. Recognition by his parents soon follows. Accompanied by his faithful squire Gandalín, he has several fantastic adventures, such as his enchantment in the palace of the wicked magician Arcalaus.

Due to a misunderstanding, Oriana accuses Amadís of unfaithfulness, and he retreats to the life of a hermit on a desert island (*Peña Pobre*) under the name of Beltenebros. Eventually they are reconciled, and Oriana gives birth to Esplandián, who is promptly snatched away by a lioness and reared by a hermit. Amadís, now called the Knight of the Green Sword, because of one of his exploits, travels seeking adventures. Oriana's father, unaware of her deep involvement with Amadís, arranges her marriage to the emperor of Rome, which Amadís prevents. Eventually, in Book 4, Oriana and Amadís are married.

Montalvo wrote a sequel, *Las sergas de Esplandián* (1508; The Deeds of Esplandián), and other authors, such as Feliciano de *Silva, continued the series. Others composed new series in imitation, such as the *Palmerín* romances.

Books of chivalry were extensively read in the sixteenth c. and their influence on the emperor Charles V, Saint *Teresa of Ávila and the *conquistadores* is widely noted. By the end of the century, professional writers no longer composed the romances, but they continued to attract a reading public even after the publication of *Cervantes' *Don Quijote* (1605 and 1615). *See also* Caballerías, Libros de.

## BIBLIOGRAPHY

### Primary Text

*Amadís de Gaula*. Ed. Edwin Place. 4 vols. Madrid: CSIC, 1971.

### English Translation

*Amadis of Gaul*. Tr. E. Place and H. Behm. 2 vols. Lexington: U of Kentucky P, 1974–75.

### Criticism

Eisenberg, Daniel. *Romances of Chivalry in the Spanish Golden Age*. Newark, DE: Juan de la Cuesta P, 1982.

O'Connor, John J. *Amadis de Gaule and Its Influence on Elizabethan Literature*. New Brunswick: Rutgers UP, 1970.

Pierce, Frank. *Amadís de Gaula*. Boston: Twayne, 1976.

Eric Naylor

***AMADÍS DE GRECIA*** (Amadís of Greece), novel of chivalry. This continuation of the *Amadís de Gaula* saga was written by Feliciano de *Silva in the sixteenth c., and is number 9 of the *Amadís* texts. *See also* Caballerías, Libros de.

## BIBLIOGRAPHY

### Primary Text

*Parte tercera de la corónica del muy excelente príncipe don Florisel de Niquea . . .* Seville: Croberger?, 1546.

**AMADO BLANCO, Luis** (1910, Avilés, Asturias–1972, Vatican City), nov-elist. The Republican and leftist affiliations of Amado Blanco made necessary his exile following the Spanish Civil War, and given the strong connections between his native village and Cuba, he established himself in Havana. As a sympathizer with Fidel Castro's successful revolution, he was rewarded with the diplomatic post of Cuban ambassador to the Vatican, where he was at the time of his death. Among his works of fiction are *Un pueblo y dos agonías* (1955; One People and Two Agonies) and *Doña Velorio* (1960; Lady Wake), a collection of nine stories and a novelette. Both of these early works belong to the *intimista* style of writing, a carefully crafted and subtly conceived psychological envi-ronment characterized by ambiguity and efforts to plumb the psychic depths. In both, there are ties between Avilés and Cuba, although the first takes place primarily in Asturias, and most of the stories of the second in Cuba. *Ciudad rebelde* (1967; Rebel City) is both a novel of adventures and a kind of homage to Fidel Castro, commemorating the struggle of the Cuban people against the Batista dictatorship. The hero, Maseda, is involved in a clandestine student organization and because suspicion falls upon him, he is followed by the police in an attempt to uncover and capture his fellow conspirators. Sent to Miami by the group in order to minimize the danger of his compromising the others, he believes his inactivity is cowardly and returns, inadvertently compromising his mentor. Maseda provokes a duel with police in which he is mortally wounded, although he lives long enough to hear of the entry of Fidel's guerrillas into the capital. One of the most distinctive notes of *Ciudad rebelde* is the number of significant roles played by Spaniards, both immigrants and refugees, who help the revolutionaries in their struggle for freedom.

BIBLIOGRAPHY

Primary Text

*Ciudad rebelde*. Barcelona: Nova Terra, 1967.
*Doña Velorio. (Nueve cuentos y una nivola)*. Havana: Universidad Central de Las Villas, 1960.
*Un pueblo y dos agonías*. México: Grijalba, 1965.

Criticism

Zelaya Kolker, Marielena. *Testimonios americanos de los escritores españoles transte-rrados de 1939*. Madrid: Cultura Hispánica, 1985. 87–98.

Janet Pérez

**AMADO CARBALLO, Luis** (1901, Pontevedra–1927, Pontevedra), Galician poet and narrator. Teacher and journalist, Amado Carballo is the author of descriptive poetry in which there is an accumulation of nature images. The school he belongs to is sometimes called neo-romantic, other times *imaginista* or "pon-tevedresa" (from Pontevedra). Although hermetic, it has been of wide influence in Galician poetic writing and shares the more traditional elements of nature, rural elements, and human traits. With its effort to be objective, Amado Carballo's verse contains images similar to those of ultraism or to those of *García Lorca. His style of avant-garde writing has been called *hilozoísta* by R. Carballo Calero, but musical rhythm is not entirely lacking. It is possible to find signs of a familiarity with *Valle-Inclán and Juan Bautista Andrade in the poetry, which like the prose is in Galician. *See also* Galician Literature.

BIBLIOGRAPHY

Primary Texts

*Ogalo*. La Coruña: Nos, 1928. (poetry)
*Maliaxe*. Pontevedra: n.p., 1922. (narrative)
*Obras en prosa e verso*. Vigo: n.p., 1970.
Nine poems in *Ocho siglos de poesía gallega*. Ed., prol. C. Martín Gaite and A. Ruiz
     Tarrazona. Madrid: Alianza, 1972. Gallego and Spanish translations.
*Os probes de Deus*. La Coruña: n.p., 1923. (narrative)
*Proel*. Ponteuedra: Alborada, 1927. (poetry)

Criticism

Carballo Calero, Ricardo. *Historia da literatura galega contemporánea*. 3rd ed. Vigo:
     Galaxia, 1981.
Méndez Ferrín, Xosé Luis. "Limiar" to *Luis Amado Carballo, Obras en prosa e verso*.
     Vigo: Castrelos, 1970.
Pena, Xosé Ramón. *Luis Amado Carballo*. La Coruña: Nos, 1982.

                                                                                                    Kathleen March

**AMADOR DE LOS RÍOS, José** (1818, Baena–1878, Seville), painter, writer, and especially, important historian. His *Historia social, política y religiosa de los judíos en España y Portugal* (1875–76; Social, Political and Religious History of the Jews in Spain and Portugal) is a veritable re-evaluation of the contribution of Jews to Spanish history, a concern which culminates in our days with the work of Américo *Castro and Claudio *Sánchez-Albornoz. Amador details the enormous participation of Jews in the history of the Iberian Peninsula in areas as diverse as politics, religion, science and literature. His concern for the artistic, folkloric and historic past of Iberia is in keeping with *Romanticism. Amador's attempts to emulate Romantic poetry yielded only mediocre verse. Another work of great significance is his *Historia crítica de la literatura española* (1861–65; Critical History of Spanish Literature), a meticulous seven-volume bibliographic study of Spanish literature to the beginning of the sixteenth c. In collaboration with Juan de Dios de la Rada and Cayetano *Rosell y López, he also wrote the *Historia de la villa y Corte de Madrid* (1860; History of the Town and Court of Madrid).

BIBLIOGRAPHY

Primary Texts

*Historia crítica de la literatura española*. 7 vols. Madrid: Gredos, 1969. Facs.
*Historia de la villa y corte de Madrid*. Madrid: López de la Hoya, 1862–64.
*Historia social, política y religiosa de los judíos de España y Portugal*. Buenos Aires:
     Bajel, 1943.

**AMANTES DE TERUEL, Leyenda de los** (Legend of the Lovers of Teruel). The historical bases of the story continue to be debated (see Sotaca García and Guardiola Alcover). Boccaccio claimed the story to be true in his version, *Girolamo y Salvestra*. Juan Yagüe de Salas produced a ms. titled *La historia de los amores de Diego Juan Martínez de Marcilla e Isabel de Segura* (1217; Story of the Love Affair of Diego Juan Martínez and Isabel of Segura) for his *Los amantes de Teruel: epopeya trágica* (1616; Lovers of Teruel: Tragic Epic); many critics judge the source to be a fabrication. The story centers around the unhappy love affair of Diego de Marcilla and Isabel de Segura. In order to obtain permission to marry Isabel, Diego must become wealthy within six years. This he accomplishes, but he is then thwarted in his attempt to return to Isabel by Queen Zulima, Moorish queen of Valencia. In love with Diego, Zulima has him ambushed by bandits. When he is finally released, Isabel has already married Diego's rival. Both lovers die as a result of their sorrow and loss. Regardless of the historical truth, the legend has served as inspiration for a rich literary tradition comprising works by *Pérez de Montalbán, *Tirso, *Hartzenbusch, Antillón, and others. Tomás Bretón also composed an opera, based on the Hartzenbusch work, which premiered in 1889.

BIBLIOGRAPHY

Criticism

Guardiola Alcover, Conrado. *La verdad actual sobre los Amantes de Teruel*. Teruel: Instituto de Estudios Turolenses, CSIC, 1988.
Sotaca García, J. L. *Los amantes de Teruel. La tradición y la historia*. Zaragoza: Librería General, 1979.

Maureen Ihrie

**AMAR Y BORBÓN, Josefa** (1752, Zaragoza–1803?, Zaragoza), translator and writer. Aragonese by birth but reared and educated in Madrid, Josefa Amar y Borbón was the product as well as an example of the enlightened elite in Bourbon Spain. She was a member of the Economic Society of Zaragoza, the Medical Society of Barcelona and the Economic Society of Madrid. A well-known translator, she devoted many years of work to the translation of works by the Jesuit Llampillas. Amar y Borbón's original literary production cataloged to date includes eight essays published between 1783 and 1787 and a book *Discurso sobre la educación física y moral de las mugeres* (1790; Discourse on the Physical and Moral Education of Women). Like her contemporaries, Josefa Amar combined the established traditions of *Siglo de Oro (Golden Age) writing with eighteenth-c. themes to begin defining a literary style later to be recognized as the modern *essay.

BIBLIOGRAPHY

Primary Texts

"Discurso en defensa del talento de las mugeres." *Dieciocho* 3 (1980): 144–61.
*Discurso sobre la educación física y moral de las mugeres*. Madrid: Cano, 1790.

Criticism

McClendon, Carmen Chaves. "Josefa Amar y Borbón: A Forgotten Figure of the Spanish Enlightenment." *Seven Studies in Medieval English History and Other Historical Essays*. Jackson: UP of Mississippi, 1983.

———. "Josefa Amar y Borbón: Essayist." *Dieciocho* 3 (1980): 138–43.

Rudat, Eva M. Kahiluoto. "La mujer ilustrada." *Letras femeninas* 2 (1976): 20–32.

Carmen Chaves McClendon

**AMO, Javier del** (1944, Madrid– ), Spanish novelist, short story writer, and essayist. Del Amo holds degrees in law and clinical psychology. His short stories have appeared in *Cuadernos hispanoamericanos*, *Revista de Occidente*, *Aulas*, *El Urogallo*, *Informaciones* and *Norte* (Amsterdam). He has also published a number of essays on psychology in various newspapers and journals. His novels include *El sumidero* (1965; The Garbage Dump), *Las horas vacías* (1968; Empty Hours), *La espiral* (1972; The Spiral), and *El canto de las sirenas de Gaspar Hauser* (1973). This fourth novel is inspired by an actual news event, the finding of a feral child or adolescent, and treats two young writers who have just completed a book on "el niño gallego" (a feral) and face the ethical dilemma of whether the "civilization" into which the symbolic savage has been unwillingly shoved represents any real improvement.

Janet Pérez

**AMORÓS, Andrés** (1941, Valencia– ), literary critic, professor of literature. His earlier works include *Introducción a la novela contemporánea* (1966; Introduction to the Contemporary Novel) and *Sociología de la novela rosa* (1968; Sociology of the Romance Novel). He has worked extensively on *Pérez de Ayala, producing various critical editions, other studies, including a prologue to the *Obras narrativas*; his edition of Pérez de Ayala's *Troteras y danzaderas* won the National Prize for Literature (Essay). During the 1970s, Amorós emerged as an increasingly influential and perceptive critic of the contemporary narrative. He has also worked in the areas of literary theory and comparative literature.

BIBLIOGRAPHY

Primary Texts

*Análisis de cinco comedias. (Teatro español de la posguerra.)* Madrid: Castalia, 1977.

*El comentario de textos, 3: la novela realista.* Madrid: Castalia, 1982.

*Introducción a la novela contemporánea.* 2nd ed. Salamanca: Anaya, 1971.

*Modernismo y postmodernismo.* Madrid: La Muralla, 1973.

*La novela intelectual de Ramón Pérez de Ayala.* Madrid: Gredos, 1972.

*Sociología de la novela rosa.* Madrid: Taurus, 1968.

*Vida y literatura en "Troteras y danzaderas."* Madrid: Castalia, 1973.

Janet Pérez

**AMORÓS, Juan Bautista.** *See* Lanza, Silverio

**ANA DE SAN BARTOLOMÉ, Sor** (1549, El Almendral, Avila–1626, Antwerp), poet, spiritual autobiographer, mystic. Daughter of a peasant family wealthy enough to employ some laborers, Ana de San Bartolomé resolved to become a nun at an early age. She professed in the first Discalced Carmelite convent, in Ávila, and there met Sta. *Teresa of Ávila. Her material and spiritual existence became inextricably intertwined with that of the Saint's. For twelve years, until Teresa's death in 1582, she was her faithful servant, an almost constant companion, and ideal nurse. Her very words—a spiritual autobiography, religious poems, letters, and reports—owe their continued existence to Sta. Teresa. Sta. Teresa commanded her to learn to write, and the previously illiterate Sor Ana was thereafter miraculously able to do so. After Teresa's death, Ana de San Bartolomé saw herself as one of the direct guardians of the Teresian Constitution and Rules of the Reform. She wrote rules for nuns, founded convents in France and the Low Countries, transcribed her visions, and narrated her own *Vida* (1624; Life). Her writings evoke a fluid movement between external and internal realities, and portray Teresa as mother, companion, prophet and intermediary.

BIBLIOGRAPHY

Primary Texts

*Autobiografía*. Transcription, intro., notes., Father Fortunato Antolín. Madrid: Espiritualidad, 1969.
*Obras completas de la Beata Ana de San Bartolomé*. Ed. J. Urkiza. 2 vols. Rome: Edizioni Teresanium, 1981, 1985.

Criticism

Arenal, E., and S. Schlau. ''More Than One Teresa: A Movement of Religious Women.'' *Untold Sisters: Hispanic Nuns in Their Own Works*. Albuquerque: U of New Mexico P, 1989. Contains selections with English translations.
Florencio del Niño Jesús. *La Beata Ana de San Bartolomé. Compañera y secretaria de Sta. Teresa de Jesús (Compendio de su vida)*. Burgos: El Monte Carmelo, 1917.
Serrano y Sanz, M. *Apuntes para una biblioteca de autoras españolas*. In BAE 270.

Stacey Schlau

***ANALES CASTELLANOS*** (Annals of Castile). A medieval chronology which covers events from 618 to 1126. *See also Crónicas*; *Cronicones*.

***ANALES TOLEDANOS*** (Annals of Toledo). A medieval chronology that encompasses events to 1391. *See also Crónicas*; *Cronicones*.

**ANDRADE, Eugénio de** (1923, Póvoa da Atalaia– ), Portuguese poet. After childhood in Lisbon and high-school level study in Coimbra, Andrade has been a government employee in Oporto. *Narciso* (1940), his first volume of poetry, follows in certain essentials the lines of traditional Portuguese verse, as is true of most of the poet's early work. He has to date published at least fifteen collections, most of them slim volumes of brief lyric compositions which come increasingly under the influence of Surrealism in metaphors and other rhetorical figures. It is probable that Andrade has been influenced more or less equally by the Surrealist movement and works in that vein by *García Lorca, whom he translated. Many of Andrade's themes are constants of universal poetry—love, sorrow, separation, nature, loneliness, longing, and solitude. Others, however, are more closely tied to contemporary circumstances, as with his poetry of social protest. Among his other collections are *Adolescente* (1942), *As Mãos e os Frutos* (1948; Hands and Fruit), *Coração do Dia* (1958; The Heart of Day), and *Obscuro domínio* (1971; Dark Dominion).

BIBLIOGRAPHY

Primary Text

*Contra la oscuridad.* Intro. and Spanish tr. F. Villar Ribot. Pamplona: Pamiela, 1988. Portuguese and Spanish.

English Translations

*Inhabited Heart.* Tr. A. Levitin. Van Nuys, CA: Perivale, 1985. Portuguese and English.
*Memory of Another River.* Intro. and tr. A. Levitin. St. Paul, MN: New Rivers, 1988.

Janet Pérez

**ANDRENIO,** pseudonym of Eduardo Gómez de Baquero (1866, Madrid–1929, Madrid), journalist and literary critic. He was book reviewer for *El Imparcial,* a position previously held by *Clarín, which offered him much influence. His most important contribution is to the study of the novel, a genre he preferred and praised in his *Novelas y novelistas* (1918; Novels and Novelists) and in *El renacimiento de la novela en el siglo XIX* (1924; The Renaissance of the Novel in the Nineteenth Century.). His essays on journalism and literature are found in *Letras e ideas* (1905; Letters and Ideas), *Cartas a Amaranta* (1924; Letters to Amaranta), *Pirandello y Compañía* (1928; Pirandello and Co.), *Nacionalismo e hispanismo* (1928; Nationalism and Hispanism), and *De Gallardo a Unamuno* (1926; From Gallardo to Unamuno). In 1925 he was accepted into the Spanish Academy (*Academia Española), presenting a speech on "El triunfo de la novela" (The Triumph of the Novel).

BIBLIOGRAPHY

Primary Texts

*Cartas a Amaranta.* Madrid: Ciudad lineal, 1924.
*De Gallardo a Unamuno.* Madrid: Espasa-Calpe, 1926.
*Letras e ideas.* Barcelona: Henrich, 1905.
*Nacionalismo e hispanismo.* Madrid: Historia nueva, 1928.
*Novelas y novelistas.* Madrid: Calleja, 1918.
*Pirandello y Compañía.* Madrid: Mundo latino, 1928.
*El Renacimiento de la novela en el siglo XIX.* Madrid: Mundo latino, 1924.

Sara Schyfter

**ANDRÉS, Elena** (1931, Madrid– ), Spanish poet. Most of this writer's verse belongs to the Surrealistic trend that began in Spain with the *Generation of 1927. Despite occasional touches of social concern, her major concerns are metaphysical and cosmic, a transcendent search for meaning. *El buscador* (1959;

The Seeker) initiates Andrés's search for the significance of the human condition, continued in a more positive vein in *Eterna vela* (1961; Eternal Candle) which rejects existential nothingness in favor of an optimistic proclamation of ultimate human victory. Andrés continues her search in *Dos caminos* (1964; Two Paths), alternating between the ancestral past and unexplored future. *Desde aquí mis señales* (1971; My Address Here) furthers the quest for ultimate meaning, but with more emphasis upon the here and now, the joys and sorrows of daily existence, and less attention to the mysterious universe. *Trance de la vigilia colmada* (1980; Trance of Fulfilled Sleeplessness) returns to exploration of a mysterious, strange and sometimes sinister universe in unreal and often night-marish surroundings and a general atmosphere of anguish.

BIBLIOGRAPHY

Primary Texts

*El buscador*. Madrid: Agora, 1959.
*Desde aquí mis señales*. Salamanca: Alamo, 1971.
*Dos caminos*. Madrid: Rialp, 1964.
*Eterna vela*. Madrid: Rialp, 1961.
*Trance de la vigilia colmada*. Barcelona: Ambito literario, 1980.

Janet Pérez

**ANDRÉS, Juan** (1740, Planes, Valencia–1817, Rome), Jesuit scholar and literary historian. Expelled from Spain with his order, he lived in Naples and worked as librarian in the king's palace. He formed part of the Italian Jesuit community that renovated itself in exile as it undertook the evaluation and defense of its homeland. Andres's *Dell' origini, progressi e stato attuale d'ogni letterature* was published in the original Italian from 1782 to 1799 and was also translated to Spanish by his brother Carlos as *Origen, progresos y estado actual de toda la literatura* (1784–1806; Origin, Development and Present State of All Literature). This seven-volume, encyclopedic work is a typical product of neoclassicism. It brings foreign literary theory to Spanish attention and serves to popularize and synthesize European ideas, even if it submits to the doctrines of its day which considered the Spanish theater of the *Siglo de Oro (Golden Age) inferior to classical French tragedy. Andrés attacks the drama of Shakespeare, Lope de *Vega and *Cervantes for failing to abide by the traditional unities. He admires Greek and Roman poetry, Rousseau, and especially Voltaire, and is able to evaluate literary merits over religious ideology. *Cartas familiares* (1786–93; Personal Letters) attempts to introduce new ideas into Spain, while the *Cartas sobre la música de los árabes* (1787; Letters on Arabic Music) reflects on the Arab influence in Europe.

BIBLIOGRAPHY

Primary Texts

*Cartas familiares*. 5 vols. Madrid: Sancha, 1786–93.
*Dell' origini, progressi e stato attuale d'ogni letterature*. 7 vols. Parma: Stamperia Reale, 1782–99. Italian

*Origen, progresos y estado actual de toda literatura.* Spanish tr. C. Andrés. 10 vols. Madrid: Sancha, 1784–1806.

Criticism

Batllori, M. "Juan Andrés y el Humanismo." *RFE* 29 (1945): 121–28.

———. "Una memoria biográfica sobre Juan Andrés por Francisco Javier Burrell y Vilanova, 1822." *Archivum Historicum Societatis Iesu.* Rome. (19—?)

Mazzeo, Guido. *The Abate Juan Andrés: Literary Historian of the XVIII Century.* New York: Hispanic Institute, 1965.

Menéndez y Pelayo, M. *Historia de las ideas estéticas.* Vol. 2. Ed. E. Sánchez y Reyes. Madrid: CSIC, 1962.

**ANDRESEN LEITÃO, Alfredo.** *See* A. Rubén

**ANDÚJAR, Juan de** (15th c., ?–?), poet. One of the authors included in the *Cancionero de *Stúñiga,* his "Visión de amor" (Vision of Love) was clearly inspired by Dante's *Inferno.* Other works of Andújar include "Cómo procede la fortuna" (How Fortune Moves) and "Loores al Señor Rey don Alfonso" (Praises to Our Lord and King Don Alphonse), which was not printed until the nineteenth c.

BIBLIOGRAPHY

Primary Texts

*Cancionero de Estúñiga.* Ed., study N. Salvador Miguel. Madrid: Alhambra, 1987.

*Cancionero de Estúñiga. Edición paleográfica.* Ed. M. and E. Alvar. Zaragoza: Institución Fernando el Católico, 1981.

*Rimas inéditas del siglo XV.* Ed. E. de Ochoa. Paris: Baudry, 1851.

**ANDÚJAR, Manuel** (1913, La Carolina, Jaén– ), novelist, poet, playwright and essayist. Before the Spanish Civil War he was a journalist and a public servant. After the defeat of the republic he was exiled in Saint-Cyprien, France. He arrived in Mexico in 1939—on the refugee ship *Sinaia*—where he remained, as a *transterrado*, with a short sojourn in Chile and travel in South America, until his return to Spain in 1967. Since then he has been associated with Alianza Editorial publishers in Madrid. He now resides in San Lorenzo del Escorial and continues to write and lecture from there. In Mexico he was co-founder, with José Ramón Arana, of *Las Españas*, an important literary periodical of the *transterrado* community. He also held executive positions in the Fondo de Cultura Económica and Editorial Mortiz. His writings reflect understanding and affection for Mexico, whose influence he sees as a shaping environment that compels the *transterrados* to incorporate an awareness of the land "donde estamos y donde somos" (where we are & where we shall be) into their ongoing self-definition. Yet, both in his essays and in his narrative, his main theme is Spain, the homeland he never doubts he will see again.

His work includes *La propia imagen* (1977; Self-Image) and *Campana y cadena* (1965; Bell and Chain), poetry; *Fechas de un retorno* (1979; Dates of a Return), poetry; *Narrativa del exilio español y literatura latinoamericana* (1975; Narratives of Spanish Exile and Latin American Literature) and *Andalucía e Hispanoamérica, crisol de mestizajes* (1982; Andalucia and Spanish America: Melting Pot of Races), essays; *El primer juicio final. Los aniversarios. El sueño robado* (1962; The First Last Judgment/The Anniversaries/The Stolen Sheep), theater; and *Cartas son cartas* (1968; Letters and Letters). He is best known for his narrative, most of which is intended as part of a cycle, *Lares y Penares*, incomplete as yet. The cycle includes *Cristal herido* (1945; Wounded Glass); the *Vísperas* (Day Before) trilogy—*Llanura* (1945; Plain); *El vencido* (1949; The Defeated One); and *El destino de Lázaro* (1959; Lazarus's Destiny); *La sombra del madero* (1968; Shadow of Wood); *Historias de una historia* (1973; Tales of a Story). His short stories are *Partiendo de la angustia* (1944; Starting from Anguish); *Los lugares vacíos* (1971; Empty Places) and *La franja luminosa* (1973; The Luminous Band). Most of this narrative has appeared in peninsular editions in recent years and has been met with an avid reception particularly among younger readers, for whom the literature of the exiles had been largely unknown. *Vísperas* is being adapted for a television miniseries in Madrid, and *Cristal herido*, first published forty years ago, has awakened much interest.

Andújar's novelistic cycle is also a puzzle the reader must put together to grasp his portrait of Spain from the beginning of this century to the last stages of Spanish republican diaspora. *Vísperas* deals with some specific social problems in three regions of Spain around the decade of 1914: *Llanura* explores *cacicazgo* (power of a political boss) in La Mancha; *El vencido* shows the rise of a labor movement in a mining town in Jaén; *El destino de Lázaro* traces the tragic consequences of a bureaucratic cover-up of a military disaster. But besides social consciousness, another common thread runs through this trilogy as well as in the rest of Andújar's fiction: the presence of an individual who sometimes reluctantly but surely abandons his personal safety and comfort to respond to an injustice he cannot ignore. Thus a frivolous law student may become the *cacique's* (political boss) antagonist and lose his home, family and fortune as a result (*Llanura*); an unlettered man will choose to devote his life to the welfare of his fellow miners (*El vencido*); or a very staid and private merchant will risk public ire, and eventually lose his life, to expose a criminal bureaucratic fraud (*El destino de Lázaro*).

Together, social injustice and individual ethical choice are ingredients of a latent social explosion: *Vísperas*, the ominous visiting pause. *Cristal herido* and *Historias de una historia* thrust the narrative to its next stages. The former chronicles the idealism and unconditional commitment of young people to the republic they identified with the birth of a true democracy for Spain. Against them the fascists, concealed at first and then quite openly, wreaked their ferocious vengeance. *Historias* focuses on family events a day or so before the fateful July 19, 1936. A wedding in a provincial town, a gathering that is not to be. Visitors and resident men alike are rounded up by "the establishment" and by some—not all—army troops. The authorities who had sworn allegiance to the republic become the executioners of those suspected of supporting the republic. The "stories" continue weaving themselves in bloody strands: people who were previously indifferent become politicized. Toward the end Andújar brings many of his threads together to show us a Barcelona at war, in the vise of fascist attacks and the political, and also violent, intolerance of the leftist cadres.

Denunciation of intolerance is another trait of Andújar's narrative. In *Cita de fantasmas* (A Date with Ghosts) the son of Spanish exiles in Mexico, a young man who has spent most of his life away from Spain, sets out to ascertain the psychological roots of the civil war that has dominated his elders' destiny, determined their exile—and his. Again, it is Andújar's procedure to delve into a personal mystery and project it to the larger historical event. The young man's inquiry shows him that during the war a man, whose name is darkly muttered among the refugees, was killed by his own republican colleagues because their fanatical local leaders could not tolerate ambiguity or dissent. His more moderate comrades did nothing to help him because they were afraid. This revelation comes to the young exile step by step, so that along with the frailties and the petty limitations of individuals he is also able to grasp the generous, heroic altruism of the times. These finds help the protagonist to make peace with his elders' past and to ready himself for his next and equally difficult task: to understand and empathize with Mexico, the country to which he has decided he now belongs. The outreach of Andújar's novelistic scheme is one of the most ambitious efforts in Spanish literature, and one of the noblest.

BIBLIOGRAPHY

Primary Texts

*Campana y cadena*. Alcalá de Henares: Aldonza, 1965.
*Cristal herido*. Mexico: Isla, 1945.
*La franja luminosa*. Las Palmas, Grand Canary: Inventarios Provisionales, 1973.
*Historias de una historia*. Madrid: Al-Borak, 1973.
*Partiendo de la angustia*. Mexico: Moncayo, 1944.
*El primer juicio final. Los aniversarios. El sueño robado*. Mexico: De Andrea, 1962.
*Saint Cyprien plage, campo de concentración*. Mexico: n.p., 1942.

Criticism

Zelaya Kolker, Marielena. *Testimonios americanos de los escritores españoles transterrados de 1939*. Madrid: Instituto de Cooperación Iberoamericana, 1985.
Marra-López, J. R. *Narrativa española fuera de España, 1939–1961*. Madrid: Guadarrama, 1963.
Nora, E. G. de. *La novela contemporánea (1939–1967)*. 2nd ed. Madrid: Gredos, 1970.

Marielena Zelaya Kolker

**ÁNGELES, Juan de los** (1536, Oropesa, Toledo–1609, Madrid), Franciscan, Court preacher, mystical writer. Among Spanish mystics, he ranks behind only two: San *Juan de la Cruz and Sta. *Teresa de Jesús. After studies at the U of Alcalá, he joined the order and steadily rose to positions of high responsibility. A productive writer, his most thorough exposition of the mystical way is *Diálogos* *de la conquista del espíritu y secreto reino de Dios* (1595; *Conquest of the Kingdom of God,* 1957). His concept of beauty and love is neoplatonic, and his thought is strongly influenced by North European mystics, especially Ruysbroeck and Tauler. In 1608 he published a continuation of the *Diálogos,* the *Manual de vida perfecta* (Manual of Perfect Life). The *Triunfos del amor de Dios* (1590; Triumphs of God's Love) is very much a *Renaissance work, with many classical allusions, again the neoplatonic conception of beauty and love, and clear influence of St. Bonaventure, Sabunde, Hugo de St. Victor, etc. He subsequently revised and shortened the *Triunfos* under the title *Lucha espiritual y amorosa entre Dios y el alma* (1600; Spiritual, Loving Struggle between God and the Soul). Other works by Father Juan include *Tratado de los soberanos misterios de la Misa* (1604; Treatise on the Supreme Mysteries of Mass), *Vergel espiritual del ánima religiosa* (1609; Spiritual Garden of the Religious Soul), *Consideraciones espirituales sobre el Cantar de los Cantares de Salomon* (1607; Spiritual Considerations on the Song of Songs by Solomon), and *Cofradía y devoción de . . . Virgen María* (1608?; Brotherhood and Devotion to . . . the Virgin Mary). His style is a model of Renaissance clarity, beauty and grace, infused with very personal, profound feeling—surpassed only by the prose of Fray Luis de *León. *See also* Mysticism; Platonism.

BIBLIOGRAPHY

Primary Texts

*Diálogos de la conquista. . . .* Ed., prol. A. González Palencia. Madrid: Aguirre, 1946.
*Obras místicas.* In NBAE 20, 24.
*Triunfos del amor de Dios.* Madrid: G. del Amo, 1901.

English Translation

*Conquest of the Kingdom of God.* Tr. C. J. Crowley. St. Louis: Herder, 1957.

                                                                Maureen Ihrie

**ANGHIERA, Pietro Martire d'.** *See* Mártir de Anglería, Pedro

**ANGLADA, Maria Àngels** (1930, Vic– ), Catalan novelist and poet. Trained in classical philology, which is often reflected in her creative writings, Anglada has also published critical essays on Italian poetry and Greek mythology. *Les closes* (1979; The Enclosed), her first novel, is historical fiction set in the nineteenth c., re-creating the difficult years prior to the liberal Revolution of 1868. Prior works included another historical foray, *Memories d'un pages del segle XVIII* (1978; Memoirs of an Eighteenth-C. Peasant), and a poetry collection done in collaboration with Núria *Albó entitled *Díptic* (1972; Diptych). A solo poetry collection entitled *Kyaparíssia* (1980) contains constant references to the Mediterranean and classical world, people, landscape, languages and atmosphere. Emphasis upon things Greek appears again in *No em dic Laura* (1981; My Name Isn't Laura), a collection of three long short stories or novelettes. *Viola d'amore* (1983; Viola of Love) is not dependent upon historical or archaeological reconstruction, but evokes the world of music in the Trio Izvorul, whose members represent opposing ideologies. *See also* Catalan Literature.

BIBLIOGRAPHY
   Primary Text
*Los cercados.* Barcelona: Destino, 1986.

Janet Pérez

**ANGLICISM,** any English word which has entered the Spanish language. Until recently, the influence of English idiom was sparse; it is increasingly apparent through the influence of industry, sports, politics and the press.

BIBLIOGRAPHY
   Criticism
Pratt, Chris. *El Anglicismo en el español peninsular contemporáneo.* Madrid: Gredos, 1980. (Contains bibliography with English sources.)
Teschner, Richard V. "A Critical, Annotated Bibliography of Anglicisms in English." *Hispania* 57 (1974): 631–78.

**ANGULO, Julio** (1902, Madrid–1967, Madrid), physician, prose writer. Author of two novels: *Lluvia de cohetes* (1933; Rain of Rockets) and *Del balcón a la calle* (1948; From The Balcony to the Street). The latter earned him a National Prize for Literature. Angulo also wrote short stories, travel chronicles, and pieces for newspapers, radio, and the theater.

BIBLIOGRAPHY
   Primary Texts
*Anoche en Montecarlo.* Madrid: Rollán, 1953.
*Los árboles del huerto.* Madrid: Cid, 1954.
*Del balcón a la calle.* N.p.: n.p., n.d.
*Lluvia de cohetes.* Avila: Medrano, 1933.

Janet Pérez

**ANTOLÍN RATO, Mariano** (1943, Gijón, Asturias– ), Spanish novelist. Associated with Spain's most radical, experimental literary vanguard, Antolín Rato is on the Editorial Board of *Zikkurath/Ficción,* which publishes some of the most extreme avant-garde fiction on the European continent. He has produced a book on Zen Buddhism, another on Bob Dylan, and many articles on literature, as well as subjects such as the mass media, the drug culture, and science fiction. Antolín Rato has translated many contemporary works from English, rendering into Spanish such writers as Malcolm Lowry, William Faulkner, Gertrude Stein, Jack Kerouac and William Burroughs. In the early 1970s, Antolín Rato was a co-founder of *"Nova-Expressionismo"*—a "movement" of limited duration whose diverse membership professed a common admiration for Burroughs and a mutual interest in renovating the language via semantic, lexical and sequential fragmentation (with the result that most of their texts communicated little or nothing). *Cuando 900 mil Mach approx*, Antolín Rato's first novel, won the New Critics' Prize in 1975. *Mundo Araña* (1981; Spider World), his fourth novel, is in the vein of works written by computers, or whose characters are programs—an abstract fantasy-adventure, an allegory of the mechanisms of power and a warning (in the vein of *Brave New World* and *1984*) against such possible abuses as thought control, manipulation of sensations via the media or control of the psyche via interplay of information and disinformation. *De vulgari Zyklon B manifestante* (1975; Manifesting from Vulgari Zyklon B) and *Entre espacios intermedios: WHAMM!* (1978; Between Middle Spaces: WHAMM!) are in much the same vein. *Campos unificados de conciencia* (1984; Unified Fields of Consciousness) alludes with its title to contemporary theoretical physics. In this piece of allegorical "philosophical fiction," the writer cultivates a style some critics have termed "psychedelic realism," unfolding an adventure of phantasmagoric or fantastic beings who attempt to "metabolize" confusion in order to impede the loss of consciousness. An extended metaphor, structured upon a musical relationship of dissonances, this experimental novel is a kind of contemporary Labyrinth of Fortune, polyphonic and multidimensional, linking together a number of timeless constants of story or plot in a pseudo-technological *roman á clef* whose intention is moral or political. *Mar desterrado* (1988; Exiled Sea), his sixth novel, begins a new manner or narrative cycle in which his former psychedelic realism or "cybernetic conceits" give way to an impure *modernism, a relative traditionalism. It is set in a bar in an urban center which might well be Madrid in the 1980s (notwithstanding its being a port). Characters include a middle-aged painter, an attractive female recording executive, an insecure model, a successful journalist, and various other characters on the verge of middle age, whose lives are dominated by material objects, drugs, sex, alcohol, and fast cars or jet-set travel—paradigms of this end of the twentieth c. which the author views as the Age of Vice.

Janet Pérez

**ANTONIO, Nicolás** (1617, Seville–1684, Madrid), bibliographer and scholar. He aimed to catalog, in the *Bibliotheca hispana vetus* (Rome, 1672; Library of Ancient Spain), all books written in Spain from the time of Augustus to 1500. The *Bibliotheca hispana nova* (Rome, 1696; Library of Modern Spain) compiled literature from 1500 to 1670. Antonio's scholarly rigor was singular for his day, making these compilations valuable sources in the history of literature and literary criticism. Antonio's quest for correct information also motivated his *Censura de historias fabulosas* (Censure of False Histories), an attempt to correct historical misrepresentations. *See also* Humanism; Renaissance.

BIBLIOGRAPHY

Primary Texts

*Bibliotheca.* Ed. Pérez Bayer. Madrid: Ibarra, 1788.
*Bibliotheca hispana nova.* Turin: Bottega d'Erasmo, 1963. Facs. of 1783–88 ed.

*Bibliotheca hispana vetus*. Turin: Bottega d'Erasmo, 1963. Facs. of 1788 ed.
*Censura de historias fabulosas*. Ed. G. Mayáns y Siscar. Valencia: Bordazar de Artazu, 1742.
*Del epistolario de don Nicolás Antonio*. Ed. E. Juliá Martínez. Madrid: Artes gráficas, 1935.

Criticism

See ed. of Juliá Martínez.

**ANTONIO DE GUEVARA.** *See* Guevara, Antonio de

**ANTUNES, António Lobo** (1942, Lisbon– ), Portuguese contemporary novelist. A psychiatrist by profession, Antunes was conscripted to serve as a medical officer in the African colonial wars for 27 months. These experiences are the backdrop for most of his novels, making him an exception among contemporary writers for whom those wars seem not to have occurred.

In his first novel, *Memória de Elefante* (1979; The Memory of an Elephant), Antunes describes the psychological and emotional dismemberment of a medical doctor wallowing in loneliness and alienation. *Os Cus de Judas* (1979; *South of Nowhere*, 1983) portrays a veteran of the colonial wars whose flashbacks are intertwined with the personal struggle to adjust the past to the present. With *Conhecimento do Inferno* (1980; Knowledge of Hell), Antunes rounds out his trilogy of despair by analogizing a psychiatric hospital and Portuguese society. *Explicação dos Pássaros* (1981; The Nature of Birds) delves into the paralyzing relationship between a father and son.

The colonial wars, in *Fado Alexandrino* (1983; the Alexandrine Fado), shadow the members of a platoon reunited for a night out on the town in Lisbon and highlight the lingering but universally denied effects of those horrors. *Auto dos Danados* (1985; Ambition: A Mystery Play) is a Faulknerian saga of a latifundist family shattered by the onset of the Revolution of 1974.

Because of his caustic irreverence for the Portuguese post-revolutionary Establishment and because of his best-seller successes, Antunes is a controversial literary figure. However, his rich, elaborate metaphors and similes and his uncompromising renditions of daily speech underscore Antunes's uncontested role as a renovator and popularizer of the novel in contemporary Portugal.

BIBLIOGRAPHY

Primary Texts

*Auto dos Danados*. Lisbon: Dom Quixote, 1985.
*Conhecimento do Inferno*. Lisbon: Vega, 1980.
*Os Cus de Judas*. Lisbon: Vega, 1929.
*Explicação dos Pássaros*. Lisbon: Dom Quixote, 1983.
*Fado Alexandrino*. Lisbon: Dom Quixote, 1983.
*Memória de Elefante*. Lisbon: Vega, 1979.

English Translation

*South of Nowhere*. Tr. Elizabeth Lowe. New York: Random House, 1983.

Criticism

Pedrosa, Inês. "António Lobo Antunes." *Jornal de Letras, Artes & Ideias* 197 (14–20 April 1986): 2–3.

Jaime H. da Silva


**APOLONIO, Libro de (Book of Apollonius)**, thirteenth-c. Spanish version of the popular medieval legend of King Apollonius of Tyre. The Spanish poem has survived in the unique ms. of a codex of the Escorial library that also contains the *Vida de Santa \*María Egipciaca* and the *Libro dels Reys doriente* (see *Reys d'Orient, Libre dels tres*). The ms. is written in a fourteenth-c. hand and consists of 656 stanzas of *\*cuaderna vía*. The plot unfolds in the manner of a typical Byzantine novel with exile from the homeland, shipwrecks, miraculous survivals, successes away from home, separation of families, and, finally, triumphant reunion of family and return to the homeland. Apollonius was forced to flee Tyre when he solved a riddle posed by the incestuous King Antioch. He lost his belongings at sea and swam to shore where a kind shepherd loaned him clothes for his nude body. He arrived at the court of King Architrastes where his courtly skills impressed everyone, including Luciana, the king's daughter, who soon became his wife. In an attempt to take his wife to Tyre, Apollonius was separated from her when she was believed to have died after giving birth to a daughter, Tarsiana. Luciana's body was placed in a casket and set adrift. It arrived on shore and was miraculously revived at Ephesus by a learned doctor and his assistants. Apollonius left Tarsiana in the care of a governess and set out for Egypt. Numerous fortuitous circumstances maneuvre the lives of Apollonius, Luciana and Tarsiana until they are reunited, but the most moving and delicately told of the three sets of adventures is that of Tarsiana whose musical skills and powers of persuasion save her from prostitution and bondage. In fact, one of the major themes of the story is the eventual triumph of non-violent, courtly, humanistic skills over brute force. In this sense Apollonius is as the antithesis of Alexander the Great; whereas Alexander conquered the world by force, Apollonius triumphed with his courtly skills in music and learning. The Spanish author pointedly omits from the story the details of Apollonius's defeat of the envoy of Antioch at Tarsus.

BIBLIOGRAPHY

Primary Text

*Libro de Apolonio.* Ed. Manuel Alvar. 3 vols. Madrid: Castalia, 1976.

English Translation

*The Book of Apollonius.* Tr. R. L. Grismer and E. Atkins. Minneapolis: U of Minnesota P, 1936.

Criticism

Deyermond, A. D. "Motivos folklóricos y técnica estructural en el *Libro de Apolonio.*" *Filología* 13 (1968–69): 121–49.

Colbert Nepaulsingh

**ARAGONÉS, Juan** (?, ?–before 1576, ?), writer. Nothing is known of his life. He is remembered for twelve brief anecdotes, titled *Doce cuentos* (Twelve Stories), which served as a sort of preface to Juan de *Timoneda's work, *Alivio de caminantes* (Relief for Travelers), which appeared in 1576.

BIBLIOGRAPHY

Primary Text

*Doce cuentos.* In BAE 3.

**ARANGUREN, José Luis [López]** (1909, Avila– ), Spanish philosopher, essayist, literary critic and educator. Especially influenced by Miguel de *Unamuno and José *Ortega y Gasset, under whose aegis he was formed, and the existential thought of Heidegger, Aranguren won a chair of ethics at the U of Madrid, but was later removed for political reasons. Perhaps his greatest offense in the early Franco era was his interest in the crises of Christianity, especially the Protestant Reformation and the Church's great reformers, especially Martin Luther, with his tragic sense of inner contradiction as studied in one of Aranguren's most original and significant treatises, *Protestantismo y catolicismo como formas de existencia* (1954; Protestantism and Catholicism as Forms of Existence). Particularly concerned with the pragmatic difficulties of being a Christian in contemporary circumstances, Aranguren in his *Etica* (1958; Ethics) dealt with the problem from an existential perspective in relation to self-fulfillment. In *El Marxismo como moral* (1968; Marxism as Morality) he attempted to establish a sort of philosophical dialogue with Marxism (insofar as both Christianity and Marxism are interested in improving society, concerns of a moral nature). Aranguren also analyzed the ethical implications of technological decisions, exploring these further in *Human Communication* (1967) and *Moralidades de hoy y de mañana* (1973; Moralities of Today and Tomorrow).

From 1953 onward, Aranguren spent a good deal of time teaching in the United States, especially at the U of California, where he continued his exploration of religio-philosophical problems, but also wrote many works of literary criticism: *Crítica y meditación* (1957; Criticism and Meditation); *La ética de Ortega* (1958; The Ethics of Ortega); and *Estudios literarios* (1976; Literary Studies). Other undated titles include: *Etica y política* (Ethics and Politics); *Implicaciones de la filosofía en la vida contemporánea* (Implications of Philosophy in Contemporary Life); *La juventud europea y otros ensayos* (European Youth and Other Essays); and *Moral y sociedad. Introducción a la moral social española del siglo XIX* (Morality and Society. Introduction to Spanish Social Morality in the 19th Century.). *See also* Essay.

BIBLIOGRAPHY

Primary Texts

*Catolicismo y protestantismo como formas de existencia.* Madrid: RO, 1952.
*La cruz de la monarquía española actual.* Madrid: Taurus, 1974.
*Erotismo y liberación de la mujer.* 2nd ed. Esplugues de Llobregat: Ariel, 1973.
*Estudios literarios.* Madrid: Gredos, 1976.
*La ética de Ortega.* 3rd ed. Madrid: Taurus, 1966.
*Moral y sociedad.* 4th ed. Madrid: Cuadernos para el Diálogo, 1970.

English Translations

*Human Communication.* Tr. F. Partridge. London: Weidenfeld and Nicholson, 1967.
"Unamuno in Person and in Faith." Tr. G. D. Schade. *Texas Quarterly* 4 (1961): 25–
31.

Janet Pérez

**ARAUJO COSTA, Luis** (1885, Madrid–1957, Madrid), lawyer, scholar and journalist. He is author of *El siglo XVIII en España. Su literatura* (1922), *Francia, el noble país* (1923) and *La emperatriz Eugenia* (1923). Also his is the *Biografía del Ateneo en Madrid* (1949; Biography of the Madrid Atheneum), and several studies on Madrid neighborhoods.

BIBLIOGRAPHY

Primary Texts

*El barrio de Palacio.* Madrid: Instituto de estudios madrileños, 1952.
*Biografía del Ateneo en Madrid.* Madrid: n.p., 1949.
*Hombres y cosas de la Puerta del Sol.* Madrid: Nacional, 1952.

Sara Schyfter

**ARBÓ, Sebastián Juan** (1902, Sant Carles de la Rápita [Tarragona]–1984?, ?), Catalan novelist and biographer who lived most of his adult life in Barcelona. His first novel, written in Catalan, was *L'inútil combat* (1931; The Futile Fight). Several additional novels were written in Catalan but later published in Castilian, including *Tierras del Ebro* (1932; Lands of the Ebro [River], awarded the Fastenrath Prize of the Royal Spanish Academy); *Notes d'un estudiant que va morir boig* (1933; Notes of a Student Who Died Mad); *Camins de nit* (1935; Paths of the Night); and *Tino Costa* (1946). All of these belong to the tradition of the Catalan rural novel as established by Víctor *Català (pseud. of Catarina Albert), a neo-Naturalist novel of the soil with somber colors and strongly etched figures. Arbó's deep love for the land of his birth continues to be evident throughout most of his literary production.

In the post-war period, with the outlawing of the vernacular languages, Arbó began to write primarily in Castilian, publishing a biography, *Cervantes* (1945), and the novels, *Sobre las piedras grises* (1948; Upon the Grey Rocks), which was awarded the Premio Nadal and marked the beginning of a series of novels of urban environment, set in contemporary Barcelona; *María Molinari* (1951), continuing Arbó's portrayal of lower middle-class life in Barcelona; *Nocturno de alarmas* (1957; A Nocturn of Alarms) and *Martín de Caretas* (1959), a neo-picaresque (see picaresque) narrative; and *Entre la tierra y el mar* (1966; Between Land and Sea), which won the Vicente Blasco Ibáñez Prize. Perhaps because his *Cervantes* was widely translated and financially successful, Arbó wrote a number of other biographies, including *Oscar Wilde* (1960); *Don Pío Baroja y su tiempo* (1963; Pio Baroja and His Times, awarded the National Prize for Literature); and a biographical study of the Catalan writer Jacinto *Verdaguer, *Verdaguer, el poeta, el sacerdote i el mon* (1952; Verdaguer, the Poet, the Priest, and the World). Among his other works are *Los hombres de la tierra y el mar* (1962; Men of the Land and the Sea); *Narraciones del Delta* (1965; Tales of the Delta); and *Hechos y figuras* (1968; Facts and Figures).

BIBLIOGRAPHY

Primary Texts

*Cervantes*. 3rd ed. Barcelona: Noguer, 1956.
*Entre la tierra y el mar*. Valencia: Prometeo, 1966.
*Los hombres de la tierra y del mar*. Barcelona: Argos, 1962.
*Memorias. Los hombres de la ciudad*. Barcelona: Planeta, 1982.
*Narraciones del Delta*. Barcelona: Selecta, 1965.
*Nuevas y viejas andanzas de Martín de Caretas*. Madrid: CID, 1959.
*Sobre las piedras grises*. Barcelona: Destino, 1949.

English Translation

*Cervantes. The Man and His Time*. Tr. I. Barea. London/New York: Thames & Hudson, 1955.

Janet Pérez

**ARCE, Manuel** (1928, San Roque del Acebal, Asturias– ), poet, novelist, bookseller, publisher. A resident of Santander from his childhood, Arce began as a poet, publishing *Llamada* (1949; The Call) and *Sombra de un amor* (1952; Shadow of a Love) in this genre before attempting the novel. In quick succession he produced *Testamento en la montaña* (1956; Testament upon the Mount) and *Pintado sobre el vacío* (1958; Painted on the Void), the latter a study of the moral dilemma of a writer after the death of his wife, to whom he had been faithful, as he wonders whether her death was an accident or suicide. A third novel, *Anzuelos para la lubina* (1962; Fishhooks to Catch the Lubina), had to be published in Mexico because of *censorship problems. This novel studies the death of a child, which may have been accidental or the result of neglect. For several years, Arce devoted himself to publishing the poetry of others.

BIBLIOGRAPHY

Primary Texts

*Anzuelos para la lubina.* 2nd ed. Barcelona: Destino, 1966.
*Oficio de muchachos.* Barcelona: Seix Barral, 1963.
*Pintado sobre el vacío.* Barcelona: Destino, 1958.

Janet Pérez

**ARCE DE LOS REYES, Ambrosio de** (1621?, Madrid–1661, Madrid), dramatist. He is the author of four plays: *Cegar para ver mejor* (Losing Sight to See Better), *El hechizo de Sevilla* (The Spell of Seville), *El Hércules de Hungría* (Hercules of Hungary), and *La mayor victoria de Constantino* (Constantine's Greatest Victory). He also collaborated with five other playwrights to compose another play, *La vida y muerte de San Cayetano* (Life and Death of St. Cayetano), and entered occasional poems in literary contests in and around Madrid. Little is known about his life except that he attended the U of Alcalá between 1637 and 1646 and that he entered a congregation of secular priests in Madrid in 1659, two years before his sudden death in February 1661.

BIBLIOGRAPHY

Primary Texts

*Cegar para ver mejor.* In *Comedias nuevas escogidas.* . . . vol. 13. Madrid: n.p., 1660.
*El hechizo de Sevilla.* Valencia: Viuda de J. de Orga, 1762.
*El Hércules de Hungría.* In *Comedias nuevas escogidas.* . . . vol. 12. Madrid: n.p., 1659.
*La mayor vitoria de Constantino Magno.* In *Comedias nuevas escogidas.* . . . vol. 14.
   Madrid: n.p., 1661.

**ARCE SOLÓRZANO, Juan de** (1576, ?–?, ?), translator, author. He composed the first Spanish translation of the novel *Barlaam and Joasaph*, the Christian version of the legend of Buddha, in 1608. Other works by Arce include the *Historia Evangélica de la Vida . . . de Cristo* (1605; Evangelical History of the Life of Christ) and the *Tragedias de amor . . . historias . . . del enamorado Acrisio, y su zagala Lucidora* (1604; Love Tragedies . . . Stories . . . of the Enamored Acrisio and His Lass Lucidora).

BIBLIOGRAPHY

Primary Texts

*Historia Evangélica.* Madrid: n.p., 1605.
*Tragedias de amor.* . . . Madrid: J. de la Cuesta, 1607.

**ARCIPRESTE DE HITA** (1283?, ?–1350 or 1351, ?), medieval lyric writer. Juan Ruiz, Archpriest of Hita, is the author of one of the greatest poetic creations of Spanish literature, the *Libro de buen amor* (14th c.; *The Book of the Archpriest (Libro de buen amor)*, 1975). So varied is the work here discussed, almost anything written in these few paragraphs will find both adherents and dissenters. Generally known (especially in the twentieth c.) as the *Libro de buen amor* (Book of Good Love) even the title produces discussion. Some scholars prefer to call it the *Libro del arcipreste*. The author is Juan Ruiz. Although scholars generally suppose that there existed a historical figure named Juan Ruiz, Max Singleton opined that the name may in fact be a "John Doe." Recently, however, Francisco J. Hernández has found new documentary reference to a "Johanne Roderici archipresbitero de Fita" (20) which confirms details derived from the *Libro de buen amor* regarding its author. The physical evidence of the text leaves little room for varied interpretation. No one can refute that the work survived in three basic mss. from the fourteenth c., and that minor portions of the text can be found scattered in other fragmentary mss., one of which is a Portuguese translation.

In the three principal mss., traditionally known as the Gayoso (G), Toledo (T), and Salamanca (S) mss., G and T represent a 1330 version, although even these two differ from each other somewhat. Another version, dated 1343, is represented by the Salamanca text. G. B. Gybbon-Monypenny has convincingly resolved that the amplifications of 1343 "in the first part of the *Libro* seem intended mainly to improve the artistic effect of the structure" (1962, 216). Roger M. Walker takes the argument further, showing how additions to the second part of the text also strengthen the overall plan of the author. All can agree that the work was not written in one sitting, but no one can be absolutely certain that only one author was involved in producing the extant versions. Consensus probably holds with the one-author theory. Although the problems of author identification and single versus multiple authorship are matters of importance, they do not in any way detract from the universally recognized fact that the *Libro de buen amor* is one of the most outstanding pieces of medieval Spanish literature.

Part of the work's greatness can be found in its daring indebtedness to many European traditions. Besides the main trunk of the text, which is written in *\*cuaderna vía*, there are both popular and religious lyrics, and also pieces reminiscent of goliardic poetry. An indebtedness to church literature (catechisms, treatises on confession, popular and learned sermon techniques) is manifest throughout. Exemplum literature plays a significant role, as does the *fabliaux*. The courtly love traditions and those of medieval Latin secular drama also contribute to the text's literary virtuosity. The entire first part is essentially an Ovidian *ars amatoria*. The various literary traditions and, more importantly, literary forms appear to be one of the aims of the book, as seen in the prose prologue: "I also composed my book as a guide to some people in the writing of verse and in rhyming and for making songs, with models of lyrics, musical setting, rhymes, verses, and poetic composition in general—all of which I have written with that perfection which the art of composition requires" (Singleton, 3). Some of the additions in the 1343 version seem to be added specifically with this purpose in mind. Because the metrical variety and virtuosity evident in the body of the text fulfill this aim, one cannot doubt the seriousness of this stated intention.

A brief review of the content of this masterpiece is in order. In general, we have as the main course the (pseudo?)-autobiographical account of a man's quest for love; it could be any man's, and therefore is every man's quest. The use of empirical versus the poetic "I" is one that is often difficult and at times impossible to distinguish. The work begins with eleven monorhymed quatrains of *cuaderna vía* which contain an introductory prayer. A prose prologue much akin to the learned sermon (*divisio intra*) follows. In this prologue, the author's intention appears to be that of being properly understood, so he warns: "First, let him diligently seek to understand and judge the intention I had in the writing of the book, and also the meaning of what is said therein; and let him heed not merely the ugly sounds of the words, for—according to the Canon Law—words serve intention, and not intention, words. And God knoweth that my intention was not to write the book to show men how to sin or use obscene words, but to persuade all men to have a memory stored with good works and also to provide them with patterns of good habits and instructions for salvation in order that they all might properly be forearmed and better able to protect themselves against the numerous deceptions which some persons employ to perpetrate lust, for St. Gregory said that darts which we know are coming strike us therefore less accurately, and we may the better protect ourselves against what we have previously discerned" (Singleton 3). This quite clear warning and statement of purpose is immediately followed by the previously cited statement on the work's purpose to illustrate metrical variety. Both intentions are equally serious.

Following the prose prologue is an invocation and a few more stanzas on the nature of the book. Lyric stanzas on the joys of the Virgin follow, then a piece in *cuaderna vía* on the need for diversion in which we are admonished: "My words examine carefully, and judge with strict critique. / Experience then you'll truly not what happened to a Greek" (Singleton, st. 46ab). The first narrative is a humorous tale of a debate between a Greek scholar and a Roman ignoramus. Through this story we are told that both the wise and the ignorant are either equally correct or equally incorrect in their interpretations, for neither Greek nor Roman understands the signs of the other. Immediately following is another request that the book be read carefully: "Most of the truths of Courtesy beneath the surface lie. / So labor well and dig them out when signals catch your eye" (Singleton, st. 68ab). With such consistent warning before the main narrative, the reader must be wary. The author now cites the authority Aristotle as saying that man strives throughout his life to satisfy two appetites—one for food and the other for female companionship. He then states that he was once in love and sent a go-between to petition his lady. Twice he was rejected. Each time the rejection is couched in one exemplum or more—a device used throughout the work. Undaunted, the protagonist seeks another would-be lover. This time the object of his quest is a baker's wife, Cruz Cruzada (Crisscross Cross), and his go-between is a male. Of course he is doublecrossed (the go-between runs off with Cruz) and the hero is left to bear his cross. The entire episode is sacriligious and loaded with obscene double entendre. It concludes with a *troba cazurra* (vulgar poem)—*cazurro* poets were the lowest kind of minstrel. In this way, the author has covered the entire spectrum of society in his literary form—from the *divisio intra* of the prose prologue to the most vulgar kind of poetry in the *troba cazurra*.

After this, there follows an interesting piece on astrology and its influence. The author stays true to Catholic orthodoxy and the church's position with regard to astrology by maintaining God's role as Prime Mover. He cleverly uses this, however, to excuse his woman-quest since he claims to have been born under the sign of Venus. His third attempt, nevertheless, ends in failure and rejection. The protagonist then proceeds to denounce traitorous Love in the form of a popular sermon laden with exempla. Without justifying himself, Lord Love answers the preceding objections by urging the grumbler to follow Ovid. Lord Love advises him to seek a trustworthy go-between, and also counsels him on proper behavior while wooing—be not slothful, be free with money, drink wine sparingly, etc.— and offers information on the ideal lady. Interspersed within and part of the advice are even more exempla. The protagonist then appeals to Venus and is given essentially the same advice and the story of Don Melón (Master Melon) and Doña Endrina (Lady Sloe) begins. This episode, based on a twelfth-c. Latin elegiac comedy, essentially summarizes Ovidian doctrine and is thus a repetition of Venus's reiteration, but now the doctrine is put into practice. The story is crucial, for it introduces one of the most important prototypes of medieval Spanish literature (see Edad Media, Literatura de la), that of the go-between. Her name is *Trotaconventos (Convent-Trotter), and although no one can prove that Fernando de *Rojas, the creator of the greatest go-between of all Hispanic literature (*Celestina), based his character on Trotaconventos, there are undeniable parallels between the two. It is also important to note here that there is no break in the first-person narrative when the story of Master Melon begins. The quest, following Ovid's advice, this time proves successful. Although the climax of the story in Spanish has been lost to defacement by prudish censorship, the story is so close to the source that the source serves well in reconstructing missing portions in the Spanish. The lovers are ultimately wed. There is, however, a warning immediately following this story: "Oh, ladies, heed my messages and follow my instructions. / Take profit from my narrative: *Beware of men's seductions!*" (Singleton, st. 892ab). And later: "From tale of Sloe to profit, then, I hope your heart's resolved. / My story is illustrative: I'm not, myself, involved" (Singleton, st. 909ab).

We return to the main autobiographical thread and find, as Roger M. Walker astutely observes, that the unifying motif now becomes the implacable force, death, although amorous sorties continue as man attempts to ignore the inevitable. There is a short pursuit of the closely guarded Urraca, who dies. After two days mourning, the author addresses his audience and begs their indulgence for the scurrilous episodes which are to follow. The action now shifts to the hill country of the Guadarrama Mountains, where the Archpriest encounters four mountain women in four separate misadventures. In general, they all offer him some sort of physical refuge from the elements, and in general, they all have their way with him. As a parody of the *pastorela*, the women are depicted as the opposite of the ideal woman previously described. The hero, who up to now has been chafing at the bit for amorous encounters, now proves to be the most reluctant of lovers. A brief survey of the appearance of the fourth *serrana* (mountain woman) will help to explain this novel reticence: "Her ears are big and cumbersome, and like a yearling ass's" (1013a); "Her mouth was like a mastiff's mouth—thick were her lips and snout; / Like hard-tack horses eat, her teeth— which wide and thick, stuck out" (1014ab); "A fuzz she wore of whiskers where a blacker beard was hatching" (1015a); "Her wrist was broader than my hand . . . ," (1017a); "Her very littlest finger—that was thicker than my thumb. / To think how big the big ones were your judgment would benumb!" (1019ab). Other parts of her anatomy are as graphically described. These grotesque descriptions and episodes are immediately followed by religious lyrics praising the Virgin and one commemorating the life of Christ. A mock epic, a battle between Doña Cuaresma (Lady Lent) and Don Carnal (Lord Carnival), ensues. In this portion the author draws on several more European traditions: (1) Carnival-Lent poems; (2) treatises of confession, as when Carnival is captured and feigns repentance; (3) goliardic satire, as when he escapes and Lady Lent is forced to flee, and then Lord Carnival and Lord Love ride victoriously through town greeted by various denominations and ranks of clergy.

We return to the autobiographical stream when the go-between suggests that the protagonist seek a nun as a lover. The quest for Dona Garoça begins. As before, it provides the framework for many exempla. Within the same episode we have a brief portrait of the male protagonist. The actual outcome of the Garoça encounter is unknown. We do know that the hero is edified by her piety and that he is sanctified by her prayers. Dona Garoça dies. In an effort to refute death, there is a short and unsuccessful attempt to secure a Moorish girl. Now his faithful go-between dies, producing a serious invective against death. In this tirade the reader is warned: "We must never feel that we are secure and protected from Death, for our enemy is great and strong. We shall never be fortunate enough to escape her . . ." (st. 1580). In order to ward off Flesh, Devil, and World (our three archenemies according to the author), we are now instructed as to the arms of the Christian against the deadly sins: the sacraments, the virtues, the gifts of the Holy Spirit, and works of charity. The common denominator throughout is the number seven. It is significant that the last comment by the hero on the subject of women is his piece in praise of little women which ends with an ironic twist: "Large girls I oft have let depart—I'd small ones hoped to win. / 'Tis wise and most expedient to flee the greatest sin! / The least of evils is the best, remarks a wise professor. / Of ladies, it must follow, then, the best ones are the lesser!" (1617a-d). The last amorous adventure involves Don Furón (Master Ferret) as a go-between and serves essentially to highlight the loss of his now-dead lady go-between. This brings us to the end of the main narrative and to some final comments about the nature of the book: "A little book I've written you that hath a little text. / The gloss, however, 's not petit that lies thereto annexed. / To every lyric segment are some deeper meanings added / With which esthetic garment hath most skilfully been padded'' (1631a-d). The statement is the same that we have heard from the very beginning in the prose prologue and in stanza 16a-d, for example: "My book is not a silly tale—no ream it is of chatter; / So never think my writing is devoid of serious matter. / As coins most rich and beautiful are kept in shabby purses, / Just so a homely binding often shieldeth fairest verses.'' After the final statement about properly understanding the text, we find more religious lyrics—joys of the Virgin, and some songs for students and blind beggars.

It is difficult to end adequately any survey on such a complex masterpiece. The author's foresight is summed up in verse 1631b above: "The gloss, however, 's not petit . . . .'' We can but follow his advice: "Most of the truths of Courtesy beneath the surface lie. / So labor well and dig them out when signals catch your eye'' (st. 68ab). For: "My book is really like a score . . . / It's melody 'twill sing for you exactly as you play it'' (70ab). This, in short, is the challenge that scholarship (the gloss) will answer accordingly to the dexterity and skill of each "musician.''

## BIBLIOGRAPHY

Primary Texts

*Libro de buen amor*. Ed. M. Criado de Val and Eric Naylor. 2nd ed. Madrid: CSIC, 1972.
*Libro de buen amor*. Ed. and tr. Raymond S. Willis. Princeton: Princeton UP, 1972. (Spanish with English trans.)

English Translation

*The Book of the Archpriest (Libro de buen amor)*. Tr. Mack Singleton. Madison: HSMS, 1975.

Criticism

Burke, James F. "Again *Cruz*, the Baker-Girl: *Libro de buen amor*, ss. 119–120.'' *Revista Canadiense de Estudios Hispánicos* 4 (1980): 253–70.
———. "Juan Ruiz, the Serranas and the Rites of Spring.'' *Journal of Medieval and Renaissance Studies* 5 (1975): 13–35.
Clarke, Dorothy Clotelle. "Juan Ruiz and Andreas Capellanus.'' *HR* 40 (1972): 390–411.
Deyermond, A. D. "The Greeks, the Romans, the Astrologers and the Meaning of the *Libro de buen amor*.'' *RN* 5.1 (1963): 88–91.
———. "Juan Ruiz's Attitude to Literature.'' In *Medieval, Renaissance and Folklore Studies in Honor of John Esten Keller*. Ed. Joseph R. Jones. Newark: Juan de la Cuesta, 1980. 113–25.
Gybbon-Monypenny, G. B. "Autobiography in the *Libro de buen amor* in the Light of Some Literary Comparisons.'' *BHS* 34 (1957): 63–78.
———. "Lo que buen amor dize con rrazon te lo pruevo.'' *BHS* 38 (1961): 13–24.
———. "The Two Versions of the *Libro de buen amor*: The Extent and Nature of the Author's Revision.'' *BHS* 39 (1962): 205–21.
———. ed. *"Libro de buen amor" Studies*. London: Tamesis, 1970.
Hernández, F. J. "The Venerable Juan Ruiz, Archpriest of Hita.'' *La Corónica* 13 (1984–85): 10–22.

Kirby, Steven D. "Juan Ruiz and Don Ximio: The Archpriest's Art of Declamation." *BHS* 55 (1978): 283–87.

Knowlton, Edgar C., Jr. "Two Oriental Analogues of Juan Ruiz's Story of the Horoscope." *RN* 15.1 (1973): 183–87.

Lecoy, Felix. *Recherches sur le "Libro de buen amor."* Paris, 1938; rpt. with prologue, bibliography and index by A. D. Deyermond. Farnborough, Hants: Gregg, 1974.

Seniff, Dennis P. "Planes of Times in the *Libro de buen amor.*" *Selected Proceedings of the 32nd MIFLC.* Ed. G.C. Martin. Winston-Salem: Wake Forest U, 1984. 313–20.

Spitzer, Leo. "Note on the Poetic and Empirical 'I' in Medieval Authors." In *Romanische Literaturstudien 1936–56.* Tübingen: Niemeyer, 1959. 100–112.

Vetterling, Mary-Anne. *A Computerized Bibliography for Juan Ruiz's "Libro de buen amor."* Cambridge, MD: Brujeril, 1981.

Walker, Roger M. "Towards an Interpretation of the *Libro de buen amor.*" *BHS* 43 (1966): 1–10.

Zahareas, Anthony N. *The Art of Juan Ruiz Archpriest of Hita.* Madrid: Estudios de literatura española, 1965.

———. "The Stars: Worldly Love and Free Will in the *Libro de buen amor.*" *BHS* 42 (1965): 82–93.

Anthony J. Cárdenas

**ARCIPRESTE DE TALAVERA** (1398?, Toledo?–1468, ?), archpriest, writer. The name by which Alfonso Martínez de Toledo, prebendary of the Cathedral of Toledo, chaplain to John II, and Archpriest of Talavera, is commonly known. Martínez also spent some two years in Italy as a member of the household of Juan de Casanova, Cardinal San Sixto. The Archpriest wrote the lives of two saints (San Ildefonso and San Isidoro), one historical work (*Atalaya de las crónicas*: Watchtower of the Chronicles), and one misogynist treatise on lust, the *Reprobación del amor mundano* or *Corbacho* (1498; *Little Sermons on Sin*, 1959), for which he is most remembered. The *Corbacho* consists of a prologue, which answers to an *accessus*, and four main parts: (1) the "reprobación de loco amor" (reprobation of mad love) in thirty-eight chapters; (2) "condiciones de las viciosas mugeres" (types of perverse women) in fourteen chapters; (3) the "complisiones de los onbres" (temperaments of men) in ten chapters; and (4) the "media parte rreprobando la común materia de fablar de los fados" (portion reprobating the common way of talking about astrology) in three chapters. It is difficult to agree with some critics who do not think that the work is misogynist when in it even the lustful crime of a necrophiliac male is blamed not on the man but on the dead body of the woman. In spite of his sometimes sordid exempla Talavera's style and language are truly masterful and deserving of analysis. As a treatise on lust the *Corbacho* can be compared with the *Collar de la Paloma* (Ibn Hazm) and with the *Libro de buen amor* (\*Arcipreste de Hita) although it is, of course, vastly different from both works. It differs from the *Collar* mainly because its racy, colloquial, dramatic style contrasts with the erudite, aristocratic, poetic style of Ibn Hazm's treatise; both authors reinforce their arguments with illustrations from real life but Talavera seems more at home

with "low life" than with the elite circles to which Ibn Hazm's characters, even
the slave girls, belong. Talavera knew the *Libro de buen amor*, which he called
a "tractado" (treatise), calling his own work a "compendio," a key word for
a particular kind of treatise. The first person narrators in the *Corbacho* and the
*Libro de buen amor* are excellent actors and they provide an entertaining performance, but whereas the author of the latter seems more concerned with his
artistry, Talavera seems more concerned with his moral. The fourth part of the
*Corbacho*, the "media parte," reproduces the debate between Fortune and Poverty found also in Boccaccio's *De casibus virorum illustrium*. The *Corbacho*
ends with a controversial epilogue of disputed authorship. The imagery contained
in this epilogue, however, links it artistically with the rest of the work. *See also*
Edad Media, Literatura de la.

BIBLIOGRAPHY

Primary Texts

*Arcipreste de Talavera*. Ed. M. Ciceri. 2 vols. Modena: Società Tipografica Editrice
    Modenese, 1975. (Critical edition of the *Corbacho*.)
*Vidas de San Ildefonso y San Isidoro*. Ed. J. Madoz. Clásicos castellanos 134. Madrid:
    Espasa-Calpe, 1962.

English Translation

*Little Sermons on Sin* (tr. of the *Corbacho*). Ed. Lesley Byrd Simpson. Berkeley and
    Los Angeles: U of California P, 1959.

Criticism

Nepaulsingh, C. I. "Talavera's Imagery and the Structure of the *Corbacho*." *RCEH* 4.3
    (Spring 1980): 329–49.
Viera, David J. "An Annotated Bibliography on Alfonso Martínez de Toledo." *KRQ*
    24 (1977): 263–79.

                                                          Colbert Nepaulsingh

**ARCO, Ricardo del** (1888, Granada–?, ?), essayist, historian and literary critic.
Arco has written on various aspects of the history and archaeology of Aragon,
and has devoted works to *La imprenta en Huesca* (1911; Printing in Huesca);
*Misterios, autos sacramentales y otras fiestas en la catedral de Huesca* (1920;
Mysteries, Sacramental Plays, and Other Celebrations in the Cathedral of
Huesca); and *Gracián y su colaborador y mecenas* (1926; Gracian and His
Collaborator and Maecenas). He has also authored extensive studies of Spanish
society as portrayed in the works of Lope de *Vega and *Cervantes.

BIBLIOGRAPHY

Primary Texts

*La catedral de Huesca (monografía histórica arqueológica)*. Huesca: Campo, 1924.
*Gracián y su colaborador y mecenas*. Zaragoza: Hospicio Provincial, 1926.
*La imprenta en Huesca*. Madrid: RABM, 1911.

**ARCONADA, César M.** (1900, Astudillo, Palencia–1964, Moscow), novelist, journalist, and translator. Self-educated, he soon established himself as a music and film critic with contributions to the then numerous avant-garde magazines, a study of Debussy (1926), and a biography of Greta Garbo (1929). His writing takes a new direction with his first novel, *La turbina* (1930; The Turbine Generator), which treats the conflict between modernity and tradition when electricity is brought to a remote area of Castile. It is followed by *Los pobres contra los ricos* (1932; The Poor against the Rich) and *Reparto de tierras* (1934; Distribution of Lands). These novels establish him as a major writer of the incipient social novel. Gil Casado considers him to be among the most lyrical writers within the current of the ''new romanticism.'' His last novel, *Río Tajo* (1938; River Tajo), which earned him the National Prize for Literature, portrays the popular struggle against fascism during the Spanish Civil War. He spent the remainder of his life in exile, first in France, then in the Soviet Union, where he translated Russian authors into Spanish and published his selected works and short stories.

BIBLIOGRAPHY

Primary Texts

*Los pobres contra los ricos.* Madrid: Izquierda, 1933.
*Reparto de tierras.* Madrid: Izquierda, 1934.
*Río Tajo.* Madrid: AKAL, 1978.
*En torno a Debussy.* Madrid: Espasa-Calpe, 1926.
*Tres cómicos del cine.* Madrid: Ulises, 1931. (Charlie Chaplin, Clara Bow, Harold Lloyd)
*Vivimos en una noche oscura.* Madrid: Izquierda, 1936. (Poems)
Several articles by Arconada are included in *Documents for the Spanish Vanguard.* Ed. Paul Ilie. UNCSRLL 78. Chapel Hill: U of North Carolina P, 1969.

English Translations

''Children of Estremadura.'' Tr. J. Cleugh. *New Writing* 3 (1937): 235–42.
''The Rabbit.'' Tr. A. Flores. In *Spanish Writers in Exile.* Ed. A. Flores. Sausalito, CA: Bern Porter, 1940s.

Criticism

Blanco Aguinaga, Carlos, Julio Rodríguez Puértolas, and Iris M. Zavala. *Historia social de la literatura española.* 3 vols. Madrid: Castalia, 1978–79.
Gil Casado, Pablo. *La novela social española (1920–1971).* 2nd ed. Barcelona: Seix Barral, 1973.
Ilie, Paul. *The Surrealist Mode in Spanish Literature.* Ann Arbor: U of Michigan P, 1968.

Porter Conerly

**ARCOS, Gabriel de los.** *See* Arróniz y Bosch, Teresa

**ARDERIU I VOLTAS, Clementina** (1899, Barcelona–1976, ?) poet. The daughter of artisans, she studied music and languages, publishing her first book of poems in 1919, the same year she married poet Carles *Riba. Her early poetry is full of joy and hope; she writes of giving birth, love for her son or husband, at times with a vision of herself as a house or enclosure, in a simple, direct and charming way. *Sempre i ara* (1946; Now and Always) won the Joaquim Folguera Prize in 1938, but the publication was delayed due to the war, and then published in a semi-clandestine way. The poems in it express Arderiu's characteristic everyday world, but a new experience has been added to it: war. Sadness and melancholy spread over the verses. Old anguishes and fears show up with a more vivid face. She fights them off, seeking in solitude and peace the strength she needs. *Es a dir* (1959; That Is to Say) won the Ossa Menor Prize in 1958 and the Lletra d'or Prize in 1960. Many poems are descriptions of nature, the sea, towns and places in Catalonia, but these descriptions often mask the deeper search into the poet's own life and memory. There is in this book a new sense of time gone by; the poet turns to a questioning of temporality in direct urging terms. *L'esperança encara* (1969; Still There Is Hope), written after her husband's death, finds her fighting against despair and loneliness, a fear of which had been present in earlier works. As the title suggests, she does find hope, mainly in the Christian faith and tradition. There are four important collections of her work: *Poesies completes* (1952; Complete Poetry); *Antología poética* (1961 and 1982; Poetic Anthology), a bilingual edition with translations into Castilian; *Obra poètica* (1973; Poetic Work), generally considered the definitive edition of her work; and *Contraclaror: Antologia Poètica* (1985; View against the Light: Poetic Anthology) with an insightful introduction by the poet Maria-Mercè Marçal. Before the Spanish Civil War she traveled through Europe; afterwards, she was exiled to France, crossing the border with Riba and Antonio *Machado. She returned to Catalonia in 1943 and collaborated in the reconstruction of Catalan literary and artistic life.

In general, Arderiu's poetry is characterized by simple language used to express difficult concepts; it shows marked influences of the Catalan Josep *Carner and the French Valéry and reflects a constrained passion. *See also* Catalan Literature.

## BIBLIOGRAPHY

### Primary Works

*L'alta llibertat*. Barcelona: Catalana, 1920.
*Antologia*. Barcelona: Lira, 1923.
*Antologia*. Barcelona: La rosa dels vents, 1938.
*Antología poética*. Madrid: Rialp, 1961; 2nd enlarged edition, Barcelona: Plaza y Janés, 1982.
*Cançons i elegies*. Barcelona: La Revista, 1916.
*Cant i paraules*. Barcelona: Lira, 1923.
*Es a dir*. Barcelona: Ossa Menor, 1959.
*L'esperança encara*. Barcelona: Edicions 62, 1969.
*Obra poètica*. Barcelona: Edicions 62, 1973.
*Poemes*. Barcelona: Proa, 1936.
*Poesies completes*. Barcelona: Selecta, 1952.
*Sempre i ara*. Barcelona: Societat Aliança d'Arts Gràfiques, 1946.

Criticism

Aleixandre, Vicente. "Clementina Arderiu de cerca." In *Los encuentros*. Madrid: Guadarrama, 1959. 99–105.
Marçal, Maria Mercè. Introducció to the collection *Contraclaror*. Barcelona: laSal, 1985. 9–61.
Molas, Joaquim. Prologue to *L'esperança encara*. Barcelona: Edicions 62, 1969. 5–15.
Roig, Montserrat. "Clementina Arderiu o l'aventura de la dona." *Serra d'Or* (Jan. 1972): 27–30.

Joan Gilabert and Kathleen McNerney

**ARDERÍUS, Joaquín** (1890, Lorca, Murcia–1969, Mexico), novelist and journalist. After studying engineering in Belgium, he established himself in Madrid as a writer and journalist. He founded the magazine *Nueva España* (New Spain) with Antonio *Espina García and José *Díaz Fernández. Of all of the novelists of the *Generation of 1927, Arderíus is the most ardently anti-bourgeois. Social criticism is a constant in his writing, which evolves from expressionism to objective realism. His protagonists are typically alienated and degenerate. *Justus the Evangelist*, subtitled "a novel of Christian and social sarcasm," typifies Arderius' contempt for and treatment of traditional values. He became increasingly a proponent of the novel which portrayed class struggle. He collaborated with José Díaz Fernández in a biography of Fermín Galán (1931). His last novel, *Crimen* (1934; A Crime), which narrates the robbery and murder of a greedy priest by a desperate speculator, is devoid of the rhetoric and poetic style associated with the "new romantics." Following the Spanish Civil War, he went into exile, first in France, and then in Mexico where he was a government employee.

BIBLIOGRAPHY

Primary Texts

*Así me fecundó Zaratustra*. Madrid: Rivadeneyra, 1923.
*El baño de la muerta*. Madrid: n.p., 1928.
*Campesinos*. Madrid: Zeus, 1931.
*El comedor de la Pensión Venecia*. Madrid: Zeus, 1930.
*Don Juan de Austria. (El emperador frustrado)*. México: Ediciones Nuevas, 1944.
*La duquesa de Nit*. Madrid: Pueyo, 1926.
*La espuela*. Madrid: Sociedad General de Librería, 1927.
*Los amadores de Manqueses*. Madrid: n.p., 1929.
*Los príncipes iguales*. Madrid: Historia Nueva, 1928.
*Lumpenproletariado*. Madrid: La Novela Roja, 1931.
*Mis mendigos*. Madrid: Hispano-Alemana, 1915.
*Ojo de brasa*. Madrid: Marineda, 1925.
*Yo y tres mujeres*. Madrid: n.p., 1924.

English Translations

"Bath of Death." In *Spanish Writers in Exile*. Tr. A. Flores. Sausalito, CA: Bern Porter, 1940s.

"Night of Frost." In *Great Spanish Short Stories*. Tr. W. B. Wells. Boston: Houghton Mifflin, 1932.

Criticism

Fuentes, Víctor. "De la novela expresionista a la revolucionaria-proletaria: En torno a la narrativa de Joaquín Arderíus." *Papeles de Son Armadans* 178 (1971): 197–215.

Gil Casado, Pablo. *La novela social española (1920–1971)*. 2nd ed. Barcelona: Seix Barral, 1973.

Ilie, Paul. *The Surrealist Mode in Spanish Literature*. Ann Arbor: U of Michigan P, 1968.

Porter Conerly

**ARENAL, Concepción** (1820, El Ferrol–1893, Vigo), social critic and humanitarian. Arenal devoted her life to the constructive study of social problems and their possible solutions. Exceptional intelligence and clarity of thought illuminate her writings, as in *La beneficencia, la filantropía y la caridad* (1861; Beneficence, Philanthropy and Charity), which received an award from the Academy of Moral and Political Sciences. Other works include *Cartas a los delincuentes* (1865; Letters to Delinquents), *La cuestión social, Cartas a un obrero y a un señor* (1880; Letters to a Laborer and a Gentleman), and *La mujer de su casa* (1883; The Woman of the House).

BIBLIOGRAPHY

Primary Texts

*Obras completas*. 22 vols. Madrid: Sucesores de Rivadeneyra, 1894–1902.

Criticism

Campo de Alange, María. *Concepción Arenal 1820–1893; estudio biográfico documental*. Madrid: RO, 1973.

Mañach, Francisco. *Concepción Arenal*. Buenos Aires: Alsina, 1907.

**ARGENSOLA, Bartolomé Leonardo de** (1562, Barbastro–1631, Zaragoza), Aragonese poet and historian. Although his classical background and interest in literature and history are similar to those of Lupercio, his older brother, Bartolomé differed from him in that he was ordained to the priesthood. After studying in Huesca, Zaragoza, and Salamanca, Bartolomé was named rector of the parish of Villahermosa and was, in fact, throughout his lifetime frequently referred to as the "Rector of Villahermosa." Later he served as chaplain to María of Austria, widow of Maximilian II and daughter of Charles V, during her residence in Madrid.

When the Count of Lemos was appointed Viceroy of Naples in 1610, he invited the Argensola brothers to accompany him to Italy, where Bartolomé served as literary advisor and court poet. After Lupercio died in 1613, Bartolomé returned to Spain. From 1615 until his death he lived in Zaragoza, where he served as canon of the cathedral and chief historian of the Kingdom of Aragon, a post Lupercio had occupied before him. As a historian Bartolomé completed

Jerónimo de *Zurita's *Anales de Aragón* (1630; Annals of Aragon) and wrote *Las alteraciones populares de Zaragoza, el año de 1591* (Popular Uprisings in Zaragoza in 1591); the *Discurso sobre las cualidades que ha de tener un perfecto cronista* (n.d.; Discourse on the Qualities of a Consummate Historian); and, at the request of the Count of Lemos, *Historia de la conquista de las Islas Molucas* (1609; *The Discovery and Conquest of the Molucco and Philippine Islands*, 1708–10).

It is as a writer of formal, often didactic poetry in the classical vein that Bartolomé will be remembered. Like Lupercio, he refused to let himself be swept up by the baroque vogue of his age, preferring instead to concentrate on the conservative, often cold, intellectual poetry which, according to the classicists of his day, epitomized "good taste." Much of his work imitates that of the great Latin poets, especially Horace, some of whose odes he translated. Indeed, the rejection of trendiness and the striving toward balance and formal perfection exhibited by the Argensola brothers led to their being labeled the "Spanish Horaces." Despite Bartolomé's reverence for classical form, his opportunity to observe life both in the court and beyond it provides to the modern reader an interesting perspective of the poet's time.

Some of his finest pieces are his moral and satirical verses, especially the "epístolas morales" (moral letters) and *Diálogos satíricos* (Satirical Dialogues). The form which best displays his considerable ability to fashion polished verse is the sonnet, two of the best examples of which are "Dime, Padre común, pues eres justo" ("Tell Me, Father of All, Since You Are Righteous") and "Estas son las reliquias saguntinas" ("Here Lie the Ruins of Sagunto").

Highly esteemed by both *Cervantes and Lope de *Vega, Bartolomé was a member of the Academia Imitatoria of Madrid, where he adopted the pseudonym of "Luis de Escatrón." During his final years in Zaragoza, he not only became an arbiter of literary taste in the city, but he exercised considerable political influence as well.

Bartolomé is universally regarded as a more accomplished stylist than his brother Lupercio, whose son, Gabriel Leonardo, published the works of both in a collection entitled *Rimas* (1634; Verses). Several of Bartolomé's compositions not included in this volume have only recently come to light.

BIBLIOGRAPHY

Primary Texts

*Bartolomé Leonardo de Argensola: Rimas*. Ed. José Manuel Blecua. 2 vols. Clásicos Castellanos 184 and 185. Madrid: Espasa-Calpe, 1974.

*Conquista de las Islas Molucas*. Ed. P. Miguel Mir. Biblioteca Nueva de Autores Aragoneses 6. Zaragoza: Biblioteca de Escritores Aragoneses, 1891.

*Rimas de Lupercio y Bartolomé Leonardo de Argensola*. Ed. José Manuel Blecua. 2 vols. Madrid: CSIC, 1950–51.

English Translations

*The Discovery and Conquest of the Molucco and Philippine Islands*. Tr. John Stevens. *New Collections of Voyages and Travels*. London: J. Knapton, 1708–10 (microfilm copy 1962 by Library of Congress Photoduplication Service).

"Firmio, at Your Age No Danger Is a Slight One" and "Tell Me, Father of All, Since You Are Righteous." Tr. Elias L. Rivers. *Renaissance and Baroque Poetry of Spain*. New York: Dell, 1966. 156–57.

"To Christ Our Lord, Praying in the Garden" and "After Suffering a Great Misfortune." Tr. J. M. Cohen. *The Penguin Book of Spanish Verse*. rev. ed. Baltimore: Penguin, 1960. 208–10.

Criticism

Aznar, J. *Los Argensola*. Zaragoza: Artes gráficas, 1939.

Green, Otis H. "Bartolomé Leonardo de Argensola, Secretario del Conde de Lemos." *BH* 53 (1951): 375–92.

———. " 'Ni es cielo ni es azul.' A Note on the 'Barroquismo' of Bartolomé Leonardo de Argensola." *RFE* 34 (1950): 137–50.

Pfandl, Ludwig. *Historia de la literatura nacional española en la Edad de Oro*. Barcelona: Gili, 1952.

C. Maurice Cherry

**ARGENSOLA, Lupercio Leonardo de** (1559, Barbastro–1613, Naples), poet, dramatist, and historian. Little is known of the early years of the Argensola brothers, other than that their mother was of the Aragonese nobility and their father was from an aristocratic Italian family. Lupercio, the older of the two, studied in Huesca and graduated from the U of Zaragoza in 1582. He served as secretary first to the Duke of Villahermosa and later to the Empress María of Austria, sister of Philip II and widow of Maximilian II. Philip III named him chief historian of the Kingdom of Aragon, a post he held until 1608, when he and his brother \*Bartolomé were invited by the Count of Lemos to Naples, where the latter held the title of Viceroy.

Lupercio was strongly influenced by the great classicists of his day, especially the renowned scholars A. Schoto and P. Simón \*Abril. As it was fashionable among the humanists of the time to belong to literary academies, Lupercio joined the prestigious *Academia Imitatoria* (Academy of Imitators) in Madrid and even founded the *Academia de los Ociosos* (Academy of Idlers) in Naples. Best remembered today as a poet, he is esteemed less than his younger brother. Lupercio strove for formal precision in his compositions, and his work shows the decided influence of Horace, several of whose odes he translated into Spanish. In addition, he composed religious and moral poems and some rather formal love poems, but his satirical verse is generally regarded as his strength.

The low esteem Lupercio felt for his own poetry is best illustrated by his having ordered that his work be destroyed; however, his son Gabriel rescued some of the compositions and published the poetry of both brothers in a volume entitled *Rimas* (1634; Verses).

Of little literary value today are the three tragedies in the Senecan mode he composed in his youth—*La Filis* (Phyllis), now lost; *La Alejandra* (Alexandra); and *La Isabela* (Isabel). Far more interesting are his contributions as a historian—the *Declaración sumaria de la historia de Aragón* (1631; Summary Declaration of the History of Aragon), the *Información de los sucesos del Reino de Aragón en los años de 1590 y 1591* (1808; Information on the Events in the Kingdom of Aragon in 1590 and 1591), and his *Historia de Carlos V* (History of Charles V). *See also* Academia.

BIBLIOGRAPHY

Primary Texts

*Antología de Lupercio Leonardo de Argensola.* Ed. Fernando Gutiérrez. Barcelona: Montaner y Simón, 1946.

*Isabela. Tesoro del teatro español: Desde su origen (Año de 1356) hasta nuestros días.* vol. 1. Ed. Leandro Fernández de Moratín. Paris: Librería Europea de Beaudry, 1838.

*Lupercio Leonardo de Argensola: Rimas.* Ed. José Manuel Blecua. Clásicos Castellanos 173. Madrid: Espasa-Calpe, 1972.

*Rimas de Lupercio y Bartolomé Leonardo de Argensola.* Ed. José Manuel Blecua. 2 vols. Madrid: CSIC, 1950–51.

English Translations

"After Persistent Rains the Bright Sun Dawns," "To Sleep," "Alarming Image of Death," "Although You May Be the Descendant of Illustrious Goths," and "October Has Taken the Vine-Leaves with It." Tr. J. M. Cohen. *The Penguin Book of Spanish Verse.* rev. ed. Baltimore: Penguin, 1960. 201–3.

"To a Woman Who Used Cosmetics and Was Beautiful" and "Your Divine Eyes, Anne . . ." Tr. Elias L. Rivers. *Renaissance and Baroque Poetry of Spain.* New York: Dell, 1966. 153–55.

Criticism

Aznar, J. *Los Argensola.* Zaragoza: Artes gráficas 1939.

Crawford, J. P. Wickersham. "Notes on the Tragedies of Lupercio Leonardo de Argensola." *RR* 5 (1914): 31–44.

Green, Otis H. *The Life and Works of Lupercio Leonardo de Argensola.* Publications of the University of Pennsylvania: Series in Romance Languages 21. Philadelphia: U of Pennsylvania, 1927.

Pfandl, Ludwig. *Historia de la literatura nacional española en la Edad de Oro.* Barcelona: Gili, 1952.

C. Maurice Cherry

**ARGOTE DE MOLINA, Gonzalo** (1548, Seville–1598, Grand Canary), politician, soldier, curator, genealogist, historian, bibliophile, editor, poet, and man of letters. He was alderman of Seville and head of that city's Holy Brotherhood. At sixteen he participated in the military expedition to the Mediterranean island of Peñón, and as lieutenant at age twenty he helped suppress the *morisco uprising in Granada. His museum, one of the first in Europe, was described by Francisco de *Pacheco in 1599 as containing so famous a collection of books, horses, weaponry, stuffed animals and paintings (including portraits of notable personages by Alonso Sánchez Coello) as to warrant a visit by Philip II. His works of genealogy and history—*Nobleza de Andaluzia* (1588; Nobility of Andalusia), *Historia de las ciudades de Ubeda y Baeza* (n.d.; History of the Cities of Ubeda and Baeza), *Historia de Sevilla* (n.d.; History of Seville)—can still be culled for valuable literary information. As poet and man of letters he is significant mainly because of his connection with the so-called School of Seville. A few of his poems were anthologized in the *Parnaso español* (Spanish Parnassus), and his *Discurso sobre la poesía castellana* (1575; Discourse on Castilian Poetry) and *Discurso de la lengua castellana* (Discourse on the Castilian Language) were taken seriously by important contemporaries like Juan de la *Cueva and Fernando de *Herrera. Argote edited the *Conde Lucanor* of *Juan Manuel, González de *Clavijo's *Historia del Gran Tamorlán* (1582; History of the Great Tamerlane) and the *Libro de Montería que mandó escrevir el muy alto rey don Alonso de Castilla y de León* (1587; Book of Hunting Which the Very Illustrious King don Alonso of Castile and Leon Ordered Written). It is perhaps his work as an editor and bibliophile that is of greatest interest today to Hispanists. Argote was a friend of Ambrosio de *Morales and thus must have been part of the circle of men like Miguel Ruiz de Azagra, Pedro Ponce de León and Juan Bautista Pérez, through whose hands passed many *incunabula* and medieval Spanish mss. now believed to be lost. The only hope of discovering these lost treasures lies in the continued intensive investigation of the lives and circumstances of men like Argote de Molina. *See also* Humanism; Renaissance.

BIBLIOGRAPHY

Primary Texts

*El 'Discurso sobre la poesía castellana' de Gonzalo Argote de Molina.* Ed. Eleuterio F. Tiscornia. Madrid: Suárez, 1926.

*Nobleza de Andalucía.* Ed. M. Muñoz y Garnica. Jaén: López Vizcaíno, 1866.

Criticism

Alonso, Dámaso. "Crítica de noticias literarias trasmitidas por Argote." *BRAE* 37 (1957): 63–81.

López Martínez, Celestino. "Gonzalo Argote de Molina, historiador y bibliófilo." *Archivo Hispalense* 58–59 (1953): 187–208.

Millares Carlo, Agustín. "La biblioteca de Gonzalo Argote de Molina." *RFE* 10 (1923): 137–52.

Palma Chaguaceda, Antonio. *El historiador Gonzalo Argote de Molina.* Madrid: CSIC, 1949.

Rodríguez Marín, Francisco. "Nuevos datos. . . ." *BRAE* 8 (1921): 64–93.

Smith, Colin. "Fernando de Herrera and Argote de Molina." *BHS* 33 (1956): 63–77.

Colbert Nepaulsingh

**ARGÜELLES, Agustín** (1776, Rivadesella, Oviedo–1844, Madrid), politician and orator. Known as the *divino* (divine one) for his eloquent defense of liberal ideas, he was author of the preamble to the Constitution of 1812. Ferdinand VII imprisoned him in Ceuta and Mayorca. When liberated by the progressive Riego, he became minister of the interior only to flee to England and remain there until the death of the king. He later was asked to serve again in parliament, and helped draft the Constitution of 1837. Best known for his oratory, he authored an account of those anguished days.

BIBLIOGRAPHY

Primary Text

*Las cortes de Cádiz Examen histórico . . . el día 24 de setiembre de 1810 hasta . . . 14 del propio mes de 1813.* Madrid: Novedades, 1865.

**ARGUIJO, Juan de** (1567, Seville–1623, Seville), poet. Also a generous patron of the arts, Arguijo is best remembered for elegant sonnets which glitter with classical erudition, although at times they are also rather cold. He also penned an amusing collection of short stories which were narrated at a *tertulia. They were saved by Ortiz de Melgarejo.

BIBLIOGRAPHY

Primary Texts

*Obras completas.* Ed. R. Benítez Claros. Sta. Cruz de Tenerife: Romerman, 1968.
*Obra poética.* Ed. Stanko Vranich. Clásicos Castalia 40. Madrid: Castalia, 1972.
*Sales españolas.* BAE 176 (1964).

English Translation

"Sonnets." In *Renaissance and Baroque Poetry of Spain.* Ed., tr., intro. E. L. Rivers. New York: Dell, 1966. 240–44.

Criticism

Cabañas, P. "Garcilaso, Góngora y Arguijo: Tres sonetos sobre el mismo tema." *BHS* 47 (1970): 210–22.

**ARIAS MONTANO, Benito** (1527, Fregenel de la Sierra–1598, Seville), brilliant theologian, orientalist, biblical scholar, professor of Hebrew, poet, friend of Fray Luis de *León. By nature a retiring man, his talents and erudition drew him repeatedly into positions of significant influence. He matriculated at the U of Seville in 1546—a moment when *Erasmism and Protestant ideas were still circulating freely. After further studies there and at the U of Alcalá and the U of Salamanca, and travel to Italy, in 1560 he became a priest in the prestigious Order of Santiago. Two years later he served as a member of the Spanish delegation to the Council of Trent. In 1586 he left for Antwerp to undertake his most illustrious accomplishment, supervision of the magnificent *Bible of Antwerp. His years in Antwerp were active and productive ones: as well as editing the Bible, he acquired many books and mss. for the Escorial Library; he wrote religious poetry, devotional books, and a collection of biographic sketches of contemporary figures; he served as a political advisor for the king. He was exposed to a wide range of ideas and undogmatic thought, as many of the leading European scholars of the day passed through Antwerp. B. Reckert documents how these years of cosmopolitan experience, combined with a close personal friendship with the publisher Plantin, personal troubles with the *Inquisition (he was denounced repeatedly for altering biblical text and challenging the authenticity of the Vulgate), and personal witness of Spanish repression and arrogance toward the Flemish, ultimately wrought a profound personal evolution, seen most clearly in Arias Montano's decision to participate in a Spiritualist sect, the Family of Love.

In 1576 Arias Montano returned to Spain, assuming the position of curator of the Escorial Library and Hebrew instructor to the monks there. He also proselytized actively, though quietly, for the sect. His writings from this period on demonstrate his adherence to the philosophy of the Family of Love. Ten years later, Arias Montano was allowed to retire from public duties and controversies. He settled in a country home outside Seville; there he wrote his two-volume masterpiece, *Anima* (1593; Soul) and *Naturae Historiae* (1601; Natural History), which presents a fundamentalist interpretation of the Bible in its scriptural history of the human race and classifies all natural phenomena. (His knowledge of botany and medicinal plants was such that peasants around his country home considered him a magician.)

Through his many duties and accomplishments, Arias Montano exerted great influence during his life. Aside from his publications, the collection of books and mss. he amassed for the king constitutes a rich legacy for later generations. Eight years after his death, however, all his works were placed on the *Index* (see *Índice de libros prohibidos*); and to date there are no modern editions of his writings. *See also* Humanism; Renaissance.

BIBLIOGRAPHY

Primary Texts

*Benito Arias Montano, extractos de su vida.* Ed. C. Doetsch. Madrid: Blass, 1920.
    (Primarily extracts from letters.)
*Correspondencia del doctor Benito Arias Montano con Felipe II . . .* No ed. Madrid: n.p.,
    1863.
*Humanae salutis monumenta.* Antwerp: Plantin, 1571. 72 odes.
*Lettre du celebre docteur . . . au *oy d'Espagne.* N.p.: n.p., 1692. French, Spanish and
    Latin.
*Monumentos sagrados de la salud del hombre.* Tr. B. Feliú de San Pedro. Valencia:
    Monfort, 1774. Latin and Spanish.
*Naturae historia.* Antwerp: Plantin, 1601.
See Reckert and Morales Oliver in Criticism for list of publications and mss.

English Translation

*Geographia Sacra illustrata: or Sacred Geography Illustrated . . . according to Arias
    Montano.* London: n.p., c.1730.

Criticism

Bell, A. F. G. *Benito Arias Montano.* London: Oxford UP, 1922.
Morales Oliver, L. "Avance para una bibliografía de obras impresas de Arias Montano."
    *Revista de Estudios Extremeños.* no vol. (1928): 171.
Reckert, B. *Benito Arias Montano (1527–1598).* London: U of London, 1972.

Vázquez, J. A. *Arias Montano "rey de nuestros escrituarios."* Madrid: Biblioteca Nueva, 1943.

Maureen Ihrie

**ARIBAU, Bonaventura Carles** (1798, Barcelona–1862, Barcelona), poet, scholar, journalist, essayist, economist and politician. He studied rhetoric and philosophy as a seminarian and later physics, hydrostatics, taquigraphy and economics at the Junta of Commerce in Barcelona, and thus became a businessman. Between 1820 and 1823 he took active part in liberal politics and was one of the founders of the newspaper-magazine *El Europeo* (The European). By 1831 he had evolved into a conservative and described himself as a man "amant d'ordre" (a lover of law and order). In 1826 he began to work full time in Madrid for the Catalan financier Gaspar de la Remisa. "Oda a la Pàtria" (Ode to the Fatherland) was written to celebrate this banker's birthday; it was first recited by Aribau himself at de la Remisa's house in Madrid and was soon thereafter published in *El Europeo*. In this rather rhetorical composition Aribau blended a series of nationalistic ideas borrowed from the Romantic movement. Its fame is mostly due to its general recognition as having officially initiated the *Renaixença* (Renaissance) of modern *Catalan literature. Around 1850 Aribau became an activist Catalan lobbying in Madrid on behalf of protectionist Catalan industrialists. Aside from his fictional writings and business activities he was also a noted literary scholar for, among other enterprises, he founded and edited through volume 12 the *Biblioteca de Autores Españoles*. Other, minor works are "Carta dirigida desde Madrid al general Prim, compte de Reus" (1843; Letter Sent from Madrid to General Prim, Count of Reus); "Odes a la señora Leticia Cortesi" (1821; Odes to Mrs. Leticia Cortesi); "Odes all'eximia artista cantante Manuela Oreira Lema de Vega, che dimorava nella casa contigua a quella dell'autore" (1840; Odes to the great singer Manuela Oreira Lema de Vega, who lived in the house next to that of the author); "A la Virgen de los Dolores" (1845; To the Virgin of Sorrows); and a beautiful sonnet dedicated to "Srta. Maria Dolors de Belza." *See also* Catalan Literature; Romanticism.

BIBLIOGRAPHY

Primary Texts

*La pàtria. Trobes.* Commentary by C. Riba. Barcelona: Biblioteca de Catalunya, 1933.
*Poesies.* Study by M. Montoliu. Barcelona: n.p., 1935.

English Translations

Casas Homs, J. M. "Aribau a través de su biblioteca." In *Documentos y estudios del Ayuntamiento de Barcelona* (Barcelona) 19 (1968): n.p.
Fontana, Josep, J. Molas, and S. Baser. "Bonaventura Carles Aribau (1798–1862)." *Serra d'Or* August-Sept. 1962: 50–59.
Montoliu, M. *Aribau i la Catalunya del seu temps.* Barcelona: Institut d'estudis catalans, 1936.

Riba, C. "Entorn de les *Trobes* d'Aribau." In *Per comprendre*. Barcelona: Institució de
les lletres catalanes, 1938.

Joan Gilabert

**ARISTOTELIANISM IN SPAIN.** During the Middle Ages Spain was of vital
importance to the transmission of Aristotelian philosophy. Many of the most
influential works of Greek thought followed the route from Greece through the
Middle East to North Africa whereupon they were brought into the Iberian
Peninsula by Arab and Jewish scholars from the late eleventh c. Previously, the
Aristotelian corpus known to the West consisted of a few of the logical works
(*Organon*) in translations attributed to Boethius. Eastern scholars were primarily
interested in the scientific works, but they also produced translations and com-
mentaries on the *Metaphysics*, *Politics*, *Ethics*, *Economics*, *Rhetoric* and *Poetics*.
The works were translated at Toledo during the twelfth and thirteen centuries.
The Toledo school attracted scholars not only from North Africa and Spain but
from the rest of Europe as well. As a result, many of the most important figures
in the transmission of Aristotelianism, such as Gerard of Cremona and Michael
Scot, first came into contact with Greek philosophy in Spain.

Aristotle became the authority for medieval scholars largely through the efforts
of Thomas Aquinas (who, in turn, worked from the commentaries of Averroes)
in his attempt to reconcile Aristotelianism and Christianity. Problems arose
concerning Aristotle's theories of metaphysics and the soul as these were not
compatible with Christian theology, and the differences were never resolved.
However, Aristotle's moral works, which, besides the *Nichomachean Ethics*,
included the *Politics*, *Economics*, *Rhetoric* and *Poetics*, were enormously popular, particularly in Spain, from the thirteenth to seventeenth centuries. The most
widely read and translated was the *Ethics*, which circulated in numerous Latin
translations and in an anonymous compendium in Spanish, the first of the works
to be rendered in the vernacular. The emphasis on moral philosophy was characteristic of Aristotelianism in the Iberian Peninsula and was a factor in sustaining
the strength of the tradition. Whereas in the rest of Europe scientific discoveries
and the rise of *Platonism were dismantling the authority of Aristotle from the
fourteenth c., Spain's unique emphasis on theology combined with popular moral
philosophy established a longer-lasting and more solid tradition of Aristotelianism
than elsewhere. Plato was not considered an influential force in Spain until the
late sixteenth c., and when Platonism did arrive it could not destroy the authority
of Aristotle. However, although Spain's tradition of Aristotelianism began earlier
and lasted longer than elsewhere, Spain was not central to the interpretation and
development of Aristotelian thought. Given the advantage that Spain initially
had over the rest of Europe as the geographical point of entry of Aristotelianism
to the West, she did little for its diffusion and interpretation, for reasons not yet
established by scholars.

Among Spanish authors influenced by Aristotle's moral philosophy we find
the *Arcipreste de Hita, Juan Ruiz; Alonso de *Cartagena; Pero Díaz de Toledo;

Alfonso de la *Torre; Fernando de *Rojas and *Cervantes. In the sixteenth c., Juan Ginés de *Sepúlveda founded his attack on Bartolomé de las *Casas's defense of the Indians on the authority of Aristotle's concept of natural slavery. From this point on, Aristotelianism began to diminish slowly. In the late sixteenth and seventeenth centuries attention focused on the *Poetics*, an influence most evident in the work of Cervantes. After the *Siglo de Oro it is difficult to detect Aristotelianism as an authoritative philosophical force. Although it remained the base on which subsequent philosophical thought was founded, Aristotelianism was no longer directly influential.

Despite growing interest, a full study of Aristotelianism in Spain remains to be published. The following bibliography contains works which deal only with specific aspects of the subject. However, much insight into the literature of the Iberian Peninsula can be gained from a reading of the *Poetics* and *Nichomachean Ethics*. *See also* Edad Media, Literatura de la.

BIBLIOGRAPHY

Criticism

Forcione, Alban K. *Cervantes, Aristotle and the 'Persiles.'* Princeton: Princeton UP, 1970.
Green, Otis H. *Spain and the Western Tradition: The Castilian Mind in Literature from 'El Cid' to Calderón*. 4 vols. Madison, Milwaukee and London: U of Wisconsin P, 1968.
Menéndez Pelayo, Marcelino. *Historia de las ideas estéticas en España*. 4th ed. 2 vols. Madrid: CSIC, 1974.
Robles Carcedo, Laureano. "El estudio de la 'Ética' en España." *Repertorio de Historia de las ciencias eclesiásticas en España*. vol. 7. Salamanca: Instituto de Historia de la Teología Española, 1979. 234–353.
Sarton, George. *Introduction to the History of Science*. 4 vols. Washington, DC: Carnegie Institution, 1931; rpt. 1950.

Leslie P. Turano

**ARITZETA I ABAD, Margarida** (1953, Valls– ), novelist, historian and teacher. She has participated in a cultural program on the radio and worked at the Escola Universitària de Tarragona. She has a degree in history and philology. Her fiction is very imaginative and fanciful, but with one foot always firmly on the ground. Her first novel, *Quan la pedra es torna fang a les mans* (1981; When Stone Turns to Mud in Our Hands), won the Víctor Català Prize. *Un febrer a la pell* (1983; A February under the Skin), winner of the Sant Jordi Prize, is set against the infamous "golpazo" of February 23, 1981. A man disappears, and the protagonist, realizing that this is not a "normal" disappearance, tries to figure out what happened, reconstructing the last days of the disappeared. We are offered a gallery of personages and events that form a puzzle for our times. The change of the normal, working man to the individual capable of breaking with everything around him, including becoming sexually different, gives rise to both comic and serious reflection. The mystery is maintained until the end, which is open enough for us to imagine different conclusions. *Vermell de cadmi* (1984; Cadmium Red) is fantastic and realistic at the same time, including political cover-ups, deceptions and blunders, and manipulations of the press, as well as physical transformations of certain people into invisible beings, persons whose gender changes and who age rapidly. At times approaching science fiction, this novel is also a platform to examine government control of our lives and sexism seen through the eyes of people who have known both genders. *See also* Catalan Literature.

BIBLIOGRAPHY

Primary Texts

*Conte d'hivern*. Valencia: Prometeo, 1980.
*Un febrer a la pell*. Barcelona: Edicions 62, 1983.
*Grafèmia*. Barcelona: Laia, 1981.
*Quan la pedra es torna fang a les mans*. Barcelona: Selecta, 1981.
*Vermell de cadmi*. Barcelona: Laia, 1984.

Kathleen McNerney

**ARIZA, Juan** (1816, Motril–1876, Cuba), novelist and dramatist. In his rather Romantic dramas, he brings to the stage many key figures of Spanish history: *Hernando del Pulgar* (1849), *Alonso de Ercilla* (1848), *Antonio de Leiva* (1849), *El primer Girón* (1850; The First Giron), and *Remismunda* (1854). The best known of his historical novels, written in the tradition of Dumas, are *Dos cetros* (1845; Two Sceptors) and *El dos de mayo* (1846; The Second of May). *Viaje al infierno* (1848; Journey to Hell) is a satirical political novel. *See also* Romanticism.

BIBLIOGRAPHY

Primary Texts

*Don Alonso de Ercilla*. Madrid: Repullés, 1848. Louisville, KY: Falls City P, 1961. Microprint copy.
*El dos de mayo*. 2nd ed. Madrid: Hortelano, 1846.
*Poesías del Excmo. Sr. D. Juan de Ariza*. Havana: Avisador Comercial, 1877.
*El primer Girón*. Madrid: Omaña, 1850.
*Un loco hace ciento*. Madrid: C. González, 1853. Louisville, KY: Falls City P, 1961. Microprint copy.

**ARJONA, Juan de** (c. 1560, Granada–1603?, ?), priest responsible for the translation into Spanish of the *Thebaid* by Statius. The translation, in elegant *octavas reales* (see Octavas), earned Lope de *Vega's praise; Lope called Arjona a new Apollo ''de pluma heroica y soberana'' (of heroic, unsurpassed pen). He died after finishing nine of the twelve books; the work was completed by Gregorio Murillo.

BIBLIOGRAPHY

Primary Text

*La thebaida.* In BAE 36.

**ARJONA Y DE CUBAS, Manuel María de** (1771, Osuna–1820, Madrid), neoclassical poet. Canon of the Corodova Cathedral, he forms part of the group of Sevillan poets active in the Academia Horaciana (Horatian Academy) and the Academia de Buenas Letras (Fine Arts Academy). His work *Las ruinas de Roma* (1808; The Ruins of Rome) was inspired by a visit to Rome and is more pagan than Christian in its content. It is still impressive for its classical erudition. *La diosa del bosque* (n.d.; The Goddess of the Forest) is striking for its musicality and metrical innovations. *See also* Academia.

BIBLIOGRAPHY

Primary Text

*Poesías.* In BAE 63.

**ARMENGOL DE BADÍA, Agnès** (1852, Sabadell–1934, ?), poet, pianist and composer. From a wealthy family, she studied in a prestigious French school where she made her first literary contacts. She wrote of nature, memory, traditions and religion. Her sources vary from local legends to the classics; her style is emotional, clear and straightforward. She compiled songs her grandmother had sung to her and gave them to her teacher, Pelay Briz, who included them in his collection, *Cançons de la Terra.* From 1900 to 1902, she addressed her *Manifest* to Catalan women, encouraging them to support the Unió Catalanista. *See also* Catalan literature.

BIBLIOGRAPHY

Primary Texts

*Els dies clars.* Sabadell: Joan Sallent, 1926.
*Ramell de Semprevives: Poesies.* Sabadell: M. Torner, 1891.
*Redempció.* Sabadell: Biblioteca Sabadellenca, 1925.
*Rosari Antic, Tradicions i Records.* Sabadell: Joan Sallent, 1926.
*Sabadellenques i Altres Poesies.* Sabadell: Biblioteca Sabadellenca, 1925.

Kathleen McNerney

**ARMIÑÁN, Jaime de** (1925, Barcelona– ), Spanish playwright born into a family closely linked to the theater for three generations (his grandmother and mother were actresses, his grandfather a writer, his father a critic). Armiñán was originally linked with Alfonso *Paso and considered by early critics to belong to the tradition of Carlos *Arniches and the *astracán* (a short, exaggerated farce). *Eva sin manzana* (1954; Eve Without an Apple), his first work, was followed by *Nuestro fantasma* (1955; Our Ghost) and *Sinfonía acabada* 1956; Finished Symphony). *Café del liceo* (1958; The Lycee Cafe), *Paso a nivel* (1960; Railroad Crossing), *Pisito de solteras* (1962; Bachelor Girls' Apartment), *Academia de* *baile* (1962; Dance Academy), *La pareja* (1963; The Couple), *El último tranvía* (1965; The Last Streetcar), *Todas somos compañeras* (1965; We're All Together) and others in the same vein are comedies of intrigue, sometimes quite ingenious, often with mild criticism of current events, but with a great deal of frivolity and superficiality.

BIBLIOGRAPHY

Primary Texts

*Las doce caras de Juan*. Barcelona: Dima, 1968.
*Tiempo y hora*. Madrid: Alcalá, 1966. Television plays.

**ARNAO, Antonio** (1828, Murcia–1889, Madrid), minor poet. A defender of traditional Spanish values, he formed part of the anti-Romantic movement of the 1850s. His sentimental, pious poetry aimed at soothing "las hondas heridas de nuestra convulsa sociedad" (the deep wounds of our disturbed society). Under the influence of his close friend, José *Selgas, he was instrumental in bringing to Spanish attention the lyrical works of Heine. The national preoccupation seen in his verses also appears in his dramas: *Don Rodrigo, Don Pelayo,* and *La muerte de Garcilaso* (Garcilaso's Death). Today, however, he is most remembered for his poetry: *Himnos y quejas* (1851; Hymns and Complaints); *Las melancolías* (1857; The Blues); *La campaña de Africa* (1860; The African Campaign), which was acclaimed by the *Academia Española; and *Soñar despierto* (To Dream While Awake), published posthumously in 1891. He was also a member of the Spanish Academy. *See also* Academia Española; Romanticism.

BIBLIOGRAPHY

Primary Texts

*La campaña de Africa*. Madrid: Nacional, 1860.
*Dramas líricos*. Madrid: Medina y Navarro, 1875.
*Guzmán el bueno, ópera*. . . . Music by T. Bretón. Madrid: Rodríguez, 1876.
*Himnos y quejas*. Madrid: Espinosa, 1851.
*Soñar despierto*. Madrid: n.p., 1891.

**ARNICHES, Carlos** (1866, Alicante–1943, Madrid), playwright and key figure in the rise and splendor of the *género chico,* the festive satellite of stage drama that delighted audiences for over 30 years with comical portrayals, usually in one act, of the language, customs, and sentiments of everyday life. With the premiere in 1888 of the first in a long series of musical satires, Arniches embarked on a steady ascent toward material comfort, having grown up in the midst of penury and social instability. His newfound prosperity enabled him to devote full time to the theater. By 1895 he had emerged as one of Spain's most popular purveyors of light musical revues. He wrote over 60 percent of his 191 plays in collaboration with more than 20 playwrights. The co-author from whom he gained his most constructive insights into the development of ingenious plots and on dialogue as the focal element of comedy was Enrique *García Alvarez. Between them they produced 25 plays in the popular tradition of one-act *zarzuelas, *sainetes, *entremeses, comedietas, revues, pasillos, and comic sketches. Arniches perfected the classical Spanish sainete and became its most distinguished architect. Such plays as El santo de la Isidra (1898; Isidra's Saint) and Las estrellas (1904; The Stars) brought him instant notoriety as country's "Illustrious Sainetero." In time he shifted away from lighthearted farces featuring local color into the domain of a more serious concern for the moral and social conscience of his protagonists. This preceptive leaning resulted in a series of protest plays concerning such issues as the misuse of idleness—La Señorita de Trevélez (1916; Miss Trevélez); political tyranny—Los caciques (1920; The Bosses); and provincial hypocrisy—La heroica villa (1921; The Heroic Town). Yet even at this most incisively didactic stage, Arniches never forsook his characteristic benevolent humor. In his last plays he introduced a new and exciting genre to his repertory: the grotesque tragedy. This term refers to the use of caricature, exaggeration, and heightened improbability to produce a tragicomic effect. This mature period includes such engaging plays as Es mi hombre (1921; That's My Man), La locura de Don Juan (1923; Don Juan's Madness), La diosa ríe (1931; The Goddess Laughs), and El casto Don José (1933; Chaste Don José). The principal source of Arniches's inspiration in depicting the joys and sorrows of common people was the simple lives of his fellow citizens of Madrid, whose speech habits and customs provided the background, dialogue, warmth, and color for most of his writings. His work paved the way for such playwrights as Enrique Jardiel Poncela, Miguel *Mihura, and Alfonso *Paso to realize many of their stage successes within the current of the Spanish theater of humor. See also Contemporary Spanish Theater.

BIBLIOGRAPHY

Primary Texts

Teatro completo. Ed. E. María del Portillo. 4 vols. Madrid: Aguilar, 1948.

Criticism

McKay, D. R. Carlos Arniches. TWAS 188. New York: Twayne, 1972.

Douglas McKay

AROLAS, Juan (1805, Barcelona–1849, Valencia), poet. A member of the religious teaching order Escuelas Pías (Pious Schools), Arolas participated ardently in the Romantic movement in Spain. There are four main themes to his verse: religion, chivalry, love, and the Oriental. The latter, with exotic sultans and slaves, was his favorite. His poems are highly emotional, colorful, musical, sensual, even erotic at times, but they generally lack depth. His impetuous temperament must have rebelled in agony against his rigid vocation, for he died insane. See also Romanticism.

BIBLIOGRAPHY

Primary Texts

*Poesías*. Ed., study José R. Lomba y Pedraja. Clásicos Castellanos 95. Madrid: Espasa-Calpe, 1958.
*Poesías: caballerescas-orientales-leyendas*. Ed. Enrique Vázquez de Aldana. 3rd ed. Madrid: Compañía ibero-americana de publicaciones, 1928.
*Poesías escogidas*. Ed. L. L. Rosselló and J. Olea. Madrid: Saenz de Jubera, 1920.

Criticism

Lomba y Pedraja, J. R. *El padre Arolas, su vida y sus versos*. Madrid: "Sucesores de Rivadeneyra," 1898.

**ARQUIMBAU, Rosa María,** also known as Rosa de Sant Jordi (1910, Barcelona– ), novelist, journalist and playwright. She collaborated in many leftist publications, and the documentary character of her work is of great interest. She suffered from the Civil War, exile, and the difficult diffusion of *Catalan literature afterwards. A certain tendency toward escapism as well as strong character analysis is apparent in her work. In *40 anys perduts* (1971; 40 Years Lost), a young dressmaker working in a popular neighborhood suddenly becomes famous and decides what the aristocrats should wear. She passes easily from her proletarian origins to her new status. The protagonist of *Història d'una noia i vint braçalets* (1934; The Story of a Girl and 20 Bracelets) reveals herself to us through the linking of her many bracelets with certain events in her life. The liberated protagonist of *Home i dona* (1936; Man and Woman), separated from her husband, becomes known to us through a series of letters written to her best friend. Arquimbau won the Joan de Santamaria Prize for her work *L'inconvenient de dir-se Martines* (1957; The Inconvenience of Being Called Martines).

BIBLIOGRAPHY

Primary Texts

*40 anys perduts*. Barcelona: Biblioteca catalana de novela, 1971.
*Es rifa un home*. Barcelona: Bonavia, 1935.
*Història d'una noia i vint braçalets*. Barcelona: Llibreria Catalonia, 1934.
*Home i dona*. Barcelona: Quaderns literaris, 1936.
*L'inconvenient de dir-se Martines*. In *Premi Joan Santamaria*. Barcelona: Nereida, 1957. 87–108.
*La pau es un interval*. Barcelona: Pòrtic, 1970.

Kathleen McNerney

**ARRABAL, Fernando** (1932, Melilla, Spanish Morocco– ), playwright, novelist and filmmaker. His traumatic childhood experiences provided the material for most of his early plays, films and novels. The Spanish Civil War divided his family; his father was arrested, and the young Arrabal never saw him again. He grew up in a conservative, female-dominated household. The chance discovery of pictures and letters of his father in 1949 effected his rebellion against his mother and her pro-Franco ideology. In the early 1950s, following a period of reading, moviegoing and attendance at intellectual gatherings, Arrabal published his first drama, *Los soldados* (1952; *Picnic on the Battlefield*, 1969). That work and the plays that followed in the 1950s are characterized by the childlike nature of his characters, who may be both tender and sadistic and who are generally crushed by the incomprehensible macrocosm that surrounds them. Elements of Surrealism and the Absurd have been identified in these works by a number of critics. Arrabal, to a degree, utilized his theater, especially in this early period, as a device for externalizing and ultimately resolving his innermost conflicts. The dominant figure in the subconscious of the author and, concomitantly, in his theater was that of the mother. A principal weapon employed by Arrabal to deal with extreme psychic pain is humor. Much of his comic inspiration is of the sort known as black humor, an integral component of the grotesque, a mode found in Arrabal's earliest works, which is enriched and expanded later. In the dreamlike atmosphere of many of the early plays, repetitions, cycles and ceremonies already play a significant role, while reality remains elusive, subjective and highly volatile. These works, because of their freshness and impact in the context of the period in Spain's history that they evoke, have already gained international recognition in the realm of contemporary avant-garde theater.

While virtually all of these early plays are of interest, several do stand out as a result of intrinsic merit and/or notable productions. *El laberinto* (1956; *The Labyrinth*, 1969) uses a Kafkaesque nightmare to depict the devious nature of the modern world. *Los dos verdugos* (1956; The Two Executioners), the author's most overtly autobiographical work, portrays the insidious influence of the author's mother, who incarnates the forces of tyranny in Franco's Spain. *El cementerio de automóviles* (1957; The Automobile Graveyard) explores the nature of good and evil, incorporating a grotesque parody of the Christ story to suggest the perverseness of our society. The central metaphor of the work, contained in its title, communicates visually the wreckage of civilization endemic to our technological age. Circularity and the metamorphosis of characters are used to an unprecedented degree, anticipating the direction to be taken by Arrabal's mature theater. The famous staging of this work by Víctor García mounted initially in Dijon, France, in 1966, has also helped to establish the reputation of this intriguing work.

Arrabal left Spain in 1955, and, after recovering from a severe case of tuberculosis, decided to settle permanently in France. In 1958 he married Luce Moreau, now a professor of Spanish literature at the Sorbonne. All of his plays have been published in French, but have always been written initially in Spanish and then translated with the assistance of his wife. His contact in Paris with a variety of artists, writers and directors led to his founding of the Panic movement in 1962 and provided the artistic stimulation necessary for the more complex Panic dramas of the 1960s.

Panic is at once a serious exposition of philosophical and aesthetic principles, emphasizing memory and chance as the preeminent forces governing human actions, and a parody of all attempts at formal literary movements and theories. The first Panic play, *Primera comunión* (1963; First Communion), projects an oneiric ambience in exploring the effect of Spain's sexually repressive society on the Spanish female. The playwright's acknowledged masterpiece, *El arquitecto y el emperador de Asiria* (1965; *The Architect and the Emperor of Assyria*, 1969) dates from this period. Ceremony, game playing, cycles and a series of dualities (ranging from dream-reality to verbal lyricism-grotesque blasphemy) structure this dazzling exploration of the human condition. Tom O'Horgan's staging of the work at La Mama in New York in 1976 became one of Arrabal's greatest successes, as evidenced by Clive Barnes's glowing review of the production in the *New York Times*.

Arrabal's third period, which accords a more profound and pervasive role to political concerns, was inspired by several traumatic incidents. In 1967, Arrabal was arrested in Spain for writing a blasphemous dedication in one of his books. He spent over a month in prison before being acquitted under rather bizarre circumstances and expelled from the country. Then in 1968 he witnessed at first hand the student rebellion in Paris. The immediate product of these events was his powerful and controversial piece of guerilla theater: . . . *Y pondrán esposas a las flores* (1969; *And They Put Handcuffs on the Flowers*, 1973). Subsequent works of high merit tended to deal with Spain and the playwright's feelings about the land from which he was exiled. These include *En la cuerda floja* (1974; On the Wire) and *La torre de Babel* (1976; The Tower of Babel).

With the demise of Franco in 1975 and with Arrabal's established international reputation and growing penchant for scandal, his *angst*, which had inspired and characterized his best works, began to dissipate. He still exhibited a marvelous sense of theatrical humor, but his political farces often lacked dramatic impact. He finally was able to return to his native Spain, and his best work of recent years, *Inquisición* (1980; Inquisition) was also the first of his plays since the 1950s to premiere in Spain and to be published initially in Spanish.

Arrabal, although essentially a dramatist, has enjoyed considerable success in other genres as well. He has made a number of significant films, beginning with the autobiographical *Viva la muerte* (1970; Long Live Death) and including the enchanting children's fantasy *Pacific Odyssey* (1981) starring Mickey Rooney. His novels include *Baal Babylon* (1959), the point of departure for *Viva la muerte* and *La torre herida por el rayo* (1983; The Tower Wounded by the Flash of Lightning), which won the prestigious Nadal Prize in Spain for 1982. The latter features a chess game that runs throughout the work and structures the entire novel. Arrabal writes a regular chess column for *L'Express* in Paris. He has designed paintings, published a book of photographs of New York, and authored various political treatises and numerous poems. Although his personality and his works have often inspired sarcasm and hostility from a multitude of critics, his international reputation as an innovative voice in avant-garde drama seems assured.

BIBLIOGRAPHY

Primary Texts

*El cementerio de automóviles. El arquitecto y el emperador de Asiria.* Madrid: Cátedra, 1984.

*Inquisición.* Granada: Don Quixote, 1982.

*Pic-Nic. El triciclo. El laberinto.* Madrid: Cátedra, 1977.

*Teatro completo.* Vol. 1. Madrid: Cuspa, 1979. (Contains: *Pic-Nic, El triciclo, Fando y Lis, Ceremonia por un negro asesinado, El laberinto, Los dos verdugos, Oración, El cementerio de automóviles.*)

*. . . y pondrán esposas a las flores.* Salamanca: Almar, 1984.

English Translations

*And They Put Handcuffs on the Flowers.* Tr. Charles Marowitz. New York: Grove, 1973.

*The Architect and the Emperor of Assyria.* Tr. Everard D'Harnoncourt and Adele Shank. New York: Grove, 1969.

*Baal Babylon.* Tr. Richard Howard. New York: Grove, 1961.

*Garden of Delights.* Tr. Helen Bishop and Tom Bishop. New York: Grove, 1974.

*Guernica and Other Plays.* Tr. Barbara Wright. 3 vols. New York: Grove, 1967–9. (Includes *The Labyrinth, The Tricycle, Picnic on the Battlefield* etc.)

Criticism

Arata, Luis. *The Festive Play of Fernando Arrabal.* Lexington: UP of Kentucky, 1982.

Berenguer, Angel. *L'exil et la cérémonie. Le premier théâtre d'Arrabal.* Paris: Union générale d'Editions, 1977.

Donahue, Thomas. *The Theater of Fernando Arrabal.* New York: New York UP, 1980.

Podol, Peter. *Fernando Arrabal.* TWAS 499. Boston: Twayne, 1978.

Torres Monreal, Francisco. *Introducción al teatro de Arrabal.* Murcia: Godoy, 1981.

Peter L. Podol

**ARRIAZA, Juan Bautista** (1770, Madrid–1837, Madrid), poet. After serving in the Spanish navy, he pursued a diplomatic career, spending some time in London. His first publication, *Primicias* (1797; First Fruits), was followed by *Ensayos poéticos* (1799; Poetic Rehearsals), *Poesías patrióticas* (1810; Patriotic Poetry), and *Poesías líricas* (1822; Lyric Poetry). His poetry is spontaneous, musical, facile at times, and reaches its maximum expression in the moving patriotic poems inspired by the War of Independence with France.

BIBLIOGRAPHY

Primary Text

*Poesías.* BAE 67.

**ARRÓNIZ Y BOSCH, Teresa,** pseudonym, Gabriel de los Arcos (1827, Cartagena–1890, Murcia-Madrid), novelist. Biographical data are scarce for this prolific, remarkable fiction writer. She began publishing in 1855, with *El Testamento de Don Juan* (The Testament of Don Juan). Except for this first novel, all her work, more than 20 novels, was published as serials in publications of Madrid, such as *Revista de España, Revista Hispano-Americana, La Corres-*

*pondencia de España*, *El Diaro Español*, *El Campo*, and *El Grano de Arena* of Seville. She left four unedited novels, which were published posthumously in the magazine *El Eco de Cartagena*. One of these, *La ley de hierro* (The Iron Law) was considered by Cejador to be her masterpiece.

Her novel *Mari-Pérez* won a prize from the Spanish Royal Academy (see Academia Española) in 1876 and was then published in the magazine *La Revista de España*. According to Ferreras her writing falls within a variety of tendencies, beginning with historical novels in 1855 and shifting toward realistic works in later years. For example, *Mari-Pérez* (1879) is still a historical novel, located in sixteenth-c. Madrid, where characters are clear-cut epitomes of "good" and "bad." *Recuerdos* (1882; Remembrances), on the other hand, relates an episode during the Carlist war in a very realistic tone, showing the divisions and suffering created by politics within Spanish families. Protagonists are still described somewhat idealistically, but secondary characters and atmosphere are very realistic, and the plot and language very effective.

BIBLIOGRAPHY

Primary Texts

*La bola negra.* In *Revista de España* (Madrid) 81 (1881): 527 + .
*La ley de hierro.* In *El Eco de Cartagena* (Cartagena) a. 1890.
*Mari-Pérez.* In *Revista de España* (Madrid) 66 (1879): 238 + .
*Recuerdos.* In *Revista Hispano-Americana* (Madrid) 9 (1882): 281 + .
*El testamento de Don Juan.* Madrid: Establecimiento tipográfico militar, 1855.

Criticism

Barceló, J. y A. Cárceles Alemán. *Escritoras murcianas.* Murcia: Academia Alfonso el Sabio, 1986. 52–53.
Cejador y Frauca, Julio. *Historia de la lengua y literatura castellana.* 14 vols. Madrid: Tipología de Archivos, 1915–22. Vol 8.
Ferreras, Juan Ignacio. *Catálogo de novelas y novelistas españoles del s. XIX.* Madrid: Cátedra, 1979.
Simón Palmer, C. "Escritoras españolas del siglo XIX." In *Censo de escritoras al servicio de los Austrias y otros estudios bibliográficos.* Madrid: CSIC, 1983. 114–15.

                                                                    Cristina Enríquez

**ARTE MAYOR,** a poetic term. *Coplas* or *versos de arte mayor* refers to lines of nine to fourteen syllables, but most often twelve, in which each hemistich contains an independent dactyl rhythm. Early examples of the form are found in the *Cancionero de *Baena,* but the form was perfected by Juan de *Mena (1411–56).

BIBLIOGRAPHY

Criticism

Clarke, D. C. *Morphology of Fifteenth Century Castilian Verse.* Pittsburgh-Louvain: Duquesne U, 1964. 51–61.
Tavani, G. "Considerazioni sulle origini dell' *arte mayor.*" *Cultura neolatina* 25 (1965): 15–33.

Tittman, Barclay. "Further Remarks on the Origins of *Arte mayor*." *Cultura neolatina* 29 (1969): 274–82.

***ARTE MENOR,*** a poetic term. *Versos de arte menor* are lines of poetry containing from two to eight syllables. Usually, they contain only one rhythmic stress, other than the final.

**ARTEAGA, Esteban de** (1747, Moraleja de Coca, Segovia–1799, Paris), aesthetician. He entered the Jesuit order, but in 1769, two years after the Jesuits were expelled from Spain, he left the priesthood. He continued to live in Italy where he had moved in 1767, studying and publishing excellent works on aesthetics, such as *Investigaciones filosóficas sobre la belleza ideal* (1789; Philosophical Investigations of Ideal Beauty) and *Le rivolucioni del teatro musicale italiano* (1783–88; The Revolution of Italian Musical Theater).

BIBLIOGRAPHY

Primary Texts

*La belleza ideal.* Ed., intro. M. Batllori, S.I. 2nd ed. Madrid: Espasa-Calpe, 1955.
*I. Lettere musico-filologiche. II. Del ritmo sonoro e del ritmo muto nella musica degli antichi.* Ed., intro. M. Batllori. Madrid: CSIC, 1944.
*Le rivoluzioni del teatro musicale italiano.* 2nd ed. 3 vols. Venice: Palese, 1785.

Criticism

Olguín, M. "The Theory of Ideal Beauty in Arteaga and Winckelmann." *Journal of Aesthetics and Art Criticism* 8 (1949): 12–33.
Rudat, Eva. *Las ideas estéticas de Esteban de Arteaga.* Spanish tr. C. Criado de Rodríguez-Puértolas. Madrid: Gredos, 1971.

**ARTIGAS, Miguel** (1887, Blesa [Teruel]–1947, Madrid). Director of the Menéndez y Pelayo Library of Santander and later of the National Library (*Biblioteca Nacional) in Madrid, he was also a member of the Royal Spanish Academy of the Language (*Academia Española). A disciple of Marcelino *Menéndez y Pelayo, Artigas devoted two works to his polyfaceted mentor, *La vida y obra de Menéndez y Pelayo* (Life and Works of M.P.) and *La España de Menéndez y Pelayo* (The Spain of M.P.), and directed the publication of the national edition of Menéndez y Pelayo's complete works. As a literary critic, Artigas also published lengthy studies of the *Libro de la *miseria del omne* (Book of Human Misery), of *Ulloa, and most importantly, *Don Luis de *Góngora y Argote, Biografía y estudio crítico* (1925; Don Luis de Góngora y Argote: Biography and Critical Study), which received a prize from the Royal Academy.

**ARTILES, Jenaro J.** (1897, Las Palmas de Gran Canaria– ), librarian, cultural attaché, essayist and translator. Artiles belonged to the corps of librarians and archivists of Madrid and was director of the Library of the *Ateneo (1924–34), cultural attaché for the Spanish Republic in Berne, and director of the bibliographic section of the major Madrid daily, *El Sol* (1928–36). Artiles's Loyalist connections resulted in his going into exile following the Civil War, first in Cuba and then in the United States, where he became a professor of Spanish language and literature. Among his publications are an edition (1927) of the *Obras Completas* (Complete Works) of *Alvarez Gato in the Clásicos Olvidados (Forgotten Classics) Series, a paleographic edition of the *Libro de acuerdos del concejo madrileño* (1932; Book of Accords of the City Council of Madrid, in collaboration with Millares Carlo), and a translation with prologue of the *Philosophia electiva* of José A. Caballero (1945; Elective Philosophy).

**ASCETICAL LITERATURE** (from the Greek ασκησις (ÁSKESIS) meaning exercise, practice, training). During the sixteenth and seventeenth centuries in Spain, monks of different religious orders produced an important body of ascetical-meditative-devotional literature which forms a distinct corpus from that of classical Spanish *mysticism. The mystical process includes three stages or phases: purgative, illuminative and unitive. The ascetical process involves the first two of these, leading up to union, which is part of the mystical or unitive stage. The ascetical *tratados* (treatises), *guías espirituales* (spiritual exercises), *abecedarios* (spiritual alphabets), *manuales* (handbooks) and *opúsculos* (booklets, brief treatises) were meant to prepare the individual for union by offering spiritual direction in the exercise of prayer and meditation.

The authors of ascetical-meditative works demonstrated the manner in which the individual would practice and exercise the Christian virtues in order to predispose the soul to seek union. Furthermore, the ascetical exercises guided the person praying in his withdrawal into the depths of his soul (*recogimiento*) so that it could more easily ascend toward God. Since each individual was presumed to be a sinner as a result of the fallen condition of humanity, these books would serve as spiritual directors. It is important to note that the ascetical process was accessible to everyone since it never involved any extraordinary (sanctifying) grace on God's part. Even into modern times, the reader may utilize ascetical literature to attain perfection.

In the final stages of the ascetical process, after the soul has been purged of all thoughts and feelings not pertaining to God (dark night), illumination takes place whereby the soul is in complete and harmonious conformity with God. Asceticism commits the memory and the intellect (first two parts of the soul) since the will is moved by love to attain union, hence entering the unitive stage which is part of the mystical process. One of the prototypes of ascetical literature is the *Contemptus Mundi* (Spanish translation Zaragoza, 1493; *Imitation of Christ*, 1898) by Thomas à Kempis. In Spain Fray Luis de *Granada's *Guía de pecadores* (Lisbon, 1556; *The Sinner's Guyde*, 1598) remains one of the classical works of asceticism (*ascetismo*). *See also* Francisco de Osuna, Cristóbal de Fonseca, Malón de Chaide, Diego de Estella, Antonio de Guevara.

BIBLIOGRAPHY

Primary Texts

*Guía de pecadores*. By Luis de Granada. Clásicos Castellanos 97. Madrid: Espasa-Calpe, 1953.

*Imitación de Cristo y menosprecio del mundo.* Tr. L. Alonso Getino. Madrid: Aguilar, 1949.

English Translations

*Imitatio Christi.* By Thomas à Kempis. No tr. Boston: United Society of Christian Endeavor, 1898.
*The Sinner's Guide.* Tr. Francis Meres. Dublin: n.p., 1803. Tr. of *Guía de pecadores.*

Criticism

Asensio, Eugenio. "El erasmismo y las corrientes espirituales afines." *RFE* 36 (1952): 31–99.
Díaz-Plaja, Guillermo. *Historia general de las literaturas hispánicas.* Barcelona: Vergara, 1968. 3: 29–56.
González Haba, M. J. "Séneca en la espiritualidad de los siglos XVI y XVII." *Revista de Espiritualidad* 10 (1951): 312–54.
Green, Otis H. *Spain and the Western Tradition.* Madison: U of Wisconsin P, 1968. 4: 169–72.
Sainz Rodríguez, Pedro. *Espiritualidad española.* Madrid: Rialp, 1961.

Angelo DiSalvo

**ASENJO BARBIERI, Francisco** (1823, Madrid–1894, Madrid), composer, musicologist. In 1847 Barbieri helped bring together a group of composers all seeking the establishment of a Spanish lyric theater independent of Italian influence. His use of the *zarzuela (spoken dialogue with musical interludes, normally in one act) met with great popular success in his very first attempt, *Gloria y peluca* (1850; Glory and Wigs). Of the sixty-odd *zarzuelas* he subsequently composed, the most notable are *Jugar con fuego* (1851; Playing with Fire), *Los diamantes de la corona* (1854; The Crown Diamonds), *Pan y toros* (1864; Bread and Bulls), and *El barberillo de Lavapiés* (1874; The Little Barber of Lavapiés).

Barbieri's music library—the richest in Spain—was ultimately bequeathed to the National Library (*Biblioteca Nacional) in Madrid. It included much data and documents on the history of Spanish music. His most important publication, the *Cancionero musical de los siglos XV y XVI* (1890; Songbooks of the Fifteenth and Sixteenth Centuries), contains transcriptions of 459 mss. in the Royal Palace Library along with biographical data. Barbieri was a member of the Spanish Academy (*Academia Española) and the Academy of Fine Arts of San Fernando.

BIBLIOGRAPHY

Primary Texts

*Cancionero musical de los siglos XV y XVI.* Ed. F. Asenjo Barbieri. Buenos Aires: Shapiro, 1945.
*Teatro completo de Juan del Encina.* Ed. F. Asenjo Barbieri. Westport, CT: Greenwood, 1969.

Criticism

Chase, G. "Barbieri and the Spanish Zarzuela." *Music and Letters* 20 (1939): 32.
———. *The Music of Spain.* New York: Norton, 1941.

Salcedo, A. S. *Francisco Asenjo Barbieri: su vida y obra*. Madrid: Biblioteca Músicos Españoles, 1920s.

D. J. O'Connor

**ASENJO SEDANO, José** (1930, Guadix, Granada– ), narrator and poet. He studied law at the U of Granada. At 18 Asenjo published his first short story collection, *Leyenda de juventud* (1984; Legend of Youth). Two of his more important novels, *Los guerreros* (1970; The Warriors) and *Crónica* (1974; Chronicle), focus on the socio-economic effects of the Spanish Civil War on the population of Guadix.

*Conversaciones sobre la guerra* (1978; Conversations on the War) is perhaps the best example of this writer's novelistic talent. The impact of the Civil War is reduced, in this case, to a family. Asenjo is one of the few authors inside Spain who have dealt with the topic of the Civil War from a strictly literary point of view. The moral and material decadence of the postwar period is narrated in *Eran los días más largos* (1982; The Days Used to Be Longer). Other volumes of fiction written by Asenjo are the novel *El ovni* (1976; The UFO) and a story collection, *Indalecio el Gato* (1983; Indalecio the Cat). He utilizes poetic prose in *Yo, Granada* (1979; I, Granada), ten sketches concerning the human, historical, and aesthetic Granadinian landscape, and *Arte Menor* (1981; Minor Art), a collection of poems in the "Modernista" vein. Anecdote prevails over style in Asenjo's narrative, and he shows special sensibility in his poetic characterization of the trauma suffered by Spanish children during the Civil War. Earlier works include *Penélope y el mar* (Penelope and the Sea) and an undated memoir, *Impresiones y recuerdos de un paisaje* (Impressions and Memories of a Landscape).

BIBLIOGRAPHY

Primary Texts

*Arte Menor*. Granada: Genil, 1981.
*Conversaciones sobre la guerra*. Barcelona: Destino, 1978.
*Eran los días más largos*. Barcelona: Destino, 1982.
*Indalecio el Gato*. Barcelona: Argos-Vergara, 1983.
*Yo, Granada*. Granada: Aljibe, 1979.

Criticism

Carenas, Francisco. "José Asenjo Sedano. *Conversaciones sobre la guerra*." *Cuadernos Americanos* 224 (1979): 177–79.

José Ortega

**ASÍN PALACIOS, Miguel** (1871, Zaragoza–1944, San Sebastián). After preparing for an ecclesiastical career, he received a doctorate in theology in the Seminary in Zaragoza. As a disciple of Julián Ribera, he undertook studies in Arabic and was steeped in the methodology of the Arabists of the school of Codera. After obtaining a chair of Arabic at the U of Madrid, he became a distinguished educator, and was later director of the Royal Spanish Academy

(*Academia Española), as well as belonging to the Academies of History and of Moral and Political Science. He founded the journal *Al-Andalús*, which has continued to be a center for his disciples who have carried on his investigations. Many philological studies by Asín appeared in the *Revista de Aragón*, *Cultura Española*, *Al-Andalús* and other reviews, ranging across Islamic, Oriental and Spanish culture, and devoted especially to Moslem and Christian thought. Among his significant books are *Averroísmo teológico de Santo Tomás de Aquino* (1904; Theological Influence of Averroes in St. Thomas Aquinas); *La escatología musulmana en la Divina Comedia* (1919; Moslem Eschatology in The Divine Comedy); *El Islam cristianizado* (1931; Islam Christianized); and *La espiritualidad de Algazel y su sentido cristiano* (1934; The Spirituality of Algazel and His Christian Significance). Asín also wrote on the practices of Moslem mystics (Aben Massara and Abentofail), and studied the Murcian philosopher Aben Arabi as a source of information for Ramón *Llull. Some of his best works on Hispano-Arabic philosophy include studies of Abén Abbad de Ronda and Abenhazam de Córdoba. One of his last projects was a glossary of medieval Spanish *romance* dialect forms included in the works of a Hispano-Moslem botanist of the 11th and 12th centuries, subsequently an extremely important source for studies of pre-literary Spanish and of Mozarabic dialect. Perhaps his most polemical and controversial work was the above-mentioned study of Islamic traditions in the *Divine Comedy*, which demonstrated his thesis that much of Dante's ultraterrestrial journeys originated in writings which can be traced back to Mohammed, although a multitude of European versions exists. Subsequent discoveries have lent added credence to his thesis. Asín Palacios was the object of a posthumous tribute when the Spanish Consejo Superior de Investigaciones Científicas named the Institute of Arabic Studies in his honor.

BIBLIOGRAPHY

English Translation

*Islam and the Divine Comedy*. Tr. H. Sunderland. 1926. Rpt. London: Cuss; New York: Barnes, 1968.

Janet Pérez

**ASQUERINO, Eduardo** (1826, Barcelona–1881, Madrid), late Romantic playwright and journalist. Alone or with his brother Eusebio or others, Eduardo wrote several plays. Among them are the dramas *El gabán del rey* (1847; The King's Overcoat) and *El tesorero del Rey* (1850; the King's Treasurer). He also directed the newspaper *El Universal* (1856; The Universal). *See also* Romanticism.

BIBLIOGRAPHY

Primary Texts

*El gabán del rey*. With Romero Larrañaga. Madrid: Repullés, 1847.
*El tesorero del rey*. With García Gutiérrez. Madrid: S. Omaña, 1850.
*San Isidro Labrador*. Madrid: Operarios, 1852.

Criticism

Portilla, Anselmo de la. "Apuntes biográficos de D. Eduardo Asquerino." *Ecos del alma.*
    Mexico: n.p., 1853.
See also Criticism for Asquerino, Eusebio.

Salvador García Castañeda

**ASQUERINO, Eusebio** (1822, Seville–1892, Madrid), playwright and journalist. A militant Republican, he composed numerous historical dramas in which
criticism of contemporary politics is barely disguised. He demagogically divides
the world into "good" characters (who embody his own ideas) and "bad" ones
(representing the government). His most important plays include *Doña Urraca*
(1838), *Gustavo Wasa* (1841), *Los dos tribunos* (1845; The Two Tribunes), *Juan
de Padilla* (1846), and *Venganza de un caballero* (1846; A Knight's Revenge).
Asquerino played an important role in the journalistic world of his day, directing
the newspapers *El Eco de la Revolución* (1843; The Echo of the Revolution),
*El tíovivo* (1844–45; The Merry-go-round), and *La América* (1857–70; America).

BIBLIOGRAPHY

Primary Texts

*Doña Urraca.* Madrid: Repullés, 1838.
*Gustavo Wasa.* Madrid: Boix, 1841.
*Juan de Padilla.* Madrid: Repullés, 1846.
*Los dos tribunos.* Madrid: Repullés, 1845.
*Venganza de un caballero y juramento de un rey.* Madrid: Repullés, 1846.

Criticism

Alonso Cortés, N. "El teatro español en el siglo XIX." *Historia general de las literaturas
    hispánicas.* vol. 4, part 2. Barcelona: n.p., 1968.
Cejador, Julio. *Historia de la lengua y literatura castellana.* vol. 7. Madrid: RABM,
    1917.
García Castañeda, S. "Los hermanos Asquerino o el uso y mal uso del drama histórico."
    *Teatro romantico spagnolo.* Bologna: n.p., 1984.
Martínez Villergas, J. *Juicio crítico de los poetas españoles contemporáneos.* Paris: Rosa
    y Bouret, 1854.

Salvador García Castañeda

**ASTRANA MARÍN, Luis** (1889, Villaescusa de Haro, Cuenca–1960, Madrid),
translator, editor and scholar. Astrana Marín's numerous publications include
editions of the complete works of *Quevedo and *Calderón; he also wrote biographies of Lope de *Vega, *Séneca, Quevedo and *Cervantes (the latter a seven-
volume study). He was the first to translate the complete works of Shakespeare
into Spanish, complementing it with a biography. In 1920, he also published a
polemical work titled *Las profanaciones literarias. El libro de los plagios* (Literary Profanations. The book of plagiarisms).

BIBLIOGRAPHY

Primary Texts

*Las profanaciones literarias. El libro de los plagios: Rodríguez Marín.* . . . Madrid: Ariel, 1920.
*Vida inmortal de William Shakespeare.* Madrid: Ediciones españolas, 1941.
*Vida ejemplar y heroica de Miguel de Cervantes Saavedra.* . . . 7 vols. Madrid: Reus, 1948–58.

**ATENCIA, María Victoria** (?, Málaga– ), contemporary Andalusian poet. Atencia is known as a poet of distance: the tranquil tone of her writing points to an intimacy which takes its point of departure from daily life and objects before progressing toward an inner realm. There is an exactness and clarity about her work which nonetheless does not indicate simplicity of meaning; the naturalness has a precisely balanced expression that elicits comparisons from at times seemingly disparate elements. Although the poems may refer to the immediate reality, they also appear as memory, acquiring a dreamlike or nostalgic quality as they filter the speaker's perceptions through a personal time. There is an impression of innocence blended with tragedy, resignation, contemplation, emptiness. One senses that Atencia's poetry obtains much of its relevance for modern readers precisely from the emptiness it embodies, a neobaroque yet accepting analysis of the author's sense of nothingness, heightened at times by fragmentation and hesitation.

BIBLIOGRAPHY

Primary Texts

*Arte y parte.* Madrid: Rialp, 1961.
*Cañada de los ingleses.* Librería ANTICUARIA El Guadalhorce, 1961.
*El coleccionista.* Seville: Calle del Aire, 1979.
*Compás binario.* Madrid: Hiperión, 1984.
*Ex libris.* Madrid: Visor, 1984.
*Marta & María.* Madrid: Caballo Griego para la Poesía, 1984.
*El mundo de M.V.* Madrid: Insula, 1978.
*Paulina, o, el libro de las aguas.* Madrid: Trieste, 1984.

Criticism

Benítez Reyes, Felipe "De la poesía como un caleidoscopio detenido." *Fin de siglo* (Jerez de la Frontera) 0 (1982): 3–4.
Morales Zaragoza, María Luisa. "Preliminar," María Victoria Atencia, *Marta & María.* Madrid: Caballo Griego para la Poesía, 1984. 9–14.

Kathleen March

***ATENEO*** (Atheneum), intellectual and cultural institution, dedicated to the encouragement of literary and scientific study. In ancient Greece, the term was used for buildings dedicated to the goddess Athena, especially one temple where learned men would gather to discuss and speak formally. The Emperor Hadrian (reign A.D. 117–141) founded the first Roman Atheneum around the year 135;

it offered formal instruction as well as a meeting place for poets, orators, etc. Though not so named, similar institutions flourished in the Middle Ages in Europe; in Spain they were declared *escuelas oficiales* (official schools) by *Alphonse X, and subsequently evolved into institutions offering formal programs of study. Two of the most important *Ateneos* in Spain are the *Ateneo científico y literario* of Madrid, founded in 1820, disbanded three years later, reinstituted in 1835 by *Mesonero Romanos and Olózaga and flourishing to this day, and the *Ateneo de Barcelona* (founded in 1860 with the name *Ateneo Catalán*). Their activities include publishing; sponsoring lectures, discussion and instruction; maintaining libraries, etc. Past and present members comprise a list of illustrious scholars, scientists and intellectual leaders. *See also* Edad Media, Literatura de la.

BIBLIOGRAPHY

Criticism

Araujo Costa, L. *Biografía del Ateneo en Madrid,* Madrid: n.p., 1949.
Ruiz Salvador, Antonio. *El Ateneo científico, literario y artístico de Madrid (1835–1885).* London: Tamesis, 1971.

Maureen Ihrie

**AUB, MAX** (1902, Paris–1972, Mexico), dramatist, novelist, literary critic and occasional poet. Although born in France of a German father and French mother, Aub became thoroughly identified with his adoptive country, Spain, where his family moved when the future writer was eleven. Well acquainted in literary circles in Madrid before the war, Aub had begun to establish his name as a narrator with a number of lyric novelettes: *Geografía* (1921; Geography), *Fábula verde* (1932; Green Fable), and *Luis Álvarez Petreña* (1934), which employs epistolary technique to depict the existential frustration of the hero, who ends a suicide. While less successful in the theater, Aub also began to experiment with vanguard, "dehumanized" drama before the war, with such works as *Narciso* (1928) and *Teatro incompleto* (1931; Incomplete Theater), with his desire for innovation being especially notable in the latter.

Aub's sympathies with the workers' cause and his association with vanguard-ists combined to drive him into exile at the close of the Civil War, briefly in France and North Africa, and more permanently in Mexico, where he settled until his death, becoming an important part of the cultural life of his home in exile. Aub's most important work was done in exile, with his novels of the Civil War figuring among the most significant writing which has been done on Spain's national tragedy. His novelistic cycle, *El laberinto mágico* (The Magic Laby-rinth), depicting the war from prelude to aftermath, is an epic achievement: *Campo cerrado* (1943; Closed Field) portrays the period immediately before the conflict, ending with the street-fighting in Barcelona during the anarchic first days of the war. The war proper, viewed from both sides and from cities as well as battlefields, appears in *Campo de sangre* (1945; Bloody Field) and *Campo abierto* (1951; Open Field). Aub portrays the final days of the desperate defense

of Madrid in *Campo del Moro* (1963; The Moor's Field), a pun alluding both
to the Moorish mercenaries in Franco's army and to the Madrid park by that
name. *Campo francés* (1965; French Field) involves another pun, since *campo*
means not only field but camp, and this novel portrays the plight of Spanish
refugees in a French concentration camp, which Aub had the misfortune to know
personally, and where he began to draft some of his novels, continuing the work
later in another camp in North Africa, before he managed to escape and make
his way to Mexico. *Campo de los Almendros* (1968; Field of Almond Trees)
focuses upon another tragic moment in the final days of the Republic, as a group
of Republicans (officials, civilians and soldiers) await the hoped-for evacuation
by ships which are to carry to them to safety in exile, only to find that they are
trapped when the ships prove to belong to the Nationalists. Many of the same
themes, together with other aspects of the war, appear in many of Aub's short
story collections: *No son cuentos (cuentos)* (1944; These Are Not Stories [Sto-
ries]); *Historias de mala muerte* (1965; Tales of Bad Deaths); and *Últimos cuentos
de la guerra de España* (1969; Last Tales of the Spanish War).

Also in exile, Aub published the following dramatic works: *San Juan* (1943;
St. John), *Morir para cerrar los ojos* (1944; Dying to Close One's Eyes),
*Deseada* (1951; The Desired One), *No* (1952); and *Obras en un acto* (1960, 2
vols.; One-Act Plays). He was more prolific in the narrative, however, also
producing several narratives of the lives of Spanish Republicans in exile, especially in the story collection *La verdadera historia de la muerte de Francisco
Franco y otros cuentos* (1960; The True Story of the Death of Francisco Franco
and Other Tales), where Aub subtly undercuts the myth of the exile's return and
satirizes the wasted lives of those who spend their time in cafés awaiting the
death of the Spanish dictator. In *Las buenas intenciones* (1954; Good Intentions)
and *La calle de Valverde* (1960; Valverde Street), Aub returns nostalgically to
pre-war Spain, re-creating a beloved past never to be regained. The latter novel
is especially interesting for its portraits of literary life under the Republic.

Although he returned briefly to Spain in 1968, Aub was doomed to die in
exile before the end of the Franco era. One of his last novels, *Jusep Torres
Campalans* (1958), an elaborate literary hoax, brought him a certain belated
notoriety: this fictional "biography" of a painter, complete with an exposition
of works by the imaginary genius, was very much in the apocryphal vein of
Borges and the vanguardist style of Ramón *Gómez de la Serna. It aptly demonstrates Aub's mastery of a variety of languages and styles, and his theoretical
control of levels of discourse. Aub was an objective and informed critic, and
his critical know-how is evident in the subtleties of this surprising novel, as well
as in his books of essays: *Discurso de la novela española contemporánea* (1945;
Discourse on the Comtemporary Spanish Novel); *La poesía española contemporánea* (1954; Contemporary Spanish Poetry); and *La gallina ciega* (1970; The
Blind Chicken—but also the name of the game, Blind Man's Bluff), reflections
on a voyage to Spain, Aub's final journey, as well as the shock between the
exile's illusions and the reality of return. Representative of Aub's mature thought,
it is of special interest in relation to his intellectual development.

BIBLIOGRAPHY

Primary Texts

*El cerco.* México: Mortiz, 1968.
*Cuentos mexicanos con pilón.* México: Universitaria, 1959.
*Enero en Cuba.* México: Mortiz, 1969.
*Hablo como hombre.* México: Mortiz, 1967.
*La obra narrativa de Max Aub.* Madrid: Gredos, 1979.
*El zopilote y otros cuentos mexicanos.* Barcelona: Hispanoamericana, 1964.

English Translations

"At Santander and Guijón." Tr. C. Muhlenberg. *Spanish Writers in Exile.* Ed. A. Flores.
     Sausalito, CA: Bern Porter, 1969?
*Josep Torres Campalans.* Tr. H. Weinstock. Garden City, NY: Doubleday, 1962.

Criticism

Irizarry, Estelle. *Writer-Painters of Contemporary Spain.* Boston: Twayne, 1984 (contains
     chapter on Aub).
Pérez, Janet. "Spanish Civil War and Exile in the Novels of Aub, Ayala and Sender."
     Reprinted in *Twentieth Century Literary Criticism.* Detroit: Gale Research Com-
     pany, 1987–88.
Ugarte, Michael. "Max Aub's Magical Labyrinth of Exile." *Hispania* 68.4 (Dec. 1985):
     733–39.
Wright, Lucinda W. "Max Aub and Tragedy: A Study of *Cara y cruz* and *San Juan.*"
     *DAI* 47.5 (Nov. 1986): 1745A.

                                                                                      Janet Pérez

***AUTO,*** dramatic term. In the Middle Ages (see Edad Media, Literatura de la),
it denoted a one-act play, religious or profane. Often performed at the feast of
Corpus Christi, the earliest precursors of the *auto* are the *\*juegos* and the *misterios,* mystery or morality plays representing allegorical struggles between vice
and virtue. By the mid-sixteenth c., the term was used only for religious plays,
and the name was extended to *autos sacramentales* (sacramental plays). The
defining characteristics of the *auto sacramental* included an allegorical nature
where realistic people are rejected in favor of ideas and concepts such as Faith,
Free Will, Sin, Desire, etc., as protagonists; an unrealistic representation of time;
and a eucharistic theme. The first authors of the developing *auto sacramental*
often were ecclesiastics associated with *\*university life. One of the earliest extant
*autos* is perhaps the *Auto de la pasión* (c.1500; Auto of [Christ's] Passion), by
Lucas *\*Fernandez. Other early known practicioners include Juan del *\*Encina,
Gil *\*Vicente, *\*López de Yangüas, and Diego *\*Sánchez de Badajoz.
    During the Counter-Reformation, the *auto sacramental,* with its strong dog-
matic and didactic possibilities, came to play a key role, reaching its apex in
the *autos* of *\*Tirso de Molina, *\*Mira de Amescua, Juan de *\*Timoneda, *\*Val-
divielso, Lope de *\*Vega, and, most of all, *\*Calderón de la Barca. Calderón
termed the *auto* a sermon in verse. Staged outdoors on *\*carros,* they were visually
elaborate, highly symbolic, impressive dramatic spectacles.
    In the eighteenth c., the influence of French neoclassicism prompted such a

reaction to these symbolic works that in 1765 the presentation of *autos* was forbidden. *See also Auto de los reyes magos; Autos viejos*; Theater in Spain.

BIBLIOGRAPHY

Primary Texts

*Autos, comedias y farsas de la Biblioteca Nacional.* 2 vols. Madrid: Gómez Menor, 1962–64.
"Autos sacramentales desde su origen hasta fines del siglo XVII." In BAE 58.
"Catálogo de Autos sacramentales, históricos y alegóricos." Ed. J. Alenda. *BRAE* 3 (1916), and subsequent vols.

English Translation

*Three Spanish Sacramental Plays.* Tr., sel. R. G. Barnes. San Francisco: Chandler, 1969.

Criticism

Arias, R. *The Spanish Sacramental Play.* TWAS 572. Boston: Twayne, 1980.
Fothergill-Payne, L. *La alegoría en los autos y farsas anteriores a Calderón.* London: Tamesis, 1977.
McKendrick, Melveena. *Theatre in Spain 1490–1700.* Cambridge: Cambridge University Press, 1989. Ch. 9.
Shergold, N. D. *A History of the Spanish Stage.* Oxford: Clarendon, 1967. Chs. 15 and 16.
Varey, J. E. "La mise en scène de l'auto sacramental à Madrid au XVI$^e$ et XVII$^e$ siècles." In *Le lieu théâtral à la Renaissance.* Ed. J. Jacquot. Paris: Centre national de la recherche scientifique, 1964.
Wardropper, B. W. "The Search for a Dramatic Formula for the *auto sacramental*." *PMLA* 65 (1950): 1196–1211.

Maureen Ihrie

*AUTO DE LOS REYES MAGOS* (Auto of the Three Wise Men, 1928), medieval theatrical piece. This fragment of 147 lines of verse from a Christmas play was composed, according to *Menéndez Pidal, in the second half of the twelfth c. It survives in a unique manuscript, written in an early thirteenth-c. hand, now housed in the National Library (*Biblioteca Nacional) in Spain. The fragment can be divided into five scenes: in the first, the Wise Men, Gaspar, Balthasar, and Melchior, enter one by one and comment in monologues on a marvelous new star in the heavens; in the second, the kings confer with each other and decide to follow the star in search of the new-born king; in the third, they meet with Herod, who demands that they share their news with him; in the fourth, Herod, alone, ponders the meaning of what he has learned from the Wise Men, and summons his advisers; in the fifth, Herod's advisers, who are rabbis, quarrel with each other and fail to agree on the meaning of the event; the fragment ends with their dispute.

Winifred Sturdevant proved that this fragment belonged to a vernacular tradition rather than a Latin liturgical one because it contains elements found in the former and lacking in the latter. Rafael Lapesa studied the language and rhyme of the fragment and decided that its author was probably of Gascon origin, whereas Solá-Solé on the other hand finds Mozarabic elements in the language.

José M. Regueiro outlines the argument for a Spanish origin (possibly in Ripoll) of the theatrical tradition to which the *Auto de los Reyes Magos* belongs.

BIBLIOGRAPHY

Primary Text

*Auto de los Reyes Magos*. In *Crestomatía del español medieval*. Madrid: Gredos, 1965. 1: 71–77.

English Translation

"A Spanish Mystery Play of the 12th Century." Tr. W. K. Jones. In *Poet Lore* 39 (1928): 306–9. Also in *Spanish One-Act Plays in English*. Ed., tr., sel. W. K. Jones. Dallas: Tardy, 1934.

Criticism

Lapesa, R. "Sobre el *Auto de los Reyes Magos:* sus rimas anómalas y el posible origen de su autor." In *De la Edad Media a nuestros días: Estudios de historia literaria*. Madrid: Gredos, 1967.
Regueiro, José M. "*Auto de los Reyes Magos* y el teatro medieval." *HR* 45 (1977): 149–64.
Solá-Solé, J. M. "El *Auto de los Reyes Magos*: Impacto gascón o mozárabe?" *RPH* 29 (1975): 20–27.
Sturdevant, W. *The 'Misterio de los Reyes Magos': Its Position in the Development of the Medieval Legend of the Three Kings*. Baltimore: Johns Hopkins UP, 1927.
Wardropper, B. "The Dramatic Texture of the *Auto de los Reyes Magos*." *MLN* 70 (1955): 46–50.

Colbert Nepaulsingh

***AUTO SACRAMENTAL.*** See *Auto*

**AUTOR,** theatrical manager of the *Siglo de Oro. This term was used in the Golden Age to designate the head of a theatrical troupe, an actor-manager. The *autor* should not be confused with the author of a play, for the playwright sold his work to these directors, and with it, all printing and performance rights and royalties. The work of the autor was wide-ranging. He decided which plays were to be performed; submitted for a license and made all necessary arrangements for the play's performance; assigned the various parts to the members of his troupe; conducted rehearsals, often playing a leading role himself; managed company finances; contracted actors; and chose machinery and special effects needed for his plays. His duties were similar to those of a modern impresario.

BIBLIOGRAPHY

Criticism

Shergold, N. D. *History of the Spanish Stage*. Oxford: Clarendon, 1967.

Deborah Compte

**AUTORIDADES** (Authorities), the term used to describe all works cited as examples or explanations of words in the first dictionary published by the Spanish Academy (*Academia Española). One of the initial efforts of the Academy, the

*Diccionario de autoridades* (Dictionary of Authorities) was first published between 1726 and 1739.

BIBLIOGRAPHY

Primary Text

*Diccionario de autoridades*. 3 vols. Madrid: Gredos, 1964. Facs.

*AUTOS VIEJOS* (Old Plays), a collection of religious drama. The designation refers to a group of plays compiled in a ms. in the National Library ("Biblioteca Nacional) of Madrid titled *Colección de autos, farsas y coloquios del siglo XVI* (Collection of Plays, Farces and Colloquies of the Sixteenth Century). The complete collection contains 96 plays, all of which are anonymous except the *Auto de Caín y Abel* (Play of Cain and Abel), attributed to Jaime Ferruz of Valencia. The term *auto* denotes a one-act play and should be distinguished from the later *auto sacramental* (see *auto*). The plays all have religious themes and appear to have been performed in the churches. The texts may be divided into certain thematic groups: those dealing with the Nativity, the Passion and Resurrection; scenes from the Old and New Testaments; the lives of saints and martyrs, the Virgin Mary. The comic characters are of great interest, presaging the "*gracioso* figure of Golden Age "theater. The collection is an important source for the history of early religious drama in Castile.

BIBLIOGRAPHY
*Colección de autos, farsas y coloquios del siglo XVI*. Ed. E. González Pedroso. BAE 58. (partial edition)
*Colección de autos, farsas y coloquios del siglo XVI*. Ed. L. Rouanet. 4 vols. Barcelona: L'Avenc, 1901.

Deborah Compte

**AVELLANEDA, Alonso F. de** (fl. 1614, ?–?, ?), pseudonym for composer of the spurious continuation of "Cervantes's 1605 *Don Quijote*. It appeared in 1614, only months before Cervantes's *Segunda parte del ingenioso hidalgo Don Quijote de la Mancha* was printed. Avellaneda's true identity has never been ascertained—his hostility toward Cervantes, sympathy for Lope de "Vega, and Aragonese linguistic traits are key clues which have tantalized critics and Cervantes himself. Possible figures include: Lope de Vega, Friar Luis de Aliaga—confessor to Philip III, Dr. Blanco de Paz—long-time enemy of Cervantes or Juan "Martí—author of a second part of Mateo "Alemán's *Guzmán de Alfarache*.

Certainly the continuation, while not devoid of merit and interest, breaks decisively with its Cervantine model: Sancho abandons his master, Don Quijote and Sancho are flat caricatures of the 1605 work, and Don Quijote repudiates his love for Dulcinea. The continuation, in some ways, served Cervantes well; his brilliant inclusion of Avellaneda's work within the fabric of his *Don Quijote II* (1615) not only pushed the mixture of fiction and reality to even greater limits, but also, Avellaneda's errors may have sharpened Cervantes's own vision of his characters in their final moments.

BIBLIOGRAPHY

Primary Text

*Don Quijote de la Mancha.* Ed. Martín de Riquer. Clásicos Castellanos 174–176. 3 vols. Madrid: Espasa-Calpe, 1972.

English Translation

*Don Quijote de la Mancha (part II): being the spurious continuation of Miguel de Cervantes' part I.* Tr. A. W. Server and J. E. Keller. Newark: Juan de la Cuesta, 1980.

Criticism

Espín Rael, J. *Investigaciones sobre "El Quijote apócrifo."* Madrid: Espasa-Calpe, 1942.
Gilman, S. *Cervantes y Avellaneda. Estudio de una imitación.* Mexico: Fondo de Cultura Económica, 1951.

**AVELLANEDA, Francisco de** (1622?, ?–1675, ?), playwright of the *Calderón cycle. He is best remembered for *entremeses such as *El hidalgo de la membrilla* (n.d.; The Nobleman of the Quince), *La hija del doctor* (n.d.; The Doctor's Daughter), and *Sargento Conchillos* (n.d.; Sargeant Conchillos). Two of his best longer works are collaborations: *El divino calabrés San Francisco de Paulo* (n.d.; The Divine Calabrian St. Francisco de Paulo) was written with *Matos Fragoso, and *Cuantas veo, tantas quiero* (n.d.; However Many Women I See, That's How Many I Love) was composed with *Rodríguez de Villaviciosa. Avellaneda was also a court censor of plays in Madrid.

BIBLIOGRAPHY

Primary Text

*Cuantas veo, tantas quiero.* In BAE 47.
Several entremeses in *Colección de entremeses* . . . Ed. A. E. Cotarelo y Mori. NBAE 17.

**AVELLANO, Cofradía del** (Avellano Brotherhood), a nineteeth-c. literary group. They met outside of Granada at Fuente del Avellano—hence the name. Participants included Angel *Ganivet, Gabriel Ruiz de Almodóvar, Antonio J. Afán de Rivera, and Matías Méndez Vellido.

**AVENDAÑO, Francisco de** (sixteenth c., ?–?, ?), dramatist. Nothing more is known of Avendaño than that he was in the service of the Marquis de Villena when he composed his *Comedia Florisea* (1553; Play of Floriseo), an allegorical work in three acts of *pie quebrado* verse in which the principal characters are a gentleman known as "the Dead One," another named Floriseo, the lady Blancaflor, the shepherds Salaver and Pedrucho, the Page Listeno, and Fortune. In the prefatory section of this Italianate work Avendaño boasts that the *Comedia Florisea* is the first theatrical piece written in three, rather than five acts. It has been shown, however, that some 20 years earlier Antonio *Díez had already composed a three-act play. *See also* Theater in Spain.

BIBLIOGRAPHY

Primary Text

*Comedia Florisea.* Ed. A. Bonilla y San Martín. *RH* 27 (1912): 398–422.

Criticism

Benavides, R. *Francisco de Avendaño y el teatro renacentista español. Boletín de Filología de la Universidad de Chile* 12 (1960): 51–64.
Crawford, J. P. Wickersham. *Spanish Drama before Lope de Vega.* rev. ed. Philadelphia: U of Pennsylvania P, 1967.

                                                                    C. Maurice Cherry

**ÁVILA, Beato Juan de** (1500, Almodóvar del Campo–1569, Montilla), pre-mystic religious writer. A principal figure of the first part of the sixteenth c., Blessed John of Avila is especially important for his influence on Luis de *Granada, on Sta. *Teresa de Jesús, and on the early Jesuit movement. Based on information furnished by his biographer, the Dominican Father Luis de Granada, and on his own remarks, we know he studied law at Salamanca from 1514 to 1518. Tired of "the acursèd law," he returned to Almodóvar and led a strict spiritual life before going to the U at Alcalá from 1520 to 1525. He studied arts, letters and theology and was a student of Domingo de *Soto. Ordained a priest in 1525, he traveled to Seville, intending to proceed to America as a missionary; the archbishop persuaded him to pursue his vocation in Andalusia instead.

Although he was noted for eloquent, efficacious preaching, his sermons are for the most part now lost. In 1530, he attracted to the faith the noblewoman Sancha Carrillo, for whom he wrote his commentary to Psalm 44:11–12 (Vulgate numbering), *Audi, filia* (Hearken, o daughter, and consider, and incline thine ear. King James, Psalms 45: 10). The best known parts of the commentary attack untrue revelation and false *mysticism, plagues of the Spanish spiritual life of the day. He became known as the Apostle of Andalusia because of his preaching, and was active in the conversion of St. Juan de Dios and St. Francis Borja, the high-ranking nobleman who later became master-general of the Jesuits. Juan de Ávila was active in the organization of the U of Baeza and of other educational institutions. He died in Montilla, where he is buried, and was beatified by Leon XIII in 1894.

Blessed John was above all a preacher, and his writing reflects this predisposition. Juan de Ávila was a pre-mystic writer, and asceticism is the dominant note in his work, although there are flashes which presage the passionate writing of the later mystic movement. His principal works are *Audi, filia* and *El epis-*

*tolario espiritual para todos estados* (1578; Spiritual Letters for All Estates). His style prefigures that of Luis de Granada. He approved of St. Theresa's work and was greatly sympathetic to the early endeavors of the Jesuits in Andalusia. *See also* Ascetical Literature.

BIBLIOGRAPHY

Primary Texts

*Epistolario espiritual.* Ed. V. García de Diego. Clásicos Castellanos 11. Madrid: Espasa-Calpe, 1951.

*Obras completas.* Madrid: Biblioteca de autores cristianos, 1952.

Criticism

Torrance, E. McClure. "Style, Themes, and Ideas in the Works of San Juan de Ávila." *DAI* 41 (1980): 1632A–33A.

Eric Naylor

*¡AY, PANADERA!* (Oh, Bakerymaid), fifteenth-c. satirical Spanish verses. Written anonymously, these *coplas recount the cowardice of the rebellious barons defeated by John II and Don Álvaro de Luna in the Battle of Olmedo (1445) and are an important document of this period. There are two extant versions of the *coplas* which carry different refrains: ¡Ay, panadera! (Oh, bakerymaid!) and ¡Di, panadera! (Tell, bakerymaid!). They have been attributed to Juan de *Mena, however almost certainly without foundation.

BIBLIOGRAPHY

Primary Text

*Coplas satíricas y dramáticas de la Edad Media.* Ed. Eduardo Rincón. Madrid: Alianza, 1968.

Criticism

Artigas, Miguel. "Nueva redacción de las coplas de la Panadera." In *Estudios eruditos in memoriam de Adolfo Bonilla y San Martín.* Ed. Faculty of Philosophy and Letters of the Central U. Madrid: n.p., 1927. 1: 75–89.

Deborah Compte

**AYALA, Francisco** (1906, Granada– ), essayist, novelist, critic. Moving to Madrid with his family in 1921, he began university studies there in 1923 and earned a law degree in 1929, receiving a scholarship to study in Germany. A precocious intellect, he had already become known literarily with his first novels, *Tragicomedia de un hombre sin espíritu* (1925; Tragicomedy of a Man Without a Spirit) and *Historia de un amanecer* (1926; Story of a Sunrise). *Tragicomedia* incorporates many literary antecedents, including *Cervantes, *Lazarillo, *Espronceda's *El estudiante de Salamanca* and others in a homage to *Don Quijote* which utilizes many Cervantine techniques (devices characteristic of the whole of Ayala's writing). *Historia,* radically different, intellectualized, abstract and experimental, treats the questions of political assassination and execution, Utopian ideals, violence and self-immolation. *El boxeador y un ángel* (1929; The

Boxer and an Angel) contains five pieces of vanguard fiction of relatively trivial content, written in brilliantly metaphorical and Surrealistic prose, as is *Cazador en el alba* (1930; Hunter at Dawn), which incorporates the novelette "Erika ante el invierno" (Erika Facing Winter).

A fourteen-year hiatus in Ayala's publication of fiction spans the years in which he married Chilean Etelvina Silva in Berlin (1931) and completed his doctorate in law at the U of Madrid, beginning to teach law there the following year. He served the Republic as a diplomat during the Spanish Civil War (1936–39), going into exile in Argentina (1939–50), Puerto Rico (1950–58) and the United States. Returning to Spain for his first visit in 1960, he continued to reside in the United States, spending part of each year in Madrid until his definitive return in the mid-1980s. In exile, he published extensively in the field of sociology and continued his diplomatic activity, serving the United States as a representative to UNESCO and other bodies of the United Nations.

Ayala's legal and teaching interests are represented by many essays: *El derecho social en la constitución de la República española* (1932; Social Law in the Constitution of the Spanish Republic); *El problema del liberalismo* (1941, rev. 1963; The Problem of Liberalism) and *El pensamiento vivo de Saavedra Fajardo* (1941; The Living Thought of Saavedra Fajardo); *Razón del mundo* (The World's Reason), *Los políticos* (Politicians) and *Histrionismo y representación* (Histrionics and Performance), all in 1944, were published before his next work of fiction, *El hechizado* (1944; The Bewitched). *Jovellanos* (1945) and *Tratado de sociología* (1947; Sociological Treatise) intervened between the first publication of this masterful tale and its reappearance as part of the collection, *Los usurpadores* (1949; The Usurpers), eight outstanding stories based upon familiar figures from Spanish history, and united by the common theme of the abuse of power. One of the truly outstanding collections of short fiction in the Spanish language, *Los usurpadores* has been highly praised by critics, and much admired by other important writers, such as Jorge Luis Borges. The work's apocryphal prologue (another frequent Ayala device) reveals that "the power exercised by one man over another is always a usurpation."

Also in 1949 appeared *La cabeza del cordero* (The Head of the Lamb), four short novels unified by their common—albeit oblique—treatment of the Spanish Civil War, with irony aesthetically disguised as objective distance. Although Ayala is careful to avoid any evidence of partisanship, the collection was prohibited in Spain for some three decades by the Franco *censorship. Together with *Los usurpadores*, *La cabeza del cordero* established Ayala as one of the foremost masters of Spanish brief fiction. Between the two collections and his next stories came more essays, *La invención del "Quijote"* (1950; The Invention of the "Quijote"), *Introducción a las ciencias sociales* (1952; Introduction to the Social Sciences), and Ayala's founding of the distinguished periodical *La torre*, in Puerto Rico (1953). *Historia de macacos* (1955; Monkey Tales) includes six stories whose common theme is the human tendency to ridicule, debase, abuse and humiliate others. *Muertes de perro* (1958; *Death as a Way of Life*,

1964) and its sequel, *El fondo del vaso* (1962; In the Bottom of the Glass), are connected novels portraying tyranny, demagoguery and alienation in an imaginary Latin American country, with a dictator dominating the first novel and, following his overthrow, the worst brand of "popular" democracy in the second. Existential preoccupations and motifs are prominent in these and Ayala's next work of fiction, *El As de Bastos* (1963; The Ace of Clubs), four pieces which were later republished with one new short story added—"El prodigio"— under the title *De raptos, violaciones y otras inconveniencias* (1966; About Rapes, Violations and Other Inconvenient Occurrences). All exemplify moral and ethical concerns, and involve some form of outrage. *El rapto* (1965; the Kidnapping) re-elaborates and updates the goatherd's story in Chapter 51 of *Don Quijote*, an elaborate intertextual exercise typical of Ayala's ironic humor. His 1971 collection of fiction, *El jardín de las delicias* (The Garden of Delights), recalls the grotesque figures of the paintings of Hieronymus Bosch, from whose works the title is drawn. These satiric vignettes received Spain's most prestigious literary recognition at that time, the Premio de la Crítica.

Many of Ayala's aesthetic, critical and pedagogical concerns are embodied in *El escritor en la sociedad de masas* (The Writer in a Mass Society) and *Breve teoría de la traducción* (Short Theory of Translation), both published in 1956, as well as in *La crisis actual de la enseñanza* (1958; The Current Crisis in Education); *Tecnología y libertad* (1959; Technology and Freedom); *Experiencia e invención* (1962; Experience and Invention); *De este mundo y el otro* (Of This World and the Next) and *Realidad y ensueño* (Reality and Daydreams), both in 1963. These essay collections frequently contain the germ of an idea which becomes the theme of a subsequent work of fiction. Essays which contain important clues to Ayala's narrative principles and his intellectual history are *Reflexiones sobre la estructura narrativa* (1970; Reflections on Narrative Structure) and *Confrontaciones* (1972; Confrontations), a sort of intellectual autobiography including previously published interviews and significant essays. He was belatedly elected to the *Academia Española in 1987. *See also* Cervantes.

BIBLIOGRAPHY

Primary Texts

*El cine: arte y espectáculo.* 2nd rev. ed. Xalapa, Mexico: Universidad veracruzana, 1966.
*Derechos de la persona individual para una sociedad de masas.* Buenos Aires: Perrot, 1953.
*Ensayos de sociología política.* Mexico: Universidad Nacional, 1952.
*El escritor y su imagen.* Madrid: Guadarrama, 1975.
*España, a la fecha.* Madrid: Tecnos, 1977.
*La integración social en América.* Buenos Aires: Perrot, 1958.
*El jardín de las Delicias; El tiempo y yo.* Prol. Carolyn Richmond. Madrid: Espasa-Calpe, 1978.
*El "Lazarillo": Nuevo examen de algunos aspectos.* Madrid: Taurus, 1971.
*Obras narrativas completas.* Ed. Andrés Amorós. Mexico: Aguilar, 1969.
*Oppenheimer.* Mexico: Fondo de Cultura Económica, 1942.

*Recuerdos y olvidos 1: Del paraíso al destierro* (memoirs). Premio Nacional de Literatura
    1983. Madrid: Alianza, 1982.
*Recuerdos y olvidos, 2: El exilio.* Madrid: Alianza, 1982.
    English Translations
*Death as a Way of Life.* Tr. Joan Maclean. New York: Macmillan, 1964.
*The Lamb's Head.* Tr. and study C. C. Fitzgibbons. Diss. U of Texas, Austin, 1971.
    Criticism
Amorós, Andrés. *Bibliografía de Francisco Ayala.* NY: Syracuse U, 1973.
Ellis, Keith. *El arte narrativo de Francisco Ayala.* Madrid: Gredos, 1964.
————. "Cervantes and Ayala's *El rapto*: The Art of Reworking a Story." *PMLA* 84
    (1969): 14–19.
Hiriart, Rosario. *Las alusiones literarias en la obra narrativa de Francisco Ayala.* New
    York: Eliseo Torres, 1972.
————. *Los recursos técnicos en la novelística de Francisco Ayala.* Madrid: Insula,
    1972.
Irizarry, Estelle. *Teoría y creación literaria en Francisco Ayala.* Madrid: Gredos, 1971.
————. *Francisco Ayala.* TWAS 450. Boston: Twayne, 1977.

                                                                       Janet Pérez

**AYGUALS DE IZCO, Wenceslao** (1801, Vinaroz, Castelón–1873, Madrid),
bourgeois serial novelist of popular social protest. In 1841, with *Martínez
Villergas, he founded an important editorial house, *Sociedad Literaria*, which
was an active force until 1856, providing an outlet for many writers of the
day. Influenced by French novelists such as Eugène Sue, he depicted the
trials and frustrations of proletarian life in Spain to the enthusiasm of his
lower-class audience. Many intellectuals spurned his work. His most famous
novel is *María o la hija de un jornalero* (1845–46; Mary, or A Day Laborer's
Daughter). It was translated into French and included a prologue by Sue in
that edition. The sequel, *La marquesa de Bellaflor, o el niño de la inclusa*
(1846–47; The Marchionesse of Bellaflor, or the Child of the Foundling Home)
was equally well received; part three was titled *El palacio de los crímenes*
(1855; The Palace of Crimes). Consistently anticlerical, he fails to delve
thoughtfully into the underlying social forces at work in the world he depicts.
By the mid 1850s his novels begin to be eclipsed by the emerging realistic
novel.

    Ayguals de Izco also wrote a great deal of poetry and several plays, he
translated various works from French to Spanish and he directed compilation of
several encyclopedic works such as *El panteón universal* (1853–54; The Universal Pantheon). Newspapers were a frequent outlet for articles. Despite these
many activities, he was silent the last seventeen years of his life, and died in
relative oblivion.

BIBLIOGRAPHY
    Primary Texts
*María o la hija de un jornalero.* Madrid: Ayguals de Izco, 1845–46.
*La marquesa de Bellaflor.* Madrid: Ayguals de Izco, 1846–47.

*El palacio de los crímenes.* Madrid: Ayguals de Izco, 1855.

*El panteón universal. Diccionario histórico.* . . . Madrid: Ayguals de Izco, 1853–54.

Criticism

Benítez, R. *Ideología del folletín español: Wenceslao Ayguals de Izco (1801–1873).* Madrid: Porrúa Turanzas, 1979.

Goldman, P. B. "Toward a Sociology of the Modern Spanish Novel: The Early Years." *MLN* 89 (1974): 173–90, and 90 (1975): 183–211.

**AZA, Vital** (1851, Pola de Lena–1912, Madrid), poet and writer of popular comedies. His original profession was medicine. In 1874 he began collaboration with Miguel *Ramos Carrión, a friend and fellow playwright. The same year marks Aza's first success, *¡Basta de matemáticas!* (That's Enough Math!). Together they composed more than a dozen plays. Aza also worked with Miguel *Echegaray and others. Among his most successful plays are *Aprobados y suspensos* (1875; Passed and Failed), *Los tocayos* (1886; The Namesakes), *El señor cura* (1890; The Priest), and the sparkling farce, *La rebotica* (1895; The Back Room at the Pharmacy).

BIBLIOGRAPHY

Primary Text

*Comedias escogidas.* Nota preliminar de N.S.R. Madrid: Aguilar, 1951.

Criticism

Alonso Cortés, Narciso. *Vital Aza.* Valladolid: S.E.U.E.R.—Cuesta, 1949.

D. J. O'Connor

**AZAÑA, Manuel** (1880, Alcalá de Henares [Spain]–1940, Montauban [France]), novelist, critic. Best known for his studies on Juan *Valera—*Vida de Don Juan Valera* (1926, unpublished), *La novela de Pepita Jiménez* (1927; The Novel *Pepita Jiménez*), *Valera en Italia* (1929), the Prologue to the Clásicos Castellanos edition of *Pepita Jiménez*—Manuel Azaña carved a niche for himself in the story of Spanish literature as an introspective writer of searching and lucid prose, best exemplified in his *El jardín de los frailes* (1927; The Friars' Garden). Often judged by critics to be autobiographical, a claim that Azaña refuted, this novel is based on the author's experience at the Real Colegio de Estudios Superiores at El Escorial, where he studied from 1893 to 1897. After completing a law degree at Zaragoza (1898) and doctoral studies at the Universidad Central (Madrid, 1900), Azaña plunged into a life of literary activity that he shared with many of his famous contemporaries (Pío Baroja, *Azorín, *Valle-Inclán, *Benavente), but he was not a member of the *Generation of 1898. He collaborated in several of the literary reviews of the time; founded, with *Ortega y Gasset, the Liga de Educación Pública (1913 Public Education League) and, with Cipriano de *Rivas Cherif, the literary review *La pluma*, short-lived (1920–23) but influential, launched with the collaboration of *Unamuno, Juan Ramón *Jiménez, Alfonso Reyes, among others. The first twelve chapters of *El jardín* were first published in the pages of *La pluma*. He was a member of the Madrid *Ateneo, the cultural center where most of the then leading intellectuals congregated and of which he was elected president in 1930. Two plays, *La corona* (The Crown) and *Entremés del sereno* (The Night Watchman's Play), the first produced in 1931 with M. Xirgu in the leading role, represent his contribution to the theater.

He associated with the pro-Republican movement that led to King Alphonse XIII's abdication in 1931. Thenceforward, he was intimately associated with the fortunes of the Second Republic, becoming successively minister of war, prime minister (1931), and president (1936). Azaña's involvement in affairs of state drastically curtailed his literary activity. His *Velada en Benicarló* (1939; Vigil at Benicarlo), an introspective Platonic dialogue, can be said to be the only creative work among the many writings of his political years.

As a writer, Azaña was unaffected by the contemporary literary movements that characterized an age of restless and brilliant innovators. His lucid prose and his eloquence owe more to the intellectual thread that runs from the spirit of the encyclopedists through the reflectiveness of *Pérez Galdós and the practitioners of the psychological novel than to avant-garde literature, which he shunned. He was, fundamentally, a thinker and an essayist, qualities that make his writing more akin to *Feijóo, Valera and, sometimes, Unamuno than to most of his contemporaries. His effectiveness as a public speaker pushed him to the forefront among the group of reform-minded ideologists that assumed the leadership of the Spanish Republic. He was not, however, a political man, a quality he shared with most of the leaders of that "Republic of Intellectuals." He discharged his duties with unwavering, occasionally disastrous, honesty. (Cf. Cipriano de Rivas Cherif. *Retrato de un desconocido*. Barcelona: Grijalbo, 1979. This is the most authoritative and accurate biography extant. It was first published in 1961 [México: Oasis]. The Grijalbo edition has been profusely annotated by Enrique de Rivas, who has added also a useful introduction and 183 pages of correspondence between Azaña and the author of the book. The best source for Azaña's writings is the monumental and deceptively titled *Obras completas*, 4 vols., edited by Juan Marichal [México: Oasis, 1966–68]. *Azaña*, a compilation of the writings of various authors, edited by Vicente-Alberto Serrano and José-María San Luciano [Madrid: Edascal, 1980], includes an appendix, "Vida de Manuel Azaña," useful as a mostly accurate source of quick-reference data.) *See also* Essay.

Alan A. González

**AZANCOT, Leopoldo** (1935, Seville– ), novelist. He studied law at the U of Seville. For many years, he served as assistant director of *Indice*, chief of services of *Features*, and director of Publicaciones del Instituto de Sociología y Desarrollo de la Región Ibérica; he is a member of the Congreso de Cultura Andaluza and of the advisory board for Nueva Estafeta. His articles on art and literature have appeared in *Pueblo, ABC, Informaciones, Saturday Review, Revista de Occidente,* and *Lectures pour tons.*

His first novel, *La novia judía* (1977; The Jewish Bride), broke new ground by defying all of the taboos that had existed under Franco's regime. It won the Premio Reseno, the Premio Zikkurath and the B'nai B'rith Award; it was also a finalist for the Premio Ateneo in Seville. Subsequent novels include *Fatima* (1979), *Ella, la loba* (1980; The Shewolf), *Los amores prohibidos* (1980; Forbidden Loves), *La noche española* (1981; The Spanish Night), and *El amante increíble* (1982; The Incredible Lover). Azancot also wrote the introduction for the Spanish translation of Leon Poliakov's study of anti-Semitism, *Histoire de l'antisémitisme: De Mahomet aux marranes.*

BIBLIOGRAPHY

Primary Texts

*El amante increíble.* Barcelona: Planeta, 1982.
*Los amores prohibidos.* Barcelona: Tusquets, 1980.
*Ella, la loba.* Madrid: Libertarias, 1980.
*Fatima.* Barcelona: Argos Vergara, 1979.
*La noche española.* Madrid: Cátedra, 1981.
*La novia judía.* Barcelona: Planeta, 1977.

Dennis Klein

**AZCÁRATE, Gumersindo de** (1840, León–1917, Madrid), Krausist thinker, politician, and educator. Along with his close friend, Francisco *Giner de los Ríos (1839–1915), and others, he was one of the founders of the Institución Libre de Enseñanza (Free Pedagogical Institute) and a leading proponent of *Krausism in Spain. His autobiographical *Minuta de un testamento* (1876; Draft of a Last Will and Testament) has been described as the most important Krausist document published up to that time.

He began his law studies in Oviedo in 1855 and completed them at the U of Madrid in 1862. He held the post of professor of comparative law at the latter institution from 1873 to 1875, when he was removed as part of a purge of Krausist influence under Alphonse XII, which suspension lasted until 1881. Azcárate has been called the one true Spanish apostle of the parliamentary system. Likewise a defender of the existence of political parties, he saw them as a means of channeling diverse public opinion in order that a society might govern itself. He was elected representative to the Cortes (Spanish Parliament) at age 46.

In economic and social theory he sought to arrive at a Krausist harmony between the freedom of the individual and the organization of society. Ultimately Azcárate held that responsibility for solving social problems would come from the individual, society, and the State, all three. He was an intensely pragmatic man interested in what was theoretical and abstract primarily for its practical applications.

## BIBLIOGRAPHY

### Primary Texts

*La cuestión universitaria, 1875; epistolario de Francisco Giner de los Ríos, Gumersindo de Azcárate y Nicolás Salmerón.* Madrid: Tecnos, 1967.
*Minuta de un testamento, publicada y anotada por W....* Madrid: Librería Victoriano Suárez, 1876. (See also the 1967 edition with preliminary study by Elías Díaz. Barcelona: Cultura Popular.)
*El "self-government" y la monarquía doctrinaria.* Madrid: Librería Alejandro de San Martín, 1877.

### Criticism

Azcárate, Pablo de. *Estudio biográfico documental; Semblanza, epistolario, escritos.* Madrid: Tecnos, 1969.
Carande, Ramón. "Azcárate en sus últimos años." *Insula* 22 (Dec. 1967): 1, 10.
Díaz, Elías. "Política y religión en la *Minuta de un testamento*." *Insula* 22 (Dec. 1967): 3.

James F. Brown

**AZCÁRATE, Patricio de** (1800, León–1886, León), philosopher. He published a 26-volume corpus of studies which includes titles such as *Veladas sobre la filosofía moderna* (1854; Soirées on Modern Philosophy) and *Exposición histórico-crítico de los sistemas filosóficos modernos* (1861; Historical-Critical Exposition of Philosophical Systems). He also translated works of Leibniz and others. The philosopher Gumersindo de *Azcárate was his son.

## BIBLIOGRAPHY

### Primary Texts

*Exposición histórico-crítico....* 4 vols. Madrid: Mellado, 1861.

**AZCOAGA, Enrique** (1912, Madrid–1985, Madrid), poet, critic and novelist. Azcoaga was the recipient of the 1933 Premio Nacional de Literatura (National Literary Prize) for the collection of literary essays *Línea y acento* (Line and Accent), and in the same year he founded the magazine *Hoja Literaria* which he edited with A. Sánchez Barbudo and A. Serrano-Plaja. From 1951 to 1963 he lived and worked in Argentina, where he founded and directed the poetry magazine *Mairena* and wrote for the Argentine press. His poetic works include *El canto cotidiano* (1952; The Daily Song), a collection of poems published between 1942 and 1951; *España es un sabor* (1965; Spain Is a Flavor); *Del otro lado* (1968; From the Other Side) and *Olmeda, poemas solidarios* (1969; Elm Grove, Solidary Poems). Many of his poems contain a strong religious element. His novels include *El empleado* (1949; The Employee) and *La arpista* (1968; The Harpist). He has also translated Verlaine, and his works of art criticism include a study of Goya.

BIBLIOGRAPHY

Primary Texts

*Del otro lado*. Madrid: Mairena, 1968.
*El canto cotidiano 1942-1951*. Buenos Aires: Losada, 1952.
*España es un sabor*. Madrid: Palabra y Tiempo, 1965.
*Olmeda, poemas solidarios*. Salamanca: Alamo, 1969.

Victoria Wolff Unruh

**AZCONA, Rafael** (1926, Logroño– ), Spanish novelist, humorist and screen-play writer. Azcona began his career writing for humor magazines, and his first books belong to the humor genre: *El repelente niño Vicente* (1955; That Repulsive Kid Vicente), *Los muertos no se tocan, nene* (1956; You Don't Touch the Dead, Little Boy), and *El pisito* (1957; The Apartment), the film version of which enjoyed international success. *Los ilusos* (1958; The Dreamers) is a satire of the habitues of Madrid's literary cafés. *Pobre, paralítico y muerto* (1960; Pauper, Paralytic, and Cadaver), three tales unified by a common intention and emphasis on "black" or "sick" humor, gave rise to a film entitled "El cochecito" (The Little Car), based on the second tale. A more sober realism imbues *Los europeos* (1960; The Europeans), a novel of critical intent, not entirely void of social satire. Somewhat crude in its descriptions, the novel attempts a moral judgment of the burgeoning tourism in the Mediterranean islands, as the Spanish isle of Ibiza is invaded by northern Europeans in search of sun and erotic satisfaction.

BIBLIOGRAPHY

Primary Text

*Chistes del repelente niño Vicente*. Madrid: Arión, 1957.

Janet Pérez

**AZORÍN,** pseudonym of José Martínez Ruiz (1873, Monóvar–1967, Madrid), critic, journalist, novelist and playwright. Born into a comfortable but provincial family of landholders in Monóvar, a small town in Alicante, he received his early education as a boarder in a Catholic school in Yecla, a city dominated by religious institutions and the clergy. He later went to Valencia to study law at the university; and it was in this comparatively enlightened and cosmopolitan Mediterrean city, where Martínez Ruiz lived from 1888 to 1896, that his vocation as a writer first emerged. Some of his earliest works, like *Buscapiés* (1894; Hints), *Anarquistas literarios* (1895; Literary Anarchists) and *Charivari* (1897; Charivari), were collections of essays characterized by satirical, often scathing, attacks on Spanish writers and culture of the times. Others, like *Notas sociales* (1895; Social Notes), *La evolución de la crítica* (1899; The Evolution of Crit-icism) and *La sociología criminal* (1899; Criminal Sociology), were attempts at more theoretical interpretations of literary criticism and sociology. As important to his future as these early pamphlets was the fact that Martínez Ruiz, during the last years of his stay in Valencia, was developing into a good journalist.

Early on he became a drama critic, a role he was to exercise constantly throughout his life. But Martínez Ruiz was to gain his first reputation as a radical social critic whose ideas were founded in anarchist thought (he translated Kropotkin's *Las prisiones* in 1897). In 1896 he went to Madrid—where he continued to live until his death—and immediately became a well-known writer for the best republican and leftist newspapers and reviews: *El País*, *El Progreso*, *El Globo*, *El Imparcial*, *Revista Nueva*, *Juventud*, etc.

During the end of the nineteenth c. and the beginning of the twentieth, Spain was suffering a historical and cultural crisis: the humiliating loss of its last overseas colonies in 1898 had symbolized for many the end of its international importance; a belated but rapid industrialization, along with a weak national economy, had brought about shifting social classes and dissatisfaction among the working class and the petite bourgeoisie; and the inadequacy of the machinery of its constitutional monarchy had led to administrative corruption. These historical factors made for a creative and lively—but often confused—intellectual scene. On the one hand, there were calls of an operative or practical nature for the "regeneration" or "Europeanization" of Spain so it could participate in the growth and success of European democratic capitalism. On the other, writers and intellectuals sought their identity through an examination of Spanish character and history or turned inward, away from historical reality, to metaphysical meditations on the human condition. The words of the writers of the so-called *Generation of 1898—a Spanish literary group of which Martínez Ruiz was a key figure and which owed its definition to an essay published by him in *Clásicos y modernos* (1913; Classics and Moderns)—are pervaded by this tension between action and contemplation, between living and thinking.

The first novels of Martínez Ruiz, *Diario de un enfermo* (1901; Diary of a Sick Person), *La voluntad* (1902; Will), *Antonio Azorín* (1903; Antonio Azorín) and *Las confesiones de un pequeño filósofo* (1904; Confessions of a Little Philosopher), are among his best works of fiction and are superb chronicles of a young man's ambivalent feelings toward his historical ciricumstances. They describe in the fragmented form of vignettes with little narrative structure the reactions of the autobiographical protagonist, Antonio Azorín (whose surname Martínez Ruiz was to assume as a definitive pseudonym in 1905), to historical events and literature of Spain and his sensations and thoughts while contemplating the life, customs and landscape of his country. The author's posture toward reality oscillates between that of a social critic and that of a skeptic who dwells on the destruction of time and the transcendence of art. The young author, influenced by Montaigne and the Goncourts, challenges the aesthetics of the traditional novel through reducing external reality to disconnected impressions which reveal his sensibility. He points to the chasm between life and the contemplation of life, between the *I* and the consciousness of the *I*. The artist concentrates his attention on the details of external reality; but since he seeks principally the sensibility produced by such observations, it constitutes a rejection of reality whose existence is justified only by its aesthetic potentialities.

By 1905, Martínez Ruiz—now definitively Azorín—seems to have resolved the tensions and contradictions implicit in his early works in favor of the artist as the "little philosopher," the writer who focuses on the apparently unimportant or commonplace and makes it transcendent. He becomes the serene contemplator of the Spanish landscape and villages and of the people who populate them. He sets out almost methodically to define the *alma castellana* (Castilian Soul), to show what is eternal or present in the past; and in the process he re-evaluates almost the whole corpus of Spanish literature in literally hundreds of essays. Indeed, most of Azorín's literary production between 1905 and 1925 falls into the category of articles and essays published first in newspapers (principally in *ABC*, the daily with the widest circulation in Spain) and then collected soon after in volumes: *La ruta de Don Quijote* (1905; Don Quixote's Route), *Los pueblos* (1905; Towns), *España* (1909; Spain), *Castilla* (1912; Castile), *Lecturas españolas* (1912; Spanish Readings), *Clásicos y modernos* (1912; Classics and Moderns), *El paisaje de España visto por los españoles* (1917; Spain's Landscape Seen by Spaniards), *Los dos Luises y otros ensayos* (1912; The Two Luises and Other Essays) and *De Granada a Castelar* (1922; From Granada to Castelar). Some exceptions, like *El licenciado Vidriera* (1915; Graduate Glass; title changed later to *Tomás Rueda*), *Un pueblecito: Riofrío de Avila* (1916; A Little Village: Riofrío de Avila), his novel *Don Juan* (1922; *Don Juan*, 1923) and *Doña Inés* (1925; Doña Inés) and his acceptance speech upon election to the Spanish Royal Academy, *Una hora de España* (1924; An Hour of Spain), share the same artistic intentions.

In these works, whose massive influence on how the contemporary Spaniard views his history and traditions is inestimable, Azorín sought to describe that basic Spanish spirit or sensibility common to all times. He defines it as a painful awareness (*el dolorido sentir*) of time and change, but one tempered by the ability to transcend historical or material reality through a grasp of the eternal or mystical. Azorín's effort to find continuity and coherence in the history of the Spanish sensibility, thus de-emphasizing or deprecating the manifestations of conflict in his country's past, was undoubtedly due to his falling under the influence of two of Spain's most notable conservatives, Antonio Maura and Juan de La Cierva. Between 1907 and 1919 he was elected on five different occasions as a deputy to the Spanish parliament from the Conservative party and twice he served as under secretary for public instruction.

Nevertheless, Azorín's constant preoccupation with the aesthetics of literature, with the interpretive relationship of the written word to reality, made it possible for him to participate with varying amounts of success in the literary innovations of the first half of the twentieth c. Already apparent in his early works, his impressionistic style, with cubist overtones, stood in marked contrast to the prose of his contemporaries. He wrote in short, simple sentences, in which he eschewed the potentialities of the verb, emphasized the noun and changed the value of adverbs and adjectives.

Between 1926 and 1936 Azorín is challenged once again by experimental fiction, this time under the aegis of surrealism and expressionism. In his novels *Félix Vargas* (1928; title changed to *El caballero inactual*; The Nonpresent Gentleman), *Superrealismo* (1929; title changed to *El libro de Levante*; Book of the Levant), *Pueblo* (1930; The People), and his short stories, *Blanco en azul* (1929; *The Sirens, and Other Stories*, 1931), he seeks to describe through attention to affective memory and evocative imagination, a strange form of existence beyond the ordinary bonds of time and space, being particularly interested in the act of creation and the splitting of the personality as states of mind which radically change perspectives on reality.

It should not be surprising then that during these same years Azorín was most active as a drama critic and wrote the majority of his plays. During the decade of the 1920s he, probably more than any other critic, initiated the Spanish public to the experimental theater in Europe. And it seems clear that his renewed interest in the theater was responsible for some of the surprising innovations in his prose fiction. His own plays are to a great extent derivative, in subject matter and technique, from the avant-garde playwrights of France, Italy and Russia. *Old Spain!* (1926; the original title is in English), *Brandy, mucho brandy* (1927; Brandy, a Lot of Brandy), *Comedia del arte* (1927; Commedia dell'arte), a trilogy of one-act plays published under the main title *Lo invisible* (1927; The Invisible), *Angelita* (1930; Angelita), *Cervantes o la casa encantada* (1931; Cervantes, or the Enchanted House), and *La guerrilla* (1936; Guerrilla Fighters), mostly fantasies or farces, made a significant critical impact in their time, although Azorín was never to be considered an important dramatist.

After the fall of the dictatorship of Primo de Rivera in 1930, Azorín became active once again as a social and political journalist, this time supporting the Spanish Republicans, albeit from the point of view of a middle-class reformist. When the Civil War started in 1936, he left Madrid for Paris, where he lived uncommitted for the duration of the war. Most of his work during this period consisted of articles, essays and short stories published in *La Prensa* of Buenos Aires, and later collected in the volumes *Españoles en París* (1939; Spaniards in Paris), *Pensando en España* (1940; Thinking about Spain), and *Cavilar y contar* (1942; To Cavil and Tell).

Upon his return to Madrid in 1939, he quietly accommodated to the regime of Franco and began to write what were to be his last novels: *El escritor* (1942; The Writer), *El enfermo* (1943; The Sick Person), *Capricho* (1943; Caprice), *La isla sin aurora* (1944; Island without Dawn), *María Fontán* (1944), and *Salvadora de Olbena* (1944). The first two are interesting in that, being autobiographical, they reveal Azorín's state of soul and some of his ideas on writing. The others are humorous, ironical fantasies in which the author attempts to remove all allusions to external reality as we normally conceive of it. The ultimate failure of these last experiments with the art of the novel finds Azorín devoting the rest of his life to writing memoirs, contributing to Madrid newspapers with a penchant for movie criticism, and publishing books of previously uncollected articles. The only edition of his complete works was published from 1947 to

1954, but since that date more than twenty volumes of articles not published in the complete works have followed.

## BIBLIOGRAPHY

### Primary Texts

*Obras Completas.* Ed. Angel Cruz Rueda. 9 vols. Madrid: Aguilar, 1947–54.

### English Translations

*Don Juan.* Tr. C. A. Phillips. London: Chapman & Dodd, 1923; New York: Knopf, 1924.
*An Hour of Spain Between 1560 and 1590.* Tr. A. Raleigh. London: Routledge, 1930.
*The Sirens, and Other Stories.* Tr. W. B. Wells. London: Partridge, 1931.
For other stories, excerpts, see Rudder. *The Literature of Spain in English Translation.* New York: Ungar, 1975. 511–35.

### Criticism

Fox, Edward Inman. *Azorín as a Literary Critic.* New York: Hispanic Institute, 1962.
————. *Azorín: guía de la obra completa.* Madrid: Castalia, 1991.
Glenn, Kathleen M. *Azorín (José Martínez Ruiz).* TWAS 604. Boston: Twayne, 1981.
Livingstone, Leon. *Tema y forma en las novelas de Azorín.* Madrid: Gredos, 1970.
Lott, Robert E. *The Structure and Style of Azorín's "El caballero inactual".* Athens: U of Georgia P, 1963.
Martínez Cachero, José María. *Las novelas de Azorín.* Madrid: Insula, 1960.
Ríopérez y Milá, Santiago. *Azorín íntegro. Estudio biográfico, crítico, bibliográfico y antológico.* Madrid: Biblioteca Nueva, 1979.
Risco, Antonio. *Azorín y la ruptura con la novela tradicional.* Madrid: Alhambra, 1980.
Valverde, José María. *Azorín.* Barcelona: Planeta, 1971.

E. Inman Fox

**AZÚA, Félix de** (1944, Barcelona– ), poet, novelist, essayist and professor. Azúa first became known as a member of the "nueve novísimos" (nine ultra-new) poets presented by José María *Castellet in his controversial 1970 anthology. His most recent publications in that genre include *Poesía 1968–1978* (1979) and *Farra.* A multifaceted intellectual, he was for a time a professor of philosophy at the U of the País Vasco, and has been a frequent and regular collaborator of the national press. Subsequently, he has held the position of professor of aesthetics in the School of Architecture in Barcelona. He is the author of two collections of essays, *Baudelaire* and *La parodoja del primitivo* (The Paradox of the Primitive Man), and at least four novels: *Las lecciones de Jena* (1972; The Lessons of Jena), *Las lecciones suspendidas* (1978; Suspended Classes), *Ultima lección* (1981; The Last Lesson), and *Mansura* (1984), a neo-chivalric or pseudo-chivalric novelized interpretation of a thirteenth-c. chronicle which treats a possible (but highly unlikely) Catalan crusade to the Holy Land.

## BIBLIOGRAPHY

### Primary Texts

*Cepo para nutria* (poems). Madrid: n.p., 1968.
*Mansura.* Barcelona: Anagrama, 1984.

*Ultima lección.* Madrid: Legasa, 1981.

*El velo en el rostro de Agamenón* (poems). Barcelona: El Bardo, 1970.

Criticism

Castellet, José María. *Nueve novísimos poetas españoles.* Barcelona: Barral, 1970. Includes a biographic note and ''poética'' plus ten poems (pp. 133–52).

Janet Pérez

# B

**BACARISSE, Mauricio** (1885, Madrid–1931, Madrid), poet, novelist and teacher of philosophy. He was known as a subtle essayist and refined critic thanks to his articles in the periodical press, and won the National Prize for Literature for his novel, *Los terribles amores de Agliberto y Celedonia* (1931; The Terrible Loves of Aglibert and Celedonia). As a poet, Bacarisse was influenced by *Modernism and especially by Juan Ramón *Jiménez. The much-admired diaphanous expression of *Mitos* (1929; Myths), his most successful lyric work, was seen as evidence of a promising talent cut short by death.

BIBLIOGRAPHY

Primary Texts

*Mitos*. Madrid: Mundo Latino, 1929.
*Los terribles amores de Agliberto y Celedonia*. Madrid: Espasa-Calpe, 1931.

**BADELL, Ana María** (1932, Santander– ), Spanish novelist and journalist. A professional landscape architect and agronomist, Badell has authored numerous articles in addition to novels including *Las monjas: esas mujeres* (1966; Those Women, the Nuns), *Sor Ada* (1967; Sister Ada), *Las nuevas colegialas* (1968; The New School Girls), *Historia de un perro* (1969; Tale of a Dog), *Monte de piedad y caja de ahorros* (1977; Pawn Shop and Savings Bank) and *¡Hasta mañana, dolor!* (1977; See You Tomorrow, Pain).

BIBLIOGRAPHY

Primary Texts

*¡Hasta mañana, dolor!* Madrid: Dólar, 1977.
*Las monjas, esas mujeres*. Madrid: n.p., 1966.
*Las nuevas colegialas*. Madrid: Iberoamericanas, 1968.
*Sor Ada*. Madrid: Iberoamericanas, 1967.

Janet Pérez

**BAENA, Cancionero de** (Baena's Songbook), poetry anthology. Around 1445, Juan Alfonso de *Baena, a court official, offered his *Cancionero* to John II of Castile. Loosely organized according to subject matter or author, it contains 576 compositions by 54 known and anonymous poets who ranged in time from the reign of Henry II (1369–79) through the middle of the fifteenth c. The *Cancionero* is a remarkable example of early editing and of literary theory, as its prologue contains general reflections on metrics, poetry and poets. ("The science of poetry is . . . received . . . by grace infused by the Lord God who grants and sends it.")

Besides the grouping of these poets by age, those flourishing before 1400 and those afterwards, one may also divide them by schools: the Galician-Castilian traditional poets and the Italianate Allegorical-Dantesque ones. The first group represents the shift from Galician to Castilian as the stylish poetic language. Its best known authors are *Macías el Enamorado, *Fernández de Gerena and *Alvarez de Villasandino. The latter (fl. 1370–c. 1442), a favorite of Baena, is an example of the slow change to Castilian, since he began his career as a professional poet writing in Galician but after 1400 commonly employed Castilian.

The innovative part of the *Cancionero* is to be found in the Allegorical-Dantesque group represented principally by its initiator in Castile Francisco *Imperial, son of a Genoese family resident in Seville. He consistently uses the long line verse (*arte mayor*) of the Italianate school, and his extensive allegories set one of the major trends of fifteenth-c. poetry.

Much of the poetry represents a late reflowering of the courtly lyric, based on the tradition of Provençal and Galician-Portuguese poetry. Courtly love conventions are much in evidence, with emphasis on devotion to one's disdainful lady, the lover's anguish, and feminine beauty. Some of the poems are debates among authors on various topics; others were written on commission, either to eulogize important persons or to attack enemies. There are also verses, which have given the anthology a bad reputation among certain Spanish critics, asking for preferment at court or for restitution to favor. In the best tradition of the troubadors, there are a number of scurrilous poems and some which are openly very lewd.

The important innovations brought to Castilian verse by the allegorizers of the Italian school, Imperial and his Sevillian followers such as Ruy *Páez de Ribera, have already been mentioned. Related to this, there is much verse on theological topics such as the problem of predestination raised in a poem by Ferrán Sánchez de *Calavera and replied to by several poets.

The *Cancionero* contains the poems of many of the important writers of the day, although Pablo de *Santa María and others are omitted, and some are overrepresented, Villasandino being the most notable example. Baena is the first in a line of anthologies such as *Stúñiga and the *Cancionero general* which collect the most stylish poets of the fifteenth c. *See also* Cancionero; Gallic Portuguese Poetry (Middle Ages); Italian Literary Influences in Spain.

BIBLIOGRAPHY

Primary Text

*Cancionero de Juan Alfonso de Baena.* Ed. J. M. Azáceta. Madrid: CSIC, 1966.
                                                                      Eric Naylor


**BAENA, Juan Alfonso de** (fl. 1445–?), poet, court historian for King John II. A converted Jew (*converso), Baena collected the works for the songbook which bears his name. Although his own contributions to the *Cancionero de *Baena* (Songbook of Baena) are of secondary merit, the collection itself is extremely valuable for having preserved a rich, representative sampling of late fourteenth- and early fifteenth-c. Spanish court poetry. Baena also composed a *Decir a Juan II* (before 1445; Poem to John II), not included in the Songbook. A long poem (1,748 lines), it is his most polished work. Baena describes political and social problems facing the monarch, and then suggests remedies.

BIBLIOGRAPHY

Primary Text

*Decir que fizo Juan Alfonso de Baena.* Ed. N. F. Marino. Valencia: Albatrós-Hispanófila, 1977. Includes study and English translation.


**BAEZA, Fernando** (1920, Madrid– ), son of Ricardo Baeza, he writes novels and short stories, some of which have been included in anthologies. In 1956 he founded the publishing house Arión. He is the editor of *Pío Baroja y su mundo*, in two volumes (1962; Pío Baroja and His World).

BIBLIOGRAPHY

Primary Text

*Baroja y su mundo.* Prol. P. Laín Entralgo. 2 vols. Madrid: Arión, 1962.
                                                                 Isabel McSpadden


**BAEZA, Ricardo** (1890–1956). He was born in Cuba but lived most of his life in Spain. He was a journalist and collaborated frequently in the most important periodicals, both Spanish and Latin American. He is the author of highly es- teemed translations of the works of D'Annunzio, Oscar Wilde, O'Neill, Ludwig, Nietzsche and others. Such translations have kept the Spanish reader up to date with the most important literary events, as well as provided accurate versions of the works of such consummate authors. He has also published *Clasicismo y romanticismo* (1930?; Classicism and Romanticism) and *La isla de los santos* (*Itinerario en Irlanda*) (1930; The Island of the Saints: Itinerary in Ireland).

BIBLIOGRAPHY

Primary Texts

*Clasicismo y romanticismo.* Madrid: Compañía iberoamericana, 1930?
*La isla de los santos.* Madrid: Renacimiento, 1930.

Isabel McSpadden

**BALAGUER, Víctor** (1824, Barcelona–1901, Madrid), prolific poet, dramatist, historian. Balaguer is one of the most distinguished figures of the *renaixença catalana* (Catalan Renaissance). His outspoken political beliefs ring in *Lo llibre de la Patria* (n.d.; The Book of the Homeland) and *La Verge de Montserrat* (n.d.; The Virgen of Montserrat). *Lo llibre del amor* (n.d.; The Book of Love) and *Tragedias* (1876; Tragedies) are lyrical in nature. Historical works include *Los frailes y sus conventos* (1851; Friars and Their Convents), *Historia de Cataluña* (1860–63; History of Catalonia), and *Historia de los trovadores* (1879; History of the Troubadours). *See also* Catalan Literature.

BIBLIOGRAPHY

Primary Texts

*Obras completas.* 39 vols. Madrid: Barc, 1882–99.
*Poesías catalanas. . . .* 2 vols. Madrid: El progreso editorial, 1892. Catalan originals with
     Spanish translations.

Criticism

Gras y Elías, F. *Siluetes de escriptors catalans del sigle XIX.* Barcelona: L'Avenç, 1909–
     13.

**BALART, Federico** (1831, Pliego, Murcia–1905, Madrid), poet, art and literary critic. His poetry is rather stilted, with the exception of *Dolores* (1894; Dolores [his wife's name]; Grief [meaning of *dolores*]), inspired by his wife's death. In 1891, he was elected a member of the Spanish Academy (\*Academia Española). Other publications include the poetry of *Horizontes* (1897; Horizons), *Sombras y destellos* (1905; Shadows and Sparks), and criticism in *Impresiones: literatura y arte* (1894; Impressions: Literature and Art) and in *El prosaísmo en el arte* (n.d.; Prosaism in Art).

BIBLIOGRAPHY

Primary Texts

*Obras poéticas.* Buenos Aires: n.p., 1946.
*Poesías completas.* Vol. 1 study by Clarín. Barcelona: Gili, 1929.

**BALBÍN LUCAS, Rafael de** (1910, Alcañices, Zamora–1978, Madrid), linguist and literary critic. For thirty years he was professor of grammar and literary criticism at the U of Madrid. He served as director of the Instituto ''Cervantes'' de Filología Hispánica (''Cervantes'' Institute of Hispanic Philology) and as an editor of the *Revista de Filología Española* (Journal of Spanish Philology). Balbín was also head of publications of the Consejo Superior de Investigaciones Científicas (Superior Council of Scientific Investigation).

As a literary critic, his research centered around the poetry of *Bécquer, while his writings in the linguistics field dealt principally with rhythm and expressiveness in the Castilian language. Balbín further published several books of his own poetry.

BIBLIOGRAPHY

Primary Texts

*Días con Dios.* Madrid: Rialp, 1951. (poems)
*Edición nacional de las obras completas de Menéndez Pelayo* (ed.). Santander: CSIC, 1940–58.
*En busca de la mañana.* Madrid: Rialp, 1965. (poems)
*Poética becqueriana.* Madrid: Prensa Española, 1969.
*Romances de cruzada.* Valladolid: Santarén, 1941. (poems)
*Sistema de rítmica castellana.* 3rd ed. Madrid: Gredos, 1975.

James F. Brown

**BALBUENA, Bernardo de** (1562, Valdepeñas–1627, Puerto Rico), lyric and epic poet. A priest, Balbuena came to Mexico from Spain as a young man in 1584. He was for years a curate in Guadalajara and chaplain to the Royal Council there. He returned to Spain and in 1607 was conferred the degree of doctor of theology. In 1608 he was appointed Abbot of Jamaica and in 1619 Bishop of Puerto Rico. In the attack of Dutch pirates on San Juan in 1625, his house and library were burned, and many of his literary works lost.

Balbuena's reputation rests chiefly on his epic poem *El Bernardo, ó Victoria de Roncesvalles* (1624; Bernardo or The Victory at Roncesvalles), and his poetic evocation of Mexico City, *Grandeza mexicana* (1604; Mexican Grandeur). It has been said that in one sense, Balbuena is perhaps not precisely an epic poet, in that his works lack the heroic emphasis typical of the epic. He is rather the creator of elegant and brilliant narratives in poetic form.

Written over a period of ten years and finished in 1602, although not published until 1624, *Bernardo* consists of some 40,000 verses. The essential element of the poem is the legend of Bernardo of Carpio, which the author himself considers false. There are, however, a number of other additions: witchcraft, allegory, elements from the romances of chivalry, references to classical antiquity as well as to contemporary historical events and geography. The main sources of *Bernardo* are in Homer, Virgil, Dante, the Spanish *Romancero*, *Barahona de Soto and Luis *Zapata. At the end of each book division of the poem is an allegorical digression, expressive of the historical period and probably added after the first version was finished.

Though *Bernardo* was undoubtedly Balbuena's major work, his *Grandeza mexicana* is perhaps most often read and studied at present. This brilliant description of the Mexican capital at the beginning of the seventeenth c. was originally a letter which the poet subsequently decided to publish. In this work, as in the *Bernardo*, Balbuena shows himself to be a Baroque poet whose verses have an unusually musical quality.

Balbuena also published a collection of eclogues, *El Siglo de Oro en las selvas de Erifile* (1607; The Golden Age in the Forests of Erifile).

## BIBLIOGRAPHY

Primary Texts

*El Bernardo ó victoria de Roncesvalles.* BAE 17
*Grandeza mexicana y fragmentos del Siglo de Oro y el Bernardo.* Ed. Francisco Monterde. México: UNAM, 1963.
*La grandeza mexicana.* Ed. Luis Adolfo Domínguez. México: Porrúa, 1980.
*El Siglo de Oro en las selvas de Erifile.* Madrid: Academia Española, 1821.

Criticism

Pascual Buxó, José. "Bernardo de Balbuena y el manierismo novohispano." *Studi Ispanici* (Pisa) no vol., 1977: 143–62.
Pierce, Francis William. *The Heroic Poem of the Spanish Golden Age.* New York: Oxford, 1947.
Rojas Garcidueñas, José J. *Bernardo de Balbuena: la vida y la obra.* México: UNAM, 1958.
Van Horne, John. *"El Bernardo" of Bernardo de Balbuena.* Urbana: U of Illinois P, 1927.

Robert E. Lewis

**BALDUQUE, Juan.** *See* Taboada, Luis

**BALLESTER I MORAGUES, Alexandre** (1934, Barcelona– ), Catalan dramatist and free-lance journalist, raised in Mallorca. *Foc colgat* (1964; Buried Fire), his first play, was not performed until 1968. Thereafter, he wrote *Jo i l'absent* (1965; The Absent One and I); *Siau benvingut* (1966; Welcome, Siau); *Un baül groc p'en Nofre Taylor* (1966; A Gilded Trunk for Nofre Taylor); *Dins un gruix de vellut* (1967; Inside a Fold of Velvet), recipient of the important Josep Maria de Sagarra Prize; *La tragedia del tres i no res* (1967; The Tragedy of Three and Nothing More); *Massa temps sense piano* (1968; A Long Time without a Piano); and *Fins al darrer mot* (1969; Up to the Last Word), awarded the Santamaria Prize. Ballester has also written poems, stories, and a novel, *La servitud* (1965; Servility), which won the City of Palma Prize. Ballester's broad acquaintance with European theater adds a depth of intertextuality and experimentalism to his essentially expressionistic works.

## BIBLIOGRAPHY

Primary Texts

*Dins un gruix de vellut.* Palma de Mallorca: Moll, 1973.
*Joc de tres.* 2nd ed. Palma de Mallorca: Moll, 1980.
*Siau benvingut.* Palma de Mallorca: Moll, 1968.

Janet Pérez

**BALLESTEROS DE GAIBROIS, Mercedes** (1913, Madrid– ), novelist, dramatist and essayist, she was born of a family of the traditional Spanish nobility. Her father, Count of Beretta, was a historian; her mother was a Colombian scholar and academic. Becoming known with newspaper and periodical articles in the 1940s, Ballesteros had already published her first works of fiction in 1939: *Paris-Niza* (Paris-Nice), *La extraña boda de Glori Dunn* (The Strange Wedding of Glori Dunn) and *La aventura de una chica audaz* (The Adventure of an Audacious Girl). She wrote several works for the theater, including *Quiero ver al doctor* (I Want to See the Doctor), in collaboration with her husband, Claudio de la *Torre; *Una mujer desconocida* (An Unknown Woman); *Tío Jorge vuelve de la India* (Uncle George Returns from India); *Las mariposas cantan* (The Butterflies Sing); and *Tienda de nieve* (Store of Snow).

Ballesteros is somewhat unique among Spanish women writers in having acquired a solid reputation as a humorist, especially in collections of sketches such as *Este mundo* (1950; This World, reprinted in 1959 in two parts, entitled *Invierno* [Winter] and *Verano* [Summer]); *Así es la vida* (1953; That's Life); and *El personal* (1975; Personnel). She is not especially feminist, being relatively conservative, but she has published a biography of one of the 19th c.'s more liberated women in her *Vida de la Avellaneda* (Life of [Gertrudis *Gómez de] Avellaneda. Among her long novels are *La cometa y el eco* (1956; The Kite and the Echo), spanning two decades in the life of the orphaned Augusta and the family with whom she lives; *Eclipse de tierra* (1954; *Nothing Is Impossible*, tr. Frances Partridge, 1956), concerning the boarding-school escapades and fantasies of a child protagonist; and *El perro del extraño rabo* (1953; The Dog with the Strange Tail), which resembles juvenile fiction with its precocious child narrator and the absurd situations into which she and her brother stumble.

*Taller* (1960; Workshop) is one of Ballesteros's successes, a novel whose main characters are all women, either seamstresses or the owner of the dressmaking shop. It was adapted for the stage in 1963 with the title *Las chicas del taller* (The Girls in the Workshop). *La sed* (1965; Thirst) refers to the symbolic thirst of Justa in her search for identity and meaning in her life. *El chico* (1967; The Boy) re-creates events in the life of an anonymous boy of about twelve, from a squalid proletarian background, ultimately drowned in an attempt to save his retarded half-sister after his stepmother has set the hovel afire. Ballesteros is a skillful narrator who is at her best in characterization of women and children. She promotes spiritual values over material success, and while not innovative, has contributed with her literary successes and the high quality of her style to enhancing the general perception of women writers in Spain.

## BIBLIOGRAPHY

Primary Texts

*Mi hermano y yo por esos mundos*. Barcelona: Destino, 1962.
*El personal*. Barcelona: Destino, 1975.

Criticism

Pérez, Janet. *Contemporary Women Writers of Spain*. Boston: G. K. Hall, 1988. 68–73.
                                                                    Janet Pérez


**BALMES, Jaume** (1810, Vic–1848, Vic), philosopher, theologian and politician. He was born into the large family of a banker, studied at the Seminary of Vic and at the College of St. Charles (in Cervera), and in 1835 obtained the doctorate in theology. In 1836 he was named to the chair of mathematics of the "Societat d'Amics del País." One of the finest intellects of Catholic-conservative Catalonia, he is best remembered for a book that in his time became rather famous throughout Europe, *El protestantismo comparado con el catolicismo en sus relaciones con la civilización* (1842–44; *European Civilization. Protestantism and Catholicity Compared in Their Effects on the Civilization of Europe*, 1875), a rather reactionary polemical diatribe which is a rebuttal to Guizot's *History of the Civilization in Europe*. Another book of somewhat dubious logic, equally famous, is *El Criterio* (1845; The Criterion). These works are interesting today only for their historical value and because Balmes became a friend to the founding fathers of the Renaixença (nineteenth-c. Catalan renaissance). At the end of his life he finally wrote a work in Catalan which reflected the conservative ideas of his Castilian writings: *Conversa d'un pages de la muntanya sobre lo papa* (1842; Conversation with a Farmer from the Mountains about the Pope). As a philosopher Balmes is not very original. Aside from his scholastic background—St. Thomas—he reflects influences of the Scottish School, Descartes and Leibnitz. His Catalan prose is stylistically superior to his writings in Castilian. *See also* Catalan Literature.

BIBLIOGRAPHY

Primary Texts

*Cartas á un escéptico en materia de religión*. Barcelona: Brusi, 1846.
*Criterio (El)*. Mexico: Porrúa, 1966.
*Escritos políticos; colección completa, corregida y ordenada por el autor*. Madrid: Sociedad de operarios del mismo arte, 1847.
*Ética*. Madrid: Hernando, 1935.
*Filosofía fundamental*. Barcelona: Brusi, 1848.
*Obras completas*. Madrid: Católica, 1948.

English Translations

*European Civilization. Protestantism and Catholicity Compared in Their Effects on the Civilization of Europe*. 15th ed. Baltimore: J. Murphy and Co., 1875.
*Fundamental Philosophy*. Tr. Henry F. Brownson. New York: Sadlier, 1856.

Criticism

*Actas del Congreso Internacional de Filosofía*. No ed. Barcelona: n.p., 1948. Several articles.

Mendoza, Juan de Dios. "Bibliografía balmesiana." In *Analecta Sacra Tarraconensia* (Barcelona) 33 (1960). Entire volume devoted to Balmes.

Joan Gilabert

**BALTÉ, Teresa** (1942, Lisbon– ), poet. She earned her secondary diploma in Faro. She studied at the universities of Hamburg and Lisbon, mastering in Germanic studies. She also studied music. She has worked as a researcher, secretary, interpreter, music critic, and translator.

Extending the line of *Poemas Livres* and *Poesia–1961*, Balté writes a classically diaphanous poetry, marked by a discontent with the universe. With frequent reference to Greek mythology and literature and reliance on the Lusitanian lyrical traditions, Balté enchants the quotidian in an idyllic imagery and decasyllabic rhythms. Her poems are personal and short in accordance with their fleeting fragile feelings. The combined disillusionments of youth and maturity often produce a religiosity of the universal passage. Her continuation of the Camonean *mudança*, change, is seen even in her idylls where time changes passion into a surprise incongruity between desire and object, resulting in a refined, ironic humor. Balté also writes children's books and has translated Büchner and Brecht.

BIBLIOGRAPHY

Primary Texts

*Horizontes portáteis* (Portable Horizons). Porto: Inova, 1977.
*Jogos* (Games). Lisbon: n.p., 1962.
*Meditações* (Meditations). Lisbon: Contexto, 1983.
*Metamórfose* (Metamorphosis). N.p.: n.p., 1977.

Robert R. Krueger

**BANCES CANDAMO, Francisco Antonio de** (1662, Avilés, Asturias–1704, Lezuza, Albacete), poet, playwright, drama critic. Bances Candamo was one of the last dramatists of the *Siglo de Oro, thus closing the *Calderón cycle. Born in the north of Spain, Bances Candamo was educated in Seville. After graduating from the U he moved to Madrid at some date between 1682 and 1685. On November 15, 1685, his *Por su rey y por su dama* (For His King and for His Lady) was performed before the King and Queen in the theater of the Palace of Buen Retiro; this is the first recorded performance of a play by Bances, and it is noteworthy that, as an obscure and penniless young man from the province, he should have been chosen to write a play for performance at court. *La restauración de Buda* (The Restoration of Buddha) was written in the following year, 1686. Both these Palace plays make elaborate use of theatrical machinery, and the plots are carefully chosen to make allusions to the political and military situation at the time of writing. In 1687 Bances was appointed official playwright to the king, Charles II, and from this date onwards concentrated his energies on the writing of court plays, and also of *autos sacramentales* (see Auto): *El primer duelo del mundo* (The World's First Duel) was performed on Corpus Christi day

in 1687, and *El maestrazgo del Toisón* (Mastership of the Order of Fleece) and
*Psiquis y Cupido* (Psyche and Cupid) date from 1691. The high point of Bances's
career as court dramatist was 1692–93. Recent studies by D. W. Moir suggest
that *El esclavo en grillos de oro* (The Slave in Golden Fetters), *Cómo se curan
los celos* (How to Cure Jealousy), and *La piedra filosofal* (The Philosopher's
Stone) have clear political purpose. According to Moir, Bances wrote these plays
with the intention of influencing the choice of successor to the childless Charles
II of Spain, and, as a result of a too overt attempt to mold the course of events,
was banished from the court in 1693–95. Further plays of Bances were performed
in the public theaters of Madrid in 1696 and 1697. In the latter year he was
appointed general administrator of royal income in Ocaña, and later transferred
to Úbeda and Baeza. Bances died in Lezuza in 1704. *Por su rey y por su dama*
is perhaps his most successful play, remaining in the repertoire throughout the
eighteenth c. Based on the Spanish defense of Amiens against the French in
1597, the play appears to suggest to the King that, just as Spain in 1598 placed
the government of the Low Countries in the hands of the Archduke Albert of
Austria, so in 1685 Charles II should hand over power to the Elector of Bavaria.
*El esclavo en grillos de oro* (1692–93) has been interpreted by Moir as a satire
on the Count of Oropesa, the fallen favorite. *Cómo se curan los celos y Orlando
furioso* (1692) is concerned with the problem of the succession to the Spanish
throne, a theme further developed in *La piedra filosofal* (1693), in which a
legendary king of Spain, Hispán, considers three possible suitors for the hand
of his daughter. Moir argues that the three suitors represent Philip of Anjou, the
Archduke Charles of Austria and the son of the Elector of Bavaria, while the
daughter Iberia clearly stands for Spain. Bances's own attitude to the theater is
recorded in the treatise *Teatro de los teatros*, existing in three versions and only
recently published. In the second version he clearly reveals that, in his view,
court plays should present a political point of view. Bances's plays are characterized by an excellent command of the staging potentialities of the court
theaters of the period and clearly fall within the literary framework of the court
play as laid down by Calderón, but for Bances Candamo, the message is more
important than the medium.

BIBLIOGRAPHY

Primary Texts

*Autos sacramentales*. Ed. study J. J. Pérez Feliú. Oviedo: Instituto de Estudios Asturianos,
    1975.
*Obras líricas*. Ed. F. Gutiérrez. Barcelona: Selecciones Bibliófilas, 1949.
*Poesías cómicas*. 2 vols. Madrid: Blàs de Villa-Nueva, 1722.
*Theatro de los theatros de los passados y presentes siglos*. Ed. D. W. Moir. London:
    Tamesis, 1970.

Criticism

Cuervo-Arango, F. *Don Francisco Antonio de Bances y López-Candamo. Estudio bio-
    bibliográfico y crítico*. Madrid: Hernández, 1916.

Shaffer, Jack W. "Bances Candamo and the Calderón Decadents." *PMLA* 44 (1929): 1079–89.

Penzol, P. "Angélica y Medora en el *Orlando furioso* de Francisco Bances Candamo." *Clavileño* 7.39 (1956): 19–23.

———. "Desde Ariosto hasta Bances Candamo." *Archivum* 6 (1956): 321–26.

———. *Francisco Bances Candamo. De la comedia a la zarzuela (1622–1709)*. Madrid: Velasco, 1932.

Rozas, J. M. "La licitud del teatro y otras cuestiones literarias en Bances Candamo, escritor límite." *Segismundo* 1 (1965): 247–73.

Rubín, A. "Un dramaturgo y poeta asturiano en la Corte de los Austrias: D. Francisco Antonio Bances Candamo." *Archivum* 12 (1962): 470–78.

John E. Varey

**BÁÑEZ, Domingo** (1528, Valladolid–1604, Medina del Campo), Dominican theologian. He taught theology and philosophy at the U of Salamanca, among other places. In 1562, Báñez defended Sta. *Teresa de Jesús when she founded the first monastery in Avila; later he became her confessor and advisor. Báñez is known for his central role in the passionate, subtle theological controversy over Divine Grace and human free will (called *De auxiliis*), carried out between himself, Luis de *Molina and other Jesuits. Báñez accused Molina and his followers of overemphasizing the power of man's free will. Molina in turn charged Báñez with Calvinistic tendencies; later scholars recognize the system under the name Bañézianism.

As one of the great commentators of St. Thomas Aquinas's *Summa Theologica*, Báñez's most important theological work is his *Scholastica Commentaria in Primam Partem Summae Theologicae S. Thomas Aquinatis* (1584).

BIBLIOGRAPHY

Primary Texts

*Comentarios inéditos a la Prima secundae de Santo Tomas*. Ed. V. Beltrán de Heredia. 3 vols. Madrid: Aldecoa, 1942–48.

*Scholastica Commentaria in Primam Partem Summae Theologicae S. Thomas Aquinatis*. Ed., intro. L. Urbano. Valencia: Vives Mora, 1934.

English Translation

*The Primacy of Existence in Thomas Aquinas; a commentary in Thomistic metaphysics*. Tr., intro., notes B. S. Llamzon. Chicago: Regnery, 1966.

Criticism

Alvarez, Paulino. *Santa Teresa y el P. Báñez*. Madrid: Lezcano, 1882.

"Bañézianism." In *Encyclopedic Dictionary of Religion*. Ed. P.K. Meagher, T.C O'Brien, C.M. Aherne. Washington, D.C.: Corpus, 1979. 1: 355–56.

Régnon, Theodore de. *Báñez et Molina*. Paris: Oudin, 1883.

Hector Medina

**BARAHONA DE SOTO, Luis** (1548, Lucena–1595, Antequera), epic and lyric poet. Barahona de Soto was a disciple of the humanist Juan de Vilches in Antequera. In Granada he attended the literary gatherings of Alonso de Granada

Venegas, and there, no doubt, came into contact with Hernando de *Acuña, Diego *Hurtado de Mendoza and Gregorio *Silvestre. He participated in the suppression of the Moorish uprising in the Alpujarras in 1569. Studying medicine in Granada, Osuna and Seville, he became a well-known physician who practiced in Archidona and Antequera.

Barahona maintained a cordial relationship with Fernando de *Herrera, to whom he dedicated a famous sonnet in which he effusively praises the great Sevillian poet. His chief work is *Las lágrimas de Angélica* (1586; The Tears of Angelica), a long epic poem which develops the episode of Angelica and Medoro from Ariosto's *Orlando Furioso*. To this episode, Barahona added many others, narrated in a delicate poetry which elicited praise from both *Cervantes and Lope de *Vega.

The author is as well a lyric poet of considerable talent. Barahona wrote in short, Italianate meters. Outstanding among his poems using traditional meter are his excellent adaptations of Ovid's *Fables of Vertum and Acteon*. Among the poems of longer meter, the "Elegía a la muerte del rey Don Sebastián" (Elegy Upon the Death of King Sebastian) and the "Muerte de Garcilaso" (Death of Garcilaso) are particularly worthy of note. The "Elegía de las hamadriads" (Elegy to the Hamadriads) is an elegant and well-wrought poem which anticipates the style of *Góngora.

In prose, Barahona wrote *Los diálogos de la montería* (1890; The Hunting Dialogues), an erudite essay on the art of hunting in Spain which has been highly praised by Rodríguez Marín. *See also* Humanism; Italian literary influences; Renaissance.

BIBLIOGRAPHY

Primary Texts

*Los diálogos de la montería*. Madrid: Sociedad de bibliófilos españoles, 1890.
*Las lágrimas de Angélica*. Ed., study J. Lara Garrido. Madrid: Cátedra, 1981.
*Romancero y cancionero sagrado*. BAE 35.

Criticism

Rodríguez Marín, F. *Luis Barahona de Soto: estudio biográfico, bibliográfico y crítico.* Madrid: Rivadeneyra, 1903. Appendix reproduces Barahona's lyric poetry.

                                                                Robert E. Lewis

**BARALT, Rafael María** (1819, Maracaibo, Venezuela–1860, Madrid), historian and poet. Baralt made Spain his home in 1843, and ten years later was admitted to the *Academia Española, occupying the chair vacated by the death of *Donoso Cortés. His poetry eschews *Romanticism and models itself on Golden Age classics by *Góngora, Fray Luis de *León, etc.; his ode "A Cristóbal Colón" (To Christopher Columbus) was much celebrated. As historian, he wrote *Historia de Venezuela* (1841; History of Venezuela), and as linguist, the valuable *Diccionario de Galicismos* (1855; Dictionary of Gallicisms).

BIBLIOGRAPHY

Primary Texts

*Antología.* Biblioteca popular venezolana 81 and 82. Caracas: Ministerio de educación, 1961–62.

*Discurso de recepción pronunciado en la Real Academia Española.* Caracas: Ediciones de la Presidencia de la República, 1982.

*Diccionario de galicismos.* Madrid: Nacional, 1980. (Microfilm)

*Obras literarias publicadas e inéditas.* BAE 204.

**BARBADIÑO,** pseud. for Luis Antonio de Verney (1713, Lisbon–1792, Rome), Portuguese philosopher, theologian, writer. Verney studied humanities and theology at the U of Evora, and in 1736 traveled to Italy, studied at the U of Rome and earned a doctorate in civil law and theology. Subsequently he was named Archdeacon of the Cathedral of Evora. As one of the key Portuguese philosophers of his day, he wrote five works, in Latin, which propose a system for the study and teaching of philosophy. He is most known for his *Verdadero método de estudiar para ser útil a la República y a la Iglesia* (1746 in Portuguese, Spanish tr. in 1760; True Method of Study in Order to Serve State and Church), which attacked the methods and state of public education, and proposed specific reforms. The work sparked great debate and earned Verney the nickname *Feijoo of Portugal.

BIBLIOGRAPHY

Primary Texts

*Verdadeiro método de estudar.* Ed. A. Salgado Júnior. 5 vols. Lisbon: Sá de Costa, 1949–52.

**BARBERO SÁNCHEZ, Teresa** (1934, Avila– ), a novelist. Barbero was one of the originators of the "El Cobaya" literary group in 1953. In 1959 she moved to Madrid and began publishing poetry. She then established her reputation as a novelist. In addition to a volume of poetry, *Muchacha en el exilio* (1959; A Girl in Exile), she is also known for her study of Gabriel Miró, *Gabriel Miró* (1974). Among her novels are *Apenas llegue el buen tiempo* (1964; As Soon As Good Weather Comes), a Premio Sésamo finalist, and *Una manera de vivir* (1965; A Way of Life), winner of the Premio Sésamo, the story of a 20-year-old woman whose family believes women should not work, that they should marry early. Unable to finance her university studies, she descends into unhappiness and anguished emptiness. Losing interest in life, unable to find a job, she slashes her wrists. The work condemns the attitudes of Spanish society toward women and their lack of preparation to face the reality of the world. *El último verano en el espejo* (1967; The Last Summer in the Mirror) is an indictment of the education of Spanish girls and portrays the mid-twentieth-c. malaise of the protagonist, Marta. As Marta recalls her childhood and adolescence in a small town, and the repression, prejudices and frustrations of that life, she sees herself reduced to a figment, dominated by the men in her life, revealed as a person only within the narrow confines of her mirror. *Un tiempo irremediablemente falso* (1973; An Irremediably False Time) portrays a loveless marriage. The wife, drowning in domesticity, has no idea that women can enjoy sex, until she leaves her husband and children to live with her lover. After the deaths of her husband and lover, she builds a career and rebuilds her relationship with her daughters. *La larga noche de un aniversario* (1982; The Long Night of an Anniversary) once again criticizes the upbringing of Spanish females. The protagonist feels fossilized at age 19 and has no interest in life, which to her is an incomprehensible hieroglyphic. Leaving her university studies, she works at dull jobs. *Y no serás juzgado* (1985; And You Will Not Be Judged) won the Premio Asturias de Novela 1982. Here the crisis in the marriage of a teacher and a successful executive represents the crisis of the entire Spanish post-war generation, a truly "lost generation," whose anguish lies in the inability to feel part of the society. The husband fears sleep, silence, darkness, old age; and he resents his wife's business success and sexual frigidity. The wife is the prototype of women who grew up in dictatorial families within a dictatorial society, and neither love, work, nor material possessions can fill the emptiness of their lives. All of the novels are noteworthy for their use of interior monologue and memory and psychological insight.

BIBLIOGRAPHY

Primary Texts

*Apenas llegue el buen tiempo.* N.p.: n.p., 1964.

*Gabriel Miró.* Madrid: EPESA, 1974.

*La larga noche de un aniversario.* Madrid: Ibérica Europea, 1982.

*Muchacha en el exilio.* Bilbao: Colección Alrededor de la Mesa, 1959.

*El último verano en el espejo.* Barcelona: Destino, 1967.

*Un tiempo irremediablemente falso.* Madrid: Sala, 1973.

*Una manera de vivir.* Madrid: AULA, 1965.

*Y no serás juzgado.* Gijón: Noega, 1985.

Carolyn Galerstein

**BARCAS** (Ships), title given the celebrated trilogy by Gil *Vicente, which ranks among the most important works of religious theater. The trilogy includes the *Barca do Inferno* (1517; Ship of Hell) and the *Barca do Purgatorio* (1518; Ship of Purgatory), both written in Portuguese, and the *Barca da Gloria* (1519; Ship of Paradise), composed in Spanish. The theme is the medieval dance of death in which figures of the most diverse social stations are judged according to their deeds on Earth before their condemnation to Hell or entrance to Paradise. The works present marked social and anti-clerical satire as the characters board the various ships leading them to their final destinations. *See also Dança General de la muerte.*

BIBLIOGRAPHY

Primary Texts

*Auto da barca do inferno.* Ed. C. D. Ley. Madrid: CSIC, 1946.

*Auto da embarcação da glória.* Ed. P. Quintela. Coimbra: Coimbra, 1941.

English Translation

*The Ship of Hell.* Tr. A.F. G. (Bell). Lisbon: Agência Geral do Ultramar, 1954.

Deborah Compte

**BAREA, Arturo** (1897, Madrid–1957, London), novelist and short story writer. Despite humble origins, Barea rose to become one of the leading Spanish writers in exile after the Civil War. His literary career began with the publication of a volume of stories, *Valor y miedo* (1939; Courage and Fear), which deals with the war. But his literary fame is due almost exclusively to his autobiography/ novel, *La forja de un rebelde* (1951; *The Forging of a Rebel*, 1946), written in England where he had fled after the Nationalist victory appeared imminent. Published first in English, with his wife, Ilsa, serving as translator, this book attained an international reputation and following due primarily to its eye-witness account of wartime Madrid. It is a trilogy composed of (1) *La forja* (The Forge), a recounting of Barea's childhood and adolescence told from a child's point of view and memorable for its graceful, simple prose; (2) *La ruta* (The Track), which treats the author's experiences as a soldier in the war with Morocco in 1921 and reveals his sympathy for the long-suffering enlisted man, who was confronted by inept and corrupt leadership; and (3) *La llama* (The Flash), which has been called perhaps the best work on the Civil War that the literature of exile has produced. The trilogy is regularly praised for its simple and direct style, vibrant humanity, and faithful re-creation of the Spanish environment.

Barea's subsequent novel, *La raíz rota* (1955; *The Broken Root*, 1952), has been criticized for its supposedly exaggerated view of conditions in postwar Spain. He is also the author of essays on *García Lorca and *Unamuno, as well as a posthumous collection of stories, *El centro de la pista* (1960; The Center of the Track).

BIBLIOGRAPHY

Primary Texts

*El centro de la pista.* Madrid: Cid, 1960.
*La forja de un rebelde.* 2nd ed. Madrid: Turner, 1977.
*Lorca, el poeta y su pueblo.* Buenos Aires: Losada, 1956.
*La raíz rota.* Buenos Aires: Santiago Rueda, 1955.
*Unamuno.* Buenos Aires: Sur, 1959.
*Valor y miedo.* Barcelona: Publicaciones Antifascistas de Cataluña, 1939.

English Translations

*The Broken Root.* London: n.p. 1952.
*The Forging of a Rebel.* Tr. Ilsa Barea. New York: Reynal & Hitchcock, 1946.
*Lorca, the Poet and His People.* Tr. Ilsa Barea. New York: Grove, 1958. New York: Cooper Square, 1973.
*Unamuno.* Tr. Ilsa Barea. Cambridge: Bowes & Bowes, 1952.

Criticism

Blanco Amor, José. "A 20 años de *La forja de un rebelde*, Arturo Barea y los valores de su obra." *Cuadernos Americanos* 185 (1972): 213–22.

Devlin, John. "Arturo Barea and José María Gironella: Two Interpretations of the Spanish Labyrinth." *Hispania* 41 (May 1958): 143–48.

Marra-López, José R. *Narrativa española fuera de España (1939–1961)*. Madrid: Guadarrama, 1963.

Ortega, José. "Arturo Barea, novelista español en busca de su identidad." *Symposium* 25 (1971): 377–91.

Rodríguez Monegal, Emir. "Tres testigos españoles de la guerra civil." *Revista Nacional de Cultura* (Caracas) 182 (1967): 3–22.

Weeden, Margaret. "Arturo Barea: An Appreciation." *Meanjin* 18 (April 1959): 96–99.

James F. Brown

**BARGA, Corpus,** pseudonym of Andrés García de la Barga y Gómez de la Serna (1887, Madrid–1975, Lima, Peru), journalist, novelist, critic. Barga, whose pseudonym commemorates his birthday, abandoned studies in mining engineering to begin a career in journalism. He first distinguished himself as a chronicler of World War I for *El Sol*, whose staff he joined at the invitation of *Ortega y Gasset. His first novel, *La vida rota* (1908, 1910; The Broken Life), in two volumes, appeared amid controversy. From 1929 to 1931, he worked in Berlin as a correspondent for *La Nación* of Buenos Aires. He also began writing literary and artistic criticism for the *Revista del occidente, España*, and other important literary journals, and became involved in a famous polemic over fascism with Ortega, which appeared in *El espectador*. His novel *Pasión y muerte. Apocalipsis* (1930; Passion and Death. Apocalypse) reflects Vanguard tendencies. Politically, Barga supported the Republican Leftists, and was arrested in a 1917 strike against Primo de Rivera. Because of the Civil War, Barga accompanied Antonio *Machado into exile in France, living there from 1939 to 1947. In 1948 he moved to Lima, Peru, to become director of the School of Journalism of the U of San Marcos, a post he held until retiring. His next novel, *La baraja de los desatinos; crónica cinematográfica de 1700* (1968; The Card Deck of Foolishness; a Movie Chronicle of 1700), a Valleinclanesque farce begun in Paris in 1947, was not published until years later in Peru. It was re-edited in Spain and issued under a new title, *Hechizo de la triste marquesa* (1971; The Enchantment of the Sad Marchioness). Barga received more critical acclaim for the four volumes of his memoirs, initiated with *Los pasos contados; una vida española a caballo en dos siglos, 1887–1957* (1963; Counted Steps; a Spanish Life on Horseback in Two Centuries). The series continued with *Puerilidades burgueses* (1765; Bourgeois Childishness), *Las delicias* (1967; Delights), and finally, *Los galgos verdugos* (1971; The Henchmen Greyhounds), for which Barga received the Premio de la Crítica (Critics' Award) in 1974. Some critics consider this final volume a reworking of the youthful *La vida rota*. The narrative structure of the memoirs makes them more novelistic than historical. Barga's prose style is typified by elegance, deliberation, and parsimony of words. His being ignored by critics for years is perhaps accounted for by his imaginative subjects, unpopular in an age of realism. His "rediscovery" in recent years adds a link between the *Generation of 1898 and their successors. Barga's death of an embolism preceded by only a few hours his planned return to Spain after an almost 40-year absence.

BIBLIOGRAPHY

Primary Texts

*Apocalipsis; Pasión y muerte; Hechizos de la triste marquesa; cuentos.* Madrid: Júcar, 1987.
*Crónicas literarias / Corpus Barga.* Ed. A. Ramoneda Salas. Madrid: Júcar, 1984.
*Los galgos verdugos* Madrid: Alianza, 1971.
*Paseos por Madrid.* Madrid: Júcar, 1987.
*Los pasos contados; una vida española a caballo en dos siglos.* Barcelona: EDHASA, 1963.

Frieda Blackwell

**BARJA, César** (1892, ?–1952, ?), writer and critic, professor at UCLA. He is the author of *Rosas y espinas místicas* (Madrid, 1921; Mystical Roses and Thorns). In the United States he published *Literatura española: libros y autores clásicos* (1923; Spanish Literature: Classical Books and Authors), a series of outstanding lectures on Rosalía de *Castro (New York, 1923), an essay on Galician lyricism, several translations, and his essays *Libros y autores contemporáneos* (1935; Contemporary Books and Authors), in which he analyzes certain aspects of the works of *Ganivet, *Unamuno, *Ortega y Gasset, *Azorín, Pío *Baroja and others.

BIBLIOGRAPHY

Primary Text

*Literatura española.* Rev. ed. Los Angeles: Campbells, 1933.

Isabel McSpadden

**BARNATÁN, Ricardo Marcos** (1946, Buenos Aires– ), poet, novelist, critic. He relocated from Buenos Aires to Madrid in 1965. Outside of Spain, he is known primarily as a scholar on the work of Jorge Luis Borges. Barnatán has also published five poetry collections, *Acerca de los viajes* (1966; On Travels), *Tres poemas fantásticos* (n.d.; Three Fantastic Poems), *Los pasos perdidos* (1968: Lost Steps), *Arcana Mayor (1970–1972)* (1973), *La escritura del vidente* (1979; The Writing of the Prophet); two novels, *El laberinto de Zion* (1971; The Labrynth of Zion) and *Gor* (1973); a study of the Jewish Cabala, *La Kabala: Una mística del lenguaje* (1974; The Cabala: The Mysticism of Language); and a historical study, *Acontecimientos que cambiaron la historia* (1975; Events That Changed History).

BIBLIOGRAPHY

Primary Texts

*Acerca de los viajes.* Madrid: Pajero Cascabel, 1966.
*Acontecimientos que cambiaron la historia.* Barcelona: Planeta, 1975.
*Arcana Mayor (1970–1972).* Madrid: Visor, 1973.

*La escritura del vidente.* Barcelona: Gaya Ciencia, 1979.
*Gor.* Barcelona: Barral, 1973.
*La Kabala: Una mística del lenguage.* Barcelona: Barral, 1974.
*El laberinto de Zion.* Barcelona: Barral, 1971.
*Los pasos perdidos.* Madrid: Azur, 1968.
*Tres poemas fantásticos.* Málaga: Cuadernos de María José, n.d.

Dennis Klein

**BAROJA, Pío** (1872, San Sebastián–1956, Madrid), novelist. Baroja was born to middle-class parents in San Sebastián. His father, a mining engineer, moved the family to Madrid when Pío was 7, and two years later they relocated in Pamplona. Baroja returned to Madrid at the age of 14, remaining there through the first years of medical studies. Another transfer took the family to Valencia, where Pío finished his degree. He returned to Madrid to complete a doctorate and then relocated to the northern Spanish town of Cestona to begin his practice. Never enthusiastic about medicine, Baroja abandoned his profession after the Cestona experience, returning once more to Madrid. There he briefly took over his aunt's bakery, publishing his first novels at the same time. Increasingly successful as an author, he gave up the bakery and devoted himself exclusively to his writing. Never married, Baroja led a quiet life, alternating between Madrid and the vacation home that he eventually purchased in Vera, Bidasoa. In 1898 he made his first trip to Paris, and in subsequent years he traveled to London, Italy, Switzerland, Germany, and northern Europe. A member of the *Generation of 1898, he was a great lover of the Spanish countryside and frequently toured the various regions of Spain on foot, by horseback, by train, and later, by automobile.

In his youth, Baroja was attracted to anarchism but his skepticism precluded any long-term acceptance of political or religious dogmas. Like other members of the Generation of 1898, he was a strong critic of Spanish society and of those institutions that he believed were detrimental to Spain's cultural, social, and economic development. Among these he included the Catholic church, the Spanish educational system, and political corruption with its manipulation of the electoral process by local bosses. An individualist, Baroja disliked those institutions that sought to regulate human conduct; thus his aversion to marriage, the army, and large groups of any kind. In his novels, he invariably presents a negative portrait of characters who have been subsumed into a larger group, be it ethnic, political, religious, or social. He has been accused of anti-Semitism, Gallophobia, misogyny, and anti–Latin Americanism because he consistently belittles those who echo the values of the group. On the other hand, individuals who retain their individuality are depicted with humor, pathos, and admiration.

The conflict between the social pressure for conformity and the individual need for freedom is a basic theme in all of Baroja's novels. In those works which examine contemporary Spanish and European society, the protagonist of the earlier novels is often successful in resolving his or her personal need for freedom, but the solution is shown to be unique and not transferrable to society at large.

*El Mayorazgo de Labraz* (1903; *The Lord of Labraz*, 1926), *Camino de perfec-ción* (1902; The Way of Perfection), and the trilogy *La lucha por la vida* (1903–4; The Struggle for Life) are examples. In later novels, the protagonist is generally defeated by the social forces that confront him or her. The novel often ends on a negative note, but the struggle is shown to have given meaning and dignity to the protagonist's life. There is increasingly a suggestion that the defeated individual might have succeeded in another time or place. *La ciudad de la niebla* (1909; The City of Mist), *El árbol de la ciencia* (1911; *The Tree of Knowledge*, 1974), and *La sensualidad pervertida* (1920; *Amorous Experiments of a Simpleminded Man in a Degenerate Age*, 1931) can be included among this group. Baroja also cultivated the historical novel and the adventure story. In both cases the protagonist is a ''man of action'' who pursues adventure for its own sake, thriving on danger and independence from social conventions. It should be noted that these novels are largely escapist; the heroes are drawn from the past, and the reader is constantly reminded of the remoteness of the world depicted, through allusions to other texts or highly visible adventure-story technique.

Baroja's novel represents a major departure from the realistic-naturalistic novel that preceded it. He objected to the ''closed'' novel, with a limited number of characters, a slow progression toward narrative climax, and a neat tying up of the ends in the final resolution. He preferred what he called the ''open novel,'' with large numbers of characters who appeared and disappeared at will. The reader is never sure if a new character will become a major personality or if he or she will disappear permanently. The same is true of the use of suspense. Often an atmosphere of tension is created so that the reader expects a climactic action, but the potential adventure never materializes. When major novelistic action does occur, it is without any of the traditional building up of tension.

Most of Baroja's novels revolve around a single central character who embarks on a philosophical, economic, or sentimental search. In many cases, the internal search is effected through a physical journey. In *La busca* (1904; *The Quest*, 1922), Manuel wanders through Madrid seeking a lifestyle that will be both personally and economically satisfactory. In *Camino de perfección*, Fernando Ossorio journeys through Castilla and Valencia in his quest for spiritual and emotional health. César Moncada of *César o nada* (1910; *Caesar or Nothing*, 1976) travels throughout Italy and Spain as he seeks a viable location to apply his political energies. The peripatetic nature of Baroja's novel led earlier critics to censure their lack of structure. Baroja himself contributed to this view, with his insistence that he wrote without a plan, following the action wherever it might lead him. More recently, critics have shown that there is a great deal of design beneath the appearance of spontaneity. Furthermore, what was once considered unorthodox Barojan novelistic technique has now become the norm; in this as in many other respects, Baroja was a forerunner of the contemporary novel.

Baroja is often described as having a ''gray'' style or of writing in a ''minor key.'' Much of his language is, in fact, stark, colorless, purposely seeking to be imperceptible. However, he also cultivates a variety of styles that are highly perceptible. In his early works, a modernistic influence can be seen in his use of sensuality, the mix of eroticism and religion, and the freezing of characters in artistically effective poses. Impressionistic touches are also evident, particularly in *Camino de perfección*. In a different vein, Baroja often employs an incredibly harsh, insulting tone that is interspersed in forceful contrast to his "gray" style. The use of the grotesque and the absurd is never entirely absent from the description of minor characters, but it is a dominant force in only a few works, such as *Paradox, rey* (1906; Paradox, King). Stream of consciousness and surrealistic techniques and style appear in *El hotel del cisne* (1946; The Swan's Hotel). In virtually all of Baroja's novels, lyrical description of landscape provides a contrasting note, at times understated and at times predominant.

The Barojan novel is a major contribution to Spanish literature. It strongly influenced post–Civil War Spanish novelists, notably Camilo José *Cela, and outside of Spain, it left a major mark on John Dos Passos and Ernest Hemingway.

BIBLIOGRAPHY

Primary Texts

*El árbol de la ciencia.* Madrid: Caro Raggio, 1983.
*La busca.* Madrid: Caro Raggio, 1983.
*Camino de perfección.* Madrid: Caro Raggio, 1972.
*Obras completas.* 8 vols. Madrid: Biblioteca Nueva, 1946–51. 2nd ed. 1974–80.
*Paradox, rey.* Madrid: Caro Raggio, 1983.

English Translations

*Amorous Experiments of a Simpleminded Man in a Degenerate Age.* Tr. Samuel Putnam. New York: Warren and Putnam, 1931.
*Caesar or Nothing.* Tr. Louis How. New York: Fertig, 1976.
*The Quest.* Tr. Isaac Goldberg. New York: Knopf, 1922.
*The Restlessness of Shanti Andía and Other Writings.* Tr. Anthony Kerrigan. Ann Arbor: U of Michigan P, 1959.
*The Tree of Knowledge.* Tr. Aubrey F. Bell. New York: Fertig, 1974.

Criticism

Barrow, Leo. *Negation in Baroja.* Tucson: U of Arizona P, 1971.
Bretz, Mary Lee. *La evolución novelística de Pío Baroja.* Madrid: Porrúa Turanzas, 1979.
Ciplijauskaite, Birute. *Baroja, un estilo.* Madrid: Insula, 1972.
González López, Emilio. *El arte narrativo de Pío Baroja: Las trilogías.* New York: Las Américas, 1971.
Patt, Beatrice. *Pío Baroja.* Boston: Hall, 1971.

Mary Lee Bretz

**BAROJA, Ricardo** (1871, Riotinto, Asturias–1953, Madrid), author, artist. Brother of Pío, Ricardo was a well-known impressionist painter and engraver who also wrote a number of adventure narratives with Basque themes: *La nao capitana (Cuento español del mar antiguo)* (1935; The Flag-Ship [Spanish Tale of the Ancient Seas]) and *Carnashu*, a tale of love and war in the 17th-c. Basque country.

BIBLIOGRAPHY

Primary Text

*Obras selectas*. Madrid: Biblioteca Nueva, 1967.

**BARRAL, Carlos** (1928, Barcelona–  ), poet and publisher. Barral is recognized not only for his post–Civil War testimonial verse but also for his promotion of literary innovation as the director of Barral publishers in Barcelona. He prefers the term *civil* rather than *social* to describe his poetry, which addresses the contemporary political issues germane to the poetic vision of his generation. His poetic themes include the alienation of contemporary man in urban life, particularly in *Metropolitano* (1957; Metropolitan); a personal documentation of the historical events of his lifetime, as in *19 figuras de mi historia civil* (1961; 19 Figures of My Civil History); and the life and landscapes of the Catalonian coast.

Despite its stark objectivity, Barral's work is also characterized by linguistic experimentation and the search for new forms, consistent with his assessment that he and his contemporaries identified both thematically and formally with the *Generation of 1927. In Barral's case, the result is a more abstract and obscure poetic idiom than is often associated with post-war poetry. The 1979 edition of *Usuras y figuraciones* (Usuries and Figurations) includes selections from his major works. He has also translated the poetry of Rilke and has published two volumes of autobiographical narrative: *Años de penitencia* (1975; Years of Penitence) and *Los años sin excusa* (1978; The Years without Excuse).

BIBLIOGRAPHY

Primary Works

*Años de penitencia*. Madrid: Alianza, 1975.
*Los años sin excusa*. Barcelona: Barral, 1978.
*Metropolitano y poemas 1973–1975*. Barcelona: Colección Ambito Poesía, 1976.
*Usuras y figuraciones*. Barcelona: Lumen, 1979.

Criticism

Gil de Biedma, Jaime. ''*Metropolitano*: La visión poética de Carlos Barral (1958).'' Prologue to *Metropolitano y poemas 1973-1975*. Barcelona: Colección Ambito Poesía, 1976.
Hernández, Antonio. *Una promoción desheredada: La poética del 50*. Bilbao: Colección ''Guérnica,'' 1978. 145–48; 312–13.

Victoria Wolff Unruh

**BARRERA, Cayetano Alberto de la** (1815, Madrid–1872, Madrid), bibliographer, biographer, literary critic. As biographer, his introduction to the Spanish Academy's (*Academia Española) edition of Lope de *Vega's works brought to light new information, using the correspondence between Lope and the Duke of Sessa. Barrera's most important effort is the *Catálogo bibliográfico y biográfico* *del teatro antiguo español, desde su origen hasta mediados del siglo XVIII* (1860; Bibliographic and Biographic Catalog of Old Spanish Theater, from Its Origins to the Mid-Eighteenth Century). As a literary scholar, he proved that the *Buscapié allegedly composed by *Cervantes for the *Quijote* was in fact written by Adolfo de *Castro.

BIBLIOGRAPHY

Primary Texts

*Catálogo bibliográfico . . . siglo XVIII.* London: Tamesis, 1968. Facs.
*Nueva biografía de Lope de Vega.* 2 vols. BAE 262 & 263.
*Obras.* Madrid: Rivadeneyra, 1890.

**BARRIONUEVO, Jerónimo de** (1587, Granada–1671, ?), letter-writer, poet, and dramatist. He studied at Alcalá de Henares and Salamanca and was engaged in Italy by the Marquis of Santa Cruz. He retired to the ecclesiastical life and became the treasurer of the Cathedral at Sigüenza in 1622. From 1653 to 1658, he lived in Madrid, during which time he wrote a copious collection of letters to the Dean of Zaragoza commenting on the customs of the day. The *Avisos* (Newsletters), dated from August 1, 1654, to July 24, 1658, are of invaluable importance as a document of the contemporary life of Madrid. They record with journalistic detail foreign and political news, revealing data about public figures, petty gossip of the court, and everyday concerns of the public, such as new plays, fashion, and social gatherings. Barrionuevo also composed poetry and wrote five plays, but the *Avisos* stand as his most interesting and significant work.

BIBLIOGRAPHY

Primary Texts

*Avisos.* Ed. A. Paz y Mélia. Colección de Escritores Castellanos, 95, 96, 99, 103. Madrid: M. Tello, 1892–93.
*Avisos.* BAE 221 & 222.

Deborah Compte

**BARRIOS, Miguel de,** alias Daniel Levi de Barrios (1635, Montilla–1701, Amsterdam), poet, playwright and essayist. A Judaizing *converso, Barrios left Spain in 1650 for fear of the *Inquisition, and went to Leghorn, where he had himself circumcised. He married in 1660, and set out with his wife for Tobago in search of a new life. She died during the voyage and he returned to Europe, this time to the Low Countries. In 1662, Barrios married again. For the next twelve years he lived a double life, as a Jew in Amsterdam with his family and as a Christian in Brussels, where he was a captain in the Spanish Army. In 1674 he settled permanently in Amsterdam.

Barrios was prolific; his works include thousands of poems, four full-length plays, ten short plays and a number of historical, religious, philosophical and political treatises in prose as well as in verse. His major works are two collections of Baroque poetry: *Flor de Apolo* (1665; The Flower of Apollo) and *Coro de las Musas* (1672; Chorus of the Muses). He admired *Góngora and *Quevedo, and as T. Oelman has pointed out, "he seems to have absorbed all the influences of the *culto* and *conceptista* styles"(221). His poetry in general cannot be appraised as great. His burlesque fables, panegyrics, occasional pieces and complementary poems have mainly a social and historical interest. Barrios is at his best in the religious poems with Jewish themes. His strongest plays are *Pedir favor al contrario* (1665; Asking a Favor of the Enemy) and *El español de Orán* (1665; The Spaniard from Oran). Both were included in *Flor de Apolo;* they are "sword and cape" dramas full of intrigues of jealousy, disguises, mixed-up identities, and other elements typical of the genre. Action dominates over character development and plots are extremely complicated. *See also Conceptismo*; *Culteranismo*.

BIBLIOGRAPHY

Primary Texts

*Coro de las Musas*. Brussels: Vivien, 1672.

*El español de Orán*. Madrid: n.p., 1720.

*Flor de Apolo*. Brussels: Vivien, 1665.

*La poesía religiosa de Miguel de Barrios*. Ed., intro., notes K. R. Scholberg. Columbus: Ohio State UP, 1962.

English Translation

*Marrano Poets of the Seventeenth Century. An Anthology of the Poetry of João Pinto Delgado, Antonio Enríquez Gómez and Miguel de Barrios*. Ed., tr., intro. T. Oelman. East Brunswick, NY: Associated UP, 1982.

Criticism

Besso, H. V. *Dramatic Literature of the Sephardic Jews of Amsterdam in the XVII and XVIII Centuries*. New York: Hispanic Institute, 1947.

Scholberg, K. R. "Miguel de Barrios and the Amsterdam Sephardic Community." *Jewish Quarterly Review* 53 (1962–63): 120–59.

Hector Medina

**BARROS, João de** (1881, Figueira da Foz–1960, Lisbon), Portuguese poet and politician. He graduated in law from the U of Coimbra in 1904 but took up secondary school teaching and worked in the three main cities, Coimbra, Porto and Lisbon. Between 1910 and 1925 he became director of primary and subsequently of secondary education and then secretary to the Ministry of Education. In 1925 he held the post of minister of foreign affairs. Politically, he was eager to revive links between Portugal and Brazil, and this concern is reflected in much of his writing and in nearly all his public speeches. Together with the Brazilian writer Paulo Barreto (pseud. João do Rio) he founded the review *Atlântida* in 1915. He was also active in *Revista Nova* and *A Arte e a Vida* and other publications.

    His literary activity centers on poetry with several volumes of verse beginning with *Versos* (1897; Poems) and *Algas* (1900; Seaweed) and continuing with *O*

*Pomar dos Sonhos* (1900; The Orchard of Dreams); *Entre a Multidão* (1902; Among the Throng); *Dentro da Vida* (1903; Inside Life); *Frente a Frente* (1903; Face to Face); *Caminho do Amor* (1904; Road to Love); *Anteu* (1912; Anteus); *Sísifo* (1923; Sisyphus). He also wrote poetry of a more propagandist bent such as *Oração à Pátria* (2nd ed. 1917; Address to the Motherland), essays in a similar vein extolling the virtues that he saw Portugal as drawing from its geographical position, essays on problems in state education and prose adaptations of *Camões's *Lusiads*, Homer's *Odyssey*, Santa Rita Durão's *Caramuru* as well as adapting Swift's *Gulliver's Travels* for younger Portuguese readers.

Stylistically he tends to a certain neo-romanticism believing in the innate power of humanity and the eventual triumph of Virtue and Justice. He was, not unexpectedly therefore, a staunch supporter of the new republican government and an admirer of poets such as Cesário Verde.

BIBLIOGRAPHY

Primary Works

*Anteu-Sísifo*. Lisbon: Livros do Brasil, 1960.
*Humilde Plenitude*. Lisbon: Livros do Brasil, 1951.

Criticism

Simões, J. G. "João de Barros." In *História da Poesia Portuguesa*. Lisbon: Empresa Nacional de Publicidade, n.d. 282–86.
Sombrio, Carlos (pseud. of António Augusto Esteves). *João de Barros Ensaio literário e bibliográfico*. Figueira da Foz: Popular, 1936.

Peter Fothergill-Payne

**BARTRA, Agustí** (1908, Tarrasa, Catalonia–1982, Tarrasa), novelist, poet, professor. Largely self-taught, Bartra was a man of vast culture with a special interest in classical literature. Most of his work is written in Catalan. Following the Civil War, he was exiled in Algeria, and wrote one of his best-known novels about imprisonment there: *Cristo de 200.000 brazos* (1958; Christ with 200,000 Arms). The characters are the four occupants of an improvised hut in a concentration camp, dreamers and men of vision whose moral superiority raises them above the surrounding misery, achieving effects of lyric suffering and ethical serenity. He published a volume of poetry, theater and prose written in Castilian with the title *Odisseu* (1953; Odyssey), structured around the figure of Ulysses, the eternal wanderer (an obvious symbol of the exile or expatriate). Bartra lived for many years in Mexico, taught as a visiting professor at the U of Maryland, and, late in life, at the U of Barcelona.

*L'Estel sobre el mar* (1942; Trail in the Sea) is a collection of short stories, while *Oda a Cataluña dels tropics* (1942; Ode to Catalunya from the Tropics) and *L'arbre de foc* (1946; Tree of Fire) are volumes of poetry, as are also *Màrsias* (1946), *Màrsias y Adila* (1948; English tr., 1962) and *Démeter* (1961). *La lluna mor amb aigua* (1968; The Moon Dies with Water) is a novel which was designed as a symbolic narration of mankind's essential history, incarnated in the figure of a Mexican woodcutter, Braulio, who lives on the slopes of Popocatepetl with his wife and his dog. The deathbed recollections of the protagonist open doors to the past, with ancestral or collective memory, which are intertwined with childhood scenes (a technique similar to that used much later by Carlos Fuentes in *La muerte de Artemio Cruz*). The dying protagonist's memories include words in forgotten languages, ancient gods and rites which he does not consciously understand, as well as the epic move of the Aztecs from Aztlán to Chalco, which lasted eighty years, mixed with incidents from the history of the Spaniards in Mexico, from the days of conquest up to the revolutionary present.

BIBLIOGRAPHY

Primary Texts

*Cristo de 200.000 brazos.* Mexico: Novaro, 1958.
*Deméter.* Mexico: Universidad Veracruzana, 1961.
*La luna muere con agua.* Mexico: Mortiz, 1968. Spanish tr.
*Odiseo.* Tr. R. Xirau and A. Bartra. Mexico: Fondo de cultura económica, 1955.
*Quetzalcoatl.* Mexico: Tezontle, 1960.

English Translations

Excerpt of *Cristo de 200.000 bracos.* Tr. E. D. Randall. In *Literary Review* 7 (1963): 77–94.
*Marsias and Adila.* Tr. E. Randall. In *El corno emplumado* 4 (1962): 1–207.

Criticism

Andújar, M. *La literatura catalana en el destierro.* Mexico: Costa-Amic, 1949.
Gironella, Cecilia. *El ojo de Polifemo. Visión de la obra de A. Bartra.* Mexico: Costa-Amic, 1957.
Marra-López, J. R. *Narrativa española fuera de España (1939–1961).* Madrid: Guadarrama, 1963. 490–93.
Zelaya Kolker, Marielena. *Testimonios americanos de los escritores españoles transterrados de 1939.* Madrid: Cultura Hispánica, 1985. 234–38.

Janet Pérez

**BARTRINA, Joaquín María** (1850, Reus–1880, Barcelona), journalist and poet. Bartrina was greatly influenced by developments in the natural sciences (he was the first to translate Darwin into Castilian) and in philosophy. His wide-ranging articles and essays written for newspapers reveal a determined effort to order his thoughts on political and social organization, on morality, on the value and significance of human life, in conformity with the findings of contemporary thinkers. His verse chronicles the painfulness of his efforts. The poems in *Algo* (1874; Something) earned him a reputation as a pessimist and a skeptic; however, his verse laments on the implications of a materialist view of life are at odds with the sanguine belief in progress advanced in his prose essays. Toward the end of his life he supported the Catalonian regional movement (*Renaixença*) by writing for newspapers such as the *Renaixensa* and *Diari Català*. He also began to favor Catalan for his poetry. Bartrina was admired by *Azorín for his poetic prose and for his sincerity in matters concerning religious unbelief. *See also* Catalan literature.

BIBLIOGRAPHY

  Primary Texts

*Algo*. Barcelona: López, 1924.
*Joaquín María Bartrina. Obras en prosa y verso*. Ed. J. Sardá. Barcelona and Madrid: Texidó y Parera, 1881.

  Criticism

O'Connor, D. J. "Darwinism in Joaquín María Bartrina 1850–1880." *KRQ* 32 (1985): 393–404.

                                                                                    D. J. O'Connor

**BASTERRA, Ramón de** (1888, Bilbao–1928, Madrid), Basque poet, diplomat, and traveler. He studied law and joined the Spanish diplomatic corps as a young man. He served as attaché in Rome and Bucharest (where he was stationed at the start of World War I) and later in Venezuela. Upon his return to Spain he worked at the State Department in Madrid. Basterra was an early and enthusiastic proponent of the concept of Hispanism; he traveled incessantly in Europe and Latin America always in search of traces left by Spanish culture. Basterra died in 1928 in a mental asylum.

   Basterra's works are permeated with his concerns for history and Spanish culture. His enthusiasm for his own Basque roots predominates in his early works: in *La sencillez de los seres* (1923; The Simplicity of the People) he evokes his native landscapes and the simple life of his countryfolk; while in *Los labios del monte* (Madrid, 1925; The Lips of the Mount) he takes a more complex approach by composing an epic poem that captures the essential traditions and symbols of the Basque country. His prose works, *La obra de Trajano* (Madrid, 1921; Trajan's Work) and *Los navíos de la Ilustración* (Caracas, 1925; The Ships of the Enlightenment), are direct results of his involvement with Spanish topics while in Rumania and Venezuela. His enthusiasm for Rome and classical culture is best exemplified by his book *Las ubres luminosas* (Bilbao, 1923; The Luminous Udders), where he exhibits a masterful control of form.

   Basterra's ideas on Hispanism are synthesized in his concept of "la Sobre-españa." "Superspain" represents his personal attempt to link Spanish culture to the past and to the future by tracing Spain's ties to Rome and the classical world and then extending its ramifications to Spanish America where, according to him, classical culture still survives in the strength of the common language and traditions.

   In poetry, Basterra gave shape to many of these cultural theories and myths through the creation of his best-known symbol, the character Vírulo. Both Basterra and Vírulo loved and exalted the strength of Rome and Hispanic traditions. His fundamental works in this line are *Vírulo, las mocedades* (1924; Young Vírulo), a book written in a baroque style that shows the influence of Gongorism, and *Vírulo, mediodía* (1927; Vírulo, High Noon), where he uses the latest Vanguardist trends, with emphasis on Futurism. Both books attempt to establish the basic unity and order of the classical world and its survival in Spanish culture. *See also* Góngora.

BIBLIOGRAPHY

Primary Text

*Llama romance.* Ed. Guillermo Díaz Plaja. Bilbao: Publicaciones de la Diputación de Viscaya, 1971.

English Translation

Four Poems. Tr. anon. In *Alhambra* 1 (1929): 57.

Criticism

Arena, Carlos Antonio. *Ramón de Basterra.* Madrid: Cultura Hispánica, 1953.

Díaz Plaja, Guillermo. *La poesía y el pensamiento de Ramón de Basterra.* Bilbao: Juventud, 1941.

Izalde, Ignacio. "Ramón de Basterra y el mundo clásico." *Letras de Duesto* 13.27 (1983): 47–66.

María A. Salgado

**BATLLÓ, José** (1939, Caldes de Montbui, Barcelona– ), poet and critic. He was educated in Andalusia, where he lived from 1943 to 1963, when he returned to Catalonia, establishing his residence in Barcelona. Although employed in industrial administration, he has accumulated many credits as a translator to Castilian of various Catalan poets, including Pere *Quart, Salvador *Espriu and Joaquim Horta, and has published poetry, stories and articles in many periodicals, including *Papeles de Son Armadans, Insula, Signo, Cuadernos Hispanoamericanos, El Corno Emplumado, Pájaro Cascabel, Avance* and others. In 1964 he founded the poetry collection "El Bardo" which he directs and which has been influential in the discovery and careers of many new poets. Batlló has published several books of his own poetry as well, including *La señal* (1965; The Signal); *La mesa puesta* (1966; The Prepared Table); and *Las raíces* (1967; Roots). He has done anthologies of the "new" poets in Castilian—*Antología de la nueva poesía española* (1968), an indispensable point of reference for the "generation" of 1956–71—and of 20th-c. Catalan poetry (bilingual edition), as well as a study of the life and works of the Catalan poet Joan *Salvat-Papasseit. *Tocaron mi corazón* (n.d.; They Touched My Heart) is another collection of original poetry.

BIBLIOGRAPHY

Primary Texts

*Antología de la nueva poesía española.* Madrid: El Bardo, 1968.

*Canción del solitario.* Málaga: Guadalhorce, 1970.

Janet Pérez

**BAYO, Ciro** (1859, Madrid–1939, Madrid), novelist, author of travel books and histories of Spanish American countries. His extensive travels through Europe and America provided the material for his largely autobiographical writings.

The life of Bayo, the illegitimate son of a banker, reads like a *picaresque novel. As a young man he ran away from home and joined up with a group of Carlists, was taken prisoner, and was released at the end of the war. In 1876 he first visited Havana, and on his return to Spain spent five years (1878–83) studying law at the U of Barcelona, although he never entered the legal profession. After traveling through Europe he went to America again—this time Argentina, where in 1889 he became a rural schoolmaster. From there he set out by land to attend the 1893 World Exposition in Chicago and got as far as Sucre, Bolivia. He visited Chile and Peru and lived for some time in eastern Bolivia before finally returning to Spain in 1900.

Once back in Madrid, he became friends with Pío *Baroja and plunged into the literary life of the capital. In times of financial hardship he earned money writing books on sexual hygiene. Bayo was of a bohemian nature, totally indifferent to money and much opposed to false vanity. He died in 1939 shortly after the end of the Civil War.

His works can be classified into five groups. First are the novels set in Spain, including his two most important ones, *El peregrino entretenido* (1910; The Pilgrim Entertained) and *Lazarillo español* (1911; Spanish Lazarillo). Both are in the picaresque vein and close to the *Generation of 1898 in their criticism of the nation. Second are the Spanish American travel accounts, notably *Por la América desconocida* (1920; Through Unknown America). The third group is composed of his historical writings, including *Historia moderna de la América Española* (1930; Modern History of Spanish America). The fourth group treats fictionally the adventures of the conquistadors and includes *Los caballeros del Dorado* (1930; The Knights of El Dorado). Finally there are the miscellaneous writings, e.g., the treatises on hygiene, poetry, and vocabularies.

BIBLIOGRAPHY

Primary Texts

*Aucafilú. Epoca de Rosas.* Madrid: Caro Raggio, 1916.
*Los caballeros del Dorado.* Madrid: Suárez, 1930.
*Higiene sexual del soltero. El amor libre y la prostitución. Alteraciones sexuales.* Madrid: Marqués, 1902.
*Historia moderna de la América Española, desde la Independencia hasta nuestros días.* Madrid: Caro Raggio, 1930.
*Lazarillo español. Guía de vagos en tierras de España por un peregrino industrioso.* Prol. Azorín. Madrid: Beltrán, 1911.
*Manual del lenguaje criollo de Centro y Sudamérica.* Madrid: Caro Raggio, 1931.
*El peregrino entretenido. Viaje romanesco.* Madrid: Hernando, 1910.
*Por la América desconocida.* 4 vols. Madrid: Caro Raggio, 1920.

Criticism

Baroja, Ricardo. *Gente del 98.* Barcelona: Juventud, 1952.
Cardenal Iracheta, Manuel. "El peregrino escritor don Ciro Bayo y de Segurola (1859–1939)." *Clavileño* 17 (1952): 33–38.

Silverman, Joseph H. "Valle Inclán y Ciro Bayo." *NRFH* 14 (1960): 73–88.
Zwez, Richard E. "Ciro Bayo y la Generación del 98." Diss. Louisiana State U, 1974.

James F. Brown

**BÉCQUER, Gustavo Adolfo,** pseudonym of Gustavo Adolfo Domínguez Bastida; also known as Adolfo García and Adolfo Rodríguez (1836, Seville–1870, Madrid), poet and prose writer. Orphaned at a very early age, he entered the aristocratic Colegio San Telmo for maritime studies in 1846, but soon after his enrollment the Colegio closed and he went to live with his childless godmother, Manuela Monnehay. In her small library he became acquainted with some classics of West European literature. His father, José Domínguez Bécquer (pseudonym of José Domínguez Insausti [1805–41]), had been a mildly successful painter whose brother, Joaquín, had achieved even greater renown both in Seville and beyond the Pyrenees. Gustavo Adolfo, when he left San Telmo, was apprenticed to another successful painter (who had been José's student), José Cabral Bejarano, and later, to his own uncle, who soon pronounced his nephew an untalented painter with mediocre writing ability; he promptly encouraged the youth to abandon palette and easel for pen and paper.

In 1854 Gustavo left Seville for Madrid, where he was soon joined by his older brother, Valeriano (1833–70), from whom he was inseparable until Valeriano's death. In Madrid Gustavo suffered the bohemian trials and tribulations of an unsponsored, fledgling writer, doing clerical work and, generally, merely existing. In 1857 he entered a working relationship with an entrepreneur whose name appears in many sources but about whom relatively little is still known: Juan de la Puerta Vizcaíno. Together they conceived an ambitious project: to trace Spanish religious history through a study of its churches, synagogues and mosques. It was to be a multi-volume work for which a roster of luminaries was recruited. A prospectus was prepared and submitted to Isabel II for her patronage, which she granted in limited form; the book was to be financed, otherwise, by public subscription. The one and only volume published (and the only work of Bécquer that appeared in book form during his life) was devoted to Toledo. Titled *Historia de los templos de España*, it appeared in installments in 1857 and 1858. Its progress was punctuated by many interruptions, a change of publishers and a lawsuit that was eventually settled in Bécquer's favor, but by 1862 all interest in it was lost and it was destined not to be reproduced again until 1979. The work merits interest because its prose already contains, in fragmentary form, many of the images and spirit that later characterize Bécquer's *rimas* (verses) and prose writings. The articles in the book follow a pattern of subjective observations that surround factual material; much of the technical information is plagiarized and only one of its many illustrations bears Bécquer's signature. The poet confesses early in the work that he has undertaken a task beyond his intellectual resources, and he often fantasizes about the past that surrounds the monuments that he is describing. It is in these subjective passages that the genesis of much of his poetry and prose can be found; because of the technical difficulties that obstructed the project, including its change of editors, it is not possible to determine to what extent Bécquer was responsible for the plagiarized sections. Among the sources are Padre Juan de *Mariana and, to a major degree, the author of a tourist handbook on Toledo, Ramón Sixto Parro.

After a frustrated romance with Julia Espín, whose elevated social class evidently intimidated and discouraged Bécquer from even approaching her, in 1861 he married Casta Esteban, the daughter of his physician. Their tempestuous marriage was interrupted by irreconcilable differences aggravated by the presence in their home of Gustavo's brother, Valeriano, who had moved in with them in 1863; however, the couple was briefly reconciled shortly after Valeriano's death. In 1864 Luis González Brabo, prime minister under Isabel II, obtained for Gustavo the post of censor of novels, a position that he held until 1865. He was later reappointed in 1866 and he held the post until the overthrow of Isabel II ended the political career of his friend and benefactor González Brabo.

Gustavo died in Madrid on December 22, 1870, a few months after his brother; his remains and Valeriano's were transferred to Seville in 1913. He left, in addition to his widow, three children, whose fate is unknown to this day.

Bécquer published only one book, as noted above; the remainder of his opus was published, during his lifetime, in journals with which often the poet himself, his brother or close friends, like Ramón *Rodríguez Correa, were affiliated: *Album de señoritas y correo de la moda*, *La España musical y literaria*, *La Crónica*, *Museo Universal*, *El nene*, *El Contemporáneo*, *El Mundo* and *La ilustración de Madrid*. The works that appeared in these journals can be divided into poetry (*rimas*), prose fiction (*leyendas*, legends), and editorials (*Desde mi celda* [From My Cell], *Cartas literarias a una mujer* [Literary Letters to a Woman]). Under the pseudonyms Adolfo García and Adolfo Rodríguez he also wrote or collaborated in *zarzuelas*, some of which were produced with negligible to mild success in his lifetime; others were never to be presented onstage.

The *rimas* are all brief and written predominantly in lines of 7 and 11 syllables, with assonant rhyme. Their most frequent themes are love, poetry and the attendant frustrations of each. The language of the *rimas* is both traditional and innovative: their simple style is reminiscent of the Spanish classics; they also contain the poet's expressed desire to create a new language replacing words with sighs, laughter, music and color. His decision to call his verses *rimas* rather than *poemas* or *versos* is only one example of his determination to change poetic language. He often writes in a painterly style visualizing objects through mist, veils and even through the soft colors of the palette; in addition, he strips reality of its commonplaces and often goes to the essence of matter (lips instead of mouth; pupils instead of eyes). Because of their dreamlike quality and brevity these poems have been linked with the poetry of other continental Romantics, mainly Heine; although Bécquer did not know German, it is possible that he had read Heine's verses when they started appearing in Spanish (1857), but by that time he had already written parts of the *Historia de los templos de España*, in which much of the imagery is already present. It is extremely difficult to determine the exact chronology of Bécquer's writings, but the early 1860s seem to have been extremely active. That would consequently make his early and final years in Madrid periods of (a) preparation for his greatest creative years and (b) the decline of his creativity, respectively. González Brabo was interested in publishing the *rimas* in book form; to that end Bécquer prepared the *Libro de los gorriones* (Book of Swallows), but with the political upheaval in which González lost his position and influence, the ms. was lost forever. The one that does exist, housed in Madrid's National Library, is Bécquer's attempt at reconstructing his earlier effort. The Roman numerals traditionally assigned to the *rimas* correspond to the order given to them in the first posthumous edition of Bécquer's works, collected, published and prefaced by Ramón Rodríguez Correa, with the assistance of other friends, in 1871. In the *Libro de los gorriones* the *rimas* are arranged differently and they are identified by Arabic numerals. In addition to expressing his ideas about creativity in some of the *rimas*, Bécquer returned to the topic in the *Cartas literarias a una mujer*, and in his equally celebrated letters *Desde mi celda*, written while convalescing in a monastery in Veruela. These prose works address the theme of poetry and express aversion to the impact of new technology upon traditional life; they profess nonetheless a faith in the future of Spain. In other prose articles he wrote about popular customs and reviewed the work of other poets; the most widely quoted of these literary reviews is the one which discusses Agusto Ferrán's *La Soledad* (1861; Solitude), for Bécquer records his own position on traditional poetry.

Bécquer also wrote over two dozen tales that he called *Leyendas* (legends), inspired by medieval lore and the Spanish *romancero, Toledo's monuments, orientalia, religion and superstition. In almost all of them the theme of unconsummated love is a leitmotif and a great body of them follows a pattern in which the author (1) states the origin and nature of the tale he is to narrate: often attributing its source to oral tradition, (2) narrates the tale itself, and (3) gives a summary of the relevancy of the tale to real life. This final aspect of the tale often takes the form of a philosophical statement. Hence, it can be said that some of the *leyendas*, besides their anecdotal value, have a didactic component. Bécquer also produced drawings that appeared in some of the journals of the day, like *Almanaque de Gil Blas* and *Almanaque de Don Diego de noche*; these are signed "G."

Bécquer's importance cannot be overestimated; even among his contemporaries, his voice was recognized as the turning point and culmination of Spanish *Romanticism; after his death major poets from Darío to *Alberti and *Aleixandre readily acknowledged their debt to him. The profound emotion that underlies the superficial simplicity of his lines has progressively attracted the recognition of scholars; in addition to being one of the most researched poets in Spanish literary history, he enjoys the greatest popularity among Spanish speakers all over the world.

BIBLIOGRAPHY

Primary Texts

*Obras completas*. 13th ed. Madrid: Aguilar, 1969. (Contains incomplete *Historia de los templos de España* and no theater.)

*Del olvido en el ángulo oscuro, Páginas abandonadas de Gustavo Adolfo Bécquer*. Ed. Dionisio Gamallo Fieros. 2nd ed. Madrid: Valera, 1948.

*Historia de los templos de España*. Ed., intro. J. R. Arboleda. Barcelona: Puvill, 1979.

*Historia de los templos de España*. Ed. Dolores Cabra Loredo. Madrid: Museo Universal, 1985. Facs.

*Libro de los gorriones*. Eds. G. G. Gallant, R. Balbín, and A. Roldán. Madrid: Ministerio de Educación y Ciencia, 1971. Facs. (Also contains Becquer's *Introducción sinfónica* and *La mujer de piedra*.)

*Rimas*. Ed., notes R. Pageard. Madrid: CSIC, 1972.

*Teatro de Gustavo Adolfo Bécquer*. Ed. study, J. A. Tamayo. Madrid: CSIC, 1949.

English Translations

*Romantic Legends of Spain, by Gustavo Adolfo Becquer*. Tr. C. Bates and K. L. Bates. New York: Crowell, 1909.

*Symphony of Love, Las Rimas, by Gustavo Adolfo Becquer*. Tr. David F. Altabe. Long Beach, NY: Regina, 1974.

Criticism

Benítez, Rubén. *Bécquer tradicionalista*. Madrid: Gredos, 1971.

———. *Ensayo de una bibliografía razonada de Gustavo Adolfo Bécquer*. Buenos Aires: U of Buenos Aires, 1961.

Billick, David, and Walter A. Dobrian. "Bibliografía selectiva y comentada de estudios becquerianos, 1960–1980." *Hispania* 69.2 (1986): 278–302.

Brown, Rica. *Bécquer*. Barcelona: Aedos, 1963.

Carpintero, Heliodoro. *Bécquer de par en par*. 2nd ed. Madrid: Ínsula, 1972.

Díaz, José Pedro. *Gustavo Adolfo Bécquer. Vida y poesía*. 3rd ed. Madrid: Gredos, 1971.

Díez Taboada, Juan María. *La mujer ideal. Aspectos y fuentes de las rimas de Gustavo Adolfo Bécquer*. Madrid: CSIC, 1965.

Entrambasaguas, Joaquín de. *La obra poética de Bécquer en su discriminación creadora y erótica*. Madrid: Vasallo de Mumbert, 1974.

*Estudios sobre Gustavo Adolfo Bécquer*. Madrid: CSIC, 1972.

King, Edmund L. *Gustavo Adolfo Bécquer; From Painter to Poet. Together with a Concordance of the Rimas*. Mexico: Porrúa, 1953.

Montesinos, Rafael. *Bécquer. Biografía e imágenes*. Barcelona: Editorial RM, 1977.

Schneider, Franz. *Gustavo Adolfo Bécquer's Leben unt Schaffen unter besonderer Betonung des chronologischen Elementes*. Borna and Leipzig: Noske, 1914.

Sebold, Russell P. *Gustavo Adolfo Bécquer*. Madrid: Taurus, 1982.

Joseph R. Arboleda

**BELLIDO, José María** (1922, San Sebastián– ), Spanish playwright, a member of the so-called Underground group, whose work dates from the late 1940s through the end of the Franco era. Like most of the Underground writers, Bellido has had difficulty publishing and producing his works in Spain, with slightly better fortune abroad (contrary to expectations of writers in this group, probabilities of productions did not improve significantly following the death of Franco). The most profound impact for Bellido's theater came as a result of his reading the works of Bertolt Brecht in 1959, which provoked an ethical crisis in Bellido as to his purpose as an author. Imagination, fantasy and bizarre irony are typical of the most characteristic Bellido works, which range from allegory to satire. Vaguely expressionistic and remotely indebted to *Valle-Inclán, Bellido's theater sometimes approaches the Kafkaesque, sometimes the absurd, without being either completely. *Tren a F . . .* (1960; *Train to H . . .* , 1970) portrays some of the inherent contradictions of conformist religiosity, while *El pan y el arroz o Geometría en amarillo* (1966; *Bread and Rice, or Geometry in Yellow*, 1970) approaches the question of world hunger, multinational trusts and the abuse or manipulation of power. Bellido anticipates the notion of chromosomal domination as the geometric self-multiplication by Oriental children proves to be an invincible resistance. In Bellido's own opinion, his most significant and original creations are 23 short plays termed "temblores" (quiverings), gathered together in *La suite fantástica* during the early 1970s, although published only in bits and pieces. Paradox, the rejection of all formal limitations, humanistic concerns, fantasy and iconoclastic originality make the *temblores* perhaps the most interesting innovation in Spanish theater since the *esperpentos* of Valle-Inclán.

BIBLIOGRAPHY

English Translations

"Fantastic Suite: Tremor No. 3: Sol-fa for Butterflies." Tr. M. C. Wellwarth. In *Modern International Drama* 6.2 (1973): 39–56.

*Train to H . . .* , tr. R. Flores, and *Bread and Rice or Geometry in Yellow,* tr. R. Lima. In *The New Wave Spanish Drama.* Ed. G. E. Wellwarth. New York: New York UP, 1970.

Criticism

Wellwarth, G. *Spanish Underground Drama.* University Park: Pennsylvania State UP; Puerto Rico: Villalar, 1978.

Janet Pérez

**BELMONTE BERMÚDEZ, Luis de** (1587?, Seville–1650, Seville), playwright, poet, biographer. As a youth he traveled to the New World and in 1605 was in Lima, according to the prologue of his play, *Algunas hazañas de las muchas de don García Hurtado de Mendoza, marqués de Cañete* (1622; Some Feats among the Many of García Hurtado de Mendoza, Marquis of Cañete). Belmonte accompanied a Captain Quirós in his travel, and a historical account, titled *Historia del descubrimiento de las regiones australes por el general Pedro Fernández de Quirós* (*The Voyages of Pedro Fernández de Quirós, 1595 to 1606*, 1904) has been attributed to him. The ms. was not published until 1876, and the attribution has been challenged, but not disproved.

Belmonte's verse includes *Vida del Padre Maestro Ignacio de Loyola* (1609; Life of Father Ignatius of Loyola), an epic poem depicting the saint's life, and

*La Hispálica* (unedited until 1921; Hispalica [Hispalis was the Roman name for Seville]). As a dramatist of the school of Lope de *Vega, Belmonte composed about 25 plays, some written in collaboration with authors such as *Mira de Amescua, *Ruiz de Alarcón, Luis *Vélez de Guevara, Guillén de *Castro, *Moreto, and *Martínez de Meneses. His most notable works include *El sastre del Campillo* (1624; The Tailor of Campillo [published in Part 27 of Lope de Vega's plays]); *La renegada de Valladolid* (1652; The Renegade of Valladolid); and *El diablo predicador y mayor contrario amigo* (1653; The Devil, Preacher and Most Contrary Friend). *See also* Siglo de Oro.

BIBLIOGRAPHY

Primary Texts

*La Hispálica.* Ed., intro. P. M. Piñero Ramírez. Seville: Diputación Provincial, 1974.
*Historia del descubrimiento de las regiones australes por el general Pedro Fernández de Quirós.* 3 vols. Madrid: Hernández, 1876 & 1881.
*El sastre del Campillo.* Intro., notes F. A. de Armas. Valencia: Soler, 1975.

English Translation

*The Voyages of Pedro Fernández de Quirós, 1595 to 1606.* Tr., ed. C. Markham. 2 vols. London: Hakluyt, 1904.

Criticism

de Armas, F. A. "La lealtad en *El sastre del Campillo.*" *Hispanófila* 43 (1971): 9–16.
Kincaid, W. A. "Life and Works of Luis de Belmonte Bermúdez (1587?–1650?)." *RH* 74 (1928): 1–260.
Piñero Ramírez, P. M. *Luis de Belmonte Bermúdez.* Seville: Diputación Provincial, 1976.

Deborah Compte

**BELO, Ruy de Moura** (1933, São João da Ribeira–1978, Queluz), Portuguese contemporary poet. While a law student at the U of Coimbra, Belo joined the Opus Dei in 1951 and, for ten years, studied both civil law and, later in Rome, canon law, in which he earned his doctorate. He also served in the bureaucratic apparatus of the Salazar regime as a censor. In 1961, he abandoned both the lay Catholic brotherhood and law, and enrolled as a student at the Faculty of Letters in Lisbon. As a translator, he rendered into Portuguese French authors and Jorge Luis Borges; and, from 1971 to 1977, he was Lecturer in Portuguese at the U of Madrid.

The evolution from dogmatic Catholicism and Salazarism to a break with both his faith-entrenched religiosity and his political and career commitments to the dictatorship marks Belo's first two volumes of verse. In *Aquele grande rio Eufrates* (1961; That Great River, the Euphrates), Belo communicates the crisis and the rupture as a clash between the metaphysical and the worldly in rather abstract language replete with biblical allusions. The subsequent *O problema da habitação—alguns aspectos* (1962; The Quandary of Living: Some Aspects) pictures the problematic as twofold: the collapse of certitude, whether religious or socio-political, and the anxiety wrought by an art unbound by strictures of form or content.

*Boca bilíngüe* (1966; Multiple Meanings) is in the tradition of the "cantiga de mal dizer," where satire and skepticism lure the poet's sensibility. *Homem de palavra[s]* (1969; A Man of [His] Word[s]) reveals an accommodation with the lost faith as in the generational poem, "Nós os vencidos do catolicismo" (We Who Were Vanquished by Catholicism), and the rise of a new aesthetic, humanistic creed based on poetry and on the word made verse. It also underscores the consolidation of a new poetic diction oriented toward the colloquial without rejecting the metaphysical.

Later books, such as *Transporte no tempo* (1973; Borne through Time), affirm solitude and alienation as the fulcrum for the poet's mission as perturber of social, intellectual, and aesthetic norms. *País possível* (1973; The Possible Country) examines Belo's being ill at ease with his nationality and the malaise of pre-Revolution Portugal. Consisting of one long poem—"Pequena História Trágico-Terrestre" (Brief Tragi-Terrestrial History)—whose title plays on the classic Shipwreck Narratives of the Portuguese Overseas Expansion, this elegy confirms Belo's refocusing on Iberian themes and literary traditions. Hence, the following *A margem da alegria* (1974; The Riverbank of Happiness) is a reworking of the historical legend of Iberia's quintessential victim of love and politics, Inês de Castro (see *Inés de Castro, Leyenda de*) with a subtext of a personal love affair. *Toda a terra* (1976; All of the Land) is divided into a first part dealing with Portugal and a second with Spain, and is influenced by an Unamunian pre-occupation with this tragic land which is the split peninsula and with an equally Unamunian nostalgia for the lost God. Again, in the valedictory *Despeço-me da terra da alegria* (1977; I Bid Farewell to the Land of Happiness), Belo dwells upon the tradition of melancholy, especially as expressed in António Nobre's *Só* (Alone) and as perceived by such as *Unamuno as a Portuguese characteristic. Yet, he also re-asserts his belief in the poet's primacy and in his craft, the word.

Although characterized mostly by free verse, Belo's poetics is one of intricate internal and assonantal rhymes and alliterations and, also, of alexandrine and decasyllabic meters. In the poetry which appears in Portugal in the latter part of this century, Belo's is a unique voice and a school unto himself.

BIBLIOGRAPHY

Primary Text

*Obra Poética de Ruy Belo.* Ed. Joaquim Manuel Magalhães. 3 vols. Lisbon: Presença, 1984.

Criticism

Guimarães, Fernando. "Acerca da poesia de Ruy Belo: Um Espaço de Sentido." *Colóquio* 73 (n.d.): 50–55.

Jaime H. da Silva

**BEÑA, Cristóbal de** (fl. 1813, ?–?, ?), poet, fabulist. He emigrated to London for political reasons. His *Fábulas políticas* (1813; Political Fables) are heavily influenced by La Fontaine and Tomás de *Iriarte. Most of his poetry appears in *La lira de la libertad* (1813; Liberty's Lyre).

BIBLIOGRAPHY

Primary Texts

*Fábulas políticas*. Prol. L. Montañés. Madrid: Suárez, 1946. Facs.
*La lira de la libertad*. London: M'Dowall, 1813.
Various poems in BAE 61 and 68.

**BENAVENTE, Jacinto** (1866, Madrid–1954, Madrid), Spanish playwright.
Benavente was born in Madrid to a wealthy upper-middle-class family. His
father, a famous pediatrician, died when Jacinto was still a university student.
The future playwright immediately abandoned his law studies and began to
cultivate the theater. A bachelor, he devoted his life primarily to travel and to
the theater, confessing that he rarely read non-dramatic literature. His success
as dramatist began with his second production (1892) and continued to the end
of his life. He was, however, strongly criticized by many intellectuals, in part
because of his refusal to support the Allied Forces in World War I and in part
because his theater was seen as excessively complaisant or negative. In spite of
this opposition he was awarded the Nobel Prize for Literature in 1922. Although
his most important plays were written in the first two decades of this c., he
continued to produce new plays throughout his life.

Benavente is generally considered the most important dramatist in Spain since
the *Siglo de Oro, although he is also criticized for not having enriched Spanish
theater more than he did. His is, in many respects, a continuation of *la alta
comedia* of *Tamayo y Baus and Adelardo *López de Ayala, with an emphasis
on bourgeois themes, such as the conflict between new and old money, or the
problem of hypocrisy in middle-class relations. At the same time, Benavente
rejects the Romantic tradition and in particular the neo-Romantic excesses of
the Spanish dramatist José *Echegaray. Benavente stresses dialogue over action,
ironic repartee over emotional revelation. Conflict is often muted in Benavente's
theater; major confrontations take place offstage and scenes end with anticli-
mactic verbal duels between characters who lack the passion to produce real
dramatic conflict. Although Benavente has been criticized for the excessive
"wordiness" of his theater, it is largely his dialogue that has contributed to his
stature as a dramatist. Witty, fast-moving, often gratuitous, it has lost none of
its vitality over the years. In many of his plays, the characters exist only to
engage in verbal play and consequently, Benavente achieved no major dramatic
characterizations.

Benavente's most important works are those written between 1900 and 1920.
It was in these years that he created Moraleda, a fictitious Castilian town that
synthesizes provincial Spanish bourgeois society of the period. Moraleda is the
setting for *La gobernadora* (1901; *The Governor's Wife*, 1918), *El primo Roldán*
(1901; Cousin Roldan), *El marido de su viuda* (1908; *His Widow's Husband*
1917), and *Pepa Doncel* (1928), among others. During the same period Benavente wrote his two well known rural plays, *Señora Ama* (1908) and *La malquerida*
(1913; *The Passion Flower*, 1917–24). With this last play, Benavente creates

one of his strongest characters, the tragic Raimunda, whose efforts to reconcile her husband and her daughter by a previous marriage fuel their incestuous passion, which subsequently destroys the entire family. *La noche del sábado* (1903; *Saturday Night*, 1918), with its fusion of fantasy and reality, is considered by some critics to be the most successful modernist play produced in Spain. *Los intereses creados* (1907; *The Bonds of Interest*, 1967), generally considered to be Benavente's best work, draws on the Italian *commedia dell'arte* as well as the Spanish Golden Age theater tradition. The play exemplifies Benavente's masterful use of dialogue, his predilection for an ironic tone and focus that reflect a skeptical, almost nihilistic vision, and his emphasis on language over action. *See also* Contemporary Spanish Theatere; Theater in Spain.

BIBLIOGRAPHY

Primary Texts

*Comedias escogidas*. Madrid: Aguilar, 1978.
*Los intereses creados*. Ed. Fernando Lázaro Carreter. Madrid: Cátedra, 1974.
*Obras completas*. 3rd ed. 7 vols. Madrid: Aguilar, 1945–46.

English Translations

*The Bonds of Interest*. Tr. John G. Underhill. New York: F. Ungar, 1967.
*The Governor's Wife*. Tr. John G. Underhill. Boston: R. G. Badger, 1918.
*Plays of Jacinto Benavente*. Tr. J. G. Underhill. 4 vols. New York: Scribner, 1917–24.
*The Prince Who Learned Everything Out of Books*. Tr. John G. Underhill. Boston: R.
      G. Badger, 1919.
*Saturday Night*. Tr. John G. Underhill. Boston: R. G. Badger, 1918.

Criticism

Borel, Jean Paul. *El teatro de lo imposible*. Madrid: Guadarrama, 1966.
Díaz, José A. *Jacinto Benavente and His Theater*. New York: Las Américas, 1972.
Ruiz Ramón, Francisco. *Historia del teatro español: Siglo XX*. Madrid: Alianza, 1971.
      2nd ed. Madrid: Cátedra, 1975.
Starkey, Walter. *Jacinto Benavente*. London: Oxford UP, 1924.
Torrente Ballester, Gonzalo. *Teatro español contemporáneo*. Madrid: Guadarrama, 1968.

Mary Lee Bretz


**BENEGASI Y LUJÁN, José Joaquín** (1707, Madrid–1770, Madrid), poet, dramatic writer. His verse was often humorous. Poems by his father are included with his own in *Poesías líricas y joco-serias* (1743; Lyric and Joco-Serious Poems). José Joaquín also narrated saints' lives in verse, as in the *Vida del portentoso negro, San Benito de Palermo* (1746?; Life of The Amazing Black Man, St. Benito of Palermo), in *seguidillas, and the *Vida de San Dámaso* (1752; Life of St. Damasus), in *redondillas*. Dramatic compositions include *Comedia (que no lo es) burlesca: Llámenla como quisieren* (1753; Burlesque Play (Which It Isn't): Call It Whatever You Like), and *La campana de descansar* (n.d.; The Rest-Time Bell).

BIBLIOGRAPHY

Primary Texts

*Comedia (que no lo es) burlesca.* . . . 2nd ed. Madrid: García, 1761.
*Obras métricas.* . . . 2nd ed. Madrid: Escrivano, n.d.
*Poesías lýricas y joco-serias.* . . . Madrid: González, 1743.
*Vida del . . . San Benito de Palermo.* Madrid: Escribano, 1763.

**BENET, JUAN** (1927, Madrid– ), engineer, novelist and essayist. By profession a hydrographic engineer, Benet is also one of the leading cultivators of the "new novel," an elitist, experimental genre, recondite in subject and style. Benet's works are typically devoid of linear plot, with deliberate confusion on temporal planes, as well as in matters of character, history, and geography. *Nunca llegarás a nada* (You'll Never be Anything) was his first collection of stories in 1961, followed by his first novel, *Volverás a Región* (1967; You Will Return to Región), a typical example of most of his writing: minimal plot in the traditional sense; fragmentation of various planes; long, convoluted sentences; confusion of facts and characters; mystery; the presence of ruins and menacing characters; atmosphere of anxiety and suspense; and disregard for logic, history, and rationality. Time as a theme is evident, but it is fragmented into cyclical or recurring segments, and is present in the form of memory (which is deemed unreliable). Several generations within a mythical place called Región—a microcosm of Spain and setting of many of Benet's works—intermingle, making individuation almost impossible, but establishing an emotional and experiential continuum that negates quantifiable time. Other examples of his fiction are *Una meditación* (1970; A Meditation, 1982), a dense novel of 329 pages, written in a single paragraph; *Un viaje de invierno* (1972; A Winter's Trip), a series of themes developed almost in musical fashion, as the allusion to Schubert's *Die Winterreise* might suggest (although the "plot" is a re-creation of the myth of Persephone and Koré); and *La otra casa de Mazón* (1973; Mazón's Other House), with its mixture of drama and novel and clear Faulknerian influence. *Una tumba* (1971; A Tomb), a venture into the Gothic narrative, infrequently cultivated by Peninsular writers, treats a theme found in many of Benet's short stories, the influence of the dead and of the spirit world on the vulnerable living. Benet has also essayed the detective genre in *El aire de un crimen* (1980; The Air of a Crime), one of his most popularly oriented works.

In addition to fiction, Benet has written theater (*Agonía confutans* [1969]), several books of essays, including *La inspiración y el estilo* (1966; Inspiration and Style), *Puerta de tierra* (1970; Earthen Door), *El ángel del Señor abandona a Tobías* (1976; The Angel of the Lord Abandons Tobias), *En ciernes* (1976; In the Bud), and *¿Qué fue la guerra civil?* (1976; What Was the Civil War?). Benet scorns critics in general and tends to avoid characteristic Spanish realism and *costumbrismo*, which he considers impoverished and pedestrian, valuing instead mystery and metaphor, myth and metaliterary allusion, as well as the cultivation of language as an end in itself. *See also* Essay; Romanticism.

BIBLIOGRAPHY

Primary Texts

*5 narraciones y dos fábulas* (short stories). Barcelona: Gaya Ciencia, 1972.
*Cuentos completos.* 2 vols. Madrid: Alianza, 1977.
*Del pozo y del Numa: Un ensayo y una leyenda* (fiction). Barcelona: Gaya Ciencia, 1978.
*En el estado* (novel). Madrid: Alfaguara, 1977.
*La moviola de Eurípides* (essay). Madrid: Taurus, 1982.
*Saúl ante Samuel* (novel). Barcelona: Gaya Ciencia, 1980.
*Sub rosa* (short stories). Barcelona: Gaya Ciencia, 1973.
*Teatro.* Madrid: Siglo XXI de España, 1970.
*Trece fábulas y media* (short stories). Madrid: Alfaguara, 1981.

English Translation

*A Meditation.* Tr. Gregory Rabassa. New York: Persea Books, 1982.

Criticism

Compitello, Malcolm A. "Juan Benet and His Critics." *Anales de la Novela de Posguerra*
     3 (1978): 123–41.
Díaz, Janet W. "Variations on the Theme of Death in the Short Fiction of Juan Benet."
     *American Hispanist* 4.36 (May 1979): 6–11.
Herzberger, David. *The Novelistic World of Juan Benet.* Clear Creek, IN: American
     Hispanist, 1976.
Manteiga, Robert, David Herzberger, and Malcolm Compitello, eds. *Critical Approaches
     to the Writings of Juan Benet.* Hanover, NH: UP of New England, 1984.
Manteiga, Robert C. "Benet Ventures beyond Región." *Denver Quarterly* 17.3 (Fall
     1982): 76–82.
Vásquez, Mary S. "The Creative Task: Existential Self-Invention in Benet's *Una me-
     ditación.*" *Selecta* 1 (1980): 118–20.

                                                        Margaret E. W. Jones

**BENEYTO, Miguel** (1560?, ?–1599, ?), poet and dramatist. Charter member
of the Academia de los Nocturnos (Academy of the Night Revelers) with the
pseudonym "Sosiego" (Serenity), Beneyto was one of the Valencian precursors
to Lope de *Vega. Extant are only a few poems and one play, *El hijo obediente*
(n.d.; The Obedient Son). *See also* Academia.

BIBLIOGRAPHY

Primary Texts
*Poetas dramáticos valencianos.* Ed. Juliá Martínez. 2 vols. Madrid: RAE, 1929.

Criticism
Weiger, J. G. *The Valencian Dramatists of Spain's Golden Age.* TWAS 371. Boston:
     Twayne, 1976.

**BENEYTO CUNYAT, María** (1925, Valencia– ), poet, novelist and literary
critic. Born in Valencia but raised in Madrid, Beneyto has published poetry and
prose in both Catalan and Spanish, and her creative writing and criticism have
appeared in Spanish and Venezuelan newspapers and literary magazines. The

recipient of numerous regional and national literary prizes, in 1956 she was awarded the Calvina Telzaroli Italian poetry prize for her *Antología general* (1956; General Anthology). The collection *Poesía* (1976; Poetry) includes selections from many of her earlier works, such as *Eva en el tiempo* (1952; Eve in Time), *Criatura múltiple* (1954; Multiple Child), *Tierra viva* (1956; Live Earth) and *Poemas de la ciudad* (1956; Poems of the City). Beneyto's poetic themes include the dehumanization and social problems of urban life, the existential condition of women, lost love, and the search for religious values. She often employs urban and rural landscape imagery.

Beneyto's novel *La invasión* (1955; The Invasion) received the Ateneo Prize. *La dona forta* (1967; The Strong Woman) is a psychological work which focuses on the relationship between a mother and her son. The strength of the mother, who is somewhat lacking in sentiments, is not found in the son.

BIBLIOGRAPHY

Primary Texts

*Antología general*. Caracas: Lírica hispana, 1956.
*Biografía breve del silencio*. Alcoy: La Victoria, 1975.
*La dona forta*. Valencia: Senent, 1967.
*Poesía 1947–1964*. Barcelona: Plaza y Janés, 1976.
*Ratlles a l'aire*. Barcelona: Faro, 1958; Valencia: Torre, 1956.
*Vidre ferit de sang*. Gandia: Ajuntament de Gandia, 1977.

Criticism

Marín, Diego. *Poesía paisajística española 1940–1970*. London: Tamesis, 1976. 65–66 & 103–5.

Victoria Wolff Unruh and Kathleen McNerney

**BENGOECHEA, Javier de** (1919, Bilbao– ), poet and critic. A lawyer in Bilbao, Bengoechea has contributed art and theater criticism to regional and national literary magazines. His published poetry includes *Habitada claridad* (1951; Inhabited Clarity), which was honored in the Adonais competition; *Hombre en forma de elegía* (1955; Man in the Form of Elegy), recipient of the 1955 Adonais award; and *Fiesta nacional* (1959; National Holiday).

BIBLIOGRAPHY

Primary Works

*Fiesta nacional*. Madrid: Agora, 1959.
*Habitada claridad*. Madrid: Rialp, 1951.
*Hombre en forma de elegía*. Madrid: Rialp, 1955.

Victoria Wolff Unruh

**BENGUEREL I LIOBRET, Xavier** (1905, Barcelona– ), novelist, poet, playwright and translator. He was born in the working-class neighborhood of Poble Nou and is of Swiss ancestry. He began to write rather early and his first novels are strongly influenced by the Anglo-Saxon and French psychological novel.

His most noted early works are *Pàgines d'un adolescent* (1929; Pages of an Adolescent), *La vida d'Olga* (1930; The Life of Olga), *El teu secret* (1932; Your Secret), *Suburbi* (1985; Working-Class Neighborhood), and a volume of short stories, *Sense retorn* (1939; No Return). He also wrote poetry (*Poemes*, 1934; Poems) and drama (*El casament de Xela*, 1936; Xela's Marriage). In this period of his literary production Benguerel was influenced by Graham Greene, Georges Bernanos and François Mauriac. In 1939 he had to exile himself, first to France and later to Chile. He returned to Catalonia in 1954. After several notable novels, namely *L'home dins el mirall* (1951; The Man Inside the Mirror), *La família Roquier* (1953; The Rouquier Family), and *El testament* (1955; The Testament), Benguerel wrote a series of masterpieces blending the traditional historical novel with personal testimony of the development of Catalan nationalism. Aside from their intrinsic literary worth this series of novels is an attempt to explain the catastrophe of 1939. *Gorra de Plat* (1967; The Concierge) is perhaps his best work. It is the story of Pep Sisquella, a Catalan of humble origin who relates to the reader the private and historical ups and downs of any archetypal business dynasty from the beginning of the century up to 1939. In its Castilian version it received the coveted Premio Planeta. In *1939* (1973) Benguerel chronicles the tragic drama of the defeat of Catalonia at the end of the Spanish Civil War and in *Els vençuts* (1972; The Defeated) he dramatizes the exodus of Catalans to the French concentration camps. *Icària, Icària* (1974) is without a doubt Benguerel's most ambitious and complex novel. It tells two simultaneous stories. One takes place in the nineteenth c. and deals with the utopian ideals and adventures of a group of Catalans, followers of Étienne Cabet in the United States of America. The other is a story of the twentieth c., depicting the same utopian Catalans, now transformed into the violent anarchists of the twenties, and the epic battles of 1939. This group of novels is among the best of the contemporary Catalan narrative. Benguerel has also translated from French and English. His final version of *The Raven* (*El corb i altres poemes*, 1982; The Raven and Other Poems) as well as his translations of the *Fables* of La Fontaine (1969- ) are simply Catalan masterpieces. Finally, Benguerel's *Memòries* (1971; Memories) are a fine tapestry of his personal views of the times in which he has lived and of insights into his literary work. *See also* Catalan literature.

## BIBLIOGRAPHY

### Primary Texts

*La máscara y El hombre en el espejo*. Prol. J. Ferrater Mora. Spanish tr. J. Pomar. Barcelona: Polígrafa, 1970. Catalan and Spanish.
*Obres completes*. Barcelona: La rosa vera, 1967.

### Criticism

Gilabert, J. "El món de Xavier Benguerel i el de la burgesia nacionalista catalana." In *Actes del IV Col·loqui d'Estudis a Nord-Amèrica*. Washington and Montserrat: n.p., 1985.

Guansé, D. "Xavier Benguerel, novel·lista." In *Miscel·lànea*. Barcelona: n.p., 1956.
Serrahima, M. "Revisió de Xavier Benguerel." *Serra d'Or* (May 1969): 51–52.

Joan Gilabert

**BENITO DE LUCAS, Joaquín** (1934, Talavera de la Reina– ), poet and
university professor, who has taught in the Middle East and Berlin. Among his
collections of lyrics are *Las tentaciones* (1964; Temptations) and *Materia de
olvido* (1967; Matter of Oblivion), which was awarded the Adonais literary prize.

BIBLIOGRAPHY

Primary Texts

*Materia de olvido*. Madrid: Rialp, 1968.
*La sombra ante el espejo*. Oltas del Rey, Toledo: Junta de Comunidades de Castilla–La
Mancha, 1987.

Janet Pérez

**BENOT, Eduardo** (1822, Cadiz–1907, Madrid), politician, mathematician,
philologist, writer. By age fourteen, he was producing political articles for the
paper *El defensor del pueblo*. He wrote plays, poetry, and articles on many
topics, but his most enduring work focused on various facets of language. They
include *Arquitectura de las lenguas* (1888–91; The Architecture of Languages);
the *Diccionario de ideas afines* (1899; Dictionary of Related Ideas), which he
directed; and the *Arte de hablar, gramática filosófica* (1910; Art of Speaking,
Philosophical Grammar). Benot considered language to be the logical, rational
product of the mind, and believed that all languages shared certain structural
features. He became a member of the Spanish Academy (\*Academia Española)
in 1887. Benot also published a translation of Shakespeare's works, with a
prologue.

BIBLIOGRAPHY

Primary Texts

*Arquitectura de las lenguas*. 3 vols. Buenos Aires: Glem, 1943.
*Arte de hablar, gramática filosófica*. Buenos Aires: Anaconda, 1941.
*Diccionario de ideas afines y elementos de tecnología*. Buenos Aires: Anaconda, 1949.
*Mi siglo y mi corazón. Drama alegórico*. Cádiz: Revista médica, 1863. Rpt. Louisville,
KY: Falls City P, 1961. Microprint.
*Obras dramáticas de Guillermo Shakespeare*. Tr., study E. Benot. Madrid: Perlado,
Páez, 1912–16.

**BERCEO, Gonzalo de** (c. 1196, Logroño–c. 1260, ?), religious poet and author.
Gonzalo de Berceo was born in the village of Berceo, near the great monastery
of San Millán de la Cogolla (Logroño) in la Rioja, a region famed for its wines.
The monastery dates from the times of Saint Emilian (San Millán, 474–574),
but it suffered much damage in 1002 when Almanzor raided la Rioja. King
García of Navarre (1035–1054) tried to restore the monastery, with work begun
in 1053 and a new series of buildings completed in 1067. The old monastery

was built around the cave where San Millán had lived and was buried, on a cramped rocky site on the mountainside, and was known as San Millán de Suso ("Upper"). The new structure, San Millán de Yuso ("Lower"), stood in the wide valley beneath. The monks followed the Benedictine rule.

The foundations existed side by side until the dissolution of the monasteries in the 1830s. Now Suso is unoccupied but kept as a national monument, while Yuso—completely rebuilt in the seventeenth and eighteenth centuries—is currently occupied by Augustinian friars.

Berceo tells us himself of his origin:

> Gonçalvo fue so nomme           qui fizo est tractado,
> en Sant Millán de Suso          fue de niñez criado,
> natural de Verco ond            sant Millán fue nado,
> Dios guarde la su alma          del poder del Peccado.
>
> Goncalvo was the name of he who wrote this tract,
> as a child he was raised in San Millán de Suso,
> born in Berceo, where San Millán was born, may
> God protect his soul from the power of sin.

*Vida de San Millán*, stanza 489

Born in Berceo, at an early age he entered the monastery school, probably as an *oblato* or child offered as a potential monk and priest. Certain documents of the year 1221 indicate that he became a deacon in that year, and since at that time the minimum age was 25, he must have been born in 1196 at the latest. It is quite probable that he studied sometime between 1221 and 1228 at the U of Palencia, founded by Alphonse VIII and Bishop Tello Téllez de Meneses of Palencia in 1210. We are also fairly sure that he was the *notario* or legal secretary of Abbot Juan Sánchez (1209–53), which may explain why Gonzalo was a priest in the village of Berceo and not a monk, despite his obvious fondness for the order.

He appears in documents in 1221, 1228, 1237, 1240, 1242, and 1246. In one of his works (*Milagros* 869) he refers to King Ferdinand the Saint as dead, so Berceo was alive after 1252. However, a document of 1264 that mentions him in reference to a document of the period 1236–42 indicates that he was dead by 1264, since he was not called as a witness.

Berceo's works (with one minor exception noted below) are all written in *cuaderna vía, the fourfold way, a series of monorhymed stanzas made up of four alexandrines. Each hemistich has a stress on the sixth syllable, so that hemistichs of six, seven or eight syllables are possible. However, the second hemistich never has eight since esdrújulo ($-\ \vee\ \vee$) rhymes are too difficult. We have ten works by him, described below in their most probable chronological order. All his works are religious in subject and tone, with one possible exception: one ms. of the *Libro de *Alexandre* ends with the following stanza:

> Si queredes saber            quien fizo esti ditado,
> Gonçalo de Berceo           es por nonbre clamado,

natural de Madrid,                    en Sant Mylián criado,
del abat Johán Sánchez                notario por nonbrado.

If you want to know who made this poem
He is called Gonçalo de Berceo by name
born in Madrid, raised in San Millán,
appointed legal Secretary to the abbot Johán Sánchez

*Madrid* is actually *Madriz*, the disappeared town of which the village Berceo
was a dependency. The data given on Berceo appears to be accurate, and Juan
Sánchez was abbot 1209–53. If Berceo did write this book, it was during his
earlier years, but the whole question of his authorship is hotly debated. However,
the evidence for Riojano authorship has grown more convincing recently.

Berceo's first work is the *Vida de San Millán*, which tells the life of the patron
saint of the monastery. Born in 474, St. Emilian was a shepherd in his youth
and then a hermit. The Bishop of Tarazona ordained him, after which he worked
as a priest for some time in the village of Berceo, but soon returned to the
wilderness. A group of followers grew up around him, and in time the monastery
of Suso was built where he lived and was finally buried in 574. Berceo based
his text on Bishop Braulio of Zaragoza's *Vita Beati Aemiliani* (590–651). Berceo
used the traditional tripartite division of the saint's story: his life, miracles while
alive and his death, and then posthumous miracles. To those miracles told by
Braulio, Berceo added a long one concerning the *Votos* or devotional offerings
to San Millán. Claiming to follow a document granted in 934 by Count Fernán
González of Castile, Berceo tells how Abdurrahman III (912–961) attacked the
Christians because they refused to continue paying the Tribute of Sixty Maidens.
The Leonese under Ramiro II (927–950) were joined by the Castilians and the
Navarrese, and after making promises of offerings to St. James and San Millán,
they joined battle with the Moors on the Campo de Toro and there defeated them
with the aid of heavenly hosts led by the two saints. The count's document
specified what the towns and villages were to pay to the monastery in money
and goods each year. Berceo's source document appears to be a forgery made
by a contemporary of his, the monk Fernandus, in an effort to change the
traditional devotional offerings into legally binding payments, since the monastery's income from these sources had dwindled in the face of competition from
the new orders and monasteries that were springing up. The work has 489
quatrains.

*The Vida de Santo Domingo de Silos* (Life of St. Dominic of Silos), written
about 1236, tells the story of a saintly hermit, born in 1000, who became a
priest and later prior of San Millán in about 1033. Since Dominic refused to let
King García of Navarre (1035–54) take large sums from the monastery, the king
forced the weak abbot to strip him of his position and finally drove him into
exile. Dominic fled to the court of Ferdinand I of Castile (1032–65), García's
brother, where he was made welcome and appointed abbot of the almost ruined
monastery of San Sebastián de Silos. The saint restored the monastery and
wrought many miracles, especially the liberation of captives. He died in 1073

and soon thereafter the monastery was named after him. Silos and San Millán were linked by a Pact of Brotherhood in 1190, which was renewed in 1236. The work, having 777 quatrains, is based in the *Vita Beati Dominici*, written about 1080 by the monk Grimaldus.

The *Sacrificio de la Misa* (Sacrament of Mass), 297 quatrains, describes the ceremonies of the Mass in terms of their development from old Hebrew rites and of their symbolism. It is based on an anonymous Latin treatise. A reference in lines 183c-d makes it clear that Berceo had already been ordained when he wrote it.

The *Duelo de la Virgen* (Sorrow of the Virgin) follows the form of a sermon wrongly attributed to St. Bernard of Clairvaux (1109–53), and while it is composed of the monorhymic quatrains in narrative style that Berceo always used, it does contain many appealingly lyrical passages. It also contains the 13 couplets of a watchers' song, with the refrain *Eya velar*—the only departure from *cuaderna vía* in all Berceo's works. The *Duelo* has 210 strophes.

There are also three hymns of seven quatrains each which translate the *Veni Creator Spiritus*, *Ave maris stella* and *Christe qui lux es et dies* respectively. Another Marian work is his *Loores de Nuestra Señora* (Praises to Our Lady), of unknown source, which sings the praises of Mary in 233 strophes. Next comes the *Signos del Juicio Final* (Signs of Judgment Day), based on a 12th-c. Latin poem, with 77 stanzas that describe the Signs and Judgment Day.

The most famous work is the *Milagros de Nuestra Señora* (Miracles of Our Lady), which Berceo probably composed over a period of time: stanza 325 refers to Bishop Tello of Palencia as still alive (he died in 1246) while stanza 869 refers to Ferdinand I (The Saint) as dead, and so was written after 1252. There is an introduction in the form of an allegorical *locus amoenus* followed by 25 miracles, all but one of which are found in several Latin collections. The work has a total of 911 quatrains.

The *Vida de Santa Oria* (Life of St. Oria) was written when Berceo was old, and is based on a lost Latin *Vita Beatae Aureae* by a certain Muño. It tells the story of a young girl whose piety was such that at the age of nine in 1052 she had herself walled up in a cell in Suso, where she died in 1070. The work describes her origins and ascetic life, but most of all the three visions that she had. The work now has 205 quatrains, but we know it originally had 219 since a folio containing 14 stanzas is missing.

The last work, the *Martirio de San Lorenzo* (Martyrdom of St. Lawrence), is incomplete since it ends at stanza 105 quite abruptly with St. Lawrence's dying words on the grill. It is based on the standard Latin life of the saint, but has an unusual introduction that makes him a companion of St. Vincent, and protégé of Bishop Valerio in Huesca. The rest of the work may have been lost or Berceo may have died before he could complete it.

In all his works we can perceive that Berceo is writing his texts in Spanish for the instruction, edification and entertainment of his public, very much in keeping with the spirit of the Lateran reforms initiated by Innocent III in the early 13th c. His public would be the general population, including in particular the pilgrims who came to visit the monastery of San Millán, and the commonest mode of presentation would have been oral performance.

Berceo's works existed in two ms. collections. The first was $Q$, the quarto manuscript of about 1260 with 32 stanzas per folio in double columns. In about 1325 an elaborate and much larger manuscript was made (in folio and hence known as $F$), having only 16 stanzas per folio and a single column. $Q$ and $F$ were lost during the movements that followed the dissolution of the monasteries in the 1820s–30s, but parts of $F$ were discovered by Marden in the 1920s, and given to the Real Academia de la Lengua (MSS 4, 4a, 4b). Two works exist in independent medieval copies: *Santo Domingo* in MS *S* (Silos, library) and *sacrificio* MS *BN* (National Library, MS 1533). There is a copy of *S* known as *H* in the Real Academia de la Historia, MS–12–4–1, ant. H–18. Fortunately a group of excellent scribes copied large parts of $Q$ in about 1775–77 under the direction of Father Ibarreta (MS *I*, Silos, MS 93). There are also 18th-c. copies of *San Millán*, *Loores*, *Santa Oria* and *San Lorenzo*. See also Hagiography.

BIBLIOGRAPHY

Primary Texts

*Cuatro poemas de Berceo*. Ed. C. Carroll Marden. *RFE* anejo 9. Madrid: RFE, 1928.
*Obras Completas*. Ed. Brian Dutton 5 vols. London: Tamesis, 1967–1981.
*Veintitrés milagros*. Ed. C. Carroll Marden. *RFE* anejo 10. Madrid: RFE, 1929.

Criticism

Artiles, Joaquín. *Los recursos literarios de Berceo*. Madrid: Gredos, 1964.
Gariano, Carmelo. *Análisis estilístico de los* "Milagros de Nuestra Señora." Madrid: Gredos, 1965.
See also vol. 1 of Dutton's *Obras Completas*.

Brian Dutton

**BERENGUER, Luis** (1923, El Ferrol–1979, Cadiz), professional naval officer, poet and novelist. Berenguer is known especially for his novel *El mundo de Juan Lobón* (1966; The World of Juan Lobon), which won the coveted Premio de la Crítica (Critics' Prize) for 1967. It has been compared, perhaps somewhat superficially, with *Pascual Duarte's Family* by Camilo José *Cela. Subsequently, Berenguer published *Marea escorada* (1969; Rough Seas).

BIBLIOGRAPHY

Primary Texts

*La noche de Catalina Virgen*. Barcelona: Dopesa, 1975.
*Obras selectas e inéditas*. Prol. A. Grosso. Barcelona: Dopesa, 1976. Contains *Juan Lobón*.
*Tamatea, novia del otoño*. Madrid: Altalena, 1980.

Janet Pérez

**BERGAMÍN, José** (1895, Madrid–1983, San Sebastián), essayist, poet, playwright, and literary critic. The son of a well-known politician, Bergamín identified himself with the *tertulias* of Ramón Gómez de la Serna and the Mexican writer Alfonso Reyes. He began his literary career under the patronage of Juan Ramón *Jiménez, but they later quarreled. His friendship with the somewhat older generation is apparent in the influences of Jiménez, *Unamuno, and *Gómez de la Serna reflected in his book of aphorisms *El cohete y la estrella* (1923; The Sky-Rocket and the Star). In Madrid, he founded a review of neo-Catholic tendencies: *Cruz y Raya* (1933–36). He emigrated to Mexico in 1939, where he founded the review *España Peregrina* (Peregrine Spain) and a publishing house, "Editorial Séneca." From Mexico he moved to Venezuela and, eventually, to Uruguay. He returned to Spain in 1959 and although he resided in Paris for extended periods, finally chose Madrid as his residence.

Bergamín is known for the high caliber of his prose and for his subjective but rigorous approach to literary criticism. His serious attitude is captured in his own expression: "To write is to think and to think is to commit oneself." His multifaceted writings are exemplified in the variety of texts he published from the start: the experimental plays *Tres escenas en ángulo recto* (1923; Three Scenes at Right Angles) and *Enemigo que huye* (1927; Enemy Who Flees); the aphorisms of *El cohete y la estrella* (1923); the masterful plays on words and paradoxes of *La cabeza a pájaros* (1925–30; Harebrained); the sketches of contemporary authors contained in *Caracteres* (1926; Characters); the defense of bullfighting in *El arte de birlibirloque* (1930; By Extraordinary Means); and the philosophical and religious essays collected in *El pozo de la angustia* (1941; The Well of Anguish). Bergamín continued to produce without decline. Some of his later works are the plays *Melusina y el espejo* (1952; Melusina and the Mirror) and *Medea, la encantadora* (1954; Medea, the Sorceress); the poetic collections *Poemas y sonetos rezagados* (1963; Straggling Poems and Sonnets) and *Duendecitos y coplas* (1963; Little Goblins and Ballads); and the essays *Fronteras de la poesía* (1959; Poetry's Infernal Frontiers), *Al volver* (1962; Upon Returning), *Beltenebros* (1969), and *Los filólogos* (1978; The Philologists). *See also* Contemporary Spanish Theater.

BIBLIOGRAPHY

Primary Texts

*Disparadero español (1936–1940). Poesía.* 3 vols. Madrid: Turner, 1983.

English Translation

*Characters.* Tr. V. Llona. In *The European Caravan.* Ed. S. Putnam. New York: Warren and Putnam, 1931.

Criticism

Alonso, Cecilio. "José Bergamín: utopía y popularismo." *Camp de l'Arp* (Barcelona) 13 (Oct. 1974): 10–16.

Dennis, Nigel. "José Bergamín and the Aesthetics of the Generation of 1927." *BHS* 58 (1981): 313–28.

————. *Perfume and Poison. A Study of the Relationship Between José Bergamín and Juan Ramón Jiménez.* Kassel: Reichenberger, 1985.

Vivanco, Luis Felipe. "El aforismo y la creación poético-intelectual de José Bergamín."
    In *Historia general de las literaturas hispánicas*. Ed. G. Díaz Plaja. 6 vols.
    Barcelona: Vergara, 1968. 6: 599–609.

María A. Salgado

**BERLANGA, Andrés** (1941, Labros [Guadalajara]– ), journalist and professor
in a school of journalism. He published a collection of short fiction, *Barruntos*
(1967; Presentiments), and in 1970 his first novel, *Pólvora mojada* (Wet Powder),
was a finalist for the Nadal Prize. Set in the contemporary university ambience
of the author's professional life, it deals with a radical group which undertakes
a violent subversive action in an atmosphere of politico-social agitation.

BIBLIOGRAPHY

Primary Texts

*Barruntos*. Madrid: AZ, 1967.
*Del más acá*. Madrid: Observatorio, 1987.
*La gaznápira*. Barcelona: Noguer, 1984.
*Pólvora mojada*. Barcelona: Destino, 1972.

Janet Pérez

**BERMÚDEZ, Jerónimo,** pseudonym, Antonio de Silva (1530?, Galicia–
1590?,?), playwright and poet. After travel through Spain, France, Africa and
Portugal, Bermúdez entered the Order of Santo Domingo and became a professor
of theology in Salamanca. His intention as a dramatist was to introduce classical
Greek tragedy to Spain in accord with Aristotelian precepts (see Aristotelianism).
Bermúdez referred to himself as the author of the first Spanish tragedies. Under
his pseudonym, he wrote the two tragedies *Nise lastimosa* (1577; Nise the Pitiful)
and *Nise laureada* (1577; Nise Crowned). The first is an adaptation of the
Portuguese tragedy *\*Inés de Castro* by Antonio Ferreira; the second is an original
work, and a continuation of the first. Bermúdez also composed a posthumous
panegyric to the Duke of Alba in Latin distichs which he later translated into
Spanish under the title *La Hesperodia*.

BIBLIOGRAPHY

Primary Texts

*La Hesperodia*. In *Parnaso español*, vol. 7. Ed. López Sedano. Madrid: Ibarra, 1772.
*Primeras tragedies españolas*. Ed. Mitchell Triwedi. Madrid: Castalia, 1975.

Criticism

Freund, M. L. "Algunas observaciones sobre 'Nise lastimosa' y 'Nise laureada' de
    Jerónimo Bermúdez." *Revista de Literatura* 19 (1961): 103–12.

Sánchez Cantón, F. J. ''Aventuras del mejor poeta gallego del Siglo de Oro, Fray Jerónimo Bermúdez.'' *Cuadernos de Estudios Gallegos* 20 (1965): 225–42.

Deborah Compte

**BERMÚDEZ DE CASTRO, Salvador** (1814, Jerez de la Frontera–1883, Rome), poet. Of an illustrious family, he fervently espoused *Romanticism. His *Ensayos poéticos* (1840; Poetry Attempts) is preceded by an introduction which attributes any perceived skepticism or sense of futility in the poems to the ambience of the day. He attained some fame for a new way of stressing octaves; the variation was called *bermudinas*. His historical work, *Antonio Pérez, secretario de estado del rey Felipe II* (1841; Antonio Pérez, Secretary of State to King Philip II), is a valuable source. Bermúdez de Castro also served as ambassador to Mexico (1844–47) and Paris (1865).

BIBLIOGRAPHY

Primary Texts

*Antonio Pérez*. . . . Madrid: Est. Tipográfico, 1841.
*Ensayos poéticos*. Orizaba, Mexico: Aburto, 1865.

Criticism

García Aráez, J. ''Don Salvador Bermúdez de Castro.'' *Revista de Literatura* 4 (1953): 73–120.

**BERNÁLDEZ, Andrés** (c. 1450, ?–after 1513, ?), historian, chaplain to the Archbishop of Seville. His *Historia de los Reyes Católicos don Fernando y doña Isabel* (n.d.; History of the Catholic Monarchs, Ferdinand and Isabella) contains valuable information concerning events between 1454 and 1513. He pays particular attention to Columbus (*Colón, Cristóbal) and the discovery of America. An inflexible, orthodox Christian who fully supported the *Inquisition and all its activities, his personal views color his assessments markedly. He is also known as *El cura de los palacios* (The Palace Priest).

BIBLIOGRAPHY

Primary Texts

*Historia de los Reyes*. . . . Prol. L. de la Calzada. Madrid: Aguilar, 1946.
*Historia de los Reyes*. . . . In BAE 70.

English Translation

*The voyages of Christopher Columbus . . . to which is added the account of his second voyage written by Andrés Bernáldez*. Ed., tr., intro., C. Jane. London: Argonaut, 1930.

**BERNARDO DEL CARPIO,** hero of legends which originated as a reaction to those about Charlemagne and Roland. Bernardo was supposedly the nephew of Alphonse the Chaste (ruled Leon 791–835), born of the secret union of the king's sister and the Count of Saldaña, whom the king ordered imprisoned. When Alphonse named Charlemagne his heir in return for help against the Moors,

Bernardo led a protest which forced the king to ally with the Moors and to attack Roland at Roncesvaux. At the death of Alphonse II, Bernardo served Alphonse III. When he requested his father's freedom, the king refused. Bernardo rebelled and forced the king's assent. His father, by this time, had just died, but the corpse was dressed and sent forth to meet Bernardo. Bernardo was exiled and emigrated to France.

The legend originated around 1200 in Spanish epic poetry. The earliest references to it are in the *Chronicon Mundi* (1236; Great Chronicle of the World) by Lucas de *Tuy and other chronicles, including the *Estoria de España* (History of Spain) of *Alphonse X the Learned. It is the subject of many ballads and of works such as Lope de *Vega's play *Las mocedades de Bernardo* (The Youthful Exploits of Bernardo), the epic *El Bernardo* (1624) by *Balbuena, and *Hartzenbusch's *Alfonso el Casto* (1841; Alphonse the Chaste).

BIBLIOGRAPHY

Criticism

Franklin, A. B. "A Study of the Origins of the Legend of Bernardo del Carpio." *HR* 5 (1937): 286–303.

                                                                    Eric Naylor

**BERTRANA, Aurora** (1899, Girona–1974, Berga), novelist. A world traveler, she used the exotic places she had visited as a background for some of her works. The stories in *Peikea, princesa caníbal i altres contes oceànics* (1980; Peikea, the Cannibal Princess and Other Oceanic Stories) show us a utopian society in which the landscape, favorable to love and tenderness, is the main source of human life. The Civil War is the background for the emotional *Tres presoners* (1957; Three Prisoners) and the Second World War for *Entre dos silencis* (1958; Between Two Silences). *Fracàs* (1966; Failure) is a novel of social criticism directed against the upper classes who, masked with respectability and religious ritual, are filled with ambition and selfishness. *La nimfa d'argila* (1959; The Clay Nymph) is a study of infantile psychology, and *Oviri i sis narracions més* (1965; Oviri and Six Other Stories) explores the relationships between people and animals. *Vent de grop* (1967; Tailwind) is a love story set in a fishing/tourist village of the Costa Brava. Daughter of the well-known Catalan writer Prudenci *Bertrana, she possessed a finely crafted style.

BIBLIOGRAPHY

Primary Texts

*Ariatea*. Barcelona: Alberti, 1960.
*Camins de somni*. Barcelona: Alberti, 1955.
*La ciutat dels joves*. Barcelona: Pòrtic, 1971.
*Edelweis*. Barcelona: La novel·la femenina, 1937.
*Entre dos silencis*. Barcelona: Aymà, 1958.
*Fracàs*. Andorra: Alfaguara, 1966.
*L'illa perduda* (with Prudenci Bertrana). Barcelona: NAGSA. n.d.

*La isla perdida*. Barcelona: Juventud, 1954. Spanish translation of *L'illa perduda*.
*El Marroc sensual i fanàtic*. Barcelona: Mediterranea, 1936.
*Memòries del 1935 fins al return a Catalunya*. Barcelona: Pòrtic, 1975.
*Memòries fins al 1935*. Barcelona: Pòrtic, 1973.
*La nimfa d'argila*. Barcelona: Alberti, 1959.
*Oviri i sis narracions més*. Barcelona: Selecta, 1965.
*Paradisos Oceànics*. Barcelona: Proa, 1930.
*Peikea, princess caníbal i altres contes oceànics*. Barcelona: Balagué, 1934; Barcelona:
    Pleniluni, 1980.
*Tres presoners*. Barcelona: Alberti, 1957.
*Vent de grop*. Andorra: Alfaguara, 1967.
*Vertigo de horizontes*. Barcelona: Torrell de Reus, 1952.

Kathleen McNerney

**BERTRANA, Prudenci** (1867, Tortosa–1942, Gerona), Catalan novelist, dramatist and painter. Bertrana belongs essentially to the ruralist novel headed by Víctor *Català (pseud. Catarina Albert), a violent and pessimistic variant of realism. His first novel, *Josafat* (1906) already displays the same crude vigor characteristic of his work as a whole. *Naufrags* (1907; The Shipwrecked) was his first important work, again with touches of savage realism. *Proses bàrbares* (1911; Barbarous Prose) is a vigorous, colorful story collection. Other works are *Els Herois* (1920; Heroes) and *El meu amic Pellini* (1923; My Friend Pellini). *L'hereu* (1931; The Heir) won the Crexells Prize, awarded annually by the Catalan government to the best novel. Among his later novels is *El vagabund* (1933; The Vagabond), while *La dona neta* (1924; The Clean Lady) and *Tieta Claudina* (Auntie Claudina) are theatrical pieces. *See also* Catalan Literature.

BIBLIOGRAPHY

Primary Texts

*La dona neta*. Barcelona: Duran Alsina, 1924.
*L'hereu*. 3rd ed. Barcelona: Selecta, 1947.
*Els herois*. Barcelona: Catalana, 1920.
*Josafat*. Barcelona: Ales Esteses, 1929?
*Naufrags*. Barcelona: Domenech, 1907.
*Proses bàrbares*. Barcelona: Societat Catalana, 1911.

Janet Pérez

**BESSA-LUIS, Agustina** (1922, Vila-Mea– ), Portuguese novelist and short story writer. The rural northern background of the area of her birth is often re-created in her fiction, which makes no pretense at objectivity. A writer more in the Modernist vein of Rosa *Chacel, Bessa-Luis minimizes action and plot in order to maximize character depiction, psychological analysis, meditation and memory. It is no accident that some critics have found analogies with Proust. Prime techniques include the internal monologue, stream of consciousness, third-person indirect narrative and a probing of motivations tending to reveal the failings of common sense. The writer's first two novels, *Mundo fechado* (1948;

Closed World) and *Os super-homens* (1950; Supermen), written in a different, tentative style, went unnoticed, by contrast with her third narrative effort, *A sibila* (1953; The Sibyl), which won two prizes and widespread popularity. This novel displays the writer's definitive style and perspective which characterize all subsequent works. She excels at the portrayal of confused or contradictory emotions, the need for intuition and psychological improvisation, the problematic nature of human relationships, as seen in a trilogy centering upon the concept of family ties, *As relações humanas* (Human Relationships), which includes *Os quatro rios* (1964; Four Rivers), *A dança das espadas* (1965; Sword Dance), and *Canção diante de uma porta fechada* (1966; Song before a Closed Door). *A bíblia dos pobres* (The Bible of the Poor), another multi-volume novelistic cycle, treats similar themes and begins with *Homens e mulheres* (1967; Men and Women) and *As categorias* (1970; Categories). Bessa-Luis is a prolific narrator with many other titles to her credit, including not only novels but at least one play and a travel book.

Janet Pérez

**BESTIARIO** (Bestiary), a collection of descriptions of real and imaginary animals; the traits attributed to each are frequently accompanied by some allegorical interpretation. The bestiary is derived from the Greek *Physiologus*, meaning "naturalist," which described some 49 animals. Its origin is believed to be Eastern, perhaps in Alexandria or Syria. By late antiquity, the *Physiologus* circulated in several Latin versions. Isidore of Seville's *Etymologiae* (Book 12) influenced the later tradition which continued well into the *Renaissance. Despite its pervasive influence in art and literature, no vernacular bestiary itself has survived in Spain.

BIBLIOGRAPHY

   Criticism

McCulloch, F. *Mediaeval Latin and French Bestiaries.* UNCSRLL 33. Chapel Hill: U of North Carolina P, 1960.

Solalinde, A. G. "El *Physiologus* en la *General Estoria* de Alfonso X." In *Mélanges d'histoire littéraire générale et comparée offerts à Fernand Baldensperger.* Paris: n.p., 1930. 2:251–54.

Porter Conerly

**BIBLE IN VULGAR TRANSLATION** (Biblia en romance [Bible in Spanish]). The history of the vernacular Bible in the Iberian peninsula is yet to be written, albeit the Bible in its multifarious forms (translations, commentaries, glosses, devout and didactic literature such as the poetry of the *mester de clerecía) was the cornerstone of culture and learning in the Middle Ages (see Edad Media, Literatura de la). There are several outstanding examples of early prose works that are directly inspired by the Bible. The first of these is the *Fazienda de Ultramar* (The Matter of Outremer), which survives in a unique, early 13th-c. ms. According to its factitious claim, it was compiled by a certain Almeric, archdeacon of Antioch, at the request of Raimundo, archbishop of Toledo, renowned for his school of translators. While in the tradition of the Latin *itineraria*, it contains a great deal from the Old Testament, believed to be translated from the Hebrew rather than from the Vulgate. The Old Testament is the principal source for *Alphonse X the Learned's *Grande e general estoria* (General History of the World). Conceived much like the French *Bible Historiale*, the General History paraphrased the Old Testament and incorporated such models as Petrus Comestor's *Historia Scholastica* and the *Antiquities of the Jews* of Josephus. In the 14th c., Pero *López de Ayala held a strong attraction to the Book of Job, which he translated along with Gregory the Great's *Moralia* and an abridged version of Gregory's commentary. The concluding part of Ayala's *Rimado del palacio* (Rhyme of the Palace) is itself a commentary on Job.

    The survival of vernacular biblical mss. in Spain is low in comparison to that of England, France, and Germany. The paucity of texts is not an uncommon phenomenon in medieval Spanish literature, but it may be misleading here in an assessment of the importance of the vernacular Bible. Margherita Morreale considers the ms. tradition in Castilian and Catalan to be very complicated. Moreover, the tradition reflects a great variety in the translations. The diversity of these texts would suggest a vaster and more deeply rooted tradition than what first meets the eye. The extant Castilian biblical mss. (excluding the translations found in Alphonse the Learned's General History of the World) now number fourteen, of which only three can be considered relatively complete: two of the Escorial bibles (MSS. I-j-3 and I-j-4) and the Alba Bible (Old Testament, 1422–33). The Valencian Bible, translated by Bonifatius Ferrer (d. 1417), brother of St. Vincent Ferrer, was printed in 1478, but is lamentably lost, in all likelihood due to the *Inquisition. The Catalan Psalter (1480) is allegedly based on Ferrer's translation. Of the Catalan Bibles surviving from the 15th century, the only complete one is the Peiresc Bible in Paris (Bibliothèque Nationale MS. esp. 2–4).

    There are additional factors which contribute to our understanding of the role of the vernacular Bible in Spain: the sources of the translations and the eventual bans on translations. Translations were derived from three sources: the Vulgate, Hebrew, and French. The various mss. of the Escorial bibles are derived from both Latin and Hebrew sources. The Alba Bible, translated by Rabbi Mosse Arragel of Guadalajara, attempts to meld Jewish and Christian biblical scholarship. Morreale judges it unique among the Bibles of the Middle Ages in its heterogeneous incorporation of rabbinic lore and Catholic exegesis. Medieval versions from Hebrew are also represented in the Constantinople Pentateuch (1547) and the Ferrara Bible (1553), for they abound in Hebraisms.

    The influence of French and Provençal scriptural texts in Spain has been studied by Samuel Berger. The 14th-c. Catalan Marmoutier New Testament in Paris (Bibliothèque Nationale esp. 486), which shares certain similarities with the Peiresc Bible, appears to descend from French and Provençal versions. The *Genesi de scriptura* (1451; Genesis of Scripture), a compendium of Holy Scripture, was translated from Provençal. The Castilian Osuna Bible has been shown to be an heir of the French genre known as the *Bible moralisée*, that is, an illustrated Bible, current in the 13th and 14th centuries. It is not illustrated, but contains detailed instructions for illumination.

The prohibitions on vernacular translations prior to the Council of Trent, which have been examined by Jesús Enciso, were enforced in varying degrees. Bartolomé Carranza de Miranda, archbishop of Toledo, observes in the prologue to his *Commentarios sobre el catechismo christiano* (1588; Commentaries on the Christian Catechism) that schools, monasteries and the nobility, who were free of suspicion, were given license to own and read vernacular bibles. The first ban, promulgated by the Council of Tarragona (1233), which was called by James I the Conqueror, coincided with the threat of the Albigensian heresy and was relatively short-lived. It was, according to Enciso, of little or no consequence in Castile. A more effective ban followed the expulsion of the Jews in 1492. Carranza also mentions a general ban during the reign of Charles V to thwart the spread of Protestantism to Spain. Enciso has shown that theologians like the Franciscan Alfonso de Castro believed vernacular translations to be a key factor in the emergence of a variety of heresies. These theologians, nevertheless, recognized the need for the liturgical Gospels and Epistles in the vernacular. Gonzalo García de Santa María (d. 1521) had earlier translated these with the *Postilla* of William of Paris. Throughout the 16th c., scriptural translations are noticeably printed outside of Spain and are found on the Indexes of the Spanish Inquisition (*see* Índice de libros prohibidos). Portions of the New Testament were translated by Juan de *Valdés (d. 1541); Francisco de *Enzinas (based on the Greek text of Erasmus); Juan Pérez de Pineda (including a Psalter, 1557). Casiodoro de *Reina translated the entire Bible, which appeared first in Basel (1569) with subsequent editions in Frankfurt (1602; 1622). A somewhat revised version by Cipriano de *Valera was printed in Amsterdam (1602); Valera's New Testament had already been printed in London (1596).

By the end of the 18th c. the Index no longer prohibited vernacular translations of the Bible. Consequently, a Spanish New Testament was produced in Valladolid (1790) by Anselmo Petite. Felipe Scío de San Miguel translated the whole Bible from the Vulgate, which appeared in Valencia (1790–93). A widely used translation was that of Torres Amat and Petisco (Madrid, 1823–25), which underwent many printings. This has been replaced by the Nácar-Colunga version, which is based on the original languages, and the Bover-Cantera version.

BIBLIOGRAPHY

Primary Texts

Alba Bible. *Biblia (Antiguo Testamento) traducida del hebreo al castellano por Rabbí Mosé de Guadalfajara.* Ed. Antonio Paz y Melia. 2 vols. Madrid: n.p., 1920–22.

Alfonso X, the Learned. *Grande e general estoria.* Part I. Ed. Antonio García Solalinde. Madrid: Centro de Estudios Históricos, 1930. Part II. Ed. A. G. Solalinde, L. A. Kasten, and V. R. B. Oelschlager. Madrid: CSIC, 1957; 1961.

———. *General estoria*. Parts I and IV. *Concordances and Texts of the Royal Scriptorium Manuscripts of Alfonso X, el Sabio*. Ed. L. A. Kasten and J. J. Nitti. Madison: Hispanic Seminary, 1978.

Escorial Bible (I-j-3; I-j-8). *Biblia medieval romanceada*. Ed. A. Castro, A. Millares Carlo, and A. J. Battistessa. Buenos Aires: Instituto de Filología, 1927.

Escorial Bible (I-j-4). *Biblia medieval romanceada judío-cristiana, versión del Antiguo Testamento en el siglo XIV sobre los textos hebreo y latino*. Ed. J. Llamas. 2 vols. Madrid: Instituto Francisco Suárez 1950; 1955.

———. *Escorial Bible I-j-4. The Pentateuch*. Ed. O. H. Hauptmann. Philadelphia: U of Pennsylvania P, 1953.

Escorial Bible (I-j-6). *El evangelio de San Mateo*. Ed. Thomas Montgomery. Anejo 7 of the *BRAE*. Madrid: Real Academia Española, 1962.

*La fazienda de ultramar. Biblia romanceada et itinéraire biblique du XII$^e$ siècle*. Ed. M. Lazar. Salamanca: U of Salamanca, 1965.

*Genesi de la scriptura. Compendi historial de la Biblia que ab lo titol de Genesi de Scriptura trellada del provençal a la llengua catalana*. Ed. M. V. Amer. Barcelona: Biblioteca Catalana, 1873.

López de Ayala, Pero. *Libro de Job*. Ed. Francesco Branciforti. Messina-Florence: Le Monnier, 1962.

———. *Las flores de los "Morales de Job."* Ed. Francesco Branciforti. Messina-Florence: Le Monnier, 1963.

Criticism

Berger, Samuel. "Nouvelles recherches sur les bibles provençales et catalanes." *Romania* 19 (1890): 505–61.

———. "Les manuels pour l'illustration du psautier au XIII$^e$ siècle." *Bulletin et mémoires de la Société Nationale des Antiquaires de France* 57 (1896): 95–134.

Enciso, Jesús. "Prohibiciones españolas de las versiones bíblicas en romance antes del tridentino." *Estudios Bíblicos* 3 (1944): 523–54.

Morreale, Margherita. "Apuntes bibliográficos para la iniciación al estudio de las Biblias medievales en castellano." *Sefarad* 20 (1960): 66–109.

———. "Apuntes bibliográficos para la iniciación al estudio de las Biblias medievales en catalán." *Analecta Sacra Tarraconensia* 31 (1960): 271–90.

———. "Vernacular Scriptures in Spain." In *The Cambridge History of the Bible*. Cambridge: Cambridge UP, 1969. 2: 465–91.

Wilson, E. M. "Continental Versions to c. 1600. Spanish" and "Continental Versions from c. 1600 to the Present Day." In *The Cambridge History of the Bible*. Cambridge: Cambridge UP, 1963. 3: 125–29; 354–55.

Porter Conerly

**BIBLE OF ALCALÁ** (Biblia políglota complutense— Polyglot Bible of Complutum [the Latin name for Alcalá]), the first published polyglot Bible. Cardinal Jiménez de *Cisneros envisioned and oversaw the historic project. In 1502 a team of Hebrew, Greek and Latin scholars first joined to begin translation of the text. Antonio de *Nebrija, Hernán *Núñez (Pinciano), Demetrio Duco and Diego López de Estúñiga handled Greek and Latin sources; Alfonso de Alcalá, Pablo Coronel and Alfonso de Zamora oversaw Hebrew texts, while Juan de *Vergara and Bartolomé de Castro coordinated treatment of textual variations.

No expense was spared in the acquisition of mss., nor in the printing which took three years (1514–17). The result was 600 six-volume copies. Volumes 1 through 4 contain translations of the Old Testament in Greek, Hebrew, Latin and Chaldean; volume 5 gives the New Testament in Greek and Latin; and volume 6 is composed of a Hebrew-Chaldean vocabulary, a Hebrew grammar, and index of names. Although it was shortly overshadowed by the *Bible of Antwerp, it served as an invaluable resource for that Bible, and is a distinguished indicator of the advanced humanistic development in Spain at that time. *See also* Humanism; Renaissance; *Siglo de Oro*.

BIBLIOGRAPHY

Primary Text

*Biblia polyglotta*. 6 vols. Alcala: Guillermo de Brocar, 1514–17.


**BIBLE OF ANTWERP** (Biblia políglota de Amberes). Under sponsorship of Philip II, Benito *Arias Montano supervised the editing and printing of the magnificent Antwerp Polyglot Bible. Using the *Bible of Alcalá as a starting point, he incorporated additional textual versions and various studies of Biblical archaeology. Printed between 1569 and 1573, the eight-volume work influenced subsequent polyglot Bibles throughout Europe. *See also* Humanism; Renaissance; *Siglo de Oro*.

BIBLIOGRAPHY

Primary Text

*Biblia Sacra, Hebraice, Chaldaice, Graece, & Latine*. Ed. B. Arias Montano. Antwerp: Plantin, 1569–72.


**BIBLIOTECA DE AUTORES ESPAÑOLES** (Library of Spanish Authors), a publication series dedicated to the printing of classical Spanish texts. The BAE, as it is commonly abbreviated, published its first volumes in 1846, under Bonaventura Carles *Aribau and Manuel Rivadeneyra, the editor. By 1880, when publication first ceased, 71 volumes had been printed. Despite the uneven quality, both with regard to purity of text and usefulness of companion notes and studies, it has been the most valuable and extensive collection of Spanish literature available. To this day, it is often cited, and certain volumes remain unsurpassed. Marcelino *Menéndez y Pelayo later continued the series, under the title *Nueva biblioteca de autores españoles* (New Library of Spanish Authors), abbreviated NBAE; certain volumes are of enormous importance, such as the *Orígenes de la novela* (Origins of the Novel) by Menéndez y Pelayo, the *Crónica general* (General Chronicle) by *Menéndez Pidal, the *Libros de caballerías* (Books of Chivalry) by Alonso de *Bonilla, etc. Publication of the NBAE ceased in 1926. A second series of the BAE began publication in 1950, with Atlas Publishers, producing re-editions and new editions which adhere to more rigorous standards than those of the original series. Over 300 volumes now exist. Volume 71 (1953) indexes vols. 1-70, and volume 226 indexes vols. 72–225.

Maureen Ihrie


**BIBLIOTECA NACIONAL** (National Library). Although there existed a collection, known as the Queen Mother's Library, in 1637, the Biblioteca Nacional (originally named Biblioteca Real, or Royal Library) was founded by Philip V in 1712. The present building, located at the Avenue of Calvo Sotelo 20 in Madrid, was begun in 1866, and opened in 1894. The collection holds 24,000 original mss., over 25,000 rare books, and over 2,500 incunabulae. By law, the National Library also receives one copy of all Spanish publications. Library directors have included figures such as Leandro Fernández de *Moratín, *Hartzenbusch, *Menéndez y Pelayo; many other illustrious representatives of Spanish letters have been associated with the institution in other capacities.

BIBLIOGRAPHY

Criticism

Ponce de León, E. *Guía del Lector en la Biblioteca Nacional.* 2nd ed. Madrid: Patronato de la Biblioteca Nacional, 1949.

Maureen Ihrie


**BIEDMA Y LA MONEDA DE RODRÍGUEZ, Patrocinio,** pseudonym, Ticiano Imab (1848, Bejigar, Jaén–c. 1917, Cadiz?), journalist, novelist, poet. From a rich and illustrious family, at fifteen she married the son of a marquis; she soon was widowed and later remarried. She led an intensely active life, editing (in Cadiz) a magazine of literature, arts and sciences called *Cádiz* (1877–81) and collaborating in many journals and magazines throughout Spain.

Her first books were poetry, *Guirnalda de Pensamientos* (1872; Garland of Thoughts) and *Recuerdos de un ángel* (1874; Reminiscences of an Angel). Then she published more than 15 novels, at least four art studies, social and philosophical essays, and a study of Spanish heraldry; most are very hard to find. A few of her books were translated into French; she published in Cadiz, Madrid, Barcelona and America.

She translated from Catalan into Spanish a tragedy of Víctor *Balaguer, *La Sombra del César* (1878; The Shadow of Caesar). Blanco García characterized her fiction as "sentimental novels." The critic Cossío mentions a costumbrist ballad, *Recuerdos de Andalucía* (Reminiscences from Andalusia), included in the *Novísimo Romancero Español* (1880; Latest Spanish Ballads) and a historical poem, *El héroe de Santa Engracia* (1874; The Hero of Santa Engracia), that relates a heroic episode of a member of her husband's family during the war against French invaders.

BIBLIOGRAPHY

Primary Texts

*La boda de la niña.* Cádiz: n.p., 1885.
*Dos hermanas.* 2nd ed. Cádiz: Tipología La Mercantil, 1884.
*El héroe de Santa Engracia.* In *Novísimo Romancero Español.* Madrid: Biblioteca En-
    ciclopédica Popular Ilustrada, 1880.
*La Marquesita.* Cádiz: Tipología La Mercantil, 1892.
*El Odio de una mujer.* Cádiz: n.p., 1882.

Criticism

Blanco García, F. *La literatura española en el S. XIX.* 3rd ed. Madrid: Saenz de Jubera
    Hermanos, 1909.
Cejador y Frauca, Julio. *Historia de la lengua y literatura castellana.* 14 vols. Madrid:
    Tipología de Archivos, 1915–22.
Ferreras, Juan Ignacio. *Catálogo de novelas y novelistas españoles del s. XIX.* Madrid:
    Cátedra, 1979. 78–79.

                                                                        Cristina Enríquez

**BLACK LEGEND, The** (*La leyenda negra.*) It could be defined as the extremely negative view which West Europeans had of Spanish institutions, Spanish behavior abroad, and especially of Spanish colonization in America. Spaniards have held that the *Leyenda negra* was a propaganda device used to deprecate all things Spanish and to paint as black an image of Spain as possible. As early as the fifteenth c., there was anti-Aragonese feeling in the Italian peninsula due to Aragonese expansion in that area. S. G. Payne notes that in the 1490s the Aragonese Pope Alexander VI Borgia was called a *marrano* (swine) by Italian enemies. In the sixteenth c., anti-Aragonese feeling in Italy changed to anti-Spanish sentiments, and anti-Spanish attitudes spread to Germany. Germany went through the Protestant Revolution beginning in 1517, and tensions between German Protestants and the Spain of the Hapsburg monarchs remained high in the sixteenth and seventeenth centuries, manifesting themselves in armed conflict between German Protestants and Catholics, the latter supported by Spain. Thus, some Germans began to launch anti-Spanish propaganda.

What really fueled the *Leyenda negra* was a book written by a Spanish monk, Bartolomé de Las *Casas. Las Casas had been an *encomendero,* that is, holder of an *encomienda* or grant of Indians forced to labor for their Spanish masters, on the island of Hispaniola and in Cuba. He grew appalled at the treatment the natives were receiving at the hands of their overlords; this suffering he witnessed moved him to devote his life to helping them, and Las Casas became a Dominican monk. In 1515, he traveled to Spain to intercede on behalf of the Indians with King Ferdinand and was sent by the Regent Cardinal Jiménez de *Cisneros to Hispaniola as protector of the Indians. He attempted to devise a model Indian village in Venezuela, but it failed (1520–21). Las Casas labored tirelessly to help terminate the institution of the *encomienda* in the New World, and was partly responsible for passage of the *New Laws* in 1542, designed for the protection of the Indians. Among other things, the *New Laws* provided for the gradual extinction of the *encomienda*; this measure met with such opposition, it could not be enforced. In 1552, Las Casas's book appeared, the *Brevíssima relación de la destruyción de las Indias* (*In Defense of the Indians against the Persecutors and Slanderers of the Peoples of the New World,* 1974). This tiny book was to be used by many Western Europeans to denounce Spanish behavior in America. Las Casas held that millions of Indians had been exterminated by the *encomienda* in the Antilles and gave some gruesome descriptions of treatment of the aborigines. Although there was no doubt some truth in his assertions, he probably indulged in exaggerations too. The book laid a solid foundation for the Black Legend. It was a huge success, and by the eighteenth c. there were three Italian editions, three Latin, four English, six French, eight German, and eighteen Dutch. A London edition of 1689 carried this title: *Popery truly Display'd in its bloody Colours; or a Faithful Narrative of the Horrid and Unexampled Massacres, Butcheries, and all manner of Cruelties, that Hell and Malice could invent, committed by the Popish Spanish Party, on the Inhabitants of West India. Composed first in Spanish by Bartholomew de las Casas, a Bishop there, and an Eye-Witness of most of these Barbarous Cruelties; afterwards translated by him into Latin, then by other hands into High-Dutch, Low-Dutch, French and now Taught to speak modern English.* Las Casas was the center of controversies until his death in 1566. He challenged the most famous humanist of his time, Juan Ginés de *Sepúlveda, who asserted that wars on the Indians were just, because God had ordained certain men to be slaves. Most of the Spanish clergy rejected Las Casas's arguments and the Spanish colonists hated him. But in the rest of Western Europe he was read with fascinated attention and applauded by most.

Another element that helped launch the Black Legend was the atrocious behavior of Spain in the Low Countries. Repression there was bloody, especially during the epoch of the Duke of Alba in the 1560s, and the Dutch were to remember this for a long time. According to Payne, "the first full-blown statement of the Black Legend was the *Apology* of the Dutch leader William the Silent, prepared in 1580 and circulated throughout Western Europe" (1,266). This document accused Spaniards of cruelty and fanaticism, emphasizing the nefarious role of the *Inquisition, the suppression of *moriscos, and the destruction of millions of Indians. How many of these accusations were accurate, and how many were the figments of the writers' imaginations? Spaniards did commit atrocities in the Indies and in the Netherlands, though the figure of many millions of Indians dead at the hands of the Spaniards is doubtless an exaggeration, as we have stated above. Yet modern research has shown that the figure of three million Indians living in the Caribbean before the arrival of Columbus should be accepted. And of course they all disappeared in a short time, and the argument that they died off because of disease is no longer tenable as there is no record of any epidemic among the Indians of the Antilles before 1518.

In the development of the Black Legend we also should not forget the role played by Antonio *Pérez, secretary of Philip II of Spain. In 1578, Pérez pre-cipitated the murder of Juan de Escobedo, secretary of Don Juan de Austria, governor of Flanders, with the possible connivance of Philip. The motives for this sinister affair were the mutual jealousies of Philip and Don Juan, which Pérez did the utmost to exploit. When the possibility arose that Escobedo, who had arrived in Madrid, would reveal Pérez's plotting, the latter had him done away with. Jailed for a number of years, Pérez was able to escape from Spain in 1591. He offered his services to Henry IV of France and Elizabeth of England, both enemies of Philip II. In England, Pérez published his *Relaciones* (1594; Accounts), which attacked Philip II and his policies. Naturally Spain's enemies saw in this work an additional weapon in their anti-Spanish campaign. Another anti-Hispanic work, in English, printed in London by Pérez and titled *Treatise paraenetical*, also contributed to English negative feelings toward Philip and Spain. The full title indicates the work's purpose: *A Treatise Paraenetical, That is to say, an Exhortation Wherein is showed by good and evident reasons, infallible arguments, most true and certaine histories, and notable examples; the right way and true means to resist the violence of the Castilian king; to break the course of his desseignes; to beat down his pride, and to ruinaate his puissance*. But even some Spaniards would in more modern times paint a negative image of the Spain of the sixteenth c. and of Philip II. A case in point is Angel de Saavedra, Duke of *Rivas, author of the famous *Romances históricos* (1841; Historical Ballads). In one of these *romances*, entitled *Una noche de Madrid en 1578* (A Madrid Night in 1578), Philip II is shown plotting the murder of Escobedo with Antonio Pérez. The king is a decidedly sinister figure:

> Melancólico era el uno,
> de edad cascada y marchita,
> macilento, enjuto, grave,
> rostro como de ictericia;
> ojos siniestros, que a veces
> de una hiena parecían,
> otras vagos, indecisos
> y de apagadas pupilas. . . .
> . . . . .
> Y escaso y rojo cabello,
> y barba pobre y mezquina
> le daban a su semblante
> rara expresión y ambigua.

(One of them was melancholic, / worn out and withered in age, / emaciated, dried up, solemn, / his face yellow like jaundice; / with wicked eyes, that at times / seemed like a hyena's / at other times, they were vacant, hesitant / with lifeless pupils / . . . / and sparse red hair, / and a poor, miserly beard / gave to his ap-pearance / a strange, ambiguous look.)

It is somewhat surprising that a nationalist, and by the time the *romances* were published, a conservative such as Rivas chose to portray Philip II in an essentially negative light, though a certain Satanic grandeur at times emanates from this figure. After all, under Philip II Spain was immensely powerful and universally feared. The answer lies perhaps in the impact made on the poet by the bad reputation which Philip II enjoyed with the eighteenth-c. European Enlightenment and with Spanish liberals—a reputation still widely accepted by the Spain of the 1830s, which had only recently suffered under another despot, Ferdinand VII. The rehabilitation of Philip II, begun in the later nineteenth c., reached a climax during the Franco dictatorship, when Philip was consistently portrayed as the good, "prudent" king.

BIBLIOGRAPHY
Primary Texts
Casas, Bartolomé de las. *Brevísima relación de la destrucción del las Indias*. Buenos Aires: Editorial Universitaria, 1966.
Pérez, A. *A treatise Paraenetical*. . . . Tr. I. D. Dralymont. London: Ponsonby, 1598.
———. *Cartas de Antonio Pérez*. In BAE 13.
———. *Las obras y relaciones de Antonio Pérez*. Geneva: Tournes, 1676.
*The Drama of William of Orange*. Ed. L. H. Lehman. New York: Agora, 1937.
    English Translation
Las Casas, B. *The Tears of the Indians; Being an Historical and True Account of the Cruel Massacres and Slaughters of Above Twenty Millions of Innocent People*. Tr. J. Philips. Williamstown, MA: Lilburne, 1970.
    Criticism
Arnoldson, S. *La conquista española de América según el juicio de la posteridad; vestigios de la leyenda negra*. Madrid: Insula, 1960.
Juderías, J. *La leyenda negra*. Madrid: Nacional, 1967.
Maltby, W. S. *The Black Legend in England*. Durham, NC: Duke UP, 1971.
Payne, S. G. *A History of Spain and Portugal*. Madison, WI: U of Wisconsin P, 1973. 1: 264–66.
Powell, Philip W. *Tree of Hate*. New York: Basic Books, 1971.
Ungerer, G. *A Spaniard in Elizabethan England: The Correspondence of Antonio Pérez's Exile*. 2 vols. London: Tamesis, 1974.

                                                        Gabriel Lovett

**BLAJOT, Jorge** (1921, Barcelona– ), poet, essayist and literary critic. Father Blajot, a Jesuit priest, has published several volumes of religious poetry. His works include *Veruela: Juventud en el claustro* (1947; Veruela: Youth in the Cloister) and two books of poetry: *Hombre interior* (1952; Interior Man) and *La hora sin tiempo* (1958; The Hour Without Time).

BIBLIOGRAPHY
Primary Texts
*Hombre interior*. Madrid: Cultura Hispánica, 1952.
*La hora sin tiempo*. Barcelona: Flors, 1958.

                                                    Victoria Wolff Unruh

**BLANCO AGUINAGA, Carlos** (1926, Irún– ), novelist, literary scholar, professor. Widely known for his books on *Unamuno (Unamuno, teórico del lenguaje, El Unamuno contemplativo* [México, 1954 and 1959 respectively]) and other authors of the *Generation of 1898 (*Juventud del 98* [Madrid, 1970]), he has authored also many articles of literary criticism ranging from the *Siglo de Oro* to contemporary writers, has written short stories and poetry (see *Presencia* [México, 1948–50], of which he was one of the founders, *Peña Labra* 35–36 [Santander, 1980]), also novels, of which one, *Ojos de papel volando*, has been published (Barcelona, 1984; Eyes of Paper Flying). He has co-authored, with Julio Rodríguez-Puértolas and Iris Zavala, the controversial *Historia social de la literatura española (en lengua castellana)* (Madrid, 1979; 2nd ed. 1981), in which, as the authors state in the "Explicación previa," the intention is to study the story of literature from a dialectical perspective and, leaving aside positivistic and avant-garde, idealistic approaches, attempt to comprehend the creative work both in itself and in its relation to other works, as well as the common relation that the sum of them has to changing social structures and ideologies. Blanco Aguinaga has also an extensive study on the poetry of Emilio *Prados (*Emilio Prados, vida y obra* [New York, 1960]) and has amply edited the work of this poet (Emilio Prados, *Poesías completas* [México, 1975]). He has held appointments at Ohio State U, Johns Hopkins U and the U of California, first at Riverside and, since 1964, at San Diego, where he now resides. From 1980, he has held, conjointly, a Professorship at the Universidad del País Vasco.

BIBLIOGRAPHY

Primary Texts

*Historia social*. 2nd ed. 3 vols. Madrid: Castalia, 1981.
*Juventud del 98*. 2nd ed. Barcelona: Crítica, 1978.
*Ojos de papel volando*. Barcelona: Grijalbo, 1984.

Alan A. González

**BLANCO AMOR, Eduardo** (1897, Orense–1979, Orense), Galician poet, short story writer, novelist, essayist. From an early age, Blanco Amor lived in Argentina, where he maintained an intense level of journalistic activity. He was editor of the newspaper of the *Federación de Sociedades Galegas* (Galician Societies' Federation) and of the journals *Céltiga* and *A Terra* (The Land). He also served as correspondent for *La Nación* (The Nation) of Buenos Aires in Spain during the 1930s. He was a member of the faculty of Humanities and Sciences in Uruguay and of the *Escuela Internacional de Temporada* in Santiago de Chile. In addition, he was the director of the Spanish Chamber Theater in Buenos Aires. Blanco Amor's major importance, however, is based on his literary creation, which includes all genres and is in both Galician and Castilian.

Blanco Amor's poetry is a masterly blend of avant-garde elements such as Cubist and Surrealist images and metaphors, with the medieval techniques found in other Galician writers as well in the twentieth c. neo-troubador tendency that is still present in Galician poetry today. His prose demonstrates an attempt at the renovation of narrative structures in Galician prose. *A esmorga* (1959; The Good Times) has been compared with Camus's *La chute*, although its author denies having read its supposed precursor. In *Xente ao lonxe* (1972; Far-away

People), the novelistic narrator is a child, a frequent feature in Galician prose. Its descriptions of human misery have been compared by Carballo Calero to *Naturalism. The short story collection *Os biosbardos* (1962; Fantasies) again maintains the child protagonist and recalls the popular tone so prevalent in much of Galician creation.

As a friend of *García Lorca, Blanco Amor is said to have played an important part in the composition of Lorca's *Seis poemas gallegos* (Six Galician Poems).

## BIBLIOGRAPHY

### Primary Texts

*A esmorga*. Buenos Aires: n.p., 1959.
*Cancioneiro*. Buenos Aires: n.p., 1955.
*La catedral y el niño*. Buenos Aires: n.p., 1949.
*Castelao*. No city: n.p., 1974.
*En soledad amena*. Buenos Aires: n.p., 1941.
*Farsas*. Buenos Aires: n.p., 1953; México: n.p., 1962.
*Horizonte evadido*. No city: n.p., 1963.
*Las buenas maneras*. No city: n.p., 1974.
*Os Biosbardos*. Vigo: n.p., 1962.
*El padre Feijoo*. No city: n.p., 1974.
*Poema en catro tempos*. Buenos Aires: n.p., 1931.
*Romances galegos*. Buenos Aires: n.p., 1928.
*Teatro pra xente*. Vigo: n.p., 1974.
*Xente ao lonxe*. Vigo: n.p., 1972.

### Criticism

Carballo Calero, Ricardo. *Historia da literatura galega contemporánea*. Vigo: Galaxia, 1982.
Casares Mouriño, Carlos, "Leria con Eduardo Blanco Amor." *Grial* 41 (1973): 337–44.
Lourenzo y Pillado Mayor, Manuel. *O teatro galego*. A Cruña: O Castro, 1979.
Vázquez Cuesta, Pilar, "Literatura gallega." In *Historia de las literaturas hispánicas no castellanas*. Ed. J. M. Díez Borque. Madrid: Taurus, 1980.

                                                           Kathleen March


**BLANCO AMOR, José** (1910, ?– ), novelist. A Spanish journalist, already established as a voluntary expatriate in Buenos Aires before the arrival of the flood of refugees from the Civil War, Blanco Amor came late to the novel, producing *La vida que nos dan* (The Life Which Is Given Us), with which he won the Premio Valle-Inclán, in 1953. Apparently a nostalgic recollection of childhood, the narrative is described as a vivid evocation of childhood in rural Spain. In later novels, Blanco Amor explores the urban problems of Buenos Aires with its latent social pathology, as in *Todos los muros eran grises* (1956; All the Walls Were Grey). The author has explained the novel's genesis as his perceptions during a bus ride through the slums of Buenos Aires at dawn one winter day in 1935, seeing the unemployed living like mice or rats in hovels of tin cans and empty boxes. The novel is divided into four parts, each of which relates a decisive moment in the psychological disintegration of Lara, a Spaniard and the protagonist, who moves from the most sordid proletarian neighborhoods to the endless landscapes of the pampas and finally to the shores of Mar del Plata. Blanco Amor pays special attention to the exploitation of workers, as well as the exploitation of some immigrants by others, and to the worst aspects of ethnic rivalries, xenophobia and prejudice.

*Antes que el tiempo muera* (1957; Before Time Dies) explores a northern Argentine province, near the Chaco, relating the disintegration of a family of large landholders of Spanish background. A conflict of violent passions results from years of struggle between father and daughter for control, culminating in apparent parricide and the later murder by the daughter of her illegitimate son. Blanco Amor contrasts the splendor of the Hispanic past with the degradation of the present, and interweaves many scenes of colonial customs, indigenous legends, tales from the period of conquest, and superstitions. *Duelo por la tierra perdida* (1959; Mourning for the Lost Land) portrays a Spanish political refugee and his struggle to adjust to and be accepted by Buenos Aires society. A successful writer who lives in a wealthy suburb, he entertains fairly lavishly as he and his second wife celebrate the wedding of his stepdaughter. His wife invites all the refugees whose names she finds in her husband's address book, a social gaffe which nonetheless permits the novelist to analyze a broad range of exile types. However, the protagonist is tormented by the secret of having abandoned his wife and children in Spain. Although aware that they had survived, for unexplained reasons he did not attempt to contact them, and in fact sold his property there, leaving them in such poverty that it causes the wife's death. Much of the novel's emphasis is upon the lack of understanding between Argentines and the Spanish exiles, a lack of Hispanic solidarity, as well as the presence of a substantial population of other ethnicities and their scorn for Hispanics. Blanco Amor describes a world in transition, without faith, where characters' lives are marked by tedium, solitude, disbelief, skepticism, and suffering, all of it intensified by the exile experience and the incompatibility between Spaniards and their lands of exile.

BIBLIOGRAPHY

Primary Texts

*Antes que el tiempo muera*. Buenos Aires: Losada, 1957.
*Duelo por la tierra perdida*. Buenos Aires: Losada, 1959.
*Todos los muros eran grises*. Buenos Aires: Losada, 1956.

Criticism

Zelaya Kolker, Marielena. *Testimonios americanos de los escritores españoles transterrados de 1939*. Madrid: Cultura Hispánica, 1985. 147–61.

Janet Pérez

**BLANCO SOLER, Carlos** (1894, Madrid–1962, Madrid), essayist and historian. A doctor who published several medical studies, Blanco Soler is also known for several historical works. These include *La duquesa de Alba y su tiempo*

BLANCO WHITE, JOSÉ MARÍA

(1949; The Duchess of Alba and Her Time), which examines the relationship between the Duchess and Goya, and *Papeles importantes del reinado de Fernando VII* (1952; Important Papers from the Reign of Ferdinand VII). Other works include *Fe y poesía de España* (1950; Faith and Poetry of Spain) and a novel, *El hijo de Don Juan* (1946; The Son of Don Juan), which presents a continuation of the story of Don Juan Tenorio.

BIBLIOGRAPHY

Primary Texts

*El hijo de Don Juan.* Madrid: Aguilar, 1946.
*Fe y poesía de España.* Madrid: Bolaños y Aguilar, 1950.
*La duquesa de Alba y su tiempo.* Madrid: EPESA, 1949.
*Papeles importantes del reinado de Fernado VII.* N.p.: n.p., 1952.

Victoria Wolff Unruh

**BLANCO WHITE, José María,** family name used interchangeably with Blanco y Crespo (1775, Seville–1841, Liverpool, England), journalist, poet, and religious polemicist. Born of devout Irish Catholic parents who settled in Andalusia, Blanco White received a thorough formal education, acquiring a knowledge of several languages. He was strongly encouraged to follow an ecclesiastical career and was ordained, but later became a liberal and a skeptic after reading *Feijoo and Fénelon. His reputation as an outstanding orator enabled him to secure a position as a chaplain in Seville, where he collaborated in editing the newspaper *Semanario Patriótico*.

In 1810, as a result of the Napoleonic invasion, Blanco White was forced to flee to Cádiz and later to London, the intellectual center for many Spanish exiles, where he met *Martínez de la Rosa. There, he founded another newspaper, *El Español* (The Spaniard), and the magazine *Variedades o el Mensajero de Londres* (Miscellany or the London Messenger). *Letters from Spain* (1822), a depiction of Spanish customs and manners published under the pseudonym Don Leocadio Doblado, established his literary reputation in England, and he became friendly with John Stuart Mill and Robert Southey. His "El Alcázar de Sevilla" (The Prison/Castle of Seville), published anonymously in *No me olvides* in 1825, is sometimes considered one of the earliest documents of Spanish *Romanticism. Tormented by religious doubts, Blanco White converted to Anglicanism while teaching at Oxford U in the 1820s, and he produced several works refuting Catholicism, including *Practical and Internal Evidence Against Catholicism* (1825) and *Second Travels of an Irish Gentleman in Search of a Religion* (1833). In the 1830s, Blanco White resided in Liverpool and converted to Unitarianism. His command of both English and Spanish allowed him to compose poetry with equal facility in either language.

BIBLIOGRAPHY

Primary Texts

Poetry. In BAE 67. 649–663.
*Letters from Spain.* London: H. Colburn, 1822.

*The Life of the Rev. Joseph Blanco White, Written by Himself.* Ed. J. H. Thom. 3 vols. London: J. Chapman, 1845.

*Practical and Internal Evidence Against Catholicism.* London: J. Murray, 1825.

*Second Travels of an Irish Gentleman in Search of a Religion.* Dublin: R. Milliken and Son, 1833.

Criticism

Alborg, Juan Luis. *Historia de la literatura española.* Madrid: Gredos, 1980. Vol. 4.

Méndez Bejarano, Mario. *Vida y obras de D. José Mª. Blanco y Crespo (Blanco White).* Madrid: RABM, 1920.

Linda Maier

**BLASCO IBÁÑEZ, Vicente** (1867, Valencia–1928, Menton, France), Valencian novelist, short story writer, and essayist. He was a precocious novelist who began his literary career at the age of fourteen. He studied law in his native city of Valencia. In Madrid he became the secretary of Manuel *Fernández y González, the popular and prolific writer of serial novels. While very young he supported the tenets of the Republican party, headed by the Catalonian Francisco *Pi y Margall. Blasco Ibáñez acquired much popularity as a politician and was congressman for seven terms. Because of his political beliefs, he engaged in street fighting, was jailed thirty times, was involved in a series of duels, and was exiled. His life of wandering through foreign lands began with his escape to Paris in 1890 to avoid prison. In 1920 George Washington U conferred upon him an honorary doctoral degree. He spent the last part of his life in Menton, on the Mediterranean coast of France.

An eclectic novelist, he was a man of action and of powerful and vivid imagination. He was the most read and translated contemporary European novelist in the first half of this century. In a 1924 contest sponsored by the *International Book Revue* of New York to determine the ten most popular writers in the United States, England, and Australia, Blasco Ibáñez placed second to H. G. Wells, author of *Outline of History* (1920). Movie versions have been made of many of his novels. In addition, he published travelogues, a collection of articles on Mexico, and countless short stories. Blasco Ibáñez, *Pardo Bazán, and Leopoldo Alas (*Clarín) form the triad of the best short story writers of Spanish realism. In some of his short stories, Blasco Ibáñez treats the same themes as those present in his novels, but with more rapid and impressionistic technique. Of great interest are the two collections of *Cuentos valencianos* (1896, 1900; Tales of Valencia) and *Novelas de amor y muerte* (1927; Tales of Love and Death).

His novels may be divided into five groups:

1. The Valencian group dealing with various aspects of the life of Blasco Ibáñez's native region: *Arroz y Tartana* (1894; *The Three Roses*, 1932), a social, economic, and moral study of the Valencian middle class; *Flor de mayo* (1895; *The Mayflower*, 1921), a study of the misery and difficult existence of the fishermen of the Valencian coast; *La barraca* (1898; *The Cabin*, 1917), the

conflict and struggle for existence among the farmers in the irrigated plain of Valencia; *Entre naranjos* (1900; *The Torrent*, 1921); *Sónnica la cortesana* (1901; *Sonnica*, 1912), a historical and archaeological perspective of Saguntum; *Cañas y barro* (1902; *Reeds and Mud*, 1928), a study of base passions unleashed in the fetid environment of the lagoon.

2. The group of the thesis novels: *La catedral* (1903; *The Shadow of the Cathedral*, 1909), the vicissitudes of an anarchist in Toledo; *El intruso* (1904; *The Intruder*, 1928), the migration of workers, their poverty and impact on the traditions and religious beliefs of the inhabitants of Bilbao; *La bodega* (1905; *Fruit of the Vine*, 1919), the workings of an anarchist among the workers of the city of Jerez; *La horda* (1905; *The Mob*, 1927), a treatment of the law and the poor classes in Madrid; *La maja desnuda* (1906; *Woman Triumphant*, 1920), a psychological study of moral destruction resulting from the struggle between the artistic temperament and the love for a woman; *Sangre y arena* (1908; *The Blood of the Arena*, 1911), a study of a bullfighter and his relationships with women, set against the background of the national institution of bullfighting; *Los muertos mandan* (1909; *The Dead Command*, 1919), the dilemma of the protagonist torn between religious traditions and social laws and the ultimate triumph of love.

3. The group of American themes: *Los argonautas* (1914; The Argonauts), a treatment of the Spanish migration to South America; *La tierra de todos* (1922; *The Temptress*, 1923), the effect of a woman's refusal to conform to local customs on a small Argentine town.

4. The fourth group, centering on the theme of World War I: *Los cuatro jinetes del Apocalipsis* (1916; *The Four Horsemen of the Apocalypse*, 1918), a novel which traces the fortunes of an Argentine family on both sides of the Atlantic during World War I and which, in its English translation and exceedingly successful film version, catapulted Blasco Ibáñez to fame, thus causing him to be the most universally renowned Spanish author of the twentieth c.; *Mare Nostrum* (1918; *Our Sea*, 1919), a powerfully descriptive treatment of the German submarine warfare in the Mediterranean; *Los enemigos de la mujer* (1919; *The Enemies of Women*, 1920), a study of the inevitable paradox of the destructive yet redemptive influence of ''woman.''

5. The fifth group, dealing with miscellaneous themes: *El paraíso de las mujeres* (1922; Women's Paradise), a novel whose characters live in a world of pure fantasy, a world beyond reality; *La reina Calafia* (1923; *Queen Calafia*, 1924), an intertwining of various periods of past history and a modern episode; *El papa del mar* (1925; *The Pope of the Sea: A Historic Medley*, 1927), a treatment of Avignon and the Aragonese antipope Pedro de Luna; *En busca del gran Khan* (1929; *Unknown Lands: The Story of Columbus*, 1929), a novelistic biography of Columbus; *El caballero de la Virgen* (1929; *The Knight of the Virgin*, 1930), a novelistic account of Alonso de Ojeda, who accompanied Columbus on his second voyage; *El fantasma de las alas de oro* (1930; *The Phantom with Wings of Gold*, 1931), a study of the international society of Monte Carlo.

By intertwining vivid, colorful, sensual, luxuriant, imaginative yet realistic techniques, Blasco Ibáñez vivifies the Valencian *huerta* and dramatizes the wretched lives of its people who viciously struggle among themselves for mere survival. Blasco Ibáñez, in his earlier works, is a true disciple of Zola. Perceiving the new developments in science, however, he causes his later novels to reflect the continuous interaction and inevitable effect of science on people and to evolve from the study of the conflict between man and his environment to the less readily apparent drama of the passions within the inner self.

BIBLIOGRAPHY

Primary Texts

*Obras completas.* 3 vols. Madrid: Aguilar, 1947.
Plaza y Janés, Barcelona, has been republishing all individual novels since 1978.

English Translations

*Blood and Sand.* Tr. F. Partridge. New York: Ungar, 1958.
*La Bodega (The Fruit of the Vine).* Tr. I. Goldberg. New York: Dutton, 1919.
*The Borgias; or, At the Feet of Venus.* Tr. A. Livington. New York: Dutton, 1930.
*The Cabin.* Tr. F. Haffkine Snow and B. M. Mekota. New York: Knopf, 1917.
*The Dead Command.* Tr. F. Douglas. New York: Duffield, 1919.
*The Enemies of Women.* Tr. I. Brown. New York: Dutton, 1920.
*The Four Horsemen of the Apocalypse.* Tr. C. Brewster Jordan. 1918. Rpt. New York: Dutton, 1962.
*The Intruder.* Tr. Mrs. W. A. Gillespie. New York: Dutton, 1928.
*The Knight of the Virgin.* Tr. A. Livingston. New York: Dutton, 1930.
*Mare Nostrum (Our Sea).* Tr. C. Brewster Jordan. New York: Dutton, 1919.
*The Mayflower: A Tale of the Valencian Seashore.* Tr. A. Livingston. New York: Dutton, 1921.
*The Mob.* Tr. M. Joaquín Lorente. New York: Dutton, 1927.
*The Naked Lady.* Tr. F. Partridge. London: Elek, 1959.
*The Phantom with Wings of Gold.* Tr. A. Livingston. New York: Dutton, 1931.
*The Pope of the Sea: An Historic Medley.* Tr. A. Livingston. New York: Dutton, 1927.
*Queen Calafia.* Tr. anon. New York: Dutton, 1924.
*Reeds and Mud.* Tr. L. Beberfall. Boston: Humphries, 1966.
*The Shadow of the Cathedral.* Tr. Mrs. W. A. Gillespie. New York: Dutton, 1909.
*Sonnica.* Tr. F. Douglas. New York: Duffield, 1912.
*The Temptress.* Tr. L. Ongley. New York: Dutton, 1923.
*The Three Roses.* Tr. S. E. Grummon. New York: Dutton, 1932.
*The Torrent.* Tr. I. Goldberg and A. Livingston. New York: Dutton, 1921.
*Unknown Lands; The Story of Columbus.* Tr. A. Livingston. New York: Dutton, 1929.

Criticism

Day, A. Grove, and Edgar C. Knowlton, Jr. *Vicente Blasco Ibáñez.* TWAS 235. New York: Twayne, 1972.
Entrambasaguas, Joaquín de. *Las mejores novelas contemporáneas (1900–1904).* Barcelona: Planeta, 1958. 3–80. Contains a good bibliography.
Esteban, Manuel A. ''Zola and Blasco Ibáñez: A New Look.'' *Nineteenth Century French Studies* 8 (1979–80): 87–100.

Fabbri, Maurizio. "Per una rilettura dell'opera di Blasco Ibáñez." *Spicilegio Moderno: Saggi e Ricerche di Letterature e Lingue Straniere* 7 (1977): 85–104.

Langston, Carol Ann Levert. "Female Primary Characters in Several of Blasco's Valencian Novels." Diss. Louisiana State U. *Dissertation Abstracts* 40 (1980): 6304A.

Pitollet, Camille. *V. Blasco-Ibáñez. Ses romans et le roman de sa vie.* Paris: Calmann-Lévy, 1921.

Smith, Paul. *Vicente Blasco Ibáñez. An Annotated Bibliography.* London: Grant & Cutler, 1976. An excellent work which contains primary and secondary bibiographic entries from 1882 through 1974.

Suárez, Bernardo. "Técnicas impresionistas en las novelas valencianas de Blasco Ibáñez." In *The Twenty-Seventh Annual Mountain Interstate Foreign Language Conference.* Eds. Eduardo Zayas-Bazán and M. Laurentino Suárez. Johnson City: East Tennessee State U, 1977. 273–79.

Swain, James O. *Vicente Blasco Ibáñez. General Study with Emphasis on Realistic Techniques.* Knoxville: n.p., 1959.

Xandro, Mauricio. *Blasco Ibáñez.* Madrid: Espesa, 1971.

Gilbert Paolini

**BLECUA TEIJEIRO, José Manuel** (1913, Alcolea de Cinca– ), critic. A professor at the U of Barcelona, he has devoted much of his professional life to the study of Spanish poetry, producing numerous scholarly editions, including Juan de *Mena's *Laberinto* (1943; Labyrinth); the *Cancionero de 1628* (1945); *Rimas inéditas de Herrera* (1948; Unpublished Poems of Herrera), and various unknown or lost poems of Fray Luis de *León, Lope de *Vega and others. He produced a critical edition of don *Juan Manuel's *Libro infinido* (1938), as well as various other editions of classical writers, anthologies of poetry, a number of student manuals, a short *Historia de la literatura española* (History of Spanish Literature) and *El mar en la poesía española* (1945; The Sea in Spanish Poetry). He has also done critical editions of the poetry of Lupercio and Bartolomé Leonardo de *Argensola (Zaragoza, 1950) and an extensive study of Jorge *Guillén's *Cántico*.

Janet Pérez

**BLEIBERG, Germán** (1915, Madrid–1990, Madrid), distinguished poet, editor scholar. He obtained his doctorate in Philosophy and Letters at the University of Madrid. Exiled to the United States following the Civil War, he taught at Vassar College, Harvard University, SUNY Albany, as well as other U.S. institutions. He drew the attention of the literary world in 1936 with the publication of his book *Sonetos amorosos* (Love Sonnets) which, together with *El rayo que no cesa* by Miguel *Hernández and *Abril* of Luis *Rosales, became the foundation of the "Garcilasista" movement. In 1938, he shared the National Prize for Literature with Miguel Hernández.

In 1947, drawing away from his earlier classicism, he published *Más allá de las ruinas* (Beyond the Ruins), which includes a selection of ten years of his work. Two volumes appeared in 1948: *El poeta ausente* (The Absent Poet) with sketches by Gregorio Prieto, and *La mutua primavera* (Mutual Spring). In 1951 appeared his *Antología de elogios de la lengua española* (Eulogies of the Spanish Language). *Selección de Poemas 1936–1973* (1975; Selected Poems 1936–1973) includes both previously published and unpublished poems.

In his capacity as scholar, Dr. Bleiberg was a major force in the growth of Hispanism in the twentieth century: he directed the edition of the three volume *Diccionario de historia de España* (1952, rpt. 1968–69; Dictionary of Spanish History); co-edited *Spanish Thought and Letters in the Twentieth Century* (1966) with Inman Fox; co-directed with Julián Marías the first four editions of the *Diccionario de literatura española* (1949, 1953, 1964, 1972; Dictionary of Spanish Literature). With John E. Varey, he founded and co-directed the distinguished publishing house Tamesis Books Limited, devoted to Hispanic letters. He was also a member of The Hispanic Society of America.

BIBLIOGRAPHY

*Antología de la literatura española.* 4 vols. Madrid: Alianza, 1970–72.

*Diccionario de historia de España.* 2nd ed. 3 vols. Madrid: RO, 1968–69.

*Diccionario de literatura española.* 4th ed. Madrid: RO, 1972.

*El "informe secreto" de Mateo Alemán sobre el trabajo forzoso en las minas de Almadén.* London: Tamesis, 1985.

*Selección de Poemas 1936–1973.* London: Grant & Cutler, 1975.

*Spanish Thought and Letters in the Twentieth Century.* Nashville: Vanderbilt UP, 1966.

Translation

B. "Eclogue of the Shipwreck: 3 and 5." Tr. E. Inman Fox. In *Chelsea* 24–25 (1968): 26–27.

Criticism

González Muela, Joaquín. "Sobre la poesía de Germán Bleiberg." *Insula* 41 (May 1986): 7.

***BOBO*** (buffoon, or dunce), a character of the sixteenth-c. Spanish drama found in both religious and secular theater. A popular figure, he is noted for his rusticity and foolishness and his use of the conventional rustic jargon, *sayagués*. The character first appears in early Nativity plays, where his principal attributes are ignorance and boorishness, yet he is also related to the medieval court fool. The figure on occasion evolves into the wise fool, particularly in the plays of *Torres Naharro where he is used as a vehicle for moralizing. Torres Naharro's depiction of the comic rustic is later imitated by Lope de *Rueda in his *pasos. See also* Theater in Spain.

BIBLIOGRAPHY

Criticism

Brotherton, John. *The "Pastor-Bobo" in the Spanish Theater.* London: Tamesis, 1975.

Salomon, Noël. *Recherches sur le thème paysan dans la 'comedia' au temps de Lope de Vega*. Bordeaux: Institut d'Études Ibériques et Ibéro-Americaines de l'Université de Bordeaux, 1965.

Deborah Compte

**BOCÁNGEL Y UNZUETA, Gabriel** (1603, Madrid–1658, Madrid), poet. He was also librarian to the Cardinal Prince don Ferdinand, to whom he dedicated his *Lira de las musas* (1635; The Muses' Lyre). In *Rimas* (1627; Verses), he states his views on learned poetry. Both collections contain ballads and sonnets which reveal his talent as a fine *culterano* poet. His lyric attempts to achieve more than sensorial effects, and reveals the influence of *Góngora and *Jáuregui. *See also* Culteranismo.

BIBLIOGRAPHY

Primary Texts

*Al invicto y serenísimo señor don Fernando de Austria, infante de España*. N.p.: Sánchez, 1637.
*Elegía en la muerte de Lope Félix de Vega Carpio, insigne poeta*. Valladolid: Donaire, 1939.
*La lira de las musas*. Madrid: Cátedra, 1985.
*Obras*. Ed. R. Benítez Claros. Madrid: CSIC, 1946.
*Sonetos*. Barcelona: Devenir, 1984.

Criticism

Dadson, T. J. "An Autograph Copy of Gabriel Bocángel's *El cortesano español*." *BHS* 53 (1976): 301–14.
———. "Gabriel Bocángel's *Consejos cristianos, morales, y poéticos:* A New, Longer and Better Text." *BHS* 61.2 (1984): 151–64.
———. "Poesías inéditas de Bocángel." *BBMP* 48 (1972): 327–57.
———. "Poesías inéditas de Bocángel: poesías nupciales." *BBMP* 52 (1976): 155–74.
———. "Some Problems Connected with the Printing and Dating of Gabriel Bocángel's *La lira de las musas*." *MLR* 77.4 (1982): 848–59.

Andrea Warren Hamos

**BÖHL DE FABER, Juan Nicolás** (1770, Hamburg, Germany–1863, Cádiz), German Hispanist established in Cádiz and father of the writer *Fernán Caballero, pseudonym of Cecilia Böhl de Faber. In 1814 he began a literary campaign promoting Schlegel's ideas on the Spanish *Romancero and the theater of the Golden Age. As initiator of romantic ideas in Spain, in 1818 he began his long polemic with the neoclassicists José Joaquín de *Mora and *Alcalá Galiano, both of whom attacked his romantic theories. He published in Germany a *Floresta de rimas antiguas castellanas* (1821–25; Anthology of Ancient Castilian Rhymes) and *Teatro español anterior a Lope de Vega* (1832; Spanish Theater before Lope de Vega) in which he sought to rehabilitate classical Spanish literature. In Cadiz he put on a number of *Calderón's plays with great success. In general, he supported a return to traditional Spanish literature which reflects popular ideals, the monarchy and Christian values. His example was followed by Agustín *Durán who in 1828 began to edit his ballad book, and who attacked neoclassical theater in favor of Lope and Calderón. *See also* Romanticism.

BIBLIOGRAPHY

Primary Texts

*Donde las dan, las toman.* Cadiz: Villegas, 1814.
*Floresta de rimas antiguas castellanas.* Hamburg: Perthes y Besser, 1821–25.
*Vindicaciones de Calderón y del teatro antiguo español contra los afrancesados en literatura.* Cadiz: Carreño, 1820.
*Teatro español anterior a Lope de Vega.* Hamburg: F. Perthes, 1832.

Criticism

Alborg, Juan Luis. *Historia de la literatura española.* Vol. 4, *El romanticismo.* Madrid: Gredos, 1980. 73–87.
Llorens, Vicente. *El romanticismo español. Ideas literarias. Literatura e historia.* Madrid: Castalia, 1979.
Peers, E. Allison. *Historia del movimiento romántico español.* Madrid: Gredos, 1954.

Phoebe Porter Medina

**BOJIGANGA,** a type of acting troupe during the *Siglo de Oro. The term referred to a rather large troupe, with two women, a boy, and six or seven men, who would travel from village to town, performing a variety of plays, *autos*, etc. *See also* Compañía.

**BOLEA, José** (1906?, Valencia?– ), novelist. Another Spanish exile who is little known, Bolea has published several books in his adoptive land of Mexico, where he arrived in 1939 after having crossed the Pyrenees on foot and having been confined in the French concentration camp of Argeles. Escaping, he reached Paris, and later obtained passage in steerage to Mexico. *La isla en el río* (1971; The Island in the River), his first novel, follows in the steps of the turn-of-the-century regional novel, re-creating Valencian characters in a fashion reminiscent of *Blasco-Ibáñez. From the perspective of Republican refugees in Mexico in 1970, through a variety of retrospective techniques, Bolea re-creates the period leading up to exile. *Viento del noroeste* (1972; Northwest Wind) is a historical narrative based upon several years of research, and carries a lengthy bibliography at the end. It relates the discovery of the route used by ships to go from the western coast of Mexico to the Philippines and return with spices, silks and perfumes of the Far East, and re-creates the risks involved: hunger, scurvy and other sicknesses, shipwrecks, pirates, storms. Bolea emphasizes the contributions of the pilot Urdaneta and, in the next generation, of Vizcaino. *Puente de sueños* (1978; Bridge of Dreams) is inspired to a considerable extent by the refugee experience and memories of the Spanish Civil War, although it is not a novel of the war per se; rather, it reconstructs the life of a family during almost a c., set in the same fictional Valencian town (Citra) as Bolea's first novel. To the naturalistic reminiscences of that work, *Puente de sueños* adds a series of apocalyptic touches.

BIBLIOGRAPHY

Primary Texts

*La isla en el río.* Mexico: Oasis, 1971.
*Viento del noroeste.* Mexico: Oasis, 1972.
*Puente de sueños.* Mexico: Xaloc, 1978.

Janet Pérez


**BONAFOUX, Luis** (1855, France–1918, Puerto Rico?), journalist, critic. Founder of the newspapers *El Español* (The Spaniard) and *El intransigente* (The Uncompromising One), Bonafoux was an astute commentator of the political situation in Spain and in the Antilles. He also participated in a heated literary polemic with *Clarín in 1887 and 1888, accusing him of plagiarizing a portion of *La Regenta* from *Madame Bovary.*

BIBLIOGRAPHY

Primary Text

*Artículos recogidos de* Puerto Rico Ilustrado. Puerto Rico: Puerto Rico Ilustrado, 1937.

Criticism

Botrel, J. F. "Últimos ataques de Bonafoux a 'Clarín'." *Archivum* 18 (1968): 177–88.
Richmond, C. "La polémica Clarín-Bonafoux y Flaubert." *Insula* 365 (1977): 1, 12.

Maureen Ihrie


**BONET, Juan** (1917, Palma de Mallorca– ), journalist and novelist. He is author of *Historia para unas manos* (1962; Story for Some Hands) and *La terraza* (1965; The Terrace), among other novels. He also writes theater in Mallorcan, and is a painter and founder of the daily *Baleares.*

BIBLIOGRAPHY

Primary Texts

*Un poco locos, francamente.* Barcelona: Destino, 1959.
*La prole.* Barcelona: Destino, 1965.

Isabel McSpadden


**BONILLA, Alonso de** (c. 1570, Baeza–1642, Baeza), silversmith and poet. Bonilla is the known author of 1,792 poems, almost all *a lo divino* and many of great length. His first volume, *Peregrinos pensamientos, de mysterios divinos en varios versos, y glosas dificultosas* (1614; Beautiful Thoughts of Divine Mysteries in Several Verses and Complex Glosses), contained 688 poems. Bonilla's Christian *conceptismo* is elegant, delicate, carefully polished in meter and rhyme.

BIBLIOGRAPHY

Primary Texts

*Ciento veintinueve poesías autógrafas e inéditas.* Ed. I. López Sanabria. Jaén: Gráficas
  Nova, 1968. Includes biography and bibliography.
*Peregrinos pensamientos de mysterios divinos en varios versos, y glosas dificultosas.*
  Baeza: Pedro de Cuesta, 1614.
*Poesías.* In BAE 35.

Criticism

Chércoles Vico, A. "Alonso de Bonilla. Breves noticias acerca de su obra." *Revista de
  Lope de Sosa* (Jaén) 5 (1917): 258–62.

Maureen Ihrie

**BONILLA Y SAN MARTÍN, Adolfo** (1875, Madrid–1926, Madrid), critic and
scholar. The holder of chairs of law and of philosophy, he was a disciple of
*Menéndez Pelayo who produced an abundance of critical editions, studies of
classical texts, and works in the history of philosophy. Especially important
critical editions include *Libro de los engannos e asayamientos de las mujeres*
(Book of the Deceits and Temptations of Women), *El diablo cojuelo* (The
Limping Devil), various books of chivalry, and the complete works of *Cervantes
(in collaboration with R. Schevill). Among his historical and critical studies in
philosophy, the following are noteworthy: *Luis Vives y la filosofía del Renacimiento* (1903; Luis Vives and Renaissance Philosophy); *Erasmo en España*
(Erasmus in Spain, in *Revue Hispanique* 17); *El mito de Psyquis* (1908; The
Myth of Psyche); and *Historia de la filosofía española* (1908; History of Spanish
Philosophy), of which he finished only the first two volumes, treating the primitive and Hispano-Roman period, and the visigothic-hispanohebraic period, ending with the 12th c.

Janet Pérez

***BONIUM O BOCADOS DE ORO*** (13th c.; Bonium or Morsels of Gold), didactic
treatise/narrative fiction in romance prose. Its source is the *Libro de las sentencias*
(Book of Maxims) of Abulwafa Mobeshir ibn Fatik (12th c.). To proverbs and
aphorisms about religion, politics, astronomy, medicine, economics, and hygiene, it adds biographical sketches and introduces a fictional device (*Calila e
Digna*). Bonium, king of Persia, travels to India to seek advice on how better
to govern his kingdom and is helped by Indian, Greek, Latin and Moslem
philosophers. *Bonium* influenced the *Siete Partidas* of *Alphonse X and possibly
don *Juan Manuel. It was popular in the fifteenth and sixteenth c. (Toledo, 1510;
Valladolid, 1527). Fifteenth-c. mss. are found at the Escorial Library, the Menéndez Pidal Library, and the *Biblioteca Nacional (National Library) in Madrid.

BIBLIOGRAPHY

Primary Texts

*Bocados de Oro, kritische ausgabe des alspanischen Textes.* Ed. Mechthild Crombach.
  Bonn: Romanisches Seminar der Universität, 1971.

*Mittheilungen aus dem Eskurial.* Ed. H. Knust. Tübingen: Litterarischen Vereins in
    Stuttgart, 1879. 141: 63–498 & 538–601.

Criticism

Goldberg, H. "Moslem and Spanish Christian Literary Portraiture." *HR* 45 (1977): 311–
    26.

Reginetta Haboucha

**BORDÓN,** a poetic term. It refers to a refrain of *verso quebrado* (a shortened,
four-syllable line), repeated at the end of each stanza of a poem.

Maureen Ihrie

**BORJA Y ARAGÓN, Francisco de.** *See* Esquilache, Príncipe de

**BORROW, George** (1803, Norfolk, England–1881, ?), polyglot, Hispanophile.
Borrow, a vigorous, singular individual, is important to Hispanism because of
his account *The Bible in Spain* (1842). It is largely a compilation of reports
Borrow remitted to the Bible Society during a five-year period (1835–40) when
he traveled through western Spain, southern Portugal and Tangiers, selling Bibles. It is a richly detailed documentation of the customs and life of the day,
infused with the author's contradictory yet disarming personality. Valuable sociological information is also found in his account of the gypsies in Spain.

BIBLIOGRAPHY

Primary Texts

*The Bible in Spain.* London: Century, 1985.
*The Zincali, or an Account of the Gypsies of Spain.* London: John Murray, 1972. [Mi-
    crofiche]

Criticism

Collie, Michael. *George Borrow: Eccentric.* Cambridge: Cambridge UP, 1982.
Williams, David. *A World of His Own: The Double Life of George Borrow.* Oxford:
    Oxford UP, 1982.

Maureen Ihrie

**BOSCÁN, Juan** (1487?, Barcelona–1542, Barcelona), poet, translator, and tutor
to the future Duke of Alba. Educated in a humanistic milieu, Boscán (Joan Boscá
Almugáver in his native Catalan) studied with Lucio *Marineo Sículo, who said
that of all the youths who served the Catholic Monarch, Ferdinand, none surpassed Boscán in his enthusiasm for matters of the spirit. Such interests would
be reflected in his friendships made in the court of Charles V with Diego *Hurtado
de Mendoza, Andrea *Navaggiero, and *Garcilaso de la Vega. Indeed, his cultured Valencian wife, Ana Girón de Rebolledo—to whom world literature owes
a great debt—would publish his lyrical works posthumously along with some
of Garcilaso's in *Las obras de Boscán y algunas de Garcilaso de la Vega* (1543;
The Works of Boscán and Some of Garcilaso de la Vega).

Two figures of the Italian Renaissance were in Spain during 1526 who, through their relationships with Boscán, would profoundly affect the development of Hispanic belles lettres. The first of these, Andrea Navaggiero, would convince him to experiment with Italian meters, thereby initiating the great period of classical Spanish lyric poetry. In a letter sent to the Duchess of Somma, Boscán narrates what transpired during his conversation with Navaggiero in Granada, who was Venetian ambassador there: he should experiment with the sonnet and other forms. The second influence, Baldassare *Castiglione, author of *Il cortegiano* and a close friend of Navaggiero, impressed Boscán sufficiently that he made a translation of these famous dialogues, *Los cuatro libros del cortesano* (1534; The Four Books of the Courtier).

Boscán quickly adapted not only the sonnet, but also the tercet and the *ottava real* (*octavas) the mainstay of *Renaissance epic verse. Yet his lyricism is impoverished, suffering in comparison to the genius of his friend, Garcilaso. Boscán, who was already acquainted with the hendecasyllable line typical of much Catalan lyric poetry, is limited to singing the sweetness of his happy home, of his wife, and of his children without attaining the supreme and universal note of poetic virtuosity. The first book of the *Obras* contains his earlier, pre-Italianate poems composed in the traditional Castilian meters found in the medieval *cancioneros*; the second, the Italianate forms (his adaptation of Ausiàs *March is inspired, the sonnets in imitation of Petrarch are not); the third, the humanistic poetry "Epístola a Mendoza" (Epistle to Mendoza), "Octava rima" (Octave Rhyme), and "Hero y Leandro"; and the fourth, the brilliant lyrics of Garcilaso de la Vega. A very successful work, the *Obras* was issued in editions including the texts of both poets until 1570. A contrafactum version as *a lo divino* poetry was prepared by Sebastián de *Córdoba, *Las obras de Boscán y Garcilaso trasladadas en materias christianas y religiosas* (1575; The Works of Boscán and Garcilaso Rephrased as Christian and Religious Material).

If Boscán's lyrical poetry in itself is perhaps less valuable than his act of metrical innovation (his first language was Catalan, after all), his translation of Castiglione's *Il cortegiano* is brilliant, offering a new compendium of Renaissance values to the Hispanic world, which alone establishes him as a major figure in the history of its national literature. *See also* Humanism; Italian Literary Influences; Renaissance.

BIBLIOGRAPHY

Primary Texts

*Juan Boscán y su cancionero barcelonés.* [MS 359 of the Central Library of Barcelona.] Ed. Martín de Riquer. Barcelona: Ayuntamiento, 1945.

*Las obras de Boscán y algunas de Garcilaso de la Vega repartidas en quatro libros* (Barcelona: Carles Amorós, 1543). Ed. F. S. R. Madrid: Aguilar, 1944.

*Las obras de Juan Boscán repartidas en tres libros.* Ed. William I. Knapp. Madrid: Librería de M. Murillo, 1875.

*Obras poéticas.* Ed. Martín de Riquer, Antonio Coma, and Joaquín Molas. Barcelona: Facultad de Filosofía y Letras, 1957.

*Los quatro libros del cortesano compuestos en italiano por el conde Balthasar Castellón y agora nuevamente traduzidos en lengua castellana por Boscán* (Barcelona: Pedro Monpezar, 1534). Ed. M. Menéndez y Pelayo. *RFE* Anejo 25. Madrid: CSIC, 1942.
*Las treinta de Juan Boscán.* Ed. Hayward Keniston. New York: The Hispanic Society of America, 1911.

English Translations

[*The Works of Juan Boscán, Divided into Three Books.*] Numerous poems are translated by David H. Darst in *Juan Boscán* (1978, see below), which also contains translations of Boscán's manifesto on the adoption of the Italianate meters, "To the Duchess of Somma," and the poem "Boscán's Conversion."
"On the Death of Garcilaso"; "A Picture of Domestic Happiness" (from "Epistle to Mendoza"). With biographical notes. *Warner's Library of the World's Best Literature.* Ed. Charles D. Warner. New York: The International Society, 1896. 4: 2203–8.

Criticism

Armisen, Antonio. *Estudios sobre la lengua poética de Boscán.* Zaragoza: Zaragoza UP, 1982.
Darst, David H. *Juan Boscán.* TWAS 475. Boston: Twayne, 1978.
Gallego Morell, Antonio. "Bibliografía de Boscán." *Revista Bibliográfica y Documental,* fasicules 1–4 (1949).
Menéndez y Pelayo, Marcelino. *Antología de poetas líricos castellanos: Boscán (Obras completas).* Vol. 26 (vol. 10 of the *Antología*). Santander: CSIC, 1945.
Morreale, Margherita. *Castiglione y Boscán: El ideal cortesano en el renacimiento español (Estudio léxico-semántico).* Anejo 1 (2 vols.) of the BRAE. Madrid: RAE, 1959.
Porter, Thaddeus C. "The Italianate Poetry of Juan Boscán." Diss. Vanderbilt U, 1968.
Simón Díaz, José. "Juan Boscán." *Bibliografía de la literatura hispánica.* Madrid: CSIC, 1973. 6: 622–34.

Dennis P. Seniff

**BOSCH, Andrés** (1926, Palma de Mallorca– ), Spanish novelist, lawyer, translator, editor and journalist. Not a mainstream novelist, Bosch belongs to a small group, variously described as "intellectual" and "metaphysical," including Carlos *Rojas (the best known and most successful), García-Viñó, and Antonio *Prieto. All are post-war writers, belonging chronologically to the mid-c. generation, but rejecting the prevailing "social realism" in favor of treatment of psychological conflicts, inner struggles and a search for intimate understanding. *La noche* (1959; Night), winner of the lucrative Planeta Prize, portrays a boxer's search for identity, finally found in defeat. *Homenaje privado* (1962; Private Homage), winner of the City of Barcelona Prize in 1961, reconstructs the life of a dead protagonist to show how injustice ruined his potential and indirectly led to his demise. Other titles include *La revuelta* (1963; Stirred Up); *La estafa* (1965; The Swindle); *Ritos profanos* (1967; Profane Rites), a collection of four novelettes; *El mago y la llama* (1970; The Magician and the Flame); *El cazador de piedras* (1974; The Hunter of Stones); and *Arte de gobierno* (1977; The Art of Government). *Arte de gobierno* creates a parallel between the bullfight (in which an unusually vicious bull dispatches several toreros) and a governmental slaughter of spectators. Characteristic of Bosch's fiction is the presentation of the objective (outer) world in counterpoint with the subjective (inner) perception of the characters via constant change of perspective.

## BIBLIOGRAPHY

### Primary Texts

*Arte de gobierno.* Barcelona: Planeta, 1977.
*El cazador de piedras.* Barcelona: Planeta, 1974.
*La estafa.* Madrid: Uriarte, 1965.
*Homenaje privado.* Barcelona: Plaza y Janés, 1962.
*El recuerdo de hoy: novela.* Barcelona: Planeta, 1982.

### Criticism

García-Viñó, M. *Novela española actual.* Madrid: Guadarrama, 1967. 175–99.

Janet Pérez

**BOTELHO, Fernanda** (1926, Lisbon?– ), Portuguese poet and novelist. As a poet, she is grouped with the generation of neo-realists appearing in the late 1950s, whose evolution is parallel to that of the "social realists" in Spain; Botelho and Urbano Tavares Rodrigues also cultivate a "new" fiction of existentialist overtones influenced by certain themes and techniques of the French *nouveau roman. As Coordenadas Líricas* (1951; Lyric Coordinates), her first book of verse, contains only twenty-eight compositions but a surprising range from a modified romanticism to a more geometric formalism. Her prose fiction is ably constructed, with even some architectural virtuosity. Early works reflect the negative attitudes of post-war youth, with something of the geometric aspects of her poetry in her first two novels, *Ângulo Raso* (1957; Flat Angle) and *Calendário Privado* (1958; Private Calendar), a lucid denunciation of sterile existence. *A Gata e a Fábula* (1960; The Cat and the Fable), which won the Camilo Castelo Branco Prize for that year, moves away from the university environment and youthful protagonists of the earlier novels toward psychological analysis of the bourgeois ambient. *Xerazade e os Outros* (1964; Scheherezade and the Others) incorporates mythic elements which are updated, but the intent is a nearly radiographic analysis of escapism in the bourgeoisie.

## BIBLIOGRAPHY

### Primary Texts

*Ângulo raso.* Lisbon: Bertrand, 1957.
*Calendário privado.* Lisbon: Bertrand, 1958.

*A Gata e a Fábula*. Lisbon: Bertrand, 1960.
*Xerazade e os Outros*. Lisbon: Bertrand, 1964.

Janet Pérez

**BOTELLA PASTOR, Virgilio** (1906, Alcoy– ), novelist. Before the Spanish Civil War, Botella Pastor obtained a degree in law and served the Navy in a legal capacity. Although chronologically he belongs to the *Generation of 1925 (or Generation of *Ortega y Gasset), he did not enter literary life until much later. As a Republican sympathizer, he went into exile following the conflict, and first began to write and publish in Mexico, where he lived for a time, and later in Paris. Above all, his novels treat the themes of defeat and exile, as can be surmised from the titles: *Porque callaron las campanas* (1953; Because the Bells Fell Silent), which deals with the Civil War; *Así cayeron los dados* (1959; That's the Way the Dice Fell) and *Encrucijadas* (1962; Crossroads), both dealing with the flight into exile; and *Tal vez mañana* (1965; Perhaps Tomorrow). *Tal vez mañana* describes the struggle of a group of Spanish Republican exiles to adjust to the Mexican environment and earn a living there from 1939 to 1941, a narrative in which the author has exaggerated the use of Mexican dialect, types and scenes. *Porque callaron las campanas* does not present the battlefront, but a civilian who is living in Barcelona during the last desperate months of the war. It is a reflexive, meditative and philosophical novel, as well as a love story, with a profoundly human and moving vision of the final disbanding of the Republican defenders. *Así cayeron los dados* is divided in two parts, "La huida" (The Flight)—an impressive depiction of concentration camps and the human types confined in them—and "La espera" (The Wait), which abounds in reflections on the bitterness of exile and the solitude of the expatriate, together with the anguished situation of the Spanish refugees in Europe faced with yet another war.

BIBLIOGRAPHY

Primary Texts

*Así cayeron los dados*. Paris: Gondoles, 1959.
*Encrucijadas*. Paris: Gondoles, 1942.
*Porque callaron las campanas*. Mexico: Libertad, 1963.
*Tal vez mañana*. Paris: Gondoles, 1965.

Criticism

Marra-López, José R. *Narrativa española fuera de España (1939–1961)*. Madrid: Guadarrama, 1963. 496–99.
Zelaya Kolker, Marielena. *Testimonios americanos de los escritores españoles transterrados de 1939*. Madrid: Cultura Hispánica, 1985. 222–26.

Janet Pérez

**BOTÍN POLANCO, Antonio** (1898, Santander–1956, Madrid), novelist. A lawyer by training, Botín Polanco earned a certain name as a novelist and refined humorist, as well as a careful stylist. Among his titles are the following: *La*

*Divina Comedia* (1927; The Divine Comedy); *El, ella y ellos* (1929; He, She and They); *Virazón* (1931; Sharp Turn); *Logaritmo* (1933; Logarithm); *Peces joviales* (1934; Jovial Fish); and the amusing essay *Manifiesto del humorismo* (1951; Humorists' Manifesto).

BIBLIOGRAPHY

Primary Texts

*El, ella y ellos.* Madrid: Renacimiento, 1929.
*Logaritmo.* Madrid: Espasa-Calpe, 1933.
*Manifiesto.* Madrid: RO, 1951.
*Virazón.* Madrid: Espasa-Calpe, 1931.

Janet Pérez

**BOTTO, António Tomás** (1897, Abrantes–1959, Rio de Janeiro), modernist Portuguese poet and playwright. Of provincial origins, Botto early entered the literary circles of the Modernists in Lisbon where he was first a bookstore employee and, subsequently, a civil servant. He also spent a brief period in Angola (1924–25) and, finally, immigrated to Brazil. In Lisbon he collaborated in such Modernist reviews as *Athena* and *Contemporânea* and was an adherent of the "Presença" movement.

Botto acquired notoriety with the publication of his *Canções* (1921; Songs), a compilation of his earlier *Trovas* (1917; Ballads), *Cantigas de Saudades* (1918; Days of Longing), *Cantares* (1919; Canticles) and additional poems. Because of their homoerotic themes and celebration of male beauty, these lyrical renderings in simple language of proscribed sexual pleasures and relationships led to the confiscation of the second edition in 1922. The affair became a "cause célèbre" and turned into a literary polemic when Fernando *Pessoa in his essay "António Botto and the Esthetic Ideal In Portugal" defended Botto as a unique example in Portuguese literature of an apologist for Hellenic Beauty. Raul Leal in *Sodoma Divinizada* (1923; Divine Sodom) counter-attacked in vitriolic tones.

Undeterred, Botto continued to elaborate upon his homoerotic sentiments and imagery, adding a new dimension to the Portuguese literary tradition of "Saudosismo." *Curiosidades Estéticas* (1924; Aesthetic Curios), *Pequenas Esculturas* (1925; Diminutive Sculptures) and *Olímpiadas* (1927; Olympics) reveal Botto's appropriation of Pessoa's defense of his work. *Dandismo* (1928; Dandyism), *Ciúme* (1934; Jealousy), *A Vida que te dei* (1938; The Life Which I Gave You) and *Baionetas da Morte* (1936; Death's Bayonets) are of a greater psychological vein with populist tendencies and vivid portrayals of Lisbon's Bohemian underground.

As a playwright, Botto examined in dramatic form the thematic predilections of his poetry. Among the plays, *Alfama* (1933; Alfama) is set in Lisbon's popular, medieval neighborhood and *António* (1933; Anthony) reconsiders the homoeroticism of *Canções*. Botto also enriched Portuguese literature with a children's series: *O Livro das Crianças* (1931; The Children's Book), *O Meu Amor Pequenino* (1934; My Little Love), and *Dar de beber a quem tem Sede* (1935;

Quenching the Thirsty). In Brazil, Botto wrote an Alphonsine *Fátima—Poema do Mundo* (1955; Fatima—A Worldly Poem).

BIBLIOGRAPHY

Primary Text

*As Canções de António Botto.* Lisbon: Presença, 1980.

Criticism

Gaspar Simões, João. "A Fatalidade na Poesia de António Botto." *O Mistério da Poesia.* Coimbra: Presença, 1931.

Jaime H. da Silva

**BOUSOÑO, Carlos** (1923, Boal, Asturias– ), poet, critic and professor at the U of Madrid. Bousoño also taught at Wellesley College in 1947, and has been a lecturer on Spanish poetry in Mexico. Bousoño has published several volumes of poetry, many of them marked by a strong religious preoccupation, including *Subida al amor* (1943; Ascent to Love); *Primavera de la muerte* (1946; Springtime of Death); *Hacia otra luz* (1952; Toward a Different Light); and *Noche del sentido* (1957; Night of the Senses [or of Sense, Meaning]). These works were collected in a single edition of *Poesías completas* (1960; Complete Poems). As critic and essayist, Bousoño is especially known for *La poesía de Vicente Aleixandre* (1950; The Poetry of Vicente *Aleixandre, 4 ed., 1977), often considered the definitive work on interpretation of the difficult and sometimes hermetic expression of this Nobel prizewinner. Other critical essays include *Seis calas en la expresión literaria española* (1951; Six Stages in Spanish Literary Expression) in collaboration with Dámaso *Alonso and *Teoría de la expresión poética* (1952; Theory of Poetic Expression, 6th ed., 1977), one of his most influential contributions to critical theory and methodology, which has gone through several editions. Later collections of poetry include *Invasión de la realidad* (1962; Invasion of Reality) and *Oda en la ceniza* (1967; Ode of Ashes), which was awarded the prestigious Critics' Prize in 1968.

BIBLIOGRAPHY

Primary Texts

*Antología poética, 1945–1973.* Esplugas de Llobregat: Plaza y Janés, 1976.
*Invasión de la realidad.* Madrid: Espasa-Calpe, 1962.
*Oda en la ceniza.* 2nd ed. Madrid: Ciencia Nueva, 1968.
*Selección de mis versos.* 2nd ed. Madrid: Cátedra, 1982.

Janet Pérez

**BOWLE, John** (1725, Wiltshire, England–1788, Wiltshire, England), eminent humanist, medieval scholar, hispanist. His English edition of *Cervantes's *Quijote* (1781) has been praised as "an eternal bibliographic monument, an endless mine in which all *cervantistas*, of Spain as well as other countries, have searched for materials—whether or not they acknowledge." *Pellicer and *Clemencín owe to him the best data of their investigations.

BIBLIOGRAPHY

Criticism

Pastor, Antonio. "Breve historia del hispanismo inglés." *Arbor* 28–29 (1948): 549–66.

Maureen Ihrie

**BOYL, Carlos** (1577, Valencia–1617, Valencia), poet and dramatist. Member of the Academia de los Nocturnos (Academy of the Night Revelers) with pseudonym "Recelo" (Distrust) and founder of the Academia de los Adorantes (Academy of the Adoring Ones). Boyl's one extant play, *El marido asegurado* (1616; The Reassured Husband) was well received in its day and still is favorably regarded. Boyl was assassinated outside the Cathedral of Valencia, perhaps in connection with a romantic intrigue. *See also* Academia.

BIBLIOGRAPHY

Primary Text

*El marido asegurado.* In *BAE* 53.

Criticism

Weiger, J. G. *The Valencian Dramatists of Spain's Golden Age.* TWAS 371. Boston: Twayne, 1976.

Maureen Ihrie

**BRANDÃO, Fiama Hasse Pais** (1938, Lisbon– ), poet, playwright, novelist, translator. She frequented courses in Germanic philology at the U of Lisbon in the fermentative 1950s. One of the most original experimentalists out of the Poesia–1961 movement, Fiama Brandão writes a sober but sensually elegant poetry. Her earlier surrealistic tendencies produced rich experiments in poetic concepts and forms with a rigorous craft and a wealth of concrete metaphors derived from her double indexing meaning, as in *O Texto de João Zorro* (1974; João Zorro's Text). Her later tendencies are more existentialist and analytical, combining an esoteric poematic plan with an anti-lyrical preoccupation with cultural issues. Brandão's more recent poetry presents a liquidity of metaphor and metaphysics in *Âmago I—Nova arte* (1986?; Pith I—New Art). She is anthologized in many collections. Besides being a prizewinning playwright (*Os Chapéus de chuva* [1962; The Umbrellas]; *Quem move as árvores* [1969; Who Moves the Trees]), she writes novels and translations of Brecht, Artaud, John Updike, O'Neill and *García Lorca. She collaborates in the leading poetry journals of Portugal and Europe, such as *Seara Nova* and *Vértice*.

BIBLIOGRAPHY

Primary Texts

*Âmago I—Nova arte.* N.p.: n.p., 1986?
*Novas visões do passado.* Lisbon: Assírio & Alvim, 1975.
*O Aquário.* Lisbon: n.p., 1959.
*Os Chapéus de chuva.* Lisbon: Minotauro, 1962.
*O Texto de João Zorro.* Porto: Inova, 1974.

English Translation

Three poems in *Contemporary Portuguese Poetry: An Anthology in English*. Selected by Helder Macedo and E. M. de Melo e Castro. Manchester: Carcanet, 1978.

Criticism

Coelho, Eduardo Prado. *A Palavra sobre a Palavra*. Lisbon: n.p., 1972.

Silveira, Jorge Fernandes da. "Poetas Leitores de [Fernando] Pessoa." In *Actas do 2º Congresso Internacional de Estudos Pessoanos*. Oporto: Centro de Estudos Pessoanos, 1985. 571–78.

Robert R. Krueger

**BRANDÃO, Raul** (1867, Foz do Duoro–1930, Oporto), Portuguese novelist, dramatist and essayist. Trained for a military career, he achieved the rank of captain before retiring in 1912. His literary career began much earlier with an apprenticeship in journalism. *Impressões e paisagens* (1890; Impressions and Landscapes), his first important narrative work, is a collection of tales about the problematic lives and suffering of the working class and the poor. His social preoccupations are lasting and central to his work, with most characters having no refuge from harsh or tragic reality save fantasy and dreams. Economic problems and social injustice form the thematic axis of *A farsa* (1903; Farce), *Os pobres* (1906; The Poor), *Húmus* (1917) and *Pobre de pedir* (1931; Poor Enough to Beg), all revolving around the pain of poverty. Although injustice does not disappear in *Pescadores* (1923; The Fishermen) and *As ilhas desconhecidas* (1927; The Uncharted Isles), the author's lyric portraits of the beauty of the Portuguese coast and landscape make the final effect less dreary and dismal. Brandão also wrote a three-volume set of memoirs (*Memórias*, 1919, 1925, 1933), chronicling the difficult last days of the monarchy in Portugal and the equally problematic early years of the republic. A hybrid genre, these memoirs are by no means limited to the author's recollections, but include interviews, documents of various kinds, statements by participants and even gossip. Brandão also wrote for the theater: *O Gebo e a sombra* (1923; Tatters and the Shadow), *O rei imaginario* (1923; The Imaginary Monarch), and *O avejão* (1929; Scarecrow).

BIBLIOGRAPHY

Criticism

Andrade, João Pedro. *Raul Brandão*. Lisbon: Arcadia, 1963. 98–99.

Ribeiro, Aquilino. *Camões, Camilo, Eça e alguns mais*. Lisbon: Bertrand, 1949. 267–70.

Schneider, Marshall J. and Irwin Stern. *Modern Spanish and Portuguese Literature*. New York: Crossroad/Ungar/Continuum, 1988. 458–62.

Janet Pérez

**BRAVO VILLASANTE, Carmen** (1918, Madrid– ), scholar, translator. She has written numerous books and articles on literary topics pertaining not only to Spain, but to other countries as well. For two decades she taught Spanish literature courses for American universities with programs in Madrid. She has demonstrated a strong and lasting interest in children's literature the world over in such works as *Historia de la literatura infantil universal* (1971; A World History of Children's Literature), *Antología de la literatura infantil universal* (1971; World Anthology of Children's Literature, 2 vols.) and *Historia y Antología de la literatura infantil iberoamericana* (1966; A History and Anthology of Spanish American Children's Literature, 2 vols.). Along with these booklength studies, she has several articles devoted to children's literature in specific countries: France, Denmark and Russia. Her work in this field brought recognition in 1980 in the form of the Premio Nacional de Investigación Sobre Literatura Infantil (National Award for Research in Children's Literature) from the Spanish Ministry of Culture.

In the realm of adult literature, she has published a number of monographic studies of Spanish writers such as Juan *Valera, Emilia *Pardo Bazán, Gertrudis *Gómez de Avellaneda and Benito *Pérez Galdós.

A broad output of translations into Spanish of Goethe, Heine, Von Kleist and E.T.A. Hoffmann merited her the Premio Fray Luis de León de Traducción (Fray Luis de León Translation Award) from the Spanish Ministry of Culture in 1976.

BIBLIOGRAPHY

Primary Texts

*Biografía de Pushkin.* Palma de Mallorca: José J. de Olañeta, 1985.
*Cuentos de E.T.A. Hoffmann.* Madrid: Alianza, 1985.
*Galdós visto por sí mismo.* Madrid: Alianza, 1985.
*Historia de la literatura infantil española.* Madrid: Doncel, 1963.
*Vida y obra de Emilia Pardo Bazán.* Madrid: Magisterio Español, 1972.

Elisa Fernández Cambria

**BRETÓN DE LOS HERREROS, Manuel** (1796, Quel, Logroño– 1873, Madrid), playwright and poet. From the small town of Quel in the wine-making region of La Rioja, Bretón's family moved to Madrid in 1806. Bretón studied there, but due to financial difficulties resulting from his father's death in 1811, he enlisted in the army the following year at age fifteen and served until 1822. In 1818, he was gravely wounded in the left eye, possibly in a duel caused by a love affair; he lost the vision in this eye and retained a prominent scar.

Bretón de los Herreros dominated nineteenth-c. Spanish theater and, along with Gorostiza and Ventura de la *Vega, is responsible for maintaining the Moratinian-style comedy throughout the Romantic period and for serving as a link to the high comedy of the second half of the c. Although his plots are simple and his technique conventional, the plays are ingeniously well executed.

Bretón's theater career, which began after his discharge from the military, may be divided into two periods. His first period (1824–30) is dominated by his translations of primarily French dramatists such as Beaumarchais, Delavigne, Marivaux, Molière, Racine, and Scribe and his modern arrangements of Spanish

Golden Age classics, decisively advancing their revival. His first original play, *A la vejez viruelas* (1817; The Young Old Codger), was performed in 1824, and his first real success came in 1828 with *A Madrid me vuelvo* (It's Back to Madrid for Me). Bretón's original production during this period is strongly marked by the influence of Leandro Fernández de *Moratín.

The premiere of *Marcela, o ¿a cuál de los tres?* (1831; Marcela, or Which of the Three?) opens Bretón's second period, in which he developed a more personal style in his continued treatment of the foibles of the Spanish middle class, for which he is best known and remembered. The theme of *Marcela*— an independent young woman faced with a choice among three suitors—is one that Bretón used many times, thus being condemned by some for monotonous repetition. This period was briefly interrupted by Bretón's attempt at Romantic drama with *Elena* (1834) and the two historical plays, *Don Fernando el emplazado* (1837; Don Fernando the Summoned) and *Vellido Dolfos* (1839). His satire on *Romanticism, *Me voy de Madrid* (1835; I'm Leaving Madrid), provoked a quarrel with *Larra, who found it personally insulting, but the two were reconciled a year later. Bretón returned to his typical comedy of manners with *Muérete ¡y verás!* (1837; Die and You Will See!) and *El pelo de la dehesa* (1840; The Country Bumpkin). He continued to turn out a large number of plays until 1867, when his last play, *Los sentidos corporales* (The Bodily Senses), appeared.

In addition to his theatrical production, Bretón published poetry and journalistic articles. His first collection of verse in the lyric tradition of the eighteenth c., *Poesías* (Poetry), appeared in 1831. He regularly contributed a column on theater, literary criticism, and music to *El Correo literario y mercantil* and occasionally wrote for *La abeja, El artista, Boletín de comercio, La ley,* and *El universal.* Several of his ''Cuadros de costumbres,'' depictions of Spanish customs and manners, were published in the *Semanario pintoresco español* and in *Los españoles pintados por sí mismos* (1851; Spaniards Portrayed by Themselves).

Bretón also served as director of the *Biblioteca Nacional* (National Library) from 1847 to 1854 and as secretary to the *Academia Española* (Spanish Academy). Despite his increasing popularity and success, Bretón's old age was bitter and cynical, and he died in 1873, after a brief illness. *See also* Theater in Spain; *Siglo de Oro.*

BIBLIOGRAPHY

Primary Texts

*A la vejez viruelas.* Madrid: Miguel de Burgos, 1825.
*Marcela, o ¿a cuál de los tres?* Ed., intro J. Hesse. Madrid: Taurus, 1969.
*Obras.* 5 vols. Madrid: Ginesta, 1883–84.
*Obras teatrales: Marcela, o ¿a cuál de los tres?; Muérete ¡y verás!; La escuela del matrimonio.* Ed. F. Serrano Puente. Logroño: Estudios Riojanos, 1975.
*El pelo de la dehesa.* Ed. J. Montero Padilla. Madrid: Cátedra, 1974.

English Translation

*One of Many.* In *Spanish One-Act Plays in English.* Tr. W. Knapp Jones. Dallas: Tardy, 1934.

Criticism

Alborg, Juan Luis. *Historia de la literatura española.* Vol. 4. Madrid: Gredos, 1980.
Chaskin, Silvia Novo Blankenship. "Social Satire in the Works of Manuel Bretón de los Herreros." Diss. U of Virginia, 1968.
Flynn, Gerard. *Manuel Bretón de los Herreros.* TWAS 487. Boston: Twayne, 1978.
Le Gentil, Georges. *Le poète Manuel Bretón de los Herreros et la société espagnole de 1830 à 1860.* Paris: Hachette, 1909.
Molíns, Mariano Roca de Togores, Marqués de. *Bretón de los Herreros: Recuerdos de su vida y de sus obras.* Madrid: Tello, 1883.
Qualia, Charles Blaise. "Dramatic Criticism in the Comedies of Bretón de los Herreros." *Hispania* 24 (1941): 71–78.

Linda Maier

**BREYNER ANDRESEN, Sophia de Mello** (1919, Lisbon– ), a classicist and Portugal's greatest woman poet of modern times. Formed under the shadow of *Modernism, she proceeds from early treatment of the universal poetic themes of love, nature, and the sea, to contemporary history and a concern with significant national problems. Books produced under the influence of notions of *engagement* and socio-political criticism are largely neo-realist in nature. Sophia de Mello's works include *Poesia* (1944), *Dia do Mar* (1947; Day of the Sea), *Coral* (1950; Chorus), *No Tempo Dividido* (1954; In Divided Times), *Mar Novo* (1958; New Sea), *O Cristo Cigano* (1961; The Gypsy Christ), *Livro Sexto* (1962; Sixth Book), *Geografia* (1967), *Grades* (1970; Prison Bars), and *Dual* (1972).

BIBLIOGRAPHY

Primary Texts

*Antología.* Porto: Figueirinhas, 1985.
*Histórias da terra e do mar.* Lisbon: Salamandra, 1984.

English Translation

*Marine Rose: Selected Poems/Sophia de Mello Breyner.* Tr. R. Fainlight. Redding Ridge, CT: Black Swan, 1988.

Criticism

Martins García, José. "Portuguese Poetry (From World War II to the 1974 Revolution)." In *Roads to Today's Portugal.* Ed. Nelson H. Viera. Providence, RI: Gávea-Brown, 1983. 67–84.
Sayers, Raymond. "Portuguese Poetry of Today and Eugenio de Andrade." *Concerning Poetry* 17.2 (Fall 1984): 137–54.
Vásquez Cuesta, Pilar. *Poesía Portuguesa Actual.* Madrid: Nacional, 1976. 37.

**BRIDOUX Y MAZZINI DE DOMÍNGUEZ, Victorina** (1835, Manchester, England–1862, Santa Cruz de Tenerife), poet and short story writer. She was the daughter of a French businessman who married a Spanish woman, Angelina

Mazzini, of Italian ancestry. After her father's death, they moved to Cádiz and then to Gibraltar, where the mother, herself a poet, taught languages (French, English and German) in a religious private school where Victorina was educated. Victorina's knowledge of languages may have afforded her firsthand contact with the German lyric trends that later surfaced in her poetry.

Mother and daughter then moved to Santa Cruz de Tenerife where Victorina married and began to publish her poems (1852–62) in local publications, such as *El Eco del Comercio*, *El Fénix*, etc. She died of yellow fever while very young. After her death her poems were gathered and published by her husband in *Lágrimas y flores* (1863; Tears and Flowers).

She was a close friend of *Pilar Sinués and other women writers of the Peninsula, and friendship figures as a major theme in her poetry, as well as the search for an ever silent, evasive, intuitively sensed presence which never reveals herself, the poet as creator of a magic inner world, and an acute sense of mystery. She uses Romantic metrics and prefers consonant rhymes. Though her poetry has many similarities with *Bécquer's, most of her poems were written before his first rhyme was published in 1858. *See also* Romanticism.

BIBLIOGRAPHY

Primary Text

*Lágrimas y flores*. Producciones literarias. 2 vols. Santa Cruz de Tenerife: n.p., 1863.

Criticism

Alonso, María Rosa. *En Tenerife, una poetisa. Victorina Bridoux y Mazzini (1835–1862)*. Santa Cruz de Tenerife: Librería Hesperides (Canarias), 1940.
Cossío, José María. *Cincuenta años de poesía española (1850–1900)*. 2 vols. Madrid: Espasa-Calpa, 1960.

Cristina Enríquez

**BRINES, Francisco** (1932, Oliva, Valencia– ), poet. Brines obtained a degree in law from the U of Salamanca and another in philosophy and letters from the U of Madrid, where he established his residence. His first volume of poetry, entitled *Las brasas* (1960; The Embers), obtained the Adonais prize in 1959. *El Santo inocente* (1965; The Sainted Innocent) may be classed with some reservations as social poetry with political overtones, as is also the case with his following collection, *Palabras a la oscuridad* (1966; Words to the Darkness), which won the Critics' Prize for that year. Subsequently Brines published *Aún no* (1971; Not Yet) and *Poesía 1960–1971: ensayo de una despedida* (1974; Poetry 1960–1971: Attempt at a Farewell) with a significant preliminary study of Brines's work by Carlos *Bousoño. Several years of silence intervened before the publication of *Insistencias en Luzbel* (1977; Insistence upon Lucifer), which makes of Lucifer a symbol for modern, existential man in his futile battle against meaninglessness and death. Even in his first work, *Las brasas*, Brines focuses upon the emptiness of human life; man's temporality threatens to reduce him to the level of object. In his next major work, *Palabras a la oscuridad*, Brines dramatizes the conflict between the vitality of nature and human life and Time the Destroyer, exalting life at the same time he underscores the threat of temporality and death. The focus upon time and death becomes clearer and still more narrow in *Aún no*, and pessimism intensifies as the negative vision of reality is expressed in most unusual language. As the poet's vision darkens with successive works, his latest volume presents God as deception, the human condition as nothingness, and Lucifer as oblivion. Reversing traditional views, this work suggests that self-destruction is the only creative act possible, the only assertion of individual existence and rebellion against oblivion.

BIBLIOGRAPHY

Primary Texts

*Poesía 1960–1971: ensayo de una despedida*. Barcelona: Plaza & Janés, 1974.
*Insistencias en Luzbel*. Madrid: Visor, 1977.

English Translation

"The Girl." Tr. anon. In *Arena* 23 (1965): 63–64.

Criticism

Bousoño, Carlos. "Prólogo." In Brines. *Poesía 1960–1971*. 11–94.
Bradford, Carole. "Francisco Brines and Claudio Rodríguez: Two Recent Approaches to Poetic Creation." *Crítica Hispánica* 2 (1980): 29–40.
———. "The Dialectic of Nothingness in the Poetry of Francisco Brines." *Taller Literario* 1.2 (1980): 1–12.
Debicki, Andrew. *Poetry of Discovery: The Spanish Generation of 1956–71*. Lexington: UP of Kentucky, 1982. 20–39.

                                                                              Janet Pérez


**BRITO, Casimiro (Cavaco Correia de)** (1938, Loulé, Algarve– ), poet. Brito was an activist-poet in the 1950s and in the Poesia–1961 movement (*Canto adolescente* [1961; Adolescent Song]); he is a world traveler, and writes with a lyrical, dramatic feeling for the land and for the people's struggles. He has a strong ideology and aesthetic for cultural liberation, while a strain of tragic optimism runs through his poetry as in *Vietnam—Em nome da liberdade* (1968; Vietnam—In the Name of Freedom), *Negação da morte* (1974; Denial of Death), and *Corpo sitiado* (1976; Body under Siege). Recently, his writing is a labyrinthian struggle with language and identity, as in *Labyrinthus* (1981; Labyrinthus). Brito's 1977 essays in *Prática da escrita em tempo de revolução* (1977; The Praxis of Writing in Revolutionary Times) express the ideals of a cultural revolution with all its naive relativity and subversive imagination. His 1983 short stories in *Contos da morte* (1983; Tales of Death) present a gallery of social types in their quotidian struggle with alienation and exploitation.

Brito lives in Lisbon, working as a bank manager. He collaborates with several poetry associations and edits publications in Portugal and Spain, such as *Cadernos do meio-dia*, *Jornal de letras e artes*, *Vértice*, and *El Molino de papel*.

BIBLIOGRAPHY

Primary Texts

*Corpo sitiado, 1955–1963*. Lisbon: Iniciativas, 1976.
*Ode & ceia*. Lisbon: Dom Quixote, 1985.
*Pátria sensível, ou, Que fazer do corpo com seus rios, margens & afluentes*. Lisbon:
    Dom Quixote, 1983. (fiction)
*Prática da escrita em tempo de revolução*. Lisbon: Caminho, 1977.
*Vietnam—Em nome da liberdade*. N.p.: n.p., 1968.

English Translation

Four poems in *Contemporary Portuguese Poetry: An Anthology in English*. Selected by
    Helder Macedo and E. M. de Melo e Castro. Manchester: Carcanet, 1978.

                                                            Robert R. Krueger

**BROSSA CUERVO, Joan** (1919, Barcelona– ), poet and dramatist. Brossa is
an important Catalan-language Vanguard poet and playwright, a self-taught writer
whose formal education was thwarted by the Spanish Civil War (1936–39) and
its chaotic aftermath. One of his earliest influences was that of the painter Joan
Miró, whose friendship he cherished. In the 1940s he was involved in the
founding of the review *Algol* and the group "Dau al set" which, led by him
and the painter Antonio Tàpies, attempted to keep up with the European artistic
experimental currents, banished from Spain by the Franco regime. In 1948 they
started the underground magazine *Dice on Seven*, considered the first manifestation of the re-emergence of the avant-garde in Barcelona. Brossa and Tàpies
have continued their collaboration, especially through the publication of *Novel·la*,
a collection of comments on official Spanish documents, punctuated by Tàpies's
satirical drawings.

Brossa's abundant poetry, characterized by irreverence, unexpected associations, and bizarre use of language, has been linked to surrealism; his dramatic
output has been placed within the currents of the Theater of the Absurd. Brossa,
however, denies both associations in several essays he has written dealing with
his "ars poetica," some of which have been collected in *Vivàrium* (Barcelona,
1972; Personal Experiences). He asserts that his works simply reflect the lack
of coherence and transcendence present in the routine actions of everyday life.

Despite Brossa's intensive poetic creation, he did not become an acknowledged
model for the younger generation of poets until the late 1970s. Partly to blame
for this delay is the fact that although he is first and foremost a poet, his dramatic
production has attracted more attention and wider critical response. Some of his
early poetic output includes *Sonets de caruxs* (1949; Sonnets of Endearment),
*Fogall de sonets* 1949; Gathering of Sonnets), *Em va fer Joan Brossa* (1951; It
Turned Out to Be Joan Brossa), *Poems civils* (1961; Civil Poems), *Pluja* (1963;
Rain), and *El saltamartí* (1969; The Tumbler). Then, in 1970 he published
*Poesia rasa* (Plain Poetry), which included some 450 poems written between
1943 and 1959. It was at this point that the full richness of his poetic vein became
apparent and that he became an influential poet in contemporary Catalan letters.

Although Brossa's first dramatic work, *Cop desert* (Desert Blow), dates from 1944, he did not become known to the public until much letter through plays like *El bell lloc* (1961; The Handsome Madman), *Or i sal* (1961; Gold and Salt), *Acció spectacles* (1962; Action Shows), and *Calç i rajoles* (1964; Whitewash and Glazed Tiles). By 1983 his dramatic works covered six compact volumes. In addition to this dramatic collection, some of his later books of poetry have been collected in *Poems de seny i cabell* (1977; Poems of Sense and Hair).

BIBLIOGRAPHY

Primary Texts

*Teatre complet*. 6 vols. Barcelona: Edicions 62, 1973–83.

English Translation

*Four Postwar Catalan Poets*. Cross-Cultural Review no. 1. Comp. and tr. David Rosenthal. Merrick, NY: Cross-Cultural Communications, 1978.

Criticism

Fábregas, Xavier. "Introductió al teatre de Joan Brossa." In *Teatre complet*, 1; 5–52.
Salgado, María A. "Joan Brossa's *La sal i el drac*: A Playwright's Reflections on Life, Theatre, Playwrighting." *Discurso Literario* 2.2 (Spring 1985): 363–76.
Terry, Arthur. "Alguns aspects de la poesia de Joan Brossa." In *Actes del 3ᵉʳ Colloqui International de Llengua i Literatura Catalanes* [Celebrat a Cambridge abril de 1973]. Oxford: Dolphin, 1976. 353–69.

María A. Salgado

**BUENDÍA, Rogelio** (1891, Huelva–1968, ?), poet and physician. Buendía collaborated in the pre-ultraísta journal *Los Quijotes* and later in avant-garde publications. He served on the editorial board of *Grecia*, founded in Seville in 1918. Publications of his appeared in *Cervantes*, *Tableros*, *Horizonte*, *Alfar*, and others. With Adriano del *Valle and Fernando *Villalón, Buendía founded *Papel de Aleluya* (Huelva, 1927–28). His *La rueda de color* (1923; Wheel of Color) is one of the most cited books of ultraist poetry, which in themselves are not numerous.

BIBLIOGRAPHY

Primary Texts

*Del bien y del mal*. N.p.: n.p., n.d.
*Diagramas del sueño*. N.p.: n.p., n.d.
*Guía de jardines*. N.p.: n.p., 1928.
*Nácares*. Sevilla: n.p., 1916.
*Naufragio en tres cuerdas de guitarra*. N.p.: n.p., n.d.
*El poema de mis sueños*. N.p.: n.p., n.d.
*La rueda de color*. N.p.: n.p., 1923.
*Vuelo y tierra*. Madrid: n.p., 1945.

Criticism

Peña, Manuel de la. *El ultraísmo en España*. Madrid: Colección Clásicos y Modernos, 1925.

Valle, Adriano del. "Algunas palabras sobre *La rueda de color*, de Rogelio Buendía."
   *Alfar* (June-July 1924): 24–25.
Videla, Gloria. *El ultraísmo*. Madrid: Gredos, 1964.

Kathleen March

**BUENO, Manuel** (1874, Pau, France–1936, Barcelona), essayist, journalist, novelist, short story writer and playwright. The works of Bueno, better known as a secondary figure of the so-called *Generation of 1898, are currently out of print. His creative writings tend to be realistic. Among his works are *Almas y paisajes* (1900; Souls and Landscapes), *Jaime el conquistador* (1912; James the Conqueror), *En el umbral del drama* (1918; On the Threshold of Drama), *El dolor de vivir* (1924; The Hurt of Living), *Los nietos de Danton* (1936; Danton's Grandchildren) and *Teatro español contemporáneo* (1910; Contemporary Spanish Theater).

BIBLIOGRAPHY

Primary Texts

*Poniente solar*. In *Las mejores novelas contemporáneas*. Ed. J. de Entrambasaguas. 3rd
   ed. Barcelona: Planeta, 1986. 8: 281–94.
*Las terceras de ABC*. Madrid: Prensa Española, 1977.

Criticism

Entrambasaguas, J. de. "Manuel Bueno (1874–1936)." In *Las mejores novelas contem-
   poráneas*. 3rd ed. Barcelona: Planeta, 1986. 8: 35–79.
Granjel, L. S. *Maestros y amigos de la generación del noventa y ocho*. Salamanca:
   Universidad de Salamanca, 1981.
Sainz de Robles, F. C. *Manuel Bueno o un intelectual irritable y ascéptico*. Madrid:
   Fundación Universitaria Española, 1975.

Luis T. González-del-Valle

**BUERO VALLEJO, Antonio** (1916, Guadalajara– ), dramatist. Generally considered the greatist living Spanish playwright, Buero is credited with the revitalization of the Spanish theater after the Civil War (1936–39). As children he and
his friends often acted out imaginary tales, complete with costumes and sets, although he preferred art to these juvenile theatrical exhibitions. Hoping to be a
painter, in 1934 he enrolled in Madrid's San Fernando School of Fine Arts. With
the outbreak of war, Buero enlisted as a medic with the Republicans, and in spite
of his non-combative role, he was sentenced to death when the conflict ended.
This sentence was later commuted, but he remained imprisoned until 1945.
   The years between 1945 and 1949 were decisive in Buero Vallejo's life, for
he then abandoned hopes of becoming a great artist and instead turned his talents
to drama. The decade immediately following the war had been a very mediocre
one on the Spanish stage. Drawing-room comedies and escapist plays dominated
the scene. In 1949 the then-unknown Buero submitted his drama *Historia de
una escalera* (1949; The Story of a Stairway) to a national competition. It not
only won the country's most prestigious theater award, the Lope de Vega Prize,
but was so popular with critics and public alike that its run was extended and

the annual production of *Don Juan Tenorio*, a perennial favorite with Spanish theatergoers, was cancelled. It also marked the beginning of a new age of realism in Spanish drama. The play chronicles the hopes and aspirations of three generations of Madrid tenement dwellers, whose social and economic immobility is symbolized by the dilapidated staircase of their apartment building.

Since then, Buero has continued to write and stage plays regularly. By the end of the 1981 theatrical season twenty-two of his dramas had been produced. His work almost invariably centers around his attempt to understand man and his destiny, and the vehicle he uses in this endeavor is tragedy, which he has defined as a conflict between liberty and necessity. Martha Halsey points out that his characters struggle against limitations imposed by their own incomprehension and the injustices of society. Yet "tragedy," for Buero, is not necessarily "tragic" at all, because it brings us closer to an understanding of the true nature of man.

He often uses the interplay of light and darkness (or vision and blindness) as symbols of man's limitations in the quest for truth. Such is the case, for example, with the blind protagonists of *En la ardiente oscuridad* (1950; *In the Burning Darkness*, 1985), which takes place in a school for the blind, or *El concierto de San Ovidio* (1962; *The Concert at Saint Ovide*, 1967), the story of a group of blind street musicians who attempt to overcome the physical obstacle of blindness and become serious musicians.

The political implications of some of his works prevented their staging during the Franco era. Notable among them is *La doble historia del doctor Valmy* (*The Double Case History of Doctor Valmy*, 1967)—first presented in England but not performed in Spain until 1976—which is centered around the torture of political prisoners in a fictitious country.

His characters are often drawn from the poor and oppressed, the socially and economically downtrodden, and although the protagonist is usually defeated in the end, we are not left without hope—at least in his earlier plays. However, it has been noted that the decade of the 1970s saw a pessimistic turn in his works which may possibly presage a new and darker orientation. Whether it will continue remains to be seen.

Buero visited the United States as guest lecturer at several universities in 1966 and again in 1970 for a symposium on Spanish theater held at the U of North Carolina. He is a member of the Spanish Royal Academy (*Academia Española) and lives and works in Madrid. Following is a complete list of his dramas (through 1981) arranged chronologically by the year they were first performed: *Historia de una escalera* (1949; The Story of a Stairway), *Las palabras en la arena* (1949; The Words in the Sand), *En la ardiente oscuridad* (1950; *In the Burning Darkness*, 1985), *La tejedora de sueños* (1952; *The Dream Weaver*, 1967), *La señal que se espera* (1952; The Awaited Sign), *Casi un cuento de hadas* (1953; Almost a Fairy Tale), *Madrugada* (1953; Dawn), *Irene o el tesoro* (1954; Irene or the Treasure), *Hoy es fiesta* (1956; Today Is a Holiday), *Las cartas boca abajo* (1957; The Cards Face Down), *Un soñador para un pueblo* (1958; A Dreamer for a People), *Las meninas* (1960; The Ladies in Waiting), *El concierto* *de San Ovidio* (1962; *The Concert at Saint Ovide*, 1967), *Aventura en lo gris* (1963; Adventure in Gray), *El tragaluz* (1967; The Skylight), *El sueño de la razón* (1970; *The Sleep of Reason*, 1985), *Llegada de los dioses* (1971; Arrival of the Gods), *La fundación* (1974; *The Foundation*, 1985), *La doble historia del doctor Valmy* (1976; *The Double Case History of Doctor Valmy*, 1967), *La detonación* (1977; The Detonation), *Jueces en la noche* (1979; Judges in the Night), *Caimán* (1981; Alligator). *See also* Contemporary Spanish Theater.

BIBLIOGRAPHY

Primary Texts

*Aventura en lo gris: Dos actos y un sueño*. Madrid: Puerta del Sol, 1955.
*El concierto de San Ovidio: Parábola en tres actos*. Madrid: Alfil, 1959.
*La doble historia del doctor Valmy: Relato escénico en dos partes*. Ed. Alfonso M. Gil. Philadelphia: Center for Curriculum Development, 1970.
*En la ardiente oscuridad: Drama en tres actos*. Madrid: Alfil, 1951.
*Historia de una escalera: Drama en tres actos*. Barcelona: José Janés, 1950.
*Un soñador para un pueblo: Versión libre de un episodio histórico, en dos partes*. Madrid: Alfil, 1959.
*El sueño de la razón: Fantasía en dos actos*. Madrid: Escelicer, 1970.
*El tragaluz: Experimento en dos partes*. Madrid: Alfil, 1968.

English Translations

*The Concert at Saint Ovide*. Tr. Farris Anderson. In *Modern International Drama I*. State College: Pennsylvania State UP, 1967.
*The Double Case History of Doctor Valmy*. Tr. F. Anderson. In *Artes Hispánicas/Hispanic Arts* 1.2 (1967): 85–169.
*The Dream Weaver*. Tr. William I. Oliver. In *Masterpieces of the Modern Spanish Theatre*. Ed. Robert W. Corrigan. New York: Macmillan-Collier, 1967.
*Three Plays/Antonio Buero Vallejo*. Tr. M. P. Holt. San Antonio: Trinity UP, 1985. Contains *The Sleep of Reason*, *The Foundation*, and *In the Burning Darkness*.

Criticism

Cortina, José Ramón. *El arte dramático de Antonio Buero Vallejo*. Madrid: Gredos, 1969.
Doménech, Ricardo. *El teatro de Buero Vallejo: Una meditación española*. Madrid: Gredos, 1973.
Donahue, Francis. "Spain's Tragic Voice: Antonio Buero Vallejo." *Revista/Review Interamericana* 9 (1979): 209–17.
*Estreno* (U of Cincinnati) 5.1 (1979). Special issue devoted to Buero Vallejo.
Halsey, Martha T. *Antonio Buero Vallejo*. New York: Twayne, 1973.
Ruiz Ramón, Francisco. *Historia del teatro español. Siglo XX*. 4th ed. Madrid: Cátedra, 1980. 337–84.

James F. Brown

**BULULÚ,** a type of acting troupe during the Golden Age. The term designated a farceur who performed alone, changing his voice for different characters. *See also* Compañía; *Siglo de Oro*.

Maureen Ihrie

**BUÑUEL, Miguel** (1924, Castellote, Teruel– ), novelist and author of children's books. Buñuel has published the following narratives for adults: *Narciso bajo las aguas* (1958; Narcissus Beneath the Waters); *Un lugar para vivir* (1962; A Place to Live); *Un mundo para todos* (1962; A World for All); and *Las tres de la madrugada* (1967; Three O'Clock in the Morning). Among the prizes he has received are the ''Selecciones Lengua Española'' and the ''Lazarillo,'' an international prize for children's fiction.

BIBLIOGRAPHY

Primary Texts

*Un lugar para vivir*. Barcelona: Caralt, 1962.
*Un mundo para todos*. Barcelona: Plaza y Janés, 1962.
*Narciso bajo las aguas*. Valladolid: Gerper, 1959.
*Las tres de la madrugada*. Madrid: Alfaguara, 1967.

Janet Pérez

**BURGOS, Francisco Javier de** (1842, Puerta de Santa María, Cadiz–1902, Madrid), playwright, librettist and journalist. After preparing himself in Madrid for a career as a highway engineer, he returned to Cádiz where he began to write for newspapers. As a playwright, he cultivated short farces and comic one-act pieces. One such comic sketch is *Los valientes* (1886; The Brave Ones). He also wrote librettos for *zarzuelas. Two of his better known works are *El mundo comedia es o El baile de Luis Alfonso* (1881; All the World is a Comedy or Luis Alfonso's Ball) and *Boda de Luis Alfonso o La noche de encierro* (1897; Luis Alfonso's Wedding or A Night of Enclosure). Both works are set to the music of Jerónimo Giménez and contain scenes of customs and manners typical of the period. He wrote some of his works in collaboration with *Luceño and *Fernández Shaw.

BIBLIOGRAPHY

Primary Texts

*A Sevilla por todo: zarzuela en dos actos*. Madrid: J. Rodríguez, 1881.
*Boda, tragedia y guateque, o El difunto de Chuchita*. Madrid: R. Velasco, 1881.
*El mundo comedia es o El baile de Luis Alfonso*. Madrid: R. Velasco, 1898.
*La boda de Luis Alfonso o La noche de encierro*. Madrid: Velasco, 1897.
*Los valientes*. Madrid: M. P. Montoya, 1886.

Criticism

Díaz, Nicomedes Pastor, and Francisco de Cárdenas. *Galería de españoles célebres contemporáneos*. Madrid: Ignacio Boix, 1841–46. 2: 1–71.

Phoebe Porter Medina

**BURGOS OLMO, Francisco Javier** (1778, Motril, Granada–1849, Madrid), poet, playwright and politician. He directed the publications *Miscelánea de Comercio, Artes y Letras*, *El Imparcial* and *El Universal*, and was elected to the Spanish Academy (*Academia Española) in 1827. He also occupied important political posts.

In the theater, Burgos modernized the classic tradition in some of his comedies such as *El heredero* (1804; The Inheritor); *El baile de las máscaras* (1832; The Masked Ball), etc. He is an elegant poet in his odes "A la razón" (To Reason), "El porvenir" (The Future), and others. A didactic tone prevails in his verse.

BIBLIOGRAPHY

Primary Texts

*Las tres iguales*. Madrid: Burgos, 1828.
His poetry is found in BAE 67: 443–50.

Criticism

Cejador y Frauca, J. *Historia de la lengua y literatura castellana*. Madrid: RABM, 1917.
    380–82.

**BURGOS SEGUÍ, Carmen de,** "Colombine" (c. 1870, Almería–1932, Madrid), journalist, translator, prose author. Born sometime between 1867 and 1879, the daughter of the Portuguese consul in Almería, Burgos married a local newspaperman at 16, initiating her lifelong contact with the world of journalism. The mother of two children, one of whom died early, she divorced her husband amid much scandal and moved to Madrid. Continuing studies begun in Almería, she won a professorship in the Escuelas Normales de Maestras in 1901. Posted to Guadalajara, she remained there until 1907 when she returned to Madrid as professor in the Escuela Normal Central where she remained as professor of language and literature until her death. Having begun to study pedagogy in the Colegio Nacional de Sordomudos y de Ciegos in 1904, she also held a position in that institution.

In addition to her teaching career Burgos was a prolific writer widely recognized in her day as a journalist, lecturer, translator, biographer, essayist and novelist. She contributed frequently to newspapers and magazines both within Spain and abroad, becoming the first woman editor on the staff of a newspaper to engage in reporting and to conduct interviews. Supported by the Junta de Ampliación de Estudios, Burgos traveled throughout Europe and later the Americas, drawing on her travels in numerous articles and books. Forthright and polemical, her essays addressed topical issues, often breaking taboos. Burgos campaigned for female suffrage, women's rights and divorce, while opposing the death penalty. At mid-century critics dismissed her non-fiction writing as ideological rather than philosophical or scholarly, but the recent interest in women's history has brought a fresh perspective to the study of her work.

Burgos published volumes ranging in subject from the obligatory women's manuals (*Arte de saber vivir* [1910; How to Live Well], *La cocina moderna* [n.d.; Modern Cooking], *Manual de cartas* [1910; Handbook for Letter Writing]), to accounts of her travels (*Por Europa* [n.d.; Across Europe], *Cartas sin destinatario* [n.d.; Letters to an Unknown Reader]), the discussion of social issues (*El divorcio en España* [1904; Divorce in Spain], *La mujer moderna y sus derechos* [1927; The Modern Woman and Her Rights]), and biographies of literary and political figures (*"Fígaro"* [1919], *Giacomo Leopardi* [1911], *Rafael de Riego* [1931]). Her literary talent manifested itself first in poetry, *Notas del alma* (1901; Songs from the Soul), and criticism, *Ensayos literarios* (Literary Essays), before she turned to prose fiction. Her impressive creativity yielded more than one dozen novels and numerous short novels, which appeared in the popular weekly magazines circulating widely in Spain. Few of these shorter works are collected into volumes or republished separately. Burgos herself compiled two collections of short fiction (*Cuentos de Colombine* [1908; Stories by Colombine] and *Mis mejores cuentos* [1923; My Best Stories]); two modern editions of short novels also exist. Burgos's fiction embraces naturalistic determinism (*Los inadaptados* [1909; The Misfits]), lingering Romanticism (*El último contrabandista* [1920; The Last Smuggler]), changing economic conditions (*"Villa-María"* [1916]), social concerns (*La malcasada* [1923; The Unhappily Married Woman], *El hombre negro* [1916; The Evil Man]), psychic phenomena (*El Retorno* [n.d.; The Reappearance], *Los espirituados* [1923; The Possessed]), and in one of her last publications, latent homosexuality (*Quiero vivir mi vida* [1931; I Want to Live My Own Life]). Her best works demonstrate an impressive talent for concise character delineation and the broad evocation of environment. She is perhaps at her strongest in the portrayal of the conflicting roles and identities of women in her shorter works.

Carmen de Burgos's long relationship with the vanguard writer Ramón *Gómez de la Serna, which began in 1909, when he was 20, brought her into close contact with the male-dominated literary scene and the world of publishing. Their attachment lasted with decreasing intensity until his marriage in 1931.

Eugenio de Nora's dismissal of Burgos as a "popularizer" has some validity to it; she saw journalism and fiction as the communication of current issues and ideas to the broadest possible public. At its weakest her fiction is formulaic, declining into a facile romanticism with heavy didactic overtones, but her finest short fiction conveys a depth of emotion and of lived experience brought to bear on the portrayal of human life. The social, economic, emotional and sexual repression of women all find expression in her fiction, often centering on the tension between a woman's experience of repression and the unexpected need to choose the future direction of her life.

BIBLIOGRAPHY

Primary Texts

*Cuentos de Colombine*. Valencia: Sempere, [1908].

*El divorcio en España*. Madrid: Romero, 1904.

*Los espirituados (novela)*. Madrid: Rivadeneyra, 1923.

*"Fígaro" (revelaciones, "ella" descubierta, epistolario inédito)*. Madrid: Alrededor del Mundo, 1919.

*Los inadaptados (novela)*. Valencia: Sempere, 1909.

*La malcasada (novela)*. Valencia: Sempere, 1923.

*Mis mejores cuentos (novelas breves seleccionadas por el propio autor precedidas de un prólogo autógrafo del mismo).* Madrid: Prensa Popular, 1923.
*La mujer moderna y sus derechos.* Valencia: Sempere, 1927.
*El retorno; novela espiritista (basada en hechos reales).* Lisbon: Lusitania, n.d.
*El último contrabandista (novela).* Barcelona: Ramón Sopena, 1920.

Criticism

Gómez de la Serna, Ramón. *Automoribundia (1888–1948).* Buenos Aires: Sudamericana, 1948. 210–12, *passim.*
Nora, Eugenio G. de. *La novela española contemporánea.* Vol. 2 (1927–1939). 2nd ed. Madrid: Gredos, 1968. 49–53.
Romá, Rosa. Introduction to *El hombre negro.* Madrid: Emiliano Escolar, 1980. 13–28.
———. Introduction to *"Villa-María."* Madrid: Emiliano Escolar, 1980. 13–28.
Starcevic, Elizabeth. *Carmen de Burgos: defensora de la mujer.* Almería: Librería-Editorial Cajal, 1976.

Maryellen Bieder

**BURGUILLOS, Tomé,** pseudonym used by Lope de *Vega for his *Rimas humanas y divinas . . . no sacadas de biblioteca ninguna* (1634; Divine and Human Rhymes . . . Not Taken from Any Library).

Maureen Ihrie

**BURLADOR.** *See* Don Juan, The Myth of

*BURLERÍA,* literary term. It denotes an imaginary tale, similar to a *conseja* or *patraña.*

*BUSCAPIÉ* (hint, explanation). As a literary term, *buscapié* denotes a "key" which reveals the true significance of obscure passages, or unknown characters, in a literary work. For example, some critics once felt that *Cervantes wrote a *buscapié* for the *Quijote,* indicating the true identities of his characters. Cayetano Alberto de la *Barrera disproved this allegation.

BIBLIOGRAPHY

Primary Text

Barrera, Cayetano Alberto de la. *El cachetero del Buscapié.* Prol. F. Rodríguez Marín. Santander: Librería Moderna, 1916.

Maureen Ihrie

**BUSCÓN.** *See* Quevedo, Francisco de; Picaresque

# C

CABA, Pedro (1900, ?–?), essayist. His most suggestive book, *Andalucía, su comunismo y su cante jondo* (1933; Andalusia, Her Communism and Her Cante Jondo), was written in collaboration with his brother, Carlos. His novel *Las galgas* (1934?) won the Gabriel Miró literary prize. After another novel, *Tierra y mujer o Lázara la profetisa* (1945; Land and Woman or Lazara the Prophetess), and a biography of Eugenio *Noel (1949), he turned to philosophical themes: *¿Qué es el hombre?* (1949; What Is Man?), *Los sexos, el amor y la historia* (1947; The Sexes, Love and History), and *Biografía del hombre* (1967; Biography of Man).

BIBLIOGRAPHY

Primary Texts

*Andalucía, su comunismo y su cante jondo*. Madrid?: Atlántico, 1933.
*Biografía del hombre*. Madrid: Nacional, 1967.
*Las galgas*. Barcelona: Juventud, 1934?
*Tierra y mujer o Lázara la profetisa*. Barcelona: Selecciones literarias y científicas, 1945.
*Los sexos, el amor y la historia*. Barcelona: Selecciones literarias y científicas, 1947.

Isabel McSpadden

CABAL, Fermín (1948, León– ), playwright and screenwriter. Unlike most of Spain's younger dramatists, Cabal has been quite successful in getting his plays staged in Madrid. Nevertheless, he is presently occupied with the cinema and is unwilling to affirm any intention of definitely returning to the theater. He began working in the theater with several groups that generated a number of collective productions. His own first staged drama, *Tú estás loco, Briones* (1978; You Are Crazy, Briones), was directed by the author with a cast culled from the collective group Tabano. His earliest works utilized some of the conventions of collective theater: experimentation, farce, satire and humor. They were quite stylized, with touches of the absurd. Cabal's greatest successes, however, represented a return to realism. *¡Vade retro!* (1982) had a successful run during the

1982–83 season in Madrid, and *Esta noche gran velada* (1982; Tonight a Great Evening Party) enjoyed a major critical and commercial success the following season. Cabal uses the term "hyper-realism" to describe his brand of theater. *¡Vade retro!* depicts the physical and psychological battle between an older priest and the rebellious younger Father Lucas during a single night. And *Esta noche gran velada* deals with a boxer's struggle against himself and the forces of corruption, climaxed by his murder for winning a championship fight he was supposed to throw. The play utilizes clichés from the American cinema, stereotypical characters and names, and a fascinating blend of pathos and humor to both distort and heighten realism. Cabal's future as a playwright remains uncertain, but the impact of the plays already staged on the theater-going public is undeniable. *See also* Contemporary Spanish Theater.

BIBLIOGRAPHY

Primary Texts

*Esta noche gran velada. Caballito del diablo.* Madrid: Fundamentos, 1983.
*Tú estás loco, Briones. Fuiste a ver a la abuela??? Vade retro!* Madrid: Fundamentos, 1982.

Criticism

Bigelow, Gary. "Fermín Cabal, cifra del teatro español actual: fragmento de una entrevists." *Estreno* 9.2 (Fall 1985); 24–27.

Peter L. Podol

**CABALLERÍAS, Libros de** (Romances of Chivalry), immensely popular genre in sixteenth-c. Spain. They narrate heroic, fantastic exploits of dashing knights-errant. Although derived in large part from medieval French Arthurian literature, one may also point to the *Gran *conquista de ultramar* (The Great Conquest beyond the Sea), the *Leyenda del *caballero del cisne* (Legend of the Swan Knight), the *Libro del caballero *Cifar* (Book of the Knight Cifar), and the *Libro del *paso honroso* (Book of the Pass of Arms) as Spanish antecedents. The first indigenous romance of chivalry was the *Amadís de Gaula* (before 1508). As D. Eisenberg states,

> Just as the writings of Aristotle defined what would later be called the field of philosophy, so the *Amadís* defined what the romance of chivalry would be in Spain. From *Amadís* the other romances took their basic framework: the traveling prince, the constant tournaments and battles, the remote setting in a mountainous, forested (never desert or jungle) land, the interest in honor and fame. (1982, p. 3)

The instant, enormous success of the original *Amadís* quickly begat continuations of the *Amadís* cycle—the *Sergas de Esplandián* (before 1510; Esplandián's Exploits), *Florisando* (1510), *Lisuarte de Grecia* (1514)—and new heroes and cycles as well: *Palmerín de Olivia* (c. 1510), *Primaleón* (1511 and 1512), *Belianís de Grecia* (1547), *Clarián de Landanis* (1518), etc. Eisenberg states that, during the reign of Charles V (1517–56)—who was a strong devotee of the genre—"new romances were published at the rate of almost one per year" (1982, p.41). Many leading figures of the day have confessed (oftentimes with chagrin) to earlier addiction to the libros de caballerías, including Juan de *Valdés, Sta. *Teresa de Jesús, and San *Ignacio de Loyola. The romances were harshly attacked by some (Joan Lluis *Vives, Juan de Valdés, some Erasmists), for their immoral moments, improbable escapism and lack of constructive examples for the reader, to little avail. The most famous lampooning of the genre, which ultimately served to preserve rather than squelch interest in the romances for the modern reader, is, of course, *Cervantes's *Don Quijote de la Mancha* (1605 and 1615), whose hero also models himself on the *Amadís*.

BIBLIOGRAPHY

Criticism

Eisenberg, D. *Castilian Romances of Chivalry in the Sixteenth Century: A Bibliography*. London: Grant and Cutler, 1979.

————. *Romances of Chivalry in the Spanish Golden Age*. Newark, DE: Juan de la Cuesta, 1982.

Mancing, H. *The Chivalric World of Don Quijote: Style, Structure and Narrative Technique*. Columbia: U of Missouri P, 1982.

Thomas, H. *Spanish and Portuguese Romances of Chivalry*. Cambridge, England: Cambridge UP, 1920. Rpt. New York: Kraus, 1969.

Maureen Ihrie

**CABALLERO, Fermín** (1800, Barajas de Melo, Cuenca–1876, Madrid), critic and journalist. Active in politics—he served in the cabinet under the presidency of Joaquín María López (1843)—Fermín Caballero is better known as a literary critic and a journalist of the liberal persuasion. His most significant contribution to Spanish letters is his *Vidas de los conquenses ilustres* (1868–75; Lives of Illustrious Citizens of Cuenca), in which he studies the personal histories of Alonso Díaz de Montalvo, Alfonso and Juan de *Valdés, Melchor *Cano, and others. Other works include *Pericia geográfica de Miguel de Cervantes* (1840; The Geographical Knowledge of Cervantes), *Memoria sobre el fomento de la población rural* (1862; Memorandum on the Support of the Rural Population), and *Fisonomía natural y política de los procuradores en las Cortes de 1834, 1835 y 1836* (1836; Natural and Political Physiognomy of the Parliamentary Proctors of 1834, 1835, and 1836). *Azorín, in commenting on this last-named volume, praises Caballero's writing as "solid, compact, and very Castilian."

BIBLIOGRAPHY

Primary Texts

*Fisonomía natural y política de los procuradores en las Cortes de 1834, 1835 y 1836.* Madrid: Boix, 1836.

*La imprenta en Cuenca.* Cuenca: El Eco, a cargo de L. Carretero, 1869.

*Memoria sobre el fomento de la población rural.* Madrid: Colegio de Sordo-mudos y de Ciegos, 1863.

*Pericia geográfica de Miguel de Cervantes.* Madrid: Yenes, 1840.

*Vidas de los conquenses ilustres.* 4 vols. Madrid: Colegio de Sordo-mudos y de Ciegos, 1868–75.

Criticism

Martín Gallardo, F. "Fermín Caballero y Menéndez Pelayo." *Boletín de la Biblioteca Menéndez Pelayo* 52 (1976): 313–29.
Martínez Ruiz, José (Azorín). "1836," *Lecturas españolas.* In *Obras completas.* Madrid: Aguilar, 1947. 2: 593–98.

Noël M. Valis

**CABALLERO BONALD, José Manuel** (1926, Jerez de la Frontera– ), poet and novelist of the second post-war generation. After four books of poetry in the fifties (*Las adivinaciones* [1952; The Divinings]; *Memorias de poco tiempo* [1954; Memorials of Little Time]; *Anteo* [1956; Anthaeus]; *Las horas muertas* [1959; Hours on End (La Critíca Prize, 1960)]), he began his novelistic career with *Dos días de septiembre* (1962; Two Days in September [Biblioteca Breve Prize]), written in Colombia where he taught briefly at the National U. A poetry anthology, *El papel del coro* (1961; The Role of the Chorus), and the volume of verse *Pliegos de cordel* (1963; Street Stories) date from this period. Two subsequent novels, *Agata ojo de gato* (1974; Cat's-eye Agate [Barral Prize, 1974]) and *Toda la noche oyeron pasar pájaros* (1981; They Heard Birds Pass All Night [Ateneo de Sevilla Prize]), and the volumes of poetry *Descrédito del héroe* (1977; The Hero's Discrediting) and *Laberinto de fortuna* (1984; The Labyrinth of Fortune [prose poems]) complete his creative work to date. He has also published studies on *flamenco* and has served both as secretary of *Papeles de Son Armadans* and as president of the PEN club of Spain.

BIBLIOGRAPHY

Primary Texts

*Agata ojo de gato.* Barcelona: Barral, 1977.
*Dos días de septiembre.* Barcelona: Argos-Vergara, 1977.
*Poesía, 1951–1977.* Barcelona: Plaza y Janés, 1979.
*Selección natural: Edición del autor.* Madrid: Cátedra, 1983. With introduction by author.
*Toda la noche oyeron pasar pájaros.* Barcelona: Planeta, 1981.

English Translation

"Waiting." Tr. C. D. Ley. In *Spanish Poetry since 1939.* Ed. C. D. Ley. Washington, DC: Catholic U of America P, 1962.

Criticism

Alvarado Tenorio, Harold. *Cinco poetas de la generación del 50: González, Caballero Bonald, Barral, Gil de Biedma, Brines.* Bogota: Oveja Negra, 1980.
Curutchet, Juan Carlos. "Caballero Bonald: Un precursor." In his *A partir de Luis Martín Santos: Cuatro ensayos sobre la nueva novela española.* Montevideo: Alfa, 1973. 11–27.
Gullón, Ricardo. "Mitologías de la ciénaga." *Cuadernos Hispanoamericanos* 297 (1975): 551–60.

Ortega, José. "Nuevos rumbos en la novelística española de posguerra: *Agata ojo de gato* de Caballero Bonald." *Anales de la Novela de Posguerra* 2 (1977): 19–29.

Villanueva, Tino. "*Pliegos de cordel*: La intención moral de J. M. Caballero Bonald en la poesía de la infancia." *BH* 84. 1–2 (Jan.-June 1982): 95–144.

Martha Miller

***CABALLERO DEL CISNE, Leyenda del*** (Legend of the Knight of the Swan). A tale which first appeared in Germany and then in other countries, its best known modern version is *Lohengrin* by Wagner. The legend, closely allied with the French epic, appeared in Spain in the pseudo-history *La gran *conquista de Ultramar* (c. 1300; The Great Conquest beyond the Sea) which tells of the ancestors and exploits of Godfrey of Bouillon (died 1100), first Latin ruler of Jerusalem. It was incorporated there to show that the Bouillon family was especially favored by God.

The Swan Knight episode relates how Princess Isomberta is miraculously guided to marry Count Eustacio, who is immediately called off to war. The princess has seven sons at a single birth. An angel comes down and places a gold collar on the neck of each. The count's wicked mother machinates for the execution of Isomberta and the children, but the order is not carried out, and the boys are abandoned in a wood where they are suckled by a hind and later taken in by a hermit. The grandmother manages to gain control of all save the eldest, but when their collars are removed to cut their throats, they turn into swans and escape to live in a pond near the hermitage. The wicked lady orders the collars melted down for a cup, but one suffices and the goldsmith, perceiving a miracle, hides the others.

Count Eustacio returns after seventeen years and Isomberta is forced to defend herself against the charge that her sons were born in adultery. An angel warns the hermit, and he sends the remaining son to be his mother's champion. After his triumph, the mother-in-law is walled in alive and the collars are placed on the swan's necks so that they regain human form. One boy remains a swan, since his collar was destroyed. The eldest is given the special grace of being victorious against those who wrongly accuse ladies or deprive them of their possessions. The swan is able to locate these women and tows the knight to them in a small boat.

They succor the Duchess of Bouillon, whose daughter the knight marries under condition that she neither ask his name nor whence he came. Unable to contain her curiosity, after she questions him he departs in the swan-boat (cf. myth of Psyche). Their daughter Ida is the mother of Godfrey of Bouillon and of his brothers Eustace and Baldwin.

BIBLIOGRAPHY

Primary Texts

*La gran conquista de Ultramar*. 4 vols. Ed. Louis Cooper. Bogota: Instituto Caro y Cuervo, 1979. Vol. 1.

*The Old French Crusade Cycle.* Ed. J. Nelson and E. Mickel. Vol. 1. University: U of Alabama P, 1977.

Eric Naylor

**CABAÑAS, Pablo** (1923, ?– ), poet, literary scholar. His poetry includes *Evocación* (1951; Evocation), *Lejos* (1953; Faraway), and *Mi tiempo se llama espera* (n.d.; My Time Is Called Wait). He has also prepared critical editions of *Jauregui's *Orfeo* (1948), and of *Pérez de Montalbán's *Orfeo en lengua castellana.* Also his is *El mito de Orfeo en la literatura española* (1948; The Myth of Orpheus in Spanish Literature).

BIBLIOGRAPHY

Primary Text

*El mito de Orfeo en la literatura española.* Madrid: CSIC, 1948.

Isabel McSpadden

**CABAÑERO, Eladio** (1930, Tomelloso, Ciudad Real– ), poet. In 1957 he won second place in the Adonais literary contest, and in 1963 he received the Premio Nacional de Poesía. He has published *Desde el sol y la anchura* (1956; From the Sun and Breadth), *Una señal de amor* (1958; A Sign of Love), *Recordatorio* (1961; Memento), and *Marisa Sabia and Other Poems* (1963), which are all collected in *Poesía, 1956–1970. Marisa Sabia* received a National Prize of Literature in 1963.

BIBLIOGRAPHY

Primary Text

*Poesía, 1956–1970.* Prol. F. Martínez Ruiz. Barcelona: Plaza y Janés, 1970.

English Translation

"You, the One I Love." Tr. anon. In *Arena* 23 (1965): 64–65.

Isabel McSpadden

**CABANYES, Manuel de** (1808, Villanueva y Geltrú, Barcelona–1833, Villanueva y Geltrú), pre-romantic poet. The influence of Byron, some classical turns of speech, clear, direct expression and true inspiration are apparent in his scant opus. His book *Preludios de mi lira* (1833; Preludes from My Lyre) appeared only weeks before his premature, sudden death from phthisis. Most memorable are the poems "A Cintio" (To Cintio), "A la Independencia de la Poesía" (To the Independence of Poetry), and "Preludios de mi lira" (Preludes of My Lyre).

BIBLIOGRAPHY

Primary Texts

*The Poems of Manuel de Cabanyes.* . . . Ed., intro. E. Allison Peers. Manchester: Manchester UP, 1923.

*Poesies completes de Manuel de Cabanyes.* Ed., prol. A. Maseres. Barcelona: Barcino, [1850s].

*Producciones escogidas.* Barcelona: Verdaguer, 1858.

Criticism

Romano Colangeli, M. *Clasicismo e romanticismo in Manuel de Cabanyes*. Lecce: Milella, 1958.

**CABEZAS, Juan Antonio** (1900, Cangas de Onís, Asturias– ), journalist, prose author. His parents emigrated to Cuba; Cabezas spent five years in Havana, returning to Spain at age twenty-four. Three years later he became director of the newspaper *El Carbayón*. His first book of stories, *Perfiles del alma* (1923; Profiles of the Soul), was published in Cuba. Currently he is an editor for the newspaper *ABC*. Aside from many journalistic pieces, Cabezas has published over fifty volumes—novels such as *Señorita 0–3* (n.d.; Miss 0–3) and *La ilusión humana* (1952; The Human Illusion); biographies of *Clarín, Concepción *Arenal, and Rubén Darío; travel books, and biographies of people and cities, such as *Madrid, Biografía de una ciudad* (1959; Madrid, Biography of a City), *Madrid, escenarios y personajes* (1968; Madrid, Settings and Characters), and *Asturias. Biografía de una región* (1956; Asturias, Biography of a Region). More recent are *La cara íntima de los Borbones* (1979?; The Private Side of the Bourbons) and *Cien años de Teléfono en España. Crónica de un proceso técnico* (1974; One Hundred Years of Telephone in Spain: Chronicle of a Technical Process).

BIBLIOGRAPHY

Primary Texts

*Asturias. Biografía de una región*. 2nd ed. Madrid: Espasa-Calpe, 1971.
*La cara íntima de los Borbones*. Madrid: San Martín, 1979?
*Cien años de Teléfono en España. Crónica de un proceso técnico*. Madrid: Espasa-Calpe, 1974.
*Señorita 0–3*. Madrid: Oriente, 1932.

Isabel McSpadden

*CABO* (tail, end), a poetic term. Used by pre–Golden Age poets, *cabo* refers to the final stanza which closes a poem or song.

*CABO ROTO* (broken end), poetry of, verses which terminate with incomplete words and rhymes, leaving off all syllables following the accented one. One of the most famous examples is found in a poem prefacing *Cervantes's masterpiece, the *Quijote*:

> Soy Rocinante el famo—
> Biznieto del gran Babie—
> Por pecados de flaque—
> Fui a poder de don Quijo—

(I am Rocinante the fam— / Great-grandson of great Babie— / Through sins of weak—/ I fell into the hands of Don Quijo—.) The technique produces a jocular, roguish effect, and is also used by some *picaresque authors.

**CABRAL, Alexandre** (1917, Lisbon– ), Portuguese short story writer, novelist, literary critic, translator and historian. Alexandre Cabral is without doubt one of the leading intellectual figures in Portugal today: quite apart from his own relatively minor, but nonetheless valuable, contribution to creative and imaginative fiction, he is a distinguished translator and historian, as well as a committed socialist, having defied official harassment and even periods of imprisonment to participate in the work of groups such as the Associação De Amizade Portugal-Cuba (Association for Portuguese-Cuban Friendship) and the Liga Para O Intercâmbio Com Os Países Socialistas (Society for Exchange with Socialist Countries). He was also deeply involved in the formation and organization of the Sociedade Portuguesa de Escritores (Portuguese Writers' Society), a group which he recalls with some regret in his semi-autobiographical *Memórias de um resistente* (1970; Memoirs of a Dissident) as having had the potential to maintain some degree of intellectual liberty during the years of the Salazar regime, if it had not allowed itself to be divided from within.

However, it is for his work as a critic and editor of literary texts, in particular those of Camilo Castelo Branco, that Cabral is most familiar. His work has included various original articles, as well as prepared editions of at least twenty-four of Camilo's novels, and similar editions of various other aspects of his work which are too often neglected: his shorter prose fiction, his polemical texts, his correspondence, his poetry and drama, and his exchange of telegrams with his lover Ana Plácido during the difficult years of 1959 and 1960.

In all of these projects, Cabral, possibly influenced by his materially based political beliefs, displays the same unfailingly thorough investigation of the social, cultural and personal backgrounds against which the respective works must be set. In this way he not only succeeds in increasing our appreciation of an author who often fails to appeal to the modern literary taste, but he also provides a refreshing alternative to the over-sentimental and uncritical attitudes which have often bedevilled studies of Castelo Branco Pérez.

In particular, he concentrates on the personal and social contexts of the works under review, thus maintaining the traditional biographical line of Camilo criticism, while also managing to prove that Camilo was not as unaware of the social developments of his time as is often believed. Indeed, Cabral always maintains a very strongly independent line in his work on Camilo, also questioning the otherwise accepted notions of Camilo as a figure aloof from all human contact, and of the "brasileiro" as a figure of unadulterated evil in Camilo's fictional world. Furthermore, his discussion of Camilo has the merit of presenting the man and the author with fair treatment of both his strengths and weaknesses, so that he does not hesitate to label some of his historical writing as dull, for example, or to criticize him for some of his more hysterical outbursts in his polemics; faults such as these have been passed over in silence too often in the past.

This tendency to de-romanticize accepted ideas is a trait of Cabral's personality which we may also trace in his own literary creation, especially in his African works, *Contos da Europa e da Africa* (1947; Tales from Europe and Africa), *Terra quente* (1953; Hot Land) and *Histórias do Zaire* (1956; Stories of the Zaire). These works are typical of Portuguese writing about Africa in the 1950s in their realistic approach to life in a colonial setting, unlike much that was written before that time.

In these works, Cabral presents us with a somewhat sordid picture of colonial life, which is seen as corrupting both the native population and their European masters. Thus, in the short novel *Terra quente*, for example, we see how power has corrupted Afonso, the self-satisfied and ruthless owner of a coffee plantation in what was untamed jungle before. This process of corruption is made particularly evident by the introduction of Afonso's naive nephew, Tiago, who is explicitly compared to Afonso as he himself was upon his first arrival in the area. Clear echoes of the legend of Eden in the depiction of pre-colonial society are set alongside the moral degradation of the native in a European-dominated civilization in order to further illustrate the alienation of the African from his own land and his own past. The story ends with the murder of Tiago by Afonso, who is insanely jealous of any challenge to his own power; this could perhaps be seen to extend the links with Genesis further to the tale of Cain and Abel.

The short stories of the collection *Histórias do Zaire* tend to concentrate more on the loss of purpose in the lives of the Africans who function purely as slaves to a society which they cannot understand. Thus, "Daba-Goma" shows us an old man who contemplates the powerlessness of his native gods to prevent the prostitution and drunkenness introduced among his people, who have no moral or spiritual order left to rely on, since their own traditional beliefs have failed them and those of the white man seem alien and unconvincing. Similarly, *Kandot era o 'boy' do Sr. Hiebler* (Kandot Was Mr. Hiebler's "Boy") presents an appalling orgy of untamed sexual license, drunkenness and violence as three slaves take advantage of their master's absence to indulge in a futile rebellion against his authority by taking over his house for the day.

In general, the African stories demonstrate a clear understanding of the dangers and tensions of colonial life, as well as a rare sensitivity to the reactions and sentiments of the native mind, typical of the internationalism which has always marked Cabral's outlook. One might also speculate that his realistic vision and sensitive treatment of the African as well as the European character helped to foster the growth in awareness of the colonial question and the subsequent development of the native literary tradition in Africa itself. What is beyond all doubt is that his own time in the colonies, where he could identify completely with neither black nor white, enabled him to observe in detail and to present with great power a strong indictment of European colonialism.

Unfortunately, Cabral's other fictional works fail to achieve the same degree of interest and conviction: *Malta brava* (1955; A Daring Gang) is set in an over-militarized church boarding-school, where a rebellion against draconian discipline imposed upon the pupils is subdued by the total destruction of all their spirit and individuality, symbolized by the widespread use of numbers rather than names to identify them. Like Vargas Llosa's similar work *La ciudad y los perros* (The City and the Dogs), the corruption and the hypocritical concern among the school authorities for its good name would appear to be a thinly veiled attack on the moral leadership and legitimacy of the political order in the country as a whole.

Both this work and *Memórias de um resistente* are too committed to retain the reader's full attention; the *Memórias* form a reasonably interesting document of what life is like for the intellectual in a society which he cannot accept, but the ability to detach oneself from a given situation proves difficult to maintain in an autobiographical account of life in one's own country. Similarly, *Margem norte* (1961; Northern Edge), which deals with the struggles of ordinary people in Lisbon at a time of great change and modernization in the city, fails to catch our attention, for, once more, Cabral is too closely involved in these matters to achieve the balance between sensitive understanding and objective detachment which distinguishes both his African stories and his work on Camilo.

Among Cabral's historical and sociological studies, all of which give clear expression to his own socialist viewpoint, are works on a popular revolt in Oporto in 1831; on the treatment in *Justiça* (Justice), a nineteenth-c. Lisbon republican journal, of alleged crimes by the Portuguese monarchy; and *Um Português em Cuba* (1969; A Portuguese in Cuba). This work is an interesting study of post-revolutionary Cuba and the progress which society has made there since Fidel Castro came to power. However, although it should not be dismissed too lightly as an idealized piece of propaganda, it undoubtedly presents a rather uncritical vision of the country, which may cause irritation to the less enthusiastic reader.

Mention should also be made of Cabral's work as a translator of foreign literature into Portuguese. From French he has translated Anatole France's *L'Ile des Pingouins* (1960; *A ilha dos pinguins*; Penguin Island), Roger Martin du Gard's *Vieille France* (1959; *Velha França*; Old France) and Claude Roy's *A Tort ou à Raison* (1960; *Com razão ou sem ela*; Right or Wrong). However, what is perhaps his most valuable contribution as a translator working in a market flooded with (often poor) translations from the more familiar languages of French and English is his interest in less obvious literary areas. Thus, he has also provided Portuguese translations of the novels *Valtagul* (1962; *A Machadinha*; The Hatchet) by the popular Romanian author, Mihail Sadoveanu, and Jaroslav Hašek's *The Good Soldier Schweik* (1961; *O valente soldado Chveik*). (An interesting footnote to this is that, of Cabral's own literary production, only *Terra quente* and *Histórias do Zaire* have attracted the attention of translators; these two works have both been translated into Polish).

Cabral is not a major literary figure in his own right. However, his African stories are without doubt among the finest works of Realist fiction in the Portuguese language, presenting a convincing critique of colonial life without lapsing into sentimentality or a superficially simplistic viewpoint. His other literary productions are unlikely to stand the test of time, but his valuable contributions to scholarship in other respects, particularly his fine work on Camilo, make Alexandre Cabral a figure who should not be forgotten in any account of modern Portuguese literature.

BIBLIOGRAPHY

Primary Texts

*Camilo Castelo Branco: Roterio Dramático dum Profissional das Letras*. Rev. Vila Nova de Famalico: Estudos Camilianos, 1989.
*Contos da Europa e da Africa*. N.p.: n.p., 1947.
*Dictionário de Camilo Castelo Branco*. Lisbon: Caminho, 1989.
*Histórias do Zaire*. 2nd ed., rev. Lisbon: Prelo, 1965.
*Terra quente*. Lisbon: n.p. 1953.

David Frier

**CABRERA, Alonso de** (1549?, Córdoba–1598, ?), Dominican professor, preacher to Philip II. He journeyed to the New World, and on his return to Spain was appointed professor of theology, preacher to Philip II and later to Philip III. Considered the best secular orator of his time, he spoke at the funeral of Philip II. Numerous sermons by Cabrera were published, as well as works such as *Consideraciones sobre todos los evangelios de la Cuaresma* (1601 & 1602; Considerations on All the Gospels of Lent) and *Sobre los evangelios del adviento* (1609 & 1610; On the Advent Gospels). His dense, sententious style is said to foreshadow that of the Baroque. *See also* Siglo de Oro.

BIBLIOGRAPHY

Primary Texts

*Antología*. Ed., sel., L. Felipe Vivanco. Madrid: Nacional, 1948.
*Sermones*. In NBAE 3.

**CABRERA, Ramón** (1754, Segovia–1833, Seville), priest, philologist. He served as director of the Spanish Academy (*Academia Española) from 1812 to 1814 and 1820 to 1823. His principal works are the *Breves consideraciones acerca de la armonía, gravedad y abundancia de la lengua castellana* (1781; Brief Thoughts on the Harmony, Gravity and Richness of the Castilian Tongue) and the *Diccionario de etimologías de la lengua castellana* (1837; Etymological Dictionary of the Castilian Language).

BIBLIOGRAPHY

Primary Text

*Diccionario de etimologías.* . . . 2 vols. Madrid: Calero, 1837.

**CABRERA DE CÓRDOBA, Luis** (1559, Madrid–1623, Madrid), historian. He participated in preparations for the Spanish Armada, aiding the Duke of Osuna, viceroy of Naples. His major work is the *Historia de Felipe II* (1619; History of Philip II); it is meticulous and precise in details, and adheres closely to historical and chronological truth. The second part of the historical narrative was not published until 1877, due to Cabrera's refusal to allow any emendation of the original as requested by the deputies of Aragón, who disliked their portrayal in the account of Antonio *Pérez.

Cabrera de Córdoba limited himself to recording the internal history of Spain under Philip II: there is a wealth of information concerning customs, founding of monuments, theaters, etc. His prose unfortunately lacks clarity, as efforts to achieve a particular style result in a certain dryness and exaggerated, inventive concision. The enigmatic figure of Philip II is at times poorly judged. The *Historia* enjoyed considerable fame and a broad circulation. *Pérez de Montalbán based his work about Philip II on Cabrera's account. Another work, *Relaciones de las cosas sucedidas en la corte de España desde 1599 hasta 1614* (1857; Account of the Events in the Royal Court of Spain from 1599 to 1614), is of similar historical interest.

Cabrera also composed an extended narrative poem titled *Laurentina* (1590?). *See also* Siglo de Oro.

BIBLIOGRAPHY

Primary Texts

*Cosas y casos de los albores del siglo XVII español: antología de hechos espigados de memorias escritas entre 1599 y 1614*. New York: Hispanic Institute, 1951.
*Felipe Segundo, rey de España*. Madrid: Aribau, 1876.
*Laurentina*. Ed. L. Pérez Blanco. Madrid: Real Monasterio, 1975.

**CADALSO, José,** pseudonym Dalmiro (1741, Cádiz–1782, Gilbraltar), dramatist, poet, essayist, and short fiction writer. Cadalso veers dramatically between the enlightened aesthetics of eighteenth c. neoclassicism and the cosmic desperation of *Romanticism, manifesting both extremes in his varied artistic production. This turbulent dialectic was not evident in Cadalso as a child—or at least in the little we know of his childhood—since he came from a distinguished family, enjoyed the benefits of a quality education (by the Jesuits in his hometown, in the Jesuit college in Paris [1750–54], and in the prestigious Royal Seminary of Nobles in Madrid [1758–60]) and traveled widely. He was, though, a rather lonely child: his mother died when he was two years old, and his father's business concerns kept him away from home for long periods of time. He was raised in part by his grandfather and an uncle. His trips to European capitals and his knowledge of several foreign languages infused him with a cosmopolitan spirit which clearly expressed itself in his writings.

A year after the death of his father in 1761, Cadalso joined the army, enlisting as a cadet in the Bourbon Horse Regiment. He was to serve his country as a soldier his entire life. It was as a soldier, in 1764, that he befriended the supreme commander of the Spanish forces, Count Aranda, who in 1766 was named president of the powerful Council of Castile. Cadalso's winning charm enabled him to befriend other individuals who would help him both literarily and socially, among them Gaspar Melchor de *Jovellanos and the beautiful Countess-Duchess of Benavente. In 1768 Cadalso was accused of writing a biting criticism of Madrid's customs, *Calendario manual y guía de forasteros en Chipre* (Handy Almanac and Foreigner's Guide to Cyprus), which earned him a six-month banishment to Aragón. His exile lasted two years, and during that time he wrote many of the poems published later as *Ocios de mi juventud* (1773; Pastimes of My Youth).

By 1770 Cadalso had returned to Madrid, in the company of the leading neoclassical writer of the day, Nicolás Fernández de *Moratín, and in the arms of his girlfriend, the actress María Ignacia Ibáñez (whom he called Filis in his writings). He formed a close and passionate friendship with Moratín. Together—and often accompanied by María Ignacia and her younger sister, Francisca (whom Moratín celebrated as Dorisa)—they attended the theater, wrote plays, discussed poetry, and attempted to bring about a renovation of Spanish letters. Cadalso frequented the *tertulia* at the San Sebastián Inn. Filis starred in Moratín's neoclassical play, *Hormesinda* (1770), and in Cadalso's heroic tragedy, *Don Sancho García* (1771), and both authors celebrated their friendship, loves, and epicurean pleasures in their poetry. In April 1771, Filis died suddenly; Cadalso was inconsolable. To soften his pain, he immersed himself in his writing. During these years he wrote several of his most important creations: additions to *Ocios*, *Los eruditos a la violeta* (1772; The Pseudo-Intellectuals), *Cartas marruecas* (finished by 1774; Moroccan Letters), and *Noches lúgubres* (1774; Mournful Nights). Only *Eruditos*, which enjoyed an enormous popular success, and *Ocios* were published during his lifetime. Other works were never published and have disappeared: *La Numantina* (The Girl from Numancia), a play; and *Observaciones* (Observations), an epistolary novel. One drama, *Solaya o los circasianos* (Solaya or the Circassians), long thought lost, has only recently been rediscovered.

In 1773 Cadalso's regiment was dispatched to Salamanca, where he developed another group of close friends and participated in a *tertulia* which included the poets José *Iglesias de la Casa, Father Diego *González, and Juan *Meléndez Valdés. From 1774 to 1782, Cadalso continued his ascent in the army, reaching the rank of colonel in early 1782. By then he was in Gibraltar, fighting for the Spanish recovery of that strategic rock, in British hands since 1704. On the night of February 26, Cadalso was killed by enemy fire; he was forty-one years old.

The *Cartas marruecas* is Cadalso's best-known work. Completed in the early 1770s, it was not published until 1789, when it appeared in installments in the serial publication *Correo de Madrid*. It is a brilliant fiction, a compilation of ninety letters exchanged between Gazel, a young man in the employ of the Moroccan ambassador in Madrid; Ben Beley, his wise confidant in Morocco; and Nuño, a Spanish Christian who befriends Gazel. Inspired by the example of the epistolary works of Montesquieu and Goldsmith, so popular in the eighteenth c., Cadalso comments satirically and didactically on the customs of his country. He aspires to an impartiality well in keeping with the scientific spirit of the Enlightenment. His criticisms reveal his concern for Spain's industrial progress, economic stability, educational system, political organization, and social welfare. The work expands upon the criticisms of customs which had long concerned him, a partial example of which he had published in the *Eruditos*. It reveals Cadalso's struggle between optimism and pessimism, reason and emotion, reform and resignation.

For years critics repeated that *Noches lúgubres* was autobiographical, and that the work's most shocking episode—Tediato's disinterment of the body of his dead lover—was a narrative reenactment of Cadalso's supposedly similar actions with the body of Filis. Such stories are discounted today, although it is accepted that *Noches* does reflect its author's tragic and "Romantic" state of mind following his lover's death, a state of emotional turbulence also seen in the poems dedicated to Filis in *Ocios*.

Cadalso was a complex, exciting and very talented observer of society. His seductive charm, his deep friendships, his broad intellectual concerns, his aesthetic creed, and his profound patriotism made him one of his century's most interesting men of letters.

BIBLIOGRAPHY

Primary Texts

*Cartas marruecas*. Ed. Manuel Camarero. Madrid: Castalia, 1984.
*Cartas marruecas*. Eds. Lucien Dupuis and Nigel Glendinning. London: Tamesis, 1966.
*Cartas marruecas*. *Noches lúgubres*. Ed. Joaquín Arce. Madrid: Cátedra, 1978.
*Escritos autobiográficos y epistolario*. Eds. Lucien Dupuis and Nigel Glendinning. London: Tamesis, 1979.
*Noches lúgubres*. Ed. Edith Helman. Madrid: Taurus, 1968.
*Solaya o los circasianos*. Ed. Francisco Aguilar Piñal. Madrid: Castalia, 1982.

Criticism

Arce, Joaquín. "Cadalso y la poesía del siglo ilustrado." *Cuadernos para la Investigación de la Literatura Hispánica* 1 (1978): 195–206.
*Cadalso*. No ed. 2 vols. Cádiz: Diputación de Cádiz, 1983.
*Coloquio internacional sobre José Cadalso*. Eds. M. DiPinto, M. Fabbri, and R. Froldi. Bologna: n.p., 1985.
*Coloquio internacional sobre José Cadalso*. No ed. Abano Terme, Italy: Piovan, 1985.
Deacon, Philip. "Cadalso: Una personalidad esquiva." *CH* 389 (1982): 327–30.
Dowling, John C. "La sincronía de *El delincuente honrado* de Jovellanos y las *Noches lúgubres* de Cadalso." *NRFH* 33 (1984): 218–23.
Glendinning, Nigel. "Sobre la interpretación de las *Noches lúgubres*." *Revista de Literatura* 44 (1982): 131–39.
———. *Vida y obra de Cadalso*. Madrid: Gredos, 1962.
Helman, Edith. "*Caprichos* and *Monstruos* of Cadalso and Goya." *HR* 26 (1958): 200–222.
Hughes, John B. *José Cadalso y las 'Cartas marruecas'*. Madrid: Tecnos, 1969.
Maravall, José A. "El pensamiento político de Cadalso." *Mélanges a la mémoire de Jean Sarrailh*. Paris: Institut d'Etudes Hispaniques, 1966. 2: 81–96.
Sebold, Russell P. *Colonel Don José Cadalso*. TWAS 143. Boston: Twayne, 1971.

Wardropper, Bruce. "Cadalso's *Noches lúgubres* and Literary Tradition." *Studies in Philology* 49 (1952): 619–30.

David Thatcher Gies

**CÁDIZ, Diego José de** (1743, Cádiz–1801, Ronda), friar, writer, playwright. José Caamaño García Texeiro, born into a distinguished family, entered a monastery for Capuchine missionaries. After ordination he spent the remainder of his life traveling throughout Spain in a persistent battle against all forms of impiety. He was especially vocal in his condemnation of what he viewed as the immoral ideas being introduced into Spain by the Enlightenment reformers. His works—sermons, treatises, and other genres of both a religious and a practical nature—attained widespread popularity, particularly among conservatives in the south and east, and were republished several times in the eighteenth and nineteenth centuries. His greatest impact was on the theater. In his *Dictamen sobre el asunto de comedias y bailes* (1790; Discourse on the Question of Plays and Dances) he roundly condemns the immorality of public stage performances. So persuasive were his arguments that theatrical productions in many cities in Andalusia and the Levante were banned during much of the latter half of the eighteenth c. Other important works include *Afectos de un pecador arrepentido* (1776; Passions of a Repentent Sinner), and *El soldado católico en guerra de religión* (1794; The Catholic Soldier in a Religious War). Two unsuccessful attempts were made to publish his complete works (1796 and 1856). Friar Diego José de Cádiz was beatified in 1894. *See also* Theater in Spain.

BIBLIOGRAPHY

Primary Texts

*Afectos de un pecador arrepentido.* Granada: n.p., 1833.
*Dictamen sobre el asunto de comedias y bailes.* N.p.: n.p., 1790?
*El soldado católico en guerra de religión.* Madrid: la Parte, 1814.

Criticism

Hardales, Serafín de. *El misionero capuchino. Compendio histórico de . . . Cádiz.* Marina: M. Segovia, 1811.
Ott, Oliver. "Prédication et violence en Espagne à la fin du XVIII$^e$ siècle: Le Vitupère des 'philosophes' chez Fray Diego de Cádiz 1786–1797." *Imprévue* 1 (1981): 41–65.

Donald C. Buck

**CAGIGAL DE LA VEGA, Fernando,** Marqués de Casa-Cagigal (1756, San Sebastián–1824, Barcelona), playwright and poet. He distinguished himself as a cavalry officer in Menorca, Gibraltar and the Rousillon, but despite his rank of lieutenant-general, he was forced to retire because King Ferdinand VII suspected him of Liberal leanings. Cagigal left several writings on plays and operas performed on the Barcelona stage, some translations, poetry, and four original plays. Cagigal was a friend of the elder *Moratín and devoted follower of his school.

*El matrimonio tratado* (1817; The Prearranged Marriage), *La sociedad sin más-cara* (1818; Society without a Mask), *La educación* (1818; Education), and *Los perezosos* (1819; The Good-for-Nothings) follow the rules of neoclassicism and have a very direct didactic and moralistic purpose. A reformer with an enlightened mind, Cagigal believed Spaniards had to be educated before reforms could be undertaken. He criticized parasites and useless members of society, attacked lazy noblemen, and stressed the important roles of merchants and farmers in contemporary society. He was in favor of progress and scientific innovations. As a poet he left *Romances militares* (1817; Military Ballads), also of a didactic nature.

BIBLIOGRAPHY

Primary Texts

*A la elocuencia.* Barcelona: Garriga y Aguasvivas, 1820.
*El matrimonio tratado.* Barcelona: Roca, 1817.
*Fábulas y Romances militares.* Barcelona: Brusi, 1817.
*La educación.* Barcelona: Roca, 1818.
*La sociedad sin máscara.* Barcelona: Roca, 1818.
*Los perezosos.* Barcelona: Roca, 1819.

Criticism

Caldera, Ermanno. *La commedia romantica in Spagna.* Pisa: Giardini, 1978.
García Castañeda, S. "El Marqués de Casa-Cagigal, escritor militar." *La guerra de la Independencia y su momento histórico.* Santander: n.p., 1979. 2: 743–56.
———. "Moralidad y reformismo en las comedias del Marqués de Casa-Cagigal." *Atti del congreso sul Romanticismo Spagnolo e Ispanoamericano.* Geneva: n.p., 1982. 25–34.

                                                          Salvador García Castañeda

**CAJAL, Rosa María** (1920, Zaragoza– ), novelist. She felt her literary vocation early, but the necessity to support herself from office employment forced her to postpone her literary career. After writing many stories and novels without intending to publish them, she moved to Madrid and finally began publishing newspaper articles and stories in various magazines. She won third prize in a *Zarzuela libretto contest and was also a finalist for the Premio Gijón for short novels in 1951. Her first published novel, *Juan Risco* (1948), was a finalist for the Premio Nadal. It is an existentialist novel in which the protagonist bitterly withdraws from human society. He helps a young woman down on her luck, but rejects her when she falls in love with him. He cynically arranges for her to meet an editor, who will be her next lover. When the editor's wife Cristina dies, Risco's past is revealed: he had been Cristina's husband and a famous journalist, but had faked suicide and taken on another identity in order to free Cristina. However, his new identity led only to emptiness and self-contempt. *Primera derecha* (1955; First Floor, Right) was a finalist for the Premio Ciudad de Barcelona. The novel depicts the life of a matriarch who lives only for her children and for her husband, whom she considers merely another child. Throughout the novel she is never shown doing anything outside the four walls of her house. After having two miscarriages and bearing and rearing seven children, she finds her very being in motherhood. *Un paso más* (1956; One Step Further) is the only one of Cajal's novels to present an unconventional woman as the protagonist. In a situation rare during the 1950s, the young woman leaves her village to build a career in business in the city. She seeks independence and, despite self-doubts, proves stronger than the men and other women against whom she is juxtaposed. As a successful bookstore owner, she employs a male friend and serves as his mother-figure but does not return his love. Her women friends and relatives are weak, dependent and shallow; but she takes step after step, in personal life and in business, until she becomes a complete woman. Cajal's most recent novel is *El acecho* (1963; The Ambush).

BIBLIOGRAPHY

Primary Texts

*El acecho*. Madrid: Bullón, 1963.
*Juan Risco*. Barcelona: Destino, 1948.
*Primera derecha*. Barcelona: Caralt, 1955.
*Un paso más*. Barcelona: Garbo, 1956.

Carolyn Galerstein

**CALAVERA, Ferrán Sánchez de** (?,?–after 1443?, ?), poet. His work, found in the *Cancionero de *Baena*, is largely pessimistic and skeptical in tone, treating profound themes such as free will versus predestination. Most famous is the *Dezyr a la muerte del almirante Ruy Díaz de Mendoza* (n.d.; Poem on the Death of Admiral Ruy Díaz de Mendoza), a source of Jorge *Manrique's *Coplas*.

BIBLIOGRAPHY

Primary Texts

*Cancionero de Baena*. Pref. H. R. Lang. New York: Hispanic Society, 1926. Facs.
*El Cancionero de Juan Alfonso de Baena. Siglo XV*. Buenos Aires: Anaconda, 1949.

**CALDERÓN DE LA BARCA, Pedro** (1600, Madrid–1681, Madrid), dramatist and poet. Calderón's life was not uneventful. He was the third child and second son born to Diego Calderón and Ana María de Henao. A third son, Joseph, and two daughters followed him. Originally from the Santander region, the family belonged to the lower ranks of the nobility, but Don Diego Calderón's chief source of income appears to have been a royal treasury office. The father was an ''escribano de cámara en el Real consejo y Contaduría mayor de Hacienda.'' One gathers, then, that he ran an intendancy of accounts for the treasury and that he had purchased his charge. However, scribal duties were held to be incompatible with noble rank in seventeenth-c. Spain, so Philip IV obtained for Pedro Calderón a dispensation from this parental blot by making the dramatist a knight of Santiago in 1936.

Calderón's mother died in 1610, his father in 1615, but not without having taken a second wife, Juana Freyle Caldera. A dispute over property involved Doña Juana in a lawsuit with her stepsons. It was finally settled out of court. But its legal documentation is the first evidence of that concert among the three Calderón brothers which was to be lifelong. Perhaps the greatest family influence on their lives was that of their grandmother, Doña Inés Riaño y Peralta, who died in 1613. In her will she established in the family's parish church of San Salvador a *capellanía*, a chantry or perpetual religious trust, and designated Diego, Pedro, and Joseph Calderón as, in that succession, its chaplains. For many years none of her grandsons was to take it up. Diego seems to have been a sort of lobbyist. He married and had one son, Joseph Antonio, who all his life was very close to his uncle Pedro. Don Pedro had an illegitimate son, born around 1648 and described as dead in 1657. Joseph Antonio brought the boy up as his own. Joseph Calderón went into the army and rose to the rank of brevet brigadier. He was killed in a skirmish in the Catalan campaign in 1645. He did not marry and left no recorded issue.

Pedro would appear to have been the Calderón destined for the chantry, and it is hard to combat the evidence that for many years he resisted it. Just after his student years, which oral tradition has him spending at the Colegio Imperial and at Alcalá, and documentation at Salamanca, he and his brothers got into several well-publicized scrapes, a murder in 1621, a wounding in 1629. Pedro's play of earliest date is *Amor, honor, y poder* (1623; Love, Honor, and Might). He soon attracted royal favor, which brought him knighthood in 1636, and which he retained beyond Philip IV's death until his own. When the king called Santiago to arms, Calderón responded by campaigning in Catalonia as a cavalry officer from 1640 to 1641 and in 1642. But the desperate 1640s disrupted Madrid's cultural and court life, bringing to a close Calderón's period of great success as a popular dramatist. With only rather uncertain royal and city commissions left to him, don Pedro was ordained in 1650 and at last took up his inheritance. In 1653 Philip presented him with the chaplaincy of the Reyes Nuevos in Toledo. However, he moved back to Madrid, where he died rich and surrounded by beautiful and costly things. He wrote about 118 three-act secular plays, over 70 brief but dense allegorical dramas (*autos sacramentales; see* auto), as well as many prefatory and comical pieces, not to mention works composed in collaboration, plus poems. He is one of the world's greatest dramatists.

But how could this truth have for so long eluded not only highly discerning Europeans and Americans but also cultivated Hispanics? To be sure, Calderón found in the Goethe of the Weimar Hoftheater and of the *Conversations with Eckermann* an ideal judge of his stagecraft and his art. Yet Goethe failed to launch Calderón, the dimness of whose reputation in Spain and outside may be ascribed to dogmatic criticism, by which he has been victimized in both a negative and a positive manner. The great negative dogmatist of Calderón is Marcelino *Menéndez y Pelayo, who in his bicentenary *Calderón y su teatro* marshaled the principal prejudices of eighteenth-c. good taste as well as those of nineteenth-c. realism and *naturalism to do the dramatist's standing an injury from which it has not yet fully recovered. True Calderonian criticism derives from efforts to undo the harm done over a century ago; and Calderón's most constructive and appreciative modern critics have until recently been British, Edward M. Wilson and his student Bruce W. Wardropper chief among them. But by a strange irony Calderón's most influential British critic has been a dogmatist of his virtues, Alexander A. Parker who, obsessed by what he has seen as the playwright's overwhelming preoccupation with morality, conscience, and an artistic unity legislated by these, has created for Calderón a kind of repellent Catholic grandeur that discourages the modern sensibility, however sympathetic. Menéndez y Pelayo's barbaric Calderón has been made better, but has become forbidding in the process, and inhuman.

The inhumanity of Calderonian drama derives from its central rite of sacrifice. Where honor is not an issue, the victim tends to be male. Where it is, and the gender of that noun in Latin and in the principal Romance languages is suggestive, the victim is female. *El príncipe constante* (1636; The Steadfast Prince) is an early (1627) masterpiece involving the sacrifice of a Portuguese royal prince who has fallen a prisoner to his Islamic enemies. But even though the person on whom the play mainly focuses is male, its principal is female: woman as a means of exchange. Thus there is a deep bond, one that goes well beyond the sexual, between the Christian prince Fernando and the Mohammedan princess Fénix. Both are objects in human barter. The prince's captors want to trade him, just as men in most cultures trade in women. The two great sonnets at the core of the drama express the common subjection of a Christian man and a Moslem woman. But the man triumphs over victimization by taking sacrifice into his own hands. He refuses to be bartered and so immolates himself. His slow progress to sainthood is a sanctioned form of suicide, holy anorexia. Yet self-sacrifice is very different from victimization by society, for though the result is the same, the gradual suicide controls the form and tempo of the process. The fully conscious suicide is, as Hedda Gabler knows, a supreme artist. And so, even in *El príncipe constante*, where the success of sacrifice is foreordained, Fernando's wresting of power over his own victimization is a major step toward a profoundly human countercurrent in the drama of Calderón, its deep aversion to sacrifice, its struggles to postpone, avoid, evade and overcome the tragic rite on which the Christian social order rests, as well as the Mohammedan.

Calderón's most famous play, *La vida es sueño* (1636; Life is a Dream), like *El príncipe constante*, pairs a female with a male victim. Men have not only abused the beautiful Muscovite Rosaura but also her mother, and Rosaura opens the play by repairing to Poland in search of redress. Just across the border, she discovers in the chained prince Segismundo her male counterpart. Both know themselves to be oppressed. The main action of the play therefore involves their joint uprising against their oppressors, Segismundo's against the father who has denied him, Rosaura's against the father and the lover who have denied her. Their revolt would naturally end in the murder of the oppressors, and Calderón gives this tragic impetus compelling force. When the play does not end in expected sacrifice, the explanation is not some failure of tragic conviction in Calderón but rather a dramatic art that puts higher value on the non-tragic than on the tragic. Segismundo succeeds in engendering in himself such a measure of moral and artistic self-fashioning that he can place his creative power in the path of a tragic train of events and deflect it, art winning out over fate and brutal circumstance.

The artist, then, figures with unprecedented prominence in Calderonian drama. Perhaps the most audacious attempt to resolve the conflict between philosophy, with its tragic and oppressive vision of human destiny, and poetry, which admits of consolation and hope, is that carried out in the auto sacramental *El gran teatro del mundo* (written 1675; All the World's a Stage) where Calderón magnificently merges opposites, diversion with a sense of direction, amusement with morality. Two devices effect this compatibility. In the first place Calderón puts God himself in charge of the revels as *autor, technically impresario, but also connotatively as the source and creator of the elements of the play. Medieval philosophy was fond of describing God as an artist, *artifex*, or painter, *pictor*, but not so much to ennoble art as to make the divine mind more comprehensible. Calderón, in contrast, apotheosizes drama by showing it to be God-inspired. He also reconciles the tendency of amusement to move away from and be forgetful of God with reverential concentration on him through the use of pilgrimage, which has all the delight of escaping from that room to which Pascal would like to confine us along with the gravity of the funeral cortege. *El gran teatro del mundo* is, however, a pilgrimage to different stations. The wayfarers reach their goals at individual points and the procession moves on without them. As each traveler dies, her or his companions genuinely regret the diminution of their number; but since this small society is a congenial one, it offers true solace on the road to the tomb by diverting, momentarily, its members' thoughts from their destination. This aversion from death constitutes *El gran teatro del mundo* as a *comedia*, any play in Spanish Golden Age parlance but with the characteristic assumption that classic Iberian drama aspires to the more fortunate rather than to the less fortunate conclusion. If they can accept any kind of play, moralists will more probably tolerate tragedy, which is intent on death, than comedy, which would, we all know how vainly, elude it. No dramatist surrenders more completely to the inevitable than Calderón. By doing so he preserves his creative strength in order to win whatever victories it is licit to win. *El gran teatro del mundo* triumphs twice, once on this side of the grave, once on the other. The good society in the play provides its pilgrims with remarkable comfort. It sustains each of them to the end. In addition, each of them, except one child and one adult, joins the better society that assembles around God's table after death. By bracketing death with a communion that both precedes and follows it, Calderón counter-attacks that tragic vision which perceives life as a flicker of interlude and converts dying itself into an isolation through which all souls will individually pass as they hope to ascend from a carnal to a spiritual commonweal. *El gran teatro del mundo* shows death to be a potentially tragic interlude from which, however, the majority of mortals will emerge intact, saved. Thus, the play is a brief Spanish mode of Dantean comedy, triumphant; and art has greatly contributed to the victory. Pascal in the *Pensées* warns that non-tragic drama (*la comédie*) is the most dangerous form of amusement of which the Christian can partake. Calderón's art, by dramatizing a metaphor, by ascribing festivity to the divine desire for diversion, by imparting to human existence a dynamic, the pilgrimage, which is both deeply secular and sacred, succeeds in reconciling the profane to the sacred, the creative to the dogmatic.

In sacramental drama, however, Calderón did have to contend with doctrine which, though susceptible of the most imaginative animation by him, could not be altogether transformed. To be sure, Calderón's dramatic sensibility required formulas against which to work, Catholic dogma in the allegorical plays, classical themes in the mythological works, strict social code in the dramas of honor. His achievement, especially in the second and third categories, is to convert the tragic implications of a given state of affairs into non-tragic circumstance. The honor plays and the mythological dramas give the greatest scope to Calderón's comic genius; but no group of his writings has been more maligned, more misunderstood, than the mythological. It is simply not defensible to see these as the product of a personal decline in an author whose last plays are among his finest, or as the product of a national decadence which is anything but firmly established. Calderón's mythological drama is in fact another, and freer, mirroring mode of the allegorical. Each category reflects the other, a function revealed by the modified presence of the mythological in the allegorical: Jason, Psyche, Cupid, Circe, Ulysses, the sibyls, Astrea, Pan, the labyrinth, Perseus, Andromeda and Orpheus.

Reciprocally, Christianity achieves euhemeristic presence in the mythological drama, nowhere more compellingly than in *La estatua de Prometeo* (1667; Prometheus the Sculptor). In the *Theogony* and again in *Works and Days* Hesiod was the first poet to describe this great antagonist, who tried to trick Zeus and who in the early Christian era came to be widely considered as a classical figure of Christ. In its essence the Prometheus myth is etiological, a Greek Genesis that tries to account for both civilization and its discontents. Calderón's masterful version is Wagnerian. It deploys drama, music, and plastic expression to create a vast synaesthetic dissonance striving for the supreme harmonic. However, the play's basic stance, like Calderón's own as an artist, is adversarial. Prometheus opposes his fellow Caucasians, his brother, and some of the gods. Conflict in Calderón always serves a higher purpose as it tragically pursues some more tolerable resolution. Art is the medium by which *La estatua de Prometeo* rises to a knowledge of evil and good just barely sufficient to allow the good to prevail. Prometheus, his imagination obsessed by the immanent or quasi-idea of Minerva, forms a statue of her to which she descends. Now more fully known to him, she helps him steal fire from Apollo so that the blessings of cookery and civilization may spread among men, along with the destruction that is fire's other function. Prometheus's devotion to Minerva kindles a feeling of passionate rivalry in her bellicose sister Pallas, who sends Pandora down among the Caucasians to incite duels, war, and the desire for revenge. Most of all, Pandora, a figure of Helen, stimulates male sexual rivalry and jealousy, particularly between the brothers Epimetheus and Prometheus, so that the prime encounter—first imaginative, next plastic, and finally personal—between a goddess and a man results in general ruin, as with Yeats's far more sexually graphic enactment in the assault on Leda by the swan: "A shudder in the loins engenders there / The broken wall, the burning roof and tower / And Agamemnon dead." Commerce between gods and humans has dire results. But even from the devastation a higher construction can rise. Yeats reaches for a new foundation among the ruins with the question, "Did she put on his knowledge with his power / Before the indifferent beak could let her drop?" For Prometheus in his contest with Pallas the answer is in the affirmative. Knowledge, as Yeats suggests, can ultimately overpower armed or feathered might. The good elements descended from the divine can be used to put down the evil also disseminated from above. Moreover, knowledge (*ciencia*) in *La estatua de Prometeo* materializes as art which pursues, captures, and contains the divine. It is the chalice of religion. Like Rilke, Prometheus can proclaim himself the vessel of a deity and in so doing imply that deity's dependence on him. Moreover, art understood as the form of religion constitutes a higher religion that abandons human sacrifice. Just as Prometheus and Pandora are about to be hurled to their death Minerva intercedes for them with Jupiter, and Apollo announces their pardon in time to save them. Long before René Girard, Calderón fully realized that sacrifice constitutes both society and religion, but his drama seeks to break the deadlock that imprisons civilization and the sacred within the precincts of endless victimization. Such is the sense in which Calderón is that inconceivable thing, a progressive, a Comtean, for whom the third stage, after superstition and religion, is art as a *ciencia* that empowers its practitioners to rise above sacrifice. *La estatua de Prometeo* is the anti-pharmacy of Calderón, the cure that abolishes both poison and antidote.

Nonetheless, as etiological myth, *La estatua de Prometeo* also is the alembic which distills that potent Golden Age venom, honor, with its female source in Pandora, over whom Prometheus and Epimetheus duel and to whom they immolate others and themselves. Calderonian honor makes the social rites of victimization contemporary to him and secular. Honor is Calderón's Oedipus complex. And it is cruelly fixated on the female who, if she can escape the cross, will attain unprecedented new human depth. Criticism has understandably concentrated on the three horrific plays—*A secreto agravio secreta venganza* (1637; Hidden Crime, Hidden Punishment), *El médico de su honra* (1637; Pharmacist to His Honor), and *El pintor de su deshonra* (1650; Depictor of His Shame)—that constitute the central triptych of crucifixion, for they frame the fundamental mystery of the secular drama, they are its Eleusinian rite. This, however, is art as murder, art as crime. Its revolting sublimity—Doña Mencía as hero ranks with Lear—voices an eloquently mute appeal that is answered in nearly all the other, more than a hundred, non-allegorical plays. Society is intent upon the sacrifice of its women, whom Calderón, with the greatest difficulty, spares. The dominant male voice of the three great and awful tragedies of honor cries out: "¡rigor!" (severity). The subdominant female voice of the multiple comedies that echo this tragic hierarchy responds with "¡piedad!" (mercy). The appeal is almost always heard, and granted, so that the legal and human result is reversal. Compassion overrules ferocity. The female subdominant replaces the masculine dominant, even and especially in harsh and cruel males. Recoiling against the barbarism of female sacrifice, on which they nonetheless concentrate with a clarity and intensity that exonerate the non-tragic plays of the slightest imputation of frivolity (although there is *always* humor in Calderón), the greatest number of the secular plays seeks relief from the strictures that artistically determine them. Initially overshadowed by tragedy, Calderonian comedy longs to subvert its rule. It rises up in revolt against established order and by disobedience transforms the ancient dispensation. The new society that each play creates is a better society, for it victimizes women less. But what the plays collectively tend to is a general pardon, an end to this terrible male rule of "law." Calderón himself, I have not the slightest doubt, was completely conventional in his idea of the role in society of each gender; but his art drove him to the ultimate audacity, as when in *El postrer duelo de España* (1672; The Final Duel in Spain), he envisages, from the male point of view, the abolition of a social rite of sacrifice on which his drama thrives. Still more daringly, in *Afectos de odio y amor* (1664; Expressions of Hatred and Love), he fashions from Queen Christina of Sweden a sovereign who legally abolishes the whole system of the exploitation of the female. She outlaws romantic love and duelling, and throws every area of achievement open to women on merit, including war and government. Under the aegis of Queen Christina, Calderonian dramaturgy would of course perish, so that the play in which she figures reverts to something like the old order. Nonetheless, much of the greatness of the drama of Calderón derives from its deep and clear-sighted desire for its own abolition. It is in many ways a magnificent appeal that has not been answered yet. But we continue to feel the power of its persuasion. *See also* Siglo de Oro; Theater in Spain; Zarzuela.

BIBLIOGRAPHY

Primary Texts

*Autos sacramentales*. Ed. P. de Pando y Mier. 6 vols. Madrid: Ruiz de Murga, 1717.
*Autos sacramentales*. Ed. A. Valbuena Prat. Madrid: Aguilar, 1959.
*Cada uno para sí*. Ed. J. M. Ruano de la Haza. Kassel: Reichenberger, 1982.
*Comedias*. In BAE 7, 9, 12, 14 (1944–45).
*Comedias*. Ed. A. Valbuena Briones. Madrid: Aguilar, 1973.
*Comedias*. Ed. D. W. Cruickshank and J. E. Varey. 19 vols. London: Gregg, 1973.
*Dramas*. Ed. A. Valbuena Briones. Madrid: Aguilar, 1969.
*La estatua de Prometeo*. Ed. M. R. Greer. Kassel: Reichenberger, 1988.
*Fieras afemina amor*. Ed. E. M. Wilson. Kassel: Reichenberger, 1984.

English Translations

*Beware of Still Waters*. Tr. D. M. Gitlitz. San Antonio: Trinity UP, 1984.
*Calderón de la Barca: Four Plays*. Tr., intro. E. Honig. New York: Hill and Wang, 1961.
*Four comedies by Pedro Calderón de la Barca*. Tr. K. Muir. Lexington: UP of Kentucky, 1980.
*Life Is a Dream*. Tr. E. Honig. New York: Hill and Wang, 1970.
*The Prodigious Magician*. Tr. B. W. Wardropper. Madrid: Porrúa Turanzas, 1982.
*Three Comedies by Pedro Calderón de la Barca*. Tr. K. Muir. Lexington: UP of Kentucky, 1985.

Criticism

Parker, A. A. *The Allegorical Drama of Calderón*. Oxford: Dolphin, 1943.
ter Horst, R. *Calderón: The Secular Plays*. Lexington: UP of Kentucky, 1982.
Wardropper, B. W. "Calderón's Comedy and His Serious View of Life." In *Hispanic Studies in Honor of Nicholson B. Adams*. Chapel Hill: U of North Carolina P, 1966.
————, ed. *Critical Essays on the Theatre of Calderón*. New York: New York UP, 1965.
Wilson, E. M. "Calderón." In *A Literary History of Spain*, vol. 3, *Drama: 1492–1700*. New York: Barnes and Noble, 1971.

Robert ter Horst

**CALDERS, Pere** (1912, Barcelona– ), Catalan novelist and short story writer. The only son of an enthusiastic amateur author and printer who published a few of his own short novels, Calders was raised in an emphatically pro-Catalan atmosphere. He worked for a few years as a commercial artist, but also began writing newspaper articles in the early 1930s, and in 1936 published his first two books, *El primer arlequí* (The First Harlequin), short stories, and *La Gloria del doctor Larén* (The Glory of Dr. Laren), a novel. As a member of the Syndicate of Professional Artists (which was responsible for all propaganda and war-related publicity during the Civil War) and a major contributor to *L'Esquella*, a widely circulated weekly of political satire, Calders was exempt from military service, but in 1937 he enlisted as a military cartographer. Calders still found time to write, and was a finalist for the Narcís Oller Prize with an unpublished collection of stories entitled *L'any de la meva gracia* (The Year of My Grace). He also won a contest with a novel entitled *La cèllula* (The Cell), which was not published and subsequently was lost; it apparently dealt with the political activities of a cell of the Catalan Socialist party. His most important literary project during the war years was a sort of war diary entitled *Unitats de xoc* (1938; Shock Troops).

During the desperate final months of the war, Calders wrote his first long novel, *Gaeli i l'home déu* (1938; Gaeli and the God-Man), a finalist for the Creixells Prize. The first of his fantasy pieces, it deliberately ignores the realities of 1938, describing a magic world where supernatural powers are used in an attempt to defeat evil in the world and create a utopia of peace and harmony. Crossing into France shortly before the war's end, Calders was interned in a concentration camp. Escaping with the aid of the local Red Cross, he reached a refuge for Republican intellectuals and later emigrated to Mexico. First working as a graphic designer, he established himself and a new family in Mexico City, collaborating enthusiastically with Catalan publications in exile. He wrote fiction regularly and in 1942 won the Concepció Rabell Prize with a collection of short stories, *Memories especials* (Special Memories), subsequently incorporated in a collection published as *Cròniques de la veritat oculta* (1955; Chronicles of the Hidden Truth).

The 1950s were especially productive, with many of Calders's best short stories being written during these years, as well as an unpublished novel, now lost, *La ciutat cansada* (The Tired City). A novella, *Ronda naval sota la boira* (Naval Round beneath the Fog), written 1954–55 and the author's personal favorite, remained unpublished for some eleven years. Meanwhile, Calders's father—still in Barcelona—gathered a group of his stories and entered them in the competition for the important Víctor Català Prize. Winning this event led to the first serious critical studies of Calders's work and publication of two more story collections, *Gent de l'alta vall* (1957; People of the High Valley) and *Demà a les tres de la matinada* (1959; Tomorrow at 3:00 A.M.), in which many tales involve humorous treatments of fantasy or science fiction themes (space travel, time travel and the like). The short novel *Aquí descansa Nevares* (1980; Here Lies Nevares) has a distinctly Mexican theme, also found in four of the five narratives in *Gent de l'alta vall*.

Fearing that his children would reach adulthood without any experience of Catalonia, Calders decided in 1962 to return to Barcelona. His employer's buying a Catalan publishing house allowed him to continue working for the same enterprise, and in 1963 Calders brought out his second long novel, *L'ombra de l'atzavara* (The Shadow of the Agave), winner of the Sant Jordi Prize, portraying Catalan exiles in Mexico. Although anthologies of his stories appeared in 1968 and 1969, Calders published no new fiction until 1978 when *L'invasió subtil i altres contes* (Subtle Invasion and Other Stories) won the Lletra d'Or Prize for 1979. This new collection demonstrating Calders's bent for science fiction was followed by a group of thirty-five stories written largely during the 1970s, *Tot s'aprofita* (1983; Everything Is Utilized). Calders is arguably the most important story-writer in Catalan today. *See also* Catalan Literature.

BIBLIOGRAPHY

Primary Texts

*Aquí descansa Nevares i altres narracions mexicanes*. Barcelona: Edicions 62, 1980.
*Cròniques de la veritat oculta*. 2nd ed. Barcelona: Edicions 62, 1978.
*Demà a les tres de la matinada*. 2nd ed. Barcelona: Edicions 62, 1980.
*El primer arlequí*. 2nd ed. Barcelona: Edicions de la Magrana, 1983.
*Gent de l'alta vall*. 2nd ed. Barcelona: ADN, 1980.
*Invasió subtil i altres contes*. Barcelona: Edicions 62, 1978.
*Tots els contes (1936–1967)*. Barcelona: Llibres de Sinera, 1968; 2nd ed., Barcelona: J. Tremoleda, 1973.

*Tot s'aprofita*. Barcelona: Edicions 62, 1983.
*Tres per cinc, quinze*. Barcelona: Moby Dick, 1984.
*Tria personal*. Barcelona: Llibres a Ma, 1984.
Criticism
Bath, Amanda. *Pere Calders: Ideari i Ficció*. Barcelona: Edicions 62, 1987.
Melcion, Joan. Prol. to *Invasió subtil i altres contes*. Barcelona: Edicions 62, 1978. 5–15.
———. Intro. to *Aquí descansa Nevares i altres narracions mexicanes*. Barcelona: Edicions 62, 1980. 7–31.
Pérez, Janet. "Three Contemporary Cultivators of Science Fiction in Catalan." *Discurso Literario* 2.1 (1984): 203–16.
Pont, Jaume. "Imaginación y paradoja en Pere Calders." *Insula* 420 (Nov. 1981): 3–4.
Triadu, Joan. "Un exili signat Pere Calders." In *Una cultura sense llibertat*. Barcelona: Proa, 1979. 108–12.

Janet Pérez

**CALÉ Y TORRES DE QUINTERO, Emilia** (1837, La Coruña–1908, Madrid), poet and writer. Her poems first appeared in local publications of Galicia. When she moved to Madrid, she extended her collaborations to Spanish and American publications, occasionally using the pseudonym Esperanza (Hope). In Madrid, she held a literary circle which included poets of the Galician Renaissance, although she always wrote in Spanish. In 1875 she returned to La Coruña and married the journalist Lorenzo Gómez Quintero.

Her first collection of poems, *Horas de inspiración* (Hours of Inspiration), appeared in 1867, and enjoyed a second edition in 1874. *Crepusculares* (Twilights) was published in 1894. Critical opinion has noted the clear affection for her motherland, Galicia, throughout *Horas de inspiración*. José María Cossío finds a new treatment of romantic themes in her poetry which points to a new lyrical attitude in Spain. Calé y Torres de Quintero also composed a sociological essay, *Cuadros sociales* (1878; Social Scenes), and two dramas, one of which, *Lazos rotos* (1883; Broken Bonds), premiered in La Coruña.

BIBLIOGRAPHY
Primary Texts
*Crepusculares*. Madrid: n.p., 1894.
*Cuadros sociales*. N.p.: n.p., 1878.
*Escenas de la vida*. La Coruña: n.p., 1890.
*Horas de inspiración*. Lugo: Soto y Freire, 1867.
*Lazos rotos*. Premiere in La Coruña, 1883.
Criticism
Cossío, José María. *Cincuenta años de poesía española (1850–1900)*. Madrid: Espasa-Calpe, 1960.

Cristina Enríquez

***CALILA E DIGNA,*** a thirteenth-c. Castilian translation of an Arabic collection of apologues called *Kalila wa-Dimna* which in turn derives from the famous third-c. Sanskrit collection, *Panchatantra*, by way of a sixth-c. Persian trans-

lation. The Castilian work survives in two fourteenth-c. copies, according to
*Menéndez Pidal; the recent edition of Keller and Linker reproduces both mss.
Although both mss. claim that Prince Alphonse, son of King Ferdinand, ordered
the translation, one of them gives the date 1261 for this order, leading some
scholars to doubt its authenticity, since Alphonse already would have been king
for nine years. Another ms., however, gave a more plausible date of 1251, and
most scholars accept that the translation was done at Alphonse's request. Gayangos demonstrated in his edition of 1860 that the Castilian translation could
not have been made from the Latin version of John of Capua, as had been
supposed, but rather directly from the Arabic of Ibn al-Muqaffa. The Castilian
and Arabic versions omit material from the original *Panchatantra* and add sections not included in the latter. The Castilian version consists of at least fifty-
six exempla in eighteen chapters. The title refers to two jackals, one of whom,
Digna, is punished with starvation for plotting against Sencebar, the favorite ox
in the court of a lion king. Discussion of Digna's offense gives rise to the book's
exempla. The work is important, as Keller and Linker point out, because these
stories have influenced, directly or indirectly, *Alphonse X, don *Juan Manuel,
the *Arcipreste de Hita, various *picaresque authors, *Cervantes, *Tirso de Molina, Lope de *Vega, Tomás de *Iriarte, el Padre *Isla, etc., to name only a few.

BIBLIOGRAPHY

Primary Text

*El libro de "Calila e Digna."* Ed. John E. Keller and Robert W. Linker. Madrid: CSIC,
    1967.

Criticism

López Morillas, Consuelo. "A Broad View of *Calila e Digna* Studies." *RPH* 25 (1971):
    85–96.

                                                           Colbert Nepaulsingh


**CALVETE DE ESTRELLA, Juan Cristóbal** (1526?, Sariñena, Huesca–1593,
Salamanca), humanist, chronicler. He accompanied Prince Philip on several trips
to Flanders and Germany, which yielded his most significant work, the *Felicísimo
viaje del príncipe don Felipe, hijo de Carlos V, a Alemania y a Flandes* (Antwerp,
1522; The Most Felicitous Journey of Prince Philip, Son of Charles V, to Germany and Flanders). Some sections clearly emulate the tone of novels of chivalry
(*caballerías). Also his is a Latin praise of the Duke of Alba, and a narration of
the conquest of a city in Berbery—which was used as a Latin school text. *See
also* Humanism.

BIBLIOGRAPHY

Primary Texts

*Felicísimo viaje del príncipe....* Ed. M. Artigas. Madrid: Sociedad de Bibliófilos Es-
    pañoles, 1930.
*Encomio del gran duque de Alba.* Tr. S. López de Toro. Madrid: Blass, 1945.

*Elogio de Vaca de Castro.* Ed., study, tr. J. López de Toro. Madrid: CSIC, 1947. Latin and Spanish.

**CALVO ASENSIO, Pedro** (1821, Mota del Marqués [Valladolid]–1863, Madrid), playwright and journalist. Educated at the Universities of Valladolid (in humanities and philosophy) and Madrid (in pharmacy and law), Calvo Asensio was a successful confectioner of well-constructed yet mediocre historical dramas, such as *La cuna no da nobleza* (1845; Blood Doesn't Always Tell), *Los disfraces* (1844; The Masks), *La escala de la fortuna* (1848; The Scale of Fortune), *Felipe el prudente* (1853; Philip the Prudent), and *Fernán González* (1847; in collaboration with Juan de la Rosa). An influential and outspoken liberal journalist, he founded *El Restaurador Farmacéutico* (1844; The Pharmaceutical Restorer), the satirical *El Cínife* (1845; The Buzzing Gnat), and finally, *La Iberia* (1854), which became the voice of the Spanish Progressive party. He also organized the coronation of the poet *Quintana in 1855.

BIBLIOGRAPHY

Primary Texts

*La cuna no da nobleza.* Madrid: Repullés, 1845.
*Los disfraces.* Madrid: Repullés, 1844.
*La escala de la fortuna.* Madrid: D. L. Cordón, 1848.
*Felipe el prudente.* Madrid: C. González, 1853.
*Fernán González.* Madrid: Repullés, 1847.

Criticism

Alonso Cortés, Narciso. "Calvo Asensio." *Miscelánea vallisoletana.* 3rd series. Valladolid: Miñón, 1955. 351–58 (orig. 1921).

Noël M. Valis

**CALVO DE AGUILAR, Isabel** (1916, ?– ), Spanish novelist and radio scriptwriter. Founder of the Asociación de escritoras españolas (Association of Spanish Women Writers), Calvo also produced an important *Antología biográfica de escritoras españolas* (1954; Biographical Anthology of Spanish Women Writers). Her novels are aimed at the broad general public, and combine fantastic adventures, Gothic elements, exotic settings and love interest with intrigue or crime. *El misterio del palacio chino* (1951; The Mystery of the Chinese Palace), a love story cast as a Chinese legend, ends tragically. *La isla de los siete pecados* (1951; The Isle of Seven Sins), set in modern Spain despite its title, is a tale of unrequited love combined with fantasy adventures. *Doce sarcófagos de oro* (n.d.; Twelve Gold Sarcophagi) involves an evil madman who kills and embalms a beautiful girl met during his travels through the Orient. The theme of necrophilia or wish to preserve eternally the body of a beautiful woman appears again in *La danzarina inmóvil* (1954; The Motionless Dancer), in which an artist changes his ballerina wife into a statue.

BIBLIOGRAPHY

Primary Texts

*El monje de los Balkanes*. Madrid: Rumbos, n.d.
*El numismático*. Madrid: Rumbos, n.d.

Janet Pérez

**CALVO SERER, Rafael** (1916, Valencia–1988, Madrid), philosopher, scholar. Professor of history of Spanish philosophy at the U of Madrid, Calvo Serer is the author of the controversial study *España, sin problema* (1949; Spain, Without Problems), for which he won the National Prize for Literature. A follower of the ideas of *Donoso Cortés, *Menéndez Pelayo, and Ramiro de *Maeztu, he wrote several other books, including *Teoría de la Restauración* (1952; Theory of Restoration), *La configuración del futuro* (1953; Configuration of the Future), *Los motivos de las luchas intelectuales* (1955; The Motives for Intellectual Conflict), *Política de integración* (1955; The Politics of Integration), and *La literatura universal sobre la guerra de España* (1962; World Literature on the Spanish Civil War). The last-named work is virulently attacked in H. R. Southworth's *El mito de la cruzada de Franco* (1963; The Myth of Franco's Crusade).

BIBLIOGRAPHY

Primary Texts

*La configuración del futuro*. 2nd ed. Madrid: Rialp, 1963.
*España, sin problema*. 3rd ed. Madrid: Rialp, 1957.
*La literatura universal sobre la guerra de España*. Madrid: Ateneo, 1962.
*Teoría de la Restauración*. 2nd ed. Madrid: Rialp, 1956.

Criticism

Southworth, H. R. *El mito de la cruzada de Franco*. Paris: Ruedo Ibérico, 1963.

Noël M. Valis

**CALVO SOTELO, Joaquín** (1905, La Coruña– ), dramatist. Trained as a lawyer, Calvo Sotelo produced his first play in 1930, but did not reach his stride as a dramatist until the late 1940s. In 1949, he won the Jacinto Benavente Prize for the lightweight but amusing play *La visita que no tocó el timbre* (The Caller Who Didn't Ring). His greatest theatrical success, however, was to be the thesis drama *La muralla* (1954; The Wall), which is a psychological and moral exploration of the themes of guilt, retribution, and redemption played against the remembered backdrop of the Spanish civil war. Another play of interest in his richly varied repertoire is the darkly satirical *El inocente* (performed 1968; The Innocent One), in which the author, according to his *autocrítica*, posits "the conflict between individual purity, rare as a hothouse flower, and the impurity of the human jungle that stifles and corrupts." Other plays among his fifty-odd works include *Criminal de guerra* (1951; War Criminal), *María Antonieta* (1952), *El jefe* (1953; The Leader), *La ciudad sin Dios* (1957; City without God), and *El proceso del* *arzobispo Carranza* (1964; The Trial of Archbishop Carranza). His plays reflect a conservative view of life, strongly influenced by his deep Catholicism, but not exempt from a critical stance toward the suspect values of modern society. Flawed at times by overblown melodrama and topicality, Calvo Sotelo's dramatic opus represents, nonetheless, a significant contribution to post-war Spanish theater, as Marion P. Holt has noted. A member of the Royal Spanish Academy (*see* Academia Española) since 1955, he is also a journalist, principally for the Spanish newspaper *ABC*. See also Contemporary Spanish Theater.

BIBLIOGRAPHY

Primary Texts

*La ciudad sin Dios*. Madrid: Alfil, 1960.
*El inocente*. Madrid: Escelicer, 1969.
*La muralla*. Ed. R. E. Henry and E. Ruiz Fornells. New York: Appleton-Century-Crofts, 1962.
*El proceso del arzobispo Carranza*. Madrid: Escelicer, 1971.
*La visita que no tocó el timbre*. 2nd ed. Madrid: Alfil, 1959.

Criticism

Holt, M. P. *The Contemporary Spanish Theater (1949–1972)*. TWAS 336. Boston: Twayne, 1975. 67–83.
Pasquariello, A. M. "*La muralla*: The Story of a Play and a Polemic." *KRQ* 4 (1957): 193–99.
Poyates, M. B. "*La muralla* de Calvo Sotelo, Auto de psicología freudiana." *Hispania* 57 (1974): 31–39.

Noël M. Valis

**CAMBA, Francisco** (1884, Galicia–1947, ?), novelist. He lived for a time in Buenos Aires, working as a journalist, and became well known among the followers of *Modernism, even before his brother Julio did. His first novel was *Camino adelante* (1905; The Road Ahead). Upon his return from America he published *Los nietos de Ícaro* (1911; Grandchildren of Icarus), based on the lives of aviators. Most of his novels, and the best one among them, depict regional themes which evoke and describe both legendary and modern Galicia. The influence of *Valle-Inclán is evident in the creation of the old Galician atmosphere as well as in the musicality of its prose. *La revolución de Laiño* (n.d.; The Revolution of Laiño) received the Fastenrath prize given by the Spanish Academy (*Academia Española). Other novels with Galician background are *El pecado de San Jesusito* (St. Jesusito's Sin), and *El tributo de las siete doncellas* (The Tribute of the Seven Damsels). The following novels have war and revolution as their main theme: *El enigma de las llamas azules* (The Enigma of the Blue Flames), *La sirena rubia* (1926; The Blonde Siren), *La noche mil y dos* (Night 1,002), *Madridgrado*. He is also the author of *Episodios contemporáneos*. (Contemporary Episodes).

BIBLIOGRAPHY

Primary Texts

*Madridgrado, documental film*. 2nd ed. Madrid: Ediciones Españolas, 1940.
*Los nietos de Icaro*. 2nd ed. Madrid: Renacimiento, 1923.
*La noche mil y dos*. Madrid: Renacimiento, 1923?
*La revolución de Laiño*. 5th ed. Madrid: Renacimiento, 1924.
*La sirena*. Madrid: Atlántida, 1926.
*El tributo de las siete doncellas*. Madrid: Atlántida, 1926.

Isabel McSpadden

**CAMBA, Julio** (1882, Villanueva de Arosa–1962, Madrid), journalist, humorist. Camba is a literary descendant of the *Generation of 1898 in his reformist stance on Spain derived from travels throughout Europe and the Americas as a correspondent for the Madrid daily *ABC*.

Camba's main literary weapon is his humor, an irony born of observable contrasts between his country and those visited in foreign travels. His style is simple, direct and unadorned. Though none of his books has been translated into English, for several years some of his works were among the most popular in Spain: *La rana viajera* (1920; The Traveling Frog) and *Aventuras de una peseta* (1924; Adventures of a Peseta), both inspired by his assignments abroad, and *La ciudad automática* (1932; The Automatic City) dealing with the automated U.S. society, as well as *La casa de Lúculo o el arte de bien comer* (1929; Luculo's House or the Art of Eating Well), a gastronomical treatise of his home region of Galicia.

BIBLIOGRAPHY

Primary Texts

*Mis páginas mejores*. Madrid: Gredos, 1969.
*Obras completas*. 2 vols. Madrid: Plus-Ultra, 1948.

English Translations

"Spanish Cooking." Tr. anon. In *Alhambra* 1 (1929): 13–15 and 48–49.
"Spanish Interlude." Tr. anon. In *Living Age* 345 (1934): 421–24.

Criticism

González López, E. *Galicia, su alma y su cultura*. Buenos Aires: Galicia, 1954. 191–204.

Ricardo Landeira

*CAMBALEO,* a type of Golden Age traveling theatrical group. *Rojas Villandrando indicates that the *cambaleo* was composed of "a woman who sings and five men who cry" (I, 153). Their repertoire would usually include one full-length play, two *autos*, and three or four *entremeses*, and they would accept food as part of their salary.

BIBLIOGRAPHY
C. Rojas Villandrando, Agustín, *El viaje entretenido*. Ed., intro., notes J. Joset. 2 vols.
Clásicos Castellanos 210–211. Madrid: Espasa-Calpe, 1977.

**CAMÍN, Alfonso** (1890, Roces, Gijón–1982, Roces), prolific poet, novelist, bohemian. He was very attached to Hispanic America, having lived most of his life there. Influenced by *Modernism, his more important poetry includes *Adelfas* (1913; Oleanders), *Crepúsculos de oro* (1914; Twilights of Gold), and *Antología poética* (1931; Poetry Anthology). The novel *Entre volcanes* (1928; Among Volcanoes) is also his. Years later he published *Los poemas del Indio Juan Diego* (1934; Poems of the Indian Juan Diego), *Aguilas de Covadonga* (1940; Covadonga Eagles), *Lienzos de España* (1941; Canvasses of Spain), and *Poemas del destierro* (1942; Poems of Exile). He returned permanently to Spain in 1967.

BIBLIOGRAPHY
Primary Texts
*Adelfas*. Havana: n.p., 1913.
*Antología poética*. Madrid: Renacimiento, 1931.
*Crepúsculos de oro*. Havana: Veloso, 1914.
*Lienzos de España*. Mexico: Norte, 1941.
*Los poemas del Indio Juan Diego*. Madrid: Revista Norte, 1934.
*Poemas para niños de 14 años*. Madrid: Nacional, 1970.

Isabel McSpadden

**CAMÕES, Luis Vaz de** (1524 or 1525, Lisbon?–1580, Lisbon), soldier, dramatist, epic and lyric poet. Three Portuguese cities claim Camões as native son: Lisbon, Coimbra and Evora. Little is documented regarding his life. Around 1547 he was a soldier in Ceuta, Africa, losing an eye there. In 1553, after a stay in jail prompted by some sort of fight, he traveled to India and the Far East, not returning to Lisbon until 1569 or 1570. His letters indicate a rather wild, rough lifestyle. Camões's great epic narrative, *Os Lusiadas* (*The Lusiads*, 1963), was published in 1572, warranting a modest yearly pension from the king. He died eight years later. All other accounts regarding Camões—noble birth, studies at the U of Ceuta, love affair with a lady-in-waiting of the court, duels, poverty in his final years—are conjecture, or second- and third-hand accounts, sometimes romanticized.

Camões left a substantial amount of lyric poetry, three plays, four letters, and the majestic national epic, *Os Lusiadas*. Patterned after the *Iliad,* the *Aeniad*, and Ovid's *Metamorphosis*, it celebrates the sons of Lusus—mythical founder of Lusitania, or Portugal—and commemorates the heroic emergence of Portugal and her empire. The work betrays a solid knowledge of Latin literature; of the contemporary poetry of Spain, Italy and Portugal; and of astronomy, botany, geography, history, and nautical sciences. A compendium of *Renaissance learning, it is a theatrical, sincere, stirring, patriotic work. *Os Lusiadas* has merited many editions and translations through the years; 1580 saw the first translation to Spanish, and the first English version dates from 1655. By the nineteenth c., it had been translated into all the major foreign languages of Europe.

Even without his epic masterpiece, Camões would be well-remembered for his lyric poetry, especially the outstanding sonnets and *canções*. Indeed, his translated lyrics were extremely popular in the United States throughout the nineteenth c. (*see* N. Andrews). Even more so than in the epic, the major theme of his lyric is love.

BIBLIOGRAPHY

Primary Texts

*Lírica completa*. Ed., pref. M. de Lurdes Saraiva. 3 vols. Lisbon: Moeda, 1980–81.
*Os Lusiadas*. Ed., intro., notes J. D. M. Ford. Cambridge, MA: Harvard UP, 1946.
*Os Lusiadas*. Ed., intro., notes F. Pierce. Oxford: Clarendon, 1973. Rpt. 1981.

English Translations

*Dante, Petrarch, Camoens, 124 Sonnets*. Ed., tr. R. Garnett. Boston: Copeland and Day, 1896.
*Luis de Camões. The Lusiads*. Tr. R. Fanshawe. Ed., intro. G. Bullough. London: Centaur, 1963.
*The Lusiads of Luis de Camões*. Tr. L. Bacon. New York: Hispanic Society, 1950.

Criticism

Andrews, N. "Toward an Understanding of Camões's Presence as a Lyric Poet in the Nineteenth-Century American Press." *Luso-Brazilian Review* 17.2 (1980): 171–86.
Bowra, C. M. "Camões and the Epic of Portugal." In *From Virgil to Milton*. London: n.p., 1945. 86–138.
"Camões and His Centuries." Special Issue of *Luso-Brazilian Review* 17.2 (1980). Contains six articles.
Figueiredo, Fidelino de. "Ainda a épica portuguesa." *Estudios Hispánicos. Homenaje a Archer A. Huntington*. Wellesley, MA: Wellesley College, 1952. 155–70.
Glaser, E. "Manuel de Faria e Sousa and the Mythology of " 'Os Lusiadas.' " *Miscelânea de Estudos a Joaquim de Carvalho* (Figueira da Foz) 6 (1961): 614–27.

**CAMÓN AZNAR, José** (1898, Zaragoza–1979, Madrid), dramatist, prose and poetry author, scholar. An art critic and historian who has held chairs of art history at the universities of Salamanca, Zaragoza. and Madrid, Camón Aznar also produced a number of interesting literary works, including *El héroe* (1930s; The Hero), a tragedy; *El pozo amarillo* (1936; The Yellow Well), a miracle; *El hombre en la tierra* (1940; Man on the Earth), poetry; *Dios en San Pablo* (1940; God in St. Paul); *El rey David* (King David) and *Hamlet, sin venganza* (Hamlet, Without Revenge), tragedies. Later tragedies are entitled *Los fuertes* (The Strong) and *Hitler*. More theoretical essays are *El arte desde su esencia* (1940; Art from Its Essence) and *Don Quijote en la teoría de los estilos* (1948; Don Quixote in the Theory of Styles). Closely related to his academic specialty are a large number of books on the history of art, including *Dominico Greco*, (1950); *El arte de Solana* and *Picasso y el Cubismo* (1956). Camón Aznar's style tends to the

Baroque, abounding in conceits, loaded with images, and often resembling writers of the seventeenth c. in its involutions and tortured syntax.

BIBLIOGRAPHY

Primary Texts

*Arte español del siglo XVIII.* Madrid: Espasa-Calpe, 1984.
*Francisco de Goya.* Zaragoza: Caja de Ahorros, 1980?
*El Greco.* Granada: Albaicín/Sadea, 1966.
*El héroe.* Zaragoza: Librería General, 1942.
*El hombre en la tierra.* 2nd ed. Madrid: EPESA, 1951.
*El pozo.* Madrid: Cruz y Raya, 1936.
*Tragedias. El héroe, El pozo amarillo, El Rey David, Los fuertes.* Madrid: Espasa-Calpe, 1952.

**CAMPILLO, Narciso del** (1835, Seville–1900, Madrid), poet and prose author. He sometimes used the pseudonym "El sacristán jubilado" (The Retired Sexton). A friend of *Bécquer, Juan *Valera, and others, his verse reveals influences both of Golden Age poets (Luis de *León, F. de *Herrera), and the *Romanticism of *Zorrilla. *Poesías* (Poetry) appeared in 1858, *Nuevas poesías* (New Poetry) in 1867. *Una docena de cuentos* (1878; A Dozen Stories) carries a prologue by Valera; it was followed by *Nuevos cuentos* (1881; New Stories). A member of the Spanish Academy (*Academia Española), his *Retórica y poética o literatura preceptiva* (1872; Rhetoric and Poetics or Preceptive Literature) has undergone many editions. *See also* Siglo de Oro.

BIBLIOGRAPHY

Primary Texts

*Nuevas poesías.* Cádiz: Revista Médica, 1867. Bound with the 1858 *Poesías.*
*Retórica y poética. . . .* 11th ed. Madrid: Hernando, 1928.
*Una docena de cuentos.* Prol. J. Valera. Madrid: Ilustración Española y Americana, 1878.

**CAMPO ALANGE, Condesa de** [María de los Reyes Lafitte y Pérez del Pulgar] (1902, Seville– ), feminist, prose author. Married to a grandee of Spain in 1922, she lived in Paris from 1931 to 1934 where she studied art and art history, resulting in her first book, a critical biography of the painter, *Maria Blanchard* (1944). Her collection of essays, *La guerra secreta de los sexos* (1948; The Secret War between the Sexes), is a philosophical study of women throughout history, emphasizing feminine psychology, women's position in society, and male-female relations. *De Altamira a Hollywood* (1953; From Altamira to Hollywood) returns to artistic themes, and is followed by *Mi niñez y su mundo* (1956; My Childhood and Its World), memoirs. *La flecha y la esponja* (1959; The Arrow and the Sponge), a short story collection, provides a fictional elaboration of themes first explored in *La guerra secreta de los sexos.* The title reflects the writer's acquaintance with Freudian symbolism, while the text re-creates masculine-feminine conflicts with great imagination and sensitivity. Other important feminist works by Campo Alange include *La mujer como mito y como ser humano* (1961; Woman as Myth and as Human Being) and *La mujer en España, cien años de su historia (1860–1960)* (1963; Woman in Spain: One Hundred Years of History [1860–1960]), a historico-literary overview of Spanish womanhood, incorporating articles, interviews, letters, polls, published and un-published memoirs, and oral tradition in an effort to reconstruct feminine socio-cultural evolution. *Concepción Arenal 1820–1893* (1973) provides a detailed study of one of Spain's pioneering feminists, her work for prison reform, and her activities as writer and educator.

BIBLIOGRAPHY

Primary Texts

*Concepción Arenal.* Madrid: RO, 1973.
*De Altamira a Hollywood.* Madrid: RO, 1953.
*La flecha y la esponja.* Madrid: Arión, 1959.
*La guerra secreta de los sexos.* 3rd ed. Madrid: RO, 1958.
*Habla la mujer.* . . . Madrid: Cuadernos para el diálogo, 1967.
*La mujer en España.* Madrid: Aguilar, 1963.

Janet Pérez

**CAMPOAMOR, Ramón de** (1817, Navia, Asturias–1901, Madrid), poet. Be-fore devoting himself to the literary life, the young Campoamor entertained the notion of becoming a Jesuit and later studied, then abandoned, medicine. He was civil governor of Alicante (1854) and Valencia (1856) and a member of the Conservative party, sometimes engaging in political and journalistic polemics. A popular literary figure, he entered the hallowed ranks of the Royal Spanish Academy (*Academia Española) in 1861.

His plays, better read than produced, include *Guerra a la guerra* (1870; War on War), *El Palacio de la Verdad* (1871; The Palace of Truth), *Cuerdos y locos* (1871; Wisemen and Madmen), and *Dies irae* (1873); his prose includes *El personalismo* (1855; Personalism), *Lo absoluto* (1865; The Absolute), and *La metafísica y la poesía* (1891; Metaphysics and Poetry). He is best known for his poetry: *Ternezas y flores* (1840; Tenderness and Flowers), *Ayes del alma* (1842; Sighs of the Soul), *Doloras* (1845; Poems of Sorrow), *Pequeños poemas* (1873–92; Small Poems), and *Humoradas* (1886; Humoresques). Campoamor himself defined the titles of these last-named volumes in this way in his prologue to the *Humoradas*: "What is an *humorada*? An intentional trait. And a *dolora*? An *humorada* converted into drama. And a *pequeño poema*? An amplified *dolora*." Uncharacteristically and less felicitously, he also wrote some long epic poems: *Colón* (1853; Columbus), *El drama universal* (1869; The Universal Drama), and *El licenciado Torralba* (1888; The Licentiate Torralba).

While his first book of poems, *Ternezas y flores*, reflects a romantic outlook and style, his later poetry shows less and less overt *romanticism, at least in the language and tone, though he retains the themes of the romantics—love and philosophical doubt (*see* D. L. Shaw). His is a more rationalistic, social poetry, representative of a utilitarian age—the era of *lo positivo* (the positive)-with its familiar, prosaic tones and sensible, realistic language. No poet of romantic rebelliousness or impossible ecstasies, Campoamor dwells on the here and now, rejecting the dreamworlds of the romantics. Still, beneath the ironic, if benevolent, acceptance of reality and its deficiencies, there lies a radical skepticism expressed in the disillusioned distance and condensed form of his better poetry, the *Doloras* and *Humoradas*.

In his *Poética* (1883), well studied by Vicente Gaos, he attacks sonorous, rhetorical poetry, expresses distaste for the concept of "art for art's sake," and emphasizes the poetry of ideas. What Campoamor wants is a "clear, precise, and correct poetry." (Gaos, 136) Thus, it is unfortunate his poetic theory and poetry are often at odds with each other, for his verse is too often verbose and redolent of the commonplace in sentiment and idea. His poetry, once extremely popular with a certain class of educated though average reader, is now outmoded, lacking the poetic thrust of essentiality. Still, later poets, perhaps even *Bécquer, owe a debt to him, as *Cernuda says, "for having stripped poetic language of all its antiquated adornments, of all the false phrases binding it." (310–11) In this sense, Campoamor can be seen as the precursor of a more realistic, less adorned poetry and of the poetry of ideas.

His complete works were published in eight volumes in 1901–3.

BIBLIOGRAPHY

Primary Texts

*Doloras, cantares, los pequeños poemas*. Buenos Aires/México: Espasa-Calpe Argentina, 1944.
*Humoradas*. Madrid: Fe, 1886.
*Obras poéticas completas*. 7th ed. Madrid: Aguilar, 1972.
*Pequeños poemas*. Madrid: F. Bueno, 1893–94.
*Poesías de Campoamor*. Barcelona: R. Sopena, 1974.

English Translations

See Robert S. Rudder, *The Literature of Spain in English Translation. A Bibliography* (New York: Frederick Ungar, 1975), pp. 294–97, for individual poems translated.

Criticism

Cernuda, Luis. *Estudios sobre poesía española contemporánea*. In his *Prosa completa*. Barcelona: Barral, 1975.
Gaos, Vicente. *La poética de Campoamor*. 2nd ed. Madrid: Gredos, 1969.
Shaw, Donald L. *A Literary History of Spain: The Nineteenth Century*. New York: Barnes and Noble, 1972. 64–67.

Noël M. Valis

**CAMPOMANES, Pedro** (1723, Sta. Eulalia de Sorribas, Asturias–1803, Madrid), public servant, and political and economic writer. He became a leading figure in Spain's judicial and political life, assuming the posts of attorney general, minister, and serving as director of the Royal Academy of History; he was also named the Count of Campomanes and Governor of the Council of Castile. His works represent the Enlightenment reform attitudes of Charles III's court, in both the political and economic spheres. He participated in the project headed by *Olavide to repopulate the Sierra Morena region of Andalusia. His interest in the development of the Sociedades Económicas de Amigos del País (Economic Societies of Patriots), whose goal was the revitalization of Spain's local economies, is reflected in two works: *Discurso sobre el fomento de la industria popular* (1774; Discourse on the Encouragement of Public Manufactory) and the anonymously published *Discurso sobre la educación popular de los artesanos y su fomento* (1775; Discourse on the General Education of Artisans and Its Support). A similar work is *Tratado de la regalía de amortización* (1765; Treatise on the Exemptions of Amortization). Writings of a historical nature include *Disertaciones históricas del Orden y Caballería de los Templares* (1747; Historical Theses on the Order and Knighthood of the Templars) and *Vida y obras de Feijoo* (1765; Life and Works of Feijoo). For many years, Campomanes was credited with the *Cartas político-económicas*; the work now is considered that of León de Arroyal. *See also* Isla, José Francisco.

BIBLIOGRAPHY

Primary Texts

*Dictamen fiscal de expulsión de los Jesuitas de España (1766–1767).* Ed., intro., notes, J. Cejudo and T. Egido. Madrid: Fundación Universitaria Española, 1977.
*Discurso sobre la educación popular.* Ed. F. Aguilar Piñal. Madrid: Nacional, 1978.

Criticism

Bustos Rodríguez, M. *El pensamiento socio-económico de Campomanes.* Oviedo: Instituto de Estudios Asturianos, 1982.
Isla, J. F. de. *Anatomía del informe de Campomanes.* Intro., notes, C. Pérez Picón. León: CSIC, 1979.
Jordán de Urries, R. *Cartas entre Campomanes y Jovellanos.* Madrid: Fundación Universitaria Española, 1975.

Donald C. Buck

**CAMPOS, Jorge** (1916, Madrid–1983, Segovia), prose author. He has written both short stories and novelettes. He is author of the selection and foreword to the following: *Poesías de Boscán* (1940; Poetry of *Boscán), *Poesía lírica castellana* (1941; Castilian Lyric Poetry), *Historia universal de la literatura* (1946; World History of Literature), *Presencia de América en la obra de Cervantes* (The Presence of America in Cervantes's Work), *Hernán Cortés en la dramática española* (Hernán *Cortés in Spanish Drama), *La literatura de Hispanoamérica* (The Literature of Hispanic America), and *Antología hispanoamericana* (1950; Hispano-American Anthology). Among his short story collections are *Seis mentiras en novela* (1940; Six Lies in Novel Form), *Eblis* (1942), *En nada de tiempo* (1949; In No Time), *Vichort, El hombre y los demás* (1953; Man and the Others). In 1955 he received the Premio Nacional de Literatura with *Tiempo pasado* (Past Tense). He has given special attention to the Spanish Romantics, and has prepared for the *Biblioteca de Autores Españoles the editions dedicated to *Espronceda,

Duque de *Rivas, *Alcalá Galiano, *Estébanez Calderón and Juan *Arolas. In 1964 his *Conversaciones con Azorín* (Conversations with *Azorín) was published.

BIBLIOGRAPHY

Primary Texts

*El atentado.* Santander: Bedía, 1951.
*Conversaciones con Azorín.* Madrid: Taurus, 1964.
*Cuentos sobre Alicante y Albatera.* Barcelona: Anthropos, 1985.
*Eblis.* Valencia: Cosmos, 1942.
*El hombre y los demás.* Valencia: Castalia, 1953.
*Tiempo pasado.* Santander: Cantalapiedra, 1956.

English Translations

"The Attempt." Tr. anon. In *Arena* 23 (1965): 9–16.
"The Autograph." Tr. G. Ayer. In *Texas Quarterly* 4 (1961): 190–97.

Isabel McSpadden

**CAMPRODÓN, Francisco** (1816, Vich, Barcelona–1870, Havana, Cuba), lyric poet and playwright. After studying at the U of Cervera in Lérida (Jaume *Balmes was a fellow student), Camprodón lived in Barcelona, writing in Catalan and in Spanish. His first work, written in two weeks and based on an early love, was first called *Lola*, but then renamed *Flor de un día* (Flower of One Day); it opened in Madrid in 1851, one month after Camprodón's arrival in the capital, and was a solid success.

Camprodón followed the formula of Eugene Scribe in his writing: "First and foremost, characters; with characters there are situations; and with characters and situations, though a common criminal write the dialogue, success is assured." He flouted syntax, yet his works moved the public. *Nombela notes his "lively imagination, exquisite delicacy of feeling and noble and well-bred Catalonian honesty."

Camprodón wrote lyric poetry in Spanish—*Emociones* (1850; Emotions)— but his poems in Catalan are considered superior. As one of the revivers of the flagging *zarzuela, he contributed *El dómino azul* (1853; The Blue Domino), *Los diamantes de la corona* (1854; The Crown Diamonds), *Marina* (1855), *El diablo las carga* (1860; The Devil Takes Them), and *Una vieja* (1860; An Old Woman).

Respected and popular, he also became wealthy, served as a representative to the Cortes (Spanish Parliament), and, after the September Revolution (1868), was named to an administrative post in the Treasury Department in Cuba, where he died.

BIBLIOGRAPHY

Primary Texts

*El diablo las carga.* Madrid: Rodríguez, 1860.
*Los diamantes de la corona.* Madrid: Rodríguez, 1854.

*Marina.* Madrid: Rodríguez, 1855.
*Una vieja.* Madrid: Rodríguez, 1860.

Merry Wheaton

**CANALES, Alfonso** (1923, Málaga– ), poet and writer of the group of poets associated with the magazine *Caracola.* With *Muñoz Rojas, he founded the collection "A quien va conmigo.'' Among his titles are *Sonetos para pocos* (1950; Sonnets for the Few); *Sobre las horas* (1950; Upon the Hours); *El Candado* (1956; The Padlock) and *Port-Royal* (1956). More recent titles include *Cuestiones naturales* (1961; Natural Issues); *Cuenta y razón* (1962; Count and Reason) and *Aminadab* (1965), which received the National Literary Prize. In 1968 he published a complete edition of *Port-Royal.*

BIBLIOGRAPHY

Primary Texts

*El año sabático.* Madrid: Nacional, 1976.
*Aminadab.* Madrid: RO, 1965.
*Cuenta y razón.* Madrid: Rialp, 1962.
*Ocasiones y réplicas.* Málaga: Diputación Provincial, 1986.
*Port-Royal.* Madrid: El Bardo, 1968.

**CÁNCER Y VELASCO, Jerónimo de** (159?, Barbastro–1655, Madrid), playwright and poet. Of noble birth, and a near relative of the jurisconsult Jaime Cáncer, he studied at Huesca and Salamanca, and practiced law in Barcelona. A clever, easy versifier, he was given to puns and word plays in the fashion of *conceptismo, approaching the humor of *Quevedo. He collaborated with writers like *Calderón, *Moreto, *Rojas Zorrilla, Luis *Vélez de Guevara, among others. Under Cáncer's direction, in collaboration with *Rosete Niño and Antonio *Martínez de Meneses, *El mejor representante, San Ginés* (The Best Representative, St. Ginés) was composed; it possesses true dramatic spirit, pathos and beauty. Cáncer also found success with the *entremés, as in *La visita de la cárcel* (1675; The Prison Visit), and the dances *Los gitanos* (The Gypsies) and *¿Qué quieres, boca?* (What Do You Want, Mouth?). *Obras varias* (1651; Selected Works) is a compilation of his poetry and also includes the burlesque play *La muerte de Baldovinos* (The Death of Baldovinos)—banned by the *Inquisition in 1790— and the one-act play *La Garrapiña* (The Grabber), with a prologue by Juan de *Zabaleta—eliminated in subsequent editions. Cancer also wrote *Vejamen* (Insult) which was read to a Madrid academy (*Academia) on August 28, 1640, at the home of Agustín de Galarza. *See also* Theater in Spain.

BIBLIOGRAPHY

Primary Texts

*Colección de entremeses, loas, bailes, jácaras y mojigangas desde fines del siglo XVI a mediados del XVIII.* Ed. E. Cotarelo y Mori. 2 vols. Madrid: Bailly-Baillière, 1911.

Entremeses. In NBAE 11.
*Obras varias de don Gerónimo de Cáncer y Velasco.* Prol. J. de Zabaleta. Madrid: n.p.,
   1651.
Plays. In BAE 14.
Poetry and *Vejamen.* In BAE 42.

   Criticism

Díaz de Escovar, N. "Don Jerónimo de Cáncer y Velasco. . . . " *Revista contemporánea*
   121 (1901): 392–409.

                                                            Andrea Warren Hamos


**CANCIO, Jesús** (1885, Comillas, Santander–1961, Madrid), poet. His preference for maritime themes has earned him the informal nickname "poet of the
sea." His poetry is unaffected, almost realistic, and despite his use of regional
and maritime expressions, he cannot be considered a regional poet. *Cejador y
Frauca is one of several critics to have praised his verse. Cancio's volumes
include *Olas y cantiles* (Waves and Cliffs), *Bruma norteña* (Northern Fog),
*Maretazos* (1947; Heavy Seas), and *Barlovento* (1951; Windward).

BIBLIOGRAPHY

   Primary Texts

*Barlovento.* Madrid: Espasa-Calpe, 1951.
*Maretazos.* Buenos Aires: Nova, 1947.
*Poesía del mar, antología.* Prol. F. C. Sáinz de Robles. Santander; Bedía, 1960.

                                                            Isabel McSpadden


*CANCIONERO* (Anthology). The Cancionero tradition of collecting into one
volume songs and lyric poetry composed by a group of poets, or an individual
poet, begins in the Middle Ages. The collections sometimes include a single
school or style of poetry; other times they are quite varied. The oldest extant
*cancionero* is that of King Denis of Portugal (1259–1325). Titled *El Cancionero
de Ajuda,* and written in Gallego-Portuguese, it shows the influence of the
Provençal school of writing. Also from this period are the *Canzionero portoghese
da Vaticana* and the *Canzioniere portoghese Colocci Brancuti*, of the thirteenth
and fourteenth c., which contain lovely *cantigas de amigo* and *de escarnio.* The
*Cancionero de *Baena* (1445) is the earliest Castilian collection; it compiles
courtly poetry. The *Cancionero de Estúñiga* (c. 1460–63) is composed of more
popular verse. The most important Castilian anthology is the *Cancionero General*
(1511) of Hernando del *Castillo, which includes 1033 pieces by 128 named,
and other unnamed, poets. The poems range from ballads and satiric poems to
love poetry and religious verse. Five years later a similar Portuguese anthology,
the *Cancionero General de Resende* (1516) appeared. The popularity and influence of these cancioneros throughout Iberian and Hispanic literature and culture
are manifest to this day. *See also* Edad Media, Literatura de la; Gallic-Portuguese
Poetry.

## BIBLIOGRAPHY

Primary Texts

Baena, Juan Alfonso de. *Cancionero.* Ed. J. M. Azaceta. Madrid: CSIC, 1966.

*Cancionero de Ajuda.* Ed. C. Michaëlis. Halle: Niemeyer, 1904.

*Cancioneiro da Ajuda.* Ed. H. H. Carter. MY: MLA; London: Oxford UP, 1941.

*Cancionero de Estúñiga.* Ed. N. Salvador Miguel. Madrid: Alhambra, 1977.

Castillo, Hernando del. *Cancionero general.* Ed., biblio., indexes, A. Rodríguez-Moñino. Madrid: n.p., 1958. Facs. of 1511 Valencia ed.

*Segunda parte del Cancionero general.* Ed., study A. Rodríguez Moñino. Valencia: Castalia, 1956.

*Canzoniere portoghese Colocci-Brancuti.* Ed. E. Molteni. Halle: Niemeyer, 1880.

Criticism

Asensio, E. *Poética y realidad en el Cancionero peninsular de la Edad Media.* Madrid: Gredos, 1957.

Dutton, Brian, and S. Fleming. *Catálogo-índice de la poesía cancioneril del siglo XV.* Madison: HSMS, 1982.

Rodríguez Moñino, A. *Manual bibliográfico de Cancioneros y Romanceros.* 4 vols. Madrid: Castalia, 1973–78.

**CANDEL CRESPO, Francisco** (1925, Casas Altas, Valencia– ), novelist, short story writer, essayist and playwright. Born to a humble family, Candel grew up in working-class neighborhoods, inspiration for his more than thirty-five volumes of novels and essays. He writes for the worker and captures the spiritual and social pulse of Barcelona's working class. His works fall into the category of social realism; anti-elitist in tone, he opposes Spain's economic system. His sincere, clear style, delicate lyricism and lucid testimony of tenement life have made him popular with the reading public. Although many of Candel's books have been translated into German, French, Flemish, Russian and other languages, critics have largely ignored his work; nevertheless, Félix Ros considers him as Dickensian. Candel has written two plays, *Sala de espera* (1964; Waiting Room) and *Richard* (1964), but is best known as a novelist. His first novel, *Hay una juventud que aguarda* (1956; There Are Young People Waiting), went unnoticed, but *Donde la ciudad cambia su nombre* (1957; Where the City Changes Its Name) and *Han matado a un hombre, han roto un paisaje* (1959; They've Killed a Man, Broken a Landscape) were resounding successes. Other important novels include *Temperamentales* (1960; Temperamental Ones), *Los importantes: pueblo* (1961; The Important Ones: The People) and its sequel *Los importantes: élite* (1962; The Important Ones: The Elite), *¡Dios, la que se armó!* (1964; Heavens, What a Ruckus!), *Richard* (1965), *Brisa del cerro* (1970; Breeze from the Hill), *Historia de una parroquia* (1971; Story of a Parish), *Los avanguardistas y la guerra* (1971; The Avante-Garde and War), *Diario para los que creen en la gente* (1973; Diary of Those Who Believe in People), *Crónicas de marginados* (1976; Chronicles of Outcasts), *Barrio* (1977; Slum), *Esa infancia desvaída* (1980; That Dull Infancy) and *Hemos sido traicionados* (1982; We Have Been Betrayed). Candel has also written many volumes of short stories, such as *¡Échate un pulso, Hemingway!*

(1959; Take your Pulse, Hemingway!), *El empleo* (1965; Employment), *Los hombres de mala uva* (1968; Men of Bad Seed), *Treinta mil pesetas por un hombre* (1969; Three Thousand Pesetas for a Man), *El perro que nunca existió y el anciano padre que tampoco* (1973; The Dog That Never Existed and the Old Man Who Didn't Either), and *El Candel contra Candel* (1981; Candel versus Candel). In his essays, Candel addresses the issues of social outcasts, slums, trade unions, immigration, in short, the social and economic plight of the working class. His "obra maestra" is *Els altres catalans* (1964; The Other Catalonians), which has been translated into Spanish and other languages. Additional books of essays include *La carne en el asador* (1966; Meat on the Spit), *Parlem-ne* (1966; Don't Speak), *Ser obrero no es ninguna ganga* (1968; Being a Worker Is No Bargain), *Fruit d'una necessitat* (1969; Fruit of Necessity), *Los que nunca opinan* (1971; Those Who Never Have an Opinion), *Inmigrantes y trabajadores* (1972; Immigrants and Workers), *Apuntes para una sociología del barrio* (1972; Notes for a Sociology of the Slums), *Algo más sobre los otros catalanes* (1973; More on the Other Catalonians), and *Viaje al rincón de Ademuz* (1977; Journey to the Corner of Ademuz).

BIBLIOGRAPHY

Primary Texts

*A cuestas con mis personajes*. Barcelona: Laia, 1975.
*Carta abierta a un empresario*. Barcelona: Plaza y Janés, 1981.
*Obras selectas*. 2 vols. Barcelona: Ahr: difusión Editorial Marín, 1974.

Criticism

Gilabert, Joan J. "Aspectos peculiares del realismo social en la obra de F. Candel." In *El perro que nunca existió y el anciano padre que tampoco* by F. Candel. Barcelona: Laia, 1973.
———. "El escritor y el elitismo: Francisco Candel cumple cincuenta años." In *Crónicas de marginados* by F. Candel. Barcelona: Laia, 1976. 9–18.
Ros, Félix. Prologue in *Obras selectas*, Vol. 1, by F. Candel. Barcelona: Ahr: difusión Editorial Marín, 1974. 11–18.

Jana Sandarg

**CANELO GUTIÉRREZ, Pureza** (1946, Madrid– ), Spanish poet. *Celda verde* (1971; Green Cell), Canelo's first book, envisions poetry as the product of an encounter between the poet and the universe. *Lugar común* (1971; Common Place) presents the problematic relationship between poet and poetry, creation and creator, as a cosmic force and form of existence. *El barco de agua* (1974; The Water Boat) has as its main theme the inner quest for self and the creation of a universe via the poetic word. *Habitable* (1979; Livable) continues the author's search for the essence of poetry. Words appear as autonomous, drifting forces, which oblige the creative writer to readjust continually. One of Canelo's most daring experimental works, it exemplifies her creation of a personal grammar and syntax which transcends logic, deepening the reader's understanding of the hidden mechanisms of language and involvement with the mysteries of the poetic word.

BIBLIOGRAPHY

Primary Texts

*El barco de agua*. Madrid: Cultura Hispánica, 1974.
*Celda verde*. Madrid: Nacional, 1971.
*Habitable*. Madrid: Rialp, 1979.
*Lugar común*. Madrid: Rialp, 1971.

Janet Pérez

**CAÑETE, Manuel** (1822, Sevilla–1891, Madrid), poet, critic, and journalist. Cañete was frequently a polemical and aggressive personality on the literary scene. Espousing conservative values in literature and politics, he contributed to many newspapers and magazines of the day, including the *Ilustración Española y Americana*, and gave a course on theater at the *Ateneo. He demonstrated a hostile, inflexible attitude toward the neo-romantic drama of José *Echegaray. Though his poetry (see *Poesías*, 1843) is generally mediocre, occasionally he was capable of better things, such as "El árbol seco" (The Withered Tree), a delicate ballad evocative of the German *lieder*. As a critic, he is known for his study of pre-Lope theater and his editing of Lucas *Fernández's *Farsas y églogas* (Farces and Eclogues). He was a member of the Royal Spanish Academy (1857). *See also* *Academia Española.

BIBLIOGRAPHY

Primary Texts

*La esperanza de la patria* (with Manuel Tamayo y Baus). Madrid: C. González, 1852.
*Farsas y églogas*, by Lucas Fernández. (edition). Madrid: Nacional, 1867.
*¡Un jesuita!* Madrid: Repullés, 1846.
*Poesías*. Granada: Imprenta de Benavides, 1843.
*Poesías*. Madrid: Rivadeneyra, 1859.

Criticism

Randolph, Donald Allen. *Don Manuel Cañete, cronista literario del romanticismo y del posromanticismo en España*. Chapel Hill: U of North Carolina P, 1972.

Noël M. Valis

**CAÑIZARES, José de** (1676, Madrid–1750, Madrid), poet, prolific dramatic author. Rather than conforming to emerging neoclassical style, his plays continued the Baroque tradition of *Calderón, and his poetry, that of *Góngora. This fact involved him in literary disputes with contemporaries, especially Juan de Maruján. Cañizares was a talented writer, very popular with the public, and his work boasts great variety, both in genre (*Loas, *Mojigangas, *Zarzuelas, *Entremeses), and in the subject matter of his longer plays. There are plays of history—*El picarillo en España* (The Rogue in Spain); saints' lives—*A cuál mejor, confesado y confesor* (Which Is Better, Penitent and Confessor), which dramatizes the lives of Santa *Teresa and San *Juan de la Cruz; *comedias de magia*, or magic plays, such as *El anillo de Giges* (Giges's Ring), etc. Many of his works refashion preexisting material from the Golden Age, such as *El dómine Lucas* (The Latin Teacher Lucas), which surpasses the model by Lope de *Vega, or *La más ilustre fregona* (The Most Illustrious Kitchen Maid), which dramatizes *Cervantes's exemplary novel. Cañizares's greatest assets are characterization and satire; he also often made music an integral part of his works. *See also* Siglo de Oro; Theater in Spain.

BIBLIOGRAPHY

Primary Texts

*El anillo de Giges.* Ed. J. Álvarez Barrientos. Madrid: CSIC, 1983.
*Entremés de Bartolo Tarasca.* Ed. A. Calderone. Messina: Peloritana, 1979.
Selected plays in BAE 49.
Selected poems in BAE 67.

Criticism

Ebersole, A. V. *José de Cañizares, dramaturgo olvidado del siglo XVIII.* Madrid: Ínsula, 1974.
Johns, K. L. *José de Cañizares, traditionalist and innovation.* Chapel Hill, North Carolina, and Valencia: Hispanófila Albatrós, 1980.

**CANO, José Luis** (1912, Algeciras– ), Andalusian poet, critic, anthologist and editor. Raised in Málaga, he received his literary education from Emilio *Prados and other poets of the magazine *Litoral*. During this time he met Vicente *Aleixandre, Federico *García Lorca, Manuel *Altolaguirre and Salvador Dalí. Between 1931 and 1936 he was in Madrid for university studies. His friendship with Aleixandre grew. For belonging to a leftist student organization, he was imprisoned in Algeciras by Francoist forces until the end of the Civil War.

During the 1940s he published three volumes of his own verse, and in 1945 began his association with Enrique Canito and the long-lived and influential literary magazine *Ínsula*; he became its editor in 1983. He has lectured widely in Europe and the United States. His principal publications include biographies of Antonio *Machado, García Lorca and Aleixandre; an important series of anthologies: *Antología de poetas andaluces contemporáneos* (1952; Anthology of Contemporary Andalusian Poets), *Antología de la nueva poesía española* (1958; Anthology of New Spanish Poetry), *El tema de España en la poesía contemporánea* (1964; The Theme of Spain in Contemporary Poetry), *Antología de la lírica española actual* (1964; Anthology of Current Spanish Lyric), and *Lírica española de hoy* (1974; Today's Spanish Lyric); numerous books of criticism and essays, such as *De Machado a Bousoño* (1955; From Machado to Bousoño), *Poesía española del siglo XX* (1960; Twentieth Century Spanish Poetry), *La poesía de la generación del 27* (3rd ed., 1986; Poetry of the Generation of 1927), and *Poesía española contemporánea: las generaciones de posguerra* (1974; Contemporary Spanish Poetry: The Postwar Generations). His own poetry is most accessible in *Poesías completas (1942–1984)* (1986; Poetry, 1942–1984).

BIBLIOGRAPHY

Primary Texts

*La poesía de la generación del 27.* 3rd ed. Madrid: Labor, 1986.
*Poesía española en tres tiempos.* Granada: Don Quijote, 1984?
*Poesías completas (1942–1984).* Barcelona: Plaza & Janés, 1986.

English Translations

"To My Loneliness" and "Portrait." Tr. H. W. Patterson. In *Antología Bilingüe (español-inglés) de la Poesía Española Moderna.* Madrid: Cultura Hispánica, 1965.

Stephen Miller

**CANO, Leopoldo** (1844, Valladolid–1934, Madrid), dramatist. A high-ranking military leader with a distinguished service record, Cano figured prominently in the Third Carlist War and held an important post in Puerto Rico. As a literary figure he is noted primarily as a dramatist and follower of José *Echegaray. Works in the Echegaray mold include *La pasionaria* (1883; The Passion Flower), *La opinión pública* (1878; Public Opinion), *La trata de blancos* (1887; White Slavery), and *Gloria* (1888). His exaggerations of Echegaray's melodramatic style reach the point of parody in *Los laureles de un poeta* (1878; A Poet's Laurels). He strays from his master's style in the symbolist work *La mariposa* (1879; The Butterfly). Cano was admitted to the *Academia Española (Spanish Academy) in 1910. *See also* Contemporary Spanish Theater.

BIBLIOGRAPHY

Primary Texts

*Gloria.* Madrid: Rodríguez, 1888. Louisville, KY: Falls City P, 1961.
*La opinión pública.* Madrid: Abienzo, 1878. Louisville, KY: Falls City Microcards, 1959.
*La pasionaria.* Madrid: Montoya, 1884. Louisville, KY: Falls City P, 1961.
*La trata de blancos.* Madrid: Rodríguez, 1887. Louisville, KY: Falls City P, 1961.

Donald C. Buck

**CANO, Melchor** (1509, Tarancón, Cuenca–1560, Toledo), brilliant Dominican theologian and professor. He professed in the order in 1525, and then studied at the U of Salamanca under Francisco de *Vitoria (1527–31). Cano then taught at St. Gregory's College in Valladolid, at the U of Alcalá, and the U of Salamanca. He represented Charles V at the Council of Trent from 1551 to 1554, and later served as adviser to Philip II, encouraging the king to break with Rome. His enmity for the Jesuits and disputes with the Archbishop Bartolomé Carranza provoked various conflicts over the years. Cano's principal theological work is the *De locis theologicis* (1563, posthumously; On Theological Sources); for it he merits a position as founder of modern fundamental theology. Scholasticism and *humanism are harmonized in his thought. Also his is the *Tratado de la* *victoria de sí mismo* (1550; Treatise on Victory over Oneself), a commentary on G. Baptista di Crema's ascetic treatise of the same name, which is superior to the source. Also extant is some commentary on St. Thomas of Aquinas's thought, and two course lectures, which were published in 1550. *See also* Renaissance.

BIBLIOGRAPHY

Primary Texts

*Opera.* . . . Rome: Forzeni, 1890.
*Tratado de la victoria de sí mismo.* In BAE 65.
*La virtud de la esperanza en Melchor Cano.* Ed., intro. F. Casado Barroso. Rome: Iglesia Nacional Española, 1969.

Criticism

Gutiérrez, C. *Españoles en Trento.* Valladolid: CSIC, 1951.
Sanz y Sanz, J. *Melchor Cano.* Monachil, Granada: Sta. Rita, 1959.

**CÁNOVAS DEL CASTILLO, Antonio** (1828, Málaga–1897, Santa Agueda [Guipúzcoa]), essayist and belletrist. Cánovas, influenced by his uncle *Estébanez Calderón, left for the capital in 1845 and had received his law degree by 1853. In Madrid, he frequented both literary (the *Ateneo and so on) and political circles, entering the Spanish Parliament for the first time in 1854. His political career soared from civil governor to minister by 1864; he capped his progress by forming a government at the end of 1874. Cánovas is credited in large part with having created and fomented the political mechanisms and ambience of the Restoration period. As the actual and moral head of the conservative party, he wielded great authority during the reign of Alphonse XII and the Regency. In order to stabilize the then messy political situation in Spain, he brought about the *turno pacífico*, the alternate sharing of power between the conservative and liberal parties, with Sagasta as the liberal head.

Intelligent and commanding, in many ways superior to the political realities surrounding him, he is often considered a prime example of the Spanish doctrinaire. His conservative position and personality, not surprisingly, garnered vituperative attacks from his contemporaries—witness Leopoldo Alas's (*Clarín) brilliant polemic, *Cánovas y su tiempo* (1887; Canovas and His Age)—as well as much praise. Yet Cánovas, for all his ideological conservatism, was a political realist, for he believed that politicians could suffer no greater lack than the inability to perceive historical reality. In August 1897, he was assassinated at the health resort of Santa Águeda by the Italian anarchist Angiolillo, an act which for many signified the end of an era.

Cánovas was a well-educated and cultivated man, a voracious reader with a penchant for both theory and belles lettres. His poetry (*Obras poéticas*, 1887) offers little of interest today, but his biography on Estébanez Calderón, *El Solitario y su tiempo* (1883; The Solitary One and His Times), still merits reading. He also wrote a rather long-winded historical novel, *La campana de Huesca*

(1852; The Bell of Huesca), which includes a prologue by Estébanez Calderón, and numerous historical studies, such as *Estudios del reinado de Felipe IV* (1888; Studies on the Reign of Philip IV) and *Historia de la decadencia de España* (1910; History of Spain's Decadence). *Problemas contemporáneos* (1884–90; Contemporary Problems) contains many of his essays and conferences, for Cánovas was a frequent speaker and orator, both in and out of Parliament.

BIBLIOGRAPHY

Primary Texts

*La campana de Huesca*. Buenos Aires: Espasa-Calpe, 1950.
*Obras*. 9 vols. Madrid: Pérez Dubrull, 1883–90.
*Problemas contemporáneos*. 3 vols. Madrid: Pérez Dubrull, 1884–90.
*El Solitario y su tiempo*. 2 vols. Madrid: Pérez Dubrull, 1883.

Criticism

Alas, Leopoldo (Clarín). *Cánovas y su tiempo*. Madrid: Fe, 1887.
Fernández Almagro, Melchor. *Cánovas: Su vida y su política*. 2nd ed. Madrid: Tebas, 1972.
Pérez Galdós, Benito. *Cánovas*. Madrid: Alianza, 1980.
Quinn, David. "Cánovas, Unamuno and Regeneration." *Hispanófila* 66 (May 1979): 53–65.
———. "Cánovas y el historicismo." *Hispanófila* 72 (May 1981): 19–30.

Noël M. Valis

**CANSINOS ASSÉNS, Rafael** (1883, Sevilla–1964, Madrid), critic, translator, and novelist. Together with Guillermo de *Torre, he was one of the foremost figures in avant-garde criticism. His most significant work, still useful to scholars today, is found in *La nueva literatura* (The New Literature); it represents the first unified treatment of diverse writers and poets in the first third of the twentieth c. In addition to a study of Concha *Espina, he has published collections of essays dedicated to such themes as Jews in Spanish literature, the novels of bullfighting, the Don Juan myth, etc. He was an accomplished translator of classic authors including Goethe, Dostoyevski, Emerson, and Dumas. The author of several full-length novels, he also cultivated with considerable success the novelette.

BIBLIOGRAPHY

Primary Texts

*Evolución de los temas literarios*. Santiago de Chile: Ercilla, 1936.
*La huelga de los poetas*. Madrid: Mundo Latino, 1921.
*Literaturas del norte; La obra de Concha Espina*. Madrid: Hernández y Saez, 1924.
*La nueva literatura*. 2nd ed. 4 vols. Madrid: Páez, 1925.
*Los judíos en la literatura española*. Buenos Aires: Columna, 1937.
*El movimiento vanguardista poético*. Madrid: n.p., 1924.
*Poetas y prosistas del novecientos*. Madrid: América, 1919.
Several articles of Cansinos Asséns are included in *Documents of the Spanish Vanguard*. Ed. Paul Ilie. Chapel Hill: UNCSRLL, 1969.

Criticism

Torre, Guillermo de. "Evocación de un olvidado: Cansinos Asséns." In *Las metamorfosis de Proteo*. Buenos Aires: Losada, 1956. 116–26.
Zuleta, Emilia de. *Historia de la crítica española contemporánea*. 2nd ed. Madrid: Gredos, 1974.

Porter Conerly

***CANTAR DE GESTA,*** literally, "song of deeds." *Gesta*, which is derived from the Latin verb *gero*, hence *gesta* = "deeds," designates the folk epic. It narrates the exploits of a hero, historical or legendary, and reached a popular audience through the dramatic recitation of a jongleur. The extant folk epics of Spain constitute only a minute part of the epic tradition which flourished there in the Middle Ages (*See* Edad Media, Literatura de la). These are the *Cantar de mio Cid*, the *Cantar de *Rodrigo*, a fragment of the *Cantar de *Roncesvalles*, and the *Poema de *Fernán González*, which is a reworking of an earlier epic in an altogether different verse form. Among several explanations that have been offered for the dearth of Spanish epic texts, which contrasts dramatically with the survival of numerous French epics, is that the latter were copied for libraries and intended to be read, while in Spain the ms. was intended as a jongleur's prompt-copy. In any case, the epic could be and was used for a variety of purposes, serving the political and economic interests of both church and state. One of the distinguishing features of medieval historiography is the incorporation of poetic material and the degree to which chroniclers relied on the *cantares de gesta*. Indeed, our knowledge of epic traditions would be extremely scant were it not for the prose versions of epic poems and the references to them which are preserved in Latin and vernacular chronicles. The intricacies of Spanish history and epic have been examined in detail by Louis Chalon. The ballad tradition (*Romancero) is an additional source for the study of epic material.

The origin, evolution, and composition of the Romance epic have been ardently debated by a host of scholars. Initial speculation centered on origin and produced two differing views. The theory of French origin was established by Andrés Bello and maintained by Gaston Paris. This was opposed by Ramón *Menéndez Pidal on the basis of metrical irregularity of the Spanish epic, the paragogic *É*, and the absence of French influence in the peninsula until the 13th c. He preferred, instead, the theory of Germanic origin from which point he would pursue much of his subsequent research. These ideas were followed in 1915 by the theory of Arabic origin of Julián Ribera. Although it did not attract many adherents, the theory has been revived recently by several scholars, most notably, Álvaro Galmés de Fuentes. From the discussion and elaboration of these theories, there have emerged two predominant schools: the individualist and the traditionalist or neo-traditionalist. Scholars' acceptance of one or the other theory was not always absolute, but rather conditional and apt to be modified in light of further considerations.

The individualist theory is based on the writings of Joseph Bédier, which posit that epic poems arose in the 11th and 12th centuries in a monastic ambience. Like *hagiography, they were the works of individual authors. The poems' air of historicity bespeaks their sources in chronicles and annals. Epics were circulated by jongleurs and flourished in connection with tomb cults along the pilgrim routes.

The essential point of the traditionalist theory is that the Romance epic is the result of a continuous evolution from Visigothic times. An epic was composed soon after the events which it describes, thus accounting for its historicity, and then underwent a series of reworkings by anonymous jongleurs in which the historical facts were amplified and embellished with fictional material.

Following the establishment of the individualist-traditionalist dichotomy, major subsequent developments in epic studies stemmed from Parry and Lord's research on oral-formulaic style and composition. Studying the craft of modern jongleurs in Yugoslavia, which is based on improvisation, Parry and Lord found definite similarities with the characteristics of both the Homeric and medieval epic. The suggestion that epic songs are independent of any written tradition corroborates analogous arguments put forward earlier by Menéndez Pidal, namely, that ballads survive independent of written tradition, just as we do not question the existence of Vulgar Latin despite the scant written testimony of it. The evidence adduced by Parry and Lord diverges from the Pidalian theory on the matter of transmission: the former proposes improvisation, the latter hinges on memorization. A final consideration concerns the nature of the text of the poem as it survives in written form. For the proponents of oral-formulaic composition, the written version represents a transcription of a jongleur's performance, a dictated text, which for some scholars accounts for the metrical irregularity of the Spanish epic.

The individualist and traditionalist theories remain current among Hispanists. The adherents to the former have questioned the ability of the Cantar de mio Cid (Song of the Cid) to meet the Parry-Lord criteria for oral composition. Moreover, the complexities and artistic sophistication which we have come to appreciate in the poem would make oral composition, for the individualists, even less likely. Salvador Martínez has recently studied the medieval Latin tradition and its role in the genesis of the vernacular epic. Despite the trend of Pidalian revisionism, Samuel Armistead has ably defended the traditionalist theory in a recent article in which he traces the evolution of the *Song of Rodrigo* and several other epics.

An inventory of Spanish epic tradition from extant texts, including those poems and references to poems that survive in the chronicles, reveals two principal cycles: the cycle of the Cid (*Cantar de mio Cid, Cantar de Rodrigo, Cantar de Sancho II* or *El Cerco de Zamora, Cantar de Fernando*) and the cycle of the Counts of Castile (*Poema de Fernán González, Los Siete Infantes de Lara, Cantar de la *Condesa Traidora, Cantar del *infante don García*). To these may be added the cycle of Carolingian epics such as the *Mainete*, concerning the youthful exploits of Charlemagne in Spain, and the *Roncesvalles* fragment. An

CANTAR [OR POEMA] DE MIO CID

indigenous creation in this same cycle, but in the tradition of the rebel vassal, is the *Bernardo del Carpio* about which Lucas de *Tuy and Rodrigo *Ximénez de Rada offer conflicting versions. *See also* Bernardo del Carpio; *Infantes de Lara, Leyenda de los.*

BIBLIOGRAPHY

Primary Texts

*Cantar de Rodrigo.* In Deyermond, Alan D. *Epic Poetry and the Clergy: Studies on the Mocedades de Rodrigo.* London: Tamesis, 1969.

*El cantar de Sancho II y cerco de Zamora.* Madrid: RFE, 1947.

*Poema de Fernán González.* Ed. Alonso Zamora Vicente. 2nd ed. Clásicos Castellanos, 128. Madrid: Espasa-Calpe, 1954.

*Poema de mio Cid.* Ed. Ian Michael. Clásicos Castalia, 75. Madrid: Castalia, 1976.

*Poema de mio Cid.* Ed. Colin Smith. Oxford: Clarendon, 1972.

*Primera crónica general.* Ed. Ramón Menéndez Pidal. 2nd ed. 2 vols. Madrid: Gredos, 1955.

*Reliquias de la poesía épica española.* Ed. Ramón Menéndez Pidal. Madrid: Espasa-Calpe, 1951.

English Translation

*The Poem of the Cid.* Ed. Ian Michael. Tr. Rita Hamilton and Janet Perry. Manchester: Manchester UP, and New York: Barnes and Noble, 1975.

Criticism

Armistead, Samuel G. "The *Mocedades de Rodrigo* and the Neo-Individualist Theory." *HR* 46 (1978): 313–27.

Chalon, Louis. *L'Histoire et l'épopée castillane du Moyen Age: Le Cycle du Cid, le cycle des comtes de Castille.* Paris: Champion, 1976.

Deyermond, A. D. *A Literary History of Spain: The Middle Ages.* London: Benn, and New York: Barnes and Noble, 1971.

———. "Medieval Spanish Epic Cycles: Observations on Their Formation and Development." *KRQ* 23 (1976): 281–303.

Faulhaber, Charles B. "Neo-Traditionalism, Formulism, Individualism, and Recent Studies on the Spanish Epic." *RPH* 30 (1976): 83–101.

Galmés de Fuentes, Alvaro. *Épica árabe y épica castellana.* Barcelona: Ariel, 1978.

Lord, Albert B. *The Singer of Tales.* Cambridge: Harvard UP, 1960.

Magnotta, Miguel. *Historia y bibliografía de la crítica sobre el Poema de Mio Cid.* UNCSRLL 145. Chapel Hill: U of North Carolina P, 1976.

Martínez, H. Salvador. *El "Poema de Almeria" y la Epica románica.* Madrid: Gredos, 1975.

Porter Conerly

***CANTAR [or POEMA] DE MIO CID*** (*Poem of the Cid*, 1984), epic poem. It has long been regarded as the oldest major work of literary merit in the Spanish language to have survived in a reasonably complete ms. copy. For the greater part of this c., until the 1970s, scholarship on the *Cantar*, or *CMC*, was virtually dominated by the views of the eminent philologist Ramón *Menéndez Pidal, who produced a classic three-volume edition (1908–11, with subsequent corrections and reprintings) and wrote seminal studies concerning the poem's historicity and the essentially oral and popular nature of the Romance epic tradition. Increasingly, these "traditionalist" views have been challenged, largely by British scholars who have contested Menéndez Pidal and his "neo-traditionalist" followers on practically every major aspect of *CMC* criticism. Some of the principal revisions concern a later date of composition (1207); learned and single authorship, attributed by Colin Smith to Per Abad (\*Abbat, Per), who heretofore was thought to be merely the copyist named in the *explicit* of the single extant ms. (*CMC*, lines 3731–33); and the essentially fictional but legalistic nature of the *CMC*. To "neo-traditionalists," the views of the "British school" (which is neither as British nor as tidy as the name suggests) represent a ghostly revival of "neo-individualist" ideas, thought to be long buried in literary history under the weight of Pidalist interpretation.

While disavowing any such "British school," Smith has extensively articulated the revisionist position, and has drawn on the work of Andrés Bello (published in 1881), Russell, Deyermond, Fradejas Lebrero, and Ubieto Arteta to argue forcefully for the 1207 date. But he has gone further than his predecessors in rejecting a prior, oral stage which might have resulted in the existing text, *CMC*. Central to Smith's professed "positivist" strategy is to gainsay Menéndez Pidal's notion of "lost intermediate texts" embedded in the prose of such chronicles as the Alphonsine *Estoria de España*—the "continuum of epic texts," whose mode of being was oral and therefore ephemeral (Armistead 1978, p. 317). In Pidalist criticism the link between historicity and hypothetical "lost intermediate texts" is a crucial one; it connects, on the one hand, events which occurred in the lifetime of Rodrigo Díaz de Vivar, el Cid, known to have died in 1099, and, on the other, the text of *CMC*, which according to Menéndez Pidal (1961) was composed as early as 1105, with the extant version dating from around 1140. Smith's sweeping rejection of all oral antecedents of *CMC* has spurred considerable debate (see Smith's response, 1985, to Armistead's theoretical statement, 1979, and Deyermond's review article, 1985). In place of the workings of a determining system—an intertextual web of formulas, themes, narrative functions and poetic diction (a Saussurean *langue*)—Smith posits an author and imagines an individual poetics (Saussurean *parole*) that can be explained as biography. But Smith's argument does not necessitate a dismissal of all oral antecedents, nor does it render impertinent the trace of oral style in epic texts (Rico; Walsh [1990]); there are, moreover, comparative studies of oral-formulaic diction which suggest that the existing ms. was composed in writing, but with a marked oral provenance (Miletich).

In Smith's estimation *CMC* is not the first literary masterpiece by a quirk of literary history, but rather, a unique and personal creation—derived from French and Latin sources—which founded epic and poetic discourses in the vernacular. Its author and a certain lawyer, Per Abad, named in legal proceedings that took place in 1223, are one and the same, conjectures Smith, despite his "positivism." In Smith's revised literary history, it is to Burgos's poetic genius, Per Abad, that *Berceo and subsequent poets are indebted, rather than to the workings of a tradition, as Menéndez Pidal argued, maintained by professional minstrels (*juglares*) who conservatively re-created, albeit with great flair, an oral poetic discourse grounded in Castile's heroic past and in the popular culture which bound performers and their audience.

Questions of authorship aside, Smith and others of a similar revisionist bent (Russell, Lacarra, Pavlović and Walker) have uncovered in *CMC* valuable information concerning legal practices and institutions of the late twelfth and early thirteenth centuries. The *CMC*'s legalistic mentality—its climax is a courtroom scene—and its fastidious depiction of legal procedure (adumbrated by Eduardo de Hinojosa in 1899) have now been traced to the displacement of customary law by Roman principles. But rather than discrediting the Pidalist model of historicity, awareness of these legal themes and contexts has infused the Pidalist notion of historicity with a more sophisticated content, which, beyond a certain geographical accuracy, was both too reductive and global.

The Cid is a pivotal literary figure, who inspired the medieval epic cycle comprised of *CMC*, *Mocedades de Rodrigo* ([*Rodrigo, Cantarde*] see Armistead 1955 and Deyermond 1968), *Cantar de Sancho II de Castilla*, and *Cerco de Zamora* (see Reig), although reasonably complete poetic texts remain of only the first two. Important examples of the Cid theme can be found in several genres—in ballad literature (*Romancero), as in the familiar "Hélo, hélo por do viene," the Golden Age epic by Diego Ximénez de Ayllón, *Los famosos y heroycos hechos del invencible y esforçado cauallero, honra y flor de las Españas, el Cid Ruy Díaz de Biuar* (1579), the dramas of Guillén de *Castro, *Mocedades del Cid* (c. 1610–15) and Lope de *Vega, *Las almenas de Toro* (c. 1615–19), and Corneille's French adaptation, *Le Cid* (1636).

## BIBLIOGRAPHY

### Primary Texts

Menéndez Pidal, Ramón, ed. *Cantar de Mio Cid: Texto, gramática y vocabulario*. 4th ed. 3 vols. Madrid: Espasa-Calpe, 1969.
———, ed. *Poema de Mio Cid*. Clásicos Castellanos, 24. 1911; rpt. Madrid: Espasa Calpe, 1971.
Michael, Ian, ed. *Poema de mio Cid*. 2nd ed. Madrid: Castalia, 1978.
Smith, Colin, ed. *Poema de mio Cid*. Oxford: Clarendon, 1972.

### English Translations

*Poem of the Cid*. Tr. W. S. Merwin. New York: New American Library, 1975.
*The Poem of the Cid*. Tr. Rita Hamilton and Janet Perry. Intro., Notes by Ian Michael. New York: Viking Penguin, 1984.

### Criticism

Aizenberg, Edna. "Raquel and Vidas: Myth, Stereotype, Humor." *Hispania* 63 (1980): 478–86.
Alonso, Dámaso. "Estilo y creación en el *Poema del Cid*." *Ensayos sobre poesía española*. Madrid: RO, 1944. 69–111.

Armistead, Samuel G. "The *Mocedades de Rodrigo* and Neo-Individualist Theory." *HR* 46 (1978): 313–27.

———. "*La Gesta de las Mocedades de Rodrigo*: Reflections of a Lost Epic Poem in the *Crónica de Castilla* and the *Crónica General de 1344*." Diss., Princeton, 1955.

Burshatin, Israel. "The Docile Image: The Moor as a Figure of Force, Subservience, and Nobility in the *Poema de mio Cid*." *KRQ* 31 (1984): 269–80.

———. "Las teorías de Ramón Menéndez Pidal ante la crítica literaria post-estructuralista: Observaciones en torno a los conceptos 'tradición' e 'intertextualidad.' " *La juglaresca: Actas del I Congreso Internacional Sobre La Juglaresca*. Ed. Manuel Criado de Val. Madrid: Edi–6, 1986. 59–64.

Burshatin, Israel, and B. Bussell Thompson. "*Poema de Mio Cid*, Line 508: The Cid as a Rebellious Vassal?" *La Corónica* 5 (Spring 1977): 90–92.

Castro, Américo. "Poesía y realidad en el *Poema del Cid*." *Tierra Firme* 1 (1935): 7–30. Rpt. in *Semblanzas y estudios españoles: Homenaje ofrecido a don Américo Castro por sus ex-alumnos de Princeton U*. Ed. Juan Marichal. Princeton: Princeton UP, 1956. 3–15.

Catalán, Diego. "Crónicas generales y cantares de gesta. El *Mio Cid* de Alfonso X y el del Pseudo Ben-Alfarâŷ." *HR* 31 (1963): 195–215; 291–306.

Chasca, Edmund de. *The Poem of the Cid*. TWAS 378. Boston: Twayne, 1976.

Coe, Ada M. "Vitality of the Cid Theme." *HR* 16 (1948): 120–41.

Deyermond, Alan D. *Epic Poetry and the Clergy: Studies on the "Mocedades de Rodrigo."* London: Tamesis, 1968.

———. "A Monument for Per Abad: Colin Smith on the Making of the *Poema de Mio Cid*." *BHS* 62 (1985): 120–26.

———. "Tendencies in *Mio Cid* Scholarship, 1943–73." *"Mio Cid" Studies*. Ed. Alan D. Deyermond. London: Tamesis, 1977. 13–47.

Dunn, Peter N. "Theme and Myth in the *Poema de Mio Cid*." *Romania* 83 (1962): 348–69.

Faulhaber, Charles B. "Recent Studies on the Spanish Epic." *RPH* 30 (1976–77): 83–101.

Fox, Dian. "Pero Vermúez and the Politics of the Cid's Exile." *MLR* 78 (1983): 319–27.

Fradejas Lebrero, José. *Estudios épicos: 'El Cid'*. Aula Magna, 3. Ceuta: Instituto Nacional de Enseñanza Media, 1962.

Garci-Gómez, Miguel. *El Burgos de Mio Cid*. Burgos: Excma. Diputación Provincial de Burgos, 1982.

———. *'Mio Cid': Estudios de endocrítica*. Barcelona: Planeta, 1975.

Gerli, E. Michael. "The *Ordo Commendationis Animae* and the Cid Poet." *MLN* 95 (1980): 436–41.

Gilman, Stephen. "The Poetry of the 'Poema' and the Music of the 'Cantar.' " *Philological Quarterly* 51 (1972): 1–11.

Hart, Thomas R. "The Infantes de Carrión." *BHS* 33 (1956): 161–73.

Horrent, Jules. "Tradition poétique du *Cantar de mío Cid* au XIIe siècle." *Cahiers de Civilisation Médiévale* 7 (1964): 451–77.

Lacarra, María Eugenia. *El 'Poema de mio Cid': Realidad histórica e ideología*. Madrid: Porrúa, 1980.

López Estrada, Francisco. *Panorama crítico sobre el 'Poema del Cid'*. Madrid: Castalia, 1982.

Magnotta, Michael. *Historia y bibliografía de la crítica sobre el 'Poema de mío Cid'* *(1750–1971)*. UNCSRLL 145. Chapel Hill: U of North Carolina P, 1976.

Marcos Marín, Francisco. *Poesía narrativa árabe y épica hispánica: Elementos árabes en los orígenes de la épica hispánica*. Madrid: Gredos, 1971.

Marín, Nicolás. "Señor y vasallo: Una cuestión disputada en el *Cantar del Cid.*" *Romanische Forschungen* 86 (1974): 451–61.

Matulka, Barbara. *The Cid as a Courtly Hero: From the "Amadís" to Corneille.* New York: Institute of French Studies, Columbia U, 1928. See rev. Emilio Alarcos, *RFE* 18 (1931): 269–71.

Menéndez Pidal, Ramón. "Dos poetas en el *Cantar de mio Cid.*" *Romania* 82 (1961): 145–200; repr. in *En torno al 'Poema del Cid'*. Barcelona: EDHASA, 1963.

Miletich, John S. "Repetition and Aesthetic Function in the *Poema de Mio Cid* and the South-Slavic Oral and Literary Epic." *BHS* 58 (1981): 189–94.

Nepaulsingh, Colbert I. "The 'Afrenta de Corpes' and the Martyrological Tradition." *HR* 51 (1983): 205–21.

Pavlović, Milija N., and Roger M. Walker. "Roman Forensic Procedure in the *Cort* Scene in the *Poema de Mio Cid.*" *BHS* 60 (1983): 95–107.

Powell, Brian. *Epic and Chronicle: The "Poema de Mio Cid" and the "Crónica de Veinte Reyes."* London: Modern Humanities Research Association, 1983.

Reig, Carola. *El 'Cantar de Sancho II' y 'Cerco de Zamora'*. RFE Anejo 37. Madrid: CSIC, 1947.

Rico, Francisco. "Çorraquín Sancho, Roldán y Oliveros: Un cantar paralelístico castellano del siglo XII." *Homenaje a la memoria de Don Antonio Rodríguez-Moñino (1910–1970)*. Madrid: Castalia, 1975. 537–64.

Rodríguez-Moñino, Antonio, and Arthur L-F. Askins, eds. *Historia y romancero del Cid (Lisboa, 1605)*. Madrid: Castalia, 1973.

Russell, P. E. "Some Problems of Diplomatic in the *Cantar de Mio Cid* and Their Implications." *MLR* 47 (1952): 340–49.

Salinas, Pedro. "La vuelta al esposo: Ensayo sobre estructura y sensibilidad en el *Cantar de mio Cid.*" *BSS* 24 (1947): 79–88; rpt. in *Ensayos de literatura hispánica*. Ed. Juan Marichal. 3rd ed. Madrid: Aguilar, 1967.

Smith, Colin. *Estudios cidianos*. Madrid: Colecciones Universitarias Planeta S.A., 1977.
———. *The Making of the "Poema de mio Cid."* Cambridge: Cambridge UP, 1983.

Spitzer, Leo. "Sobre el carácter histórico del *Cantar de mio Cid.*" *NRFH*, 2 (1948): 105–17. Rpt. *Sobre antigua poesía española*. Buenos Aires: U. of Buenos Aires, 1962. 9–25.

Thompson, B. Bussell. "Diego Ximénez de Ayllón and Chivalric Renditions of the Cid." Paper read at MLA convention, New York, NY, 1983.

Ubieto Arteta, Antonio. *El 'Cantar de Mio Cid' y algunos problemas históricos*. Valencia: Anubar, 1973.

Walker, Roger M. "A Possible Source for the 'Afrenta de Corpes' Episode in the *Poema de Mio Cid.*" *MLR* 72 (1977): 335–47.

Walsh, John K. "Epic Flaw and Final Combat in the *Poema de mio Cid.*" *La Corónica* 5 (Spring 1977): 100–109.
———. "Performance in the *Poema de mio Cid.*" *RPH* 44 (1990): 1–25.
———. "Religious Motifs in the Early Spanish Epic." *RHM* 36 (1970–71 [1974]): 165–72.

Waltman, Franklin M. *Concordance to "Poema de mio Cid."* University Park: Pennsylvania State UP, 1972.

Webber, Ruth House. "Narrative Organization of the *Cantar de Mio Cid*." *Olifant* 1
     (1973): 21–34.

Israel Burshatin

**CANTAR DE RODRIGO.** *See Rodrigo, Cantar de*

**CANTIGA,** a type of poetic composition. The *cantiga* was once much in style
in the Middle Ages (*see* Edad Media, Literatura de la), reaching its apogee in
Galician-Portuguese lyric poetry. The term may be accented either on the first
syllable, a pronunciation now considered antiquated by the Dictionary of the
Real Academia (*Academia Española) but still used by many, or on the penultimate syllable.

Three kinds of *cantigas* are clearly identifiable in the *cancioneros*: (1) the
*cantiga de amor*, or love song, addressed to a woman; (2) the *cantiga de amigo*,
or song to a (male) friend; and (3) the *cantiga de escarnio* or *cantiga de maldizer*,
satirical pieces.

The first of these three is characterized by a male voice as the poet lover who
is singing to his lover, normally about the torments of love and punishments
inflicted on him by the lack of compassion and/or reciprocity of the woman.
Most critics believe this genre to be directly linked to the poetry of the troubadours
of Provence, and the songs do indeed show basic similarities in forms and themes.

The second of the three, the *cantiga de amigo*, is characterized by a female
voice as the plaintiff, singing to her lover about her unhappiness in love. The
oldest forms of this subgenre are believed to be the Mozarabic *kharjas*. Many
critics believe that while the *cantigas de amor* are of courtly origins, these
reverse-role poems are of popular origins, although it must be pointed out that
there are many overlaps in themes as well as forms and that the entire discussion
is part of the highly complex picture of the origins of lyric poetry in the ver-
naculars in Europe, a discussion over which there continues to be much debate
and disagreements (*see* Boase).

The third group of *cantigas* is satirical pieces purporting to combat moral
vices. On occasion, however, they also address themselves to the issue of the
defects, moral and physical, of poor poets and the *juglar* (jongleur), a theme
which can also be found, in different forms, in the *cantigas de amor* and *amigo*,
usually in the guise of complaints about malicious and/or defective "others."

One of the first authors of *cantigas* in Galician-Portuguese was King Sancho
I of Portugal (1154–1211) and one of the most famous was King Denis (Diniz)
of Portugal (1279–1325). The most famous collection of *cantigas* is of a religious
nature: that of *Alphonse X the Wise (the Learned, the Sage), who gave that
name to his collection of 420 compositions, written in Galician, describing the
miracles of the Virgin Mary. The meter of these compositions, whose musical
notation has been conserved, is varied: verses vary from a length of 4 to 16
syllables. The thematic connection between the religious *cantigas* of Alphonse

and the secular love varieties of *amor* and *amigo* is also much debated. *See also* Gallic Portuguese Poetry.

BIBLIOGRAPHY

Criticism

Boase, Roger. *The Origin and Meaning of Courtly Love.* Manchester: Manchester UP, 1977.

María Rosa Menocal

**CANTIGAS DE SANTA MARÍA** (Songs of the Virgin Mary), a collection of 420 compositions dedicated to the Virgin Mary, composed by *Alphonse X the Learned.

**CAPMANY, Maria Aurèlia** (1918, Barcelona–1991, Barcelona), novelist, playwright and essayist. Daughter of the Catalan folklorist Aureli Capmany, she grew up in a cultured environment. She studied philosophy at the U of Barcelona but never finished her doctorate. She began to write quite early, under the strong influences of the modern Anglo-Saxon writers James Joyce, Katherine Mansfield, Dashiell Hammett, Ernest Hemingway and, above all, Virginia Woolf. A leading feminist and leftist politician, Capmany is best known for *Un lloc entre els morts* (1967; A Place among the Dead), but she had begun writing novels in 1947—*Necessitem morir* (We Need to Die)—and continued writing quite regularly up to her death. Among her best works are *L'altra ciutat* (1955; The Other City), *Betúlia* (1956), *Tana o la felicitat* (1956; Tana or Happiness), *Feliçment, jo sóc una dona* (1969; Fortunately, I Am a Woman), and *Vitrines de Amsterdam* (1970; Showcases of Amsterdam). Capmany was also one of the leading figures of Catalan feminism, and she wrote exhaustively on this topic in several magazines and newspapers—*Serra d'Or*, *Presència*, etc. Her books on this subject—*La dona a Catalunya* (1966; Woman in Catalonia), *El feminismo ibérico* (1970; Iberian Feminism), and with Carmen Alcalde, *El feminisme a Catalunya* (1973; Feminism in Catalonia)—are considered cornerstones of feminism in the Iberian Peninsula. She was equally outstanding as an essayist of literary criticism and sociopolitical subjects, as in *Pedra de toc I* (1970; Cornerstone, I) and *Pedra de toc II* (1975; Cornerstone, II). She did several masterly Catalan translations of contemporary Italian writers (Pavese, Pratolini, Pirandello and others). Capmany wrote several plays: *Tu i l'hipòcrita* (1959; You and the Hypocrite), *El desert dels dies* (1960; The Desert of the Days), and with Xavier Romeu the very successful *Preguntes i respostes sobre la vida i la mort de Francesc Layret, advocat dels obrers de Catalunya* (1970; Questions and Answers about the Life and Death of Francesc Layret, Advocate of the Workers of Catalonia). *See also* Catalan Literature.

BIBLIOGRAPHY

Primary Texts

*Antifémina.* Madrid: Nacional, 1977.
*El comportamento amoroso de la mujer.* Barcelona: Dopesa, 1974.

Criticism

Haro Tecglen, Eduardo. Prologue to *Obres selectes i inèdites.* Barcelona: Dopesa, 1975.
Triadú, Joan. Prologue to *Necessitem morir.* Barcelona: Proa, 1977.

Joan Gilabert

**CAPMANY I MONTPALAU, Antoni de** (1742, Barcelona–1813, Cádiz), soldier, politician, historian, essayist and philologist. He studied humanities in the Episcopal College of Barcelona, and at age eighteen he entered the military service. He later went into politics and belonged to the liberal wing of the eighteenth-c. Enlightenment. In 1808, after the Napoleonic invasion, he left Madrid and became a member of the Junta Central, which opposed the French. He was extremely active as a representative of Catalonia in the promulgation of the Constitución de Cádiz (The Cádiz Constitution). In this southern city he died of the plague.

Although he did not write in Catalan nor believe in the renaissance of that language—"idioma provincial muerto hoy para la república de las letras" (a provincial language dead now for use in literature)—from 1777 and through the Junta de Comerç barcelonina (Barcelona Trade Commission) he was a tireless defender of Catalan financial interests and national entity vis-à-vis the central power. As a result of this struggle he published *Memorias históricas sobre la marina, comercio y artes de la antigua ciudad de Barcelona* (4 vols. 1779–92; Historical Memories of the Merchant Marine, Commerce and Industrial Arts of the Old City of Barcelona), a work of enormous importance for understanding modern Catalan nationalism and specifically the nineteenth-c. Renaixença. This encyclopedic work is, incidentally, the first economic history of any country in Europe and a true monument to reason. Another facet of Capmany's importance is his keen interest in Hispanic folklore, that is, the search for national character in unique ways of life but always interrelated to economic developments. The title of one of his books speaks for itself: *Discurso económico-político de defensa del trabajo mecánico de los menestrales, y de la influencia de sus gremios en las costumbres populares, conservación de las artes y honra de los artesanos* (1778; Economic-political treatise in defense of the mechanical work of the workers and of the influence of their guilds on popular customs, the preservation of the arts and the honor of the artisans). His linguistic investigations were more controversial. His *Filosofía de la elocuencia* (1777; Philosophy of Eloquence) is a theoretical work which points out the deficiencies of Spanish in scientific terminology, and favors the revitalization of Spanish through expanding the lexicon with new Latin and Greek derivations and with foreign borrowings. However, his enthusiastic acceptance of French and other foreign influences in the language was completely rejected in his 1812 revision of the *Filosofía*, which espouses a radical stance for the purity of the Spanish language. The companion piece to the *Filosofía*, the *Teatro histórico-crítico de la elocuencia española* (5 vols., 1786–94; Historical-Critical Anthology of Spanish Eloquence) projects a more moderate balance between purity and stagnation on the one hand, and foreign influence and degeneration on the other; it has been termed the most important philological work of the eighteenth c. Capmany's most lasting and influential work in hispanic philology is the *Diccionario francés-español* (1801; French-Spanish Dictionary). *See also* Catalan Literature.

## BIBLIOGRAPHY

### Primary Texts

*Antiguos tratados de paces y alianzas entre algunos reyes de Aragón y diferentes príncipes infieles de Asia y Africa, desde el siglo XIII hasta el XV.* Madrid: Imprenta Real, 1786. Facs. ed., Valencia, 1974.

*Compendio cronológico-histórico de los soberanos de Europa.* Madrid: D. Miguel Escribano, 1784.

*Descripción política de las soberanías de Europa.* Madrid: D. Miguel Escribano, 1786.

*Filosofía de la elocuencia.* London: Longman, Hurst, Rees, Orme and Brown, 1812.

*Libro del Consulado del Mar. [Código de las costumbres marítimas de Barcelona, hasta aquí vulgarmente llamado Libro del Consulado.]* Ed. A. M. de Saavedra. Barcelona: Cámara Oficial de Comercio y Navegación de Barcelona, 1965.

*Memórias históricas sobre la marina, comercio y artes de la antigua ciudad de Barcelona.* Ed. E. Giralt y Raventós. Barcelona: Cámara Oficial de Comercio y Navegación de Barcelona, 1961.

*Teatro histórico-crítico de la elocuencia española.* 5 vols. Madrid: A. de Sancha, 1786–94.

### Criticism

Abbott, Don. "Antonio de Capmany: Human Nature and the Nature of Rhetoric." *Quarterly Journal of Speech* 69 (1983): 75–83.

Alvarez Junco, José. "Capmany y su informe sobre la necesidad de una Constitución." *CH* 210 (1967): 520–53.

Baquero Goyanes, Mariano. "Prerromanticismo y retórica: Antonio de Capmany." *Studia Philológica* [Homenaje ofrecido a Dámaso Alonso] 1 (1960): 171–89.

Giralt, Emili. *Ideari d'Antoni de Capmany.* Barcelona: Ediciones 62, 1965.

Glendinning, Nigel V. "A Note on the Authorship of the 'Comentario sobre el Doctor festivo y maestro de los eruditos a la violeta, para desengaño de los españoles que leen poco y malo.' " *BHS* 43 (1966): 276–83.

Juretschke, Hans. *Los afrancesados en la guerra de la Independencia.* Madrid: Rialp, 1962.

Montoliú, M. *Homenaje a Capmany en el II centenario de su nacimiento.* Barcelona: Biblioteca Central, 1945.

Vilar, Pierre. *L'obra de Capmany, model de métode històric.* In *Butlletí del centre Excursionista de Catalunya.* vol. 43. Barcelona: n.p., 1933.

―――. "Antonio de Capmany. Des lumière et des ombres." *Actes du IX Congrès des Hispanistes Français*. Dijon: U of Dijon, 1973. 174–95.

Joan Gilabert and Kathleen McNerney

**CAPUA, Juan de** (13th c., ?–?), *converso* translator. John of Capua translated the collection of moral fables *Calila e Digna* from Hebrew to Latin, using the title *Directorium Vitae Humanae*. His version became very popular in medieval Europe and was the source for all Occidental translations other than the Spanish one. The anonymous Spanish translation appeared in 1493.

**CARANDELL, Luis** (1929, Barcelona– ), journalist and essayist. He is an assiduous collaborator of the liberal periodical *Triunfo* and has published a number of successful books of political satire and humor. Among his better-known works are *Vivir en Madrid* (1967; To Live in Madrid); *Los españoles* (1968; The Spaniards); and *Celtiberia Show* (1970).

BIBLIOGRAPHY

Primary Texts

*Celtiberia bis.* Madrid: Guadiana, 1972.
*Celtiberia Show.* Madrid: Guadiana, 1970. Selections from his "Celtiberia Show" column in *Triunfo* from 1951 to 1970.
*Democracia, pero órganica.* Barcelona: Laia, 1974.
*Los españoles.* Barcelona: Cultura Popular, 1968.
*Vida y milagros del monseñor Escrivá de Balaguer, fundador del Opus Dei.* Prol. A. Conim. Barcelona: Laia, 1975.

**CARBALLO CALERO, Ricardo** (1910, El Ferrol– ), professor, critic. One of the most distinguished Galician critics of this c., Carballo Calero's production also includes the novel *A xente da Barreira* (1951; The People from Barriera), poetry both in Galician *O silenzo axianllado* (1934; Hoped for Silence) and in Spanish *La soledad confusa* (1931; Confused Solitude), and drama, *Catro pezas* (1971; Four Pieces). Yet his most important work has been done from his professorship at the U of Santiago de Compostela. *Sete poetas* (1955; Seven Poets), *Historia da literatura galega contemporánea* (1962; A History of Contemporary Galician Literature), *Gramática elemental del gallego común* (1966; Elementary Grammar of Everyday Galician) and *Sobre lingua e literatura galega* (1971; Essays on Galician Language and Literature) are the best known and most useful. Carballo Calero's academic style and method have set the standard for all those who follow in his footsteps in the research and scholarship of Galician letters. *See also* Galician Literature.

BIBLIOGRAPHY

Primary Texts

*Aportaciones a la literatura gallega contempóranea.* Madrid: Gredos, 1955.
*Historia da literatura galega contemporánea.* Vigo: Galaxia, 1955.

*Sete poetas galegos.* Vigo: Galaxia, 1955.
*O silenzo axianllado.* Santiago: Nós, 1934.
*La soledad confusa.* Santiago: Nós, 1932.
*A xente da Barreira.* Santiago: Bibliófilos Gallegos, 1951.

Criticism

Díaz Plaja, G. *Literatura gallega.* Madrid: Magisterio Español, 1974. 161–63.

Ricardo Landeira

**CARDILLO DE VILLALPANDO, Gaspar** (1527, Segovia–1581, Alcalá de Henares), humanist. A staunch Aristotelian, he taught at the U of Alcalá and participated in the Council of Trent. *See also* Aristotelianism; Humanism; Renaissance.

BIBLIOGRAPHY

Primary Text

*Apologia Aristotelis.* In *Clarorum Hispanorum opúscula selecta.* Ed. Cerdá y Rico. Madrid: n.p., 1781. 271–346.

**CARNER, Josep** (1884, Barcelona–1970, Brussels), poet, playwright, translator and prose writer. Carner was the son of a literary family. His father was the director of the magazine *La Hormiga de Oro* and a very well-known journalist for the newspaper *El Correo Catalán.* Carner was a precocious child; at twelve years he published his first poems and articles in the drama review *L'Aureneta* (The Little Swallow). He received the degree of law and humanities from the U of Barcelona in 1904. From the beginning of the c. until 1939 he was extremely active, writing on politics and art in the most important magazines and newspapers of Catalonia, notably in the *Veu de Catalunya* (Voice of Catalonia). He was the most feared polemicist of his time, usually defending conservative causes within Catalan nationalism. He used a number of pseudonyms: Two, Caliban, Bellafilla, Tuduri and others. Around 1919, however, he began to lose faith in Catalan conservatism and gradually eased into leftist politics, socialism and trade unionism. In 1921 he entered the diplomatic service and during the Spanish Civil War represented the Republic in Brussels where he married the distinguished writer Emilie Noulet. After the Nazi conquest of Belgium, they exiled themselves to Mexico, where he taught in the College of Mexico. After World War II he returned to his beloved Brussels, where he taught at the Free U. The last years of his life were spent in Barcelona.

Carner is one of the truly great poets of modern Catalonia; a true polyglot, he is an archetypal example of the universal Catalan. Aside from Catalan, he also wrote in Castilian, French and Italian, and his work as a translator is astonishing: *Lluna i llanterna* (1935; Moon and Lantern), Chinese poets, Shakespeare (perhaps the best in any European language), the Bible, Saint Francis, Molière, Milton, Mark Twain, Dickens, Arnold Bennett, Andersen, Musset, La Fontaine, Defoe, Lewis Carroll, La Bruyère, Leopardi and others. As a renovator of Catalan poetry and language he is a master, ranking only after Jacinto *Verdaguer and *Maragall. His work exemplifies how a commonplace theme, treated by a great poet, can acquire profound human interest. In different phases of his poetic life, Carner was influenced by various masters: Ibsen, Maeterlinck, Verhaeren, Ruskin, Samain, Petrarch, Keats, Ronsard, Baudelaire, the Provençal troubadors, Shakespeare, the great medieval epic writers and many more. The thematic range of his works is equally awesome: popular poetry, existentialism, objectivism, fantasy, dreams, love, passion, the harmony of Paradise Lost, carpe diem, humor, political satire, Catalan nationalism, the landscape, family life, longing for Catalonia (''anyorança''), loneliness, etc. Carner's irony is the dominant characteristic of his work, but his generous and free spirit makes it smooth and sympathetic in spite of its barbs. His unusual control of poetic devices (he is a great sonneteer) allows him to make the Catalan language a servant of his intuition and his contained emotion in the best classical tradition, and like the true classics he causes the difficult to appear easy. In chronological order, his best books of poetry are *Llibre dels poetes* (1904; Book of Poets), *Primer llibre de sonets* (1905; First Book of Sonnets), *Els fruits sabrosos* (1906; The Tasty Fruits), *Segon llibre de sonets* (1907; Second Book of Sonnets), *La paraula en el vent* (1911; The Word in the Wind), *Auques i ventalls* (1914; Cartoons and Fans), *Bella terra, bella gent* (1918; Beautiful Land, Beautiful People), *La inútil ofrena* (1924; The Useless Gift), *El cor quiet* (1935; The Quiet Heart), *Nabí* (1941), *Llunyania* (1952; Far Away), *Arbres* (1953; Trees). He is equally excellent as a theorist of poetry: *Teoria de l'ham poètic* (1970; Theory of the Poetic Hook); or as a prose writer: *Deu rondalles de Jesús infant* (1904; Ten Tales of the Baby Jesus), *Misterio de Quanaxhuata* (1943; Mystery of Quanaxhuata). *See also* Catalan Literature.

## BIBLIOGRAPHY

Primary Texts

*Nabí, poema.* Mexico: Séneca, 1940.
*Obres completes.* Barcelona: n.p., 1968.
*Seis poetas catalanes: Josep Carner, Carles Riba, Joan Salvat-Papasseit, J. V. Foix, Pere Quart, Salvador Espriu.* Sel. prol. and notes by José Batlló. Madrid: Taurus, 1969.

English Translations

*Poems.* Tr. Pearse Hutchinson. Oxford: Dolphin, 1962.

Criticism

Busquets, Loreto. *Aportació lèxica de Josep Carner a la llengua literaria catalana.* Barcelona: n.p., 1977.
Calders, Pere. *Josep Carner.* Barcelona: n.p., 1964.
Cardona, Osvald. *El temps de Josep Carner.* Barcelona: n.p., 1967.

Plà, Josep. "Josep Carner, un retrat." In *Homenots. Tercera sèrie*. Barcelona: n.p., 1972.
*Serra d'Or* 7 (1965). Special issue devoted to Carner with articles by various authors.

Joan Gilabert

**CARNER-RIBALTA, Josep** (1898, Balaguer– ), poet, novelist, historian and essayist. He studied various subjects in several countries: the United Kingdom, France and the United States. An ardent and uncompromising Catalan nationalist, he has devoted his life to politics and literature. Very early in his hometown of Balaguer he founded the Catalanist weekly *Flama* (The Flame) and was chief editor of the bulletin *Estat Català* (The Catalan State) between 1920 and 1923. He was exiled to Paris as a result of the aborted attempt by Macià (later, president of the Autonomous Government of Catalonia, 1931–35) to proclaim the independence of Catalonia at Prats del Molló in 1926. After the Spanish Civil War he was again exiled and resided in several countries before settling in the United States. In New York in 1942, together with J. A. Gibernau and others, he founded the bulletin *Free Catalonia* (1924–44). He presently lives in California where he has written exhaustively in Catalan on the colonization of that state: *Els catalans en la descoberta i colonització de Califòrnia* (1946; The Catalans in the Discovery and Colonization of California); *Gaspar de Portolà Conqueridor de Califòrnia* (1971; Gaspar de Portolà conqueror of California). Although he has spent most of his life exiled to foreign countries (today he is a U.S. citizen), his literature is full of passion and life. Carner's literary production is prodigious and scattered throughout many countries. In his poetry one can detect some influences of *Maragall, *Carner, *Salvat-Papasseit and a number of foreign poets: Valéry, Longfellow, Tagore and others. He is also the author of several film scenarios and adaptations of American films produced mainly in Hollywood and Mexico. A truly universal Catalan, Carner-Ribalta feels at home almost anywhere; his literature, although of the highest quality, is difficult to appraise because it is scattered throughout the world. *See also* Catalan Literature.

BIBLIOGRAPHY

Primary Texts

*Poetry*
"Les ades de Montmur." In *Al legoria*. Balaguer: Romeu, 1973.
"L'alegre vianant." In *Geopoemes*. Barcelona: R. Dalmau, 1969.
"Càntic d'amor." *La Revista* 125 (1931).
*Poetry in translation*
*L'etern adolescent*. Barcelona: La Novel la d'ara, 1926.
"Gitanjali" by Rabindranath Tagore. With Ventura Gassol. Barcelona: L'arc de Berà, 1928.
*Nits de lluna a l'Orinoco*. Barcelona: l'Atzar, 1983.
"Poesies completes" of Paul Valéry. Barcelona: Biblioteca Selecta, 1961. (Prose fiction).
"Poetes russos de la Revolució." Barcelona: Com. de Lletres, 1937.
*Prose fiction in translation*
*Almayer's Folly* by Joseph Conrad. Barcelona: Col. Literaria, 1928.

*Memoirs*
*De Balaguer a Nova York passant per Moscou i Prats de Molló.* Paris: Ed. Catalanes de
    Paris, 1972.
*Theater*
*El plaer de viure.* (Premi Ignasi Iglesies 1933). Barcelona: Col. Nostre Teatre, 1936.
*Theater in translation*
*L'Emperador Jones* by Eugene O'Neill. Barcelona: Ed. 62, 1984.
*El misteri de la 4 ª avinguda* by Donald Ogden Stewart. Premiere in Romea, 1934.
*La tràgica història de D. Faust* by Christopher Marlow. Barcelona: Ed. 62, 1981.
*Biography and history*
"Contribució a una biografia de Gaspar de Portolà." Barcelona: Episodis de la Història,
    Dalmau, 1966.
*Francesc Macià.* Barcelona: L'arc de Berà, 1931.
*Gaspar de Portolà conqueridor de California.* Barcelona: Biblioteca Selecta, 1971.

English Translation

*Facts about Catalonia.* New York: Free Catalonia, 1943.

Joan Gilabert

**CARNERO, Guillermo** (1947, Valencia– ), poet, critic and professor of Spanish literature. His first book of poems, *Dibujo de la muerte* (1967; Sketch of
Death), was acclaimed as one of the most important works of his generation.
He was included in J. M. Castellet's *Nueve novísimos poetas españoles* (1970;
Nine Very New Spanish Poets) and since then has usually been identified with
the *novísimos* group. His other poetry collections include *El Sueño de Escipión*
(1971; Scipio's Dream), *Variaciones y figuras sobre un tema de La Bruyère*
(1974; Variations and Figurations on a Theme of La Bruyère), *El Azar Objectivo*
(1975; Objective Chance) and his complete works, *Ensayo de una teoría de la
visión* (1979; Trying Out a Theory of Vision). Selected poems have been translated into English, German, French, Italian and Czech.

BIBLIOGRAPHY

Primary Texts

*El Azar Objectivo.* Madrid: Visor, 1974.
*Dibujo de la muerte.* 2nd ed. Barcelona: Ocnos, 1971.
*Ensayo de una teoría de la visión.* 2nd ed. Madrid: Hiperion, 1983.
*El Sueño de Escipión.* Madrid: Visor, 1971.
*Variaciones y figuras sobre un tema de La Bruyère.* Madrid: Visor, 1974.

English Translations

*Recent Poetry of Spain.* Tr. Louis Hammer and Sara Schyfter. Old Chatham, NY: Sachem,
    1983. 300–315.

Criticism

Bousoño, Carlos. "La poesía de Guillermo Carnero." *Ensayo de una teoría de la visión.*
    2nd ed. Madrid: Hiperion, 1983. 11–68.
Jiménez, José Olivio. "Estética del lujo y de la muerte." *Diez años de poesía española,
    1960–1970.* Madrid: Insula, 1972. 375–85.

Jover, José Luis. "Nueve preguntas a Guillermo Carnero (En torno a *Ensayo de una teoría de la visión)." *Nueva Estafeta* 9–10 (1979): 148–53.
López, Ignacio-Javier. "Ironía, distancia y evolución en Guillermo Carnero." *Insula* 408 (1980): 1, 10.
Martín, Salustiano. "La teoría de la visión de Guillermo Carnero." *Insula* 404–5 (1980): 24.

Kay Pritchett

**CARNICER, Ramón** (1912, Villafranca del Bierzo, León– ), novelist. His stay as a visiting professor at the City U of New York inspired one of his books, *Nueva York. Nivel de vida, nivel de muerte* (1970; New York. Level of Life, Level of Death). He has published *Vida y obra de Pablo Piferrer* (1960; Life and Works of Pablo Piferrer), and a collection of stories, *Cuentos de ayer y hoy* (1961; Stories of Yesterday and Today), a collection which won the Leopoldo Alas prize in 1961. He has also written a novel, *Los árboles de oro* (1962; The Golden Trees), and a travel book *Donde las Hurdes se llaman Cabrera* (1964).

BIBLIOGRAPHY

Primary Texts

*Los árboles de oro.* Esplugas de Llobregat: Plaza y Janés, 1975.
*Cuentos de ayer y hoy.* Barcelona: Rocas, 1961.
*Donde las Hurdes se llaman Cabrera.* Barcelona: Seix Barral, 1964
*Las personas y las cosas.* Barcelona: Península, 1973.
*Nueva York. Nivel de vida, nivel de muerte.* Esplugas de Llobregat: Plaza y Janés, 1970
*Vida y obra de Pablo Piferrer.* Madrid: CSIC, 1963

Isabel McSpadden

**CARO, Rodrigo** (1573, Utrera–1647, Seville), priest, antiquarian, archaeologist, poet, and friend of many eminent writers of the day. His own poetry is infused with much wisdom and culture, though it lacks true genius. His most famous piece is "Canción a las ruinas de Itálica" (Song to the Ruins of Italica). Extremely valuable today are his research efforts, such as *Antigüedades, y principado de la ilustríssima ciudad de Sevilla . . .* (1634; Antiquities, and Preeminence of the Illustrious City of Seville); *El Santuario de Nuestra Señora de la Consolación* (1622; The Sanctuary of Our Lady of Consolation); *Los días geniales o lúdicros* (1626; Pleasant Games Days)—which, in six dialogues, compares games from antiquity to those popular in Golden Age Spain, providing much folklore; and *Varones insignes en letras* (n.d.; Illustrious Men in [Their] Letters), which offers correspondence by many leading literati of the day. *See also* Siglo de Oro.

BIBLIOGRAPHY

Primary Texts

*Adiciones al libro de las Antigüedades.* Prol. J. Hazañas y la Rúa. Seville: Aleman, 1932. Also in *Memorial histórico español* 1 (1851): 345–458.

*Antigüedades y principado.* . . . Ed., notes A. Gali. Lassaletta. 2 vols. Seville: Bergali,
    1895.
*La Canción a las ruinas de Itálica.* Intro., notes, Latin tr., M. A. Caro. Bogota: Voluntad,
    1947.
*Días geniales o lúdicros.* Ed., study, notes J. P. Etienvre. Clásicos Castellanos 212 and
    213. Madrid: Espasa-Calpe, 1978.
*Varones insignes en letras.* Ed., study S. Montoto. Seville: Real Academia Sevillana de
    Buenas Letras, 1915.

   Criticism

Morales, M. *Rodrigo Caro. Bosquejo de una biografía íntima.* Seville: n.p., 1947.

**CARO BAROJA, Julio** (1915, Madrid– ), distinguished historian, ethnographer, folklorist, and member of the Royal Academy of History. Caro Baroja is
an excellent essayist and one of the most original scholars of Spain's regional
cultures and variety of subcultures. He has done extensive studies of the Basques
and other ethnic groups in the peninsula, including *Los pueblos de España* (1946;
The Peoples of Spain); *Los pueblos del norte de la Península Ibérica* (1943;
The Peoples of the North of the Iberian Peninsula); *Razas, pueblos y linajes*
(1957; Races, Peoples and Lineages); *Las brujas y su mundo* (1961; Witches
and Their World); and a three-volume investigation, *Los judíos en la España
moderna y contemporánea* (1962; The Jews in Modern and Contemporary Spain).
More recent works include *Vidas mágicas e Inquisición* (1967; Magical Lives
and the Inquisition); *El señor inquisidor y otras vidas por oficio* (1968; The
Grand Inquisitor and Other Lives by Position), and an erudite, original and
intriguing *Ensayo sobre la literatura de cordel* (1969; Essay on Literature of
Popular Fairs). *See also* Essay.

BIBLIOGRAPHY

   Primary Texts

*Algunos mitos españoles.* 3rd ed. Madrid: Centro, 1974.
*Las brujas y su mundo.* Madrid: Alianza, 1968.
*Ensayo sobre la literatura de cordel.* Madrid: RO, 1969.
*Las formas complejas de la vida religiosa: religión, sociedad y carácter en la España
    de los siglos XVI y XVII.* Madrid: Akal, 1978.
*Los judíos en la España moderna y contemporánea.* 2nd ed. 3 vols. Madrid: Istmo, 1978.
*Los pueblos de España.* Barcelona: Barna, 1946.
*Los pueblos del norte de la Península Ibérica.* Madrid: CSIC, 1943.
*Razas, pueblos y linajes.* Madrid: RO, 1957.
*El señor inquisidor y otras vidas por oficio.* Madrid: Alianza, 1968.
*Vidas mágicas e Inquisición.* Madrid: Taurus, 1967.

   English Translations

*The World of the Witches.* Tr. O.N.V. Glendinning. Chicago: U. of Chicago Press, 1964.

**CARO MALLÉN DE SOTO, Ana** (1569?, ?–after 1645, ?), poet, playwright.
Praised by *Matos Fragoso and Luis *Vélez de Guevara, two plays by her have
survived. *Valor, agravio y mujer* (1653; Valor, Insult and Woman) is a cape-

and-sword adventure featuring a strong heroine. *El Conde de Partinuples* also stars an atypical woman, Princess Rosaura. The latter was very popular in its day. Also by Caro Mallén de Soto are various poems and descriptions of contemporary celebrations and people.

BIBLIOGRAPHY

Primary Texts

*El conde de Partinuples.* In BAE 49.
*Valor, agravio y mujer.* In BAE 268.

Criticism

Galerstein, Carolyn, and K. McNerney. *Women Writers of Spain.* Westport, CT: Greenwood, 1986.

**CARO ROMERO, Joaquín** (1940, Seville– ), poet. He became known publicly through his book *Espinas en los ojos* (1960; Thorns in the Eyes) and *El transeúnte* (1962; The Pedestrian). He received the Adonais prize for *El tiempo en el espejo* (1966; Time in the Mirror), and in 1970 he published an anthology of his works entitled *Vivir sobre lo vivido* (Living on Past Experience).

BIBLIOGRAPHY

Primary Texts

*El tiempo en el espejo.* Madrid: Rialp, 1966.
*Tiempo sin nosotros.* Madrid: Prensa Española, 1969.
*Vivir sobre lo vivido.* Prol. J. Guillén. Madrid: Ínsula, 1970.

Isabel McSpadden

**CARRANQUE DE LOS RÍOS, Andrés** (1902, Madrid–1936, Madrid). A journalist who died young, he authored three novels about life in Spain during the Second Republic: *Uno* (1934; One); *La vida difícil* (1935; The Hard Life), a work which presents the worlds of the down-and-out and of the well-to-do, apparently different but both characterized by the emptiness and frustration of life in a dehumanized society; and *El cinematógrafo* (1936; The Movie Theater), which combines social criticism with a protest against bourgeois art. Joaquín de Entrambasaguas includes the latter in the ninth volume of *Las mejores novelas contemporáneas* (The Best Contemporary Novels), and José Luis Fortea has studied this largely forgotten author whose work shows the influence of Pío *Baroja and anticipates the ''social novel'' of the 1950s.

BIBLIOGRAPHY

Primary Texts

*El cinematógrafo.* Madrid: Espasa-Calpe, 1936.
*Uno.* Madrid: Espasa-Calpe, 1934.
*La vida difícil.* Madrid: Espasa-Calpe, 1935.

Criticism

Fortea, J. L. *La obra de Andrés Carranque de los Ríos*. Madrid: Gredos, 1973.

Merry Wheaton

**CARRASCAL, José María** (1930, Madrid– ). He earned three separate degrees in philosophy, navigation and journalism. After working for the Merchant Marine, he moved to Berlin and worked as a journalist for *Diario de Barcelona* and *El Pueblo* of Madrid. Since 1966, he has lived in the United States, where he combines his creative endeavors with his career as a journalist.

His novels express his concern with the problems of contemporary man in an alienating society. He has said that the main function of a writer is to show the irrationalities of our modern existence. He is the author of five novels and three books of essays. The novels are *El capitán que nunca mandó un barco* (1972; The Captain That Never Commanded a Ship), *Groovy* (1973; winner of the Nadal Prize, 1972), *La muerte no existe* (1974; Death Does Not Exist), *Mientras tenga mis piernas* (1975; As Long As I Have Legs), *Cuatrocientos años triunfales* (1982; Four Hundred Years of Triumph). His books of essays are titled *USA Superstar* (1973), *La aventura americana* (1982; The American Adventure), and *La revolución del PSOE* (1985; The Revolution of the Spanish Socialist Workers Party).

BIBLIOGRAPHY

Primary Texts

*La aventura americana*. Barcelona: Planeta; Madrid: Instituto de Estudios Económicos, 1982.
*El capitán que nunca mandó un barco*. Barcelona: Destino, 1972.
*Groovy*. 2nd ed. Barcelona: Destino, 1973.
*Mientras tenga mis piernas*. Barcelona: Destino, 1975.
*USA Superstar*. Barcelona: Destino, 1973.

Criticism

Bejel, Emilio F. "El lenguaje de *Groovy* de José María Carrascal." *Cuadernos Americanos* 209 (Nov. 1976): 222–36.
Gómez López-Egea, Rafael. "*Groovy*, el lamento de una juventud que muere." *Arbor* 86 (Sept.-Oct. 1973): 81–89.
Hiriarte, Rosario. "*Groovy* de José María Carrascal." *Cuadernos Americanos* 199 (March-April 1975): 239–43.
Lezcano, Margarita M. "Las novelas ganadoras del premio Nadal 1970–1979." Diss., Florida State U, 1984.
Quiñonero, Juan Pedro. "José María Carrascal, premio Nadal: 'Nuestro idioma no es bueno para hablar de angustia.' " *Informaciones* 11 (January 1972): 10.

Margarita Lezcano

**CARREDANO, Vicente** (1920, Santander– ), journalist, essayist and writer of fiction. Carredano is an assiduous contributor to the media, ranging from newspapers to periodicals and radio programs. In 1951 he published *Un hombre sin* *caballo* (A Man Without a Horse), and in 1956 received the Sésamo Prize for his novelette, *No quiero quedarme solo* (I Don't Want to Stay Alone). *Los ahogados* (1953; The Drowned) is a collection of his short stories.

BIBLIOGRAPHY

Primary Texts

*Los ahogados*. Madrid: Sociedad General Española de Librería, 1953.
*Un hombre sin caballo*. Santander: Nieto, 1951.
*No quiero quedarme solo*. Barcelona: Planeta, 1958.

**CARRERE, Emilio** (1881, Madrid–1947, Madrid), poet, translator. Educated at the U of Madrid, Carrere, after an initial period of respectability, embraced the bohemian life of the lower depths of Madrid. He became one of the most popular personalities of the capital and, for his prolific publishing, was known in literary circles as the Rey del Refrito (King of the Reprint). He also chronicled the life and times of the city in the newspaper *Madrid*. Though he wrote fiction (*La tristeza del burdel*, 1913; Tristesse of the Bordello) and plays (*La canción de la farándula*, 1912; Song of the Strategem), Carrere is remembered more as a poet and a translator of Verlaine, whose influence is patent in the Spaniard's work. In such volumes as *El caballero de la muerte* (1909; The Knight of Death), *Dietario sentimental* (1916; Sentimental Diet), *Del amor, del dolor y del misterio* (1915; On Love, Grief, and Mystery), and *Nocturnos del otoño* (1920?; Autumn Nocturnes), he writes of decay, the bohemian life, and the popular lower-class neighborhoods of Madrid. His complete works were published in a collection of 15 volumes (1921–25?).

BIBLIOGRAPHY

Primary Texts

*Del amor, del dolor y del misterio*. Madrid: Renacimiento, 1915.
*Obras*. 15 vols. Madrid: Mundo Latino, 1921–25?

English Translations

"The Mantilla." Tr. T. Walsh. In *Literary Digest* 69 (1921): 34.
"The Three Hussars." Tr. J. Perlman. In *Poet Lore* 61 (1966): 202–3.

Criticism

Sáinz de Robles, F. C. *Raros y olvidados*. Madrid: Prensa española, 1971.

Noël M. Valis

**CARRILLO Y SOTOMAYOR, Luis** (1581 or 1582, Córdoba–1610, Puerto de Santa María), poet and literary theorist. His brief but productive life was divided between arms and letters: educated at Salamanca, he became a knight of the Order of Santiago and *cuatralbo* (commander of four galleys) in the Spanish navy. Carrillo's poetry vividly evokes the sea and navigation, and is pervaded by the theme of absence and nostalgia. He engaged in literary debate with the critic Francisco de *Cascales, and won the rare praise of the acerbic Cristóbal

*Suárez de Figueroa. His literary friendships included the Murcian writers led by Cascales, and the Conde de Niebla, patron of Luis de *Góngora and Pedro de *Espinosa. It was to the Conde de Niebla that both Carrillo and Góngora dedicated their long poems in *octava rima* based on the Ovidian account of the myth of Polyphemus and Galatea. Carrillo's *Fábula de Acis y Galatea* (Myth of Acis and Galatea), however, as Dámaso *Alonso points out, was not a model for Góngora's *Fábula de Polifemo y Galatea*: the former has the delicate subtlety of *Garcilaso de la Vega, in contrast to the Baroque exuberance of Góngora's poem. As in the *Metamorphoses*, Carrillo's narrator is Galatea; in some passages the text resembles a free translation rather than a creative imitation of the Latin original.

Carrillo's poetry and poetic theory is a major link between Fernando de *Herrera's conscious crafting of the poetic work of art and elevation of literary language to the level of classical models, and the cultivation of extremely complex and allusive structures in the poetry of Góngora. Although Carrillo's development as a poet was cut short by his early death, his *Libro de la erudición poética* (ms. written 1607; Book of Poetic Erudition) is an important manifesto of *culteranismo*, the cultivation of a learned and difficult style directed toward learned readers that would culminate in the work of Góngora and his followers. Carrillo's poems occasionally exceed Góngora's in difficulty, in both the sonnet and the popular verse forms of romance (*romancero*) and *redondilla*.

Carrillo's poetry displays a versatility of theme and tone ranging from melancholy to heroism to witty wordplay. Despite the promise of his technical skill and sensibility, he had not yet found a characteristic voice. After Carrillo's death, his works were collected and printed by his brother Alonso in 1611; a substantially corrected edition appeared in 1613.

BIBLIOGRAPHY

Primary Texts

*Libro de la erudición poética.* Ed. Manuel Cardenal Iracheta. Madrid: CSIC, 1946.
*Poesías completas.* Ed. Dámaso Alonso. Madrid: Signo, 1936.
*Poesie I: Sonetti.* Ed. Fiorenza Randelli Romano. Messina-Florence: D'Anna, 1971.

Criticism

Orozco Díaz, Emilio. *Amor, poesía y pintura en Carrillo de Sotomayor: comentarios e investigaciones en torno a un poema inédito.* Granada: U of Granada, 1967.
Randelli Romano, Fiorenza. "La poesia di Carrillo attraverso i sonetti." *Quaderni Ibero-Americani* 31 (1965): 451–71.

Emilie Bergmann

**CARRO** (cart), a portable stage mounted on wheels that was used during the performance of the *autos sacramentales*, religious plays of Corpus Christi. Don Quixote encounters one of these vehicles and exclaims, " 'Wagoneer, coachman, devil, or whoever you may be, tell me at once who you are, where you are bound, or who are the people in your coach, which looks more like Charon's boat than the type of cart in common use.' Stopping the cart, the devil civilly replied, 'Sir, we are the travelling players of Angulo el Malo's company. This morning, which is the octave of Corpus Christi, we have performed a theatrical piece called *The Parliament of Death* in the village which lies beyond that hill. This afternoon we are to give it again in that village which you can see from here. Since it is so close and to save ourselves the trouble of undressing and dressing again, we are travelling in the costumes of our parts. That young man represents Death, the other an angel; that woman, who is the author's wife, plays a queen; the other a soldier; that one an emperor, and I am a devil, one of the principal characters of the play, for in this company I take the leading roles.' " (DQ part II, Ch. 11)

The carts contained a platform mounted on wheels and carried all the necessary accoutrements for the performance—stage equipment, costumes, etc. The portable stage was pulled by oxen. The directors of flourishing theater companies adorned the animals with flowers and decorative blankets and painted their horns in gold. The more elaborate plays used several stages simultaneously; *Calderón needed at least five portable stages for his religious plays. *See also* auto; Theater in Spain.

BIBLIOGRAPHY

Criticism

Shergold, N. D. *A History of the Spanish Stage from Medieval Times until the End of the Seventeenth Century.* Oxford: Clarendon, 1967.

Deborah Compte

**CARTAGENA, Alonso de,** also known as Alfonso de Santa María (1385?, Burgos–1456, Villasandino), humanist, theologian, and jurist. A member of the influential neo-Christian family Santa María, he succeeded his father, Pablo de *Santa María, as bishop of Burgos (1435). He was educated at Salamanca and was considered one of the most learned men of his age; his writings in Latin and Spanish reflect the deep roots of scholasticism and traditionalism in 15th-c. Spanish *humanism. His often cited polemic with Leonardo Bruni D'Arezzo concerning the Italian humanist's translation of Aristotle's *Nicomachean Ethics* only accentuates the late arrival of *Renaissance humanism in Spain. His works can be divided into three general areas: juridical, moral, and historico-literary. The most notable among the first is his *Defensorium Unitatis Christianae* (1449), a defense of the neo-Christians directed to John II. The *Doctrinal de caballeros* (Code of Chivalry), which is based upon the *Siete Partidas* (The Seven Parts of the Law) of *Alphonse X and other legal compilations, is a prescriptive analysis of the second estate. Other writings record his participation in the Council of Basel (1431–47). From his moral writings come the *Oracional* (1453–54; Treatise on Prayer), written for Fernán *Pérez de Guzmán; translations and glosses of several essays from *Seneca, commissioned by John II; translations from Cicero (*De Officiis* and *De Senectute*, 1422); and Boccaccio's *De Casibus Virorum Illustrium.* Among his historico-literary works is the *Anacephaleosis,* an epitome of Spanish history; it was translated from Latin into Spanish in 1463 as the *Genealogía de los reyes de España* (Genealogy of The Kings of Spain) by Fernán Pérez de Guzmán and Juan de Villafuerte. He also translated Cicero's *De Inventione Rhetorica*. Several unfinished works of Cartagena were completed by Diego *Rodríguez de Almela.

BIBLIOGRAPHY

Primary Texts

*Defensorium Unitatis Christianae*. Ed. Manuel Alonso. Madrid: Instituto Arias Montano, 1945.
*Proposición contra los ingleses. Sobre el acto de caballería*. See *Prosistas castellanos del siglo XV*. In BAE 116.

Criticism

Camillo, Ottavio di. *El humanismo castellano del siglo XV*. Valencia: Torres, 1976.
Cantera Burgos, Francisco. *Alvar García de Santa María y su familia de conversos. Historia de la judería de Burgos y de sus conversos más egregios*. Madrid: Instituto Arias Montano, 1952.
Penna, Mario. Introduction to *Prosistas castellanos del siglo XV*. BAE 116.
Serrano, Luciano. *Los conversos D. Pablo de Santa María y D. Alfonso de Cartagena. Obispos de Burgos, gobernantes, diplomáticos y escritores*. Madrid: Instituto Arias Montano, 1942.
Tate, R. B. "The *Anacephaleosis* of Alfonso García de Santa María, Bishop of Burgos, 1435–1456." In *Hispanic Studies in Honour of González Llubera*. Ed. F. Pierce. Oxford: Dolphin, 1959. 387–401.

                                                          Porter Conerly

**CARTAGENA, Teresa de** (before 1435, Cartagena–?), nun, religious writer. She may have been a granddaughter of Pablo de *Santa María, bishop of Burgos and patriarch of the influential and literary neo-Christian family of the same name. A nun, she studied several years at Salamanca. Stricken with total deafness, she converted her affliction into a major force in her life and writings. In her first work, *Arboleda de los enfermos* (1453–60; Grove for the Sick), she discusses her own affliction and isolation which subsequently led to spiritual enrichment. The grove, a variant of the *locus amoenus*, symbolizes the books in which she sought consolation and respite. While this consolatory treatise is in the Boethian tradition (see Deyermond), the editor of her works, L. J. Hutton, finds a more immediate source of inspiration in Pedro de Luna's (d. 1423) *Libro de las consolaciones humanas* (Book of Life's Consolations). Her second work, *Admiraçión operum Dey* (The Wonder of God's Works), written at the request of the wife of Gómez *Manrique, treats God's granting of spiritual favors to Souls, and also reflects the surprise and disbelief with which her first work was received; it is an apologia for women writers. Sincerity and psychological insights characterize her work. For her felicitous style and expression she frequently recurs to images from the Bible, medicine, and scenes of daily life.

BIBLIOGRAPHY

Primary Text

*Arboleda de los enfermos. Admiraçión operum Dey.* Ed., study L. J. Hutton. *BRAE*
    Anejo 16. Madrid: RAE, 1967.

Criticism

Cantera Burgos, F. *Alvar García de Santa María y su familia de conversos; historia de
    la judería de Burgos y de sus conversos más egregios.* Madrid: Instituto Arias
    Montano, 1952.
Deyermond, A. "El convento de dolençias': The Works of Teresa de Cartagena." *Journal
    of Hispanic Philology* 1 (1976): 19–29.
Hutton. L. F. See *Arboleda de los enfermos,* above.

Porter Conerly

**CARVAJAL, Antonio** (1943– ) [Albolote-Granada], poet. Carvajal studied
philosophy and letters at the U of Granada, where he presently teaches Spanish
language and literature. *Tigres en el jardín* (1968; Tigers in the Garden) constitutes a metaphoric celebration of love in precise classical verse. In *Serenata
y navaja* (1973; Serenade and Knife) the initial skepticism of the poetic speaker
is overcome by an exultation of life. The use of baroque stylistic and rhetorical
devices receives an ample treatment in *Siesta en el mirador* (1979; Siesta in the
Balcony). The most recent books of verse written by Carvajal include *Servidumbre de paso* (1982; Passing Servitude); *Del viento en los jazmines* (1984;
Of Wind and Jasmines), and *Noticia de septiembre* (1984; September News).
    *Extravagante jerarquía* (1983; Extravagant Hierarchy) integrates Carvajal's
production between 1968 and 1982. In Carvajal's poetry we find a wide range
of theme and meter, utilized with excellent technical control. In his poems he
integrates the best of Spanish poetic tradition, especially the Baroque, with
contemporary poetic forms.

BIBLIOGRAPHY

Primary Texts

*Del viento en los jazmines.* Madrid: Hiperión, 1984.
*Extravagante jerarquía.* Madrid: Hiperión, 1983.
*Serenata y navaja.* Barcelona: "El Bardo," 1973.
*Siesta en el mirador.* San Sebastián: "Ancia," 1979.
*Tigres en el jardín.* Barcelona: "El Bardo," 1968.

Criticism

Prat, Ignacio. "Cuatro artículos." In *Extravagante jerarquía.* Madrid: Hiperión, 1983.
    291–307.

José Ortega

**CARVAJAL, Micael de** (c. 1480, Plasencia–c. 1530, ?), priest and poet. Scant
and extremely conflicting biographical information is available concerning Carvajal, who is best known as the author of one of the finest examples of religious

drama in the early Spanish theater, the *Tragedia llamada Josephina* (c. 1535; The Tragedy of Joseph). The piece incorporates freely the Old Testament account and several later versions of the story of Joseph and stands out for the emotional and lyrical qualities rarely found in the works of Carvajal's contemporaries. In *Las cortes de la muerte* (1557; The Court of Death), a brief episodic piece composed in *quintillas* and completed by Luis *Hurtado de Toledo, Carvajal dealt with the medieval Dance of Death (*Dança General de la Muerte) and the vanity of temporal existence. Decidedly anti-Protestant in sentiment, this became one of the most popular works of the latter half of the sixteenth c.

BIBLIOGRAPHY

Primary Texts

*Cortes de casto amor* and *Cortes de la muerte*. Facs. ed. of 1557 Toledo ed. Valencia: Andrés Ortega del Alamo, 1963.

*Las cortes de la muerte*. *Romancero y cancionero sagrados*. Ed. Justo de Sancha. BAE 35 (1950).

*Tragedia Josephina*. Ed. Joseph E. Gillet. Elliot Monographs in the Romance Languages and Literatures 28. Princeton: Princeton UP, 1932.

Criticism

Crawford, J. P. Wickersham. *Spanish Drama before Lope de Vega*. Rev. ed. Philadelphia: U of Pennsylvania P, 1967.

Gitlitz, David M. "La actitud cristiano-nueva en *Las cortes de la muerte*." *Segismundo* 17–18 (1973): 141–64.

———. "*Conversos* and the Fusion of Worlds in Micael de Carvajal's *Tragedia Josephina*." *HR* 40 (1972): 260–70.

Rodríguez Puértolas, Julio. "*Las cortes de la muerte*, obra erasmista." *Homenaje a William L. Fichter: Estudios sobre el teatro antiguo hispánico y otros ensayos*. Ed. A. David Kossoff and José Amor y Vázquez. Madrid: Castalia, 1971. 647–58.

Ruiz Ramón, Francisco. *Historia del teatro español (Desde sus orígenes hasta 1900)*. vol. 1. Madrid: Alianza, 1967.

C. Maurice Cherry

**CARVAJAL Y MENDOZA, Luisa de** (1566, Jaraicejo, Cáceres–1614, London), religious poet. Her voluminous writings, which include an autobiography, a collection of letters, and spiritual poetry, reveal her to be one of the most significant women in the wars of religion between England and Spain. Born to a noble family and raised for a time at court, Carvajal wrote tirelessly of her "great desires for martyrdom," leaving for England as a Catholic lay missionary in 1605. Twice jailed for her public support of the church, she died in London of a prolonged illness in 1614; Philip III ordered her body returned to Spain, where proceedings for her beatification began in 1625. Although influenced by Luis de *Granada, Saint Ignatius (*Ignacio) of Loyola, and Saint John of the Cross (*Juan de la Cruz), Carvajal's poetry discloses distinctly feminine characteristics in its imagery and poetic voice.

322CARVALHO, MARIA JUDITE DE

# BIBLIOGRAPHY

Primary Texts

*Epistolario y poesías.* BAE 179.

*Escritos autobiográficos.* Barcelona: Juan Flors, 1966.

Criticism

Abad, S. J., Camilo María. *Una misionera española en la Inglaterra del siglo XVII.* Santander: Pontificia Comillas, 1966.

Anne Cruz

**CARVALHO, Maria Judite de** (1921, Lisbon– ), Portuguese short story writer, novelist and journalist. Maria Judite de Carvalho has published excellent work in three different genres. However, in two of these, her production amounts to one volume only: her one full-length novel is *Os armários vazios* (1966; The Empty Cupboards), although "novel" is a purely formal characteristic as this work is not noticeably different in character from her longer short stories; while *A janela fingida* (1975; The Imitation Window), a collection of short columns which originally appeared, in most cases, in the newspaper *O Diário de Lisboa*, is a jumbled assortment of more trivial but nonetheless enjoyable and observant articles, ranging from memories of childhood and impressions gained while traveling around Portugal to discussions of topical matters of the day.

However, it is her work as a writer of short stories which has gained her the greatest critical acclaim. *As palavras poupadas* (1961; The Unspoken Words) was awarded the Prémio Camilo Castelo Branco, and although any of her collections would be worthy of such an honour, it seems appropriate that she should have been recognized for this title, for the inadequacy of words, and the problems of interpersonal communication in general, constitute one of the central concerns of her work as a whole.

Although she has been classified in the past, not without some reason, as an existentialist writer, her concerns are always centered around the difficulties created by living in the world with others, from whose consciousnesses we are irrevocably separated. Even when the superficial characteristics of her work change from the prosaic realism of collections such as *Paisagem sem barcos* (1963; Sea Without Boats) to the more adventurous science-fiction style of *Os idólatras* (1969; The Idol-Worshippers), these predominant, underlying aspects of her work remain the same.

Her fiction is marked by the seemingly total impossibility of building meaningful bridges between the self and the outside world: parents do not understand their children; the children are perplexed by the breakdown in communication between their parents; husbands show no signs of awareness of their wives' concerns; friends, if they are to be found, fail to see the necessary course of action in a given situation; and even the happiest of marital relationships can be destroyed irreparably.

This deeply pessimistic view of life is closely linked to the nature of modern society: the stories are usually set in Lisbon—various references to landmarks of the capital make this clear—but this setting is very weak; for Lisbon we could substitute any modern, industrialized city.

The twentieth-c. world is seen as a soulless body where people exist purely in terms of their function at work, a theme which is developed most fully in the later collection, *Os idólatras*. But even in the most characteristic works, such as *Os armários vazios*, we find characters who are so dominated by the tedium of their daily routine that they have no time left for enjoying life itself.

This applies most particularly to men. Male characters in Carvalho's work tend to be cold and unresponsive; the need to submit continually to the oppressive routine of work in order to meet the material needs of the household limits their ability to respond adequately to the needs of the domestic environment; or, sometimes, the male wishes to enjoy the security of a relationship without endangering his own freedom. As a result, the desire of the female protagonist to enrich her life with a family is often forgotten or ignored, which frequently brings about the complete breakdown of marriage.

The passing of time is also an important theme. Female protagonists usually reach their point of crisis in their mid- or late thirties, the age when youth finally gives way to middle-age, and hopes of a family, if they have not already been fulfilled, must be forgotten. It is at this age, too, that frustration at the attitudes of career-minded husbands or uncommitted boyfriends tends to set in. As a result, it is usually at this age that we find characters contemplating the meaning of life and finding that it involves a pain worse than the emptiness of death.

But, even if relationships are fulfilling, the experience of them is no less painful. They may decay in time, and a love once possessed is lost as characters go their separate ways and lose the flower of their youth: this is, for example, what happens in "Uma história de amor" (Love-Story from *Flores ao telefone*), and it is for fear of this that Amélia kills her beloved Karl in "O homem voador e a mulher que não tinha asas" (The Trapeze-Artist and the Woman without Wings from the same collection), significantly using for this purpose the chest in which she keeps her photographs of him as he is and has been.

Again, one may find a life crushed by the sudden intervention of events beyond human control or of actions of incalculable consequences: thus road or air accidents are frequent events in Carvalho's work, often occurring at the moment when success seems to be within reach—"Tudo vai mudar" (Everything Will Change from *Paisagem sem barcos*) and "A noiva inconsolável" (The Inconsolable Bride from *As palavras poupadas*) are only two examples among many; and the tragic endings of stories such as "Um diário para Saudade" (A Diary for Saudade from *Flores ao telefone*) are attributable to individual actions which, in themselves, are normal or not particularly blameworthy (in this case, one child reporting another to a teacher who then confiscates her diary), but which, within a given context and given the total impossibility of knowing others' thoughts and feelings, can have disastrous results.

Or, again, a seemingly fulfilling relationship may be destroyed by the sudden discovery of facts hitherto unknown. Thus, the title of *Os armários vazios* refers to a line from Paul Eluard: "J'ai conservé de faux trésors dans des armoires vides." The quotation refers to the tragedy of the protagonist, Dora Rosário, whose life is shattered twice by placing excessive faith in the men in her life: after her husband's death she devotes her life to mourning him, thus wasting what remains of her youth and losing the chance to know her daughter as she grows up. It is only then that she discovers the awful truth, that her husband had seriously contemplated leaving her before his death; she then turns for fulfillment to Ernesto, who abandons her for her own daughter, Lisa, who is totally unaware of the relationship which he has had with her mother.

This story is typical of Carvalho, emphasizing as it does the enormous gap which exists between reality and our limited awareness or perceptions of reality; the total mental isolation of the individual; as a result of this fact, the damage which our every action may unwittingly create for others; and yet, despite this bleakly cynical view of human relationships, the need for these as the only source of purpose in an otherwise lonely and soulless world.

However, this is far from being Carvalho's best work: it struggles to maintain the quality of her short stories over the length of a full-scale novel, and, in particular, the use of the first-person narrative form fails to achieve conviction. This technique is employed to accentuate the bleakness of the work by reflecting the protagonist's sad experience of life through the eyes of a character who is equally world-weary; however, it is only at rare intervals that the narrator's own comments add an extra dimension to the work, for too often they strike the reader as gratuitous insertions of little relevance.

Rather, it is in the genre of the short story that Carvalho excels: the recurrent themes of her work, as set out above, are simple and far from original. Yet it is the sobriety and concision of her writing which give it its emotional power, a quality which is lost in longer stories such as *Os armários vazios*.

She possesses in abundance all the gifts required to create a successful narrative in condensed form. Her stories do not indulge in long passages of exposition; rather we find ourselves placed, by means of the technique of internal focalization, into the thought processes of an individual in a given situation, so that often it is only late in the text that we discover a character's identity or his relationship to others. This has the further advantage of enabling us to experience life through the eyes of the central protagonist, sharing all his doubts and anxieties, and, of course, we also experience the essential mental loneliness of the human condition—the inaccessibility of the minds of others is thus further highlighted.

She has achieved considerable mastery of the concise but telling and evocative image or phrase. Thus, in *Paisagem sem barcos*, for example, we find that the following sentence—"Há como que um pequeno elevador hidráulico que desce, quando é necessário, do seu cérebro à sua boca, carregando dentro de si palavras que entram serenas no mundo"—not only provides us with an original and humorous characterization of the person in question, but also tells us as much about the sensitivity and loneliness of the focused center of consciousness as it does about the explicit object of description. Furthermore, for the reader who is aware already of the significance of words and communication in Carvalho's writing, this one sentence helps us to place the character in question directly into the framework of the author's cynical view of the relationship between the sexes.

Symbols and images also develop their own semantic significances within the context of Carvalho's work as a whole. Thus, for example, the telephone, the instrument which is usually regarded as having eased communication, becomes the symbol of distant and meaningless communication. It is hardly to be found surprising, therefore, in the story *Flores ao telefone* (1968; Flores on the Phone), that Flores's suicide is due to her use of the telephone to make a last despairing attempt to relate to the outside world; the people whom she contacts fail, quite understandably given their respective situations, to appreciate her urgent need of assistance, a need which would be more apparent given direct contact.

Similarly, words and speech have their own special significance. We have already quoted an example from *Paisagem sem barcos* to illustrate Carvalho's gift for achieving the striking phrase or image, but the way in which this sentence is couched illustrates also her view of language: words are not just words; they are events like any other and actions of incalculable significance. Each word spoken can have enormous effects on people in a given situation, as in "Adelaide" (from *Flores ao telefone*), where a casual, impulsive suggestion completely ruins a woman's life; but man's dilemma is such that words left unspoken can be equally disastrous, an idea that is constant to the stories in *As palavras poupadas*. Man must communicate to survive, but language, his major means of communication, is fragile and unreliable.

Dreams, too, are important. Beautiful dreams of travel to exotic places, or simpler but equally valuable dreams of fulfillment through a happy domestic life, find fulfillment only in the imagination, in a fantasy world rather akin to that of Walter Mitty. Indeed, in "A vida é o sonho" (Life is Dreaming; from *Tanta Gente, Mariana*, 1959, So Many People, Mariana), Calderón's religious speculation is evoked by the title, only to be replaced by the concept of a world of fantasy within the self as a welcome escape from the drudgery of everyday reality. In this story the protagonist deliberately avoids the possibility of fulfilling his dreams in order to avoid disappointment. Meanwhile, in "Tudo vai mudar" (Everything Will Change from *Paisagem sem barcos*), the hero is actually destroyed by his own dreamworld, as he is too immersed in his thoughts to notice the traffic in the street. Dreams, then, have their value as an escape from the realities of existence, but only negatively, as long as they remain dreams; they must not intrude upon real life.

One of the principal characteristics of Carvalho's earlier writing is its dependence upon the familiar world of big-city life in an ordinary environment. *Os idólatras*, however, marks a major break from this approach, although the themes remain essentially the same: the mechanized, coldly functional society which she presents in a recognizably realistic world is now merely projected into a world of fantasy, where characters nonetheless have the same concerns as in her more characteristic stories—finding some sort of purpose to a life which is beyond their own control, as in "As mãos ignorantes" (The Ignorant Hands); or facing up to the fact that the passing of time destroys all things, especially love, as in "O meu pai era milionário" (My Father Was a Millionaire).

In this respect, the stories of this collection bear some resemblance to E. M. Forster's *The Machine Stops* or to certain stories of Arthur C. Clarke, but, above all, the reader is reminded of Kafka's *Verwandlung* ("Metamorphosis") or some of J. L. Borges's *Ficciones* (Fictions) by the skillful way in which he is led to perceive a realism of experience within an unrealistic framework of science fiction.

However, this change in presentation should not be seen as being entirely unexpected. There are signs in some of the stories of *Flores ao telefone* (published only one year before *Os idólatras*) that the familiar formula is becoming exhausted: some stories lack convincing resolution, and there are fewer of the strikingly concise and evocative images of previous works. However, two stories point the way forward: in "O homem voador e a mulher que não tinha asas" the narrative is not set in the usual world of insignificant clerks or schoolteachers but in the domestic environment of a circus trapeze artist; and, perhaps less convincingly, *O casamento* ("The Marriage") ends with a priest having a nervous breakdown and accusing his sacristan of being an alien and not the Son of God. Nevertheless, these two stories do indicate a search for a new formula, and yet they too preserve Carvalho's overriding concern for very familiar social and emotional problems.

Carvalho tends to use short and simple sentences, as if her awareness of the problem of communication impelled her to use language as sparingly and as unambiguously as possible. Her stories open abruptly and are usually focused upon one mind whose every thought and feeling are reported to us, so that we share the perplexity of that individual in a world where his destiny is beyond his own control and where it is impossible to gain access to the equally private thoughts of others. At the same time, because the reader finds himself in possession of this "impossible" insight, but only temporarily so, he cannot share fully in the knowledge of the focused mind, and he therefore experiences the events of the narrative like a spectator at a drama with no exposition, in that he has no knowledge of inter-relationships among characters or of situations taken for granted by the focused mind. This achieves two particular effects: the bewilderment of the reader is greater than that of the protagonist, thus accentuating the gaps in all processes of communication; and relationships are reduced to questions of interpersonal reactions so that ties of blood or marriage become no more significant than any casual encounter, an effect which is consistent with the author's pessimistic view of human contact.

Similarly, because of the technique of internal focalization, different time scales often overlap without any warning in the course of the narrative, just as they may often be intermingled in everyday thought processes. Although this often results in some temporary confusion on the part of the reader, clarity is always ultimately achieved and the bewilderment caused often serves to accentuate the contrast between the crushed hopes and dreams of youth and the sad realities of middle-age.

Carvalho suffers from the same fate of anonymity outside her own country as all but the greatest of writers in Portuguese; and yet the concision, precision and elegance of her written style, as well as the profundity and sincerity of emotion with which she gives fresh expression to the twentieth-c. commonplaces of nihilistic angst and man's existential loneliness, must surely earn her a place among the finest writers to have appeared in Portugal in the last thirty years.

BIBLIOGRAPHY

Primary Texts

*Além do Quadro*. Lisbon: O Jornal, 1983.
*As palavras poupadas*. Rev. Mem-Martins: Europa-América, 1988.
*Os armários vazios*. 2nd ed. Amadora: Bertrand, 1978.
*Os idolátras*. Lisbon: Prelo, 1969.
*Paisagem sem barcos*. Lisbon: Arcâdia, 1963.
*Tanta gente, Mariana*. Rev. Mem-Martins: Europa-América, 1988.

Criticism

Lúcia Lepecki, Maria. "Maria Judite de Carvalho: circularidade de acção, procura de palavra." In *Meridianos do Texto*. Ed. Maria Lúcia Lepecki. Lisbon: Assírio e Alvim, 1979. 71–96.

David Frier

**CARVALHO, Raul de** (1920, Lisbon– ), Portuguese poet. Carvalho belongs to a surrealist group which appeared after 1950, characterized by the exercise of automatism, a concentration of the subconscious, the use of "black" or "sick" humor, and various techniques of interference with verbal association. The poetry of Carvalho is especially notable for its rhythmic qualities. Among his collections are *As Sombras e as Vozes* (1949; Shadows and Voices), *Poesia* (1955), *Mesa da Solidão* (1955; Table for One), *Parágrafos* (1956; Paragraphs), *Versos* (1958), and *Poesia, 1949–58* (1965).

BIBLIOGRAPHY

Primary Texts

*Parágrafos*. Lisbon: n.p., 1956.
*Poesia*. Lisbon: Portugália, 1955.
*Poesia 1949–58*. Lisbon: Ulisseia, 1965.
*Tampo vazio*. Lisbon: Moraes, 1975.
*Versos*. (Poesia II) Lisbon: Author ed., 1958.

**CASANOVA DE LUTOSLAWSKI, Sofía** (1862, Almeiras, La Coruña–1958, Warsaw), Spanish poet and short story writer. Casanova married a Polish nobleman in 1887 and thereafter lived mostly outside Spain, but continued to collaborate in the Spanish press. This, combined with her frequent visits to Spain, and her work to improve the lot of women everywhere, led to her receiving the Cross of Alfonso XII and becoming a member of the Royal Galician Academy. Besides her work on the situation of Spanish women abroad, she wrote on behalf of working women throughout Europe, and advocated better hygiene. In addition to her poems and short stories, Casanova published many volumes on Poland and Russia, including works originally written in Polish. She wrote travelogues, histories, novels, and essays relevant to the turn-of-the century feminist movement. *Poesías* (1885; Poems), Romantic in tone and subject, also contains some social notes in its treatment of Galician miners and sailors. *Fugaces* (1898; Fleeting) contains youthful poems, and others of the collection "Ausencia" (Absence), composed from 1887 to 1897, are largely incidental in nature. *El cancionero de la dicha* (1911; The Songbook of Good Fortune) reproduces many poems from earlier collections, but contains new compositions of anguished, frustrated love, and life as a desperate, doomed search.

Narratives by this prolific writer include *Lo eterno: narración española* (1907; The Eternal, A Spanish Tale), novelette; *Más que amor; cartas* (1909; More Than Love; Novels), an epistolary novel; *El pecado* (1911; Sin), a collection of short stories set mostly in Galicia; *Exóticas* (1912), a collection of sketches and short stories; *La madeja* (1913; The Skein), described by the author as a frivolous comedy; *El doctor Wolski. Páginas de Polonia y Rusia* (1914; Doctor Wolski. Pages from Poland and Russia), an early treatment of the theme of genetic engineering; *De Rusia. Amores y confidencias* (1927; From Russia. Love and Confidences), a collection of essays and short stories; and *Las catacumbas de Rusia roja* (1933; The Catacombs of Red Russia), which reflects the struggle of revolutionary and counter-revolutionary forces in the aftermath of the Bolshevik revolt.

BIBLIOGRAPHY

Primary Texts

*Idilio epistolar*. Madrid: Aguilera, 1931.

*Princesa rusa*. Madrid: Publicaciones Prensa Gráfica, 1922.

*Sobre el Volga helado; narración de viajes*. Madrid: Librería de Fernando Fe, 1903.

*Viajes y aventuras de una muñeca española en Rusia*. Burgos: Hijos de Santiago Rodríguez, 1920.

Janet Pérez

**CASARES, Julio** (1877, Granada–1964, Madrid), lexicologist and literary critic. Casares was also secretary of the Royal Spanish Academy (*Academia Española) and, at one time, in charge of language interpreting in the Ministry of State. He is known in particular for two studies on contemporary authors: *Crítica profana* (1915; Profane Criticism), dealing with such literary figures as *Azorín, *Valle-Inclán, Ricardo *León, among others, and *Crítica efímera* (1918; Ephemeral Criticism), lighting on such subjects as Blanco Fombona, Mariano de *Cavia, Julio *Cejador, and Antonio de *Valbuena. He excelled in lexicological and grammatical studies, for which he was greatly esteemed. *Cosas del lenguaje* (1943; Bits on Language), for example, deals with spoken and written discourse. He also wrote a *Diccionario inglés-español y español-inglés* (1936), as well as a *Diccionario ideológico de la lengua española* (1942; Ideological Dictionary of the Spanish Language) and the *Nuevo concepto del Diccionario de la lengua y otros problemas de lexicografía y semántica* (1921; A New Concept of the Dictionary of the Language and Other Problems of Lexicography and Semantics). The latter includes his acceptance speech for the Royal Spanish Academy. Casares was, in addition, a talented violinist.

BIBLIOGRAPHY

Criticism

Zuleta, E. de. *Historia de la crítica española contemporánea*. Madrid: Gredos, 1966. 176–77.

Noël M. Valis

**CASAS, Bartolomé de Las** (1474, Seville–1566, Valladolid), historian of the conquest and colonization of the New World and passionate defender of the American Indians. Son of a Sevillian merchant who accompanied Columbus (\*Colón) on his second voyage, Las Casas came to America in 1502, participated in conquests in Santo Domingo and Cuba, and for a number of years administered land and slaves as an *encomendero*. He was ordained a priest and by 1510 underwent a crisis of conscience which convinced him that the slavery of the Indians was unjust. This fundamental conviction afforded him a cause which he never abandoned in the course of his long life: the protection of the Indians from the excesses of the Spanish colonial enterprise. When his own efforts to found a Utopian community of Indians and Spanish peasants came to nothing, Las Casas took Dominican orders and retired to a monastery to write his *Historia de las Indias* (1868; *History of the Indies*, 1971), which began with the discoveries of Columbus and continued through 1520, remaining unfinished at the time of the author's death in 1566. During the same period he began writing a separate work, the *Apologética historia de las Indias* (1909; Apologetic History of the Indies), initially a treatise on certain aspects of Indian civilization, which evolved into a lengthy history in its own right that has recently come to be viewed as an embryonic "program for comparative ethnology." Appointed Bishop of Chiapas and officially designated as Procurador de los indios (Defender of the Indians), he journeyed repeatedly to Spain to speak for Indian causes, and intervened decisively in the adoption of the enlightened "New Laws" (1542) of colonial administration. In 1548 he returned definitively to Spain, and in 1550 he participated in a celebrated debate in Valladolid before royal officials in which he proposed, in opposition to the humanist Juan Ginés de \*Sepúlveda, that the American Indians were by nature free men who could not justly be enslaved. On this same occasion he presented his other fundamental theses: that the Spanish claim to dominion over the New World territories could be based solely on the imperative to propagate the Christian Gospel; and that the evangelization of the Indians was properly carried out not by armed force, but rather through peaceful means. This latter view he had developed previously in a Latin treatise, *De unico vocationis modo omnium gen-*

*tium ad veram religionem* (1942; On the Only Way of Bringing All Peoples to the True Religion). By far the most influential of Las Casas's works, and the only one to be printed in his lifetime, was his *Brevíssima relación de la destruyción de las Indias* (1552; *The Devastation of the Indies: A Brief Account*, 1974), which portrayed the Indians as being victims of barbarous atrocities perpetrated by the Spaniards. This little book, quickly translated into all the major European languages, was instrumental in the creation of the anti-Spanish *Black Legend, used to advantage by Spain's enemies and rivals for centuries.

Las Casas's defects as an historian are directly attributable to his overriding polemical orientation. An incorrigible scholastic, he wields his erudition with a heavy hand, and the constant repetition of a limited number of ideas, all leading to the same point, tends to tire. Though Las Casas was a prolific author, his lasting influence is to be found not in his prose style, which is labored and difficult, but rather in his controversial role in the shaping of Spanish and Latin American history.

BIBLIOGRAPHY

Primary Texts

*Apologética historia sumaria.* Ed. Edmundo O'Gorman. 2 vols. Mexico: UNAM, 1967.
*Brevísima relación de la destrucción de las Indias.* Ed. André Saint-Lu. Madrid: Cátedra, 1982.
*Historia de las Indias.* Ed. Agustín Millares Carlo. México: Fondo de Cultura Económica, 1951.
*Obras escogidas.* Ed. Juan Pérez de Tudela Bueso. BAE 95, 96, 105, 106, 110.
*Tratados de fray Bartolomé de las Casas.* Prol. Lewis Hanke and M. G. Fernández. México: Fondo de Cultura Económica, 1965.

English Translations

*Bartolomé de las Casas: A Selection of His Writings.* Tr. & ed. George Sanderlin. New York: Knopf, 1971.
*The Devastation of the Indies; A Brief Account.* Tr. Herma Briffault. Intro. Hans Magnus Enzenberger. New York: Seabury, 1974.
*History of the Indies.* Tr. and ed. Andrée Collard. New York: Harper & Row, 1971.

Criticism

Bataillon, Marcel. *Études sur Bartolomé de Las Casas.* Paris: Centre de recherches de l'Institut d'études hispaniques, 1965.
Fried, Juan, and Benjamin Keen, eds. *Bartolomé de las Casas in History: Toward an Understanding of the Man and His Work.* DeKalb: Northern Illinois UP, 1971.
Hanke, Lewis. *All Mankind in One: A Study of the Disputation between Bartolomé de Las Casas and Juan Ginés de Sepúlveda in 1550 on the Intellectual and Religious Capacity of the American Indians.* DeKalb: Northern Illinois UP, 1974.
————. *Bartolomé de Las Casas: An Interpretation of His Life and Writings.* The Hague: Martinus Nijhoff, 1951.
Pagden, Anthony. *The Fall of Natural Man.* London: Cambridge UP, 1982.

Robert E. Lewis

**CASCALES, Francisco de** (1564, Murcia–1642, Sto. Domingo, Murcia), professor, translator, humanist. Of *converso lineage, his father was burned at the stake. Cascales served as a soldier in France and the Netherlands. His poetry is of scant merit, but his translation of Horace's *Poetics* is masterful. In 1634 he published *Cartas filológicas* (Philological Letters), an erudite piece which criticizes *Góngora harshly. As official historian of Murcia he wrote *Discursos históricos de la muy noble ciudad de Murcia* (1621; Historical Discourses on the Noble City Murcia). He also composed a *Tablas poéticas* (1617; Poetry Tables), a complete, concise, correct *Renaissance interpretation of classical poetics; it is the first Spanish precept to document the fusion of Horatian and Aristotelian poetics. *See also* Aristotelianism in Spain.

BIBLIOGRAPHY

Primary Texts

*Cartas filológicas*. Ed. J. García Soriano. Clásicos Castellanos 103, 117, and 118. Madrid: Espasa-Calpe, 1930–41.

*Discursos históricos*. . . . 3rd ed. Murcia: Tornel y Olms, 1874.

*Tablas poéticas*. Ed., notes B. Brancaforte. Clásicos Castellanos 207. Madrid: Espasa-Calpe, 1975.

Criticism

García Berrio, A. *Introducción a la poética clasicista: Cascales*. Barcelona: Planeta, 1975.

García Servet, J. *El humanista Cascales y la Inquisición murciana*. Madrid: Porrúa Turanza, 1978.

García Soriano, J. *El humanista Francisco Cascales: su vida y sus obras*. Madrid: RABM, 1924.

**CASONA, Alejandro,** pseudonym of Alejandro Rodríguez Álvarez (1903, Besullo [Oviedo]–1965, Madrid), Asturian playwright. Casona began his career as an educator, contributing humanitarian service first in the Valle de Arán, where he founded a children's theater. Later (1931), he received an appointment from the Inspección Provincial de Madrid (Madrid's Provincial Inspection Bureau) to lead several cultural missions to Spain's provinces. In 1936, the Civil War forced him, a Republican and an intellectual, into exile. In 1937, he left Europe with the Díaz/Collado theatrical company to tour Latin America, eventually establishing residence in Argentina. In 1963, he returned to Spain, where the plays that had won him fame in Latin America were received warmly.

Though Casona disowned his first original work, a book of poems entitled *La flauta del sapo* (1930; The Toad's Flute), it clearly marks his poetic inclinations. *Flor de leyendas* (1932; Legendary Gems), a collection of legends, earned him the Premio Nacional de Literatura (National Literary Prize). Success as a playwright came with his winning the Lope de Vega prize in 1933, with *La sirena varada* (Mermaid Aground), followed by the premiere of *Otra vez el diablo* (1935; The Devil Again), and *Nuestra Natacha* (Our Natacha), premiering in Barcelona in 1935 and in Madrid's Teatro Victoria in February of 1936. The balance of his plays, with the exception of *El caballero de las espuelas de oro* (1964; The Knight with the Golden Spurs) and his version of Fernando de *Rojas's *La *Celestina* (1965), had their birth in Latin America.

Among the plays that have their roots in tradition and are redolent with Calderonian symbols and values, though clearly in a modern idiom, are *Otra vez el diablo*, *La dama del alba* (1944; *Lady of the Dawn*, 1972), *La barca sin pescador* (1945; *Boat Without a Fisherman*, 1970) and *Siete gritos en el mar* (1952; Seven Cries at Sea). The latter play, along with a *La llave en el desván* (1951; The Key in the Attic) and *La casa de los siete balcones* (1957; The House of the Seven Gables), resonates with suggestions of the paranormal, notably extra sensorial perception. The plays most directly concerned with the solipsistic, illusion/ reality theme are *La sirena varada*, which also carries strong traditional values, *Prohibido suicidarse en primavera* (1937; *Suicide Prohibited in Spring-time*, 1968), *Las tres perfectas casadas* (1941; The Three Perfect Wives), and *Los árboles mueren de pie* (1949; Trees Die Standing). His historical plays are *Sinfonía inacabada* (1939; Unfinished Symphony, a version of the Franz Schubert story), *Corona de amor y muerte* (1955; *Love, Death, and a Crown*, 1972, a revival of the passionate and tender story of Inés de Castro), and *El caballero de las espuelas de oro*, Casona's interpretation of Francisco de *Quevedo's life.

Other plays include *El crimen de Lord Arturo* (1929; a dramatic version of Oscar Wilde's *Lord Arthur Savile's Crime*, 1887), *Romance de Dan y Elsa* (1938; Ballad of Dan and Elsa), *La molinera de Arcos* (1947; The Miller's Wife), *La tercera palabra* (1953; The Third Word), and *Tres diamantes y una mujer* (1961; Three Diamonds and One Woman). Casona also wrote plays for children, some plays in collaboration with other authors (with limited success), translations of Voltaire, Lenormand, and De Quincey, and numerous essays. He spent several years working in Argentina's motion picture industry and delivered lectures in many countries, but always felt, and indeed proved, that the theater was his true world.

Critics have remarked on the prevalence of fantasy and illusion in Casona's works, which allies readily with the author's tacit plea for an imaginative approach to life. A non-abrasive humor is ever present, serving a gentle satire, calculated to effect, humanely and poetically, the balance of human values in society.

Critics have also noted Casona's contribution to the renovation of Spanish theater, but a few have turned bitter in their denunciation of him, averring that he ignored Spain's current social stresses, giving his public a theater mainly literary, indifferent to social urgencies. Their objections are clearly ideological and not aesthetic. *See also* Contemporary Spanish Theater.

BIBLIOGRAPHY

Primary Text

*Obras completas.* Ed. Federico C. Sáinz de Robles. 6th ed. 2 vols. Madrid: Aguilar, 1969; rpt. 1974.

English Translations

*Boat without a Fisherman.* Tr. Richard Dalmar. In *Modern Spanish Stage.* Ed. Marion Holt. New York: Hill and Wang, 1970.

*Lady of the Dawn* and *Love, Death, and a Crown*. Prol. and tr. by Graciela Miranda de
   Graves. Valencia: Albatrós, 1972.
*Suicide Prohibited in Springtime*. Tr. A. D. Horvath. In *Modern Spanish Theatre*. Ed.
   M. Benedikt and G. E. Wellwarth. New York: Dutton, 1968.
Criticism
Bernal Labrada, Hilda. *Símbolo, mito y leyenda en el teatro de Casona*. Oviedo: Instituto
   de Estudios Asturianos, 1972.
*Boletín del Instituto de Estudios Asturianos*, no. 57 (April 1966). This entire number is
   dedicated to Alejandro Casona.
Moon, Harold K. *Alejandro Casona*. TWAS 748. Boston: Twayne, 1985.
Plans, Juan José. *Alejandro Casona*. Oviedo: Richard Grandío, 1965.
Saínz de Robles, Federico C. "Prólogo" to the *Obras completas de Alejandro Casona*.
   6th ed. 2 vols. Madrid: Aguilar, 1969; rpt. 1974.

Harold K. Moon

**CASTAÑÓN, Luciano** (1926, Gijón– ), novelist, poet and folklorist. His novels
include *El viento dobló la esquina* (1958; The Wind Turned the Corner); *Los
días como pájaros* (1962; Days Like the Birds); and *Vivimos de noche* (1964;
We Live by Night). His play *El detenido* (The Arrested Man) received the 1964
Guipúzcoa Theater Prize. He has published at least one collection of poems,
*Barrio de Cimadevilla* (1967; Uptown Neighborhood), and from his investiga-
tions of northern folklore, has compiled *Refranero asturiano* (1962; Asturian
Proverbs and Folk-Sayings).

BIBLIOGRAPHY
   Primary Texts
*Barrio de Cimadevilla*. Barcelona: El Bardo, 1967.
*Los días como pájaros*. Barcelona: Caralt, 1962.
*Refranero asturiano*. Oviedo: Diputación de Oviedo, CSIC, 1962.
*Vivimos de noche*. Barcelona: Caralt, 1964.

**CASTELAO, Daniel Rodríguez** (1886, Rianxo, La Coruña–1950, Buenos
Aires), Galician cartoonist, essayist, humorist, author of short stories, novels,
theater, lectures and political articles. As a child he emigrated to Argentina to
join his father there and began his drawings. He studied medicine at the U of
Santiago (Compostela), but soon abandoned the profession, later working as a
technical draftsman in the Institute of Geography and Statistics. He became
identified with the cause of the people of Galicia, and is considered a paradigm
of the purest Galician spirit. Circumstances forced him into exile, and he traveled
in various European countries, lived in several Latin American countries, and
finally established himself in Buenos Aires. His entire artistic and literary production is an affirmation of his essential *galleguismo* (Galician nationalism):
stories, theater, cartoons, travel impressions, novels, criticism of art, historico-
political essays, and erudite studies—all are imbued by the same folkloric,
intimate Galician spirit. His best-known works include the album of sketches

*Nós* (first exhibited in 1915), as well as the lyrical, humorous collections *Cincoenta homes por dez reás* (Fifty Men by Ten Lines), *Galicia mártir*, and *Atila en Galicia*, and his most admired literary work, *Cousas da vida* (Things of Life). Other prose compositions include the strange, original, macabre tale *Un ollo de vidro* (1920; The Glass Eye), the short story collection *Retrincos* (1934; Bits and Pieces), and the novel *Os dous de sempre* (1934; The Same Two). The literary works reflect Castelao's vocation as a cartoonist, as his characters tend to be caricatures, with the whole drawn rapidly and with large brush strokes.

BIBLIOGRAPHY

Primary Texts

*Cousas da morte antoloxia.* Vigo: Castrelos, 1973.
*Cousas da vida II.* Vigo: Galaxia, 1962.
*Cuatro obras: teatro, relatos, fantasía macabra, ensayos.* Spanish tr., study S. Alonso Montero. Madrid: Cátedra, 1974.
*Un ollo de vidrio.* Vigo: Galaxia, 1964.
*Retrincos.* 2nd ed. Madrid: "Celta," 1961.

                                                                                        Janet Pérez


**CASTELAR, Emilio** (1832, Cádiz–1899, San Pedro del Pinatar, Murcia), essayist, novelist, orator. Professor of Spanish history at the U of Madrid beginning in 1858, Castelar was one of the great Republican statesmen and orators of the first Spanish republic (1873), and he remained faithful to his republican principles throughout his political career. Never a radical or revolutionary, he espoused a liberal and moderate form of republicanism. He was also a prolific writer, contributing to many European and American newspapers and magazines, and producing all manner of books during his daily eight- to ten-hour writing stints. Castelar was, as *Azorín and others have observed, one of the outstanding European figures of his time and was perhaps more appreciated abroad than in his own country.

His works, informative and free-flowing, are of a historical-philosophical bent, with a tendency to generalize and to introduce flowery figures of rhetoric. His, however, is not an intellectually rigorous mind, it must be admitted. Representative of his studies are *La civilización en los cinco primeros siglos del cristianismo* (1859; Civilization during the First Five Centuries of Christianity), *La fórmula del progreso* (1867; The Formula for Progress), *Tragedias de la historia* (1881; Tragedies of History), *Galería histórica de mujeres célebres* (1888–89; A Historical Gallery of Celebrated Women), and *La revolución religiosa* (1880–83; The Religious Revolution). He also wrote novels: *La hermana de la caridad* (1857; Sister of Charity), *El suspiro del moro* (1885; The Moor's Sigh), *Nerón* (1891; Nero), and *Fra Filippo Lippi* (1877); and personal reminiscences: *Recuerdos de Italia* (1875; Memories of Italy), *Un año en París* (1876; A Year in Paris), and *Autobiografía* (1922; Autobiography). And of course, there are volumes and volumes of discourses, for which he is justly renowned; see, for example, *Discursos y ensayos*, ed. J. García Mercadal (1964) and *Discursos parlamentarios*, ed. Carmen Llorca (1973).

A man of vast, multifaceted culture and refined sensibility, Castelar waxed enthusiastic quickly, a trait which his tender and benevolent nature transposed into a lyrical and too often verbose prose style, akin to *Zorrilla's. His undisciplined mind was easily influenced by such writers as Hegel, Victor Hugo, Michelet, Renan, Quinet, Girardin, Strada, and *Clarín. But he was a pre-eminent disseminator of European ideas, of the swirl and mix of intellectual and political currents of his times. His republicanism is streaked with a vague though authentic religious spirit, hardly orthodox but consistent throughout, and a very real patriotism, a passion for his country.

Everything is molded to the oratorical flow in his prose style. Eloquent and musical in tone and rhythm, he penned extremely long paragraphs, replete with such rhetorical devices as enumeration, repetition, antithesis, and comparisons. This blown-up though harmonious style evidences a marvelous plasticity of imagery and a euphoniousness of sound. Here is a well-known example of Castelar's ample, flexible, and musically fluid prose, taken from an 1869 speech in which he defended the principle of religious freedom:

> Great is the God of Sinai; thunder precedes him, lightning accompanies him, light envelops him, the earth trembles, mountains break apart; but there is an even greater God, who is not the majestic God of Sinai, but the humble God of Calvary, nailed to the cross, wounded, taut, crowned with thorns, the bile of betrayal on his lips, and yet withal, saying: "Father, forgive them, forgive my executioners, forgive my persecutors, for they know not what they do!" Great is the religion of power, but greater is the religion of love; great is the religion of implacable justice, but greater is the religion of merciful forgiveness; and I, in the name of that religion; I, in the name of the Holy Gospel, I come here today to ask you to write at the head of your code, the words, religious freedom, that is, freedom, fraternity, equality among all men.

His carefully constructed sentences—he apparently rarely improvised—with their romantic undertones, finely tuned resonances, and deliberate climaxes, anticipate in some ways the modernism of Rubén Darío. *See also* Essay.

BIBLIOGRAPHY

Primary Texts

*Un año en París*. Madrid: El Globo, 1875.
*Discursos parlamentarios*. Ed. Carmen Llorca. Madrid: Narcea, 1973.
*Discursos. Recuerdos de Italia. Ensayos*. Ed. Arturo Souto Alabarce. México: Porrúa, 1980.
*La hermana de la caridad*. Buenos Aires: Sopena Argentina, 1943.
*Obras escogidas*. 12 vols. Madrid: Gráfica Universal/ A. de San Martín, 1922–23.

English Translations

*Life of Lord Byron, and Other Sketches*. Tr. Mrs. Arthur Arnold. New York: Harper, 1876. (*Vida de Lord Byron*)

*Old Rome and New Italy.* Tr. Mrs. Arthur Arnold. New York: Harper, 1873. (*Recuerdos de Italia*)
*The Republican Movement in Europe.* Tr. John Hay. New York: n.p., 1872–75. (*Historia del movimiento republicano en Europa*)
Criticism
Jarnés, Benjamín. *Castelar, hombre del Sinaí.* Madrid: Espasa-Calpe, 1935.
Llorca, Carmen. *Castelar, precursor de la democracia cristiana.* Madrid: Biblioteca Nueva, 1966.
Martínez Ruiz, José (Azorín). *De Valera a Miró.* Madrid: Aguado, 1959. 53–144.
Picón, Jacinto Octavio. *Discursos leídos ante la Real Academia Española.* Madrid: Fortanet, 1900.

Noël M. Valis

**CASTELLANOS, Juan de** (1522, Alanís, Seville–1607, Tunja, Colombia), soldier, priest, and writer. After traveling through much of the New World as a soldier, he became a priest at age thirty-seven. In 1589 he published the poem *Elegías de varones ilustres de Indias* (Elegies of Illustrious Men of the Indies), which, with almost 150,000 verses, is the longest epic poem in Castilian. It is of mediocre poetic worth but great, wide-ranging historical and philological value. The *Elegía VI*, for example, is the first poem about Puerto Rico ever written; M. T. Babín equates it with the *Cantar de mio Cid* in terms of its historical meaning to Puerto Rico. Castellanos also wrote the *Discurso del Draque* (n.d., Drake's Discourse), of equal historical merit.

BIBLIOGRAPHY
Primary Texts
*Discurso del Draque.* Ed. González Palencia. N.p.: n.p., 1921.
*Elegías.* In BAE 4.
*Obras.* Ed., intro., C. Parra. 2 vols. Caracas: Suramérica, 1930–32.
*Obras.* Ed., prol. M. A. Caro. 4 vols. Bogota: ABC, 1955.
*Juan de Castellanos. "Elegías de varones ilustres de Indias."* Ed., study I. J. Pardo. Caracas: Italográfica, 1962.

English Translation
*Elegía a la muerte de Juan Ponce de León.* Study, M. T. Babín. English tr. M. Lee. Puerto Rico: Instituto de Cultura Puertorriqueña, 1967.

Criticism
Rojas, U. *El Beneficiado d. Juan de Castellanos Cronista de Columbia y Venezuela.* Tunja: Biblioteca de Autores Boyacenses, 1958.
Romero, M. G. *Juan de Castellanos: un examen de su vida y de su obra.* Bogota: n.p., 1964.

**CASTELLANOS Y VELASCO, Julián.** *See* Escamilla, Pedro

**CASTELLET, José María** (1926, Barcelona– ), Catalan essayist and editor. An eminent figure in Castilian and Catalan criticism, Castellet is best known for his study of the contemporary Spanish novel, *La hora del lector* (1957; The

Moment of the Reader), and several major anthologies of poetry. In *Veinte años de poesía española, 1939–1959* (1960; Twenty Years of Spanish Poetry; published in 1966 as *Un cuarto de siglo de poesía española, 1939–1964*; A Quarter-Century of Spanish Poetry), he approached the poetry of the post–Civil War period from a modified Marxian perspective. A significant controversy resulted when a second anthology, *Nueve novísimos poetas españoles* (1970; Nine Very New Spanish Poets), announced the end of social or testimonial poetry and predicted a more elitist trend for the 1970s. He has published several anthologies of Catalan poetry including *Poesía catalana del segle XX* (1963; Twentieth-Century Catalan Poetry) and, in collaboration with Joaquim Molas, *Antología general de la poesía catalana* (1979; General Anthology of Catalan Poetry). *See also* Catalan Literature.

BIBLIOGRAPHY

Primary Texts

*Antología general de la poesía catalana.* Ed. J. M. Castellet and Joaquim Molas. Barcelona: Edicions 62, 1979.
*La hora del lector.* Barcelona: Seix Barral, 1957.
*Nueve novísimos poetas españoles.* Barcelona: Barral, 1970.
*Un cuarto de siglo de poesía española, 1939–1964.* Barcelona: Seix Barral, 1973.
*Veinte años de poesía española, 1939–1959.* Barcelona: Seix Barral, 1962.

Criticism

Broch, A. "Analisi i evolucio de l'obra critica de José María Castellet Segona etapa: 'El realisme historic 1958–1968.' " *Taula de Canvi* 11 (1978): 93–116.
Cerda, Jordi Pere. "Sur l'essai de Castellet et Joaquim Molas: 'Poesie catalane du vingtieme siecle.' " *La litterature catalane. Europe* 464 (1967): 46–49.
Oliver, M. A. "J. M. Castellet, lector ingenu." *Serra d'Or* 229 (1978): 35–39.

                                                                Kay Pritchett

**CASTIGLIONE, Baldassare** (1478, Casatico, Mantua–1529, Toledo), Italian author, diplomat and soldier. He was one of the pivotal figures of the Italian Renaissance. His renowned *Libro del Cortegiano* (1528; *The Book of the Courtier*, 1967) is one of the most influential productions of the *Renaissance. It helped diffuse Italian *humanism throughout all of Europe and influenced profoundly the concept of what a gentleman should be.

Castiglione was an apostolic nuncio to Spain from 1525 until his death. The Emperor Charles V, who admired Castiglione and had great trust in his knightly expertness, honored him with the grant of the diocese of Ávila.

Castiglione's lyrics, in Latin and Italian, reveal him as a sensitive and talented poet. His diplomatic reports and his letters constitute important historical documents. However, Castiglione's great monument is his *Book of the Courtier*, a work of high literary merit which presents a philosophy of life as well. The work, in four books, is a treatise in dialogue form on the training and function of the court gentleman. In refined and elegant prose spiced with humor, the speakers, prominent nobles and literati in the court of Urbino (the Duchess

Elizabetta Gonzaga, Emilia Pia, Giuliano de Medici, Ludovico da Canossa, Pietro Bembo, Bernardo Bibbiena and others), describe the ideal courtier. He should be nobly born; well-versed in classical and modern languages, painting and music; skilled in military arts, sports and dancing; and gracious in conversation. An immediate success, *The Book of the Courtier* was a major influence on Spanish culture, literature and ideas. Spanish was, in fact, the first foreign language into which it was translated, by Juan *Boscán, who published it in 1534. *See also* Humanism; Italian literary influences.

BIBLIOGRAPHY

Primary Texts

*El Cortesano.* Tr. into Spanish by Juan Boscán. Intro. Marcelino Menéndez Pelayo. Ed., notes, A. González Palencia. RFE Anejo 25. Madrid: Aguirre, 1942.
*Il Libro del Cortegiano, con una scélta delle opere minori.* Ed., intro., and notes by Bruno Maier. Torino: Unione Tipogràfico-Editrice Torinese, 1955.

English Translation

*The Book of the Courtier.* Tr., intro. George Bull. Baltimore: Penguin, 1967.

Criticism

Croce, Benedetto. *La Spagna nella vita italiana durante la Rinascenza.* Bari: Laterza, 1949.
Hanning, Robert W., and David Rosand, ed. *Castiglione: The Ideal and the Real in Renaissance Culture.* New Haven: Yale UP, 1983.
Mades, Leonard. *The Armor and the Brocade: A Study of Don Quixote and the Courtier.* New York: Las Américas, 1968.
Morreale, Margherita. *Castiglione y Boscán: El ideal cortesano en el Renacimiento.* 2 vols. BRAE 1. Madrid: Aguirre, 1959.
Woodhouse, J. R. *Baldesar Castiglione: A Reassessment of "The Courtier."* Edinburgh: Edinburgh UP, 1978.

Hector Medina

*CASTIGOS E DOCUMENTOS.* Complete title: *Castigos e documentos para bien vivir ordenados por el rey don Sancho IV* (Teachings and Treatises for Right Living Arranged by King Sancho IV), a collection of moral advice, sermons and stories about allegorical or miraculous events, all with didactic intent, derived from Latin sources—both pagan and Christian—and from traditional vernacular works. Although the ms. now in the Escorial Library states that Sancho IV composed the *Castigos* for his son between 1292 and 1293, some modern scholars do not accept this as fact. *See also* Edad Media, Literatura de la.

BIBLIOGRAPHY

Primary Text

*Castigos e documentos para bien vivir ordenados por el Rey Don Sancho IV.* Ed. A. Rey. Bloomington: Indiana UP, 1952.

Criticism

Keller, J. E., and R. P. Kinkade. *Iconography in Medieval Spanish Literature*. Lexington:
U of Kentucky P, 1984. 52–59.

James Ray Green

**CASTILLA DEL PINO, Carlos** (1922, Córdoba– ), Spanish psychiatrist, popular essayist and sociologist. Castilla works especially in the area of interface between sociology and psychiatry, both in the popular arena via the periodical press, and in professionally oriented monographs. In the tradition of *Ortega y Gasset, he uses the newspapers as a forum for educating the populace on a variety of issues; as did Karl Marx in early writings, he also utilizes his essays to acquaint readers with aspects of socialist ideology. Among his significant titles destined for specialized audiences are *Un estudio sobre la depresión: fundamentos de antropología dialéctica* (1966; A Study of Depression: Fundamentals of Dialectical Anthropology) and *La culpa* (1968; Guilt). By dialectical anthropology is meant primarily the understanding of mental and emotional problems within a specific social context; thus, depression and guilt, for example, would be analyzed and explained within the precise social circumstances in which they occur. *Psicoanálisis y marxismo* (1969; Psychoanalysis and Marxism) carries the same principles a step further, seeing alienation and most neurotic behavior as sociogenic. Castilla has also written an autobiographical novel, *Discurso de Onofre* (1977; Discourse of Onofre). *See also* Essay.

BIBLIOGRAPHY

Primary Texts

*La culpa*. Madrid: RO, 1968.
*La cultura bajo el franquismo*. Barcelona: Anagrama, 1977.
*Discurso de Onofre*. Barcelona: Peninsula, 1977.
*Un estudio sobre la depresión*. 7th ed. Barcelona: Península, 1974.
*Psicoanálisis y marxismo*. Madrid: Alianza, 1969.

Janet Pérez

**CASTILLEJO, Cristóbal de** (1492?, Ciudad Rodrigo–1550, Vienna), poet. At fifteen he began serving at the court of Ferdinand and Isabella, as page to the Archduke Ferdinand, brother of Charles V. Sometime after 1515 he entered the Cistercian order but left the monastery in 1525 to become secretary to Ferdinand, then king of Bohemia and later of Hungary. His life in Vienna was characterized by the meagerness of his salary, scarcely augmented by a small pension from Charles V, and by his casual attitude toward his religious vows. He wrote love lyrics to a number of women, most notably the young Anna von Schaumburg. Only two of Castillejo's works were published during his lifetime: the burlesque *Sermón de amores* (1542; Sermon on Love), similar to the *Libro de buen amor* (*Arcipreste de Hita) in its comic approach to the topic; and *Diálogo de las condiciones de las mugeres* (1544; Dialogue on the Qualities of Women), less harshly misogynistic than the medieval *Corbacho* (*Arcipreste de Talavera). Both poems by Castillejo were censored by the *Inquisition, even changing the title of the *Sermón* to *Capítulo* (Chapter or Treatise).

Although Castillejo is best known for his "nationalist" or traditionalist opposition to the Italianate meters and stylistic innovations of *Boscán and *Garcilaso de la Vega, his only direct attack is *Contra los que dexan los metros castellanos y siguen los italianos* (Against Those Who Leave Castilian Meters and Follow the Italian Ones), a series of poems in Castilian and Italian meters, including sonnets, meant to demonstrate the superiority of the former and mildly ridicule the latter. Rather than engage in polemics, he demonstrated the lively flexibility and spontaneity of octosyllabic verse in his compositions. He found the new style ponderously serious and premeditated, and defended the *cancionero* style as appropriate for emotional expression and conceptual wit. Cast in *pie quebrado* (octosyllables alternating with a tetrasyllable every fifth line), his *Canto de Polifemo* (Song of Polyphemus) is an earthy translation from Ovid that displays the colloquial vitality of traditional Castilian poetry. As José F. Montesinos pointed out in his 1935 edition of the poem, "Castillejo could not imagine the Ovidian Cyclops without making him a Castilian shepherd or goatherd, and his vocabulary gives legitimacy to this vision." Other translations from Latin, such as Catullus's "Dame basia mille" (Kiss me a thousand times), the "Fábula de Acteón, traducida de Ovidio, moralizada" (Myth of Actaeon, translated from Ovid and moralized), and the "Historia de Píramo y Tisbe, traducida de Ovidio" (Myth of Pyramus and Thisbe), dedicated to Anna von Schaumburg, have a similar quality. The division between the traditional, essentially oral, *cancionero* style and the Italianate innovations, conducive to self-conscious composition of written texts, is not a definitive one, and medieval elements continue throughout Spanish *Renaissance poetry. Castillejo, whose love lyrics are strongly reminiscent of the *cancionero* poets', represents the peculiarly medieval currents of conceptual wit, moralizing and misogyny while his translations "paganize the octosyllable," as Rafael Lapesa observed. The edition of his poetry published in 1573 was censored by the Inquisition. It is divided into *Obras de amores* (Love Poetry), *Obras de conversación y pasatiempo* (Topical Poetry; glosses of ballads, and the "Dialogue between the Author and His Pen"), and *Obras morales y de devoción* (Moral and Devotional Poetry, the Dialogues between Truth and Flattery and between Memory and Oblivion). Except for a few fragments, his dramatic works have been lost. *See also* Italian literary influences.

## BIBLIOGRAPHY

### Primary Text

*Obras completas.* Ed. J. Domínguez Bordona. Clásicos Castellanos 72, 77, 88, 91. Madrid: Espasa-Calpe, 1926–28.

### Criticism

Chevalier, Maxime. "Castillejo, poète de la Renaissance." *Travaux de l'Institut d'Études Ibériques et Latino-américaines* (Strasbourg) 15 (1975): 57–63.

Cinti, Bruna. "Erasmismo e idee letterarie in Cristóbal de Castillejo." *Annali di Ca' Foscari* 3 (1964): 65–80.
Foulché-Delbosc, R. "Deux oeuvres de Cristóbal de Castillejo." *RH* 36 (1916): 489–620.
Lapesa, Rafael. "Poesía de cancionero y poesía italianizante." In *De la Edad Media a nuestros días*. Madrid: Gredos, 1967. 145–71.
Nicolay, Clara Leonor. *Life and Works of Cristóbal de Castillejo*. Philadelphia: U of Pennsylvania, 1910.

Emilie Bergmann

**CASTILLO PUCHE, José Luis** (1919, Yecla, Murcia– ), novelist, journalist and essayist. Castillo Puche first became known with a volume about [Pío] *Baroja, *Memoria íntimas de Aviraneta* (1952; The Intimate Memoirs of Aviraneta [a Baroja character and alter ego]). The protagonist of *Con la muerte al hombro* (1953; With Death on Your Back), his first novel to be published, is an invalid (as much spiritually as physically), filled with psychological unrest, which is aggravated by the gloomy shadow of his native village. The anguished life and strange personality of the protagonist serve to link past and present. *Sin camino* (1956; Without a Road), his second novel, the story of a religious vocation beset by worldly temptation, was followed in the same year by *El vengador* (The Avenger), the drama of those who return from the war soul-sick with the thirst for revenge, a noble attempt to treat fairly the tragic division of Spaniards in the Civil War. *Hicieron partes* (1957; They Divided the Spoils) was awarded the Laurel Prize for Catholic novels in the year of its appearance, and the following year received the coveted National Literary Prize "Miguel de Cervantes." *Hicieron partes* provides an illustration of the saying that money is the root of evil via the history of six humble families which are disrupted and come to hate each other because of a large inheritance. Money for them is not a solution, but the destruction of their small world as diabolical interests enter the picture.

*Misión en Estambul* (1958; Mission in Istanbul) is an early variant of the spy thriller. Castillo Puche began to travel extensively, and published travel books such as *América de cabo a rabo* (1959; America from Head to Tail) and *El Congo estrena libertad* (1961; The Congo Gains Freedom). *Paralelo 40* presents a description of the American neighborhood in the "new" Madrid, inhabited primarily by families of men at the Torrejón air base, contrasting their lifestyle with the surrounding poverty. *Jeremías el anarquista* (Jeremiah the Anarchist) is a stark denunciation of social and political inequities, while *Como ovejas al matadero* (1971; Like Sheep to the Slaughter) returns to the problem of the priest and the intimate human and personal conflicts of those consecrated to a religious life but torn by human needs (an obsessive theme with Castillo Puche and one with some autobiographical substrata, since he himself left the seminary). It is the first volume of a projected trilogy entitled *El cíngulo* (The Priest's Girdle).

Castillo Puche is a devotee of Hemingway and frequented his company when Hemingway lived in Madrid. Castillo Puche has published a number of essays on the American writer's impact in Spain, as well as a biography, *Hemingway entre la vida y la muerte* (1968; Hemingway between Life and Death).

Many of Castillo Puche's novels are set in Hécula (the fictional counterpart of his native Yecla), a symbolic village of La Mancha, halfway between the gardens of Valencia and the aridity of the Castilian high plains. His so-called trilogy of liberation includes *El libro de las visiones y las apariciones* (1977; The Book of Visions and Apparitions); *El amargo sabor de la retama* (1979; The Bitter Taste of Broom) and *Conocerás el poso de la nada* (1982; You Will Know the Dregs of Nothingness), all set in Hécula and emphasizing its religious fanaticism, obscurantism and hypocrisy. The novel is a denunciation of rigid social and educational schemes and their repression of individual needs and expression. In its sequel, the same world appears, mixed with memories of a cruel adolescence, at once rebellious and submissive. The cycle as a whole is a sort of *bildungsroman*, the protagonist's search for personal freedom and a catharsis which will break the hold of a childhood and youth marked by ignorance, oppression and fanaticism. In the final novel of the trilogy, a clean break comes, symbolized by the death of the protagonist's mother. *See also* Essay.

BIBLIOGRAPHY

Primary Texts

*El amargo sabor de la retama*. Barcelona: Destino, 1979.
*Como ovejas al matadero*. Barcelona: Destino, 1971.
*Con la muerte al hombro*. 3rd ed. Barcelona: Destino, 1972.
*Conocerás el poso de la nada*. Barcelona: Destino, 1982.
*Hicieron partes*. 2nd ed. Barcelona: Destino, 1967.
*El libro de las visiones y las apariciones*. Barcelona: Destino, 1977.
*Sin camino*. 2nd ed. Barcelona: Destino, 1983.
*El vengador*. 2nd ed. Barcelona: Destino, 1960.

                                                                        Janet Pérez

**CASTILLO SOLÓRZANO, Alonso de** (1584, Tordesillas, Valladolid–1648, ?), prolific writer. His father was chamberlain to the Duke of Alba. Although his novels contain detailed descriptions of student life, it is unknown whether he was a student. By 1619, he was already active in the literary life of Madrid. As majordomo for the Marquis de los Vélez, Castillo Solórzano traveled to and lived in Valencia during the latter's viceroyalty. Upon the death of the marquis, Castillo continued in the service of his son and successor, viceroy of Aragon and ambassador to Rome, traveling with him.

Castillo Solórzano's fame was established with the rise of the short novel in the seventeenth c. Author of fifty-four short novellas, he is the most prolific novelist of the century. His works fall into two general categories: the *novela cortesana,* or courtesan novel, constructed around a love intrigue, and the *pic-aresque novel, reflecting the decline of society into appearances. *Tardes entretenidas* (1625; Pleasant Evenings) is the title given to a collection of six novels, constructed rather like the *Decameron;* the theme is love and the myriad variations and adventures it inspires. *Las harpías en Madrid* (1631; The Harpies of Madrid) was his first separate picaresque work, featuring a group of female tricksters. The female rogue also stars in *La niña de los embustes, Teresa de Manzanares* (1632; The Child of Hoaxes, Theresa of Manzanares), and in *El bachiller Trapaza* (1634?; The Bachelor Trapaza) and its continuation, *La garduña de Sevilla y anzuelo de las bolsas* (1634?; *Spanish Amusements or the Adventures of That Celebrated Courtezan Seniora Rufina*, 1727). These works became best-sellers. Castillo Solórzano also wrote five interludes and seven plays, including an adaptation of his novel *Los alivios de Casandra*, as well as *entremeses which he integrated into his novels (e.g., *La castañera, El casamentero, La prueba de los doctores* [The Chestnut Ventor, The Go-Between, The Test of the Doctors]). His *Sagrario de Valencia* (1635; Sacrarium of Valencia) detailed the lives of saints from that kingdom. Lope de *Vega praised Castillo Solórzano's talent in the *Laurel de Apolo*.

## BIBLIOGRAPHY

### Primary Texts

*Alonso de Castillo Solórzano's "Sala de recreación."* Eds. R. F. Glenn and F. G. Very. Chapel Hill/Madrid: Castalia, 1977.

*Aventura del bachiller Trapaza.* Madrid: Cátedra, 1986.

*Fiestas del jardín; que contienen tres comedias, y cuatro novelas.* Hildesheim: G. Olms, 1973.

*La garduña de Sevilla y anzuelo de las bolsas.* Madrid: Espasa-Calpe, 1972.

*Las harpías en Madrid.* Madrid: Castalia, 1985.

*Jornadas alegres.* Madrid: Librería de los bibliófilos españoles, 1909.

*La niña de los embustes, Teresa de Manzanares, natural de Madrid.* Mexico: Aguilar, 1964.

### English Translations

*La pícara, or the triumphs of a female subtelty display'd in the impostures of a beautiful woman.* Tr. John Davies. London: W. W., 1665. Microfilm: U Microfilms, 1964.

*Spanish Amusements, or the Adventures of That Celebrated Courtezan Seniora Rufina call'd the poet-cat of Seville. Being a detection of the articles used by such of the fair sex, as aimed more at thy purses than at the hearts of their admirers.* In six novels. 2nd ed. London: Curll, 1727 & 1741.

### Criticism

Armistead, S. G., and J. H. Silverman. "Una variación antigua del romance de Tarquino y Lucrecia." *Thesaurus* 33 (1978): 122–67.

Bernadach, Moise. "Castillo Solórzano et ses fantaisies prosodiques (a propos d'une ingénieuse utilisation des romances)." *Revue des langues romanes* 80 (1972): 149–75.

Dunn, Peter. *Castillo Solórzano and the Decline of the Spanish Novel.* Oxford: Blackwell, 1952.

García Gómez, E. "Boccaccio y Castillo y Solórzano." *RFE* 15 (1928): 376–78.

Soons, A. *Alonso de Castillo Solórzano*. TWAS 457. Boston: Twayne, 1977. Includes tr. of poetry.

Andrea Warren Hamos

**CASTRESANA, Luis de** (1925, Bilbao– ), journalist and novelist. Castresana has published a biography of Dostoyevski and several novels, including *Gente en el hotel* (People in the Hotel); *Un puñado de tierra* (1958; A Handful of Earth); and *La muerte viaja sola* (1953?; Death Travels Alone). Pío *Baroja furnished the prologue for a collection of Castresana stories entitled *Cuentos del dolor de vivir* (Tales of the Pain of Living).

BIBLIOGRAPHY

Primary Texts

*La muerte viaja sola*. Madrid: La Nave, 1955
*Obras selectas de Luis de Castresana*. 5 vols. Bilbao: Enciclopedia Vasca, 1968–71.
*El otro árbol de Guérnica*. Ed., intro., L. Hickey. London: Harrap, 1972. Intro., and notes in English.
*Un puñado de tierra*. Barcelona: Caralt, 1953.

English Translation

*The Sower*. Tr. M. David. London: Four Square, 1961.

**CASTRO, Carmen** (1911, Madrid– ), essayist. A doctor of philosophy and letters, she wrote a dissertation entitled *Los personajes femeninos en la obra de Cervantes* (Feminine Characters in the Work of Cervantes). She is the daughter of the historian, philologist and essayist Américo *Castro, and the wife of philosopher Xavier *Zubiri. She is known for her essays on Proust, especially *Marcel Proust o el vivir escribiendo* (1952; Marcel Proust or, A Life of Writing).

BIBLIOGRAPHY

Primary Text

*Marcel Proust o el vivir escribiendo*. Madrid: RO, 1952.

Janet Pérez

**CASTRO, Cristóbal de** (1878, Iznajar, Córdoba–?, ?), poet, journalist. A modernist poet, he published in 1903 *Cancionero galante* (Gallant Songbook) and *El amor que pasa* (Love Which Passes). He also collaborated with *López Alarcón on the dramatic poem *Gerineldo* (1908). Among his novels, special mention is due *La interina* (1921; The Replacement). His journalistic activities, for which he is best known, appeared in leading Madrid papers; they reveal an uninterrupted contact with the literary world in their critiques.

BIBLIOGRAPHY

Primary Texts

*El amor que pasa*. Madrid: Romero, 1903.
*Cancionero galante*. Paris: n.p., 1903.

*Gerineldo.* Madrid: Sociedad de Autores Españoles, 1909.
*La interina.* Madrid: Sanz Calleja, n.d.

Isabel McSpadden

**CASTRO, Ernesto Manuel de Melo e** (1923, Lisbon?– ), Portuguese poet and critic. In collaboration with Maria Alberta Meneres, Castro published a most significant *Antologia da Novíssima Poesia Portuguesa* (1961; Anthology of the Newest Portuguese Poetry). This group of experimental poets displays a wide variety of influences, operative in the case of Castro as well, ranging from the mathematical combinations of Max Bense and the Stuttgart school, Mallarmé's reflections upon the importance of graphic space, Pound's efforts to assimilate archaic ideographic writing with Oriental phonetic writing, the studies of Empson on poetic ambiguity and Umberto Eco's concept of the "open" work to the theories of Brazilian *concretismo* (concrete poetry). A collective manifesto by a group including Castro, M. S. Lourenço, Gastão Cruz and Antonio Ramos Rosa appeared in *Poesia 61*, with Castro authoring *A Proposição 2.01* (1961; Proposition 2.01). Other collective publications of this group are found in *Poesia e Tempo* (1962; Poetry and Time), and the series *Pedras Brancas* (White Stones) begun in 1961. Castro's own publications include *Entre o som y o sul* (1960; Between Sleep and the South), *Queda Livre* (1961; Remaining Free), *Ideogramas* (1962); and *Poligonia do Soneto* (1963; Polygon of the Sonnet). His works incorporate the interest of Portugal's poetic theorists in the scientific, mathematical and linguistic theorization of the Stuttgart school.

BIBLIOGRAPHY

Primary Texts

*Antología do conto fantástico portuguès.* 2nd ed. Lisbon: Afrodite, 1974.
*Contemporary Portuguese Poetry: An Anthology in English.* Ed., sel. H. Macedo and
    E. M. de Melo e Castro. Manchester; Carcanet, 1978.
*Ideogramas.* Lisbon: Guimaraes, 1962.
*Literatura portuguesa de invenção.* Sao Paolo: DIFEL, 1984.
*As palabras só-lidas.* Lisbon: Horizonte, n.d.
*Poligonia do Soneto.* Lisbon: Guimarães, 1963.
*A Proposição 2.01.* Lisbon: Ulisseia, 1965.

Janet Pérez

**CASTRO, Eugénio de** (1869, Coimbra–1944, Coimbra), Portuguese poet and dramatist. Castro lived most of his life in Coimbra, in whose university he taught Romance literature. His poetry collection, *Oaristos* (1890), which reveals his proximity to Mallarmé, features exquisitely polished, sonorous verse, varied forms and a virtuoso command of metrics. Castro is identified with a renewal of Portuguese poetry under the aegis of symbolism. The influence of Schopenhauer and Baudelaire infuses the volume of poetry *Horas, Silva, Interlunio* (1894; Horas, Blackberries, Dark of the Moon) and the drama *Belkiss* (1894), as well as the dramatic poem, *Sagramor* (1895), and the verse legend *Salome* (1896), all darkened by pessimism and anguish. *Constança* (1900) retells the tragic love of *Inés de Castro (see Inés de Castro, Leyenda de) and the crown prince, Dom Pedro, Portuguese literature's equivalent of Romeo and Juliet. A subsequent move in the direction of classicism is evident in several books of poetry published after the turn of the century: *Depois da ceifa* (1901; After the Reaping), *A Sombra do Quadrante* (1905; In the Shadow of the Quadrant), *A Fonte do Sátiro* (1908; Fountain of the Satyr), and the drama *O Anel de Polícrates* (1907; Polycrates's Lamb). Castro's professional specialization as a linguist is evident in his introduction (in *Camafeus Romanos* [1921; Roman Cameos]) of Latin themes in Portuguese poetry and his translations of Goethe (1909). Later works include *Cançoes desta negra vida* (1922; Songs of This Dark Life), *Cravos de papel* (1922; Paper Nails), *Descendo a encosta* (1924; Descending the Cliff), and *Chamas d'uma candeia velha* (1925; Flames of an Aged Candle).

BIBLIOGRAPHY

Primary Texts

*Cristalizações da Morte*. Lisbon: José Luís da Costa, 1884.
*Jesus de Nazaré*. Lisbon: Académica, 1885.
*Per Umbram*. Lisbon: Nacional, 1887.
*Os sete Dormentes*. Lisbon: n.p., 1895.
*A nereide de Harlém*. Lisbon: n.p., 1886.
*Obras poeticas*. 10 vols. Lisbon: Lumen, 1927–44.

Criticism

Fein, John M. "Eugenio de Castro and Modernism in Spain." *PMLA* 73 (1959): 556–61.

**CASTRO, Fernando Guillermo de** (1927, Madrid– ). He won the Café Gijón prize with his story "Las horas del día" (The Hours of the Day) and the Sésamo prize in 1958 with "Madrid, 1936." He has published other short stories, "El zapato" (The Shoe) and "Dos novelas de amor" (Two Love Stories) in 1958. He also wrote essays (*Baroja, historiador romántico*) and has collaborated regularly in newspapers and magazines.

Isabel McSpadden

**CASTRO, Guillén de** (1569, Valencia–1631, Madrid), playwright and poet. He is the best of the Valencian dramatists, and one of the most talented of Lope de *Vega's generation and school. We have no definite knowledge of the first twenty years of his life, but his career as a writer must have begun early for there are several references to him in the records of a literary society founded in 1591, the Academia de los Nocturnos (Academy of the Night Revelers; *Academia). The military profession also attracted him at an early age; in 1593 he was a cavalry officer in the coast guard, which was organized to protect Valencia against pirates. He was apparently involved in an unsavory romance some time before his marriage to doña Marquesa Girón de Rebolledo in 1595. His wife died a few years later. In 1607 Castro went to Italy and was appointed governor of Scigliano by the Count of Benavente, viceroy of the Kingdom of

Naples. By 1616 he was in Valencia, and there organized a literary society, Los montañeses del Parnaso (Dwellers of Mt. Parnassus), and became its president. In 1618, he left Valencia for Madrid and found a powerful patron, don Juan Téllez Girón, son of the Duke of Osuna. Castro took an active part in the city's literary life, marrying again in 1626. A friend of Lope de Vega, he was praised by Lope, *Cervantes, *Ruiz de Alarcón, Agustín de *Rojas, and many others.

Castro's plays span a wide range of subjects; his forty-three plays include those of character and customs, "sword and cape" dramas, historical and mythological works, plays of chivalry and romance, and dramas on biblical subjects and saints' lives. The usual motives of action are love, personal honor, loyalty, jealousy and envy. Plots are usually very complicated, and often are developed without great skill; in some the endings are abrupt and even illogical. His most famous plays are *Las mocedades del Cid* (1618; *The Youthful Deeds of the Cid*, 1969), and *Las hazañas del Cid* (1618; The Feats of the Cid), drawn from ballad cycles. *Las mocedades del Cid* revolves around the love between Rodrigo and Jimena, the violent separation of the lovers, and their ultimate marriage. Unlike the vast majority of Golden Age plays, the work does not have a *gracioso*. Nevertheless, as L. Mades points out, "it is a typical product of *Siglo de Oro* drama in that it draws upon national tradition, features the theme of honor, and exercises the technical liberties established by Lope." The play was Corneille's source for his *Le Cid* (1636). *Las hazañas del Cid* is overshadowed by its predecessor. Its central theme is the struggle between Sancho and Urraca for possession of Zamora and the efforts of the Castilian champion, Don Diego Ordóñez de Lara, to avenge the king's death. The title of the play is misleading since Rodrigo is no longer the central figure.

Other notable plays by Castro are two of character and customs; *Los malcasados de Valencia* (1618; The Ill-Mated Couples of Valencia), a bitter satire on married life, and *El Narciso en su opinión* (1625; The Self-Styled Narcissus), model for one of *Moreto's masterpieces (*El lindo en su opinión*); three plays based on Cervantine works, titled *Don Quijote de la Mancha* (1618), *La fuerza de la sangre* (1618; Kinship's Powerful Call), and *El curioso impertinente* (1618; Dangerous Curiosity); the powerful epic drama *El conde Alarcos* (1618; Count of Alarcos); two plays inspired by classical literature, *Progne y Filomena* (1618; Procne and Philomela) and *Dido y Eneas* (1625); and one provoking family tragedy, *El amor constante* (1608; Constant Love), which ends with a justification of tyrannicide. *See also* Cantar del Cid; Siglo de Oro; Theater in Spain.

BIBLIOGRAPHY

Primary Texts

*Obras de don Guillén de Castro y Bellvis.* Ed. E. Juliá Martínez. 3 vols. Madrid: RABM, 1925–27.
*Las mocedades del Cid.* In *Diez comedias del Siglo de Oro.* Ed. H. Alpern and J. Martel. Rev. L. Mades. New York: Harper and Row, 1968.

English Translation

*The Youthful Deeds of the Cid*. Tr. R. R. La Du, L. Soto-Ruiz, and G. A. Daeger. Intro., J. G. Weiger. New York: Exposition P, 1969.

Criticism

García Lorenzo, L. *El teatro de Guillén de Castro*. Barcelona: Planeta, 1976.

Wilson, W. E. *Guillén de Castro*. TWAS 253. New York: Twayne, 1973.

Hector Medina

**CASTRO, José María Ferreira de** (1898, Oliveira de Azemeis–1973, Lisbon), Portuguese novelist. Emigrating at the age of twelve to Belem at the mouth of the Amazon, he spent some four years working among the rubber harvesters, which provided the basis for his most famous and probably greatest novel, *A selva* (1930; *The Jungle*, 1935), translated into fourteen languages. Ferreira de Castro began his literary career in Belem with *O criminoso por ambição* (1916; Criminal through Ambition). Returning to Portugal in 1919, he settled in Lisbon where he became a free-lance journalist, with considerable hardship; days of privation and hunger undoubtedly strengthened his burgeoning sociological motivation and bent for social criticism. Between 1921 and 1928, he published numerous novels and short stories in addition to his articles and essays. *Emigrantes* (1928; *Emigrants*, 1962) is a socially conscious portrayal of Portuguese driven by poverty to seek their fortunes in Brazil—a narrative based, as is *The Jungle*, on the writer's own years along the Amazon. The jungle darkness, depredations of the hostile Indian tribes, fevers, insects and reptiles, exploitation by brutal management and perennial debt are depicted against vivid descriptions of the flora and fauna of the Amazon wilderness which at times becomes almost a protagonist.

Later novels include *Eternidade* (1933; Eternity), *Terra fria* (1934; Cold Highlands), *A tempestade* (1940; The Storm), and the more significant *A lã e a neve* (1947; The Wool and the Snow), which follows the fortunes of a shepherd who despairs of his life without a future, abandoning his pastoral existence to struggle as an apprentice and then a weaver in a spinning factory in Covilha. *A curva da estrada* (1950; The Bend in the Road) centers upon an aging Spanish socialist leader, corrupted by the struggle for power, as he struggles against human frailties, political disillusionment, and his own moral ambivalence to decide whether or not to abandon the party. *A missão* (1954; *The Mission*, 1963) contains three novellas, with the title tale referring to another battle of conscience (whether to identify a monastery by painting the name on its roof to protect it from bombing, while thus facilitating the identification of a neighboring factory as the desired target). *O instinto supremo* (1968; The Supreme Instinct), again set in Brazil, narrates an expedition which attempts to pacify and civilize a tribe of Parintintins Indians, against the backdrop of the Amazon jungle. Natural determinism and the theme of man's exploitation by his fellow man, rather than the exoticism of the jungle, dominate Ferreira de Castro's novels of Brazil. The numerous translations have made him one of Portugal's best-known writers of the twentieth c.

BIBLIOGRAPHY

Primary Texts

*Carne faminta.* Lisbon: n.p., 1922.
*O éxito fácil.* Lisbon: n.p., 1923.
*Ferreira de Castro A sua vida.* . . . Sel., intro. A. Salema. Lisbon: Europa-América, 1974.
*Obra completa.* 5 vols. Rio de Janeiro: Aguilar, 1958—.

English Translations

*Emigrants.* Tr. D. Ball. New York: Macmillan, 1962.
*Jungle, a Tale of the Amazon Rubber Tappers.* New York: Viking, 1935.
*The Mission.* Tr. A. Stevens. London: Hamilton, 1963.

                                                            Janet Pérez

**CASTRO, Rosalía de** (1837, Santiago de Compostela–1885, Padrón), Galician poet and novelist. Castro was the natural child of Teresa de Castro Abadía and José Martínez Viojo, a priest who therefore could not recognize his daughter. Various critics have pointed out that her illegitimacy may lie at the root of her view of life as desolate and hopeless. Brought up by her mother and her paternal aunts, she received little schooling as a child. She began writing poetry as a child and published her first volume of poems when she was twenty years old, *La flor* (1857; The Flower), which consists of six poems written in Castilian. In 1858 she married Manuel *Martínez Murguía, a noted critic and historian. Murguía destroyed his wife's letters to him before he died, leaving the nature of their relationship in the dark. They had seven children, two of whom died in infancy. She died of cancer in 1885; before her death she requested to have all her unpublished mss. burned.

Her first book of poetry, *La flor,* is romantic in tone and style; it was praised by Murguía, who claimed later not to have known his future wife when he wrote his review of her poetry. In 1863 she published two volumes of poetry, *A mi madre* (To My Mother), written on the death of her mother, and *Cantares gallegos* (Galician Songs), one of her most important works. *Cantares gallegos* was written while Castro was living in Castile and was inspired by her love and homesickness for her homeland. In it she glosses popular Galician songs and evokes the landscape, customs and people of Galicia with tender, nostalgic emotions in her native tongue. Other themes dealt with are the social injustices committed against Galicians, the plight of the laborers who must leave Galicia to work in Castile, and the typical holidays and pilgrimages of Galicia described in a more festive tone. *Follas novas* (1880; New Leaves), also written in Galician, is a more intimate and subjective volume which shows Castro's desolate view of human existence. This collection also contains compositions of a social character which deal with the problem of emigration from Galicia, the women abandoned by their husbands and their strength of spirit in the face of loneliness, hardships and suffering. *En las orillas del Sar* (1884; *Beside the River Sar,* 1937) was published a few months before her death and contains poetry written in Castilian years before the publication date. The verses in this collection are highly intimate evocations of her feelings of solitude, nostalgia, hopelessness and sorrow. The poet oscillates between her belief in God, her doubt of his existence and her feelings of despair. She seeks to reconcile her belief in God with the suffering of existence; she appears to need to believe in order to give meaning to her existence. Many of the ideas that she develops in her poetry foreshadow those of Antonio *Machado, *Unamuno and the existentialists. She uses flexible metrical combinations and original rhyme schemes; she avoids rigidly structured stanzas and favors assonance to consonant rhyme. She also wrote novels such as *La hija del mar* (1859; The Daughter of the Sea), a romantic novel which is interesting from a biographical point of view for the light it sheds on her attitudes; *Flavio* (1861), a study of two romantic characters; *Ruinas, Desdichas de tres vidas ejemplares* (1864; Ruins, Misfortunes of Three Exemplary Lives), which is made up of a group of *cuadros de costumbres* or scenes of local color; *El caballero de las botas azules* (1867; The Gentleman with the Blue Boots), her longest novel and considered her best by some critics; and *El primer loco* (1881; The First Madman), one of her better novels which explores the mysterious nature of love. All in all, she is best remembered for her poetry; her lyricism, sincerity, originality and lack of affectation place her alongside *Bécquer in nineteenth-c. Spanish poetry.

BIBLIOGRAPHY

Primary Texts

*El caballero de las botas azules (cuento extraño)*. Buenos Aires: Emecé, 1942.
*Obras completas*. Ed. V. García Martí. Madrid: Aguilar, 1952.
*El primer loco (cuento extraño)*. Madrid: Moya y Plaza, 1881.
*Ruinas*. Prol. Armando Cotarelo Valledor. La Coruña: Moret, 1928.

English Translation

*Beside the River Sar; Selected Poems from En las orillas del Sar*. Tr., annotations and preface by S. Griswold Morley. Berkeley: U of California P, 1937.

Criticism

*Actas do Congreso internacional de estudios sobre Rosalía de Castro e o seu tempo, I, II & III*. Santiago de Compostela, Spain: Consello da Cultura Galega, Universidad de Santiago de Compostela, 1986.
Alberto Robatto, Matilde. *Rosalía de Castro y la condición femenina*. Madrid: Partenon, 1984.
Alonso Montero, Jesús. *Rosalía de Castro*. Madrid: Júcar, 1972.
Azorín. *Clásicos y modernos*. Madrid: Renacimiento, 1913.
Cortina, A. Prologue to *Obra poética de Rosalía de Castro*. Buenos Aires: Espasa-Calpe, 1942.
Costa Clavell, Javier. *Rosalía de Castro*. Barcelona: Plaza y Janés, 1967.
Kulp, Kathleen K. *Manner and Mood in Rosalía de Castro: A Study of Themes and Style*. Madrid: Porrúa Turanzas, 1968.
Kulp-Hill, K. *Rosalía de Castro*. TWAS 446. Boston: Twayne, 1977.
Mayoral, Marina. *La poesía de Rosalía de Castro*. Madrid: Gredos, 1974.

Naya Pérez, Juan. *Inéditos de Rosalía*. Santiago: Publicaciones del Patronato de Castro, 1953.

Varela, José Luis. *Poesía y restauración cultural de Galicia en el siglo XIX*. Madrid: Gredos, 1958.

Phoebe Porter Medina

**CASTRO CALVO, José María** (1903, Zaragoza– ), professor of Spanish literature at the U of Barcelona. His academic career has been enhanced by his excellent edition of Don *Juan Manuel's *Libro de la caza*, and his edition of the works of Gertrudis *Gómez de Avellaneda for the *Biblioteca de Autores Españoles, vols. 272, 278–79, and 287–88.

Isabel McSpadden

**CASTRO QUESADA, Américo** (1885, Río de Janeiro–1972, Gerona, Spain), literary critic and historian. A distinguished and often controversial scholar, Américo Castro is best known for his work on *Cervantes, on the Islamic and Judaic elements of Spanish society and literature, and in historiography. He has been variously celebrated as the instigator of the renaissance in Hispanic studies in the United States in the latter half of the twentieth c. and decried as being obsessed with the Jewish and Arabic components (*converso) of Spanish history.

Castro was involved with Don Ramón *Menéndez Pidal in the Centro de Estudios Históricos from its foundation in 1910, and taught at the Universidad Central in Madrid from 1911 on, obtaining the chair in the history of the language in 1915. During his early years as a scholar, much of Castro's work was published in the *Revista de filología española* (Review of Spanish Philology), established in 1914 as the official organ of the Centro de Estudios Históricos. Until the beginning of the Civil War, Castro flourished in this ambience and traveled extensively in both Europe and the New World. His publications and scholarly interests during this period of time were primarily philological and literary. In 1925 he published *El pensamiento de Cervantes* (The Thought of Cervantes), considered by some to be his best work.

At the outbreak of the Civil War, Castro went to Argentina briefly and then to the United States, where he taught in Wisconsin, Texas, and finally at Princeton, where he was to remain until his retirement. His inaugural lecture, *The Meaning of Spanish Civilization*, signaled a new focus in his work: Spanish history and a radically new approach to it, distinguished primarily in the positive approach he took toward the non-Christian elements in Spanish society. Castro rapidly established himself as one of the major figures in Hispanic studies in the United States, and in 1948 he published *España en su historia (Cristianos, Moros y Judíos)* extensively revised and published as *La realidad histórica de España* and translated as *The Structure of Spanish History*. A "sequel" was published in English as *The Spaniards, An Introduction to Their History*. In these works, Castro develops his theory of what created the Spaniards and what constitutes "Spanishness," rejecting the previous popular notion that Spain and

Spaniards were Iberian, Roman and Visigothic and maintaining that it is not possible to speak of Spain until after 711. As the first modern historian to create a theory of Spanish history in which Muslims and Jews played a decisive and positive role and in which it was the *interaction* among the three castes of believers which produced the distinctive features of Spanish society, Castro earned himself many enemies, among them the historian *Sánchez-Albornoz and others to whom Castro's interpretation of Spanish Christianity and culture in a Semitic, rather than west European, context was anathema.

His success as a scholar and teacher who provided a dramatically different focus for Hispanic studies, and who was successful in cultivating a very eclectic group of Castristas, is well attested to in the 1965 *Collected Studies in Honour of Américo Castro's 80th year*. A succinct exposition of Castro's place in twentieth-c. historiography, and Spanish thought on its medieval heritage, may be found in chapter 10 of James Monroe's *Islam and the Arabs in Spanish Scholarship*. A selection of his essays which can serve as an introduction to the wide range of his scholarly interests is *An Idea of History, Selected Essays of Américo Castro*.

BIBLIOGRAPHY

Primary Texts

*España en su historia (Cristianos, Moros y Judíos)*. Buenos Aires: Losada, 1948; rev. and pub. as *La realidad histórica de España*. Mexico: Porrúa, 1954.
*El pensamiento de Cervantes*. Madrid: Centro de estudios históricos, 1925. 2nd ed., substantially rev., with updated bibliography. Ed. J. Rodríguez Puértolas. Barcelona: Noguer, 1971.
*Semblanzas y estudios españoles*. Princeton and Madrid: Ínsula, 1956. (Contains complete bibliography of Castro's work through 1955, including reviews thereof.)

English Translations

*An Idea of History, Selected Essays of Américo Castro*. Tr. and ed. Stephen Gilman and Edmund L. King. Columbus: Ohio State UP, 1977.
*The Meaning of Spanish Civilization*. Princeton: Princeton UP, 1940.
*The Spaniards, An Introduction to Their History*. Tr. Willard F. King and Selma Margaretten. Los Angeles: U of California P, 1971.
*The Structure of Spanish History*. Tr. Edmund L. King. Princeton: Princeton UP, 1954.

Criticism

*Collected Studies in Honour of Américo Castro's 80th Year*. Ed. M. P. Hornik. Oxford: Lincome Lodge Research Library, 1965.
Monroe, James. *Islam and the Arabs in Spanish Scholarship*. Leiden: Brill, 1970. (Ch. 10)

María Rosa Menocal

**CASTRO Y ROSSI, Adolfo de** (1823, Cádiz–1898, Cádiz), literary and historical scholar. The appearance of Castro's *Buscapié* (1848; *The Squib or Searchfoot*, 1849), a work attributed to *Cervantes, caused a tremendous uproar in literary circles not only in Spain, but in the rest of Europe as well. Castro pretended that the *Buscapié*, which contains 64 pages of text and 194 of notes, was a copy of an original ms. by Cervantes that he had found in a bookstore. The *Buscapié* was immediately translated into various European languages, and with his hoax Castro managed to deceive many scholars. Among those not taken in by the fake document were *Martínez Villergas, Ticknor and *Gallardo; the latter kept up a lively polemic with Castro. Castro responded to Gallardo's scathing condemnation of his literary hoax by writing a burlesque biography titled *Aventuras literarias del iracundo extremeño Don Bartolo Gallardete* (1851; Literary Adventures of the Irate Extremaduran Don Bartolo Gallardete). Although remembered for his *Buscapié*, Castro also engaged in literary work of a more serious nature. He edited numerous volumes of the *Biblioteca de Autores Españoles. His historical studies include a history of the Jews in Spain and another of the Spanish Protestants during the reign of Philip II.

BIBLIOGRAPHY

Primary Texts

*Aventuras literarias del iracundo extremeño Don Bartolo Gallardete.* Cádiz: Pantoja, 1851.
*El Buscapié. Opúsculo inédito que en defensa de la primera parte del ''Quijote'' escribió Miguel de Cervantes Saavedra. Publicado con notas históricas, críticas y bibliográficas por Don Adolfo de Castro.* Cádiz: Revista Médica, 1848.
*Curiosidades bibliográficas. Colección escogida de obras raras de amenidad y erudición con apuntes biográficos de los diferentes autores por don A. de Castro.* Madrid: Rivadeneyra, 1855.
*Poetas líricos de los siglos XVI y XVII.* Madrid: M. Rivadeneyra, 1854–57.

English Translations

*History of Religious Intolerance in Spain.* Tr. Thomas Parker. London: Cash, 1853.
*The History of the Jews in Spain.* Tr. Rev. Edward Kirwan. Cambridge, England: Deighton, 1851.
*The Spanish Protestants and Their Persecution by Phillip II.* Tr. Thomas Parker. London: C. Gilpin, 1851.
*The Squib or Searchfoot.* Cambridge, England: Deighton, 1849.

Phoebe Porter Medina

**CASTRO Y SERRANO, José de** (1829, Granada–1896, Madrid), novelist and essayist. He studied at Granada Seminar, was a member of the Cuerda granadina group and of the Spanish Academy (1899 *Academia Española). *La novela de Egipto; viaje imaginario a la apertura del Canal de Suez* (1870; The Novel of Egypt; Imaginary Trip to the Opening of the Suez Canal) is based on a series of letters written by Castro that appeared in the newspaper *La época*. Didacticisms and humor characterize his best writings, such as *El marido de la condesa* (1856; The Countess's Husband) and *La cura de los deseos* (1862; The Remedy of Desires).

*Historias vulgares* (1887; Ordinary Stories) constitutes a vivid and amusing testimony of daily life in the second half of the nineteenth c. Among the pieces included in this volume are "Antonio Sánchez," "Juan de Sidonia," "El frac azul" (The Blue Tuxedo), "El reloj de arena" (The Hourglass), etc.

BIBLIOGRAPHY

Primary Texts

*Cartas transcendentales escritas a un amigo de confianza.* Madrid: Fontanet, 1862–65.
*La cura de los deseos.* Madrid: Fontanet, 1862.
*Historias vulgares.* Madrid: Fontanet, 1887.
*La novela de Egipto; viaje imaginario a la apertura del Canal de Suez.* Madrid: Fontanet, 1870.

José Ortega

**CASTROVIEJO BLANCO-CICERÓN, Concha** (1912, Santiago de Compostela– ). A novelist, Concha Castroviejo studied at the university of her native city in addition to her study of French literature at the U of Bordeaux. From 1939 to 1950 she lived in Mexico, where she taught in the capital city, in Tijuana and at the U of Campeche. Upon her return to Spain she completed a course of study at the Official School of Journalism in Madrid and has since maintained an active journalistic career, publishing articles and criticism in both Spanish and foreign periodicals and winning a number of journalism prizes. Her first novel, *Los que se fueron* (1957; Those Who Went Away), follows a group of post–Civil War Spanish exiles to Paris and then to Mexico. The heroine, a widow with a young son, refuses to waste her time with other expatriates who sit around in cafés bemoaning the loss of their homeland. Refusing to marry a wealthy Mexican, she develops a successful career and gives up hope of returning to Spain, realizing that her son's future lies in Mexico. *Víspera del odio* (1959; Eve of Hate) is a psychological novel which received the Premio Elisenda de Montcada. The novel explores the development of a woman's hatred for her husband, but the Civil War provides the impetus for the narrative structure. Two themes are developed: the woman's sacrifice of herself and the safety of her illegitimate child for the sake of the lover, and the chaos of war as an excuse for personal vindictiveness and revenge by the cruel husband who represents the greed of the old order. Castroviejo has also published short stories and detective novels and is known for her children's books: *El jardín de las siete puertas* (1962; The Seven-Gated Garden), which won the Premio Doncel; *Los piratas* (1962; The Pirates); *El zopilote* (1962; The Vulture); and *Los días de Lina* (1971; Lina's Days).

Her works have been translated into Czech, English and French.

BIBLIOGRAPHY

Primary Texts

*Los días de Lina.* Madrid: Magisterio Español, 1971.
*El jardín de las siete puertas.* Madrid: Doncel, 1962.
*Los piratas.* Madrid: Doncel, 1962.
*Los que se fueron.* Barcelona: Planeta, 1957.

*Víspera del odio.* 2nd ed. Madrid: Círculo de Amigos de la Historia, 1970.
*El zopilote.* Madrid: Doncel, 1962.

Criticism

Domínguez Rey, A. "Concha Castroviejo." *La Estafeta Literaria* 528 (1973): 15–17.
Galerstein, C. "The Spanish Civil War: The View of Women Novelists." *Letras Femininas* 10.2 (Fall 1984): 12–18.

Carolyn Galerstein

**CASTROVIEJO Y BLANCO-CICERÓN, José María** (1909, Santiago de Compostela–1983, Vigo), Galician poet, essayist and prose writer. After graduating from the U of Santiago, Castroviejo studied in Lyon and became professor of political economics in Santiago, while also serving as adviser for cultural affairs to the Ministry of the Exterior. He also taught in Palermo, Italy. Editor of the newspaper *El Pueblo Gallego* (The Galician People), he received several prizes for his journalistic and creative work. His poetry has symbolist and avantgarde elements.

BIBLIOGRAPHY

Primary Texts

*Altura.* Vigo: Cartel, 1938 (poetry)
*La burla negra.* Madrid: EMESA, 1973.
*El Conde de Gondomar: un amor entre ocasos.* Madrid: Prensa Española, 1967.
*Los paisajes iluminados.* Barcelona: Destino, 1963
*El pálido visitante.* Santiago: Galí, 1960.
*Tempo de outono e outros poemas.* Vigo: Faro de Vigo, 1964.
*Las tribulaciones del cura de Noceda.* Barcelona: Taber 1970.
*Viajes por los montes y chimeneas de Galicia.* Madrid: Espasa-Calpe, 1962.

Criticism

Camino, T. del. "Estrena idioma." In *La Noche* (Santiago) Nov. 4, 1964.
Cunqueiro, Alvaro. "*Tempo de outono.*" In *Faro de Vigo* Oct. 2, 1964.

Kathleen March

**CATALÀ, Víctor,** pseudonym of Catarina Albert (1869, L'Escala–1966, L'Escala), novelist, poet and playwright. Her family belonged to the rural gentry. She spent most of her life in L'Escala, a small town on the Costa Brava. Autodidactic and rather shy, she began to write as a very young woman but was not known as a writer until 1898, when she received a prize at the Jocs Florals (Floral Games) of Olot with a prose monologue, *La infanticida* (Infanticide), and the poem *El llibre nou* (The New Book), both published in the same year. Her knowledge of French and Italian and her travels throughout Europe allowed her to acquire a vast culture. A woman of quiet and deep sensitivity, she started writing poetry and drama, but she is better remembered as one of the best Catalan prose writers of all times. She was one of the very few Catalan novelists who praised Narcís *Oller when the members of the literary movement called "modernisme" (*modernism) rejected him. Her work can be ascribed to rural naturalism, for she went beyond the picturesque and rural folklorism of the early Catalan romantics. In this respect Víctor Català's work is very similar to that of the Countess of *Pardo Bazán in Castilian literature. Her influences, however, are from the great master of the nineteenth-c. Catalan novel, Narcís Oller, and by association from the French writers of the same century, especially Émile Zola. In general, Català has a very dark and pessimistic view of the rural world; most characters of her novels are primitive, brutal and, above all, alienated and compelled by a fatalistic force to a tragic end. Nonetheless, in certain works, as in her best-known novel *Solitud* (1908; Solitude), some of the most notorious naturalistic characteristics (detailed descriptions, verisimilar material, fateful vision of life, etc.) are confronted with idealism (lyric prose, high and unselfish hopes, legends, mythical elements, etc.). Also, one can find a clear effort to achieve aesthetic beauty in her descriptions, as crude and terrible as they might be. Most important, Català, like her predecessor Oller, inserts into her work the everyday language of the common people. She is without a doubt the greatest prose writer of the first quarter of twentieth-c. Catalonia.

Aside from *Solitud*, she wrote a number of noteworthy novels and short stories: *Dramas rurals* (1902; Rural Dramas), *Ombrívoles* (1904; Shady Places), *Caires vius* (1908; Living Aspects). From 1907 until 1918, Català did not write anything at all, possibly resentful of the furious and unjust attacks by the modernist and "noucentistes" (twentieth-c. neoclassicists) on her literature and on herself personally since, according to them, a woman should not be permitted to write "crude" and "violent" art. Those were the years when—to the shock of the conservative literary mandarins—it was revealed that behind the famous pseudonym Víctor Català was a woman. In 1918 she tried an urban novel, *Un film (3.000 metres)* [A Film (3,000 meters)]. Finally, there appeared *La Mare balena* (1920; The Mother Whale), *Vida molta* (1950; A Lot of Life) and her last work *Jubileu* (1951; Jubilation). The last two books are collections of short stories. *See also* Catalan Literature; Naturalism.

BIBLIOGRAPHY

Primary Text

*Obres completes*. Barcelona: Selecta, 1951.

Criticism

Bloomquist, Gregori. "Notes per a una lectura de Solitud." *Els marges* 3 (1975): 104–7.

Capmany, M. A. "Els silencis de Catarina Albert." Epilogue to *Obres Completes*. Barcelona: Selecta, 1972.

Miracle, Josep. *Víctor Català*. Barcelona: n.p., 1963.

Oller i Rabassa, Joan. *Biografia de Víctor Català*. Barcelona: Dalmau, 1967.

Serrahima, M. *Víctor Català a Dotze mestres*. Barcelona: n.p., 1973.

Joan Gilabert

**CATALAN LITERATURE.** It is believed that the transition from Latin into rudimentary Catalan took place gradually around the ninth c. However, the first preserved text documenting the usage of Catalan is the *Homilies d'Organyà*

(The Homilies of Organyà), from the end of the twelfth c. or possibly the beginnings of the thirteenth. This relatively late date may be attributed to the fact that what is today Catalonia was very early and intensely romanized, and thus Latin was used there longer than in other parts of the Roman world. The *Forum iudicum*, for example, was translated into Catalan around the twelfth c. and the *Usatici*, in the thirteenth c. The very beginnings of what we properly call Catalan literature must be placed with the troubadors who wrote in Provençal and flourished between the twelfth and thirteenth centuries; poets like Guillem de Berguedà or King Alphonse the Pure himself are considered among the best troubadors of early medieval Europe. With respect to educated narrative poetry, Catalonia equally provided distinguished masters of the "roman courtois," such as Ramon Vidal de Besalú and the anonymous author of the *Jaufré*. Catalan literature, however, does not have a tradition of medieval epic poetry like that of Castile-Leon, France, or the Nordic countries of Europe.

The true Golden Age of Catalan literature began characteristically with the rapid rise of the bourgeoisie and its imperial expansion throughout the Mediterranean at the end of the thirteenth c. With the chronicles, the natural literary genre of this new laic world, Catalan letters made the definite transition from Latin and Provençal to Catalan proper. For instance, *Muntaner in his famous *Chronicle* wrote proudly in "lo bell catalanesc" (beautiful Catalan), and his linguistic nationalism was shared by several of the great Catalan kings: Jaume I the Conqueror ordered the production of the chronicle bearing his name and likewise Pere el Ceremoniós (Peter the Ceremonious) dictated personally to a team of writers. Another chronicle is the one written by Bernat Desclot on the reign of Pere el Gran (Peter the Great). Equally brilliant is what we can very loosely denominate "religious literature." Arnau de Vilanova is known for his apocalyptic treatises written in mature and incisive prose. Above all, the Majorcan Ramón *Llull is probably one of the giants of European medieval literature. He singlehandedly compiled enormous scientific encyclopedias, devised systems of philosophy, and wrote pamphlets on religious politics, passionate mystical confessions, and poems and novels in several languages. Known as the Doctor Il·luminat (Enlightened Master) throughout the medieval world, Llull drew upon all the disciplines of his time in order to realize his great ideal, the reorganization of all the world's religions into the Christian God. His *Blanquerna* is possibly one of the first modern European novels; for the first time, the protagonist is not a knight, a nobleman or a king. Blanquerna rises from commoner to bishop and then to pope only to become, in the end, a hermit. The Italian Renaissance arrived very early in Catalonia (the Catalan royal court resided for a time in Naples), and one of Catalonia's kings, Martí l'Humà (Martin the Human), gave it royal impetus. But even before that, the Catalan Renaissance had already produced great masters. Bernat *Metge, skeptic and rationalist, deeply influenced by Cicero and Petrarch, was the greatest Catalan humanist of the time. *Lo somni* (The Dream) was written in extremely refined Catalan. The rationalist spirit was very strong in one of the most outstanding writers of this age, Anselm *Turmeda.

Defrocked by the Franciscan order, he became one of the most corrosive Islamic writers. He embraced the religion of Islam, changed his name to 'Abd-dallàh al-Taryuman, and died in Tunis (c. 1430). *Eiximenís was another writer of note who compiled the knowledge of the Middle Ages and preached that "seny" (common sense) is the proper behavior of a true Christian and Catalan. But most of the great masters of the Catalan fifteenth-c. Renaissance came from Valencia, including Jordi de *Sant Jordi, one of the most exquisite poets of fifteenth-c. Europe, and Ausiàs *March, the great poet of life and death, and sublime and sensuous love. He had enormous importance in Castilian Renaissance poetry. However, the Catalan literature of this period excels most in the narrative genre. Some critics say that the foundations of the modern European novel are in fifteenth-c. Catalonia. L'espill (The Mirror) by Jaume *Roig is one of the key precedents of the *picaresque novel, and Tirant lo Blanc (masterfully translated into English by David Rosenthal) by J. *Martorell and J. *Galba is considered by everyone, including *Cervantes, a true masterpiece of the fifteenth c. Catalonia also produced one of the best European novels of chivalry, the *Curial y Güelfa, of unknown authorship.

Several national cataclysms, notably the devastating recurrences of the black plague and its sequel of diminishing population, civil wars and the union with Castile, had a direct bearing on the decadence of Catalan litera- ture. Between the end of the fifteenth c. and the beginning of the nineteenth, the Catalan language seemed to be doomed forever. The national spirit shone through several times (e.g., rebellions in 1654 and in 1714), but only disaster resulted, and very little of outstanding literary value was produced. With the industrial revolution at the end of the eighteenth c. and very clearly at the be- ginning of the nineteenth, Catalonia once more revived its literary glories un- der the auspices of the Catalan bourgeoisie. The modern Renaixement (Renaissance) of Catalan letters began with *Romanticism and the writing in 1859 of the famous poem "La pàtria" (The Fatherland) by a banker, Carles *Aribau. The first phase of this literary movement was dominated by the writer-scholars: *Milà i Fontanals, a polyglot who studied the glorious past in order to regain a needed cultural continuity to the present; Pons i Gallarza, who revived the Italian and Latin classics; and *Rubió i Ors (Lo Gayter del Llobregat), who urged all Catalan writers to use their native tongue. These men set the stage for the three literary masters of the end of the nineteenth c.: the playwright Àngel *Guimerà, the novelist Narcís *Oller and the poet Ja- cint *Verdaguer i Santaló. From then on Catalonia's literature continued to develop similarly to any other European literature, except for two peculiari- ties: the almost exclusive dominance of middle-class values and aesthetics and the lack of a national government. Thus, Catalan literature in many ways mirrored the social divisions of the country. On one side were moderate to conservative middle and upper classes and, on the other, a radical proletariat increasingly formed by immigrants from the poorest parts of Spain. The former were mostly Catalan speaking and the latter, mostly Castilian. Catalonia's response to the socio-political crises of the last decade of the nineteenth c. (the loss of the last Spanish colonies where Catalans had invested heavily, the crisis of the monarchy, etc.) was the literary movement known as Modernisme (*Modernism), which rejected the preceding realist aesthetics, championed new and daring forms, exalted the will of the individual, and showed strong influences of German culture, especially of Nietzsche and Goethe. The best representative of this movement is the poet and essayist Joan *Maragall, one of the greatest poets of his time and indeed of all Catalan poetry. He was the creator of the "paraula viva" (the living word) and in his essays on the Tragic Week of 1909 he was one of the first modern Catalan writers to point out the long-range dangers of social inequalities and the deep divisions within Catalan culture. Santiago *Rusiñol represented in his plays the more decadent aspects of the movement. Finally, purely social literature, strongly influenced by Ibsen, can be found in the dramas of Ignasi *Iglèsies. In narrative, Víctor *Català (pseudonym of Catarina Albert) and Joaquim *Ruyra mixed modernist individuality and stylist prose with positivist and naturalist ruralism. During the first decade of the twentieth c. the literary pendulum again swung to neoclassicism with "noucentisme," preaching cosmopolitan intellectualism and in general defending the principles of literary purity and formalism. Two of the greatest poets of contemporary Catalonia came out of this movement: Josep *Carner, a stylist with a great sense of irony, and Carles *Riba, one of the truly great humanists of the Iberian Peninsula. Above all, it was Eugenio d'*Ors who would act as high priest of the movement. The European avantgarde movement of the first quarter of the century also flourished in Catalan literature. Its best known and most valuable representatives are Joan *Salvat-Papasseit, of working-class origin, who tried to blend revolutionary content and form, and J. V. *Foix (the first Catalan to win Spain's National Literary Award), who tried to synthesize the neoclassical formalism of "noucentisme" and surrealism. Josep *Plà and Gaziel are contemporary narrators whose extensive work spans the Spanish Civil War, as does that of two of the best novelists of the twentieth century, Llorenç *Villalonga and, above all, Mercè *Rodoreda, the latter of international fame. Pere *Quart, Gabriel Ferrater, Joan *Brossa, Xavier *Benguerel, Joan Sales, Maria Aurèlia *Capmany, Agustí *Bartra, and Manuel de *Pedrolo are among the best writers of post-war Catalonia; Salvador *Espriu is perhaps the greatest and most representative of those writers who had to weather the most repressive years of the Franco dictatorship. Among the younger generations are excellent poets like Pere *Gimferrer, narrators like Pere *Calders, Terenci *Moix, Montserrat *Roig, Baltasar *Porcel, A. Artís-Gener and many others. At present, Catalan literature appears alive and vigorous, having survived the cultural genocide of the Franco years; in fact, one can even detect a healthy euphoria reminiscent of the first years of the Renaixença. See also Crónicas.

## BIBLIOGRAPHY

Criticism

Fuster, Joan. *Literatura Catalana Contemporània*. Barcelona: Curial, 1972.

Riquer, Martí de. *Literatura Catalana Medieval*. Barcelona: Ayuntamiento de Barcelona, 1972.

Riquer, Martí de, and A. Comas. *Història de la literatura catalana*. 2nd ed. 4 vols. Barcelona: Ariel, 1980.

Roca-Pons, Josep. *Introduction to Catalan Literature*. Bloomington: Indiana UP, 1977.

Ruiz-Calonge, Joan. *Història de la Literatura Catalana*. Barcelona: Teide, 1954.

Terry, Arthur. *Introducción a la lengua y literatura catalanas*. Barcelona: Ariel, 1977. The second part of the book is a Spanish translation of *Catalan Literature* by A. Terry.

Joan Gilabert

**CATECHETICAL LITERATURE** (Catechetics, from the Greek [KATEX-EIN] κατηχειν—to teach or instruct about the law of God). Catechetical literature involves the art of instructing on Christian doctrine often by means of questions and answers. The term *catecismo* (catechism) refers to the specific type of works, whereas *catequesis* (catechetics) is the art of writing these works. During the Middle Ages (*see* Edad Media, Literatura de la) catechetics followed rather closely the development of philosophy and theology. The rediscovery of the Aristotelian corpus (*Aristotelianism) significantly influenced catechetics since it helped bring about a logical ordering of its contents. During the sixteenth and seventeenth centuries Spain witnessed a flowering of this type of religious literature. *Catecismos* were composed for the purpose of explicating Catholic dogma, Christian morals and the Sacraments; hence, they were not meant to be meditative or devotional. These works took on diverse forms and focused on various aspects of doctrine. Some were more general in scope, covering the full gamut of Catholic doctrine. Others, for example, Eusebio *Nieremberg's *Aprecio y estima de la divina gracia* (Madrid, 1638; Appreciation and Esteem of Divine Doctrine) expatiated on one particular point of dogma. Works such as Pedro de *Medina's *Libro de verdad* (Valladolid, 1555; Book of Truth) were encyclopedic in scope. The great sermons preached at the important cathedrals and at the royal court, many of which were transcribed and incorporated into collections, also constitute an important segment of catechetical literature.

## BIBLIOGRAPHY

Primary Texts

Carranza de Miranda, Bartolomé. *Comentario sobre el catecismo cristiano*. Anvers: Martín Nucio, 1558.

Medina, Pedro de. *Libro de verdad*. Valladolid: Fernández de Córdoba, 1555.

Nieremberg, Juan Eusebio. *Aprecio y estima de la divina gracia*. Madrid: Sánchez, 1638.

Pineda, Juan de. *Treinta y cinco diálogos familiares de la agricultura cristiana*. Salamanca: Adurça y López, 1589.

Criticism

Guerrero García, J. R. *Catecismos españoles del siglo XVI.* Madrid: Instituto Superior de Pastoral, 1969.
Huerga, A. "Sobre la catequesis en España durante los siglos XV y XVI." *Analecta Sacra Tarraconensia* 41 (1968): 299–345.

Angelo DiSalvo

**CAVESTANY, Juan Antonio** (1861, Sevilla–1924, Madrid), poet, dramatist and conservative statesman. He served as representative to several legislative assemblies and as senator from the province of Salamanca. His first drama, *El esclavo de su culpa* (A Slave to His Guilt), was staged in 1877 while he was still in his teens. Later works include *Grandezas humanas* (1878; Great Human Feats), *Salirse de su esfera* (1879; Getting Out of One's Class), *Despertar en la sombra* (1881; To Wake Up in the Shade), *Nerón* (1901; Nero), *Farinelli* (Farinelli)—an opera for music by Bretón—and two volumes of lyric poems, *Versos viejos* (Old Verses) and *Al pie de la Giralda* (1908; At the Foot of the Giralda).

An eloquent orator, he was named in 1902 to the Royal Spanish Academy of the Language (*Academia Española).

BIBLIOGRAPHY

Primary Texts

*El esclavo de su culpa.* Madrid: Velasco, 1902.
*Grandezas humanas.* Madrid: Rodríguez, 1878. Rpt. Louisville, KY: Falls City P, 1961.
*Nerón.* Madrid: Velasco, 1901. Rpt. Louisville, KY: Falls City P, 1961.
*Salirse de su esfera.* Madrid: Gutlon, 1879. (Vol. 38, #7 of the Spanish Plays Collection.)

Merry Wheaton

**CAVESTANY, Pablo** (1886, Madrid–?), poet and novelist. Son of Juan Antonio *Cavestany, he has published the novel *Mario Gracián* (1946) and a collection of poems, *Collar de armonías* (1941; Ring of Harmonies). Other titles are the novel *A la orilla del tiempo* (1952; On the Shore of Time) and *Fuego en la aldea; poema dramático* (1953; Fire in the Village; dramatic poem). His style is clear and personal.

BIBLIOGRAPHY

Primary Texts

*Collar de armonías.* Barcelona: Juventud, 1941.
*A la orilla del tiempo; novela.* Madrid: Escelicer, 1952.

*Mario Gracián.* Barcelona: Juventud, 1946.
*Fuego en la aldea; poema dramático.* Madrid: Gráficas reunidas, 1953.
Isabel McSpadden

**CAVIA, Mariano de** (1855, Zaragoza–1919, Madrid), journalist. He often used the pseudonym Sobaquillo. His articles appeared in leading Madrid papers; some were subsequently collected and published in book form. Many can still be read with enjoyment, as they possess a timeless quality not always found in such articles. In 1923, his works were collected under the title *Chácharas* (Baubles).

BIBLIOGRAPHY
Primary Text
*Chácharas.* Prol. J. Ortega Munilla. Madrid: Renacimiento, 1923.

**CECILIA DEL NACIMIENTO Sor** (1570, Valladolid–1646, Valladolid), poet, theologian, and dramatist. Daughter of a university family—her father was secretary of the U in Valladolid and her mother was a well-known humanist of the day— Cecilia del Nacimiento, with her sister *María de San Alberto, transferred her learning and artistic abilities to the relatively safe environment of the Discalced Carmelite convent in her native city, founded a generation earlier by Sta. *Teresa de Jesús. She took the veil in 1587, and except for a ten-year period during which she was sent to Calahorra to help with the foundation of another convent, she remained within its walls until her death. There, protected by her brothers' important positions within the church hierarchy, she wrote, painted, held convent offices, and engaged in meditative practices that led to mystical ecstasy.

Her extant work, a good portion of which has been published as her *Obras completas* (1971; Complete Works), includes several prose pieces: a fragment from her spiritual autobiography; treatises on the transformation of the soul in God, on the soul's union with God, on the Immaculate Conception, and on the mysteries of the faith; two narratives of mystical favors; two exegeses of lines from the Song of Songs; an account of the foundation of the convent in Calahorra; a response to a questionnaire regarding her brother Antonio Sobrino's beatification; and several letters, mostly to members of her family. She also wrote approximately one hundred religious poems in a variety of meters, as well as at least one play to celebrate a novice's taking full vows. *See also* Mysticism.

BIBLIOGRAPHY
Primary Texts
"Aviendo yo quedado sola de la familia. . . . " In *Relación de cosas memorables de la vida y muerte del Sr. D. Francisco Sobrino, obispo del Valladolid, y de sus padres y hermanos. . . .* Ms. Valladolid: Convent of the Carmelitas Descalzas de la Concepción, 1640.
*Obras completas.* Ed., study, P. J. Díaz Cerón. Madrid: Editorial de la Espiritualidad, 1971.

"Poesías de las MM. María de San Alberto y Cecilia del Nacimiento." Ms. 89. Valladolid: Convent of the Carmelitas Descalzas de la Concepción, n.d.

Criticism

Alonso Cortés, B. *Dos monjas vallisoletanas poetisas*. Thesis, U of Madrid, 1941. Contains selected texts and commentary.

Arenal, E., and S. Schlau. "Two Sisters among the Sisters: Intellectual Servants, Ecclesiastic Upper Crust." In *Untold Sisters; Hispanic Nuns in Their Own Works*. Albuquerque: U of New Mexico P, 1989. Contains selections with English translations.

Reverendo Padre Emeterio de Jesús María, ed. *El Monte Carmelo: Revista de Estudios Carmelitanos* 47 (April-Sept. 1946): n.p. Contains selected texts and commentary.

Padre Gerardo de San Juan de la Cruz. *Obras del místico doctor San Juan de la Cruz*. Toledo: Peláez, 1912–14. Vol. 3: 339–438.

Petronila de San José. "Virtudes de la madre Cecilia del Nacimiento, religiosa Carmelita Descalza del Convento de Valladolid." Ms. Valladolid: Convent of the Carmelitas Descalzas de la Concepción, n.d.

Stacy Schlau

**CEJADOR Y FRAUCA, Julio** (1864, Zaragoza–1927, Madrid), professor and scholar. He taught at the U of Madrid and was an eminent, productive literary critic. Among his most significant works are the fourteen-volume *Historia de la lengua y literatura castellana* (1915–20; History of Spanish Language and Literature); annotated editions of the *Lazarillos,* the *Celestina,* and works by *Gracián y Morales, Mateo *Alemán, and others; and the posthumously published *Vocabulario medieval castellano* (1929; Medieval Spanish Vocabulary).

BIBLIOGRAPHY

Primary Texts

*Historia de la lengua y literatura castellana*. Madrid: Gredos, 1972–73. Facs.

*Tesoro de la lengua castellana*. Madrid: Perlado, 1908–14.

*Vocabulario medieval castellano*. New York: Olms, 1971. Rpt. of 1929 ed.

**CELA, Camilo José** (1916, Iria Flavia, Galicia– ), novelist, short story writer, essayist; winner of a Nobel Prize in literature in 1989. The eldest of seven children of a conservative, upper middle-class family, Cela was a twenty-year-old university student when the Spanish Civil War broke out, and he experienced the siege of Madrid (which colors much of his first collection of poetry, *Pisando la dudosa luz del día* [1945; Treading Doubtful Daylight]. He was subsequently mobilized into the Nationalist (Franco) army, thus entering the post-war period in the advantageous company of the victors, although much of his work is a covert subversion of regime principles. Known primarily as a novelist, Cela has also authored many travel books, numerous collections of short stories, and several volumes of essays, as well as having tried his hand at drama and returning periodically to poetry. His first novel, *La familia de Pascual Duarte* (1942; *The Family of Pascual Duarte*, 1946), is his most famous piece of fiction, the purported autobiographical memoir of an Extremaduran peasant awaiting execution. Pascual's matter-of-fact recital of crimes, murders and atrocities (prototype of the post-war movement known as *tremendismo*) has been somewhat inexactly compared to *The Stranger*, by Camus. The work's success spawned a host of imitators who blended neo-naturalism with elements of the *esperpento* of *Valle-Inclán, as well as touches of existential alienation, solitude, absurdity and despair. *Pabellón de reposo* (1943; *Rest Home*, 1961) is ostensibly the diaries of several terminally ill patients suffering from tuberculosis, and reflects Cela's own pair of confinements in tubercular sanatoriums. *Nuevas andanzas y desventuras de Lazarillo de Tormes* (1944; New Wanderings and Misadventures of Lazarillo de Tormes) resurrects the classic sixteenth-c. rogue and transports him to the twentieth (an instance of *picaresque influence which can be found in the first chapter of *Pascual Duarte*, several of the travel books, and some of Cela's short stories). *La colmena* (1951; *The Hive*, 1953), a complex orchestration of hundreds of characters without plot or protagonist, offers a cross-section of Madrid life during the winter of 1942–43, a time of near-famine, filled with hunger, misery, moral bankruptcy and man's inhumanity to man. *Mrs. Caldwell habla con su hijo* (1953; *Mrs. Caldwell Speaks to Her Son*, 1968), radically experimental, fragmentary, lyrical and unorthodox, consists of some two hundred "chapters" written in the second person by Mrs. Caldwell to her son. The reader slowly realizes that Mrs. Caldwell is unbalanced and her son long since dead. *La Catira* (1955), set in Venezuela and incorporating Cela's observations of Venezuelan regional dialect, is less a biography of the female protagonist (as purported) than a catalog of horrible deaths and of sexual aberrations and perversions (motifs which abound in Cela's work, and constitute a constant thematic characteristic).

Many critics consider Cela essentially a stylist, and some of the best examples of his style can be found in the early story collections and such early travel books as *Viaje a la Alcarria* (1948; *Journey to the Alcarria, 1964*), *Del Miño al Bidasoa* (1952; From the Miño River to the Bidasoa) and *Avila* (1952), as well as *Judíos, moros y cristianos* (1956; Jews, Moors and Christians). Collected essays appear in the volumes *Mesa revuelta* (1945; Cluttered Desk), *Cajón de sastre* (1957; Tailor's Box) and *La rueda de los ocios* (1957; Round of Idleness). Cela's literary criticism, sometimes opinionated and polemical, may be sampled in *Cuatro figuras del '98* (1960; Four Figures of the Generation of 1898). *La cucaña* (1959; The Cocoon) purports to be the title of a multi-volume autobiography, of which only the first volume, *La rosa* (The Rosebud), treating the author's early childhood, has appeared.

Cela has also produced a large number of miscellaneous works, of which the following may be considered typical: a four-volume *Enciclopedia del erotismo* (Encyclopedia of Eroticism), properly researched scholarship of pornography and erotic art, and the several volumes of his *Diccionario de palabras secretas* (Dictionary of Secret Words), an erudite study of the derivations, etymology and morphology of obscenities and vulgarities. This lengthy project might be viewed as an ironic reaction by Cela to his early election (1957) to the Real Academia Española de la Lengua, and the activities and deliberations of that ostensibly august body. In 1956, Cela founded the literary monthly *Papeles de Son Armadans* (Papers from Son Armadans, i.e., the district where Cela lives in Palma de Mallorca), an important intellectual and artistic outlet until its suspension in 1979.

Cela's best achievements as a narrator are found in his short fiction, including the story collections *Esas nubes que pasan* (1945; Those Clouds Passing By), *El bonito crimen del carabinero y otras invenciones* (1947; The Guard's Pretty Crime and Other Tales), *El gallego y su cuadrilla* (1951; The Galician and His Gang), *Baraja de invenciones* (1953; Deck of Fictions), *El molino de viento y otras novelas cortas* (1956; The Windmill and Other Short Novels) and *Nuevo retablo de Don Cristobita* (1957; New Triptych of Don Cristobita). Much of Cela's unflaggingly prolific output from the 1950s and 1960s is of limited interest, being in the nature of "potboilers" or pastiches, or of deluxe, limited-edition printings designed for the collectors' market.

Of greater significance are his relatively recent experimental novels, *San Camilo 1936* (1969) and *Oficio de tinieblas, 5* (1973; Office of Darkness). Both are written principally in the second person, the former being an interminable monologue by the protagonist-narrator, who chronicles events in Madrid during the week preceding the outbreak of the Civil War (most of which appear to have transpired in the brothels). *Oficio*, consisting of nearly twelve hundred "monads" or fragments ranging from a few words to three pages is an atemporal anti-novel without protagonist, plot, character delineation or development, lacking sustained action, and identifiable time or place, held together by the reiteration of certain themes: boredom, sexuality, absurdity, eroticism, death, bestiality, war, violence, fear, betrayal, defeat, pain, excrement—with unexpected lyric intervals as counterpoint.

With the transition to democracy following the death of Franco in November of 1975, Cela served for a time as a senator by royal appointment, representing the interests of the intelligentsia. Having "abdicated" his novelistic position and trade publicly following the release of *Oficio de tinieblas*, Cela wrote regularly for the newspapers during the next decade and periodically produced volumes of essays, but did not return to the novel until *Mazurca para dos muertos* (1983; Mazurca for Two Cadavers), a pseudo-mythic treatment of the Civil War in rural Galicia. *See also* Censorship.

BIBLIOGRAPHY

Primary Texts

*El juego de los tres madronos*. Barcelona: Destino, 1983. Newspaper articles.
*Maria Sabina*. Madrid: Alfaguara, 1970. Oratory.
*El solitario*. 3rd ed. Barcelona: Noguer, 1976. Surrealist sketches.
*Tobogán de hambrientos*. Barcelona: Noguer, 1962. Novel.
*Viaje a U.S.A.*. Madrid: Alfaguara, 1967. Ballads.

*Vuelta de hoja.* Barcelona: Destino, 1981. Political essays.
See also *Revista Hispanica Moderna* in Criticism.

English Translations

*The Family of Pascual Duarte.* Tr. A. Kerrigan. Boston: Little, Brown, 1964.
*The Hive.* Tr. J. M. Cohen. New York: Farrar, Straus, 1953.
*Journey to the Alcarria.* Tr. F. M. López-Morillas. Madison: U of Wisconsin P, 1964.
*Mrs. Caldwell Speaks to Her Son.* Tr. J. S. Bernstein. Ithaca, NY: Cornell UP, 1968.
*Rest Home.* Tr. H. Briffault. New York: Las Americas, 1961.
*San Camilo, 1936; the Eve, Feast, and Octave of St. Camillus of the Year 1936 in Madrid.*
    Tr. J.H.R. Polt. Durham: Duke UP, 1991.

Criticism

"Camilo José Cela: Vida y Obra." *Revista Hispánica Moderna* 38. 2–4 (1962): 107–
    275. Includes criticism, bibliography, and a selection of items published pre-
    viously.
*Cuadernos Hispanoamericanos* 337 and 338 (July-August 1978). Issue devoted to Cela.
Foster, D. *Forms of the Novel in the Work of Camilo José Cela.* Columbia, MO: U of
    Missouri P, 1967.
Henn, D. *Camilo José Cela: Critical Guide to Spanish Texts (La colmena).* London:
    Grant and Cutler, 1974.
Kirsner, R. *The Novels and Travels of Camilo José Cela.* Chapel Hill, NC: U of North
    Carolina P, 1963.
McPheeters, D. W. *Camilo José Cela.* TWAS 67. New York: Twayne, 1969.
*Review of Contemporary Fiction* 4.3 (Fall, 1984). Issue devoted to Cela.

                                                                            Janet Pérez


**CELA TRULOCK, Jorge** (1932, Madrid– ), writer and publisher. The youngest brother of novelist Camilo José *Cela, Cela Trulock usually signs his works
"Jorge Trulock" to avoid any appearance of taking advantage of the more famous
brother's reputation. His first novel, *Las horas* (1956; The Hours), is similar in
a number of ways to Joyce's *Ulysses* (i.e., it is the novel of a city, closely tied
to a specific, limited time-span, and relies heavily on internal monolog). The
focus is upon minute daily events in the lives of lower-class Madrid residents
and workers. *Blanquito, peón de brega* (1958; Whitey, Bullfighter's Pawn)
presents the bitter disillusionment of a would-be matador who has spent the best
years of his life hoping to triumph in the bullring and thereby become rich and
famous. In reality, however, he is little better than the servant of a mediocre
matador, badly paid and worse treated. Finally allowed to fight, he is killed his
first day. *Trayecto Circo-Matadero* (1965; Bus from Circus to Slaughterhouse)
is a novel about prostitution, although it includes other themes as well. A ka-
leidoscopic vision of poverty and misery, its characters are motivated by an
enormous thirst for life and an obsessive desire for happiness, in spite of the
cruel and crushing circumstances of their present existence. Their suffering and
humiliation lead them to ignore the present, projecting themselves toward the
future and its one bright ray of hope.

BIBLIOGRAPHY

Primary Texts

*Blanquito, peón de brega.* Valladolid: Gerper, 1958.
*Las horas.* Barcelona: Destino, 1958.
*Trayecto Circo-Matadero.* Madrid: Alfaguara, 1965.

Janet Pérez

**CELAYA, Gabriel,** pseudonym of Rafael Gabriel Múgica Celaya (1911, Hernani, San Sebastián– ), poet, prose author, essayist. Son of a wealthy Basque industrial family, Celaya was trained as an engineer, but his lifelong desire was to be a writer. While studying in Madrid, he lived from 1927 to 1935 in the famous Residencia de Estudiantes at a time when some of the most brilliant intellectuals of the c. were in residence there. Although he attempted to fulfill his family duties and run the business, serious personal conflicts arose, especially after the publication of *Marea de silencio* (1935; High Tide of Silence) and the winning of a literary prize with the unpublished ms. of *La soledad cerrada* (written 1935, published 1947; Closed Solitude). Celaya's pre-war writings show the influence of vanguardist experimentation and Surrealism, anathema to the post-war "social" poets and the Franco regime alike (thus, some of Celaya's works of the 1930s remained unpublished for decades, e.g., *Los poemas de Rafael Múgica*, written in 1934, published 1967). The poet spent the war years and the immediate post-war period working for the family firm until 1946, completing several books which were not published: *Avenidas* (1939; Avenues, included in *Poesías completas* [1939]); *Objetos poéticos* (1944; Poetic Objects, published 1948); *Movimientos elementales* (published 1947; Elementary Movements) and *El principio sin fin* (1944; Beginning without End, published 1949). His struggles to write in hostile circumstances produced a severe depression and led to hospitalization. Amparo Gastón, whom he met at this time, became his lifelong companion, and after his convalescence, they founded the publishing house, Norte, which became influential in the area of post-war poetry. Celaya began to translate important European poets to Spanish, including Rilke, William Blake and Rimbaud. *Tranquilamente hablando* (1947; Speaking Calmly), Celaya's first significant post-war work, abandons the earlier vanguardism for a low-key neo-realism and everyday language, which became the hallmarks of his works for more than a decade.

The next several years were of intense productivity, including lectures and writing for newspapers as well as these books of poetry: *Se parece al amor* (1949; It Looks Like Love), *Las cosas como son* (1949; Things As They Are), *Deriva* (1950; Drifting), *Las cartas boca arriba* (1951; Cards Face Up), *Lo demás es silencio* (1952; The Rest Is Silence), *Paz y concierto* (1953; Peace and Concert), *Vía muerta* (1954; Dead Way), and *Ciento volando* (1953; One Hundred [Poems] Flying), his first book in collaboration with Amparo Gastón. By the mid–1950s, Celaya had become very involved in political issues, and had written several books of poetry demanding social justice, thereby widening the rift between him and his family, with whom he broke definitively in 1956. *Cantos iberos* (1955; Iberian Songs) is one of his key works from the mid-century period. With Blas de *Otero, Celaya is a founder or leader of the "social poets" of the 1950s and 1960s (a politically mixed group that coincided primarily in opposition to Franco and their expressions of protest). Under the influence of Marxist theorists, many of these poets came to view literature as justifiable only insofar as it served to effect social change; Celaya defined poetry as "an instrument to change society."

*De claro en claro* (1956; From Clearing to Clearing) received the Critics' Poetry Prize, one of Celaya's most significant awards; from this time on, he began to be recognized abroad, with bilingual editions in France and Italy, and several anthologies as well as new collections 1957–60: *Entreacto* (1957; Between the Acts), *Las resistencias del diamante* (1957; The Resistance of the Diamond), *Cantata en Aleixandre* (1959), *El corazón en su sitio* (1959; Heart in the Right Place), *Para vosotros dos* (1960; For the Two of You), *Poesía urgente* (1960; Urgent Poetry), and *Música celestial* (1958; Celestial Music). Many works of these years had to be published abroad because of problems with the Franco *censorship. Further poetry collections from the 1960s include *La buena vida* (1961; The Good Life), *Rapsodia éuskara* (1961; Basque Rhapsody), *Episodios nacionales* (1962; National [Historic] Episodes), *Mazorcas* (1962; Ears of Corn), *Versos de otoño* (1963; Autumnal Verses), *Dos cantatas* (1964; Two Cantatas), *La linterna sorda* (1964; Blind Lantern), *Baladas y decires vascos* (1965; Basque Ballads and Sayings), *Lo que faltaba* (1967; All That Was Missing), *Los espejos transparentes* (1968; The Transparent Mirrors), and *Canto en lo mío* (1968; I Sing of My Own).

By the end of the 1960s, Celaya and many other writers of "social" literature were growing disillusioned with the lack of results from the use of their pens to transform society, and were frustrated by the pedestrian sameness of the themes and forms to which they had restricted themselves. A new experimentalism began to emerge, with attributes of contemporary Baroque. In Celaya's case, it became clear in *Lírica de cámara* (1969; Chamber Lyrics), whose title suggests stately, traditional chamber music, but whose content clarifies that the allusion is to the chamber of an atomic reactor. Although the first (incomplete) edition of Celaya's *Poesías completas* appeared in 1969, and anthologies which also represented earlier periods, the new direction is clearly reaffirmed in *Operaciones poéticas* (1971; Poetic Operations) and *Campos semánticos* (1972; Semantic Fields), as well as *Función de Uno, Equis, Ene* (1973; Function of One, X, N). Although some new collections of poetry were completed during the 1970s, Celaya produced more essays and new editions of earlier works.

He has also written fiction: *Tentativas* (1946; Attempts); *Lázaro calla* (1949; Lazaro Is Silent); *Penúltimas tentativas* (1960; Next to Last Attempts), *Lo uno y lo otro* (1962; One Thing and Another), *Los buenos negocios* (Good Business Deals), and a drama, *El revelo* (1963; The Manifestation). Beginning in the

1960s, Celaya began to publish numerous essays and literary studies as well: *Poesía y verdad* (1960; Poetry and Truth); *Exploración de la poesía* (1963; Exploration of Poetry); *Inquisición de la poesía* (1972; Inquisition for Poetry); *La voz de los niños* (1972; Children's Voices); *Bécquer* (1972).

BIBLIOGRAPHY

Primary Texts

*Los poemas de Juan Leceta* (includes *Avisos, Tranquilamente hablando, Las cosas como son*). Barcelona: Colliure, 1961.

*Poesía (1934–1961)*. Madrid: Giner, 1962.

*Poesías completas*. Madrid: Aguilar, 1969.

*Dirección prohibida* (includes *Las resistencias del diamante, Poemas tachados, Episodios nacionales, Cantata en Cuba*). Buenos Aires: Losada, 1973.

English Translations

Four poems tr. by José Yglesias. In *Massachusetts Review* 3 (1962): 403–8.

"Last Encounter with Lorca." Tr. J. Yglesias. In *Massachusetts Review* 5 (1964): 635–39.

Two poems tr. by H. W. Patterson. In *Antología Bilingüe*. Madrid: Cultura Hispánica, 1965.

Criticism

Brooks, Zelda Irene. "Major Themes in the Poetry of Gabriel Celaya." Diss., U of Oklahoma, 1968.

Cohen, J. M. "Since the Civil War. New Currents in Spanish Poetry." *Encounter* 12.2 (Feb. 1959): 44–53. Daydí-Tolson, Santiago. *The Post–Civil War Spanish Social Poets*. Boston: Twayne, 1983. 70–89.

Seirra, Pierre-Olivier. *Gabriel Celaya*. Paris: Seghers, 1970. (In French.)

Ugalde, Sharon Keefe. *Gabriel Celaya*. TWAS 483. Boston: Twayne, 1978. (In English.)

Janet Pérez

**CELESTINA.** Popular title, often preceded by the definite article "la," for a Spanish classic, taken from the name of one of the central characters. It originally circulated in sixteen acts, as the *Comedia de Calisto y Melibea* (first extant edition, Burgos, 1499?; *The Celestina: A Novel in Dialogue*, 1955), then in twenty-one, as the *Tragicomedia de Calisto y Melibea* (many of whose earliest survivors bear the date 1502, but see below; *Celestina or the Tragicke-Comedy of Calisto and Melibea*, 1631; rpt. 1967). Although modern editors have discounted the twenty-two act version (oldest extant form Toledo, 1526), the most recent authority on such matters, Miguel Marciales, believed the additional so-called *Auto de Traso* (Traso's Act) was an authentic part of the complete early *Tragicomedia*.

The plot of this early best-seller is simple, revolving around a love affair between the young heirs of two noble families. Aided by his servants and the clever old go-between Celestina (who is known to traffic in sorcery), Calisto manages to win over the initially reluctant Melibea. After one night of love (in the *Comedia*)—or many, in the *Tragicomedia*—both lovers perish: he, by falling from Melibea's garden wall; she, by throwing herself down from a tower. Their deaths bring the total count of fatal victims to five, the other three being Celestina and her murderers (and former allies), two of Calisto's servants, who had argued bitterly with her over the reward paid out by the young nobleman. Among the remaining characters, including the servants' girlfriends, other servants, the ruffian Centurio, and Melibea's parents, the girl's father has a special importance, since it is he who pronounces the work's closing monologue. In this *planctus* Pleberio rails against the world, fortune, and love and stresses his desperate sense of isolation, with no hint of the consolation that might be expected to come from a merciful God. Neither this apparently unorthodox ending nor the open portrayal of sexual actions and occasional accompanying obscenities called down the fury of the *Inquisition (which did, however, act later to expurgate a few anti-clerical passages).

Among the series of vexing problems surrounding *Celestina* scholarship, the question of authorship looms large. Since Marcelino *Menéndez y Pelayo's influential proclamation of a single author, many readers have been persuaded to attribute the work to Fernando de *Rojas, from Puebla de Montalbán, who is named in the book's acrostic verses, despite the indication in the opening letter that the first act and the beginning of the second were written by a separate author. Today many critics favor dual authorship (Rodrigo de *Cota being the leading contender for the work's seminal portion), considering the *converso* (convert) Rojas to be the one who elaborated the remaining part of the *Comedia*, and later, according to some, the additions and changes that produced the *Tragicomedia*. The latter part of this theory, however, is disputed by others, who contend that someone else (the elusive Sanabria?) was responsible for the sequence in the *Tragicomedia* known as the *Tratado de Centurio* (Centurio's Treatise). Scholars struggling with this important question have based their conclusions on the study of sources, syntax, characterization, etc., as well as on information gleaned from the work's peripheral pages.

In addition to the problem of many editions presumed lost, there is one concerning the numerous surviving *Tragicomedias* bearing the date 1502. None of these, it seems, was printed prior to 1510 (as shown by F. J. Norton's careful study of their typography and watermarks). Whether or not there was a first printing in 1500, then, and despite the many "1502" editions, the oldest surviving text of the work is an Italian translation (Rome, 1506), followed by the recently (1965) rediscovered Jorge Coci printing (Zaragoza, 1507).

*Celestina* proved to be of universal appeal, despite its original setting (possibly Salamanca, or, though less likely, Toledo). Having been translated quickly (and repeatedly) into the major European languages, it also exerted powerful influence in Spain. There, *Celestina*'s imitations include verse renditions by Pedro Manuel Jiménez de *Urrea (1513) and Juan Sedeño (1540); a trio of anonymous *comedias* published together (1521): *Tebaida*, *Hipólita*, and *Serafina*; and six early sequels: Feliciano de *Silva's *Segunda comedia de Celestina* (1534; Second Comedy of

Celestina), Gaspar Gómez de Toledo's *Tercera parte de la tragicomedia de Celestina* (1536; Third Part of the Tragicomedy of Celestina), Sancho de Muñón's *Tragicomedia de *Lisandro y Roselia* (1542; Tragicomedy of Lisandro and Roselia), the anonymous (sometimes attributed to Sebastián *Fernández) *Tragedia Policiana* (1547; The Policiana Tragedy), Juan Rodríguez Florián's *Comedia Florinea* (1554; The Florinea Comedy), and Alonso de *Villegas Selvago's *Comedia Selvagia* (1554; The Selvagia Comedy). Other works reminiscent (in style, characterization, etc.) of the *Tragicomedia* were produced by Juan del *Encina, Gil *Vicente, Bartolomé de *Torres Naharro (*Himenea*, 1517), Juan de la *Cueva, Lope de *Vega—*La Dorotea* (1632) and *El caballero de Olmedo* (c. 1620–25; *The Knight from Olmedo*, 1961)—and such novelists as *Cervantes, *Quevedo, and *Salas Barbadillo.

This c. has seen an international profusion of adaptations of *Celestina* for the stage. Nevertheless, not all critics agree that the work belongs to the genre of theater (to be read, probably aloud to a group, not performed), some of them preferring instead to assign it to the category of dialogue novel. Not in dispute, however, is its generic model: medieval Latin humanistic comedy, bolstered by the sentimental romance. Foremost among the work's sources are Petrarch's Latin works. Other important sources that have been identified include Aristotle, Boethius, Ovid, Andreas Capellanus, and Boccaccio, as well as El Tostado (Alfonso de *Madrigal), the *Arcipreste de Talavera (Alfonso Martínez de Toledo), Diego de *San Pedro, Jorge *Manrique, and Juan de *Mena.

In attempting to account for the extraordinary initial success of *Celestina* and for its enduring appeal, some critics have pointed to its harmonious amalgamation of opposites, stemming from its birth at the critical juncture between the Middle Ages (*Edad Media, Literatura de la) and the Renaissance. On the one hand, for example, we have the medieval habit of citing traditional *sententiae*; on the other, Renaissance creativity, which produced such novelties as a linguistic scheme in which the stylistic register is determined not by a character's social class but rather by that of his interlocutor and by the topic of conversation: medieval renunciation vs. Renaissance freedom, etc. Perhaps a more helpful way to view the situation is to focus, with Lida de Malkiel, on the book's artistic originality. If it continues to fascinate and stir controversy today, small wonder that it took Europe by storm when it first appeared. This remarkably vivid portrait of an entire social constellation of city dwellers must have delighted contemporary readers. The cautionary lesson notwithstanding, they must have stayed caught up in the love story. Finally, they must have been bedazzled by the personage of Celestina, whose centrality was confirmed by generations of printers who were the first to refer to the book with her name (initially, in Italy, in 1519). Equally at home with her peers and with her superiors (not to mention her underworld companions), this social subversive has survived admirably, despite her ignominious, and well deserved, fictional death. *See also* Censorship; Edad Media, Literatura de la; Renaissance; Siglo de Oro; Theater in Spain.

## BIBLIOGRAPHY

### Primary Texts

*Celestina: Tragicomedia de Calisto y Melibea. Fernando de Rojas.* Intro. and ed. by Miguel Marciales. Prepared by Brian Dutton and Joseph T. Snow. Illinois Medieval Monographs, 1–2. 2 vols. Urbana/Chicago: U of Illinois P, 1985.

*La Celestina.* Ed. Julio Cejador y Frauca. 3rd ed. Clásicos Castellanos 20 and 23. 1945; rpt. Madrid: Espasa-Calpe, 1984.

*La Celestina.* Intro. by M. Menéndez Pelayo. Ed. Eugenio Krapf. 2 vols. Vigo: Eugenio Krapf, 1899–1900.

*Comedia de Calisto y Melibea.* Ed. Jerry R. Rank. Chapel Hill, NC: Hispanófila, 1978.

*Comedia de Calisto y Melibea.* Facs. of the 1st ed. (Burgos: Fadrique de Basilea, 1499?). Ed. Archer M. Huntington. 1909; rpt. New York: Hispanic Society of America, 1970.

*Tragicomedia de Calixto y Melibea: Libro también llamado "La Celestina."* Ed. M[anuel] Criado de Val and G. D. Trotter. 3rd ed. Clásicos Hispánicos, 2: 3. 1970; rpt. Madrid: CSIC, 1984.

### English Translations

*Celestina: A Play in Twenty-One Acts Attributed to Fernando de Rojas.* Tr. Mack Hendricks Singleton. 1958; rpt. Madison: U. of Wisconsin P, 1968.

*Celestina or the Tragicke-Comedy of Calisto and Melibea.* Translated to the English from the Spanish of Fernando de Rojas by James Mabbe, anno 1631. Reprint, with the intro. by James Fitzmaurice-Kelly, of the 1894 London ed. New York: AMS Press, 1967.

*Celestina or the Tragi-Comedy of Calisto and Melibea.* Translated from the Spanish by James Mabbe, anno 1631. Also an Interlude of Calisto and Melibea (For the first time accurately reproduced from the Original Copy) Printed by John Rastell, circa 1530. Ed. H. Warner Allen. Broadway Translations. 1908; rpt. London: Routledge; New York: Dutton, 1923.

*Celestina or the Tragi-comedy of Calisto and Melibea.* Tr. Phyllis Hartnoll. Everyman's Library, 100. London: Dent; New York: Dutton, 1959.

*Celestine or the Tragick-Comedie of Calisto and Melibea: Translated by James Mabbe.* [MS. c. 1603–1611.] Ed. Guadalupe Martínez Lacalle. Colección Támesis, Serie B, Textos, 14. London: Tamesis, 1972.

*La Celestina: Tragicomedy of Calisto and Melibea.* Tr. Wallace Woolsey. New York: Las Américas, 1969.

*The Celestina: A Novel in Dialogue.* Tr. (of the *Comedia de Calisto and Melibea*) Lesley Byrd Simpson. 1955; rpt. Berkeley/Los Angeles: U of California P, 1966.

*The Spanish Bawd: La Celestina. Being the Tragi-Comedy of Calisto and Melibea.* Tr. J. M. Cohen. Penguin Classics, L142. Harmondsworth, England/Baltimore: Penguin, 1964. Also New York/London: New York UP, 1966.

### Criticism

Bataillon, Marcel. *"La Célestine" selon Fernando de Rojas.* Études de Littérature Étrangère et Comparée, 42. Paris: Didier, 1961.

Castro, Américo. *La Celestina como contienda literaria (castas y casticismos).* Madrid: RO, 1965.

Criado de Val, Manuel, ed. *"La Celestina" y su contorno social: Actas del I Congreso Internacional sobre* La Celestina. Barcelona: Hispam and Borrás, 1977.

Deyermond, Alan D. "La Celestina." In *Edad Media*. Vol. 1 of *Historia y crítica de la literatura española*. Ed. Francisco Rico. Colección Páginas de Filología. Barcelona: Crítica, 1980. 485–97, with excerpts from major works of *Celestina* criticism, 498–528.

———. *The Petrarchan Sources of "La Celestina."* 1961; rev. rpt. Westport, CT: Greenwood, 1975.

Gilman, Stephen. *The Art of "La Celestina."* 1956; rpt. Westport, CT: Greenwood, 1976.

———. *The Spain of Fernando de Rojas: The Intellectual and Social Landscape of "La Celestina."* Princeton: Princeton UP, 1972.

Heugas, Pierre. *"La Célestine" et sa descendance directe*. Bordeaux: Institut d'Études Ibériques et Ibéro-Américaines de l'Université, 1973.

Lida de Malkiel, María Rosa. *La originalidad artística de "La Celestina."* 2nd ed. Buenos Aires: Editorial Universitaria de Buenos Aires, 1970.

———. *Two Spanish Masterpieces: The "Book of Good Love" and "La Celestina."* Illinois Studies in Language and Literature, 49. Champaign-Urbana: U. of Illinois P, 1961.

Maravall, José Antonio. *El mundo social de "La Celestina."* 3rd ed. Biblioteca Románica Hispánica, Estudios y Ensayos, 80. 1972; rpt. Madrid: Gredos, 1976.

Menéndez Pelayo, M[arcelino]. *La Celestina*. In his *Orígenes de la novela*, 3. 1910; rpt. Madrid: CSIC, 1962. Printed separately in Colección Austral, 691. 1947; rpt. Madrid: Espasa-Calpe, 1979.

Norton, F[rederick] J[ohn]. *Printing in Spain, 1501–1520, with a Note on the Early Editions of the "Celestina."* Cambridge: UP, 1966.

Penney, Clara Louisa. *The Book Called "Celestina" in the Library of the Hispanic Society of America*. New York: Hispanic Society of America, 1954.

Russell, Peter E. *Temas de "La Celestina" y otros estudios: Del "Cid" al "Quijote."* Colección Letras e Ideas, Maior, 14. Barcelona: Ariel, 1978.

Snow, Joseph T. *"Celestina" by Fernando de Rojas: An Annotated Bibliography of World Interest 1930–1985*. Madison, WI: HSMS, 1985.

———, ed. *Celestinesca: Boletín informativo internacional* (Dept. of Romance Languages, U. of Georgia), biannual journal devoted to *Celestina*, with running bibliography, since 1977.

Kathleen Kish

**CENSORSHIP IN SPANISH LITERATURE.** The function of censorship within a given political, religious, or social group is to declare and to maintain the values of the community as perceived by the censors. Every community or society at some time engages in censorship of one kind or another. The literary history of any nation should include an account of the censorial practices which helped to structure the prevailing values, tastes and styles of the culture. For Spanish literature, censorial activities of most wide-ranging significance began in the early modern period. With the proclamation of the Papal Bull of 1478 establishing the Spanish *Inquisition, restrictions were placed on what was written about or by Jews and Judaizing converts (\*conversos). The significance of that proclamation would not become fully evident until the sixteenth c. when all the forces limiting biblical studies, philological methodology and humanistic inquiry in general had altered the course of \*Renaissance culture in Spain. In that period, major censorial activities were necessarily associated with the rapidly growing new print technology. A 1502 proclamation by the Catholic Monarchs Isabel and Ferdinand required that a ms. receive approval of the Royal Council before a printing permit would be finally issued. Accompanying the secular control of unprinted works were the ecclesiastical and Inquisitorial printing permits and the church's *Índices*, the lists of printed works which were deemed to be morally or spiritually damaging to potential readers. The first Spanish *Index* (1551; See *Índice de libros prohibidos*) was a variant of the Louvain *Index* (1550–51), and it included no works that were literary in the strict sense. Although the 1559 Valdés Index was predominantly a list of prohibited theological and devotional works, it did include some literary works by Juan del \*Encina, Bartolomé de \*Torres Naharro, Gil \*Vicente, Alfonso and Juan de \*Valdés, Luis de \*Granada, Garci \*Sánchez de Badajoz and Jorge \*Manrique as well as two editions of *Lazarillo de Tormes* (See *Lazarillos*). In effect, the early Renaissance experimentation of some of Spain's most important writers of literary and humanistic works was curtailed by the *Index's* prohibitions on their writing. The Quiroga *Indices* of 1583 and 1584 added few literary works to the prohibited list, but they initiated the listing of expurgated works, a practice that would be expanded in the seventeenth-3. *Indices* of Sandoval (1612), Zapata (1632), and Sotomayor (1640). The expurgation of works in Spain became a somewhat liberalizing alternative to the total prohibition practiced by the Roman Inquisition: it legalized the reading of certain works after objectionable passages were deleted. The acts of expurgation which effectively saved works from total prohibition ranged from one word, as in the case of Gregorio \*Silvestre, or a sentence as in \*Cervantes's *Don Quixote*, to several hundreds of pages in Luis de Granada's case. It is significant that among the secular and regular clerics and the doctors of theology and canon law who typically served as censors were Spanish humanists such as Benito \*Arias Montano and Juan de \*Mariana, strong advocates for expurgation as an alternative to the absolute prohibition of works.

One method of assessing the effect of censorial activity on Spanish literature is to consider the types and numbers of literary works which were included on prohibitory or expurgatory *Indices*. Theater works and religious essays were the most prohibited literary genres, the novel second, and poetry the least. As times changed, the censors' perception of what was morally or spiritually dangerous resulted in the addition of some previously approved older works to a new *Index* or supplement. Two cases in point are the 1632 expurgation of the \*Celestina and the 1801 prohibition of Lope de \*Vega's *La fianza satisfecha* (A Bond Honored). In an analysis of all the *Indices* and their corresponding supplements published between 1551 and 1848, Antonio Márquez reports that only eighty-two writers among the entire number censured were authors of literary works. By way of comparison, he notes that while 1,500 nonliterary writers were added to Zapata's 1632 *Index*, only eighteen names of literary authors were included (Márquez, 159). However, the statistical testimonies of the *Índices* describe only one aspect of the censorial activity that ruled in Spain from the sixteenth c. onward. An author's works could be censured without inclusion on an *Index*. Antonio de *Nebrija, Cristóbal de *Castillejo, and Lope had works of prose or poetry confiscated, and the representation of certain plays by Lope and Pedro *Calderón de la Barca were prohibited although no *Index* listed the condemned works. The threat of a possible Inquisitorial investigation and the danger that a book once written might not be printed combined to create a climate of fear and suspicion in which writers, publishers and bookdealers attempted to work (see Kamen, Pinto Crespo, and Márquez). Indirectly, by its impact on cultural attitudes in general, the censorial atmosphere predominating in Spain affected Spanish literature in ways which have yet to be revealed. It is assumed that in order to survive, authors practiced undetermined types of self-censorship, whose profound psychological and literary complications need to be fully studied (*see* Alcalá). Other unanswered questions concern the development of certain genres, especially the *picaresque novel, whose evolution might have been furthered by the official disapproval of less realistic works such as chivalric or pastoral romances. In addition, there is room for speculation about what unknown effects were wrought on Spanish culture by the prohibition of foreign authors such as Rabelais and Boccaccio or John Locke, Adam Smith and Alexander Pope. While limited numbers of prohibited works from neighboring lands did reach some Spanish readers despite the Inquisition's inspection of imported goods, the deprivation of innumerable religious and literary works constitutes a missing force that could have shaped Spanish culture.

Repressive Inquisitorial acts are usually associated with sixteenth and seventeenth-c. Spain, but the powerful Holy Office remained as a strong determinant of what eighteenth-c. Spaniards were allowed to write and read. It could be said that censorship was more severe since fewer enlightened individuals were enlisted as censors. In addition, fewer works could be "saved" by expurgation since the new *Indices* listed only prohibited works. As a whole these *Indices* contained fewer theological works but many more books and authors whose political philosophy threatened the *ancien régime*. For example, one volume of Benito Jerónimo *Feijóo's 1739 *Teatro crítico universal* was listed on the 1747 Pérez de Prado *Index*. The regime of Charles III brought more enlightened control to the censorial process. In 1762 the king abolished the *tassa*, the required government license to print a work, and in 1768 he established a liberalized state system of hearings to process works for approval. A 1773 proclamation removed the bishops' powers to issue *imprimatur* documents, but the Inquisition was still able to maintain some censorial powers. The forces of the status quo and liberalization continued to battle over the issue of censorship from the time of the French Revolution through the first decades of the nineteenth c. The 1790 *Index* of Rubín de Cevallos was followed by an 1805 supplement that included works by Nicolás Fernández de *Moratín, Diego de *Torres Villarroel, and José *Cadalso. Inquisitorial restraints often consisted of informal legal actions against Enlightenment supporters such as Mauricio de Iriarte in 1776, Félix María *Samaniego in 1793 and Mariano Luis de Urguijo in 1796. Pablo de *Olavide was the only author to be fully processed by the Inquisition in the eighteenth c. (1776–78), and he was the last Spanish author to undergo a complete Inquisitorial trial. In the main, those who suffered most censorial pressures or Inquisitorial processes in that century were the editors and directors of periodic publications with whom the major literary figures collaborated.

During the first twenty years of the nineteenth c. the Inquisition continued to exercise active censorial powers while liberal forces fought against its control. In 1808, Gaspar Melchor de *Jovellanos—a censor himself—suffered legal action against his *Informe sobre la ley agraria* (*Agrarian Law Report*). In 1810, however, the Cortes de Cádiz (Parliament) issued a declaration of freedom of the press. By 1834 the Spanish Inquisition was abolished by María Cristina in the name of young Queen Isabel II. The *Index* continued to appear, but only in the form of supplements and additions. For example, an 1844 summary index was followed by an 1848 appendix which prohibited Leandro Fernández de *Moratín's *El sí de las niñas* (The Brides' Consent), and Bartolomé José *Gallardo's *Diccionario crítico-burlesco*. The Spanish *Indices* of 1866 and 1880 are merely Spanish versions of the Roman Index. For the remainder of the nineteenth c. and in the early decades of the following one, enforcement of the *Indices* and other censorial practices no longer functioned through formal bureaucratic structures specifically organized to censure. Censorial standards were more randomly applied as local bishops and functionaries placed strictures on specific works as the occasion might arise. Although a prelate might declare certain books dangerous, readers managed to acquire such works without fearing the widespread inspection of private libraries and bookstores, the seizure of imported books, and the rigorous prosecution techniques that characterized the Inquisition's control during the sixteenth and seventeenth centuries. Nevertheless, even before the Civil War, representations of theater works could be prohibited, and outspoken writers continued to exercise auto-censorship.

For nearly thirty years after the Civil War, official censorship in Spain was based on the Press Law of 1938. In effect, what had been an exceptional wartime measure became the institutionalized norm as the Franco regime created a censorial bureaucracy reminiscent of that of the seventeenth c. A Book Inspection Service functioned to enforce the 1938 code until the Ministry of Information and Tourism was formed under the direction of Gabriel Arias Salgado in 1951. The total rigidity of censorial control under his regime was followed in 1962 by eight years of somewhat less severe vigilance under the supervision of Manuel Fraga Iribarne. During his administration, a new Press Law (1966) was established in an attempt to loosen censorial control established in 1938. While the results for the media were slightly positive, for authors and book publishers

Fraga's measures resulted in more detailed examination of works. Consequently, under the Press Law's facade of liberalization, more works were expurgated and detained by Fraga's censorial practices than during other periods of Franco's rule. The brief administrations of Alfredo Sánchez Bella (1970–73) and of Pío Cabanillas Gallas (1974–75) were characterized by progressively fewer denunciations of books and more open control as the Franco regime waned and advocates of civil freedom continued to gain influence.

During the Franco era, administrators censured works which were not supportive of (1) the regime or its institutions, (2) the church or its ministers, (3) strict moral standards, and (4) proper and non-provocative language. Our knowledge of the manner in which these general criteria were applied has benefited greatly from a survey of Spanish authors conducted by Manuel Abellán. According to his 1980 study, Spanish writers were unanimous in reporting that censorial practices were extremely inconsistent. For the writers, Spanish censorship was like the Franco regime itself: lacking a precise definition of which traditional values were to be defended, it imposed itself by negating its ill-defined contrary (Abellán, p. 135). The survey of authors determined that the most censured genre was clearly the novel with some 13 percent of works having been considerably detained for three or more years by the censors. Most poetry publications, however, were detained one year or less. Theater works appear to have been subject to more local restrictions against performances, but dramatic mss. were often detained for lengthy periods. Contributing to the official functions exercised by censors were the paracensorial activities of those outside the bureaucracy. The auto-censorship practiced by writers and their agents was accompanied by the considerable censorial activities of their editors. After the 1966 Press Law, editors openly consulted with censors even before works were officially submitted for final censorial approval. The most typical case of censorial pressure for any author consisted of delays in publication. For others, such as Juan *Marsé in the case of his prize-winning *Si te dicen que caí* (The Fallen), an alternative was to publish his work in another Spanish-speaking nation. In an extreme case, Ana María *Matute chose to renounce totally her novel *Luciérnagas* (Fireflies) when the censors banned it in 1953. As in earlier periods, well-known Spanish authors and intellectuals served as censors. Abellán lists the examples of José Antonio *Maravall and Martín de Riquer (p. 110) and the case of José Camilo *Cela who had published *La colmena* (1951; The Beehive) in Argentina to avoid censorship but who had served as a censor of Spanish periodicals and had been granted unusual clemency for his later novels (pp. 69, 113–14) through his personal association with censors. Since the era of Franco censorship ended in 1976, Spanish readers and writers have experienced the same general freedom of expression and information as the citizens of other Western democracies. Previously prohibited works of foreign and Spanish authors are now widely available as Spain enjoys a cultural renaissance. *See also* Printing in Spain.

BIBLIOGRAPHY

Criticism

Abellán, Manuel. *Censura y creación literaria en España 1939–1976*. Barcelona: Península, 1980.

Alcalá, Angel "Control inquisitorial de humanistas y escritores." *Inquisición española y mentalidad inquisitorial*. Ed. A. Alcalá. Barcelona: Ariel, 1984.

Anon. "Spain: *Índice*: 20 Years of Censorship." *Index on Censorship* 1.4 (1972).

Beneyto, Antonio. *Censura y política en los escritores españoles*. Barcelona: Euros, 1975.

Burns, James. "The Wrinkled New Face of Spain." *Index on Censorship* 6.3 (1977).

Cisquella, G., J. L. Erviti, and J. A. Sorolla. *Diez años de represión cultural. La censura de libros durante la Ley de Prensa (1966–76)*. Barcelona: Juvenil, 1977.

Cramsie, Hilde F. *Teatro y censura en la España franquista*. New York: Peter Lang, 1984.

Diéguez, Diego. "Spain's Golden Silence." *Index on Censorship* 2.1 (1973).

Domergue, Lucienne. *Le livre en Espagne au temps de la Révolution Française*. Lyon: Presses Universitaires, 1984.

Journeau, Brigitte. "Problèmes de censure entre 1844 et 1854." *Culture et société en Espagne et en Amérique latine au XIXe siècle*. Lille: Centre d'Études Ibériques et Ibéro-américaines, 1980.

Kamen, Henry. *The Spanish Inquisition*. New York: New American Library, 1965.

Márquez, Antonio. *Literatura e Inquisición en España (1478–1834)*. Madrid: Taurus, 1980.

Morón Arroyo, Ciriaco. "La Inquisición y la posibilidad de la gran literatura barroca española." *Inquisición española y mentalidad inquisitorial*. Ed. A. Alcalá. Barcelona: Ariel, 1984.

Pinto Crespo, Virgilio. *Inquisición y control ideológico en la España del siglo XVI*. Madrid: Taurus, 1983.

Rumeu de Armas, Antonio. *Historia de la censura gubernativa en España*. Madrid: M. Aguilar, 1940.

Sierra Corella, Antonio. *La censura de libros y papeles en España y los índices y catálogos españoles de los prohibidos y expurgados*. Madrid: Cuerpo Facultativo de Archiveros, Bibliotecarios y Arqueólogos, 1947.

Catherine Swietlicki

**CENTENO, Yvette Kace** (1940, Lisbon– ), novelist, playwright, poet, essayist, director of programs for radio and television, translator. Although known more as a novelist (especially, *Não só quem nos odeia* [1966; Not Only He Who Hates Us] and *As Palavras, que pena* [1972; The Words, What a Pity]), Yvette Centeno is an emerging figure in Portuguese theater and poetry. Her 1983 novel, *No Jardim das Nogueiras* (In the Walnut Grove), is a mystical experiment of the *novas escritas*. She writes an alchemical poetry concerned with noncommunication in human relations and with the absurd in life's discontinuities. Jungian symbologies pervade her poetry since her first publications in the 1960s to today. Her 1984 poems in *Perto da :erra* (Close to the Earth) are a personal, intertextual (Paul Celan) preoccupation with the "conjunção/conjunction" of past-present, life-death, thought-being, and Centeno's tropic attraction to the occult and mysterious. The 1974 revolution helped bring out the dramaturge in Centeno with *Teatro aberto* (1974; Open Theater), whose dramatic exercises, though still tied to the old declamatory theatrical axioms, are struggles for a new drama. Her plays also show a neo-Baroque game of reversals in words and deeds as in *Saudades do Paraíso* (1979; Nostalgia for Paradise).

Yvette Centeno also publishes critical essays on the symbological in Peter Weiss, Fernando *Pessoa, Hermann Hesse (see *5 Aproximações* [1976; *5 Approximations*]), in *Camões (see *A Viagem de "Os Lusíadas": Símbolo e Mito* [1981; The Voyage of *The Lusiads*: Symbol and Myth]), and in *A Alquimia do amor* (1982; The Alchemy of Love).

She earned a master's degree in Germanic philology at the U of Lisbon, and taught for four years at the Universidade Nova de Lisboa. Her essays and columns appear in many Portuguese and European journals and newspapers, such as *Colóquio: Letras*, *Biblos* and *Humboldt*. She directs children's programs for radio and television, besides translating Shakespeare, Brecht, C. Sternheim, and H. Lange.

BIBLIOGRAPHY

Primary Texts

*O Barco na cidade*. Lisbon: Guimarães, 1965.

*Irreflexões*. Lisbon: Atica, 1974.

*Perto da terra*. Lisbon: Presença, 1984.

*Teatro aberto*. Lisbon: Atica, 1974.

*5 Aproximações: Peter Weiss—A. Ramos Rosa, Alquimia e misticismo, Fernando Pessoa—Hermann Hesse*. Lisbon: Ática, 1976.

English Translations

Three poems in *Micromegas: A Poetry Magazine: Portuguese issue* 12.1 (1985): 5–6.

Robert R. Krueger

***CENTÓN*** (Cento), literary term. The word derives from the Latin *Cento*, or "patchwork." Popular during the *Renaissance, Centones are poetry compilations of quotes and excerpts by famous authors. There is one such title in Spanish literature, the *Centón epistolario*. It was published around 1650, but bore the false date of 1499. It was a falsification, but the perpetrator remains a mystery. The pseudonym used was El Bachiller *Gómez de Cibdarreal.

**CERDÁ Y RICO, Francisco** (1739, Castalla, Alicante–1800, Madrid), humanist, bibliophile. He attended the U of Valencia, graduating in 1760 with a bachelor's degree in civil law. In 1776, he was appointed to the staff of the Royal Library. There, for the next seventeen years, he dedicated himself to editing near-forgotten works and mss. of medieval and *Siglo de Oro Spanish literature—works such as F. de *Moncada's chronicle, *Expedición de los catalanes y aragoneses contra turcos y griegos* (1777; Expedition of the Catalans and Aragonese against the Turks and Greeks), a twenty-one volume collection of Lope de *Vega's loose, or uncollected works, and writings by Pedro de *Valencia, Juan de *Vergara and Luisa *Sigea, in the two-volume *Clarorum Hispanorum opuscula selecta et rariora* (1776–78; Selected Rare Works by Illustrious Spaniards).

BIBLIOGRAPHY

Primary Texts

*Clarorum hispanorum opuscula selecta et rariora*. Madrid: Sancha, 1781.
*Colección de las obras sueltas de Lope Félix de Vega Carpio*. Madrid: Sancha, 1781.
*Expedición de los catalanes y aragoneses contra turcos y grigos*. By F. de Moncada. Madrid: Sancha, 1777.

Criticism

González Palencia, A. *Don Francisco Cerdá y Rico. Su vida y sus obras*. Madrid: Tip. de Archivos, 1928.

**CERNUDA, Luis** (1902, Sevilla–1963, Mexico), poet and critic. Cernuda's first collection, *Perfil del aire* (1927; The Air's Profile), announced an accomplished craftsman with a gift for clarity and concision. This collection became *Primeras poesías* (First Poems) upon the publication in 1936 of the poet's assembled verse as *La realidad y el deseo* (1936; Reality and Desire), a title that he would henceforth use for all subsequent editions. Cernuda's principal prose poetry is gathered in two collections, *Ocnos* (1942; Ocnos) and *Variaciones sobre tema mexicano* (1952; Variations on a Mexican Theme). His wide-ranging critical works include two collections of essays, *Poesía y literatura I & II* (1971; Poetry and Literature I & II), *Estudios sobre poesía española contemporánea* (1957; Studies on Contemporary Spanish Poetry), *Crítica, ensayos y evocaciones* (1970; Criticism, Essays and Evocations), *Pensamiento poético en la lírica inglesa (siglo XIX)* (1958; Poetic Thought in English Lyricism [XIXth Century]).

In the late 1920s and early 1930s, the influence of surrealism liberated Cernuda from formal and emotional constraints. In the two books written at that time, *Un río, un amor* (1929; A River, A Love, 1971) and *Los placeres prohibidos* (1931; Forbidden Pleasures, 1971), Cernuda abandons the strictures of formal verse in favor of a freer, discursive line.

From the first moment of his poetry, to *Invocaciones* (1935; Invocations, 1971), Cernuda investigates problematic areas of his existence: a dissatisfaction with social circumstance ranging from the general concerns of politics (he embraces communism for a short period) through a rejection of conventional religion to the feeling of alienation from customary mores rooted in his homosexuality. This multi-faceted rebelliousness caused Cernuda to feel isolated at times, though more often than not he saw this isolation as the necessary condition of the poet.

Cernuda achieves his mature voice with *Las Nubes* (1940; The Clouds, 1971). His principal themes are now time and its corollary ideas: death, the supreme evidence of man's temporality; memory, a generally insufficient ally; desire, or love, both the means to arrest decay and at the same time the most painful reminders of its inevitability. The presence of Spain is significant in *The Clouds* but will diminish in the next collection *Como quien espera el alba* (1947; *Like Someone Waiting for the Dawn*, 1971), to be replaced by the nostalgia of exile.

The years between the Spanish Civil War and his departure from England were Cernuda's most tumultuous period and his most productive. Besides the collections just mentioned he completed *Ocnos*, a volume of prose poems. He brings the dramatic monologue to a high degree of polish with such pieces as "Quetzalcoatl." He is determined now to salvage out of his own past, his present, and the nature of his art a system of values, ethical and esthetic, from which he can contemplate disaster with some hope. He will turn with insistence to an examination of art as an instrument of investigation and as a means to achieve, at times, moments of eloquent serenity.

*Vivir sin estar viviendo* (1949; *Living without Being Alive*, 1971), completed in the United States, also belongs to this period. Here, the poet explores the discontinuities of time and of the self. His expression tends toward ever greater simplicity, while the flow of his verse seeks the inner music of the language, achieving an active tension between its flow and the stresses of the poetic line.

Cernuda's meditative poems develop from material to abstract evidence. They ponder the concreteness of circumstance according to a near cosmic plane of being. But in the last phase of his poetry encompassed by *Con las horas contadas* (1956; *With Time Running Out*, 1971) and *Desolación de la Quimera* (1962; *The Disconsolate Chimera*, 1971), the poet finds this plane of being within himself as an immediate apprehension of continuity. Such meditative pieces include a note of irony that now tempers the attraction of any harmonizing vision. The self-examination is often engaged in through the second person form of address—dialogue with himself—favored by the poet since *The Clouds* and achieving now its most sophisticated form, as in "Nocturno Yanqui" (Yankee Nocturne), one of the great poems of Cernuda's last phase.

*The Disconsolate Chimera*, Cernuda's final collection, shows no change of direction. The exploration of love is still important: love re-creating reality, narcissism—and its corollary, homosexual passion, the chasm between the beloved and the lover. Time and the body remain terms of reference with respect to the resistance of desire to aging as well as in the memory of past love. The memory of Spain reappears, and the theme of the bitterness of exile resurges. This last book also contains some of Cernuda's greatest poems in which he interrogates the nature of art: "Mozart (1756–1956)," "Ninfa y pastor, por Tiziano" (Nymph and Shepherd, by Titian) and perhaps the greatest of his longer compositions, "Luis de Baviera escucha *Lohengrin*" (Louis of Bavaria Listens to *Lohengrin*), an intense pondering of music and representation as an enhancing mirror to Narcissus.

Because of Cernuda's clarity, his total involvement in his task, his view of poetry as an instrument for investigating reality and the self, recent generations of Spanish poets have turned to him as their mentor. They acknowledge him as the first of the group of 1925 to express with impassioned logic the paradoxes of duration and to have made of ethical introspection the methodological cornerstone of his poetry.

BIBLIOGRAPHY

Primary Texts

*La realidad y el deseo*. Mexico: Fondo de Cultura Económica, 1965.
*Poesía completa*. Barcelona: Barral, 1977.
*Prosa completa*. Barcelona: Barral, 1975.

English Translations

*The Poetry of Luis Cernuda*. Ed. A. Edkins and D. Harris. New York: New York UP, 1971.
*Selected Poems of Luis Cernuda*. Ed. and tr. R. Gibbons. Berkeley: U of California P, 1977.

Criticism

Harris, Derek. *Luis Cernuda: A Study of the Poetry*. London: Tamesis, 1973.
Talens, Jenaro. *El espacio y las máscaras. Introducción a la lectura de Cernuda*. Barcelona: Anagrama, 1975.
Jiménez-Fajardo, Salvador. *Luis Cernuda*. TWAS 455. Boston: Twayne, 1978.

Salvador Jiménez Fajardo

**CERVANTES DE SALAZAR, Francisco** (1514?, Toledo–1575, México), historian and author. A student at Salamanca and professor at the U of Osuna (1546), he left for México in 1551, was rector of the university there, and canon of the cathedral when he died.

His *Obras* (Complete Works) were published in Alcalá in 1546 and re-edited, with a prologue, by \*Cerdá y Rico (Madrid, 1772). Among them are the continuation of \*Pérez de Oliva's *Diálogo de la dignidad del hombre* (Dialogue on the Dignity of Man); Luis \*Mexía's *Labricio Portundo (Apólogo de la ociosidad y el trabajo* (Labricio Portundo, Fable on Idleness and Work) glossed and moralized; and Luis \*Vives's *Introducción y camino para la sabiduría* (Introduction and Path to Knowledge), expanded and with commentary. These *Obras* are dedicated to Hernán \*Cortés, the major personage in Cervantes de Salazar's great work, *Crónica de Nueva España* (Chronicle of New Spain). A narrative of greatest historical value for knowledge of the conquest of México, it was based on the *Relaciones* (Accounts) of Cortés, whom he knew personally, and on the works of \*López de Gómara. The *Crónica*, which consists of six books, has been edited by Manuel Magallón (Madrid, 1914), and served as a source for Antonio de \*Herrera's *Historia*. It is of much interest for the study of the customs, rites, witchcraft, ceremonies, etc., of the Indians. Cervantes de Salazar also wrote the *Túmulo imperial de la gran ciudad de México* (Imperial Sepulcher of the Great City of Mexico), in which he relates the posthumous honors dedicated to the memory of Charles V in New Spain.

BIBLIOGRAPHY

Primary Texts

*Crónicas de la Nueva España.* Ed. M. Magallón. BAE 244 and 245.
*México en 1554: tres diálogos latinos.* Mexico: Jesús Medina, 1970.
*México en 1554 y Túmulo imperial.* Mexico: Porrúa, 1972.
*Obras que Francisco Cervantes de Salazar ha hecho, glosado, y traduzido. La primera
     es la introducción y camino para la sabiduría.* Alcalá de Henares: n.p., 1546.

English Translation

*Life in the Imperial and Loyal City of Mexico in New Spain, and the Royal and Pontifical
     University of Mexico, as Described in the Dialogues for the Study of the Latin
     Language.* Tr. Minnie Lee Barrett. Westport, CT: Greenwood, 1970.

                                                              Catherine Larson

**CERVANTES SAAVEDRA, Miguel de** (1547, Alcalá de Henares–1616, Madrid), novelist, dramatist, and poet. Cervantes was one of seven children in what may well have been a *converso family (i.e., of Jewish blood) of very modest means; his father was a practical surgeon. Little is known of his early years except that in Madrid in the late 1560s he was a favored pupil of the Erasmian educator *López de Hoyos. At the age of twenty-four, after military service probably in Flanders and in Italy, Cervantes fought valiantly in the battle of Lepanto on October 7, 1571. The serious wounds he received on this occasion, particularly that which disabled his left hand, were for him a proud reminder that he had taken part in one of the great events in history, the battle that kept Europe safe from the Turkish hordes.

In 1575 Cervantes was returning to Spain when his ship was captured by Turkish pirates; for the next five years he was held as a slave for ransom in Algiers. His genuinely heroic efforts to organize escape attempts and the respect with which he was treated by his captors are the stuff of legend.

After a dramatic last-minute ransom that saved him from being shipped to Constantinople and perhaps lost forever to posterity, Cervantes arrived in Spain in 1580 only to learn that ex-soldiers often receive less than the admiring welcome and support of a grateful society that they might have expected. Upon his return Cervantes settled in Madrid, where he turned from arms to letters and became a significant figure in the formative era of the Spanish *theater. During this period Cervantes had a liaison with an actress, which led to the birth of his only child, his daughter Isabel. In 1584 he married the respectable Catalina de Salazar from Esquivias, in La Mancha. Long periods of separation in their married life, together with the fact that they had no children, have suggested that the marriage was less than successful, although some biographers also point out that Cervantes's frequent stays in Esquivias can also suggest a more stable family situation.

Cervantes's first substantial work of prose fiction, the *pastoral romance entitled *Galatea*, was published in 1585. Shortly thereafter Cervantes was employed as a civil servant, first requisitioning supplies for the Spanish Armada, and then as a tax collector, performing tasks that required constant travel, mostly in southern Spain. On at least two occasions, in 1597 and 1602, he was jailed when his accounts did not balance. By 1604 Cervantes was living in Valladolid, then the site of the court, writing some of the fiction that was to be published subsequently.

After the appearance of the first part of *Don Quixote* in 1605, Cervantes moved with the court to Madrid in 1606; there he was to reside for the remainder of his life. Little is known of his activities (besides writing) during this period. After a surprising eight-year lapse of time, Cervantes's final years saw the publication of a brilliant series of works: 1613, *Exemplary Tales*; 1614, the poetic *Voyage to Parnassus*; 1615, *Don Quixote* II and *Eight Plays*. On April 23, 1616, having recently taken Franciscan vows and been administered last rites, Cervantes died, probably of dropsy. He was buried in an unmarked grave in the Trinitarian convent on what is today the Street of Lope de Vega in Madrid.

Cervantes's life, with its classic mixture of glory and failure, as a model for the artist who was not appreciated by his contemporaries as he would be by posterity, and as an example of how one can maintain humanity and optimism in the face of repeated setbacks and disappointments, is almost as much a source of inspiration as are his greatest literary efforts. Biographers, novelists, poets, dramatists (e.g., as in the case of the American musical comedy *Man of La Mancha*) have often fused Miguel de Cervantes and Don Quixote into a single character. In the most literal sense, Cervantes's own words, "Each man is the child of his own works," are true in his case.

Cervantes's literary works include the following: *La Galatea* (1585; *Galatea*, 1833); *El ingenioso hidalgo Don Quijote de la Mancha* (1605; *The History of the Valorous and Wittie Knight-Errant, Don Quixote of the Mancha*, 1612); *Novelas ejemplares* (1613; *Exemplarie Novells*, 1640); *Viaje del Parnaso* (1614; *Voyage to Parnassus*, 1870); *Segunda parte del ingenioso caballero Don Quijote de la Mancha* (1615; *The Second Part of the History of the Valorous and Wittie Knight-Errant, Don Quixote of the Mancha,* 1620); *Ocho comedias y ocho entremeses* (1615; Eight Plays and Eight Interludes [See Bibliography Section B-Honig and Starkie.]); *Los trabajos de Persiles y Sigismunda* (1617; *The Trials of Persiles and Sigismunda,* 1619); miscellaneous poetry, especially the "Epístola a Mateo Vázquez" (Letter to Mateo Vazquez); and two plays from the 1580s, *Los tratos de Argel* (*The Commerce of Algiers*, 1870) and *La Numancia* (*Numantia*, 1885). In addition, several works have been attributed to Cervantes: the story "La tía fingida" (The Feigned Aunt), several interludes, various poems, and a fragment of dialogue entitled "La vida del campo" (Country Life), which has been proposed either as part of the sequel to *Galatea* or as a section from the projected *Semanas del jardín* (Weeks in the Garden).

### Poetry

Like most of his contemporaries, Cervantes would have aspired to greatness as a poet more than as anything else. He wrote verse all his life, and most of his major prose works include embedded poetry. But in spite of his love for the genre, Cervantes seldom achieved excellence as a lyric (or dramatic) poet, a fact which he recognized on several occasions.

Cervantes comes closest to significant achievement when writing in a humorous or satiric vein. Without doubt his most enduring single poem is the sonnet that begins "Voto a Dios, que me espanta esta grandeza" (I swear to God that all this grandeur frightens me), a sharp satire on the opulent tomb of Philip II in the cathedral of Seville, which Cervantes himself read dramatically at the scene in 1598. Also worthy of note are another pair of sonnets in the same vein, especially the one on the English raid on Cádiz, the *romance* entitled "Los celos" (Jealousy); the sonnet "Cuando Preciosa el panderete toca" (When Preciosa plays the tambourine) from "The Little Gypsy Girl"; Grisóstomo's song and Cardenio's *ovillejos* from *Don Quixote* I, 14 and 27 respectively; and some of the burlesque poetry found throughout *Don Quixote*. Not without interest, especially in some vivid and moving passages, is the "Letter to Mateo Vázquez," a plea for military intervention to rescue Christian slaves in Africa; the poem's authenticity, however, has been seriously questioned. His most sustained effort, the *Voyage to Parnassus*, is a long allegory and satire; the best passage is the penetrating self-presentation at the beginning of ch. 4.

**Theater**

Cervantes's contribution to the shaping of the Spanish theater in the 1580s can probably never be judged adequately, as all but two of the twenty to thirty plays he states he wrote during that period are lost. His claims to have been the first Spanish dramatist to reduce the number of acts from five to three and to use allegorical figures on stage, as well as to have been well received by the theater-going public, may be somewhat exaggerated, but probably contain at least some literal truth. *The Commerce of Algiers* is dramatically clumsy but occasionally interesting for its autobiographical glimpses and presentation of the daily life of Christian captives in northern Africa. *Numantia* is Cervantes's best-known and most admired full-length play. This grand and genuinely moving— though sometimes ponderous and long-winded—story of the heroic resistance of a single Celtiberian town under siege by Roman troops has had great patriotic and romantic appeal.

Late in life Cervantes revised a few earlier dramatic works, wrote some new ones and published his *Eight Plays and Eight Interludes* in 1613. In the prologue he writes of his long-standing fondness for the theater, recalls having seen as a child the famous Lope de *Rueda and his primitive traveling theater, makes the claims for himself cited above, and states that he was at work on yet another drama. Cervantes returns to Algiers for the setting of some of these generally undistinguished works, others are based on legendary or literary themes, some are love intrigues, and a few have more realistic elements. The best of them is *Pedro de Urdemalas*, the story of a *pícaro* (*picaresque) who eventually becomes an actor.

It is really only in the short, comic interludes (*entremeses) that Cervantes's genius consistently shines. None of his contemporaries who wrote in this popular genre produced better works than these. All eight interludes have their comic and satiric moments, but three are absolute gems. In "El viejo celoso" (The Jealous Old Husband) a young wife deceives and mocks her elderly spouse. "La cueva de Salamanca" (The Cave of Salamanca) also deals with marital deception, as a student poses as a magician in order to turn the lovers of a woman and her maid into "devils," allowing the adulterers and lovers to escape the husband's wrath. "El retablo de las maravillas" (The Wonder Show) is a variant on the theme of the emperor's new clothes. In order to see the invisible drama staged by two traveling *pícaros*, the audience (including the town's most distinguished citizens) must be of legitimate birth and of pure Christian stock (i.e., neither bastards nor of Jewish blood). In order to preserve their social status, of course, all pretend to see the non-existent marvels being "presented."

### Galatea

*Pastoral literature was popular throughout the *Renaissance, and in the wake of the models provided by Sannazaro's *Arcadia* (1504) and Montemayor's *Diana* (1559) the pastoral romance replaced the romance of chivalry as the most popular form of fiction in the second half of the sixteenth century. It was only natural that a young ex-soldier and aspiring dramatist should take a turn at the genre: Cervantes's first published work was *Galatea*, 1585. The conventions of the pastoral—the stylized vocabulary, settings, themes, and characters—had an irresistible appeal to Cervantes throughout his career and appear from time to time in several of his works, especially both parts of *Don Quixote*. On the other hand, no writer of the time satirizes more sharply these very conventions, especially in the canine pastoral episode of "El coloquio de los perros" (The Dogs' Colloquy).

*Galatea* may be the least appealing of Cervantes's novels, but is by no means ordinary as a pastoral romance. Cervantes, as was his custom, expanded the limits within which such romances were normally written. The main characters Galatea and Elicio are not among the most moving pastoral creations, the bucolic and amorous poetry scattered throughout is rarely distinguished, the plot is characteristically not very coherent, the long interpolated "Song" of the muse Calíope is an unattractive panegyric, and the work's acknowledged inconclusiveness is unsatisfying. Yet there are in the text moments of brilliance, and Cervantes's introduction of Italianate and Byzantine elements in some of the interpolated narrations, together with a surprising degree of violence and emphasis on death, clearly set his romance apart from others in the tradition.

### Don Quixote I

The premise of the 1605 *Don Quixote* is intertextual. The book is a parody and satire on the romances of chivalry; it contains an ongoing commentary, both literal and metaphorical, on all types of fiction, as well as popular and erudite poetry and the theater; it is an intensely self-conscious literary artifact. Everything Don Quixote does in the early part of the novel is in conscious imitation of his literary models: *Amadís de Gaula, Belianís de Grecia, and other heroes of chivalric romances. Other characters such as Sancho Panza, friends and relatives from the village of La Mancha, and various innkeepers, travelers and brief acquaintances made along the way, all participate, with greater or lesser enthusiasm and will, in the knight-errant's world of chivalry.

The opposition between the mad, book-inspired, idealistic knight and his sane, pragmatic, materialistic squire appears to be absolute at the beginning of their relationship. But this simple truth—as is the case with all other facile statements about this novel—obscures the subtle, constantly shifting and evolving, relationship between the two as the book progresses. Early in the novel Sancho distracts Don Quixote from his chivalric enterprise, brings out his humanity through humor, and constantly points out—and sometimes forces his master to acknowledge—reality. Meanwhile, the knight-errant broadens the simple farmer's horizons, introducing him to a variety of literature, intellectual discourse, and social interaction that he had never before experienced. Don Quixote begins as an absolute madman, transforms reality to fit his aesthetic construct, is supremely confident in his physical prowess, admits no compromise, and acts before he reflects. By the end of the book he is physically exhausted from the beatings he has received and emotionally and spiritually sapped from the lies and deceits of both friends and casual acquaintances; when he is defeated in the battle with the penitents in ch. 52 he offers no excuse, and returns home amid scorn and derision in absolute silence, his chivalric career brought to a close. Sancho, meanwhile, slowly assumes an increasingly responsible role in the relationship and even sallies forth in quixotic defense of his master when the latter's supposed friends enviously humiliate and demean him (chs. 47 and 52). The Sancho who returns home at the end of the book and assures his wife that it is a lovely thing to search for adventures and visit castles is virtually a new man.

The structure of *Don Quixote* is episodic and has appeared simple and arbitrary to many readers. Such, however, is not the case. The work is carefully modulated to swing between action and reflection, primary and secondary narration. There is ample evidence that Cervantes revised the structure of his text in order to achieve a greater variety and balance of tone, rhythm and theme. An episode from early in the book, such as Don Quixote's battle with the Basque squire (chs. 8–9), could not be interchanged with one from the midpoint, such as the episode of the galley slaves (ch. 22), and much less with one from the final section, such as Don Quixote's defeat by the penitents (ch. 52). A complex web of intratextual allusion to events and concepts is used to develop character, theme and style in such a way that to remove or modify any part would be to jeopardize the whole. The turning point in the book is Don Quixote's withdrawal to the wilderness of the Sierra Morena (ch. 25) in order to perform a gratuitous penance in imitation of Amadís de Gaula and Orlando Furioso. Until this point the comic adventures of knight and squire have been the dominant mode. But with the reintroduction of the curate and barber (ch. 26), who take control of the action in the remaining chapters, the book becomes quite something else. The increased prominence of embedded narration and various secondary characters who dominate the reader's attention make the latter half of the book substantially different from the first.

The major thematic concerns include some of those most characteristic of modern literature: the relationship between art and life; reality versus appearance; literary theory and aesthetics; the nature of truth; role playing; and the problems of narration. And all the while the work remains supremely comic. Virtually every type of verbal and conceptual humor is to be found in the text: Don Quixote's archaic speech in imitation of his literary models, and his inappropriate rhetoric, both forms of parody; other sorts of literary satire and burlesque; Sancho Panza's rustic speech and strings of proverbial clichés; some metafictional incongruities and paradoxes of narration; situational comedy and slapstick humor; practical jokes and tricks; and more. *Don Quixote* is a funny book, but at the same time it raises serious questions and explores subtle psychological relationships.

The popularity of the book was enormous and immediate. Literary and anecdotal references both from Spain and the New World make it clear that the main characters from the book became immediate and indelible features of popular culture. Thomas Shelton's English translation was published in 1612; the translations into French, Italian, German and Dutch soon followed. Contemporary readers seized on the comic and burlesque features that are most prominent in the first half of the book, reacted with mixed feelings to the interpolated narrations, and generally overlooked the more serious or potentially serious aspects of the work. The early image of the mad Don Quixote ridiculously attacking windmills (in ch. 8) overshadowed the later, more serene, defeated and pathetic knight-errant.

### Exemplary Tales

By critical consensus, Cervantes's *Exemplary Tales*, published in 1613, can be divided into three groups. The first group consists of the realistic, often satiric, stories that have appealed most to modern taste; these are the stories most often published, translated, studied, read, and enjoyed today. "Rinconete and Cortadillo" is a picaresque tale of two youths in the context of organized crime in Seville. "El licenciado vidriera" (The Glass Licenciate) is a pathological tale of a man who literally believes that he is made of glass and spouts philosophical and satiric maxims. "El celoso extremeño" (The Jealous Extremaduran) deals with obsessive protectionism and infidelity within the context of a May-December marriage. The highlight of the whole collection is the linked pair of "El casamiento engañoso" (The Deceitful Marriage) and "El coloquio de los perros" (The Dogs' Colloquy) which brings the volume to a close. The former is a brief picaresque episode of mutual deceit that ends with the reading of the ms. of the latter, a satiric tale consisting of the life and opinions of two talking dogs. The sophistication, complexity and ambiguity of this framed narrative provide as intriguing a piece of self-conscious narration as Cervantes ever wrote.

The second group contains those tales generally called idealistic or romantic.

These stories tended to be the most popular and influential with Cervantes's contemporaries, but are less frequently published or read today. They are much more conventional and clearly related to the type of short fiction practiced by Italian Renaissance writers such as Bandello, featuring characters of noble birth, love intrigue, extraordinary coincidence and adventures, a rhetorical style, and a happy resolution. Though all of these stories can be read with pleasure, probably the best of the group is "La fuerza de la sangre" (The Power of Blood), a violent tale of rape and redemption, and a literal demonstration of the power of (spilled) blood to assert itself.

More transitional in nature are the two stories in the third group: "La gitanilla" (The Little Gypsy Girl) and "La ilustre fregona" (The Illustrious Kitchen Maid). Both tales begin in the context of a realistic and marginal subculture, those of gypsies and the picaresque servant class, but both ultimately give way to more conventional plots involving wealthy nobles, hidden identities and happy marriages. These stories are intriguing, but ultimately unsatisfying, narrative experiments.

Overall, the *Exemplary Tales* have usually been ranked second to *Don Quixote* among Cervantes's works. There is no question that they represent a milestone in the development of short fiction in European letters. No previous collection contained a greater variety of style, theme, character, or narrative technique; no previous practitioner of the genre wrote with comparable subtlety, profundity or originality. Not until the nineteenth c. were Cervantes's accomplishments in short story to be matched.

### Don Quixote II

One of the early readers of Cervantes's novel was the unknown person who published a sequel under the pseudonym of Alonso Fernández de *Avellaneda in 1614. Avellaneda accepted Cervantes's explicit invitation at the end of Part I and followed approved literary tradition in continuing another author's unfinished work. Typically, Avellaneda's reading of *Don Quixote* focused on the most superficial comic features of the earliest presentation of the characters. His Don Quixote is absurdly comic, unchanging in his madness, with little or no psychological depth; Sancho Panza is an inferior buffoon. The spurious sequel is well written, clever and amusing, but in every way inferior to Cervantes's continuation. Avellaneda's main contribution was to have spurred Cervantes to complete his own second part, which appeared in 1615, less than a year before his death. In his prefatory material and, more important, in his text, Cervantes devastates his literary rival: he has his characters change course in order not to appear in cities where the false chronicler placed them; devils play tennis in hell with his rival's book; a prominent character from Avellaneda's version signs an affidavit that his previous experiences were false.

"Second parts were never good," says Sansón Carrasco early in Cervantes's continuation of his novel (ch. 4). Literary tradition and the example of Avellaneda lend truth to that affirmation. Cervantes accepted the challenge, however, of competing with himself, and consciously avoided repeating his earlier work. If in Part I the romances of chivalry provided the point of departure, here it is the 1605 *Don Quixote* itself that plays that role. Left alone, the protagonist would not have taken to the road again as a knight-errant, for after his absolute defeat (in I.52) he had no internal motivation for such an effort. The meddling and urging of his friends and—above all—the fact that a history of his adventures has been published, in which it is announced that he made another sally, conspire to force the role of knight-errant back upon him. *Don Quixote* II is not so much the self-generated exploits of a comic madman as it is a chronicle of the existential anguish of a man caught in a role he rejected, trapped by his former self. Don Quixote rarely or never transforms reality as he had early in Part I, talks consciously in imitation of his literary models, or rejects the reality-based advice of Sancho and others in order to undertake fantastic adventures. Instead, he engages in normal discourse, accepts the standard version of reality, is often brooding and introspective, and generally acts poorly in the chivalric tricks and masquerades perpetrated by others. It is only necessary to juxtapose the protagonist's words and deeds in an episode early in Part I, such as the encounter with the silk merchants (ch. 4) or the windmill adventure (ch. 8), with those of one from early in Part II, such as the enchantment of Dulcinea (ch. 10) or the scene with the acting troupe (ch. 11), to see how radically different Cervantes's sequel really is. The most important secondary characters in Part II have read the earlier version of the knight's exploits and, following the example of the curate and others in the second half of that work, deceive and manipulate Don Quixote for their own amusement.

If Don Quixote is an increasingly serious character who receives the reader's growing pity and sympathy, he is proportionally less comic. That is not to say that he is a noble or tragic figure in 1615, but that he has evolved far from the comic madman of the beginning of the first part of the novel. In order to compensate for the knight's diminished importance overall, maintain comedy at the forefront, and provide alternate points of interest, Cervantes introduces several major factors. First of all, Sancho Panza is at least as important as, if not more important than, his master. He speaks more often and more confidently, directs the action to a greater degree, and occupies center stage much more frequently. The long section of the novel that is devoted to his successful governorship (chs. 44–53) is the high point in his intellectual and spiritual development. Comedy is sustained throughout, with slapstick scenes and gratuitous violence still frequent, but much of the comic focus is shifted to the work's narrative structure. Cide Hamete Benengeli, the sometimes omniscient, sometimes very fallible, historian who is supposed to be the primary source of the text's narration, is increasingly put forth in a comic context. He misunderstands and misjudges his characters, engages in flawed logic and philosophizing, and generally distracts the reader from more substantial and serious matters. Meanwhile, social themes (generally only alluded to in passing in the first part) are very prominent in this book. Important contemporary issues such as the responsibilities of society's privileged classes, the expulsion and persecution of the

*Moriscos (converted Muslims) in 1609, and Catalonian banditry are all probed in intriguing detail.

Cervantes's victory over his rival was absolute. While Avellaneda's text was not published in Spain again until well into the eighteenth c., Cervantes's *Don Quixote* II had three editions in the seventeenth c. and the two parts together were published more than a dozen times in that period. Part II was also translated into English by Shelton and published in 1620. The novel's popularity has not waned in any subsequent age.

### Persiles

Cervantes probably began writing his Christian allegory *Persiles and Sigismunda* at some relatively early point, perhaps around the turn of the century, may have worked on it from time to time, and rushed to finish it as he was dying. His last recorded words are those he penned for the dedication and prologue of this book, in late April of 1616; the work was published by his widow in 1617. In *Don Quixote* I, 48, the Canon of Toledo discusses the aesthetics of prose fiction and concludes that an epic can be written in prose as well as it can in verse. *Persiles* is Cervantes's epic in prose and should be read in the light of the ongoing debate over aesthetics—both explicit and metaphorical—that permeates Cervantes's works. Heliodorus's *Ethiopian History* is the acknowledged model upon which the romance is based.

The story is a simple one. Persiles, Prince of Thule, and Sigismunda, Princess of Frisland, in the disguise of Periandro and Auristela, supposedly brother and sister, make a pilgrimage from the dark and barbaric northern regions to Rome, where they reveal their true identities, receive papal blessing and marry. Along the way they have a series of marvelous and dangerous adventures, are separated and reunited several times, undergo numerous physical and spiritual tests, and encounter a large number of extraordinary individuals with interesting stories of their own to tell. Chaos gives way to order, darkness to light, doubt to certainty, conflict to resolution, and paganism to Christianity.

In his dedication to *Don Quixote* II Cervantes stated that he was completing *Persiles* and predicted that it would be either the worst or the best novel written in Spanish. It is, of course, neither. Extremely popular in its own c. (there were eleven editions in the seventeenth c.), translated to all major European languages, the romance was widely read and appreciated through the eighteenth c. After a long period of neglect and scorn in the nineteenth c. and first half of the twentieth c., *Persiles* today is the topic of lively critical debate and the subject of some of the best contemporary Hispanic scholarship. Some consider it Cervantes's supreme achievement.

Cervantes's contributions in poetry, theater and the pastoral novel would at best rank him among the second rate. The significance and influence of the *Exemplary Tales* and *Persiles*, however, would have sufficed to place him at the forefront of his contemporaries as one of Spain's great writers. It is only the towering achievement of *Don Quixote* that moves Cervantes into the hallowed company of Homer, Dante, Shakespeare, and Goethe. No literary genre is so pervasively influenced by a single paradigmatic text as is the novel—the dominant modern genre, one that came into being in sixteenth- and seventeenth-c. Spain— by *Don Quixote*. Great characters created consciously in imitation of Cervantes's knight-errant include such disparate figures as Fielding's Parson Adams, Dickens's Mr. Pickwick, Dostoyevski's Prince Myshkin, *Pérez Galdós's Isidora Rufete, Sinclair Lewis's George F. Babbitt, and Saul Bellow's Eugene Henderson. The basic Cervantine premise of an individual who, as a result of reading books (or watching movies or television), rejects reality in favor of a literature-inspired model is a timeless story told over and over by authors such as Jane Austen, Henri Stendhal, Gustave Flaubert, Henry James, Joyce Carol Oates, John Irving, and many others. As all modern students of metafiction have recognized, *Don Quixote* is the point of departure for this major tradition in fiction. All the great writers in this line—Laurence Sterne, *Unamuno, Roland Barthes, Jorge Luis Borges, John Fowles, and Robert Coover, to name but a few—pay homage to the first and greatest of all ludic novelists—Miguel de Cervantes.

BIBLIOGRAPHY

Primary Texts

*Don Quijote de la Mancha*. Ed. Juan Bautista Avalle-Arce. 2 vols. Madrid: Alhambra, 1979.
*Don Quijote de la Mancha*. Ed. Martín de Riquer. Barcelona: Planeta, 1975.
*Entremeses*. Ed. Eugenio Asensio. Madrid: Castalia, 1970.
*Entremeses*. Ed. Nicholas Spadaccini. Madrid: Cátedra, 1982.
*La Galatea*. Ed. Juan Bautista Avalle-Arce. 2 vols. Madrid: Espasa-Calpe, 1961.
*El ingenioso hidalgo Don Quijote de la Mancha*. Ed. John Jay Allen. 2 vols. Madrid: Cátedra, 1977.
*El ingenioso hidalgo Don Quijote de la Mancha*. Ed. Luis Andrés Murillo. 3 vols. Madrid: Castalia, 1978.
*Novelas ejemplares*. Ed. Harry Sieber. 2 vols. Madrid: Cátedra, 1983.
*Novelas ejemplares*. Ed. Juan Bautista Avalle-Arce. 3 vols. Madrid: Castalia, 1982.
*Obras completas*. Ed. Angel Valbuena Prat. 2 vols. Madrid: Aguilar, 1975.
*Poesías completas*. Ed. Vicente Gaos. 2 vols. Madrid: Castalia, 1973–81.
*Los trabajos de Persiles y Sigismunda*. Ed. Juan Bautista Avalle-Arce. Madrid: Castalia, 1969.

English Translations

*The Adventures of Don Quixote*. Tr. J. M. Cohen. Baltimore: Penguin, 1950.
*"The Deceitful Marriage" and Other Exemplary Novels*. Tr. Walter Starkie. New York: New American Library, 1963.
*Don Quixote of La Mancha*. Tr. Walter Starkie. New York: Signet, 1964.
*Don Quixote*. Tr. John Ormsby. Rev. and ed. Joseph R. Jones and Kenneth Douglas. New York: Norton, 1981.
*Exemplary Stories*. Tr. C. A. Jones. Harmondsworth: Penguin, 1972.
*Galatea*. Tr. H. Oelsner and A. B. Welford. Glasgow: Gowans and Gray, 1903.
*The Ingenious Gentleman Don Quixote de la Mancha*. T. Samuel Putnam. New York: Modern Library, 1949.
*Interludes*. Tr. Edwin Honig. New York: Signet, 1964.

*The Wanderings of Persiles and Sigismunda.* Tr. Louisa Dorothea Stanley. London: Joseph Cundall, 1854.

Criticism

Allen, John J. *Don Quixote: Hero or Fool?: A Study in Narrative Technique.* 2 vols. Gainesville: U of Florida P, 1969–79.

Amezúa y Mayo, Agustín G. de. *Cervantes, creador de la novela corta española.* 2 vols. Madrid: CSIC, 1956–58.

*Anales Cervantinos* 1–9 (1951–62), 10- (1971- ).

Avalle-Arce, Juan Bautista. *Don Quijote como forma de vida.* Madrid: Fundación Juan March/Castalia, 1976.

———. *Nuevos deslindes cervantinos.* Barcelona: Ariel, 1975.

Avalle-Arce, Juan Bautista, and E. C. Riley, eds. *Suma Cervantina.* London: Tamesis, 1973.

Bandera, Cesáreo. *Mímesis conflictiva: Ficción literaria y violencia en Cervantes y Calderón.* Madrid: Gredos, 1975.

Bjornson, Richard, ed. *Approaches to Teaching Cervantes' "Don Quixote."* New York: MLA, 1984.

Byron, William. *Cervantes: A Biography.* New York: Doubleday, 1978.

Castro, Américo. *El pensamiento de Cervantes.* New ed. Ed. Julio Rodríguez-Puértolas. Barcelona: Noguer, 1972.

*Cervantes: Bulletin of the Cervantes Society of America* 1- (1981- ).

Church, Margaret. *Don Quixote: Knight of La Mancha.* New York: New York UP, 1971.

Close, Anthony. *The Romantic Approach to "Don Quixote": A Critical History of the Romantic Tradition in "Quixote" Criticism.* New York: Cambridge UP, 1977.

Criado de Val, Manuel, ed. *Cervantes: Su obra y su mundo. Actas del I Congreso Internacional sobre Cervantes.* Madrid: Edi–6, 1981.

Drake, Dana B. *"Don Quijote" (1894–1970): A Selective Annotated Bibliography.* Vol. 1 UNCSRLL 138. Chapel Hill: U of North Carolina P, 1974. Vol. 2, Miami: Universal, 1978. Vol. 3, *"Don Quijote" in World Literature.* New York: Garland, 1980. Vol. 4, *Extended to 1979*; with Frederick Viña. Lincoln: Society of Spanish and Spanish-American Studies, 1984.

Durán, Manuel. *Cervantes.* TWAS 329. New York: Twayne, 1974.

Efron, Arthur. *"Don Quixote" and the Dulcineated World.* Austin: U of Texas P, 1971.

El Saffar, Ruth. *Distance and Control in "Don Quixote": A Study in Narrative Technique.* UNCSRLL 147. Chapel Hill: U of North Carolina P, 1975.

———. *Beyond Fiction: The Recovery of the Feminine in the Novels of Cervantes.* Berkeley: U of California P, 1984.

———. *Novel to Romance: A Study of Cervantes's "Novelas ejemplares."* Baltimore: Johns Hopkins UP, 1974.

Flores, Angel, and M. J. Benardete, eds. *Cervantes across the Centuries.* New York: Dryden, 1947.

Flores, R. M. *The Compositors of the First and Second Madrid Editions of "Don Quixote," Part I.* London: Modern Humanities Research Association, 1975.

———. *Sancho Panza through Three Hundred Seventy-five Years of Continuations, Imitations, and Criticism, 1605–1980.* Newark: Juan de la Cuesta—Hispanic Monographs, 1982.

Forcione, Alban K. *Cervantes, Aristotle, and the "Persiles."* Princeton: Princeton UP, 1970.

————. *Cervantes and the Mystery of Lawlessness: A Study of "El casamiento engañoso" y "El coloquio de los perros."* Princeton: Princeton UP, 1984.

————. *Cervantes and the Humanist Vision: A Study of Four "Exemplary Novels."* Princeton: Princeton UP, 1982.

————. *Cervantes' Christian Romance: A Study of "Persiles y Sigismunda."* Princeton: Princeton UP, 1972.

Friedman, Edward H. *The Unifying Concept: Approaches to the Structure of Cervantes' "Comedias."* York, SC: Spanish Literature Publications, 1981.

Gaos, Vicente. *Cervantes: Novelista, dramaturgo, poeta.* Barcelona: Planeta, 1979.

Haley, George, ed. *El "Quijote" de Cervantes.* Madrid: Taurus, 1980.

Hatzfeld, Helmut. *El "Quijote" como obra de arte del lenguaje.* 2nd ed. Madrid: CSIC, 1972.

Ihrie, Maureen. *Skepticism in Cervantes.* London: Tamesis, 1982.

Johnson, Carroll B. *Madness and Lust: A Psychoanalytical Approach to Don Quixote.* Berkeley: U of California P, 1983.

Labrador Herraiz, José J., and Juan Fernández Jiménez, eds. *Cervantes and the Pastoral.* Cleveland: Penn State U–Behrend College, Cleveland State U, 1986.

Madariaga, Salvador de. *"Don Quixote": An Introductory Essay in Psychology.* Rev. ed. London: Oxford UP, 1961.

Mancing, Howard. *The Chivalric World of "Don Quixote": Style, Structure and Narrative Technique.* Columbia: U of Missouri P, 1982.

Márquez Villanueva, Francisco. *Fuentes literarias cervantinas.* Madrid: Gredos, 1973.

————. *Personajes y temas del "Quijote."* Madrid: Taurus, 1975.

McGaha, Michael D., ed. *Cervantes and the Renaissance: Papers of the Pomona College Cervantes Symposium, November 16–18, 1978.* Easton, PA: Juan de la Cuesta— Hispanic Monographs, 1980.

McKendrick, Melveena. *Cervantes.* Boston: Little, Brown, 1980.

Molho, Maurice. *Cervantes: Raíces folklóricas.* Madrid: Gredos, 1976.

Morón Arroyo, Ciríaco. *Nuevas meditaciones del "Quijote."* Madrid: Gredos, 1976.

Murillo, Luis A. *The Golden Dial: Temporal Configuration in "Don Quijote."* Oxford: Dolphin, 1975.

Nelson, Lowry, Jr., ed. *Cervantes: A Collection of Critical Essays.* Englewood Cliffs, NJ: Prentice-Hall, 1969.

Ortega y Gasset, José. *Meditations on "Quixote."* Tr. Evelyn Rugg and Diego Marín. New York: Norton, 1961.

Percas de Ponseti, Helena. *Cervantes y su concepto del arte: Estudio crítico de algunos aspectos del "Quijote."* 2 vols. Madrid: Gredos, 1975.

Predmore, Richard. *Cervantes.* New York: Dodd, Mead, 1973.

————. *The World of Don Quixote.* Cambridge: Harvard UP, 1967.

Riley, E. C. *Don Quixote.* London: Allen & Unwin, 1985.

————. *Cervantes's Theory of the Novel.* Oxford: Clarendon P, 1962.

Riquer, Martín de. *Aproximación al "Quijote."* 2nd ed. Barcelona: Teide, 1967.

Rodríguez-Luis, Julio. *Novedad y ejemplo de las "Novelas" de Cervantes.* 2 vols. Madrid: Porrúa Turanzas, 1980.

Rosenblat, Angel. *La lengua del "Quijote."* Madrid: Gredos, 1971.

Russell, P. E. *Cervantes.* Oxford: Oxford UP, 1985.

Serrano-Plaja, Arturo. *"Magic" Realism in Cervantes: "Don Quixote" as Seen through "Tom Sawyer" and "The Idiot."* Tr. Robert S. Rudder. Berkeley: U of California P, 1970.

Van Doren, Mark. *Don Quixote's Profession.* New York: Columbia UP, 1958.
Varo, Carlos. *Génesis y evolución del "Quijote."* Madrid: Alcalá, 1968.
Weiger, John G. *The Substance of Cervantes.* Cambridge: Cambridge UP, 1985.
Welsh, Alexander. *Reflections on the Hero as Quixote.* Princeton: Princeton UP, 1981.
Williamson, Edwin. *The Half-way House of Fiction: "Don Quixote" and Arthurian Romance.* Oxford: Clarendon P, 1984.

Howard Mancing

**CESARINY, Mario** (1923, Lisbon– ), Portuguese poet and painter. With António Pedro and Alexandre O'Neill, he was one of the founders of the first surrealist group in Portugal in 1947, the Grupo Surrealista de Lisboa. Cesariny soon left it to form another group, usually known as Os Surrealistas, which was very active in the Lisbon literary scene between 1949 and 1951, with exhibitions, public sessions, manifestos, etc. In general, surrealism came late to Portugal. It attracted a few poets earlier, such as António Pedro, who belonged to the London Surrealist Group, and Edmundo de Bettencourt, but it is instructive to note that Bettencourt's *Poemas Surdos, 1934–1940* could not find a publisher until the early sixties. Cesariny, like some who eventually joined the surrealist credo, first associated with the neo-realists who dominated Portuguese letters in the *resistant* atmosphere of the war and immediate post-war years, but he broke away when neo-realism, with its humanitarian concerns, seemed to him too narrow to afford the possibility of practicing poetry and art as a real *adventure* in living. Although clearly influenced by French surrealism, whose techniques he generously adopted, from automatic writing to "collage," his poetry cannot be understood apart from a Portuguese modern tradition, especially the *Orpheu* poets (e.g., Fernando *Pessoa, Mario de *Sá-Carneiro and Almada Negreiros). One of Cesariny's best-known poems is a highly creative pastiche in praise of Álvaro de Campos's manner, *Louvor e Simplificacão de Álvaro de Campos* (1953; Eulogy and Simplification of Álvaro de Campos). The devastating irony and humor he abundantly uses can also belong to a very old tradition of Portuguese poetry—one which begins with the *cantigas de escarnio e maldizer* (songs of vilification) found in the medieval *Cancioneiros.*

One of the most important living Portuguese poets, Cesariny has recently collected most of his poetry into three volumes: *Primavera Autónoma das Estradas* (1980; Autonomous Spring of the Roads), *Manual de Prestidigitação* (1980; Handbook of Prestidigitation) and *Pena Capital* (1982; Capital Punishment). In both his poetry and painting he is an artist who starts by depriving himself, as he says, from all "truths," first from "big ones," then from "small ones," in order to attain the meaning of life, only to be recaptured, in the end, in the "surreality" dreamed of by all visionaries.

BIBLIOGRAPHY

Primary Texts

*As mãos na água a cabeça na Água.* Phala: n.p., 1972.
*Manual da Prestidigitação.* Lisbon: n.p., 1980.

*Pena Capital*. Lisbon: n.p., 1982.
*Primavera Autónoma das Estradas*. Lisbon: n.p., 1980.
*Textos de afirmação e de combate do movimiento surrealista mundial*. Lisbon: Perspectivas e Realidades, 1977.

Criticism

Leal, R., N. Correia, and L. de Freitas. *Mario Cesariny*. Lisbon: Secretario de Estado da Cultura, 1978.
*Le Surréalisme Portugais and Surréalisme Périphérique*. Montreal: n.p., 1984.

Fernando J. B. Martiñho

**CÉSPEDES, Pablo de** (1548, Cordova–1608, Cordova), architect, painter, sculptor, writer. After studies at the U of Alcalá, he made the first of two trips to Rome, returning to Spain in 1575. His admiration for Italian Renaissance culture was enormous. Céspedes's literary opus includes sonnets, a heroic poem, letters, and a fragmentary *Arte de la pintura* (n.d.; Art of Painting). He dedicated his *Discurso de la comparación de la antigua y moderna pintura y escultura* (n.d., Discourse on the Comparison of Ancient and Modern Painting and Sculpture) to another vibrant *Renaissance figure, Pedro de *Valencia. *See also* Italian literary influences.

BIBLIOGRAPHY

Primary Texts

*Fragmentos poéticos*. In BAE 32.
*La pintura. Poema*. Segovia: Espinosa de los Monteros, 1786.

**CÉSPEDES Y MENESES, Gonzalo** (1585, Madrid–1638, Madrid), historian, novelist. Unexplained events and biographical gaps characterize our knowledge of Céspedes. He attempted to pass to the New World, but before embarking was incarcerated in Seville for several years for unknown reasons. Next, he was transferred to a prison in Granada, and finally released. In 1614 he was in Madrid, and there published his first work, Part 1 of *Poema trágico del español Gerardo y desengaño del amor lascivo* (1615; *Gerardo the Unfortunate Spaniard*, 1622), a *picaresque narrative. Part 2 followed in 1618. Partly written in prison, this racy account may include autobiographical data. Its characters are victims, and the tone is pessimistic and fatalistic. By 1619, Céspedes was again in prison, in Madrid (cause unknown), and subsequently exiled from Castile for ten years. He lived in Zaragoza for a long period, but disappeared from there, presumably to avoid harassment which had dogged his life. He continued to write, publishing in 1622 the *Historia . . . de los sucesos de Aragón* (1622; History of Events in Aragon), which attempts to clarify events surrounding the Antonio *Pérez affair. The following year the *Historias peregrinas y ejemplares* (1623; Beautiful, Exemplary Stories) appeared. This collection of six short stories includes one, *La constante cordobesa* (The Steadfast Cordova Woman), which is a precursor of *Tirso's *Burlador de Sevilla*. In 1626, a picaresque narrative, quite possibly with many autobiographical moments, was published with the title *El soldado*

*Píndaro* (1626; The Soldier Pindaro). After he published the *Historia de Felipe IV* (1631; History of Philip IV), which covers the early years of the king's reign and defends him against French and Belgian attacks, Céspedes's exile from Castile was lifted. In 1635 Céspedes published his final work, the political statement *Francia engañada, Francia respondida* (1635; France Deceived, France Answered). Using the obvious pen name Gerardo Hispano, Céspedes gives a passionate refutation of French charges against the Spanish nation.

BIBLIOGRAPHY

Primary Texts

*La constante cordobesa y El desdén del Alameda.* Seville: Hispalense, 1947.
*Historia apologética en los sucesos de Aragón.* Seville: Rodríguez Muñoz, 1978. Facs.
*Historia de don Felipe IV.* Barcelona: Cormellas, 1634.
*Historias peregrinas y ejemplares.* Ed., study Y. R. Fonquerne. Clásicos Castalia 23. Madrid: Castalia, 1970.
*Poema trágico del español Gerardo* and *Varia fortuna del soldado Píndaro.* In BAE 18.
*Varia fortuna del soldado Píndaro.* Ed., prol., A. Pacheco. Clásicos Castellanos 202, 203. Madrid: Espasa-Calpe, 1975.

English Translation

*The Famous History of Auristella.* Tr. W. B. London: Hundmarsh, 1683. Contains part 1, discourse 2 of *El español Gerardo.*
*Gerardo the Unfortunate Spaniard.* Tr. L. D. London: Blount, 1622.

Criticism

See Fonquerne and Pacheco, in Primary Texts.

Maureen Ihrie

**CETINA, Gutierre de** (before 1520, Seville–1557?, Mexico), soldier and poet. He received a well-founded classical instruction in Seville. As a soldier, he traveled in Italy and Germany. A friend of *Hurtado de Mendoza, the Prince of Ascoli, Jorge de *Montemayor, etc., he left for the New World and was seriously injured in Puebla de Los Ángeles, Mexico. There are various accounts of his death. The biography presented by Hazañas in his edition of Cetina's works is not universally accepted. All of the most recent biographical data concerning Cetina has been meticulously compiled by R. Lapesa.

Within the tradition of Spanish *Renaissance lyric, Cetina's verse occupies an intermediate step between the poetry of *Garcilaso de la Vega and Fernando de *Herrera. He adopted the contemporary Italianate poetic forms and also was influenced strongly by Ausiàs *March. He translated Petrarch and Ariosto, and also Italian poets of secondary importance: Transilbo, Aquilano, Gesueldo, etc. Cetina very ably adapted the madrigal, but his experiments with the sestina and the capitolo were less successful.

Among his madrigals, his most famous is *A unos ojos* (To Certain Eyes). He composed an extensive collection of sonnets (244 in the Hazañas edition), eleven love songs, nine *estancias*, seventeen epistles, and one ode. Herrera imputed a lack of vigor to Cetina, describing his poetry as dispirited; others, however, praise Cetina's characteristic gentleness and delicacy of expression.

Cetina wrote *Epístolas* (Epistles) in tercets; many contain interesting autobiographic data. His prose works include *Diálogo entre la cabeza y la gorra* (Dialogue between the Head and the Cap), and *Paradoja* (Paradox), which is a version of one of Pandolfo Colleruccio's dialogues. *See also* Italian literary influences; Renaissance.

BIBLIOGRAPHY

Primary Texts

*Obras*. Ed. J. Hazaña y la Rúa. 2 vols. Seville: Díaz, 1895.
*Obras*. In BAE 32.

Criticism

Lapesa, R. "Gutierre de Cetina. Disquisiciones biográficas. In *Estudios hispánicos. Homenaje a Archer M. Huntington*. Wellesley, MA: Wellesley College, 1952. 311–26.
Withers, A. M. *The Sources of the Poetry of Gutierre de Cetina*. Philadelphia: U of Pennsylvania, 1923.

Deborah Compte

**CHABÁS Y MARTÍ, Juan** (1893? 1898? 1900?, Denia, Alicante–1954, La Habana), writer and literary critic. A prolific writer, Chabás collaborated in the *Revista de Occidente* and was a member of the Centro de Estudios Históricos (Center of Historical Studies) of Madrid. G. Videla notes that he sympathized with the avant-garde writing of *ultraísmo* and in fact published in the journal *Ultra*. His book *Espejos* (1921; Mirrors) shows not only the influence of this movement but also that of Juan Ramón *Jiménez. In exile after the Spanish Civil ar, Chabás was a professor in Cuba. In this same country, his *Historia de la literatura española* (1932; History of Spanish Literature) was re-edited several times.

BIBLIOGRAPHY

Primary Texts

*Agor sin fin*. Madrid-Buenos Aires: Iberoamericana, 1930.
*Antología general de la literatura española*. Havana: Cultural, 1955.
*Espejos* (verso, 1919–1920). Madrid: Alejandro Pueyo, 1921.
*Fábula y vida*. Santiago de Cuba: Universidad de Oriente, 1955.
*Historia de la literatura española*. Madrid: Iberia, 1932.
*Italia fascista (política y cultura)*. Barcelona: Mentora, 1928.
*Juan Maragall, poeta y ciudadano*. Madrid: Espasa-Calpe, 1935.
*Literatura española contemporánea, 1898–1950*. Havana: Cultural, 1952.

*Madrid*. Barcelona: Cervantes, 192?.
*Vuelo y estilo; estudios de literatura contemporánea*. Madrid: GEL, 1934.

Kathleen March

**CHACEL, Rosa** (1898, Valladolid– ), novelist, essayist, poet. A member of the *generation of 1927 and a literary disciple of *Ortega y Gasset, Chacel studied painting and sculpture before beginning a career as a writer. From the age of eight she attended art classes in Valladolid. After her family moved to Madrid in 1908, she studied at the Escuela de Artes y Oficios and at the Escuela Superior de Bellas Artes de San Fernando. When her bad health prevented her from continuing at the unheated school of fine arts in 1918, she became a member of the *Ateneo (the Atheneum) of Madrid, thus beginning her formal association with the world of letters.

Chacel and her husband, painter Timoteo Pérez Rubio, lived and studied in Rome at the Spanish Academy from 1922 to 1929, where she wrote her first novel, *Estación, ida y vuelta*, which was greatly influenced by Joyce's *Portrait of the Artist as a Young Man* and by Proust's *Remembrance of Things Past*. This novel is an important antecedent of the French new novel. The title is difficult to translate, for *estación* means both (train) station and season; thus, the title refers to a round trip (Station, Round Trip) made by the protagonist as well as to the cyclic nature of the work (Return of the Season).

During this period, Chacel collaborated on several literary magazines, among them *Revista de Occidente*, *Hora de España*, and *Ultra*, and she published a book of sonnets, *A la orilla de un pozo* (At the Well's Edge) in 1936. She was preparing a biographical novel about Teresa Mancha, the lover of the Romantic poet José de *Espronceda—a work commissioned by Ortega for the series Extraordinary Lives of the Nineteenth Century— when the Spanish Civil War began, delaying its publication indefinitely.

During and after the war she lived and traveled in Europe, including Germany, Greece, and France, before finally emigrating with her family to Río de Janeiro in 1940. She and her son, Carlos, divided their time between Brazil and Buenos Aires, spending the school year in the latter city, while her husband remained in Brazil. *Teresa* was finally published in Buenos Aires in 1941 (Ediciones Nuevo Romance). Her third novel, *Memorias de Leticia Valle* (Memories of Leticia Valle) was begun during her sojourn in Italy prior to 1930, but it was completed and published in Buenos Aires in 1945 (Editorial Emecé).

One of her most ambitious and, undoubtedly, one of her best novels, *La sinrazón* (Lack of Reason), was published in Buenos Aires in 1960 (Premio de la Crítica—National Critics' Prize of Spain—1977). Chacel had won the 1976 Premio de la Crítica as well for her novel *Barrio de Maravillas* (1976; The Maravillas Parish), the first volume in a trilogy which Chacel has described as a history of her literary generation. *Barrio* covers the period from the turn of the century until World War I. The second part of the trilogy was published under the title *Acrópolis* (1984), although Chacel had often indicated that the title would be *La escuela de Platón* (The Platonic School).

A collection of short stories, *Icada, nevda, diada*, published in Barcelona in 1971 included the stories from two earlier collections, *Sobre el piélago* (1951; On the High Sea) and *Ofrenda a una virgen loca* (1961; Offering to a Crazy Virgin), plus an additional selection of stories. Another work of short fiction is *Novelas antes de tiempo* (1981; Novels before Their Time), a collection of novels Chacel has started but fears she will not live long enough to finish.

Her essays include *La confesión* (1971), *Saturnal* (1972; *Saturnalia*), written with support from the Guggenheim Foundation, and a collection of critical essays edited by Clara *Janés, *Los títulos* (1981; Titles).

Chacel returned to Spain permanently after her husband's death in 1977. Her first book-length work after that tragedy was a study of her husband's paintings: *Timoteo Pérez Rubio y sus retratos del jardín* (1980; Timoteo Pérez Rubio and His Portraits of the Garden).

In Madrid Chacel continues to write novels, short stories, poetry, and essays as she has done since 1930. Chacel has published an autobiography of her first ten years, *Desde el amanecer* (1972; Since Dawn), and a two-volume diary under the general title *Alcancía* (1984) which refers to a catch-all container into which miscellaneous items are cast. Volume 1 is called *Ida* (Departure) and the second is *Vuelta* (Return).

Most critics consider Chacel's fiction to be of exceptional quality. If the tragedy of the Spanish Civil War had been avoided, and Rosa Chacel had continued to write and publish in Spain—*Teresa* was her second novel to appear in Spain, thirty-three years after her first novel—she would almost certainly be one of the most respected novelists of contemporary Spain. She was a Cervantes Prize finalist in 1985.

BIBLIOGRAPHY

Primary Texts

*Acrópolis*. Biblioteca Breve. Barcelona: Seix Barral, 1984.
*Barrio de Maravillas*. Barcelona: Seix Barral, 1976.
*Estación, ida y vuelta*. Barcelona: Bruguera, 1980.
*Memorias de Leticia Valle*. Barcelona: Bruguera, 1980.
*La sinrazón*. Bilbao: Albia, 1977.
*Teresa*. Barcelona: Bruguera, 1980.

Criticism

Aguirre, Francisca. "Rosa Chacel, como en su playa propia." *CH* 296 (1975): 298–315.
Joly, Monique, Jean Tena, and Ignacio Soldevila-Durante. *Panorama du roman espagnol d'après-guerre (1939–1975)*. Montpellier: Université de Montpellier, 1979. 112–17, 175–84, 321–30.
Marra-López, José R. "Rosa Chacel: La búsqueda intelectual del mundo." *Narrativa española fuera de España (1939–1961)*. Madrid: Guadarrama, 1963. 134–47.
Myers, Eunice D. "*Estación, ida y vuelta*: Rosa Chacel's Apprenticeship Novel." *Hispanic Journal* 4.2 (Spring 1983): 77–84.

Porlán, Alberto. *La sinrazón de Rosa Chacel*. De palabra, 5. Madrid: Anjana, 1984. (Interviews)

Eunice D. Myers

**CHACÓN, Gonzalo** (?, ?–1517, ?), historical author. Called ''el Viejo'' (The Old Man), he served as Isabella's majordomo. The *Crónica de don Alvaro de Luna* (Chronicle of Álvaro de Luna), which probably was written between 1445 and 1460, has been attributed to him. As a youth, Chacón served Luna as a page and servant. The *Crónica* was first printed in Milan, Italy, in 1546—the first printing inside Spain was not made until 1784. *See also* Luna, Alvaro de; Renaissance.

BIBLIOGRAPHY

Primary Texts

*Crónica de don Alvaro de Luna*. Ed. J. de Mata Carriazo. Madrid: Espasa-Calpe, 1940.

**CHAMIZO, Luis** (1888, ?, Extremadura–1944, ?), poet. The influence of *Gabriel y Galán is apparent in Chamizo's *Poesías extremeñas* (n.d. Extremaduran Poems) and in his *El miajón de los castúos* (1921; The Essence of The Pure Ones). Also his are the drama *Las brujas* (presented in 1930; The Witches), and the book *Extremadura 1942*.

BIBLIOGRAPHY

Primary Texts

*Las brujas*. 2nd ed. Madrid: Sociedad general española, 1942.
*Extremadura*. Madrid: Sociedad General, 1942.
*El miajón de los castúos*. 2nd ed. Madrid: Pueyo, 1921.

Criticism

Barros, Pedro. ''Luis Chamizo, un poeta olvidado.'' In *Estudios sobre literatura y arte: dedicados al profesor Emilio Orozco Díaz*. Ed. A. Gallego Morell et al. Granada: U of Granada, 1979. 1: 93–107.
Cañellas Rey de Viñas, A., and R. Cañellas Rodríguez. ''El color en la obra de Chamizo.'' *Revista de Estudios Extremeños* 35 (1979): 281–91.

Isabel McSpadden

**CHAMPOURCÍN, Ernestina de** (1905, Vitoria– ), poet and novelist. The wife of the poet Juan José *Domenchina, she accompanied him into exile at the end of the Civil War, living in Mexico where she worked as a translator and interpreter. After his death in 1959, she returned to Spain in 1972, and has since resided in Madrid. Besides her poetry and a novel, she has published an anthology, a good deal of literary criticism, and her memoirs of Juan Ramón *Jiménez, a major influence on her poetry: *La ardilla y la rosa (Juan Ramón en mi memoria)*. The obsessive nucleus of her poetry is the theme of love, and her varying treatment of it permits division of her lyric works into three periods: (1926–36) human love; (1952–74) divine love; (1978-present), retrospective.

*En silencio* (1926; In Silence) is her first book of poetry, published when Champourcín was only twenty-one. *Ahora* (1928; Now) is very much in the vein of the *Generation of 1927, written in free verse which combines traces of the *Generation of 1898, strong Modernist tendencies and overblown exoticism with anticipations of surrealist imagery. *La voz en el viento* (1931; The Voice in the Wind) continues to reflect the influence of Juan Ramón Jiménez (who contributed a handwritten introduction to the volume) and prolongs the theme introduced in the previous volume of neo-mystic longing to unite with the infinite through contemplation of nature. In *Cántico inútil* (1936; Futile Canticle) the poet takes leave of her Modernist and Generation of 1898 tendencies, but continues her pursuit of the theme of love via the fantastic quest for mystic unions ranging from platonic to cosmic, sexual to divine. It is Champourcín's last book before exile and initiates a lapse in all poetry publication until 1952. However, in that same year, in which she also married Domenchina, Champourcín published a novel entitled *La casa de enfrente* (1936; The House across the Street). Utilizing the diary format, it recounts a girl's memories of childhood, adolescence and her first love affair.

*Presencia a oscuras* (1952; Presence in Darkness) appeared after a sixteen-year lapse and includes poems written from 1948 to 1950 and initiates the period which the poet has termed *amor divino* (divine love). Using prose-like structures and citing biblical passages, this work incorporates invocations, prayers and litanies. *El nombre que me diste* (1960; The Name You Gave Me) includes twenty-one poems which are thematically similar to those of *Presencia a oscuras*, but differ in using an approximation of the traditional *romance* (ballad) form with assonantal rhyme. *Cárcel de los sentidos* (1964; Prison of the Senses) reiterates the themes and forms of the divine love period of Champourcín's work, and expresses the desire to escape earthly sensation and finitude to devote the self to Light, Truth, Eternity, God. *Cartas cerradas* (1968; Closed Letters) conveys the notion that it is of the essence of poetry to sustain a dialogue with God. Some of the "letters," longer than most other compositions of the period, contain autobiographical echoes, while others reiterate the divine love themes. *Poemas del Ser y del Estar* (1974; Poems of Being and State), the first book written after Champourcín's return to Spain, brings to a close her second period.

*Primer Exilio* (1978; First Exile) initiates the poet's third, retrospective period, which includes echoes of both earlier periods, introduces a more philosophical perspective, and at the same time allows for more intrusion of worldy realities such as war, exile, friends, travel, and a variety of human problems and anxieties. *La pared transparente* (1984; The Transparent Wall), again philosophical and retrospective, reflects in particular Champourcín's Mexican experience, but sounds a new note of alienation, symbolized by the title image: "walls" exist wherever there is loneliness, desperation, lack of communication, dehumanization and spiritual isolation.

Champourcín was the best-known woman poet of the Generation of 1927, and was included by Gerardo *Diego in his significant *Anthology* in 1934; after thirty-three years in Mexico, however, she was largely unknown in Spain, which may intensify the sense of exile and alienation expressed in her last two books.

BIBLIOGRAPHY

Primary Texts

*Antología poética.* Madrid: Torremozas, 1988.
*Hai-Kais espirituales.* México: Ecuador 0° 0' 0″— Finisterre, 1967.
*Primer exilio.* Madrid: Rialp, 1978.

Janet Pérez

**CHANZONETA,** a poetic term. It refers to festive songs or verses which are sung or recited as a part of religious holidays.

**CHICHARRO BRIONES, Eduardo** (1905, Madrid–1964, Madrid) poet. Son of a well-known painter, he studied painting in Rome and at the Escuela de Bellas Artes de San Fernando in Madrid, where he was a professor. An original writer, after the Civil War he founded ''postismo'' with Carlos-Edmundo de Ory. With Ory he also wrote the book of poems titled *Las patitas de la sombra* (n.f., The Little Paws of Shade). Also his is *Akebedonys* (1935), a theatrical piece, and *Cuadernos de Poemas en Prosa* (n.f., Notebooks of Prose Poems), in Italian.

Isabel McSpadden

**CHORDÀ I REQUESENS, Mari** (1942, Amposta– ), poet, screenwriter and director. She studied education and fine arts at Sant Jordi in Barcelona and for ten years earned her living by painting and teaching art. She taught film at the U of Barcelona and wrote and directed three films. In 1975 she opted for writing as the easiest means of communicating with the public, since paper and pencil are the only technical equipment necessary. Her poetry is varied and rich; . . . *i moltes altres coses* (1975; and Many Other Things) speaks the words suppressed for many years which are finally pronounced with rage. The verses gather together the cry of women to reclaim as their own the streets, the city, and all other spaces. *Quadern del cos i de l'aigua* (1978; Notebook of the Body and of Water), with drawings by Montse Clavé, is a book of very sensual poetry, reclaiming the body from drudgery for pleasure, and is a song for the discovery of one's own body.

BIBLIOGRAPHY

Primary Texts

. . . *i moltes altres coses.* Barcelona: laSal, 1975
*Quadern del cos i de l'aigua.* Barcelona: laSal, 1978.

Isabel Segura

**CHUECA Y GOITIA, Fernando** (1911, Madrid– ), architect, art historian, essayist and member of the Royal Academy of History. He has published several studies on Ventura Rodríguez, a book titled *Invariantes castizos de la arquitec-*

*tura española* (1947; Indigenous Constants of Spanish Architecture), several works on the cathedrals of Valladolid (1947) and Salamanca (1951), and an analytical essay, "Nueva York, Forma y Sociedad" (1953; New York, Form and Society). Other books by Chueca include *Semblante de Madrid* (1951; Countenance of Madrid), *La arquitectura del siglo XVI* (1953; Sixteenth-C. Architecture), *Resumen histórico del urbanismo en España* (1954; Historical Review of Urbanism in Spain), *Madrid y Sitios Reales* (1958; Madrid and Royal Sites), *Breve historia del urbanismo* (1958; Brief History of Urbanism), and the poetry collection, *Materia de recuerdos* (1968; Questions of Memories).

BIBLIOGRAPHY

Primary Texts

*La arquitectura del siglo XVI.* Madrid: Plus-Ultra, 1953.
*La destrucción del legado urbanístico español.* Madrid: Espasa-Calpe, 1977.
*Invariantes castizos de la arquitectura española.* Madrid: Dessat, 1947.
*Resumen histórico del urbanismo en España.* Madrid: Instituto de Estudios de Administración Local, 1954.
*El semblante de Madrid.* Madrid: RO, 1951.

Isabel McSpadden

**CID, El.** Rodrigo Díaz de Vivar (c. 1043–1099), the greatest figure from Spain's heroic age, is better known in history and legend by the honorific title *mio Cid* (my lord, from the Arabic *sidi*). The deeds of Rodrigo in the service of Sancho II, as the faithful exile of Alphonse VI, and as the conqueror of Valencia, have been celebrated in epic poetry, chronicles, and ballads. His military career, never tainted by defeat, led to his consecration as the symbol of the spirit of Castile. The epithet *El Campeador* (the victor, the master of the battlefield) was his by antonomasia. Even before his death, he was the subject of the Latin poem *Carmen Campidoctoris* (c. 1094). In an age when chronicles were devoted almost exclusively to royalty and saints, we nevertheless have a limited biography of the Cid, the Latin *Historia Roderici* (1145–65?), the most trustworthy account of his career, whose author apparently had access to pertinent documents and letters. The treatment of Rodrigo by contemporary Arab historians (Ibn Alcama, Ibn Bassam, and others) is, as can be expected, negative. These historians' views later became the foundation for Reinhardt Dozy's negative and erroneous biography of the Cid (1849). The most comprehensive biography of the Cid remains Ramón *Menéndez Pidal's monumental *España del Cid.*

The heroic character of Rodrigo is best portrayed in the *Cantar de mio Cid (Song of the Cid)*, a poetic account of his banishment and the recovery of his honor. The faithful vassal, the just lord, the devoted husband and paterfamilias are other facets of his character depicted by the poet. The *Cantar de *Sancho II [y el cerco de Zamora]* (Song of Sancho II, or The Siege of Zamora), which is in prose in several chronicles, forms an important part of the poetic cycle of the Cid. The *Cantar de *Rodrigo* (Song of Rodrigo, or The Youthful Deeds of Rodrigo) is a reworking of an earlier epic and reflects the epic in decline. The deeds attributed to Rodrigo are wholly fictitious; character portrayal has deteriorated considerably.

The deeds of Rodrigo were quickly incorporated into the chronicle (*Crónica) tradition, first in Latin and later in the vernacular. Notable, besides the chronicles of *Ximénez de Rada and *Alphonse X the Learned, are the *Crónica de veinte reyes* (Chronicle of Twenty Kings), the *Crónica de los reyes de Castilla* (Chronicle of Castile), and the *Crónica particular del Cid* (Chronicle of the Cid). Several of these accounts were popularized in printed editions in the sixteenth c.

There are over two hundred extant ballads on the Cid, created in the fifteenth and sixteenth centuries, which focus on dramatic and popular episodes in the legend. They are derived from late versions of the epic and from the chronicles. The collection by Juan de Escobar (1611) enjoyed an enduring popularity. The ballad tradition was brought to the stage by Guillén de *Castro in his *Mocedades del Cid* (1618; *Youthful Deeds of the Cid*) and *Las hazañas del Cid* (1618; Deeds of the Cid); the first of these was the model for Corneille's famous and controversial play. During the Romantic period and throughout the nineteenth c., the legend of the Cid was revitalized in Spain and the rest of Europe through translations and a variety of adaptations. Menéndez Pidal has surveyed these in *La epopeya castellana a través de la literatura española*. Noteworthy in this century are Eduardo *Marquina's *Las hijas del Cid* (1908; The Daughters of the Cid) Antonio *Gala's *Anillos para una dama* (performed 1973; Rings for a Lady) and the Hollywood movie *El Cid*, with Charlton Heston in the title role.

BIBLIOGRAPHY

Primary Texts

Alfonso X, the Learned. *Primera Crónica General de España*. 3rd ed. 2 vols. Ed. Ramón Menéndez Pidal. Introd. Diego Catalán. Madrid: Gredos and Seminario Menéndez Pidal, 1982.
Song of Rodrigo. In *Epic Poetry and the Clergy: Studies on the Mocedades de Rodrigo*. Ed. A. D. Deyermond. London: Tamesis, 1969.
Song of Sancho II. In *El cantar de Sancho II y cerco de Zamora*. Ed. Carola Reig. Madrid: RFE, 1947.
Song of the Cid. *Poema de mío Cid*. Ed. Ian Michael. Madrid: Clásicos Castalia, 1976. *Poema de mío Cid*. Ed. Colin Smith. Oxford: Clarendon, 1972.
*Spanish Ballads*. Ed. C. Colin Smith. 3rd ed. Oxford: Pergamon, 1971.

English Translation

*The Poem of the Cid*. Ed. Ian Michael. Tr. Rita Hamilton and Janet Perry. Manchester: Manchester UP; New York: Barnes and Noble, 1975.

Criticism

Menéndez Pidal, Ramón. *La España del Cid*. 7th ed. 2 vols. Madrid: Espasa-Calpe, 1969. (Vol. 2 contains the *Carmen Campidoctoris*, the *Historia Roderici*, and other pertinent documents.)
———. *The Cid and His Spain*. Tr. Harold Sunderland. 1934; rpt. London: Cass, 1971.
———. *La epopeya castellana a través de la literatura española*. Buenos Aires: Espasa-Calpe Argentina, 1945.

Milá y Fontanals, Manuel. *De la poesía heroico-popular castellana.* Ed. Martín de Riquer and Joaquín Molas. Barcelona: CSIC, 1959.

Porter Conerly

**CIEZA DE LEÓN, Pedro de** (c. 1520, Seville–1554, Seville), chronicler of the New World. Cieza journeyed to America in 1535, and did not return to Spain until 1550 or 1551. His *Crónica del Peru* (1553; first partially translated as *The Seventeen Years Travels of Peter de Cieza Through the Mighty Kingdom of Peru, and the large Provinces of Cartagena and Popayan in South America:* . . . , 1709) contains invaluable first-hand reports on the deeds of the conquering soldiers, the history and geography of the region, the rituals and customs of the Inca, and the civil wars among the conquerors. Divided into four parts, not all of which have been published in their entirety, the information it contains and its admirable clarity and organization make it one of the most valuable documents about the New World. Unfortunately, the English translations are both incomplete and filled with errors and mistranslations, rendering them at best harmless, and often, a dangerous distortion. *See also* Renaissance.

BIBLIOGRAPHY

Primary Texts

*Crónica del Perú.* 3rd ed. Madrid: Espasa-Calpe, 1962. Contains part 1.
*La Crónica del Perú.* BAE 26.
*Del Señorío de los Incas.* Prol. Alberto Mario Salas. Buenos Aires: Solar, 1943. Contains part 2.
Consult León in Criticism for sources for parts 3 and 4.

English Translation

*The Incas.* Tr. Harriet de Onís. Ed. V. W. von Hagan. Norman: U of Oklahoma P, 1959.

Criticism

León, Pedro R. *Algunas observaciones sobre Pedro de Cieza de León y la "Crónica del Perú."* Madrid: Gredos, 1972. Contains biography, critical summary of the *Crónica*, editions and translations of Cieza's work, and bibliography.

Maureen Ihrie

**CIFAR,** *Libro del caballero* (Book of the Knight Cifar) a long chivalric novel. Composed in the late thirteenth or early fourteenth c., probably by the Archdeacon of Madrid at the Cathedral of Toledo, Ferrand Martines, the work consists of a prologue and three main parts: (1) "El Caballero de Dios y el Rey de Mentón" (The Knight of God and the King of Menton); (2) "Castigos del Rey de Mentón" (Teachings of the King of Menton); and (3) "Los Hechos de Roboán" (The Deeds of Roboan). The first part tells how the knight Cifar is separated from his wife Grima and from their sons Gargín and Roboán, and how after many Byzantine adventures they are reunited in the Kingdom of Mentón. In the second part Cifar, now king of Mentón, instructs his sons with doctrinal material drawn from the *Flores de Filosofía,* *Alphonse X's second *Partida,* and the *Castigos e documentos*. In the third part, one of the sons, Roboán, endures a series of adventures that parallel those of his father in part one until he, like his father, wins a kingdom. King Roboán returns with his queen to Mentón for a seven-day family reunion with his father; during the visit the sun did not set. The word *Cifar* means *traveler* in Arabic and has the same root as *safari*. The motif of man (*homo viator*) traveling through hell and purgatory to paradise is the basic structural element of the novel, and is found in the prologue as well as in each of the three parts. This motif is also made explicit by the Ribaldo (who is sometimes called an antecedent of *Cervantes's Sancho Panza):

> Cavallero—dixo el ribaldo—así va ome a paraíso, ca primeramente ha de pasar por purgatorio e por los lugares mucho ásperos ante que allá llegue. E vos, ante que lleguedes a grant estado al que avedes a llegar, ante avedes a sofrir e a pasar muchas cosas ásperas.

> (Knight—said the Ribaldo—this is how man reaches paradise, for first he must pass through purgatory and many harsh places before he arrives there. And you, before you reach the great position to which you shall arrive, you must first suffer and endure many harsh things.)

Hell in the prologue is the exile to Rome; purgatory, the indoctrination and struggle in Rome; and paradise, the triumphant return to Spain. In the three main parts hell corresponds to Tarta, the enchanted lake, and the Islas Dotadas; purgatory corresponds to Cifar's struggles at Grades, Garfín's struggles with Nasón, and Roboán's struggles with Farán; paradise corresponds to Mentón, Nasón's county, and Tigrida. *See also* Caballerías, Libros de; Edad Media, Literatura de la.

BIBLIOGRAPHY

Primary Texts

*Libro del cavallero Cifar*. Ed. M. A. Olsen. Madison, WI: HSMS, 1984.

Criticism

Burke, J. F. *History and Vision*. London: Tamesis, 1972.
Keightley, R. G. "The Story of *Zifar*." *MLR* 73 (1978): 308–27.
Walker, R. M. *Tradition and Technique in "Libro del Caballero Cifar."* London: Tamesis, 1974.

Colbert Nepaulsingh

**CIGES APARICIO, Manuel** (1873, Enguera, Valencia–1936, Ávila), essayist. He was a soldier in the Spanish-American War, and related, both in spirit and in style, to the *Generation of 1898. An editor of *El Imparcial*, his novels include *El vicario* (1905; The Vicar), and *Villavieja* (1914). He also wrote a biography titled *Joaquín Costa, el gran fracasado*. (1930; Joaquín Costa, the Great Failure).

BIBLIOGRAPHY

Primary Texts

*Joaquín Costa, el gran fracasado.* Madrid: Espasa Calpe, 1930.
*El vicario.* Madrid: n.p., 1905.
*Villavieja.* Madrid: Ratés Martín, 1914.

Criticism

Fuentes, V. "La literatura comprometida de Manuel Ciges Aparicio." *Insula* 27 (April n. d.): 13.
Meneses, C. "Ciges Aparicio vuelve del olvido." *La palabra y el hombre: Revista de la universidad veracruzana* 19 (1976): 92–93.

                                                                        Isabel McSpadden

**CIRIA Y ESCALANTE, José de** (1904, ?–1924, Madrid), avant-garde poet. Ciria y Escalante was director of the journal *Reflector*, whose only issue appeared in Madrid, in December 1920. He was a participant in the ultraist literary *velada* (encounter) of January 28, 1921, "Del Madrid funambulesco," held in the Parisiana salon. In April of that same year, he took part in the ultraist meeting of the \*Ateneo (Madrid). Called a *creacionista* by Gerardo \*Diego, Ciria y Escalante died very young, but his work is remembered for its avant-garde nature and appearance at a time when Spanish literature was undergoing radical changes. Guillermo de \*Torre termed him ultraist. At the suggestion of M. \*Fernández Almagro, a group of friends published his short literary production as *Poemas*. Ciria y Escalante is the "Giocondo, Amigo mío" in a poem by \*García Lorca.

BIBLIOGRAPHY

Primary Texts

*Poemas póstumos.* Santander; not found, 1924.

Criticism

"José de Ciria y Escalante, Madrid 1924." *Alfar* 47 (Feb. 1925): 31.
Videla, Gloria. *El ultraísmo.* Madrid: Gredos, 1964.

                                                                        Kathleen March

**CIRLOT, Juan Eduardo** (1916, Barcelona–1973, Barcelona), poet and critic of literature, art and architecture. Cirlot was a leading theoretician and spokesman for the School of Barcelona. His poetry includes *Seis sonetos y un poema del amor celeste* (1943; Six Sonnets and a Poem of Celestial Love); *Canto de la vida muerta* (1945; Song of Dead Life); and *Lilith* (1949). He also authored *Introducción al surrealismo* (1953; Introduction to Surrealism). Among his studies of painting are *Juan Miró* (1949); *La Pintura abstracta* (1951; Abstract Painting); *La Pintura surrealista* (1955; Surrealist Painting); *Cubismo y figuración* (1957; Cubism and Imagination); *Arte contemporáneo* (1958; Contemporary Art); and *Del Expresionismo a la abstracción* (1958; From Expressionism to the Abstract). *Tapies* (1960) and *Significación de la pintura de Tapies* (1962; The Meaning of Tapies' Painting) interpret the Barcelona painter Antonio Tapies.

Additional art criticism includes *La Pintura contemporánea* (1963; Contemporary Painting); *Hieronymous Bosch* (1967); *El Espíritu abstracto* (1970; The Abstract Spirit); *Arte del siglo XX* (1972; Twentieth-Century Art); *La Pintura de Monserrat Guidol* (1972; The Painting of Monserrat Guidol); *La Pintura gótica europea* (1972; European Gothic Painting); and *El Nacimiento de un genio* (1972; *Picasso: Birth of a Genius*, 1972). Major architectural studies are *El Arte de Gaudí* (1950; Gaudí's Art) and *Introducción a la arquitectura de Gaudí* (1966; *The Genesis of Gaudian Architecture*, 1967). Fascinated by symbology, Cirlot authored *El Ojo en la mitología: su simbolismo* (1954; Eye Symbolism in Mythology). His *Diccionario de símbolos tradicionales* (1958; *A Dictionary of Symbols*, 1962) is a renowned study of symbolism in all its aspects.

BIBLIOGRAPHY

Primary Texts

*Diccionario de símbolos*. 2nd ed. Barcelona: Labor, 1982.

*Introducción a la arquitectura de Gaudí*. Barcelona: R M, 1966.

*El nacimiento de un genio*. Barcelona: Gustavo Gili, 1972.

*Obra poética*. Ed. Clara Janés. Madrid: Cátedra, 1981.

*Poesía de J. E. Cirlot (1966–1972)*. Ed. Leopoldo Azancot. Madrid: Nacional, 1974.

English Translations

*A Dictionary of Symbols*. Tr. Jack Sage. 2nd ed. New York: Philosophical Library, 1982.

*The Genesis of Gaudian Architecture*. Tr. Joyce Wittenborn. New York: G. Wittenborn, 1967.

*Picasso: Birth of a Genius*. Tr. Paul Elek, Ltd., New York: Praeger, 1972.

Criticism

Dietz, Bernd. "La necesaria presencia de Juan Eduardo Cirlot." *CH* 302 (1975): 473–78.

Janés, Clara. "Cirlot y el surrealismo: El material poético." *Nueva Estafeta* 53 (1983): 55–61.

———. "Cirlot y el surrealismo: El tema de amor" *CH* 363 (1980): 494–514.

Robert Sandarg

**CIRRE, José Francisco** (1905, Granada– ), professor, scholar. Secretary of the magazine *Tierra Firme* and manager of the publishing house Cruz y Raya, he was also secretary of the Institut d'Etudes Hispaniques of the U of Brussels (1937–39). Since 1946 he has taught at Wayne State U in Detroit. He has analyzed the generation of Jorge *Guillén–*García Lorca in *Forma y espíritu de una lírica española* (1950; Form and Spirit of Spanish Lyricism).

BIBLIOGRAPHY

Primary Texts

*Forma y espíritu de una lírica española*. Mexico: Gráfica Panamericana, 1950.

*El mundo lírico de Pedro Salinas*. Granada: Don Quijote, 1982.

Isabel McSpadden

**CISNEROS, Francisco Jiménez de** (1436, Torrelaguna, Madrid–1517, Roa, Burgos), Franciscan, cardinal, inquisitor general, patron of education. A figure of enormous political importance, he became confessor to Queen Isabella in

1492, Archbishop of Toledo in 1496, and later, inquisitor general and cardinal. The *Catholic Encyclopedia* deems him the reformer and renewer of the Spanish church before the Council of Trent. He vigorously sponsored several singular cultural achievements of *Renaissance Spain: he founded and nurtured the U of Alcalá; he founded the Major College of San Ildefonso; he financed and arranged publication of the great *Biblia políglota complutense* (1514–17; *Bible of Alcalá); and he stimulated printing of books in general by subvening publication of many religious and secular works, such as Aristotle's writings, biographies of St. Thomas, etc., and the *Agricultura general* (1513; General Agriculture) by G. Alonso de *Herrera, arranging for free distribution of the latter to farmers. *See also* Humanism; Inquisition.

BIBLIOGRAPHY

Criticism

Ceballos Piñas, E. *Cisneros, un gran español*. Madrid: Publicaciones españolas, 1973.

Maureen Ihrie

**CLARAMONTE, Andrés de** (1580, Murcia?–1626, Madrid), dramatist, actor, *autor* of plays. The negative judgments of Marcelino *Menéndez y Pelayo have until very recently obstructed proper recognition and evaluation of Claramonte's work. *Rojas Villandrando referred to him as one of the most successful *autores* of the day. A. Rodríguez López Vázquez has recently begun to rectify modern critical neglect of Claramonte, tracing his peripatetic life as actor and director throughout Spain (with gaps), from about 1602 to 1626. He estimates that Claramonte probably composed about 50 plays. Ascertaining authorship is a knotty problem, however, as Claramonte left no will itemizing his writings, and his published works were, for the most part, either unauthorized editions or included in collections attributed to others, such as Lope de *Vega. The *Estrella de Sevilla* (Star of Seville) may be his, and also *Dineros son calidad* (Money Is Class)—attributed to Lope; López Vázquez even argues that the *Burlador de Sevilla* (*Tirso de Molina) may be by Claramonte. Plays certainly by him include *La infelice Dorotea* (Unfortunate Dorothy), *El valiente negro en Flandes* (The Brave Black in Flanders) and *Deste agua no beberé* (I Will Not Drink This Water). *See also* Theater in Spain.

BIBLIOGRAPHY

Primary Texts

*El burlador de Sevilla*. Ed., intro., A. Rodríguez López-Vázquez. Kassel: Reichenberger, 1987.
*Comedias de Andrés de Claramonte*. Ed. María del Carmen Hernández. Murcia: Academia Alfonso el Sabio, 1983.
"A Critical Edition and Study of Andrés de Claramonte's *La infelice Dorotea*." C. A. Ganelin. *DAI* 44 (1984): 3395A (U of Chicago).
*Deste agua no beberé*. Ed., intro. A. Rodríguez López-Vázquez. Kassel: Reichenberger, 1984.

"Edición crítica de *El valiente negro en Flandes* de Andrés de Claramonte." A. T. Trejo. *DAI* 38 (1978): 4873A (U of Southern California).
*Púsoseme el sol salióme la luna.* Ed., intro. A. Rodríguez López-Vázquez. Kassel: Reichenberger, 1985.

Criticism

Leavitt, S. *The "Estrella de Sevilla" and Claramonte.* Cambridge: Harvard UP, 1931.

Maureen Ihrie

**CLARASÓ, Noel** (19-, Alexandria– ), prose author. Trained as a lawyer, he writes in Spanish and Catalan, sometimes using the pseudonym León Daudí. He has published more than one hundred books and eight thousand articles—mostly humorous—since the Civil War. Eugenio De Nora has described him as a manufacturer of second-rate works. Typical are the novels *Seis autores en busca de un personaje* (1951; Six Authors in Search of a Character), *Fruta prohibida* (1964; Forbidden Fruit), and a short story collection, *Siga perdiendo el tiempo con Noel Clarasó* (1947; Keep Wasting Time with Noel Clarasó).

BIBLIOGRAPHY

Primary Texts

*Departamento Diez.* Barcelona: Sagitario, 1968.
*Seis autores en busca de un personaje.* 2nd ed. Madrid: Aguilar, 1959.
*Seis vidas al margen de la ley.* Barcelona: MYNE, 1965.

Merry Wheaton

**CLARIMÓN, Carlos** (1920, Zaragoza– ), author of novelettes such as *Aquel día* (That Day), *Los bancos son de piedra* (Stone Benches), and *La trampa* (The Trap). He also collaborates in several literary journals, and has been recognized for the originality of his short stories.

BIBLIOGRAPHY

Primary Text

*Hombre a solas.* Madrid: Taurus, 1961.

Isabel McSpadden

**CLARÍN,** pseudonym of Leopoldo Alas (1852, Zamora–1901, Oviedo), novelist, short story writer, and critic. "Me nacieron en Zamora" ("They had me born in Zamora"), Clarín once said of his birthplace. Zamora notwithstanding, Alas is thoroughly identified with the Asturian capital of Oviedo, the "Vetusta" of his masterpiece *La Regenta* (1884–85; *La Regenta*, 1984). His work as educator—professor of law at the U of Oviedo—critic, and narrator cannot be separated from the people and ambience of Asturias; yet isolated and provincial as he appeared to be, Leopoldo Alas exercised a profound influence on the Spanish capital. Greatly feared, often maligned as a critic, Clarín's acerbic pen, from the 1870s till the end of his life, wielded merciless satire on unsuspecting amateurs of belles lettres, soon to be cringing mediocrities of the Madrid literary scene, and even supposed giants of Spanish Restoration culture, in such volumes as *Solos de Clarín* (1881; Solos by Clarín), *Sermón perdido* (1885; Lost Sermon), *Nueva campaña* (1887; New Campaign), *Mezclilla* (1889; Mélange), *Ensayos y revistas* (1892; Essays and Reviews), *Palique* (1893; Small Talk), and a series of eight *Folletos literarios* (1886–91; Literary Pamphlets). His youthful immersion in the philosophical-moral doctrines of *Krausism and later exposure to positivism, *naturalism, spiritual idealism, and other ideological trends of the nineteenth c. were instrumental in fashioning out of the daily pettiness and shortsightedness of Restoration life a more thoughtful and profound critic of his times than might have been expected. Amid the lightweight banter of his *paliques* and *solos*, Clarín wrote many serious essays, on Baudelaire (a kindred spirit in many ways), Zola (a major influence), *Pérez Galdós (his primary Spanish model), naturalism (exploited as a technique in his fiction), faith within doubt (anticipating *Unamuno), and the moral, political, and literary decadence of Spanish Restoration society (perhaps the major theme of his work).

Indeed, one of the keys to understanding Alas lies in his criticism, or more accurately, in his critical attitude toward reality. Objects and persons are subjected to an often harsh and inevitably questioning scrutiny which frequently functions through the use of irony or satire. The few exceptions to this rule are his short story treatments of animals (as protagonists), as in "El Quin" (1895), and of "gentes humildes," as Francisco García Pavón labels them ("Gentes humildes en la obra narrativa de 'Clarín,' " *Arbor*, 1952), the humble, modest poor of the country (Rosa and Pinín in "¡Adiós, Cordera!," 1892) and, occasionally, of the city (Pipá in the 1879 story of the same name), who are viewed as victims of society. Nothwithstanding this deviation from the norm, Clarín's entire production, both critical and narrative, is permeated with the irony and satire of the critical realist, tempered at times by humor, it is true, but often ferocious and pitiless in intent. Witness his major novel, *La Regenta*, now considered by Gonzalo Sobejano, Mario Vargas Llosa, and others as the most significant novel of the last century (along with the quite different *Fortunata y Jacinta*, by Galdós). A novel which depicts through the decline and fall of an individual—Ana Ozores—the profound pervasiveness of evil and decay in Spanish Restoration society, *La Regenta*, in using a neurotic, yet poignantly affecting outsider (Ana) as the central protagonist in order to manifest not only the individual's physiological-mental decline but, indirectly, the degeneration of a society, follows a pattern frequently utilized by realists and naturalists alike (as in Zola's Rougon-Macquart series, Galdós's *La desheredada* and *La de Bringas*). But Clarín's parallel development of individual and collective decadence differs considerably from the naturalist mold in two significant aspects. First, in contrast to the Zolaesque emphasis on the physiological etiology of the neurotic and of degeneration in general, Alas's view looks forward to the Freudian conception of neurosis and, specifically, of hysteria as a mental malady. But second and more important, Clarín's psychological analysis of a dissolving, fragmented soul in torment attains far more complexity and depth than previous naturalistic novels. And this sensitive exploration of the individual psyche, which seems far more Baudelairean than naturalistic, is intimately and profoundly tied to an adept analysis of the social body.

Clarín's second long novel, *Su único hijo* (1891; tr., *His Only Son*, 1981) has been, traditionally, a somewhat unclassifiable and less appreciated work for both critics and readers. After *La Regenta*, reviewers evidently expected the second novel to resemble its predecessor by adhering to the detailed, realist-naturalist bent of the first novel. But by 1891 Zolaism was on the decline and the psychological novel in the forefront. In response to contemporary idealistic aspirations and to his own inner unrest, Clarín in *Su único hijo* shed much of this heavy, detailed framework and concentrated more on inner realities. As in *La Regenta*, the protagonist of *Su único hijo*, Bonifacio Reyes, reveals a dissatisfaction with life and a quest for a deeper reality that will give meaning to his existence, a search which takes the form of dreams and dream making. A transitional novel, *Su único hijo* reflects the peculiar ambience of the *fin de siècle* in all its indecisive yet very suggestive contours and is streaked with ambiguous tonalities, due in large part to its ambivalent authorial point of view and a double-edged mood with its soft side of reverie and a cutting underside of satire and irony.

Clarín's short stories (and short novels), collected in such volumes as *Pipá* (1879), *Doña Berta, Cuervo, Superchería* (1892; Doña Berta, Crow, and Superstition), *El Señor, y lo demás son cuentos* (1892; The Good Lord, and All the Rest Mere Tales), *Cuentos morales* (1896; Moral Tales), and *El gallo de Sócrates* (1901; Socrates' Rooster), offer additional first-rate examples of a remarkable writer and personality.

BIBLIOGRAPHY

Primary Texts

*¡Adiós, Cordera! y otros cuentos*. 8th ed. Madrid: Espasa-Calpe, 1979.
*Clarín político*. Ed. Yvan Lissorgues. 2 vols. Toulouse: Université de Toulouse–Le Mirail, 1980–81.
*Cuentos morales*. Madrid: Alianza, 1973.
*Ensayos y revistas*. Madrid: Manuel Fernández y Lasanta, 1892.
*Folletos literarios*. 8 vols. Madrid: Fernando Fe, 1886–91.
*Galdós*. Madrid: Renacimiento, 1912.
*El gallo de Sócrates y otros cuentos*. Madrid: Espasa-Calpe, 1973.
*Mezclilla*. Madrid: Fernando Fe, 1889.
*Nueva campaña*. Madrid: Fernando Fe, 1887.
*Obra olvidada*. Ed. Antonio Ramos-Gascón. Madrid: Júcar, 1973.
*Palique*. Ed. José María Martínez Cachero. Barcelona: Labor, 1973.
*Pipá*. Ed. Antonio Ramos-Gascón. 6th ed. Madrid: Cátedra, 1983.
*Preludios de Clarín*. Ed. Jean-François Botrel. Oviedo: Instituto de Estudios Asturianos, 1972.
*La Regenta*. Ed. Gonzalo Sobejano. 2 vols. Madrid: Castalia, 1981.
*Sermón perdido*. Madrid: Fernando Fe, 1885.
*Solos de Clarín*. Madrid: Alianza, 1971.

*Su único hijo.* Ed. Carolyn Richmond. Madrid: Espasa-Calpe, 1979.
*Superchería, Cuervo, Doña Berta.* 2nd ed. Madrid: Taurus, 1980.
*Teresa. Avecilla. El hombre de los estrenos.* Ed. Leonardo Romero. Madrid: Castalia, 1975.
*Treinta relatos.* Ed. Carolyn Richmond. Madrid: Espasa-Calpe, 1983.
English Translations
*Doña Berta.* Tr. Zenia Da Silva. In *Great Spanish Stories.* Ed. Angel Flores. New York: Modern Library, 1956. (*Doña Berta*).
*His Only Son.* Tr. Julie Jones. Baton Rouge/London: Louisiana State UP, 1981.
*La Regenta.* Tr. John Rutherford. Athens: U of Georgia P; New York Penguin, 1984.
"What Naturalism Is Not." Tr. George J. Becker. In *Documents of Modern Literary Realism.* Ed. George J. Becker. Princeton: Princeton UP, 1963. 266–73. (Prologue to Emilia Pardo Bazán's *La cuestión palpitante.*)
See also Robert S. Rudder, *The Literature of Spain in Translation. A Bibliography* (New York: Ungar, 1975), pp. 276–77, for additional translations of individual stories.
Criticism
*Archivum* (Oviedo), 2 (1952). Homage volume.
Baquero Goyanes, Mariano. *Prosistas españoles contemporáneos.* Madrid: Rialp, 1956.
Beser, Sergio. *Leopoldo Alas, crítico literario.* Madrid: Gredos, 1968.
———, ed. *Leopoldo Alas, teoría y crítica de la novela española.* Barcelona: Laia, 1972.
Blanquat, Josette, and Jean-François Botrel, ed. *Clarín y sus editores (65 cartas inéditas de Leopoldo Alas a Fernando Fe y Manuel Fernández Lasanta, 1884–1893).* Rennes: Université de Haute Bretagne, 1981.
Cabezas, Juan Antonio. *Clarín, el provinciano universal.* Madrid: Espasa-Calpe, 1936.
*Los Cuadernos del Norte* (Oviedo) 2.7 (1981); and 5.23 (1984). Homage volumes.
Durand, Frank. "Structural Unity in Leopoldo Alas's *La Regenta.*" *HR* 31 (1963): 324–35.
*Insula* 39. 451 (June 1984). Homage volume.
Kronik, John W. "La modernidad de Leopoldo Alas." *Papeles de Son Armadans* 41 (May 1966): 121–34.
Lissorgues, Yvan. *La Pensée philosophique et religieuse de Leopoldo Alas (Clarín), 1875–1901.* Paris: Editions du Centre Nacional de la Recherche Scientifique, 1983.
Martínez Cachero, José María. *Las palabras y los días de Leopoldo Alas.* Oviedo: Instituto de Estudios Asturianos, 1984.
———, ed. *Leopoldo Alas "Clarín."* Madrid: Taurus, 1978.
Rivkin, Laura M. "Extranatural Art in Clarín's *Su único hijo.*" *MLN* 97 (1982): 311–28.
Rutherford, John. *Leopoldo Alas: La Regenta.* London: Grant and Cutler, 1974.
Sobejano, Gonzalo. *Clarín en su obra ejemplar.* Madrid: Castalia, 1985.
Valis, Noël M. *The Decadent Vision in Leopoldo Alas.* Baton Rouge/London: Louisiana State UP, 1981.
———. "Order and Meaning in Clarín's *La Regenta.*" *Novel* 16 (1983): 246–58.

Noël M. Valis

**CLAVERÍA, Carlos** (1909, Barcelona–1974, ?), professor, scholar. He taught around the world—Hamburg, Upsala, Frankfurt, Stockholm, Pennsylvania, Los Angeles, and served as director of the Spanish Institute in Munich, and the

Spanish Institute in London. Besides journalistic collaborations, he wrote *Cinco estudios de literatura española moderna* (1945; Five Studies of Modern Spanish Literature), *"Le Chevalier Delibéré" de la Marche y sus versiones españolas del siglo XVI* (1950; La Marche's *Chevalier Delibéré* and Its Spanish Versions in the Sixteenth C.), *Estudios sobre los gitanismos del español* (1951; Studies on Gypsyisms in Spanish), *Temas de Unamuno* (1952; Themes of Unamuno), and *Ensayos hispanosuecos* (1954; Hispano-Swedish Essays). He also belonged to the Spanish Academy (*Academia Española).

BIBLIOGRAPHY

Primary Texts

*"Le Chevalier Delibéré" de la Marche y sus versiones españolas del siglo XVI.* Zaragoza: Instituto Fernando el Católico, 1950.
*Cinco estudios de literatura española moderna.* Salamanca: CSIC, 1945.
*Estudios hispanosuecos.* Granada: U of Granada, 1954.
*Estudios sobre los gitanismos del español.* RFE Anejo 53. Madrid: RFE, 1951.
*Historia del Reino de Navarra.* Pamplona: Gómez, 1971.
*Temas de Unamuno.* 2nd ed. Madrid: Gredos, 1970.

Isabel McSpadden

**CLAVIJO, Ruy González de** (?, Madrid–1412, Madrid), historical author. He was the first Spaniard to document his journey to the Far East with a book. Sent by Henry IV to Persia in 1403, he recounts his three-year trip in the entertaining *Historia del gran Tamorlán* (1582; *Embassy to Tamorlane 1403–1406*, 1928). In addition to descriptions of customs and of cities such as Constantinople, Trebizond, Tehran, etc., there are accounts of political struggles between Tamerlane and Bagazit. Composed shortly after 1406, it circulated in ms. form for many years before being published.

BIBLIOGRAPHY

Primary Text

*Embajada a Tamorlán.* Ed., study F. López Estrada. Madrid: CSIC, 1943.

English Translation

*Embassy to Tamerlane, 1403–1406.* Ed. E. Ross and E. Powell. Tr., intro. G. Le Strange. London: Routledge, 1928.

**CLAVIJO Y FAJARDO, José de** (1730, Canarias–1806, Madrid). Although born in the Canary Islands, Clavijo was educated in France, where he developed strong neo-classic attitudes through friendships with Voltaire, Buffon and others. A liaison with Beaumarchais's sister Louise Caron served as the inspiration for both Goethe's *Clavigo* and Beaumarchais's own *Eugénie*. (The latter was subsequently translated into Spanish by Ramón de la *Cruz.) After returning to Spain he came under the protection of the Count of Aranda, who named him director of the Royal Theaters in Madrid. He also served as secretary of the Cabinet for Natural History, and editor of the government-sponsored periodical *El Mercurio*.

In 1762 he founded and directed *El Pensador* (The Thinker), a series of eighty-six essays published in periodical form and modeled after *The Spectator* of Addison and Steele. From this vantage point he launched a campaign against what he saw as contemporary society's stagnation in seventeenth c. traditions and values. To him this was particularly evident in the theater. He participated in various attempts to reform Spanish theater along strict neo-classic lines and led the attack against the *auto sacramental* as the epitome of the decadent baroque theater still popular among the theater-going masses. His efforts and those of Nicolás Fernández de *Moratín in his *Desengaños al teatro español* (1763; Setting Right the Errors of Spanish Theater) contributed to the prohibition of *auto sacramental* performances by royal decree on June 11, 1765. In recent years, however, Alborg and Andioc have downplayed somewhat the significance of the role played by Clavijo and Moratín in the demise of the *auto sacramental* in the theaters. As a translator, Clavijo's monumental achievement was the twenty-one volume Spanish version of the *Histoire naturelle* by Buffon (1785–1805). In addition, he translated the *Sermones* of Massillon (1769–73) and, in conjunction with *Olavide, Tomás de *Iriarte and others, produced Spanish versions of several plays from classical French drama, including *Andromaque* by Racine. Clavijo is best remembered as a major figure in the development of the essay and of periodical literature in Spain, and as an ardent defender of the neo-classic ideals of the Enlightenment. *See also* Auto; Essay; Theater in Spain.

BIBLIOGRAPHY

Criticism

Doreste, V. "Estudio sobre Clavijo y Fajardo." *Anuario de Estudios Atlánticos* 12 (1966): 201–19.
Espinosa, Antonio. *Don José Clavijo y Fajardo*. Las Palmas: Cabildo Insular, 1970.
Petersen, H. "Notes on the Influence of Addison's *Spectator* and Marivaux's *Spectateur Français* upon *El Pensador*." *HR* 4 (1936): 256–63.

                                                                        Donald C. Buck

**CLEMENCÍN, Diego** (1765, Murcia–1834, Madrid), priest, scholar, and critic. A member of the Academies of the Spanish Language, of History, and of San Fernando, he also served as foreign minister and minister of governmental affairs (in 1822). Upon Ferdinand VII's return to power, he retired to Murcia. With the end of the absolutist government in 1833, he was named librarian to María Cristina, Regent to Isabel II. Clemencín died shortly thereafter, the victim of a cholera epidemic. His many erudite works include a study of the chronicle by Rasis the Moor and the *Elogio de la reina Isabel la Católica* (1821; Panegyric to Isabella the Catholic). His most ambitious work was an annotated edition of *Don Quijote* (1833–39; rpt. Madrid: Castalia, 1947). *See also* Academia; Academia Española.

BIBLIOGRAPHY

Criticism

Puyol y Alonso, J. *Don Diego Clemencín, Ministro de Fernando VII. (Recuerdos del Ministerio de 7 de julio de 1822.)* Madrid: "Revista de archivos," 1929.

Donald C. Buck

**COBOS, el padre.** *See* Nocedal, Cándido

**CODERA ZAIDÍN, Francisco** (1836, Fonz, Huesca–1917, Fonz), distinguished classicist, Hebraist, Arabist. He taught Arabic at the Central U, and was a driving force in the growth of Arabic studies in Spain. Notable publications include the *Tratado de numismática arabigoespañola* (1879; Treatise on Hispanoarabic Numismatics), and the ten-volume *Biblioteca arabigohispana* (1882–95; Hispano-Arabic Library).

BIBLIOGRAPHY

Primary Texts

*Biblioteca arabigohispana*. 10 vols. Madrid: n.p., 1882–95.
*Estudios críticos de historia árabe española*. Zaragoza: Uriarte, 1903–17.
*Tratado de numismática.* . . . Madrid: Murillo, 1879.

**COELLO, Antonio** (1611, Madrid–1682, Madrid), dramatist. A member of the group of writers influenced by *Calderón, Coello has been acclaimed for *El celoso extremeño* (n.d.; The Jealous Extremaduran), the religious play *La cárcel del mundo* (n.d.; The Prison of the World), and *Yerros de naturaleza y aciertos de fortuna* (n.d.; Nature's Errors and Fortune's Successes). The latter was written in collaboration with Calderón and is a possible precursor to *La vida es sueño*. Very few works written exclusively by Coello have survived, although he collaborated with writers such as *Rojas Zorrilla, Juan *Vélez de Guevara, Antonio de *Solís, *Pérez de Montalbán, and his brother Juan Coello. Antonio also wrote *El conde de Sex o dar la vida por su dama* (n.d.; The Earl of Essex, or Giving One's Life for One's Lady), which was attributed to Philip IV. As Cotarelo has observed, Coello was the first to dramatize the story of the love between Elizabeth of England and the Earl of Essex, a theme later imitated by Corneille (1678) and many others. *See also* Theater in Spain.

BIBLIOGRAPHY

Primary Texts

*El conde de Sex o dar la vida por su dama*. BAE 45.
*Yerros de naturaleza y aciertos de la fortuna*. Ed. E. Juliá Martínez. Madrid: Hernando, 1930.

Criticism

Cotarelo y Mori, E. *Dramáticos españoles del siglo XVII: Don Antonio Coello y Ochoa.* BRAE 5. Madrid: RABM, 1919. 550–600.

Deborah Compte

**COIMBRA, Leonardo José** (1883, Lixa–1936, Porto), Portuguese philosopher and poet or, in the opinion of some, poetic philosopher. He started out training for the navy but transferred to education studies at the U of Porto. A talented and charismatic personality, he made a place for himself among his fellow students pressing his republican convictions and campaigning for free universal education. In 1908, together with Jaime *Cortesão and Alvaro Pinto he founded the Grupo ABC, a voluntary organization that took up the task of teaching illiterates. Adult illiteracy was then generally claimed to exceed 80 percent of the population. Once again with Cortesão and others of like mind he was instrumental in founding the Universidade Popular (People's University) and a politico-literary group Nova Seara (to be distinguished from *Seara Nova* in which the latter was also involved) and later, a similar group Renascença Portuguesa. Their publication *A Águia* propagated the views of the movement and of Coimbra himself. After unsuccessfully competing for a university post in Lisbon on the basis of his philosophical text *O Criacionismo* (1912; Creationism), he returned to secondary teaching until 1919 when he was appointed to head the newly created philosophy department in Porto, a post he filled until 1925. He was also active in politics, being elected to the Chamber of Deputies and twice holding the post of minister of education. He was killed in an automobile accident in 1936.

His philosophical system, which he formulated under the title of Criacionismo, embodies a somewhat starry-eyed, optimistic extension of the positions of Descartes, Leibniz, and various others, together with a generous admixture of the basic tenets of Saudosismo. Essentially, his system strives to reject the limits, as he sees them, imposed by observable fact in order to substitute or revitalize the "creative" metaphysical power of the human spirit. The terms of opposition that he uses are "cousismo" or "reification" to define the passive, analytic mode of thinking that he sees as dead-ended and "criacionismo" or "creationism" to define the new state of mind capable of "creating" a new outlook beyond the facts. He published many works and often lectured on his system, exerting strong influence on his contemporaries and students who studied under him and doing much to move them toward the mystic nationalism and orthodox catholicism that he himself increasingly supported.

BIBLIOGRAPHY

Primary Texts

*Obras Completas.* 14 vols. Porto: Tavares Martins, 1956.
Of particular interest are vol. 2, *O Criacionismo*, and vol. 6, which contains the analyses of the works of Luís de Camões, Antero de Quental, Guerra Junqueiro and Teixeira de Pascoaes.

Criticism

Alves, Angelo. *O Sistema filosófico de Leonardo Coimbra*. Porto: Tavares Martins, 1962.

Peter Fothergill-Payne

**COLINAS, Antonio** (1946, La Bañeza, Leon– ), poet and novelist of the third post-war generation. His poetry, though incorporating abundant cultural references (some of them reflecting his four years' residency in Italy), is primarily notable for its air of cosmic meditation. A strong poetic vocation has resulted in steady production since 1967, when *Poemas de la tierra y la sangre* (Poems of Earth and Blood) appeared. Subsequent volumes include *Preludios a una noche total* (1969; Preludes to a Total Night), *Truenos y flautas en un templo* (1971; Thunderclaps and Flutes in a Temple), *Sepulcro en Tarquinia* (1975; Sepulcher in Tarquinia; La Crítica Prize, 1976), *Astrolabio* (1979; Astrolabe), *En lo oscuro* (1981; In the Darkness), and *Noche más allá de la noche* (1982; Night beyond the Night). He is also the author of two novels, *Un año en el sur (Para una educación estética)* (1985; A Year in the South [For an Aesthetic Education]), and *Larga carta a Francesca* (1986; Long Letter to Francesca), as well as critical works on *Aleixandre, Leopardi, and others.

BIBLIOGRAPHY

Primary Texts

*Larga carta a Francesca*. Madrid: Seix-Barral, 1986.
*Poesía, 1967–1981*. Madrid: Visor, 1984.
*Un año en el sur (Para una educación estética*. Madrid: Trieste, 1985.

Criticism

Cano, José Luis. "La poesía de Antonio Colinas." *Insula* 399 (1980): n.p.
Jiménez, José Olivio. "Prólogo." *Poesía, 1967–1981*. By Antonio Colinas. Madrid: Visor, 1984. 9–49.

Martha Miller

**COLL Y VEHÍ, José** (1823, Barcelona–1876, Gerona), poet, journalist, theorist and critic. As a poet, he wrote various compositions in imitation of Fray Luis de León. His elegy "A la muerte de Aribau" (Upon Aribau's Death) and his ode "La belleza ideal" (Ideal Beauty), a sort of *ars poetica*, stand out in his poetic work. In Madrid he worked as a correspondent for the *Diario de Barcelona*, and he taught rhetoric and poetry at the Instituto de San Isidro. He wrote a number of important studies on rhetoric and poetry: *Elementos de literatura* (1856; Elements of Literature), *Compendio de retórica y poética* (1883; Compendium of Rhetoric and Poetics), *La sátira provenzal* (1861; Provençal Satire), *Diálogos literarios* (1866; Literary Dialogues), and *Refranes del Quijote ordenados y glosados* (1874; Proverbs from the Quijote Arranged and Glossed). His literary studies represented the dawn of a new literary science that broke with neoclassical theory of the eighteenth c., and his teachings influenced later generations of scholars.

BIBLIOGRAPHY

Primary Texts

*Compendio de retórica y poética, o Nociones elementales de literatura.* Barcelona: Barcelonesa, 1883.
*Diálogos literarios.* Barcelona: J. Bastinos, 1866.
*Elementos de literatura.* Madrid: Rivadeneyra, 1856.
*Los refranes del Quijote ordenados y glosados.* Barcelona: Diario de Barcelona, 1874.
*La sátira provenzal.* Madrid: Rivadeneyra, 1861.

Phoebe Porter Medina

**COLMENARES, Diego de** (1586, Segovia–1651, Segovia), chaplain, historian. He wrote the informative *Historia de la Insigne Ciudad de Segovia* (1637; History of the Renowned City of Segovia).

BIBLIOGRAPHY

Primary Text

*Historia de . . . Segovia.* Ed. T. Baeza González. Rev. M. María Vergara. Segovia: Academia de Historia y Arte de San Quirce, 1969–70.

Criticism

Vera, Juan de. "Biografía de Diego de Colmenares." *Estudios segovianos* 3 (1951): 5–115.

Phoebe Porter Medina

**COLOMA, Carlos** (1573, Alicante–1637, Madrid), historian, politician, soldier. Of noble birth, his elegantly written *Guerras en los Estados Bajos desde el año 1588–1599* (1625; Wars in the Low Countries from 1588 to 1599) benefits from his personal involvement in and witness to events there. Coloma also translated Tacitus's works.

BIBLIOGRAPHY

Primary Text

*Las guerras en los Estados Bajos. . . .* In BAE 28.

**COLOMA, Luis** (1851, Jerez de la Frontera–1915, Madrid), novelist, essayist, and short story writer. A law student at the U of Seville, Coloma associated with the elegant drawing-room society of Seville and Madrid. He also wrote for the newspapers *El Tiempo* of Madrid and *El Porvenir* of Jerez. In 1873, after suffering a serious self-inflicted but accidental pistol wound, he entered the Society of Jesus. Encouraged by the famous Andalusian novelist *Fernán Caballero, he entered the literary world by writing novels and short stories. In 1910 in *Recuerdos de "Fernán Caballero"* (Remembrances of Fernán Caballero), he published his collection of personal notes, anecdotes, and letters which he had exchanged with her. Luis Coloma was a prolific short story writer. He published his first stories in *El Mensajero del Corazón de Jesús* (1880; The Messenger of the Sacred Heart of Jesus); they were later collected in several volumes entitled

*Lecturas recreativas* (1884–87; Recreational Readings). Later volumes of stories are *Al natural* (1888; True to Life), *El cazador de venados* (1888; The Deer Hunter), *¿Qué sería?* (1888; What Could It Be?), and *Nuevas lecturas* (1902; New Readings). He wrote *Solaces de un estudiante* (1884; A Student's Solace), *La Gorriona* (1887; Miss Sparrow), *Juan Miseria* (1888; *John Poverty*, 1911), *Por un piojo* (1889; For a Louse), *Retratos de antaño* (1895; Men of Yore), *La reina mártir* (1902; The Martyr Queen), *El Marqués de Mora* (1903; The Marquis of Mora), and *Fray Francisco* (1914; Friar Francis).

Padre Coloma also wrote several novels. Those of lesser importance are *Jeromín* (1905; *The Story of Don Juan of Austria*, 1912) and *Boy* (1910; *A True Hidalgo*, 1911). His most successful novel, which caused a great deal of scandal, was *Pequeñeces* (1890–91; *Currita, Countess of Albornoz: A Novel of Madrid Society*, 1900). *Pequeñeces* is a satire of the aristocratic society of Madrid in the years which preceded the Restoration. It reveals the web of political, economical, and amorous intrigues in which nobility were caught in their attempt to restore the Bourbons to the throne of Spain. The action centers on the corrupt lives of Currita Albornoz and the ladies of the aristocracy. The novel was considered a *roman à clef*, and much effort was spent in trying to uncover the identities of the principal characters. *See also* Essay.

## BIBLIOGRAPHY

### Primary Texts

*Obras completas*. Ed. Rafael María de Hornedo. 4th ed. Madrid: Razón y Fe, 1960.
*Pequeñeces*. Ed. Rubén Benítez. Madrid: Cátedra, 1975.
*Pequeñeces*. Ed. Joaquín Antonio Peñalosa. México: Porrúa, 1968.

### English Translations

*Boy. A True Hidalgo*. Tr. Harold Binns. London: Herder, 1911.
*Jeromín. Estudios históricos sobre el siglo XVI. The Story of Don Juan of Austria*. Tr. Lady Moreton. London and New York: Lane, 1912.
*Juan Miseria. John Poverty*. Tr. E. M. Brooks. Philadelphia: Kilner, 1911.
*Pequeñeces. Currita, Countess of Albornoz: A Novel of Madrid Society*. Tr. by Estelle H. Atwell. Boston: Little, Brown, 1900.
Rudder, Robert S. *The Literature of Spain in English Translation. A Bibliography*. New York: Frederick Ungar, 1975. In addition to the translations of individual works listed above, this volume also includes translations of collections of short stories.

### Criticism

Alas, Leopoldo (Clarín). *Ensayos y revistas*. Madrid: n.p., 1892.
Dendle, Brian J. "Blasco Ibáñez and Coloma's Pequeñeces," RN 8 (1967): 200–203.
———. *The Spanish Novel of Religious Thesis. 1876–1936*. Princeton: Princeton UP, 1968.
Pardo Bazán, Emilia. "La algarada de *Pequeñeces*." *La Ilustración Artística* 488 (1891): 276–77.
———. *El Padre Luis Coloma: biografía y estudio crítico*. Madrid: Saenz de Jubera, 1891.

Peñalosa, Joaquín Antonio. "Prólogo." *Pequeñeces, Jeromín*. México: Porrúa, 1968. ix-xxii.
Schumacher, John N. "Integrism: A Study in Nineteenth-Century Spanish Political-Religious Thought." *Catholic Historical Review* (Washington) 67 (1962): 343–64.

Gilbert Paolini

**COLÓN, Cristóbal** (1451?, Genoa, Italy–1506, Valladolid), explorer, discoverer and historian. Colón, or Columbus, was the first historian of the New World. His surviving logbooks, letters and dispatches are of enormous historical interest. Though they are written in a Spanish which Columbus had learned in Portugal (his native Genoese tongue had no written form), fragments of great stylistic beauty surface nonetheless. *See also* Renaissance; Siglo de Oro.

BIBLIOGRAPHY

Primary Texts

*La carta de Colón anunciando.* . . . Transcription, notes, study C. Sanz. Madrid: Hauser y Menet, 1956. Facs.
*Cartas de relación de la conquista de América*. Ed. J. Le Riverend. 2 vols. Mexico: Nueva España, 1945.
*Diario de a bordo*. Ed. L. Arranz. Madrid: Historia 16, 1985.

English Translation

*The Four Voyages of Christopher Columbus*. Ed., tr. J. M. Cohen. Harmondsworth: Penguin, 1969.

Criticism

Menéndez Pidal, R. *La lengua de Cristóbal Colón*. . . . 3rd ed. Madrid: Espasa-Calpe, 1947.
Milani, V. I. *The Written Language of Christopher Columbus*. Buffalo, NY: SUNY Buffalo, 1973.

**COLUMBUS, Christopher.** *See* Colón, Cristóbal

**COMELLA, Luciano Francisco** (1751, Vich–1812, Madrid), playwright. Although born in Catalonia, he spent his entire career as one of Madrid's leading popular dramatists. He wrote over 200 works in virtually every dramatic genre. Representative plays include *Dona Inés de Castro* (c.1794), a lyric tragedy; *Federico II, Rey de Prusia* (1794; Frederick II, King of Prussia), a historical drama; *La Cecilia*, a drawing-room melodrama; *El matrimonio secreto* (The Secret Marriage), and *Hércules y Deyanira,* both *zarzuelas; El pueblo feliz* (The Happy Peasants), a comedy; and *El menestral sofocado* (The Suffocating Mechanic), a *sainete. He is noted today more for his extended polemic with Leandro Fernández de *Moratín than for his theater. Moratín's *La comedia nueva* satirizes the type of dramatist which, in his view, Comella epitomized—a hack writer who pandered to the ignorant public's desire for improbable stories filled with action and spectacle. The neoclassicist's assessment became the standard critical

viewpoint of Comella and his works. Recent studies, notably that of I. Mc-
Clelland, have pointed to Comella's acute sense of theatricality and his growth
as a dramatist sensitive to social concerns. His contribution to popular drama
can best be found in the genres of melodrama, and domestic and historical drama,
where he introduced some of the ideas projected by the neoclassical reform
movement and yet maintained the essentially baroque character of traditional
popular theater. *See also* Theater in Spain.

BIBLIOGRAPHY

Primary Texts

*La Cecilia*. Madrid: Cano, 1786.
*Federico Segundo, rey de Prusia*. Valencia: Hermanos de Orga, 1795.
*Hércules y Deyanira*. Barcelona: P. Nadal, 1968. Microopaque.
*El matrimonio secreto*. Madrid: Librería de Cerro, 1800.

Criticism

Cambronero, Carlos. "Comella, su vida y sus obras." *Revista Contemporánea* 102
    (1896): 567–82; 103 (1896): 41–58, 187–99, 308–90, 479–91, 637–44; 104
    (1896): 49–60, 206–11, 288–96, 398–405, 497–509.
Cave, Michael. "Comella and the Spanish Baroque Drama." *Revista/Review Intera-
    mericana* 3 (1974): 340–50.
———. "La obra dramática de Luciano Francisco Comella." Diss., U of Connecticut,
    1972.
McClelland, Ivy L. *Spanish Drama of Pathos (1750–1808)*. 2 vols. Liverpool: Liverpool
    UP, 1970.
Subirá, José. "Músicos al servicio de Calderón y de Comella." *Anuario Musical* 22
    (1967): 197–208.

                                                            Donald C. Buck

**COMPAÑÍA** (Company), the general term used since the Golden Age to refer
to an organized troupe of performers and the technical staff needed to mount
theatrical performances. *Rojas Villandrando, in his *Viaje entretenido* (Entertaining Journey), describes eight distinct types of performing groups: *bululú,
*ñaque, *gangarilla, *cambaleo, *garnacha, *bojiganga, *farándula and *com-
pañía*. These classifications were made according to the number of actors in the
troupe and the type of performances offered, with the *compañía* being the most
sophisticated. Rojas relates that "in the companies there are all types of low-
lifes who, nonetheless, are quick to learn genteel ways; there are also morally
upstanding people—well-born into society—distinguished men, and even honorable women . . . ; they have a repertory of fifty plays, an extensive wardrobe
of costumes, sixteen people who perform, thirty who eat, one who takes in the
money and God only knows which ones steal." By the early seventeenth c.,
under the influence of Lope de *Vega's *comedia nueva* style, the companies had
developed a rigid hierarchy of role casting according to the prominence of the
part and the character type to be portrayed. There were six to eight *damas*
(leading ladies), and four to six *galanes* (leading men), two *graciosos* for the

male comic parts (the female comic roles were played by the third and fifth *damas*), one or two *barbas* (bearded-ones, i.e., father-figure roles), and a *vejete* ("old fool"). Salaries were ranked according to the performer's position in the system, the highest paid being the leading *dama*, *galán*, and *gracioso*. In addition to their daily fixed stipend, the performers also received a portion of the receipts taken in from a specified area of the theater. In this manner the performers' incomes were partially determined by the success of the production. This hierarchical system for the performing companies lasted well into the nineteenth c. *See also* Siglo de Oro; Theater in Spain.

BIBLIOGRAPHY

Primary Texts

Buck, Donald C. "Theatrical Production in Madrid's Cruz and Príncipe Theaters during the Reign of Felipe V." Diss., U Texas Austin, 1980.
Shergold, N. D. *A History of the Spanish Stage from Medieval Times until the End of the Seventeenth Century*. Oxford: Clarendon, 1967.

Donald C. Buck

**CONCEPTISMO,** a literary style of the Baroque. *Conceptismo* is the name given to the complex and intentionally difficult style prevalent in Spanish poetry and prose during the late sixteenth and the seventeenth centuries. It is analogous to Italian *Marinismo*, French *préciosité*, and British *euphuism* and "metaphysical" poetry, and was cultivated by writers of the first rank, such as *Quevedo, *Góngora, Lope de *Vega, *Gracián, and *Calderón. The term derives from the style's emphasis on the subtlety and complexity of novel metaphor and Latinism in allusion, lexicon, and syntax, as in Gongorism or *culteranismo*, and from the style's basis on the *concepto* (conceit), which underlies the wordplays, paradoxes, antitheses, parallelisms and comparisons which abound in it. The *concepto* is cataloged and studied in all its possible varieties and defined as a "concordance or harmonious correlation expressed by the intellect between two or more recognizable extremes" in the *Agudeza y arte de ingenio* (The Art of Clever Expression and Wit) of Baltasar Gracián. Gracián's work is virtually the only contemporary formal examination of Baroque style and aesthetics in Spain, and is often considered the poetics of *conceptismo*.

Although distinguishable from each other in their emphasis on substance and content, and image and cultivated expression respectively, *conceptismo* and *culteranismo* frequently function together in literary works, especially poetry, responding to the same predilection for complication and difficulty and readily combining abstruse metaphor, classical reference, and conceptual complexity. Although in the seventeenth c, the two tendencies produced opposing literary camps of *culteranos* and *anti-culteranos*, dominated respectively by Góngora and Quevedo (and constituting the literary component of a bitter *ad hominem* polemic between the two authors), Góngora's poetry is as conceptista as it is culturanista, and both authors are cited frequently as examples in Gracián's

*Agudeza*. The verses from stanza 13 of Góngora's "Fábula de Polifemo y Galatea" (Fable of Polyphemus and Galatea),

> si roca de cristal no es de Neptuno
> pavón de Venus es, cisne de Juno

> (If not Neptune's shining crystal rock
> she is Juno's swan or Venus's peacock)

describing the nymph Galatea, well demonstrate the natural fusion of the two techniques. Possessing a swan's whiteness, from which her eyes shine, because the tail of a peacock is also said to possess eyes, Galatea is a swan with attributes of a peacock, and a peacock with attributes of a swan. This complex notion is expressed in terms of a paradoxical reversal of the conventional mythological association of the swan with Venus and the peacock with Juno to combine classical allusion with antithesis and paradox in several elaborate metaphors.

*Conceptismo* has distant roots in part in a philosophical tendency and predilection for wordplay present in fifteenth-c, *cancionero* poetry and retained in an attenuated form and with expressive simplicity in the work of Spain's greatest *Renaissance poet, *Garcilaso de la Vega. Hence, it is more a natural evolution or intensification of previously existing tendencies than a radical departure, and developed more immediately from one of the two poetic schools that derived from differing emphases in carrying on Garcilaso's poetic tradition in the work of his poetical heirs. These schools are those of Sevilla and Salamanca, represented by the poets Fernando de *Herrera and Fray Luis de *León respectively, both followers of Garcilaso. Herrera cultivates the classical elements, imaginative metaphors, and syntactic variation present in Garcilaso's work; and Luis de León develops its meditative quality, simplicity of expression, and profundity of thought. A line of development is traceable from Garcilaso to Fray Luis to the *conceptismo* of Quevedo, who in 1631 published for the first time an edition of Fray Luis's poetry. Thus, *conceptismo* may be said to have derived from the Salamanca school.

*Conceptismo* lends itself to both a concise elliptical form in prose and poetry, and a more copious form in prose, corresponding to what Gracián, alluding to Aristotle, calls the "laconic" and "asiatic" styles, It effects either elegant philosophical depth or biting satire and humor in the works of writers such as Quevedo or Gracián, and ultimately is the style of some of Spain's greatest literature. Poems such as Quevedo's "¡Ah de la vida!" (What of life), "Miré los muros de la patria mía" (I looked at the walls of my country), and "A una nariz" (To a Nose) typify the two strains of philosophy and satire, as do such prose works of the period as his *Sueños* (*Dreams*), Alemán's *Guzmán de Alfarache*, (*Guzman of Alfarache*), and Gracián's *Criticón*. The first tercet from Quevedo's sonnet "¡Ah de la vida!" exemplifies *conceptismo* in poetry at its laconic, philosophical peak:

> Ayer se fué, mañana no ha llegado,
> hoy se está yendo sin parar un punto;

soy un fué, y un seré y un es cansado.

(Yesterday went off, tomorrow has not arrived
today is slipping away without stopping at all;
I am a was and a will be and a tired is.)

The three lines, speaking (as does the entire sonnet) of the rapidity with which
life passes, make subtle use of nominalized adverbs of time and verbs employed
in a variety of tenses to express with laconic intensity a profound concept.

In writers of lesser stature, what began as cultivation of the idea became, in a welter
of puns, antitheses, parallels, and paradoxes, a complexity more verbal than conceptual and more superficial than profound. *See also* Escuela Salmantina; Escuela Sevillana.

BIBLIOGRAPHY

Criticism

Borghini. *Baldassar Gracián, scritore morale e teorico del concettismo*. Milan: Ancora,
    1947.
Collard, A. *Nueva Poesía: conceptismo, culteranismo en la crítica española*. Waltham,
    MA: Brandeis U, 1967.
Croce, B. "I Trattatisti Italiani del concettismo e Baltasar Gracián." *Atti e Memorie
    della R. Academie di Scienze Lettere Ed Arti in Padova* 29 (1899). Spanish tr.
    in *La Lectura*. Vol. 2. Madrid, 1912.
Green, O. H. *Spain and the Western Tradition*. Vol. 4. Madison: U of Wisconsin P,
    1963.
Hernández, María Teresa. "La teoría literaria del conceptismo en Baltasar Gracián."
    *Estudios de Lingüística* 3 (1985–86): 7–46.
Milner, Z. "Le Cultisme et le conceptisme dans l'oeuvre de Quevedo." *Lingua nostra*
    54.153 (1960): n.p.
Parker, A. A. "La buscona piramidal: Aspects of Quevedo's *conceptismo.*" *Innere Reich*
    1 (1969): n.p.
———. " 'Concept' and 'Conceit': An Aspect of Comparative Literary History." *MLR*
    77.4 (Oct. 1982): xxi-xxxv.

                                                                Theodore L. Kassier

**CONCEPTO,** a pithy flash of wit, the cornerstone of *conceptismo. The concepto
is born of a novel joining of two terms which customarily seem opposed, but
in fact share some quality or characteristic. Brevity is also an essential part of
the *concepto.*

**CONDE, Carmen** (1907, Cartagena– ), poet, novelist, critic. Conde has the
unique honor of being the first and only woman admitted to the Royal Spanish
Academy (*Academia Española) founded in 1784. Conde's first poems appeared
in the local press in 1925, and her first book *Brocal* (1929; Opening) shortly thereafter. After completing studies in the Normal School of Albacete, Conde married
poet Antonio Olivar in 1931, and together they founded the Popular U of Cartagena. Critical acclaim came first in 1934 with *Júbilos* (Murcia, 1934; Jubilations),

surrealistic and ultraistic poems, prologued by the Chilean poet Gabriela Mistral, and with the inclusion of poems in a Belgian anthology. During the Civil War, Conde followed her husband in the Republican army and studied at the U of Valencia. After the war, Conde took refuge with friends in Madrid and resumed her poetic career with *Ansia de gracia* (1945; Desire for Grace), followed by *Mujer sin edén* (1947; *Woman without Eden,* 1986), and *Sea la luz* (1947; Let There Be Light), all containing a more personalized poetry, although with surrealistic echoes. In the next decade, her prolific poetic production included *Iluminada tierra* (1951; Illuminated Land), whose publication coincided with a lecture tour to Paris; *Mientras los hombres mueren* (1953; While Men Die), her reaction to the Civil War; and *Vivientes de los siglos* (1954; Survivors of the Centuries), winner of the Simón Bolívar Award. *Los monólogos de la hija* (1959; The Daughter's Monologue) reflects a transition to a more personalized, lyrical poetry, continued in *Derribado arcángel* (1960; Fallen Archangel), with its passionate spiritualism; and *Poemas del Mar Menor* (1962; Poems of the Mar Menor) and *Jaguar, puro, inmarchito* (1963; Pure, Unspotted Jaguar), reactions to a trip to America. An anthology of Conde's poetry, *Obra poética (1929–1966)* (1967; Poetic Works), received the National Literary Award. Conde's later poetry, in *A este lado de la Eternidad* (1970; This Side of Eternity), *Cita con la vida* (1976; Date with Life), *El tiempo es un río lentísimo de fuego* (1978; Time Is a Slow River of Fire), and *La noche oscura del cuerpo* (1980; The Dark Night of the Body), alluding to San Juan, focus attention on women's role in a changing society, time, and death. Conde's poetry offers a vision of the world simultaneously universal and uniquely feminine. In 1943, under the pen name "Florentina del Mar," Conde began writing prose. Her first children's work, *Don Juan de Austria* (1943; Don Juan of Austria), was followed by a dozen juvenile stories, novels, and plays. In 1961, she and her husband produced the children's drama *A la estrella por la cometa* (To the Star by Comet), winner of the Doncel Award. Conde's adult novels began with *Vidas contra su espejo* (1944; Lives against Their Mirror), and include *En manos de silencio* (1950; In Silent Hands), *Las oscuras raíces* (1953; Dark Roots), recipient of *Garbo* magazine's Elisenda de Moncada Award, and *Soy la madre* (1980; I Am the Mother), winner of the Ateneo de Sevilla Award. Conde has edited anthologies of poetry and published short stories, meditations, biographies, and literary essays. Conde's life and works have been the subject of several books, such as Leopoldo de Luis's volume in the "España, escribir hoy" series (number 13, 1982), and numerous magazine articles in English and Spanish. She has also recorded readings of her poetry. In 1978, Carmen Conde's lifetime accomplishments were recognized by her admission to the Royal Spanish Academy. Her entrance address was entitled "Poesía ante el tiempo y la inmortalidad" (Poetry in the Face of Time and Immortality). Conde's great versatility and universal appeal make her the "grand dame" of twentieth-c. Spanish letters.

BIBLIOGRAPHY

Primary Texts

*A este lado*. Madrid: Biblioteca Nueva, 1970.
*Cita con la vida*. Madrid: Biblioteca Nueva, 1976.

*Obra poética.* Madrid: Biblioteca Nueva, 1967.
*Las oscuras raíces.* Barcelona: Garbo, 1953.
*Vidas contra su espejo.* Madrid: Alhambra, 1944.

English Translations

"The Joy of Living" and "Invocation." Tr. H. W. Patterson.
In *Antología Bilingüe (Español-Inglés) de la Poesía Española Moderna.* Madrid: Cultura Hispánica, 1965.
*Woman without Eden-Mujer sin Edén.* Tr. J. R. de Armas and A. Levitin. Miami: Universal, 1986.

Frieda H. Blackwell

**CONDE, Francisco Javier** (1908, Burgos–1974, Bonn) professor, ambassador, diplomat. A professor of political law at Madrid's Central U, he composed outstanding treatises on law and noteworthy essays on political theory and sociology. Best-known are *Teoría y sistema de las formas políticas* (Theory and System of Political Forms) and *El saber político de Maquiavelo* (n.d.; Machiavelli's Political Wisdom). A founding member of the International Association, he directed their publication *Clavileño* (1950–57). His skill as a lecturer brought him teaching invitations throughout Europe and the United States.

BIBLIOGRAPHY

Primary Texts

*Escritos y fragmentos políticos.* 2 vols. Madrid: Instituto de Estudios Políticos, 1974.

Isabel McSpadden

**CONDE, José Antonio** (1765, Peraleja, Cuenca–1820, Madrid), historian and philologist. Conde studied in both the seminary at Cuenca and the U in Alcalá de Henares, where he obtained degrees in canonic and civil law. He became the director of the library in El Escorial, and later served as head of the Royal Library in Madrid. It was from the collection at El Escorial that he obtained the ms. to the *Cancionero de *Baena* (Songbook of Baena), which was sold by his heirs and now resides in the National Library in Paris. A committed neo-classicist and friend of Leandro Fernández de *Moratín, he was exiled in 1813, but soon returned to Madrid. Conde was a philologist of questionable merit. His major work, *Historia de la dominación de los árabes en España sacada de varios manuscritos y memorias arábigas* (1820–21, posthumously; *History of the Dominion of the Arabs in Spain*, 1854–55), has largely been discredited. The nineteenth-c. Arabist Dozy pointed out Conde's paucity of source materials, his faulty understanding of Arabic grammar, and his lack of historical sensitivity. In addition to his work in Arabic, he translated works from Hebrew, Greek and Latin. Using the pseudonym "El cura de Montuerga" (Father Montuerga), he also engaged in a polemic with Astarloa and Juan Bautista Erro over the origins of the Basque language.

BIBLIOGRAPHY

Primary Texts

*Historia de la dominación de los árabes en España sacada de varios manuscritos y memorias arábigas.* 3 vols. Madrid: García, 1820–21.

English Translation

*History of the Dominion of the Arabs in Spain.* Tr. Mrs. Johnathon Foster. London: H. G. Bohn, 1854–55.

Criticism

Manzanares de Cirne, M. "Gloria y descrédito de D. José A. Conde." *Anuario de Estudios Medievales* (Barcelona) 6 (1969): 553–63.
Roca, P. "Vida y escritos de D. José A. Conde." *RABM* 8 (1903): 378–92 & 458–69; 9 (1904): 279–91 & 338–54; 10 (1905): 27–42 & 139–48.

Donald C. Buck

**CONDESA TRAIDORA, Cantar de la** (Song of the Traitorous Countess), medieval legend. It recounts the ill-fated marriages—with their dire consequences—of Count Garci Fernández, the son of Fernán González. In the first, the handsome young count, famous for his beautiful hands, is abandoned by his French wife (Doña Argentina), whom he had met when she journeyed to Santiago de Compostela. She returns to her homeland in the company of a French count, a widower, also on a pilgrimage. Garci Fernández, bent on revenge, sets out for France (the shrine at Rocamador) disguised as a pilgrim. There he conspires with his rival's daughter, the beautiful Doña Sancha, to carry out his vengeance: the beheading of Doña Argentina and the French count in their bed. Garci Fernández returns to Castile with Sancha, who bears him a son, Sancho. Doña Sancha, eventually disenchanted, devises a scheme to rid herself of her husband: she maintains his horse on bran alone; the weakened horse fails in battle; the wounded Garci is captured and dies shortly thereafter. Sancha then attempts to realize her desire to marry a Moorish king (according to one account Almanzor) by poisoning her son. Discovering the plot, Sancho forces his mother to drink the poisoned wine. The legend, which does not survive in the ballad tradition, is commonly believed to be a vestige of an epic, though this has recently been questioned. It survives in several different versions: the *Crónica Najerense* (c. 1160; Chronicle of Najera); *Ximénez de Rada's De rebus Hispaniae* (13th c.; History of Spain); and *Alphonse X the Learned's Primera Crónica General* (13th c.; First General Chronicle). The latter is the most complete. While none of the accounts is historically true (Garci Fernández had only one wife), with the exception of his capture and death, some have suggested that the vilification of the countess is a mythical distortion of the historical rebellion of Sancho against his father, which may have been supported by his mother. *See also* Edad Media, Literatura de la.

## BIBLIOGRAPHY

Primary Texts

Alfonso X, the Learned. *Primera Crónica General de España.* Ed. R. Menéndez Pidal. 3rd ed. 2 vols. Madrid: Gredos and Seminario Menéndez Pidal, 1982.

Anon. *Crónica Najerense.* Ed. A. Ubieto Arteta. Textos Medievales 15. Valencia: Anúbar, 1966.

Ximénez de Rada, R. *De rebus Hispaniae.* 1793; Facs. rpt. Ed. María D. Cabañes Pecourt. Textos Medievales 22. Valencia: Anúbar, 1968.

Criticism

Chalon, Louis. "La historicidad de la *Leyenda de la Condesa traidora.*" *Journal of Hispanic Philology 3* (1978): 153–63.

Martínez, Salvador. "Tres leyendas heroicas de la *Najerense* y sus relaciones con la épica castellana." *Anuario de Letras* 9 (1971): 115–77.

Menéndez Pidal, Ramón. "Realismo de la epopeya española, la *Condesa traidora.*" In *Idea imperial de Carlos V.* 5th ed. Madrid: Espasa-Calpe, 1955. 37–72.

Porter Conerly

*CONGRUISMO* (Congruism), a theological doctrine. It is very similar to the one developed by Luis de *Molina in his attempt to harmonize an individual's free will and the efficacious power of God's grace. Congruism was the doctrine followed by sixteenth-c. Jesuits such as Luis de Molina and Francisco *Suárez. Even though God has foreknowledge of whether a person cooperating with His grace will be saved, this does not in any way interfere with the operation of the will. In other words, although God gives grace in order to assist one in choosing to do good and thus be saved, this efficacious grace does not counteract free will. Efficacious grace has the power to bring an individual to salvation and God knows this fact beforehand through His middle knowledge (*scientia media*). Nevertheless, free will allows the individual to have the choice to cooperate or not with God's grace. The word *congruo* (congruous) implies the cooperation of the human will with God's grace.

## BIBLIOGRAPHY

Criticism

*The Catholic Encyclopedia.* Vol. 4. New York: McGraw-Hill, 1967. 176–77.

Angelo DiSalvo

*CONQUISTA DE ULTRAMAR, GRAN* (The Great Conquest Beyond the Sea), medieval recounting of the Crusades. It is a Castilian translation, probably done in the late thirteenth-c. scriptorium of Sancho IV, of various French historical and fictional accounts of the Crusades. It survives in one complete printed text (Salamanca 1503), and three incomplete mss. from the thirteenth, fourteenth and fifteenth centuries, respectively. The complete work consists of four books with a total of 1,320 chapters (231, 265, 395, and 429, respectively), whereas the longest ms. contains only approximately 561 chapters, so that more than half the surviving text is available only in the late printed version. The bulk of the complete text (some 1,100 chapters) is a translation of French versions of William of Tyre's *Historia rerum in partibus transmarinis gestarum*, the most widely read medieval history of the Crusades. Between these historical accounts are interspersed translations of French chivalric fiction about the Swan Knight *Caballero del Cisne, Geoffrey of Bouillon, the siege of Antioch, *Li Caitif*, the Conquest of Jerusalem, *Bertes aux grans pies*, and Charlemagne. *See also* Edad Media, Literatura de la.

BIBLIOGRAPHY

Primary Text

*La Gran Conquista de Ultramar*. Ed. P. de Gayangos. BAE 44.

Criticism

Gumbrecht, H. U. "Four Spanish Romance Texts of the 13th Century." *YFS* 51 (1974): 205–22.

Northrup, G. T. "*La Gran Conquista de Ultramar* and Its Problems." *HR* 2 (1934): 287–302.

Colbert Nepaulsingh

**CONTEMPORARY SPANISH THEATER.** More than other genres, theater is a reflection of the socio-historical context in which it is created. Its very existence is dependent upon the tastes of the theater-going public. Because it has traditionally been viewed as a dangerous medium—a potential corruptor of public morals or an instrument for political propapanda—theater is also more likely to be subject to *censorship than are poetry or narrative. It is therefore not surprising that theater in twentieth-c. Spain has undergone periods of great change as the nation itself has moved from relative freedom early in the century, to the dictatorship of Primo de Rivera, to the social and political upheaval of the Second Republic and the Civil War, to the repression of the Franco era, to renewed freedom under a democratic monarchy. At times the Spanish stage has developed in consonance with the wider currents of European drama, but at others, principally during the moments of greatest censorship, it has been out of phase with other national theaters.

At the turn of the c., the Spanish stage was marked by a concerted effort to break with the melodramatic theatrical style epitomized by the neo-romantic drama of José *Echegary (1832–1916). The leaders in the realistic movement were Benito *Pérez Galdós (1843–1920), one of Spain's greatest novelists, and Jacinto *Benavente (1866–1954). Galdós's plays in the last decade of the nineteeth c. scandalized bourgeois theatergoers for their daring themes, their everyday language, and their natural acting. *Electra*, which opened in January 1901, proved to be a scandal in a political sense as well. Widely interpreted as a statement against fanaticism and repression, it ultimately led to a change in the government.

Galdós's work, in the form of dramatized versions of his novels and revisions of his plays, has continued to be staged in Spain throughout the twentieth c., often with considerable success, but there is no doubt that Benavente was the superior theatrical craftsman. Indeed Benavente, initially hailed by contemporary intellectuals for his satirical vision of middle-class morality, eventually fell into writing formula dramas, and his name became synonymous with pejorative allusions to the ''well-made play.'' When Echegaray was awarded the Nobel Prize in 1904, the young writers of the *Generation of 1898 organized a protest. Benavente's Nobel Prize in 1922 was greeted with similar dismay.

While the term *Benaventine* evokes a kind of realistic, representational drama that appeals to the bourgeois society it mirrors, Benavente's major contributions to theater repertory are both atypical. *Los intereses creados* (1907; The Bonds of Interest), a theatrical satire of universal human foibles, is built on stock elements of the *commedia dell'arte*. *La malquerida* (1913; The Passion Flower) is a rural tragedy that has all the intensity of human passions of the classic model on which it is structured.

The trend toward realistic, representational theater, characteristic of Galdós and Benavente, was a reaction against the bombastic style that dominated the Spanish stage in the final quarter of the nineteenth c. and hence was out of step with the innovative currents in other national theaters, which were moving away from realism/*naturalism. At the beginning of the twentieth c., the Spanish stage also gave rise to a kind of poetic drama, but one that was rooted in romantic tradition. Typical of this movement was the theater of Eduardo *Marquina (1879–1946) and such works as *En Flandes se ha puesto el sol* (1910; The Sun Has Set in Flanders), a historical verse drama that idealized Spain's past. A third movement, one that has always had a strong following on the Spanish stage, was that of comedy, ranging from the Andalusian comedies of manners of the *Álvarez Quintero brothers, Serafín (1871–1938) and Joaquín (1873–1944), to the popular farces of Pedro *Muñoz Seca (1881–1936) and Carlos *Arniches (1866–1943).

It is a critical commonplace to deplore the preference of Spanish audiences for light comedy rather than serious drama, but the *sainete, or popular farce, in its various forms has been a mainstay of the Spanish stage for centuries, the chief attraction for the working-class playgoer, and in many cases has withstood the test of time. In the 1980s, Muñoz Seca and Arniches were still being staged regularly in Madrid.

In addition to popular farce, Arniches was the author of grotesque tragicomedies. His *La señorita de Trevélez* (1916; Miss Trevelez) is a clear forerunner of the *esperpento* of Ramón del *Valle-Inclán (1866–1936), perhaps Spain's greatest playwright of the twentieth-c. Valle-Inclán's major plays—beginning with *Divinas palabras* (Divine Words) in 1920—went largely unstaged during his lifetime. In fact his expressionistic, grotesque tragicomedies with their spatial fluidity and the cinematic approach of their stage directions were considered unstageable. But his subject matter was also taboo, both during the Primo de Rivera dictatorship of the 1920s and the first decades following the Civil War. *La hija del capitán* (1922; The Captain's Daughter) and *Los cuernos de don*

*Friolera* (1925; Don Friolera's Horns), for example, subjected the military to Valle-Inclán's systematic deformation of Spanish reality. The original texts were prohibited on the Spanish stage until after Franco's death. The successful 1984–85 production in France and Spain of *Luces de bohemia* (1924; Bohemian Lights) highlighted the enduring and innovative quality of Valle-Inclán's theater.

To Valle-Inclán may be attributed both a distancing technique that relates his work to Bertolt Brecht and a view of the human condition that links him to a later theater of the absurd. Clearly his use of the expressionistic mode was contemporaneous with a similar anti-realistic movement of the German-language stage. Various writers of Valle-Inclán's generation, notably Miguel de *Unamuno (1864–1936) and *Azorín (José Martínez Ruiz, 1873–1967), were keenly aware of European experimental theater and attempted to create related works of their own. It must be noted that in the period from World War I through the 1930s, Spain was open to cultural interaction with other countries and contributed its own share of genius to emerging avant-garde movements in art and cinema (e.g., Luis Buñuel, Salvador Dalí, Pablo Picasso). If theater lagged behind in Spain, it did elsewhere, too, because of the preferences of the audiences on which the mainstream, commercial stage depends.

While Valle-Inclán's major contribution to world theater was to go unrecognized until years after his death, two younger playwrights, both of whom were involved during the Second Republic in efforts to take theater to the people, quickly achieved national and even international fame. Alejandro *Casona (Alejandro Rodríguez Alvarez, 1903–65) broke with realism/naturalism by writing a kind of poetic fantasy that linked his theater with the reality/illusion themes of the Italian Luigi Pirandello and the theatricalized life of the Russian Nikolai Evreinov. Following the Civil War, Casona became active in the Argentine stage; with works such as *Los árboles mueren de pie* (1949; Trees Die Standing), he has become part of international repertory. When he returned from exile in the 1960s, however, a younger generation of Spanish intellectuals became disillusioned upon discovering that Casona's theater eschewed social and political questions.

The twentieth-c. Spanish playwright of greatest international fame is Federico *García Lorca (1898–1936), whose assassination at the beginning of the Civil War has come to symbolize that Spanish national tragedy. Like Casona, Lorca belonged to an international theater movement that attempted to break away from realism/naturalism and the restraints of the representational theater so admired by middle-class audiences. He is widely considered to be the most successful European exponent of poetic drama, a drama not marked by the superficial use of verse like Marquina's but rather by the poetic essence of its characters, situations, language, and staging.

Lorca's fame as a dramatist rests primarily on his trilogy of poetic tragedies: *Bodas de sangre* (1933; Blood Wedding), *Yerma* (1934), and *La casa de Bernarda Alba* (1936; The House of Bernarda Alba). This last work received its premiere in Argentina in 1945, and all three have become part of international repertory. They are not, however, Lorca's most innovative works. His early farces, like Valle-Inclán's *esperpento* and German expressionism, reflected a fascination with silent films and with puppet theater, both art forms that reinforced a perception of progressive dehumanization in the modern world. Like his friend Salvador Dalí, Lorca was also a surrealist, but he considered his key text in this mode, *Así que pasen cinco años* (1931; When Five Years Pass), to be unperformable and called off its scheduled premiere in 1936. His even more experimental *El público* (1930; The Audience), a work that would have placed him at the forefront of the European avant-garde, was not published until 1978.

Before the outbreak of the Civil War, the Spanish stage was actively involved in exploring all of the major currents of Western theater and, in some cases, was in a position to assume a leadership role. The war and the period of political and cultural repression that followed effectively severed Spain from the outside world. In the early post-war years, the stage was dominated by poetic idealizations of the past and Benavente's formula bourgeois dramas. The first new playwright to emerge in the 1940s was Víctor *Ruiz Iriarte (1912–82), a writer of comedies ranging from poetic fantasy in the Casona/Evreinov mold to comedies of manners to satires of middle-class morality. His *El landó de seis caballos* (1950; The Six-Horse Landau) is considered the prototype of the post-war *teatro de evasión*, that is, an escapist theater that ostensibly avoided society's problems. It must be noted that escapist plays—those in which the characters themselves create fantasies to help them retreat from unpleasant realities—did, in fact, faithfully mirror the ideology of the times, namely, the audience's desire to forget the war and its aftermath.

It is certainly true that the most popular genre on the commercial Spanish stage during the Franco years was comedy—often of high quality and literary merit. Enrique *Jardiel Poncela (1901–52) wrote ingenious farces that self-consciously parodied theatrical and film conventions. His *Eloísa está debajo de un almendro* (1940; Eloise Is Under an Almond Tree) was successfully revived in Madrid in 1984, thus proving its enduring interest for a new generation of theatergoers. Like the latter play, the absurdist comedies of Miguel *Mihura (1905–77) have withstood the test of time. His *Tres sombreros de copa* (1952; Three Top Hats), would have figured prominently in the European avant-garde had it been staged twenty years earlier when it was written. José *López Rubio (b. 1903) achieved his fame for works of poetic fantasy, often written in the Pirandellian mode, but also was successful at creating more serious dramas.

The literary quality of the comedies of these writers has not yet been matched by later generations. Like Mihura, Alfonso *Paso (1926–78) began by writing experimental, absurdist comedies, but soon fell into a formula. He was so prolific that in many seasons he premiered several new plays. His comedies are still popular with certain audiences and are regularly staged in Madrid, along with revivals of Muñoz Seca, Jardiel, Mihura, a variety of younger Spanish authors, and innumerable translations of French and British bedroom farces. With respect to the predominance of light comedy, the commercial stage of Madrid is no different from that of Paris or London.

In 1949, with the premiere of *Historia de una escalera* (Story of a Stairway) Spain witnessed the arrival of a new playwright whose name has become synonymous with the nation's socially committed drama. Antonio *Buero Vallejo (b. 1916) is generally considered Spain's greatest living dramatist and her only real tragedian. He has initiated several important and innovative trends on the Spanish stage. *Historia de una escalera* led the way for serious theater, structured on the *sainete*, that could reveal realistically the situation of Spain's lower classes. *Un soñador para un pueblo* (1958; A Dreamer for a People) introduced a new kind of Spanish history play, one that demythified the past and hence, indirectly, was able to present a critical view of the present as well. In *El tragaluz* (1967; The Basement Window), *El sueño de la razón* (1970; The Sleep of Reason), and *La fundación* (1974; The Foundation), he refined his use of an "immersion" technique, reminiscent of the psychological expressionism of Arthur Miller. His major contribution to world theater lies in this technique that forces the audience to identify with a handicapped character and thus experience his deafness or madness. Into the 1980s, Buero has continued to produce new plays at the rate of one every two or three years. His theater has been widely staged throughout Europe and Latin America; he clearly ranks with Valle-Inclán and García Lorca as one of twentieth-c. Spain's major playwrights.

Buero's groundbreaking *Historia de una escalera* was soon followed by socially committed works of several younger playwrights who came to be known as the "Realistic Group." The first of these, Alfonso *Sastre (b. 1926), has also acquired an international reputation and is his generation's foremost theorist on theater. His plays, however, were generally unacceptable to the censor and therefore seldom staged in Spain during the Franco years.

Although the dramatists who have been classified together as "Realists" varied considerably in their approaches to theater, they shared Sastre's fate. Such plays as *Escuadra hacia la muerte* (1953; Condemned Squad), an existentialist view of a possible third world war, by Sastre; *El tintero* (1961; The Inkwell), an expressionistic portrayal of the dehumanizing impact of capitalist bureaucracy, by Carlos *Muñiz (b. 1927); and *La camisa* (1962; The Shirt), a *sainete* dealing with the forced emigration of Spain's poor, by Lauro *Olmo (b. 1922), are seen as landmarks of the Spanish stage by specialists in the field but did not open the doors of Spain's theaters to their authors. Nor did those doors swing open for them immediately upon the dictator's death. Nevertheless, the Realistic Group has achieved some notable successes in democratic Spain. Examples include the historical *Las arrecogías del Beaterio Santa María Egipcíaca* (1977; The Inmates of the Convent of St. Mary Egyptian) by José *Martín Recuerda (b. 1922) and the esperpentic *Bodas que fueron famosas del Pingajo y la Fandanga* (1978; The Famous Nuptials of Pingajo and Fandanga) by José María *Rodríguez Méndez (b. 1925). Sastre himself has finally gained official recognition for his *La taberna fantástica* (The Fantastic Tavern), which received the National Theater Prize for 1985.

The difficulties confronted by the Realistic Group during the Franco years emanated not from their use of realism but rather from their critical stance. Spanish audiences, like theatergoers in other Western nations, have a strong preference for realism/naturalism. They also tend to favor plays that probe psychological or moral questions of guilt and retribution. Two of the longest-running dramas of the 1950s and 1960s, both of them dealing with moral dilemmas posed by the Civil War, fall within this category: *La muralla* (1954; The Wall) by Joaquín *Calvo Sotelo (b. 1905), and *La casa de las chivas* (1969; The House of the "Chivas") by Jaime *Salom (b. 1925).

The Realistic Group may be compared with the contemporaneous "Angry Young Men" of the British stage. Another group of playwrights in Spain may be compared to the French theater of the absurd and other European avant-garde movements. In Spain, however, such playwrights, who approached theater from diverse aspects of anti-realism, were unlikely to have their works staged, except in small, experimental theaters or in the theater festivals that began to appear in the early 1960s. (Perhaps the best known of these is the one held annually in Sitges on the Costa Brava.) These dramatists, who tended toward political allegory and absurdist tragifarce, were variously called the "Underground" or "Silenced" Theater. After Franco's death, when their works were no longer prohibited by official censorship, they came to be labeled the "New Authors."

Related to this Spanish avant-garde is one playwright of international stature. Fernando *Arrabal (b. 1932) left his native country in the 1950s and became actively involved in the French stage. His plays, which have been produced around the world, were originally published and staged in French. While the theater world at large considered Arrabal to be French, the playwright himself has never lost sight of his Spanish roots. Since Franco's death, he has been staged in Spain with some regularity, although not always with success. Among his works that have been well received is his *El arquitecto y el emperador de Asiria* (1967; The Architect and the Emperor of Assyria), which had its Madrid premiere in 1983.

Like Arrabal, Manuel *Pedrolo (b. 1918), a native of Catalonia, has been identified with the French theater of the absurd. Outside Spain he is the best known of the contemporary dramatists who write in Catalan rather than Castilian Spanish.

The dual problem faced by the New Authors in Spain was official censorship— having their texts prohibited by the government—and unofficial censorship— being turned away by theater impresarios who feel that anti-realist plays lack box-office appeal. Thus the transition from dictatorship to democracy has not guaranteed them access to the boards. Only a handful have, in fact, achieved national recognition. This group includes some, like Luis *Riaza (b. 1925) and Luis Matilla (b. 1938), who have been staged in government-subsidized theaters and two who have had commercial successes: Manuel *Martínez Mediero (b. 1939) and Francisco Nieva (b. 1927).

Nieva in several respects is a case apart. An exponent of the neo-surrealist "theater of the marvelous" who does not hesitate to debunk Spain's most cherished traditions and myths, he established his reputation as a playwright with the box-office triumph in 1976 of *La carroza de plomo candente* (The Carriage of White Hot Lead). But he is also well known as a stage designer and director and was honored with the National Theater Prize of 1979 for his total contribution to the Spanish stage. In 1986 he was named to the Spanish Royal Academy (*Academia Española), an action that symbolically set aside the division between the traditional and the avant-garde.

Another case apart is Antonio *Gala (b. 1936), whose theater defies ready classification into any of the dominant groups. The premiere of his first play, *Los verdes campos del Edén* (1963; The Green Fields of Eden), was a major theatrical event. The play itself is a curious blend of expressionism, à la Muñiz's *El tintero*, and a kind of poetic idealism that evoked the praise of Casona and the wrath of the leftist intellectuals. With *Anillos para una dama* (1973; Rings for a Lady), a debunking of the Jimena-Cid historical myth, Gala established himself as a major voice on the Spanish stage. In the 1970s and 1980s, he has proved to be the most commercially successful of Spain's serious playwrights. His works are marked by a surface level of wit and humor, generally requiring the skills of top-notch comedic actresses, but are underscored by an allegorical commentary on contemporary Spain and the universal human condition. Often his characters are in search of a paradise that they are doomed not to find. Always they present an impassioned plea for freedom, particularly the freedom to live one's own life and love the person of one's own choice.

While it is useful to place individual playwrights within certain general tendencies, many dramatists have moved during their careers from one subgenre or approach to another. For example, Muñiz is usually identified as part of the Realistic Group but his best-known work, *El tintero*, bears a strong resemblance to the anti-realistic theater of the New Authors. Salom, who began as a conservative in both political and religious terms, by the 1970s had shifted to the opposite spectrum. His *La piel del limón* (1976; Bitter Lemon), one of the longest-running plays of the decade, was a plea for divorce reform and a rejection of the Franco era "National Catholicism." Its innovative use of psychological expressionism also separated it quite distinctly from the same playwright's earlier use of representationalism.

In keeping with the times, a number of playwrights, including Gala, Salom, and Nieva, began writing works that lent themselves easily to feminist interpretations. Women dramatists, however, are few and far between in twentieth-c. Spanish theater. The only one of note in recent years is Ana *Diosdado (b. 1938), whose prize-winning *Olvida los tambores* (1970; Forget the Drums) gained her national recognition. In the 1970s she staged five original plays, ranging from the traditional "well-made play" of her first efforts to much more innovative works.

The transitional period following Franco's death in 1975 brought a number of changes to the Spanish stage. Some of these, like the delayed stagings of previously forbidden plays and the gratuitous introduction of nudity, proved to be temporary. Others, like the open discussion of previously taboo topics (divorce, homosexuality, political and sexual repression), have had a lasting impact. With the advent of the Centro Dramático Nacional and other government-subsidized theater ventures, the quality of stage productions has improved. Spanish theater professionals, who had lived and worked in other countries, returned to Spain, bringing with them the insights gained from their training abroad. Individual companies, like Els Joglars and the Lliure in Catalonia, gained international stature. Spain, however, still awaited the emergence of new dramatists, hidden talent that theoretically had been waiting in the wings until censorship lifted.

The expectation for a group of "New New Authors" was finally fulfilled in the 1980s. Fernando *Fernán Gómez (b. 1921), the first to gain recognition, is one of Spain's best-known film actors; his bittersweet drama of the Civil War, *Las bicicletas son para el verano* (1982; Bicycles Are for Summer), was enthusiastically received by critics and public alike. Also acclaimed have been the works of two younger playwrights, Fermín *Cabal (b. 1948) and José Luis Alonso de Santos (b. 1942), both of whom began their careers in the small independent groups that specialize in collective theater. Cabal's greatest success to date has been ¡*Esta noche gran velada! ¡Kid Peña contra Alarcón por el título europeo!* (1983; Big Match Tonight! Kid Peña vs. Alarcon for the European Title!), a "hyperrealistic" look at the boxing world that owes as much to American movies as it does to reality. Alonso de Santos was awarded the National Theater Prize of 1985 for his *Bajarse al moro* (Going Down to Marrakesh), a realistic play that deals with young people and the drug subculture. *Bicicletas son para el verano* and the plays of Cabal and Alonso de Santos are generally marked by a surface humor that was seldom found in the realistic plays of the 1960s. Moreover, they are openly metatheatrical, replete with intertextual references to the movies and with cinematographic staging techniques. They do deal with real contemporary problems, but their approach is much more playful than that of the socially committed dramatists of the Franco era.

In the last half of the 1980s, the Spanish stage was beset by all of the same difficulties that face theater everywhere: the high cost of staging productions, rising ticket prices, increasing competition from videocassettes as well as from television and movies. Nevertheless there is hope for the future. That hope resides in the talent and versatility of productive playwrights of varying ages and approaches to theater.

BIBLIOGRAPHY

Primary Texts

*Estreno*. University of Cincinnati, 1975- . Semi-annual scholarly journal. Publishes contemporary Spanish play in each issue.
O'Connor, Patricia W., and Anthony M. Pasquariello, eds. *Contemporary Spanish Theater: Seven One-Act Plays*. New York: Charles Scribner's Sons, 1980.
*Primer Acto*. Madrid, 1957- . Monthly drama journal. Publishes new Spanish play or translation of foreign play in each issue.

Sáinz de Robles, Federico Carlos, ed. *Teatro español*. Annual anthology of selected Spanish plays staged in seasons 1949–50 and 1973–74. Madrid: Aguilar, 1951–75.

Salvat, Ricard. *Años difíciles: 3 testimonios del teatro español contemporáneo*. Barcelona: Brughera, 1977.

*Teatro representativo español*. Madrid: Escelicer, 1972. (Includes eight plays of twentieth-c.)

*El teatro y su crítica: Reunión de Málaga de 1973*. Málaga: Instituto de Cultura de la Diputación Provincial de Málaga, 1973. (Includes four contemporary plays.)

English Translations

Benedikt, Michael, and George E. Wellwarth, eds. *Modern Spanish Theatre: An Anthology of Plays*. New York: E. P. Dutton, 1969.

Corrigan, Robert W., ed. *Masterpieces of the Modern Spanish Theatre*. New York: Macmillan, 1967.

Holt, Marion Peter, ed. *DramaContemporary: Spain*. New York: Performing Arts Journal Publications, 1985.

———. *The Modern Spanish Stage: 4 Plays*. New York: Hill and Wang, 1970.

O'Connor, Patricia, tr. *Contemporary Spanish Theater: The Social Comedies of the Sixties*. Madrid: Sociedad General de Librería, 1983.

———. *Plays of Protest from the Franco Era*. Madrid: Sociedad General de Librería, 1981.

Wellwarth, George E., ed. *The New Wave Spanish Drama: An Anthology*. New York: New York UP, 1970.

Criticism

Brown, Gerald G. *A Literary History of Spain: The Twentieth Century*. London and New York: Ernest Benn and Barnes and Noble, 1972. 110–34; 157–61.

Edwards, Gwynne. *Dramatists in Perspective: Spanish Theatre in the Twentieth Century*. New York: St. Martin's, 1985.

Holt, Marion P. *The Contemporary Spanish Theater (1949–1972)*. TWAS 336. Boston: Twayne, 1975.

McKay, Douglas R. "Forty Years of Titillation: The Absurdist Trend in Spanish Theater Humor." *Estreno* 7.1 (1981): 11–13.

Newberry, Wilma. *The Pirandellian Mode in Spanish Literature from Cervantes to Sastre*. Albany: SUNY, 1973.

O'Connor, Patricia W. "Post-Franco Theater: From Limitation to Liberty to License." *Hispanic Journal* 5.2 (1984): 55–73.

———. "Torquemada in the Theater: A Glance at Government Censorship." *Theater Survey* 14.2 (1973): 33–45.

Ruiz Ramón, Francisco. *Historia del teatro español, siglo XX*. 2nd ed. Madrid: Cátedra, 1975.

Wellwarth, George E. *Spanish Underground Drama*. University Park and London: Pennsylvania State UP, 1972.

———. *The Theatre of Protest and Paradox*. New York: New York UP, 1971. 353–84.

Zatlin-Boring, Phyllis. "Expressionism in the Contemporary Spanish Theatre." *Modern Drama* 26 (1983): 555–69.

————. "Theatre in Madrid: The Difficult Transition to Democracy." *Theatre Journal* 32 (1980): 459–74.
————. "Three Dramatists in Search of Their Youth." *Estreno* 11.2 (1985): 4–6.

Phyllis Zatlin

**CONTIJOCH PRATDESABA, Josefa** (1940, Manlleu Osona, Catalunya–   ), poet and prose author. Contijoch's early interest in writing, beginning with diaries and poems written during adolescence, stemmed in part from her father's business, a bookstore and print shop. She studied a commercial course in a private religious school in the village of Manlleu and later continued with studies of French and English, subsequently taking courses in philology at the U of Barcelona. Although early writing in a local literary supplement, *Cau Faluga*, beginning in 1964, included some essays in Castilian, since 1967 she has written only in Catalan. Early books were poetry, including *De la soledad primera* (1964; About First Solitude), *Aquello que he visto* (1965; What I've Seen), *Tombstone Blues* (1967; title only in English), and *Quadern de vacances (Una lectura de "El Segon Sexe")* (1983; Vacation Notebook [A Reading of "The Second Sex"]). Other poetry received awards in ms. form but has not appeared in print (La corda de l'arpa i el coll de l'artista, 1972 [The Chord of the Harp and the Artist's Neck]; Orient-Express, 1980 [title in English]). In 1983, she turned to the narrative, writing *Potala* (1986), a novel of irony and humor incorporating a politico-literary mythology and utilizing the voyage topos (symbol of life) in combination with that of the quest (symbolizing uncertainty). *No em dic Raquel* (1989; My Name Isn't Rachel) is narrated from the viewpoint of a dead protagonist—Rachel—who has been strangled and dismembered with an electric saw by her erstwhile lover, Enric, who disposes of the remains in the city dump. In the ensuing investigation, involving several others who knew her, Rachel proves to have been a drug smuggler and transvestite, a homosexual male with bisexual affairs. Contijoch represents the "new" feminist novelists in Catalan, who deliberately tackle taboos, eroticism and a wide range of "masculine" topics, often parodically or subverting another genre (here, the murder mystery).

Janet Pérez

**CONTRERAS, Alonso de** (1582, Madrid–after 1641, ?), soldier, adventurer, author. His friend Lope de *Vega apparently induced him to set down an account of his many travels and adventures. The resulting *Vida* (Life), which he began writing around 1630, is a lively, vivid, unpretentious and at times disorganized account, detailing his departure from Madrid to Italy in 1595, battles there, imprisonment and torture (for he was for a while believed to be a secret king of the *moriscos* in Hornachos), and subsequent adventures in Flanders and the New World. *See also* Siglo de Oro.

BIBLIOGRAPHY

Primary Texts

*Vida del capitán Alonso de Contreras*. Prol. Ortega y Gasset. Madrid: RO, 1943. Also in *BRAH* 37 (1900): 129–270.

Criticism

Benítez Claros, R. "La personalidad de Contreras." In *Visión de la literatura española.* Madrid: Rialp, 1963. 117–29.
Morel-Fatio, A. "Soldats espagnols du XVIIᵉ siècle: Alonso de Contreras." *BH* 3 (1901): 135–58.

María Teresa Pajares

**CONTRERAS, Jerónimo de** (c. 1520, Aragón?–c. 1585, ?), writer. His Byzantine love story of Luzmán and Arbolea, titled *Selva de aventuras* (1565; Forest of Adventures), served as source for Lope de *Vega's *El peregrino en su patria*. Contreras also wrote a eulogy of famous Spaniards, *Dechado de varios subjectos* (1572; Some Model People). *See also* Humanism; Renaissance.

BIBLIOGRAPHY

Primary Texts

*Dechado de varios subjectos.* Alcalá: Querino Gerardo, 1581.
*Selva de aventuras.* In BAE 3.

**CONTRERAS Y LÓPEZ DE AYALA, Juan de** (1893, Segovia–1978, Segovia), Marquise of Lozoya, professor of art history, poet. He published *Poemas arcaicos* (1913; Archaic Poems), *Poemas de enseñanzas* (1915; Poems on Teaching), and *Poemas castellanos* (1920; Castilian Poems); the latter volume won the Fastenrath prize in that year. His poetry displays a lyricism unaffected by *modernism. He also wrote the well-documented, five-volume *Historia del arte hispánico* (1931–49; History of Hispanic Art).

BIBLIOGRAPHY

Primary Texts

*Historia del arte hispánico.* 5 vols. Barcelona: Salvat, 1931–49.
*Poemas castellanos.* Segovia: Lozano, 1920.

Isabel McSpadden

**CONVERSO** (Convert), significant cultural group of medieval and Golden Age Spain and Portugal. Although *converso* could denote either Muslim or Jewish converts to Christianity, in fact it was usually reserved for the latter group of new Christians. The Jewish presence in Spain, up to the expulsion of 1492, has been eloquently narrated by Yitzhak Baer. Although the majority of Jews, and conversos, were working-class artisans, shopkeepers, etc., a small, highly visible minority attained noticeable wealth, position, and/or influence in the cities and in the court. Some Spanish kings, as far back as *Alphonse X, John II, and Peter I, and Portuguese Kings João I and Afonso I, openly favored Jewish and/or converso minorities. For the Jew, conversion at the least afforded official access to offices and careers in the church and in government, and other advantages. A converso presence in Spain became important around the thirteenth c., and there gradually arose a growing resentment and hostility on the part of many urban Christians, especially of the lower class. Although sporadic waves of anti-Semitism had occurred over the centuries, 1391 marks the onset of the most vigorous, extensive violence against Jews, and some *conversos,* producing thousands of forced conversions among survivors. Subsequent anti-Semitic outbreaks occurred in Spain (as in the rest of Europe): Toledo in 1449 and 1467; Cordova in 1473; Seville in 1481. Unlike the rest of Europe, which resolved the situation with expulsion, Spain pursued the path of assimilation and increased her considerable ranks of forced conversions even further, opting for expulsion only in 1492. Portugal followed suit in 1496. Thus the *converso* group in Spain was unmatched by any other nation. Of course, the sincerity of the forced conversions was questioned, to a certain extent with legitimacy. In 1478, the Spanish *Inquisition began the task of questioning sincerity of belief among *conversos.* In Portugal, the Inquisition was established in 1536 for the same purpose. The word *converso* took on an increasingly pejorative connotation over the years, and *converso* lineage became an obstacle to advancement and privilege of all sorts in society, only abating in the late seventeenth to eighteenth centuries.

The short- and long-term consequences of the significant converso presence in Spain are numerous and complex. With regard to literature, it is a fact that the anti-converso movement coincided with Spain's greatest literary flowering, the *Siglo de Oro. It is also a fact that many of the finest writers of the Middle Ages and also The Golden Age were of converso lineage: Pablo de *Santa María, Alonso de *Cartagena, Joan Luis *Vives, Fernando de *Rojas, Luis de *León, *Arias Montano, Felipe *Godínez, Sta. *Teresa de Jesús, Mateo *Alemán are but a few examples that come to mind. Some critics (Bataillon, *Castro Quesada) argue that the converso group provided fertile territory for *Erasmism, *Mysticism, and, in a smaller way, Illuminism (*Alumbrados) to take such profound root in Spain. Américo Castro forcefully contended that the singular living situation of the converso—a rejected member of society, acutely aware of the hypocrisy of professions to faith by some Christians and new-Christians alike—gave rise to a singular worldview which voiced itself in the literary blossoming of the *picaresque, the *pastoral, and the above-mentioned authors and currents of thought. Not all critics concur. Most would agree that the converso presence and legacy is a vexing, rich area of study.

BIBLIOGRAPHY

Criticism

Baer, Yitzhak. *A History of the Jews in Christian Spain.* Tr. from Hebrew, L. Schoffman. 2 vols. Philadelphia: Jewish Publication Society, 1961.
Bataillon, M. *Erasmo y España.* 2 vols. Mexico: Fondo de cultura económica, 1950.
Castro, A. *The Structure of Spanish History.* Tr. E. L. King. Princeton: Princeton UP, 1954. Based on 1948 ed. of *España en su historia.*
Sánchez Albornoz, Claudio. *España, un enigma histórico.* 2nd ed. Buenos Aires: Sudamericana, 1962.

Maureen Ihrie

*COPLA,* a poetic term. It may mean or refer to (1) a folk ballad, with verses of 8 to 12 syllables and stanzas of 3 to 5 lines; (2) a popular lyric; (3) in the late fifteenth c., satiric verses, as in the *Coplas de *Mingo Revulgo;* or (4) as practiced in the *Renaissance, 8- to 12-line stanzas with 8 to 11 syllables per line. One of the most famous of this type is Jorge *Manrique's *Coplas por la muerte de su padre.*

**CÓRDOBA, Martín Alonso de** (c. 1398, Cordova–c. 1468 or 1476, Cordova), Augustinian preacher, writer. He taught at the U of Toulouse and the U of Salamanca. Many of his writings are lost, known only by title. What has survived is didactic in nature and directed to specific audiences. The *Jardín de las nobles doncellas* (written before 1467; Garden of Noble Maidens) was composed for the then Princess Isabella; it defends her right to the throne and is an antecedent of Fray Luis de *León's *La perfecta casada.* For Alvaro de *Luna, Córdoba penned *De próspera y adversa fortuna* (written 1440–53; On Prosperous and Adverse Fortune); it was later edited with the title *Compendio de la fortuna.* He also wrote a *Tratado de la predestinación* (n.d.; Treatise on Predestination), and a *Libro del regimiento de los señores* (n.d.; Book of Conduct for Gentlemen), and an *Ars praedicandi* (n.d.; Art of Preaching).

BIBLIOGRAPHY

Primary Texts

*Ars praedicandi.* In *La Ciudad de Dios* 172 (1959): 327–48.
*Compendio de la fortuna.* Ed. P. F. Rubio Alvarez. Madrid: El escorial, 1958.
*Jardín de nobles donzellas.* . . . Ed., study H. Goldberg. UNCSRLL 137. Chapel Hill: U of North Carolina P, 1974.
*Obras.* In BAE 171.
*Tratado del siglo XV sobre la predestinación.* Ed. A. Sánchez Fraile. Salamanca: Centro de Estudios Salmantinos, 1956.

Maureen Ihrie

**CÓRDOBA, Paulus Álvaro de** (c. 800, Córdoba–c. 861, ?), Latin author, lay defender of the Christian faith and culture living in Moslem-controlled territory. A disciple of St. Elogius and one of the most learned men of his day, Córdoba was familiar with certain classical works as well as the Bible. He wrote religious poetry, letters, and a *Vida de San Eulogio* (Life of St. Elogius). In his *Indiculus luminosus* (854) he follows his mentor in attacking Christians who have fallen into Arabic ways and praising the Christian martyrs. The main focus of his twenty extant letters is religious disputes. Córdoba follows the tradition of St. Isidore, but uses a rhetorical Latin style replete with barbarisms.

BIBLIOGRAPHY

Primary Text

*Epistolario.* Ed., study J. Madoz. Madrid: CSIC, 1947.

Criticism

Sage, C. M. *Paul Albar of Cordoba; Studies on His Life and Writings*. Washington: Catholic U of America, 1943.

Lucy Sponsler

**CÓRDOBA, Sebastián de** (1545?, Ubeda–1604, ?), poet. Córdoba's version *a lo divino* of *Garcilaso de la Vega and *Boscán's Italianate poetry responded to the preoccupations of the austere Counter-Reformation moralists in Spain. The extraordinary diffusion of Boscán and Garcilaso's works inspired other writers of the period to experiment with analogous literary themes. Córdoba transformed the incomparable verse in his *Obras de Boscán y Garcilaso trasladadas en materias cristianas y religiosas* (1575; The Works of Boscan and Garcilaso Transposed to Christian and Religious Matters). It was well received; a second edition followed in 1577. The work would be little known today had it not been carefully read and appreciated by San *Juan de la Cruz.

BIBLIOGRAPHY

Primary Texts

*Garcilaso a lo divino*. Ed., study G. R. Gale. Madrid: Castalia, 1971.

*Obras de Boscán y Garcilaso trasladadas en materias cristianas y religiosas*. BAE 35.

Criticism

Alonso, Dámaso. *La poesía de Juan de la Cruz*. Madrid: CSIC, 1942.

Deborah Compte

**COROMINAS, Joan** (1905, Barcelona– ), philologist. One of the all-time great Catalan philologists, Corominas was a pupil and disciple of Pompeu Fabra, *Menéndez Pidal and Jakob Jud. He held chairs of Romance philology in Barcelona, and later in Argentina and at the U of Chicago. Linguists are indebted to him for the important *Diccionario Crítico Etimológico de la Lengua Castellana*, 4 vols. (1954–57; Critical and Etymological Dictionary of the Castilian Language) and several works on Catalan philology, including *L'Estil i Manera de M. J. de Galba i el de Joanot Martorell* (1953; The Style and Manner of M. J. de Galba and that of Joanot Martorell). He rendered into Catalan the complete works of Terence (4 vols., 1936–59), and produced an amply documented *Introducció a l'estudi de la Toponímia Catalana i altres assaigs toponomastics* (1962; Introduction to the Study of Catalan Toponymics and Other Essays on Toponomy). Especially important for students of Spanish literature is his excellent critical edition of the *Libro de Buen Amor*. *See also* Catalan Literature.

BIBLIOGRAPHY

Primary Texts

*Diccionario Crítico Etimológico de la Lengua Castellana*. 4 vols. Madrid: Gredos, 1954–57.

*Libro de buen amor*. Madrid: Gredos, 1967.

**COROMINES, Pere** (1870, Barcelona–1939, Buenos Aires), Catalan journalist, essayist, short story writer and political philosopher. Coromines studied law, but his romantic anarchism landed him in prison, after which he wrote *Les presons imaginàries* (1899; Imaginary Prisons). His idealism and almost mystical desire for goodness are evinced by the title, and completely imbue the later *Vida austera* (1911; Austere Life), which expresses a sort of modern search for saintliness. Coromines was a founder of the Esquerra Catalana (Catalan Left, a party devoted to Catalan nationalism). Numerous writings in the journal *Poble Català* attest to his political enthusiasm, although serious errors led to his withdrawal from political life during a prolonged period of ostracism spent in writing and the practice of law. With the establishment of the Spanish Republic in 1931, he contributed to the drafting of the Catalan statute of autonomy and served as an adviser to the new government. His unfailingly idealistic, philosophically oriented texts include *Les hores d'amor serenes* (1912; Serene Hours of Love), *Cartes d'un visionari* (1921; Letters from a Visionary); *Estudi sobre el pensament filòsofic dels jueus espanyols a l'Edat Mitjana* (1921; Studies on the Philosophical Thought of Spanish Jews in the Middle Ages); *A recés dels Tamarius* (1925; In the Shade of the Tamarind Tree); a trilogy, *En Tomàs de Bajalta*, comprising *Silén* (1925), *Rigmalió* (1928), and *Prometeu* (1934); and *Interpretació del vuit-cent català* (1937; Interpretation of the Catalan Penny). Coromines joined the exodus of refugees from Spain at the end of the Civil War, writing his final works in France and Argentina, including the unfinished *Diari de la Diàspora* (published fragmentarily by the journal *Catalunya* in Buenos Aires), in which he viewed the Republican exodus as similar to the Hebrew diaspora.

BIBLIOGRAPHY

Primary Texts

*Cartes d'un visionari.* Barcelona: López, 1921.
*Diaris i records.* Ed. M. Cahner and J. Coromines. 2 vols. Barcelona: Curial, 1974–75.
*Obra completa en castellano.* Madrid: Gredos, 1975.
*Por Castilla adentro.* Madrid: Compañía iberoamericana, 1930.
*El sentimiento de la riqueza en Castilla.* Madrid: Fortanet, 1917.

Janet Pérez

**CORONADO, Carolina** (1823, Badajoz–1911, Lisbon), novelist, poet. Given her long life, Coronado was witness to the height of \*Romanticism, the rise and decline of realism and \*naturalism, and the apogee of the \*Generation of 1898. She was a precocious writer whose talent was commemorated by \*Espronceda when she was only sixteen. Although she lived most of her youth in rural solitude, by the age of twenty she was collaborating in Spanish and American periodicals. Later she married an American diplomat whose wealth enabled her to keep one of the nineteenth-c.'s most fashionable literary and political salons. She offered asylum in her home to progressives who participated in the failed revolution of 1866. Although she was politically traditional (and enjoyed a cordial relationship with the queen), she was more progressive concerning the treatment of women and children, and took a stand against intolerance and religious fanaticism in her novel *Jarilla* (1875), which presents an unhappy love affair shipwrecked on the rocks of religious principle. Earlier, in her two-volume historical novel, *La Sigea* (1854), Coronado criticized the fanaticism which led to the *Inquisition, as well as the lack of tolerance which brought persecution of the 16th-c. Latinist and poet Luisa *Sigea. *La Rueda de la Desgracia. Manuscrito de un conde* (1873; The Wheel of Misfortune. Manuscript of a Count) treats moral decline in a thesis novel exposing the dangers of lack of patriotism and national integrity, supposedly as a result of Spain's succumbing to foreign influence and capital and materialistic philosophies.

Although she frequently lived outside Spain because of her husband's diplomatic posts, she always returned, and from 1873 onward was usually in Spain. Later in life, however, sorrowed by the deaths of her husband and one of her daughters, she retired to a place she owned near Lisbon, where she remained until her death. Coronado's poems are largely collected in *Poesías de la señorita Doña Carolina Coronado* (Madrid, 1852). Many are lyrical meditations on flowers and trees, solitude and various aspects of nature, often linked via a variant of the pathetic fallacy with human emotions. The pangs of love, regret for lost childhood, the horrors of civil war, admiration for scientific progress, and personal expressions of suffering are combined with poems of a more social or political nature, some dedicated to monarchs, but others protesting the limitations imposed upon women. Some exhibit a melancholic sentimentalism, while others, treating human love, become almost mystic.

Coronado also wrote a number of works for the theater, but without success. Her dramas include *Alfonso IV de León*, *Petrarca* and *El divino Figueroa*, all with historical themes. Miscellaneous works are *Paseos desde el Tajo al Rhin* (Trips from the Tagus to the Rhine); *Quevedo y Lord Byron*; and *Safo y Santa Teresa de Jesús*. She also published several other novels, among them *Paquita*; *La luz del Tajo* (The Light of the Tagus); and *La enclaustrada* (The Cloistered Woman). The vanguard writer Ramón *Gómez de la Serna devoted a book of personal and biographical reminiscences to her: *Mi tía Carolina Coronado* (1942; My Aunt Carolina Coronado).

BIBLIOGRAPHY

Primary Texts

*Jarilla*. Barcelona: Montaner y Simón, 1943.
*Poesías*. . . . Madrid: n.p., 1852.
*La Rueda de la Desgracia. Manuscrito de un conde*. Madrid: Tello, 1873.
*La Sigea*. 2 vols. Madrid: Anselmo Sta. Coloma, 1854.

Criticism

Gómez de la Serna, R. "Mi tía Carolina Coronado." In *Biografías Completas*. Madrid: Aguilar, 1959. 869–980.
Hara, Jacqueline. "Carolina Coronado (1820–1911): Her Life and Work." *DAI* 47 (1986) 1742A. Ohio State U.

Kirkpatrick, Susan. "Gertrudis Gómez de Avellaneda, Carolina Coronado y Rosalía de Castro: Estudios recientes." *Insula* 44.516 (Dec. 1989): 12–13.

Janet Pérez

**CORPUS BARGA.** *See* Barga, Corpus

*CORRAL,* an open-air theater. The transformation from medieval religious drama to *Renaissance secular forms meant that the physical locations of the performances themselves had to be disassociated from the churches and related environs. Theatrical performances were moved, first to the public squares, where large numbers of people could congregate freely, and later to the interior patios or *corrales* formed by the adjoining walls of the buildings within a given block. The early *corrales* were frequently set up in the patios of the hospitals and other charitable institutions for whose benefit the profits from the performances were donated. The first corrales were extremely primitive: an open space where the audience stood and a curtainless platform for a stage. Viewing space from the windows and balconies of the contiguous buildings was often rented out by the property owners. The performances were done in the open air, although a cumbersome canvas awning could be rigged to protect the stage, and occasionally the audience, in the event of inclement weather. By the end of the sixteenth c, a few cities, with Madrid leading the way, established more or less permanent sites for the *corrales*. The Madrid *corrales* of the Príncipe (est. 1579) and the Cruz (est. 1583), named for the streets where they were located, quickly established the capital city as the theatrical center of Spain. Madrid attracted and developed from among its own talent the leading dramatists, performers and musicians of the period. Indeed, the fame of Golden Age drama rests primarily on those plays produced in the Madrid *corrales*.

The Cruz and the Príncipe had similar physical features. The stage was fairly large: wide enough to accommodate additional seating at either side, and deep enough to be partitioned by a curtain toward the back. The resulting space could be used either as a dressing area or for quick scene changes. The public space in the *corrales* was divided according to admission price as well as social boundaries. There were at least three distinct entrances: to the main floor and galleries, frequented by the lower and middle classes; to the box seats of the wealthy patrons; and to the lower balcony, known as the *cazuela* (literally "stewpan"), which was reserved for women only. The general admission audience paid twice—once to the management and again to the company representative. The spectator who wished to sit in one of the side galleries paid again for his seat. The ecclesiastics and well-educated men dominated the *tertulia*, the name given to the top-most balcony. The expensive side boxes, which could be rented for a single performance or for an entire season, were the only part of the *corral* where women were permitted in the company of men. Until the mid-eighteenth c., when the *corrales* were converted into enclosed theaters (the Cruz in 1736, the Príncipe in 1743), performances took place in the afternoon: at four o'clock during the spring and at two o'clock during the winter. The theatrical season lasted from Easter to Corpus Christi and from early September to Lent. By the early eighteenth c., performances were offered during the summer months as well. At first, the companies performed only on Sundays and official holidays, but soon began daily performances throughout the season.

The *corrales* in Madrid, as in other cities, began under the auspices of fraternal organizations which sponsored performances as a way of funding various charitable institutions. From the beginning, the city government was closely involved in the administration of the *corrales*, and by 1638, Madrid's city council had total control over them. The day-to-day management was in the hands of a lessee who paid a fixed sum each year for the rights to the *corrales*. This system of city administration lasted well into the nineteenth c. The public exercised considerable influence on performances in the *corrales*; numerous contemporary accounts describe the power of the *mosqueteros* (the name for the men who stood in the patio area), who could make or break a performance, an entire production, or even the career of an actor or dramatist by their applause or derisive whistles and protests. In his "Arte nuevo de hacer comedias . . . " (The New Way to Write Plays), Lope de *Vega states, "I write in that style which was invented by those who sought the public's approval; because, as it is the public who is paying, it is only just that we dramatists pander to its crude tastes in order to please it." Notwithstanding Lope's seemingly cynical attitude, he recognized the importance of popular opinion and succeeding generations of dramatists heeded his advice.

The popular success of the *corrales* and their dramatists even influenced the development of court theater. In 1607, a *corral* was installed in a patio of the palace so that the royal family could view this kind of popular theater. When the theater at the Buen Retiro was opened in 1640, productions were patterned after those in the *corrales*, and utilized many of the same actors and production resources as the public facilities. After a few private performances to the court, the theater opened its doors to the general public and functioned as an additional *corral* in Madrid, subject to the same administrative practices as were the Cruz and the Príncipe. *See also* Autor; Compañía; Siglo de Oro; Theater in Spain.

BIBLIOGRAPHY

Criticism

Allen, John J. *The Reconstruction of a Spanish Golden Age Playhouse. El Corral del Príncipe 1583–1744.* Gainesville: U Florida P, 1983.
Arróniz, Othón. *Teatros y escenarios del siglo de oro.* Madrid: Gredos, 1977.
Rodrigo, A. *Almagro y su Corral de Comedias.* Ciudad Real: CSIC, 1971.
Shergold, N. D. *A History of the Spanish Stage from Medieval Times until the End of the Seventeenth Century.* Oxford: Clarendon P, 1967.

Donald C. Buck

**CORRAL, Pedro del.** Little is known about the life of this fifteenth-c. author. He wrote the *Crónica sarracina* (Saracen Chronicle) or *Crónica del rey don Rodrigo con la destruyción de España* (Chronicle of King Rodrigo with the

Destruction of Spain), probably around 1440, though it was not published until 1499. Corral initially based his work on sources such as the *Crónica general* (General Chronicle) and *Crónica troyana* (Trojan Chronicle), but soon abandoned any attempt at historical writing by inventing fictitious sources, such as Eleastras, Alanzuri, and Carestas. The resulting *Crónica* may be more properly termed a romance, though some have called it the first Spanish historical novel. Its literary merits are few, but it has given us the oldest ballads about Rodrigo and inspired plays by the Romantic dramatists *Hartzenbusch and *Zorrilla. *See also Crónica.*

BIBLIOGRAPHY

Primary Text

Menéndez Pidal, Juan. *Leyendas del último rey godo.* Madrid: Revista de Archivos, 1906.

Criticism

Tate, Robert B. *Ensayos sobre la historiografía peninsular del siglo XV.* Madrid: Gredos, 1970.

James Ray Green

**CORREA CALDERÓN, Evaristo** (1899, Neira de Rey, Lugo–?), professor of literature, scholar. In 1924 he published his first novel, *El milano y la rosa* (The Goshawk and the Rose); he has also written works in Galician. His excellent annotated edition of *Gracián's Complete Works appeared in 1945, followed by his anthology *Los costumbristas españoles* (1950–51; Spanish Costumbrismo Writers), which includes a well-documented foreword. *See also* Romanticism.

BIBLIOGRAPHY

Primary Texts

*Baltasar Gracián: su vida y su obra.* 2nd ed. Madrid: Gredos, 1970.
*Los costumbristas españoles.* Madrid: Aguilar, 1950–51.
*Obras completas de Baltasar Gracián y Morales.* Madrid: Aguilar, 1944.

Isabel McSpadden

**CORREAS, Gonzalo** (c. 1571, Jaraiz, Plasencia–1631, Salamanca), humanist, translator, professor of Greek and Hebrew, philologist. He received his bachelor of arts in 1592, and then taught for forty years at the U of Salamanca. His valuable proverb collection, *Vocabulario de refranes proverbiales y otras fórmulas comunes de la lengua castellana* (Vocabulary of Proverbs and Other Common Locutions of the Castilian Language), was not published until 1906. Correas translated Epictetus's *Encheiridion* and the *Cebetis Tabula*, publishing them with his *Ortografía castellana nueva i perfecta* (1630; New, Perfect Castilian Orthography). His works of grammar include the *Arte de la lengua española castellana* (written 1626, not published until this c.; Art of the Castilian Spanish Language), and the *Gramática trilingüe de las tres lenguas castellana, latina y griega* . . . (1627; Trilingual Grammar of the Three Languages, Spanish, Latin and Greek . . . ). *See also* Humanism; Renaissance; Siglo de Oro.

BIBLIOGRAPHY

Primary Texts

*Arte de la lengua española castellana.* Ed., intro. E. Alarcos. RFE Anejo 56. Madrid: CSIC, 1954.

*Arte Kastellana.* Ed., intro. M. Taboada Cid. Santiago: U of Santiago de Compostela, 1984. Spanish section of the *Trilingüe.*

*Vocabulario de refranes.* Ed. L. Combet. Bordeaux: Institut d'Études Iberiques . . . de l'Université de Bordeaux, 1967.

**CORREIA, Natália** (1923, Lisbon?– ), Portuguese poet and playwright. Among her poetic collections are *Comunicação* (1949; Communication), *Poesia* (1955), *Dimensão Encontrada* (1957; Discovered Dimension), *Cántico do Pais Emerso* (1961; Canticle of the Immersed Land), *O Homúnculo* (1964; The Humunculus) and *O Vinho e a Ira* (1965; Wine and Ire). While theater does not appear to be her primary vocation, Correia has also written dramatic works, collaborating with Manuel de Lima on a Surrealist piece entitled *Sucubrina ou a teoria do Chapéu* (1953; Sucubrina or the Chapeu Theory), and authoring other works in the same vein without a collaborator.

BIBLIOGRAPHY

Primary Texts

*As maças de Orestes.* Lisbon: Dom Quixote, 1970.

*Dimensão Encontrada.* Lisbon: n.p., 1957.

*O homúnculo.* Lisbon: Contrapunto, 1964.

*O Vinho e a Ira.* Lisbon: Ribeiro de Mello, 1966.

Janet Pérez

**CORRO, Antonio del** (1527, Seville–1591, London), religious convert to Protestantism. Marcelino *Menéndez y Pelayo considers him a freethinker rather than a Calvinist or Lutheran. A Hieronymite monk, he fled Spain to France in 1557 with eleven other brothers, including Cipriano de *Valera. In 1560, he was a Protestant minister in Aquitaine; by 1567 he was preaching in Antwerp. In 1569 he arrived in England. In 1573 he published an explanation of Paul's Letter to the Romans. It was very well received and won him a chair in theology at the U of Oxford. He was still in England in 1583.

In 1567 Corro wrote, in French, to Philip II, giving an explanation of his départure from Spain. Titled *Lettre envoiée a la Maiesté du Roy des Espaignes (A Supplication Exhibited to the Most Mightie Prince Philip King of Spain,* 1577), it advocates universal religious tolerance. In 1586, he published a Spanish and French grammar; it was translated into English in 1590.

BIBLIOGRAPHY

Primary Texts

*Dialogus theologicus.* London: T. Purfoote, 1574.

*Epistola beati.* London: n.p., 1581.

*Reglas gramaticales para aprender la lengua española y francesa.* Oxford: Barnes, 1586.

English Translations

*An epistle or godlie admonition.* . . . Tr. from French by G. Fenton. London: Bynneman, 1569.
*The Spanish grammar.* . . . Tr. J. Thorie. London: Wolfe, 1590.
*A supplication exhibited to the Moste Mightie Prince Philip King of Spaine.* . . . London: Coldoche and Bynneman, 1577.

Criticism

Hauben, Paul J. *Three Spanish Heretics and the Reformation.* Geneva: Droz, 1967.

Maureen Ihrie

**CORTÉS, Hernán** (1485, Medellín, Extremadura–1547, Castilleja de la Cuesta, Seville), soldier of fortune and conqueror of the New World Indians. After studying law at the U of Salamanca, he went to Cuba under Diego de Velásquez, from whom he broke away. Subsequently, Cortés led the conquest of Mexico, and described it in his *Cartas y relaciones* (1523–25; *Dispatches from Mexico to Charles V*, 1957). To reward Cortés's military victories, Charles V knighted him in the Order of Santiago, naming him Marquis del Valle de Oaxaca. Histories of the day which portrayed Cortés include those of *Lopez de Gómara and Bernal *Díaz del Castillo. *See also* Renaissance; Siglo de Oro.

BIBLIOGRAPHY

Primary Texts

*Cartas de relación.* Mexico: Porrúa, 1969.
*Cartas y documentos de Hernán Cortés.* Ed. M. Hernández Sanches-Barba. Mexico: Porrúa, 1963.
*Cartas y relaciones.* Ed. P. de Gayangos. BAE 22

English Translations

*Dispatches from Mexico to Charles V.* Ed. A. Grove Day. New York: American Book Co., 1935.
*His Five Letters of Relation to the Emperor Charles V (1519–1526).* Tr. and Ed. F. A. MacNutt. Glorieta, NM: Rio Grande, 1977.

Criticism

Johnson, W. W. *Cortés.* Boston: Little, Brown, 1975.
Prescott, W. H. *History of the Conquest of Mexico.* New York: Random House, 1979.
Reynolds, W. A. *Romancero de Hernán Cortés. Estudio y textos de los siglos XVI y XVII.* Madrid: Alcalá, 1967.
Valle, R. H. *Bibliografía de Hernán Cortés.* New York: B. Franklin, 1970.

Veronica Sauter

**CORTESÃO, Jaime Zuzarte** (1884, Ançã near Coimbra–1960, Lisbon), Portuguese historian, poet at and playwright. He graduated in medicine at the U of Lisbon in 1910, thereafter teaching (1912–15), entering politics (1915–17) and serving as a volunteer military doctor with the Portuguese expeditionary force in Flanders (1917–19). Subsequently he held the post of director of the National Library in Lisbon (1919–27) when, together with Raul *Proença and Câmara

Reys he formed the group known as the Grupo da Biblioteca, which included among its number at various times, Aquilino *Ribeiro, António *Sérgio, Afonso Lopes *Vieira, José de Figueiredo and Reinaldo dos Santos. In 1921, together with Raul Proença, Aquilino Ribeiro and Câmara Reys he founded *Seara Nova*, an influential and remarkably long-lived critical review. When the military took power in 1926–27, he was forced into exile, going first to Spain and then France and England. In 1940 he moved to Brazil, returning to Portugal in 1950 where he lived out the remainder of his life.

His early involvement with the Saudosismo movement and its Seara Nova and Renascença Portuguesa offshoots brought contributions to *A Águia* and *Seara Nova*. Indeed, most of his writing was published under the aegis of these organizations, conforming to and arguing for their position.

Understandably, his historical work centers on figures and periods that illustrate the high points of Portuguese expansion, such as the voyages of discovery or the history of the Republic, of which he was an ardent supporter. The same can be said of his plays, particularly *O Infante de Sagres* (1916; Henry the Navigator), and *Egas Moniz* (1918; The Faithful Vassal).

In common with his companions in *Seara Nova* and the Grupo da Biblioteca he was more rationalistic in his approach to and conviction in the specificity of the Portuguese national character, avoiding the enthusiasm and emotionalism of the hard-line Saudosistas. He also shared *Seara Nova*'s abhorrence for the anti-democratic attitudes and actions of the armed forces and the government that they implanted. He also felt very strongly that intellectuals should be active participants in the political life of their country.

BIBLIOGRAPHY

Primary Texts

*Obras Completas* Pref. and ed. Victor Magalhães Godinho. Lisbon: Portugália, 1964.

Criticism

Águas, Neves, *Bibliografia de Jaime Cortesão*. Lisbon: Arcádia, 1962.
Lopes, Oscar, *Jaime Cortesão*. Lisbon: Arcádia, 1962.
Saraiva, Ricardo, *Jaime Cortesão*. Lisbon: Seara Nova, 1953.

Peter Fothergill-Payne

**CORTEZ, Alfredo** (1880, Estremoz–1946, Lisbon), Portuguese playwright. A judge by profession, Cortez thus had a privileged view of social problems and human shortcomings. He came to literature rather late, with his first play *Zilda* (1921), a naturalistic satire of materialism and sensuality. Later satires (e.g., *Batón* [Lipstick] and *Lá-lás*, 1939) were censored. Among his best-known works are *A la fe* (1924; In Faith), a lyric treatment of legendary, historical loyalty; *Gladiadores* (1934; The Gladiators), a farcical lampoon of machismo, feminism, the media and the law; and *Tá-Mar* (1936; High Seas), another verse drama exalting the honest fisher folk. During the 1930s, he pioneered the use of expressionistic techniques, provoking scandals with his plays and manifestos.

Janet Pérez

**CORTEZÓN ÁLVAREZ, Daniel** (1927, Ribadeo, Lugo– ), Galician critic, novelist, and dramatist. After his first years in Andalucía, Cortezón and his family were forced by the Civil War to go to France, later returning to Ribadeo, where until 1963 he worked in a pharmacy. He presently resides in Madrid, writing in Galician and Spanish in almost every genre. Cortezón's themes reveal an interest in the historical aspects of Galician culture, particularly those of the earliest period.

BIBLIOGRAPHY

Primary Texts

*Os anxos cómense crus.* Vigo: n.p., 1972.
*Aspeitos histórico-socrolóxicos do ser de Europa.* Buenos Aires: Centro Gallego de Buenos Aires, 1961.
*O cabaleiro da lus.* Buenos Aires: Centro Gallego de Buenos Aires, 1956. (novel)
*Compañero presidente, compañero.* N.p.: n.p., 1974. (theater)
*As covas do rei Cintolo.* Vigo: Galaxia, 1956. (novel)
*Danza, contradanza y metamorfosis de moros y cristianos.* N.p.: n.p., 1975.
*Detrás de los pilares del Este.* N.p.: n.p., 1961. (novel)
*Encuentro en Selene.* N.p.: n.p., 1962. (theater)
*Gelmírez o la gloria de Compostela.* Buenos Aires: n.p., 1972. (theater)
*Las ideas-fuerzas históricas.* N.p.: n.p., 1951.
*El obispo ciego.* N.p.: n.p., 1962. (theater)
*Pantocrítica Galiciana y otras cuestiones.* N.p.: n.p., 1956. (essay)
*Prisciliano.* Vigo: Galaxia, 1970.
*De la saudade y sus formas.* NY: Casade Galicia, 1960.
*A vila sulagada.* Sada: O Castro, 1981. (novel)

Kathleen March

**COSAUTE,** a courtly dance. Eugenio Asensio has convincingly corrected the term *cosante* in his commentaries on J. Romeu Figueroas's study, *El Cosante en la lírica.* Asensio states, "*Cosaute*—and not *cosante*—is a word of French origin which signified a courtly dance accompanied by song." He bases his evidence on the rhyme between *cosaute* and *faraute*, offering examples from the works of Rodrigo *Cota and Antón de *Montoro. The word appears in the form of *corsaute* and *corsaote*, and is derived from *coursault.* He traces the evolution of the term to *cosante* in the book cited below.

BIBLIOGRAPHY

Criticism

Asensio, E. *Poética y realidad en el Cancionero peninsular de la Edad Media.* Madrid: Gredos, 1957. 186 ff.

Romeu Figueroas, J. "El cosante en la lírica de los *Cancioneros* musicales españoles de los siglos XV y XVI." *Anuario Musical* 5 (1950): 15–61.

Deborah Compte

**COSSÍO, Francisco de** (1887, Sepúlveda, Segovia–1975, Segovia), distinguished journalist. He was awarded the Mariano de Cavia Prize in 1929 and lived in Valladolid, contributing regularly to *Norte de Castilla*. Also a novelist of sensibility, he published his first fiction, *La casa de los linajes* (The House of the Ancestors), when he was only 19. His best-known novels are *Clara* (1948), outstanding psychological fiction of his time, and *Taxímetro* (1940; Taxicab), his work most favorably received by critics, with a good plot, journalistic events, and semi-vanguardist literary technique in the form of an unreal biography of a fantastic character. Other novels are *El estilete de oro* (1814; The Golden Chisel); *Las experiencias del Doctor Henson* (1931?; Doctor Henson's Experiences); *El caballero de Castilnuovo* (1925; The Gentleman from Castilnuovo); *La rueda* (1927; The Wheel); *Elvira Coloma o Al morir de un siglo* (1942; Elvira Coloma or At the Turn of a Century); *Aurora y los hombres* (1951; Aurora and Men); *Cincuenta años* (1952; Fifty Years). Cossío was also a dramatist of diverse success; noted plays include *En el limpio solar* (In the Noble Manor House); *Román el rico* (Wealthy Román); *Maniquí* (Manikin); *La casa de cristal* (The Glass House); *La mujer de nadie* (No One's Woman).

BIBLIOGRAPHY

Primary Texts

*Aurora y los hombres*. Buenos Aires: Espasa-Calpe, 1950.
*Clara*. Barcelona: Janés, 1948.
*Elvira Coloma*. Barcelona: Juventud, 1942.
*Manolo*. 2nd ed. Valladolid: Santarén, 1939.
*La rueda*. 2nd ed. Valladolid: Santarén, 1939.
*Taxímetro*. Madrid: Juventud, 1940.

Pilar Sáenz

**COSSÍO, José María de** (1893, Valladolid–1977, Madrid), journalist, literary critic, essayist. A member of the group Cruz y Raya, and later of Escorial, he was admitted to the Spanish Academy (*Academia Española) in 1948. An acute connoisseur of Spanish poetry, he wrote a valuable study of nineteenth-c. poets, *Cincuenta años de poesía española, 1850–1900* (1960; Fifty Years of Spanish Poetry). Other important literary criticism by Cossío includes *Poesía castellana: notas de asedio* (1936; Spanish Poetry, Brief Annotations), *La obra literaria de Pereda* (1934; Pereda's Work), *El Romanticismo a la vista* (1944; On Romanticism), *Fábulas mitológicas de España* (1952; Mythological Fables of Spain), and *Los toros en la poesía española* (1931; Bulls in Spanish Poetry). He is even more known for his monumental encyclopedia on bullfighting, *Los toros* (1943–83; The Bulls). With regard to his own creative writing, the most celebrated is *Epístolas para amigos* (n.d.; Epistles to Friends). *See also* Essay.

BIBLIOGRAPHY

Primary Texts

*Cincuenta años de poesía española, 1850–1900.* 2 vols. Madrid: Espasa-Calpe, 1960.
*Fábulas mitológicas de España.* Madrid: Espasa-Calpe, 1952.
*La obra literaria de Pereda.* Santander: Martínez, 1934.
*Los toros.* 4 vols. Madrid: Espasa-Calpe, 1943–83.
*Los toros en la poesía española.* 2 vols. Madrid: CIAP, 1931.

Pilar Sáenz

**COSSÍO, Manuel Bartolomé** (1858, Haro, Logroño–1935, Madrid), professor, scholar. He taught art history at the U of Barcelona; later he became a professor of pedagogy at the U of Madrid, the director of the Pedagogy Museum, and a main figure at the Institución Libre de Enseñanza after the death of Francisco *Giner de los Ríos (1839–1915). He was an outstanding authority in the field of pedagogy, and his writings on this subject were published in several journals, including the *Boletín de la Institución Libre de Enseñanza.* Some of these articles were later collected in the volume *De su jornada* (1929; On His Day). With J. Pioján, he edited a great, 26-volume treatise on art history titled *Summa artis* (n.d.). In 1908, Cossío also published a significant biography and artistic analysis of El Greco's work, with added valuable new data, and set forth a new appreciation of El Greco for this c., which is quite different from that which prevailed in previous centuries.

BIBLIOGRAPHY

Primary Texts

*De su jornada.* Madrid: Blass, 1929.
*El Greco.* 2nd ed. Buenos Aires: Espasa-Calpe, 1948.
*Summa artis.* 4th ed. 26 vols. Madrid: Espasa-Calpe, 1955—.

Isabel McSpadden

**COSTA I LLOBERA, Miguel** (1854, Palma de Mallorca–1922, Palma de Mallorca), Catalan poet, essayist, orator and theologian. After beginning the study of law in Madrid, he discovered that his true vocation was poetry. Being of a wealthy family, he retired to Mallorca to devote himself to literature, publishing his first volume of poems, *Poesies*, in 1885. After studying in the Gregorian U in Rome, he was ordained a priest in 1888, obtaining his doctorate in theology in 1889. Thereafter he again devoted himself to poetry, participating repeatedly in the Jocs Florals (poetic contests), and in 1902 won the title of *mestre en gai saber* (master troubador) for having won the first prize in each of the Jocs' essential thematic areas, faith, love, and country. His most important volumes include *De l'agre de la terra* (1897; Of the Bitterness of Earth); *Tradicions i fantasies* (1903; Traditions and Fantasies); *Horacianes* (1906; Poems after Horace); and *Visions de Palestina* (1908; Visions of Palestine). Some of these titles clearly suggest the strong classical bent of his writing, but perhaps fail to communicate the strong emotional quality and almost ecstatic reaction to the beauties of the Mallorcan countryside. Costa i Llobera was very influential in *Catalan literature, and especially in the formation of the Mallorcan school of poets. *See also* Catalan Literature.

BIBLIOGRAPHY

Primary Texts

*Antología poètica.* 2nd ed. Barcelona: Selecta, 1981.
*Horacianes.* Palma de Mallorca: Moll, 1938.
*Tradicions i fantasies.* 3rd ed. Palma de Mallorca: Moll, 1976.
*Visions de la Palestina.* Palma de Mallorca: Moll, 1977.

**COSTA Y MARTÍNEZ, Joaquín** (1844, Monzón–1911, Graus), Aragonese politician and writer on legal, literary, historical, sociological, political, agricultural and geographic topics.

While it has been common to call him a precursor to the *Generation of 1898, Costa should be viewed as what he is: a distinguished member of the Generation of 1868 whose work *Unamuno, *Azorín and, later, *Ortega continued in their own way. As did *Pérez Galdós, he visited and wrote about the Parisian International Exposition of 1867. There he too realized how far behind the rest of Europe Spain was. From that time his mission was to work for national regeneration, making his name synonymous with all republican and progressive activity. His single best-known and most representative work may be *El colectivismo agrario* (1898; Agrarian Collectivism). In the present context the following should be also mentioned: *La poesía popular* (1881; Popular Poetry of Spain), and *Mitología y literatura celto-hispana* (1888; Celtic-Hispanic Mythology and Literature).

BIBLIOGRAPHY

Primary Texts

*Obras completas.* 21 vols. Huesca: Campo, 1911–24.

Criticism

Cheyne, George J. G. *A Bibliographic Study of the Writings of Joaquín Costa.* London: Tamesis, 1972.
———. *Joaquín Costa, el gran desconocido.* Esplugas de Llobregat: Ariel, 1972.
Martín Retortillo, Cirilio. *Joaquín Costa, Propulsor de la reconstrucción nacional.* Barcelona: Aedos, 1961.
Pérez de la Dehesa, Rafael. *El pensamiento de Costa y su influencia en el 98.* Madrid: Sociedad de Estudios y Publicaciones, 1966.

Stephen Miller

**COSTUMBRISMO.** *See* Romanticism

**COSTUMBRISTAS.** *See* Romanticism

**COTA, Rodrigo** (?, Toledo?–after 1504, ?), poet. A Toledan of Jewish ancestry, Rodrigo Cota wrote *Epithalamium*, a burlesque denouncing Diego Arias de Avila, the treasurer of the Catholic Kings, because he was not invited to the wedding of Arias's son or nephew. The work is of historical interest in its allusions to customs of Spanish Jews.

His most acclaimed work, *Diálogo entre el amor y un viejo* (Dialogue between Love and an Old Man, 1964), was edited for the first time in 1511 in the *Cancionero general*. In this work an old man reproaches Love, but Love reveals its alluring character and succeeds in persuading him; as the old man succumbs, Love mocks him for his folly. The dialogue possesses remarkable dramatic potential; for that reason it was published by Leandro Fernández de *Moratín in *Orígenes del teatro* (Origins of the Theater). The strictly dramatic part is the last, since the first adheres to the medieval literary debate tradition. The dialogue is simply and masterfully written.

The *Coplas del provincial* (Verses of the Provincial), the *Coplas de *Mingo Revulgo* (Verses of Mingo Revulgo), and the first act of the *Celestina* have been attributed to Cota without substantial evidence.

BIBLIOGRAPHY

Primary Texts

*Diálogo entre . . . un viejo.* Ed., intro., E. Aragone. Firenzie: Le Monnier, 1961.
*Las coplas del provinciano.* Ed. Foulché-Delbosc. In NBAE 22.

English Translation

"Dialogue between Love and an Old Man." Tr. L. Newton. In *Early Spanish Plays.* Ed. R. O'Brien. 2 vols. New York: Las Americas, 1964.

Criticism

Cantera Burgos, F. *El poeta Ruy Sánchez Cota (Rodrigo Cota) y su familia de judíos conversos.* Madrid: U of Madrid, 1970.
Cotarelo, E. "Algunas noticias nuevas acerca de Rodrigo de Cota." *BRAE* 13 (1926): 11–17.

                                                                Deborah Compte

**COTARELO VALLEDOR, Armando** (1879, Vegadeo, Asturias–1950, Madrid), playwright, professor. Professor of Spanish language and literature at the U of Santiago, Cotarelo Valledor played an important role as an intellectual during the crucial years of the Generación Nós (We Generation) and the Instituto de Estudios Gallegos (Institute of Galician Studies). Starting in 1939 he held the same position at the U of Madrid. A member of the *Academia Española, he also belonged to the Royal Academy of History and was perpetual secretary of the Instituto de España (Spain Institute).

A versatile and prolific writer, Cotarelo Valledor was more than anything an essayist of literary and historical themes, yet for Galician literature his importance rests on his theatrical creation and on his compilations of popular literature, among the latter *Contos de Nadal colleitos do pobo* (1927; Christmas Stories Taken from the People).

BIBLIOGRAPHY

Primary Texts

*Beiramar*. La Coruña: n.p. 1931.
*El gabán*. Ribadeo: n.p. 1900.
*Hóstia*. La Coruña: n.p. 1926.
*Lubicán*. Santiago: n.p. 1924.
*Memorias de un escolar de antaño, 1808–1809*. Madrid: Pueyo, 1919–21.
*Mourenza*. Santiago: n.p. 1931.
*El pazo*. Santiago: Ecode Santiago, 1923.
*Sinxebra*. Santiago: n.p. 1923.
*Trebón*. Santiago: U. de Santiago de Compostela, 1984.

Criticism

Various Authors. *A presencia de Armando Cotarelo en Galicia*. Santiago: Xunta de
    Galicia, 1984.

Luis Martul Tobío

**COTARELO Y MORI, Emilio** (1857, Vega de Ribadeo, Asturias–1936, Madrid), literary scholar, secretary of the *Academia Española. His erudite investigations clarified many aspects of literary history by unearthing a great quantity of bibliographical data. He published studies on *Villamediana, Enrique de *Villena, Rodrigo *Cota, Diego de *San Pedro, Antón de *Montoro and *Alvarez Gato. His book on Tomás de *Iriarte (1897) received the literary prize given by the Academia Española, and gained him acceptance into the institution. Cotarelo's literary studies centered around the history of theater, producing works such as *Bibliografía de las controversias sobre la licitud del teatro en España* (1904; Bibliography of the Controversies Concerning the Legitimacy of Theater in Spain), and studies on *Tirso, *Rojas Zorrilla, *Jiménez de Enciso, *Diamante, *Vélez de Guevara, *Cubillo de Aragón, *Coello, *Calderón de la Barca and Agustín *Moreto. Cotarelo also directed publication of texts by Juan del *Encina, Lope de *Rueda, three volumes of Tirso's plays, ten volumes of Lope de *Vega's works, and two volumes of *entremeses*. He also studied dramatic art in the eighteenth c., bringing to light information concerning well-known actors, and publishing the *sainetes of Ramón de la *Cruz. Cotarelo also possessed a background in music, which he applied in his works *La ópera en España* (n.d.; Opera in Spain), and *Ensayo sobre la zarzuela* (n.d.; Essay on the Zarzuela).

BIBLIOGRAPHY

Primary Texts

*Bibliografía de las controversias sobre la licitud del teatro en España*. Madrid: RABM,
    1904.

*Colección de entremeses, loas, bailes, jácaras y mojigangas desde fines del siglo XVI a mediados del XVIII.* NBAE 17–18.
*Orígenes y establecimiento de la ópera en España hasta 1800.* Madrid: RABM, 1917.

Isabel McSpadden

**COVARRUBIAS Y OROZCO, Juan.** *See* Orozco, Juan de

**COVARRUBIAS Y OROZCO, Sebastián de** (1539, Toledo–1613, Cuenca), lexicographer, Canon of the Cuenca Cathedral. Son of Sebastián de *Horozco, and brother to Juan de *Orozco, he wrote *Emblemas morales* (1610; Moral Emblems), and, more important, the *Tesoro de la lengua castellana o española* (1611; Treasury of the Castilian or Spanish Language), which is the most important dictionary between that of *Nebrija (1492), and the Spanish Academy's *Diccionario de autoridades* (1726–39). It continues to be a valuable resource in the study of Golden Age literature. *See also* Academia Española; Humanism; Siglo de Oro.

BIBLIOGRAPHY

Primary Texts

*Emblemas morales.* Ed., intro., D. Moir. Menston: Scolar, 1973.
*Tesoro de la lengua castellana o española.* Ed. M. de Riquer. Barcelona: Horta, 1943.

Criticism

González Palencia, A. "Sebastián de Covarrubias y Orozco (datos biográficos)." In *Historias y leyendas.* Madrid: CSIC, 1942. 285 and ss.

**CRÉMER, Victoriano** (1908, Burgos– ), largely self-taught poet and dramatist. A typographer by profession, Crémer has lived most of his life in León. In the immediate post-war years, he was a founder, with Antonio G. de Lama and Eugenio G. de *Nora, of the literary review *Espadaña*, which for its several years' existence was quite influential in Spanish letters. Before the war, he published *Tendiendo el vuelo* (1928; Taking Flight). The books which made him best known came in the 1940s, and express social preoccupations and a concern for life's problems: *Tacto sonoro* (1944; Sonorous Touch); *Caminos de mi sangre* (1947; Roads of My Blood); and *Las horas perdidas* (1949; The Lost Hours). Crémer's collected dramatic works are published under the title of *En la escalera* (1940; On the Stairway). In 1967, his complete poetic works up to that time were brought out in a single edition as *Poesía total (1944–1966)*.

BIBLIOGRAPHY

Primary Texts

*Caminos de mi sangre.* Madrid: n.p., 1947.
*Las horas perdidas.* Barcelona: Porter, 1949.
*Poesía.* 2 vols. León: CSIC, 1984.
*Poesía total 1944–1966.* Buenos Aires: Plaza y Janés, 1967.

*Los trenes no dejan huella: historia secreta de una ciudad, novela.* Madrid: Santiago García, 1986.

English Translation

Four poems. Tr. L. Lowenfels and J. Braymer. In *Literary Review* 7 (1964): 617–23.

Janet Pérez

**CRESPO, Ángel** (1926, Ciudad Real– ), poet. He was the founder and director of the poetry magazines *Decaulión* (1951–53) and *El Pájaro de Paja*. His first five books of poetry apppeared between 1950 and 1957, and during the early 1950s he participated in the *Postismo* movement. Crespo has a distinct poetic voice, making poetic use of humor, while at the same time striving to find or create meaning and significance in the everyday minutiae. His style is essentially anti-rhetorical, but does incorporate intertextual references to literature and art. Early poetry collections include *Una lengua emerge* (1950; A Tongue Emerges); *Quedan señales* (1952; Signs Remain); *La pintura* (1955; The Painting); *Todo está vivo* (1956; Everything Is Alive); and *La cesta y el río* (1957; The Basket and the River). Three books were published in 1959: *Junio feliz* (Happy June); *Júpiter*; and *Oda a Nanda Papiri*. An anthology of Crespo's poetry of the 1950s appeared in 1960, entitled simply *Antología poética*. *Puerta clavada* (1961; Nailed Door) was followed by *Suma y sigue* (1962; Total and Continue Adding), apparently a cumulative or selected edition of poetry to that point. *Pausa en otoño* (1962; Pause in Autumn) appeared in the same year, and in 1964, *Cartas desde un pozo* (Letters from a Well) and *Poésie* (an anthology with translations into Italian). *No sé cómo decirlo* (1965; I Don't Know How to Say It) and *Docena florentina* (1966; Florentine Dozen) both appeared in time to be incorporated into the most significant and widely used collection of Crespo's lyrics, *En medio del camino: Poesía 1949–1970* (Halfway Down the Road: Poetry from 1949 to 1970), Crespo's collected works to that date, reorganized by the poet. His works for the next five years appear in *Claro, oscuro: (1971–1975)* (1978; Clearly, Dark: [1971–75]). In the same year, Crespo published a new work, *Colección de climas* (1978; Collection of Climates), and more recently, *Donde no corre el aire* (1981; Where the Air Doesn't Flow). Crespo is an excellent translator, having won the 1957 Adonais Prize for his rendering from the Portuguese of Fernando *Pessoa's *Poemas de Alberto Caeiro*.

BIBLIOGRAPHY

Primary Texts

*El aire es de los dioses (1978–1981).* Zaragoza: Olifante, 1982.
*El ave en el aire.* Barcelona: Plaza y Janés, 1985.
*Claro, oscuro: (1971–1975).* Zaragoza: Porvivir, 1978.
*En medio del camino.* Barcelona: Seix Barral, 1971.

English Translation

Three poems. Tr. A. Terry. In *The Sacrifice.* Belfast: Queens U of Belfast, 1967.

Criticism

Albi, José. "Introducción a la poesía de Angel Crespo." In Crespo, *Antología poética*.
    Valencia: Ed. de la Revista Verbo, 1960. 8–93.
Bertelloni-Baggicki, María Teresa. "El sentido del tiempo en la poesía de Angel Crespo."
    *Nueva Estafeta* 11 (1979): 59–64.
Capecchi, Luisa. "Un viaje por la poesía de Angel Crespo." *Insula* 35.402 (May 1980):
    7.
Debicki, Andrew P. *Poetry of Discovery: The Spanish Generation of 1956–71*. Lexington:
    UP of Kentucky, 1982. 183–92.
Gómez Bedate, Pilar. "La contestación de la realidad en la poesía de Angel Crespo."
    *Revista de Letras* 4 (1969): 605–45.
Metzler Linda. "The Poetry of Angel Crespo." Diss., U of Kansas, 1978.
Rica, Carlos de la. "Vanguardia de los años cincuenta (desde el ismo a la generación."
    *Papeles de Son Armadans* 37.109 (1965): i–xvi; 37.110: xxv–xlviii; 37.112: iii–
    xv.

Janet Pérez

**CRÒNICA OF MUNTANER.** *See* Muntaner, Ramon

**CRÓNICAS** (Chronicles). From the decline of the Roman Empire and the Germanic invasions to the end of the Middle Ages, Spanish historiography underwent
several distinctive periods of development in the conception of history, the use
of sources, and the eventual use of the vernacular. The first departure from Greek
and Roman historiography was made by Paulus Orosius, who, at the behest of
St. Augustine, wrote the *Seven Books of History against the Pagans*, a work of
enormous influence on later historians and intellectuals. Its providential view of
history provides the basis for a reconciliation of classical and Christian beliefs.
*The Cronicón de Idacio* (Chronicle of Idatius, d. 470), by Idatius, bishop of
Chaves, recounts the Germanic invasions of the peninsula, in particular, the
ravages of the Suevi in Galicia. Notable is Idatius's reckoning of time according
to the "Roman era" or "era of Caesar," i.e., from the year 38 B.C. when
Augustus imposed a tribute on the Roman provinces of *Hispania*. This system
of dating continued well into the fourteenth c. The sixth c. represents a period
of relative calm with the conversion from Arianism of the Suevi and their
successors, the Visigoths. The *Chronicon Monumenta Germaniae Historica*
(Chronicle of John of Biclaro, d. 621) by John, the bishop of Gerona, is dedicated
to the reign of Leovigild and leads up to the conversion of Recared (589). It
was St. Isidore (d. 636), bishop of Seville, who first conceived of a truly national
history. His work, translated as *History of the Kings of the Goths, the Vandals,
and the Suevi* (1970), recognizes the role of the Visigoths in forging a monarchy
out of Hispania. Indicative of this new spirit is the famous "Praise of Spain"
with which he begins the *History*: "Of all the lands which stretch from the West
to India, you are the most beautiful, O Spain, sacred and ever-blessed mother
of leaders and of nations."
    During the early period of Islamic domination the writings of Christian his-

torians appear sketchy and generally repeat their sources in an impoverished annalistic prose or, at best, resemble the epitomes of Roman history. The earliest of these is the *Continuatio Hispana*, also known as the Mozarabic Chronicle of 754, which contains the chronicles of Idatius, John of Biclaro, and St. Isidore. Arab historians, on the other hand, have been recognized for their detail, variety of sources, and lively anecdotal narrative. The great flourishing of historiography coincides with the caliphate of Cordova, which in its greatest moment became the cultural center of the Islamic world. Many of these works have been lost or survive in fragments. The first general history of Spain by a Muslim was that of Ahmad ibn Muhammad al Razi (d. 955). Later known as the *Crónica del moro Rasis* (Chronicle of the Moor Rasis), it was incorporated into the *Crónica de 1344* (Chronicle of 1344). His son, Isa al-Razi, compiled the *Anales palatinos del Califa de Córdoba* (Annals of the Caliph Al-Hakam II). From the same period have come the *Historia de los jueces de Córdoba* (History of the Judges of Cordova) by Al-Khusani (d. 971) and the *Historia de la conquista de España de Abenalcotía el cordobés* (History of the Conquest of Spain) by Ibn al-Qutiyya (d. 977), who was of Gothic ancestry.

Historians have long recognized that the revival of the Isidorean perspective in historiography is peculiar to Asturias and León. This aspect of neo-Gothicism was clearly in the interest of the early Reconquest and is present in the *Crónica Albedense* (Chronicle of Albelda, c. 883), which dedicates sections to universal history, Arab history, and to the kings of Asturias, León, and Navarre as the heirs of the Visigoths. Neo-Gothic ideals are confirmed in the *Crónica de Alfonso III* (Chronicle of Alphonse III) which, in scope, is exclusively national. Initiating the tradition of official, royal chronicles, it spans the reigns of Wamba to Ordoño I (672–866). *Sampiro: su crónica* (Chronicle of Sampiro, d. 1041) written by the bishop of Astorga, though sorely lacking in detail, is a principal source for the tenth c. and for the events surrounding the famous count of Castile, Fernán González. The so-called *Historia Silense* (c. 1115), believed to be the work of a Mozarab in Toledo, records events until the death of Fernando I (1065). Noteworthy are its condemnation of the Goths for their responsibility in the destruction and loss of Spain, and its decidedly anti-French spirit. Diego Gelmírez (d. 1140), archbishop of Santiago de Compostela, commissioned the extensive *Historia compostelana* (History of Compostela) to record his own achievements and to document the privileges of his diocese. A storehouse of details and documents, it relates the discovery of the tomb of St. James, whose cult would be a major phenomenon in the history of medieval Spain. The eulogistic *Chronica Adefonsi Imperatoris* (c. 1147) divides its attention between Alphonse VII's wars with other Christian princes, chiefly Alphonse I of Aragon, and the wars with the Muslims. It concludes with the incomplete Poem of Almería, which compares Alphonse with Charlemagne and is frequently noted for its controversial yet suggestive reference to the Cid as a hero in song. Of considerable importance for our understanding of the *Song of the Cid* (*Cantar del Cid*) is the *Historia Roderici* (c. 1144), the biography of Rodrigo Díaz de Vivar. While it is somewhat fragmentary, focusing on the two banishments of Rodrigo, his service to the Moorish king of Saragossa, and his subsequent victories in the eastern regions of the peninsula, it is undoubtedly the most trustworthy account of the Cid.

A new phase in Spanish historiography begins with the *Crónica Najerense* (Chronicle of Najera, c. 1160), which relates events from Creation to the reign of Alphonse VI. According to Benito Sánchez Alonso, a clear historical perspective emerges that is universal for antiquity; national for the Visigothic period; and Leonese-Castilian for the Reconquest. Moreover, among its numerous sources is material from several *chansons de geste*. The incorporation of poetic sources may lessen the historical accuracy of such chronicles, yet they remain one of our most valuable resources for the study of the epic and the age.

Historiography advances clearly, respective of organization and variety of sources, in the first half of the thirteenth century with Lucas de *Túy (d. 1249), called *el Tudense*, and Archbishop Rodrigo *Jiménez de Rada (d. 1247), known as *el Toledano*. Lucas's *Chronicon Mundi* (Chronicle of the World) covers, in four books, the history from creation to the conquest of Cordova. Much more ambitious and influential among later historians was Archbishop Rodrigo's *De rebus Hispaniae* (History of Spain or History of the Goths), which studies the Visigoths, the Islamic conquest, and the Reconquest up to his own time. The number of sources used by the *Toledano* as well as his integration of Arabic chronicles has led to his recognition as the foremost historian before *Alphonse X, the Learned. In addition to forming the core of Alphonse's History of Spain, the *Toledano* was widely diffused in several vernacular versions and amplifications well into the fourteenth c. The anonymous *Crónica latina de los reyes de Castilla* (Latin Chronicle of the Kings of Castile) belonging to this period is noted for its accuracy.

The use of the vernacular is firmly established by Alphonse X, the Learned and his collaborators in the *Primera crónica general de España* (History of Spain) and the *Grande e general estoria* (General History of the World). Moreover, it freed Spanish historiography from a limited public. It was, as Diego Catalán has noted, a decisive step in the secularization of Spanish history, which henceforth would be a more vital component of medieval Spanish culture. The initial efforts of Alphonse's collaborators focused on translations (1250–60) and continued the tradition of the "school of translators" in Toledo. The historical compilations were produced between 1269 and 1280. Alphonse builds on the work of his immediate predecessors, Lucas de Túy and, especially, Rodrigo Jiménez de Rada, yet he extends considerably his use of literary sources. The first work underway was the History of Spain, which begins with Genesis and ends with the reign of Fernando III, his father. Though not completed until c. 1289 during the reign of Sancho IV, evidence indicates that the Alfonsine plan was complete in a rough draft. The part dealing with the Reconquest, which was completed by Sancho's collaborators, underwent, according to Diego Catalán, changes which did not affect the content, but were limited to amplifications and style. Alphonse's failure to finalize the History of Spain is explained by the diversion of his efforts to other projects, in particular, the General History of the World, which incorporated an even greater number and variety of sources. It too, in spite of its enormity, fell short of Alphonse's design, for it breaks off at the birth of the Virgin.

The History of Spain became the canon for historians well into the fourteenth c. The first example of this is the *Crónica abreviada* (1330–32; Abridged Chronicle) by Alphonse's nephew Don *Juan Manuel. The principal continuer of Alfonsine historiography was the Portuguese, Pedro of Barcelos, the illegitimate son of King Dinis. His *Crónica Geral de Espanha de 1344* (Chronicle of 1344— named for the year of its undertaking) was based primarily on an earlier Galician-Portuguese translation of the History of Spain, and was, in turn, translated again into Castilian; it was subsequently more influential in the fifteenth and sixteenth centuries than the Alfonsine History of Spain. The *Crónica de veinte reyes* (Chronicle of Twenty Kings) and the *Crónica de los reyes de Castilla* (Chronicle of the Kings of Castile) belong to this period and are derived from a new lost abridgment of the History of Spain.

Also in the Alfonsine tradition is the Aragonese *La Grant Crónica de Espanya* (Great Chronicle of Spain) compiled toward the end of the fourteenth c. under the auspices of Juan *Fernández de Heredia (d. 1396). While they may have been conceived as part of this Alfonsine tradition, the so-called *Crónicas de los reyes de Castilla: Alfonso X, Sancho IV, Fernando IV* (Three Chronicles of Alphonse X, Sancho IV and Ferdinand IV) are probably the work of one author, Fernán Sánchez de Valladolid, commissioned by Alphonse XI. They have all been criticized for their inaccuracies, bias, and lack of style. The *Gran crónica de Alfonso XI* (Great Chronicle of Alphonse XI, 1376–79) is notable for the interpolation of the Poem of *Alphonse XI by Rodrigo Yáñez.

Independent are the Catalan chronicles of this period which are considered to be among the monuments of the Middle Ages. The *Crònica de Jaume I* (Chronicle of James I), Desclot's *Crónica del rey de Aragón* (*Chronicle of the Reign of King Pedro III of Aragón,* 1928–34), the *Crònica* (Chronicle) of Ramón *Muntaner, and the *Crónica del rey de Aragón* (Chronicle of Pedro IV), written by the king in collaboration with Bernat Desclot, are the testimony of a dynasty recording the feats of the crown of Aragon in its expansion into the Mediterranean. They use a variety of sources ranging from Provençal *chansons de geste* to eyewitness accounts and royal documents. The *Crónica de San Juan de la Peña* (Chronicle of St. John de la Peña, c. 1359), commissioned by Pedro IV with versions in Latin, Catalan, and Aragonese, is a history of the kings of Aragon and the counts of Barcelona.

The fifteenth c. produced a plethora of historical writings throughout the peninsula. Chroniclers essayed new genres, including individual and collective biographies and travel books. The partisan writing in many of these chronicles reflects the political factionalism which prevailed during the greater part of the century. The court of John II, noted for its literary patronage, produced a chronicle of his reign by several authors, in particular, Alvar García de Santa María.

Equally important for this reign is the Falconer's Chronicle by Pedro Carrillo de Huete, which was later reworked by Lope Barrientos. Diego Enríquez del Castillo's Chronicle is an apologia for Henry IV, who, nonetheless, is denounced by Alfonso de *Palencia in his *Gesta Hispaniensia*. The chroniclers of the Catholic Kings include Diego de *Valera, Andrés *Bernáldez, and Hernando de *Pulgar.

The noteworthy contributions in the realm of individual biography are the *Crónica de Don Pero Niño* (c. 1446; *Chronicle of the Deeds of Pero Niño*, 1928); the *Crónica de Alvaro de Luna* (c. 1460; Chronicle of Alvaro de Luna), a justification of the actions of the outstanding figure of the period; and the *Hechos del Condestable Miguel Lucas de Iranzo* (c. 1471; Deeds of the Constable Miguel Lucas de Iranzo), attributed to Pedro de *Escavias. The initiator of collective biography is Fernán *Pérez de Guzmán with his brief *Generaciones y semblanzas* (1450; Portraits and Sketches), which in turn inspired Hernando del Pulgar's *Claros varones de Castilla* (c. 1485; Illustrious Men of Castile). The first original travel book in Spanish is the *Historia del gran Tamorlán* (Narrative of the Embassy to the Court of Timour by Ruy Gonzálo de *Clavijo). From the court of John II comes the *Andancas e viajes* (1454; Travels and Adventures) of Pero *Tafur.

While several historians wrote in Latin (Alonso de *Cartagena, Rodrigo Sánchez de Arévalo, Alfonso de *Palencia), a truly humanist perspective is considered to be a late development appearing first in writers like Joan Margarit (d. 1484), bishop of Gerona, and Gonzalo García de Santa María with his Latin *Crónica de Juan II* (Chronicle of John II of Aragon). *See also* Edad Media, Literatura de la; Escuela de Traductores de Toledo.

BIBLIOGRAPHY

Primary Texts

Alfonso X, the Learned. *Primera crónica general*. Ed. R. Menéndez Pidal. Intr. D. Catalán. 3rd ed. 2 vols. Madrid: Gredos and Seminario Menéndez Pidal, 1982.

———. *Grande e general estoria*. Part I. Ed. Antonio García Solalinde. Madrid: Centro de Estudios Históricos, 1930. Part II. Ed. Antonio García Solalinde, Lloyd A. Kasten, Victor R. B. Oelschlager. Madrid: CSIC, 1957; 1961.

———. *General estoria*. Parts I and IV. *Concordances and Texts of the Royal Scriptorium Manuscripts of Alfonso X, el Sabio*. Ed. Lloyd A. Kasten and John J. Nitti. Madison: Hispanic Seminary, 1978.

Al-Khushani, Muhammad ibn Harith. *Historia de los jueces de Córdoba*. Ed. and Tr. Julián Ribera. Madrid: Ibérica, 1914.

Anonymous. *Chronica Adefonsi Imperatoris*. Ed. Luis Sánchez Belda. Madrid: CSIC, 1950.

Anonymous. *Chronica Adefonsi Imperatoris*. Spanish tr. M. Laza Palacio. In *La España del poeta de "Mio Cid." Comentarios a la "Crónica de Alfonso VII."* Malaga: n.p., 1964.

———. *Continuatio Hispana*. In *Monumenta Germaniae Historica Auct. Antiq. XI, Chronica Minora* 2:323–68.

———. *Crónica Albeldense*. In *España Sagrada*. 13: 417–66.

CRÓNICAS

466

CRÓNICAS

———. *Crónica anónima de Abd al-Rahman III al-Nasir*. Ed. and tr. E. Levi-Provençal and Emilio García Gómez. Madrid: CSIC, 1950.

———. *Crónica de Alfonso III*. Ed. A. Ubieto Arteta. Valencia: Textos Medievales, 1961.

———. *Crónica de Álvaro de Luna*. Ed. Juan de Mata Carriazo. Madrid: Espasa-Calpe, 1940.

———. *Crónica de Juan II*. See Pérez de Guzmán.

———. *Crónicas de los reyes de Castilla: Alfonso X, Sancho IV, Fernando IV*. BAE 66.

———. *Crónica de 1344*. Ed. Diego Catalán and María Soledad de Andrés. Madrid: Seminario Menéndez Pidal and Gredos, 1971.

———. *Crónica del moro Rasis*. Ed. D. Catalán and M. Soledad de Andrés. Madrid: Gredos and Seminario Menéndez Pidal, 1982.

———. *La traducción gallega de la Crónica General y de la Crónica de Castilla*. 2 vols. Ed. Ramón Lorenzo. Orense: Instituto de Estudios Orensanos, 1975–77.

———. *Crónica latina de los reyes de Castilla*. Ed. María D. Cabanes Pecourt. Valencia: Textos Medievales 11, 1964.

———. *Crónica Najerense*. Ed. Antonio Ubieto Arteta. Valencia: Textos Medievales, 1966.

———. *Gran crónica de Alfonso XI*. Ed. Diego Catalán. Madrid: Seminario Menéndez Pidal and Gredos, 1977.

———. *Historia Compostelana*. In *España Sagrada*. 20:1–598.

———. *Historia Compostelana*. Spanish tr. by M. Suárez. Intro., notes by J. Campelo. Santiago de Compostela: n.p., 1950.

———. *Historia Silense*. Ed. Justo Pérez de Urbel and A. González Ruiz-Zorrilla. Madrid: CSIC, 1960.

Barrientos, Lope. *Refundición de la Crónica del Halconero*. Ed. Juan de Mata Carriazo. Madrid: Espasa-Calpe, 1946.

Bernáldez, Andrés. *Memorias del reinado de los Reyes Católicos*. Ed. M. Gómez Moreno and J. de Mata Carriazo. Madrid: RAH, 1962.

Carrillo de Huete, Pedro. *Crónica del halconero de Juan II*. Ed. Juan de Mata Carriazo. Madrid: Espasa-Calpe, 1946.

Clavijo, Ruy González de. *Historia del gram Tamorlán*. Ed. Francisco López-Estrada. Madrid: CSIC, 1943.

Desclot, Bernat. *Crònica*. Ed. M. Coll i Alentorn. 5 vols. Barcelona: Barcino, 1949–51.

Díez de Games, Gutierre. *Crónica de Don Pero Niño, Conde de Buelna*. Ed. Juan de Mata Carriazo. Madrid: Espasa-Calpe, 1940.

Enríquez del Castillo, Diego. *Crónica del rey Don Enrique IV*. BAE 70.

Escavias, Pedro de. *Hechos del Condestable Miguel Lucas de Iranzo*. Ed. Juan de Mata Carriazo. Madrid: Espasa-Calpe, 1940.

Fernández de Heredia, Juan. *La Grant Crónica de Espanya. Libros I-II*. Ed. Regina af Geijerstam. Uppsala: Studia Romanica Upsaliensia, 1964.

Garcia de Santa María, Alvar. See Pérez de Guzmán.

Ibn al-Qutiyya, Muhammad ibn 'Umar. *Historia de la conquista de España de Abenalcotía el cordobés*. Trans. Julián Ribera. Madrid: Real Academia de la Historia, 1926.

Idatius. *Cronicón de Idacio*. Trans. Marcelo Macías. Orense: Otero, 1906.

Isa al-Razi. *Anales palatinos del califa de Córdoba al-Hakam II*. Trans. Emilio Garcia Gómez. Madrid: Sociedad de Estudios y Publicaciones, 1967.

Jaume I. *Crònica de Jaume I*. Ed. J. M. de Casacuberta and E. Bague. 9 vols. Barcelona: Barcino, 1926–62.

Jiménez de Rada, Rodrigo. *De rebus Hispaniae*. Ed. María D. Cabanes Pecourt. Valencia: Textos Medievales 22, 1968.

John of Biclaro. *Chronicon*. *Monumenta Germaniae Historica*. Auct. Antiq. XI, Chronica Minora, 2; 211–20.

Juan Manuel. *Crónica abreviada*. Ed. Raymond and Mildred Grismer. Minneapolis: Burgess, 1958.

López de Ayala, Pedro. *Crónica del rey Don Pedro*. BAE 66.

——. *Crónicas de los reyes de Castilla: Enrique II, Juan I, Enrique III*. BAE 68.

Lucas de Túy. *Chronicon Mundi. Crónica de España*. Ed. and Spanish tr. Julio Puyol. Madrid: RABM, 1926.

Muntaner, Ramon. *Crònica*. Ed. J. M. Casacuberta and M. Coll i Alentorn. Barcelona: Barcino, 1927–52.

Palencia, Alonso de. *Crónica de Enrique IV*. Trans. Antonio Paz y Melia. 5 vols. Madrid: Colección de Autores Castellanos, 1904–9.

Pedro, conde de Barcelos. *Crónica Geral de Espanha de 1344*. Ed. Luis Lindley Cintra. Lisbon: Academia Portuguesa da História, 1951.

Pérez de Guzmán, Fernán. *Crónica de Juan II*. BAE 68.

——. *Generaciones y semblanzas*. Ed. R. B. Tate. London: Tamesis, 1965.

Pulgar, Fernando del. *Claros varones de Castilla*. Ed. R. B. Tate. Oxford: Oxford UP, 1971.

——. *Crónica de los Reyes Católicos*. Ed. Juan de Mata Carriazo. Madrid: Espasa-Calpe, 1943.

Sampiro. *Sampiro: su crónica y la monarquía leonesa en el siglo XI*. Ed. Justo Pérez de Urbel. Madrid: CSIC, 1952.

Tafur, Pedro. *Andanças e viajes*. Ed. José M. Ramos. Madrid: Hernando, 1934.

Valera, Diego de. *Crónica de los Reyes Católicos*. Ed. Juan de Mata Carriazo. Madrid: Molina, 1927.

English Translations

Clavijo, Ruy González de. *Embassy to Tamerlane*. Tr. Guy Le Strange. London: Routledge, 1928.

Desclot, Bernat. *Chronicle of the Reign of Pedro III of Aragon*. Tr. F. L. Critchlow. Princeton: Princeton UP, 1928–34.

Díez de Games, Gutierre. *The Unconquered Knight: A Chronicle of the Deeds of Pero Niño, Count of Buelna*. Tr. J. Evans. London and New York: Routledge, 1928.

Isidore of Seville. *History of the Kings of the Goths, the Vandals, and Suevi*. Tr. G. Donini and G. Ford. 2nd ed. Leyden: Brill, 1970.

Jaume I. *The Chronicles of James I, King of Aragon*. Trans. John Forster. London: Chapman and Hall, 1883.

Orosius, Paulus. *Seven Books of History against the Pagans*. Tr. Irving Woodworth Raymond. New York: Columbia UP, 1936.

Pedro IV of Aragon. *Chronicle. Pere III of Catalonia (Pedro IV of Aragón)*. Tr. Mary Hillgarth. 2 vols. Toronto: Pontifical Institute of Mediaeval Studies, 1980.

Tafur, Pedro. *Travels and Adventures*. Trans. Malcolm Letts. London: Routledge; New York: Harper, 1926.

Criticism

Armistead, Samuel G. ''New Perspectives in Alfonsine Historiography.'' *Romance Philology*. 20 (1966); 204–17.

Avalle-Arce, Juan B. *El cronista Pedro de Escavias*. UNCSRLL 127. Chapel Hill: U of North Carolina P, 1972.

Catalán, Diego. *De Alfonso X al Conde de Barcelos*. Madrid: Gredos, 1962.

――――. "El Toledano romanzado y las estorias del fecho de los godos del siglo XV." In *Estudios dedicados a James Homer Herriott*. Ed. Lloyd Kasten. Madison: U of Wisconsin, 1966. 9–102.

――――. *La tradición manuscrita en la Crónica de Alfonso XI*. Madrid: Gredos, 1974.

――――. "Don Juan Manuel ante el modelo alfonsí: testimonio de la Crónica abreviada." In *Don Juan Manuel Studies*. Ed. Ian Macpherson. London: Tamesis, 1977. 17–51.

Deyermond, A. D. *A Literary History of Spain. The Middle Ages*. London: Benn; New York: Barnes and Noble, 1971.

Eisenberg, Daniel. "The *General estoria*: Sources and Source Treatment." *Zeitschrift für Romanische Philologie* 80 (1973); 206–27.

Hillgarth, J. N. *The Spanish Kingdoms (1250–1516)*. 2 vols. Oxford: Clarendon, 1978.

Lomax, Derek W. "Rodrigo Jiménez de Rada como historiador." *Actas del quinto Congreso Internacional de Hispanistas*. Bordeaux: Presse Universitaire, 1977. 587–92.

Martínez, Salvador. "Tres leyendas heroicas de la *Najerense* y sus relaciones con la épica castellana." *Anuario de Letras* 9 (1971); 115–77.

Meregalli, F. *Cronisti e viaggiatori castigliani del quattrocento (1400–1474)*. Milan: Instituto Cisalpino, 1957.

O'Callaghan, Joseph F. *A History of Medieval Spain*. Ithaca, NY, and London: Cornell UP, 1975.

Rico, Francisco. "Las letras del siglo XII en Galicia, León y Castilla." *Ábaco*. 2 (1969): 11–91.

――――. *Alfonso el Sabio y la General estoria*. Barcelona: Ariel, 1972.

Russell, J. C. "Chronicles of Medieval Spain." *HR* 6 (1938): 218–35.

Sánchez Alonso, Benito. *Historia de la historiografía española*. 2nd ed. Madrid: CSIC, 1947.

Tate, R. B. "A Humanistic Biography of John II of Aragon." *BHS* 39 (1962): 1–15.

――――. *Ensayos sobre la historiografía peninsular del siglo XV*. Madrid: Gredos, 1970.

――――. "López de Ayala, humanist historian?" *HR* 25 (1957): 157–74.

――――. "Mythology in Spanish Historiography of the Middle Ages and the Renaissance." *HR* 22 (1954): 1–18.

――――. "Nebrija the Historian." *BHS* 34 (1957): 125–46.

――――. "Rodrigo Sánchez de Arévalo (1404–1470) and His *Compendiosa Historica Hispanica*." *Nottingham Medieval Studies* 4 (1960): 58–80.

――――. "The *Anecephaleosis* of Alfonso García de Santa María, Bishop of Burgos (1435–1456)." In *Hispanic Studies in Honor of González Llubera*. Oxford: n.p., 1959. 387–401.

――――. "The *Paralipomenon Hispaniae* of Joan Margarit, Cardinal Bishop of Gerona." In *Bulletin of the John Rylands Library* 34 (1951): 137–65.

Porter Conerly

**CRONICONES.** The term *cronicones* (annals) as distinguished from *\*crónicas* (chronicles) has not, in the past, been applied consistently or rigorously. Notwithstanding, the *cronicón* (late Latin *chronicon*) is essentially a year-by-year record of events which, for the most part, is devoid of historical criteria. The spare and sketchy narratives which are associated with the *cronicones* are, to a certain extent, characteristic of Christian historians in general during the early period of Islamic domination until the twelfth c. Typical of these are: the *Continuato hispana*, or the Mozarabic Chronicle of 754; the *Crónica Albedense*, or Chronicle of Albelda (c. 883); and *Sampiro. Su Crónica*, the Chronicle of Sampiro (d. 1041). An extreme example in the early twelfth c. is the Chronicle of Pelayo, bishop of Oviedo (1101–29). It ignores the political importance of Ferdinand I and the ensuing dynastic struggle as well as the role of Alphonse VI in the capture of Toledo. Pelayo, who appears oblivious of the Cid, is chiefly concerned with the diocese of Oviedo. *Cronicones*, which continued to be written well into the fourteenth c., constituted valuable sources for later chronicles. The customary attention which is given to dates in citing a battle, a natural disaster, the death of a saint, and so forth, and also to royal genealogies, makes these annals useful for establishing the chronology of events during this period. There are additional characteristics shared by many *cronicones*. The point of departure is usually some significant event, frequently the birth of Christ or the entrance of the Goths into Spain. Another could be an important battle or the taking of a city by the Muslims. Outside of Catalonia, time is generally reckoned according to the Spanish or Roman era. The *cronicones* may evidence multiple authorship and several stages of compilation. There is a demonstrated interest in ecclesiastic and monastic affairs. Many of these annals were collected and published by Father Enrique *Flórez and his successors in the series *La España sagrada* (Sacred Spain). The best survey of the *cronicones* is found in Benito Sánchez Alonso's *Historia de la historiografía española*.

From the region of Castile came the first *Anales castellanos* (Castilian Annals), which began with the spread of Islam and ended with the celebrated victory of Ramiro II at Simancas (939). The second *Anales castellanos* reached to the reign of Alphonse VII (1126) and were later continued to the year 1219 and translated into Spanish as the first *Anales toledanos* (Annals of Toledo). The *Chronicon Villarense*, generally known as the *Liber Regum* and considered the first vernacular chronicle, was compiled between 1194 and 1211. It is written in Aragonese and offers a genealogy from Adam to Christ; the succession of Roman emperors and Visigothic kings; and the Leonese kings of the Reconquest with their counterparts in Navarre, Aragon, and France. Under the title *Efemérides riojanas* are gathered the *Chronicon Ambrosianum*, *Chronicon Burgense*, and the *Annales Compostellani*. The *Compostellani*, though found in Santiago de Compostela, deal only with the events of Castile and Navarre; it reaches to the capture of Seville (1248). In all likelihood, a *Morisco compiled the second *Anales toledanos*, which holds no relation to the first of this name and is noteworthy for its interest in the Muslims: time is reckoned from the hegira instead of in accordance with the Spanish era; important Christian victories are omitted; and the lexicon is rare. The *Cronicón del Cerratense*, compiled by the Dominican Rodrigo del Cerrato, spans the years 618 to 1252, the death of

Fernando III. The first *Cronicón de Cardeña* begins with the settling of Amaya (856) and reaches the year 1327. Oddly enough, there is no mention of the Cid. The second *Cronicón de Cardeña* summarizes the successive reigns from Alfonso II to Fernando IV (791–1312). The third *Anales toledanos* reaches the year 1391.

The first significant annals from Catalonia are the *Chronicon Rivipullense* (1191) from the monastery at Ripoll, whose point of departure is the appointment of Pontius Pilate. Its twelfth-c. chronology is especially detailed; as with most chronicles of eastern provenance, it favors the computation of years from the birth of Christ rather than according to the Spanish era. In this respect the *Necrologio de Roda* or *Chronicon Rotense* is different, making use of the Spanish era. It is more than a necrology, for it provides summaries of the reigns of the kings of Navarre from Sancho I Garcés (925) to Sancho III Garcés (1035); it continues with the kings of Aragon until 1209. The *Chronicon Dertusense* has been linked to the *Chronicon Rivipullense*; it uses the Spanish era together with the Christian era. The *Chronicon Ulianense* records events in Aragon during the twelfth and thirteenth centuries. The two *Chronicones Barcinonenses* cover the years 985–1308, beginning with the Islamic conquest of Barcelona. The *Chronicon* or *Necrologium Gerundense* (1102–1311) is based on two necrologies of ecclesiastic interest. The most heterogeneous annals, according to Sánchez Alonso, are *Chronicon Dertusense* (1323), which is written in Provençal and concerned with the events in Catalonia and Aragon.

Events from Galicia and Portugal are recorded in the *Chronicon Complutense*, so-called for having been found in Alcalá de Henares; it ends with the death of Fernando I (1065). Three *Chronicones Conimbricenses* list events from the twelfth century. The *Chronicon Lusitanum* begins with the migration of the Goths and their arrival in Spain and focuses eventually on Portugal, extolling the reign of Afonso I Henriques. The *Chronicon Alcobacense*, beginning with the birth of Afonso I and concluding in 1355, is devoted exclusively to Portugal. The fourth *Chronicon Conimbricense* (1326) begins with the Goths and continues sporadically; the greatest detail is given to the first quarter of the fourteenth century. The fifth *Chronicon Conimbricense* is written in Portuguese and spans the years 1296–1406; its entries are more amply explained than in most annals. *See also* Edad Media, Literatura de la.

BIBLIOGRAPHY

Criticism

Sánchez Alonso, B. *Historia de la historiografía española*. 3 vols. Madrid: CSIC, 1941–50.

                                                                    Porter Conerly


**CRUSAT, Paulina** (1900, Barcelona– ), Spanish novelist, poet and critic. Most of her fiction appeared during the 1950s and 1960s. *Mundo pequeño y fingido* (1953; Small, Feigned World), subjective and non-mimetic, rejects the documentary style of social realism then in vogue, portraying a group of aristocrats belonging to the first era of *Romanticism, who meet in Switzerland early in the past c. An excellent psychological analysis expresses Crusat's belief in the essential similarity of human problems throughout time. Two linked novels, jointly titled *Historia de un viaje* (Story of a Voyage), are *Aprendiz de persona* (1956; Apprentice Person) and *Las ocas blancas* (1959; The White Geese); they work with a probable autobiographical basis, describing the childhood and adolescence of the female protagonist in turn-of-the-century Barcelona.

BIBLIOGRAPHY

Primary Texts

*Aprendiz de persona*. Barcelona: Destino, 1956.
*Las ocas blancas*. Barcelona: Destino, 1959.
*Relaciones solitarias*. Barcelona: Plaza y Janés, 1965.

Janet Pérez

**CRUZ, Juan de la.** *See* Juan de la Cruz, San

**CRUZ, Ramón de la** (1731, Madrid–1794, Madrid), dramatist. Don Ramón de la Cruz Cano y Olmedilla was one of the most popular and prolific writers for the Spanish stage during the second half of the eighteenth c. Born to a family of modest circumstances but higher aspirations, he entered government service in 1759 as a functionary in the accounting section of the Justice Department, where he served until his death. As a literary figure he received encouragement from the Duke of Alba, but it was in the Countess of Benavente, in whose palace he lived and worked, that he found a strong patron for his talent. In spite of his aristocratic supporters and the fame which his works gained for him, Cruz died in relative poverty. His wife, Dona Margarita Beatriz de Magán, petitioned his superiors in the government for financial aid in paying for the funeral; the Countess of Benavente granted Cruz's wife and daughter a pension in recognition of his long service to the Benavente family.

Cruz began his literary career in the neo-classic atmosphere fomented by the Conde de Aranda during the 1750s. A member of the Academy of Arcadians (*Academia), using the name Larissio Dianeo, he counted among his early backers the journalist Mariano Nipho, with whom he would later break over questions of popular style. In his formation as a dramatist Cruz began by translating or adapting a number of foreign works in the classic mold, including *Bajazet* by Racine, *Eugénie* by Beaumarchais, and *L'Ecossaise* (The Scots Woman) of Voltaire; Apostolo Zeno's *Sesostris*, and Metastasio's *Aecio*. He even produced a version of *Hamlet*, taken not from the original English, but from the French translation by Ducis. In his prologue to *Quien complace a la deidad acierta a sacrificar* (1757; Whoever Pleases the Gods Succeeds in Sacrifice), Cruz criticized the practice of writing solely for the entertainment of the public, the carelessness of style found in traditional theater, and the shameless spectacle of the *sainete, the short, comic pieces with which he would later find his greatest success. He did point out, however, that although he would like to write in the new neo-classic style, to bring honor to Spain and to be an example to other Spanish dramatists, the classic forms of pure tragedy and comedy would never become popular in Spain. His insight into the public's tastes in theatrical entertainment and his developing common-sense approach to the problem of writing for that audience soon led him away from the neo-classic school. The decision to embrace popular theater, and his growing fame in this field, earned him the undying enmity of the neo-classicists. Cruz was embroiled in continual polemics with Nicolás Fernández de *Moratín, who attributed the failure of his plays *La Petimetra* (1762; The Society Lady) and *Lucrecia* (1763) to Cruz's enormous influence over performers in Madrid. Both Nipho and Tomás de *Iriarte wrote attacks against Cruz and his works, and considered him a major obstacle to the success of neo-classic drama in Spain. A more moderate viewpoint was expressed by Leandro Fernández de *Moratín, who saw in Cruz a natural comic talent, and pointed to his ability to portray contemporary social customs and character types in his comic vignettes.

Cruz's transformation from neo-classic sympathizer to popularist can be seen in two genres: the *sainete* and related short, comic works which earned him the title "Maestro de hacer sainetes" (Master Sainete-Writer) from colleague Luceno; and the *zarzuela*. What had begun as a courtly form of music drama with dialogue, whose protagonists were gods and goddesses of Greek and Roman mythology, was transformed by Cruz, and composer Rodríguez de Hita, into a truly native lyric-dramatic genre which portrayed everyday people, using traditional Spanish themes. Two works, *Las Segadoras de Vallecas* (1768; The Reapers from Vallecas) and *Las labradoras de Murcia* (1769; The Working Women from Murcia), are considered landmark achievements in the *zarzuela*.

It was as "Master Sainete-Writer," however, that Cruz earned his place among the principal figures of Spanish *theater. Attempts to classify the enormous variety and prodigious quantity of *sainetes*—Cruz wrote over 400—have resulted in two distinct approaches: by subject (Durán, Hartzenbusch, Arturo García) and by structure (Pérez Galdós, Gatti). Categories of the first method generally include: (1) works depicting specific locales and customs of Madrid, such as *El Rastro por la mañana* (The Fleamarket by Morning) or *La pradera de San Isidro* (The Meadow of San Isidro); (2) *sainetes* satirizing social mores or particular character types, as in *El Sarao* (The Dance) and *La presumida burlada* (The Presumptuous Woman Undone); (3) works in which Cruz defends himself against his critics, as in *El pueblo quejoso* (The Nagging Public) or *¿Cuál es tu enemigo?* (Which One Is Your Enemy?); and (4) works which parody classic tragedy, such as *Manolo*, *Inesilla la de Pinto*, and *La Zara*. José Gatti in his introduction to his edition of *Doce Sainetes* has suggested a bipartite division based on structural features: (1) those "which lack an organic plot: the author is content with displaying a parade of characters in a succession of scenes and dialogues''; and (2) "*sainetes* which outline a possible comedy'' (12). The first category embraces the majority of the works; the second describes those which approach the structure and continuity of a full-length comedy, such as *Los picos de oro* (The Gadflies).

The general view of Cruz's *sainetes* has been that they are an accurate reflection of life in Madrid during the latter half of the eighteenth c. Cruz stated that he tried to copy faithfully the people and traditions of Madrid, but he also affirmed the satirical intentions of much of his work. Cotarelo points out that, by the end of the 1760s, Cruz had established a clear pattern of portraying society with a definite satirical purpose: to ridicule and condemn society's vices and defects. In the majority of Cruz's *sainetes*, their comic atmosphere belies the concept of a mere portrayal of Madrid's society and its customs. The derisive nature of comedy tends to reduce to the absurd and expel any element in society not in keeping with the norm. Cruz's *sainetes* select those excesses and aberrations in Madrid's social order and lay bare their faults. In that sense the society portrayed is not always the everyday world but a special "comic" world full of eccentrics and social outcasts. Through his comic view of society Cruz was successful in popularizing the very type of social criticism which the neo-classicists were unable to make work in their own dramatic style. While his critics discounted his works for their lack of cohesiveness, and especially for their plebeian style which forsakes poetic quality for comic effect, Cruz's *sainetes* are firmly rooted in the traditions of the minor theatrical genres, from the *pasos of Lope de *Rueda to the *entremeses of *Cervantes, *Quiñones and *Moreto, and the *sainetes* of Juan de Castro and *Cañizares. Cruz defended his own populist style by affirming that in order to reproduce faithfully the atmosphere inherent to the vices in society and ridicule them, "the poet should think like the sages and speak like the common people." That Cruz's works dominated the Madrid stage, both during his long career and on into the nineteenth c., attests to his affinity for and understanding of the society in which he lived.

Of the hundreds of *sainetes* and longer plays, only some 250 of the former and a handful of the latter have been published. Many of those *sainetes* appeared in *suelta* (pamphlet) form during the late eighteenth and early nineteenth centuries. Cruz himself published a valuable collection of his works in the *Teatro o colección de los sainetes y demás obras dramáticas de D. Ramón de la Cruz*. The collection includes nineteen full-length plays and a mere forty-seven *sainetes*. His own emphasis on the longer works shows his desire to be considered a more serious dramatist rather than a writer just of minor works. *See also* Theater in Spain.

BIBLIOGRAPHY

Primary Texts

"Cinco sainetes inéditos de Don Ramón de la Cruz con otro a él atribuido." Ed. C. E. Kany. *RH* 60 (1924): 40–185.
*Colección de sainetes, tanto impresos como inéditos, de D. Ramón de la Cruz*. Ed. A. Durán. 2 vols. Madrid: Yenes, 1843.
*Doce Sainetes*. Intro. J. F. Gatti. Barcelona: Labor, 1972.
"Más sainetes inéditos." Ed. C. Kany. *RH* 76 (1929): 360–571.
*Ocho sainetes inéditos de Don Ramón de la Cruz*. Ed. C. Kany. U of California Publications in Modern Philology 13, no. 1. Berkeley: U of California P, 1925.

*Sainetes I.* Ed. John C. Dowling. Madrid: Clásicos Castalia, 1981.
*Sainetes de Don Ramón de la Cruz en su mayoría inéditos.* Ed. Emilio Cotarelo y Mori. 2 vols. NBAE 23 and 26.
*Teatro, o Colección de los sainetes y demás obras dramáticas de D. Ramón de la Cruz y Cano.* 10 vols. Madrid: Imprenta Real, 1786–91.
*Ten Unedited Works by Ramón de la Cruz.* Ed., intro E. Coughlin, Madrid: Albatrós Hispanófila, 1987.

Criticism

Buck, D. C. "Comic Structures in the *Sainetes* of Ramón de la Cruz." *Studies in Eighteenth-Century Spanish Literature and Romanticism.* Ed. D. Barnette and L. Barnette. Newark, DE: Juan de la Cuesta, 1985. 65–76.
Caro Baroja, J. "Los majos." *CH* 299 (1978): 281–349.
Carrasco, H. "*Manolo*: Una tragedia paradójica." *Nueva Revista del Pacífico* 21 (1982): 31–45.
Cotarelo y Mori, E. *Don Ramón de la Cruz y sus obras: ensayo biográfico y bibliográfico.* Madrid: José Perales y Martínez, 1899.
Coughlin, E., Fernando Jiménez, and B. Jiménez. "Una obra inédita de D. Ramón de la Cruz: Su *Introducción* para la tragedia *Numancia destruida*." *BBMP* 53 (1977): 307–16.
Gatti, J. F. "La fuente literaria de *Inesilla la de Pinto*." *RFH* 5 (1943): 368–73.
———. "Las fuentes literarias de dos sainetes de don Ramón de la Cruz." *Filología* 1 (1949): 59–74.
———. "Sobre las fuentes de los sainetes de Ramón de la Cruz." *Studia Hispanica in Honorem R. Lapesa.* Ed. Eugenio de Bustos et al. 3 vols. Madrid: Gredos, 1972. 1; 243–49.
Hamilton, A. "Ramón de la Cruz's Debt to Molière." *Hispania* 4 (1921): 101–13.
———. "Ramon de la Cruz, Social Reformer." *RR* 12 (1921): 168–80.
———. *A Study of Spanish Manners, 1750–1800, from the Plays of Ramón de la Cruz.* U of Illinois Studies in Lge. and Lit. 11. Urbana: U of Illinois, 1926. 357–428.
Martín, Gregorio. "Cervantine Discretion in Ramón de la Cruz." *Estudios Ibero-Americanos* 4 (1978): 235–37.
Moore, John A. *Ramón de la Cruz.* TWAS 179. Boston: Twayne: 1972.
Pérez Galdós, B. "Don Ramón de la Cruz y su época." *Revista de España* 17 (1870): 200–227; 18 (1871): 27–52.
Salá, José M. "Ramón de la Cruz entre dos fuegos: literatura y público." *CH* 277–78 (1973): 350–60.
Vilches de Frutos, M. F. "El habla popular en los sainetes de Ramón de la Cruz." *Dieciocho* 6.1–2 (1983): 116–37.

Donald C. Buck

**CRUZ RUEDA, Ángel** (1888, ?–1961, ?), literary critic, novelist. His main critical works are *Examen crítico de B. López García y don Armando Palacio Valdés.* His novels include *Dolor sin fin* (Pain without End), *Huerto silencioso* (Quiet Garden), and *Leyendas de la Historia de España* (Legends of Spanish History), which won the National Prize for Literature in 1930. Cruz Rueda also published some didactic writings, a volume of essays titled *Peregrinaje de estío (por Aragón, Francia y Guipúzcoa)* (Summer Pilgrimage [through Aragon,

France and Guipuzcoa]), and completed various editions of *Azorín's works, with detailed biographies and bibliographies.

Isabel McSpadden

*CUADERNA VÍA* (Fourfold way), a poetic term. Also called *alejandrinos* and *mester de clerecía*, it is the most important "educated" verse form of the Middle Ages. Four-line stanzas, each line being composed of fourteen syllables with caesura precisely in the middle, comprise the *cuaderna vía*. Consonant rhyme unites each stanza. This form was used by *Berceo and in the *Libro de * Alexandre*, the *Libro de *Apolonio*, the *Poema de *Fernán González*, etc. Popular from the thirteenth to fifteenth centuries, it was eventually superseded by the poetry of *arte mayor. See also* Edad Media, Literatura de la; *mester de juglaría*.

BIBLIOGRAPHY

Primary Texts

Fitzgerald, J. D. *Versification of the 'cuaderna vía' as found in Berceo's.* . . . New York: Columbia UP, 1905.
Saavedra Molina, J. "El verso de clerecía." *Boletín de Filología* 6 (1950–51): n.p.

Maureen Ihrie

**CUBILLO DE ARAGÓN, Álvaro** (c. 1596?, Granada–1661, Madrid), minor poet and dramatist. He held the position of notary most of his life, first in Granada, later for the court in Madrid, where he moved in 1641. Father to eleven children, he found his economic woes a lifelong condition; much of his poetry was penned to cultivate potential patrons. By the early 1630s he was active as a dramatist. Author of about forty extant plays, he is often classified with the school of *Calderón, but many works attest also to the influence of Lope de *Vega. He wrote all types of drama, religious, "sword and cape farces," etc., but his best works, and the largest type, are historical. *La mayor venganza de honor* (before 1626; Honor's Greatest Revenge) is a worthy treatment of the legend which also inspired Lope's *Los comendadores de Córdoba*. *La tragedia del Duque de Verganza* (c. 1640?; The Tragedy of the Duke of Braganza) examines the bases of royal authority. Although Cubillo de Aragón's works are uneven and often suffer from clumsy plot development, they exhibit vigorous characterizations, witty dialogue, and moments of sparkling lyricism.

BIBLIOGRAPHY

Primary Texts

*La mayor venganza de honor*. In *Nuevo teatro de comedias varias de*. . . . Madrid: Imprenta Real, 1658.
*La tragedia del duque de Verganza*. In *El enano de las musas*. Madrid: María de Quiñones, 1654. Rpt. Hildesheim: Olms, 1971.
Seven plays are also found in BAE 51.

Criticism

Whitaker, S. B. *The Dramatic Works of Álvaro Cubillo de Aragón*. UNCSRLL 149. Chapel Hill: U of North Carolina P, 1975.

José Ortega

**CUÉLLAR, Jerónimo de** (1622, Madrid–after 1665,?), dramatist. A dramatist of the *Calderón school, Cuéllar lived at the Royal Court as a valet of King Philip IV, and was a knight of the Order of Santiago. His most notable plays include *Cada cual a su negocio* (Each One to His Own Business) and *El pastelero de Madrigal* (The Pastry-Cook of Madrigal), which treats the disappearance of the Portuguese King Sebastián, a theme also dramatized by *Zorrilla in *Traidor, inconfeso y mártir*.

BIBLIOGRAPHY

Primary Texts

*Cada cual a su negocio*. In BAE 47.
*El pastelero de Madrigal*. Madrid: Cuesto, n.d.

Deborah Compte

**CUENCA, Carlos Luis de** (1849, Madrid–1927, Avila), dramatist, librettist, poet. Aside from contributions to popular magazines, he wrote plays and *zarzuelas*, the most memorable of which is *La divina zarzuela* (1885; The Divine Zarzuela).

BIBLIOGRAPHY

Primary Text

*La divina zarzuela*. Madrid: Montoya, 1885.

*CUESTIÓN DE AMOR*, an anonymous narrative. The *Cuestión de amor de dos enamorados* (The Amatory Debate of Two Lovers) was written in Naples about 1508–12. It follows the pattern of Diego de *San Pedro's *Cárcel de amor*, but also includes intercalated poems. According to the anonymous author, "the major portion of this work is a true story; the work was composed by a gentleman who witnessed it all." The narrative depicts the courtly life of Naples and has been unjustly classified as a "drawing room chronicle." The names of the royal characters are disguised by pseudonyms and anagrams, many of which have been clarified by Benedetto Croce.

BIBLIOGRAPHY

Primary Text

*Cuestión de amor*. Ed. M. Menéndez y Pelayo. NBAE 7.

Criticism

Croce, B. *Di un antico romanzo spagnuolo relativo alla storia di Napoli: "La Questión de Amor."* Naples: n.p., 1894.

Deborah Compte

**CUETO, Leopoldo Augusto de** (1815, Cartagena–1901, Madrid), Marquis of Valmar, palace majordomo, poet, scholar and critic. Cueto's tragedy, *Cleopatra*, attempts to portray cultural history, but is not a significant contribution to the theater. His enduring literary contributions are his scholarly studies, such as *Bosquejo historicocrítico de la poesía castellana en el siglo XVIII* (1860; Historical-Critical Outline of Spanish Poetry in the Eighteenth C.), or his edition of *Alphonse X the Learned's "Cantigas."* He contributed to *Las mujeres españolas, portuguesas y americanas* (1872, 1873, 1876; Spanish, Portuguese and Latin-American Women), a three-volume *costumbrista* work which studies in some depth representatives of different geographic regions.

A member of the Spanish Academy (\*Academia Espada), and its treasurer at one point, he delivered before it a eulogy for the Duke of \*Rivas, his brother-in-law, in which he unjustly accused the duke of having plagiarized from Próspero Mérimée his immensely popular Romantic tragedy, *Don Alvaro. See also* Romanticism.

BIBLIOGRAPHY

Primary Texts

*Obras.* 4 vols. Madrid: Rivadeneyra, 1893–1906.

*Discurso necrológico literario en elogio del Excmo. Sr. duque de Rivas.* Madrid: Rivadeneyra, 1866.

Merry Wheaton

**CUEVA, Juan de la** (1550?, Seville–1610?, Seville), dramatist. As a precursor of Lope de \*Vega and the greatest c. of the Spanish theater, Cueva's principal importance lies in his pioneering use of national historical themes in his plays. Three of these—*La muerte del rey don Sancho y reto de Zamora* (The Death of King Sancho and the Challenge of Zamora—\*Sancho II de Castilla), *La libertad de España por Bernardo del Carpio* (The Liberation of Spain by Bernardo del Carpio), and *Los siete infantes de Lara* (The Seven Infants of Lara)—draw for the first time upon the considerable dramatic possibilities of the \*Romancero and the old chronicles (\*Crónicas); these three plays were published in Seville in 1583, together with eleven other plays of Cueva's, including three on classical themes.

In Leucino, the protagonist of Cueva's *El infamador* (The Slanderer), some critics have seen a forerunner of \*Tirso de Molina's Don Juan, antihero of *El burlador de Sevilla* (The Seducer of Seville). *El infamador* is clearly a prefigurement of the type of drama called *de capa y espada* (cloak and dagger), but unlike the later works, it includes startling supernatural and mythological elements. Cueva also used contemporary events as dramatic subjects; in *El saco de Roma* *y muerte de Borbón* (The Sacking of Rome and the Death of the Duke of Bourbon), he dramatized the invasion and pillaging of the Eternal City by Spanish troops in May of 1527. Cueva's talent as a playwright is inconsistent; he is capable of flat writing, his dramatic conceptions sometimes border on the ridiculous, and yet, in the midst of these flaws, we regularly find passages of considerable poetic merit.

Though his importance is primarily as a dramatic poet, Cueva also wrote lyrics (adopting and later rejecting the Petrarchan mode, like many of his contemporaries); especially notable is his *Coro febeo de romances historiales* (1587; Apollonian Chorus of Historical Ballads). He also produced allegorical, mythological, and didactic verse, with one attempt at an epic, the *Conquista de la Bética* (1603; Conquest of Beatica). A burlesque poem also survives: the *Batalla entre ranas y ratones* (Battle between the Frogs and the Mice). In a genealogical poem, *Historia de la Cueva* (History of the "Cave," that is, the family history of the Cuevas), the poet records a wealth of information about his antecedents.

Cueva's dramatic and poetic theories are expounded in his *Ejemplar poético* (1606; a treatise on poetry). He may have been the first, as he claims here, to have used Italianate meters in dramatic dialogue. *See also* Italian literary influences; *Infantes de Lara, Leyenda de los*; Don Juan, the Myth of.

BIBLIOGRAPHY

Primary Texts

*Bernardo del Carpio*. Ed. A. Watson. Exeter, Eng.: Exeter UP, 1974.
*Comedias y tragedias*. Ed. F. A. de Icaza. 2 vols. Madrid: Maestre, 1917.
*Conquista de la Bética: poema heroyco*. 2 vols. Madrid: Imprenta Real, 1795.
*El infamador. Los siete infantes de Lara. Ejemplar poético*. Ed. Fr. A. de Icaza. Clásicos Castellanos 60. Madrid: Espasa-Calpe, 1953.
*El infamador*. Ed. J. Caso González. Salamanca: Anaya, 1965.
*Los inventores de las cosas*. Ed. Beno Weiss and Louis C. Pérez. University Park: Pennsylvania State UP, 1980.
*Poèmes inédits, publiés d'après des manuscrits autographes conservés à Séville dans la Bibliothèque Colombine*. Ed. F. A. Wulff. Lund: C. W. K. Gleerup, 1887.

English Translation

"To Cassius" ["A Casio"]. In *Spanish Lyrics*. Tr. K. S. Craig. London: J & E Bumpus, 1929.

Criticism

Bataillon, Marcel. "Simples réflexions sur Juan de la Cueva." *BH* 36 (1935): 329–36. A Spanish translation of the preceding is included in M. Bataillon, *Varia lección de clásicos españoles*. Madrid: Gredos, 1964. 206–13.
Caso González, José. "Las obras de tema contemporáneo en el teatro de Juan de la Cueva." *Archivum* 19 (1969): 127–47.
Crawford, J. P. Wickersham. *Spanish Drama before Lope de Vega*. Philadelphia: U of Pennsylvania P, 1968. 164–70.
Glenn, Richard F. *Juan de la Cueva*. TWAS 273. New York: Twayne, 1973.
Silveira y Montes de Oca, Jorge A. "El *Romancero* y el teatro nacional español: de Juan

de la Cueva a Lope de Vega.'' In *Lope de Vega y los orígenes del teatro español.* Madrid: EDI–6, 1981. 73–81.

Wardropper, Bruce W. ''Juan de la Cueva y el drama histórico.'' *NRFH* 9 (1955): 149–56.

William Ferguson

*CULTERANISMO,* a literary style of the Baroque. This term, and others related to it (*culterano* and *culteranista*), was first used in the early seventeenth c. to refer to poetry characterized by a highly Latinate syntax and a wealth of classical allusions. The origin of all these words is in the word *culto,* which means cultured or learned. Juan de Corominas's dictionary suggests that the word *culterano* may have been formed by analogy with *luterano* (Lutheran) since this kind of poetry was felt by its critics to have an un-Spanish or even heretical novelty. The nineteenth edition of the Royal Academy Dictionary (1971) defines the term as a poetic vice. But it seems clear that the word, coined apparently by the humanist Bartolomé \*Jiménez de Patón, was used at first without the pejorative connotations that it and *gongorismo* (Gongorism) later came to have.

The enrichment of medieval Spanish by the adoption of classical syntax and neologisms was a natural and even necessary aspect of \*Renaissance culture in Spain, although excesses in this direction were always resisted. The first poet to cultivate a poetic style which openly and systematically imitated Latin was Juan de \*Mena (1411–1456). A century later, Fernando de \*Herrera criticized \*Garcilaso de la Vega for expressions that were too plain or vulgar, insisting on the avoidance of the language of everyday prose.

*Culteranismo* had counterparts in other cultures. John Lyly's prose in England, the work of the *précieux* poets in France, and Marino's mannerist poetry in Italy are examples of similar tendencies all over Europe in the late Renaissance.

*Culturanismo* found theoretical support in Spain in Luis \*Carrillo y Sotomayor's *Libro de la erudición poética* (1611; Book of Poetic Erudition). Baltásar de \*Gracián y Morales's *Agudeza y arte de ingenio* (1648; The Art of Clever Expression and Wit) also defends ''difficult'' poetry, particularly that of Luis de \*Góngora, whom he admired.

It is with Góngora that this movement is carried to controversial extremes. Góngora was a learned man and prided himself on being incomprehensible to the majority. His major poems, which appeared in about 1613, are enormously complex syntactically and are full of classical references, particularly to mythology and astrology. Although this poetry for the minority had its detractors, its influence can be seen even in Góngora's sternest critics. In reaction to Góngora's *Soledades* (Solitudes), for example, Francisco de \*Quevedo composed a ''Receta para hacer Soledades en un día'' (Recipe for Making Solitudes in a Day), part of which follows:

Quien quisiere ser culto en solo un día:
la jeri-(aprenderá) gonza siguiente:
fulgores, arrogar, joven, presiente,

candor, construye, métrica armonía;

(He who wants to be cultured in only one day
the following jar (will learn) gon: . . . )

None of the words that follow, apparently so scandalous then, would seem out of place in modern Spanish. Lope de *Vega makes fun of Góngora's uncompromising use of hyperbaton in these lines, in which a cat,

en una de fregar cayó caldera,
*trasposición* se llama esta figura,
de agua acabada de quitar del fuego.

(into a for dishes fell cauldron,
*transposition* is called this figure,
of water just taken from the fire.)

Nevertheless, both Lope and Quevedo wrote at times with the very language that they mocked in their adversary.

Although Góngora is generally recognized to be a major poet, his influence in the long run was perhaps more pernicious than otherwise. In poets of talent, like Francisco de *Medrano and Pedro *Soto de Rojas, or, in the New World, Carlos de Sigüenza y Góngora and Sor Juana Inés de la Cruz, the erudite tradition produced some authentic poetry. But a great deal of later seventeenth-c. poetry is full of high-sounding verbiage, and its erudition is second- or third-hand. *See also* conceptismo; Siglo de Oro.

BIBLIOGRAPHY

Criticism

Green, O. H. *Spain and the Western Tradition.* vol. 4. Madison: U of Wisconsin P, 1966.
Mackenzie, Anne L. "The Individuality of the Baroque Style in Spain: Some Aspects of Gongorismo." In *Aureum Saeculum Hispanum.* Ed. Karl-Herman Korner and Dietrich Briesmeister. Wiesbaden: Franz Steiner, 1983. 187–201.

John Turner

**CUNQUEIRO, Álvaro** (1911, Mondonedo–1981,?), essayist, journalist, novelist. Cunqueiro began his literary career as a vanguard poet in Galician with the book *Mar ao norde* (1932; Sea to the North), followed by the first surrealist verse in Galicia titled *Poemas de sí e non* (1933; Yes and No Poems). Following the Civil war, Cunqueiro switched to the realm of fiction in *Merlín e familia* (1955; Merlin and Family), *Escola de mencineiros* (1960; School for Witchdoctors) and *Tesouros novos e vellos* (1964; Old and New Treasures), all written in Galician. In 1968 he received the prestigious Nadal prize for his novel in Spanish, *Un hombre que se parecía a Orestes* (1968; A Man Much Like Orestes). In all of his writings Cunqueiro displays an enduring fondness for the magical and the fantastic.

BIBLIOGRAPHY

Primary Texts

*El año del cometa con la batalla de los cuatro reyes.* Barcelona: Destino, 1974. (novel)
*Boticas y curanderos.* Barcelona: Destino, 1976. (vignettes).
*La crónicas del Sochantre.* 2nd ed. Barcelona: Destino, 1966.
*Cuando el viejo Sinbad vuelva a las islas.* 2nd ed. Barcelona: Destino, 1971.
*Merlín y familia.* Barcelona: Destino, 1969. In Spanish.
*Las mocedades de Ulises.* 2nd ed. Barcelona: Destino, 1970.
*La otra gente.* Barcelona: Destino, 1975.
*Vidas y fugas de Fanto Fantini.* Barcelona: Destino, 1971.

Criticism

Fernández del Riego, F. *Historia da literatura galega.* Vigo: Galaxia, 1971. 209–10, 250–52, 259.
Kronik, J. *"Un hombre que se parecía a Orestes."* Review in *Hispania* 53 (March 1970): 152.
Thomas, M. D. *"Un hombre que se parecía a Orestes:* A Humorous Revitalization of an Ancient Myth." *Hispania* 61.1 (March 1978): 35–45.

                                                    Ricardo Landeira

**CURA DE LOS PALACIOS, El.** *See* Bernáldez, Andrés

*CURIAL Y GÜELFA,* a fifteenth-c. Catalan romance. This anonymous work combines the features of the Italianate sentimental novel and the chivalric romances of the Breton cycle. Curial is a humble military commander encouraged by his young patroness Güelfa to become the perfect knight and lover. After numerous adventures, Curial's triumphs prove him worthy of Güelfa, and he finally marries her. The plot is drawn from novel 61 of the *Cento novelle antiche,* an Italian collection of short tales written in the thirteenth c. The anonymous author was surely a learned man, and clearly influenced by Dante and Boccaccio. *See also* Italian Literary Influences.

BIBLIOGRAPHY

Primary Text

*Curial y Güelfa.* Ed. Marina Gustà. Barcelona: Edicions 62, 1979.

                                                    Deborah Compte

**CURROS ENRÍQUEZ, Manuel** (1851, Celanova–1908, Havana), poet. Together with Rosalía de *Castro and Eduardo *Pondal, Curros Enríquez ranks as one of the three greatest poets of nineteenth-c. Galician letters. He wrote prose and verse, in Gallego as well as Castilian. A rebel from his youth, Curros ran away from home as a child and from Spain as a young man. He was jailed for the anti-clerical nature of his first poems. Earning his livelihood as a newspaperman, Curros traveled far and wide, from Rome to Havana, where he died. His verse is moved by a dual impetus: social commitment and love for his native Galicia. *Aires d'a miña terra* (1880; Memories of the Motherland) and *O Divino* *sainete* (1888; The Holy Play) are the two books that best exemplify the ideological poetry for which he is best known. Curros inaugurated in Galician letters the notion that literature can and should be used as a weapon. The power of the church, the plight of the emigrant, the insensitivity of government, the uselessness of the aristocracy were all themes that Curros, in his "épater le bourgeouis" manner, proved were not alien to good poetry.

BIBLIOGRAPHY

Primary Texts

*Aires d'a miña terra.* 5th ed. Madrid: Peña Cruz, 1929.
*El divino sainete.* Spanish tr. A. Curros Vázquez. Madrid: Peña Cruz, 1918.
*Obras completas.* 6 vols. Madrid: Hernando, 1910–29.

Criticism

Ferreiro, Celso Emilio. *Curros Enríquez.* La Coruña: Moret, 1954.
Vilanova Rodríguez, A. *Vida y obra de Manuel Curros Enríquez.* Buenos Aires: Galicia, 1953.

Ricardo Landeira

# D

DA CAL, Ernesto Guerra. *See* Guerra da Cal, Ernesto

DALMIRO. *See* Cadalso, José

*DANÇA DE GALANES* (Suitor's Dance), title to a small *cancionero* (song-book). First published in 1612, it contains charming responsive songs and dances suitable for weddings and other festivities.

BIBLIOGRAPHY

Primary Text

*Cancionero llamado dança de galanes*. Valencia: Castalia, 1949.

*DANÇA GENERAL DE LA MUERTE* (*The General Dance of Death, 1896*), anonymous didactic poem. Probably derived from the French *Danse macabre*, the Spanish *Dança general de la muerte* dates from the late fourteenth or fifteenth c. and is preserved in ms. b-iv–21 of the Escorial Library. Its anonymous author follows the standard European pattern, in use since the early fourteenth c., of arranging Death's victims in two hierarchies, one ecclesiastical and the other lay. Key figures from both realms are presented alternately, giving the poem a coherent structure and also giving the poet the opportunity to present a critique— at times bitingly satirical—of contemporary society. The Spanish version lacks the often gruesome illustrations that accompanied many European Dances of Death, but retains the decidedly pessimistic worldview typical of the late Middle Ages.

The dialogue form suggests dramatic possibilities though there is no evidence that the *Dança* was represented. The poem opens with a friar's sermon and ends with a collective resolve to repent, but the actual dance is characterized by a consistently despondent tone, as no one escapes under the guidance of a per-sonified Death.

An expanded version of the *Dança* was printed in 1520 in Seville, but its author attempted to cover a broader spectrum of society, with emphasis on laymen as opposed to clergy. As a consequence his amplified version lacks the coherent alternating structure of the original. The theme was still popular in the sixteenth c. and was incorporated into several dramatic works, among them Gil *Vicente's *Trilogía de las Barcas* (The Trilogy of the Ships) and the *Farsa llamada Danza de la Muerte* (Farce Called Dance of Death) of Juan de *Pedraza, published in 1551. *See also* Edad Media, Literatura de la.

BIBLIOGRAPHY

Primary Texts

*Dança general de la muerte.* Ed. Josep María Solá-Solé. Barcelona: Puvill, 1981.
*Dança general de la muerte (siglo XV–1520).* Ed. Víctor Infantes. Madrid: Visor, 1982.

English Translation

*The Dance of Death.* In *Poets and Poetry of Europe.* Tr. H. W. Longfellow. Boston: Houghton, 1896.

Criticism

Deyermond, Alan D. "El ambiente social e intelectual de la *Danza de la muerte.*" In *Actas del II Congreso Internacional de Hispanistas.* Mexico: El Colegio de México, 1970. 267–76.
Hood, D., and J. R. Williamson. " 'Pensaste el mundo por vos trastornar': The World Upside Down in the *Dança general de la Muerte.*" *Medium Aevum* 48 (1980): 90–101.
Mikus, Patricia F. "The Spanish 'Dança general de la muerte" in the European Context of the Theme." *Mid-Hudson Language Studies* 1 (1978): 35–50.
Whyte, Florence. *The Dance of Death in Spain and Catalonia.* Baltimore: Johns Hopkins UP, 1931.

James Ray Green

**DANVILA, Alfonso** (1879, ?–?, ?), novelist, diplomat. He traveled throughout Europe and Spanish America, serving as ambassador to Argentina and France. His early works include novels of manners such as *Lully Arjona* (1901) and eighteenth-c. historical monographs like *Luisa Isabel de Orleans* (1902) and *Fernando VI y Doña Bárbara de Braganza* (1905; Ferdinand VI and Barbara of Braganza). His most noteworthy literary contribution was some fourteen historical novels concerning the early eighteenth-c. Peninsular War; all were published as part of the series *Luchas fratricidas de España* (1923–30; Fratricidal Struggles in Spain). Following the model of *Pérez Galdós's *Episodios nacionales,* the works are well documented, entertaining, and filled with anecdotes.

BIBLIOGRAPHY

Primary Texts

*Fernando VI y Doña Bárbara de Braganza, 1713–1748.* Madrid: Ratés Martín, 1905.
*Las luchas fratricidas de España.* Madrid: Espasa-Calpe, 1950–57.

*Luisa Isabel de Orleans.* Madrid: Fe, 1902.
*Lully Arjona.* Madrid: Hernández, 1901.

Merry Wheaton

**DE RIVAS, Enrique** (1931, Madrid– ), poet and essayist. In 1939 he left Spain and went to Mexico after a brief sojourn in France. His formative years were spent in Mexico (where he attended the Universidad Nacional Autónoma), Puerto Rico (where he received his bachelor's degree in 1951 from the U of Puerto Rico), and the United States, where in 1956 he was awarded his doctorate from the U of California, Berkeley. After four years on the faculty of the U of the Americas, he received a United Nations appointment (Food and Agricultural Organization) in Rome, where he now resides. A growing awareness of the recent history of Spain and Europe affected him strongly in his formative years. His humanistic concerns, which he shares with members of his generation (Manuel *Durán, Luis Rius, Ramon Xirau, et al.), are revealed in early work such as *Primeros Poemas* (1940; First Poems), and *Diario de octubre* (1961; October Diary). Most of his verse, including *Las puertas de la noche* (1965; Doors of Night), *Tiempo ilícito* (1981; Illicit Time), and *El espejo y su sombra* (1985; The Mirror and Its Shadow), reveal wide inspirational scope stemming from De Rivas's ample and varied experience. His style possesses a metaphorical freshness and a delicate sensorial awareness of the possibilities of lyrical expression and verse form. Other noteworthy publications are *En la herencia del día* (1966; Inheriting the Day) and *Como quien lava las cosas* (1984; As One Who Washes Things). He has published a volume of essays on medieval literature titled *Figuras y estrellas de las cosas* (1969; Figures and Stars of Things), and has been a frequent contributor in prose and verse to literary journals such as *Papeles de Son Armadans, The New Morality, Elsinore, Settanta* (Rome), *Sur* (Buenos Aires), *Diálogos,* and *Revista mexicana de literatura* (Mexico). *See also* Essay.

BIBLIOGRAPHY

Primary Texts

*El espejo y su sombra.* Valencia: Pre-Textos/Poesía, 1985.
*Figuras y estrellas de las cosas.* Maracaibo: U of Zulia, 1969.
*En la herencia del día.* Maracaibo: U of Zulia, 1966.

Alan A. González

*DÉCIMA,* a popular form of verse. Also called the *espinela* after its supposed creator Vicente *Espinel (1550–1624), the *décima* is a ten-line, octosyllabic stanza with an *abbaaccddc* rhyme scheme. The importance of the *décima* for popular verse may be compared to that of the sonnet for learned poetry.

BIBLIOGRAPHY

Criticism

Clarke, D. C. "Sobre la 'espinela.' " *RFE* 23 (1936): 293–304.
Millé y Giménez, J. "Sobre la invención de la décima o espinela." *HR* 5 (1937): 40–51.

**DECIR,** a poetic term. In the Middle Ages and *Renaissance, *decir* was the term given in titles of poems, such as the *Decir de las siete virtudes* (Poem on the Seven Virtues) by Francisco *Imperial. Oftentimes they were rather short and didactic, political or courtly. *See also* Edad Media, Literatura de la.

**DEJADOS.** *See* Alumbrados

**DELAFÓN, Remigio Andrés.** *See* Acuña y Villanueva de la Iglesia, Rosario de

**DELGADO, Jaime** (1923, Madrid– ), professor, poet. A professor of American history at the U of Barcelona, he has written several studies in this field. Poetry publications by Delgado include *Hombre de soledad* (1950; Man of Solitude), *Memoria del corazón* (1957; Memory of the Heart), *Lo nuestro* (1966; Ours), and *Bajo el signo de Aries* (1969; Under the Influence of Aries). His poetry has received several prizes, including the Hermanos Machado national prize in 1966.

BIBLIOGRAPHY

Primary Texts

*Bajo el signo de Aries.* Madrid: Nacional, 1969.
*España y México en el siglo XIX.* 3 vols. Madrid: CSIC, 1950.
*La independencia de América en la prensa española.* Madrid: n.p., 1949.
*Lo nuestro.* Madrid: n.p., 1966.

Isabel McSpadden

**DELGADO, Sinesio** (1859, Támara, Palencia–1928, Madrid), Castilian critic and dramatist. He received a degree in medicine, but soon abandoned the medical profession. The journalist and lyricist Ramos Carrión lured him to Madrid, where Delgado began his literary career as a writer for *Madrid Cómico* (Comical Madrid). His intense desire to help his fellow writers resulted in his founding the Sociedad de Autores Españoles (Society of Spanish Writers), which provided financial support to writers in need. In *Mi teatro* (1905; My Theater) he gives a personal account of the origins and purpose of the society. Ultimately, Delgado was forced out of the society due to personal and ideological rivalries. While known for his abundant humorous and satirical articles, Delgado earned fame as a prolific librettist and playwright, with over one hundred *comedias,* *zarzuelas and *sainetes to his credit. Among his most popular works were *La zarzuela nueva* (1897; The New Zarzuela), *La baraja francesa* (The French Deck of Cards), *El ama de llaves* (The Keeper of the Keys), and *El retablo de Maese Pedro* (1916; Master Peter's Puppet Show). His comedy *Nuestro compañero en la prensa* (Our Friend in the Press) was particularly well received. As a poet Delgado published three volumes: *Pólvora sola* (1888; Solitary Powder), *Almendras amargas* (1893; Bitter Almonds), and *Lluvia menuda* (1895; Light Rain).

BIBLIOGRAPHY

Primary Texts

*El ama de llaves*. Madrid: Administración lírica dramática, 1893.
*Nuestro compañero en la prensa*. Madrid: Hernández, 1911.
*Obras completas*. Madrid: Hernández, 1919.
*Mi teatro*. Madrid: Hernández, 1905.
*La zarzuela nueva*. Madrid: Hernández, 1897.

Donald C. Buck

**DELGADO BENAVENTE, Luis** (1915, Getafe, Madrid– ), playwright. He has received several prizes (Calderón de la Barca, Ciudad de Barcelona, Lope de Vega) for his plays: *Días nuestros* (1951; Our Days), *Tres ventanas* (1952; Three Windows), *Media hora antes* (1955; Half an Hour Before), *Presagio* (n.f.; Foreboding), *Jacinta y Humo* (1952). He has also published short stories in various magazines and a collection of ten stories entitled *El samovar hierve* (1952; The Samovar Is Boiling).

BIBLIOGRAPHY

Primary Texts

*Presagio*. N.p.: n.p., 1954?
*El samovar hierve*. Madrid: RO, 1952.
*Tres ventanas*. Madrid: Puerta del Sol, 1955.

Isabel McSpadden

**DELIBES, Miguel** (1920, Valladolid– ), novelist, publisher, lawyer, professor and journalist. Delibes has managed the equivalent of three careers: he holds the Intendencia de Comercio degree, the equivalent of a doctorate in business, and has taught mercantile law for many years at the School of Commerce in Valladolid. Longtime editor and director of *El Norte de Castilla*, one of Spain's oldest and most prestigious daily newspapers, he is unquestionably one of Spain's foremost novelists and intellectuals today. Delibes is a spokesman for conservation, for the ecology, and for myriad things sacrificed, irretrievably lost, in the name of progress. As an avid amateur sportsman, trout fisherman and small-game hunter, Delibes is intimately acquainted with every meter of the terrain which so often appears in his fiction, as well as with the ''backward,'' laconic, earthy peasants who populate many of his works. With few exceptions, his works are realistic, a realism often attenuated by a lyric vision or symbolic intent. His first two novels, *La sombra del ciprés es alargada* (1948; Long Is the Cypress's Shadow), winner of the Nadal Prize, and *Aun es de día* (1949; Still It Is Day) are traditional in concept and execution, the first seen as bitter, pessimistic and ''Proustian,'' the second seen either as *tremendista* (neonaturalistic) or as optimistic by critics who judged the works mainly from the psychology of their respective protagonists.

*El camino* (1950; *The Path*, 1961) is the first novel to exhibit that style later inseparably associated with Delibes: colloquial, conversational, ironic, sprinkled with aphoristic pronouncements in regional Castilian dialect, and laced through with humorous tag lines, folkloric toponomy and nicknames. In this third novel, also, Delibes explores a less traditional structure, dispensing with plot and linear action in favor of anecdotal evocation and experimenting with time via flashbacks, non-sequential action and disjointed events. He initiates use of the technique of point of view, submerging his own personality, vision and awareness in those of a character with a limited, primitive, distorted or elemental perspective—a technique subsequently considered another Delibes trademark. *Mi idolatrado hijo Sisí* (1953; My Adored Son, Sisi) reverts to linear chronology, sequential action and a fairly traditional plot: because of its exceptional scope and length, *Sisí* was some five years in the writing. A novel with an anti-Malthusian thesis, this work presents some three decades of the twentieth c. (ending with the Spanish Civil War) as the novelist analyzes how a wealthy businessman's egotistical refusal to have more than one son first ruins the son who is spoiled beyond belief, and ultimately leads to the father's suicide when the boy is killed in the war.

Two of Delibes's works from this period are linked by common technique and the same narrator-protagonist. *Diario de un cazador* (1953; Diary of a Hunter) and *Diario de un emigrante* (1959; Diary of an Emigrant) are both presented from the viewpoint of Lorenzo, a *bedel* (glorified janitor) in an institution of higher education, assumed by many to be the same one where Delibes taught. At the same time the novelist conceals his culture and ampler vision behind the pen of a relatively uneducated and prejudiced narrator, he explores the hitherto unexploited richness of popular, colloquial expression, indulging his growing interest in language per se in the sequel (a spin-off of a lecture tour by Delibes in Chile: Lorenzo spends over a year in Chile, but returns disillusioned with both the hunting and the chances of quick riches). In the interim between the two diaries, the novelist published *Siestas con viento sur* (1956; Naps with the Southern Breeze), a collection of four novelettes, three of which utilize the point-of-view technique, and which won for him the Fastenrath Prize of the *Academia Española.

In *La hoja roja* (1959; The Red Leaf), Delibes treats material seldom touched by Spanish novelists, the loneliness of the elderly in the face of approaching death, the quiet desperation of society's aged rejects, the low-key lyricism of the humble, poor and unwanted. While some lyric motifs verge upon the pedestrian, Delibes captures the underlying poetry of the trials, difficulty and pathos of the miracle of life. Repetition exercises a structuring function in the essentially plotless narrative, even more so than in *The Path*, underscoring the cyclic monotony of daily rituals. Because there are only two major characters, an old retired civil servant and his illiterate young maid, Desi, the novel often resembles parallel monologues. It was adapted by the author for theatrical production in 1986. The technique of point of view is used with deepening mastery in *Las ratas* (1962; The Rats; tr. Alfred Johnson, *Smoke on the Ground*, 1972) as Delibes returns to the isolated Castilian village setting of some of his most memorable achievements. With two main characters—a retarded hunter of rats and his almost clairvoyant son—this short novel is set in a small cave outside the village and the minutely described terrain immediately surrounding it. Although Delibes by no means invented the use of caves as dwellings by the poor, he does utilize the cavern with deliberate allegorical intent to convey the embedded message that life in the impoverished and forgotten Castilian countryside has changed little in millennia. This work earned Delibes the prestigious Premio de la Crítica (Critics' Prize) in 1962.

Allegory is more extensively developed in *Cinco horas con Mario* (1966; Five Hours With Mario), wherein marital conflict symbolically incarnates the social and ideological strife which led to the Spanish Civil War. Among Delibes's most self-consciously experimental works, this novel is almost entirely an uninterrupted first-person interior monologue, directed by Carmen to the dead body of her husband. The dead protagonist, Mario, never appears directly before the reader, but is presented through the eyes and mind of Carmen, a perspective which is also a distorting lens. The widow is clearly the antagonist. Irony and self-contradiction are utilized with such skill that the reader ends fully aware of Carmen's hypocrisy and deceptions. Still more allegorical is *Parábola del náufrago* (1969; Parable of the Shipwrecked Man) in which Delibes represents the plight of the individual imperiled by a dehumanized technocracy. Peculiar to this novel are the three distinct styles or narrative voices, corresponding to an omniscient, ironic narrator, a more or less lucid, laconic Jacinto, and the hallucinatory, delirious mind of Jacinto in process of disintegration. The wildly fluctuating chronology is unique in Delibes's works to date, as is the incorporation of an apocryphal language and experiments with punctuation (quite probably a parody of the "new novel"). Reminiscent of *Brave New World* as well as the atmosphere associated with Kafka, *Parábola* uses the device of metamorphosis to symbolize the degradation and "neutralizing" of individuals who dare to think for themselves.

In 1973, Delibes, who had won a National Prize for Literature in 1955, was elected to the Royal Spanish Academy, in recognition both of his novelistic accomplishments and his contributions to the preservation of the rural Castilian lexicon. His interest in language appears not only in his fiction, but in an extensive list of books on his hunting and fishing avocations: *La caza de la perdiz roja* (1960; Hunting the Red Partridge); *El libro de la caza menor* (1964; The Book of Small Game Hunting); *Con la escopeta al hombro* (1970; With My Gun on My Shoulder); *Aventuras, venturas y desventuras de un cazador a rabo* (1977; Adventures, Ventures and Misadventures of a Tracking Hunter); *Mis amigas las truchas* (1977; My Friends the Trout); *Las perdices del domingo* (1981; Sunday Partridges); and others. Delibes has also written many travel books, collections of short fiction, and several books of essays.

*El príncipe destronado* (1973; The Dethroned Prince) and *Las guerras de nuestros antepasados* (1975; Our Forefathers' Wars) are superficially very different, yet similar in their extensive use of concealed parallels, ironic symbolism, and anti-war messages. In each, Delibes employs a peculiarly limited, distorted narrative consciousness, one that of a little boy not yet four, and the other that of a mentally disturbed young prisoner. Although the pretext of tape-recorded psychiatric sessions, lending a semblance of question-answer format to *Las guerras*, is new for Delibes, the remaining elements of style are not. In both novels, although in very different environments and social milieus, Delibes explores the effects of parents' belligerence and bellicose attitudes upon the young. *El príncipe destronado* was made a highly successful motion picture entitled *La guerra de Papá* (Papa's War).

Delibes's concern with the abandonment of Castilian farms and villages, already present in *Las ratas* and *Las guerras de nuestros antepasados* and books of essays such as *SOS* (1976) and the meditative, philosophical *Viejas historias de Castilla la vieja* (1964; Old Tales of Old Castile), reappears in his first fully post-Franco novel, *El disputado voto del señor Cayo* (1978; The Disputed Vote of Mr. Cayo), a humorous yet very serious satire of election issues and non-issues in the new democracy. His concern for the rural poor and those in forgotten villages similarly underlies *Los santos inocentes* (1981; The Blessed Innocents) and *El tesoro* (1986; The Treasure), while his preoccupation with the lasting divisions which produced the Civil War and have survived to the present is the primary inspiration for *377a, madera de héroe* (1988; 377A, The Stuff of Which Heroes Are Made), perhaps the most important work on the war by a member of Delibes's generation. In 1982, Delibes was awarded the Prince of Asturias Prize for Letters, and in 1985, that of Castille and León.

## BIBLIOGRAPHY

### Primary Texts

*Cartas de amor de un sexagenario voluptuoso*. Barcelona: Destino, 1983.
*La mortaja*. Madrid: Alianza Editorial, 1970. Short stories.
*La partida*. Barcelona: Luis de Caralt, 1954. Ten stories.
*Los santos inocentes*. Barcelona: Planeta, 1981.
*USA y yo*. Barcelona: Destino, 1966. Travel.

### English Translation

*The Path*. Tr. John and Rita Haycraft. New York: John Day, 1961.
*Smoke on the Ground*. Trans. Alfred Johnson. Garden City, NY: Doubleday, 1972.

### Criticism

Díaz, Janet. *Miguel Delibes*. TWAS. New York: Twayne Publishers, 1971. In English.
Hickey, Leo. *Cinco horas con Miguel Delibes. El hombre y el novelista*. Madrid: Prensa Española, 1968.
Pauk, Edgar. *Miguel Delibes: Desarrollo de un escritor (1947–1974)*. Madrid: Gredos, 1975.

Rey, Alfonso. *La originalidad novelística de Delibes*. Santiago de Compostela: Universidad, 1975.

Sobejano, Gonzalo. Introduction to *La mortaja*. Madrid: Cátedra, 1984. 11–75.

Janet Pérez

**DELICADO, Francisco** (1480?, Diocese of Cordova–1534, Venice?), novelist and editor. Little biographical data is known beyond what he himself reveals. Raised in Peña de Martos (Jaén), he was a vicar, a disciple of *Nebrija, and of possible marrano (*converso) descent. He lived in Italy, leaving Rome for Venice in 1528, after the sacking by the Spanish imperial troops. In Venice, he published, anonymously, the *Retrato de la lozana andaluza* (1528; *Portrait of the Lusty Andalusian Woman*, 1979), a precursor of the *picaresque novel, with the only female protagonist until *La pícara Justina*. In dialogue form like La *Celestina*, it depicts, without idealization, a depraved lower class of 125 lively and lewd characters, Spanish or Italian ruffians, bawds, panders, courtesans, go-betweens, scoundrels, as well as noblemen and priests. With journalistic realism and in a rich and dynamic Castilian prose interspersed with Italianisms, it gives a forceful historical documentation of moral and social corruption in early Renaissance Italy, combining the sensuality of the Boccaccian novel with the glorification of obscenity, lascivious love, and the lowest forms of life. Despite the apparent lack of moral preoccupation, Delicado, in fact, looks retrospectively at the sacking as the providential punishment against the sinful Romans. He calls his dialogues *mamotretos* (notebooks) and intervenes as a friend and confidant of the heroine. In 1845, Ferdinand Wolf discovered the only ms. at the Imperial Library in Vienna; it remained anonymous until Pascual de Gayangos identified it, in 1857. Delicado published two editions of *La Celestina* (1531; 1534), and excellent critical editions of the chivalric novels *Amadís* (1533) and *Primaleón* (1534), revealing his authorship of *La Lozana* in the prologue to Book III of *Primaleón*. He wrote in Italian on the healing of *Il Mal Franceso* (The French Disease, or Syphilis) with *palo santo* (lignum vitae) and gave the only known mention of his cure for melancholy, *De consolatione infirmorum*.

BIBLIOGRAPHY

Primary Texts

"Francisco Delicado. El modo de apoderare el legno de India Occidentale. A Critical Transcription." *RHM* 36 (1970–71): 251–71.

*Retrato de la Lozana andaluza*. Ed. B. Damiani and G. Allegra. Madrid: Porrúa, 1975.

English Translation

Lee, Ann A. "Portrait of Lozana. The Lusty Andalusian Woman by Francisco Delicado: Translation, Introduction, and Notes." *DAI* 40 (1979): 1453 A (U of South Carolina).

Criticism

Allegra, G. "Sobre una nueva hipótesis en la biografía de Francisco Delicado." *BRAE* 56 (1976): 523–35.

Bagby, A. I., Jr. "La primera novela picaresca española." *Torre* 68 (1970): 83–100.

Damiani, B. M. "La Lozana andaluza: Tradición literaria y sentido moral." In *Actas del Tercer Congreso Internacional de Hispanistas*. Ed. Carlos H. Magis. Mexico: El Colegio de México por la Asociación Internacional de Hispanistas, 1970. 241–48.

———. "Delicado y Aretino. Aspects of a Literary Profile." *KRQ* 17 (1970): 309–24.

———. "Un aspecto histórico de *La Lozana Andaluza*." *MLN* 87 (1972): 178–92.

———. *Francisco Delicado*. TWAS 335. New York: Twayne, 1974.

———. "*La Lozana Andaluza*: Ensayo bibliográfico II." *Quaderni Ibero-Americani* 51–2 (1978–79): 121–52.

Díez Borque, J. M. "Francisco Delicado, autor y personaje de *La Lozana andaluza*." *Prohemio* 3.3 (1972): 455–66.

Hernández Ortiz, J. A. *La génesis artística de* La Lozana Andaluza: *El realismo literario de Francisco Delicado*. Madrid: Aguilera, 1974.

Hughes, J. B. "Orígenes de la novela picaresca: *La Celestina* y *La Lozana andaluza*." In *La picaresca: Orígenes, textos y estructura. Actas del I Congreso Internacional sobre la Picaresca*. Ed. M. Criado de Val. Madrid: Fundación Universitaria Española, 1979. 327–34.

Ugolini, F. A. *Nuovi dati ritorno all biografia di Francisco Delicado desunti da una sconosciuta operetta*. Perugia: Di Salvi, 1975.

Wardropper, B. "La novela como retrato: el arte de Francisco Delicado." *NRFH* 7 (1953): 475–88.

Reginetta Haboucha

***DENUESTOS DEL AGUA Y EL VINO*** (Debate between Water and Wine), early thirteenth-c. poem. An example from among the many medieval poems in which two opposing elements (good and evil, the scholar and the soldier, etc.) conduct a debate. This particular version proceeds from one of various Latin or French poems on the theme composed during the Middle Ages (*see* \*Edad Media, Literatura de la). It is found at the end of *Razón feita de amor* (Lyric Poem about Love) when a glass of water is accidentally spilled into a glass of wine. This provokes a somewhat burlesque debate between the two, with each pointing out the weaknesses of the other. The water accuses the wine of destroying man's reason and the wine retorts by accusing the water of spoiling and weakening the wine. The wine further boasts that in the Eucharist it is converted into the blood of Christ while the water revels in the fact that it is holy since it is needed for baptism. *See also Razón de amor*.

BIBLIOGRAPHY

Primary Texts

London, G. H. "The *Razón de amor* and the *Denuestos del agua y el vino*. New Readings and Interpretations." *RPH* 19 (1965–66): 28–47.

Menéndez, Pidal R. "*Razón de amor* con los *Denuestos del agua y el vino*." *RH* 13 (1905): 602–18.

Morel Fatio, A. "Textes Castillans Inédits." *Romania* 16 (1887): 364–82.

Criticism

Pacheco, Arsenio "*¿Razón de amor o Denuestos del agua y el vino?*" *BHS* 51 (1974): 1–15.

Lucy Sponsler

**DIAMANTE, Juan Bautista** (1625, Madrid–1687, Madrid), dramatist. Born into a prosperous merchant-class family, of Greek and Sicilian heritage, Diamante studied at the U in Alcalá de Henares, receiving a degree in canon law. Despite progressing through the ranks of the clergy and attaining the titles of Knight of the Order of Jerusalem and Prior of the Morón Convent, Diamante acquired a notorious reputation for his bellicose nature. His nefarious exploits notwithstanding, he was a successful dramatist, popular with court and public audiences alike. Two volumes containing twenty-four of his plays were published in Madrid (1670 and 1674). In addition to writing more than forty plays himself, Diamante collaborated on works with many contemporaries, including Lanini, *Matos Fragoso and *Villaviciosa. Although his plays represent several different types of *comedia*, Diamante is best known for those which involve traditional Spanish themes, among them *El cerco de Zamora* (The Blockade of Zamora), *Juan Sánchez de Talavera*, and *Santa Teresa de Jesús*.

Three works have attracted the attention of critics because of their successful reworking of older plays: *El valor no tiene edad y Sansón de Extremadura, Diego García de Paredes* (Valor Is Ageless and Samson the Extremaduran, Diego García de Paredes) is based on a play by Lope de *Vega; *La judía de Toledo* (The Jewess of Toledo) recasts a play of the same name by *Mira de Amescua. Of particular interest is *El honrador de su padre* (His Father's Honorer), a play about the young *Cid which seems to draw on both the original Guillén de *Castro work (*Las mocedades del Cid*) and the French version by Corneille. *See also* Theater in Spain.

BIBLIOGRAPHY

Primary Texts

See *Dramáticos posteriores a Lope de Vega*. BAE 49.

Criticism

Cotarelo, E. *Don Juan Bautista Diamante y sus comedias*. *BRAE* 3. Madrid: RABM, 1916. 272–97 and 454–97.
Guellouz, S. "Une Nouvelle Lecture des Mocedades et du Cid: *El Honrador de su padre* de J. B. Diamante." In *Pierre Corneille*. Ed. A. Niderst. Paris: PUF, 1985. 83–92.
Paulson, M. G. "The Genesis of an Anachronism: The Mary Stuart Plays of Diamante and Boursault." *USF Language Quarterly* (Tampa, Florida), 21.3–4 (Spring-Summer 1983): 40–42.

Soons, Alan. Four Transpositions of the Theseus Legend in the Hispanic Theater.''
   *Cithara* 24.2 (May 1985): 3–21.

                                                                    Donald C. Buck

**DIANA, Manuel Juan** (1814, Seville–1881, Madrid), dramatist and novelist.
A little-known Romantic writer, he composed two novels which were awarded
prizes by the Spanish Academy (*Academia Española) in 1876: *La calle de la
Amargura* (n.d.; Bitterness Street), and *El rostro y la condición* (n.d.; The Face
and the Character). His plays include *Receta contra las suegras* (n.d.; Recipe
for Mother-in-laws), *La cruz de la torre blanca* (n.d.; The Cross from the White
Tower)—in collaboration with Gregorio *Romero Larrañaga, and *La vieja del
candilejo* (n.d.; The Old Lady with the Kitchen Lamp)—in collaboration with
Larrañaga and González Elipe. *See also* Romanticism.

BIBLIOGRAPHY

   Primary Texts

   *La cruz de la torre blanca.* Madrid: Lalama, 1847.
   *Receta contra las suegras.* Madrid: Rodríguez, 1864.
   *La vieja del candilejo.* Madrid: Repullés, 1838.

*DIARIO DE LOS LITERATOS DE ESPAÑA* (1737–42; Journal for the Learned
Men of Spain), the first periodical in Spain to attempt a serious survey and
analysis of all the current scientific and literary books printed in Spain. Its
founders, Francisco Manuel Huerta y Vega, Juan Martínez Salafranca and Leopoldo Jerónimo Puig, modeled their publication after the *Journal des Savants*
(Journal of Learned Men) from Paris. Although conceived as a trimester publication, only seven volumes actually appeared during its five-year existence.
The first volume (April 1737) was dedicated to Philip V, and in appealing for
royal patronage, the editors compared themselves with those forward-thinking
scholars of Spain whom Philip had supported in such endeavors as the *Academia
Española. From the first issue the *Diario* came under constant and vociferous
attack from its critics. Internal dissent also plagued the journal, and after the
third volume Huerta resigned his editorship. The *Diario* seemed doomed after
the fifth volume, and it was only through the intervention of the Minister José
de Campillo y Cosío that the last two volumes were published, under the auspices
of the Royal Press. Owing to the erudition of many of the defenses and counter-
attacks which appeared in the introductions of the *Diario*, Marcelino *Menéndez
Pelayo wondered whether the inexperienced editors, whose own writings betray
an undistinguished intellect, received help from outside sources. Certainly their
collaborators on the various articles in the *Diario* held more distinguished rep-
utations: they included Juan de *Iriarte, *Mayáns y Siscar and José Gerardo de
*Hervas, who published his satirical piece *Jorge Pitillas* in the *Diario*. Although
the title implies a more literary bent, the *Diario* reflects the emphasis on religious
and historical publications during the first half of the eighteenth c. The *Diario*
also announced significant foreign publications.

BIBLIOGRAPHY

Criticism

Castañón Díaz, J. A. "El *Diario de los Literatos de España*. Juicios críticos e ideas literarias." *Estudios* (1958): 33–101, 321–72, and 553–86.

———. "Ideas eruditas en el *Diario de los Literatos*." *Burgense* 31 (1971): 193–264.

Quirk, R. J. "Two Problems Concerning the Literary Criticism of the *Diario de los Literatos*." *RN* 21 (1979): 205–10.

Ruizveintemilla, J. M. "El *Diario de los Literatos* y sus enemigos." *Actas del Sexto Congreso Internacional de Hispanistas*. Toronto: U of Toronto P, Dept. of Spanish and Portuguese, 1980. 655–59.

———. "La fundación del *Diario de los Literatos* y sus protectores." *BBMP* 52 (1976): 229–58.

Tomisch, M. G. "Intento de delineación del buen gusto en el *Diario de los Literatos de España* (1737–1742)." *Cahiers du Monde Hispanique et Luso-Brésilien* 31 (1978): 47–58.

Donald C. Buck

**DIAS, João Pedro Grabato.** *See* Quadros, António

**DÍAZ, Nicomedes Pastor.** *See* Pastor Díaz, Nicomedes

**DÍAZ-CAÑABATE, Antonio** (1898, Madrid–1980, Madrid), genre writer of sketches of Madrid, and taurine journalist. He was the bullfight critic for the Madrid weekly magazine *El Ruedo* (The Bullring), from 1944 to 1958, as well as for the daily newspaper *ABC* (from 1958 to 1972), during which time he showed himself to be witty, impartial and absolutely honest in his judgments. He was an extraordinary conversationalist, listener and observer of those around him, which led to *Historia de una taberna* (1944; History of a Tavern), the first in a series of picturesque genre works whose sketches constitute a type of nostalgic memorial to the Madrid of his youth, combined with details of the present which will endure for generations to come.

BIBLIOGRAPHY

Primary Texts

*La fábula de Domingo Ortega*. 2nd ed. Madrid: Juan Valero, n.d.
*Historia de una taberna*. 5th ed. Madrid: Espasa-Calpe, 1976.
*Historia de una tertulia*. Madrid: Espasa-Calpe, 1978.
*Madrid y los madriles*. 3rd ed. Madrid: Prensa Española, 1975.
*Paseíllo por el planeta de los toros*. Madrid: Salvat-Alianza, 1970.

English Translations

*The Magic World of the Bullfighter*. Tr. R. H. Stevens. London: Burke, 1956.
*The World of Bullfighting*. Tr. of *El mundo de los toros*. 3rd ed. Leon: Everest, 1979.

Criticism

Luján, Néstor. "Los toros y el periodismo." *Los toros*. Vol. 7. Madrid: Espasa-Calpe, 1982.

Zabala, Vicente, "Adiós, maestro." *ABC Edición Semanal Aérea*, September 25, 1980·
28–29.

Rosario Cambria

**DÍAZ CANEJA, Guillermo** (1876, Madrid–1933, ?), actor, dramatist, novelist.
He studied commerce and declamation, and became an actor. He collaborated
on several Spanish and American newspapers and journals. For the theater he
wrote *Un beneficio* (A Benefit) and *Pilar Guerra*. The latter is also the title of
one of his novels. Other novels of note are *El sobre en blanco* (n.d.; The
Unaddressed Envelope), which received the *Academia Española's Fastenrath
prize in 1918, and *El carpintero y los frailes* (The Carpenter and the Friars),
which combines humor with social and religious concerns. His style is clear,
precise, realistic, and unintentionally moralizing.

BIBLIOGRAPHY

Primary Texts

*El carpintero y los frailes*. Madrid: Pueyo, 1927.
*El sobre en blanco*. 8th ed. Madrid: Pueyo, 1929.
*Pilar Guerra; novela*. 2nd ed. Madrid: Cosane, 1920.

Isabel McSpadden

**DÍAZ DE ESCOBAR, Narciso** (1860, Málaga–1935, Málaga), playwright,
poet, literary scholar. He studied in the seminary in Málaga, but abandoned it
for a law degree. He founded the Academia de Declamación (Declamation
Academy). His scholarly essays include *Don Francisco de Leiva y Ramírez de
Arellano* (1899), *Historia del teatro español* (1925; History of Spanish Theater),
various *Anales del teatro* (1910–1917; Theater Annals), *Biografías de actrices*
(Actresses' Biographies), and *El teatro en Málaga* (1896; The Theater in Málaga). He also wrote some plays: *María la malagueña* (Maria of Málaga), *El
autor del crimen* (The Author of the Crime), *Monje y emperador* (Monk and
Emperor). Other works are *Curiosidades malagueñas* (Malagan Curiosities) and
*Galería literaria malagueña* (Malagan Literary Gallery). He is also a poet and
the author of popular songs compiled in *Guitarra andaluza* (c. 1908; Andalusian
Guitar [Music]), *Malagueñas*, and *Cantares del soldado* (Soldiers' Songs), and
likewise published *Chascarrillos andaluces* (Andalusian Witty Tales).

BIBLIOGRAPHY

Primary Texts

*El autor del crimen*. Tuy: Tipografía regional, 1913.
*Curiosidades malagueñas*. Málaga: Zambrana, 1899.

*Guitarra andaluza.* Barcelona: Granada, 1911.
*Siluetas escénicas del pasado.* Barcelona: Tasso, 1949.

Isabel McSpadden

**DÍAZ DE LAMARQUE, Antonia** (1827, Marchena, Seville–1892, Dos Hermanas, Seville), poet short story writer. Both she and her husband, José Lamarque de Novoa, belonged to the lyrical school of Seville. Her first book, *Poesías de . . .* (Poems of . . . ) appeared in 1867, though her fame was established much earlier by journal publications. In 1861 Pilar *Sinués wrote an enthusiastic article about her in the *Correo de la Moda.* By 1890 she had published three more books of poems: *Flores marchitas* (1877; Withered Flowers), a collection of ballads and legends; *Poesías religiosas* (1889; Religious Poems); and *Aves y flores* (1890; Birds and Flowers), moral fables. Two novels also appeared by 1890.

In two poems, "La poetisas españolas" (Women Poets from Spain) and "Epístola a una amiga" (Letter to a Friend), she sets forth her ideas about women's intellectual work: if women wish to avoid society's scorn, they should write only as a hobby. Her poetry possesses the academic tone characteristic of the Seville school and a strong moral bent. Expressions of her personal religious feelings approach *mysticism, but poems which treat aspects of Christian dogma are rather cold. She avoided all extremes of pathos.

Her social position afforded contact with many Spanish and foreign intellectuals. Fastenrath, for example, translated and published a few of her compositions in German.

BIBLIOGRAPHY

Primary Texts

*Aves y flores.* Barcelona: Pons, 1890.
*Flores marchitas.* Sevilla: n.p., 1877.
*Poesías de Antonia Díaz de Lamarque.* Sevilla: M.P. Salvador, 1867.
*Poesías religiosas.* Preface by Joaquín Rubió y Ors. Barcelona: Fidel Giró, 1889.
*El precio de una dádiva.* N.p.: n.p., 1881.
*Tres flores.* N.p.: n.p., 1881.

Criticism

Cossío, José María. *Cincuenta años de poesía española (1850–1900).* Madrid: Espasa-Calpe, 1960.

Cristina Enríquez

**DÍAZ DEL CASTILLO, Bernal** (1492, Medina del Campo–1582, Guatemala), soldier and historian of the conquest of Mexico. A typical Spanish adventurer of his time, Bernal Díaz came to the New World as a youth and participated in a number of explorations and conquests before joining the expedition of Hernan *Cortés to Mexico in 1519. Rewarded for his role in the conquest, he settled in Guatemala as a landowner and city councilman, but he was dissatisfied with his lot and returned to Spain on two separate occasions to seek greater recognition and royal concessions. Only when he was past the age of seventy did he begin to write his *Verdadera historia de la conquista de la Nueva España* (1632; *The Conquest of New Spain*, 1976), which narrates not only the events of the conquest but also developments in Mexico through 1568. Conceived in large measure as a response to the *History of the Conquest of Mexico* written by the humanist *López de Gómara, in which the figure of Cortés stands out in clear relief above the other actors in the drama, Bernal Díaz's history underscores the importance of the role of the common soldier, and particularly his own participation, in the decisive events of the conquest. As Iglesia has shown, the actual corrections of facts in Gómara's history are few and of relative inconsequence, while Bernal Díaz owes to the humanist an important and unacknowledged debt: the borrowing of Gómara's structure and organizational plan for his own history. Fully aware that he cannot compete with Gómara's disciplined literary style, Bernal Díaz stresses that his writing follows the usage of "our common Castilian speech, which many learned men hold to be the best style," and that the truth contained in his history is more important than the polished rhetoric of the humanist. His work is in fact a pleasant, eminently readable account, full of the digressions and significant human detail of oral storytelling which makes it attractive to the modern reader. Writing not from notes but from vivid memories of events which in some cases had occurred over fifty years before, Bernal Díaz constructed a highly personal narrative which often takes on an almost novelesque character. In this c., it has become the most widely read and most often republished account of the conquest of Mexico. *See also* Renaissance; Siglo de Oro.

BIBLIOGRAPHY

Primary Text

*Historia Verdadera de la conquista de la Nueva España.* Ed. Joaquín Ramírez Cabañas. México: Porrúa, 1974.

English Translation

*The Conquest of New Spain.* Tr. and ed. J. M. Cohen. Harmondsworth, Middlesex, England: Penguin, 1963.

Criticism

Cascardi, Anthony J. "Chronicle toward Novel: Bernal Díaz' *History of the Conquest of Mexico.*" *Novel* 15.3 (Spring 1982): 197–212.

Cerwin, Herbert. *Bernal Díaz: Historian of the Conquest.* Norman: U of Oklahoma P, 1963.

Iglesia, Ramón. "Bernal Díaz del Castillo y el popularismo en la historiografía española." In *El hombre Colón y otros ensayos.* México: El Colegio de México, 1944. 53–116.

Sáenz de Santa María, Carmelo. "Bernal Díaz del Castillo: historia interna de su crónica." *Revista de Indias* 66 (Oct.-Dec. 1956): 585–604.

Todorov, Tzvetan. *La Conquête de l'Amérique.* Paris: Editions du Seuil, 1982.

Robert E. Lewis

**DÍAZ FERNÁNDEZ, José** (1898, Aldea del Obispo, Salamanca–1940, Toulouse), journalist, critic, and novelist. An active journalist in Madrid, he was the director of *Nueva España* (New Spain), which he founded with Joaquín

*Arderíus and Antonio *Espina. His first novel, *El blocao* (1928; *The Blockhouse*, 1930), is based upon his experiences in the Moroccan War. It represents a new response to realism amid the vogue of dehumanized art. Víctor Fuentes and Pablo Gil Casado have recognized the significance of Diaz Fernández's essay *El nuevo romanticismo* (1930; The New Romanticism) for any understanding of the social novelists of the *Generation of 1927, whose works offer a radical dramatic alternative to the prevailing elitist ideas of those influenced by *Ortega y Gasset. *La venus mecánica* (1929; The Mechanical Venus), his second and last novel, is also autobiographical; it is an indictment of Madrid society during the last years of the dictatorship of Primo de Rivera, seen through the eyes of a prostitute and a journalist as they awaken to revolutionary ideals.

BIBLIOGRAPHY

Primary Texts

*El blocao*. Madrid: Turner, 1976.
*El nuevo romanticismo*. Ed., study J. M. López de Abiada. Madrid: Esteban, 1985.
*La venus mecánica*. Ed., study J. M. López de Abiada. Barcelona: Laia, 1983.
*Vida de Fermín Galán*. (biografía política) Madrid: Zeus, 1930 (in collaboration with Joaquín Arderíus).

English Translation

*The Blockhouse*. Tr. Helen B. Newsome. London: M. Hopkinson, 1930.

Criticism

Blanco Aguinaga, Carlos, Julio Rodríguez-Puértolas, and Iris M. Zavala. *Historia social de la literatura española*. Madrid: Castalia, 1978.
Fuentes, Víctor. "De la literatura de vanguardia o la de avanzada: en torno a José Díaz Fernández." *Papeles de Son Armadans* 162 (1969): 243–60.
———. Prologue to *El blocao* (1976). Gil Casado, Pablo. *La novela social española (1920–1971)*. Barcelona: Seix Barral, 1973.

                                                                  Porter Conerly

**DÍAZ MAS, Paloma** (1954, Madrid– ), Spanish philologist, critic, and writer of fiction. A specialist in Sephardic literature, she has published a number of technical studies, and a book-length essay, *Los sefardíes: Historia, lengua y cultura* (1986; The Sephardic Jews: History, Language and Culture), a finalist for the National Essay Prize. Díaz Mas holds a doctorate in Romance philology from the U of Madrid, as well as a degree in journalism; she currently resides in Vitoria, where she is a professor of Spanish literature at the U of the País Vasco (Basque Country). Among her professional critical writings are studies of traditional Spanish poetry and the *Romancero (medieval ballad collections).

At the age of nineteen she published her first book of short stories, *Biografías de genios, traidores, sabios y suicidas, según antiguos documentos* (1973; Biographies of Geniuses, Traitors, Wise Men and Suicides, According to Ancient Documents) and ten years later won the City of Toledo Prize for a theatrical piece, *La informante* (1983; The [Female] Informer). Two novels were published in 1984, *El rapto del Santo Grial* (The Sequestering of the Holy Grail), a finalist for the Herralde Prize, and *Tras las huellas de Artorius* (Following the Footsteps of Artorius). *El rapto del Santo Grial* is extremely amusing in its erudite parody of the chivalric tales of the Arthurian cycle, re-created from a subversive, feminist viewpoint, capturing the essentials of the language of legend and chivalric romance at the same time the adventures related are subtly stripped of all epic stature. *Nuestro milenio* (1987; Our Millennium) is a collection of short stories destined for the intellectual delight of well-informed readers, acquainted with the full range of literary development from the early Apocalyptic and earlier Greek myths through medieval and Renaissance texts and several modern European literatures. Interweaving complex intertextual allusions with subtle irony, Díaz Mas offers brilliant style, lexical abundance and a feast for the mind.

BIBLIOGRAPHY

Primary Texts

*El rapto del Santo Grial*. Barcelona: Anagrama, 1984.
*Nuestro milenio*. Barcelona: Anagrama, 1987.

Janet Pérez

**DÍAZ-PLAJA, Fernando** (1918, Barcelona– ), professor, historian and publisher. He has written several meritorious historical essays: *Teresa Cabarrús* (1943); *La vida española en el siglo XVIII* (1946; Spanish Life in the Eighteenth Century); *La historia de España en la poesía* (1946; Spain's History in Her Poetry), and a great number of documentary compilations and anthologies. One of his most successful works in Spain, and also popular abroad, is *El español y los siete pecados capitales* (1966; Spaniards and the Seven Capital Sins), which has gone through numerous editions.

BIBLIOGRAPHY

Primary Texts

*La España franquista en sus documentos*. Esplugas de Llobregat: Plaza & Janés, 1976.
        (Published in 1970 under the title *La posguerra española en sus documentos*.)
*La España que sobrevive*. Madrid: Espasa-Calpe, 1987.
*La vida española en el siglo XVIII*. Barcelona: Martín: 1946.

English Translation

*The Spaniard and the Seven Deadly Sins*. Tr. J. Inderwick. Palmer, NY: Scribner's, 1967.

**DÍAZ-PLAJA, Guillermo** (1909, Manresa–1984, Barcelona), professor of literature and author of didactic works related to literature, he was also a poet: *Primer cuaderno de sonetos* (1941; First Notebook of Sonnets), *Intimidad* (1946; Intimacy). His most important books belong to the field of historico-literary research and essays: *El arte de quedarse solo y otros ensayos* (1936; The Art of Being Alone and Other Essays), *Rubén Darío* (1930), *Introducción al estudio del romanticismo español* (1936, 2nd ed. 1942; Introduction to the Study of Spanish Romanticism), which won the Primer Premio Nacional de Literatura in

1936; *La poesía lírica española* (1937, 2nd ed. 1948; Spanish Lyrical Poetry) and *El espíritu del barroco* (1940; The Spirit of the Baroque). A most prolific man, he directed *Historia de las literaturas hispánicas* (Barcelona, 1950 and following years in several volumes). He published a collection of essays entitled *Poesía y realidad* (1952; Poetry and Reality), and a keen analysis entitled *Modernismo frente a Noventa y Ocho* (1951; Modernism vs. Ninety Eight). He also directed the four-volume *Antología Mayor de la literatura española*. Díaz-Plaja distinguished himself as a brilliant lecturer both in Europe and America. Among his final books one should mention *Memoria de una generación destruida* 1930–1936 (1966; Memory of a Broken Generation), *Las estéticas de Valle-Inclán* (1965; The Aesthetics of Valle-Inclán) and *El oficio de escribir* (1969; The Profession of Writing). He was also director of the Instituto del Libro Español, and a numerary member of the *Academia Española.

BIBLIOGRAPHY

Primary Texts

*Antología Mayor de la literatura española.* 4 vols. 2nd ed. Barcelona: Labor, 1970.
*Historia de la literatura española.* 13th ed. Mexico: Porrúa, 1977.
*Modernismo frente a noventa y ocho.* Madrid: Espasa-Calpe, 1951.
*Memoria de una generación destruida, 1930–1936.* Barcelona: Delos-Aymá, 1966.
*Poesía junta 1941–1966.* Buenos Aires, Losada, 1967.

Criticism

Carrero Eras, Pedro. "Las 'repúblicas' de Torbado y Díaz-Plaja." *Arbor* 390 (n.d.): 99–110.

Isabel McSpadden

**DÍAZ RENGIFO, Juan.** *See* Rengifo, Juan Díaz

**DÍAZ TANCO DE FREGENAL, Vasco** (149?, Fregenal, Extremadura–1560?, ?), actor, writer and printer. Díaz traveled widely as an actor and was known all over Portugal and Castile, as well as in France, Italy and Greece. He probably lived in Turkey at one point in his life, and was apparently held captive for a time (before 1547) in "tierras de infieles" (land of infidels). By his own testimony Díaz was a cleric in the diocese of Badajoz. His first known work, *Los veinte triumphos* (c. 1530; Twenty Triumphs), is a narrative poem which recounts the lives of twenty Spanish noblemen. The text contains much valuable information about Charles V and the early years of his reign. Díaz worked for a while as a printer in Orense (Galicia). While there he published his own account of the Turkish Empire, *Palinodia de la nefanda y fiera nación de los turcos* (1542; Palinode on the Nefarious and Fierce Nation of the Turks), for which he drew on his experiences in that country. In his time he was a famous dramatist and wrote tragedies in the classic mold on biblical themes, such as *Absalón, Amón y Saúl* and *Jonatás en el monte de Gelboé* (Johnathan on Mount Gilboa). None of his dramatic works has survived intact. The prologue of his *Jardín del alma cristiana* (1552; Garden of the Christian Soul) states that Díaz had written, compiled or translated some forty-eight different books. Díaz's extant works display a style which recalls certain Latinate aspects of early *Renaissance authors such as Juan de *Mena. In recent years his works have been studied by the historian and bibliophile Rodríguez-Moñino.

## BIBLIOGRAPHY

### Primary Texts

*Palinodia de los turcos*. Intro. Antonio Rodríguez-Moñino. Badajoz: Institución de Servicios Culturales de la Excelentísima Diputación Provincial de Badajoz, 1947. Facs.

*Los veinte triumphos*. Ed. Antonio Rodríguez-Moñino. Madrid: Gráficos Ultra, 1945.

### Criticism

Rodríguez-Moñino, Antonio. "Díaz Tanco en Bolonia durante la coronación de Carlos V." *Filología* 8 (1962, publ. 1964): 221–40.

Donald C. Buck

**DICENTA, Joaquín** (1863, Calatayud–1917, Alicante), dramatist who also wrote poetry and novels. Dicenta began his career as a playwright with *El suicidio de Werther* (1880; Werther's Suicide), a play in verse belonging to the post-romantic tradition exemplified by the bourgeois dramas of José *Echegaray. His later plays presented ordinary people as protagonists and drew upon class conflict and social injustice as motives for dramatic action. In addition, Dicenta provided his working-class characters with sources of conflict usually reserved for their social superiors—rivalry in love leading to questions of honor, the need for vengeance—and, more significantly, the characters were not objects of comic derision. Dicenta's most famous play, *Juan José* (1895; *Juan José*, 1919), revealed these innovations in an elementary but powerful action. Despite its primary emphasis on sexual rivalry and its recourse to the traditional solution (murder) to problems of honor, the implication that social injustice was inherent in the contemporary class structure was apparent and made *Juan José* the precursor of the social drama in Spain. *El señor feudal* (1897; The Feudal Lord) set its tale of social injustice in Andalusia. *Daniel* (1906) dealt with the organization of mine workers. *El lobo* (1914; The Wolf) reverted to the romantic theme of the criminal transformed by love. *See also* Contemporary Spanish Theater.

## BIBLIOGRAPHY

### Primary Text

*Juan José*. Ed. J. Mas Ferrer. Madrid: Cátedra, 1981.

### English Translation

*Juan José*. In *Contemporary Spanish Dramatists*. Tr. and intro. C. A. Turrell. Boston: Badger, 1919.

Criticism

García Pavón, F. *El teatro social en España*. Madrid: Taurus, 1962. 36–62.
Mas Ferrer, J. *Vida, teatro y mito de Joaquín Dicenta*. Alicante: Instituto de Estudios
    Alicantinos, 1978.
Peak, Hunter J. *Social Drama in Nineteenth Century Spain*. Chapel Hill: U of North
    Carolina P, 1964. 106–18.
                                                                    D. J. O'Connor


**DICENTA, Joaquín, [Jr.]** (1893, Madrid–1967, Madrid), modernist poet, playwright, and journalist. Son of the playwright by the same name, he started writing for the stage and the press at a young age. His modernist poems are characterized by musicality and delicate tones; typical are his early volumes, *El libro de mis quimeras* (1912; The Book of My Whims) and *Lisonjas y lamentaciones* (1913; Flatteries and Lamentations), a book prologued by Benito *Pérez Galdós. As a playwright Dicenta Junior is associated with the poetic theatre cultivated by several other modernist writers, among them *Marquina, *Villaespesa, and the *Machado brothers. All of them used a musical versification that depended on the power of rhyme and rhythm for evoking a vision suggestive of a romantic, idealized past. His plays were extremely popular and were given official recognition: *Son mis amores reales* (1927; My Royal Love) won the Piquer prize of the Academia de la Lengua, and *Leonor de Aquitania* (1933) won the Lope de Vega prize of the Ayuntamiento de Madrid. Both plays are included in his *Obras dramáticas* (1933; Dramatic Works). Despite their artistic merit, however, these plays became dated rather quickly. They were too escapist in nature. Their characters, situations, and language showed total disregard for the socio-political concerns of their time. In addition to the short novel *El baile de los panaderos* (The Bakers' Dance), Dicenta is the author of several other plays such as *El bufón* (1913; The Buffoon), *La leyenda del yermo* (1915?; The Legend of the Wilderness), *El idilio de Pedrín* (1916; Pedrín's Idyll), and the dramatic trilogy titled *Hernán Cortés*. He wrote a large number of plays in collaboration with Antonio Paso: *La casa del señor cura* (1922; The Priest's House), *La casa de salud* (1922; The Rest Home), *Simón y Manuela* (1923), *El tenedor* (1925; The Fork), and even a *zarzuela, *Contrabandista valiente* (1928; Brave Smuggler). In 1956, and with José Jobos, he wrote a *comedia de santos* (religious play), *La zarza sin espinas, Vida y milagros de San Francisco Solano* (1970; The Thornless Bush. Life and Miracles of Saint Francis Solano). *See also* Contemporary Spanish Theater.

BIBLIOGRAPHY

Primary Texts

In *Spanish Plays Collection*; *La casa de salud*, vol. 391; *La casa del señor cura*, vol. 377; *Contrabandista valiente*, vol. 16; *Simón y Manuela*, vol. 16; *Son mis amores reales* vol. 16 and vol. 407; *El tenedor*, vol. 377.

*Obras dramáticas.* Madrid: Reus, 1934.
*La zarza sin espinas.* Cordoba: Real Academia de Ciencias, 1970.
Criticism
Saínz de Robles, Federico. *Ensayo de un diccionario de la literatura.* Madrid: Aguilar,
    1964. 2: 324–25.
Valbuena Prat, A. *Historia del teatro español.* Barcelona: Noguer, 1956. 617.

María A. Salgado

*DICHOS DE SABIOS ET PHILOSOPHOS, Libro de* (Sayings of Wise Men
and Philosophers), early fifteenth-c. unpublished ms. Found at the Escorial Library (b.ij.19 fol. 127), this book is representative of the didactic literary production in prose, from Oriental sources, which began under Ferdinand the Saint
and *Alphonse X the Learned in the thirteenth c. and is known as *catecismos
político-morales* (political and moral catechisms). Translated from the Catalan
to the Castilian vernacular in 1402, this ms. is based on a compilation prepared
by Rabbi Judah b. Astruch, almost a c. earlier, and filled with sententious sayings.

BIBLIOGRAPHY
Criticism
Amador de los Ríos, J. *Historia crítica de la literatura española.* Madrid, 1865. Facs.
    Madrid: Gredos, 1969. 6: 304, n.1.

Reginetta Haboucha

**DIEGO, Gerardo** (1896, Santander– ), poet and critic. Gerardo Diego Cendoya
is one of seven children born to Manuel Diego Barquin, a shopkeeper of modest
means, and Angela Cendoya Uría, his second wife. Gerardo studied arts at a
Jesuit school in Deusto (Bilbao) and philosophy and letters at the Universities
of Salamanca and Madrid, earning a doctorate from the latter. From 1920 to his
election in 1948 to the *Academia Española, Diego taught school in Soria, Gijón,
Santander, and Madrid. He broke into the Spanish literary scene in 1918, after
winning a pedagogical literary contest sponsored by a local journal. That same
year he met *Cansinos Asséns, considered by many the spiritual father of the
Ultraist movement in Spain. It was through Cansinos's chronicles that Diego
was first introduced to the poetry of Vicente Huidobro. Shortly thereafter his
own poems began to appear in many of the Spanish literary journals. Diego
became actively involved in the literary circles of Madrid and Santander, sharing
his ideas on poetry with Eugenio *Montes, Juan *Larrea, Guillermo de *Torre,
Pedro *Garfias, and Huidobro himself. His outspokenness earned him the reputation of ''l'enfant terrible'' of the Spanish poetic Vanguard, and his name
became synonymous with the terms *ultraísmo* and *creacionismo* (revolutionary
poetic movements in Spain during the 1920s). Diego's literary career began
modestly with some prose writings in local journals, but soon blossomed into
one of the richest collections of prose and poetry in the history of Spanish letters.
His articles alone—which number in the hundreds and range from literary criticism to essays on art, music, history and religion—have prompted one frustrated

critic to apologize for not listing them all in the bibliography of his book on the poet. For his work Diego has been awarded nearly every major literary prize: 1925, National Literature Prize for *Versos humanos* (Human Verses); 1961, Literature Prize of the Juan March Foundation; 1967, Grand Cross of Alphonse X; 1968, Gold Medal of Merit for Work; 1980, Cervantes Prize for Literature, the Spanish version of the Nobel Prize. An inquisitive traveler, astute critic, accomplished pianist, and, above all, a talented and sensitive poet, Gerardo Diego could justifiably be called "a man for all seasons."

**Works**

*El Romancero de la novia* (1920; The Ballads of the Bride), *Imagen* (1922; Image), *Soria, Galería de estampas y efusiones* (1923; Soria. Gallery of Prints and Effusions), *Manual de espumas* (1924; Manual of Foam), *Versos humanos* (1925; Human Verses), *Víacrucis* (1931), *Fábula de Equis y Zeda* (1932; Fable of X and Z), *Poemas adrede* (1932; Poems on Purpose), *Ángeles de Compostela* (1940; Angels of Compostela), *Alondra de verdad* (1941; Lark of Truth), *Primera antología* (1941; First Anthology), *Romances (1918–1941)* [1941; Ballads (1918–1941)], *Poemas adrede* (1943; Poems on Purpose), *El Romancero de la novia*, rev. ed. (1943; The Ballads of the Bride), *La sorpresa* (1944; The Surprise), *Soria*, rev. ed. (1948), *Hasta siempre* (1949; Goodbye Forever), *La luna en el desierto y otros poemas* (1949; The Moon in the Desert and Other Poems), *Limbo* (1951), *Versos divinos* (1952; Spiritual Verses), *Biografía incompleta* (1953; Incomplete Biography), *Segundo sueño* (1953; Second Sleep), *Variación* (1954; Variation), *Amazona* (1955; Amazon), *Égloga de Antonio Bienvenida* (1956; Eclogue to Antonio Bienvenida), *Paisaje con figuras* (1956; Landscape with Figures), *Evasión* (1958; Escape), *Amor solo* (1958; Lonely Love), *Canciones a Violante* (1959; Songs to Violante), *Tántalo* (1960; Tantalus), *Ángeles de Compostela*, versión completa (1961; Angels of Compostela, complete version), *Glosa a Villamediana* (1962; Gloss to Villamediana), *La suerte o la muerte* (1963; Luck or Death), *El jándalo* (1964; The Andalusian), *El cerezo y la palmera* (1964; The Cherrytree and the Palmtree), *El cordobés dilucidado* (1966; The Elucidated Cordovan), *Vuelta de peregrino* (1966; The Return of the Traveler), *Odas morales* (1966; Odes of Morality), *Variación 2* (1966; Variation 2), *Poesía amorosa (1918–1969)* (1970; Love Poetry [1918–1969]), *La fundación del querer* (1970; The Foundation of Love), *Cementerio civil* (1972; Civil Cemetery), *Palma de mano abierta* (1973; Open Palm), *Poesía de creación* (1974; Creative Poetry), *Primera antología de sus versos (1918–1941)* (1976; First Anthology of Verses [1918–1941]), *Segunda antología de sus versos (1941–1967)* (1976; Second Anthology of Verses [1941–1967]), *Soria sucedida* (1977; Soria Revisited), *Poemas mayores* (1980; Major Poems), *Poemas menores* (1980; Minor Poems). In addition to these collections of original poetry, Diego has published several editions of his *Poesía española, Antología* (1934; Anthology of Spanish Poetry), and *Antología poética en honor de Góngora* (1927; Poetic Anthology in Honor of Góngora). He has also published countless articles on diverse topics.

Gerardo Diego has been called the personification of the Spanish Vanguard.

506                                                    DIEGO, GERARDO

Not only is he the author of two of the outstanding examples of Ultraist and Creationist poetry, *Imagen* (Image) and *Manual de espumas* (Manual of Foam), but was always one of the staunchest defenders of these poetic movements. Like many of his contemporaries, he flirted with *gongorismo* (poetry in the style of the famous seventeenth-c. poet Luis de *Góngora y Argote). His *Fábula de Equis y Zeda* (Fable of X and Z) is a harmonious blend of Baroque forms and devices defined by a spirit of inventiveness and playfulness characteristic of the new poetry. While Diego's *creacionista* poetry is perhaps his most original and personal poetic contribution, his reputation does not rest on this single facet of his work, but on the depth and breadth of his poetic production. He has made use of nearly every poetic form from the classical odes, eclogues, sonnets, elegies and epistles to the more traditional songs and ballads. The poet himself has said that he cannot help being simultaneously attracted to the country and the city, to the past and the future; that he loves the new art forms as well as the old; that traditional rhetoric is fine, but what truly excites him is the idea of reshaping it to satisfy his own particular whims. In his poetry we find traces of the classics (Homer, Aeschylus, Shakespeare, *Cervantes, *Ignacio de Loyola, San *Juan de la Cruz, *Garcilaso de la Vega) as well as the more modern writers (*Machado Ruiz, Juan Ramón *Jiménez, Cansinos, Ramón *Gómez de la Serna, Huidobro, the Modernists, Purists and French Symbolists). But the dominant influences have been Lope de *Vega and music. Diego considers Lope the greatest of all Spanish poets, and finds in his work a constant source of poetic inspiration. He sees music as a paradigm for what he believes poetry in its purest state should be: a number of diverse elements that combine to form one entity sufficient unto itself. While a poem might have a basis in reality, it aspires to a pure or ideal form which should be judged on its own merit as a work of art. This dehumanized poetry, as *Ortega y Gasset defined it, is what Diego has sought to achieve. For him, the most important dehumanizing element in poetry is, without a doubt, the metaphor, specifically the extended metaphor.

Flowing water is perhaps the most popular of Diego's images, but prevalent also in his poetry are the clock, which symbolizes not so much the passing of time as the interruptions in time, and the butterfly or angel, a dual symbol representing the poet's elusive dreams and his lost innocence.

The predominant themes in Diego's poetry are painting, religion, the bullfight, mythology, the landscape, and, of course, music. Biblical stories are poetically recounted in ''Salmo de la Transfiguración'' (Psalm of the Transfiguration), ''La voz de Isaías'' (The Voice of Isaiah), and ''La doncella de Judit'' (The Maid-servant of Judith). The bullfight is colorfully depicted in *La suerte o la muerte* (Luck or Death). The poet's music is forever with him, be it in the melodious flow of water from a babbling brook or in the sweet song of a lark that reminds him of Chopin. Landscape and travel are also repetitive themes.

Diego's more recent poetry is marked by a tone of nostalgia. This added emotional touch, which Diego had always shunned, lends yet another charming dimension to the poet's verse.

Unfortunately, Gerardo Diego has not been given the critical attention that other members of his poetic generation have received, yet "his work," as King Juan Carlos stated as he presented Diego with the Cervantes Prize, "adds immortality to us all."

## BIBLIOGRAPHY

Primary Texts

*Ángeles de Compostela*. Madrid: Gráficas Valera, 1961.

*Poemas mayores*. Madrid: Alianza, 1980.

*Poemas menores*. Madrid: Alianza, 1980.

*Poesía amorosa (1918–1969)*. 2nd ed. Barcelona: Plaza y Janés, 1970.

*Poesía de creación*. Barcelona: Seix Barral, 1974.

*Poesía española contemporánea (1901–1934)*. Madrid: Taurus, 1974. Anthology of poems by other poets.

*Primera antología de sus versos (1918–1941)*. 7th ed. Madrid: Espasa-Calpe, 1976.

*Segunda antología de sus versos (1941–1967)*. 2nd ed. Madrid: Espasa-Calpe, 1976.

*Soria sucedida*. Barcelona: Plaza y Janés, 1977.

*La suerte o la muerte*. Madrid: Gráficas Valera, 1963.

*Versos divinos*. Madrid: Fundación Conrado Blanco, 1970.

English Translations

8 poems. In *Contemporary Spanish Poetry*. Ed. E. L. Turnbull. New York: Greenwood, 1968.

See also Rudder, R.S. *The Literature of Spain in English Translation*. New York: Ungar, 1975. 397–99.

Arriso, Miledda C. *Gerardo Diego*. Torino: G. Giappichelli, 1955.

Dehenin, Elsa. *La résurgence de Góngora et la génération poétique de 1927*. Paris: Didier, 1962.

Gallego Morell, Antonio. *Vida y poesía de Gerardo Diego*. Barcelona: Editorial Aedos, 1956.

Manrique de Lara, José Gerardo. *Gerardo Diego*. Madrid: EPESA, 1970.

Villar, Arturo del. *Gerardo Diego*. Madrid: Ministerio de Cultura, 1981.

———. *Imagen múltiple*. Madrid: Toro de Barro, 1980. An anthology of poems dedicated to Gerardo Diego and written by other contemporary Hispanic poets.

Robert Manteiga

**DIEGO, Luis de** (1919, Oviedo– ), short story author. He has published a good book of travels entitled *Un velero en el Atlántico* (1957; A Sailboat on the Atlantic), which compiles the experiences and impressions of his sailing aboard the vessel *Elcano*.

## BIBLIOGRAPHY

Primary Text

*Un velero en el Atlántico*. Madrid: Arión, 1957.

Isabel McSpadden

**DIEGO DE ESTELLA.** *See* Estella, Diego de

**DIESTE, Rafael** (1899, Rianxo–1981, La Coruña), Galician writer and philosopher. Dieste's earliest writings were journalistic pieces published in his native Galicia, followed by a book of short stories in the Galician vernacular, *Dos* *arquivos do trasno* (1926; From the Goblin's Archives), which was subsequently revised and augmented on his return from exile in 1963. His second major work, a play written in Galician, *A fiestra valdeira* (1927; The Empty Window), was highly praised by Eugene O'Neill.

Dieste was a sponsor of the Pedagogical Missions, introduced by the Spanish Republic in 1931 to expand cultural activities to the provinces, and was in charge of its guignol (puppet) theater, for which he wrote several pieces. He emigrated to Argentina in 1939, where he published an expanded version of his 1933 book of poetry, *Rojo farol amante* (1940; Loving Red Lantern), and revisions of earlier plays in a trilogy entitled *Viaje, duelo y perdición* (1945; Journey, Duel, and Perdition). He published his masterwork, *Historias e invenciones de Félix Muriel* (Stories and Inventions of Félix Muriel), in Buenos Aires in 1943. It is an exploration of memory with magical and poetic realism and extraordinarily lyrical prose. Félix Muriel serves as either narrator, observer or actor of the ten stories set in Galicia, which include stories, folktales, and vignettes. Some seem disarmingly simple, about childhood incidents, but their recollection has mythical, philosophical and surrealistic overtones that turn them into unforgettable and transcendental experiences, both for the narrator and the reader. Self-encounter, the passing of time, the pleasures and dangers of memory, the human values of friendship and charity, and the wonders and small miracles of life and nature are major motifs. A new edition was published in Spain after Dieste's return in 1961 and was received by critics as an extraordinary work. A new annotated edition in 1985 incorporated another Félix Muriel story that belonged to the same period, and *El País* (December 16, 1985, p. 2) hailed it as "one of the most important books of narrative in Spanish history in the last half-century."

Dieste's writings also include several books on mathematics and philosophical essays: *Luchas con el desconfiado* (1948; Struggles with the Distrustful) and *Diálogo de Manuel y David* (1966; Dialogue of Manuel and David, about Kant and Hume). He authored a book on tragedy and history, *La vieja piel del mundo* (1936; The Old Skin of the World), and other works on language, orthography, and painting.

Posthumous publications include a previously unpublished, highly original narrative re-creating the world "on the other side" that some call the afterlife, *La isla* (1985; The Island), in the same volume with a philosophical essay, *Tablas de un naufragio* (Boards of a Shipwreck); two volumes of theater (1981); a revised edition of earlier philosophical essays called *El alma y el espejo* (1981; The Soul and the Mirror); Dieste's early journalism in Galician; and *Antre a terra e o ceo* (1981; Between Earth and Sky), a collection of letters and essays: *Testimonios y homenajes* (1983; Testimonies and Tributes).

Dieste stands out among twentieth-c. writers as a philosopher-narrator who translates his own ontological and epistemological concerns into creative literature in different genres. He combines a profoundly Galician spirit with universal themes and myths, particularly in his masterpiece, *Félix Muriel*.

BIBLIOGRAPHY

Primary Texts

*El alma y el espejo.* Madrid: Alianza, 1981.
*Dos arquivos do trasno.* Vigo: Galaxia, 1973.
*Historias e invenciones de Félix Muriel.* Ed. E. Irizarry. Madrid: Cátedra, 1985.
*La Isla—Tablas de un naufragio.* Barcelona: Anthropos, 1985.
*Viaje, duelo y perdición.* Pamplona: Peralta, 1979.

English Translations

"The Bishop's Blessing." Tr. C. Preston. In . . . *And Spain Sings.* Ed. J. J. Benardete
    and R. Humphries. New York: Vanguard, 1937. (Poem)
"The New Spectacle of Wonders." Tr. A. L. Lloyd. In *New Writing* 4 (1938): 232–44.
"The Stuffed Parrot." Tr. Z. Da Silva. In *Great Spanish Stories.* Ed. A. Flores. New
    York: Modern Library, 1956.

Criticism

*Grial* (Vigo) 78 (1982). Special issue devoted to Dieste.
Irizarry, E. *La creación literaria de Rafael Dieste.* Sada–La Coruña: Castro, 1980.
———. *Rafael Dieste.* TWAS 554. Boston: Twayne, 1979. In English.

                                                            Estelle Irizarry

**DÍEZ, Antonio** (fl. 1535–?), book vendor, dramatic author. In about 1535, the *Auto llamado de Clarindo* (Clarindo's Play) appeared under his name. Of minor literary value, it is a love story between two pairs of lovers, in the tradition of the *Celestina. It is, however, the first three-act play written in Spanish, despite claims of dramatists such as *Avendaño, *Cervantes and *Virués.

BIBLIOGRAPHY

Primary Text

*Auto de Clarindo.* In *Obras dramáticas del siglo XVI. Primer serie.* Ed. G. Ochoa.
    Madrid: n.p., 1914. Facs.

**DÍEZ-CANEDO, Enrique** (1879, Badajoz–1944, Mexico), poet, translator, critic. He initiated several post-modernism trends in Spanish lyricism. An essential constant of his verse is the perfect balance between intellectual and artistic faculties. His poetry books are *Versos de las horas* (1906; Poems of the Hours), *La visita del sol* (1907; The Visit of the Sun), *La sombra del ensueño* (1910; The Shadow of the Dream), *Imágenes* (1910; Images), *Algunos versos* (1924; Some Verses), and *Epigramas americanas* (1928; American Epigrams). He has masterfully translated both French and English modern poets such as Verlaine and Francis Jammes to Spanish, as well as works by Montaigne, Webster and Wells. For years he was a literary critic and collaborator on *El Sol* and other newspapers. Current on both European and Latin American literature, he traveled as a diplomat throughout most of South America. In Madrid he was both the director and a professor of the Escuela Central de Idiomas (Central Language

School). His main prose works are *Sala de retratos* (1920; Portrait Room), *Conversaciones literarias* (1921; Literary Conversations) and *Los dioses del Prado* (1931; The Gods of the Prado). He was a numerary member of the *Academia Española.

BIBLIOGRAPHY

Primary Texts

*Conversaciones literarias.* Mexico: Mortiz, 1964.
*Estudios de poesía española contemporánea.* Mexico: Mortiz, 1965.
*Sala de retratos.* San José, Costa Rica: García Monge, 1920.
*El teatro español de 1914 a 1936.* Mexico: Mortiz, 1968.
*El teatro y sus enemigos.* Buenos Aires: Ver, 1963.
*La visita del sol.* Madrid: Pueyo, 1907.

English Translations

"The Contemporary Spanish Theatre." Tr. S. P. Underhill. In *The Theatre in a Changing Europe.* Ed. T. H. Dickinson. New York: Holt, 1937.
"Prayer in a Garden." Tr. E. Allison Peers. *Translation (London).* Ed. N. Braybrooke and E. King. London: Phoenix, 1945.

Criticism

Poylo, Anne. "Enrique Díez-Canedo, traductor de Valery Larboud." *Insula* 396–97 (1979): 26.

                                                                                    Isabel McSpadden

**DÍEZ CRESPO, Manuel** (1911, Seville– ), poet connected with the group Mediodía (Noon). He has published *La voz anunciada* (1941; The Announced Voice), with a foreword by Father Justo Pérez de Urbel, and *Yo y mi sombra (Poemas de Sevilla)* (1974; Me and My Shadow [Poems of Seville]).

BIBLIOGRAPHY

Primary Texts

*Memorias y deseos, poesía, 1941–50.* Madrid: Nacional, 1951.
*Yo y mi sombra (Poemas de Sevilla).* Sevilla: Municipal, 1974.

                                                                                    Isabel McSpadden

**DÍEZ DE GÁMEZ, Gutierre** (1378?, Galicia–1450, ?), lieutenant and aide of Don Pero Niño and author of *El victorial: Crónica de don Pero Niño, conde de Buelna* (n.d.; *The Unconquered Knight*, 1928). This chivalric chronicle does not completely cover the life of Don Pero since it ends in 1446 and he died in 1453. It portrays the count as a model knight, forceful and gallant, while describing his life of tournaments and naval battles. There are quotations from the *Libro de *Alexandre*, aphorisms, morals, and songs. Unusual judgments on Englishmen, Frenchmen, and Spaniards are also made, and there is an interesting passage on arms and learning similar to that in the *Quijote* (I, 38). Don Pero's character comes through by means of the grandeur of his deeds, though he does acquire a somewhat idealized stature from the extensive praise he receives. He himself showed his appreciation of the chronicle by providing in his will that a copy be kept in the coffer of a church treasury. *See also* Crónicas.

BIBLIOGRAPHY

Primary Text

*El victorial: Crónica de don Pero Niño, conde de Buelna.* Ed. Juan de Mata Carriazo. Colección de Crónicas Españolas. Madrid: Espasa-Calpe, 1940.

English Translation

*The Unconquered Knight. A Chronicle of the Deeds of Don Pero Niño.* Tr. Joan Evans. London: Routledge, 1928.

Criticism

Giménez, Antonio. "El arquetipo de caballero en la *Crónica de Don Pero Niño.*" *CH* 326–27 (1977): 338–52.

Surtz, Ronald E. "Díez de Games' Deforming Mirror of Chivalry: The Prologue to the *Victorial.*" *Neophilologus* 65 (1981): 214–18.

Lucy Sponsler

**DÍEZ DEL CORRAL, Luis** (1911, Logroño– ), renowned essayist. He has written historical and sociological essays for various journals, as well as *Ensayos sobre arte y sociedad* (1955; Essays on Art and Society), *La función del mito clásico en la literatura contemporánea* (1957; The Function of Classical Myths in Contemporary Literature), and *Del viejo al nuevo mundo* (1963; From the Old to the New World). He has also written a noteworthy book of direct impressions, *Mallorca* (1942), and an extensive *essay titled *El liberalismo doctrinario* (1945; Doctrinary Liberalism). His *El rapto de Europa* (1954; *The Rape of Europe,* 1959) won him recognition as one of the most accurate interpreters of Occidental culture; it has been translated to English, Italian, French, German, Dutch and Japanese. He has also successfully translated Hölderin.

BIBLIOGRAPHY

Primary Texts

*La función del mito clásico en la literatura contemporánea.* Madrid: Gredos, 1957.
*El liberalismo doctrinario.* 3rd ed. Madrid: Instituto de Estudios Políticos, 1973.
*Mallorca.* Barcelona: Juventud, 1942.
*La monarquía hispánica en el pensamiento político europeo: de Maquiavelo a Humboldt.* Madrid: Alianza, 1983.
*Perspectivas de una Europa raptada.* Madrid: Seminarios y Ediciones, 1974.
*El rapto de Europa.* Madrid: RO, 1954.

English Translation

*The Rape of Europe.* Tr. H. V. Livermore. New York: Macmillan, 1959.

Isabel McSpadden

*DIEZ MANDAMIENTOS* (Ten Commandments), a brief thirteenth-c. guide for priests hearing confession. The work lists each commandment with a short explanation of how each may be violated, and then gives other questions to be asked of the penitent. It is one of the earliest examples of Castilian prose.

BIBLIOGRAPHY
Primary Text
*Diez mandamientos.* Ed. A. Morel-Fatio. *Romania* 16 (1887): 379–82.

**DIONÍSIO, Mário** (1916, Lisbon– ), Portuguese poet. Dionísio belongs to the group of the *Novo Cancioneiro*, although he is also associated with a number of other Lisbon poetic groups. *Riso Dissonante* (1950; Dissonant Laughter) combines lyric and combative tones, opposing the senses of hope and despair, loss of things past and hope for the future. Early works are somewhat schematic, as in *Dia Cinzento* (1944; Day of Ashes), with later books tending toward formalism. *Poesia Incompleta, 1936–1965* (1966; Incomplete Poems) brings together all of Dionísio's poetry up to that date. He has also cultivated the essay and literary criticism, as well as serving as an art critic. His criticism can be classified as generally neo-realistic, as in *A Paleta e o mundo* (2 vols., 1956–62; The Palette and the World) and several other works devoted to interpretation and problems of the plastic arts.

BIBLIOGRAPHY
Primary Texts
*Monólogo a duas vozes, histórias.* Lisbon: Dom Quixote, 1986.
*A paleta e o mundo.* 2nd ed. 5 vols. Lisbon: Publicações Europa-América, 1973–74.
*Poesia incompleta, 1936–65.* Lisbon: Europa-América, 1966.
                                                           Janet Pérez

**DIOSDADO, Ana** (1938, Buenos Aires– ), Spanish playwright, novelist, and actress. Daughter of Spanish actor-director Enrique Diosdado, she began her acting career as a child in Argentina before the family returned to Spain, where she completed her education. She began writing in the 1960s, publishing two novels, but her real importance as an author resides in her theater. In the 1970s she had five original plays produced in Madrid and became the most prominent woman playwright on the contemporary Spanish stage. Two of her works, *Olvida los tambores* (1970; Forget the Drums) and *Usted también podrá disfrutar de ella* (1973; You, Too, Can Enjoy Her), number among the dozen longest-running Spanish plays of the decade and were awarded major theater prizes.

Underlying all of Diosdado's plays is a humanitarian plea for greater communication, understanding, and freedom, but the individual works vary considerably in structure, tone, and setting. *Olvida los tambores* deals with diametrically opposed lifestyles of two young couples in the present. It requires a representational stage setting, conforms to the three unities, and may be considered a traditional well-made play. *Usted también podrá disfrutar de ella* also is a realistic play dealing with a contemporary situation—the exploitation of individuals by capitalist enterprises—but calls for a nonrepresentational staging to facilitate the free flow among six locations at five moments in time. *El okapi* (1972; The Okapi) has a surface level of realism, revolving around the stagnated life of the elderly, but also functions as an allegory extolling freedom. *Los comuneros* (1974; The Commoners) is an ambitious history play, dealing with the execution of the leaders in a popular revolt against Charles I. The mode is that of psychological expressionism; the action is an extended flashback, screened through the consciousness of the king. Her most completely allegorical work, *Y de Cachemira, chales* (1976; And Shawls from Kashmir), presents four survivors of a nuclear war trapped within a department store but is, in fact, a metaphorical commentary on the end of the Franco era.

Diosdado has also prepared Spanish adaptations of several foreign plays, including Tennessee Williams's *Cat on a Hot Tin Roof*, 1979, and Ibsen's *A Doll's House*, 1983, and was the author of a television series, "Trece anillos de oro" (1983; Thirteen Wedding Bands), in which she starred in the role of a divorce lawyer. *See also* Contemporary Spanish Theater.

BIBLIOGRAPHY

Primary Texts

*El okapi*. Madrid: Escelicer, 1972.
*Olvida los tambores*. Madrid: Escelicer, 1972.
*Usted también podrá disfrutar de ella*. Madrid: MK, 1975.
*Los comuneros*. Madrid: Preyson, 1983.
*Y de Cachemira, chales*. Madrid: Preyson, 1983.

Criticism

Anderson, Farris. "From Protest to Resignation." *Estreno* 2.2 (1976): 29–32.
Zatlin-Boring, Phyllis. "The Theater of Ana Diosdado." *Estreno* 3.1 (1977): 13–17.
———. "Ana Diosdado and the Contemporary Spanish Theater." *Estreno* 10.2 (1984): 37–40.

Phyllis Zatlin

*DISPUTA DE ELENA Y MARÍA* (Debate between Elena and Maria), poem. This thirteenth-c. debate poem from León, also known as the debate between the cleric (scholar) and the knight, was found in a fourteenth-c. ms. The incomplete text consists of 402 metrically irregular lines in which the eight-syllable line predominates in couplet form. Occasionally, the anonymous poet employs assonance. Maria, the girlfriend of an abbot, and Elena, a knight's sweetheart, argue about which of their lovers is superior. In the popular style of the medieval debate or dispute, Maria praises the material comforts of the cleric's life while Elena prefers life with a man of action. Eventually the young ladies appear before the king so that he can decide the issue, but here the ms. ends. The question of whether a life dedicated to letters is preferable to one devoted to arms or vice versa is a frequent theme in both Latin and medieval French poetry. The Spanish poem represents the ultimate evolution of the theme and is believed to have as its source a French poem called *Le Jugement d'amour*. *See also* Edad Media, Literatura de la.

BIBLIOGRAPHY

Primary Texts

Menéndez Pidal, R. "Disputa de Elena y María." *RFE* 1 (1914): 56–96.

Pinto, Mario di. *Due contrasti d'amore nella Spagna medievales.* (Razón de amor e Elena y María). Pisa: Goliardica, 1959.

Criticism

Blanco-González, B. *Del cortesano al discreto. Examen de una "decadencia."* Vol. 1. Madrid: Gredos, 1962.

Menéndez Pidal, R. *Tres poemas primitivos: Elena y María, "Roncesvalles," Historia troyana polimétrica.* Buenos Aires: Espasa-Calpe, 1958.

Tavani, G. "Il dibattito sul chierico e il cavalière nella tradizione mediolatina e volgare." *Romanistiches Jahrbuch* 15 (1964): 73–79.

Lucy Sponsler

***DISPUTA DEL ALMA Y DEL CUERPO*** (Debate between the Body and the Soul), poem. In this fragment (37 lines) of a poem in *mester de juglaría*, dating from the end of the twelfth or beginning of the thirteenth c., the soul and body of a dead man blame each other for sins committed during life. The parchment ms., dated 1201, was found by Tomás Muñoz Romero in the monastery of Oña and contains only the soul's part of the debate. It is a translation of a French poem, *Débat du corps et de l'âme*, which in turn derives from a Latin one, *Rixa animi et corporis*. The topic had a long life and even appears as the theme of *Calderón's *auto sacramental, *El pleito matrimonial del alma y el cuerpo* (The Matrimonial Quarrel between the Body and the Soul). *See also* Auto.

BIBLIOGRAPHY

Primary Texts

*Débat de l'âme et du corps.* Ed. C. de Roche. Basel: Kreis, 1980.

"La disputa del alma y del cuerpo." Ed. R. Menéndez Pidal. *RABM* 4 (1900): 451–53. Includes ms. facs.

"La disputa del alma y del cuerpo." Ed. A. G. Solalinde. *HR* 1 (1933): 196–207. Includes text and comparison with French poem.

Criticism

Groult, P. "*La disputa del Alma y del Cuerpo.* Sources et originalité." In *Linguistic and Literary Studies in Honor of Helmut A. Hatzfeld.* Ed. A. Crisafulli. Washington, DC: Catholic U of America P, 1964. 221–29.

Von Kraemer, E. *Dos versiones castellanas de la "Disputa del Alma y el Cuerpo."* Helsinki: n.p., 1956.

Lucy Sponsler

**DOBLADO, Don Leocadio.** *See* Blanco White, José María

***DOCTRINA DE LA DISCRICIÓN*** (Doctrine of Discretion), treatise on Christian doctrine. It is found in the same ms. as the *Proverbs* of Rabbi Sem *Tob, now located in the Escorial Library. This text is comprised of 154 stanzas in monorhymed octosyllabic tercets and was written by Pedro de Veragüe, as stated in the final stanza. The treatise explains the Ten Commandments, the Credo, the seven mortal sins, etc. It was widely read until the early sixteenth c. and represents the oldest Spanish catechism. *See also* Catechetical Literature.

BIBLIOGRAPHY

Primary Texts

*Doctrina de la Discrición.* BAE 58.
*Doctrina de la Discrición.* Ed. R. Foulché-Delbosc. *RH* 14 (1906): 565–97.

Lucy Sponsler

**DOMENCHINA, Juan José** (1898, Madrid–1959, Mexico), poet, journalist and essayist. Although he studied pedagogy, Domenchina never taught. He took part in politics during the Second Republic, and subsequently went into exile for the remainder of his life. As a newspaper critic, he published many articles in the prominent Madrid daily *El Sol* during the 1930s. Books of poetry include *Del poema eterno* (1917; Of the Eternal Poem); *Las interrogaciones del silencio* (1918; Interrogations of Silence); *La corporeidad de lo abstracto* (1929; The Corporeal Abstract); *El tacto fervoroso* (1930; The Fervent Touch) and *Margen* (1933; Margin). Domenchina wrote at least a pair of novels, *La túnica de Neso* (1919; Neso's Tunic) and *Dédalo* (1932; Daedalus), the latter with a prologue by Juan Ramón *Jiménez. Domenchina's works of the 1920s and 1930s show typical vanguardist influence and the "dehumanized" traits characteristic of the period; his earlier poetry is the product of a disciple of Juan Ramón Jiménez, but with more Baroque elements in the form. Other discernible influences include Valéry, and Spanish classics, especially *Quevedo. His last book of poetry, published in exile in Mexico, is *Exul Umbra* (1948).

BIBLIOGRAPHY

Primary Texts

*La corporeidad de lo abstracto.* Madrid and Buenos Aires: Renacimiento, 1929.
*El estrañado y otros poemas.* Madrid: Rialp, 1969.
*Perpetuo arraigo. Destierro. Pasión de sombra. Tres elegías jubilares. Exul Umbra. La sombra desterrada (1939–1949).* Mexico: Signo, 1949.
*Poesías completas (1915–1934).* Madrid: Signo, 1936.

Criticism

Zardoya, Concha. "Juan José Domenchina, poeta de la sombra." In her *Poesía española contemporánea.* Madrid: Guadarrama, 1961. 397–410.

**DOMÈNECH I ESCUTÉ DE CAÑELLAS, Maria,** also known as Josep Miralles (1877, Alcover–1952, Barcelona), novelist. She advocated better education for women and founded the Federació sindical d' obreres, a union for working women. The nine stories in *Confidències* (1946; Confidences) are about nine women who tell us their intimate feelings through monologues and dialogues. *Contrallum* (1917; Against the Light) is a psychological novel about a young man who suffers from the strictures of tradition, a small town, his social class, and an unhappy marriage.

BIBLIOGRAPHY

Primary Texts

*Confidències*. Barcelona: NAGSA, 1946.
*Contrallum*. Barcelona: Publicació Catalana, 1917.
*Els gripaus d'or*. Valencia: Fidel Giro, 1919.
*Herències*. Barcelona: Societat catalana d'edicions, 1925.
*Neus*. Barcelona: Joventut, 1914.
*Al rodar del temps*. Barcelona: NAGSA, 1946.

Kathleen McNerney

**DOMÍNGUEZ BERRUETA, Juan** (1866, Salamanca–1958, Salamanca), historian, educator, essayist. A professor of mathematics in Salamanca, his works include *La cientificomanía* (1895; Scientificomania), *Música nueva* (1900; New Music), *La canción de la sombra* (1910; Shadow's Song), *Fray Juan de los Angeles* (1927), *El cardenal Cisneros* (1929; Cardinal Cisneros), and *Un cántico a lo divino* (1931; Song to the Divine).

BIBLIOGRAPHY

Primary Texts

*La canción de la sombra*. Madrid: Espasa-Calpe, 1935.
*Un cántico a lo divino; vida y pensamiento de San Juan de la Cruz*. Barcelona: Araluce, 1931.
*El cardenal Cisneros*. Madrid: Aguilar, 1929.
*Filosofía mística española*. Madrid: CSIC, 1947.
*Fray Juan de los Angeles*. Madrid: Voluntad, 1927.

Isabel McSpadden

**DON JUAN, The myth of.** The figure of Don Juan has emerged through the centuries as the most enduring and influential produced by the literature of any nation. The mythic dimension of that quintessential Spanish character has been firmly established and is widely recognized by a number of critics from Spain as well as from a number of other countries. In examining literary manifestations of the legend in Spain, the possibilities of illuminating different cultures, periods and artistic movements by comparing the treatments of a common character and legend across chronological and national boundaries become apparent. The growing awareness on the part of each subsequent Don Juan character of his own mythic nature is influenced by each of his predecessors. The two primary components of the Don Juan legend are the character as the seducer of women and an element of the supernatural which involves a reciprocal invitation to dinner extended by Don Juan and a representative of the other world. While other countries have legends which incorporate some of these features, the double invitation appears to be unique to Spain. Its earliest manifestations are found in several *romances* (See *Romancero*) discovered by the renowned medievalist Ramón *Menéndez Pidal. One ballad tells of a man who goes to church not to pray but to look at pretty girls. En route one Sunday, he comes across a skull in the street. He kicks it and invites it to his home. The skull comes and invites the young man to visit his tomb at midnight. The man does so and is able to leave alive. This third meeting with death is only because he is wearing a religious relic. In another version, which approximates more closely what will become the first formal literary work, the young rake pulls the beard of a statue. There is a clear suggestion of a previous hostile relationship between the young man and the representative of the dead. The second ballad then follows the plot line of the first except that the reason the young man escapes unpunished is that he went to confession before appearing in response to the statue's return invitation.

Although several problems remain unresolved in determining the direct influence of these ballads on *Tirso de Molina, they are generally accepted as having provided him with the basis for his drama *El burlador de Sevilla* (1630; *The Playboy of Seville*, 1963). The two key motifs of the drama, which define both its theme and its dramatic energy, are "esta noche he de gozalla" (I shall possess her this very night) and "tan largo me lo fiáis" (there is plenty of time for me to repent). The former communicates the energy of the play and its protagonist, suggesting both his dynamism and his total commitment to the present moment. And the latter suggests the religious theme that was of paramount importance to the author who was, after all, a priest. Tirso's Don Juan is not an atheist; he simply chooses to ignore religious and moral considerations. He does, however, call for confession when confronted with death. Despite Tirso's theme that man must lead a virtuous life and be prepared to meet his maker at any moment, the dramatist's admiration for the daring and bravery of his character, especially in his encounters with the supernatural, infuses the climactic scenes of the work with dramatic energy and impact. The appeal of the work lies more in the fascination and wonder generated by the presence of supernatural forces than in the impact of the seduction scenes. Although there is certainly some truth in the contention that the character of Don Juan is of greater interest as a mythic figure than he is in any individual work of literature, the merits of Tirso's drama should not be discounted.

The most widely known and beloved of the Don Juan plays in Spain is José *Zorrilla's version of 1844 entitled *Don Juan Tenorio*. A distinguishing feature of that drama is the use of the inn where Don Juan and his rival Don Luis first make their bet as to who is the more virile as evidenced by the number of women they can seduce in a year and the number of men they can kill in duels. That setting, which functions as a theater within a theater, sets the tone for the heightened theatricality of the play, which is further distinguished from Don Juan plays of other periods by allowing Don Juan to fall in love. His feelings for Doña Inés cause him to prostrate himself at the feet of her father and ultimately result in his salvation at the moment of his death because of the intervention of

Inés's soul. This Romantic rendition undermines the central theme of Tirso's original drama completely. The work suffers from a diffuseness, self-indulgence and heavy-handedness in imagery and plot construction. Despite these flaws, its tremendous appeal—enhanced to a large degree by the lush, palpably evocative verses of Zorrilla and its association with the religious holiday of All Souls Day—has assured its position of pre-eminence in Spanish theater. Zorrilla's Don Juan has become a character conscious of the role he is playing, and Zorrilla's text enables him to portray himself with verve and to embody the ideals of Spanish *machismo* in a manner that continues to appeal to many Spaniards.

The contemporary work that comes closest to the spirit of the original play by Tirso is Jacinto *Grau's *El burlador que no se burla* (1930; The Seducer who Doesn't Seduce). The myth of Don Juan is manifested not merely in the actions of the protagonist and his expressed awareness of the role he is playing, but also in the reference to a series of lectures on the subject that appears in the play itself. One character explains Don Juan in terms of the affirmation of polygamy introduced into Spanish culture by the Moors. The play combines action with sections of static discourse. But there is appeal in the scenes of sexual conquest and in Don Juan's confrontation with the forces of the supernatural. Rather than a statue, Grau utilizes the Devil himself who urges the protagonist to rebel against God as he did. Don Juan refuses, however, asserting that he is his sole master. In that sense, he is quite different from the devout hero created by Tirso and the uncertain agnostic placed on the stage by Zorrilla. Still, the valor of the unrepentant hero generates dramatic impact. The epilogue of the play presents three of Don Juan's victims; they all express no regrets for their actions and assert their admiration for Don Juan.

Numerous works in Spain and in other countries have incorporated the figure of Don Juan. His honor as reputation based on sexual exploits and his unrivaled egocentricity link him with Spain, but do not diminish his universal appeal. Works of international renown devoted to his adventures include a Molière drama, Mozart's opera *Don Giovanni*, a Lord Byron poem and Richard Strauss's tone poem. In Spain numerous authors, abandoning the formal legend but presenting a clearly identifiable Don Juan figure, have sought to adapt the myth to their particular thematic or aesthetic purposes. Within the *Generation of 1898 alone, we encounter *Azorín's poetic novel *Doña Inés* (1925), *Unamuno's drama *El hermano Juan* (1929; Brother Juan) and Ramón del *Valle-Inclán's *esperpento*, *Las galas del difunto* (1926; The Dead Man's Finery). This broad range of works attests to the vitality of the myth and to the enduring fascination that the figure of Don Juan has continued to exert on artists and writers everywhere.

## BIBLIOGRAPHY

Primary Texts

Grau, Jacinto. *El burlador no se burla*. Buenos Aires: Losada, 1941.
Tirso de Molina. *El burlador de Sevilla y convidado de piedra*. Ed. Gerald Wade. New York: Scribner's, 1968.

Zorrilla, José. *Don Juan Tenorio*. Ed. Lewis Brett. In *Nineteenth Century Spanish Plays*. New York: Appleton-Century Crofts, 1963.

English Translation

Tirso de Molina's *The Playboy of Seville* and José Zorrilla's *Don Juan Tenorio*. In *The Theater of Don Juan*. Ed. Oscar Mandel. Lincoln: U of Nebraska P, 1963.

Criticism

Baquero, Arcadio. *Don Juan y su evolución dramática*. 2 vols. Madrid: Nacional, 1966.
Ebersole, Alva. *Disquisiciones sobre "el Burlador de Sevilla" de Tirso de Molina*. Salamanca: Almar, 1980.
Feal, Carlos. "Conflicting Names, Conflicting Laws: Zorrilla's Don Juan Tenorio." *PMLA* 96.3 (May 1981): 375–87.
———. *En nombre de don Juan (Estructura de un mito literario)*. West Lafayette: Purdue UP, 1986.
Grescioni Neggers, Gladys. *Don Juan* (Hoy). Madrid: Turner, 1977.
Weinstein, Leo. *The Metamorphoses of Don Juan*. Stanford: Stanford UP, 1959.

Peter L. Podol

**DONOSO CORTÉS, Juan** (1809, Valle de la Serena, Badajoz–1853, Paris), professor, politician, essayist and orator. After studying in Cáceres and Seville, he became a professor at the Colegio de Humanidades in Seville. Later, having moved to Madrid, he took part in politics and began to write and speak publicly. In 1851 he was named plenipotentiary minister in Paris, after having been named Marquis of Valdegamas and having served on the Spanish legation in Prussia. In Paris he gained great notoriety and the friendship of Catholic writers such as Veuillot and Montalembert.

His most important work is his *Ensayo sobre el catolicismo, el liberalismo y el socialismo* (1851; Essay on Catholicism, Liberalism and Socialism), which gave rise to polemics inside Spain and in other European countries as well. In 1856 *Valera wrote a penetrating commentary about Donoso's *Ensayo*. His other writings include lectures in the Atheneum (*Ateneo), articles, letters and speeches. He was a brilliant orator whose speeches are characterized by their use of rhetoric and expressive force. His religious ideas, presented with the vehemence of a recent convert, are marked by an extremely traditional attitude which contrasts with his original doctrinarianism. He defends Catholicism and authoritarian politics. Stylistically, he delights in oratorical antithesis, comparisons and contrasts; his tone is passionate and grandiloquent. Marcelino *Menéndez y Pelayo says that Donoso was more a polemicist than philosopher, and more an orator than polemicist.

BIBLIOGRAPHY

Primary Texts

*Obras completas*. Ed. Juan Juretschke. Madrid: Católica, 1946.

English Translation

*An Essay on Catholicism, Authority and Order Considered in Their Fundamental Principles*. Tr. Madeleine Vincent Goddard. New York: J. F. Wagner, 1925.

Criticism

Caturelli, Alberto. *Donoso Cortés. Ensayo sobre su filosofía de la historia*. Córdoba: Universidad, 1958.

Galindo Herrero, S. *Donoso Cortés y su teoría política*. Badajoz: Diputación, 1957.

Sánchez Abelenda, Raúl. *La teoría del poder en el pensamiento político de Juan Donoso Cortés*. Buenos Aires: Universitaria, 1969.

Schramm, Edmund. *Donoso Cortés. Su vida y su pensamiento*. Madrid: Espasa-Calpe, 1936.

Suárez, Federico. *Introducción a Donoso Cortés*. Madrid: Rialp, 1964.

Valera, Juan de. "Estudios criticos sobre filosofía y religión." In *Obras completas*. Madrid: Aguilar, 1961. 2: 1377–93.

Phoebe Porter Medina

**DOTOR, Ángel** (1898, Argamasilla de Alba, Ciudad Real–?), essayist, author of travel books. He has written books and essays about several cities, cathedrals, paintings, painters, and New World conquerors such as Hernán *Cortés.

BIBLIOGRAPHY

Primary Texts

*Catedrales de España*. 2nd ed. Gerona: Carles, 1952.

*Don Quijote y el Cid: el alma de Castilla*. Rev., expanded ed. Madrid: Nacional, 1945.

Isabel McSpadden

**DUARTE, Afonso** (1884, Ereira–1958, Ereira), Portuguese poet. Afonso Duarte's poetical itinerary begins under the sign of *saudosismo*, which Fernando *Pessoa defined as "pantheistic transcendentalism," and some influence of António Nobre and Guerra Junqueiro, two recognized masters of poets associated with the literary review *A Águia* (The Eagle), which advanced the ideals of *saudosismo*. The *saudosist* phase of Afonso Duarte's poetry covers the books collected in *Os 7 Poemas Líricos* (1929; The Seven Lyrical Poems) and, in general terms, is guided by a poetics in which such aims as a "sublime art," through an exaltation of the "cosmic beauty of life" and an elevated and noble style, stand out. In a second phase, initiated by *Ossadas* (1947; Bones) and comprised of such titles as *Post-Scriptum de um Combatente* (1949; Postscript of a Warrior), *O Anjo da Morte e Outros Poemas* (1956; The Death Angel and Other Poems), and *Lápides e Outros Poemas* (1960; Tombstones and Other Poems), Afonso Duarte leaves behind the "long" poems of the first phase and their "entangled style" and now composes "brief poems/like the instant of the flower/which opened up to die," the rude and austere "epigramatic style," which, however, makes use of "words" puddled in the "clay of his humanity." The love for the "people" that could already be perceived in his first books, takes, from *Ossadas* on, new tones, often by means of his condition as a farmer, which makes him the brother of the "poor who ploughs the land / with his arm," and at the same time emphasizes the different look he now casts at the landscape, far from the "abstract lines" in which he spoke about "Things" as "ghosts praying.'' The proud denouncement of Salazar's authoritarian rule (he envisions the country as a ''prison''), the ''tough fighting spirit'' that puts him close to the ''young poets'' animated by ''faith'' in the future (the neo-realist poets in Coimbra, in the late thirties and the early forties), does not prevent him from signing a maxim in which, opposite to Manichean simplifications common at the golden period of neo-realism, it is proclaimed that ''there is as much humanity / in the one who looks after a flower / as in the one who repairs / the dynamic lines of an engine.'' Afonso Duarte is, in the period after World War II, one of the first poets in Portugal to call attention to the ''atomic fright'' and to fix in verse ''the new mystique which burns the world.'' In the triptych written between 1950 and 1952—*Sibila* (1950; Sybil), *Canto de Babilónia* (1952; Song from Babylonia) and *Canto de Morte e Amor* (1952, Song of Death and Love)— Duarte, under the suggestion of Bandarra'a ballads and engaging in a grave dialogue with other prophetic voices (especially *Camões, who, incidentally, is a constant presence in his work from the beginning), sings of the approach of the ''Apocalypse Beasts'' and the ''descent to Hell.'' For Duarte, this ''sad'' fate—witness the ''confusion of Babel'' and longing for the ''land of Zion''— is the ''modern poet's lot.''

BIBLIOGRAPHY

Primary Texts

*Canto de Morte e Amor*. Coimbra: n.p., 1952.
*Canto de Babilónia*. Coimbra: n.p., 1952.
*Lápides e Outros Poemas*. Lisbon: Iniciativas, 1960.
*Obra Poética*. Lisbon: Iniciativas, 1956. Includes all previously published books and *O Anjo da Morte e Outros Poemas, 1952–56*.
*Os 7 Poemas Líricos*. Coimbra: Gráfica Conimbricense, 1929. Includes three verse collections published between 1912 and 1916, and unpublished poems.
*Ossadas*. Lisbon: Seara Nova, 1947.
*Poesias de Afonso Duarte*. Intro. M. Madalena Gonçalves. Lisbon: n.p., 1984.
*Post-Scriptum de um Combatente*. Coimbra: n.p., 1949.
*Sibila*. Coimbra: Atlantida, 1950.

Criticism

See M. Madalena Gonçalves, above.
Oliveira, Carlos de, and J. José Cochofel. ''Afonso Duarte e a Sua Obra—Apontamentos Bibliográficos.'' Appendix to *Obra Poética*, above.

Fernando J. B. Martiñho

**DUEÑAS, Juan de** (?, ?–1460?, ?), soldier, courtier, poet. His was a tumultuous life—he alienated John II and was forced to flee to Naples. There, he was captured in the Battle of Ponza (1425), and taken prisoner. Eventually released, he returned to Spain, living at the court of Doña Blanca de Navarra. His works are found in the *Cancionero de *Stúñiga*, as well as many mss. *Cancioneros*. Two of his most famous poems are ''Nao de amor'' (Ship of Love) and ''El pleito que ovo

Juan de Dueñas con su amiga'' (The Suit Which Juan de Dueñas Had with His Lady Friend).

BIBLIOGRAPHY

Primary Text

*Poesías*. In NBAE 22.

Criticism

Vendrell, F. "La corte literaria de Alfonso V y tres poetas de la misma." *BRAE* 19 (1932): n.p.; 20 (1933): 67–92.

**DUQUE, Aquilino** (1931, Sevilla– ), poet and novelist. He has spent many years in Italy working as a translator and interpreter for an agency of the United Nations. He studied law in Seville and later continued his studies in Cambridge and in Dallas, where he perfected his knowledge of English. His first books of poetry appeared in 1958, *La calle de la Luna* (Street of the Moon) and *El campo de la Verdad* (The Field of Truth). In 1966, he published two novels, *La operación Marabú* (Operation Marabu) and *Los consulados del más allá* (Consulates of the World Beyond). With his poetry collection *De palabra en palabra* (1968; From Word to Word), Duque won the Leopoldo Panero Poetry Prize. In 1970, he won the Washington Irving Prize for short stories, as well as the City of Seville Prize for *La rueda de fuego* (1971; Wheel of Fire). Another novel, *La linterna mágica* (1971; The Magic Lantern), which appeared almost simultaneously, was inspired by the death of the Cuban writer Calvert Casey, a close friend of Duque's who died in Rome in 1969, destroyed by the macabre and grotesque world he inhabited. *El mono azul* (1973; The Blue Coverall), a finalist for the Nadal Prize, refers to the symbolic ''uniform'' of the popular militia that defended the Loyalist cause in the Spanish Civil War. Duque follows the vicissitudes of a gallery of archetypal characters in an effort to exorcise phantoms of the conflict which continue to haunt the present. In addition to his own creative writing, he has rendered into Spanish a variety of works by Dylan Thomas, Henrich Böll, Thomas Mann, Bertolt Brecht and William Saroyan.

BIBLIOGRAPHY

Primary Texts

*La linterna mágica*. Barcelona: Plaza & Janés, 1971.
*La Operación marabú*. Madrid: Alfaguara, 1966.
*De palabra en palabra*. Madrid: Cultura hispánica, 1968.
*El mono azul*. Barcelona: Destino, 1973.
*Los consulados del más alla*. Barcelona: Destino, 1976.
*La rueda de fuego*. Barcelona: Planeta, 1971.

English Translation
"Vindication of Espronceda." Tr. anon. In *Arena* 23 (1965): 66–67.

Janet Pérez

**DUQUE DE ESTRADA, Diego** (1589, Toledo–1647, Caller, Cerdeña), poet, autobiographer. His *Comentarios del desengaño de sí mismo* (n.d.; Commentary on Undeceiving Oneself) is an action-filled tale of passion, military prowess and adventures which most critics judge to be more invention than fact, perhaps including the author's pretensions to nobility. His only extant poetry is *Octavas rimas a la insigne victoria que la Serenísima Alteza del Príncipe Filiberto ha tenido . . .* (n.d.; Octave on the Renowned Victory Which His Most Serene Highness Prince Philbert Had . . . ).

BIBLIOGRAPHY

Primary Texts

*Comentarios*. Ed. P. de Gayangos. Madrid: Nacional, 1860.
*Comentarios*. In *Autobiografías de soldados, siglo XVII*. Ed., study J. M. Cossío. In BAE 90 (1956).

Criticism

Croce, B. *Fantasía y realidad en las memorias de Diego Duque de Estrada*. Tr. C. Pérez Bustamante. Santiago: El Eco franciscano, 1934.

**DURÁN, Agustín** (1793, Madrid–1862, Madrid), bibliographer and critic. Durán received a degree in law from the U of Seville. His initial literary formation was heavily influenced by the early nineteenth-c. "pre-romantic" writers, principal among them Alberto *Lista and Manuel *Quintana. His friendship with Bartolomé *Gallardo y Blanco, however, left the most profound impression on Durán and solidified his lifelong interest in bibliography and literary history. Although they later parted ways, Gallardo's influence on Durán is very evident in the latter's approach to historical investigation and in his methodology in re-editing early Hispanic texts. Durán was identified with the liberal movement and as a result lost his position with the government in 1823. After the death of Ferdinand VII he received an appointment to the National Library (*Biblioteca Nacional) in Madrid. Dismissed by the conservative government in 1840, he returned in 1843. He became the director of the National Library in 1854 and retired the following year. Durán was a partisan of the views of *Böhl de Faber on Spanish *theater and popular poetry. Their ideas sprang from a fervent nationalistic attitude toward literature which defined the classical and romantic concepts in terms of religious, political, and social characteristics. To Durán, Romanticism in literature "emanated from Christian spirituality, from the heroic customs of the Middle Ages, and from the individualistic approach to the consideration of man." He saw in the *Siglo de Oro school of drama, as represented by Lope de *Vega and *Calderón, a principal example of Spanish *Romanticism. In his *Discurso sobre el influjo que ha tenido la crítica moderna en la decadencia* *del teatro antiguo español* (published anonymously in Madrid, 1828; Discourse on the Influence of Modern Criticism on the Decadence of Golden Age Spanish Theater) Durán attacks the classical precepts of dramatic unities and defends the superiority of Golden Age theater over the neo-classic drama of the late eighteenth and early nineteenth centuries, which he characterizes as anti-nationalist. Durán wrote monographs on Lope de Vega and on *El condenado por desconfiado* (Condemned through Mistrust) by *Tirso de Molina. In 1826 Durán began collaborating on an edition of several Golden Age plays, published as *Thalia Española* (1834; Spanish Thalia). He also collected and published in 1843 two volumes of *sainetes* by Ramón de la *Cruz. Durán's greatest bibliographic achievement was his five-volume *Colección de romances antiguos* (1828–32; Collection of Old Ballads) which, in a revised and amplified form, was published in two volumes of the *Biblioteca de Autores Españoles* (1849–51). His collection was the largest and most important source of Spanish ballads at that time. Although his ideas on the origins of these ballads have been superseded by later critics, interest still continues over the texts which he brought to light, as well as over many of the scholarly and bibliographic notes included with the poems. Durán also wrote a few original legends, imitating the language of old ballads, among them *La infantina de Francia y sus amores con el Rey de Hungría* (1856; The French Princess and Her Love Affair with the Hungarian King's Daughter) and *Leyenda de las tres toronjas del vergel de amor* (1856; Legend of the Three Grapefruit in the Orchard of Love).

BIBLIOGRAPHY

Primary Text

*Discurso sobre el influjo que ha tenido la crítica moderna en la decadencia del teatro antiguo español*. Intro. Donald L. Shaw. Exeter: U of Exeter P, 1973.

Criticism

Gies, David Thatcher. *Agustín Durán: A Biography and Literary Appreciation*. London: Tamesis, 1975.

———. "El romance y el romanticismo: Perspectivas de Agustín Durán." *Dieciocho* 3 (1980): 62–68.

Romero Tobar, Leonardo. "Textos inéditos de Agustín Durán, Gallardo, Böhl, Quintana y Martínez de la Rosa." *RABM* 78 (1970): 409–28.

                                                                    Donald C. Buck

**DURÁN, Manuel** (1925, Barcelona– ), poet and critic. The son of a lawyer father and librarian mother, Durán was born into an educated and intellectual family of the Catalan bourgeoisie. Their home was destroyed in an aerial bombardment of Barcelona; his father occupied important posts on the Republican side during the war, and became a political refugee. Young Durán, who was arrested by the Franco regime and jailed briefly at the age of fourteen, fled with his mother and siblings through the Pyrenees to France, living for a time in Montpellier. With the advance of Hitler into France, the Durán family moved to Mexico, where the writer began studying law and literature simultaneously, while continuing to write poetry (which he began at the age of ten). With other Spanish emigrés, he founded a literary review, *Presencia*. After finishing his university studies, he worked as a radio announcer, translator and simultaneous translator for various organisms of the United Nations. He also translated more than twenty books from French, Italian and English. His first volume of poetry, *Puente* (1946; Bridge), was written in Castilian; a second collection, *Ciutat i figures* (1952; City and Figures), is in Catalan. Following his marriage and a year of bohemian existence in Paris, Durán did his doctorate in Romance languages at Princeton under the direction of the distinguished Hispanist Américo *Castro and subsequently taught at Smith College. For many years, he has been a professor of Spanish literature at Yale U, and has published a large number of critical studies, including *El superrealismo en la poesía española contemporánea* (1925; Surrealism in Contemporary Spanish Poetry); *La ambigüedad en el Quijote* (1960; Ambiguity in ''Don Quixote''); *Lorca, A Critical Anthology* (1962); *Voces españolas de hoy* (1965; Voices of Spain Today); and an anthology, *Ortega y Gasset, sus mejores páginas* (1966; The Best Pages of Ortega y Gasset). In collaboration with Agustí *Bartra, he did another anthology, *Panorama de la literatura española* (1967; Panorama of Spanish Literature).

Additional books of poetry by Durán include *Ciudad asediada* (1954; City Besieged); *La paloma azul* (1959; The Blue Dove); *El lugar del hombre* (1965; A Man's Place); *La piedra en la mano* (1970; The Stone in One's Hand); and *Cámara oscura* (1972; Dark Chamber). His poetry has been divided into three stages, the first comprising only the first book, *Puente*, and characterized by simple versification and traditional themes: love, solitude, human destiny, country landscapes. His style changes in the next three books, which abound in verses replete with cynicism, sarcasm and irony, very evident in choice of syntax. There is a sense of internal rebellion, accompanied by a rejection of forms of punctuation (such as the lack of periods), in what is essentially a poetry of censure rich in conceits and metaphor. In later books, beginning with *La piedra en la mano*, there appears a distinctly intellectual emphasis, replete with intertextual allusions, and a deliberate modernization of traditional poetic lexicon via the incorporation of words from many languages as well as ultramodern vocabulary. Although Durán does not belong fully to any movement, he often coincides with aspects of surrealism.

BIBLIOGRAPHY

Primary Text

*Cervantes.* TWAS 329. Boston: Twayne, 1974.

Criticism

Semprún Donahue, Moraima de. *La poesía de Manuel Durán.* Prol. Jorge Guillén. Pittsburgh: Latin American Literary Review Press, 1977.

Janet Pérez

**DUYOS, Rafael** (1906, Valencia– ), poet. His verse is colorful, with a simple rhythm, and his key themes are related to bullfighting. Among his works are *Toros y pan* (1932; Bulls and Bread), *Cabanyal* (1933), *Fragmentos de cartas* *jamás escritas* (1936; Fragments of Letters Never Written), *Junto al Plata* (1941; By the Plata), *Romances de la Falange* (1939; Falangist Ballads), and *Los ángeles hacen palmas: Romancero taurino* (1946: The Angels Clap Their Hands: Bullfighting Ballads).

BIBLIOGRAPHY

Primary Texts

*Cabanyal*. 2nd ed. Valencia: Levante de España, 1933.
*Romances de la Falange*. Buenos Aires: Libro de Romances de la Falange, 1937.

Isabel McSpadden

# E

---

**ECHEGARAY, José** (1832, Madrid–1916, Madrid), playwright. Of Basque heritage, intelligent and multifaceted, he succeeded as an engineer, economist, playwright and politician. In politics, he was initially a liberal, then a republican, and later a dynastic; as minister of finance, he founded the Bank of Spain. Echegaray's fondness for the theater began in his early youth; his neo-Romantic dramas were successfully performed from 1874 on. In 1894, he became a member of the *Academia Española, and in 1904, he was awarded the Nobel Prize in literature, sharing it with the Chilean poet Gabriela Mistral.

Most of Echegaray's plays do not follow the customary norms of Spanish *Romanticism. A notable exception is the legendary tragedy *En el seno de la muerte* (premiere, 1879; In the Grip of Death). Ibsen, Dumas, Bjöernson and Sudermann all left their mark on his work. Echegaray depicted human passions; his dramatic conflicts included problems of conscience, adultery, and duels. Suicide was at times the end result. The literary merit of his theater varies widely; he tailored some works to the personal characteristics of the actors who would perform them—actors such as Antonio Vico, Rafael and Ricardo Calvo, Elisa Mendoza Tenorio, María Guerrero and Fernando Díaz de Mendoza. His Romanticism sometimes welcomed social issues, as well as the positivist trend characteristic of the last third of the nineteenth c. His works are always thesis dramas. Of all his plays, *El gran galeoto* (Premiere, 1881; *The Great Galeoto*, 1969) is the most famous; also worthy of memory are *O locura o santidad* (1877; *Madman or Saint*, 1912) and *El hijo de don Juan* (1892; Don Juan's Son)— clearly shaped by Ibsen's *Ghosts*. His passionate language and exaggerated situations thrilled the public of his day, but seem excessive to contemporary tastes. In the strictest sense, his theater belongs to the genre of melodrama. After his death, his *Recuerdos* (1917; Memories) was printed. Echegaray's legacy, in the final analysis, rests more on his tremendous force of personality and success in many areas of life than on his contribution to literature. *See also* Contemporary Spanish Theater.

BIBLIOGRAPHY

Primary Texts

*En el seno de la muerte.* In Spanish Plays 83.
*El gran galeoto.* Rev. ed. Intro., notes, A. M. Espinosa. New York: Crofts, 1931.
*El hijo de Don Juan.* 2nd ed. Madrid: Yagues, 1892.
*Obras dramáticas escogidas.* 12 vols. Madrid: Tello, 1884–1905.

English Translations

*The Great Galeoto.* In *Masterpieces of Modern Spanish Drama.* Ed. B. H. Clark. New York: Kraus Rpt., 1969.
*The Son of Don Juan.* Tr. J. Graham. London: Unwin, 1895.
*Madman or Saint.* Tr. R. Lansing. In *Poet Lore* 23 (1912): 161–220.

Criticism

La John, L. *Azorín's Criticism of José Echegaray (Occasional Papers in Language, Literature and Linguistics).* Columbus: Ohio U Modern Lges. Dept., 1968.
Mathías, J. *Echegaray.* Madrid: EPESA, 1970.

Isabel McSpadden

**ECHEGARAY, Miguel** (1848, Quintanar de la Orden, Toledo–1927, Madrid), playwright, librettist. Brother to José *Echegaray, Miguel wrote his first play, *Cara y cruz* (1864; Heads and Tails), at age sixteen. He was a popular librettist for *género chico works; his finest librettos include *Gigantes y cabezudos* (1898; Giants and Pigheads), *La viejecita* (1898; The Little Old Lady), and *El dúo de la Africana* (1893; The Duet of the African Woman). He became a member of the Spanish Academy (*Academia Española) in 1913.

BIBLIOGRAPHY

Primary Texts

*Cara y cruz.* In *Teatro español* 32.
*El dúo de la Africana.* Madrid: Unión Musical Española, 1939.
*Gigantes y cabezudos.* Madrid: Unión Musical Española, 1927.
*La viejecita.* Madrid: Velasco, 1909.

**ECLOGUE.** *See* Égloga

**EDAD DE ORO.** *See* Siglo de Oro

**EDAD MEDIA, Literatura de la** (Literature of the Middle Ages). Vernacular Spanish literature begins with the thirteenth c. Before this time, there were Latin chronicles, writings of early Christian authors, and an Hispano-Arabic lyric, which combined a main part of a poem written in Arabic or Hebrew (*muhwash-shaha*) with the ending of the final stanza written in Spanish *romance* (jarchas; *see* Kharja). Thirteenth-c. Spain witnessed the development of Galician-Portuguese love poetry, *cantigas de amigo* and *cantigas de amor* (*Cantigas); debate poems, *Disputa del alma y del cuerpo,* *Disputa de Elena y María*; a curious hybrid, *Razón de amor y Denuestos del agua y del vino*; saints' lives such as *Vida de Santa *María Egipcíaca*; and the first vernacular poet whose identity is known to us, Gonzalo de *Berceo. Religious themes—*Milagros de Nuestra Señora* and saints' lives—characterize his work, the first in Spanish to employ what became known as *cuaderna vía, a fourteen-line Spanish alexandrine in four-line, single-rhymed stanzas. The anonymous *Libro de *Alexandre*, a 10,700-line poem, often has been attributed to Berceo by critics, but the attribution remains unproven.

Another major work is the anonymous *Poema* (or *Cantar) de mio Çid,* the story of Rodrigo Díaz de Vivar, the Spanish hero exiled by King Alphonse VI. Critics have attempted to reconstruct lost epics from the chronicles that deal with such legends as *Siete Infantes de Lara* (*see Infantes de Lara, Leyenda de los*), the Counts of Castile, and Sancho II and to determine if the epics were of learned or popular origin, a topic which is still hotly debated. The degree of historicity of the legends found in the chronicles varies greatly.

By far, the single most important figure of the thirteenth c. is Alfonso el Sabio (*Alphonse X the Wise, or Learned) of Castile, who reigned from 1252–1284. Under Alphonse's direction, Latin, Arabic and Hebrew scholars gathered in Toledo and compiled codes of law, known as *Siete Partidas*, scientific and mathematical treatises, a history of Spain, *Estoria de España* or *Primera crónica general* and an unfinished history of the world, *General estoria*. Alphonse himself composed, in Galician-Portuguese, many poems in honor of the Virgin Mary, *Cantigas de Santa María,* and some satirical poetry as well.

Fourteenth-c. Spain produced the first indigenous romance of chivalry, *Libro del caballero *Cifar*, and a long prose work on the Crusades, *La gran *conquista de Ultramar,* both anonymous. Two major figures are Juan Ruiz, *Arcipreste (Archpriest) of Hita, and Don *Juan Manuel, nephew of Alphonse X and grandson of Ferdinand III. Juan Ruiz's *Libro de buen amor* documents in a series of parodic, satiric episodes the archpriest's life as an unsuccessful lover. The notorious go-between *Trotaconventos is often cited by critics as the prototype for the fifteenth-c. Fernando de *Rojas's *La *Celestina,* a novel in dialogue that offers a bridge between the literatures of medieval and *Renaissance Spain. Don Juan Manuel based his most famous work on stories of Arabic, Oriental and European origins, a collection of fifty-one didactic tales called *Libro de Patronio o el Conde Lucanor* (1330–35).

In the second half of the fourteenth c., Spain experienced political and social disasters, some of which are reflected in works such as Pero *López de Ayala's *Rimado de Palacio,* the anonymous *Libro de *miseria de omne* and another anonymous poem in the *danse macabre* tradition, *Dança General de la Muerte.*

The nature of Spanish *Humanism and the influence of Italian Humanism constitute a continuing debate, but it is undeniable that Spanish letters flowered and diversified in the fifteenth c., especially in poetry. An oral ballad tradition enjoyed widespread popularity; the ballads, known as *romances*, highlight dramatic and lyrical moments from the lives of legendary and historical figures, among a great many other themes. Romance ballads from other countries are being collected even today.

The reign of John II of Castile (1406–54) witnessed the emergence of great Castilian poetry of Italian influence. Along with Jorge *Manrique (*Coplas que fizo por la muerte de su padre*), and his uncle Gómez *Manrique (author of a liturgical drama called *Representación del nacimiento de Nuestro Señor*), the two poets of renown are Íñigo López de Mendoza, Marqués de *Santillana (1398–1458) and Juan de *Mena (1411–56). The former wrote, besides poetry, a treatise on poetic composition, *Carta o Prohemio al condestable don Pedro de Portugal*. Juan de Mena created a political allegory of contemporary society, *Laberinto de Fortuna* (1444), and both poet and poem enjoyed great popularity well into the sixteenth c. The works of many poets, major and minor, can be found in collections called *cancioneros, the most famous of which is the *Cancionero de *Baena* (1511).

If fifteenth-c. poetry was sophisticated and innovative, the prose was no less so: didactic prose continued, such as Alfonso Martínez de Toledo's *Arcipreste de Talavera o Corbacho* (1438); travel literature and chronicles flourished, as did treatises on the nature of mankind (debates on the vices and virtues of men and women) and exemplary portraits of contemporary figures. A major group is the prose romances, chivalric and sentimental. The chivalric romances, such as *Amadís de Gaula*, were wildly popular in the sixteenth c.; the sentimental romances, tales of unhappy or tragic love, are unusual because they are peculiarly Spanish, not translated from French or Italian sources, although they are somewhat reminiscent of Boccaccio's *Fiammetta* and Aeneas Sylvius Piccolomini's (Pope Pius II) *Historia de duobus amantibus*.

The earliest *romance* is *Siervo libre de amor* (early 1440s) by Juan *Rodríguez de la Cámara (or del Padrón). The two other important authors are Juan de *Flores (*Grisel y Mirabella* and *Grimalte y Gradissa*) and Diego de *San Pedro (*Tractado de amores de Arnalte y Lucenda* and *Cárcel de amor*), both of whose works were published in the 1490s. The c. closes with *La Celestina* (1499 and 1502), a masterpiece that reflects themes of the Middle Ages (e.g., fortune and courtly love) and, by its structure, form and character portrayal, looks ahead to the Renaissance and Spain's literary Golden Age. *See also* Arcipreste de Talavera; *Crónicas*; *Cronicones*; Gallic-Portuguese love poetry; Italian literary influences; Hagiography; Hispano Judaic Literature; Romancero; Siglo de Oro.

BIBLIOGRAPHY

Criticism

Blanco Aguinaga, C., et al. *Historia social de la literatura española.* Vol. 1. Madrid: Castalia, 1978.

Deyermond, A. *A Literary History of Spain: The Middle Ages.* London: Benn, 1971.

López Estrada, F. *Introducción a la literatura medieval española.* 4th ed. Madrid: Gredos, 1979.

                                                                    Patricia Grieve

*ÉGLOGA* (eclogue), a *pastoral composition. Of classical origin, these bucolic poems were most popular in the *Renaissance. Leading practitioners in Spain include *Garcilaso de la Vega, Lucas *Fernández, Juan del *Encina, F. de *Herrera, Lope de *Vega, Pedro de *Espinosa, *Meléndez Valdés, and Leandro Fernández de *Moratín.

**EGUÍLAZ, Luis de** (1830, Sanlúcar de Barrameda–1874, Madrid), playwright and novelist. Historical erudition is the hallmark of his dramatic works such as *Una aventura de Tirso* (1855; Tirso's Adventure) which deals with *Tirso de Molina's love affair with a poet named doña Feliciana. Other plays were inspired by medieval history: *Las querellas del rey sabio* (1858; The Wise King's Complaints) and *La vaquera de Finojosa* (1858; The Milkmaid of Finojosa). Works with a moralizing intent include *Verdades amargas* (1863; Bitter Truths), *Mentiras dulces* (1859; Sweet Lies) and *La cruz del matrimonio* (1860; The Cross of Marriage). He also composed librettos for *zarzuelas, of which the most famous is *El molinero de Subiza* (1860; The Miller from Subiza). One of his historical novels is titled *La espada de San Fernando* (1852; St. Ferdinand's Sword). In general, his work describes local customs, types and manners, and his tone is sentimental and moralistic.

BIBLIOGRAPHY

Primary Texts

*Obras dramáticas de don Luis de Eguílaz*. Paris: Dramard-Baudry, 1864.

Phoebe Porter Medina

**EIXIMENIS, Francesc** (1330/35, Girona–1409, Perpinyà), a Franciscan monk who traveled extensively throughout Europe, residing at various times in Italy, France and, above all, England, where he studied at Oxford. Being very close to the Catalan royal court, he was appointed to a chair at the U of Lleida and subsequently in Toulouse (Languedoc). The exact date on which he started to write his monumental work *Lo Crestià* (The Christian) is not known. He intended to expound, in thirteen volumes, the principal bases of Christianity, the forces of evil in the temptations of man and the way of salvation through Christian virtues, divine grace, the Catholic church and the imitation of Christ by leading a life marked by the absence of excesses, or *seny* (common sense). It is noteworthy to point out that salvation was as easily obtained by a priest as by a laic; *seny*, justice and humanism were above dogma. The first volume, *El Primer* (1381; The First), was written in Barcelona, and *El segon* (The Second), in Valencia. There, in 1383, he wrote a small and extremely interesting volume devoted to ''good government,'' the *Regiment de la Cosa pública* (Laws of Public Life) with materials destined for volume 12 of *Lo Crestià*. In 1384 he composed *El Terc* (The Third), of 1,600 chapters, a moral treatise in the form of a sermon (probably his last work) to exalt in a very modern manner the virtues of the Catalans and their differences from other European nationalities. Thence he proceeded to write *El Dotze* (The Twelfth) dealing with the *Regiment de prínceps i de comunitats* (Laws of Princes and Communities), an ethical and political treatise earmarked for civil and military administrators and, in general, the leaders of Catalonia. Eiximenis did not complete *Lo Crestià*, but in the *Llibre de les Dones* (c. 1386; The Book of Women) he alludes, in 300 chapters, to the themes of the other projected volumes of *Lo Crestià*: the virtues, the Ten Commandments, penitence and confession, prayer and contemplation, paradise. Other important works are *El llibre dels àngels* (1392; Book of the Angels), *Vida de Jesucrist* (c. 1394; Life of Christ), and some minor works in Latin.

Eiximenis was probably one of the most knowledgeable people of medieval culture. Not a speculative theologian or a mystic, he followed St. Paul and St. Francis, devoted all his work to giving practical and realistic advice based on personal experiences. He also criticized the injustices of the mighty, the pettiness of the swelling burgeoisie and the stupidity of mankind. In this sense he remains a true classic. *See also* Catalan Literature

BIBLIOGRAPHY

Primary Texts

*Com usar bé de beure e menjar*. From the *Terç del Crestià*. Ed., intro. Jorge E. J. Gracia. Barcelona: Curial, 1977.
*Contes i faules*. Ed. M. Olivar. Barcelona: Els Nostres Clàssics, 1925.
*Doctrina compendiosa*. Ed. P. Martí de Barcelona. Barcelona: Els Nostres Clàssics, 1929.
*El Naixement de l'Infant Jesús* (fragment of the *Vida de Jesucrist*). Barcelona: n.p, 1951.
*Regiment de la Cosa pública*. Barcelona: Els Nostres Clàssics, 1927.
*Terç del Crestià*. Eds. P. P. Martí de Barcelona and Norbert d'Ordal. 3 vols. Barcelona: Els Nostres Clàssics, 1929–32.

Criticism

Gracia, J. J. "Francesc Eiximenis' Sources." In *Catalan Studies. Estudis sobre el català. Volume in memory of Josephine de Boer*. Ed. J. Gulsoy and J. M. Solá Solé. Barcelona: Hispam, 1977. 163–71.
Nougaard, E. J. "A Motiv-Index study of the 'Faules' of Francesc Eiximenis." In *Catalan Studies*, op. cit. 189–94.
Paláez, Manuel J. "Notas críticas a cuatro recientes estudios sobre Francesc Eiximenis." *Estudios Franciscanos* 80 (1979): 67–74.
Viera, David J. "A Partial Bibliography of the Works and Studies on Francesc Eiximenis (1340?–1409?)." In *Catalan Studies*, op. cit. 163–71.
Webster, J. R. "The Works of Francesc Eiximenis as a Historical Source." In *Catalan Studies*, op. cit. 195–201.

Joan Gilabert

**ELUCIDARIO** (Clarifier), literary term. To paraphrase R. Kinkade, the name and concept *lucidario* come from a Latin work of Honorius Augustodunensis (c. 1095; *Elucidarium*) written to preserve St. Anselm's commentaries regarding the Church Fathers. In the Middle Ages *lucidarios* were didactic works intended to clarify difficult concepts. The *Lucidario* attributed to Sancho el Bravo is a good example. Composed of 106 chapters, it treats topics such as where God was before Creation, the heavenly regions and elements, the devil and his knowledge, why all men are different, why hares and rabbits sleep with their eyes open, etc. *See also* Edad Media, Literatura de la.

BIBLIOGRAPHY

Criticism

Kinkade, Richard. *Los 'lucidarios' españoles*. Madrid: Gredos, 1968. Edition and study.

Maureen Ihrie

**ENCINA, Juan del** (1468?, Encinas, Salamanca?–1529/30, León), poet, musician/composer, and playwright. The son of a Salamancan shoemaker, Juan de Fermoselle, Encina was a multi-faceted genius, and is generally recognized as the father of Spanish *theater. A chorister at the Cathedral of Salamanca, he received the bachelor of law degree from the U of Salamanca, took minor orders, and between 1492 and 1495, entered the household of the Duke of Alba, whom he served for several years as actor, courtier, musician, and playwright. In 1498 he competed for the post of cantor at the Cathedral of Salamanca, which was given to his rival and dramatic disciple, Lucas *Fernández; on losing, he left Spain for Rome, where he became a favorite of the Spanish pope, Alexander VI. In 1500, he was granted benefices in the diocese of Salamanca, even being appointed cantor at the cathedral there although Fernández apparently continued to hold the post. In 1509, Pope Julius II appointed him archdeacon of Málaga Cathedral, despite the fact that he was not a fully ordained priest. After three trips between Spain and Rome during 1512–18, Encina obtained the post of prior to León Cathedral from Pope Leo X. In 1519, around the age of fifty, he was ordained and went on a pilgrimage to Jerusalem, where he celebrated his first Mass. Residing in León from 1523 on, he died there in late 1529 or early 1530.

In Encina's works, traditional Medieval themes and metrical forms are filtered through a creative genius that guides Hispanic literature and music into the *Renaissance period. His *Cancionero* (1496; Songbook), which was published in Salamanca, contains all his poetry and his first eight dramatic eclogues (he was the pioneer in Spanish Renaissance literature to adapt these Classical *pastoral poems). The *Cancionero* is preceded by an *Arte poética castellana* (The Art of Castilian Poetics) that departs from the doctrines of Antonio de *Nebrija, Encina's contemporary, in taking as models and authorities for the Castilian lyric its poets of the fifteenth c., especially Juan de *Mena. The eclogues, produced for the pleasure of the Duke of Alba while at Alba de Tormes, lack Italianate influence beyond the pastoral convention itself; their themes are now religious, now secular. They are quite brief: the longest has 557 verses. The 1507 edition of the *Cancionero* adds two new dramas: the *Égloga de las grandes lluvias* and the *Representación de Amor* (1498?; The Eclogue of the Great Rains and the Power of Love).

Only three of the eclogues follow medieval European Christmas dramatic tradition: the second, featuring evangelists John and Matthew as well as shepherds Luke and Mark; and the third and fourth, on the Passion and the Resurrection

of Christ. These works, or *Autos de Navidad* (Christmas One-Act Plays), sec-
ularize the old medieval mystery plays, endowing them with safe passage through
the world at the same time that they are imbued with lyricism and action. If the
brief *Representaciones* of Gómez *Manrique (c. 1412-c. 1490) are excluded, we
find little in the way of dramatic art in Castilian literature between the late
twelfth-c. *Auto de los Reyes Magos* (Play of the Three Kings) and the works
of Encina. Departing from the traditional religious *officium pastorum*, Encina
creates in his works a Castilian pastoral world, complete with a conventional
language (the rustic speech known as *sayagués*, which is sprinkled with abundant
Portuguese and Leonese terms) and a series of equally conventional characters
(shepherds) who embody fictional entities as well as real people—including
Encina himself. The other eclogues, secular in nature, are known for their
comicality and sense of contrast and tension: the *Égloga de Carnaval* (Eclogue
of the Feast before Lent) and the *Antruejo* (which depicts the medieval tradition
of the struggle between Lady Lent and Lord Flesh) are somewhat neo-pagan in
character, with their shepherds gormandizing before the arrival of Lent; these
works were produced between 1494 and 1496. Of a similar character is the *Auto
del repelón* (The Hair-Pulling Play), in which two shepherds narrate how they
were the victims of students' practical jokes at the marketplace.

Encina's travels to Italy doubtless influenced his dramatic production, for the
impact of Italian poets can be noted in the *Egloga de Fileno, Zambardo y
Cardonio* (c. 1500; Eclogue of Fileno, Zambardo, and Cardonio), a close adaptation from the work of Antonio Tebaldeo; and in the *Egloga de Plácida y
Vitoriano* (1514; Eclogue of Placida and Vitoriano). The *Fileno*, which may
have been a source of *Garcilaso de la Vega's *Egloga segunda*, concerns the
desperation of Fileno over his unrequited love for Cefira, his two friends' inability
to help him in his plight, and his consequent suicide; written in eighty-eight
*coplas de *arte mayor*, it is the first tragedy in the drama of the Golden Age.
The *Plácida,* a complex polymetric work, is the most ambitious of Encina's
eclogues, and is almost as long (2,578 verses) as a three-act *comedia* of the
seventeenth c.

Encina's best poems in the 1496 *Cancionero* are clearly of popular inspiration,
and his glosses on songs and fragments of traditional ballads make his contribution all the more memorable. Notable among these are "Pues no te duele mi
muerte" (Since My Death Doesn't Bother You); "No te tardes que me muero,
/ carcelero" (I'm Dying, Jailer, So Don't Tarry); "Vencedores son tus ojos"
(Your Eyes Conquer [Me]); and "Ojos garzos ha la niña" (The Girl Has Blue
Eyes). *See also* Italian literary influences; Siglo de Oro; Theater in Spain.

## BIBLIOGRAPHY

### Primary Texts

"El *arte de poesía castellana* de Juan del Encina (Edición y notas)." Ed. Juan Carlos
  Temprano. *BRAE* 53 (1973): 321–50.
*Cancionero de las obras de Juan del Enzina (Salamanca, 1496)*. Facs. ed. by Emilio

Cotarelo y Mori. Madrid: RAE, 1928. The fourth edition (Salamanca, 1507) contains Eclogues 9 and 10; the fifth (Salamanca, 1509), Eclogues 12 and 13.

*Cancionero de las obras de Juan del Enzina (Salamanca, 1496): Edición y concordancias.* Ed. Juan Carlos Temprano. [Microfiche Publication.] Madison, WI: HSMS, 1983.

*Obras completas.* Ed. Ana María Rambaldo. 4 vols. Madrid: Espasa-Calpe, 1978–83.

*Poesía lírica y cancionero musical.* Eds. R. O. Jones and Carolyn R. Lee. Madrid: Castalia, 1972 [1975].

*Viage y peregrinación a Jerusalem.* Madrid: Pantaleón, 1786.

English Translation

Various passages and verses from the *Cancionero* of 1496 appear in Henry W. Sullivan's *Juan del Encina* (1976; see Criticism).

Criticism

Andrews, Richard J. *Juan del Encina: Prometheus in Search of Prestige.* Berkeley and Los Angeles: U of California P, 1959.

López Morales, Humberto. *Tradición y creación en los orígenes del teatro castellano.* Madrid: Alcalá, 1968.

Menéndez Pelayo, Marcelino. *Antología de poetas líricos castellanos.* Vol. 7. Madrid: Hernando, 1898.

Sullivan, Henry W. *Juan del Encina.* TWAS 399. Boston: Twayne, 1976.

Terni, Clemente. *Juan del Encina: L'òpera musicale.* Transcription and Study. Messina/Firenze: Editrice d'Anna, 1974.

Van Beysterveldt, Anthony. *La poesía amatoria del siglo XV y el teatro profano de Juan del Encina.* Madrid: Insula, 1972.

Dennis P. Seniff

**ENCINAS, Pedro de** (c. 1530, Burgos–1595, ?), Dominican, religious poet. He studied at Salamanca. He wrote *Églogas espirituales* (1597; Spiritual Eclogues), which is comprised of six eclogues, *a lo divino.*

BIBLIOGRAPHY

Primary Text

*Églogas.* Ed., intro., J. M. Aguado. Madrid: Santísimo rosario, 1924.

**ENCISO, Pilar** (c. 1930, Madrid– ), Spanish playwright and director. Enciso studied at Madrid's Royal School of Dramatic Arts, where she obtained the Lope de Vega Prize in stage direction for 1951. In 1954, together with Lauro *Olmo and other members of the Grupo Literatura de Juglaría—socially and politically committed authors, artists, and musicians—she founded a group that staged plays for children in a tent theater in Madrid's Tetuán district. She subsequently directed puppet theater for children during the annual Madrid Book Fair on the Paseo del Prado and during the annual Festival of St. Isidro, in Madrid's Retiro Park. Enciso's efforts revived the interest in children's theater that had waned since the activities of such figures as *Valle-Inclán, *Casona, and *García Lorca.

In collaboration with Olmo, Enciso has authored five plays for children and youth, some of which are inspired by tales from the *Panchatantra*, Aesop, and

La Fontaine. All have a clear social message. Through lively action, song and dance, humor and poetry, mime and imaginative visual effects, these plays show how, through solidarity and union, the oppressed can win their freedom. Most of these plays formed part of the repertoire of Enciso's Teatro Popular Infantil (Popular Children's Theater) and were first performed during the 1960 Book Fair and St. Isidro Festival.

*El león engañado* (1969; The Lion That Was Deceived) and *El león enamorado* (1969; The Lion That Fell in Love), performed at Valencia's Quart Theater, in 1972, and at Madrid's Arniches Theater in 1973–74, oppose the all-powerful Lion to the alliance of his victims, whose wits enable them to triumph. *Asamblea general* (1965; General Assembly) is based on La Fontaine's "Les animaux malades de la peste," which opened in 1968 at Castellón's major theater. The play dramatizes the judgment and condemnation of the humble Donkey by the tyrant Leónidas, the lion, because the former dared to taste the grass belonging to an abbey. The innocent Donkey is to be the scapegoat, the sacrifice demanded by the gods, who are offended by the sins of the people. *Asamblea general*, which has become a children's classic, was a highlight of the 1978 meeting in Madrid of the ASSITEJ (L'Association Internationale du Théâtre pour L'Enfance et la Jeunesse) and won the Manuel Espinosa y Cortina Theater Award of the *Academia Española for the best play premiered in 1977–81. Other plays by Enciso and Olmo include *La maquinita que no quería pitar* (1969; The Little Machine That Refused to Whistle) and *El raterillo* (1965; The Pickpocket), which was awarded the Prize of the Critics' Circle of Uruguay after a Montevideo performance in 1967. *See also* Contemporary Spanish Theater.

BIBLIOGRAPHY

Primary Texts

(co-authored with Lauro Olmo)

*Asamblea general y dos piezas más: Teatro para la infancia y la juventud/ Asambrea xeral e duas pezas mais: Teatro para os nenos e a mocedade*. Madrid: Universidad Internacional Menéndez y Pelayo, 1981. Bilingual edition. Contains *El león engañado* and *El león enamorado*.

*El raterillo* and *Asamblea general*. In *Primer Acto*, no. 71 (1965).

*Teatro infantil*. Madrid: Escelicer, 1969. Contains *El león engañado*, *El león enamorado*, *La maquinita que no quería pitar*, *El raterillo*, and *Asamblea general*.

Criticism

Cervera, Juan. *Historia crítica del teatro infantil español*. Madrid: Nacional, 1982.

Fernández Cambria, Elisa. "Teatro desconocido de Sastre, Olmo y Muñiz: piezas para niños y jóvenes." *Estreno* 9.1 (Spring 1983): 15–19.

Lázaro Carreter, F. "Asamblea general de Pilar Enciso y Lauro Olmo." *Gaceta Ilustrada* (June 11, 1978): 97.

Tames, R. L. *Introducción a la literatura infantil*. Santander: Instituto de Ciencias de la Educación de la Universidad de Santander, 1985.

Zatlin, Phyllis. "Children's Theater in Contemporary Spain." *Estreno* 9.1 (Spring 1983): 7–10.

Martha T. Halsey

***ENDECHA***, a short lyric dirge or lament. Sometimes referred to as a *romancilla*, the customary form is a five-, six-, or seven-syllable line with assonant rhyme in the even lines. The *endecha real*, however, usually employs four lines (three seven-syllable lines with one eleven-syllable line) with assonance in the second and fourth lines. The *endecha* appeared in the fifteenth c., the *endecha real* in the sixteenth c.

**ENRÍQUEZ DE GUZMÁN, Feliciana** (late 16th c., ?–?), playwright. Little is known of her. One main work by her has survived, the *Tragicomedia los jardines y campos sabeos* (Tragicomedy of the Gardens and Sabaean Fields). In two parts, it narrates the story of Maya, daughter to Atlantis and Clarisel.

BIBLIOGRAPHY

Primary Text

*Tragicomedia los jardines y campos sabeos*. In BAE 269. 358–87.

Criticism

Galerstein, Carolyn, and Kathleen McNerney. *Women Writers of Spain*. Westport, CT: Greenwood, 1986.

**ENRÍQUEZ DE PAZ.** *See* Enríquez Gómez, Antonio

**ENRÍQUEZ DEL CASTILLO, Diego** (1433, Segovia–1504?, ?), chaplain, counselor of Henry IV, biographer. He composed a *Crónica del Rey don Enrique IV* (Chronicle of King Henry IV), a favorably biased account of Henry's life up to 1467. The first ms. was lost in the Battle of Olmedo, in which Enríquez del Castillo was captured. He rewrote it; while his memory fully recaptured characterizations, dates are often erroneous. His account is as well-disposed to the king as Alfonso Fernández de *Palencia's narrative is negative.

BIBLIOGRAPHY

Primary Text

*Crónica del Rey don Enrique IV*. In BAE 70.

Criticism

Puyol, J. "Los cronistas de Enrique IV." *Boletín de la Academia de Historia* 78 (1921): 399–415.

**ENRÍQUEZ GÓMEZ, Antonio,** pseudonyms Enríquez de Paz and Fernando de Zárate (1600?, Cuenca/Segovia–1663, Seville), lyricist, playwright, epic poet, and satirist. Of *converso* descent, he was a wholesale cloth merchant before moving to France in 1635, in fear of the *Inquisition. He had a distinguished military career and became a Knight of the Order of Saint Michael. He was secretary to Louis XIII and dedicated a treatise on political morality to young Louis XIV, *Luis dado a Luis y Ana* (1645; Louis Given by God to Louis and Anne). Most of his works were published in France. He later moved to Amsterdam, where he became a Jew and a protégé of the wealthy and powerful Sephardic community. He is thought to have returned to Spain in 1649, assumed the name Fernando de Zárate, and written numerous plays. He was executed in absentia at an auto-da-fé in Seville on April 13, 1660, and is believed to have attended the burning of his own effigy. Recently produced documents reveal his arrest by the Inquisition in 1661, as a Judaizer, and his confession and death of natural causes in the cells of Seville on March 18, 1663. *Academias morales de las Musas* (1642; Moral Academies of the Muses), his best lyric poems, express yearning for Spain and deep sadness about his exile. They enjoyed great popularity in Spain. As a dramatist, Enríquez Gómez was influenced by *Calderón. He treated themes of love, honor, and friendship, as in *Celos no ofenden al Sol* (Jealousy Does Not Offend the Sun) and *A lo que obliga el honor* (That to Which Honor Compéls), and used the Bible to borrow from its style, language, and themes. *La prudente Abigail* (Wise Abigail), *La soberbia de Nembrot* (The Pride of Nimrod), and two epic poems, *La Culpa del primer peregrino* (1644; The Sin of the First Pilgrim), a metaphysical work about the Fall of Adam, and *Sansón Nazareno* (1644; Samson the Nazirite), are based on the Old Testament. The prologue to the Samson poem includes a catalog of twenty-two plays, from among which two stand out: a criticism of the Inquisition, artfully disguised behind orthodox theology, *Política angélica* (1647; Heavenly Politics) and *La Torre de Babilonia* (1649; The Tower of Babylon), a satire reprinted in Madrid in 1670. Enríquez Gómez dedicated a ballad to Lope de Vera y Alarcón, who was burned at the stake in Valladolid on July 25, 1644, *Romance al divín mártir, Judá Creyente* (Ballad to the Divine Martyr, Judah the Believer). This ms. is found in the Bodleian Library at Oxford. His major work, *El siglo pitagórico y vida de don Gregorio Guadaña* (1644; The Pythagorean Century and the Life of Don Gregory Guadaña), is a social satire in two parts. *El siglo pitagórico*, in verse with some prose segments, presents brilliant and acerbic transformations of a soul in various bodies, based on the Pythagorean idea of transmigration. In its depictions of the greedy, the talebearer, the lady, the royal favorite, the hypocrite, the miser, the physician, the haughty, the thief, the schemer, the nobleman, and the virtuous, it ridicules various classes and types of seventeenth-c. society. *La vida de don Gregorio Guadaña* is a novel of adventure, in prose, inserted after the fourth transmigration. Its protagonist is a Sevillian of some means who travels to Madrid in search of pleasure and amorous affairs. Of an erotic and, at times, obscene character, it gives detailed descriptions of the physical attributes of female characters and an analysis of their psyche. As a social satire, it is more entertaining than bitter, with sly mockery and wit as well as lyric sincerity. Written after the manner of the *picaresque (*Quevedo's *El Buscón*), its tone is light, pleasant, ingenious, and often mischievous, but at times the plot becomes dense.

## BIBLIOGRAPHY

Primary Texts

"Antonio Enríquez Gómez's 'Romance al divín mártir, Judá Creyente.' " Ed. by T. Oelman. *Journal of Jewish Studies* 26 (1975): 113–31.
*Celos no ofenden al sol* and *A lo que obliga el honor*. BAE 47. (Other plays appear in same volume under the authorship of Fernando de Zárate.)
"Dos versiones de un texto de Antonio Enríquez Gómez: Un caso de auto-censura." By Constance Rose. *NRFH* 30.2 (1981): 534–45.
*Enríquez Gómez, Antonio. Fernán Méndez Pinto: Comedia famosa en dos partes.* Eds. L. G. Cohen, F. M. Rogers and C. Rose. Harvard Studies in Romance Lges. 5. Cambridge, MA: Dept of Romance Lges. and Lits., 1974.
*Enríquez Gómez, Antonio. Romance al divín mártir, Judá Creyente (don Lope de Vera y Alarcón) martirizado en Valladolid por la Inquisición.* Ed. T. Oelman. Rutherford, NJ: Fairleigh Dickinson UP; London: Associated U Presses, 1986.
*Las "Academias morales" de Antonio Enríquez Gómez.* Ed. J. G. García Valdecasas. Seville: Universidad Hispalense, 1970.
*El Siglo Pitagórico y Vida de Don Gregorio Guadaña, édicion critique avec introduction et notes.* Ed. Charles Amiel. Paris: Ediciones Hispanoamericanas, 1977.

English Translation

*Marrano Poets of the 17th Century: An Anthology of the Poetry of João Pinto Delgado, Antonio Enríquez Gómez, and Miguel de Barrios.* Ed. and Tr. T. Oelman. Rutherford, NJ: Fairleigh Dickenson UP; London: Oxford UP, 1982.

Criticism

Amador de los Ríos, J. *Estudios históricos, políticos y literarios sobre los judíos de España.* Madrid: n.p., 1848. 569–88.
Dille, G. F. "Antonio Enríquez Gómez's Honor Tragedy, *A lo que obliga el honor*." *Bulletin of the Comediantes* 30.2 (Fall 1978): 97–111.
———. "Notes on Aggressive Women in the *Comedia* of Enríquez Gómez." *RN* 21 (1980–81): 215–21.
———. "The Tragedy of Don Pedro: Old and New Christian Conflict in *El Valiente Campuzano*." *Bulletin of the Comediantes* 35.1 (Summer 1983): 97–109.
Oelman, T. "The Religious Views of Antonio Enríquez Gómez: Profile of a Marrano." *BHS* 60.3 (July 1983): 201–9.
Profeti, Maria Grazia. "Un esempio di critica 'militante': Il prologo al *Sansón Nazareno* de Enríquez Gómez." *Quaderni di Lingua e Letterature* 7 (1982): 203–12.
Révah, I. S. "Un pamphlet contre l'Inquisition d'Antonio Enríquez Gómez: la seconde partie de la 'Política angélica' (Rouen, 1647)." *Revue des études juives* 121 (1962): 81–168.
Rose, C. "Antonio Enríquez Gómez and the Literature of Exile." *Romanische Forschungen* 85 (1973): 63–77.
———. "Las comedias políticas de Enríquez Gómez." *Nuevo Hispanismo* 2 (Spring 1982): 45–55.
———. "Who Wrote the *Segunda Parte* of *La hija del aire?*" *Revue belge de philologie et d'histoire* 54.3 (1976): 797–822.
———, with M. Gendreau-Massaloux. "Antonio Enríquez Gómez et Manuel Fernandes de Villareal: Deux destins parallèles, une vision politique commune." *Revue des études juives* 136 (1977): 368–86.

Thacker, M. J. "Gregorio Guadaña: *Pícaro francés* or *Pícaro galán?*" *Hispanic Studies in Honor of Frank Pierce*. Ed. John England. Sheffield: Dept. of Hispanic Studies, U of Sheffield, 1980. 149–68.

Reginetta Haboucha

**ENTRAMBASAGUAS, Joaquín de** (1904, Madrid– ), professor at the Universities of Murcia and Madrid. He has published essays, anthologies, poetry and numerous articles on literary criticism in several journals and newspapers. He has done studies on Cristóbal *Lozano, Adán de la Parra and *Moreto and has contributed to Spanish erudition with his book *Una familia de ingenios: los Ramírez de Prado* (1943; A Family of Geniuses). His most outstanding contribution to Spanish literature is his extended research on Lope de *Vega and his time. He has brought to light several unpublished works of Lope de Vega and has also published *Una guerra literaria del Siglo de Oro: Lope de Vega y los preceptistas aristotélicos* (1932; A Golden Age Literary War: Lope de Vega and the Aristotelian Preceptists) and *Vida de Lope de Vega* (1936; The Life of Lope de Vega), which reveals many details and information unknown until its publication.

BIBLIOGRAPHY

Primary Texts

*Estudios sobre Lope de Vega*. 2nd ed., rev. expanded. 3 vols. Madrid: CSIC, 1967.
*Estudios y ensayos sobre Góngora y el barroco*. Madrid: Nacional, 1975.
*Una familia de ingenios*. RFE Anejo 26. Madrid: RFE, 1943.
*Una guerra literaria*. Madrid: Archivos, 1932.
*Vida de Lope de Vega*. Barcelona: Labor, 1942.

Isabel McSpadden

**ENTREMÉS,** a type of *Siglo de Oro theatrical work. They were brief, comic representations, usually burlesque or farcical in nature, performed between acts of a play. Like the *loa, they arose from the pressing need to entertain and pacify the impatient audience of the day, which was comprised of all sectors of society. E. Asencio has observed how the *entremés* functions as a counterpoint to the *comedia* (play): (1) while the *comedia* moves from perturbed order to order restored, the *entremés* embraces chaos and the imperfections of the world; (2) the personalities of the *comedia* are superior to the audience—even the *gracioso*'s quick wit and verbal facility is to be envied, but in the *entremés* the public is superior to the players; (3) jocose moments in the *comedia* serve to highlight the noble sentiments or suffering of the protagonists, whereas in the *entremés*, the jocose colors all—suffering is transformed to cause for hilarity; and (4) the poetic language of the *comedia* evokes wondrous landscapes and horizons, but the language of the *entremés* moves toward physicality— gestures, song, dance, etc.

Lope de *Rueda (1505?–65) is credited with creation of the *entremés*; subsequent practitioners adopted his use of rapid, colloquial dialogue, with regional accents, and a host of "types"—the fool, the cowardly braggart, the go-between, talky blacks, gypsies, shady Valencians, country hicks from Extremadura, the Biscayan, etc. From 1550 to 1600, the *entremés* slowly became more literary and sophisticated in construction, and music was used more. The first part of Lope de *Vega's plays (1609) included twelve *entremeses*—eleven in prose and one in verse (it is not certain who authored them). And, in 1615, *Cervantes published *Ocho comedias y ocho entremeses* (Eight plays and Eight *entremeses*)—with six in prose and two in verse. From this point, verse began to be preferred over prose. Later practitioners of this highly indigenous flowering include *Hurtado de Mendoza (1586–1644), *Quiñones de Benavente (1589–1651), Ramón de la *Cruz (1731–94), and the *Alvarez Quintero brothers (1871–1938 and 1873af02–1944).

BIBLIOGRAPHY

Primary Text

*Colección de entremeses, loas, bailes, jácaras y mogigangas desde fines del siglo XVI.* Ed. A. Cotarelo, 2 vols. In NBAE 17 and 18.

Criticism

Asencio, E. *Itinerario del entremés.* Madrid: Gredos, 1965.
Jack, W. S. *The Early Entremés in Spain: The Rise of a Dramatic Form.* Publication of the U of Pennsylvania Series in Romance Languages and Literature 8. Philadelphia: U of Pennsylvania, 1923.

Maureen Ihrie

***ENTREMÉS DE LOS ROMANCES*** (*Entremés* of Ballads), anonymous *entremés, written c. 1597. This brief farce, which pokes fun at the excessive popularity of the *Romancero at the close of the sixteenth c., presents the story of Bartolo who, addicted to ballads, finally goes mad from excessive reading of them, and sets out, imitating the heroes of whom he has read. Many critics feel it may have sparked *Cervantes's creation of *Don Quijote de la Mancha*, in which the hero's delusions proceeded from excessive reading of chivalric novels. Adolfo de *Castro y Rossi erroneously attributed the *entremés* to Cervantes.

BIBLIOGRAPHY

Primary Text

*Cuatro entremeses atribuidos a Miguel de Cervantes.* Ed. A. de Castro. 1877. Rpt. Barcelona: Guarro Casas, 1957.

Criticism

Menéndez Pidal, R. *Un aspecto en la elaboración del "Quijote."* Madrid: RABM, 1924.

**ENXEMPLOS, Libro de los.** *See* Exenplos, Libro de los

**ENZINAS, Francisco de** (1520, Burgos–1552, Strasbourg), humanist, professor, historian, Lutheran reformer. He fully embraced Luther's doctrines, and thus fled Spain, studied in Louvain, changed his surname to Dryander, and later taught Greek at Cambridge. He wrote the *Breve y compendiosa institución cris-tiana* (1540; Brief and Concise Christian Institution), a Spanish translation of the New Testament (1543), for which he was jailed, a translation of Plutarch's *Lives,* and translations of Livy, Lucan, etc. He also penned a significant historical work titled *Historia del estado de los Países Bajos y de la Religión de España* (1558; History of the Low Countries and Religion in Spain), under the name Francisco du Chesne, and an autobiographical work, *Memorias 1543–45* (n.d.; Memoirs).

BIBLIOGRAPHY

Primary Texts

*Historia de la muerte de Juan Díaz.* Madrid: n.p., 1865.

*Mémoires de Francisco de Enzinas: texte latin inédit, avec la traduction française du XVIe siècle en regard 1543–1545.* Brussels: Société de l'histoire de Belgique, 1862–63.

*Memorias: Historia del estado.* Tr. from French by A. F. Sosa. 2 vols. Buenos Aires: Aurora, 1943–44.

*El Nuevo Testamento de Nuestro Redentor y Salvador Jesucristo.* Bio., notes, B. F. Stockwell. Buenos Aires: Aurora, 1943.

Criticism

Bataillon, M. *Erasmo y España.* Mexico City: Fondo de Cultura Económica, 1950.

Maureen Ihrie

**EPÍSTOLA MORAL A FABIO** (Moral Epistle to Fabio), seventeenth-c. moral poem. Written in tercets and numbering only 205 lines, it has been acclaimed as the most significant poem of the c., for its clear, intensely sincere, Stoic expression of the value of human life—so deceptive and fleeting. In melancholy tone, yet with serenity and dignity, it evokes the quintessence of Spanish values at that moment in history. Various authors have been suggested— *Medrano, Francisco de *Rioja—but the most likely candidate is that proposed by Dámaso *Alonso, Andrés *Fernández de Andrada.

BIBLIOGRAPHY

Primary Text

*La "Epístola moral a Fabio" de Andrés Fernández de Andrada.* Ed., study D. Alonso. Madrid: Gredos, 1978.

Criticism

Alonso, D. *Dos españoles del Siglo de Oro.* Madrid: Gredos, 1960.

**ERASMISM,** a spiritual movement of sixteenth-c. Spain which generated pro-found cultural, political and philosophical repercussions, which reached into the seventeenth c. and beyond. Although the Dutch humanist Desiderius Erasmus (1465–1536) never set foot in Spain, his thought took stronger root there than in any other part of Europe, in part because of aspects it shared with *humanism, *mysticism, and church reforms underway at the same time. Erasmus advocated an "inner Christianity." Critical of ceremonies and outward (hypocritical) manifestations of religious piety, he espoused instead the daily virtues of love, charity, self-knowledge, humility, and a direct knowledge of God and his law through reading the Scriptures and through the use of silent, mental prayer. Peace was another cornerstone of his thought; he deplored war, particularly between Christian nations. Although Erasmus felt an enormous need for reform in the church, he also saw the need to preserve the authority of the church, in the final analysis. Erasmus's reforms met with rapid acceptance among the contemplative Franciscans, Hieronymites, *conversos, and *alumbrados in Spain, in part because they echoed reforms initiated by Cardinal *Cisneros.

The first translation of Erasmus's writings appeared in Spain in 1516, but the most significant translation came ten years later with the *Enchiridion* or *Manual del caballero christiano* (1526; Enquiridion or Manual of the Christian Knight). A second edition was published in 1527, and in 1528 no fewer than nine editions were printed. Erasmus's thought spread rapidly in the court, in many religious orders, among the aristocracy, and to other social classes as well. A backlash inevitably arose. In 1527, a challenge to Erasmus's orthodoxy was resoundingly defeated, but after Erasmus's death in 1536, and the death of the supportive Archbishop Manrique two years later, a change of atmosphere prevailed. Increasing inquisitorial hostility and persecutions made advocates more prudent; some Erasmists fled the country. In 1559, some of Erasmus's works were placed on the Index (*see* Índice de libros prohibidos). Others were expunged of offending passages. Nonetheless, Erasmist attitudes and ideas had been so firmly planted in the earlier years that they could not be smothered.

Marcel Bataillon, among others, has studied eloquently the development of Erasmism in Spain and its profound mark on the culture. José Luis Abellán summarizes the essence of Spanish Erasmism as a reaction against the immorality of church abuses; the advocation of Christianity as a religion of love, peace and charity; and the espousal of an "inner Christianity" which does not depend on church structure. As such, Erasmus's influence in Spain endured well into the seventeenth c. Juan de *Avila, Domingo de *Soto, Luis de *Granada, Juan and Alfonso de *Valdés, Andrés *Laguna, Cristóbal de *Villalón, Luis de *León and *Cervantes are but a few of the many *Siglo de Oro figures whose writing reflects Erasmist thought in Spain. *See also* Inquisition; Renaissance.

BIBLIOGRAPHY

Primary Text

*El enquiridión o manual del caballero cristiano.* Ed. D. Alonso. Prol. M. Bataillon. Madrid: CSIC, 1971.

Criticism

Abellán, J. L. *El erasmismo español.* Madrid: Espejo, 1976.
Bataillon, M. *Erasmo y España.* Mexico: Fondo de Cultura Económica, 1966.

Maureen Ihrie

**ERAUSO, Catalina de** (1592, San Sebastián–1650?, Mexico), singular historical figure, dubbed the Monja Alférez (Nun-ensign). Erauso's amazing exploits served as inspiration for an alleged autobiography and a play by *Pérez de Montalbán. Born to a noble family, she entered a convent at a very young age. In 1607, disguised as a man, she abandoned the nunnery, traveled to the New World and lived as a soldier, participating in campaigns against the Indians. Only in 1623, when wounded in battle, was her true identity revealed. She later returned to Spain, a legend in her own time, and went on to Rome; Pope Urban VIII granted her special permission to wear male clothes. She subsequently returned to America and died years later in Mexico.

Recent criticism argues that a brief, original ms., dated 1624, was composed by Erauso, but then elaborately recast with fictitious additions and alterations by another author, in 1625 and 1653, and published.

BIBLIOGRAPHY

Primary Text

*Memorias de la monja alférez.* Madrid: Felmar, 1974.

English Translation

*The Nun Ensign.* Tr. J. Fitzmaurice-Kelly. London: Unwin, 1908.

Criticism

Vallbona, Rima-Gretchen Rothe. "Historic Reality and Fiction in *Vida y Sucesos de la Monja Alférez.*" *DAI* 43 (1982): 1161A. Middlebury College. Also contains critical edition of 1624 ms.

Maureen Ihrie

**ERCILLA Y ZÚÑIGA, Alonso de** (1533, Madrid–1594, Madrid), soldier and epic poet of the conquest of Chile. Of a noble family from the town of Bermeo in the Basque region, Ercilla accompanied Prince Philip as a page in travels to England, Flanders, Italy, and Germany. In 1555 he embarked for the Indies with the expedition of the ill-fated *adelantado* (governor) of Chile, Jerónimo de Alderete. For four years he fought in the battles against the Araucan Indians, while beginning to write the poem that was to bring him fame. Returning to Spain in 1563, he published the first part of *La Araucana* (*The Araucaniad*, 1945) in 1569 at his own cost, and in 1570 married María de Bazán, a woman of considerable wealth. In 1571 Ercilla was knighted in the Order of Santiago. In 1574 he undertook a lengthy trip in which he visited the papal court in Rome and was present in Prague at the coronation of Rudolf II as king of Bohemia. He later traveled to the Azores and to Portugal, where he met *Cervantes, before returning definitely to Madrid. In 1578 he published the second part, and in 1589 the third, of *La Araucana*. An immensely wealthy man toward the end of his life, Ercilla lent large sums of money to nobles and individuals of the court. He had an illegitimate son, Juan de Ercilla, who died in the Invincible Armada in 1588.

*La Araucana* is generally recognized as the most important epic poem of the Spanish *Siglo de Oro. Its thirty-seven cantos evoke the history of the conquest of Chile, from the initial defeats of the Spaniards, through the reorganization of their forces and renewed offensive under García Hurtado de Mendoza, to their final victory over the Araucans and exploratory expeditions to the South.

While the historical reliability of the work with regard to the general outline of events of the conquest has been firmly established by José Toribio Medina and others, *La Araucana*, more than a chronicle, is primarily a poetic creation in the epic tradition of Ariosto's *Orlando Furioso* (1516–32) and of *Os Lusiadas* (1571) of Luis de *Camões. Although Ercilla was influenced by the classical Latin authors Virgil, Lucan and *Seneca, his greatest inspiration is undoubtedly Ariosto, whose stylistic devices he frequently imitates.

Dedicated to Philip II, *La Araucana* incorporates the theme of the Indies into Spanish poetry within the canons of the *Renaissance epic. Rather than an individual protagonist, the collective hero of Ercilla's epic is the Araucan people. The Indian leaders, Lautaro, Tucapel, Galvarino, the aged counselor Colocolo, and above all Caupolicán, embody variations of the same primitive heroism admired by the poet. Caupolicán, especially in the scene of his stoic death, is the prototype of valor and daring; Lautaro is more sober and measured; Colocolo represents the wisdom of age. No Spanish captain, on the other hand, is portrayed as being an equal counterpart to the most outstanding Indian *caudillos* (chiefs). In spite of his declarations to the contrary, the poet does not strictly limit himself to treatment of military actions. He also adds the personal histories of the Indian leaders, describing the love between husband and wife: Guacolda and Lautaro, Tegualda and Crepino, Glaura and Cariolano, Fresia and Caupolicán. In the last two parts, Ercilla even manages to include descriptions in his American narrative of contemporary European events—the battles of San Quentin and Lepanto, and the war with Portugal—the presence of which disrupt the thematic unity of the poem.

Ercilla excels in the description of military actions, portraying them in all their movement, color and dramatic quality. His treatment of geography and plant and animal life, when he is able to avoid imitating the landscapes of the Latin poets, is occasionally vivid and realistic, conveying the violence and untamed character of the American continent.

*La Araucana* exercised great influence over the literature of its time, particularly in America, where many imitations and continuations of the poem appeared. Some of these include *El Arauco domado* (1596; Arauco Tamed) of Pedro de *Oña; *Purén indómito* (late 16th-c. ms.; published 1862 as Unconquered Purén) of Hernando *Álvarez de Toledo; *La Argentina* (1602; The Argentiniad) of Barco Centenera; *Guerras de Chile* (1610; Wars of Chile), attributed to Juan de Mendoza y Monteagudo. In México, this genre produced *Nuevo mundo y conquista* (1594; New World and Conquest) of Gabriel Lobo Lasso de la Vega; and *Historia del Nuevo México* (1610; History of New Mexico) of Gaspar Guzmán. *See also* Italian Literary Influences.

BIBLIOGRAPHY

Primary Text

*La Araucana*. Ed. Marcos A. Moríñigo and Isaías Lerner. 2 vols. Madrid: Castalia, 1979.

English Translation

*The Araucaniad; a Version in English Poetry of Alonso de Ercilla y Zúñiga's "La Araucana."* Tr. Charles Maxwell Lancaster and Paul Thomas Manchester. Nashville: Vanderbilt UP, 1945.

Criticism

Águila, August J. *Alonso de Ercilla y Zúñiga: A Basic Bibliography*. London: Grant & Cutler, 1975.

Brunet, Hugo Montes. *Estudios sobre La Araucana*. Valparaiso: n.p., 1975.

Caillet-Bois, Julio. *Análisis de La Araucana*. Buenos Aires: Centro de Editores de la América Latina, 1965.

Iglesias, Augusto. *Ercilla y La Araucana*. Santiago de Chile: Academia Chilena, 1969.

Pierce, Francis William. *The Heroic Poem of the Spanish Golden Age*. New York: Oxford P, 1947.

                                                                    Robert E. Lewis

**ESCALANTE Y PRIETO, Amós de,** pseudonym Juan García (1831, Santander–1902, Santander), journalist, novelist and poet. His travel books—*Del Manzanares al Darro* (1863; From the Manzanares to the Darro), *Del Ebro al Tíber* (1864; From the Ebro to the Tiber), and, particularly, *Costas y montañas* (1871; Coasts and Mountains) and *En la Playa* (1873; At the Beach)—were valued for the range of the author's interests and information as well as for their purity of language. His historical novel *Ave, Maris Stella* (1877; Hail, Star of the Sea) recounts a seventeenth-c. legend with scant emphasis on action. In 1890 Escalante published his *Poesías*, a collection untouched by contemporary trends, evocative of local sea and landscapes.

BIBLIOGRAPHY

Primary Text

*Obras escogidas*. Preliminary study by Marcelino Menéndez Pelayo; Intro. to bibliography, Helen S. Nicholson. Madrid: Atlas, 1956.

Criticism

Cossío, J. M. de. *Amós de Escalante*. Madrid: Tip. de Archivos, 1933.

                                                                    D. J. O'Connor

**ESCAMILLA, Pedro,** pseudonym of Julián Castellanos y Velasco (?, Madrid–1891, ?), dramatist, author of *folletines* (novels published in serials), and director in 1865 of the Madrid periodical *El Fisgón* (The Spy). His dramatic and narrative fiction was characterized by inventive plots and melodramatic effects. His theater pieces were popular successes; the literary historian *Cejador y Frauca lists no fewer than twenty-one titles from among *folletines* Escamilla published between 1876 and 1886. In addition to adventure novels, for example, *Un drama al pie* *del cadalso* (1878; A Drama at the Foot of the Gallows), Escamilla wrote historical novels, such as *El sacristán de las monjas* (n.d.; The Nuns' Sacristan), and novels of local customs, such as *Las chulas de Lavapiés* (1881; The Girls from Lavapiés).

BIBLIOGRAPHY

Primary Texts

*Un gallego: comedia original en un acto.* Madrid: Lalama, 1861.
*El orángutan: juguete cómico.* . . . Madrid: Arregui, 1879.
*Ruperto el pobre diablo: parodia de la ópera.* . . . Madrid: Montoya, 1883.

Criticism

Ferreras, Juan Ignacio. *La novela por entregas 1840–1900.* Madrid: Taurus, 1972. 221–
    22.

                                                        D. J. O'Connor

**ESCAVIAS, Pedro de** (c. 1417, Andújar–shortly after 1482, Andújar), soldier, historian, poet, mayor of Andújar. J. B. Avalle-Arce has recently rescued Escavias from relative obscurity, clarifying many literary and biographical points. Of noble birth, Escavias was educated at the court of John II, also serving as a page. A loyal supporter of Henry IV, he closely assisted Constable Miguel Lucas de Iranzo, the last heroic soldier of Spain, in various military campaigns and stratagems. The literary fruits of this association include various poems, most of which are published in the *Cancionero de Oñate-Castañeda,* including "Coplas al Condestable Miguel Lucas" (c. 1463; Poems to Constable Miguel Lucas), which are lyrical narrative praises; the *Hechos del Condestable Don Miguel Lucas de Iranzo* (1473–74; Deeds of Constable . . . Iranzo), a rich historical account of events in the constable's life from 1458 to 1471; and the *Reportorio de príncipes* (after 1474; Almanac of Princes), which is a history of Spain. The theme of loyalty underlies each of these works. Escavias is an exemplary model of the arms/letters tradition, as seen in *Garcilaso de la Vega, *Boscán, *Cervantes, and so many others.

BIBLIOGRAPHY

Primary Texts

*Hechos del condestable don Miguel Lucas de Iranzo (crónica del siglo XV).* Ed. and
    study, J. de Mata Carriazo. Madrid: Espasa-Calpe, 1940.
"Reportorio de Príncipes, Caps. CXLVI y CXLVII." In *El cronista Pedro de Escavias.*
    Ed., study, J. B. Avalle-Arce. UNCSRLL 127. Chapel Hill: U of North Carolina
    P, 1972. Final chapters of the *Reportorio.*
"Un cancionero del siglo XV con varias poesías inéditas." Ed. F. R. de Uhagón. *RABM*
    4 (1900): 516–35.

Criticism

*See* Avalle-Arce, above.

Maureen Ihrie

**ESCOBAR, Luis** (1908, Madrid– ), theater director, playwright. He collaborated with Hans Rothe on *La voz amada* (The Beloved Voice), with Arvid de Budisco on *Los endemoniados* (The Demon-Possessed), and with Juan Ignacio Luca de Tena on *El vampiro de la calle Claudio Coello* (The Vampire on Claudio Coello Street). *Elena Ossorio* (1955), not written in collaboration, offers a successful evocation of Lope de *Vega's life. In 1959, *El amor es un potro desbocado* (Love Is a Bolting Colt), written with Luis Saslawski, successfully revived the theme of the *Cid's youthful days. *Un hombre y una mujer* (A Man and a Woman), which appeared in 1962, was inspired in part by M. *Fórmica's *La ciudad perdida*.

BIBLIOGRAPHY

Primary Texts

*El amor es un potro desbocado.* Madrid: Alfil, 1959.
*Elena Ossorio.* Madrid: Alfil, 1959.
*Fuera es de noche.* Madrid: Escelicer, n.d.
*Un hombre y una mujer.* Madrid: Alfil, 1962.

Criticism

"La primera obra de un gran director; *Elena Ossorio*, de Luis Escobar." *Teatro* (May-
    Aug. 1955): 22.

Isabel McSpadden

**ESCOBAR Y MENDOZA, Antonio de** (1589, Valladolid–1669, Valladolid), Jesuit religious poet. His ornate, fully Baroque verse was ridiculed by French author Pascal in *Lettres provinciales.* Escobar y Mendoza may have written about 150 plays, none of which survived. His two long, extant poems are *San Ignacio* (1613; St. Ignatius), and *Historia de la Virgen Madre de Dios María* (1618; Story of Mary the Virgin Mother of God)—which was revised with the title *Nueva Jerusalén María* (1625; New Jerusalem Mary). It is an effusive, elaborate comparison between the Virgin and a new, ideal Holy City.

BIBLIOGRAPHY

Primary Texts

*Historia de la Virgen Madre de Dios María.* New York: De Vinne, 1903. Facs.
*Historia de la Virgen Madre de Dios María.* Ed., study J. Salas. Santiago, Chile: Revista
    Católica, 1904.
*Nueva Jerusalén.* Mexico: Biblioteca Mexicana, 1759.

Criticism

Wyzewa, T. "Le Père Escobar et les Lettres Provinciales." *Revue des Deux Mondes*
    (March 1872): n.p.

**ESCOBEDO, Joana** (1942, Barcelona– ), Catalan critic, novelist and author of language texts. A curator of special collections at the Biblioteca de Catalunya, Escobedo has written numerous erudite articles in specialized journals, as well as imaginative fiction. *Silenci endins* (1979; The Silence Around), her first novel, utilizes a sleepless night and the female protagonist's half-dreaming consciousness to reveal the effects of her rigid formal education and years of repressive conditioning. *Amic, amat* (1980; Friend, Lover) continues the feminist preoccupation, focusing on a couple's problematic relationship set against the background of Barcelona in counterpoint with memories of New York. In both, Escobedo experiments with interior monologue and multiple time planes.

BIBLIOGRAPHY

Primary Texts

*Amic, amat.* Barcelona: Edicions 62, 1980.
*Silenci endins.* Barcelona: Edicions 62, 1979.

Janet Pérez

**ESCOSURA, Patricio de la** (1807, Madrid–1878, Madrid), poet, critic, playwright and novelist. He pursued a military career and twice had to emigrate because of political activities. As a friend of *Espronceda, he took part in the secret society of the Numantinos and in the literary circle of the Parnasillo. He became a member of the Royal Spanish Academy (*Academia Española) in 1847.

As a poet, he imitated Espronceda and is best known for his composition "El bulto vestido del negro capuz" (1835; The Figure in the Black Hood), an epic-lyric poem which brought him great fame in his day. First published in *El Artista*, it takes place in Simancas during the period of the comuneros. His historical novels, *Ni Rey ni Roque* (1835; Not a Single Living Soul) and *El conde de Candespina* (1832; The Count of Candespina), were written in imitation of Walter Scott. His later novel, *El patriarca del valle* (1846–47; The Patriarch of the Valley), deals with the historical events between 1815 and 1839 and prefigures *Pérez Galdós's *Episodios nacionales*. Other novels include *La conjuración de Méjico* (1850; The Conspiracy of Mexico) and an autobiographical work, *Las memorias de un coronel retirado* (1868, The Memoirs of a Retired Colonel).

Escosura dedicated himself with most perseverance to theater. As a minister of government, he proposed the renovation of the Príncipe Theater in Madrid and the rehabilitation of Spanish theater in general. His first drama, *La corte del Buen Retiro* (1837; The Court of the Buen Retiro [well-known park in Madrid]), deals with the love affair between *Villamediana and Queen Isabel, wife of Philip IV. The second part of this drama, *También los muertos se vengan* (1838; The Dead Also Take Revenge), possesses brilliant scenography. One of his better works, *Don Jaime el conquistador* (1838; Sir James the Conqueror), deals with a conqueror's love affairs with three different women and the intrigue involved in his opposition to the church and the nobility. Historical plays presenting American themes are *Las mocedades de Hernán Cortés* (1844; Hernando

Cortez's Youth) and *Higuamota* (1838). *El amante universal* (1847; The Universal Lover), generally considered to be his masterpiece, was inspired by Leandro Fernández de *Moratín and is neo-classical in its three unities, uniform metrical scheme, upper-middle-class characters and moral lesson. Because of his great admiration for *Calderón, he wrote two dramas in which the Golden Age dramatist appears as a character in the works: *¿Cuál es mayor perfección?* (1862; What Is Greater Perfection?) and *Pedro Calderón* (1867). He also wrote scholarly works such as *Estudios históricos sobre las costumbres españolas* (1851; Historical Studies of Spanish Customs), *Manual de mitología* (1845; A Manual of Mythology) and a two-volume study on Calderón's theater edited by the Royal Spanish Academy. Although Escosura left no single work of top quality, in total his general literary production is representative of the ideas and tendencies of the first half of the nineteenth c.

BIBLIOGRAPHY

Primary Texts

*El amante universal.* Madrid: Jordán, 1847.
*La corte del Buen Retiro.* Madrid: Piñuela, 1837.
*¿Cuál es mayor perfección?* Madrid: Rojas, 1862.
*Ni rey ni roque. Episodio histórico del reinado de Felipe II.* Madrid: Repullés, 1835.
*También los muertos se vengan.* Madrid: Nacional, 1844.

Criticism

Alborg, Juan Luis. *Historia de la literatura española, El romanticismo.* Madrid: Gredos, 1980. 4:618–27.
Brown, Reginald F. "Patricio de la Escosura as Dramatist." *Liverpool Studies in Hispanic Literature.* Ed. E. Allison Peers. Liverpool: Institute of Hispanic Studies, 1940. 175–201.
Cano Malagón, María Luz. "Los *Recuerdos literarios* de Escosura: Otras memorias del siglo XIX." *Castilla* 13 (1988): 35–42.
Ferrer del Río, Antonio. *Galería de la literatura española.* Madrid: Mellado, 1846. 187–201.
Iniesta, Antonio. *Don Patricio de la Escosura.* Madrid: Fundación Universitaria Española, 1958.

Phoebe Porter Medina

**ESCRIVÁ, El Comendador** (c. 1450, ?–c. 1520, ?), Valencian poet. He was ambassador for Ferdinand and Isabel at the Vatican in 1497—nothing else is known of his life. He wrote, in Castilian and Valencian, poems both witty and serious. Most famous is "Ven muerte tan escondida" (Come Death So Covert); it was often glossed by later Golden Age writers, including *Cervantes, Lope de *Vega, and others. Also his is a sentimental, courtly novella in dialogue, *Queja que da a su amiga ante el dios de amor, por modo de diálogo en prosa y verso* (Complaint He Gives to His Lady before the God of Love, in a Prose and Verse Dialogue), which first appeared in the second edition (1514) of the *Cancionero* of Hernando del Castillo. *See also* Siglo de Oro.

BIBLIOGRAPHY

Primary Text

*Cancionero general de Hernando del Castillo.* Ed. J. de Balenchana. 2 vols. Madrid: Genesta, 1882. Contains 29 works by Escrivá.

**ESCUELA DE TRADUCTORES DE TOLEDO** (Toledo School of Translators), twelfth-c. translation center. It is important to know that this so-called Toledo School of Translators is not a ''school'' in the strict sense of the word. Translation of Arabic science did become intense from about the beginning of the second quarter of the twelfth c. and continued unabatedly on to the end of the reign of King *Alphonse X (1284). Although much of the translation actually occurred in Toledo, other translations associated with this period occurred in Barcelona, Tarazona, Segovia, León, Pamplona and beyond the Pyrenees as well. The main patron and catalyst was Archbishop *Raimundo of Toledo (1126–52), but Michael, Bishop of Tarazona in Aragon (1119–51), was also a patron, specifically of Hugh of Santalla. This ''school'' was not an isolated historical phenomenon. It served as the great bridge between a scientifically impoverished West and a West enriched by Arab-modified Greek learning filtered through Arabic enhancements, which ultimately led to the great *Renaissance.

A quick synopsis of historical events will make it obvious that, ironically, it was man's inhumanity to man—intolerance and war—which caused in large part the transmission of knowledge.

Because Rome had been more concerned with practical matters and less so with Greek science, the West received this science through a circuitous route. In brief, contact between Greek and Middle Eastern cultures occurred when Greek savants fled eastward in retreat from religious disputes raging in Byzantium. The closing of Greek schools in the fifth and sixth centuries augmented the eastward exodus of scholars. The Middle East, aware of Greek culture since the days of Alexander the Great, readily accepted Greek science, translating it into Semitic tongues, one of which ultimately was Arabic. When the Arabs invaded Spain in 711, along with the bloodshed came the science. Christians, Jews, and the dominant Arabic culture peacefully cohabited in the Iberian Peninsula, and specifically in Toledo until 1085 when Alphonse VI reconquered it from the infidel. The population in Toledo was of necessity at least bilingual—Spanish or Hebrew plus the dominant Arabic. The mixed population and the wealth of Arabic texts made possible the increase in translation. Even though translation was not restricted to Toledo, this city soon became a major center of this activity, which became very intense with Archbishop Raimundo's largess.

The process of translation is interesting since it would be used as much as a c. later in the royal scriptorium of Alphonse X. One scholar, better versed in Arabic, would translate the Arabic into a lingua franca, in this case Spanish; a second scholar, better versed in Latin, would then take the Spanish translation and render it into the scholarly lingua franca, Latin. Since there was no demand for it, the Spanish translation was apparently discarded. Translations of this period made available to Western Europe, and especially to the incipient studia generalia, both the works by Greek masters—Ptolemy, Aristotle, Hippocrates, Galen, Euclid—and also those of Arabic masters— Averroes, Avicenna, Messahala, and others. These translators were John of Seville; Ibn David (Avendaut); Dominicus Gundissalinus (died post–1190); and perhaps most important of all, the Italian Gerard of Cremona (1114–87), considered the greatest translator of all. Finally, Mark of Toledo takes us into the thirteenth c. Also associated at one point or another with the translation activity centered in Toledo are Plato of Tivoli, Daniel of Morely, Adelard of Bath, Hugh of Santalla, Robert of Ketton, Hermann of Carinthia (or the Dalmatian, not to be confused with Hermann Contractus—the cripple), and Hermann's student, Rodolfo of Brujas. We cannot leave Toledo without mentioning that Michael Scot, eventually the court astrologer of Frederick II, spent some time in Spain and in Toledo where he learned the Arabic that was to serve him well later.

It is interesting to note that this great center of translation became associated in the minds of many with the black arts. "In the mediaeval mind the science of magic lay close to the magic of science" (Haskins, p. 19).

*See also* Edad Media, Literatura de la.

BIBLIOGRAPHY

Criticism

Burnett, C. S. F. "A Group of Arabic-Latin Translators Working in Northern Spain in the Mid-12th Century." *Journal of the Royal Asiatic Society* (1977): 62–108.

González Palencia, A. *El arzobispo don Raimundo de Toledo.* Barcelona: Labor, 1942.

Haskins, C. H. *Studies in the History of Mediaeval Science.* Cambridge: Harvard UP, 1924. Rpt. New York: Ungar, 1960.

Menéndez Pidal, R. "España y la introducción de la ciencia árabe en Occidente." In *España, Eslabón entre la cristiandad y el islám.* Colección Austral 1280. Madrid: Espasa-Calpe, 1956. 33–60.

Millás Vallicrosa, J. M. "Translation of Oriental Scientific Works (To the End of the Thirteenth Century)." Tr. D. Woodward. In *The Evolution of Science: Readings from the History of Mankind.* Ed. G. S. Métraux and F. Crouzet. New York: New American Library of World Literature, 1965. 128–67.

Anthony J. Cárdenas

**ESCUELA SALMANTINA** (Salamancan School), the name given a school of poets, headed by Fray Luis de *León, that cultivated sober, balanced, and restrained poetry relatively free of pomposity and grandiloquence. This school of poets has traditionally been seen as opposed to the Sevillian school, led by Fernando de *Herrera, whose characteristics include bombast and the cultivation of ornate external forms and poetic figures. Today, these distinctions are generally viewed as superficial and invalid attempts at categorization; the concept of two separate poetic schools is seen by many critics as a notion that should be abandoned. That concept had originally offered a pretext for contrasting the two poetic geniuses associated with Salamanca and Seville, respectively: Fray Luis and Herrera, but disagreement concerning which poets should belong to each school and the difficulties of defining the limits and characteristics of the groups have led to a re-evaluation of the concept.

An alternative approach combining these differing viewpoints would entail exploring the various generations of Petrarchan poets in Spain, since the two schools reflect the poetic ideals of Petrarch filtered through the genius of *Boscán and *Garcilaso de la Vega and then infused into the poetry of Spanish writers of the last half of the sixteenth c. The basic tenets of Petrarchan poetry—platonic love, melancholy, the importance of nature (although in a stylized, pastoral sense)—served beautifully to express the poetic messages of the young poets of the end of the century. These writers then attempted to inculcate their own personalities into the framework of the Italianate topics, grouping themselves in two of the major Spanish cultural centers of the time. Salamanca, at the height of its prestige as a university city (see Universities), was one of those centers, and the poets linked with the Salamancan school were associated with the university.

As noted above, the Salamancan school exhibits a tendency toward intimacy and subjectivity; restraint, somber expression, moral seriousness, and a strong Horatian influence are characteristics traditionally associated with the school, leading to the perception that the poetry of these poets offers a classical, harmonious balance between form and content. Fray Luis de León, the Salamancan school's greatest representative, was able to express a great number of emotions with a small number of poetic elements, using the richness of nuance and shades of meaning to replace grandiloquence of expression. Other poets associated with this school include Francisco de *Figueroa and Francisco de *Aldana; all three were termed ''divine'' by the critics for their *Renaissance serenity and relaxed cultivation of form. Apart from these three poets, critics are divided on whether or not anyone else should be added to the list; possible candidates include Jerónimo de *Lomas Cantoral and Ramírez Pagán, who are closer to the Salamancan than to the Sevillian school. There is much disagreement as to where to place Francisco de *Medrano, a Horatian poet who is also termed a transition figure between the two schools because of the rich color of his poetic language. Also included in the list of possible members of the Salamancan school are a number of rather distant imitators of Fray Luis: *Malón de Chaide, Juan de Almeida, *Arias Montano, among others. It is clear that traditional groupings must be revised. Fray Luis de León's dazzling personality is not sufficient to justify the term *school*, which incorporates the notions of discipline and adherence to rules and which is not profoundly characteristic of this group of poets.

### Salamancan School (Eighteenth Century)

Some literary historians speak of an eighteenth-c. Salamancan School, attempting to categorize the members of the Arcadia or Parnaso Salamantino, founded by Fray Diego *González. They associate this school, which was against *Culteranismo* and in favor of maximum lyric purity in the style of Fray Luis, with *Cadalso, *Jovellanos, *Meléndez Valdés, *Iglesias, *Quintana, Sánchez Barbero, and González Carvajal, among others. Nevertheless, in spite of the coincidences of their literary environment, these poets are actually quite diverse; they should not be studied as a unified school. *See also* Italian literary influences.

BIBLIOGRAPHY

Criticism

Bonneville, Henry. "Sur la poésie à Séville au Siècle d'Or." *BH* 66 (1964): 311–48.
Gallego Morell, Antonio. *Estudios sobre poesía española del primer siglo de oro.* Madrid: Insula, 1970.
Jones, R. O. *A Literary History of Spain. The Golden Age: Prose and Poetry.* New York: Barnes and Noble, 1971.
Rivers, Elías L., ed. *Poesía lírica del Siglo de Oro.* 5th ed. Madrid: Cátedra, 1983.
Valbuena Prat, Ángel. *Historia de la literatura española.* 2 vols. Barcelona: Gili, 1950.

Catherine Larson

**ESCUELA SEVILLANA** (Sevillian School). As noted in the description of the Salamancan school (*Escuela Salmantina), the term *school* is extremely problematic with regard to grouping the late sixteenth-c. poets from Seville and Salamanca. Nevertheless, a general classification of the works of the Sevillian school would incorporate a number of similar features, including the use of rich imagery, neologisms, pomposity, color, and extraordinary erudition and grandiloquence. Great interest in adjectives and accents, hyperbaton, ornate metaphors, and the cultivation of form for its own sake are salient characteristics of the school. The brief, somber, and balanced poems of Fray Luis de *León may be contrasted with Fernando de *Herrera's long elegies; these meditative, weighty elegies were written in accordance with the poetic theory expounded in Herrera's *Anotaciones* (1580; Annotations) to the poetry of *Garcilaso de la Vega. This tendency toward the Baroque seems to be a constant in Andalusian poets; see, for example, Juan de *Mena and *Góngora.

As with the Salamancan school, it is difficult to classify the other members of the school. One member might be Juan de *Mal Lara, at whose famous humanities school many of the Sevillian poets met. Other candidates are Mal Lara's successor in the direction of the school, Diego *Girón, Francisco de *Medina, Francisco de *Rioja, Juan de *Arguijo, and Pedro de *Espinosa. A Sevillian poet whose work moves in another direction is Baltasar del *Alcázar, whose satiric poems show the classical influence of Martial and Horace more than the bombast and grandiloquence associated with the other Sevillian poets. Pablo de *Céspedes and Francisco de *Pacheco are also debated members of the Sevillian school. As in the case of the Salamancan school, the glowing personality of one poet—here, Herrera—is really what has motivated the classification of these poets as a distinct school, although some critics suggest that the Sevillian group maintained more contact and mutual influence.

### Escuela Sevillana (Eighteenth Century)

The Andalusian poets who were grouped in the *Pléyade poética* (Poetic Pleiad), included *Arjona, *Reinoso, and, especially, *Lista.

BIBLIOGRAPHY

Primary Text

*Fernando de Herrera y la escuela sevillana*. Ed. G. Chiappini. Madrid: Taurus, 1985.

Criticism

Lasso de la Vega, Angel. *Historia y juicio crítico de la escuela poética sevillana en los siglos 16 y 17*. Madrid: Galiano, hijos de Galiano, 1871.

Sánchez, Alberto, ed. *Poesía sevillana en la Edad de Oro*. Madrid: Clásicos Castilla, 1948.

Catherine Larson

**ESLAVA, Antonio de** (1570?, Sanguesa, Navarre–?), novelist. He wrote eleven Italianate novellas, in dialogue, published under the title *Primera parte del libro intitulado Noches de invierno* (1609; First Part of the Book Titled Winter Nights). Shakespeare may have used the novella "Do se cuenta la soberbia del rey Nicíforo y encendio de sus naves" (Where Is Told of the Pride of King Nicephorus and Burning of His Boats) as inspiration for his play *The Tempest*. *See also* Italian Literary Influences.

BIBLIOGRAPHY

Primary Text

*Noches de invierno*. Ed. González Palencia. Madrid: SAETA, 1942.

English Translation

*The Fountain of Youth*. In *The Spanish Novelists*. T. Rosco. London: n.p., 1832. 2: 272–97.

Criticism

José y Prades, J. "*Las noches de invierno* de Antonio de Eslava." *Revista bibliográfica y documental* 3 (1949): 163–96.

**ESPANCA, Florbela de Alma da Conceição** (1894, Vila-Vicosa–1930, Matosinhos), Portuguese poet. After a youth spent in the country she spent three years enrolled in the Faculty of Law of the U of Lisbon. Her first two collections of poems, *Livro de Mágoas* (1922; Book of Sorrows) and *Livro de Soror Saudade* (1923; The Book of Sister Longing), were published during her student years. Her adult life was marked or possibly marred by three equally unhappy marriages. The first two (1913 and 1921) ended in divorce and the third concluded with her death in somewhat unclear circumstances. The remainder of her work was published posthumously largely due to the efforts of Guido Battelli, professor of Italian at Coimbra U. The remaining corpus consists of a sonnet sequence, *Charneca em Flor* (1930; Barrens in Flower); *Juvenília* (1930), gathering together her poetry dating between 1916 and 1917; a volume of short stories,

*Máscaras do Destino* (1932; Masks of Destiny), dedicated to her brother Apeles Espanca, painter and aviator, killed in an air crash in 1927 and to whom she was intensely attached. A second set of short stories, *O Dominó Negro* (1931; The Black Mask), and a volume of letters (*Cartas de Florbela Espanca*, 1981) have been recovered and published. She was also a sporadic contributor to *Seara Nova* but without sharing the political commitment of that journal.

Her poetry is all in sonnet form, often influenced as to composition and content by António Nobre, particularly in *Mágoas*, and by Antero de Quental in *Soror Saudade*.

Her reputation as a poet was slow in building, but she is now often seen as the "great feminine voice" of modern Portuguese lyric poetry. Particularly striking is the way in which her poems often paint her psyche and its tribulations on a day-by-day basis, offering the reader a poetic personal diary. Her prose style is evocative rather than concretely descriptive and has a distinct *art nouveau* flavor to it. This is clearly evidenced in "O Aviador" (The Aviator), the first short story in *Máscaras*, and "Amor de Outrora" (Love from the Past) in *Dominó Negro*.

BIBLIOGRAPHY

Primary Text

*Obras Completas de Florbela Espanca*. 6 vols. Lisbon. Dom Quixote, 1985–86.

Criticism

Bessa Luís, Agustina. *Florbela Espanca*. Lisbon: Arcádia, 1979.
Guedes, Rui. *Florbela Espanca* (Fotobiografia). Lisbon: Dom Quixote, 1985.
Sena, Jorge de. "Florbela Espanca." In Sena's *Da Poesia Portuguesa*. Lisbon: Ática, 1959. 115–43.

Peter Fothergill-Payne

**ESPÉCULO DE LOS LEGOS** (Guide for Laymen), fourteenth-c. didactic work dealing with moral questions. This book includes ninety-one chapters translated from the *Speculum laicorum* attributed to John Howden or Hoveden (thirteenth c.). In order to make learning more palatable, it was common practice in the Middle Ages to include a mixture of parables, lives of the saints, religious elements derived from the Holy Scriptures, etc. As examples this work additionally draws from Oriental themes (some fables are from the stories of Don *Juan Manuel's *El Conde Lucanor*) and includes much other miscellaneous subject matter. *See also* Edad Media, Literatura de la.

BIBLIOGRAPHY

Primary Text

*Espéculo de los legos*. Ed. José María Mohedano. Madrid: CSIC, 1951.

Criticism

La Granja, Francisco de. "Eco de un poeta árabe antiguo en la literatura española." *Al-Andalús* 41 (1976): 179–93.
Russell, P. E. Review of Mohedano edition above, *MLR* 49 (1954): 94.

Lucy Sponsler

**ESPINA, Concha** (1869, Santander–1955, Madrid), Spanish novelist, playwright, and poet, generally associated with realism. Her early novels are set in rural Santander, with the misty, sunless terrain serving as background to tales of unrequited love. Later novels move beyond the local scene, with greater emphasis on contemporary social reality and its impact on the individual, in particular, women. In all of her work, Espina presents suffering as a fundamental law of human existence. One of her best novels, *La esfinge maragata* (1914; *Mariflor*, 1924), describes life in the isolated, culturally independent area of Maragatería and masterfully analyzes the individual as well as collective responses of the Maragatan women to their environment. *El metal de los muertos* (1920; The Metal of the Dead) is set in the Río Tinto copper mines in the Andalusian province of Huelva. For the first time Espina's protagonists are drawn from the working class, and the need for moderate social reform is suggested. With the outbreak of the Civil War, Espina's social preoccupation is displaced by strident defense of fascism and Falangism. This tone continues through the 1940s, but in her last novels (1947–52) she abandons ideological rhetoric and creates some of her most intriguing characters. With respect to form, Espina shows little evolution; she consistently employs a rich, dense style with a tendency toward long, complex sentences. Most of her novels are structured around the life history of a single character and follow strict chronological order. Typically she stresses the sentimental aspect of her characters, and almost without exception, exalted sentimentality leads to personal disillusionment. Writing essentially independently of the major literary currents of the day, Espina achieved several major successes as a novelist but did not leave a significant mark on the Spanish novel and its subsequent development.

BIBLIOGRAPHY

Primary Texts

*La esfinge maragata.* Madrid: Aguilar, 1962.
*El metal de los muertos.* Madrid: Afrodisio Aguada, 1941.
*Obras completas.* Madrid: FAX, 1972.

English Translations

*Mariflor.* Tr. Frances Douglas. New York: Macmillan, 1924.
*The Red Beacon.* Tr. Frances Douglas. New York: Appleton, 1924.
*The Woman and The Sea.* Tr. Terrell Louise Tatum. New York: R. D. Henkle, 1934.

Criticism

Boyd, Ernest. *Studies from Ten Literatures.* New York: Scribner's, 1925.
Bretz, Mary Lee. *Concha Espina.* Boston: G. K. Hall, 1980.

558ESPINA GARCÍA, ANTONIO

Canales, Alicia. *Concha Espina*. Madrid: EPESA, 1974.
Nicholson, Helen Schenck. *The Novel of Protest and the Spanish Republic*. Tucson: U of Arizona P, 1939.
Nora, Eugenio de. *La novela española contemporánea*. Madrid: Gredos, 1963.

Mary Lee Bretz

**ESPINA GARCÍA, Antonio** (1894, Madrid–1972, Madrid), Vanguardist biographer, poet, and novelist. After completing his *bachillerato* he entered the School of Medicine, which he abandoned four years later to pursue his literary interests. He became a journalist and collaborated in some of the more important Madrid journals: the newspapers *El Sol* and *El Heraldo de Madrid* and the magazine *La Revista de Occidente*. He also co-directed the Republican weekly *Nueva España* (1929–33). He was civil governor of Alava and the Balearic Islands at the outbreak of the Civil War (1936), an event that forced him to seek exile in France and Mexico. He did not return to Spain until 1960.

As a poet, Espina identified himself with Ultraism; his books *Umbrales* (1918; Thresholds) and *Signario* (1923; Sign) appeared at the height of the movement. For some critics, his interest in the unusual and the bizarre makes him a direct heir of *Gómez de la Serna; for others, his black humor and deformed, grotesque vision of the world can be traced to Goya and *Gutiérrez Solana. His novels, rather than telling a story or developing characters, aim at surprising the reader with a style full of daring metaphors, arbitrary paradoxes, learned allusions, and bizarre vocabulary. These traits were already present in his first book of prose, *Divagaciones* (1919; Wanderings), a collection of articles and tales, but they become more obvious and an actual impediment to narrative unity in *Pájaro pinto* (1927), a novel which deals in part with the frivolous European world of the post–World War I era. His second novel, *Luna de copas* (1929; Moon of Goblets), shares the same dehumanizing characteristics. Espina's work as a biographer is more successful: his novelized account *Luis Candelas, el bandido de Madrid* (1929; Luis Candelas, Madrid's Bandit) captures effectively the atmosphere of Madrid; while the even more historically accurate *Romea, o el comediante* (1935; Romea, or the Actor) succeeds in re-creating a lively and vigorous portrayal of life in the same city. His additional biographies on Espartero, *Quevedo, *Cánovas, etc., are of lesser interest. Espina was also able to exercise his wit in a series of incisive and extremely personal essays. Among his important early works in this genre are *Lo cómico contemporáneo* (1928; Contemporary Humor) and *El nuevo diantre* (1934; The New Devil); among his late ones mention must be made of *El alma garibay* (1964; Garibay Soul) and *El genio cómico y otros ensayos* (1965; The Comic Genius and Other Essays).

BIBLIOGRAPHY

Primary Texts

*El genio cómico y otros ensayos*. Madrid: Cruz del Sur, 1965.
*Luis Candelas, el bandido de Madrid*. Buenos Aires/ Mexico: Espasa-Calpe, 1964.
*El nuevo diantre*. Madrid: Espasa-Calpe, 1934.

*Romea, o el comediante.* Madrid: Espasa-Calpe, 1935.
*Umbrales.* Madrid: Alcoy, 1918.

Criticism

Crispin, John. "La novela de la generación de 1925: Antonio Espina." *Archivum* 16 (1966): 213–22.
Nora, Eugenio de. *Historia de la novela española contemporánea.* Madrid: Gredos, 1962. 2.1: 192–95.

María A. Salgado

**ESPINEL, Vicente Martínez** (1550, Ronda–1624, Madrid), poet, musician and novelist. His years as a student at Salamanca (1570–72), where the musicians Francisco Salinas and Juan de Navarro taught and performed, were important to his musical development. His departure from the university coincided with the imprisonment of Fray Luis de *León. Adventures from his fictionalized autobiography have been attributed, without convincing evidence, to the years between 1572 and 1581. During this time he became a part of the Sevillian cultural circles frequented by the painter Francisco *Pacheco and the poets Fernando de *Herrera and Luis *Barahona de Soto. He accompanied the Duke of Medina-Sidonia to Italy, where he remained from 1581 to 1584, a period that enriched his knowledge of Italian poetic forms. Returning to Spain to study for the priesthood, he obtained a half-benefice in Ronda which he held from 1587 to 1599. He found provincial life increasingly frustrating and his relations with church authorities in Ronda were turbulent, culminating in a fine for neglect of ecclesiastical duties. Fortunately, in 1599 he was appointed chapelmaster of the Chapel of the Bishop of Plasencia in the church of San Andrés in Madrid, where he flourished in the active cultural life to which he belonged. Espinel's disappointments in Ronda are reflected in some poems of his *Diversas rimas* (1591; Miscellaneous Verse). Espinel's gift for lyricism, clarity and sensitivity to the color and moods of nature is evident in these poems. They are representative of a transitional aesthetic bridging that of *Garcilaso de la Vega, Fray Luis de León, and Herrera, and of *Góngora, Lope de *Vega and *Quevedo. He displays a technical command of Italianate stanzas and his facility with traditional peninsular forms reflects his talents as a composer and musician. Lamentably, texts of his music have not survived. Lope de Vega claimed him as his literary mentor, and attributed to him the invention of the *espinela* (*see* décima), an octosyllabic ten-line verse form rhyming *abba:accddc* with a pause after the fourth line, a form which Lope used increasingly in his plays. The sonnet-like structure of the ten-line stanzas of the *espinela* is exploited by *Calderón in *La vida es sueño* (Life Is a Dream). Gonzalo de *Céspedes y Meneses was the first to attribute the form to Espinel in print in 1615, although earlier examples have been found; he is also apocryphally credited with the addition of a fifth string to the guitar. It is Espinel's development of the new forms' expressive possibilities, however, that justifies his importance.

His poem "La casa de la memoria" (The House of Memory) praises many of his contemporaries including those with whom he associated in the literary academies (*Academia) of Madrid: Lope de Vega, *Cervantes, the *Argensola brothers, *Salas Barbadillo, Quevedo, *Liñán de Riaza, Pedro de *Padilla and Calderón. His repertoire of figurative language favors metaphor, anaphora, antonomasia, and apostrophe over the elaborate periphrasis, paronomasia, chiasmus, hyperbaton, synecdoche and metonymy favored by Luis de Góngora and his followers. Espinel's poetry tends to combine lyricism and narrative, and suggests a serene attitude of tolerance and Christian Stoic resignation that can also be found in his fictionalized autobiography, *La vida del escudero Marcos de Obregón* (1618; *Account of the Life of the Squire Marcos de Obregon*, 1816). The narrative is divided into three *relaciones* (accounts) and each of these larger sections into *descansos* (pauses or stages). Although it is one of the sources for episodes in Lesage's *picaresque *Gil Blas de Santillane*, Espinel's work is not strictly picaresque. It lacks the typical anti-hero: Marcos is no alienated and rejected half-outsider driven by hostile circumstances to deceive others for his own benefit, nor do his moral reflections on remembered errors constitute mere hypocritical self-aggrandizement. Marcos's experience does not embitter him but allows him the perspective to advise moderation and tolerance in other characters. The work is a complex play of memory and narrative voice, combining events in the author's life, portraits of his literary friends in Madrid, and a view of youthful impulsiveness from the wisdom of age, with fictional episodes and structures from the picaresque novel, chronicles (*crónicas), and chivalresque and Byzantine romances. It offers a middle ground between the hostile world of the picaresque and the idealized one of romance, and explores the relationship between fiction and autobiography, Marcos serving as alter ego for Espinel. Although no proof exists that Espinel received a university degree, he enjoyed a reputation for erudition and literary taste, upholding Horatian and neo-Aristotelian precepts in his work as book censor for the *Inquisition from 1609 until the year before his death. *See also* Humanism; Italian literary influences.

BIBLIOGRAPHY

Primary Texts

*Diversas rimas.* Ed. Dorothy Clotelle Clarke. New York: Hispanic Institute, 1956.
*Relaciones de la vida del escudero Marcos de Obregón.* Ed. María Soledad Carrasco de Urgoiti. 2 vols. Madrid: Clásicos Castalia, 1972.

English Translation

*Account of the Life of the Squire Marcos de Obregón.* Tr. Major Algernon Langton. 2 vols. London: John Booth, 1816.

Criticism

Clarke, Dorothy Clotelle. "Sobre la espinela." *RFE* 33 (1936): 293–304.
Conant, Isabel Pope. "Vicente Espinel as Musician." *Studies in the Renaissance* 5 (1958): 133–44.
Haley, George. *Vicente Espinel and "Marcos de Obregón."* *A Life and Its Literary Representation.* Providence, RI: Brown UP, 1959.

Heathcote, A. Anthony. *Vicente Espinel.* TWAS 440. Boston: Hall, 1977.

Millé y Giménez, Juan. "Sobre la invención de la décima o espinela." *HR* 5 (1937): 40–51.

Emilie Bergmann

**ESPINELA.** *See* Décima

**ESPINOSA, Pedro de** (1578, Antequera–1650, Sanlúcar de Barrameda), poet, prose author, anthologist. He attended some university, retreated to live as a hermit for three years after being bitterly disappointed in love, and became a priest (c. 1612–14). In 1618 he entered the service of the Duke of Medina Sidonia, retiring from service in 1637. Friend to many writers of the day, he visited various cities when compiling his outstanding anthology of contemporary poets, *Las flores de poetas ilustres* (1605; Flowers of Illustrious Poets). Virtually all the major poets of the day—including some recently deceased—are represented, attesting to Espinosa's keen aesthetic sensibilities and judgment.

F. López Estrada discerns three main tendencies in Espinosa's poetry: profane verse—treating mythological, burlesque or love themes; religious, spiritual verse, the most significant category; and panegyric pieces. The influence of *conceptismo* is more apparent than that of *culteranismo*. A fine lyricist, he invests his work with strong personal emotion and a painterly vision.

López Estrada further notes that the same tendencies organize Espinosa's prose works. He wrote profane novels such as *El perro y la calentura* (1625; The Dog and the Fever), an imaginative satirical dialogue with moralizing intent. It was published along with *Quevedo's *Cartas del caballero de la Tenaza* and thereby for a time was attributed to Quevedo. Also profane is the *Pronóstico judiciario* (1627; Judicial Prediction), which cleverly ridicules astrology, again with a moralizing bent. Religious in nature is *El espejo de cristal* (1625; The Glass Mirror), which counsels on the art of dying well. Panegyric works include an homage to his birthplace, *Panegírico a la ciudad de Antequera* (1626; Panegyric to the City of Antequera), filled with patriotic affection, and the *Panegírico del duque de Medina Sidonia* (1629; Eulogy of the Duke of Medina Sidonia), whom he served. As with his poetry, his prose works are relatively brief and carefully revised.

BIBLIOGRAPHY

Primary Texts

*Obras de Pedro Espinosa.* Ed. F. Rodríguez Marín. Madrid: RABM, 1909.

*Poesías completas.* Ed., prol., F. López Estrada. Clásicos Castellanos 205. Madrid: Espasa-Calpe, 1975.

Criticism

*Homenaje a Pedro Espinosa*. Seville: U of Seville, 1953.
Rodríguez Marín, F. *Pedro de Espinosa: estudio biográfico, bibliográfico y crítico*. Madrid, 1907. Rpt. Netherlands: Philo, 1975.
Terry, A. *Pedro Espinosa and the Praise of Creation*. BHS 38 (1961): 127–44.

Maureen Ihrie

**ESPRIU, Salvador** (1913, Santa Coloma de Farners–1985, Barcelona), poet, playwright, prose writer and critic. Son of a notary public, he studied law and classical history at the U of Barcelona and in 1933 took an important study trip throughout the Mediterranean visiting the ancient countries (Greece, Italy, Palestine, Egypt, etc.) where the great classical myths of antiquity had originated. This vital experience together with his continual readings of the classical myths would have a lasting influence in his writings, on theme as well as form. As early as 1929, at the age of sixteen, he published his first book, *Israel*, and until the Spanish Civil War prose writing dominated his literary production. Novels like *El doctor Rip* (1931; Doctor Rip) and *Laia* (1932) are a clear break with the then-dominant literary formulas of the "noucentisme" (a literary movement that defended the strictly classical interpretation of culture and rejected the anarchistic and romantic vision of art). These books, together with *Ariadna al laberint grotesc* (1935; Ariadna in the Grotesque Labyrinth) and *Miratge a Citerea* (1935; Mirage in Citerea), are perhaps the most significant of Espriu's first period, fluctuating from the grotesque to sublime lyricism. His early influences were the Castilian modernists, but also *Valle-Inclán and Gabriel *Miró, and later on, more profoundly, the Catalan masters, Joaquim Ruyra and Víctor *Català. However, the constant sources of Espriu's inspiration were the Bible, with special emphasis on the Old Testament, and the classical epic. This phase of Espriu's literature ended with the Civil War. Right after the occupation of Barcelona in 1939 by Franco's armies, he wrote one of his dramatic masterpieces, *Antígona* (published much later in 1955 and staged in 1958). Though inspired by the classical play of the same title, Espriu's drama concentrates on Christian compassion for the defeated. Profoundly embittered and shocked by the cultural genocide committed by the victors, he was silent until 1946. But then Espriu turned fully to poetry for some years and wrote a block of five books of poetry considered among the best ever written in Catalan: *Cementiri de Sinera* (1946; Cemetery in Sinera), *Les cançons d'Ariadna* (1949; Songs of Ariadna), *Les hores i Mrs. Death* (1952; Hours and Mrs. Death), *El caminant i el mur* (1954; The Wanderer and the Wall), and *Final del laberint* (1955; The End of the Labyrinth). These are books of stoic and yet classical serenity alternating with touches of Goya-esque satire, but always within a formal symmetry, gradually striving toward a mystical experience. Since Joan *Maragall no other Catalan poet had reached such heights. Espriu blends the elegiac, the satirical and the political elements of his poetry into a solid, well-rounded unity. In 1957, Espriu turned to theater and dramatic poetry, producing several masterpieces: *Primera història d'Esther* (1957; The First Story of Esther), a satirical farce on death, power and war, implying a clear link between the tragic fate of the Jewish and Catalan peoples; *La pell de brau* (1960; The Skin of the Bull, tr. under Catalan title, 1987), in which the Hebrew word *sheparad* is a metaphor for the Iberian Peninsula, and he condemns hate, war, and especially war among brothers (like Maragall, Espriu in this book opens his arms to all Hispanic peoples on biblical terms, preaching tolerance and understanding among them; controlled rage and classical eloquence are the trademarks of this work which had enormous success all over Spain); and the play *Ronda de mort a Sinera* (1978; Death Watch in Sinera), a meditation on death, a recurrent theme in all of Espriu's works. Espriu is considered today the most important figure of *Catalan literature. This second brilliant period is also strongly influenced by some of the great and most somber masters of Anglo-American literature: Poe, Blake, Melville, Eliot, Joyce, Pound and others.

BIBLIOGRAPHY

Primary Texts

*Antología de Salvador Espriu*. Castilian tr. and intro. E. Badosa. Barcelona: Plaza y Janés 1978.
*Narracions*. Intro. Francesc Vallverdú. Barcelona: Edicions 62, 1965.
*Obra poètica*. Intro. Joan Fuster, note on Espriu's books by M. A. Capmany. Barcelona: Albertí, 1963.
*Obres completes*. Intro. J. M. Castellet. 4th ed. Barcelona: n.p., Edicions 62, 1981.

Criticism

Capmany, María Aurèlia. *Salvador Espriu*. Barcelona: n.p., 1971.
Castellet, J. M. *Iniciación a la poesía de Salvador Espriu*. Madrid: n.p., 1971.
*La pell de brau*. Tr. B. Raffell. Marlboro, VT.: Marlboro, 1987.
*Lord of the Shadow: poems*. Intro., sel. J. M. Castellet. Eng. tr. K. Lyons. Oxford: Dolphin, 1975. Catalan and English.
Plà, Josep. "Salvador Espriu." In *Homenots. Quarta sèrie*. Barcelona: n.p., 1975. 205–42.
Porcel, Baltasar. "Salvador Espriu, foc i cendra." *Serra d'Or*. No vol. (May 1966): no pages.
Teixidor, Joan. "Salvador Espriu." In *Cinc poetes*. Barcelona: n.p., 1969.

Joan Gilabert

**ESPRONCEDA, José de** (1808, Almendralejo, Extremadura–1842, Madrid), Romantic poet. Espronceda symbolizes the lyric daring of Spanish *Romanticism. His poems are moving, painful, bitter and tender all at once: the tragedies embodied in his words are those experienced in his life, or as J. Casalduero has written, "the pain of life becomes lyricism."

Espronceda was born just as the War of Independence was about to devastate the Iberian Peninsula; his whole existence was an extension of those turbulent years. His father was a soldier of some renown, actively engaged in the conflicts. It is not clear where José and his mother lived during the war or during the years following Ferdinand VII's return. By 1820 the family was installed in the capital, and José met several of the people who would influence him greatly: his friend

Patricio de la *Escosura and his teachers José *Gómez Hermosilla and Alberto *Lista. The influence of Lista on Espronceda cannot be overemphasized. Lista, who had recently opened his famous Colegio de San Mateo, served as formative guide to a number of the next generation's leaders, young men like Ventura de la *Vega, Eugenio de *Ochoa, Gregorio *Romero Larrañaga, and the future Counts of Cheste and Molins. Lista taught from a liberal neo-classical perspective, encouraging his students to think independently, challenge received ideas, and write. Many of them reacted to the volatile political realities of the day. Espronceda, along with Vega and several others, formed a secret society called "Los numantinos" (in honor of the ancient Spanish town of Numantia, which had heroically resisted Roman invasion). They witnessed Riego's execution and vowed to avenge the death of that revolutionary leader. In the meantime, Lista's school had been closed by the government, and classes were being conducted in his house, where the students formed another society—this one significantly less "dangerous"—the literary Academia del Mirto (Academy of the Myrtle). Espronceda composed his first verses for that group. In late 1824 "Los numantinos" were denounced for their activities, and Espronceda was sentenced to a three-month confinement in the Convent at Guadalajara (he was seventeen years old). In this prison-like atmosphere he began to write his first long poem, *Pelayo* (significantly, on the theme of a heroic resistance to foreign oppression). Espronceda, in consort with his friends, enjoyed life in Madrid's cafés (in particular the Café Príncipe) and continued working on *Pelayo* as well as other poems. But Ferdinand VII was tightening his absolutist grip on Spain, and Espronceda, long the object of police surveillance for his suspicious activities, left Madrid and traveled to Lisbon in 1827. The exact reasons for his departure remain unknown, but this self-imposed exile lasted until 1833.

In Portugal Espronceda first met Teresa Mancha, the woman who was to inspire his most passionate—and most romantically bitter—verses. Their relationship was stormy: she married another man in 1829, but conducted a scandalous love affair with Espronceda for several years, crossing national boundaries and giving birth to their daughter, Blanca. Teresa's sudden abandonment of José and her untimely death in 1839 stimulated Espronceda's astonishing elegy, the "Canto a Teresa" (1839; Song to Teresa). From Lisbon Espronceda went to London, where a sizeable population of Spanish emigrés lived. He increased his political activities, moving to Brussels in 1829 and then to France. The July 1830 revolt in Paris intensified his revolutionary leanings, and later that year he participated in Chapalangarra's failed attempt to overthrow the regime of Ferdinand VII. His agitation in the name of freedom kept him in constant motion, traveling to London again and then back to Paris in 1832. The limited Spanish amnesty of that year enabled him to return to his country, which he did in March of 1833. Teresa followed him, and he installed her in a little house on the same street where he lived with his mother.

In Spain, Espronceda continued to behave in ways which linked him closely to the exalted faction of Spanish Romantic authors. One denouncement of government policies earned him yet another period of exile, this time in Cuéllar, where he began his historical novel *Sancho Saldaña o el castellano de Cuéllar* (1834; Sancho Saldaña or the Castilian from Cuéllar). In early 1834, together with his old Numantian friends, he began publication of *El Siglo* (The Century), a newspaper that ran into *censorship problems and was silenced after fourteen issues, but Espronceda continued to contribute to the newspapers: *El Artista* (The Artist), voice of the liberal Romantics, published his famous "La canción del pirata" (1835; The Pirate's Song), and *El Español* (The Spaniard) published two important political tracts, "Libertad, Igualdad, Fraternidad" (1835; Liberty, Equality, Fraternity) and "El Gobierno y la Bolsa" (1836; The Government and the Treasury). Espronceda also wrote three plays during the 1830s: *Blanca de Borbón* (1831?); *Ni el tío ni el sobrino* (1834; Neither the Uncle Nor the Nephew), written in collaboration with *Ros de Olano; and *Amor venga sus agravios* (1838; Love Avenges Its Insults), in collaboration with Eugenio Moreno López. Espronceda's dramas were largely unsuccessful.

The Pirate's Song is the best known of Espronceda's series of poems which champion society's rejected, marginal types and turn them into heroes of the Romantic world. His pirate fears nothing, lives freely (his God is "liberty"), and laughs at death. In "El reo de muerte" (1835; The Condemned Prisoner), "El mendigo" (1835; The Beggar), "El verdugo" (1835; The Executioner), "El cosaco" (1838; The Cossack), and especially "A Jarifa, en una orgía" (1839–40; To Jarifa, in an Orgy), Espronceda makes it clear that he identifies with—and stands by—those whom society vicitimizes and scorns.

The epitome of his exaltation of those who live alienated from the social status quo is Félix de Montemar, the hero of *El estudiante de Salamanca* (written in 1836–39, published in 1840; *The Student of Salamanca*, 1953), Espronceda's shocking explosion of Romantic rebellion. This masterpiece of lyrical *angst* is a mixture of legend, fantasy, and sustained lyrical genius in which Montemar, a "second Don Juan Tenorio" (*see* Don Juan, The Myth of), loves and abandons the innocent Elvira, then is led by a mysterious veiled figure (the spectre of the dead Elvira) into a phantasmagorical, chilling nightmare of confrontation with her and with his own death. Even in his darkest moments, when eternal damnation threatens to engulf him, Montemar refuses to abandon his rebellious stance. His body surrenders to inevitable death, but his "spirit" is "never vanquished." It is a brilliant tale of hallucinatory agony, one in which the true essence of revolutionary Romanticism—man's refusal to let his spirit be conquered by the arbitrary restrictions of existence—is given breathtaking poetic expression.

It seems as though Espronceda was engaged in writing his long, complex poem *El diablo mundo* (1840; Devil World) when he learned of Teresa's death in 1839. Although their affair had ended by then, Espronceda was devastated by her death, and his mind was flooded with memories of his days with her. Those memories, however, were not pleasant. He was tragically aware that their innocent and blissful (if stormy) past would dissolve into an ugly and unhappy present. He wrote the deeply disturbing "Canto a Teresa," which appeared as part two of *El diablo mundo*. In it, Espronceda reviews the trajectory of their relationship, going beyond mere sadness to a posture of pain so deep that the only response possible is sardonic laughter, a posture which hides his true suffering from an uncaring society (''so there is one cadaver more . . . / what does the world care!'').

*El diablo mundo* is Espronceda's most ambitious poem. Begun in 1839, portions of it appeared in local newspapers, but Espronceda died before it was completed (his friend Miguel de los Santos *Álvarez finished it). He wrote seven sections, attempting a new myth of creation to explain his anguished Romantic cosmos. Critics have argued about the poem's thematic coherence, but its artistic coherence is undeniable—the subjective, pessimistic, frustrated and mysterious tone synthesizes Espronceda's entire literary life.

In 1841, together with Ros de Olano and Santos Álvarez, the poet founded another newspaper, *El Pensamiento* (Thought), but this endeavor was as shortlived as the other. The government sent him off to the Low Countries on a diplomatic assignment (to keep him out of the capital?), but he was soon back in Madrid as a member of Parliament, loudly demanding the same progressive reforms he had always championed. Espronceda's political activity was as intense as his poetic activity. Throughout his life his militant agitation for progressive republican ideals earned him banishments and conflicts with censors. His bitter rejection of society's indifference to man's suffering, his quest for individual freedom, and the passion of his volcanic and constant movement fused his politics to his poetics. His Romantic hero destroyed himself in his rebellion, cut off from the future, angrily protesting cosmic injustice. His was a world of shattered dreams. In May 1842, at the age of thirty-four, Espronceda contracted a serious throat infection. It proved fatal; within eight days he was dead.

BIBLIOGRAPHY

Primary Texts

*El estudiante de Salamanca*. Ed. Benito Varela Jácome. Madrid: Cátedra, 1980.
*El estudiante de Salamanca*. *El diablo mundo*. Ed. Robert Marrast. Madrid: Castalia, 1978.
*Obras completas*. Ed. Jorge Campos. Madrid: Atlas, 1954.
*Poesías líricas y fragmentos épicos*. Ed. Robert Marrast. Madrid: Castalia, 1970.

English Translation

*The Student of Salamanca*. Tr. E. O. Lombardi. San Francisco: Cunningham, 1953.

Criticism

Carnero, Guillermo. *Espronceda*. Madrid: Júcar, 1974.
Casalduero, Joaquín. *Espronceda*. Madrid: Gredos, 1961.
Gies, David T. ''Visión, ilusión y el sueño romántico en la poesía de Espronceda.'' *Cuadernos de Filología* 3 (1983): 61–84.
Hafter, Monroe Z. ''*El diablo mundo* in the Light of Carlyle's *Sartor Resartus*.'' *RHM* 37 (1972): 46–55.
Ilie, Paul. ''Espronceda and the Romantic Grotesque.'' *Studies in Romanticism* 11 (1972): 94–112.

ESSAY															567

Landeira, Luis. *José de Espronceda*. Lincoln, Nebraska: Society of Spanish and Spanish
    American Studies, 1985.
Marrast, Robert. *Espronceda y su tiempo*. Barcelona: Crítica, 1989.
———. *José de Espronceda et son temps*. Paris: Klincksick, 1974.
Rees, M. A. *Espronceda: El estudiante de Salamanca*. London: Grant and Cutler, 1979.
Sebold, Russell P. "El infernal arcano de Félix de Montemar." *HR* 46 (1978): 447–64.
Wardropper, Bruce. "Espronceda's *Canto a Teresa* and the Spanish Elegiac Tradition."
    *BHS* 40 (1963): 89–100.

David Thatcher Gies

**ESQUILACHE, Príncipe de** (1581, Madrid–1658, Madrid), poet. Francisco
de Borja y Aragón descended from the Italian Borgia family on the paternal
side; he was Prince of Squillace, Italy, and Viceroy of Peru (1615–21). He
founded the U of San Marcos in Lima. A good friend of both *Argensola brothers,
he generally eschewed *culteranismo*. An accomplished poet, he composed some
300 ballads, court poetry, and some religious verse. His *Obras en verso* (Works
in Verse) appeared in 1639.

BIBLIOGRAPHY

Primary Texts

*Égloga a la serenísima señora infanta doña María. . . .* Buenos Aires: Granada, 1941.
*Obras*. In BAE 16, 29, 42 and 61.

Criticism

Arco, R. del. "Don Francisco de Borja, poeta anticulterano." *Archivo de Filología
    Aragonesa* (Zaragoza) 3 (1950): 83–126.
Dios Barros, J. *Don Francisco de Borja: su vida y sus obras*. Valencia: n.p., 1954.

**ESSAY.** Originally and most properly a short piece of expository prose which
can treat a wide variety of subjects, particularly those which do not fall under
readily recognized disciplines; its purpose is to explore and hypothesize rather
than to document and to prove rigorously. But with increasing specialization
forming the typical intellectual during the last c., there is a certain tendency for
discursive writers to collect shorter writings in thematic volumes in which individual pieces are more or less integrated into book form. *Ortega y Gasset,
perhaps the most significant Spanish essayist of the twentieth c., has said that
"el ensayo es la ciencia, menos la prueba explícita" (the essay is science less
explicit proofs). Montaigne is considered the first modern essayist. English writers of the eighteenth c. such as Addison, Steele, Samuel Johnson and Goldsmith
set the balance between highly personal, whimsical writing and reasoned, informed writing, especially that treating matters of social interest.

    The Spanish tradition of the essay seems to center about writers of the end
of the nineteenth c. and of the first three and a half decades of our c. This is
probably because, as in so many things, the broad crisis of cultural *modernism
had the effect of creating an almost new starting point for subsequent thought.
Nonetheless, many of Mariano José de *Larra's sketches of national manners,
albeit written in fictive-narrative form, are highly analytic and critical works

which clearly establish the precedent and necessity for writing about the most important theme of Spanish modernist thought: the origins and character of Spanish national life. Important writings by *Unamuno (*En torno al casticismo* [1895; Concerning Spanishness]), *Ganivet (*Idearium español* [1897; Spanish Idearium]), Ramiro de *Maeztu (*Hacia otra España* [1899; Toward Another Spain]), *Azaña (*La invención del Quijote y otros ensayos* [1935; The Invention of *Don Quijote* and Other Essays]), *Ors (*El arte de Goya* [1928; The Art of Goya]), Ortega (*España invertebrada* [1921; Invertebrate Spain]), *Castro Quesada (*El pensamiento de Cervantes* [1925; Cervantes's Thought]), *Madariaga (*España*, 1931), *Marañón (*Cuatro comentarios a la revolución española* [1931; Four Commentaries Concerning the Spanish Revolution]) and others develop and expand on Larra's preoccuppation with Spanish character, culture, historico-political experience and organization. It is characteristic of Spanish intellectual life that any person pretending to be part of it develops his or her own theory of it while studying and being able to discuss others' theories. The essay, whether appearing in book form or in such leading Spanish dailies as *El País*, *ABC*, and *La Vanguardia*, performs today still this function of recalling past discussions of national themes while exploring and advancing new explanations. Well-known contemporary men of letters such as Francisco *Ayala, Ricardo Gullón, Pedro *Laín Entralgo, José Luis *Aranguren, Gonzalo *Torrente Ballester, Julián *Marías, José Luis Abellán, Juan *Goytisolo, Juan *Benet and many, many others have made this type of very public writing a significant part of their overall activity.

Another variety of the essay is less directly or indirectly nationalistic. Unamuno's philosophical-religious writings are especially worth citing in this regard: *La vida es sueño* (1898; Life is a Dream), *Mi religión y otros ensayos* (1910; My Religion and Other Essays), *Del sentimiento trágico de la vida en los hombres y los pueblos* (1912; The Tragic Sense of Life), and *La agonía del cristianismo* (1925; The Agony of Christianity). Ortega adds to the range of the essay through well-known and much-translated works of sociological and aesthetic discussions such as *El tema de nuestro tiempo* (1923; The Theme of Our Time), *La deshumanización del arte* (1925; The Dehumanization of Art), and *La rebelión de las masas* (1930; The Rebellion of the Masses). Finally, the work of Marañón in which he places his medical and psychological knowledge at the service of wider cultural topics should serve to indicate that there is no limit on the subject matter of the essay; the following titles should be consulted: *Estudio biológico sobre Enrique IV de Castilla* (1930; Biological Study of Henry IV of Castile), *Amiel: un estudio sobre la timidez* (1932; Amiel: A Study about Timidness), and *El conde-duque de Olivares, o la pasión de mandar* (1936; The Count-Duke of Olivares, or The Passion for Being the Boss).

Despite the center of gravity of the essay residing in the forceful, well-reasoned writing of notable stylistic character, it is apparent that much scholarly writing, especially on literary and socio-historic themes, enjoys the benefits of association with the great tradition constituted by the authors and works cited above. In this regard it is interesting to note that José Luis Gómez-Martínez's journal *Los Ensayistas: Georgia Series on Hispanic Thought* began a new editorial policy in 1985; special numbers on Brazil, Chile and Argentina, for example, bring together specialists from many academic disciplines who contribute short, but often heavily documented academic pieces to the forum created by the special number of the journal. Taken in the context of the kind of essay work discussed previously, this development serves to demonstrate that the essay, perhaps as does the novel, admits of many variations according to the audience for which the author writes.

Stephen Miller

**ESTALA, Pedro** (c. 1740, Madrid–c. 1820, France), influential humanist, translator, literary critic. He sometimes used the pseudonyms Ramón Fernández (his barber's name), or Claudio Bachiller Rosillo. In Madrid, he was a close friend and mentor to *Forner and Leandro Fernández de *Moratín, and other poets of the day. Protected by Godoy, Estala also was persecuted when the latter fell. An *afrancesado* (French sympathizer in the Napoleonic invasion), he published a journal, *El Imparcial* (1809; The Impartial One), for the French. He later was forced to move to France. As an anthologist, Estala compiled six volumes, with thoughtful prologues, for the *Colección de poetas españoles* (1786–98; Collection of Spanish Poets); the series eventually numbered twenty volumes. His translations of *Oedipus Rex* (1793) and *Pluto* (1794) included influential, original essays on Greek tragedy and comedy. Also extant are *Veintiuna cartas inéditas dirigidas a don J. P. Forner* (n.d.; Twenty-One Unpublished Letters to J. P. Forner), and *Cuatro cartas de un español a un anglómano en que se manifiesta la perfidia del gobierno de la Inglaterra* (1805; Four Letters from a Spaniard to an Anglomane in Which Is Made Evident the Perfidy of the Government of England).

BIBLIOGRAPHY

Primary Texts

*Colección de poetas españoles.* 20 vols. Madrid: Imprenta Real, 1792–1825. Vols. 1–6 edited by Estala.

*Cuatro cartas de un español. . . .* Madrid: Villalpando, 1805.

*Veintiuna cartas inéditas. . . .* Ed. J. Pérez de Guzmán. *BRAH* 63 (1911): 5–36.

*ESTANCIA* (stanza, strophe), a literary term. Introduced from Italy and very popular during the *Renaissance, the *estancia* often employed seven- and eleven-syllable lines. The number of lines in a stanza could vary, but the first stanza would always determine the length of all subsequent stanzas in a given composition. *See also* Italian literary influences.

**ESTÉBANEZ CALDERÓN, Serafín** (1799, Málaga–1867, Madrid), politician, poet, prose author. After studying law, he played an important role in public life, serving as a robed minister in the Supreme Court of War and in the

marines, and as counselor of state and senator. These activities were complemented by various literary and cultural endeavors. He maintained correspondence
with his great friend Juan *Valera—these letters have been preserved and published. An avid bibliophile, he amassed an important library of rare and antique
books. He studied and taught Arabic, recognizing its importance in Spanish
culture and literature. In Cádiz, he organized the art museum, expanded the
city's library, and founded a lyceum. He composed a historical and geographical
study of Morocco, the *Manual del oficial en Marruecos* (1844; The Officer's
Manual of Morocco), which gained him entry to the Academy of History. He
was never to complete his greatest project, a history of the Spanish infantry;
what he did write has been collected by Jorge *Campos in his edition of Estébanez
Calderón's *Obras* (Works).

Initially, Estébanez used the pseudonym Safino; later he became known by
the pen name El Solitario (Solitary One). In 1831, he published a historical
novel, *Cristianos y moriscos* (Christians and Moors), which recounts the love
affair between a Moorish woman and a Christian man during the period of Charles
V. Estébanez is best known, however, for his *Escenas andaluzas* (1846; Andalusian Scenes), which originally appeared as separate articles in the journals
*Cartas españolas* and *Semanario Pintoresco Español*. Inspired in part by Estébanez's reading of Jouey, it is a collection of scenes which capture the Andalusian language, color, and picturesqueness during the Romantic period. His
use of archaic vocabulary and idioms in these descriptions stems from his interest
in Golden Age literature. The lengthiness of description, lack of action and
exaggerated verbosity make reading these *Escenas* somewhat slow and taxing.
Better-known articles are "Pulpete y Balbeja," "La rifa andaluza," "La feria
de Mairena" and "Un baile en Triana"—all treat typical Andalusian types,
customs and folklore. *See also* Romanticism; Siglo de Oro.

## BIBLIOGRAPHY

### Primary Texts

*Juan Valera—Serafín Estébanez Calderón (1850–1858). Crónica histórica y vital de*
    *Lisboa, Brasil, París y Dresde*. Ed. Carlos Sáenz de Tejada Benvenuti. Madrid:
    Moneda y Crédito, 1971.
*Obras de Don Serafín Estébanez Calderón*. Intro. Jorge Campos. 2 vols. BAE 78 and
    79.

### Criticism

Cano, José Luis. "Actualidad de El Solitario." *Clavileño* 7 (1956): 51–55.
Cánovas del Castillo, Antonio. *El Solitario y su tiempo. Biografía de Don Serafín Es-*
    *tébanez Calderón y crítica de sus obras*. 2 vols. Madrid: A. Pérez Dubrull, 1883.
Manzanares, M. "El arabismo romántico de Estébanez Calderón." *PMLA* 67 (1962):
    414–18.
Montesinos, José F. *Costumbrismo y novela*. Valencia: Castalia, 1960.
———. "Nota a El Solitario." *Studia Philológica*. Homenaje a Dámaso Alonso. Madrid:
    Gredos, 1962. 475–92.
Pavieso, Luisa. "En torno a unas notas de Montesinos sobre el lenguaje de las *Escenas*

*andaluzas* de Estébanez Calderón." In Caldera, Ermanno, intro. *Romanticismo 3–4: Atti del IV Congresso sul romanticismo spagnolo e ispanoamericano (Bordighera, 9–11 aprille 1987): La narrative romántica.* Genoa: Biblioteca di Letteratura, 1988. 175–78.

Phoebe Porter Medina

**ESTEBANILLO GONZÁLEZ,** *La vida y hechos de Estebanillo González, hombre de buen humor, compuesto por él mismo* (1646; The Life and Deeds of Estebanillo González, Good-Humored Man, Written By Him), *picaresque novel. One of the final picaresque works of the seventeenth c., it is considered by some critics a genuine autobiography, whether or not the name Esteban González is authentic. The narrative details Esteban's peripatetic life and misadventures during the Thirty Years War of Europe (1618–48). The narrative weds a high level of historical accuracy to the customary topics of the picaresque genre. A cynical, shameless, at times crude work, it usually is also very funny.

BIBLIOGRAPHY

Primary Texts

*Vida y hechos de Estebanillo González.* Ed. J. Millé y Jiménez. Clásicos Castellanos 108 and 109. Madrid: Espasa-Calpe, 1956.
*Vida y hechos de Estebanillo González.* Ed., intro., biblio., N. Spadaccini and A. Zahareas. Clásicos Castalia 86 and 87. Madrid: Castalia, 1978.

English Translation

*The Life of Estevanillo Gonzalez. . . .* In *The Spanish Libertines.* Tr. Captain J. Stevens. London: n.p., 1709.

Criticism

Bataillon, M. "Estebanillo González, buffon pour rire." In *Studies in Spanish Literature of the Golden Age Presented to E. M. Wilson.* London: Tamesis, 1973. 25–44.
Bjornson, R. "Estebanillo González: The Clown's Other Face." *Hispania* 60 (1977): 436–42.
Spadaccini, N. *Estebanillo González and the New Orientation of the Picaresque Novel.* New York: New York UP, 1971.

Maureen Ihrie

**ESTELLA, Diego de,** religious name of Diego Ballesteros y Cruzas (1524, Estella, Navarra–1578, Salamanca), Franciscan monk, orator-preacher in the court of Philip II, reformer of the Spanish pulpit and influential writer of ascetical-devotional works. Fray Diego spent several years in Portugal as spiritual director to Princess Juana.

His ascetical work called *Libro de la vanidad del mundo* (Toledo, 1562; *The Contempt of the World and the Vanity Thereof,* 1584) exerted a major influence, enjoying numerous reprintings within Spain and translations into all major languages of Europe as well as Czech, Polish and Arabic. The first English translation by the Jesuit William Creighton appeared as early as 1584. Subsequent English editions were adapted for use in the Anglican liturgy in 1586 and 1608.

In 1574 Diego de Estella published a second edition of this book with 180 additional chapters.

The book, which is replete with biblical quotations and references to the writings of both the Greek and Latin Fathers, advises readers to shun the things of the world in order to enjoy (gozar) God's presence. The work is strictly ascetical, making evident the influence of Thomas à Kempis as it reminds the individual to keep the life of Christ in mind as a perfect model. Estella wrote a "vida de santo" (life of a saint) called *Tratado de la vida de San Juan Evangelista* (Lisbon, 1554; Treatise on the Life of St. John the Evangelist). He also made a contribution to meditative literature with the *Meditaciones devotíssimas del amor de Dios* (Alcalá, 1597; *A Hundred Meditations on the Love of God*, 1873). These devotional meditations are said to be his masterpiece not only for their eloquent literary style, but also for their contribution to affective theological principles common to the Franciscan school of religious thought. *See also* Ascetical Literature.

BIBLIOGRAPHY

Primary Texts

*Libro de la vanidad del mundo*. Madrid: Aranzazu, 1980.
*Meditaciones devotíssimas del amor de Dios*. Madrid: Gil Blas, 1920.
*Tratado de la vida de San Juan Evangelista*. Lisbon: n.p., 1554.

English Translations

*The Contempte of the World and the Vanitie Thereof*. Tr. George Cotton. St. Omer, France: John Heigham, 1622.
*Meditations on the Love of God*. Tr. Julia Pember. New York: Sheed and Ward, 1939.

Criticism

Allison Peers, Edgar. *Studies of the Spanish Mystics*. Vol. 2. London: Sheldon, 1930.
Groult, Pierre. "Un disciple espagnol de Thomas à Kempis: Diego de Estella." *Lettres Romanes* 5 (1951): 287–304; 6 (1952): 82–88, 142–40, 275–82, 335–42.

Angelo DiSalvo

**ESTELRICH, Juan** (1896, Felanitx, Mallorca–1958, Paris), Catalan humanist, prose writer. He represented Spain in UNESCO, and directed the Bernat Metge Institution for the publication of Greek and Latin texts. His writings include *Entre la vida y els llibres* (1926; Between Life and Books), *Un nuevo humanismo* (1928; A New Humanism), *La falsa paz* (1949; False Peace) and *Las profecías se cumplen* (1948; Prophecies Fulfill Themselves).

BIBLIOGRAPHY

Primary Texts

*Entre la vida y els llibres*. Barcelona: Llibreria Catalonia, 1926.
*La falsa paz*. Barcelona: Montaner y Simón, 1949.

*Las profecías se cumplen.* Barcelona: Montaner y Simón, 1948.
*La qüestió de les minories nacionals.* Barcelona: Llibreria Catalonia, 1929.

Isabel McSpadden

**ESTÉVEZ DE GARCÍA DEL CANTO, Josefa** (c. 1830, Valladolid–after 1889, Vitoria), poet, fiction writer. In 1845 she married the army officer, novelist and poet Antonio García del Canto. They subsequently moved to the Philippines, where he served as governor of Davao. Widowed in 1886, she professed in Vitoria three years later.

Her most important poetic work is *Mis recreos. Poesías religiosas* (1888; My Entertainments. Religious Poetry); the general style and tone recalls that of the *Escuela Sevillana poets. Besides glosses of prayers (*glosa) and romances (*see Romancero*), there are poems devoted to her husband, more personal and lyrical. She also published a popular romance, *El Romancerillo de San Isidro* (1886; The Little Romance of San Isidro), and two novels, *Memorias de un naúfrago* (1885; Memoirs of a Shipwreck) and *El zapatito* (1889; The Little Shoe)—the latter was awarded a prize in 1883 from the Montreal Academy of Tolosa (France), and was published in 1889 in the magazine *El Correo de la Moda*. Other prizes awarded to Doña Josefa include ones from contests in Alba de Tormes, Avila (1882), Valladolid (1879 and 1883), and Salamanca (1884). Her poem "El amor de los amores" (The Love of All Loves) was included in the *Novísimo Romancero Español.*

BIBLIOGRAPHY

Primary Texts

*Máximas y reglas de conducta aplicables a los diversos estados y condiciones de la vida sacadas de las obras de Santa Teresa.* . . . Salamanca: J. Hidalgo, 1888.
*El mejor amigo. Libro para los niños.* Salamanca: Jacinto Hidalgo, 1888.
*Memorias de un naúfrago.* Salamanca: J. Hidalgo, 1885.
*Mis recreos. Poesías religiosas.* Salamanca: J. Hidalgo, 1888.
*El Romancerillo de San Isidro.* Madrid: Hernando, 1886.
*El Zapatito.* In *El Correo de la Moda* (Madrid), 1889.

Criticism

Alonso Cortés, N. *Miscelánea Vallisoletana.* 2 vols. Valladolid: Miñón, 1965. 2: 755–58.
Cossío, J. M. *Cincuenta años de poesía española (1850–1900).* 2 vols. Madrid: Espasa-Calpe, 1960. 1: 634–36.

Cristina Enríquez

**ESTREMERA, Antonio** (1884, Madrid–1938, Barcelona), dramatic author. He composed scripts for *zarzuelas, and collaborated with Antonio *Paso, Carlos *Arniches, and others on various plays. Among his works are *La atropellaplatos* (The Clumsy House Servant), *Noche de Cabaret* (Cabaret Night), and *Sixto Sexto.* With Arniches and Guerrero y Torres he wrote the *sainete "Don Quintín el Amargao" (1925; Don Quentin the Bitter).

BIBLIOGRAPHY

Primary Texts

*La atropellaplatos.* Madrid: Ducazcal de González, 1928.
*Sixto Sexto.* Madrid: Ducazcal, 1929.
*Don Quintín el amargao.* Madrid: Unión musical española, 1925.

Isabel McSpadden

**EXENPLOS, Libro de los** (Book of Object Lessons). A collection of object lessons compiled early in the fifteenth c. by Clemente *Sánchez de Vercial (1370?–1434?), a canon of León Cathedral, who also wrote a devotional manual, the *Sacramental*, which was widely used in Spain until it was condemned by the *Inquisition in the sixteenth c. Following a pattern very popular in Latin and vernacular story collections, Sánchez de Vercial arranged his collection alphabetically, thus the complete title *Libro de los exenplos por a.b.c.* Two manuscripts survive—one in the *Biblioteca Nacional (National Library) and the other in the Bibliothèque National in Paris. In 1961 John Keller published a critical edition which incorporates both. The complete text has 456 divisions, each headed by a Latin *sententia* with an accompanying Spanish translation, usually in verse. Many of the divisions contain more than one exemplum, and there is a total of 548 exempla in the work, making it the largest such collection in Spanish. The stories are drawn from diverse sources, among them the *Disciplina clericalis*, the *Gesta Romanorum*, and *The City of God*, and Sánchez may have intended his collection as a source book for preachers.

BIBLIOGRAPHY

Primary Text

Sánchez de Vercial, Clemente. *Libro de los exenplos por a.b.c.* Ed. John E. Keller. Madrid: CSIC, 1961.

Criticism

Goldberg, Harriet. "Deception as a Narrative Function in the *Libro de los exenplos por a b c.*" *BHS* 62 (1985): 31–38.
Krappe, A. H. "Les sources du *Libro de los Exenplos.*" *BH* 39 (1937): 5–54.
Sturm, Harlan. "A Note on the Sources of the *Libro de los exenplos por a.b.c.*" *KRQ* 17 (1970): 87–91.

James Ray Green

**EZQUERRA, Ramón** (1904, Almuniente [Huesca]– ). A scholar and professional educator specializing in history, Ezquerra received the National Literary Prize in 1933 for his excellent historiographic essay *La conspiración del duque de Híjar, 1648* (1934; The 1648 Conspiracy by the Duke of Híjar). As an historian, Ezquerra showed an enduring interest in America, and produced many studies of the American West. Another sub-specialty, travel literature, also led to publication of several studies, including one of Badía. His work on the 18th-c. writer, padre *Isla, is also noteworthy, particularly his *Obras y papeles perdidos del padre Isla* (Lost Works and Papers of Father Isla).

# F

**FABLIELLA,** diminutive of *fabla* in medieval vernacular of Castile. It meant *fábula* (novel, tale) as well as *refrán* (popular saying, proverb). As *fábula*, it appears in don *Juan Manuel's prologue to the *Libro Del Caballero y del Escudero* (Book of the Knight and the Squire): ''fiz lo en una manera que llaman en esta tierra fabliella'' (I did it in the manner which, in this land, is called novel). As *refrán*, it appears in *El Conde Lucanor* (Count Lucanor, 36): ''El mercadero tovo que aprendiendo tales fabliellas podria perder quantas doblas traya'' (The merchant considered that, if he kept learning such sayings, he could waste all his doubloons). In *El Libro de Buen Amor* (*Book of Good Love*, 179), Juan Ruiz (*Arcipreste de Hita) writes: ''Rredréme de la dueña e crey la fabrilla, / que diz: 'por lo perdido non estés mano en mexilla' '' (I gave up the lady and paid heed to the proverb which says: for what is lost don't sit grieving with your hand on your cheek). *Fabliella* is found also in the *Libro de *Alexandre* (Book of Alexander, 520d), and in *Alphonse X's *General Estoria* (General History, 9.45).

BIBLIOGRAPHY

Primary Texts

*Don Juan Manuel. Obras completas.* Ed. J. M. Blecua. Madrid: Gredos, 1983.

*Juan Ruiz, Arcipreste de Hita. El Libro de Buen Amor.* Ed. J. Cejador y Frauca. Madrid: Espasa-Calpe, 1970.

*El Libro de Alexandre. Texts of the Paris and the Madrid Manuscripts Prepared with an Introduction.* Princeton: Princeton UP, 1934.

English Translation

*Libro de Buen Amor.* Ed. and Tr. R. S. Willis. Princeton: Princeton UP, 1972.

Criticism

de Gorog, R. ''La sinonimia y el vocabulario del *Libro de Alexandre.''* *HR* 38 (1970): 353–67.

Huerta Tejada, Félix. *Vocabulario de las obras de Don Juan Manuel (1282–1348).* Madrid: RAE, 1956. *Prólogo general* 447, 17; *Lucanor* 162, 18.

Sas, Louis F. *Vocabulario del "Libro de Alexandre."* Madrid: Academia Española, 1976. 271.

Valbuena Prat, A. *Historia de la literatura española.* Barcelona: Gili, 1981. 1: 236–38.

Reginetta Haboucha

**FABRA, Pompeu** (1868, Barcelona–1948, Barcelona), Catalan grammarian and a very influential figure of twentieth-c. Catalan culture. He developed the *Normes ortogràfiques* (Orthographic Norms of 1913, the basis for modern Catalan spelling) in association with the Institut d'Estudis Catalans. As president of the Philological Section of the Institute for Catalan Studies, Fabra oversaw the compilation of the *Diccionari General de la Llengua Catalana* (1932; General Dictionary of the Catalan Language), the work of many years for many collaborators. Often called the "Fabra Dictionary," it has become the great normative dictionary of Catalan. Fabra also produced a *Diccionari Ortogràfic* (1937; Orthographic Dictionary), including words as yet undefined. *See also* Catalan Literature.

BIBLIOGRAPHY

Primary Texts

*Diccionari General de la Llengua Catalana.* 2nd ed. Barcelona: Lopéz Llausàs, 1954.

*Diccionari Ortogràfic.* 4th ed. Barcelona: Institut d'Estudis Catalans, 1937.

*Introducció a la gramàtica catalana.* Rev., expanded by R. Aramon y Serra. Barcelona: Edicions 62, 1968.

**FAGUNDO, Ana María** (1938, Tenerife, Canary Islands– ), poet, short story writer, essayist and critic. After studying business in Tenerife, she came to the United States to study English and literature, earning her doctorate in comparative literature at the U of Washington (she published a book on Emily Dickinson in 1972). *Brotes* (1965; Sprouts), her first book of poetry, treats life, love, solitude, and the problems of poetry. *Isla adentro* (1969; Within the Island) concentrates upon the relationship between the poet and poetry, expressed in mystical terms of divine union. *Diario de una muerte* (1970; Diary of a Death) is an elegy to the poet's father, an anguished yet elegant and eloquent lament. *Configurado tiempo* (1974; Configuration of Time) affirms the inseparable union of life and poetry, and returns to love, recollections of Tenerife, and spiritual themes. *Invención de la luz* (1978; Invention of Light) won the Carabela de Oro (Golden Caravel) Prize for Poetry in Spain in 1977. This collection equates lyrics and luminosity, and abounds in colorful imagery. Affirming the inseparability of poetry and love, the poems are hope-filled, vivid and replete with metaphors. *Desde Chanatel, el canto* (1982; Chant from Chanatel), Fagundo's sixth collection, was a finalist in the Angaro Prize competition. Chanatel is the name of a symbolic point of departure; the book is a reiteration of the major themes of previous volumes, as well as a return to origins, a journey through memory which unites and synthesizes universal themes: life, love, hope, death, poetry, sorrow, light. Fagundo is also editor of the literary review *Alaluz*.

BIBLIOGRAPHY

Primary Texts

*Brotes.* Sta. Cruz de Tenerife: n.p., 1965.
*Configurado tiempo.* Madrid: Oriens, 1974.
*Desde Chanatel, el canto.* Seville: Angaro, 1982.
*Invención de la luz.* Barcelona: Vosgos, 1978.
*Isla adentro.* Sta Cruz de Tenerife: Gaceta Semanal de Las Artes, 1969.

Janet Pérez

**FALCÓN O'NEILL, Lidia** (1935, Madrid– ), lawyer, novelist, journalist, feminist leader. Lidia Falcón has been the guiding intellectual and activist force in Spanish feminism for over twenty years. She is the founder of the first Feminist party in Spain (1979) and the founder of Spain's first feminist magazine, *Vindicación Feminista* (1976–79; Feminist Vindication). She is a nationally known journalist and has published fourteen books of fiction as well as socio-political treatises on women and society. As a product of the Spanish Civil War, a child of the defeated Republicans, she documents this silenced and anguished chapter in Spanish history in her autobiographical books and articles. Falcón has experienced torture and interior exile for her staunch support of women's rights and human freedom. *Mujer y sociedad* (Women and Society) constituted a ground-breaking study in women's history, sociology, anthropology and politics when it was first published in 1967. The militant tone, as well as the content of the book, caused it to be detained by the censors for over two years. *Cartas a una idiota española* (1974; Letters to a Spanish Idiot) is an irreverent and humorous criticism of male exploitation of women using the literary device of letters from a female lawyer (Falcón) to her friend. *Es largo esperar callado* (The Long and Silent Wait) is a realistic portrayal of over twenty years of clandestine struggle in Spain, fictionally re-creating key historical figures such as Santiago Carrillo, Dolores Ibarruri and Enrique Lister. The novel is also significant for its portrayal of the lives of Spanish exiles in France and in the socialist countries, and for its picture of the difficulties women have had to endure in Spanish society at large, as well as in the supposedly progressive circles of leftist politics. *En el infierno, Ser mujer en las cárceles de España* (1977; In Hell: To be a Woman in Spanish Prison) is a novelized account of the situation of women in Spanish jails, reformatories, psychiatric and prison hospitals which was written while the author was in prison and smuggled out to her children. The following are both autobiographical works: *Los hijos de los vencidos* (1979; Children of the Defeated) and *Viernes y trece en la Calle del Correo* (1981; Friday and Thirteen on Correo Street). *Los hijos de los vencidos* documents post–Civil War Spain and Falcón's own first fourteen years as a child of the defeated Republicans. *Viernes y trece* recounts in novel form the judicial process against various political activists and intellectuals accused of collaborating with the Basque terrorist organization— the ETA—in September 1974. Falcón was arrested, along with twenty others, and remained imprisoned in Yeserías, the women's penitentiary in Madrid, for nine months. Dramatist Antonio *Buero Vallejo has called this mystery, detective and political novel "the last word on the subject of terrorism." In her two-volume treatise, *La razón feminista* (1981–1982; Feminist Reason), Falcón analyzes the material causes of the exploitation of women throughout history and in all types of communities. In volume 2 she demythifies the taboos concerning motherhood and discusses genetic experiments and fertilization *in vitro* as tools for liberation.

BIBLIOGRAPHY

Primary Texts

*El alboroto español.* Barcelona: Fontanella, 1984.
*Cartas a una idiota española.* 4th ed. Barcelona: Plaza & Janés, 1980.
*Los derechos civiles de la mujer.* Barcelona: Nereo, 1963.
*Los derechos laborales de la mujer.* Madrid: Montecorvo, 1965.
*Es largo esperar callado.* 3rd ed. Barcelona: Vindicación Feminista–Hacer, 1984.
*Los hijos de los vencidos.* N.p · Pomaire, 1979.
*En el infierno, ser mujer en las cárceles de España.* N.p.: Feminismo, 1977.
*El juego de la piel.* Barcelona: Argos-Vergara, 1983.
*Mujer y sociedad.* 3rd ed. Barcelona: Fontanella, 1984.
"Las mujeres caminaron con el fuego del siglo." Unpublished play. Barcelona, 1985.
*La razón feminista. La mujer como clase social y económica, el modo de producción
       doméstica.* Barcelona: Fontanella, 1981.
*La razón feminista. La reproducción humana.* Barcelona: Fontanella, 1982.
*Rupturas.* Barcelona: Círculo de Lectores, 1985.
*Viernes y trece en la Calle del Correo.* Barcelona: Planeta, 1981.

Criticism

Starcevic, Elizabeth. "*Rupturas*: A Feminist Novel." *ALEC* 12(1.2) 1987: 175–189.
Waldman, Gloria F. "Vindicación Feminista: Lidia Falcón, Ester Tusquets y Mercé
       Rodoreda." *La Torre* (U of Puerto Rico) 115 (Jan. - March 1982): 10–25.
———. "Tres novelistas españolas." *Linden Lane Magazine* (New Jersey) 3.2 (April-
       June 1983): 36–37.
———. "*Con el fuego del siglo*: visto desde dentro." *Estreno* (U of Cincinnati) 10.2
       (Fall 1984): 1–2.

                                                                   Gloria Feiman Waldman

**FANER, Pau** (1949, Ciutadella, Menorca– ), novelist. He obtained his doctorate in Romance philology and has taught English at the pre-university level in Spain. Beginning with *Contes menorquins, L'Arcàngel* (1972; The Archangel, Menorcan Tales) and including *Un regne per a mi* (A Kingdom for Me), winner of the Sant Jordi Prize for Catalan Fiction in 1975 and the prestigious Critics' Prize of 1977, Faner has written steadily. He produced in rapid succession *El camp de les tulipes* (Tulip Field), *Potser nomes la fosca* (Perhaps Only the Smoke), *Amb la mort al darrera* (With Death Behind), *El violi magic* (The Magic Violin), *La vall d'Adam* (Adam's Valley), *Lady Valentine* (title only in English; Víctor Català Prize, 1983), and *Fins al cel* (Heaven at Last, Josep Pla Prize for 1983, also Joan Creixells Prize, 1984).

With *Caballos de carga* (1985; Pack Horses), Faner experiments with novelistic perspective, situating the narrative consciousness in the mind of a carriage horse whose forebears and descendants have served the same family for generations. Faner exploits this original viewpoint to present a chronicle of three or four generations of the Menorcan bourgeoisie, following the example of the *Picaresque novel in utilization of a pseudo-innocent perspective through which to criticize social shortcomings. In *Flor de sal* (1985; Salt Flower), Faner offers a historical novel based upon the civil conflicts of Menorca in the period 1706–1802, a century of seesaw predominance of British, French and Spanish influences on the island. In addition to a collection of swashbuckling freebooters, sensuous lady mercenaries and more serious historical characters, Faner presents the contemporaneous development of modern social structures and economic activities and organizations on the island during the eighteenth c. Divided into twenty-four chapters with quasi-Cervantine headings that summarize the content, *Flor de sal* combines fantasy (appearances by ghosts and intervention by the dead in the lives and destinies of the living) with matter-of-fact realism and a substratum of historical research for uncommon literary impact. Irony, humor and a superior style are attributes of Faner which—in combination with excellent narrative skills—augur favorably for his literary future.

BIBLIOGRAPHY

Primary Texts

*L'Arcàngel*. Barcelona: Nova Terra, 1974.
*El camp de les tulipes i altres narracions*. Barcelona: Pòrtic, 1976.
*Flor de sal*. Barcelona: Destino, 1986.
*Un regne per a mi*. Barcelona: Proa, 1976.

                                                                    Janet Pérez

**FARÁNDULA,** a type of traveling theater troupe of the Golden Age. According to *Rojas Villandrando, it was composed of three well-dressed women with two chests of goods who were able to perform ten to twelve plays for Corpus Christi festivals for 200 ducats. *See also* Siglo de Oro; Theater in Spain.

**FARIA, Benigno Almeida** (1943, Lisbon– ), Portuguese novelist. Faria began writing at an early age, with *Rumor Branco* (1962; White Rumor) composed in an innovative vein, but suffering from a certain prolixity and immaturity. *Paixão* (Countryman) is an essayistic novel of great strength and transcendent realism portraying the world along the Tagus River.

**FARIA, Pedro.** *See* Hurtado de la Vera, Pedro

**FARIÑA Y COBIÁN, Herminia** (1904, Santiago de Compostela–1966, ?), Galician writer. From her youth, Fariña y Cobián maintained an active literary life. Her first book of verses, *Cadencias* (1922; Pontevedra), was written in Spanish and has seen various editions. *Seara* (1924; Harvest) is her only book of poetry in Galician. Romantic in content, its meter and style were more similar to modernism. In Vigo her plays *Margarida a Malfadada* (Margaret the Misfortunate) and *O saldado froita* (Happy Ending?) were staged during the 1920s. She traveled to America after her marriage, and her later books were in Spanish. Fariña y Cobián collaborated in both Spanish and Latin American publications. The most frequent theme of her writing is rural Galicia, presented in a style that may be exaggeratedly "native." *See also* Galician Literature.

BIBLIOGRAPHY

Primary Texts

*Bajo el cielo porteño.* Buenos Aires: n.p., 1930.
*Cadencias.* Pontevedra: n.p., 1922.
*Hosanna.* Buenos Aires: n.p., 1931.
*Por España y para España.* N.p.: n.p., n.d.
*Seara.* Pontevedra: Celestino Peón, 1924.

Criticism

Carballo Calero, Ricardo. *Historia da literatura galega contemporánea.* Vigo: Galaxia, 1981.
Couceiro Freijomil, Antonio. *Diccionario bio-bibliográfico de escritores.* Santiago: Bibliófilos Gallegos, 1951–54.

Kathleen March

**FAZIENDA DE ULTRAMAR, La** (The Matter of Outremer), medieval prose narrative. Only recently discovered, this pilgrim's guide to the Holy Land combines geographic descriptions and historical excerpts from the Old Testament. The ms. dates from the thirteenth c.; its Castilian text may be based on a Latin translation of a twelfth-c. Hebrew text. *See also*: Bible in Vulgar Translation.

BIBLIOGRAPHY

Primary Text

*La fazienda de Ultramar.* Ed., intro M. Lazar. Salamanca: Acta Salmantina, 1965.

**FEIJOO Y MONTENEGRO, Benito Jerónimo** (1674, Orense–1764, Oviedo), early Enlightenment critic and essayist. Born into a moderately well-to-do family (which he remembered as having had a strong interest in books), Feijoo, instead of exercising his right as eldest son to inherit the family estate, became a Benedictine friar. He studied in Salamanca, and in 1710 he went on to gain a professorship in theology at the U of Oviedo, where he spent the rest of his life. An exceedingly intelligent man, he read widely and dedicated his life to a campaign to combat what he considered to be errors propagated by the unenlightened or the ill-informed. To that end he wrote prodigiously against ignorance, superstition, and distorted doctrine, while remaining faithful to his own firmly established Christian beliefs. In his attempt to discover the varied "truths" of human existence, he defended the value of direct observations and experience, ideals which he wished to see integrated into Spain's educational system. He opposed received opinion and so-called truths based solely on authority, and he championed free scholarly inquiry.

The core of Feijoo's production rests in his encyclopedic eight-volume *Teatro crítico universal* (1726–40; Universal Theater of Criticism) and his five-volume *Cartas eruditas* (1742–60; Erudite Letters). Both works contain an early panorama of man's knowledge as interpreted in 261 articles by Feijoo. The subjects covered include art, astronomy, geography, economics, political law, physics, mathematics, natural history, medicine, biology, literature, aesthetics, Christian morals, philosophy, superstition, folklore, and philology. Many essays were translated into English throughout the eighteenth c. His books are invaluable sources of information, even when the information in them has been updated or corrected by modern science. His belief in the open pursuit of knowledge led him to consult, and to integrate, the ideas of the leading European intellectuals of his day—including, frequently, writers forbidden in Spain. Great thinkers of the past and present (Bacon, Descartes, Erasmus, Gessner, La Bruyère, Liebnitz, Montaigne, Montesquieu, More, Newton, Pascal, Rousseau) are represented in Feijoo's works. He wrote in Spanish, as opposed to the Latin which other teachers and churchmen tended to use, and his works attracted national and international attention. They were as vociferously condemned by his enemies as praised by his admirers.

Polemics over his works began immediately after the publication of his first treatise, a defense of Dr. Martín Martínez's *Medicina scéptica* (1725; Skeptical Medicine). He followed this with an *Ilustración apologética* (1729; Illustrative Apologetics) and a later *Justa repulsa a las inicuas acusaciones* (1749; Just Repudiation of Iniquitous Charges), but his critics refused to be silenced. Controversy surrounded Feijoo to such an extent that in 1750 King Ferdinand VI was forced to issue a decree prohibiting further attacks on Feijoo or on his writings. Still, while he spent the majority of his life surrounded by his rich library in his monastery cell in Oviedo and seeking only intellectual stimulation and solitude (ill health forced him to retire from teaching in 1739), his fame and influence increased. Writers from all over Europe came to Oviedo to see him. By the time he died in 1764 it is thought that some 500,000 volumes of his various works had been sold at home and abroad. The *Teatro* alone went through twenty editions; the *Cartas*, eleven. Several miscellaneous works were published posthumously in a collection called *Adiciones* (1783; Additions). His poetry was less successful and has not been adequately studied.

Feijoo's monastic quietude contrasted with the aggressive fervor of his ideas, a contrast which merely underscores the greatness of his achievements: he is credited with having begun Spain's Enlightenment almost singlehandedly. His broad interests, clear writing style, intellectual curiosity, encyclopedic knowledge, sense of skeptical inquiry, and courageous commitment to the ideals in which he believed place him above any other Spanish figure—and most Europeans—of the first half of the eighteenth c. *See also* Essay.

BIBLIOGRAPHY

Primary Texts

*Feijoo: Obras (selección)*. Ed. I. L. McClelland. Madrid: Taurus, 1985.
*Obras completas*. Ed. José Miguel Caso González. Oviedo: Centro de Estudios del Siglo XVIII, 1981.
*Obras completas*, I. Oviedo: Cátedra Feijoo, 1981.
*Teatro crítico universal. Cartas eruditas*. Ed. Carmen Martín Gaite. Madrid: Alianza, 1970.
*Teatro crítico universal*. Ed. Giovanni Stiffoni. Madrid: Castalia, 1986.
*Teatro crítico universal*. Ed. Angel R. González Fernández. Madrid: Cátedra, 1980.

English Translation

*Essays or Discourses Selected from the Works of Feijoo*. Tr. J. Brett. London: H. Payne, 1780.

Criticism

Alvarez de Miranda, Pedro. "Aproximación al estudio del vocabulario ideológico de Feijoo." *CH* 347 (1979): 367–93.
———. "La Fecha de publicación del primer escrito de Feijoo." *Dieciocho* 9 (1986): 24–34.
Browning, John. "Fray Benito Jerónimo Feijoo and the Sciences in Eighteenth-Century Spain." *The Varied Pattern: Studies in the Eighteenth Century*. Toronto: U of Toronto P, 1971.
Cameron, William J. *A Bibliography in Short-Title Catalog Form of Editions 1719–1764 of the Writings of Feijoo*. 3 vols. Ontario: U of Western Ontario, 1985.
Caso González, José. "Feijoo, hoy." *CH* 106 (1976): 723–35.
Cerra Suárez, S. "Doscientos cincuenta años de Bibliografía Feijoniana." *Studium Ovetense* 2 (1976).
Deply, G. *Bibliographie des Sources françaises de Feijoo*. Paris: Hachette, 1936.
McClelland, I. L. *Benito Jerónimo Feijoo*. TWAS 51. New York: Twayne, 1969.

David Thatcher Gies

**FELIPE, León,** pseudonym León Felipe Camino Galicia (1884, Tabara, Zamora–1968, Mexico), Spanish poet. The son of a notary who lived in several small cities in northern Spain, Felipe obtained a degree in pharmacy and practiced this profession in Spain's Basque country. An avid theater buff, he became an actor and traveled about the peninsula with a small company, and began to write, publishing his first book, *Versos y oraciones de caminante* (1920; Verses and Prayers of a Traveling Man), shortly before going to North Africa, where he spent two years as a hospital administrator in Guinea. Impulsively going to Mexico, he went on to New York and Columbia U, where he studied with Federico de Onís in 1924, then taught at Cornell (1925–29), becoming familiar with English poetry, especially that of Whitman and Eliot. An enlarged second edition of his first book appeared in New York in 1929, followed by *Drop a Star* (1930; title only in English), a lengthy poem in three cantos with prologue and epilogue. *Drop a Star* reflects the clash between the poet's spirit and capitalism, his hostility to Anglo-Saxon civilization and all that is symbolized by

Hollywood and Wall Street. With the proclamation of the Republic, Felipe returned to Spain, but was jailed for dubious financial transactions. He returned to the New World in 1933, visiting Madrid in 1935, then going to Panama as a cultural attaché of the Spanish embassy. During the Civil War, he returned to the peninsula to devote his poetry to defending the Republic, especially in *La insignia* (1937; Insignia), which he recited publicly as he did with *Oferta* (1938; Offering), included in his next book, *El payaso de las bofetadas y el pescador de caña* (1938; The Buffeted Clown and the Fisherman with the Cane Pole). That same year he returned to Mexico, where he lived for the remainder of his life.

In 1939, two significant works appeared, *El hacha (Elegía española)* (The Axe: Spanish Elegy) and *Español del éxodo y del llanto* (Spaniard of Exodus and Weeping), the latter one of his best-known titles. These books are a high point of Felipe's production, although perhaps surpassed by *Ganarás la luz* (1949; You Will Earn the Light) and *El ciervo* (1958; The Deer). The latter is a very existential work, filled with anguish and despair as the poet contemplates human existence as absurdity and being unto death. Conceiving of himself and humanity as abandoned by God and adrift in a meaningless universe, León Felipe meditated upon man's inhumanity to man, stressing social aspects of Christianity. A wanderer and itinerant by nature, he resumed his vagabondage in 1945, traveling throughout Latin America as a kind of modern pilgrim or troubadour, reciting his poetry and lecturing. Felipe translated works of Waldo Frank, Whitman, and Shakespeare, and helped to found the literary review *Cuadernos Americanos*.

The epic and dramatic quality of Felipe's poetic language echoes his youthful experiences as an actor, while his vision of himself as a modern prophet explains the declamatory and emphatic accent of much of his verse, as well as the exhortative patterns and preachy repetitiveness reminiscent of certain biblical passages. God and prophecy or the prophet are almost leitmotifs in his work, and thus the biblical echoes are no accident: Felipe sought inspiration in the Bible, and much of his pre-war poetry reflects a search for salvation, an attempt to attune himself to what is most essential in Catholicism. After the war, there is fury and grief at the defeat of justice and freedom, the horror of fratricidal slaughter, the pain and longing of exile. At one and the same time, Felipe is humble and Promethean, a solitary mystic and a somewhat anarchic egalitarian. His expression is blunt and direct, sometimes to the extreme. Felipe viewed the poet's mission as the defense of human freedom. His basic concepts are few and elementary, communicated via free verse abounding in rhetorical figures, grandiloquence and emotional outbursts: it is poetry to be declaimed. Felipe is the poet par excellence of the Spanish Civil War and of the exile experience, the poet of Spain's tragedy, the bard without a country.

BIBLIOGRAPHY

Primary Text

*Obras completas*. Buenos Aires: Losada, 1963.

Criticism

Murillo González, Margarita. *León Felipe. Sentido religioso de su poesía*. Mexico: Colección Málaga, 1968.

Rivera, Tomás. "La teoría poética de León Felipe." *Cuadernos Americanos* 186 (1973): 193–214.

Torre, Guillermo de. "Interpretaciones de León Felipe." *Insula* 23.265 (December 1968): 1, 10.

Villavicencio, Laura. "Estructura, ritmo e imaginería en *Ganarás la luz* de León Felipe." *Cuadernos Americanos* 183 (1972): 167–91.

Zardoya, Concha. *Poesiá española del 98 y del 27*. Madrid: Gredos, 1968. 194–95.

Janet Pérez

**FELIÚ Y CODINA, José** (1847, Barcelona–1897, Barcelona), Catalan dramatist. Feliú was a follower of José *Echegaray and a champion of the neoromantic school of late nineteenth-c drama. His works are characterized by a vivid *naturalism which focused on various regional locales both within and outside Catalonia. His plays depicted such diverse areas of Spain as Catalayud, in *La Dolores* (1892; The Sorrowful One); Murcia, in *María del Carmen* (1895); and Andalucía, in *La real moza* (1896; A Real Dame). *La Dolores* is his most famous work, and its protagonist's character is particularly well delineated. The play was extremely popular and was made into a hugely successful *zarzuela* by Tomás de Bretón (1895). The character of Dolores was continued by other writers, such as the sequel by Luis *Fernández Ardavín, *La hija de la Dolores* (The Daughter of the Sorrowful One). Feliú wrote both in verse, as in *La Dolores*, and in prose, as with *María del Carmen*. His verse plays sometimes suffer from a mannered poetic style. Although he occasionally resorted to scenes of questionable taste, Feliú was at his best in portraying picturesque regional customs.

BIBLIOGRAPHY

Primary Texts

*La Dolores*. Madrid: Velasco, 1892.
*María del Carmen*. 2ed. Madrid: Velasco, 1896.

Donald C. Buck

**FERNÁN CABALLERO,** pseudonym of Cecilia Böhl de Faber (1796, Morges, Switzerland–1877, Seville), novelist. She was the daughter (and, in many ways, the literary product) of the distinguished German Hispanist, Johann Nikolaus Böhl von Faber, and early feminist (and Catholic traditionalist) Francisca Ruiz de Larrea, of Cádiz. Her personal circumstances were filled with almost as much drama as a work of fiction. She was married and widowed three times: first, in 1816, to a Captain Planels, a brute of a husband, who fortunately died soon after the marriage; then, in 1822, to the Marquis of Arco-Hermoso, who loved her but left her saddled with debts; and finally, in 1837, most probably out of a sense of compassion, to Antonio Arrom de Ayala, seventeen years her junior, whose financial and business difficulties eventually drove him to suicide. She suffered passionately in 1836 over an unhappy love affair with an English aristocrat identified in letters as Federico Cuthbert. And in her last years, she experienced economic deprivation—the loss of her residence at the Alcázar of Seville, which had been provided by Queen Isabel II, for example—and emotional depression over her own life and the fall of the Bourbon monarchy in 1868.

Fernán Caballero is best known for her novel *La Gaviota* (1849; *The Sea Gull*, 1965), in which she re-elaborates the age-old conflict between city and countryside and, in the process, idealizes her rural setting, Villamar, as a kind of lost earthly paradise free of foreign influence and the corrupting effects of modern-day liberalism. *La Gaviota*, like some of Fernán Caballero's other work, is streaked with lachrymose *romanticism and even melodrama, but is significant for its attempt to depict realistically—within the limitations of her moralizing, traditionalist stance—the customs and character of the Spanish people, in particular, the Andalusians. Much of her fiction, as J. Herrero has pointed out, originated in her enthusiastic and indefatigable *costumbrista* efforts to collect Andalusian folkways and traditional beliefs. She was, in addition, an admirer of Honoré de Balzac's *roman de moeurs*. Writing in a rather barren literary period—1850–1870—Fernán Caballero, though no ''Spanish Sir Walter Scott,'' as Eugenio de *Ochoa once hailed her, must be taken seriously as the initiator of both the regional novel and the thesis novel of ideological conflict. Though her great popularity declined and she was eclipsed by such up-and-coming— and artistically superior—writers as *Pérez Galdós, Juan *Valera, and *Pereda, she remains a significant figure in the renaissance of nineteenth-c. Spanish narrative, both for what she did—fashion novels out of *costumbrista* sketches and observation—and for what she failed to do—free the novel from that very same *costumbrismo* and from the subjective confines of her own ideology. Some of her other novels include *La familia de Alvareda* (1856; *The Family of Alvareda*, 1872), the autobiographical *Clemencia* (1852), *Elia, o La España treinta años ha* (1849; *Elia, or Spain Thirty Years Ago*, 1868), *Un servilón y un liberalito, o tres almas de Dios* (1859; *A Loyalist and a Liberal, or Three Souls of God*, 1882), and *Un verano en Bornos* (1855; A Summer in Bornos). Two of many collections are *Cuadros de costumbres populares andaluzas* (1852; Sketches of Popular Andalusian Customs), and *Relaciones* (1857; Tales). There are six Madrid editions of her complete works, none reliable (the first in 1855–58, and the latest in 1917–28). Likewise, the oft-cited 1910 biography by novelist Father Luis *Coloma, *Recuerdos de Fernán Caballero* is not to be trusted (*see* J. Herrero, under Criticism). *See also* Romanticism.

BIBLIOGRAPHY

Primary Texts

*Cecilia Böhl de Faber (Fernán Caballero) y Juan Eugenio Hartzenbusch. Una correspondencia inédita*. Ed. T. Heinermann. Madrid: Espasa-Calpe, 1944.
*Clemencia*. Ed. J. Rodríguez-Luis. Madrid: Cátedra, 1975.

*Cuentos de encantamiento y otros cuentos populares.* Ed. Carmen Bravo-Villasante. Madrid: Emesa, 1978.

*Elia.* Ed. J. Montesinos. Madrid: Alianza, 1968.

*La familia de Alvareda.* Ed. J. Rodríguez-Luis. Clásicos Castalia 88. Madrid: Castalia, 1979.

*La Gaviota.* Ed. J. Rodríguez-Luis. Barcelona: Labor, 1972.

*Obras de Fernán Caballero.* Ed. J. M. Castro Calvo. 5 vols. BAE 136–40.

English Translations

*Alvareda Family.* Tr. V. Pollington. London: Newby, 1872.

*Elia or, Spain Fifty Years Ago.* Tr. anon. New York: Appleton, 1868.

*The Old and the New.* Tr. H. and A. Zimmern. In *Half-Hours with Foreign Novelists.* London: Chatto and Windus, 1882. *Un servilón y un liberalito.*

*The Sea Gull.* Tr. Joan Maclean. Woodbury, NY: Barron's, 1965.

Criticism

Gullón, G. "El costumbrismo moralizante de Fernán Caballero." In *El narrador en la novela del siglo XIX.* Madrid: Taurus, 1976. 29–42.

Herrero, J. "El testimonio del padre Coloma sobre Fernán Caballero." *BHS* 41 (1964): 40–50.

———. *Fernán Caballero: Un nuevo planteamiento.* Madrid: Gredos, 1963.

Kirkpatrick, S. "On the Threshold of the Realist Novel: Gender and Genre in *La Gaviota.*" *PMLA* 98 (1983): 323–40.

Klibbe, L. H. *Fernán Caballero.* TWAS 259. New York: Twayne, 1973.

Montesinos, J. F. *Fernán Caballer. Ensayo de justificación.* Berkeley: U of California P, 1961.

Valis, N. "Eden and the Tree of Knowledge in Fernán Caballero's *Clemencia.*" *KRQ* 29 (1982): 251–60.

Noël M. Valis

**FERNÁN GÓMEZ, Fernando** (1921, Lima, Peru– ), playwright and novelist. He was born into a family dedicated to the theater. His mother, Carola Fernán Gómez, was an actress for the renowned theatrical company of María Guerrero and Fernando Díaz de Mendoza. Born in Lima, Peru, while the company was on a tour and registered in Buenos Aires, Argentina, he was not granted Spanish nationality until recently. He was a man of many talents (actor, movie and theater director, scriptwriter, columnist, novelist, and playwright). In his youth he gained fame particularly as an actor, even though he also directed several films. His first literary attempt dates from 1961, when he published his novel *El vendedor de naranjas* (The Orange Seller), which did not make any impact. It was printed in small numbers and, according to the author, he gave most of them away to his friends. It was not until the eighties that Fernán Gómez's literary production received the recognition it deserved. In 1978 he was awarded the Lope de Vega Theater Prize for his play *Las bicicletas son para el verano* (Bicycles Are for the Summer). The play was staged at the Teatro Español in Madrid in 1982 and became one of the greatest theatrical successes among both public and critics. *Las bicicletas son para el verano* was published in 1984, followed by two other plays in 1985: *La coartada* (The Alibi) and *Los domingos, bacanal* (Sundays, Bacchanal), which were actually the first ones he had written. That same year he published his second novel, *El viaje a ninguna parte* (The Trip to Nowhere), and in 1986, *El vendedor de naranjas* was re-edited. His literary career during the eighties has not kept Fernán Gómez from his other activities. He has co-written filmscripts with Jaime de Armiñán and Carlos Saura, acted in and directed several movies and plays, and has been a regular contributor to the press. His plays have been staged, generally with great success: *Los domingos, bacanal* in 1980, *Las bicicletas son para el verano* in 1982, *Del rey Ordás y su infamia* in 1983 (King Ordás and his Infamy) and *La coartada* in 1985. He has also written children's literature: *Los ladrones* (1986; The Thieves).

BIBLIOGRAPHY

Primary Texts

*Las bicicletas son para el verano*. Intro. E. Haro Tecglen. 2nd ed. Madrid: Espasa-Calpe, 1984.
*Impresiones y depresiones*. Barcelona: Planeta, 1987.
*El vendedor de naranjas*. Madrid: Espasa-Calpe, 1986.

Criticism

Haro Tecglen, E. Introduction to *Las bicicletas son para el verano* (1984).
———. Introduction to *La coartada. Los domingos, bacanal*. Madrid: Espasa-Calpe, 1985.
Tébar, Juan. *Fernando Fernán Gómez, escritor (Diálogo en tres actos)*. Madrid: Anjana, 1984.
———. Introduction to *El vendedor de naranjas* (1986).

Samuel Amell

***FERNÁN GONZÁLEZ, Poema de*** (Poem of Fernán González), a poem in approximately 752 stanzas of *cuaderna vía* composed about the middle of the thirteenth c. by an unknown monk of the monastery of San Pedro de Arlanza. It has survived in a fifteenth-c. codex together with four other works. The poet used material from historical and legendary accounts of the life of one of the earliest counts of Castile, Fernán González (915–70), who is credited in the poem with having miraculously saved Castile from the Moors, the Navarrese, and the Leonese. The first 172 stanzas of the poem purport to be a historical account of Spain from the creation of the earth through the invasion of the Moors in 711 and the years of the early leaders of Castile before Fernán González; in this section is inserted (stanzas 144–60) the well-known "Elogio de España" (Praise to Spain) patterned upon a tradition of chauvinistic descriptions which leads back to Isidore of Seville's *Historia Gothorum*. Sections of this poem are clearly reminiscent not only of medieval Spanish chronicles but also of the works of *Berceo and the *Libro de *Alexandre*; its many miraculous episodes stand in contrast to the *Cantar de mio Cid* with which it might otherwise be compared as Castilian literary propaganda; and the episode of the "mal arcipreste" (bad archpriest) brings to mind *Arcipreste de Hita's *Libro de buen amor*. *See also* Crónicas; Edad Media, Literatura de la.

BIBLIOGRAPHY

Primary Text

*Poema de Fernán González.* Ed. Erminio Polidori. Rome: Semerano, 1962.

Criticism

Toro-Garland, Fernando de. "El arcipreste, protagonista literario del medioevo español." In *El Arcipreste de Hita.* Ed. Manuel Criado de Val. Barcelona: SERESA, 1973. 327–36.

Colbert Nepaulsingh

**FERNÁNDEZ, Lope de** (mid 15th c., ?–?), Augustinian prose author. Father Fernández wrote the brief treatise on penitence titled *El espejo del alma* (The Soul's Mirror). Some critics also consider him the author of *Libro de las tribulaciones* (Book of Tribulations). Both remain in ms. form in the Escorial Library.

**FERNÁNDEZ, Lucas** (1474?, Salamanca–1542, Salamanca), priest, professor of music, playwright. Most of his life revolved around either the Cathedral of Salamanca—where he was choirboy, cantor (1498), priest, abbot (1520)—where some of his compositions were performed, or the U of Salamanca, which he attended, where he became professor of music (1522), and where he organized festival programs over the years. Along with Juan del *Encina and Gil *Vicente, Fernández was a pioneer of Spanish *Renaissance theater. In 1514 he published seven pieces under the title *Farsas y églogas al modo y estilo pastoril y castellanos* (Farses and Eclogues in the Pastoral and Castilian Style). Three compositions are secular, two are semi-religious, one is a musical dialogue, and one—his masterpiece—is a Passion play. Of the non-religious plays, *La comedia* (performed 1496; The Comedy) is a racy, rustic wedding farce; *Farsa de la doncella* (performed 1496–97; The Maiden's Farce) depicts a love triangle, in which a shepherd vainly attempts to woo a maiden's affections from her knight; and the *Farsa de Prabos y el soldado* (performed c. 1497–99; The Farce of Prabos and the Soldier) presents another episodic love story where love is discussed in poetic and general terms, and the plot ends with marriage between one shepherd and his woman. The caricature of the soldier is quite memorable. The *Égloga del nacimiento* (performed 1500; Nativity Eclogue) and *Auto del nacimiento* (performed 1500–1502; Nativity Play) both treat Christ's birth. *Diálogo para cantar* (performed c. 1496–97; Dialogue for Singing) is a unique song drama about unrequited courtly love. Recurring features of these works include rustic scenes of daily life used as a backdrop, fine character development, and the use of *sayagués*, a regional, colloquial dialect, in the dialogues. Fernández's masterpiece, the *Auto de la Pasión* (performed 1500–1503; The Passion Play), boasts a vigorous, elegant lyricism in its vivid narration of Christ's passion; it is a jewel of Renaissance theater and a clear forerunner—if not first example—of the *auto sacramental* (*see* auto). *See also* Theater in Spain.

BIBLIOGRAPHY

Primary Texts

*Lucas Fernández, "Farsas y églogas."* Ed. E. Cotarelo y Mori. Madrid: RAE, 1929. Facs.

*Lucas Fernández, "Farsas y églogas."* Ed. J. Lihani. New York: Las Americas, 1969.

*Teatro selecto clásico de Lucas Fernández.* Ed., prol., A. Hermenegildo. Madrid: Escelicer, 1972.

Criticism

Hermenegildo, A. *Renacimiento, Teatro y Sociedad. Vida y obra de Lucas Fernández.* Madrid: Cincel, 1975.

Lihani, J. *Lucas Fernández.* TWAS 251. New York: Twayne, 1973.

Maureen Ihrie

**FERNÁNDEZ, Sebastián** (16th c., ?–?), dramatist. He has been revealed to be the author of the *Tragedia Policiana* through introductory acrostics of the work. The play recasts the legend of Pyramus and Thisbe, in twenty-nine acts. Influence of the *\*Celestina* is also apparent.

BIBLIOGRAPHY

Primary Text

*Tragedia Policiana.* In NBAE 14.

**FERNÁNDEZ ALMAGRO, Melchor** (1893, Granada–1966, Madrid), historian, literary critic, essayist and biographer. He collaborated on some of the most prestigious journals and newspapers in Spain (*El Sol, ABC, Revista de Occidente, La Gaceta Literaria*), and is the author of some excellent studies such as *Vida y obra de Angel Ganivet* (1925; Life and Works of Angel Ganivet), *Vida y literatura de Valle-Inclán* (1943; Life and Literature of Valle-Inclán) and *En torno al 98* (1948; The Generation of 98). Books on history and political science include *Orígenes del régimen constitucional en España* (1928; Origins of the Constitutional Regime in Spain), and *Historia del reinado de Alfonso XIII* (1933; History of the Reign of Alphonse XIII). In collaboration with the Duke of Maura he wrote *¿Por qué cayó Alfonso XII?* (2nd ed. 1948; Why Did Alphonse XII Fall?), *La emancipación de América y su reflejo en la conciencia española* (1944; America's Emancipation and Its Reflection in the Spanish Conscience), and *Política naval en la España moderna y contemporánea* (1946; Naval Policy in Contemporary Modern Spain). He collaborated on W. Oncken's world history series by writing the section on Central and South American republics. In 1951 he published his most accomplished historical work: *Cánovas, su vida y su política* (Canovas, His Life and Politics), which presents the life and works of Cánovas and a detailed analysis of the second half of the nineteenth c. in Spain. A member of the Academies of History and of Language, he initiated publication of the *Historia política de la España contemporánea* (Political History of Contemporary Spain). His *Viaje al siglo XX* (Journey to the Twentieth Century), which combined personal experiences with literary creativity, was published in 1962.

BIBLIOGRAPHY

Primary Texts

*Historia política de la España contemporánea.* 3 vols. Madrid: Alianza, 1968.
*Política naval en la España moderna y contemporánea.* Madrid: Instituto de Estudios políticos, n.d.
*Vida y literatura de Valle-Inclán.* Madrid: Taurus, 1966.
*Vida y obra de Angel Ganivet.* Madrid: RO, 1953.

                                                                    Isabel McSpadden

**FERNÁNDEZ ARDAVÍN, Luis** (1892, Madrid–1962, Madrid), modernist poet and playwright. His first book was a poetry collection titled *Meditaciones* (n.f.; Meditations). His theater is written in verse and exhibits traces of the style of *Marquina. Representative plays include *La vidriera milagrosa* (1925; The Miraculous Stained-Glass Window), *La hija de la Dolores* (1927; Dolores's Daughter), *La florista de la reina* (1939; The Queen's Florist), and *La dama del armiño* (1922; The Lady in Ermine), a play which evokes the city of Toledo in the sixteenth c. and was one of his most successful works. He also wrote scripts for *zarzuelas. Several critics criticized the lack of balance between his intentions and his accomplishments, as his verse could not fully compensate for various dramatic defects.

BIBLIOGRAPHY

Primary Text

*La dama del armiño; la florista de la reina; la dogaresa rubia.* Madrid: Aguilar, 1944.
                                                                    Isabel McSpadden

**FERNÁNDEZ BREMÓN, José** (1839, Gerona–1910, Madrid), dramatist, editor, journalist. His drama was not well received by critics, but his *Cuentos* (1879; Stories) was much praised. The editor of important periodicals (*La España*), *La Época, Ilustración Española y Americana*), he also wrote clever weekly commentaries of current events.

BIBLIOGRAPHY

Primary Text

*Cuentos.* Madrid: Ilustración Española y Americana, 1879.

**FERNÁNDEZ CASTRO, José** (1912, Granada– ), novelist and journalist. He has received numerous literary prizes: Antonio de Alarcón, Angel Ganivet, etc. *La sonrisa de los ciegos* (1950; The Smile of the Blind) is a series of episodes in prose and poetry dealing with the mysterious world of the blind. He is also the author of two novels: *Balada del amor prohibido* (1978; Ballad of the Forbidden Love) and *La tierra lo esperaba* (1974; The Land Was Waiting for Him). The latter constitutes a rural tragedy triggered by class conflict. Fernández Castro's style, rooted in traditional nineteenth-c. Spanish realism, is direct and lively.

He has also published short stories (1960; *El chaqué y otros relatos*; The Tuxedo and Other Stories); theater (1971; *Olite Víspera de San José*; Olite. Saint Joseph's Eve); poetry (1967; *Antes del último instante*; Before the Last Instant), and essays (1950; *Sentido estético del amor*; The Aesthetic Meaning of Love).

BIBLIOGRAPHY

Primary Texts

*A la sombra del árbol de los besos*. Madrid: Colección "Palma," 1952.
*Antes del último instante*. Granada: Gráficas del Sur, 1967.
*Balada del amor prohibido*. Granada: U of Granada, 1978.
*La sonrisa de los ciegos*. Madrid: Rumbos, 1950.
*La tierra lo esperaba*. Madrid: Espasa-Calpe, 1974.

José Ortega

**FERNÁNDEZ CUBAS, Cristina** (1945, Arenys de Mar, Barcelona– ), journalist and fiction writer. She makes her living primarily through journalism, but began publishing stories during the 1970s. *Mi hermana Elba* (1980; My Sister Elba) is a collection of four long short stories or novellas, the title tale being a remembrance of childhood and adolescent cruelty and self-centeredness which apparently causes the death of the narrator's visionary little sister. Another, "Lúnula y Violeta," tells of the encounter, relationship and death of two women who are probably two aspects of a split personality. A certain amount of fantasy or the marvelous can be found in all four stories. *El vendedor de sombras* (1982; The Seller of Dreams) is apparently children's fiction, and has been translated into Catalan and Basque. *Los altillos de Brumal* (1983; The Highlands of Brumal), another short story collection, is not easy to interpret: like her first volume, this one abounds in ambiguity, abnormal and alcoholic characters, mirror symbols and incomprehensible passages (others must be read through a mirror). Time in the title tale is fluid, unreal, and many perceptions seem inside out or backwards. The title tale creates unresolvable doubt as to the main character's sanity, and many others raise similar questions. *El año de Gracia* (1985; The Year of Grace) is the writer's first full-length novel, an adventure story in the classic vein, recalling especially such precedents as *Sinbad the Sailor* and *Robinson Crusoe*, both of which are frequently evoked via intertextual allusions. Essentially a voyage of initiation, the narrative concerns a totally innocent young seminarian whose adventures lead eventually to his decision to abandon the seminary and marry. Points of contact with the writer's earlier fiction are the oneiric atmosphere, the interweaving of marvelous and fantastic elements with the normal or realistic, and the problems of communication and perception.

BIBLIOGRAPHY

Primary Text

*Mi hermana Elba y Los altillos de Brumal.* Barcelona: Tusquets, 1988.

Criticism

Bellver, Catherine G. "Two New Women Writers from Spain." *Letras Femeninas* 8.2
    (1982): 3–7.
Zatlin, Phyllis. "Tales from Fernández Cubas: Adventure in the Fantastic." *Monographic
    Review/Revista Monográfica* 3.1–2 (1987): 107–18.

Janet Pérez

**FERNÁNDEZ CUENCA, Carlos** (1904, Madrid–1977, Madrid), actor, movie
critic, and authority. Before the Civil War he was an actor; after it he occupied
various high positions in the movie industry. He wrote many biographies of such
movie personalities as Elia Kazan, Antonioni, Greta Garbo, and Chaplin; and
in 1948 he published the first part of a history of film. Although it remained
unfinished at his death, it is a valuable repository of information. Also his are
*Historia anecdótica del cinema* (1930; Anectodal History of the Cinema) and
*La guerra civil y el cine* (1972; The Civil War and the Movies).

BIBLIOGRAPHY

Primary Texts

*La guerra civil y el cine.* Madrid: Nacional, 1972.
*Historia anecdótica del cinema.* Madrid: ibero-americana, 1930.
*Historia del cine.* 2 vols. Madrid: Aguado, 1948—.
*Panorama del cinema en Rusia.* Madrid: ibero-americana, 1930.

Isabel McSpadden

**FERNÁNDEZ DE ANDRADA, Andrés** (17th c., Seville ?–?), soldier, poet.
He is credited with the seventeenth-c. gem, *Epístola moral a Fabio.* He may
have emigrated to Mexico.

BIBLIOGRAPHY

Criticism

Alonso, Dámaso. *Dos españoles del siglo de oro.* Madrid: Gredos, 1960.

**FERNÁNDEZ DE CÓRDOBA, Fernando** (1809, Buenos Aires–1883, Madrid), soldier, politician, historian. After many years in the political arena, he
directed his attention to historical research. He wrote two accounts of the tumultuous events he witnessed and in which he participated: *Memoria sobre los
sucesos políticos ocurridos en Madrid los días 17, 18 y 19 de julio de 1854*
(1855; Account of Political Events Which Occurred in Madrid the 17th, 18th
and 19th of July, 1854), and the three-volume *Mis memorias íntimas* (1886–89;
My Personal Memoirs), which covers events from the accession of Ferdinand
VII to the throne up to the dethroning of Isabella II. His eyewitness testimony
is supplemented by valuable documentation.

BIBLIOGRAPHY

Primary Texts

*Memoria sobre los sucesos. . . . de 1854.* Madrid: Rivadeneyra, 1855.
*Mis memorias íntimas.* 2nd ed. 3 vols. Madrid: Rivadeneyra, 1899–1903.

**FERNÁNDEZ DE GERENA, Garcí,** or Ferrando de Jerena (14th c., Castile–
15th c., Castile), poet of the *Cancionero de *Baena.* Well regarded by John I,
he was disgraced and scorned by other poets for marrying a Moorish female
minstrel, assuming her wealthy. He retired to a hermitage near Gerena, then
moved to Granada to become an apostate. Returning to Castile in 1391, he
reverted to Catholicism, but his old friends never forgave him. A poet of transition
like *Macías and *Álvarez de Villasandino, he wrote in Galician and used themes
of the Provençal school, while exhibiting changes in form and language. His
verses include a poem in praise of the Virgin Mary and ''Despedida del amor''
(Love's Farewell). They display originality and imagination and are the sole
source of information about him.

BIBLIOGRAPHY

English Translation

*Love's Farewell.* In *Blind Man's Boy.* Tr. J. M. Cohen. London: New English Library,
1962.

Criticism

de los Ríos, Amador. *Historia crítica de la literatura española.* Madrid, 1865. Facs.,
Madrid: Gredos, 1969. 5:187.
Dollfus, L. *Études sur le Moyen Âge espagnol.* Paris: Leroux, 1894. 287–309.

Reginetta Haboucha

**FERNÁNDEZ DE HEREDIA, Juan** (1310, Munébrega (Calatayud)–1396,
Avignon), political adviser, diplomat, historian, bibliophile. By 1328 he was a
member of the Knights Hospitalers of St. John of Jerusalem. Ambitious, he rose
quickly in the order and became in 1338 a personal adviser to Peter IV the
Ceremonious. His long career as diplomat-soldier includes: the battle of Crécy
(1346); several extended missions to the papal court in Avignon; as a trusted
adviser of Gregory IX, the command of the fleet which returned the papal
entourage to Rome; as Grand Master (1377), the charge of an expedition against
the Turks in Morea which resulted in his capture and ransom after three years.

Although the first evidence of Heredia's bibliophilism is 1362, the majority
of the translations and historical compilations produced by his scriptorium
were executed during his tenure as Grand Master (1377–96). The extant works
attributed to Heredia are *La Grant Crónica de Espanya* (The Great Chronicle
of Spain), in the tradition of *Alphonse X the Learned; the *Crónica de los
conquistadores* (Chronicle of Conquerors) including such figures as Hercules,
Alexander, Hannibal, the two Scipios, Pompey, Caesar, Charles Martel, Charlemagne, Ferdinand II and James I; the *Crónica de los Emperadores* (Chroni-

cle of Emperors), based on the last four books of the *Epitome Historiarum* of John Zonaras; the *Libro de los fechos et conquistas de la Morea* (Chronicle of Morea); the *Crónica Troyana* (Chronicle of Troy) from Guido delle Colonne's *Historia Destructionis Troiae*; the *Eutropius,* named for the Roman historian, but based on Paul the Deacon's *History of Rome* and *History of the Lombards*; the *La flor de las ystorias de Orient* (Flower of Histories of the East), from the *Historia Orientalis* of Hed'own Patmic'; the *Libro de Autoridades* (Book of Authorities), a collection of maxims from Valerius Maximus and the Church Fathers; the *Marco Polo* (Book of Marco Polo); the *Orosius,* from Paulus Orosius; the *Plutarch,* from the *Parallel Lives*; the *Secreto Secretorum* of the Pseudo-Aristotle; and the speeches from Thucydides. Regina af Geijerstam has recently attributed to Heredia the translation of Lucas de *Tuy's *Chronicum Mundi.* The mss., with the exception of the *Orosius* and the *Plutarch,* which are later copies, were produced in Avignon. Evidence suggests some collaboration by the Aragonese court of Peter IV in the translations. The Heredia corpus is, linguistically, of special interest; its Aragonese betrays both the phenomenon of languages in contact and the intervention of several translators. It is a bountiful source for fourteenth-c. neologisms.

BIBLIOGRAPHY

Primary Texts

*Chronique de Morée aux XIIIᵉ et XIVᵉ siècles.* Ed. A. Morel-Fatio. Geneva: Société de l'Orient Latin, 1885.

*Concordances and Texts of the Fourteenth-Century Aragonese mss. of Juan Fernández de Heredia.* Ed. L. A. Kasten. Intro. by *A. Luttrell. Madison, WI: HSMS, 1982.*

*La Flor de las ystorias de Orient.* Ed. W. Robertson Long. Chicago: U of Chicago P, 1934.

*La Grant Crónica de Espanya. Libros I-II.* Ed. Regina af Geijerstam. Uppsala: Studia Romanica Upsaliensia, 1964.

*Juan Fernández de Heredia's Aragonese Version of the Libro de Marco Polo.* Ed. John J. Nitti. Madison, WI: HSMS, 1980.

*Tucídides romanceado en el siglo XIV.* Ed. Luis López Molina. Madrid: RAE, 1960.

Criticism

See R. af Geijerstam, Nitti, and Kasten/Luttrell, above.

Porter Conerly

**FERNÁNDEZ DE LA REGUERA, Ricardo** (1916, Barcenillos, Santander–), novelist. A prolific writer, popular for his direct, realistic style, Fernández de la Reguera spent part of his childhood in Chile and at age thirteen returned to Spain. He won a civil post in Barcelona, where he returned after fighting in the Civil War in the Nationalist Army. He married poet and writer Susana *March. After earning his degree in philosophy and letters, he began teaching and resumed literary activities. His hard-hitting first novel, *Cuando me voy a morir* (1950; *In the Darkness of My Fury,* 1959), recipient of the City of Barcelona Award, was a huge commercial success, especially in Germany. *Cuerpo a tierra* (1952;

*Reach for the Ground*, 1964), which dealt with the Civil War, confirmed his commercial success, with translations into German, Russian, Ukrainian, etc. This popularity continued with *Perdimos el paraíso* (1955; We Lost Paradise), chronicling the transition from childhood to maturity, winner of the Club España de México's international competition, and *Bienaventurados los que aman* (1956; Blessed Are Those Who Love), contrasting life in pre- and post-war Spain, recipient of the Concha Espina Award. Not quite so successful were *Vagabundos provisionales* (1959; Provisional Tramps), a travelogue, *Maestros ingleses* (1961; English Teachers), and *Un hombre llamado Roni* (1982; A Man Called Roni). Interspersed with the novels, Fernández also published collections of short stories, such as *Espionajes* (1963; Spying), and *Experimentos* (1974; Experiments), more pyschologically realistic. Since the 1960s, Fernández de la Reguera has centered on publishing with Planeta a series of *Episodios nacionales contemporáneos*, whose title pays homage to *Pérez Galdós. Written in collaboration with his wife, the series was begun with *Héroes de Cuba* (1963; Heros of Cuba) and *Héroes de Filipinas* (1963; Heros of the Philippines). It now extends to ten volumes and includes *Fin de una regencia* (1964; End of a Regency), *La boda de Alfonso XIII* (1965; Alfonso XIII's Wedding), *La semana trágica* (1966; The Tragic Week), *España neutral* (1967; Neutral Spain), *El desastre de Annual* (1968; The Disaster of Annual), *La cabida de un rey* (1972; Room for a King), *España sin corona* (1977; Spain without a King), and *La República* (1979; The Republic). This series covers Spanish history from the Regency into the twentieth c. Fernández de la Reguera's works have enjoyed a widespread readership, and adhere to traditional conventions of Spanish realism.

BIBLIOGRAPHY

Primary Texts

*Bienaventurados los que aman*. 3rd ed. Barcelona: Planeta, 1963.
*Cuando me voy a morir*. 2nd ed. Barcelona: Planeta, 1967.
*Espionajes: relatos*. Madrid: Taurus, 1963.
*La república de los soñadores*. Barcelona: Bruguera, 1977.

English Translations

*In the Darkness of My Fury*. Tr.? London: Wolff, 1959.
*Reach for the Ground*. Tr. I. Barea. London/New York: Abelard-Schuman, 1964.

                                                          Frieda H. Blackwell


**FERNÁNDEZ DE NAVARRETE, Martín** (1765, Abalos, Logroño–1844, Madrid), sailor, historical and literary researcher. Nicknamed "Merlín de los papeles" (Merlin of Documents), he, with two others, was commissioned by the navy to collect all mss., documents and material relating to maritime affairs of Spain. He amassed some forty-four volumes of material; among his finds was the previously unknown journal of Christopher Columbus (*Colón). Some 2,657 pieces make up the collection, which bears his name and is housed in the Naval Museum. The documents also functioned as sources for his *Colección de viajes* *y descubrimientos . . . por los españoles desde fines del siglo XV* (1825; Collection of Voyages and Discoveries by Spaniards since the End of the Fifteenth C.). Alexander Humbold deemed it the most interesting monument of contemporary geography. Fernández de Navarrete also collected documents concerning *Cervantes's life, published in 1819 as *Vida de Miguel de Cervantes* (Life of Miguel de Cervantes). From 1825 until his death, he served as director for the Academy of History.

BIBLIOGRAPHY

Primary Texts

*Colección de documentos y manuscritos compilados por Fernández de Navarrete.* Prol. J. G. Tato. 32 vols. Nedeln, Lichtenstein: Kraus-Thomson, 1971.
*Colección de los viajes y descubrimientos. . . .* Prol. J. N. González. 5 vols. Buenos Aires: Guaranía, 1945–46.
*Indice de la colección . . . que posee. . . .* Madrid: Instituto Histórico de Marina, 1946.
*Vida de Miguel de Cervantes Saavedra.* Madrid: Arlas, 1943.

English Translations

*The Life and Writings of Miguel de Cervantes.* London: Tegg, 1861.
*Narrative of the Voyage of the pinnace Santiago. . . .* In *Early Spanish Voyages to the Strait of Magellan.* Ed. C. R. Markham. London: Hakluyt, 1911. 102–7.

Criticism

*Primer centenario de don Martín Fernández de Navarrete.* N.p.: n.p., 1945.

Maureen Ihrie

**FERNÁNDEZ DE OVIEDO Y VALDÉS, Gonzalo** (1478, Madrid–1557, Santo Domingo), historian of the conquest and colonization of the New World. A descendant of Asturian nobility, Oviedo in his youth witnessed the fall of Granada to Christian forces and served as a page to Prince John, son of Ferdinand and Isabel. He lived in Italy for a time and briefly was secretary to Gonzalo de Córdoba, the Great Captain, before accompanying Pedrarias Dávila to the Indias in 1514. Though he returned to Spain on a number of occasions, he spent the majority of his life in the New World, where he held positions in the colonial administration, including governor of Cartagena and *alcaide* (mayor) of the fortress of Santo Domingo.

Oviedo's gifts as an historian were early recognized by Ferdinand, who in 1505 commissioned him to collect information on the kings of Spain. From 1532 Oviedo held the title Cronista de Indias (Chronicler of the Indies) and in this privileged position was able to solicit documents and reports from explorers and soldiers pertaining to geography, natural history and military encounters in the different regions.

Oviedo's most important work, the *Historia general y natural de las Indias* (1535; *The Natural History of the West Indies*, 1959), was not published in a complete edition until 1855. Gómara claims that this was due to the influential opposition in the court of Bartolomé de las *Casas. The first writer to compile a history of the Indies in the vernacular, Oviedo was a historian by avocation rather than by training. His history has virtually no organizational structure and often includes several versions of the same event, in the desire to leave out no detail which may be significant. What the book lacks in historical rigor due to this attitude of the author, however, it gains in spontaneity and richness. Oviedo's history is an immense repository of information regarding the flora, fauna, and human inhabitants of the New World, which reveals his acute powers of observation as an amateur naturalist and ethnologist.

In 1526, Oviedo published a summary of the first part of his history, which he presented to Charles V, the *Sumario de la natural historia de las Indias* (Summary of the Natural History of the Indies). A prolific author, he also wrote a romance of chivalry, *Don Claribalte* (1519; Sir Claribalte); a book of memoirs from his time of service to Prince John, the *Libro de la Cámara del Príncipe Don Juan* (1870; Book of the Chamber of Prince John); and a biographical encyclopedia on the nobility of Spain, the *Quinquagenas de la nobleza de España* (1880; Portraits of the Nobility of Spain). A number of his other writings remain unpublished at present, including his *Batallas y quinquagenas* (Battles and Portraits), *Catálogo real de Castilla* (Royal Catalog of Castile), *Respuesta a la epístola moral del Almirante de Castilla* (Response to the Moral Epistle of the Admiral of Castile), and the *Relación de lo sucedido en la prisión del Rey Francisco de Francia* (Narrative of Events in the Imprisonment of King Francis of France.)

BIBLIOGRAPHY

Primary Texts

*De la natural historia de las Indias*. Ed. Enrique Alvarez López. Madrid: Summa, 1942.
*Historia general y natural de las Indias*. Ed. Juan Pérez de Tudela Bueso. 5 vols. BAE 117–21.
*Libro de la cámara del príncipe Don Juan e officios de su casa e servicio ordinario. . . .* Madrid: Galiano, 1870.
*Libro del muy esforzado e invencible caballero Don Claribalte (1519)*. Facs. ed. Madrid: RAE, 1956.
*Las memorias de Gonzalo Fernández de Oviedo*. Ed. Juan Bautista Avalle-Arce. 2 vols. Chapel Hill: U of North Carolina P, 1974. An abridgement of the *Quinquagenas de la nobleza de España*.
*Sumario de la natural historia de las Indias*. Ed. Juan Bautista Avalle-Arce. Salamanca: Anaya, 1963.

English Translations

*The Conquest and Settlement of the Island of Borinquen or Puerto Rico, by Captain Gonzalo Fernández de Oviedo*. Tr., ed. Daymond Turner. Avon, CT: Limited Editions Book Club, 1975.
*The Discovery of the Amazon According to the Account of Friar Gaspar de Carvajal and Other Documents*. Tr. Bertram T. Lee. Ed. H. C. Heaton. 1st ed. 1934. Rpt. New York: AMS Press, 1970.
*The Expedition of Pánfilo de Narváez*. Tr. Gerald Theisen. Albuquerque: Theisen, 1974.
*The Journey of the Vaca Party: The Account of the Narváez Expedition, 1528–1536, as*

*Related by Gonzalo Fernández de Oviedo*. Tr. Basil C. Hedrick and Carroll L. Riley. Carbondale: U Museum, Southern Illinois U, 1974.
*The Natural History of the West Indies*. Tr., ed. Sterling A. Stoudemire. Chapel Hill: U of North Carolina P, 1959.

Criticism

Esteve Barba, Francisco. *Historiografía indiana*. Madrid: Gredos, 1964.
Iglesia, Ramón. *Cronistas e historiadores de la conquista de México: el ciclo de Hernán Cortés*. México: El Colegio de México, 1942.
O'Gorman, Edmundo. *Cuatro historiadores de Indias del siglo XVI*. México: Sepsetentas, 1972.
Pérez de Tudela, Juan. Introductory study to *Historia general y natural de las Indias*. BAE 117.
Salas, Alberto M. *Tres cronistas de Indias: Pedro Mártir de Anglería, Gonzalo Fernández de Oviedo, Fray Bartolomé de las Casas*. México: Fondo de Cultura Económica, 1959.

Robert E. Lewis

**FERNÁNDEZ DE RIBERA, Rodrigo** (1579, Seville–1631, Seville), minor baroque poet and social satirist. He first published volumes of religious poetry: *Las lágrimas de San Pedro* (1609; St. Peter's Tears), *El escuadrón humilde* (1616; The Meek Squadron), as well as satirical works: *Epitalamio en las bodas de una viejísima viuda . . . y un beodo soldadísimo de Flandes* (1625; Epithalamium for the Wedding of a Most Ancient Widow and a Drunken Flemish Soldier). More classical in tone are the moralizing *Lecciones naturales contra el común descuido de la vida* (1629; Sermons on the Widespread Negligence in Human Affairs), and the unpublished *La Asinaria* (The Ass's Story), a feeble imitation of Apuleius. He is best known for his exposure of the hypocrisies of contemporary society in a short prose anatomy, *Los anteojos de mejor vista* (1620/25; The Eyeglasses of Perfected Vision), which foreshadows novelistic techniques perfected by a contemporary, Luis *Vélez de Guevara in his longer prose work *El diablo cojuelo* (1641; The Hobbling Devil). From the tower of the cathedral of Seville, Master Disillusion observes his countrymen through lenses which expose lawyers, doctors and others in their true guise as vultures and birds of prey. Exaggerated puns and conceits in the vein of *Quevedo and Baltasar *Gracián predominate in this work and in the allegorical *El mesón del mundo* (1631; At the Inn of Life). Lope de *Vega made light of the metaphor of life as an inn as well as the literary credos which Fernández de Ribera formulates in the work.

BIBLIOGRAPHY

Primary Texts

*Los anteojos de mejor vista. El mesón del mundo*. Ed. Víctor Infantes de Miguel. Madrid: Legasa, 1979.
*El mesón del mundo*. Study, notes by Edward Nagy. New York: Las Americas, 1963.

Criticism
See Nagy ed.

Richard Glenn

**FERNÁNDEZ DE ROJAS, Juan** (1750?, Colmenar de Oreja, Madrid– 1819, Madrid), poet and satirist. Fernández was one of the five principal members of the so-called Salamancan School (*Escuela Salmantina) of poets, which flourished in that U city during the latter half of the eighteenth c. Although *Cadalso's arrival in Salamanca in 1773 helped to solidify the aesthetic direction of the group, their spiritual and intellectual leader was the Augustine Friar Diego *González. Fernández and González, joined by Father Andrés del Corral, *Meléndez Valdés and *Forner, developed their interest in *pastoral, idyllic poetry, and anacreontic verse, inspired by Cadalso as their model. Fernández adopted the poetic pseudonym Liseño. His poetry, though overshadowed by the more successful efforts of Meléndez and Forner, is a solid example of the Salamancan School's style. Perhaps his most important contribution to eighteenth-c. poetry was his work to collect and edit the poetry of the group's leader, Diego González, who had wished that his poems be destroyed after his death. Around 1780, Fernández was transferred to a convent closer to Madrid, where he turned his literary efforts to social satire. His satirical prose was far more successful as it seemed more suited to his temperament. He wrote many articles for the *Diario de Madrid* (Madrid Daily) under various pseudonyms: El Censor Mensual (The Monthly Censor), Un Filósofo Currutaco (A Philosopher-Dandy), or Don Extravagante (Sir Extravagant). He published several mordant essays, all under pseudonyms, which satirize the exaggerated social mannerisms of the day. Among the most popular were the *Crotalogía o arte de tocar las castañuelas* (1792; Crotology, or the Art of Playing the Castanets), with the pseudonym Licenciado Francisco Agustín Florencio; and its sequel, *Impugnación literaria de la Crotología* (1793; Literary Impugnation of the Crotology), under the name Juanito López Polinario. Other works in this vein are *El pájaro en la liga* (1798; The Bird in the Trap) by Cornelio Suárez de Medina; and *El currutaco por alambique* (1799; The Penurious Dandy) by Don Currutaco (Sir Dandy). One of the most famous satires of the period which was published under Fernández's pseudonym Licenciado Francisco Agustín Florencio, *Libro de moda o ensayo de la historia de los currutacos, pirracas y madamitas del nuevo cuño* (1795; Book of Manners, or Essay on the History of the Dandies, Fops and Mademoiselles of the New Mold), has now been attributed to Juan Antonio de *Iza Zamácola, better known by his own pseudonym Don Preciso (Mister Precise). Later in life Fernández collaborated on the monumental *España Sagrada* (Sacred Spain), begun in 1747 by Friar Enrique *Flórez.

BIBLIOGRAPHY

Criticism

Helman, Edith F. "Fray Juan Fernández de Rojas y Goya." In *Jovellanos y Goya*. Madrid: Taurus, 1970. 273–92.

Donald C. Buck

**FERNÁNDEZ FLÓREZ, Darío** (1909, Valladolid–1977, Madrid), Spanish novelist, playwright, literary historian. The son of a well-to-do family, Fernández Flórez studied law and philosophy at the U of Madrid, where he witnessed the downfall of the monarchy and dictatorship of Primo de Rivera, and the advent of the Second Republic (1931–36) without much interest in politics. Having lost a leg at the age of seventeen, he wrote his first novel, *Inquietud* (1931; Restlessness), before finishing his university studies, and the following year published *Maelstrom* (1932). After the war, *Mío Cid y Roldán* (1939; The Cid and Roland) marked his return to the novel. Most of the decade of the 1940s was spent as a critic for a variety of newspapers and magazines, although he did produce a pair of plays, *La dueña de las nubes* (Landlady of the Clouds) and *La vida ganada* (Earned Life) in 1944, as well as another novel, *Zarabanda*, of folkloric cut. One of the best-sellers of the post-war novel was his *Lola, espejo oscuro* (1950; Lola, Darkened Mirror), the "memoirs" of a prostitute, a neo-picaresque narrative which brought him considerable notoriety. Other novels include *Boda y jaleo de Titín Aracena* (1952; The Wedding and Dance of Titin Aracena); *Frontera* (1953; Border); *La hora azul* (1953; The Blue Hour); *Alta Costura* (1954; High Fashion Tailoring); *Memorias de un señorito* (1956; Memoirs of a Playboy); *Los tres maridos burlados* (1957; Three Deceived Husbands); *Señor Juez* (1958; His Honor, the Judge); *Yo estoy dentro* (1961; I'm Inside); and an attempt to capitalize again on the success of his previous best-seller, *Nuevos lances y picardías de Lola, espejo oscuro* (1971; New Adventures and Deceptions by Lola, Darkened Mirror). Among his works of literary history are *Drama y aventura de los españoles en Florida* (1963; Drama and Adventures of the Spaniards in Florida), *The Spanish Heritage in the United States* (1968), and *La novela actual española (De Zunzunegui a Gironella)* (1950; Today's Spanish Novel [From *Zunzunegui to *Gironella]).

BIBLIOGRAPHY

Primary Text

*El cauce logrado*. Madrid: Afrodisio Aguado, 1944.

*The Spanish Heritage in The United States*. 3rd ed. Madrid: Publicacions Españolas, 1971.

Criticism

Alborg, Juan Luis. *Hora actual de la novela española*, II. Madrid: Taurus, 1962. 289–309.

                                                                    Janet Pérez

**FERNÁNDEZ FLÓREZ, Wenceslao** (1885, La Coruña–1964, Madrid), novelist. Largely forgotten today, Fernández Flórez was the best-selling novelist of his generation. His renown is derived from an association with the daily *ABC* which lasted nearly half a century and produced small masterpieces of subtle humor. Alongside his newspaper columns Fernández Flórez wrote a long list of novels in the same ironic vein displayed in the former but endowed with a lyrical quality that is endearing both in character portrayal and in the depiction of the soft and green Galician landscape. Many of the earlier ones (1910–29) are fairly tinged with a slight and appealing eroticism. Of the twenty-four novels to come from his pen, those which to this day retain undeniable merit are *Volvoreta* (1917; Butterfly), *Ha entrado un ladrón* (1920; There Is a Burglar in the House), *La casa de la lluvia* (1925; Rainhouse), and *El bosque animado* (1944; The Living Forest).

BIBLIOGRAPHY

Criticism

Mainer, José Carlos. *Análisis de una insatisfacción: Las novelas de Wenceslao Fernández Flórez*. Madrid: Castalia, 1976.

Ricardo Landeira

**FERNÁNDEZ Granell.** *See* Granell, Eugenio Fernández

**FERNÁNDEZ GRILO, Antonio** (1845, Córdoba–1906, Madrid), poet, journalist. A court favorite of Isabella II and Alphonse XII, his more memorable poems include "El dos de mayo" (May Second), "La nochebuena" (Christmas Eve), "La chimenea campesina" (The Country Chimney), and "Siglo XX" (Twentieth Century). His formal expertise surpasses the quality of sentiments he expresses.

BIBLIOGRAPHY

Primary Texts

*Ideales. Poesías escogidas*. Paris: Sánchez, 1891.
*Poesías*. 2nd ed. Madrid: Fe, 1879.

**FERNÁNDEZ GUERRA Y ORBE, Aureliano** (1816, Granada–1891, Madrid), playwright, poet, historian and critic. He studied law and philosophy at the Colegio del Sacro Monte in Granada, and was elected to the Spanish Academy (*Academia Española) in 1856. Active in literary circles of the day, Fernández Guerra co-founded the magazine *La Alhambra* and used the pseudonym Pipi. He began his literary career with lyric poetry, but excelled as a playwright, especially with the plays *La peña de los enamorados* (1839; The Lovers' Rock); *La hija de Cervantes* (1840; Cervantes's Daughter), and *Alonso Cano o la Torre de Oro* (1854; Alonso Cano, or the Golden Tower). With *Tamayo y Baus he wrote *La ricahembra* (1854; The Noblewoman), a historical and romantic drama in verse. One of his major literary accomplishments was an edition of *Quevedo's works for the *Biblioteca de Autores Españoles (1852–59).

BIBLIOGRAPHY

Primary Texts

*Alonso Cano o la Torre de Oro*. Madrid: Repullés, 1854.
*La ricahembra*. Madrid: Abienzo, 1854.

Criticism

Cejador y Frauca, J. *Historia de la lengua y literatura castellana.* Madrid: Gredos, 1972.
  7: 298–99.
Fernández Cruz, J. *Don Juan Varela y Don Aureliano Fernández Guerra.* Cabra (Córdoba): n.p., 1969.

José Ortega

**FERNÁNDEZ MONTESINOS, José** (1897, Granada– ), professor, critic,
scholar. He has taught in several Spanish and foreign universities, and is an
outstanding critic and scholar of literary history in Spain. His studies on Lope
de *Vega are especially noteworthy; in addition to editing and providing fore-
words and notes to various plays by Lope, he has studied the *gracioso* in Lope,
prepared an edition with a study of Lope's lyric poetry, and examined other
aspects of his theater. *Estudios sobre Lope* (1951; Studies on Lope) is a compilation of all his research work on the "monstruo de la naturaleza." Also his
is an edition of Juan de *Valdés's *Diálogo de la lengua,* various articles on the
Valdés brothers, and many other subjects. His research extends also to the
nineteenth-c. novel with *Introducción a una historia de la novela en España,
en el siglo XIX* (1955; Introduction to the History of the Novel in Spain, in the
Nineteenth Century). *Costumbrismo* (*see* Romanticism) in *Fernán Cabellero and
*Pereda is the subject of other research, and he has dedicated three volumes to
*Pérez Galdós's writing. Montesinos also wrote *Ensayos y estudios de literatura
española* (1959; Essays and Studies on Spanish Literature).

BIBLIOGRAPHY

Primary Texts

*Ensayos y Estudios de literatura española.* Ed., prol., biblio., J. F. Silverman. Mexico:
  Andrea, 1959.
*Estudios sobre Lope de Vega.* 9th ed. Salamanca: Anaya, 1969.
*Introducción a una historia de la novela.* 3rd ed. Madrid: Castalia, 1973.

Criticism

Gallego Morell, A. "Los primeros artículos de José F. Montesinos (1915–1917)." *CH*
  302 (n.d.): 260–90.

Isabel McSpadden

**FERNÁNDEZ-SANTOS, Francisco** (1928, Los Cerralbos, Toledo– ), Spanish
essayist. With a law degree in hand, he began his literary career in Madrid as
the head editor of the newspaper, *Indice.* He moved to Paris in 1959, where he
writes stories and essays, such as *El hombre y su historia* (1961; Man and His
History). His recent works have tended to be political and philosophical in nature,
as indicated by the titles: *Historia y filosofía: ensayos de dialéctica* (1966; History
and Philosophy: Dialectical Essays), *España y el marxismo* (1966; Spain and
Marxism), and *Cuba: una revolución en marcha* (1967; Cuba: A Revolution in
Progress). *See also* Essay.

BIBLIOGRAPHY

Primary Texts

*Cuba: una revolución en marcha*. Paris: Ruedo Ibérico, 1967.
*España y el marxismo*. Buenos Aires: Theoría, 1966.
*Historia y filosofía: ensayos de dialéctica*. Madrid: Península, 1966.

Jana Sandarg

**FERNÁNDEZ SANTOS, Jesús** (1926, Madrid–1988, Madrid), Spanish novelist, short story writer, journalist, critic and cinematographer. Fernández Santos studied philosophy and letters at the U of Madrid, where he directed the university experimental theater. One of Spain's leading post-war narrators, Fernández Santos became known as a member of the "mid-century generation," the so-called writers of "social" literature, a neo-realist or neo-naturalist current which presented its criticism of the Franco regime beneath a facade of impersonal objectivism. *Los bravos* (1951; The Angry Ones), an experimental novel or collection of short stories and novelettes, marked the first literary success for Fernández Santos and constitutes a keystone in the emerging neo-realist social literature, a denunciation of inequality and economic injustice. The focus is on poverty in the backward rural province of León, together with the resignation and apathy fostered by misery. With a preponderance of dialogue, found in many of the works of the objectivists, its cinematic style both reflects the author's other pursuits and coincides with the best of the non-judgmental narratives of the generation. *En la hoguera* (1957; In the Bonfire), of similarly critical bent, won the Gabriel Miró prize. The best of Fernández Santos's early period of social realism is the collection *Cabeza rapada* (1958; Shaven Head), which won the coveted Critics' Prize. The formula is midway between the short story and novel, comprising independent tales related by a common setting, theme, and characters who reappear in various tales. The emphasis on social problems and objectivist narrative continues through *Laberintos* (1964; Labyrinths), a portrait of Holy Week in Segovia, in which lavish religious celebrations contrast with the moral impoverishment of characters, especially those representing the system.

Beginning with *El hombre de los santos* (1970; The Man of Saints), Fernández Santos enters a new phase characterized by greater preoccupation with style, language, technique and construction. The "man of saints" is an expert in restoration of paintings, especially those masterpieces located in abandoned or deteriorating village churches. Extensive descriptions of technical aspects of his trade are interspersed with the protagonist's thoughts and memories, his artistic sensibilities contrasting with his lack of sensitivity as a husband, father and human being. *El hombre de los santos* won a second Critics' Prize for the author, who the same year published two other works of religious environments: *Las catedrales* (1970; The Cathedrals), a collection of independent tales or episodes united by the cathedral motif, presents characters whose lives are conditioned by their dwelling in the shadow of the cathedral walls. *Libro de las memorias de las cosas* (1970; The Book of Memoirs of Things), awarded the Nadal Prize, treats the unusual topic of Protestantism in Spain, emphasizing the difficulties and suspicion faced by Protestants, together with their evangelizing zeal and human weaknesses. The technique of constant interplay between past and present appears in many works by this author. *Paraíso encerrado* (1973; Enclosed Paradise), another collection of stories linked by a common setting, presents various unrelated characters who all live around or frequent the Retiro Park in Madrid (to which the title alludes). Psychologically profound and rich in symbolism and fantasy, this is an experimental work in which the silences are as significant for the action as are the words.

*Europa y algo más* (1977; Europe and Something More) offers a varied group of brief narratives, travel memoirs and impressions, meditations on the past, literary criticism, commentary on famous personages, books, art, and even such topics as urban development. *La que no tiene nombre* (1977; She Who Has No Name) again creates a temporal counterpoint, contrasting present time with the Middle Ages via the old ballad of a father enamored of one of his daughters who, having no brothers, must go off to war. Sustained interplay between the story told in the ballad and echoes of Spain's Civil War in the world of the present is unusually effective. The suggestion of taboo in the implicitly incestuous passion reappears in another form in *Extramuros* (1978; Beyond the Walls), where the illicit passion was the homosexual love of one nun (the narrator) for another. Fernández Santos is a narrator of uniformly high levels of artistry who constantly strives to perfect his craft. Strangely enough, despite his unusual achievement in capturing the Critics' Prize on two separate occasions, Fernández Santos has not attracted the attention of Hispanists which one might expect.

## BIBLIOGRAPHY

### Primary Texts

*A orillas de una vieja dama*. Madrid: Alianza, 1979.
*Cuentos completos*. 2nd ed. Madrid: Alianza, 1985.
*El Griego*. Barcelona: Planeta, 1986.
*Los jinetes del alba*. Barcelona: Seix Barral, 1984.

### Criticism

Alborg, Concha. "El lenguaje teresiano en la obra de Jesús Fernández Santos." In *Santa Teresa y la literatura mística hispánica: Actas del I Congreso Internacional sobre Santa Teresa y la mística hispánica*. Ed. M. Criado de Val. Madrid: n.p., 1984. 793–99.
Domingo, José. "Narrativa española: Análisis de una sociedad conformista." *Insula* 274 (October 1969): 7.
Herzberger, David. *Jesús Fernández Santos*. TWAS 687, Boston: Twayne, 1983. In English.
Navajas, Gonzalo. "Confesión, sexualidad, discurso: *Extramuros* de Jesús Fernández Santos." *Hispania* 68.2 (May 1985): 242–51.
Núñez, Antonio. "Encuentro con Jesús Fernández Santos." *Insula* 275–76 (November-December 1969): 20.

Rodríguez Padrón, Jorge. "Jesús Fernández Santos y la novela española de hoy." *CH* 242 (February 1970): 437.

Schwartz, Ronald. *Spain's New Wave Novelists.* Metuchen, NJ: Scarecrow Press, 1978. 74–86.

Zamora, Carlos. "Tiempo e ideología en dos novelas sociales españolas." *REH* 19:2 (May 1985): 71–86.

Janet Pérez

**FERNÁNDEZ SHAW, Carlos** (1865, Cádiz–1911, Madrid), poet and librettist. His poetry is marked more for its brilliant versification than for its ideas, and at times is somewhat declamatory without much serious content. An exception to this generalization is his nature poetry in *Poesía de la sierra* (1908; Poetry of the Mountain Range). Other books of nature poetry include *Poesías del mar* (1909; Poems of the Sea) and *Poemas del pinar* (1912; Poems of the Pine Wood). He also composed librettos for various *zarzuelas such as *Margarita la Tornera* (1909; Margaret the Turner), which was set to music by Chapí. In collaboration with José *López Silva he wrote the librettos for *La chavala* (n.d.; the Girl), *El gatito negro* (1900; The Little Black Cat), *Los buenos mozos* (n.d.; The Good Boys), and the well-known *zarzuela La revoltosa* (1897; The Rebellious One).

BIBLIOGRAPHY

Primary Texts

*Margarita la tornera.* Madrid: Revista de Archivos, 1909.
*Poesías del mar.* Madrid: Sucesores de Hernando, 1909.
*Poemas del Pinar.* Madrid: Sucesores de Hernando, 1912.
*Poesía de la sierra.* Madrid: Sucesores de Hernando, 1908.

Phoebe Porter Medina

**FERNÁNDEZ Y GONZÁLEZ, Manuel** (1821, Seville–1888, Madrid), serial novelist. He wrote over two hundred novels, most of which were published in installments. His vast novelistic production brought him fame and fortune; he lived opulently and, during his last years, dictated his novels to his secretaries, Tomás *Luceño and *Blasco Ibáñez, in order to speed up his literary output. He squandered his money and died in poverty.

Fernández y González's novels may be divided into four periods. Between 1845 and 1857 he wrote historical adventures such as *Alla-Akbar (¡Dios es grande!)* (1849; Alla-Akbar [God is Great!]), which deals with the conquest of Granada and is based on fifteenth-c. legends and chronicles; *Obispo, casado y rey* (1850; *Hermesenda; or Bishop, Husband and King,* 1888); *El condestable don Alvaro de Luna* (1851); *Men Rodríguez de Sanabria* (1853), about the period of Peter the Cruel; *Los monfíes de las Alpujarras* (1856; The Highwaymen of the Alpujarras), and *El cocinero de Su Majestad* (1857; His Majesty's Cook), about the period of Philip III. Alborg considers the novels of this period to be among his best. After 1857 Fernández y González dedicated himself to rapid production of serial novels. He abandoned medieval themes and wrote about the

Spain of the Austrias. Novels of this period include *Los hermanos Plantagenet* (1858; The Plantagenet Brothers) and *El pastelero de Madrigal* (1862; The Confectioner of Madrigal). Works of this period are full of action, dialogue, love intrigues, duels, beautiful heroines and wicked traitors.

With the publication of *Los siete niños de Ecija* (The Seven Children of Ecija) in 1863, he initiated a third period of works which depict the Andalusian world with famous bandits, contrabandits, gypsies, gamblers and street urchins. Such novels include *Los grandes infames* (1865; The Great Villains), *Los piratas callejeros* (1866; The Street Pirates) and *Diego Corrientes* (1866–67), based on the famous bandit of the same name. The lively dialogue of such works captures the slang of underworld types and gypsies. After 1867 he wrote novels about the working class, portraying the nobility of the hard-working proletariat exploited by heartless patrons as in *La honra y el trabajo* (1867; Honor and Work). In general, in Fernández y González's novels action and dialogue dominate over description and psychological analysis. He also wrote short stories and several dramas, but is best known for historical novels of adventure. *See also* Romanticism.

BIBLIOGRAPHY

Primary Texts

*Allah-Akbar (¡Dios es Grande!): Leyenda de las tradiciones del sitio y conquista de Granada*. Barcelona: El Albir, 1982.

*El cocinero de Su Majestad*. Buenos Aires: Sopena, 1939.

*El condestable don Alvaro de Luna*. Madrid: Pueyo, 1930.

*Men Rodríguez de Sanabria*. Madrid: Tesoro, 1953.

*Los monfíes de las Alpujarras*. Madrid: Tesoro, 1951.

*El pastelero de Madrigal*. Madrid: Tesoro, 1952.

English Translation

*Hermesenda; Or Bishop, Husband and King*. Tr. J.R. and J.A.G. London: n.p., 1888.

Criticism

Alborg, Juan Luis. *Historia de la literatura española*. Vol. 4. *El romanticismo*. Madrid: Gredos, 1980. 693–94.

Contrait, René. "Pour une Bibliographie de Fernán González: A propos d'une oeuvre conyecturale introuvée de Blasco Ibáñez et d'une autre de Fernández y González redecouverte." *BH* 71 (1969): 591–603.

Ferreras, Juan Ignacio. *La novela por entregas: 1840–1900*. Madrid: Taurus, 1972. 137–44.

Hernández-Girbal, F. *Una vida pintoresca: Manuel Fernández y González*. Madrid: Biblioteca Atlántico, 1931.

Zavala, Iris M. *Ideología y política en la novela del siglo XIX*. Salamanca: Anaya, 1971. 154–62.

Phoebe Porter Medina

**FERNANDO DE ZÁRATE.** *See* Enríquez Gómez, Antonio

**FERNANFLOR,** pseud. of Isidoro Fernández Flores (1840, Madrid–1902, Madrid), journalist, politician, satirist. Fernanflor founded the literary supplement *Los lunes de el Imparcial,* and *El liberal.* His writing delineates and satirizes the foibles of the aristocracy and the bourgeoisie. His publications include *El teatro de Tamayo, estudio biográfico* (1882; Tamayo's Theater, a Biographical Study), *Cuentos* (1904, posthumously; Stories), *Cuentos rápidos* (1886; Quick Stories). His journal articles were collected posthumously under the title *Cartas a mi tío* (1903–4; Letters to My Uncle).

BIBLIOGRAPHY

Primary Texts

*Cartas a mi tío*. Madrid: Romero, 1903.
*Cuentos*. Prol. B. Pérez Galdós. Madrid: Romero, 1904.
*Cuentos rápidos*. Barcelona: Baseda, 1886.
*El teatro de Tamayo*. Madrid: Impresores y libreros, 1889.

**FERRÁN, Augusto** (1830, Madrid–1880, Madrid), poet. He studied in Germany in the late 1850s. After his return to Spain in 1859 (prompted by his mother's ill health), he founded a short-lived magazine, *El sábado* (Saturday), whose mission was the dissemination of the new German poetry in Spain. Around 1860, he also became an intimate friend of *Bécquer. Shortly thereafter, Ferrán's first volume of poetry, *La soledad; colección de cantares* (1861; Solitude, A Collection of Songs), appeared, with an enthusiastic critical prologue by Bécquer. Shortly after Bécquer's death in 1870, Ferrán's second and final book of poems, *La pereza; colección de cantares originales* (1871; Laziness; A Collection of Original Songs), was published. In 1872, Ferrán emigrated to Chile for five years, marrying there. He returned to Spain in 1877, but before his wife could join him, he was struck with bouts of insanity, was institutionalized, and died in 1880. Aside from the two volumes of poetry, he left various prose legends, translations of Heine's work, and imitations of Heine, published in various journals and magazines. *See also* Romanticism.

BIBLIOGRAPHY

Primary Text

*Obras completas*. Ed., intro. J. Pedro Diáz. Clásicos Castellanos 164. Madrid: Espasa-Calpe, 1969.

**FERRÁN, Jaime** (1928, Cervera, Lérida– ), doctor of law, poet, translator and scholar. His collection of poems *Desde esta orilla* (1954; From This Shore) was a runner-up for the Adonais Poetry Prize of the previous year. Ferrán won the City of Barcelona Prize for *Poemas del Viajero* (1954; Poems of the Traveler) and in 1957 published his collection *Descubrimiento de América* (Discovery of America). *Canciones para Dulcinea* (1959; Songs for Dulcinea) was followed by his *Libro de Ondina* (1964; Book of Ondine). Two collections appeared in 1966, *Tarde de circo* (Afternoon at the Circus) and *Historias de mariposas* (Stories of Butterflies). *Nuevas cantigas* (1967; New Canticles) is considered his most mature and best-executed collection.

Ferrán's translation of a collection of poetry by Yeats was published in Spain in 1957, and he has also written books in prose, including juvenile fiction. In the latter genre, there are several titles which follow the adventures of the young protagonist, Angel: *Angel en España* (1960; Angel in Spain), *Angel en Colombia* (1967; Angel in Colombia), winner of the Lazarillo Prize for Children's Fiction, and others. He is also known for his studies of the Catalan essayist and art critic, Eugenio d' *Ors.

BIBLIOGRAPHY

Primary Texts

*Angel en España*. Madrid: Doncel, 1965.
*Descubrimiento de América*. Madrid: Nacional, 1957.
*J. V. Foix*. Madrid: Júcar, 1987.
*Lope de Vega*. Madrid: Júcar, 1984.
*Nuevas cantigas*. Madrid: Rialp, 1966.

Janet Pérez

**FERRARI, Emilio** (1850, Valladolid–1907, Madrid), poet, dramatist. A member of the *Academia Española, he first received recognition with his philosophical poem *Pedro Abelarde* (1884). Greatly influenced by *Zorrilla and *Núñez de Arce, his best compositions include *Dos cetros y dos almas* (1884; Two Sceptors and Two Souls), *En el arroyo* (1885; In the Stream), *Las tierras llanas* (n.d; The Plains). His address upon induction into the academy discussed *modernism. Plays by Ferrari include *La justicia del acaso* (1881; The Justice of Chance) and *Quien a hierro mata* . . . (n.d.; He Who Kills without Mercy . . . ).

BIBLIOGRAPHY

Primary Text

*Obras completas*. 2 vols. Madrid: RABM, 1908–10.

**FERRATER MÓRA, Josep** (1912, Barcelona–1991, Barcelona), philosopher and essayist. A disciple of Ramon Xirau, he collected his early writings in *Cóctel de verdad* (1935; A True Cocktail). After 1939 he resided in France, Cuba, Chile and finally in the United States, where he became a professor of philosophy at Bryn Mawr College in Pennsylvania. He was first recognized in international circles with the publication in Buenos Aires of the *Diccionario de filosofía* (1941; Dictionary of Philosophy), which was greatly expanded in successive editions and translated into several languages. Through a number of pivotal books— *Unamuno: bosquejo de una filosofía* (1944; *Unamuno: A Philosophy of Tragedy*, 1962), *El hombre en la encrucijada* (1952; *Man at the Crossroads*, 1968), *El llibre del sentit* (1947; Book of Meaning), *Ortega y Gasset; An Outline of Philosophy* (1956), *Philosophy Today* (1960), *Els mots i els homes* (1970; Of Words and Man) and above all *El ser y la muerte* (1962; *Being and Death*, 1965) and *El ser y el sentido* (1967; The Human Being and Its Meaning)— Ferrater Móra developed the philosophical theory called ''integralist,'' which tries to bring together opposing systems of thought by believing that these are not absolute concepts but rather "limit-concepts." His philosophy searched for a bridge between the theories that are based on human existence and those based on nature. As a philosopher and essayist of Catalan themes he was equally outstanding. In *Formes de vida catalanes* (1944; Catalan Ways of Life) Ferrater Móra tried to reach the essences of Catalonia: continuity, "seny" (common sense), and irony. The essays "Reflexions sobre poesia" (Reflections on Poetry) in *Homenatge a Carles Riba* (1955; Homage to Carles *Riba) and "El ben cofat i l'altre" (1959; The Well Contended and the Other) in *L'obra de Josep Carner* (The Works of Josep *Carner) are definitive critical pieces. As a writer of prologues he also wrote with unusual finesse in Benguerel's *Obres completes* (1966; Complete Works). Other excellent works in Catalan include *De Joan Oliver a Pere Quart* (1967; From Joan Oliver to Pere *Quart) and, probably the best, *Una mica de tot* (1961; A Little Bit about Everything). Finally, his writing on pure literary theory should be noted: "Los escritores y sus mundos" (Writers and Their Worlds) in *El mundo del escritor* (1983; The World of the Writer).

BIBLIOGRAPHY

Primary Texts

*Les formes de la vida catalana i altres assaiys*. Barcelona: Edicions 62, 1980.
*El hombre en la encrucijada*. Buenos Aires: Sudamérica, 1952.
*Ortega y Gasset: An Outline of His Philosophy*. Rev. ed. New Haven: Yale UP, 1963.
*Unamuno. Bosquejo de una filosofía*. Buenos Aires: Losada, 1944.

English Translations

*Being and Death: An Outline of an Integrationist Philosophy*. Tr. J. Ferrater Móra. Berkeley: U of California P, 1965.
*Man at the Crossroads*. Tr. W. R. Trask. New York: Greenwood, 1968.
*Unamuno: A Philosophy of Tragedy*. Tr. P. Silver. Berkeley and Los Angeles: U of California P, 1962.

Criticism

Abellán, José Luis. *Filosofía española en América 1936–1960*. Madrid: Guadarrama, 1967.
————. *La cultura en España*. Madrid: Cuadernos para el diálogo, 1971.
Porcel, Baltasar. "Ferrater Móra o l'anàlisi viva." *Serra d'Or* (Jan. 1967): 25–33.
Roig, Montserrat. "Josep Ferrater i Móra, més enllà de la frontera." In *Retrats paral · lels, III*. Montserrat: l'Abadia de Montserrat, 1978. 101–128.

Joan Gilabert

**FERREIRA, José Gomes** (1900, Porto– ), Portuguese poet, short story writer and playwright. He has had an exceptionally long career spanning what has proved to be a period of immense political shift and literary development in Portugal. He was brought up in Lisbon and, while still a schoolboy, wrote and composed the music for a symphonic poem, "Idílio Rústico" (Rustic Idyll), which was given public performance when he was seventeen. At school he was a pupil of Leonardo *Coimbra, who influenced him toward the Saudosista poets and Raúl *Brandão in particular. At that time he wrote and put out two collections of poetry, *Lírio do Monte* (1918; Lily of the Mountain) and *Longe* (1921; Far Away). He went on to study law at the U of Lisbon, graduating in 1924 and entering the world of journalism, in which he has remained active until recently. Thereafter, insofar as literary writing is concerned, he was silent for a decade and in 1931 shifted to the *modernista* camp (\*Modernism) with the publication of his poem "Viver sempre tambem cansa" (Living tires you out too) in *Presença*. With this poem he rejected his literary past and espoused the outlook of the neo-realist movement and adopted the role of "poeta militante" (militant poet)—the overall title given to his poetry in the new collected edition.

In this second, activist part of his career, Ferreira has seen the role of the writer as that of a committed participant in the social reality of his time whose task it is to give expression to the common lot and to the aspirations of his fellow human beings. This attitude has inspired his collections of short stories and fictional and real diaries as their titles readily suggest, among them: *O Mundo Desabitado* (1960; The Deserted World); *O Irreal Cotidiano* (1971; Daily Unreality); *O Sabor das Trevas* (1976; The Taste of Shadows).

He has also been progressively moving away from the firm constraints of neo-realism and his purely militant stance to enhance universal themes and problems, with the result that his writing has developed a more reflective, oneiric and less time-bound quality.

Much of present interest in his work results from the fact that he has experienced the paradox of Portuguese existence during the preceding half c. and speaks to that condition.

BIBLIOGRAPHY

Primary Text

*Obras Completas de José Gomes Ferreira*. 14 vols. Lisbon: Moraes, 1984–86. (4 vols., poetry; 10 vols., fiction.)

Criticism

Moíses, C. F. *Poética da Rebeldia*. Lisbon: Moraes, 1983.
Torres, A. P. *Vida e Obra de José Gomes Ferreira*. Lisbon: Bertrand, 1975.

                                                    Peter Fothergill-Payne


**FERREIRA, Vergílio** (1916, Melo– ), Portuguese novelist and essayist. Abandoning his studies for the priesthood, he obtained a degree in classics, and became a secondary schoolteacher at about the same time he turned to writing fiction. His first novel, *O caminho fica longe* (1943; The Road Is Far Away), was followed by others in a similar social realist vein, including *Vagão "J"* (1946; Boxcar J). With *Mudança* (1949; Change) came a change in the writer's orientation from the realistic to the philosophical, experimental and existential, with echoes of Jean-Paul Sartre. Ferreira's profound moral, social and political concerns are closely linked to criticism of the Salazar dictatorship in Portugal (which ended in 1974). Among his better-known works are *Aparição* (1954; Apparition); *Estrela Polar* (1962; North Star); *Alegria breve* (1965; Short-lived Joy); and

*Nítido nulo* (1971; Neat Nullity). Ferreira emphasizes the unreal nature of reality through an emphasis on absurdity of situation and dialogue, or extensive use of internal monologue which intensifies alienation. Among this writer's significant literary and philosophical essays is his introduction to the Portuguese rendering (1962) of Sartre's *L'Existentialisme est un humanisme*.

BIBLIOGRAPHY

Primary Texts

*Aparição*. 10th ed. Lisbon: Arcádia, 1976.
*Conta-corrente*. 2 vols. Amadora: Bertrand, 1980—. Works.
*Nítido nulo*. 3rd ed. Amadora: Bertrand, 1983.
*Para sempre*. Lisbon: Bertrand, 1984.
*Vergílio Ferreira, um escritor apresenta-se*. Lisbon: Moeda, 1981.

Janet Pérez

**FERREIRO, Celso Emilio** (1914, Celanova–1979, Madrid), poet. It is no wonder that one of the best biographies on the social poet Curros Enríquez was written by Celso Emilio Ferreiro in 1954. Like his subject, Ferreiro eventually became the leading poet of his generation and the most visible apologist for the type of verse concerned with social and ideological themes. Aside from his essayistic production Ferreiro also wrote in Spanish several books of poetry, one of which, *Antipoemas* (1972; Anti-poems), forbidden publication by the censor in Spain, was awarded the Alamo prize in Venezuela. His greatest work is *Longa noite de pedra* (1962; Long Night of Stone). A dense work of ethical concerns, its poems soon became models for all of the young Galician poets still writing today. Ferreiro has grown to folk-hero proportions, his book achieving unheard-of sales in the realm of poetry. Following his six-year exile to Caracas, the volumes *Viaxe ao país dos ananos* (1968; Journey to the Land of Dwarfs), *Terra de ningures* (1969; No Man's Land) and *Poesía galega completa* (1975; Complete Galician Verse), among others, continue to enlarge his fame within Galicia and all of Spain as the most influential poet of his native region. *See also* Galician Literature.

BIBLIOGRAPHY

Primary Text

*Celso Emilio Ferreiro: antología*. Madrid: Júcar, 1982. Gallegan and Spanish.

Criticism

Barreiro Fernández, X. R., et al. *Los Gallegos*. Madrid: Istmo, 1976. 312–14.
Freixones, Victor F. *Unha ducía de galegos*. Vigo: Galaxia, 1976. 136–61.

Ricardo Landeira

**FERRER DEL RÍO, Antonio** (1814, Madrid–1872, El Molar), poet, editor, literary critic and history scholar. During his youth he composed mediocre poetry and tried his hand at writing plays; later he dedicated himself to historical and literary scholarship. As editor, he published critical studies in *El laberinto* and

*La Revista española de ambos mundos*. As a literary critic, he is remembered for an extensive prologue to *Ercilla's *Araucana*, edited by the Spanish Academy (*Academia Española) in 1846. The same year, his *Galería de la literatura española* (Gallery of Spanish Literature) appeared; in it he wrote about the principal literary figures of the period, more in an anecdotal than critical fashion, and included selections of their writing. *Espronceda; Ángel de Saavedra, the Duque de *Rivas; *Hartzenbusch; and Patricio de la *Escosura are among those treated. Ferrer's historical studies include *Examen histórico crítico del reinado de don Pedro de Castilla* (1851; A Critical Historical Examination of the Reign of Peter of Castile) and *Historia del reinado de Carlos III* (1856; History of the Reign of Charles III), a lengthy four-volume work composed at the request of Isabel II. He became a member of the Spanish Academy in 1853, delivering a lecture on sacred Spanish oratory.

BIBLIOGRAPHY

Primary Texts

*Examen histórico crítico del reinado de don Pedro de Castilla*. Madrid: Nacional, 1851.
*Galería de la literatura española*. Madrid: Mellado, 1846.
*Historia del reinado de Carlos III*. 4 vols. Madrid: Matute y Compagni, 1856.
*La oratoria sagrada española: Discursos leídos ante la Real Academia Española*. Madrid: Matute, 1853.

Phoebe Porter Medina

**FERRER-VIDAL, Jorge** (1926, Barcelona– ), lawyer, novelist. Typical works are *El trapecio de Dios* (1954; God's Trapeze) and *El carro de los caballos blancos* (1957; The Chariot with the White Horses), which was a finalist for the Ciudad de Barcelona Prize. His collection of short stories, *Sobre la piel del mundo* (1957; Over the Skin of the World), won the Leopoldo Alas Prize in 1956, *Sábado, esperanza* (Saturday, Hope) received the Café Gijón Prize in 1960, and *Caza mayor* (Big-Game Hunting) merited the Ciudad de Oviedo Prize in 1961.

BIBLIOGRAPHY

Primary Texts

*El carro de los caballos blancos*. Barcelona: Rumbos, 1957.
*Caza mayor*. Oviedo: Grandio, 1961.
*Sobre la piel del mundo*. Barcelona: Rocas, 1957.

Isabel McSpadden

**FERRES, Antonio** (1925, Madrid– ), novelist and short story writer. He worked as an assistant engineer until 1956 and taught literature between 1967 and 1977 at several institutions in the United States and the Universidad Veracruzana in Mexico. Ferres won the Sésamo Prize in 1956 for his short story "Cine de barrio" (Neighborhood Theater). *La piqueta* (1959; The Pickaxe), the best example of this author's social realism, is the dramatic story of a Spanish migrant family whose shanty is demolished to make way for urban renewal. In *Caminando por las Hurdes* (1960; Walking through the Hurdes), written in collaboration with Armando *López Salinas, the travelogue technique is used to expose the misery of the Hurdes area in the province of Cáceres, while the socio-economic conditions of southern Spain are the theme of *Tierra de olivos* (1964; Land of Olive Trees).

His trilogy "Las semillas" (Seeds) includes *Los vencidos* (1965; The Defeated), *Al regreso del Boiras* (1975; On Boiras' Return), and *Los años triunfales* (1978; The Triumphal Years). These novels describe the social and psychological effects of the Spanish Civil War and contain an underlying criticism of Franco's regime. This first stage of Ferres's social criticism is characterized by a direct, sober, and colloquial style. Some of his other works, such as *En el segundo hemisferio* (1970; In the Second Hemisphere) and *Ocho, siete, seis* (1972; Eight, Seven, Six), are rooted in the writer's American experience and feature characters who suffer from alienation, neurosis, and a lack of identity. Ferres's recent narratives include *El colibrí con su larga lengua* (1977; The Long Tongue of the Humming Bird); *El gran gozo* (1979; The Great Pleasure); and *La vorágine automática* (1982; Automatic Vortex). His recent novels utilize more sophisticated technical devices as well as more imaginative themes, but they lack the emotion and vigor that characterize his social realist novels of the 1950s and 1960s.

BIBLIOGRAPHY

Primary Texts

*En el segundo hemisferio*. Barcelona: Seix Barral, 1970.
*Ocho, siete, seis*. Barcelona: Barral, 1972.
*La piqueta*. Barcelona: Destino, 1959.
*Tierra de olivos*. Barcelona: Seix Barral, 1984.
*Los vencidos*. Paris: Librairie du Globe, 1965.

Criticism

Ortega, José. *Antonio Ferres y Martínez Menchén, novelistas de la soledad*. Caracas: Universidad A. Bello, 1973.
Schraibman, Joseph. "Antonio Ferres y el nuevo realismo crítico en la novela española." In *Homenaje a Sherman H. Eoff*. Ed. J. Schraibman. Madrid: Castalia, 1970. 247–59.

José Ortega

**FERRÚS, Pero** (fl. 1379, ?–?), poet. He, Pero *López de Ayala and *Macías, El Enamorado are the most famous poets in the *Cancionero de *Baena*. A resident of Alcalá, his best-known composition is a debate with López de Ayala on the relative merits of summer and winter.

**FIGUEIREDO, Antero de** (1866, Coimbra–1953, Foz do Douro), Portuguese novelist and poet. He began studying medicine but had to give up for reasons of ill health. Later he returned to the university to take a degree in literature.

He was a man of extreme sensitivity and was won over to the decadentist movement, being much influenced by Antero de Quental and António Nobre. Their influence can be noted in his prose poems *Tristia* (1893; Sadness) and *Além* (1895; Beyond) in the way in which he portrays his melancholy, pessimistic outlook on life. His *Doída de Amor* (1910; Driven Mad by Love) was also in all probability influenced by the love letters of Sister Mariana Alcoforado, the seventeenth-c. nun who fell in love with Noel Bouton, Marquis de Chamilly. He next wrote a series of historical novels taking well-known episodes of Portuguese history and devoting a great deal of attention to the accuracy of his characterizations and descriptions. These were *D. Pedro e D. Inês* (1913; The story of the love between Pedro the Cruel and Inês de Castro); *Leonor Teles* (1916) and *D. Sebastião* (1914)—Sebastian was a cult figure and the king of Portugal whose death in battle at Alcacer-Kebir opened the way for the accession of Philip II of Spain in 1580.

The latter part of his career was devoted to accounts of travel and writing of a proselytizing religious bent. Such are *Jornadas em Portugal* (1918; Portuguese Journeys); *Toledo* (1932; Toledo); *O Último Olhar de Jesus* (1928; The Last Glance of Jesus); and *Fátima* (1936; Fatima). His work was always greeted by critical acclaim, but public appreciation faded when his writing took a more overtly religious turn. *See also* Inés de Castro, Leyenda de.

BIBLIOGRAPHY

Primary Texts

*A Estrada Nova*. Lisbon: Rodrigues, 1900. Theater.
*Além*. Lisbon: Nacional, 1895. Poetry.
*Doída de Amor*. Lisbon: n.p., 1910.
*D. Sebastião*. Lisbon: Aillaud & Bertrand, 1924.
*Espanha*. Lisbon: Aillaud & Bertrand, 1924. Travel.
*Jornadas em Portugal*. Lisbon: Aillaud & Bertrand, 1918. Travel.
*Leonor Teles*. Lisbon: Aillaud & Bertrand, 1916.
*Tristia*. Lisbon: Nacional, 1893. Poetry.

Criticism

Domingos, Maurício. *A Mensagem Artística de Antero de Figueiredo*. Lisbon: Pro Domo, 1945.
Sérgio, António. *Ensaios*. Vol. 3. Lisbon: Sá da Costa, n.d.

Peter Fothergill-Payne

**FIGUEIREDO, Fidelino de Sousa** (1888, Lisbon–1967, Lisbon), Portuguese literary critic and historian, essayist and politician. Conservative and traditionalist, he brought together a group of like-minded historians to write for his *Revista de historia* (1912–28). A member of the cabinet of the dictator-general Sidonio Pais during 1918–19, Figueiredo went into exile following the assassination of Pais, living in Rio de Janeiro, Madrid (1927–30), and in Berkeley, California, as a visiting professor. He taught Portuguese literature at the U of Sao Paulo (1938–51), and, when in declining health, returned to Portugal. As a literary critic, Figueiredo followed the ideas of Benedetto Croce and Sainte-Beuve, employing psychological methodology for the authors analyzed in his critical studies. One result of his theories was *A história literaria como ciencia* (1912; Literary History as Science). He also authored a *História da literatura portuguesa* (1913–24; History of Portuguese Literature), and translated works of Miguel de *Unamuno and Marcelino *Menéndez Pelayo. Original essays on Spain include *As duas Espanhas* (1932; The Two Spains) and *Pirene* (1935). *Sob a cinza do tédio* (1925; Under the Ashes of Tedium) is a youthful autobiographical novel, but his more characteristic works are essays in the humanistic vein, including *Música e pensamento* (1954; Music and Thought), *Diálogo ao espelho* (1957; Dialogue before the Mirror), *Símbolos e mitos* (1964; Symbols and Myths), and *Paixão e ressurreição do homem* (1967; Agony and Resurrection of Man). He is remembered for his contributions to the theoretical base of Portuguese criticism.

BIBLIOGRAPHY

Primary Texts

*História d'um "vencido da vida."* Lisbon: Pereira, 1930.
*Literatura portuguesa.* Rio de Janeiro: Noite, 1941.
*Sob a cinza do tédio.* Coimbra: n.p., 1944.

**FIGUEIREDO, Tomaz de** (1902, Braga–1970, Lisbon), Portuguese novelist. He was raised in Arcos de Valdevez in a rural environment surrounded by northern traditionalism. He studied law in Coimbra and Lisbon, became a notary, and subsequently turned to fiction. A writer of satiric talent, he has been compared to the late nineteenth-c. romantic Camilo Castelo Branco, and he shows a romantic preference for the medieval past and for evil. *A toca do lobo* (1947; The Wolf's Lair) is somewhat in the vein of the Spanish *Generation of 1927, being an experimental novel with little or no action. It was followed in fairly rapid succession by *Nó Cego* (1950; Tangled Knot), *Fólego* (1950; Vitality), *Uma Noite na Toca do Lobo* (1952; A Night in the Wolf's Den); *Procissão dos defuntos* (1954; Procession of the Dead); *A Gata Borralheira* (1961; Cinderella); *D. Tanas de Barbatanas* (2 vols., 1962, 1964), *Vida de Cão* (1964; A Dog's Life, a story collection), the romance *Cycle Monólogo em Elsenor* (1965–69?; Monologue in Elsinore), and *Tiros de Espingarda* (1966; Shotgun Blasts, stories). Figueiredo has also published memoirs, *Conversa com o Silêncio* (1960; Conversing with Silence); poetry, *Guitarra* (1956; Guitar); and plays, *Teatro* (1965).

BIBLIOGRAPHY

Primary Texts

*A Gata Borralheira.* Lisbon: Guimarães, 1961.
*A má estrela.* Lisbon: Verbo, 1969.
*Monólogo em Elsenor.* Lisbon: Verbo, 1965–1969.
*Teatro.* Lisbon: Verbo, 1965.
*Tiros de Espingarda.* Lisbon: Verbo, 1966.

Criticism

Bento, José. "Tomaz de Figueiredo dez anos depois da sua morte." *Colóquio: Letras*
58(1980): 36–42.

Peter Fothergill-Payne


**FIGUERA AYMERICH, Ángela** (1902, Bilbao–1984, Madrid), Spanish poet,
teacher, and author of children's stories. After the death of her father while she
was a university student, a paternal uncle brought her to Madrid, where she
finished her degree in philosophy and letters, and in 1930 she moved her family
to Madrid, teaching as well as giving private classes to support her younger
siblings. In 1933 she was able to obtain the equivalent of a high-school teaching
certificate and was given a position in Huelva, moving there shortly after her
marriage to a cousin. After the death of her first child in 1935 (very significant
for her future poetry), they returned to Madrid but were separated by the Civil
War. In the early post-war years, Figuera devoted herself to her second son,
born in 1936, writing in her spare time. Her first book, *Mujer de barro* (1948;
Clay Woman), was followed quickly by *Soria pura* (1949; Pure Soria), the result
of a bicycle vacation through that province. The next several books by Figuera
belong to the social poetry movement, motivated above all by the protest against
injustice and lack of freedom under the Franco regime. *Vencida por el ángel*
(1950; Conquered by the Angel), *El grito inútil* (1952; The Useless Shout),
*Víspera de la vida* (1953; Vespers of Life) and *Los días duros* (1953; The Difficult
Days) are the result of her heightened consciousness of the persecutions and
inequities in Spanish society. Her next book, *Belleza cruel* (1958; Cruel Beauty),
was published in Mexico, no doubt as a result of problems with the Franco
*censorship. With a foreword by exiled poet León *Felipe, it received the Nueva
España poetry prize given by the Union of Spanish Intellectuals in Mexico. *Toco
la tierra* (1962; I Touch the Earth) was Figuera's last significant poetry collection;
after writing it, family circumstances took her away from Madrid and literary
contacts, and as a new grandmother, she began to write more for children,
although her stories were not collected and published in book form until several
years later. *Cuentos tontos para niños listos* (1979; Stupid Stories for Bright
Children) appeared just before the death of Figuera's sister and the onset of her
own final illness. *Canciones para todo el año* (1984; Songs for the Whole Year),
also for children, did not appear until after her death.

Figuera's major themes are human, rather than feminist; in her early poetry
she assumes the traditional woman's role, writing an intimate, subjective and
sometimes erotic poetry in traditional forms. Her reading of *Las cosas como son*
by Gabriel *Celaya in 1950 changed her aesthetics, so that she thereafter rejected
both aestheticism and injustice: some of her later works are in free verse, and
almost always she identifies with those who suffer in silence. In one famous
poem, she uses the theme of maternity to suggest an access to political power:
women should refuse to have sons if they must be sent to war. Her principal

difference with respect to other social poets is the absence of specific ideological tendencies and the use of a woman's perspective.

BIBLIOGRAPHY

Primary Texts

*Antología de Angela Figuera Aymerich.* Prol. Afredo Gracia Vicente. Monterrey: Sierra Madre, 1969.
*Antología total.* Prol. Julián Marcos. Madrid: Videosistemas, 1973.
*Obras completas.* Biographical note by Julio Figuera, intro. Roberta Quance. Madrid: Hiperion, 1986.
*Primera antología.* Caracas: n.p., 1961.

Criticism

Ley, Charles David. *Spanish Poetry since 1939.* Washington, DC: Catholic UP of America, 1962.
Mandlove, Nancy. "*Historia* and *Intra-historia*: Two Spanish Women Poets in Dialogue with History." *Third woman* 2.2 (1984):84–93.
Villa-Fernández, Pedro. "La denuncia social en *Belleza cruel* de Angela Figuera Aymerich." *REH* 7 (n.d):127–38.
Wright, Eleanor. *The Poetry of Protest under Franco.* London: Tamesis, 1986. 154–57.

Janet Pérez

**FIGUEROA, Francisco de** (1536, Alcalá de Henares–1617?, Alcalá de Henares), soldier, poet. He served in the military in both Italy and the Netherlands. Dubbed "el Divino" (Divine One) by peers, his poetry belongs to the *Escuela Salmantina tradition. Especially clear is the influence of *Garcilaso de la Vega. Figueroa wrote sonnets, *glosas*, songs, and elegies, both in Spanish and in Italian. On his deathbed, he ordered his works burned, but some were saved; an edition appeared in Lisbon in 1625, with a second edition the following year, adding a few additional poems. *See also* Renaissance; Siglo de Oro.

BIBLIOGRAPHY

Primary Texts

*Obras de Francisco de Figueroa.* New York: Hispanic Society, 1903. Facs. of 1626 Lisbon ed.
*Poesías.* Ed. A. González Palencia. Madrid: Sociedad de Bibliófilos, 1943.
"Poesías." Ed. R. Foulché-Delbosc. *RH* 25 (1911): 317–44.
*Poesías.* In BAE 42.

Criticism

Mele, E., and A. González Palencia. "Notas sobre Francisco de Figueroa." *RFE* 25 (1941): 333–82.

**FIGUEROA GAMBOA, Natalia** (1939, San Sebastián– ), Spanish essayist, journalist and poet. She knows several languages and has frequently worked for Spain's national radio and television networks, winning important prizes. *Decía el viento* (1957; As the Wind Was Saying) is a collection of prose poems in diary form, written under the aesthetic influence of Juan Ramón *Jiménez. *Palabras nuevas* (1960; New Words), also in lyric prose, expresses many of the day's social concerns for the poor, the underprivileged and the backwardness of Spain's provinces. *El caballo desvanecido* (1968; The Faint Horse) is her translation-adaptation of Françoise Sagan's play *Le Cheval évanoui*. *Tipos de ahora mismo* (1970; Characters of This Very Minute) portrays more than fifty contemporary types, from the movie star and tour guide to directors, writers, etc. *Los puntos sobre las íes* (1975; Dotting the I's) is a compilation of some three dozen short articles written in the five years previous, some of them written while the author was in Russia and in London. Subject matter is varied, as the writer moves from the sociological to the linguistic, the domestic to the cultural.

BIBLIOGRAPHY

Primary Texts

*El caballo desvanecido.* Madrid: Alfil, 1968.
*Decía el viento.* Madrid: Espejo, 1957.
*Palabras nuevas.* Madrid: Círculo, 1960.
*Los puntos sobre las íes.* Madrid: Prensa Española, 1975.

                                                                      Janet Pérez


**FIGUEROA Y CÓRDOBA, Diego and José** (1619?, Seville–?, Madrid and 1625?, Seville–?, Madrid), dramatists and poets. In discussions of minor Golden Age (*Siglo de Oro) dramatists, the brothers Diego and José Figueroa are invariably mentioned in the same breath—a link which has earned them the nickname of the *Quintero Brothers of the Golden Age. Scant information exists concerning their lives. Born in Seville, they studied in Salamanca and lived the remainder of their lives in Madrid, where their names figure among prizewinners of various poetry competitions held at court during the mid seventeenth-c. Diego and José were apparently from a distinguished family; the former was a Knight of the Order of Alcántara, the latter a Knight of the Order of Calatrava. They wrote plays both separately and in collaboration with each other; their works possess a fundamentally comic tone, with broad, unsophisticated humor and inevitable happy endings. At best the plays are lively, good-natured comedies of manners, although their predilection for reworking existing material lends a facile, unoriginal bent. Individually, each brother has noteworthy plays: Diego is remembered for *La hija del mesonero* (The Innkeeper's Daughter—a stage version of *Cervantes's novella, *La ilustre fregona*) and *La dama capitán* (The Lady Captain); José is known for *Muchos aciertos de un yerro* (Many Rights from One Wrong) and a half dozen *entremeses. Their team efforts, however, were even more successful, and include *A cada paso un peligro* (Danger at Every Step), *Leonicio y Montiano,* and *Rendirse a la obligación* (Yield to Duty). For publishing history regarding these plays, consult Cotarelo (Criticism).

BIBLIOGRAPHY

Primary Text

See BAE 47 for two plays.

Criticism

Cotarelo, E. *Los hermanos Figueroa y Córdoba.* Madrid: RABM, 1919.

**FLORANES, Rafael de** (1743, Liebana, Santander–1801, Madrid), historian. Floranes exercised considerable influence on the intellectual life of Valladolid through his *tertulia.* Although he received a degree in law from the university in his adopted city, Floranes dedicated his life to research on widely divergent aspects of Spanish history. His works seem to have been well known by his contemporaries, even though his mss. remained unpublished at his death. Many of these have been lost, such as his description of the *Cancionero* (Songbook) of Fernán Martínez de Burgos and his additions to Nicolás *Antonio's *Bibliotheca hispana nova* (New Hispanic Library). Among Floranes's works which have been published posthumously are *Memorias históricas de las Universidades de Castilla* (n.d.; Historical Accounts of Castilian Universities), *Las historias más principales de España puestas por orden cronológico* (1837; The Principal Histories of Spain Placed in Chronological Order), *Supresión del obispado de Alaba y sus derivaciones en la historia del País Vasco* (1919; The Suppression of the Bishopric of Alava and Its Derivations in the History of the Basque Country), and *Memorias y privilegios de la ciudad de Vitoria* (1922; Records and Franchises for the City of Vitoria). Floranes's extraordinary intellectual perception can be seen in his treatise on Spanish poetry.

BIBLIOGRAPHY

Primary Texts

"Dos opúsculos inéditos sobre los orígenes de la poesía castellana." Ed. M. Menéndez Pelayo. In *RH* 18 (1908): 295–431.

*La supresión del obispado de Alaba y sus derivaciones en la historia del País Vasco.* Madrid: Mateu, 1919.

Donald C. Buck

**FLORES, Antonio** (1818, Elche, Alicante–1865, Madrid), journalist, editor, prose writer. His funny, sometimes crude *costumbrismo* focused on lower-class Madrid society. *Ayer, hoy y mañana, o La fe, el vapor y la electricidad* (1853; Yesterday, Today and Tomorrow, or Faith, Steam and Electricity) contains sketches set in 1800, 1850, and the future 1899. *Doce españoles de brocha gorda* (1846; Twelve Spaniards by a Second-Rate Painter) is equally satirical, and was warmly praised by E. de *Ochoa. Marriage is the theme of *Historia del matrimonio* (1858; The History of Marriage). Flores translated E. Sue's *Les mystères de Paris* into Spanish, and wrote the novel *Fe, esperanza y caridad* (1857; Faith, Hope and Charity) in imitation of Sue. *See also* Romanticism.

BIBLIOGRAPHY

Primary Texts

*Ayer, hoy. . . .* 3 vols. Barcelona: Montaner y Simón, 1892–93.
*Doce españoles de brocha gorda.* 2nd ed. Madrid: Mellado, 1848.
*Fe, esperanza y caridad.* Madrid: Mellado, 1857.
*La historia del matrimonio.* Madrid: Berenguillo, 1876.
*La sociedad de 1850.* Madrid: Alianza, 1968.

Criticism

Benítez Claros, R. *Antonio Flores. Una visión costumbrista del siglo XIX.* Santiago de Compostela: U of Santiago de Compostela, 1955.

**FLORES, Juan de** (fl. 1500, Seville– ), author. Along with Diego de *San Pedro and Juan *Rodríguez de la Cámara (or del Padrón), Juan de Flores is the best known of the authors of the fifteenth-c. sentimental romances, whose theme was unhappy or tragic love affairs. Nothing is known about Flores, although recent investigations indicate that he probably wrote in the early 1480s. His two romances, *Grisel y Mirabella* and *Grimalte y Gradissa*, were published in Lérida in 1495; *Grisel y Mirabella* was enormously popular, inspiring translations and adaptations in French, English and Italian. *Grisel y Mirabella*, or more specifically, the Italian version of it, *Historia de Aurelio e Isabella*, served as a model for Lope de *Vega's play, *La ley ejecutada* (The Law Executed). *Grimalte y Gradissa*, a combination of prose and poetry—the latter composed by a collaborator, Alonso de *Córdoba—reworks Boccaccio's *Fiammetta*.

Another title long attributed to Flores, *Triumpho de Amor* (Triumph of Love), had been presumed to be a translation of Petrarch, if indeed it had ever existed, until 1977 when a ms. was found in Barcelona. Flores's long-lost work is a hybrid of sentimental romance and debate on the nature and rights of men and women. The story ends with a topsy-turvy world of courtly love in which the women do the pursuing and the men are the anguished waiting to be chosen. *See also* Italian Literary Influences.

BIBLIOGRAPHY

Primary Texts

*Grimalte y Gradissa.* Ed. Pamela Waley. London: Tamesis, 1971.
*The Novels of Juan de Flores and Their European Diffusion: A Study in Comparative Literature.* By Barbara Matulka. New York: Institute of French Studies, 1931; rpt. Geneva: Slatkine, 1974. Contains editions of the two romances.
*Triunfo de amor.* Ed. Antonio Gargano. Collana di Testi e Studi Ispanici, Sezione I, No. 2. Pisa: Giardini, 1981.

English Translation

*Histoire de . . . The Historie of. . . .* Antwerp: Juan Latio, 1556. (A four-language ed.: Italian, Spanish, French, English.) Copy in the Library of the U of Minnesota.

Criticism

Waley, Pamela. "Love and Honour in the *Novelas sentimentales* of Diego de San Pedro and Juan de Flores." *BHS* 43 (1966): 253–75.

Patricia Grieve

**FLORES ARENAS, Francisco** (1801, Cádiz–1877, Cádiz), soldier, physician, dramatist and poet. His theater follows the example of *Bretón de los Herreros. Typical dramatic works are *Coquetismo y presunción* (1831; Coquetry and Presumption), and *Hacer cuenta sin la huéspeda* (1849; To Count One's Chickens Before They Are Hatched).

BIBLIOGRAPHY

Primary Texts

*Coquetismo y presunción.* Madrid: García, 1831. Rpt. Louisville, KY: Falls City Microcards, 1960.

*Hacer cuenta sin la huéspeda.* 2nd ed. Madrid: Operarios, 1852.

*Obras escogidas.* Cádiz: Revista médica, 1878. Poetry.

**FLORES DE FILOSOFÍA** (thirteenth c.; Flowers of Philosophy), an early manifestation of Castilian didactic prose. The original work, *El libro de los çient capítulos* (Book of 100 Chapters), found at the Madrid National Library, has only 50 chapters. Prepared under *Alphonse X to educate kings and the public, *Flores* contains 38 chapters of moral, religious, and political maxims told by *Seneca and 36 other sages. Becoming very popular, it was later included in the *Libro del Caballero *Cifar* (The Knight Cifar). The oriental apologue, introduced earlier to Latin works by Petrus Alfonsí (*Alfonso, Pero), appears here in Castilian for the first time. Fifteenth-c. mss. of *Flores* are found at the Library of the Escorial and at the Madrid National Library.

BIBLIOGRAPHY

Primary Text

*Dos obras didácticas y dos leyendas.* Ed. Hermann Knust. Madrid: Sociedad de bibliófilos españoles, 1878.

Criticism

Zapata y Torres, Miguel. "Breves notas sobre el *Libro de los çient capítulos*, como base de las *Flores de filosofía.*" *Smith College Studies in Modern Languages* 10.2 (1929): 41–54.

Reginetta Haboucha

**FLORES Y BLANCAFLOR,** chivalric romance. Although the theme of Flores y Blancaflor is referred to in Castilian literary texts from the thirteenth c. on, no edition of this anonymous chivalric romance has been found dating prior to the mid-sixteenth c. The story, which reveals aspects of both the novel of adventure and the novel of chivalry, deals with Flores, a Moorish knight, and Blancaflor, a Christian damsel, who fall in love. With the help of Our Lord and with the intercession of Blancaflor, Flores converts to Christianity, and the two lovers marry. Subsequently they become king and queen of Spain and convert all inhabitants to their faith. Finally they even achieve the status of emperor and empress of Rome. The topic spread to many literatures, and there has been considerable debate as to whether the theme came to Spain from France or from Italy. The Spanish version appears to be more closely related to a Tuscan poem and to Boccaccio's *Filocolo. See also* Caballerías, Libros de.

BIBLIOGRAPHY

Criticism

Sharrer, H. L. "Eighteenth-Century Adaptations of the *Historia de Flores y Blancaflor* by Antonio da Silva, Mestre de Gramática." *HR* 2.1 (1984): 59–74.

Lucy Sponsler

**FLÓREZ, Alonso** (?, ?–1476, ?), probable author. He served the Duke of Alba, and thus may well have composed the anonymous *Crónica de los Reyes Católicos* (Chronicle of the Catholic Monarchs), which records events from the final years of Henry IV (1469) up through the war with Portugal (1476).

BIBLIOGRAPHY

Primary Text

*Crónica incompleta de los Reyes Católicos.* Ed., intro., J. Puyol y Alonso. Madrid: Archivos, 1934.

**FLÓREZ, Enrique** (1702, Villadiego, Burgos–1773, Alcalá?), theologian and historian. Enrique Flórez de Setién y Huidobro was born into a family with an illustrious heritage. He entered the Augustinian order in Salamanca at the age of seventeen and continued his religious studies in Valladolid, Ávila and at the university in Alcalá de Henares, where he was subsequently named professor of theology. Although he began his career as a preacher and theologian, Flórez was soon attracted to more scholarly research, particularly in ecclesiastical history. During his early investigations at the Royal Library in Madrid, he met and befriended many of the leading scholars of the day, among them *Mayáns y Siscar, *Sarmiento, *Nasarre and both Juan and Tomás de *Iriarte. As his interests in historical research grew, Flórez gave up his position at the university and pursued his research activities full-time, traveling all over Spain to gather a wealth of documentation and important mss. pertaining to both civil and ecclesiastic history. His first work, *Teología escolástica* (6 vols., 1732–38; Scholastic Theology), reflects his initial vocation as theologian. His second major work, *Clave historial con que se abre la puerta a la historia eclesiástica y política* (1743; Historical Key with Which To Open the Door to Ecclesiastic and Political History), demonstrates his eclectic interests as well as his surprisingly rigorous historiographic methodology, given his relatively narrow educational background. The book was extremely popular and was re-edited fifteen times during the second half of the c. Two other works of a purely historical nature are worthy of mention: *Medallas de las colonias, municipios y pueblos antiguos de España* (3 vols., 1757, 1758, 1773; Medals of the Colonies, Municipalities and Historic Towns of Spain), a work which earned him an international reputation and an honorary membership in the Royal Academy of Inscriptions and Fine Arts, in Paris, and *Memorias de las reinas católicas, historia genealógica de la Casa Real de Castilla y León* (2 vols., 1761; Accounts of the Catholic Queens: A Genealogical History of the Royal House of Castile and Leon), in which Flórez published a considerable amount of new historical data.

It was the monumental *España Sagrada* (1747- Sacred Spain) that became Flórez's life work and masterpiece. Flórez originally conceived the project as an ecclesiastic geography of Spain, but eventually expanded its scope under the persuasive urgings of Juan de Iriarte and others, who saw the value of such a comprehensive work. Similar ecclesiastic histories had been produced in Belgium, France, Italy and England, but Flórez's mammoth project was unique in two respects. First, *La España Sagrada* incorporated data on both ecclesiastic and secular history, including valuable information on each diocese's founding, its major religious figures, churches and convents, the region's political and economic development and its principal historical monuments. Second, Flórez reproduced a wealth of ms. material from medieval chronicles, such as the *Anales Toledanos* (Annals of Toledo) and the *Crónica compostelana* (Chronicle of Santiago de Compostela), as well as innumerable municipal acts and privileges. In addition, *La España Sagrada* was the first work of its kind to be written in the vernacular rather than in Latin. The first two volumes of *La España Sagrada* appeared in 1747, closely followed by volumes 3 and 4, in 1748 and 1749. These four serve as an introduction to the work as a whole: the first two outline Flórez's conception of history along geographic and chronological lines; the second two volumes provide the necessary background information on the origins of Christianity in Spain. The succeeding volumes present a diocese-by-diocese account of Spanish history. Flórez had completed twenty-seven volumes at his death in 1773 and left two more unedited. That task was undertaken by Father Manuel Risco, who was named by Charles III to succeed Flórez in the directorship of the project. Risco, along with fellow Augustinians Merino, *Fernández de Rojas and La Canal, produced another seventeen volumes, bringing the total to forty-six. When the monasteries were closed in 1836, the project was turned over to the Academy of History, which published another three volumes under the editorship of Sainz de la Baranda. Two more volumes were produced by Vincente de la Fuente, and another appeared in 1917, expanding the series to fifty-two volumes. The following year the indispensable Index to *La España Sagrada* was published by Ángel González Palencia. The latest additions to the series, two volumes edited by Father Angel Custodio Vega, appeared in 1961. Flórez's work, in spite of its now outdated and at times questionable methodology for historical investigation, continues to be an invaluable reference work for medieval Spanish history. *See also* Hagiography.

BIBLIOGRAPHY

Criticism

Martínez Cabello, G. *Biografía del R. P. Maestro Fray Enrique Flórez*. Burgos: Diputación Provincial, 1945.

Rodríguez-Moñino, Antonio. "Epistolario del P. Enrique Flórez con don Patricio Gutiérrez Bravo (1753–1773)." *BRAH* 134 (1954): 395–454.

Sagredo Fernández, F. "Enrique Flórez y su *España Sagrada*." *Homenaje a Millares Carlo*. Las Palmas, Grand Canary: Caja Insular de Ahorros de Gran Canaria, 1975. 1; 517–35.

Donald C. Buck

**FLORIT, Eugenio** (1903, Madrid– ), Spanish poet and critic. Florit spent most of his childhood in Port-Bou; the landscape of this region, the mountains, and especially the Mediterranean Sea, appear repeatedly in his poetry. As an adolescent, he moved with his family to Cuba, and continued to live there until 1940. Association with the *Revista de Avance* and some of the poets who collaborated on it, mainly Mariano Brull and Emilio Ballagas, was decisive in the direction that Florit's poetry took. After experimenting with futurism and other avant-garde poetic modes, he devoted himself to creation of a "pure poetry," a tendency which he would never completely abandon. Juan Ramón *Jiménez wrote the prologue to *Doble acento* (1937; Dual Accent), a cornerstone in Florit's production. In 1942, Florit began teaching at Columbia U, abandoning a consular career in 1945 to devote himself fully to teaching and writing. He taught at Barnard College, Middlebury College and Columbia U.

Florit's first book, *Treinta y dos poemas breves* (1927; Thirty-Two Brief Poems), is a synthesis of the literary trends of the day with reminiscences of European avant-garde and Latin American post-modernist poetry. *Trópico* (1930; Tropic) has as its main theme the Cuban landscape, the countryside and the sea. The form chosen by Florit is the *décima, consisting of ten octosyllabic verses, preferred by the Cuban peasant-composers, the "poetas guajiros." In his following book, *Doble acento*, there still appears an obvious distance between the island and the poet. Florit's vision of the Cuban landscape would change many years later, when, in his voluntary exile in New York, he looked back at the island as his second Paradise lost (the first being Port-Bou). But what is most relevant about *Doble acento* is the poetic expression of an inner being which reveals itself through long free verses. From here on, death and religiousness—sometimes bordering on a profound *mysticism— become recurrent themes in his poetry. Certain lines from "Viejos versos de hoy" (Old Verses of Today) can be compared to St. *Teresa de Ávila's best mystic poetry.

*Reino* (1938; Kingdom), *Cuatro poemas* (1940; Four Poems), *La estrella* (1947; The Star [a nativity play]), and *Poema mío* (1947; My Poem) follow. A very interesting section of the latter book is "Niño de ayer" (Child of Yore), in which the poet evokes his childhood in Port-Bou and those things that are deeply imprinted in his memory: the sea, first readings, the mountain, music, teachers, friends. In another section of the book there is a rather unique definition of poetry in his "Palabra poética" (Poetry), which summarizes Florit's aesthetic views. He claims in this text that truth, beauty and the exact word are essential in the poetic creative process, and tells us that his only passion is "a work of art."

Florit's *Conversación a mi padre* (1949; Conversation with My Father) is, without any doubt, one of the poet's masterpieces. Published as a single work, it was later included in *Asonante final y otros poemas* (1955; Final Assonant and Other Poems). "Conversación" is, as the title implies, a conversational text in which the poet talks to his dead father about the changes that have taken place in the world, of the terrifying and imminent atomic catastrophe. *Asonante final* concludes with a similar text which begins as a sort of soliloquy and then becomes a candid speech addressed to God.

*Hábitos de esperanza* (1965; Habits of Hope) contains poems written between 1936 and 1964. "Recuerdos" (Remembrances) was written in New York in 1946 and presents a view of Cuba and its landscape (its rivers) different from that of his early works. Florit is now like a native evoking the Cuban land which has become the object of his love.

Two important collections of Florit's poetry have been published in recent years: *Antología penúltima* (1970; Penultimate Anthology) and *Obras completas* (1982; Collected Works) in three volumes. In 1974 he published *De tiempo y agonía (Versos del hombre solo)* (About Time and Agony [Verses of a Lonely Man]); *Versos pequeños* (Short Poems) appeared in 1979, and in 1984, *Donde habita el recuerdo* (Where Recollections Dwell) was printed. Florit has also published books of literary criticism, edited anthologies of works by other authors and written a vast number of critical literary essays throughout his academic career.

BIBLIOGRAPHY

Primary Texts

*Antología penúltima*. Madrid: Plenitud, 1970.
*Asonante final y otros poemas*. Havana: Orígenes, 1955.
*Doble acento*. Havana: Ucar y García, 1937.
*Obras completas*. 3 vols. Lincoln: Society of Spanish and Spanish-American Studies of the U of Nebraska, 1982.
*Trópico*. Havana: Revista de Avance, 1930.

Criticism

Collins, María Castellanos. *Tierra, mar y cielo en la poesía de Eugenio Florit*. Miami: Universal, 1976.
Parajón, Mario. *Eugenio Florit y su poesía*. Madrid: Insula, 1977.
Pollin, Alice M. *Concordancias en la obra poética de Eugenio Florit*. New York: New York UP, 1967.
Saa, Orlando E. *La serenidad en las obras de Eugenio Florit*. Miami: Universal, 1973.

Servodidio, Mirella D'Ambrosio. *The Quest for Harmony: The Dialectics of Communication in the Poetry of Eugenio Florit*. Lincoln: Society of Spanish and Spanish-American Studies of the U of Nebraska, 1979.

                                                                    Luis F. González-Cruz

**FOIX, J. V.** (1893, Sarrià, Barcelona–1987, Barcelona), poet and essayist. The son of a sheep business family, he worked in his father's business for a short time. After a brief experience with law studies, he entered the world of literature. He was very active with several magazines in the teens and twenties: *La Revista*, *Trossos*, *Terramar*, *Amic de les Arts*; finally in 1935 he became chief editor of the important poetic review *Quaderns de poesia*. Though in the mainstream of Catalan surrealist poetry, Foix's poems are strongly influenced by the language of the most refined Catalan poets of the Middle Ages but also by the European tradition of elegant and obscure poetry: Licofró, *Góngora and Mallarmé, among others. Above all, Foix is a very personal and original poet who defies any specific classification. He has referred to himself, rather modestly, as an "investigador de la poesia" (a researcher of poetry) and insists that the poet is like a magician who has the power to crystallize his feelings in language. As a careful and steady architect Foix has been building his poetic tower bit by bit, always obsessed with two aims: achievement of unity (therefore his reference to "U") and of classical order. The few times that Foix reaches his avowed perfection he produces true masterpieces like the sonnets of *Sol i de Dol* (1947; Alone and in Mourning) or *Les irreals Omegues* (1948; The Unreal Omegas). Like that of his friend and long-time collaborator Joan Miró, Foix's art is difficult, intellectualized and refined, yet at the same time accessible through its many levels to a broad public; "És per la ment que se m'obra la natura" (It is through my mind that nature opens herself to me). Foix's poetry is mature and serene like the zenith of any great literature; together with *Carner, *Riba, *Salvat-Papasseit and *Espriu he forms the five most precious jewels of twentieth-c. Catalan verse. He is an equally important prose writer, ranging from politics in *Revolució Catalana* (1934; Catalan Revolution, with Jordi Carbonell), to architecture or urbanism in *Mots i maons o cascú el seu* (1971; Words and Bricks or To Each His Own), to personal memories in *Catalans de 1918* (1965; Catalans of 1918). An exquisite writer, his essays and articles in the newspaper *La Publicitat*, for instance, are not only an aesthetic delight but also an excellent survey of twentieth-c. European civilization. Foix's lack of passion or "pathos" is easily matched by the refinement of his poetic abilities and by his immense and solid culture. He is the only Catalan recipient of the Spanish National Prize of Literature (1984).

Other works of poetry are *On he deixat les claus* (1953; Where I Left the Keys), *Onze Nadals i un Cap d'Any* (1960; Eleven Christmases and One New Year's Eve), and *Desa aquests llibres al calaix d'abaix* (1964; Put Away These Books in the Lower Drawer), first published in the *Obres poètiques* (1964; Poetic Works). *See also* Catalan Literature.

BIBLIOGRAPHY

Primary Texts

*Antología lírica.* Ed., study, E. Badosa. Madrid: Rialp, 1963.
*Catalans de 1918.* Barcelona: Edicions 62, 1965.
*KRTU.* Ed. J. Vallcorba Plana. Barcelona: Crema, 1983.

English Translations

Tr. of seven poems, by M. L. Rosenthal. In *As for Love. Poems and Translations.* New York/Oxford: Oxford UP, 1987. 28–36.
*When I Sleep, Then I See Clearly.* Selected poems of J.V. Foix. Intro., tr. D.H. Rosenthal. NY: Persea, 1988.

Criticism

Ferrán, Jaime, *J.V. Foix.* Madrid: Júcar, 1987.
Gimferrer, Pere. *La poesia de J. V. Foix.* Barcelona: n.p., 1974.
Morris, C. B. *Surrealism and Spain. 1920–1936.* Cambridge: n.p., 1972.
*Serra d'Or.* Special issue dedicated to Foix. Jan. 1973.
Teixidor, Joan. "La poesia de J. V. Foix" In *Entre les lletres i les arts.* Barcelona: n.p., 1957.
Terry, Arthur. "Sobre les *Obres poètiques* de J. V. Foix." *Serra d'Or* (May 1968): 47–52.

Joan Gilabert

**FOLE SANCHEZ, Ánxel** (1903, Lugo–1986, Lugo), Galician short story writer. Fole began his career as a journalist, but also published creative efforts prior to the Civil War in such journals as *Yunque* (Anvil) and *Resol* (Glare). After the war, he spent long periods in the remote Incio Mountains, the site from which he derived many of the legendary or mythic-like materials for his short stories. In these works the geographical setting is fundamental to the overall effect. Fole was a member of the Royal Galician Academy.

BIBLIOGRAPHY

Primary Texts

*Cartafolio de Lugo.* Lugo: n.p., 1981. (journalism)
*Contos de lobos.* Vigo: n.p., 1985.
*Contos da neboa.* Vigo: n.p., 1973.
*¿E decímolo ou non o decimos?* Lugo: n.p., 1972.
*Historias que ninguén cre.* Vigo: n.p., 1981.
*Á lus do candil.* Vigo: n.p., 1952.
*Pauto do demo.* Buenos Aires: n.p., 1958. (theater)
*Santo oficio.* (unpublished poetry)
*Terra Brava.* Vigo: n.p., 1955.

Criticism

Rodríguez Fer, Claudio. *A Galicia misteriosa de Anxel Fole*. La Coruña: Sada, 1981.
————. Introduction to *Contos de lobos*. Vigo: n.p., 1985.

Luis Martul Tobío

**FONSECA, António José Branquinho da,** occasional pseudonym António
Madeira (1905, Mortágua–1974, Cascais), Portuguese novelist, short story writer
and playwright. He studied law at the U of Coimbra, coming into contact with
José *Régio and João Gaspar Simões, with whom he founded the review *Presença*. He fell out with them, and together with Miguel *Torga and Edmundo
de Bettencourt he broke with the Presença group. They felt that Régio and Simões
were no longer being true to the founding principles of the group. Their position
is set out in the June 6, 1930, issue of *Presença*.

His literary career opened with a collection of poetry, *Poemas* (1926; Poems),
which was followed by another, *Mar Coalhado* (1932; Curdled Sea). It is,
however, to his prose that he owes his position as one of the foremost writers
in the Portuguese Modernista (*Modernism) and Presença movements of this c.
This includes four collections of short stories: *Zonas* (1931; Zones), *Caminhos
Magnéticos* (1938; Magnetic Paths), *Rio Turvo* (1945; Murky River) and *Bandeira Preta* (1966; The Black Flag); two longer short stories or novellas: *O Barão*
(1943; The Baron) and *Mar Santo* (1952; The Holy Sea); and one full-length
novel, *Porta de Minerva* (1947; Minerva's Gate), set in Coimbra.

There are a number of short and largely static theatrical dialogues (one hesitates
to call them plays) which appeared in the periodical press and in volume form
under the titles *Posição de Guerra* (1929; State of War) and *Teatro* (1939;
Theater).

His writing is carefully structured, offering an interior realism which, when
confronted with currently accepted notions of reality, gives rise to a surreal
dreamlike ambient in which his protagonists find meaning and to which they
convert outsiders who, in other respects, inhabit the "real" world. *O Barão* is
probably the clearest example of this technique.

BIBLIOGRAPHY

Primary Texts

*Bandeira Preta*. 2nd ed. Lisbon: Portugália, 1966.
*O Barão*. 4th ed. Lisbon: Portugália, 1962.
*Caminhos Magnéticos*. 2nd ed. Lisbon: Guimarães, 1959.
*Mar Santo*. Lisbon: Europa-América, 1952.
*Porta de Minerva*. Lisbon: Ática, 1947.
*Posição de Guerra*. Coimbra: Presença, 1929.
*Rio Turvo*. 2nd ed. Lisbon: Inquérito, 1963.
*Zonas*. Coimbra: Universidade, 1931.

Criticism

Monteiro, Adolfo Casais. *O Romance (Teoria e Crítica)*. Rio de Janeiro: José Olympio, 1964. 373–79.

Régio, José. Postface to *O Barão*. Ed. cited above. 125–55.

Peter Fothergill-Payne

**FONSECA, Cristóbal de** (c. 1550, Santa Olla, Toledo–1621, Madrid), Augustinian writer and preacher. He wrote an important religious work called *Tratado del amor de Dios* (Salamanca, 1592; *Theion Enŏtikon: A Discourse of Holy Love*, 1652). He is classified as a mystical writer, yet this work is more a treatise on the numerous manifestations of love than on the attainment of divine union. The English subtitle claims that the treatise is a discourse through which the soul is assisted in reaching its goal of union with God. Perhaps it is because of this that Fonseca is considered by some to be a mystic. The religious tract not only discusses the nature and effects of the love that one has for God, but it treats every conceivable type of love: neighbor, women, family, honor, wisdom, country, etc. It contains ascetical elements in that it admonishes the reader to eschew the vanity of longing for the material objects of this world. Fonseca reflects on what Allison Peers calls "infused contemplation." Not only has this writer been immortalized by *Cervantes in the prologue to *Quijote* I, but he has been suggested as a possible author of Alonso F. de *Avellaneda's *Quijote*. *See also* Asceticism; Mysticism.

BIBLIOGRAPHY

Primary Texts

*Dictionario de vocablos castellanos, aplicados a la propiedad latina*. Salamanca: Juan y Andrés Renaut, 1587.

*Primera y segunda parte del Amor de Dios*. Madrid: Luis Sánchez, 1620.

Criticism

Allison Peers, Edgar. *Studies of the Spanish Mystics*. Vol. 2. London: Sheldon, 1930.

Cortés, Alonso. *El falso "Quijote" y Fray Cristóbal de Fonseca*. Valladolid: n.p., 1920.

Pérez Pastor, Cristóbal. "Documentos sobre Fr. Cristóbal de Fonseca." *Bibliografía madrileña*. Madrid: Tipografía de los Huérfanos, 1891–1907. 2 (1906): 7, 37–38; 3 (1907): 373.

Angelo DiSalvo

**FONSECA, Manuel da** (1911, Santiago do Cacem, Baixo Alentejo– ), Portuguese poet, novelist and short story writer. The backward rural area of his early upbringing appears frequently in the writer's first works of fiction, composed in neo-realist style, with emphasis upon the economic injustice and difficult living conditions. The hard life in rural areas and small towns is portrayed harshly, almost violently, suggesting the critic and reformer. However, Fonseca is less dualistic, less black-and-white in portrayals of the evil rich and suffering poor than many fellow writers of his day. His poetry also belongs to the social realist vein, evident in the unadorned, straightforward language of his early collections, *Rosa dos ventos* (1940; The Compass) and *Planicie* (1954; The Plains). His *Poemas completos* (1958; Complete Poems) were enlarged in 1963. *Aldeia Nova* (1941; New Village) is a collection of short stories. *Cerromaior* (1943; Big Hill) and *Seara de vento* (1958; Harvest of Wind) are social novels, while *O fogo e as cinzas* (1951; The Fire and the Ashes) is a story collection, as are *Un anjo no trapézio* (1968; Angel on the Trapeze) and *Tempo de solidão* (1969; Time of Solitude).

BIBLIOGRAPHY

Primary Texts

*Aldeia nova*. Lisbon: Livraria Portugália, 1942.
*Cerromaior*. Lisbon: Inquérito, 1943.
*El fuego y las cenizas*. Havana: Arte y literatura, 1978.
*O fogo e as cinzas*. Lisbon: Portugália, 1965.
*Poemas completos*. 2nd ed. Lisbon: Portugália, 1963.
*Seara de vento*. 4th ed. Lisbon: Forja, 1975.

                                                                                  Janet Pérez

**FOREST, Eva** (1928, Barcelona– ), Spanish psychiatrist, feminist, essayist and story writer. Forest studied medicine at the U of Madrid and subsequently worked with a famous psychiatrist, José López Ibor. She is married to the revolutionary dramatist Alfonso *Sastre. She is especially concerned with social justice, and her narratives range from the autobiographical to revolutionary agitation to philosophical preoccupations. One of her most widely distributed and translated works is *Diario y cartas desde la cárcel* (1978; *From a Spanish Prison*, New York, 1975; also *From a Spanish Jail*, trans. from the French, 1975). Accused of complicity in the terrorist assassination of one-time prime minister Admiral Carrero Blanco, she was imprisoned and tortured, an experience which also inspired another essay, *Operación Ogro: cómo y por qué ejecutamos a Carrero Blanco* (1974; *Operation Ogro: The Execution of Admiral Luis Carrero Blanco*, 1975). Perhaps the only woman writer with whom Forest can be compared is Lidia *Falcón; they share the prison experiences, involvement in seditious activities, and militant feminism. *Operación Ogro, diez años después: edición popular en la que se revela que "Julien Agirre" fue el seudónimo de Eva Forest* (1983; Ten Years after Operation Ogro: A Popular Edition in Which It Is Revealed That "Julien Agirre" was the Pseudonym of Eva Forest) re-creates the episode of the Basque commandos' "execution" of the prime minister. Authorship of the original pseudonymous work was one of the charges on which Forest was jailed from September 1974 to May 1977. Another testimonial of her prison experience appears in *Testimonios de lucha y resistencia: Yeserías 75–77* (1977; Testimonies of Struggle and Resistance: Yeserías [Women's Prison] 1975–77). A major theme is the use of torture by the modern state, supported by statements from Forest and thirty other women prisoners. *Onintze en el país de la democracia* (1985; Onintze in the Land of Democracy) is Forest's first strictly "literary" (i.e., not autobiographical) narrative, but it is closely related to her prison experience and the theme of torture: Onintze, a

Basque schoolteacher arrested (apparently by mistake) on suspicion of political subversion is tortured, and subsequently decides to throw in her lot with the revolutionaries. The message is that police brutality and institutionalized methods of
interrogation do not change from the dictatorial regime to the putative democracy.
Although the writing is at times almost embarrassingly bad, the force of what Forest
has to say is overwhelming.

BIBLIOGRAPHY

Primary Texts

*Diario y cartas*. Paris: Femmes, 1975. French and Spanish.
*Operación Ogro.: Cómo y por qué ejecutamosa Carrero Blanco*. Hendaye: Mugalde,
    1974.
*Testimonios de lucha y resistencia*. Hendaye: Mugalde, 1977.

English Translations

*From a Spanish Prison*. Berkeley: Moon Books; New York: Random House, 1975.
*Operation Ogro*. Tr., intro. B. Probst Solomon. New York: Quadrangle/New York Times
    Book Co., 1975.

Janet Pérez

**FÓRMICA, Mercedes** (1918, Cádiz– ), Spanish lawyer, novelist, journalist
and feminist. Fórmica's membership in the Falange from her university days
before the Civil War undoubtedly facilitated her post-war career, but even so,
her problems with the male-dominated legal profession led to a journalistic
campaign favoring legal and professional equality for women. She first began
to publish fiction under the pseudonym Elena Puerto, with *Monte de Sancha*
(1950; Sancha's Mount) being the first to appear under her own name. This
novel also holds the distinction of being the first in post-war Spain to view the
Civil War in the light of the motives of both sides, rather than being simply
another instance of self-glorification by the victors. *La ciudad perdida* (1951;
The Lost City) is set in Madrid at the time of writing, and portrays the ill-fated
foray of a clandestine anti-Franco guerrilla fighter who kidnaps a wealthy young
widow and holds her hostage. *A instancia de parte* (1954; On Behalf of the
Third Party), Fórmica's most pro-feminist piece of fiction, indicts the *machista*
society which not only exploits women but victimizes men as well. *La hija de
don Juan de Austria. Ana de Jesús en el proceso al pastelero de Madrigal* (1973;
Don Juan de Austria's Daughter, Ana de Jesus, at the Trial of the Pastry-Cook
of Madrigal) is a historical investigation of a legendary topic which was awarded
the Fastenrath Prize by the *Academia Española. Visto y vivido, 1931–1937;
Pequeña historia de ayer* (1982; Seen and Lived, 1931–1937; Short History of
Yesterday) and *Escucho el silencio. Pequeña historia de ayer II* (1984; I Listen
to the Silence) are memoirs, the first recalling Fórmica's childhood and university
days, the second depicting the war and immediate post-war years, with emphasis
upon the intellectual toll exacted by the conflict.

BIBLIOGRAPHY

Primary Texts

*A instancia de parte.* Madrid: Cid, 1954.
*La ciudad perdida.* Barcelona: Caralt, 1951.
*La hija de don Juan de Austria.* Madrid: RO, 1973.
*Monte de Sancha.* Barcelona: Caralt, 1950.
*Visto y vivido, 1931–1937.* 2nd ed. Barcelona: Planeta, 1983.

Janet Pérez

**FORNER, Juan Pablo** (1765, Mérida–1797, Madrid), polemicist and critic. Of Valencian heritage, Forner's father Francisco was a respected physician, with an interest in antiquities, manifested in his book on ancient artifacts of Mérida. His mother, María Manuela Piquer, was the niece of Andrés Piquer, a famous professor of medicine. Forner studied for a time in Salamanca, where he joined with other student-poets, under the guidance of Father Diego *González, in forming the so-called Salamancan School of poetry (*see* Escuela Salmantina). He continued his studies in civil and canon law in Toledo, though it is uncertain whether or not Forner received his degree. He arrived in Madrid in 1778 and worked for a time as the assistant to a lawyer, Miguel Sarralde. In 1790 he was appointed prosecuting attorney for the Royal Court in Seville. While in this post he married María del Carmen Carraso. He returned to Madrid in 1796 as the attorney general for the Council of Castile, and although elected as the president of the Academy of Law, Forner died before he could assume the post.

Whereas Forner's personal and professional life remains relatively obscure, he was constantly in the public eye among Spanish writers and intellectuals as one of the most provocative and controversial polemicists of his time. The general characteristic of his works is one of aggressive arrogance, and his satiric diatribes against many of the front-ranking writers of the period frequently stoop to vituperous personal slander. Writing under various pseudonyms—Pablo Ignocausto, Pablo Segarra, Tomé Cecial and Lorenzo Garrote principal among them—Forner attacked such diverse figures as *García de la Huerta, Cándido María *Trigueros, Tomás Antonio *Sánchez, *Vargas Ponce, and above all, Tomás de *Iriarte. For Forner, Iriarte represented the worst excesses of French neo-classic influence in Spanish literature. Beginning with his *Cotejo de las églogas que ha premiado la Real Academia de la Lengua* (1778; Comparison of the Prize-Winning Eclogues Cited by the Royal Academy of the Language), wherein Forner questioned the literary merits of Iriarte's second-place entry, the two engaged in a vociferous "war of words," in which each attack was met with an even stronger counter-attack. Iriarte's mildly satirical *Fábulas literarias* (1782; Literary Fables) was ridiculed by Forner in his acerbic parody, *El asno erudito* (1782; The Erudite Ass). In this work, as in his *Sátira contra los abusos introducidos en la poesía* (1782; Satire against the Abuses Introduced into Spanish Poetry), which won first prize in a competition sponsored by the Royal Academy, Forner championed the cause of Golden Age literature as the true expression of the Spanish literary tradition, in contrast to the antiseptic and prosaic style of the French-influenced neo-classicists. The Forner-Iriarte polemic reached the boiling point with Forner's satirical allegory, *Los gramáticos. Historia chinesca* (1782; The Grammarians. A Chinese Story), a thinly veiled personal attack against Iriarte. Forner portrays Iriarte as a hack writer of little literary merit who has become the puppet-like spokesman for foreign tastes. Forner furthered his defense of traditional Spanish culture with his *Oración apologética por la España y su mérito literario* (1786; Apologetical Oratory for Spain and Her Literary Merits), commissioned by Floridablanca as an official response to Nicolas Masson de Morvilliers's article on Spain in the *Encyclopédie Méthodique* (1782; Systematic Encyclopedia). Morvilliers posed the question ''What is owed to Spain?'' as a means to encapsule his general dismissal of Spanish culture as inconsequential in the development of European culture. Forner's revisionist approach, particularly his condemnatory attitude toward eighteenth-c. advancements in the natural and social sciences and his aggressive oratorical style, severely detracted from his main argument and caused further controversy among his contemporaries. Two other works demonstrate Forner's talents and limitations as an independent thinker. In his *Discurso sobre el modo de escribir y mejorar la historia de España* (1787; Discourse on the Way to Write and Better the History of Spain), Forner formulates the basis for a true theory of history founded on an aesthetic relationship between history and poetry, in the exposition of a reality—be it one historically or poetically ''true.'' Forner's most important work is generally considered to be the *Exequias de la lengua castellana, Sátira Menipea* (1789; Obsequies for the Spanish Language, a Menipean Satire). An allegory on the order of *Saavedra Fajardo's *República literaria* (1655; Literary Republic) or Leandro Fernández de *Moratín's *La derrota de los pedantes* (1789; The Rout of the Pedants), in it the author recounts a trip to Parnassus, during which he meets most of the important figures of Spain's literary history. Through his allegorical frame Forner surveys the evolution of Spanish literature, counterposing its past glories with its present nadir, especially in what Forner sees as the corruption of the Spanish language. The *Exequias* demonstrates his brilliant stylistic ability, which bears comparison to *Quevedo's satiric prose. Above all, Forner asserts himself as one of the most original and perceptive literary critics of his age.

## BIBLIOGRAPHY

### Primary Texts

*El asno erudito*. Ed. Manuel Muñoz Cortés. Valencia: Castalia, 1948.

*Cotejo de las églogas que ha premiado la Real Academia de la lengua*. Ed. Fernando Lázaro Carreter. Salamanca: Universidad de Salamanca, 1951.

*Discurso sobre el modo de escribir y mejorar la historia de España* and *Informe fiscal sobre los estudios universitarios*. Ed. François López. Madrid: Labor, 1973.

*Exequias de la lengua castellana*. Ed. Pedro Saínz Rodríguez. Clásicos Castellanos 66. Madrid: Espasa-Calpe, 1956.

*Los gramáticos. Historia chinesca*. Ed. John H. R. Polt. Madrid: Castalia, 1970.

*Oración apologética por la España y su mérito literario.* Ed. Alonso Zamora Vicente. Badajoz: Centro de Estudios Extremeños, 1945.

Criticism

Alvarez Gómez, Jesús. *Juan Pablo Forner (1756–1797), preceptista y filósofo de la historia.* Madrid: Nacional, 1971.

Fernández González, Jesús. "Presencia agustiniana en Juan Pablo Forner: Un modelo de antropología agustiniana en la filosofía española del siglo XVIII." *Augustinus* 26 (1981): 139–68.

Jiménez, José. "Repercusiones del pleito con Iriarte en la obra literaria de Forner." *Thesaurus* 24 (1969): 228–77.

Laughrin, Sister Mary Fidelia. *Juan Pablo Forner as a Critic.* Washington, DC: Catholic UP, 1943.

López, François. *Juan Pablo Forner et la crise de la conscience espagnole au XVIIIᵉ siècle.* Bordeaux: Institut d'Etudes Iberiques, 1976.

Maravall, José A. "El sentimiento de nación en el siglo XVIII: la obra de Forner." *La Torre* 57 (1967): 25–56.

Smith, Gilbert. *Juan Pablo Forner.* TWAS 377. Boston: Twayne, 1976.

Donald C. Buck

**FOULCHÉ-DELBOSC, Raimond** (1864, Toulouse–1929, Paris), French Hispanist and professor of Spanish at the U of Paris whose particular interest lay in the period spanning the fifteenth and seventeenth centuries. He was founder and editor of the *Revue Hispanique* (1894–1933). More than 200 of his articles and 171 texts, many published for the first time, appeared in his journal. Eminent European and American scholars wrote for it from the outset, making consultation of its 80 volumes indispensable to the student of Spanish literature. The *Revue Hispanique* also published the *Biblioteca hispánica*, of which Foulché was editor. The 22-volume series is comprised of critical editions including several prepared by Foulché, notably, *Cárcel de amor*, *Vida de *Lazarillo de Tormes*, the *Comedia de Calisto y Melibea* (*Celestina) and the *Obras poéticas de D. Luis de *Góngora*. He prepared an edition of the *Cancionero castellano del siglo XV* (Castilian Songbooks of the fifteenth c.) for the NBAE between 1912 and 1915. His *Essai sur les origines du romancero. Prélude* (Essay on the Origins of the Ballads), which appeared in 1912, was an attempt to distinguish truth from error in "recent affirmations of *Menéndez Pidal." In collaboration with Barrau-Dihigo, he compiled a bibliography for Hispanists, the *Manuel de l'hispanisant* (1920–25 Manual for the Hispanist).

BIBLIOGRAPHY

Primary Texts

*Cancionero castellano del siglo XV.* 2 vols. Madrid: Bailly-Bailliére, 1912–15.

*Essai sur les origines du romancero. Prélude.* Paris: Paillart, 1912.

*Manuel de l'hispanisant.* With L. Barrau-Dihigo. 2 vols. New York: Hispanic Society of America, 1920–25.

D. J. O'Connor

**FOX MORCILLO, Sebastián** (1526?, Seville–1560, at sea), philosopher. He studied at the U of Alcalá and the U of Louvain. His principal work is the *De naturae philosophia* (1551; On the Nature of Philosophy), which attempts to reconcile the thought of Plato and Aristotle. Eloy Bullón finds skeptical leanings which prefigure Descartes in Fox Morcillo's *Filosofía natural* (1553; Natural Philosophy). Philip II summoned Fox Morcillo to Spain to supervise education of his son Prince Charles. En route, his vessel was shipwrecked, and he perished at sea. *See also* Aristotelianism; Platonism.

BIBLIOGRAPHY

Primary Text

*De naturae philosophia.* Louvain: Colonaeum, 1554.

Criticism

Bullón, E. *De los orígenes de la filosofía moderna.* Salamanca: Calatrava, 1905.

González de la Calle, P. U. *Sebastián Fox Morcillo. Estudio histórico-crítico de sus doctrinas.* Madrid: Asilo de huérfanos, 1903.

Solana, M. *Historia de la filosofía española.* Madrid: Real Academia, 1941. 1: 573–617.

Maureen Ihrie

**FOXÁ, Agustín de** (Conde de Foxá) (1903, Madrid–1959, Madrid), Spanish diplomat, poet, novelist and dramatist. *El almendro y la espada* (1940; The Almond Tree and The Sword), a collection of poems, ranges from the intimate to the warlike, as suggested by the title. *Madrid de Corte a Cheka* (1938; Madrid from Royal Court to Kangaroo Court) is the best known of his novels. Written from a pro-Nationalist or pro-Franco stance, it portrays Madrid from the final days of the monarchy through the period of Republican government to the days of terror and social revolution which preceded and followed the outbreak of hostilities. Among his works for the theater are *Cui-Pin-Sing*, 1940, and *Baile en Capitanía*, 1944 (A Dance at General Headquarters).

BIBLIOGRAPHY

Primary Texts

*El almendro y la espada.* San Sebastián: López, 1940.

*Cui-Pin-Sing.* Madrid: Escelicer, 1940.

*Baile en capitanía.* Madrid: Aldus, 1944.

*Madrid de Corte a Cheka.* Madrid: Jerarquía, 1938.

Janet Pérez

**FOZ, Braulio** (1791, Fórnoles, Teruel–1865, Borja), classics professor, poet, novelist, historian. A student at the U of Huesca when Napoleon invaded Spain (1808), Foz joined the military. In 1810 he was taken prisoner and brought to

France, where he resumed studies and also taught. By 1814, he had returned to Spain, teaching at the U of Huesca, and then the U of Zaragoza. Author of various humanistic works and a poet of minor merit, he published anonymously the novel *Vida de Pedro Saputo* (Life of Pedro Saputo) in 1844. Its protagonist is a proverbial comic figure of oral history; he appeared, for example, in Melchor de *Santa Cruz's *Primera parte de la floresta española* of 1574. In Foz's work, Saputo becomes the voice of common sense and practical reason, as he moves through the rural society of Aragon. The work combines elements of *costumbrismo*, realism, intercalated stories, satire, etc., in an original, entertaining fashion. *See also* Romanticism.

BIBLIOGRAPHY

Primary Text

*Vida de Pedro Saputo*. Ed., intro. F. and D. Ynduráin. Madrid: Cátedra, 1986.

Criticism

See Ynduráin, above.

**FRAILE, Medardo** (1925, Madrid– ), dramatist, professor, and writer. A member of La Carátula, he has published two one-act plays: *Los de enfrente* (The Ones across the Street) and *Capítulo de sucesos* (Events Chapter). In 1954 he won the Sésamo Prize and also published his first book of stories, *Cuentos con algún amor* (1954; Stories with Some Love). Subsequently he published *Año de cuentos* (Year of Stories) and *A la luz cambian las cosas* (1959; Things Look Different in the Light), and most recently, *Autobiografía* (1986; Autobiography). He also published an edition of one-act plays in Spanish. He currently lives in Glasgow.

BIBLIOGRAPHY

Primary Texts

*A la luz cambian las cosas*. Torrelavega: Cantalapiedra, 1959.
*Autobiografía*. Madrid: Iberoamericana, 1986.
*Cuentos con algún amor*. Madrid: Bachende, 1954.
*Teatro español en un acto. (1940–1952)*. Madrid: Cátedra, 1989.

Isabel McSpadden

**FRANCÉS, José** (1883, Madrid–1965, Madrid), novelist, art critic, playwright. He collaborated on several magazines and journals, using the pen name Silvio Lago. His first public success was the novel *Alma viajera* (1907; Traveling Soul); typical works which followed include *La muerte, danza* (1916; Death, a Dance), which takes as its main theme the war of 1914; *El misterio del Kursal* (1916; The Mystery of the Kursaal), *La raíz flotante* (1922; The Floating Root), *Rostros en la niebla* (1927; Faces in the Fog), *Miedo* (1907; Fear), and *Cuentos del mar y de la tierra* (1920; Stories of Land and Sea). Francés contributed to art criticism with *El año artístico* (The Year in Art), published from 1916 to 1928; *Pintura* *española* (Spanish Painting); and *La caricatura española contemporánea* (1915; Contemporary Caricature in Spain).

BIBLIOGRAPHY

Primary Texts

*El alma viajera.* 5th ed. Madrid: Mundo latino, 1923.
*La caricatura.* Madrid: CIAP, 1930.
*El misterio del Kursal.* 2nd ed. Madrid: Mundo latino, 1923.
*La muerte, danza.* Madrid: Sociedad española de librería, 1916.

Isabel McSpadden

**FRANCO, Dolores** (1912, Madrid–1977, Madrid), essayist. Pursuing a degree in philology at the U of Madrid, and deeply interested in philosophy, she was a student of *Ortega y Gasset, Américo *Castro, Montesinos, Dámaso *Alonso and Salinas. She taught literature and philosophy at several Spanish institutions as well as for American universities having programs in Spain. Her critically selected anthology *La preocupación de España en su literatura* (1944; The Concern for Spain as Expressed in Its Literature) had a revised second edition entitled *España como preocupación* (1960; Spain as a Concern). A third edition of 1980 bears the same title and includes an epilogue by the author's husband of more than three decades, the Spanish philosopher Julián *Marías. *See also* Essay; Preocupación de España.

BIBLIOGRAPHY

Primary Texts

*La preocupación de España en su literatura.* Madrid: Adán, 1944.
*España como preocupación.* 3rd ed. Barcelona: Vergara, 1980.

Elisa Fernández Cambria

**FRANCOS RODRÍGUEZ, José** (1862, Madrid–1931, Madrid), politician, physician, prose writer. He wrote for several newspapers, directed some of them, and ultimately became president of the Press Association (Asociación de la Prensa). In the world of politics, he began as a councilman, and progressed to governor, minister, state adviser, and senator. His literary production is varied, and includes: scientific studies like *Cuestiones antropológicas* (Anthropology Questions); dramatic works like *Los plebeyos* (The Plebeians) and *El señorito* (The Master)—which was written as a *zarzuela; critical and historical studies such as *El teatro en España* (1908; Theater in Spain), *La vida de Canalejas* (1918; The Life of Canalejas), *En tiempos de Alfonso XII* (1917; In Alphonse XII's Time), *Días de la regencia* (The Regency Period), and *Cuando el rey era niño* (1925; When the King Was a Boy); and political and social studies such as *El escepticismo político de la clase obrera* (Political Skepticism among the Working Class) and *La mujer y la política española* (1920; Women and Spanish Politics).

BIBLIOGRAPHY

Primary Texts

*Cuando el rey era niño.* Madrid: Morales, 1895.
*Cuestiones antropológicas.* Madrid: Ruiz, 1895.
*La mujer y la política española.* Madrid: Pueyo, 1920.
*La vida de Canalejas.* Madrid: RABM, 1918.

Isabel McSpadden

**FRASSO, Antonio Lo.** *See* Lofraso, Antonio de

**FREIRE, Natércia** (1920, Lisbon?– ), Portuguese poet. Her works include *Poemas* (1957) and *Poesias Escolhidas* (1959; Selected Poems), composed with a certain delicacy but within a fairly conventional vein.

BIBLIOGRAPHY

Primary Texts

*Poesias Escolhidas.* Lisbon: Portugália, 1959.
*Poemas.* Lisbon: Bertrand, 1957.

**FRERE, John Hookham** (1769, London–1846, London), British diplomat. Frere represented Great Britain as ambassador to the court in Madrid on two different occasions: 1802 to 1804, and 1808 to 1809. His association with Spanish culture led him to translate into English various fragments of the *Cantar de mio Cid* as well as excerpts from *Berceo and two *romances* (*see* romancero). In addition, Frere was well known for his witty translations of Aristophanes and as a competent scholar of Theocritus. Frere's most important contribution to Hispanic letters was his influence on the Duque de *Rivas, whom he met and befriended during the latter's stay in Malta (1825–30). Frere is credited with being a major factor in Rivas's developing interest in the romantic movement. *See also* Romanticism.

Donald C. Buck

**FRÍAS, DUQUE DE,** Bernardino Fernández de Velasco y Pimentel (1783, Madrid–1851, Madrid), soldier, politician and poet. As a true patriot he took part in the Madrid uprising of May 2, 1808, against French occupation forces. He served as a soldier until 1811. Due to his liberal orientation, he was watched with suspicion by Ferdinand VII and had to emigrate to France in 1828. After the death of the monarch in 1833, he defended the constitutional system in his writings. During the first years of the reign of Isabel II he served as Spanish ambassador in Paris.

A lyrical poet of classical tendencies, he imitated both *Quintana and Juan Nicasio *Gallego. He wrote sonnets such as ''Al Duque de Wellington'' (To the Duke of Wellington) and ''A la muerte de la reina Doña María Isabel de Braganza'' (On the Death of the Queen Doña Maria Isabel de Braganza). ''Llanto del proscrito'' (The Outlaw's Lament) was written during his period of exile, and "Llanto conyugal" (Conjugal Lament), an elegy much admired by Juan *Valera, was written upon the death of his wife in 1828. His best known compositions are "La muerte de Felipe II" (The Death of Philip II) and the ode "A las nobles artes" (To the Noble Arts). He was a member of the Royal Spanish Academy (*Academia Española), which published his *Obras poéticas* (1857; Poetic Works) with a prologue by the Duque de *Rivas.

BIBLIOGRAPHY

Primary Text

*Obras poéticas*. Madrid: Rivadeneyra, 1857.

Criticism

Valera, Juan. "Bernardino Fernández de Velasco, Duque de Frías." *Obras completas.* Vol. 2, *Crítica literaria*. Madrid: Aguilar, 1949. 1290–93.

Phoebe Porter Medina

**FUENTES BLANCO, María de los Reyes** (1927, Seville– ), Spanish poet. Long active in municipal cultural life and social work, Fuentes Blanco has received several prizes for her lyrics. Collections of poetry include *Sonetos del corazón adelante* (1960; Sonnets Forward from the Heart); *Elegías del Uad-el-Kebir* (1961; Elegies of the Guadalquivir); *Romances de la miel en los labios* (1962; Ballads of the Honey on my Lips); *Elegías Tartessias* (1964; Elegies from Tartessos); *Oración de la verdad* (1965; Prayer of the Truth); *Concierto para la Sierra de Ronda* (1966; Concert for the Sierra of Ronda); *Acrópolis del testimonio* (1966; The Acropolis of Testimony); *Pozo de Jacob* (1967; Jacob's Well) and *Aire de amor* (1977; Air of Love).

BIBLIOGRAPHY

Primary Texts

*Acrópolis del testimonio*. Seville: Ayuntamiento, 1966.
*Aire de amor*. Madrid: Rialp, 1977.
*Concierto para la Sierra de Ronda*. Málaga: Guadalhorce, 1966.
*Romances de la miel en los labios*. Seville: Muestra, 1962.

Janet Pérez

*FUERO JUZGO* (Legal Code of the Judges), law code. This code of laws evolved during the reigns of four Visigothic monarchs before reaching its final form under King Recesvinto. It was approved by the Council of Toledo in 653–54 and was called *Liber* or *Forum Judiciorum* (Book of the Judges), since it was compiled for the use of judicial tribunals. Soon after Cordova was reconquered from the Moslems, Ferdinand III the Saint gave the city this legal code in 1241. It was then translated from the Latin into Castilian with the title *Fuero Juzgo* and is thus one of the oldest examples extant of a written, Romance language. Considered the masterpiece of Visigothic law, it is a blend of Roman and Germanic law with the Roman elements particularly noticeable in the areas of inheritance and contracts. The code has a well-developed sense of justice, but with some harshness and cruelty in law enforcement and treatment of slaves as well as inequities in the treatment of women as compared to men. On the other hand, there is much enlightenment, particularly in the treatment of the poor.

BIBLIOGRAPHY

Primary Texts

*Códigos españoles*. Madrid: Administración, 1890.
*Fuero juzgo o libro de los jueces: cotejado con los más antiguos y preciosos códices*. Ed. RAE. Valladolid: Gráficas Andrés Martín, 1980.

Criticism

Van Kleffens, E. N. *Hispanic Law until the End of the Middle Ages*. Edinburgh: Edinburgh UP, 1968.

Lucy Sponsler

**FUERTES, Gloria** (1918, Madrid– ), poet and children's author. Born and educated in Madrid, where she has lived and worked all of her life, Fuertes published her first book of poems, *Isla ignorada* (Ignored Island), in 1950. The high popularity of her work is consistent with her view of poetry, which she sees as a means of direct communication with humanity, particularly the worker and the poor, and as a way of improving the world, both socially and existentially.

In addition to her own autobiography, which she says provides a basis for identification with her reader and listener, Fuertes's themes include the street life and popular wisdom of Madrid, the protest of war and injustice, lost love, alienation and solitude. Her direct and colloquial language, narrative brevity and ironic humor, as well as her public recitations in the provincial villages of Spain, reflect her belief that "useful expression" is more important than "useless perfection" and her aversion to pure poetry and obscure forms. Her *Obras incompletas* (1975; Incomplete Works) includes poems from many of her earlier books; other important collections include the *Antología poética* (1970; Poetic Anthology) and *Historia de Gloria* (1980; History of Gloria). She has also written poems, stories and plays for children and has produced children's records and worked for Spanish radio and television. She has taught literature in Spain and the United States.

BIBLIOGRAPHY

Primary Texts

*Aconsejo beber hilo*. Madrid: Arquero, 1954.
*Antología poética (1950–1969)*. Barcelona: Plaza y Janés, 1975.
*Historia de Gloria*. Ed. Pablo González Rodas. Madrid: Ediciones Cátedra, 1980.
*Obras incompletas*. Autobiographical intro. by Gloria Fuertes. Madrid: Ediciones Cátedra, 1975.
*Sola en la sala*. Zaragoza: Javalambre, 1973.

English Translations

Selected poems. In *Twentieth-Century Women's Poetry in Translation*. Ed. Joanna Bankier et al. New York: W. W. Norton, 1976. 16–17.

Selected poems. In *A Book of Women Poets from Antiquity to Now*. Ed. Alik; Barnstone and Willis Barnstone. New York: Schocken Books, 1981.

Criticism

Bellver, Catherine G. "Gloria Fuertes, Poet of Social Consciousness." *Letras Femeninas* 4.1 (n.d.): 29–38.

Cano, José Luis. "La poesía de Gloria Fuertes." *Insula* 269 (1969): 8–9.

González Muela, Joaquín. "Gloria Fuertes, 'Poeta de guardia.' " *La nueva poesía española*. Madrid: Alcalá, 1973. 13–29.

Yndurain, Francisco. *Prólogo a Antología poética*. Barcelona: Plaza y Janés, 1970.

Victoria Wolff Unruh

**FUSTER, Jaume** (1945, Barcelona– ), novelist, screenwriter, translator and journalist. He has collaborated in a number of newspapers and journals, among them *El País*, *Avui*, *Serra d'Or* and *Canigó*. His interest in the dramatic arts manifests itself in his work in theater criticism and in film, both for television and the movie industry. Film has also had a direct influence on his novels, for example, *Tarda, sessió contínua, 3:45* (1976; Matinee, Continuous Showings, 3:45), which evokes *Red Harvest* by Dashiell Hammett and includes characters such as Humphrey Bogart, Lauren Bacall, John Wayne and Ronald Reagan, and which has been made into a film. Fuster has excelled in detective novels; other successful books in this genre are *De mica en mica s'omple la pica* (1972; Drop by Drop the Bucket is Filled) and *La corona valenciana* (1982; The Valencian Crown), both featuring the same character, Enric Vidal. In *Les cartes d'Hèrcules Poirot* (1983; The Letters of Hercules Poirot), originally a screenplay which aired in 1979, Poirot explores an assassination in a small town in the Pyrenees which he went to visit and explains his findings through a series of letters to Agatha Christie. *Les claus de vidre* (1984; The Glass Keys), a collection of short stories, also invokes the work of Dashiell Hammett. Fuster creates a new fantasy world in *L'Illa de les Tres Taronges* (1983; The Island of the Three Orange Trees) and *L'Anell de Ferro* (1985; The Iron Ring). The first takes place in an imaginary land resembling Majorca, and the second in a place invoking La Cerdanya; both are populated by historico-literary-mythical creatures and events. Fuster uses a wealth of previous literature in these works; from the old chroniclers such as Ramon *Muntaner and the novels *Tirant lo Blanc* and *Don Quixote* to *La Chanson de Roland* and the Greek epics with perhaps even a touch of *One Hundred Years of Solitude*. These narratives are delightful in their originality, evoking myths from our collective conscious and unconscious to arrive at a kind of proto-history, with good humor and a subtle irony that often leaves us smiling ruefully as we recognize the truths of his vision. A third volume in this series is promised for the future, making it a trilogy some might compare with *The Lord of the Rings*, except that each of these novels is independent, forming a saga rather than an interdependent series of adventures leading to a single goal. His most recent work, *La matèria dels somnis* (1986; Such Stuff as Dreams Are Made On), is a collection of fantastic narrations with a title that refers to the novel and film *The Maltese Falcon* as well as the quotation from Shakespeare's *The Tempest*. Fuster has translated various novels from French and Italian into Catalan. He is married to the Majorcan writer Maria Antònia *Oliver; they live in Barcelona and sometimes La Cerdanya.

BIBLIOGRAPHY

Primary Texts

*Abans del foc*. Barcelona: Edicions 62, 1971.
*L'Anell de Ferro*. Barcelona: Planeta, 1985.
*Breu història del teatre català*. Barcelona: Bruguera, 1967.
*Les cartes d'Hèrcules Poirot*. Barcelona: Edicions 62, 1983.
*Les claus de vidre*. Barcelona: Edicions 62, La Magrana, 1984.
*El Congrés de Cultura Catalana. Què és i què ha estat*. Barcelona: Laia, 1978.
*La corona valenciana*. Valencia: 3 & 4, 1982.
*De mica en mica s'omple la pica*. Barcelona: Edicions 62, 1972.
*L'Illa de les Tres Taronges*. Barcelona: Planeta, 1983.
*La matèria dels somnis*. Barcelona: La Magrana, 1986.
*Tarda, sessió contínua, 3:45*. Barcelona: Edicions 62, 1976.

Kathleen McNerney

# G

GABRIEL Y GALÁN, José María (1870, Frades de la Sierra–1904, Guijo de Granadilla), poet. José María Gabriel y Galán was born into a family of prosperous peasant farmers. He studied in Salamanca and Madrid and became a rural teacher. In 1877 he moved to Guijelo, where he combined teaching and farming with literary creation. The inspiration for his work came from his intimate involvement with his beloved rural life.

Gabriel y Galán achieved fame during his lifetime and was admired by other writers, among them the Condesa de *Pardo Bazán. His first popular recognition came in 1901 when he won the Flor Natural in the *Juegos Florales with his poem "El ama" (The Lady of The House), which initiates his book *Castellanas* (1901; Castilian Poems). The poem owes its inspiration to his mother. Following that, other books were published: *Extremeñas* (1902; Extremaduran Poems) and *Campesinas* (1904; Peasants), and after his death two new posthumous books: *Nuevas Castellanas* (1905; New Castilian Poems) and *Religiosas* (1906; Religious Poems).

Gabriel y Galán's poetry reflects the life and character of the rural peasants. His main themes are the family, affection, love of nature and the life of the common people. He found inspiration in the small things of daily life, but his very conservative position and Franciscan world view ignored the misery and unfairness of the rural sector. He was an apostle of conformity, exalting its spiritual values. The characters of his poetry—peasants, shepherds, day laborers, goatherders—are used to incarnate the purest and most idealized forms of religious life.

Forgotten today, the poetry of Gabriel y Galán was very popular during the first half of the twentieth c. Scores of his poems were memorized and recited by people in the regions of Castile and Extramadura. His poetry popularized the usage of vernacular languages and dialects, and remained apart from the centrifugal movements of the Iberian Peninsula initiated in 1868. He used a colloquial-style dialect of Extremadura, along with forms of literary Castilian. He liked to say that he wrote as people talked, and is best remembered for his directness and powerful descriptions.

BIBLIOGRAPHY

Primary Texts

*Obras completas.* Ed. Arturo Sauto Alabarde. México: Porrúa, 1981.
*Obras completas.* Madrid: Aguilar, 1973.
*Castellanas. Nuevas castellanas. Extremeñas.* Madrid: Espasa-Calpe, 1973.
*Poesía y Prosa.* Madrid: Magisterio Español, 1970.
*Cartas y poesías inéditas de Gabriel y Galán.* Madrid: Francisco Núñez, 1905.

English Translations

"To a Rich Man." Tr. Thomas Walsh. *Hispanic Anthology.* New York: Kraus, 1969.
"The Lord." Tr. Thomas Walsh. *The Catholic Anthology.* New York: Macmillan, 1932.

Criticism

Alonso, M. *El canto de Castilla. Estudio crítico sobre José María Gabriel y Galán.* Buenos Aires: Amorrortu, 1930.
Chico y Pello, Pedro. *Gabriel y Galán, maestro de escuela.* Madrid: Lemos, 1971.
Gutiérrez Macías, V. *Biografía de Gabriel y Galán.* Madrid: Publicaciones Españolas, 1956.
Montero Padilla, J. "La actitud de la crítica ante la obra de Gabriel y Galán." *Revista de Literatura* 8 (1955): 339–48.
Revilla, Marcos. *José María Gabriel y Galán, Su vida y sus obras. Estudios críticos.* Prol. by Miguel de Unamuno. Madrid: n.p., 1923.

Fernando Operé

***GAITA GALLEGA*, poetry of,** a form of verse. Adapted to the rhythm of the popular *muiñeira* dance of Galicia, these verses have any syllabism within a stanza, in contrast with the isosyllabic learned meter. Thus the rhythm is created by the distribution of generally four accents per line, influenced by music and with a varying number of unstressed syllables.

The poetry of the *gaita gallega* has ten to twelve syllables in Italo-Spanish versification, or nine to eleven in Luso-Galician, where the final unstressed syllable is discounted. Cultured decasyllabic lines have a regular OOÓ OOÓ OOÓ (O) scheme, with anapestic rhyme and three fixed stresses, as in

Velei *te*des, to*can*do o pan*dei*ro
(Xoan Manuel Pintos)
There are also false dactylic decasyllables of the pattern

ÓOO ÓOO OOÓ (O): *Mi*ña mon*tei*ra *ri*bere*ta*da.

The endecasyllable, which is the best known, has four accents, as in *Lé*valle un *gran* ó teu *fi*llo na *bi*ca (Rosalía de *Castro), and is thus endecasyllabic with dactylic rhythm. Also frequent in this poetry of popular origin are dodecasyllabic lines such as this one from Rosalía: As *có*chegas *bran*das, as *loi*tas a*le*gres. This two-part line, when not accompanied by music, resembles the twelve-syllable Castilian *arte mayor*, which is actually an imitation of *gaita gallega* poetry.

The role of caesura is important. Popularly, the basic *muiñeira* rhythm is two-part, often (O)ÓOOÓO//OÓOOÓ(O). When the caesura word is stressed on the next-to-last syllable, there is no problem, but if it has final stress, an extra syllable must be counted, as in Has de cantar//que che hei de dar zonchos (Rosalía). If the stress is on any other syllable, one less syllable is counted, so that what appears to be a dodecasyllabic verse is actually endecasyllabic. Thus, since in oral poetry anacrusis is possible, the endeca and dodecasyllabic lines become the same. The decasyllabic may also fit the scheme, with the irregularity that falls on the first hemistich made possible by the fact that the *muiñeira* rhythm allows for the first hemistich to be tetrasyllabic with anapestic meter.

When repeated, such hemistichs often take the form of refrains which are octosyllabic verses of *gaita gallega* style and are found in popular songs. A general scheme, which shows how lines of ten, eleven, and twelve syllables may fit the *gaita gallega* pattern, is

$$
\begin{array}{ccccccc}
\text{O} & \text{Ó} & \text{O} & \text{O} & \text{Ó} & \text{O} & // & \text{O} & \text{Ó} & \text{O} & \text{O} & \text{Ó} & \text{O} \\
 & 1 & 2 & 3 & 4 & & & 5 & 6 & 7 & 8 & 9 & 10 \\
 & 1 & 2 & 3 & 4 & 5 & & 6 & 7 & 8 & 9 & 10 & 11 \\
1 & 2 & 3 & 4 & 5 & 6 & & 7 & 8 & 9 & 10 & 11 & 12 \\
\end{array}
$$

In this manner, it is the main accent which gives unity to the poem. There are two principal stresses in *gaita gallega* verse, one on the first hemistich (third, fourth or fifth syllable), and the other over the second (ninth, tenth or eleventh syllable). Secondary accents may be displaced to any position.

Latin versification was quantitative, resting on long and short vowels, but subsequently the appearance of a stress based on intensity helped create a new metric system, based essentially on rhythm. The musical character of poetry from the late Latin era also had an effect, and in the Middle Ages ballads were seen to have a basis solely on stress derived from a melody. The principle is similar to that of Germanic poetry developing simultaneously. The medieval poets often used the *gaita gallega* cadence, although Provençal influence contributed to the loss of the practice among many Galician writers. In the Galician *Rexurdimento* or nineteenth-c. Renaissance, a number of poets again composed *muiñeiras*, among them Rosalía de Castro, Alberto Camino, and F. de la Iglesia. In the fourteenth c., this verse style had entered Castile and given origin to the *arte mayor* of the fifteenth-c. *cancioneros. In the seventeenth c. it was used by Lope de *Vega and, much later, by both *Valle-Inclán and Rubén Darío. It is still evident in the popular poetry of León and Asturias. *See also* Galician Literature; Gallic Portuguese Poetry.

BIBLIOGRAPHY

Criticism

Ríos, María Xesús, and Camilo Flores. "Versos de gaita gallega." *Gran Enciclopedia Gallega*. Gijón: Silverio Cañada, 1974 ff. 14: 211–12.

Kathleen March

**GALA, Antonio** (1936, Córdova– ), Spanish poet, journalist and dramatist. Gala studied law in Seville, and later philosophy and letters, with a specialization in history, in Madrid, contributing to the poetry review, *Aljibe*. He was runner-up for the Adonais Poetry Prize with *Enemigo íntimo* (1959; Intimate Enemy), but his important successes have been in the theater, and to some extent, with works written for television. Although he has not found comparable favor with the critics, Gala is without question the most popular dramatist in Spain in the 1980s in the eyes of the public. For several years, before his theatrical successes, Gala lived by teaching language classes and managing small art galleries. In 1963, he received the Calderón de la Barca National Theater Prize for *Los verdes campos del Edén* (Green Fields of Eden), which became a great success in 1964. In 1966, *El sol en el hormiguero* (Sun on the Anthill) was produced, and Gala lectured at U.S. universities including Oklahoma and Indiana. *Noviembre y un poco de yerba* (November and a Bit of Grass) followed at the end of 1967. During these years Gala produced translations and adaptations of works by Paul Claudel, Edward Albee and Sean O'Casey. The completion of *Cantar de Santiago para todos* (1971; Song of St. James for All) was followed in 1972 by the television series, "Si las piedras hablaran" (If the Stones Could Speak) and a new play, *Los buenos días perdidos* (The Good Old Days), one of Gala's most popular works, which received the National Prize for Literature a year later. In 1973, his *Suerte, campeón* (Good Luck, Champ) was prohibited by the *censorship, but *Anillos para una dama* (Rings for a Lady) premiered at the end of September. *Las cítaras colgadas de los árboles* (Zithers Hanging from the Trees) opened in 1974, and *¿Por qué corres, Ulises?* (Why Are You Running, Ulysses?) in 1975; at the same time there were revivals of *Los buenos días perdidos* and *Anillos para una dama* (produced in New York in 1981). A television series, "Paisaje con figuras" (Landscape with Figures), written by Gala was interrupted and withdrawn due to governmental prohibition, and he was brought to trial for an article written for *Sábado Gráfico*. It was falsely reported that Gala had been assassinated. The following year, however, there were several editions of his works, and he began various series of articles, most importantly the equivalent of a syndicated column, "Charlas con Troylo" (Chats With Troylo [his dog]) in *El País*, the most important daily in the post-Franco era. Two new plays opened in 1980, *Petra Regalada* and *La vieja señorita del Paraíso* (The Old Maid from Paradise). *El cementerio de los pájaros* (Bird Cemetery) premiered in 1982, and several books appeared, including the book versions of newspaper columns, *Charlas con Troylo* (1981), and *En propia mano* (1983; In One's Own Hand). *Samarkanda* opened in 1985, and *Séneca o el beneficio de la duda* (Seneca, or the Benefit of the Doubt) in 1987. More than ideas, the theater of Gala has feelings, sentiments, heart: love, hope, human contact. There is criticism of consumerism, of the search for success, the thirst for money, the Catholic church as an institution and bureaucracy. Gala's works suggest fear of fanaticism, intolerance, irrationalism, and uniforms (whether ecclesiastical or military); ridicule of the narrow and hypocritical sexual education; defense of divorce; and hope for a better future for Spain. *See also* Contemporary Spanish Theater.

BIBLIOGRAPHY

Primary Texts

*El caracol en el espejo*. Madrid: Taurus, 1970.
*Obras escogidas*. Madrid: Aguilar, 1980.
*Trilogía de la libertad (Petra Regalada, La vieja señorita del Paraíso, El cementerio de los pájaros)*. Notes, study, Carmen Díaz Castañón. Madrid: Espasa-Calpe, 1983.

Criticism

Amorós, Andrés. "Introducción." *Los buenos días perdidos* and *Anillos para una dama*. Madrid: Castalia, 1987. 9–116.
Anderson, Farris. "From Protest to Resignation." *Estreno* 1.2 (Fall 1976): n.p.
Holt, Marion P. *The Contemporary Spanish Theater (1949–1972)*. TWAS 336, Boston: Twayne, 1975.
Padilla-Mangas, Ana María. *Tipología en la obra dramática de Antonio Gala*. Córdoba: Diputación-Universidad, 1985.
Zatlin, Phyllis. "The Theater of Antonio Gala: In Search of Paradise." *KRQ* 24 (1977): n.p.

Janet Pérez

**GALBA, Martí Joan de** (?, ?–1490, ?), writer. He revised Joanot *Martorell's *Tirant lo Blanch*; the extent of his creativity is unknown, but many critics feel it to be clearly secondary to that of Martorell.

**GALICIAN LITERATURE.** Following the medieval flourishing of the Galician-Portuguese school of poetry which ended in the middle of the fourteenth c. (*see* Gallic-Portuguese Poetry), the use of Galician as a literary language was abandoned for almost five hundred years. Only with the coming of *Romanticism in the early 1830s did Galician become once again a belletristic reality. Its stirrings were faint, initially, when Nicomedes *Pastor Díaz (1811–63) published his volume *Poesías* (1840; Poems) that included several melancholy compositions written in Galician. Twenty-two years later, however, enough Galician poetry had appeared so that the important *Album de la caridad* (1862; Album of Mercy) verse anthology was published with much fanfare, marking an acknowledged renaissance of Galician literature. This anthology of nineteenth-c. Galician verse was followed almost immediately by the publication of Rosalía de *Castro's (1837–85) *Cantares gallegos* (1863; Galician Songs) and subsequently by other verse collections from Eduardo *Pondal (1835–1917) and Manuel *Curros Enríquez (1851–1908). These three, the greatest Galician poets of the nineteenth c. and, in the case of Rosalía de Castro, perhaps of all time, gave an impetus to Galician literature that would help it survive a second period of silence—this one imposed by a dictatorial *censorship—stretching from 1936 to 1975. Their themes, vaguely reminiscent of the medieval *cancioneros (solitude, love of the land, and the role of fate in man's life), constitute, as well, leitmotifs that endure in the writings of every important author to follow, not just in poetry but in the narrative and dramatic genres.

## Poetry

Twentieth-c. Galician poetry began with a reformist vengeance on the part of young writers who railed against their immediate literary ancestors in the 1922 manifesto *Máis Alá* (Further Out). Largely the work of the poet Manuel Antonio *Pérez Sánchez (1900–1928) and the artist Alvaro Cebreiro, *Máis Alá* not only demythified Curros Enríquez, Rosalía de Castro and Eduardo Pondal but, as positive notes, espoused Galician regionalism and identification with the common people as virtues to be pursued.

Manuel Antonio, the name by which he is known, was the leader of this vanguardist movement. He left behind only one book, *De catro a catro. Follas dun diario d'abordo* (1928; In Fours. Pages from a Naval Diary). It is a volume of modernist verse visibly under the spell of the French Cubist and the Spanish-American *creacionismo* aesthetics. In it Manuel Antonio, a friend of poets of the *Generation of 1927, wrote poems of protest though personal in tone using the sea as the backdrop and as the source of his metaphors. Given the stridency of his iconoclasm, the paucity of his production and the brevity of his existence, Manuel Antonio left no followers.

Luis *Amado Carballo (1901–27), though equally determined to establish a new order of Galician poetry, did so only in a structural or formalist sense. His verse is simple and short; however, its themes, tone and subjects are thoroughly familiar and traditional. Amado Carballo's two books of poems *Proel* (1927; Vigil) and, posthumously, *O Galo* (1928; The Rooster) clearly echo the sentiments of Rosalía de Castro and Pondal in the pastoral vision of Galicia's rural regions, their idyllic and melancholic pantheism, and their fondness for regional folklore. Amado Carballo's bucolic brand of poetry endured in its influence up to the 1960s when protest verse denounced its easy and uncommitted formulas. Eduardo *Blanco Amor (1905), friend and editor of Federico *García Lorca's (1898–1936) *Seis poemas galegos* (1935; Six Galician Poems), is perhaps Amado Carballo's best and closest disciple. His books *Romances galegos* (1928; Galician Ballads), *Poema en catro tempos* (1931; Poems in Four Tempos) and *Cancioneiro* (1956; Songbook) espouse an equally eclogue-like, nostalgic version of his native Galicia. They stem not only from Amado Carballo's influence but from Blanco Amor's almost lifelong exile in Buenos Aires. Other less known figures belonging to this traditionalist line are Agusto María Casas (1906), author of *O vento segrel* (1932; Lulling Wind), *Alén* (1963; Far Away) and *Servidumbre na treva* (1965; Serfdom in Darkness), and Manuel Prieto Marcos (1905–45) in *Versos en gama de gaita* (1943; Poems in Bagpipe Rhythm).

Not dissimilar in his glorification of rural landscapes and traditions is the renowned classics scholar Antonio Noriega Varela (1869–1947), also author of four books of poetry. In his best one, titled *Do ermo* (1946; Fallow), the humble characteristics of the Galician countryside take on Virgilian aspects. Its landscape of country roads and humble inns populated by poor peasants cannot be bested in an almost beatus-ille vision. Gonzalo López Abente's (1878–1958) sixty sonnets which make up *De Outono* (Autumn) are equally focused on themes of the rural landscapes of mountains and forests. And his *Centileo nas ondas* (Shimmering Waves), published when in his eighties, tends to that other great Galician theme—the sea.

Students of seminaries, like Noriega Varela had been, were Ramón Cabanillas Enríquez (1873–1959) and Aquilino Iglesia Alvariño (1909–61). Cabanillas, considered for a long time one of Galicia's best modern poets, was a prolific writer who essayed almost every type of poetry from the lyric (*A rosa de cen follas* [1927; The Rose of One Hundred Leaves]) to the narrative (*Na noite estrelecida* [1925; Starry Night]) and from the epic (*Caminos no tempo* [1949; Roads of Time]) to the dramatic (*O bendito San Amaro* [1926; Blessed St. Amarus]). Today one realizes that Cabanillas's significance is likely due as much to his voluminous output as to any other virtue of his works. Indeed Cabanillas is overshadowed by Aquilino Iglesia Alvariño, the greatest of the Latinist poets to fix their attention on the themes of landscape and solitude. Decidedly influenced by Virgil, translator of Horace and Plautus into vernacular Galician, Iglesia Alvariño produced the first significant book of Galician poetry after the Civil War, *Cómaros verdes* (1947; Green Pastures). *Corazón ao vento* (1933; Heart to the Wind), *De día a día* (1960; From Day to Day) and *Lanza de soledá* (1961; Lance of Solitude) exhibit an almost scholarly attention to structure. In Iglesias Alvariño as well as in his followers, Xosé Crecente Vega (1896–1948) and Xosé María Díaz (1914), we see a poetry where the land personifies solitude and vague longing, and its presence the existential nature of man's lot on earth.

A poet alone, unlike any of his contemporaries, was Luis Vázquez Pimentel (1895–1958). Born and raised in the arch-Galician city of Lugo, he lived and died there and it was about this city, its stones, its trees, its history, and its people that Pimentel wrote. *Sombra do aire na herba* (1959; Shadows of the Air on the Grass) contains all of his Galician verse. Written in a slow impressionist fashion, Pimentel's deeply humanistic poetry shows a readily identifiable and uncomplicated reality of people and places. There is a pleasant and comfortable sameness in all of his verses: everyday life in a small provincial capital.

The archaeologist Fermín Bouza Brey (1901–73) is the initiator of a poetic vein which survives to this day. Labeled by some *neotrovadorismo*, it is distinguished by a fondness for medieval lyric structures, archaic language and the perennial themes of minstrels. Bouza's only two published volumes *Nao senlleira* (1933; Solitary Ship) and *Seitura* (1955; Shape), written in the neo-troubadour fashion, prompted a wide and lasting following. Without a doubt its foremost practitioner remains Alvaro *Cunqueiro (1911–81), one of the most prolific and protean of all the twentieth-c. Galician writers. It is perhaps due to his other literary interests, above all prose fiction, that Cunqueiro's best known poetry had been written by mid-c. In *Cantiga nova que se chama riveira* (1933; New Song Called *riveira*) and *Dona do corpo delgado* (1950; Thin Woman) Cunqueiro exhibits an uncanny ability to clothe in a centuries-old-speech identifiable themes, all in a natural manner totally devoid of any artificiality.

Aside from Luis Pimentel's *Sombra do aire na terra*, another key work in post-war Galician poetry is Celso Emilio *Ferreiro's (1914–79) *Longa noite de pedra* (1962; Long Night of Stone). A collection of poems with a clear social and political intention, *Longa noite* has become a best-seller in all Galicia and a literary primer for all of its young poets. Unfortunately, most of Ferreiro's followers noted only his reformist ideology and little of the subtleties, the ironies and the structural mastery of *Longa noite*. While in exile in Venezuela, Ferreiro continued the writing of *engagé* poetry, poems that, while intrinsically merito-rious in a literary sense, also decried humanity's ills, such as forced emigration in *Viaxe ao país dos ananos* (1968; Journey to the Land of the Dwarf), and other types of protest verse such as *Antipoemas* (1972; Anti-poems). One of his last books, *Cimenterio privado* (1973; Private Cemetery), published upon his return to Spain, is reminiscent of the medieval lyrics in tone and structure but its ethics continue to be unmistakably Ferreiro's in their humanistic bent.

In 1950 a new generation of poets slowly began to make its way into bookstores and magazines. Manuel María Fernández Teixeiro's (1931) first two collections of poems, *Muiñeiro de brétemas* (1950; Miller of Fog) and *Advento* (1954; Advent), and Manuel Cuna Novas's (1926) *Fabulario novo* (1952; New Fables) all betray a vague existentialist despair borne of the fundamental Galician sense of *saudade* (nostalgia and solitude). Fernández Teixeiro, however, continues to explore different modes of poetic expression to such an extent that he has become the most prolific of his contemporaries. *Libro de pregos* (1962; Book of Prayers), *Terra cha* (1967; Flatlands), *Versos pra un país de minifundios* (1969; Verses for a Land of Small Parcels) and others denote by their very titles that Fernández Teixeiro's later ideological concerns parallel in many ways Celso Emilio Fer-reiro's. Uxío Novoneira's (1930) brand of poetry is *pastoral, anguished and personal, belonging to Iglesia Alvariño's type of rural and anthropomorphic landscapes. *Os Eidos* (1955; The Yards), *Os Eidos 2* (1974) and *Elegías do Caurel* (1966; Elegies from Caurel) are his best known works.

Finally we have a host of writers, better known in other genres (prose fiction), such as Xosé Luis Méndez Ferrín (1938) and Xoanna *Torres Fernández (1940), who under the spell of Ferreiro's watershed *Longa noite de pedra* have produced creditable social poetry which is typical of contemporary Galician letters. Méndez Ferrín's *Antoloxía popular de Heriberto Bens* (1972; Heriberto Bens's Popular Anthology) and Torres's *Do Sulco* (1957; Furrows) are both good examples of this tendency. Other writers, though older than either of the two foregoing, and better known in other genres but who have also produced important volumes of poetry, are the scholars Ricardo *Carballo Calero (1910), author of the sober and conceptual *Anxo da terra* (1950; Nostalgia for the Land) and *Salteiro de Fingoy* (1961; The Shoemaker from Fingoy), Ernesto *Guerra da Cal (1911), author of the rhythmic and melancholy *Lúa de alén mar* (1959; Moon of a Far Away Sea) and *Río de sombro e tempo* (1963; River of Sleep and Time) and Miguel González Garcés (1916), author of one of the best collections of con-temporary Galician poems titled *Nas faíscas do sono* (1972; In the Sparks of Sleep).

## Narrative Fiction

*O porco de pé* (1928; The Standing Pig) by Vicente *Risco (1884–1963), *Os camiños da vida* (1928; Life's Roads) by Ramón *Otero Pedrayo (1888–1976), and *Os dous de sempre* (1934; The Usual Two) by Daniel Rodríguez Castelao (1886–1950) highlight narrative Galician fiction prior to the Civil War. Before them, several so-called Galician novels, largely the works belonging to Marcial Valladares Núñez (1821–1903), such as *Maxima, ou a filla espuria* (1880; Mary, or the Illegitimate Daughter), and the priest Antonio Lopez Ferreiro's (1837–1910) *A tecedeira de Bonaval* (1894; The Weaver from Bonaval), *O castelo de Pambre* (1895; The Castle of Pambre), and *O niño das pombas* (1905; Where the Doves Nest), merit little more than a historical footnote. The formulaic structures and Byzantine plots of this early fiction subtract much from their literary worth.

Otero Pedrayo wrote a larger number of novels than any other Galician author before or since. From the above-cited title to the last one published before his death at age eighty-eight, *O señorito da Reboraina* (1960; The Lord of Reboraina), Otero Pedrayo produced upwards of twenty novels. It is an impressive number when taking into account the thousands of journalistic articles he also wrote, together with the nearly fifty volumes of poetry, theater, geography, short stories, and criticism. Otero Pedrayo's importance, however, does not stem exclusively from the enormous amount of his output but from the authentic ring of his language, the vague romanticism of his plots and his intimate knowledge of Galicia and its people. All of these things have made him the most widely read Galician author of the twentieth c.

Once the Civil War broke out in 1936, for powerful political reasons, no Galician novel was published until 1951. Ricardo Carballo Calero's *A xente da Barreira* (The People from Barreira) not only inaugurated the new era but was awarded an important and economically meaningful literary prize. Yet, narrative fiction cannot be said to have gained the significance that poetry had in the third quarter c. of Galician letters. From *A xente da Barreira*'s date of 1951 until 1975, only twenty-nine novels were published in Galicia, many of them of a hybrid and suspect novelistic format. Novellas and short stories have had more success and thus more practitioners; among them Alvaro Cunqueiro clearly stands out. Prolific and diverse in the tradition of Otero Pedrayo, this writer from Mondoñedo has published dozens of slim prose volumes ranging from the re-visiting of old myths such as *Merlín e familia* (1955; Merlin and Family) and *Si o vello Sinbad volviese as illas* (1961; If Old Man Sinbad Returned to the Isles) to the collection of fantastic tales and essays under the title *Tesouros novos e vellos* (1964; Old Treasures and New). Alvaro Cunqueiro's critical and popular successes are equally deserved.

The whole of the narrative fiction belonging to the fifties and the sixties follows very traditional patterns without innovations of any sort. It falls within the reach of a large readership and constitutes merely a stage of literary realism devoid of any technical prowess and even fewer ideological dares. The first dissonant note in the Galician novel is not sounded until 1965 with the publication of the book *Adiós, María* by Xohana Torres. She, Dora *Vázquez Iglesias (*Bergantiña* [1971; The Girl from Bergantino]), and María Xosé *Queixán (1938) (*A orella na buraco* [1965; Ear to the Ground]) are the only known female Galician novelists of the last twenty-five years.

Yet, while the updating of fictional techniques as well as the impact of European, American and South American writers has made the recent Galician novels creditable contemporary works of fiction, these novels have become increasingly cryptic, complicated and almost inaccessible to the lay reader. This, the most popular of all the genres, has nearly closed itself off from its public. Other writers belonging to Torres's and Vázquez's generation, such as Xosé Luis Méndez Ferrín and Carlos Casares (1941), seem equally intent in shaking off past traditional and realistic modes. Though social realism continues in their novels, narrative structure becomes more elastic, its characters less identifiable, its themes more *engagé*, their styles and language more personalized. It is true that a few authors, such as Xosé *Neira Vilas (1928) (*Memorias dun neno labrego* [1961; Memoirs of a Country Boy]) and Ramón de Valenzuela Otero (?) (*Non aguardei por ninguén* [1957; I Waited for No Man]), continue writing in the social realism vein, but they are in the minority. Eduardo Blanco Amor, especially in his best known work of fiction, *A esmorga* (1959; The Party), with appreciable existentialist overtones, and *Xente ao lonxe* (Far Away People), of a clear autobiographical nature, belongs to an intermediate or transitional group.

The vanguard movement is thus led by Xohana Torres, Carlos Casares and Xosé Luis Méndez Ferrín. The former's *Adiós, María* gained a very early success after it was awarded the Galicia Prize by the important Centro Gallego of Buenos Aires. And though its novelistic technique and style are new, its idée maîtresse is the oldest and most constant of all Galician literature, reverting to the medieval verse of the *cantigas: that of exile from the beloved birthplace. Winner also of several important literary prizes (Editorial Galaxia in 1975, and Premio de la Crítica in 1976) which have consolidated his renown is Carlos Casares. His initial novel, *Cambio en tres* (1969; Change by Threes), left him unsatisfied, but having tried his hand at short stories in 1967 with the twelve included in *O vento ferido* (The Wounded Breeze), Casares brought out a truly singular novel in 1975 titled *Xoguetes pra un tempo prohibido* (Toys for a Forbidden Time). Xosé Luis Méndez Ferrín, chronologically the oldest and the most mature novelist of his generation as well, began his writing career quite energetically but in the past decade has slowed down his efforts due to other interests. His three collections of short stories—*Percival e outras historias* (1958; Parsifal and Other Tales), *O crepúsculo e as formigas* (1961; Evening and the Ants) and *Elipsis e outras sombras* (1974; Ellipsis and Other Shadows)—create a magical microcosm where pure fantasy at times collides with everyday reality but which the narrator rescues amusingly. Méndez Ferrín's novels, on the other hand, adopt a more critical and less escapist stance. One of them, *Os corvos, a figueira e a* *fouce de ouro* (Ravens, the Fig Tree and the Golden Sickle), which cost its author two years in jail, remains unpublished. Others, among them *Arrabaldo do norte* (1964; Northern Suburbs), *Retorno a Tagén-Ata* (1971; Return to Tagén-Ata) and *Antón e os inocentes* (1976; Anthony and the Innocent Ones), met with repeated warnings by the censors during the final years of Franco's dictatorship. They all represent very committed ideological positions from which Méndez Ferrín has refused to retreat.

**The Essay**

The true initiators of the modern Galician essay are a group of men who on October 30, 1920, published in the city of Orense the first number of the journal *Nós: Boletín mensual da cultura galega* (We: Monthly Bulletin of Galician Culture). Vicente Risco became its literary editor and Alfonso Castelao its artistic editor. Among the journal's most assiduous collaborators, Ramón Otero Pedrayo and Florentino Cuevillas (1886–1958) are the most prominent names. These four writers, together with a large number of intermittent collaborators, were called the Generación Nós and are acknowledged as the teachers of today's Galician literary essayists. While *Nós* was guided by Risco it remained a literary magazine; once its direction passed on to Anxel Casal, *Nós* took on a more mixed cultural nature. Its last issue was number 137–138 published in May-June 1935.

Vicente Risco was the most intellectual member of the group. His interests in philosophy carried him to some elitist positions, and he has been faulted for his disdain of the rural bourgeois elements of Galicia. Once the Civil War was over in 1939, Risco stopped writing in Galician and moved to Madrid, where he lived until shortly before his death. The three major works of Risco, a first-rate anthropologist and ethnographer, are *Leria* (Idle Talk), a collection of essays written over twenty-five years; *Mittleeuropa* (Central Europe), which relates his travels throughout Central Europe in the 1930s; and *Teoría do nacionalismo galego* (Theory of Galician Nationalism), a survey of Galician culture.

Alfonso Castelao, a wit and a cartoonist (also a practicing physician), wrote six volumes of moralistic caricatures, *Cousas da vida* (Life in General), as well as a novel and a theater piece. His volumes of essays, *Sempre en Galiza* (1944; Always in Galicia) and *As cruces de pedra na Galiza* (1949; Stone Crosses in Galicia), are masterpieces of narrative and essayistic prose detailing pilgrimages carried out in his native land. He died while in exile in Buenos Aires.

The longest-lived member of the Generación Nós was Otero Pedrayo. Fondly known as the patriarch of contemporary Galician letters, he produced an enormous opus in every one of the four literary genres, but he excelled in the essay. The amorphousness of this genre lent itself well to Otero Pedrayo's boundless energy and dedication. Of a general nature are his *Síntexe xeográfica de Galicia* (1926; Geographical Synthesis of Galicia), *Pelexinares* (1929; Pilgrimages), *Ensaio sobre a cultura galega* (1933; Essays on Galician Culture), and *Guía de Galicia* (1965; Travel Guide to Galicia), in which his fondness for the idealized, extinct Galician countryside and its history is evident. Otero Pedrayo mistrusted liberalism and progress, believing that such forces would forever destroy the essential spirit of his beloved region.

Little was done in Galician studies during the Civil War period. In the decade 1936–46 not a single volume was published in Galician, and from the latter date up to 1950 only seven were issued—five of them slim verse collections. The year 1950 truly represents the birthdate of the contemporary Galician essay; in that year the large publisher Galaxia was founded in the city of Vigo. Some important volumes—such as *Antífona da cantiga* (1951; Anthology of Popular Songs), *Sete ensaios sobre Rosalía* (1952; Seven Essays on Rosalía), *La saudade* (1953; Nostalgia) and *Paisaxe e cultura* (1955; Landscape and Culture)—established this publishing house as a major outlet of Galician literature. Galaxia attracted a large group of authors and encouraged them to write and publish in their native tongue, and to collaborate in several projects. In fact, the last three works cited are all team efforts.

Among the best known essayists associated with Galaxia is Ramón Piñeiro (1915), its director and author of *Olladas do futuro* (1974; Views of the Future). Others are Francisco Fernández del Riego (?), Celestino Fernández de la Vega (1914), Domingo *García Sabell (1909), Juan *Rof Carballo (?) and Ricardo Carballo Calero. Fernández del Riego wrote the first *Manual de historia de la literatura gallega* (1951; A History of Galician Literature) for Galaxia, as well as *Cos ollos do noso espírito* (1949; Through our Soul's Eyes), *Galicia no espello* (1954; Galicia in the Mirror), *Crásicos e románticos* (Classics and Romantics) and *Letras do noso tempo* (1974; Letters of Our Time). Celestino Fernández de la Vega tends toward the philosophic side of the essay, having translated into Galician works by Heidegger and Pokorny. His main work is *O segredo do humor* (1963; The Secret of Humor), an extensive theoretical treatise on the nature and evolution of humor in European literary and artistic thought. García Sabell and Rof Carballo are medical doctors though both are better known as humanists. Rof Carballo studies in his *Patología psicosomática* (Pychosomatic Pathology) the infirm as an anthropological dilemma. His most often cited book in Galician, *Mito e realidade da Terra Nai* (1957; Myth and Reality of the Motherland), contains four of Rof Carballo's best essays on Galician folklore. García Sabell's Galician essays have hardly begun to appear in book form. Two volumes titled simply *Ensaios* were published in 1963 and 1976. Their subject matter ranges from art to medicine and from anthropology to literature. Though Carballo Calero has distinguished himself in other genres, his most significant contribution to Galician letters is to be found in the critical and literary essay. A former university professor, Carballo Calero has dominated for decades the field of literary scholarship in Galician studies. From his initial contribution to the watershed volume *Sete ensaios sobre Rosalía*, Carballo Calero has published hundreds of essays in the field of Galician literature. Among the twenty-some volumes published, his masterwork is without a doubt the monumental 900-page *Historia da literatura galega contemporánea* (1975; History of Contemporary Galician Literature), today in its second edition. Other equally fundamental works by Carballo Calero are *Gramática elemental del gallego común* (1966; Elementary Grammar of Everyday Galician), today in its seventh edition, and *Sobre lingua e literatura galega* (1971; On Galician Language and Literature).

Today's younger essayists have begun to look back and write on their literary ancestors, such as Ramón Lugrís (1932) in his *Vicente Risco na cultura galgea* (1963; Vicente Risco in Galician Culture), Celso Emilio Ferreiro in his biography of *Curros Enríquez* (1954), or Benito Varela Jácome in his *Estructuras de la novela de Castelao* (1973; Structure in the Novels of Castelao). Others have taken to gathering verse collections into anthologies such as Miguel González Garcés has done with *Poesía gallega contemporánea* (1974; Contemporary Galician Poetry) and *Poesía gallega de posguerra* (1976; Post-war Galician Poetry), or César Antonio Molina's (1952) *Antología de la poesía gallega contemporánea* (1984; Anthology of Contemporary Galician Poetry). And finally there exists yet another group of writers whose use of Galician as a language tool for their essays can best be described as a form of protest. Their bent is socio-linguistic and their concern is to decry the precarious state that their native language and culture are passing through currently. Xesús Alonso Montero, a high school teacher at the Instituto de Enseñanza Media of Lugo perhaps represents best this third, leftist, tendency. The very titles of his most widely quoted books, *Informe dramático sobre la lengua gallega* (1973; Dramatic Bulletin on the Galician Language), *Realismo y conciencia crítica en la literatura gallega* (1968; Realism and Critical Consciousness in Galician Literature), and *Lengua, literatura e sociedade en Galicia* (Language, Literature and Society in Galicia) clearly illustrate his reformist concerns.

**Drama**

To this, the most social of all literary genres, Galician writers of the twentieth c. have not contributed any works of lasting worth. Prior to the Civil War there exists a historical theater perhaps descendant of the legendary romantic dramas of the nineteenth c. penned by *Zorrilla and the Duque de *Rivas. More in a realist vein than their forerunners are *O Mariscal* (1926; The Field Marshal) by Ramón Cabanillas, and Armando Cotarelo Valledor's (1879–1950) two dramas titled *Beiramor* (1931) and *Hostia* (1926). Bridging the gap between historical drama and melodrama or comedy we have Alvaro Cunqueiro's *O incerto señor don Hamlet* (1956; An Uncertain Mr. Hamlet) and *A noite vai como un río* (1965; Night Flows Like a River) and Bernardino Graña's *Vinte mil pesos crimen* (1962; The Twenty-thousand Dollar Crime). Most, however, would consider Alfonso Castelao's farce *Os vellos non deben de namorarse* (1953; Old Folks Shouldn't Fall in Love) as the most representative piece in Galician theater. *A fiestra valdeira* (1927; The Idle Feast), a comedy by Rafael *Dieste and Blanco Amor's *Farsas para títeres* (1973; Farces for Puppets) and *Teatro pra xente* (1974; Theater for People) are equally popular and enduring. In the decades of the sixties and seventies there has been a return to historical drama, though updated and intellectualized, but still not very successful in terms of either public or critical success. Two of its practitioners are Daniel *Cortezón with *Nicolás*

*Flanel* (1956), *Prisciliano* (1970) and *Xelmírez*(1974), and Xohana Torres's *A outra banda do Iberr* (1965; On the Other Side of the Iberr) and *Un hotel de primeira sobre o río* (1968; A First-Class Hotel on the River). Only more accessible works such as *A revolta* (1965; The Upheaval) and *A obriga* (1965; The Vow) by the young Genaro Mariñas have had any measure of acceptance.

Ricardo Landeira

**GALINDO, Beatriz** (1475, Salamanca–1535, Madrid), humanist, poet. Her singular erudition earned her the nickname la Latina (The Latin Lady). Commentaries to Aristotle, notes to classics and poetry, are attributed to her; none has survived. She taught Latin to Queen Isabella, and seems also to have provided counsel in political affairs over the years. After the death of her husband in 1501, and of her beloved queen three years later, Galindo dedicated the rest of her life to charity, founding a hospital and two convents. Her portrait is found in the Lázaro Galdiano Museum in Madrid. *See also* Humanism; Renaissance.

BIBLIOGRAPHY

Criticism

"Galindo, Beatriz de." In BAE 269. Contains various documents.
Llanos y Torriglia, F. *Una consejera de estado. Doña Beatriz Galindo, la Latina*. Madrid: Reus, 1920.

**GALLARDO Y BLANCO, Bartolomé José** (1776, Campanario, Badajoz– 1852, Alcoy, Alicante), politician, bibliographer, scholar. Today he is most remembered for his collection of scrupulous bibliographic data, which was collected and arranged posthumously under the title *Ensayo de una biblioteca española de libros raros y curiosos* (1863–89; Essay of a Library of Rare and Unusual Books). In his own day, his caustic pen earned him many enemies, both political and literary; he was libeled by Adolfo *Castro y Rossi twice, and by *Estébanez Calderón and others; he was also jailed and exiled for his writings. Some of Gallardo's papers were lost, but many writings, including correspondence and some poetry, survive. A. Rodríguez-Moñino has studied in great detail the scholarship of Gallardo and his victimization by contemporaries.

BIBLIOGRAPHY

Primary Texts

*Cartas inéditas . . . a don Manuel Torrighi, 1824–1833*. Ed. A. Rodríguez-Moñino. Madrid: Maestre, 1955.
*Diccionario crítico burlesco . . .* and *Cartazgo al Censor General*. In *Don Bartolomé José Gallardo*. Ed., study A. Rodríguez-Moñino. Madrid: Sancha, 1955.
*Ensayo de una biblioteca española de libros raros y curiosos*. Madrid: Gredos, 1968. Facs.
*Obras escogidas*. 2 vols. Madrid: iberoamericana, 1928.

Criticism

Rodríguez-Moñino, A. R. *Goya y Gallardo, noticias sobre su amistad*. Madrid: Sánchez-Ocaña, 1954.

————. *Historia de una infamia bibliográfica. La de San Antonio de 1823. Realidad y leyenda de lo sucedido con los libros y papeles del don Bartolomé José Gallardo.* Madrid: Castalia, 1965.

**GALLEGO, José Luis** (1913, Valladolid–1980, Madrid), poet. Among his works are *Noticia de mi* (1947; News about Me), *Los sueños reunidos* (Gathered Dreams), and *Prometeo XX* (1970 Prometheus XX). In 1980 *Voz última* (Last Voice) was published posthumously. It was written in 1946, when Gallego was in prison.

BIBLIOGRAPHY

Primary Texts

*Prometeo XX y Prometeo liberado.* Madrid: Orígenes, 1983.
*Voz última.* Madrid: Ayuso, 1980.

Isabel McSpadden

**GALLEGO, Juan Nicasio** (1777, Zamora–1853, Madrid), poet of the Salamancan school (*Escuela Salmantina). He studied in Salamanca where he was ordained priest and where he befriended *Meléndez Valdés, *Quintana, and *Cienfuegos. During the French invasion of 1808 he fled to Seville and Cádiz. In 1810 he took part in the Cortes de Cádiz. When Ferdinand VII returned to power, Gallego was imprisoned for eighteen months because of his liberal ideas. He was elected to the Royal Spanish Academy (*Academia Española) in 1830, and served as its secretary from 1839 on.

Gallego is best known for his patriotic compositions such as his ''Al dos de mayo'' (1808; To May Second), in which he expresses his love of liberty and hatred of the invaders with genuine emotion and dramatic force. The structure of this poem is classical, but the enthusiastic fervor and lugubrious atmosphere point to Gallego's Romantic inclinations. He may be considered a transitional poet from neo-classicism to *romanticism: the polished form, perfect musicality and harmony of his verse is neo-classical in taste; his grandiloquent tone and resounding vocabulary are Romantic. ''Elegía a la Duquesa de Frías'' (1830; Elegy to the Duchess of Frías) evinces such a mixture of classical and romantic elements: mythological allusions, personal memories, a lugubrious setting and passionate sincerity of expression. Juan de *Valera considers it the most beautiful elegy of Spanish poetry. Among Gallego's better known compositions are ''A la defensa de Buenos Aires'' (1807; To the Defense of Buenos Aires), ''A Quintana por su oda al Combate de Trafalgar'' (1805; To Quintana for His Ode to the Battle of Trafalgar), ''A la memoria de Garcilaso'' (To the Memory of Garcilaso), ''Los hoyuelos de Lesbia'' (Lesbia's Dimples) and ''La última cena'' (The Last Supper). The number of his poems is small and characterized by a formal elegance and correct versification. In the manner of Fernando de *Herrera and Quintana, he tends to use long stanzas to achieve harmonious effects. Besides his elegies he wrote anacreontic poetry and a series of sonnets.

BIBLIOGRAPHY

Primary Text

*Obras poéticas de Don Juan Nicasio Gallego.* Madrid: RAE, Diccionario Universal, 1854.

Criticism

González Negro, E. *Estudio biográfico de don Juan Nicasio Gallego* (Doctoral thesis). Zamora: n.p. 1901.
Martiel, Isidoro. "Juan Nicasio Gallego, traductor de Ossian." *Revista de Literatura* 69–70 (1969): 57–77.

Phoebe Porter Medina

**GALLIC-PORTUGUESE POETRY (Middle Ages).** Medieval Gallic-Portuguese lyric and medieval Provençal lyric poetry are the two lyrics which are most abundant and of the most interest among all medieval poetry in the Romance languages. The first known example of Gallic-Portuguese medieval lyric poetry dates from 1199, the probable date of a canticle by don Sancho of Portugal, and continues until the middle of the fourteenth c.

The language is *gallego* (Galician), a medieval Romance dialect with several variants spoken in Galicia, León, Austurias and northern Portugal. In the twelfth through the fourteenth centuries *gallego* was almost identical to the Portuguese language of the time. The dialect had great prestige since Provençal influence and the cultivation of poetry at the court of King Denis (Diniz) of Portugal (1259–1325) had enabled the troubadour lyric to flourish in Galicia. *Gallego* more or less became the standard poetic language for Castilians as well as for Portuguese poets for almost two centuries as a result of being the medium of expression for troubadour poetry in Spain. Critical study has made it clear that this poetry evolved from an indigenous folkloric pre-troubadour base whose locale was Galicia. The theory proposed by Jeanroy, Lollis, Pellegrini and others that France or Provence was the source of all Romance lyric thus has been disproven. The discovery of the famous Mozarabic *kharjas*, dating prior to 1100, has supplied definitive, documented proof that a peninsular romance lyric existed prior to the Provençal and that this peninsular lyric has a clear thematic relationship to the Gallic-Portuguese canticles. However, the actual connection of the two lyrics suggested by *Ménendez Pidal and Dámaso *Alonso continues to be problematic as critics such as Costa Pimpão and Rodrigues Lapa have shown. The folkloric background joins the Provençal troubadour current in the Gallic-Portuguese *cancioneros*; the result is an enormously rich ensemble. Apart from the late thirteenth-c. Marian Canticles (in the Galician dialect) by *Alphonse X the Wise (some 453 *Cantigas de Santa María*, Songs to the Virgin Mary), the three most important known collections have preserved a total of 1,711 different poems. There are 310 in the *Cancionero de Ajuda* (CA), 1,205 in the *Cancionero de la Biblioteca Vaticana* (CV) and 1,567 in the *Cancionero da Biblioteca Nacional* (CBN) (formerly Colocci-Brancutti).

The richest collections (CV and CBN) include the three most representative lyric genres: *cantigas de amigo* (songs to a lover), *cantigas de amor* (songs of love), and *cantigas de escarnio y maldizer* (songs of mockery and slander) (*See* Cantiga). However, in these two collections the poems are late copies made by Italian scribes in the late sixteenth c. from originals now lost and dating most probably from the fourteenth c. Although the CA is of less interest since it contains only *cantigas de amor*, the most courtly genre, it holds the honor of being the oldest text, dating from the end of the thirteenth c.

## The Genres

The CBN is preceded by a fragment of a Gallic-Portuguese *Ars Poetica* probably dating from the fourteenth c., in which the *cantigas* are divided into the three genres mentioned above. According to this fragment, the difference between the *cantigas de amigo* and those *de amor* lies in the fact that in the former it is always a woman who is speaking whereas in the latter it is the troubadour speaking in the first person. The *cantigas de escarnio* and *maldizer* are of satiric character: the former use irony and double entendre while the latter attack openly and specifically. These are not the only differences, as will be seen.

### Las Cantigas de Amigo

From the point of view of form, this type is characterized by a versification scheme called "parallelistic." This term has supplanted the medieval term, *leixa pren* (leave and take). In this format the rhythmic unity is not the stanza but rather a pair of stanzas, the latter constituted typically by pairs of lines in which both stanzas express the same idea in almost identical language, with the only change being in the rhyme. The two rhymes of the first pair of stanzas are repeated alternately in the following pairs, and the final line of each stanza is the first line of each corresponding stanza and is followed by a refrain. An example is this lovely *cantiga de amor*, by Martín Codax:

> stanza 1   A:  Ondas do mar de Vigo,
>             B:  se vistes meu amigo!
>        REF:  E. ai, Deus, se verrá cedo!
> stanza 2   A:  Ondas do mar levado,
>             B:  se vistes meu amado!
>        REF:  E. ai, Deus, se verrá cedo!
> stanza 3   B:  Se vistes meu amigo,
>             C:  o por que eu sospiro!
>        REF:  E. ai, Deus, se verrá cedo!
> stanza 4   B:  Se vistes meu amado,
>             C:  o por que ei gram cuidado!
>        REF:  E. ai, Deus, se verrá cedo!
>      I.   A.  Waves of the Vigo Sea,
>            B.  Have you seen my lover?

> REF: Oh, Lord, if only he is safe!
> II. A. Waves of the turbulent sea,
> 　　B. Have you seen my beloved?
> REF: Oh, Lord, if only he is safe!
> III. B. If you have seen my love,
> 　　C. The one I sigh for!
> REF: Oh, Lord, if only he is safe!
> IV. B. If you have seen my love,
> 　　C. The one for whom I worry so!
> REF: Oh, Lord, if only he is safe!

The simple metric scheme of this poem can become much more complex with additional stanzas and more lines per stanza. The poems of simplest theme or mood tend to use a simpler form which has led to the theory that the latter are of older or at least of more archaic inspiration (return to traditional forms). The *CBN* preserves some 510 *cantigas de amigo*. Their parallelistic structure makes one think of two alternating courses or two alternating voices which would unite to sing the refrain together. (We only know the melodies of six *cantigas* by Martín Codax, which can be found in . . . *Las siete Canciones de amor*. By Martín Codax. Ed. P. Vindel. Madrid: Minuesa de los Ríos, 1915.) In all the protagonist is a young maid who, in a monologue or in dialogue with her lover, mother, friends or nature, reveals a whole gamut of amorous sentiments. With ingenuousness and grace she expresses such feelings as elation, pride in loving and being loved, timidity, anxiety, sadness, nostalgia, impatience, jealousy and anger. As for themes, the most frequent are the following:

a. *cantigas de romería* (pilgrimage songs), in which the pilgrimage can serve as a pretext for jubilation since it implies meeting the beloved, or there can be a prayer for the quick return of the absent lover. Even vengeance for a lie can appear. Fifty-three *cantigas de romería* survive with nineteen authors, among them Medinho, Arias Corpancho, Fernando de Lago, and João de Cangas. Among the shrines alluded to are San Simón, San Servando, San Clemenço, San Mamede, Santa María de Lago, Santa María das Leiras, and Santa Cecilia.

b. *cantigas marineras* (seafaring songs), in which we find the young maid going down to the sea to search for her beloved in the returning boats. These are thus almost always songs of absence and loneliness. The best poets to compose this type were Pai Gomes Charinho, Martín Codax, Nuno Fernandes Torneol and João Zorro.

c. those which have a river or fountain as their setting, with the damsel there to bathe or wash her hair, hoping at the same time to meet her lover. Pero Meogo and Martín Codax are perhaps the best cultivators of this type. Alongside these themes of rural atmosphere can be found others of a more bourgeois or even courtly nature. The latter manifest Provençal influence in their manner of expression, their psychology and their metrics. Some even lack the refrain.

### Las cantigas de amor

Luckily there are more than 700 of these lyrics extant, and they reveal the influence of the Provençal lyric on Gallic-Portuguese poetry. In this type it is the man who speaks, and his language is filled with Provençal vocabulary (mesura, sen, endurar, druro, cor, prez). Similarly, the themes also evidence the Provençal ideal of courtly love: unrequited adoration of an aristocratic lady who exemplified perfection. This love scheme is regulated by a well-defined code of courtly laws, among them fidelity, secrecy and dignity, which apply equally to the lover and his lady. In comparison to the freshness and naiveté of the *cantiga de amigo*, the *cantiga de amor* can sometimes seem cold and artifical. In the words of Carolina Michaëlis de Vasconcellos (*Cancioneiro da Ajuda*, 2: 939), they are "artificial, conventional, cold and arrogantly aristocratic," an opinion generally shared by Rodrigues Lapa (*Liçoes de Literatura Portuguesa*, 1952). However, the latter also has made an effort to vindicate them by defending their psychological and emotional truth in comparison to the Provençal lyric (in which the intellect and sentimental diversion play a greater role). On the other hand, the Provençal influence, however important, did not eliminate many of the characteristics of the indigenous lyric. With reference to the form, the *cansó* (typical form of the Provençal stanza) never became completely assimilated in Spain, so that the parallelistic form with the refrain persists in the *cantiga de amor*, giving it that repeated, insistent tone so typical of Gallic-Portuguese lyric. Those *cantigas de amor* which lack both parallelistic structure and a refrain (called *de meestria*) are in the minority. Among the outstanding composers of *cantigas de amor* are King Denis, João García de Guilhade, Arias Nunes, Pero da Ponte. Without reaching the artificial mastery evident in the Provençal song, the *cantiga de amor* nevertheless reveals the entire gamut of poetic recourses: the *dobre* (repetition of a word one or more times in each stanza, always putting it in the same places and playing with its various meanings); the *mozdobre* (an analogous technique, in which the word unfolds in its many morphological or etymological forms); the *palavra perduda* (line without rhyme); the *ata-finda* (a type of relationship among lines in which the last verse of a stanza did not end until the first line of the stanza immediately following); the *finda* (defined by the *Poética* as a termination of a thought), a stanza of one to four lines which served as a completion and conclusion to the poem.

### Las cantigas de escarnio y maldizer

These poems represent the other side of the coin in terms of Gallic-Portuguese literature. Co-existent with a lyrical tendency there has always been a predisposition toward satire, and the poems under the above heading represent an important part of the CV and the CBN (398 compositions). In the fragmentary *Poética* already alluded to, the descriptive terminology is quite varied. After distinguishing between the *cantigas de escarnio* and the *cantigas de maldizer*, the *Poética* alludes to other forms: The *jorguete de arterio* (which could be identified with the *cantigas de escarnio*, according to the composer of the

*Poética*); the *cantigas de risadilha* (laughter), probably a traditional genre which preceded the courtly ones, given the name because "at times they cause laughter, although they are not without wisdom and other benefits." Another variant was the *cantiga de seguir* (songs to follow) which parodied a previous poem which it followed. The *cantigas de escarnio* and those of *maldizer* are closely related to the Provençal *sirventés*. Although there are fewer in *gallego* than in Provençal, nevertheless there are quite a number of general moral, political or religious themes (Arias Nunes, Martín Moxa). More frequent is anecdotal and personal satire: the poor, hungry, ostentatious noble troubadour, the fickle camp-follower, the poet devoted to wine, all with a barroom realism not lacking in obscenities, but of great importance not only as a social document of the period but also from the point of view of expression and language. The satire at times takes on an anti-clerical and political character. In order to stop this wave of poetic abusiveness, Alphonse the Wise's legal code *Las siete partidas* (VII, 3, 9) prohibited the composing or singing of any poem which would dishonor or insult another person, a prohibition which even the king himself did not follow, along with a large number of troubadours and minstrels of all social classes, many of whom at the same time also wrote exquisite *cantigas de amor* and *de amigo*: Joao Soares de Paiva, Martín Soares, Nuno Peres Sandeu, Fernand-Esguio, João Zorro, Arias Corpancho and Arias Peres Vuiturom. Many of these poems offer the traditional parallelistic structure with a refrain which varies in complexity. The influence of the Provençal *sirventés* form is most visible in the work of those poets most affected by Provençal poetry (*see* the "Randglossen" of C. Michaëlis de Vasconcellos, in *Zeitschift für romanische Philologie* 25(1901): 129–74, 278–321, 533–60, 669–85; 26(1902): 56–75; 206–29; 27 (1903): 153–72, 257–77, 414–36, 708–37; 28 (1904): 385–434; 29 (1905): 683–711.)

### Metric

The stanza (*cobla, cobra,* or *talho*) varies between two and ten lines, with the four-line stanza predominating for those poems with a refrain and the seven-line stanza typical of those poems with no parallelism or refrain. Those *cantigas* which do not have parallelistic construction are generally not more than three stanzas in length. The *Póetica* calls each line a *palavra* (although the terms *ves* and *vesso* were also known). Uniform stanzas and rhyme seem to be the rule (except in the case of the *palavra perduda* defined above); the problem of number of syllables in cases of feminine rhyme persists. Masculine rhyme, however, does predominate. The rhyme varies greatly, oscillating between four and sixteen syllables per line (refrains of two lines even exist). Nevertheless, the most common lines are those of ten, eight and seven syllables.

### Periods

Carolina Michaëlis de Vasconcellos makes a six-period division: (1) Prehistoric (up to 1188); (2) Protohistoric (up to 1245); (3) Alphonsine or Golden Age (up to 1280); (4) Dionisiac (up to 1300); (5) Imitators (up to 1350); (6) Transition to the second period (from 1350 on). The Count of Barcelos, son of King Denis (who held his son in great esteem), compiler of a lost poetry collection, died in 1354. This year is generally chosen as representing the end of the Gallic-Portuguese poetic cycle. Subsequently two schools of this poetry evolved: the Gallic-Castilian, lasting until 1445 (*Cancionero de *Baena*) and the Castilian-Portuguese (Cancionero Geral de García de Resende), at the beginning of the sixteenth c.

## BIBLIOGRAPHY

### Primary Texts

Alfonso X, King of Castile and Leon, *Cantigas de Sta. María*. Prol. and modern version by A. Cunqueiro. Vigo: Galaxia, 1980.
————. *Cantigas de Sta. María*. Facs. of Escorial ms. Madrid: Edilán, 1979.
*Cancioneiro da Ajuda*. Ed. Carolina Michaëlis de Vasconcellos. 2 vols. Halle: Niemeyer, 1904. Microfilm. Ann Arbor, MI: U Microfilms, 1978?
*Cancioneiro da Biblioteca Nacional, antigo Colocci-Brancuti*. Notes, commentary, glossary by E. Paxeco Machado and J. Pedro Machado. 8 vols. Lisbon: Revista de Portugal, 1949–64.
*Cancionero da Vaticana*. Critical ed. based on diplomatic ed. by Halle. Lisbon: Imprensa Nacional, 1878.
"Las traducciones castellanas de las Cantigas de Sta. Maria." By J. E. Keller and R. W. Linker. *BRAE* 54 (1974): 221–93. Prose Spanish translations with Galician-Portuguese originals.

### Criticism

Asensio, Eugenio. *Poética y realidad en el Cancionero peninsular de la Edad Media*. Madrid: Gredos, 1957.
Bras, José Gomes. *A cantiga de amigo; fonte puríssima do lirismo português*. Santarém: Reis Brasil, 1957.
Dutton, B. "Spanish Fifteenth Century *Cancioneros*: A General Survey to 1465." *KRQ* 26 (1979): 445–60.
Filgueira Valverde, J. *Sobre lírica medieval gallega y sus perduraciones*. Valencia: Bello, 1977.
Hernández Serna, J. "Las Cantigas CCCLXXV y CCCLVII de Alfonso el Sabio: Anotaciones históricas, filológicas y artísticas." *Estudios Románicos* (U of Murcia, 1981): 137–85.
López Aydillo, E. *Los cancioneros gallego-portugueses como fuentes históricas*. New York and Paris: n.p., 1923.
Michaëlis de Vasconcellos, Carolina. *Das origens da poesia peninsular*. Lisbon: J. Fernandes Júnior, 1931.
Rodrigues Lapa, M. *Das origens da poesia lírica em Portugal na Idade Media*. Lisbon: n.p., 1929.
————. *Liçoes da literatura portuguesa*. 3rd ed. Coimbra: Coimbra Editora, 1952.
Tinnell, R. D. "Authorship and Composition: Music and Poetry in *Las cantigas de Santa María* of Alfonso X el Sabio." *KRQ* 28.2 (1981): 189–98.

Lucy Sponsler

**GALVARRIATO, Eulalia** (1905, Madrid–   ), novelist. Galvarriato is the author of one novel, *Cinco sombras* (1947; Five Shadows), which was a finalist for the prestigious Nadal Prize in 1946, and several essays. She was married to Dámaso *Alonso. *Cinco sombras* represented a radical departure from post–Civil War *tremendismo*, with its tender and lyrical story narrated by a male friend of five sisters whose intimate drama, a series of misfortunes, unfolds within their house, a world apart from the political and social upheavals of the time. It is a novel of sentiment more than action, reminiscent of the "sentimental novel" genre that flourished in fifteenth-c. Spain, in another decisive period of Spanish history and civil wars. It is also comparable to Louisa May Alcott's *Little Women*, about five women left at home during the American Civil War. The relevance of the novel to its times, however, reveals itself implicitly in the problem of noncommunication and incomprehension and in the elegiacal tone about truncated young lives, and provides a positive example of the affection of the five sisters as a family. The lyrical prose style, with its attention to small details and sensation of time standing still, seems influenced by *Azorín and *Miró.

BIBLIOGRAPHY

Primary Texts

*Cinco sombras*. 4th ed. Barcelona: Destino, 1967.
"Raíces bajo el agua [short story]." *Clavileño* 21 (June 1953): 53–64.

Criticism

Irizarry, E. "*Cinco sombras*, de Eulalia Galvarriato: Una novela singular de la posguerra." *Novelistas femeninas de la posguerra española*. Ed. J. W. Pérez. Madrid: Porrúa, 1983. 47–56.
Martínez Cachero. *La novela española entre 1939 y 1969: Historia de una aventura*. Madrid: Castalia, 1973. 115.
Nora, E. de. *La novela española contemporánea*. 2nd ed. 3 vols. Madrid: Gredos, 1970. 3: 206–9.

Estelle Irizarry

**GÁLVEZ DE CABRERA, María Rosa** (1768, Málaga–1806, Madrid), poet and dramatist. From an illustrious, well-to-do family, she married an army officer, D. José Cabrera y Ramírez. It was an unhappy marriage, and although it is not clear whether they divorced, they did not live together. It has been assumed that she was the mistress of Godoy (the king's favorite) and that his influence secured publication of her works at the expense of the Spanish government. This statement and the charge of plagiarism, however, is often imputed to nineteenth-c. women writers. Therefore it should be assumed that Godoy supported her just as he supported Leandro Fernández de *Moratín and other artists.

Her poetry and tragedies belong to the neo-classical tradition. Gálvez de Cabrera clearly considered herself a precursor; she stated that she was "the first woman in Spain who ever wrote a whole collection of tragedies." Censors presented numerous difficulties: the tragedy *Ali-Bek* was criticized for being "harsh and gory"; the comedy *La familia a la moda* (The Fashionable Family) was censored as "immoral and a model of corruption and profligacy"; *Un loco hace ciento* (One Fool Is One Too Many) was banned for its mockery of French customs—a dangerous attitude in a moment when Spain was under French rule. *Los figurones literarios* (The Pretentious Writers) is a delicious comedy that mocks the extravagances of those who take the postulates of literary tendencies to extremes.

BIBLIOGRAPHY

Primary Texts

*Ali-Bek*. In *Teatro Nuevo Español*. Madrid: Benito García, 1800–1801.
*El Califa de Bagdad*. National Library in Madrid, Xx–564.
*Un loco hace ciento*. Madrid: Benito García, 1801.
*Obras poéticas*. Madrid: Imprenta Real, 1804.

Criticism

Blanco García, P. *La Literatura española en el s. XIX*. 3rd ed. Madrid: Saénz de Jubera Hermanos, 1909.
Díaz Plaja, Guillermo. *Historia general de las literaturas hispánicas*. 6 vols. Barcelona: n.p., 1949–57.
Serrano Sanz, Manuel. *Apuntes para una biblioteca de escritoras españolas, desde 1401– 1833*. Madrid: Sucesores de Rivadeneyra, 1975.

Cristina Enríquez

**GÁLVEZ DE MONTALVO, Luis** (1546?, Guadalajara–1591?, Palermo), writer. A gentleman of the court in the service of Don Enrique de Mendoza, Gálvez de Montalvo's most notable work, *El Pastor de Fílida* (1582; The Shepherd of Filida), is a *pastoral romance which introduces the models of courtly narratives. *Cervantes and Lope de *Vega praised the work wholeheartedly. Like many pastoral romances, it is a *roman á clef* in which the author includes real personages under literary disguise in the narrative. His patron, Don Enrique de Mendoza, is Mendino; the author, Siralvo, who is enamored of Fílida. Attempts have been made to identify Fílida with the sister of the Duke of Osuna. The work follows faithfully the customary patterns of pastoral literature; one of its most outstanding features is the poetry Gálvez de Montalvo includes, in particular the verse written in accordance with the old Castilian school. Of great interest to literary criticism is the debate in the sixth part between the defenders of the rival schools of poetry: the traditional Castilian and the Italianate. In this same debate is included a poem in praise of noble ladies, *El Canto de Erión* (The Song of Erion). *El Pastor de Fílida* was a total success, attaining five editions in a short time. Gálvez de Montalvo also composed other works of slight importance, such as an unedited translation of Tasso's *Jerusalem* and a translation of Tansillo in double *quintillas*, *Las lágrimas de San Pedro* (1587; The Tears of St. Peter). *See also* Humanism; Italian Literary Influence; Renaissance; Siglo de Oro.

BIBLIOGRAPHY

Primary Text

*El Pastor de Fílida.* NBAE 7.

Criticism

Fucilla, Joseph. "On the Vogue of Tansillo's 'Lagrime di San Pietro' in Spain and Portugal." *Rinascita* 1 (1939): 73–85.

Rodríguez Marín, F. "La Fílida de Gálvez de Montalvo." *Discursos leídos ante la Real academia de la historia en la recepción pública del excmo. señor don Francisco Rodríguez Marín el día 10 de abril de 1927.* Madrid: RABM, 1927.

Deborah Compte

**GAMA, Sebastião** (1924, Lisbon?–1952, Lisbon?), Portuguese poet. During his brief life, Gama produced several books of poems, many of them in neo-historicist vein, or tinged with a certain *Romanticism as seen in his cult of the past and of nature. His works include *Cabo da Boa Esperança* (1947; Cape of Good Hope), *Campo Aberto* (1950; *Open Land*, 2nd ed. 1962), *Pelo Sonho é que vamos* (1953; Through Dreams We Go), *Serra-Mãe* (1954) and *Diário* (1961; Diary). He was associated with the *Távola Redonda* (Round Table) group to which Fernanda *Botelho and Mourão-Ferreira also belonged.

BIBLIOGRAPHY

Primary Text

*Obras.* 7 vols. Lisbon: Atica, 1957–1971.

**GAMALLO FIERROS, Dionisio** (1914, Ribadeo– ), Galician professor and literary investigator. Since collecting, in the 1940s, early verse written in Seville by *Bécquer, this classmate of *Torrente Ballester and disciple of *Menéndez Pidal has published similar materials, mostly unedited letters, by other outstanding figures of nineteenth-c. literature such as *Pereda, *Clarín, *Pardo Bazán and *Pérez Galdós. Unfortunately these publications represent only a part of the materials he possesses and are normally made public in provincial newspapers of difficult access. He is also editor of *Obras completas de Bécquer. See also* Galician Literature.

BIBLIOGRAPHY

Primary Text

*Obras completas de Bécquer.* Madrid: Aguilar, 1969.

Stephen Miller

**GANGARILLA,** a type of acting troupe of the *Siglo de Oro. The term designated a troupe of three or four actors, and a young boy to play female roles, that traveled from village to town performing farces, etc. *See also* Compañía.

**GANIVET, Ángel** (1865, Granada–1898, Riga, Latvia), essayist, novelist, journalist, diplomat. A brilliant student, he earned degrees in arts (1888) and law (1890) from the U of Granada and a doctorate in philosophy (1890) from the Central U of Madrid with a dissertation on *La importancia de la lengua sánscrita* (1889; The Importance of the Sanskrit Language). His first dissertation, *España filosófica contemporánea* (1889; Contemporary Philosophical Spain), which was rejected by the examining committee, provided an analysis of Spain's ills. The young author attributed these ills to a lack of *ideas madres*, or directing ideas. In 1891 Ganivet failed to win appointment by competitive exam to the chair in Greek at the U of Granada. During the exam period, however, he became friendly with Miguel de *Unamuno, who won the chair in Greek at the U of Salamanca. In 1892 Ganivet was named vice consul in Antwerp, Belgium. Here, he began to write. In 1896, Ganivet assumed the post of consul in Helsinki and held it until 1898 when he was transferred to Riga. There, on November 29, 1898, he drowned himself.

Much of Ganivet's work was written in Helsinki, although he completed most of his first novel, *La conquista del reino de Maya por el último conquistador español, Pío Cid* (The Conquest of the Kingdom of Maya by the Last Spanish Conquistador, Pío Cid), in Antwerp from 1893 to 1895. This novel is a biting satire of European colonialism in Africa with its absurd attempts to impose a hollow civilization and worthless, material progress on other nations. The work ridicules Spanish institutions such as the Parliament, the army, the civil service, and the church. For Ganivet, material progress is of no value; what must be achieved is spiritual regeneration. An epilogue, the allegorical "Sueño de Pío Cid" (Pío Cid's Dream), was written two years after the rest of the novel; in it Ganivet seems to consider the bloody destruction of old cultures to make way for new and superior ones a positive step in human development.

In *Granada la bella* (1896; Granada the Beautiful) Ganivet urges a restoration of Granada's communal spirit, with no concern for the difficult material realities the city faced. This work is in some ways a preview of his most famous book, a treatise on the Spanish character entitled *El idearium español* (1896; *Spain, an Interpretation*, 1946). Here, in a key text of the *Generation of 1898, Ganivet analyzed the disease which afflicted Spain and, to his mind, caused her general state of decline, and then proposed a remedy. He declared the Spanish character to be one of independence and individualism formed by the influences of Senecan stoicism and the "territorial spirit" of independence (produced by the geographical fact of being a peninsula). Spain was in the grip of what Ganivet termed *abulia*, a state of lassitude and inaction, engendered by the absence of guiding ideas. What Spain had to do was recover her sense of mission, her *ideas madres*, and thus regenerate herself. Ganivet's method, as the critic Herbert Ramsden has pointed out, is borrowed from Taine, and the influence of Hegel and the Romantics' mystique of national character is also apparent. Critics have also found the very idea of national character to be an unverifiable and potentially dangerous concept, and have considered the *Idearium*, in spite of its enormous appeal, to be a simplification of reality, overly optimistic and naive. During 1898 Ganivet and Unamuno engaged in an exchange of open letters in the Granada newspaper *El Defensor de Granada* (Granada's Defender) which were later published in book form as *El porvenir de España* (1912; The Future of Spain). In this written conversation about various ideas in the *Idearium*, Ganivet affirmed his conviction that Spain must seek her strength exclusively within herself, while Unamuno counseled against such a withdrawal.

*Cartas finlandesas* (1898; Finnish Letters) first appeared in the same newspaper from October 1896 to July 1897 and in two issues in April 1898. These essays explore Finland's "spirit" as manifested in her literature and political institutions. Ganivet was one of the first Spaniards to write about Scandinavian culture from firsthand experience.

After spending the summer of 1897 in Granada, Ganivet wrote eight short pieces, poetry and prose, about life there. They became part of a book-length homage to his native city; *El libro de Granada* (1899; The Book of Granada). *Hombres del norte* (1905, posthumously; Men of the North) is a series of essays concentrating on the ideological content of works by Scandinavian authors such as Jonas Lie, Henrik Ibsen, and others. These essays originally appeared in *El Defensor de Granada* between February and August of 1898.

Ganivet's second novel, *Los trabajos del infatigable creador, Pío Cid* (1898; The Labors of the Tireless Creator, Pío Cid), appeared in 1898. Originally projected to contain twelve labors, or chapters, like the labors of Hercules, it remained unfinished with only six at the time of his death. *Los trabajos* is dominated by the autobiographical character Pío Cid, who, despite his own profound skepticism, intervenes in the lives of a series of other characters (each of which represents a different level of Spanish society) in order to further their spiritual progress. Each character is significantly transformed by this encounter with Pío Cid. Ganivet also re-elaborates and sums up earlier themes, such as Spain and its destiny; the Spanish character and its need to cultivate the qualities of charity, sacrifice, and spirituality; pedagogy and education; skepticism; and a philosophical concern for existential problems. The novel, with its paucity of plot, descriptions, dramatic conflict and characterization (excepting Pío Cid), is a major break with the conventions of the late nineteenth-c. Spanish novel and may be considered the first novel of the Generation of 1898.

Ganivet's last work is the verse play *El escultor de su alma* (1898; The Sculptor of His Soul). Following the form of the *auto sacramental* (*auto) he presents a sculptor, the autobiographical Pedro Mártir, and his struggle to create himself and attain artistic immortality. The ambiguity of the work has given rise to diverse critical interpretations. Javier Herrero sees the play as representing the artist's reconciliation with religious faith, part of an illumination that this critic has traced through Ganivet's earlier works. Other critics disagree, finding in the work a rejection of the human struggle in favor of existence as a piece of stone, an inanimate object untroubled by the mysteries of the unknown.

In addition to the work he completed for publication, Ganivet is the author of an interesting correspondence with friends, most notably Francisco Navarro Ledesma and Nicolás María López, and family, beginning in 1888 when he left Granada, and ending shortly before his death. Much of the correspondence has been published. *See also* Essay.

BIBLIOGRAPHY

Primary Texts

*La Cofradía del Avellano: Cartas de Angel Ganivet.* Ed. Nicolás María López. Granada: Luis F. Pinar Rocha, 1935.
*Correspondencia familiar de Angel Ganivet: 1888–1897.* Ed. Javier Herrero. Granada: Anel, 1967.
*Juicio de Angel Ganivet sobre su obra literaria (Cartas* inéditas). Ed. Luis Seco de Lucena y Paredes. Granada: Universidad de Granada, 1962.
*Obras completas de Angel Ganivet.* 3rd ed. Madrid: Aguilar, 1961.
*Los trabajos del infatigable creador, Pío Cid.* Ed. Laura Rivkin. Madrid: Cátedra, 1983.

English Translation

*Spain: An Interpretation.* Tr. J. R. Carey, intro. R. M. Nadal. London: Eyre and Spottiswood, 1946.

Criticism

Ginsberg, Judith. *Angel Ganivet.* London: Tamesis, 1985.
Herrero, Javier. *Angel Ganivet, un iluminado.* Madrid: Gredos, 1966.
Jeschke, Hans. "Angel Ganivet. Seine Persönlichkeit un Hauptwerke." *RH* 72 (1928): 102–246.
Ramsden, Herbert. *Angel Ganivet's "Idearium espanol": A Critical Study.* Manchester: U of Manchester, 1967.
Shaw, Donald L. *The Generation of 1898 in Spain.* London: Benn, 1975.

Judith Ginsberg

**GAOS, Alejandro** (1908, Valencia–1958, Valencia), professor of literature, poet. In his book *Tertulia de campanas* (1932; Literary Gathering of Bells) he declared himself against "pure poetry." Traces of this first lyrical attempt appear in his next works, *Ímpetu del sueño* (1947: Dream Impetus) and *Vientos de la angustia* (1949; Anguish Winds). The poet achieved greater human presence in *La sencillez atormentada* (1951; Tormented Simplicity).

BIBLIOGRAPHY

Primary Text

*La sencillez atormentada.* Valencia: Abril, 1951.

Isabel McSpadden

**GAOS, José** (1902, Ablana, Oviedo–1969, Mexico), Spanish professor, translator, philosopher and critic. He held chairs in the universities of Zaragoza and Madrid before the Civil War, and later in Mexico. He translated into Spanish many of the important works of Husserl, Heidegger, and other contemporary philosophers, and his own work is also primarily philosophical, as in *La crítica* *del psicoanálisis en Husserl* (1933; The Critique of Psychoanalysis in Husserl); *La filosofía de Maimónides* (1940; The Philosophy of Maimonides); *El pensamiento hispanoamericano* (1944; Spanish American Thought); *Pensamiento de lengua española* (1945; Thought in the Spanish Language); *Dos exclusivas del hombre: la mano y el tiempo* (1945; Two Human Exclusives: The Hand and Time); *Filosofía de la filosofía e historia de la filosofía* (1947; Philosophy of Philosophy and History of Philosophy); *Introducción a "el ser y el tiempo" de Martin Heidegger* (1951; Introduction to "Being and Time" of Martin Heidegger); *En torno a la filosofía mexicana,* 2 vols. (1952–53; Concerning Mexican Philosophy); *Filosofía mexican de nuestros días* (1954; Mexican Philosophy in Our Day); *Sobre Ortega y Gasset* (1957; About Ortega y Gasset); *Confesiones profesionales* (1958; Professional Confessions); *Discurso de la filosofía* (1959; Discourse of Philosophy); and *Orígenes de la filosofía y de su historia* (1960; Origins and History of Philosophy).

BIBLIOGRAPHY

Primary Texts

*Confesiones profesionales.* Mexico: Fondo de Cultura Económica, 1958.
*Filosofía contemporánea.* Caracas: Universidad Central de Venezuela, 1962.
*Introducción a . . . Heidegger.* Mexico: Fondo de Cultura Económica, 1951.
*Pensamiento de lengua española.* Mexico: Stylo, 1945.
*En torno a la filosofía mexicana.* 2 vols. Mexico: Porrúa y Obregón, 1952–53.

Janet Pérez

**GAOS, Vicente** (1919, Valencia–1980, Valencia), Spanish poet, translator and professor of Spanish literature in several American universities. His collection of poetry *Arcángel de mi noche* (1944; Archangel of My Night) won the Adonais Poetry Prize, and was followed the next year by *Sobre la tierra* (1945; Upon the Earth). Other poetic collections include *Luz desde el sueño* (1947; Light from Sleep) and *Profecía del recuerdo* (1956; Prophecy of Memory). He has translated to Spanish a variety of French and English poems, including those of Peguy, Rimbaud, Shelley and Eliot. Gaos also published an essay of critical theory, *Poesía y técnica poética* (1955; Poetry and Poetic Technique), studies of classical literature, and an analysis of the stylistics of *Campoamor, *La poética de Campoamor* (1955; The Poetics of Campoamor). In 1963 he won the Agora Poetry Prize for *Mitos para un tiempo de incrédulos* (Myths for an Age of Unbelievers).

BIBLIOGRAPHY

Primary Texts

*Antología del grupo poético de 1927.* Salamanca: Anaya, 1965.
*Claves de literatura española.* Madrid: Guadarrama, 1971.
*Diez siglos de poesía española.* Madrid: Alianza, 1975.
*Obra poética completa.* Intro. D. Alonso. 2 vols. Valencia: Alfonso el Magnánimo, 1982.
*Poesía y técnica poética.* Madrid: Ateneo, 1955.

English Translation

"Incomplete Beauty" and "Revelation of Life." Tr. J. M. Cohen. In *The Penguin Book of Spanish Verse*. Ed. J. M. Cohen. Baltimore: Penguin, 1960.

Criticism

García de la Concha, V. *La poesía española de postguerra*. Madrid: Prensa Española, 1973. 423–30.

Janet Pérez

**GARAGORRI, Paulino** (1916, San Sebastián– ), literary scholar. A disciple of *Ortega y Gasset, he has been involved in editing Ortega's works, and has studied him in great depth. Garagorri's writing boasts superior clarity and organization, as in *Ortega. Una reforma de la filosofía* (1958; Ortega. A Reform of Philosophy), *La paradoja del filósofo* (1959; The Philosopher's Paradox), *Del pasado al porvenir* (1965; From the Past to the Future), *Introducción a Ortega* (1970; Introduction to Ortega), and *La tentación política* (1971; The Temptation of Politics). He also has served as secretary of the distinguished journal *Revista de Occidente*.

BIBLIOGRAPHY

Primary Texts

*Del pasado al porvenir*. Barcelona: Hispanoamericana, 1965.
*Introducción a Miguel de Unamuno*. . . . Madrid: Alianza, 1986.
*La paradoja del filósofo*. Madrid: RO, 1959.
*La tentación política*. Madrid: Seminario, 1971.
*Unamuno y Ortega*. Estella: Salvat, 1972.

Isabel McSpadden

**GARCÉS, Jesús Juan** (1917, Madrid– ), poet. He began collaborating with the Garcilaso group after the Civil War. His poetry has been published in a volume titled *He venido a esta orilla* (1949; I Came to This Shore), and in *Lo nuestro es pasar* (1963; Ours Is to Carry On).

BIBLIOGRAPHY

Primary Text

*Lo nuestro es pasar*. Madrid: n.p., 1963.

Isabel McSpadden

**GARCÉS, Julio** (1917, Soria–1978, Lima, Peru), poet. He received a law degree from the U of Barcelona. A friend of *García Lorca, he was a surrealist poet, living most of his adult life in Lima, Peru, and returning infrequently to Spain. His works include *Peregrinaje* (1937; Pilgrimage), *Primer romancero del re-*

*cuerdo* (1938; First Ballad Book of Memory), *Gris* (1942; Gray), *Odas* (1943; Odes), and *Poesía sin orillas* (Poetry without Shores [Limits]).

Isabel McSpadden

**GARCÍA, Carlos** (c. 1575, ?–c. 1630, ?), prose author, expatriate. Virtually nothing is known of his life; he seems to have resided in France for a while. *La oposición y conjunción de los dos grandes luminares de la tierra* (Paris, 1617; The Antipathy between the French and Spaniard, 1641) is attributed to him. His most important work is *La desordenada codicia de los bienes ajenos* (1619; The Lawless Greed for the Possessions of Others, translated as *The sonne of the rogue,* 1638); it is a curious, didactic mix of *picaresque and ascetic in which the author, pondering prison and hell as he sits in jail, is interrupted by Andres, a thief, who proceeds to recount his life.

BIBLIOGRAPHY

Primary Texts

*La desordenada codicia. . . .* In *La novela picaresca española.* Madrid: Aguilar, 1962.
*La desordenada codicia . . . y La oposición y conjunción de los dos grandes luminares de la tierra.* Ed. J.M.E. Madrid: Fé, 1877.

English Translations

*The Antipathy between the French and Spaniard.* Tr. R. Gentilys. London: Martine, 1641.
*The sonne of the rogue.* Tr. W. McElvin. London: Dawson, 1638. (Tr. of *La desordenada codicia.)*

Criticism

Carballo Picaza, A. "Datos para la historia de un cuento." *Revista Bibliográfica y Documental* 1 (1947): 425–66.
———. "El doctor Carlos García, novelista español del siglo XVIII." *Revista Bibliográfica y Documental* 5 (1951): 5–46.
Pelorson, J. E. "Le docteur Carlos García et la colonie hispano-portugaise de Paris, 1613–1619." *BH* 71 (1969): 518–76.

Maureen Ihrie

**GARCÍA ÁLVAREZ, Enrique** (1873, Madrid–1931, Madrid), a minor playwright of the Spanish theater of absurd humor. He exercised a paramount role in the development of the kind of incongruous comedy for which *Jardiel Poncela, Miguel *Mihura, and Alfonso *Paso gained later distinction. García Alvarez was an indefatigable collaborator. He shared over 100 titles with some 12 other playwrights, exchanging most of his aesthetic precepts with Carlos *Arniches and Pedro *Muñoz Seca. Before the age of twenty, he had written about 25 plays for the *género chico* with Antonio Paso. Thereafter, for 15 years, he collaborated almost exclusively with Arniches, writing another 25 plays. Following an irretrievable personal rift with Arniches, he then joined Pedro *Muñoz Seca, Antonio Casero, Joaquín *Abati, among others, to write 50 additional comedies. García Alvarez is the acknowledged creator of a comic prescription that bears the name *astracán* (astrakhan), a farcical composition, usually of one act, which deliberately eschews verisimilitude and promotes zany dialogue as central to the comic situation. His *astracán* formulas employed deviation and incoherence to combat the banality and dullness of everyday communication; his contrived sketches depended entirely on puns, jests, plays on words, absurd repartee, and dislocated speech for their effect, rather than on slapstick, character delineation, or clever plot line. *See also* Contemporary Spanish Theater.

BIBLIOGRAPHY

Primary Texts

*La alegría de la huerta*. With A. Paso. Rpt. Louisville, KY: Falls City Microcards, 1965.
García Alvarez's plays are also found in many volumes of the Spanish Plays collection.

Douglas McKay

**GARCÍA BACCA, Juan David** (1901, Pamplona– ), Spanish philosopher and essayist. As a professor, he taught in the Universities of Barcelona, Quito and Caracas. Philosophically, his interests have been in problems of logic, epistemology and language. He translated many Greek philosophical texts into Spanish, with commentaries. His principal works include *Introducción a la logística* (1934; Introduction to Logistics), *Introducción a la lógica moderna* (1936; Introduction to Modern Logic), *Invitación a filosofar* (1940; Invitation to Philosophize), *Filosofía de las ciencias* (1941 and 1962; Philosophy of Science), *Tipos históricos del filosofar físico desde Hesíodo hasta Kant* (1941; Historical Types of Physical Philosophy from Hesiod to Kant), *Filosofía en metáforas y parábolas* (1945; Philosophy in Metaphors and Parables), *Nueve grandes filósofos contemporáneos y sus temas* (1947; Nine Great Contemporary Philosophers and Their Themes), and *Metafísica natural estabilizada y problemática metafísica espontánea* (1963; Natural Stabilized Metaphysics and Problematic Spontaneous Metaphysics). *See also* Essay.

BIBLIOGRAPHY

Primary Texts

*Autobiografía intelectual y otros ensayos*. Caracas: U Central de Venezuela, 1983.
*Cosas y personas*. Caracas: Fondo de Cultura Económica, 1977.
*Ensayos*. Barcelona: Península, 1970.
*Fragmentos filosóficos de los presocráticos*. Caracas: Ministerio de Educación, 1963.
*Introducción a la lógica moderna*. Barcelona: Labor, 1936. Spanish translation of 1934 version in Catalan.
*Invitación a filosofar*. 2 vols. Mexico: Colegio de México, 1940–42.

Criticism

Pérez Perazzo, E. E. de, *Bibliografía de Juan d. García Bacca*. Caracas: Universidad Central de Venezuela, 1981.

**GARCÍA BADELL, Gabriel** (1943, Madrid– ), novelist. He studied law at the U of Madrid before beginning a varied literary career which included the novel *Las manos de mi padre* (1968; My Father's Hands) and several other works: *La tierra* (Earth), *El columpio* (The Swing), *A cielo abierto* (1972; Open Skies), *Lou, Un largo bostezo* (A Long Yawn) and others, all of them finalists for, but not winners of, national literary prizes. His first work to attract critical attention, *De las Armas a Montemolín* (1971; From Arms Street to Montemolin), takes its name from two streets in Zaragoza which marked the extremes of the city at the time of writing. The author attempts a sort of X-ray of this important provincial capital, while avoiding the pitfalls of regionalism and *costumbrismo* (*romanticism). The protagonist, an exiled Republican, returns to a vastly altered and unexpectedly immoral environment, which serves as a thinly veiled critique of the ethics of the Franco regime. García Badell was again finalist for the Nadal Prize with his next novel and a number of its successors, obtaining favorable notice with *Las cartas cayeron boca abajo* (1972; The Cards Fell Face Down), which examines an Aragonese village during the Civil War and studies the psychology of several characters, with special attention to their morality, ideologies and internal contradictions, their alienation, and the despair of liberal survivors in the post-war period. In *Funeral por Francia* (1975; Funeral in France), set in a Spanish prison in the post-war years, García Badell studies the effect of the admitting of a strange new prisoner, whose wife has just died. The altered internal situation is presented via examinations of the ideology, personality and internal conflicts of guards and convicts, utilizing a sort of internal dialogue between the protagonist and his late wife. *De rodillas al sol* (1976; Kneeling before the Sun) parodies the Falangist hymn "Cara al sol," to present the alienation and desperation of certain sectors of post-war Spanish society, their insecurity and lack of orientation. With *La zarabanda* (1978; The Dance), the author presents a more subtle form of violence, a spiritual transgression personified in the premeditated provocation of fear and moral terror in the psyches of supposed offenders by false Christians and their priests. The novel explores the protagonist's discovery of the origins of guilt and the obstacles to "innocence" or psychological felicity. Impelled by his mother's death and his subsequent remorse to return to ancient and abandoned religious practices, the protagonist futilely seeks absolution, which is denied him for political reasons by a church and state coalition. In *Nuevo auto de fe* (1980; Another Inquisitorial Trial of Faith), another novel and the author's eleventh volume to appear, García Badell turns more philosophical. This work's protagonist seeks a sort of Nirvana, searching for transcendent meaning beyond youthful enthusiasm or excess. Recognizing the constraints upon individual political activity or achievement, the author nonetheless maintains a certain intellectual loyalty to anarchy (on the ideal level espoused by Pío *Baroja, rather than that of activism or terrorism).

BIBLIOGRAPHY

Primary Texts

*Nuevo auto de fe.* Barcelona: Destino, 1980.
*De rodillas al sol.* Barcelona: Destino, 1976.
*La zarabanda.* Barcelona: Destino, 1978.

Janet Pérez

**GARCÍA BAENA, Pablo** (1923, Cordoba– ), poet. With Ricardo Molina, he founded the magazine *Cántico.* He has published various collections of poetry, including *Rumor oculto* (1946; Hidden Rumor), *Mientras cantan los pájaros* (1948; While the Birds Sing), *Antiguo muchacho* (1950; Old Boy), *Junio* (1957; June), and, in 1961, *Óleo* (Oil).

BIBLIOGRAPHY

Primary Text

*Poesía completa (1940–1980).* Madrid: Visor, 1982.

Criticism

Miró, Emilio. "Pablo García Baena y Justo Jorge Padrón." *Insula* 394 (1979): 6.
Villena, Luis Antonio de. "Sobre *Antiguo muchacho,* de Pablo García Baena: Sensualidad, mocedad, imperios antiguos." *CH* 367–68 (Jan.-Feb. 1981): 319–26.

Isabel McSpadden

**GARCÍA BLÁZQUEZ, José Antonio** (1940, Cáceres– ), novelist. He received his doctorate in literature from the U of Madrid, with a dissertation titled "El pensamiento estético de Oscar Wilde" (The Aesthetic Thought of Oscar Wilde), published in 1969. Since 1970 he has worked for the World Organization of Tourism, first in Geneva and later in Madrid. Due to the experimental nature of his novels, critics have considered him a member of the generation of 1966, also known as the "novísimos." His novels frequently have esoteric and obscure plots. *Los diablos* (1966; The Devils) was followed by *No encontré rosas para mi mamá* (1968; I Didn't Find Roses for My Mommy), which was later made into a movie. *Fiesta en el polvo* (1971; Party in the Dust) was followed by *El rito* (Rite), winner of the 1973 Nadal Prize. An ambitious and disconnectedly structured novel, *El rito* presents the pathological drama of a man obsessed by his own internal phantoms, torn by the creations of his delirious imagination and a repressed incestuous passion. These conflicting emotions drive him to deny the real world and to take refuge in the ideal paradise of childhood, with its perversely magical rites of childhood games. In *Señora muerte* (1976; Mrs. Death), García Blázquez delves even more deeply into the psychic world of his characters. On the level of plot, the novel relates a tale of revenge born of envy, as the protagonist attempts to destroy the love relationship of two other characters after failing in his own attempt to break into society. At the same time, the author explores hidden aspects of the lives and psyches of other personages of the novel. His most recent work is titled *Rey de ruinas* (1981; King of Ruins).

BIBLIOGRAPHY

Primary Texts

*Los diablos.* Barcelona: Plaza & Janés, 1966.
*Fiesta en el polvo.* Esplugas de Llobregat: Plaza & Janés, 1971.
*No encontré rosas para mi mamá.* Madrid: Alfaguara, 1968.
*Rey de ruinas.* Esplugas de Llobregat: Plaza & Janés, 1981.
*Señora muerte.* Barcelona: Destino, 1976.

Criticism

Domingo, José. "Novelas de Manuel Ferrand, José Antonio García Blázquez y Aquilino Duque." *Insula* 334 (Sept. 1974): 5.
Lezcano, Margarita M. "Las novelas ganadoras del premio Nadal 1970–1979." Diss., Florida State U, 1984.

                                                        Margarita Lezcano

**GARCÍA CERECEDA, Martín** (16th c., Córdoba–?), soldier and historian. He wrote a judicious *Tratado de las campañas y otros acontecimientos de los ejércitos del Emperador Carlos V* (n.d; Treatise on the Battles and Other Events of the Armies of Emperor Charles V). It covers the years 1521–45, and is an account of what he witnessed as Charles's harquebusier.

BIBLIOGRAPHY

Primary Text

*Tratado de las campañas y. . . .* Sociedad de Bibliófilos Españoles 12. 3 vols. Madrid: Aribau, 1873–76.

**GARCÍA DE LA BARGA Y GÓMEZ DE LA SERNA, Andrés.** *See* Barga, Corpus

**GARCÍA DE LA HUERTA, Vicente** (1734, Zafra [Badajoz]–1787, Madrid), dramatist and critic. García de la Huerta came from a poor but noble family, raised in the traditional atmosphere of rural Spain; he studied for a brief period in Salamanca, but soon moved to Madrid. The Duke of Alba named him official archivist of the House of Alba. With the duke's patronage, Huerta received the post of senior official at the Royal Library. He was also given membership in the Spanish Academy (*Academia Española) and the Academies of History and of San Sebastián. An amorous intrigue won him the enmity of the Count of Aranda, against whom Huerta engaged in an ill-considered series of libelous satires. For this Huerta was exiled from Madrid in 1767 and sentenced to seven years of confinement at the penitentiary in Orán. Upon Aranda's fall from power in 1777 Huerta was permitted to return to Madrid, where he spent the last ten years of his life trying to regain the favor and esteem he had held before his exile. During the first decade of his literary career in Madrid, Huerta was well known as a poet, and was considered the unofficial court poet. He wrote all manner of solemn and festive verses for court celebrations, and his eclogues were well received by his peers. One of them, *Endimión* (1755), was one of his first works to appear in print. He also wrote elegiac verse, sonnets, and ballads in which he sought to imitate *Góngora's style. Another early work, the *Biblioteca militar española* (1760; Spanish Military Library), seems to have been the result of Huerta's participation in the festivities associated with the arrival of Charles III in Madrid in 1760.

García de la Huerta's first stay in Madrid coincided with the first major confrontations between the partisans of traditional Golden Age *theater, as symbolized by *Calderón and his followers, and those reformers who wished to introduce in Spain a classically styled theater in the French manner. Although the neo-classic style was much esteemed by those literary reformers, it was generally rejected by the mass theater audience. Huerta, a man of considerable intelligence and talent, though possessed by a fiery, and occasionally foolhardy temperament, was an outspoken critic of the French influence. On the other hand, the debates over the relative merits of traditional Spanish or classic French drama led Huerta to consider the possibility of creating a truly nationalistic form of tragedy, fusing the dynamism of traditional Golden Age drama with the rigid structure and weighty style of classic tragedy. The result of his efforts over some six years was *Raquel*, first performed by an amateur troupe of actors in Orán in 1772. The play was subsequently produced in Barcelona in 1775, and received its Madrid premiere in 1778. From that point Huerta's fame was assured as the author of the most recognized dramatic work of its type from the eighteenth c. In the introductory verses which he composed for the Madrid premiere, published along with the text of the play shortly after its performance, Huerta invoked the classic muse of tragedy, but a Spanish Melpomene, ''vestida sí de ropajes Castellanos'' (dressed in Castilian raiments). Huerta yearned to create a uniquely Spanish tragedy, fulfilling all the requirements of structure and tone necessary for a classic tragedy, but with a theme which was Spanish in its origins and sentiment. Accordingly, he selected the tragic story of Raquel, the Jewish mistress of the medieval King Alphonse VIII. The theme had been used previously by several Golden Age writers: by Lope de *Vega, in his epic poem *Jerusalén Conquistada* (1609; Jerusalem Conquered), and in his play *Las paces de los reyes y judía de Toledo* (1617; Treaties of the Kings and the Jewess of Toledo); by *Mira de Amescua, in *La desgraciada Raquel y Rey Don Alfonso* (1625; The Hapless Raquel and King Alfonso); by Luis de *Ulloa Pereira, in his well-known poem *La Raquel* (1650); and in the play *La judía de Toledo* (1667; The Jewess of Toledo), attributed to *Diamante. Critics have established Huerta's sources primarily in the Ulloa poem and the Diamante play. Huerta's work is similarly imbued with a patently Spanish atmosphere, at once eloquent and vibrant. On the other hand, Huerta limited the story to coincide with the neo-classic unities of time, place and action, and cast the entire verse play in hendecasyllabic lines, the closest Spanish equivalent to the alexandrine meter of French neo-classic tragedy. Nonetheless, his use of the assonant rhyme characteristic of the traditional Spanish ballad form allowed a further indigenous quality to his work. Huerta was not so successful with subsequent efforts in tragic drama: *Agamenón vengado* (Agamemnon Avenged), based on Sophocles through an intermediate version by Fernán Pérez de Oliva; and *Xaira*, a version of Voltaire's *Zaïre*.

After the premiere of *Raquel*, Huerta intended to support his defense of traditional Spanish theater by publishing an extensive collection of Golden Age plays. It was an excellent idea, and an opportune moment for such a collection to appear, but the results of his sixteen-volume *Theatro Hespañol* (1785–86; Spanish Theater) were so erratic as to invalidate his own intentions. Among all the plays in the collection, none are to be found by such authors as Lope, *Tirso, *Ruiz Alarcón, *Guillén de Castro, Luis *Vélez de Guevara, or *Pérez de Montalbán—in short, the entire first generation of Golden Age dramatists. Instead, Huerta concentrated on Calderón and the many secondary figures who followed in the master's footsteps. Huerta's numerous enemies took advantage of his lack of judgment and launched a full-scale attack on his work. Among his most vocal critics were *Samaniego, Ezquerra, *Forner, *Jovellanos, Nicolás Fernández de *Moratín and Juan de *Iriarte, as well as myriad anonymous figures. Huerta began an equally vociferous counter-attack, but his failing health soon removed him from the center of the controversy.

Marcelino Menéndez y Pelayo characterized Huerta as ''a man with more intelligence than judgment, with better instinct than taste, with more imagination than foresight.'' This assessment coincides with that of Huerta's contemporaries, who saw in Huerta a considerable intellect which was severely undermined by an arrogantly defensive attitude that clouded his sense of judgment. *See also* Theater in Spain; Siglo de Oro.

BIBLIOGRAPHY

Primary Texts

*Raquel*. Ed. René Andioc. Madrid: Castalia, 1971.
*Raquel*. Ed. Joseph G. Fucilla. Madrid: Cátedra, 1974.

Criticism

Aguilar Piñal, Francisco. ''Las primeras representaciones de la *Raquel* de García de la Huerta.'' *Revista de Literatura* 63–64 (1967): 133–35.
Andioc, René. ''La *Raquel* y el Antiabsolutismo.'' In *Teatro y sociedad en el Madrid del siglo XVIII*. Madrid: Fundación Juan March y Castalia, 1976. 259–344.
———. ''La *Raquel* y la censura.'' *HR* 43 (1975): 115–39.
Deacon, Philip. ''García de la Huerta, *Raquel*, y el motín de Madrid de 1766.'' *BRAE* 56 (1976): 369–87.
Johnson, Jerry L. ''The Relevancy of *La Raquel* to Its Times.'' *RN* 14 (1972): 86–91.
Sebold, Russell P. ''Neoclasicismo y creación en la *Raquel* de García de la Huerta.'' *El rapto de la mente. Poética* y poesía dieciochescas. Madrid: Prensa Española, 1970. 235–54.

Schurlknight, Donald E. ''La *Raquel* de Huerta y sus 'sistema particular.' '' *BH* 83.1–
2 (1983): 65–78.

Donald C. Buck

**GARCÍA DE PRUNEDA, Salvador** (1912, Madrid– ), Spanish novelist and
diplomat. He studied in a French private school in Tours, and then at the U of
Madrid (1928–32), after which he received a grant to go to London. Later he
lectured on art at Oxford. He participated in the Civil War on the Franco side,
reaching the rank of captain. In 1943 he entered the diplomatic corps, with posts
in Paris, Oslo, and Bonn, later serving as Spanish ambassador in Tunis, in
Ethiopia and in Budapest. *La soledad de Alcuneza* (1961; The Loneliness of
Alcuneza) treats the theme of the Spanish Civil War from the viewpoint of a
soldier who loses all of his family during the conflict. *La encrucijada de Carabanchel* (1963; The Carabanchel Crossroads) was actually written first but published later, winning the Miguel de Cervantes National Literary Prize. Two other
novels, *La puerta falsa* (1969; The False Door) and *El Corpus Christi de Francisco Sánchez* (1971; The Corpus Christi of Francisco Sánchez), are also tangentially related to the war. *La primavera triste* (1976; Sad Spring) is set in
Germany and France during World War II.

BIBLIOGRAPHY

Primary Texts

*El Corpus Christi de Francisco Sánchez.* Barcelona: Caralt, 1971.
*La encrucijada de Carabanchel.* 2nd ed. Madrid: Cid, 1963.
*La puerta falsa.* Madrid: Prensa Española, 1969.
*La soledad de Alcuneza.* 3rd ed. Madrid: Cid, 1965.

Janet Pérez

**GARCÍA DE RESENDE.** *See* Resende, García de

**GARCÍA DE STA. MARÍA, Álvar.** *See Juan II, Crónica de*

**GARCÍA DE VILLALTA, José** (1801, Seville–1846, Athens), novelist. A
liberal, Villalta emigrated to England when the Duke of Angouleme's army
invaded Spain in 1823. He fought in the Greek War of Independence and later,
with *Espronceda, took part in Chapalangarra's ill-fated expedition. After Ferdinand VII's death, Villalta returned to Spain and directed the newspapers *El
Labriego* (1849; The Farmer) and *El Español* (1848; The Spaniard). Appointed
to represent Spain in Greece, he died in Athens shortly after his arrival. His
novel *El golpe en vago* (1835; The Dons of the Last Century), among the best
novels of the Romantic period, is a slightly veiled attack on the Jesuits, and it
offers a vivid gallery of scenes and types of Andalusian popular life. *See also*
Romanticism.

BIBLIOGRAPHY

Primary Text

*El golpe en vago*. 6 vols. Madrid: Repullés, 1835.

Criticism

Torres, Elías. *La vida y la obra de José García de Villalta*. Madrid: Acies, 1959.
*Tres estudios en torno a García de Villalta*. Madrid: Insula, 1965.

David Thatcher Gies

**GARCÍA DIEGO, Begoña** (1926, Madrid– ), Spanish essayist and short story
writer. García's first significant literary success came with her winning the Café
Gijón Prize for her novelette *Bodas de plata* (1958; Silver Wedding Anniversary).
The point of departure is the death of a young wife, with the present tense being
the night of the wake, although via the husband, the past is evoked along with
a hypothetical future which vanishes as the widower awakes. *Chicas solas* (1962;
Girls on Their Own) is a compilation of columns originally written for the
conservative magazine *Blanco y negro* during the 1950s, including several short
stories. In common is the witty, perceptive style of the creative journalist with
her observations of bourgeois Madrid society, the developing social change and
its critical effects for women of the middle and upper classes. *Los años locos*
(1972; The Crazy Years) is another collection of articles and short stories, again
portraying the woman's point of view to change and sameness in daily life in
Spain during the 1960s. *See also* Essay.

BIBLIOGRAPHY

Primary Texts

*Los años locos*. Madrid: Prensa Española, 1972.
*Bodas de plata*. Madrid: Afrodisio Aguado, 1958.
*Chicas solas*. Madrid: Prensa Española, 1962.

Janet Pérez

**GARCÍA GUTIÉRREZ, Antonio** (1813, Chiclana, Cádiz–1884, Madrid), romantic dramatist and poet. Verdi's well-known operas *Il trovatore* (1851) and
*Simon Boccanegra* (1857) are based on two of García Gutiérrez's most popular
dramas. Little is known of García Gutiérrez's early life in the provinces except
that he was born in 1813 in a small town near Cádiz and that he was attracted
to writing as a young boy. He unenthusiastically began medical studies at the
U of Cádiz, a career which was happily terminated when Ferdinand VII closed
the universities in 1833. A perhaps apocryphal tale recounts that García Gutiérrez
then walked all the way to Madrid in order to embark on a literary career. He
befriended *Espronceda, Mariano José de *Larra, and Ventura de la *Vega, and
later wrote several plays in collaboration with Isidoro Gil and *Zorrilla.

In 1835 he penned *El trovador* (*The Troubadour*, 1964). The play was so
disliked by his peers and by the acting company assigned to play it that García
Gutiérrez, discouraged, went off to join the army. But the Madrid stage was

ever in need of new plays, so it was decided that *El trovador* would be produced by an acting troupe, and the author managed to return to Madrid on March 1, 1836, to attend its opening. The rest, as they say, is history: the reception was so clamorously favorable that the author was called out onstage—for the first time in Spanish theatrical history—to receive the wild applause of the audience. They cheered the play's vivid characters, passionate love story, rebellion in the name of freedom, tragic denouement, and melodramatic staging. García Gutiérrez combined prose and verse, time and place, and two different but related plots to create one of Spain's most fully accomplished Romantic dramas. Manrique, the brave troubadour, fights on one level to marry Leonor (who has been promised to someone else) and on another level to free Aragón from the tyranny of the Count of Luna. Manrique's mother (who is revealed to be not his real mother) is the play's most moving character, a figure who vacillates between the role of vengeful gypsy crone and delicate maternal protector. The ambiguity of her character gives emotional depth to a play which could easily have become a mere series of shocking stage tricks.

García Gutiérrez's success with *El trovador* led him to pursue his literary career, and in the next six years alone he published fifteen works (eight original pieces and seven translations from French). Among the original works were *El paje* (1837; The Page Boy) and *El rey monje* (1837; The Monk King), as well as two volumes of verse. *Simón Bocanegra*, presented early in 1843, achieved another huge popular success; like *El trovador*, it contains a historical plot, a case of tyrannical rule, a frustrated love affair, and the death of the play's titular hero. Numerous other plays followed, most based on historical occurrences and possessing complex plots. Most were performed and published, thus increasing García Gutiérrez's fame. His work as a translator was likewise constant, and kept his name before the public. This recognition was not attenuated by his residence in Mexico and Cuba from 1844 to 1850. He demonstrated his ability to satirize some of the excesses of *Romanticism in 1850 (many of them of course encouraged by his own plays) when he published a one-act verse parody of *El trovador*, entitled *Los hijos del tío Tronera* (1850; Uncle Tronera's Children).

García Gutiérrez spent several years in Spain writing *zarzuelas before embarking for England in 1855 on a government commission; he remained in London until 1858. During his absence from Spain, a fire destroyed many of his mss., but he continued to produce plays and his fame continued to increase: he was awarded the prestigious Carlos III medal (1856), a seat in the Spanish Royal Academy (1862; *Academia Española), and several other national honors. In 1864 another of his best plays appeared in Madrid. *Venganza catalana* (Catalan Revenge) contained many of those elements which had become both the hallmarks of Romanticism and of García Gutiérrez: medieval setting, complex plotting, accomplished verse, mystery, exalted expressions of love and hate, incarceration, murder, and, as the title promises, revenge. It reached four editions in its first year in print, attesting to its considerable popularity. The following year the last of the four plays to be remembered today appeared. While *Juan Lorenzo* (1865) was not a huge success when produced in Madrid, it was the author's favorite play, and it is considered by modern critics to be subtle and interesting, perhaps García Gutiérrez's best piece. In 1868 García Gutiérrez served the government as consul in Bayonne, moving to Genoa in 1869, and finally returning to Madrid to become director of the Museum of Archeology in 1872, a position he held until his death in 1884. Surprisingly, no complete collection of his works was ever published, but he was deservedly celebrated during his lifetime. His plays unfailingly underline his concern for Spain's history and future, while his lyrical artistry, when combined with his ability to handle convoluted plots, his sensitive depiction of female characters, and his creation of powerful dramatic situations make him one of the most accomplished authors of Spanish romanticism. *See also* Theater in Spain.

BIBLIOGRAPHY

Primary Texts

*Obras escogidas*. Madrid: Rivadeneyra, 1866.
*Poesías*. Ed. Joaquín de Entrambasaguas. Madrid: Aldus, 1947.
*El trovador*. Ed. L. A. Blecua. Barcelona: Labor, 1972.
*El trovador. Los hijos de tío Tronera*. Ed. Jean-Louis Picoche. Madrid: Alhambra, 1979.
*Venganza catalana. Juan Lorenzo*. Ed. José R. Lomba. Madrid: Espasa-Calpe, 1941.

English Translations

*The Troubador*. Tr. Rachel Benson. In *Spanish Plays of the Nineteenth-Century*. New York: Las Américas, 1964.
*The Troubadour. El trovador*. Tr. Luis Soto-Ruiz and Georgia Pappanastos. In *Three Spanish Romantic Plays*. Milwaukee: Marquette UP, 1990.

Criticism

Adams, N. B. *The Romantic Dramas of García Gutiérrez*. Columbia: Instituto de las Españas, 1922.
Johnson, Jerry. "Azucena, Sinister or Pathetic?" *RN* 12 (1970): 114–18.
Lamb, N. G. *Characterization in Some Early Dramas of García Gutiérrez*. Liverpool: Liverpool Studies, 1940.
Ruiz Silva. "*El trovador*, de García Gutiérrez: drama y melodrama." *CH* 335 (1978): 251–72.
Siciliano, Ernest A. "La verdadera Azucena del *El trovador*." *NRFH* 20 (1971): 107–14.

David Thatcher Gies

**GARCÍA HORTELANO, Juan** (1928, Madrid– ), novelist. He combines the thematic concerns of the social novelists with the *objetivista* technique (less evidence of author intrusion, more reliance on "facts," description, conversation). Best known for his prize-winning novels *Nuevas amistades* (New Friendships [Biblioteca Breve Prize, 1959]) and *Tormenta de verano* (1962; *Summer Storm*, 1962 [Formentor Prize, 1961]), he attacks the vacuous, dull, boring existence of the monied middle class. Both novels center around a crime (a supposed abortion in the first, and the discovery of a body on a resort beach in the second), an event that is secondary to the revelation of the people connected to it. Tedium, lack of values, hypocrisy, class consciousness, and a ''dolce vita'' lifestyle soon become apparent. Both groups seek to escape boredom in various ways, but are incapable of any real action or act that would save them. *El gran momento de Mary Tribune* (1972; Mary Tribune's Great Moment) was hailed as a departure from the strictly behavioristic procedure of the earlier works, with the introduction of more subjective elements. The group dynamics which are disrupted with the presence of a stranger in their midst reflect the same themes as the earlier novels. García Hortelano has also written short stories, such as in *Gente de Madrid* (1957; People from Madrid).

BIBLIOGRAPHY

Primary Texts

*Apólogos y milesios*. Barcelona: Lumen, 1975.
*Gente de Madrid*. Madrid: Sedmay, 1977.
*Gramática parda*. Barcelona: Argos Vergara, 1982.
*El gran momento de Mary Tribune*. Barcelona: Barral, 1972.
*Nuevas amistades*. 5th ed. Barcelona: Formentor, 1967.
*Tormenta de verano*. Barcelona: Seix Barral, 1962.
*Los vaqueros en el pozo*. Madrid: Alfaguara, 1979.

Margaret E. W. Jones

**GARCÍA LORCA, Federico** (1898, Fuente Vaqueros–1936, Viznar, Granada), poet and dramatist. García Lorca was born, raised, and ultimately killed in and near the Andalusian city of Granada. His family was of comfortable means, and Lorca was afforded the luxury of devoting his life primarily to artistic pursuits, which included painting and music as well as literature. He moved to Madrid in 1919, and within a few years established a national reputation as a poet and dramatist.

Lorca achieved international recognition with the publication of his *Romancero gitano* (*Gypsy Ballads*, 1953) in 1928. The following year, troubled by personal conflicts, he left Spain for a year in the United States, where he lived in New York and attended Columbia U. However, the experience of New York was nightmarish for Lorca. His internal and external struggles and anguish are expressed in *Poeta en Nueva York* (*Poet in New York*, 1968), which, although written 1929–30, was first published posthumously in 1940. The collection is a powerful indictment of modern civilization and alienation, and is generally esteemed as Spain's greatest work of surrealist poetry.

Upon his return to Spain in 1930, Lorca's interests began to evolve in the direction of the theater. His most widely read and frequently performed dramas date from the 1930s, particularly the dramas that comprise the so-called rural trilogy: *Bodas de sangre* (1933; *Blood Wedding*, 1953), *Yerma* (1934; *Yerma*, 1953), and *La casa de Bernarda Alba* (written 1936; *The House of Bernarda Alba*, 1953). Also during these years, Lorca became increasingly active in the social and cultural affairs of the Spanish Republic. His most publicized venture was to direct a traveling theatrical company called La Barraca (The Cabin). The troupe was made up largely of university students and performed works from the Golden Age of Spanish drama for the benefit of the populace in the provinces. Lorca's goal was to acquaint the people with their own cultural heritage, and he presented none of his own works.

It is important to take note of Lorca's social awareness and activities during the 1930s for the sake of historical accuracy. This is because of a systematic propaganda effort of several decades' duration by the Franco government to portray Lorca as wholly apolitical, and thus deny the regime's responsibility for his assassination.

The 1930s were a period of increasing public triumph for Lorca, and his work developed in radical new directions. He examined and decried social injustice— particularly as directed toward women as an oppressed social class—while continuing to experiment with symbolic and surrealist drama. One work, *El público* (written 1930; The Public), a surrealist treatment of homosexuality in society, went unpublished in complete form until 1978 because of its subject matter.

In July 1936, Lorca traveled to Granada for a visit with his family; the outbreak of hostilities of the Spanish Civil War occurred almost simultaneously with his arrival. Lorca was forced into hiding within weeks, but was found and arrested on August 16. He was held without charges or trial, and on August 19 was assassinated near the village of Viznar.

There has been much popular legend surrounding Lorca's death. Recent research has shown that he was but the most famous of thousands of Granada citizens who were systematically murdered by Falangist forces. In the context of the military fanaticism and terrorism of the Civil War, Lorca's "crimes" were that he was known as a leftist intellectual and a homosexual. The order for his execution came from the Falangist military commander of Granada. Contrary to much popular belief, the Civil Guard was not involved in his murder.

There are two basic attitudes that characterize Lorca's work. These are an uncompromising affirmation of human vitality in the most fundamental, biological sense; and a distinct tendency to think in terms of diametrical opposites. While there are numerous themes in Lorca's work, notably the use of folkloric material and the rural ambience of his native Andalusia, vitality and intrinsic opposition are underlying tendencies that pervade virtually his entire literary output. These currents fall into three major categories: (1) individual freedom and its suppression by societal norms, (2) minority groups oppressed by soulless majorities, and (3) life itself confronted by death.

The motif of freedom versus suppression is seen most vividly in Lorca's best-known dramas, the tragedies of the rural trilogy. In these works, individual freedom is dramatized as sexual vitality suppressed by social convention. In *The House of Bernarda Alba*, the conflict arises between the imperious Bernarda and her youngest daughter Adela. The drama ends tragically when Adela hangs herself, after Bernarda announces triumphantly but untruthfully that she has shot

Adela's illicit lover. The work is notable for its feminist overtones and sympathies. The fatal conflict in *Blood Wedding* occurs between the male protagonist, Leonardo, and the villagers who choose murderous vengeance to his deviance from the status quo. Lorca underscores the rigidly conventional attitudes of the villagers by not giving them proper names, only social labels (Mother, Father, etc.). *Blood Wedding* contains Lorca's most powerful stage symbolism, and is his most frequently performed work. Yerma is arguably Lorca's single most interesting character, in that the clash between sexual freedom and societal suppression takes place within the protagonist herself. *Yerma* is not a proper name in Spanish, but an adjective meaning "barren." Barrenness—lack of children—is the perceived struggle in Yerma's life. A deeper examination of the drama and its symbolism reveals that Yerma's barrenness is the external manisfestation of her inability to resolve her internal erotic conflicts. The work ends tragically (as do all Lorca's dramas) when Yerma's husband approaches her in a state of drunken sexual desire and she strangles him.

The conflicts that Lorca explores through individual characters in his dramas, he applies to minority groups in his most widely read poetry collections. In the *Gypsy Ballads*, there is a central conflict between the gypsies with their unfettered lifestyle, and the Civil Guard, a sort of national police force that enforces the will of an oppressive government. In *Poet in New York*, the same clash occurs between the blacks and their spontaneous vitality, and the intolerant society of the majority. Understandably, the *Gypsy Ballads* comprise Lorca's most esteemed collection in Spanish-speaking countries, while American readers tend to be somewhat more attracted to *Poet in New York*.

Given Lorca's emphasis on human vitality and his tendency to think in terms of polar opposites, the confrontation of life and death is a central underlying motif in much of his work. Nowhere is this confrontation more dramatically presented than in the long, elegiac poem *Llanto por Ignacio Sánchez Mejías* (*Dirge for Ignacio Sánchez Mejías*, 1937). The poem is grounded in fact. Sánchez Mejías (1891–1934) was a bullfighter and close friend of Lorca who was fatally gored in the ring. The poet extols the extreme vitality of a man who walks the tightrope between life and lurking death in the figure of the bull, and laments the death of a dear friend in classic elegiac form. The work is considered by many readers to be Lorca's crowning achievement in poetry.

Like many creative artists, Lorca was ahead of his time in areas of thought that intrigued him. In particular, the international feminist movement and the American civil rights movement would not have surprised him, and his social criticism in these areas continues to be valid and relevant. Still, the notion of vitality and its opposing forces is Lorca's most fundamental theme. In this larger context, his only limits are those of human essentials. *See also* Theater in Spain.

BIBLIOGRAPHY

Primary Texts

*Obras completas*. Ed. Guillermo de Torre. 8 vols. Buenos Aires: Losada, 1938–46.

*Obras completas*. Ed. Arturo del Hoyo. Prol. Jorge Guillén. Epilogue by Vicente Aleixandre. Madrid: Aguilar, 1954, and numerous subsequent editions and printings.

English Translations

*The Gypsy Ballads of Federico García Lorca*. Tr. Rolfe Humphries. Intro. L. R. Lind.
  Bloomington: Indiana UP, 1953.
*Lament for the Death of a Bullfighter: And Other Poems*. Tr. A. L. Lloyd. London: W.
  Heineman, 1937; rpt. New York: AMS Press, 1978.
*Poet in New York*. Tr. Ben Belitt. Magnolia, MA: Peter Smith, 1968.
*Three Tragedies of Federico García Lorca*. Tr. Richard L. O'Connell and James Graham-
  Luján. Prol. Francisco García Lorca. New York: New Directions, 1953; rpt.
  Westport, CT: Greenwood, 1977. (*Blood Wedding*; *The House of Bernarda Alba*;
  *Yerma*.)

Criticism

Allen, Rupert C. *Psyche and Symbol in the Theater of Federico García Lorca: Perlimplín,
  Yerma, Blood Wedding*. Austin: U of Texas P, 1974.
————. *The Symbolic World of Federico García Lorca*. Albuquerque: U of New Mexico
  P, 1972.
Cobb, Carl W. *Federico García Lorca*. TWAS 23. New York: Twayne, 1967.
Durán, Manuel, ed. *Lorca: A Collection of Critical Essays*. Englewood Cliffs, NJ:
  Prentice-Hall, 1962.
Gibson, Ian. *The Assassination of Federico García Lorca*. London: W. H. Allen, 1979.
MacCurdy, G. Grant. *Federico García Lorca: Life, Work, and Criticism*. Fredericton,
  NB: York, 1986.
Morris, C. B. *Surrealism and Spain, 1920–1936*. Cambridge: Cambridge UP, 1972.
Predmore, Richard L. *Lorca's New York Poetry: Social Injustice, Dark Love, Lost Faith*.
  Durham: Duke UP, 1980.

G. Grant MacCurdy

**GARCÍA LUENGO, Eusebio** (1905, Puebla de Alcocer, Badajoz– ), dramatist
and literary critic. A frequent contributor of articles to journals such as *La Estafeta
Literaria*, García Luengo is also known for his dramatic works which include
such titles as *Por primera vez en mi vida* (For the First Time in My Life), *El
pozo y la angustia* (The Well and Anguish) and *Las supervivientes* (1955; The
Survivors), most of which have been staged privately and have been described
as existentialist plays. He is also the author of a novel, *El malogrado* (1945;
The Failure) and was the 1950 winner of the Café Gijón Prize for his narration,
*La primera actriz* (1950; The First Actress).

BIBLIOGRAPHY

Primary Texts

*Cuadernos de las Extremaduras*. Illus. José Zalamea. Madrid: Ediciones Arión, 1962.
*La primera actriz*. Madrid: Gráficas Uguinas, 1950.
*Las supervivientes*. Prol. J. Fernández Figueroa. Madrid: Índice, 1955.
*Revisión del teatro de Federico García Lorca*. Madrid: Política y Literatura Cuaderno
  3, 1951.

"Teatro, *Soledad* de Unamuno. Drama inédito." *Indice de Artes y Letras* 68–69 (1953): 27.

Porter Conerly

**GARCÍA MARTÍ, Victoriano** (1881, Puebla de Caramiñal, La Coruña–1966, Madrid), Galician essayist. A lawyer by profession, García Martí was widely known principally for his essays and to a lesser degree for other writings, which include short stories, novels, dramatic works, and history. A Galician, he often centers his essays on this region of Spain and its inhabitants. He was for many years a contributor to Barcelona's *La Vanguardia Española* (The Spanish Vanguard), and he served as secretary general of the *Ateneo of Madrid. In 1964 the *Academia Española named him a corresponding member, and he was also an honorary member of the Galician Academy.

His best known essays are *La voz de los mitos* (1941; Voice of the Myths), *Climas de misterio* (1947; Climates of Mystery), and *La vida no es sueño* (1949; Life Is Not a Dream). García Martí also edited the complete works of the Galician poetess Rosalía de *Castro. *See also* Galician Literature.

BIBLIOGRAPHY

Primary Texts

*Climas de misterio*. Madrid: Aguilar, 1947.

*Don Quijote y su mejor camino*. Madrid: Dossat, 1947.

*Ensayos: La voluntad y el destino; España, una punta de Europa; El amor; La muerte*. Madrid: Aguilar, 1950.

*La tragedia de todos*. Madrid: Mundo Latino, 1928.

*Tres narraciones gallegas: La tragedia del caballero de Santiago; El emigrante; Don Severo Carballo*. Madrid: Dossat, 1950.

Porter Conerly

**GARCÍA MORENTE, Manuel** (1886, Arjonilla, Jaén–1942, Madrid), philosopher and educator. The youngest of three children of a distinguished Andalusian physician, García Morente began his studies in Granada but from 1894 until 1905 was educated in France, first in Bayonne and later in Paris, where he studied under Boutroux, Rauch, Lévy-Bruhl, and Bergson. He was then named professor of philosophy at the Institución Libre de Enseñanza (Free Pedagogical Institute); however, he soon obtained a scholarship to study in Germany, where he became a disciple of Cohen, Natorp, and Cassirer in Marburg. It was there that he became interested in Kant, the subject of his doctoral thesis, *La estética de Kant* (1912; Kant's Aesthetics).

Morente was only twenty-six years old when he obtained the ethics professorship at the U of Madrid, making him the youngest professor in the country. Thus began a brilliant academic career which included his being elected dean of the Facultad de Filosofía y Letras in 1931, a post he held until 1936. During his years at the university he also served as under secretary of the Ministry of Public Instruction, secretary-general of the Academy of Moral and Political

Sciences, and as a collaborator for the journal *Revista de Occidente*. Morente's work as a translator (Descartes, Kant, Rickert, Simmel, Husserl, Spengler, Keyserling) earned him widespread recognition and admiration; indeed, his translations are considered some of the most valuable portions of his work.

With the outbreak of Civil War in 1936, García Morente, fearing for his life, fled to France. From there he continued to Argentina, where he served as professor of philosophy at the U of Tucumán in 1937–38. While in Argentina he underwent a spiritual revival that led him to become a priest. On his return to Spain he resumed his university teaching career until his death in 1942.

Julián *Marías has commented that Morente was not, and never pretended to be, an original philosopher in the sense of a thinker who devises his own philosophical system. Yet Morente's contribution to twentieth-c. Spanish philosophy is considerable. His early interest in neo-Kantism and Bergson gradually gave way to a preference for *Ortega y Gasset, who was friend and mentor to García Morente for many years and who to a large degree determined his mature thought. Most of his books originated as class lectures. Such is the case, for example, with what is perhaps his most important tome, *Lecciones preliminares de filosofía* (1938; Preliminary Lessons in Philosophy). Other noteworthy volumes include *La filosofía de Henri Bergson* (1917; Henri Bergson's Philosophy) and *Idea de la hispanidad* (1938; The Idea of Hispanism). Over forty years after his death he remains one of the most important university figures of contemporary Spain.

BIBLIOGRAPHY

Primary Texts

*La filosofía de Henri Bergson*. Madrid: Espasa-Calpe, 1972.
*Fundamentos de filosofía e historia de los sistemas filosóficos*. 7th ed. Madrid: Espasa-Calpe, 1973.
*Idea de la hispanidad*. Madrid: Espasa-Calpe, 1961.
*Ideas para una filosofía de la historia de España*. Madrid: Rialp, 1957.
*Lecciones preliminares de filosofía*. 4th ed. México: Porrúa, 1971.

Criticism

Alonso-Pueyo, Sabino. *Filosofía y narcismo: En torno a los pensadores de la España actual*. Valencia: Guerri, 1953.
Guy, Alain. *Les philosophes espagnols d'hier et d'aujourd'hui*. Toulouse: Privat, 1956. (Tr. to Spanish as *Los filósofos españoles de ayer y de hoy*. Buenos Aires: Losada, 1966.)
Iriarte, Mauricio de. *El profesor García Morente, sacerdote*. Madrid: Espasa-Calpe, 1953.
Marías, Julián. *La filosofía española actual*. Madrid: Espasa-Calpe, 1948.

Porter Conerly

**GARCÍA NIETO, José** (1914, Oviedo– ), Spanish critic and poet who has lived in Madrid since the age of fifteen. He is a member of the *Academia Española and of the Royal Academy of Bellas Letras of Toledo. Known especially as founder (1943) and director of the post-war poetry review *Garcilaso*, important as initiator of the "humanized" trend which reacted against the "dehumanized" (vanguardist, experimental) poetry of the *Generation of 1927, he also directed other poetry journals such as *Acanto*, and *Poesía española* and the news and culture magazine, *Mundo hispánico*. He has lectured in many cities of Spain, as well as Lisbon, Rome, London, Ghent, Caracas, and many others. His poetic works include *Víspera hacia ti* (1940; Vespers Toward You); *Poesía (1940–43)* (1944); *Versos de un huésped de Luisa Esteban* (1944; Versos of a Guest of Luisa Esteban); *Tú y yo sobre la tierra* (1944; You and I Upon the Earth); *Retablo del ángel, el hombre y la pastora* (1945; Retable of the Angel, the Man and the Shepherdess); *Toledo* (1945); *Del campo y soledad* (1946; Of the Country and Solitude); *Juego de los doce espejos* (1951; Game of Twelve Mirrors); *Primer libro de poemas* and *Segundo libro de poemas* (1951; First Book of Poems, and Second Book . . . ); *Tregua* (1951; Truce); *Sonetos por mi hija* (1953; Sonnets for My Daughter); *La red* (1956; The Net); *El parque pequeño* and *Elegía en Covaleda* (1958; The Little Park, and Elegy in Covaleda); *Geografía es amor* (1961; Geography Is Love); *Corpus Christi y seis sonetos* (1962; Corpus Christi and Six Sonnets); *Circunstancia de la muerte* (1963; Circumstances of Death); *La hora undécima* (1963; The Eleventh Hour); *Memorias y compromisos* (1966; Memories and Obligations); *Hablando solo* (1968; Talking to Myself); *Los tres poemas mayores* (1970; The Three Greatest Poems); *Facultad de volver* (1970; Capacity to Return); *Toledo* (1973); *Sonetos y revelaciones de Madrid* (1976; Sonnets and Revelations of Madrid); *Súplica por la paz del mundo y otros collages* (1977; Prayer for Peace in the World and Other Collages); *Los cristales fingidos* (1978; Pretended Crystals); *El arrabal* (1980; The Slum); *Sonetos españoles a Bolívar* (1983; Spanish Sonnets for Bolivar); *Nuevo elogio de la lengua española* and *Piedra y cielo de Roma* (1983; New Eulogy of the Spanish Language, and Stones and Skies of Rome). García Nieto has also published several works of literary criticism. His poetry is simple and direct, and his favorite themes are eternal and universal, love and friendship, time and death, Spain and its landscape, and the dialogue of man with God.

BIBLIOGRAPHY

Primary Texts

*Circunstancias de la muerte*. Seville: La Muestra, 1963.
*Geografía es amor.* Madrid: Osca, 1961.
*Hablando solo*. 2nd ed., expanded. Madrid: Cultura Hispánica, 1971.
*Memorias y compromisos*. Madrid: Nacional, 1966.
*Sonetos y revelaciones de Madrid*. Madrid: Ayuntamiento, 1976.

Criticism

Garfias, Francisco. "El taller que no cesa de José García Nieto." *Arbor* 336 (n.d.): 137–39.
———. "Los 'Tres poemas mayores' de José García Nieto." *Arbor* 312 (1971): 124–28.

Janet Pérez

**GARCÍA PAVÓN, Francisco** (1919, Tomelloso, Ciudad Real– ), short story writer, novelist, and drama critic. Since he received his doctorate from the U of Madrid, García Pavón has served as professor of dramatic literature at the

Real Escuela Superior de Arte Dramático (Royal School of Dramatic Art), director-general of the publishing house of Ediciones Taurus, and theater critic for the Madrid newspaper *Arriba*. Recognition of his literary talent first came in 1945, when his novel *Cerca de Oviedo* (1946; Close to Oviedo) was named a finalist in the prestigious Nadal competition. A later novel, *El reinado de Witiza* (1968; The Reign of Witiza), was likewise a finalist in 1968, and his novel *Las hermanas coloradas* (The Red Sisters) won the Nadal Prize in 1970.

García Pavón has been credited with raising detective literature to a position of respectability in Spain with a series of novels whose protagonist, Plinio, is police chief of the town of Tomelloso. A ''rural Sherlock Holmes,'' as Patricia O'Connor has described him, Plinio's adventures have been translated into several European languages, including French, Danish, and Polish. However, García Pavón's talent as a fiction writer is best seen in his short stories, a genre whose demands the author handles admirably with his clear, refreshing prose style. Among his most important collections are *Cuentos de mamá* (1952; Mother's Stories) and *Cuentos republicanos* (1961; Republican Stories).

As essayist and literary critic García Pavón is the author of such volumes as *El teatro social en España* (1962; Social Theater in Spain) and editor of an *Antología de cuentistas españoles contemporáneos* (1959; Anthology of Contemporary Spanish Short Story Writers), the introduction to which is considered a fine example of García Pavón's excellence as a critic. *See also* Essay.

BIBLIOGRAPHY

Primary Texts

*Cerca de Oviedo*. 3rd ed. Barcelona: Destino, 1972.
*Cuentos de mamá*. 2nd ed. Barcelona: Destino, 1972.
*Cuentos republicanos*. 3rd ed. Barcelona: Destino, 1971.
*Las hermanas coloradas; Plinio en Madrid*. 10th ed. Barcelona: Destino, 1972.
*Historias de Plinio*. Esplugas de Llobregat: Plaza & Janés, 1972.

Criticism

Bensoussan, Albert. ''Rencontre avec Francisco García Pavón'' (Interview). *Les Langues Modernes* 65 (n.d.): 374–76.
O'Connor, Patricia W. ''Francisco García Pavón's Sexual Politics in the Plinio Novels.'' *Journal of Spanish Studies: Twentieth Century* 1 (1973): 65–81.
———. ''A Spanish Sleuth at Last: Francisco García Pavón's *Plinio*.'' *Hispanófila* 48 (1973): 47–68.

Porter Conerly

**GARCÍA PELAYO, Manuel** (1909, Corrales, Zamora– ), essayist, sociologist, professor of political law. He has taught at the U of Puerto Rico and is professor at the Central U of Caracas, Venezuela. He is author of the manual *Derecho constitucional comparado* (Comparative Constitutional Law), which has been reprinted several times, and of *El reino de Dios, arquetipo político* (1957; The Kingdom of God, Political Archetype). Most of his essays are collected in two volumes: *Mitos y símbolos políticos* (1964; Political Myths and

Symbols), and *Del mito y de la razón en el pensamiento político* (1968; About Myth and Reason in Political Thought).

BIBLIOGRAPHY

Primary Texts

*Los mitos políticos.* Madrid: Alianza, 1981.
*Mitos y símbolos políticos.* Madrid: Taurus, 1964.
*Las transformaciones del estado contemporáneo.* Madrid: Alianza, 1977.

Isabel McSpadden

**GARCÍA SABELL, Domingo** (1908, Santiago de Compostela– ). Eminent physician who in the line of other doctors of medicine like Gregorio *Marañón, Roberto *Nóvoa Santos, Juan *Rof Carballo and Pedro *Laín Entralgo has dedicated much of his life to belletristic pursuits. García Sabell's Galician opus is barely collected in the two voluminous tomes of *Ensaios* (1963, 1976; Essays) containing treatises on art, medicine, philosophy, anthropology, and letters. A friend of *Valle-Inclán, García Sabell has produced several works on his countrymen, among them the posthumous edition of Valle's *La cara de Dios* (1974; God's Face), as well as various other essays of the poet Rosalía de *Castro. *See also* Essay; Galician Literature.

BIBLIOGRAPHY

Primary Texts

*Ensaios* I and II. Vigo: Galaxia, 1963 and 1976.
*Testimonio personal.* Madrid: Seminarios y Ediciones, 1971.

Criticism

Varela Jácome, Benito. *Historia de la literatura gallega.* Santiago de Compostela: Porto, 1951. 368.
Fernández del Riego, F. *Historia da literatura galega.* Vigo: Galaxia, 1971. 264–66.

Ricardo Landeira

**GARCÍA SÁNCHIZ, Federico** (1887, Valencia–1964, Madrid), prose author. In 1905 he wrote a book on Pío *Baroja. Part of the modernist movement, he attained recognition with his short story "Color" (1898; Color). After 1923, he cultivated a form of rhetoric both descriptive and lyrical in nature, called "la charla," which became popular in Latin America. One of his best works, *El viaje a España* (Trip to Spain), appeared in 1929. In 1959 he published two volumes of recollections titled *Tierras, tiempos y vida* (Lands, Times and Life), followed by a third volume, titled *América, españolear* (America, Get Spanish), in 1963. It was his final work.

BIBLIOGRAPHY

Primary Texts

*América, españolear.* Madrid: Cultura hispánica, 1963.
*Del robledal al olivar.* San Sebastián: Española, 1939.
*Tierras, tiempos y vida.* Madrid: Altamira, 1959.

Isabel McSpadden

**GARCÍA SERRANO, Rafael** (1917, Pamplona– ), Spanish novelist, essayist and journalist. He was the founder of the Falangist S.E.U. (Syndicate of University Students), the only student organization legalized by the Franco government. A student at the war's outbreak, García Serrano volunteered for the Franco army and spent some five years in hospitals following the decisive battle of Teruel. His first novel, *Eugenio o la proclamación de la primavera* (1938; Eugene or the Proclamation of Springtime), written early in the war, lyrically exalts Falangist heroics and the warlike spirit. Characters are abstract and idealized, and the entire work abounds in demagoguery. *La fiel infantería* (1943; The Loyal Infantry), his first post-war novel, paints a crude and dramatic portrait of life in the Nationalist trenches. Too skewed to be considered a historical document, it is an indicator of moral and psychological attitudes. *La fiel infantería* received the José Antonio Primo de Rivera National Literary Prize (named for the founder of the Falange) in 1943, and is García Serrano's most significant critical and popular success. *Plaza del Castillo* (1951; The Castle Square), set in the author's native Pamplona immediately prior to the war, is more controlled in its passions and probably his best literary achievement. Other treatments of the Civil War include *Los ojos perdidos* (1958; Lost Eyes), in which combat is relegated to the background during a sentimental interlude, and *La paz dura quince días* (1960; Peace Lasts Two Weeks), a novelized chronicle of the 7th Navarre Brigade during a brief respite after successful conclusion of the Nationalist campaign in northern Spain in the fall of 1937. In this work and the others mentioned above, there is a considerable autobiographical basis, and almost unfailingly a fascist ideology. In the novels and in the remainder of at least fifteen volumes of fiction and more than a dozen movie scripts, García Serrano presents his personal recollections of historical events, thinly disguised as fiction or presented as confessional testimony. His personal view of art and literature is one which downplays the well-constructed narrative and convincing, rounded characters in favor of apologia for war and violence.

BIBLIOGRAPHY

Primary Texts

*El domingo por la tarde.* Madrid: Taurus, 1962.
*La fiel infantería.* 2nd ed. Madrid: Eskua, 1958.
*El pino volador* (collected essays). Madrid: Nacional, 1964.

Criticism

Nora, E. G. de. *La novela española contemporánea.* 3 vols. Madrid: Gredos, 1967. 3:
    89–94.

Janet Pérez

**GARCÍA TASSARA, Gabriel** (1817, Seville–1875, Madrid), Romantic poet
and journalist. Tassara's father was an official of the Spanish Crown, and his
mother an Andalusian aristocrat. Proud of his classical training, he was also
influenced by *Romanticism, especially by *Espronceda; his poetry represents a
transition from Romanticism to a grandiloquent, political poetry. He considered
himself a Romantic poet with eyes toward the future rather than the past, yet
his themes match those of *Zorrilla: God, nature, history. García Tassara's most
intimate production is his religious poetry, which gives voice to a search for a
sincere form of expression. His last works reflect a return to neo-classical style.
The prologue to his collection *Poesías* (1872; Poems) is a conservative political
and poetic manifesto. His second collection *Corona poética* (Poetic Crown) was
published posthumously in Seville in 1878.

BIBLIOGRAPHY

Primary Text

*Poesías de D. Gabriel García Tassara.* Madrid: Rivadeneyra, 1880.

Criticism

Galán, R. "Tassara, Duque de Europa." *BBMP* 12 (1946): 132–69.
Herrero, J. "Un poema desconocido de Gabriel García Tassara a F. Caballero." *BHS*
    42.2 (1965): 117–19.
Laffon, A. "Un poeta olvidado: el sevillano García Tassara." *Archivo Hispalense* 8
    (1948): 97–101.
Méndez Bejarano, M. *Tassara: Nueva biografía crítica.* Madrid: Pérez, 1928.

Fernando Operé

**GARCÍA-VALDECASAS, Alfonso** (1904, Granada– ), essayist and professor
of civil law. Among his works is *El hidalgo y el honor* (1948; The Nobleman
and Honor).

BIBLIOGRAPHY

Primary Text

*El hidalgo y el honor.* 2nd ed. Madrid: RO, 1954.

Isabel McSpadden

**GARCÍA VELA, José** (1885, Oviedo–1913, Las Navas del Marqués, Ávila),
post-modernist poet with a short literary career and one book to his name:
*Hogares humildes* (1909; Humble Homes). Federico de Onís includes him in
his *Antología* and comments that ''his premature death cut short his literary
career after having published only one book which promised an excellent poet,

well versed in *modernism and French poetry. His poetry was inspired by an interior life and the idealization of everyday life.'' (648)

BIBLIOGRAPHY

Primary Text

*Antologia de la poesía española e hispanoamericana*, Ed. Federico de Onís. New York: Americas, 1961.
*Hogares humildes*. Madrid: Pueyo, 1909.

Isabel McSpadden

**GARCÍASOL, Ramón de,** pseudonym of Miguel Alonso Calvo (1913, Guadalajara– ), lawyer and poet. His existentialist verse echoes both *Unamuno and Antonio *Machado. Among his works are *Canciones* (1952; Songs), *Palabras mayores* (1952; Words), *Tierras de España* (1955; Spanish Lands) and *Del amor de cada día* (1956; About Every Day's Love). He won the Escálamo Poetry Prize in 1954, and in 1955 received the Pedro Henríquez Ureña Prize for his book *Presencia y lección de Rubén Darío* (Presence and Lesson from Rubén Darío). Garcíasol has also written an essay titled ''Una pregunta mal hecha. ¿Qué es la poesía?'' (An Ill-Formed Question. What Is Poetry?). His collection of sonnets, *La madre* (The Mother), was published in 1958, and his *Antología provisional* (Temporary Anthology) in 1967.

BIBLIOGRAPHY

Primary Texts

*Antología provisional*. Madrid: Aguilar, 1967.
*Canciones*. Madrid: n.p., 1952.
*Decido vivir*. Luesia, Zaragoza: Porvivir, 1976.
*Tierras de España*. Madrid: Rialp, 1955.

English Translations

Four poems. Tr. H. W. Patterson. In *Antología Bilingüe (Español-Inglés) de la Poesía Española Moderna*. Madrid: Cultura hispánica, 1965.

Isabel McSpadden

**GARCILASO DE LA VEGA** (1501/1503?, Toledo–1536, Nice), soldier, courtier and poet. The most brilliant of Spanish poets was the son of an ambassador to Rome for the Catholic monarchs and a mother who counted the Marqués de *Santillana among her ancestors. Tradition depicts him as universally admired. He accompanied the study of classics with fencing, riding, and music playing, developing into a perfect model of the *Renaissance courtier. Unlike his elder brother, Garcilaso remained loyal to the young King Charles I during the uprising of the Spanish *comuneros*, and was wounded at the decisive victory of Olías in 1521. The following year he participated in the abortive expedition to Rhodes along with the Catalonian poet Juan *Boscán, who became his lifetime friend. In 1525 he married Elena de Zúñiga, a union of convenience apparently suggested by the king. When in 1526 a Portuguese lady of extraordinary beauty named

Isabel Freyre joined the court as the queen's lady-in-waiting, Garcilaso turned his attention to her. How successful he was, we do not know, but eventually she married someone else. To this event Garcilaso may allude in his *Copla* 2 (Poem 2) and in Salicio's song in the first eclogue. Though she was not the first of his loves nor was she to be the last, Isabel Freyre impressed him deeply and is perhaps behind much of Garcilaso's poetry. To her untimely death these well-known lines from Nemoroso's song in the first eclogue may refer:

> Divina Elissa, pues agora el cielo
> con inmortales pies pisas y mides,
> y su mudança ves, estando queda,
> ¿por qué de mí te olvidas y no pides
> que se apresure el tiempo en que este velo
> Rompa del cuerpo y verme libre pueda,
>      y en la tercera rueda,
>      contigo mano a mano,
>      busquemos otro llano,
> busquemos otros montes y otros ríos,
> otros valles floridos y sombríos
> donde descanse y siempre pueda verte
>      ante los ojos míos,
> sin miedo y sobresalto de perderte?

(Divine Elisa, since now the heavens you tread and measure with immortal feet and see their changes as you stand still, why do you forget me and not pray for the time to be hastened when I shall break the veil of this body and find myself free, and in the third sphere [i.e., the planet Venus] hand in hand with you we can seek another meadow, we can seek other mountains and other rivers, other valleys full of flowers and shade, where I can rest and always see you before my eyes, without the fear and shock of losing you?)

In 1529 Garcilaso accompanied Charles I to Italy, where the king was crowned Holy Roman Emperor under the name of Charles V. This visit marks the beginning of his immersion in Italian culture, which was decisive for his development as a writer. In Italy he would experience the rich tradition of the Accademia Napoletana, would befriend many poets, such as Luigi Tansillo, Bernardo Tasso, and Giulio Cesare Carracciolo, and would even become an object of praise for Pietro Bembo. After a successful diplomatic mission to France, in 1531 he fell into disgrace for serving as witness to a marriage that Charles V opposed. Punished with exile to an island in the Danube, he wrote there one of his better known *canciones*, the *Canción 3* (Song 3). By 1533, however, Garcilaso seems to have recovered much of the emperor's favor. From this point until his death, only some of his incessant journeys can be mentioned here. In 1533 he was in Barcelona, where he encouraged Boscán's famous translation of *Il Corteggiano*. In 1534 he visited Avignon, dating a verse epistle to Boscán with an allusion to Petrarch's Laura:

Doze del mes d'otubre, de la tierra
do nació el claro fuego del Petrarca
y donde están del fuego las cenizas.

(The twelfth of October, from the land where the bright fire of Petrach was born,
and where the ashes of the fire do lie.)

In 1535 he was wounded twice during the capture of Tunis. Back in Naples,
he traveled in several missions to Rome, Florence, and Genoa. His end was now
close. In July of 1536 the imperial troops invaded Provence, but the expedition
did not go well and the whole army eventually had to withdraw. On September
19, during an unimportant skirmish at the little village of Le Muy, Garcilaso
was mortally wounded, dying a few weeks later. He was thirty-five years old.
As in the case of Sir Philip Sidney, tradition has it that Garcilaso had neglected
to put on a piece of his armor (a helmet in his case) before attacking the enemy.
His devotion to Charles V had cost him his life and often disturbed his writing.
But on the other hand his service had allowed him to gain a direct knowledge
of the most influential literature of his time; and as a courtier of the Holy Roman
Emperor, Garcilaso had moved in a multilingual, truly international culture, such
as the world has never seen before or later.

### The Work

Although Garcilaso left a few Latin odes and some Castilian *coplas, his best
poems are written in Italian meters: five *canciones*, two elegies, one epistle,
thirty-eight sonnets, and three eclogues. His adaptation of hendecasyllable to
Spanish was far superior to anything attempted earlier by Santillana or Boscán.
Well before those of Sidney or Ronsard, Garcilaso's sonnets and *Canciones*
competed with Italian paradigms. His eclogues, however, are his masterpieces
and grant him a place of honor among *pastoral poets. Openly challenging Virgil's
eighth eclogue, Garcilaso's first eclogue synthesizes utterances of bereavement
and unrequited love with Virgilian and Petrarchan structures. No less ambitious
is the second eclogue, where Garcilaso takes as a model the Italian *ecloga
rappresentativa*, but turns it into a huge pastoral piece; long narratives, which
would normally weaken the lyric import of any other poem, are integrated in
such a way that the second eclogue ends up as a poetic study of love and death.
In his third eclogue, an intricate yet harmonious construction blends an amoebean
pastoral song with mythological passages to objectify feelings of loss; and the
result is probably the most exquisite pastoral of the *Renaissance. As a whole,
Garcilaso's three eclogues assimilate many centuries of European literary experience, and turn an objective mode into a powerful vehicle for subjective
poetry.

Although essentially a love poet, Garcilaso's range is surprisingly wide. In
one of his elegies he can show a satiric vein:

Yo voy por medio, porque nunca tanto
quise obligarme a procurar hazienda,

que un poco más que aquellos me levanto;
  ni voy tampoco por la estrecha senda
  de los que cierto sé que la otra vía
  buelven, de noche al caminar, la rienda. (Elegy 2)

(I take the middle road, for I have never been quite so eager to acquire wealth, and hence I rise a little higher than the former; nor do I follow the straight and narrow path of those who, I surely know, shift over from one path to the other in the dark of night.)

Nor is he devoid of humor, as his contemporaries attest and this passage confirms:

A mi señor Durall estrechamente
  abraçá de mi parte, si pudierdes.

(Epistle to Boscán)

(Embrace Durall for me, if you could. [Durall was Grand Treasurer of Barcelona])

More often than not a tender lyricist, at times he reveals an almost ferocious vigor that reminds us of Lucan or Ercilla:

Unos en bruto lago de su sangre,
  cortado ya el estambre de la vida,
  la cabeça partida rebolcavan;
  otros claro mostravan, espirando,
  de fuera palpitando las entrañas

(Some in the brutish lake of their own blood, / the thread of life already cut, / their heads split open, wallowed; / others, dying, clearly revealed / their entrails quivering.)

Over Garcilaso's idyllic descriptions there lurks a gravity, a certain darkness, which tradition mentions as one of the traits of his character. The delightful pastoral *topos* of the *locus amoenus* is never enjoyed in Garcilaso for its own sake, but as a thematic contrast to feelings of unrequited love or bereavement, as in these lines from the third eclogue:

cerca del agua, en un lugar florido,
  estava entre las yervas degollada
  qual queda el blanco cisne quando pierde
  la dulce vida entre la yerva verde.

(Near the water, in a flowery spot, she lies among the grass with severed throat as the white swan lies when he loses his sweet life among the green grasses.)

But whatever the sentiment, his form is usually harmonious and faultless, the very clash between limpidity and earnestness contributing to his lyric strength. Garcilaso is a learned author. His readings, though largely confined to poetry, were vast for a man of his profession and of his youth. He had an effortless command of the best in Latin, Catalan, and Italian lyric, ranging from Catullus to Virgil, Ausiàs *March, Petrarch, and Sannazaro. He could therefore easily integrate his literary reminiscences with his own writing, turning into *poesía vera* what in less sensitive hands remained at the level of *poesia d'arte*. Like those of no other Spanish poet, Garcilaso's lines linger in the reader's memory, proof of his uncanny feeling for the acoustic and visual possibilities of his language:

> Escrito está en mi alma vuestro gesto
>
> (your countenance is written on my soul)
>
> (Sonnet 5)
>
> verme morir entre memorias tristes
>
> (to see me die among sad memories)
>
> (Sonnet 10)

To his importance as a major European lyricist, Garcilaso unites his decisive impact on the literature of Spain. His immensely successful handling of the Italian meters determined their quick adoption by the writers of the *Siglo de Oro. With one single work, the *Oda a la flor de Gnido* (Ode to the Flower of Gnido), he Hispanized the Horatian ode, which became the principal medium for San *Juan de la Cruz and Fray Luis de *León. He rendered in Spanish, for the first time, the Italian elegy and epistle in *terza rima*. He composed Italianate *canciones* that set standards of excellence from Fernando de *Herrera to Lope de *Vega. He wrote such perfect sonnets that even the most skilled among later poets, such as Lope, *Quevedo, and *Góngora, had to compete with him when writing their own. His characteristically secular poetry was often adapted for devotional purposes. Even *Cervantes shows Garcilaso's mark. But his influence does not end with the Spanish Golden Age. One of his lines, for instance, has given title to a book by Pedro *Salinas, and others have entered the works of Vicente *Aleixandre. Once the subject of a poem by *Sá de Miranda in the sixteenth c., he has become the subject of another poem by Rafael *Alberti in the twentieth. Writers who are most unlike Garcilaso may be characterized precisely insofar as they deviate from his own path. It might not be too adventurous to say that, as in the case of Petrarch in Italy, a history of the Spanish lyric could be written by following the avatars of Garcilaso across the centuries.

Garcilaso's poems were published after his death by Boscán's widow, as an appendix to those of her husband (Barcelona, 1543). As the superiority of Garcilaso's poems became apparent, he was edited separately in 1570. Soon he was both published and commented upon as a classic: by Francisco *Sánchez de las Brozas (Salamanca, 1574), Fernando de Herrera (Seville, 1580), Tomás *Tamayo de Vargas (Madrid, 1622), and José Nicolás de Azara (Madrid, 1765). Their important glosses may be consulted in Antonio Gallego Morell. *See also* Italian Literary Influences.

## BIBLIOGRAPHY

Primary Texts

*Garcilaso de la Vega: Obras completas.* Ed. Elías Rivers. Columbus: Ohio State UP, 1974.

*Garcilaso de la Vega: Poesías completas.* Ed. Germán Bleiberg. Madrid: Alíanza, 1980.

*Obras.* Ed. Tomás Navarro Tomás. 3rd ed. Clasicos Castellanos 3. Madrid: Clásicos Castellanos, 1935.

*Obras completas.* Ed. Amancio Labandeira Fernández. Madrid: Fundación Universitaria Española, 1981.

*Works: A Critical Text with a Bibliography.* Ed. Hayward Keniston. New York: Hispanic Society of America, 1925.

English Translation

*The Works of Garcilaso de la Vega, Surnamed the Prince of Castilian Poets.* Tr. Jeremiah H. Wiffen. London: Hurst Robinson, 1823.

Criticism

Barnard, Mary E. "Garcilaso's Poetics of Subversion and the Orpheus Tapestry." *PMLA* 102 (1987): 316–25.

Fernández-Morera, Dario. *The Lyre and the Oaten Flute: Garcilaso and the Pastoral.* London: Tamesis, 1981.

Gallego Morell, Antonio. *Garcilaso de la Vega y sus commentaristas.* 2nd ed. Madrid: Gredos, 1972.

Ghertman, Sharon. *Petrarch and Garcilaso: A Linguistic Approach to Style.* London: Tamesis, 1985.

Gicovate, Bernard. *Garcilaso de la Vega.* TWAS 349. Boston: Twayne, 1975. (Includes translations)

Lapesa, Rafael. *La trayectoria poética de Garcilaso.* Madrid: RO, 1948.

Dario Fernández-Morera

**GARCILASO DE LA VEGA, "El Inca"** (1539, Cuzco, Peru–1616, Córdoba, Spain), soldier, priest, translator, historian of the Incan empire and of the conquest of Peru. Garcilaso was the son of the *ñusta* Isabel Chimpu Occlo, descended from a brother of Huayna Capac, and of the Extremaduran captain Sebastián Garci Lasso de la Vega, whose family lineage included the Marqués de *Santillana, Jorge *Manrique and the poet *Garcilaso de la Vega. The young mestizo, who for a time took the name Gómez Suárez de Figueroa, grew up in Cuzco with a dual cultural and linguistic heritage which was to determine the unique perspective of his historical writing. From his mother and her family he learned Quechua, the interpretation of the *quipus*, and heard the oral tradition of the Incas. With his tutors Juan de Alcobaza and Juan de Cuéllar he studied Latin and received a humanistic education in the European tradition. At age twenty, upon the death of his father, he went to Spain, serving as a captain in the army for ten years, including service in Italy, where he learned the Tuscan dialect. Frustrated in his efforts to obtain royal favors based on his father's service in Peru, he settled in Córdoba to write. Toward the end of his life he became a priest, taking minor orders.

His first venture in literature, published when Garcilaso also was over fifty, was a translation from Italian of the Neoplatonic *Diálogos de amor* (1590; Dialogues of Love) of León *Hebreo. The following year he completed his history of the conquest of Florida by Hernando de Soto, although it was not published until 1605, with the title *La Florida del Inca* (*The Florida del Inca*, 1951). The author's fame, however, rests chiefly on his *Commentarios reales de los Incas* (*Royal Commentaries of the Incas*, 1966), the first part of which appeared in Lisbon in 1609, and the second part posthumously in 1617 in Córdoba under the title *Historia general del Perú* (General History of Peru).

For the first part of his history, dealing with Incan civilization before the arrival of the Spaniards, Garcilaso made extensive use of the papers of the Jesuit Blas Valera, who was himself a mestizo. For the second part, which concerns the conquest and ensuing civil wars between rival Spanish factions, the author depended on the chronicles of *Cieza de León, *Acosta, *López de Gómara, Agustín de *Zárate and others. In both cases, the Inca drew information as well from his own memories, experiences and acquaintances.

While Garcilaso is acknowledged to be a master of Spanish prose style, the value of his *Commentaries* as historical writing has been a more controversial issue. In the nineteenth c., the Inca was thought by some to be unreliable as an historian, a cultivator more of his own imagination than of the discipline of history. In this c., critical opinion has tended to be much more favorable toward the author, who has been portrayed on the one hand as a transmitter of Incan oral tradition, and on the other as a writer deeply influenced by European Renaissance thought, who saw in the lost civilization of his New World ancestors the embodiment of the Utopias envisioned by his humanist contemporaries. Recent studies have emphasized the value of the "imaginative amplifications" and the interpolated stories in Garcilaso's works, as literary enrichments of, rather than distractions from, the material of the historical text. *See also* Humanism; Italian Literary Influences; Renaissance; Siglo de Oro.

BIBLIOGRAPHY

Primary Texts

*Los comentarios reales de los Incas.* Ed. Aurelio Miró Quesada. 2 vols. Caracas: Biblioteca Ayacucho, 1976.
*La Florida del Inca.* Ed. Emma Susana Speratti Piñero. Mexico: Fondo de Cultura Económica, 1956.
*Obras completas del Inca Garcilaso de la Vega.* Ed. Carmelo Sáenz de Santa María. 4 vols. BAE 132–35.

English Translations

*The Florida del Inca; A History of the Adelantado Hernando de Soto, Governor and Captain General of the Kingdom of Florida.* . . . Tr. and ed. John Grier Varner and Jeannette Johnson Varner. Austin: U of Texas P, 1951.
*Royal Commentaries of the Incas and General History of Peru.* Tr. and ed. Harold Livermore. 2 vols. Austin: U of Texas P, 1966.

Criticism

Crowley, Frances G. *Garcilaso de la Vega, el Inca, and His Sources in the "Comentarios Reales de los Incas."* The Hague: Mouton, 1971.

Durand, José. *El Inca Garcilaso: clásico de América.* Mexico: Sep-setentas, 1976.

Miró Quesada, Aurelio. *El Inca Garcilaso y otros estudios garcilasistas.* Madrid: Cultura Hispánica, 1971.

Pupo-Walker, Enrique. "Las amplificaciones imaginativas en la crónica y un texto del Inca Garcilaso." *La vocación literaria del pensamiento histórico en América.* Madrid: Gredos, 1982. 96–122.

Varner, John Grier. *El Inca: The Life and Times of Garcilaso de la Vega.* Austin: U of Texas P, 1968.

Robert E. Lewis

**GARFIAS, Francisco** (1921, Moguer, Huelva– ), poet. After his first book, *Caminos interiores* (Interior Roads), he combined criticism with literary creation. His second book of poems, *El horizonte recogido*, (Found Horizon), was published in 1949, followed by *Magnificat* (1951), and then *Cerro del Tío Pío* (1964; Tío Pío's Hill). He then turned to the study of Juan Ramón *Jiménez and his works, and has published several editions of Jiménez's unpublished writings.

BIBLIOGRAPHY

Primary Texts

*Cerro del Tío Pío.* Barcelona: Chapultepec, 1964.
*Entretiempo.* Málaga: Guadalhorce, 1970.
*El horizonte recogido.* Madrid: Versal, 1949.
*Magnificat.* Madrid: Aguirre, 1951.

Isabel McSpadden

**GARFIAS ZURITA, Pedro** (1901, Salamanca–1967, Mexico), poet. Pedro Garfias, raised in Andalusia (Osuna, Ecija), moved to Madrid in 1918, and for a time participated in *ultraísta* activities. Once an admirer of *Cansinos Asséns, his attitude changed and by 1921 he left the group. However, in an article from 1934, he recalls this early literary experience with fondness. After a stay in Osuna, Garfias founded the journal *Horizonte* (Madrid, 1922–23), which lasted three issues and which, even with projects for future publication, he abandoned. He published his first book of poetry in Seville—*El ala del sur* (1926; The Wing of the South), and from 1934 until the Civil War, collaborated in *El Heraldo de Madrid* (The Madrid Herald). With the outbreak of the war, Garfias, a communist, went to the province of Córdoba and from there to Valencia and Barcelona, escaping in April 1939 to England. Before leaving, he had been awarded the National Prize for Literature (1938) for *Poesías de la guerra* (War Poems).

From England, Garfias went to Mexico, where he continued to publish and struggle in a losing battle against alcohol. Unable to maintain a steady job at the university, he acquired a reputation as composer and reciter of poems which others then collected for him. He never came to terms with exile.

Garfias's writings appear in the magazines *Los Quijotes, Cervantes, Grecia, Ultra, Alfar* and *Litoral*, in Spain, and in *Romance, Universidad, Novedades,* and *Héroes,* of Mexico.

BIBLIOGRAPHY

Primary Texts

*El ala del sur.* Seville: Herrero, 1926.
*Héroes del Sur.* Madrid-Barcelona: Nuestro Pueblo, 1938.
*Poesías de la guerra.* Valencia: Subcomisionario de Propaganda, 1938.
*Poesías de la guerra española.* Mexico: Minerva, 1941.
*Primavera en Eaton Hasting.* Mexico: Tezontle, 1941.
*Río de aguas amargas.* Guadalajara: n.p., 1953.
*De Soledad y otros pesares.* Mexico: Internacionales, 1941.
*Viejos y nuevos poemas.* N.p.: Universidad de Nuevo León, 1948.

English Translation

"Villafranca de Córdoba." Tr. K. Porter. In *The Poetry of Freedom.* Ed. W. R. Benet and N. Cousins. New York: Random House, 1945.

Criticism

Gracia Vicente, Alfredo. *Pedro Garfias, pastor de soledades.* Monterrey: n.p., 1967.
Sánchez Pascual, Angel. *Pedro Garfias, vida y obra.* Barcelona: Anthropos, 1980.

                                                                        Kathleen March

**GARIBAY Y ZAMALLOA, Esteban de** (1533, Mondragón, Guipuzcoa–1599, Madrid), historian, librarian. He studied Classics at Salamanca and Alcalá de Henares. His *Los cuarenta libros del compendio historial de las chronicas . . .* (1571; Forty Books of the Historical Compendium of the Chronicles . . . ) persuaded Philip II to appoint him librarian in 1576, and historian in 1592. After twenty-four years of research he published *Ilustraciones genealógicas de los Cathólicos Reyes de España . . .* (1596; Genealogical History of the Monarchs of Spain . . . ).

BIBLIOGRAPHY

Primary Texts

*Ilustraciones genealógicas de los Cathólicos reyes. . . .* Valencia: Artes Gráficas Soler, 1974. Rpt. of 1596 ed.
*Memorias de Garibay* and *Refranes vascongadas.* In *Memorial histórico español.* Madrid: n.p., 1854. 7: 1–660.

**GARNACHA,** traveling theater group of the *Siglo de Oro. Composed of five or six men, one woman and one young boy, with their baggage. They would usually spend a week in a town, and were prepared to perform about four plays, three *autos, and several *entremeses.

**GASPAR, Enrique** (1842, Madrid–1902, Olona, France), playwright. He quickly freed his writing from the reigning sentimentalism of the day, and composed realistic, satiric, sometimes pessimistic comedies treating contemporary mores and situations. His most mature work succeeds in presenting serious social criticism which prefigures that of *Benavente. Poyán Díaz cites the year 1867 as a watershed, after which Gaspar abandoned poetry for prose and his works became increasingly didactic. Gaspar's most memorable writing includes *La levita* (1868; The Frock Coat), *El estómago* (1874; The Stomach), *Las personas decentes* (1890; Decent People), and *La eterna cuestión* (1895; The Eternal Problem).

BIBLIOGRAPHY

Primary Texts

*La eterna cuestión.* Louisville, KY: Falls City Microcards, 1962. Rpt.

*El estómago.* Louisville, KY: Falls City Microcards, 1959. Rpt.

*La levita.* Louisville, KY: Falls City Microcards, 1959. Rpt.

*Las personas decentes.* Louisville, KY: Falls City Microcards, 1962. Rpt.

Criticism

Kirschenbaum, L. *Enrique Gaspar and the Social Drama in Spain.* Berkeley and Los Angeles: U of California P, 1977.

Poyán Díaz. *Enrique Gaspar, medio siglo de teatro español.* 2 vols. Madrid: Gredos, 1957. Includes extensive bibliography of Gaspar's works.

**GATELL, Angelina** (1926, Barcelona– ), Spanish poet. The Spanish Civil War, which Gatell experienced as a child, has colored much of her work which, like that of Ana María *Matute and others of the same generation, belongs to the movement of social protest (actually veiled political protest) of the 1950s and 1960s. The predominant mode is realistic, the tone sincere, the major themes the lack of political freedom, of justice and equality. In addition, her work conveys a horror of war and a sense of identification with the suffering of humanity. *El poema del soldado* (1954; The Soldier's Poem) is inspired by the memory of Miguel *Hernández, Spain's soldier-poet who died in a Franco jail. The work is constructed as a soliloquy, a denunciation of violence, injustice and war. *Esa oscura palabra* (1963; That Obscure Word) is another veiled protest against oppression, as well as an expression of hope for a better future. *Las claudicaciones* (1969; Surrenders) reiterates the themes of injustice and lack of freedom common to Gatell's writings of the 1950s and 1960s, this time focusing especially upon the plight of those who lost the Civil War in Spain. *El hombre del acordeón* (1984; The Accordion Man) represents a change of genre, tone and audience: this book of short stories for children is narrated by an accordion player who tells of circus life in a mixture of realism and fantasy.

BIBLIOGRAPHY

Primary Texts

*Las claudicaciones.* Madrid: Biblioteca Nueva, 1969.

*El hombre del acordeón.* Madrid: Espasa-Calpe, 1984.

*El poema del soldado.* Valencia: Diputación de Valencia, 1954.
*Esa oscura palabra.* Santander: Isla de los Ratones, 1963.

Janet Pérez

**GATOS, Libro de los** (Book of Cats). This curiously named fourteenth- or fifteenth-c. collection of apologues, most of which are beast fables, including
several that feature wily cats ("Who Will Put the Bell on The Cat's Neck,"
etc.), was rendered from the *Narrationes* or *Fabulae* of the thirteenth-c. English
preacher Odo of Cheriton. Thematically, the *Narrationes* and its heir draw from
the common stock of folktales. Nevertheless, the Book of Cats, in its amplifi-
cation of Odo and in its many new moralizations, sounds an original note. In
his sympathy for the "third estate" and hostility toward those advantaged at
court, the author frequently denounces the injustice of a feudal lord, both secular
and ecclesiastic. Concerning the title, the word *cat* is used figuratively in tale
42 of *Juan Manuel's *Conde Lucanor* to mean "hypocrite." John Keller, who
showed from a paleographic standpoint that there was no basis for the ms. reading
of *quentos,* that is, *cuentos* (stories or tales) instead of *gatos,* was led to speculate
on an Arab source. James Burke, in his summary of the controversy surrounding
the title, has suggested the Arabic etymon *qattu* ("lying," or "uttering a false-
hood"), which would have entered the language via the Mozarabs. The title is
then, for Burke, to be understood as the Book of Falsehoods.

BIBLIOGRAPHY

Primary Texts

*Libro de los gatos.* Ed. Bernard Darbord. Annexes des Cahiers de linguistique hispanique
        médiévale 3. Paris: Klincksieck, 1984.
*Libro de los gatos.* Ed. J. E. Keller. Madrid: CSIC, 1958.

Criticism

Artola, G. T. "El libro de los gatos. An Orientalist's View of Its Title." *RPH* 9 (1955):
        17–19.
Burke, James F. "More on the Title *El libro de los gatos.*" *RN* 9 (1967): 148–51.
Keller, John Esten. See *Libro de los gatos.*
———. "*Gatos* not *Quentos.*" *Studies in Philology* 50 (1953): 437–45.
Zelson, L. G. "The Title *Libro de los gatos.*" *RR* 21 (1930): 237–38.

Porter Conerly

**GAYA CIENCIA** (Gay Science), literary term. It denotes the rules and precepts
for composing poems. The term originated in Provence, and from there passed
to Catalonia. In 1323 the Catalán Raimon Vidal de Besalu founded the Consistory
of Gay Science; he also left a treatise on composition. A century later Enrique
de *Villena composed the *Arte de trobar* (n.d.; The Art of Composing). These
formalized procedures contrast with the relaxed verse of the *mester de juglaría.*

BIBLIOGRAPHY

Primary Text

*Arte de trobar.* Ed. F. Sánchez Cantón. Madrid: Suárez, 1923. Also in *RFE* 6 (1919).

**GAYA NUÑO, Juan Antonio** (1913, Soria–1976, Madrid), Spanish art critic, art historian, author. He was incarcerated for some four years after the Civil War, and was repeatedly denied a teaching position at the university level, for political reasons. His works include the following books: *El románico en la provincia de Soria* (1947; The Romanesque [Style] in the Province of Soria); *La pintura románica en Castilla* (1954; Romanesque Painting in Castile); *Escultura española contemporánea* (1957; Contemporary Spanish Sculpture); and *La pintura española fuera de España* (1958; Spanish Painting Outside of Spain). Personal recollections and impressions of the Sorian landscape are collected in *El Santero de San Saturio* (1965; The Pilgrim of St. Saturio). He also published a most original essay, *Tratado de mendicidad* (1962; Treatice on Mendacity) and a short story collection titled *Los gatos salvajes* (1968; The Wild Cats). More recent was his *Historia de la crítica de arte en España* (1975; History of Art Criticism in Spain).

BIBLIOGRAPHY

Primary Texts

*Los gatos salvajes.* Madrid: Taurus, 1968.
*La pintura española fuera de España.* Madrid: Espasa-Calpe, 1958.
*El santero de San Saturio.* Madrid: Espasa-Calpe, 1965.
*Tratado de mendicidad.* Madrid: Taurus, 1962.

English Translation

*Juan Gris.* No tr. NY: Rizzoli, 1986.

**GEDEÃO, António,** pseudonym of Rómulo Vasco Gama de Carvalho (1906, Lisbon– ), poet, dramatist, prose author. He majored in physics and chemistry, and was an expert teacher at a secondary school in Lisbon. Under his real name he wrote several pedagogical works, some aimed at youth, including *A Ciência Hermética* (Alchemy), *Que é a Física* (What's Physics), *História da Energia Nuclear* (History of Nuclear Energy), and *História do Átomo* (History of the Atom).

His poetic gift only revealed itself in 1956 when he published *Movimiento Perpétuo* (Perpetual Movement). Seven years later he produced a two-act play, *R.T.X.78/24.* This play depicts the victory of Love—in its profoundest universal meaning—over Hate, the hero being the Man who cannot adapt to the corrupt society in which he lives and who tries in every possible way to challenge and avoid it. Traditional morality, absurd and archaic values (honor, chauvinism, virtue in the abstract)—the very foundations of that society—the incompetence and lethargy of certain public services, the immoderate ambition that leads to small and big wars, all are masterly caricatured through a strongly ironic or even sarcastic tone of writing and the portrayal of ridiculous situations.

Gedeão also wrote stories and short novels such as *A Poltrona e outras Novelas* (The Armchair and Other Short Novels), which was his first book in this genre. In general, they are characterized by an ironic, clever, corrosive and humorous form of social criticism and an implicit sense of human kindness and understanding. After this first book, he published *Teatro do Mundo* (Theater of the World) and *Máquina de Fogo* (Fire Machine) in 1958 and 1961.

Poetry, however, is the principal genre of expression for Gedeão. At the end of the 1960s he collected his verse in *Poesias Completas* (Complete Poems). The preface, composed by Jorge de *Sena, analyzes the basic characteristic of Gedeão's poetic production: his viewpoint as a teacher of applied sciences, which is something completely new in the history of Portuguese literature. This combination of a scientific culture, which founds his world vision and social attitudes, and a gifted, penetrating, artistic sensitivity are singularly effective. Gedeão thereby brings a breath of innovation and challenge to Portuguese poetry of the second half of this c. through his unique vocabulary, metaphors, themes and formal processes, which he combines with the most beautiful elements of traditional Portuguese lyric poetry.

BIBLIOGRAPHY

Primary Text

*Poesias completas. (1956–1967).* 9th ed. Lisbon: Sá de Costa, 1983.

Criticism

Belo, Ruy. *Senda da Poesia.* Lisbon: União Gráfica, 1969.

Sena, Jorge de. *Dialécticas Aplicadas da Literatura.* Lisbon: Edições 70, 1978.

Natércia Fraga

**GEFAELL, María Luisa** (1918, Madrid– ), short story author. She writes primarily for children, and has published *Las hadas* (Fairies), *Cuentos de Antón Retaco* (Anton Retaco's Tales), and *La princesita que tenía los dedos mágicos* (The Princess with Magic Fingers)—winner of the Premio Nacional de Literatura in 1950. She has also translated works of Rilke and Bergson into Spanish.

BIBLIOGRAPHY

Primary Text

*Antón Retaco.* Barcelona: Noguer, 1983.

Isabel McSpadden

**GENER, Pompeyo** (1848, Barcelona–1921, Barcelona), critic, essayist, historian, and philosopher. Gener, a polyglot who wrote extensively on many subjects, especially in French and Spanish, was a graduate from both the U of Madrid in pharmacy and the natural sciences and the U of Paris in medicine. Influenced by the ideas of Renan, Comte, Littré, and Taine, he ably wrote on topics in psychology, sociology, literature, art, pathology, criminology, anthropology, philosophy, and history. He was a frequent contributor to *Revista Contemporánea* (Madrid), *La Renaixensa* (Barcelona), *La Nación* (Buenos Aires), and *Le Livre* (Paris), and he wrote several books in Catalan. As a result of a famous polemic with the critic Leopoldo Alas (*Clarín), he wrote *El caso Clarín*.

*Monomanía maliciosa de forma impulsiva. Estudio de psiquiatría* (1894; The Clarín Case Study. Malicious Monomania of an Impulsive Nature. A Psychiatric Study). He is well known today for the role his book *Literaturas malsanas* (1894; Sick Literatures) played in the debate and controversies surrounding naturalism. By applying the scientific method, he analyzed certain movements (*naturalism, decadence, Russian nihilism, etc.) which he considered to be literary manifestations of the pathological behavior and ills of his times. He concluded that these pathological phenomena were not symptoms of decadence but of progress and of energetic, ascending evolution.

BIBLIOGRAPHY

Primary Texts

*El caso Clarín.* Madrid: Paciano Torres, 1894.
*Literaturas malsanas.* Madrid: Fernando Fe, 1894.
*La muerte y el diablo.* Barcelona: Atlante, 1883.

Gilbert Paolini

**GENERATION OF 1898.** The term *Generation of 1898* is used to designate a group of writers generally characterized by their intense concern for Spain and desire for a program of national regeneration in the social, political, educational and aesthetic spheres. The name of the generation comes from the immediate stimulus that was the War of 1898 (called in Hispanic countries the War of Cuba), which brought to an end the vestiges of once-imperial Spain, and seemed like the final blow to a country that had lost the prestige, dynamism and even moral fiber it once had. The first allusions to such a generation are attributed to the historian Gabriel *Maura y Gamazo, but the designation was legitimized in a series of articles written for the magazine *ABC* beginning in February 1913 by one of its members, *Azorín, who continued to define the generation in subsequent essays and articles. Since then disagreements and polemics have arisen with regard to which writers should be included and which theory of a "generation" should be applied. These questions were further complicated by the fact that even those most widely recognized to be part of the generation, like Pío *Baroja, *Valle-Inclán and Ramiro de *Maeztu at one time or another denied being members or even that it existed. In addition, the supposed members of the group represent such a diversity of ideas, aesthetic philosophies and points of view that it is difficult to perceive similarities, and yet there is a cohesive element in that all recognized the need to carry out reforms to correct "the problem of Spain" (*preocupación de España), which they felt deeply.

Pedro *Salinas, *Ortega y Gasset, Pedro *Laín Entralgo and Julián *Marías have proposed or followed historical methodologies to apply a concept of "generation" to define the Generation of 1898. Ortega's attribution of a span of fifteen years to a generation leads him to distinguish two historical generations contributing to the group, around the central dates 1857 (to include *Ganivet and *Unamuno) and 1872, which includes most of the others. Azorín, on the other hand, had from the beginning insisted that defining the Generation of 1898 was not a question of scientific distinctions but rather of aesthetics. For Azorín it is the public, and not the members of a generation, that can best perceive a shared block of sentiments, ideas, aspirations and moral climate despite apparent contradictions and even controversies among individual members. In fact, it can be said, paradoxically, that one of the outstanding characteristics that unites them as a generation is precisely their diversity and staunch individualism. In the absence of any definite consensus about the conformity of the designation Generation of 1898 to scientific theories of generations, it seems justified to use the term rather loosely to include those authors who belong to the same historical period, were moved by the national crisis of 1898 to a spirit of national concern, and exhibit certain affinities in their writings. Pedro Salinas finds Azorín's early intuitions reinforced by the criteria proposed by the German literary historiographer Peterson for distinguishing a literary generation: proximity of birth dates, formative elements (self-education of the writers of 1898), personal contact among the members, generational experience or event, a "generational language" (*Modernism, and rupture with the previous generation (repudiation of extreme realism and *naturalism). The important factor of leadership, however, is missing; Salinas resolves this by suggesting the influence of Nietzsche.

Angel Ganivet (1865–98) is generally considered a precursor of the Generation of 1898, since his work was cut short by his suicide precisely in the traumatic year of 1898. His *Idearium español* (1897; *Spain: An Interpretation*, 1964), an examination of the national character and Spain's relationship to Europe, traces Spain's current problems to its historical depletion of energy in outside undertakings. He sees a need for reconstruction from within, especially to overcome *abulia*, apathy or weakness of will, which was to be one of the major themes of 1898. He ends on a generally optimistic note with regard to the spiritual future of Spain. The undisputed authors of the generation, or what might be called its nucleus, are its senior members Miguel de Unamuno (1864–1936), Ramón María del Valle-Inclán (1866–1936), Pío Baroja (1872–1956), the journalist Ramiro de Maeztu (1874–1936) and the poet Antonio *Machado (1875–1939). Some critics find the dramatist Jacinto *Benavente (1866–1954) too European and relatively unconcerned with Spanish themes, but Azorín and other commentators include him in the Generation of 1898 because of his irony and his renovation of Spanish theater. Azorín also includes Rubén Darío and cites the important role of Luis Ruiz Contreras, founder of *La Revista Nueva*, which offered a forum for the early writings of Unamuno, Maeztu, Baroja and Darío. Salinas notes that the generation seemed to coalesce in 1903 with the magazine *Alma Española* where Baroja, Unamuno, Valle-Inclán, Maeztu and Benavente all collaborated. A number of painters who were also writers may be considered part of the Generation of 1898, such as Picasso (1881–1973), co-founder of the magazine *Arte Joven* (Young Art) in which Unamuno and Baroja published articles. In fact, his early "blue paintings" may represent an expression of preoccupation for the state of his country as he often depicted the 1898 themes of misery, infirmity and the effects of war. Azorín mentions the painter and writer Ricardo

*Baroja (1871–1953), brother of Pío, as part of the generation. José *Gutiérrez Solana (1886–1945), whose book *España negra* (1920; Black Spain) and paintings express a pessimistic and critical view of Spain, shared many characteristics of the group, although he was born later than the rest.

Certain attitudes characterize the members of the generation, notably a spirit of altruism, unselfishness and idealism in the desire to change and better Spanish society. At the same time their writings are marked by a vague melancholy, pessimism and gravity that links them to Mariano José de *Larra, and their preferred painter El Greco. Humor is very rare in these authors, and when it does appear, it is more like traditional Spanish "black humor."

### Spanish Precedents and Precursors

For Azorín, the Generation of 1898 was formed and influenced by the critical efforts of the previous generation and their writings between 1870 and 1898, and in fact he sees the generation as a prolongation of the reconstructionist aspirations present from the seventeenth c., in the spirit of *Saavedra Fajardo. The principal influences of the previous generation in that of 1898 are the poet *Campoamor, for his corrosive critical spirit and "subversive sentimentalism"; the dramatist *Echegaray, whose passion incited the public; and *Pérez Galdós, whose novels confronted readers with the realities of Spain. Liberal writers like Juan *Valera, Emilia *Pardo Bazán and *Clarín encouraged the older members of the generation. A number of books by lesser known authors treating "the problem of Spain" appeared in the years preceding the trauma of 1898, among them *Herejías* (1887; Heresies), by Pompeyo *Gener, which discusses "the national decadence," and *Los males de la Patria* (1890; The Ills of the Country), by the engineer Lucas Mallada, friend of Baroja's father. In the very year 1898 Darío de Regoyos published his *España negra* (Black Spain), recounting a trip through Spain in company of the Belgian poet Emile Verhaeren, with his own illustrations depicting the sad scenes he observed. One year after the crisis, *Macías Picavea published a widely read book entitled *El problema nacional* (The National Problem) and Maeztu his first book, *Hacia otra España* (Toward Another Spain).

### Foreign Influences

In reacting to the plight of their country, the writers of 1898, particularly Unamuno, Baroja and Maeztu, were profoundly influenced by European thinkers. The increased availability of foreign books and magazines and improvements in travel and communications toward the end of the last century encouraged contact with European countries. Verlaine and other French poets influenced the modernists Darío and Valle-Inclán, while another Frenchman, Theophile Gautier, who wrote a book about his trip to Spain, inspired Spanish writers to appreciate their own landscape. Unamuno was familiar with the philosophies of Schopenhauer, Kant and Nietzsche. By far the most important influence was that of Nietzsche, whose philosophy was really received secondhand by Baroja, Maeztu and Azorín through books about him (particularly *La Philosophie de Nietzsche*

[1898; The Philosophy of Nietzche]) by Henri Lichtenberger and through Pablo Schmitz, a Swiss doctor who read pages of the German philosopher's correspondence to Baroja and Azorín in the garden of the monastery at Paular, a scene that Baroja re-creates in his novel *Camino de perfección* (1902; Way to Perfection). Other European writers who influenced individual writers were Ibsen, Tolstoy, Shakespeare (Benavente), Dickens, Poe, Balzac, Gautier, and Stendhal.

One of the polemical themes of the Generation of 1898 is the question of whether Spain's regeneration could best be accomplished by making Spain more European or by "Hispanicizing" Europe, as Unamuno suggested. Maeztu, who lived abroad for many years, was an early proponent of "Europeanizing" Spain and one of the first to divulge European theories of phenomenology and values in his books, but later turned ultraconservative and traditional. For Azorín and Baroja, European influences were seen as a way of enriching and vitalizing Spanish culture, not to supplant it but rather to be assimilated into it. Valle-Inclán interspersed works set in Spain with abundant classical and universal allusions, and later opened his horizons to Latin America in his novel *Tirano Banderas* (1926; *The Tyrant*, 1929).

### Aesthetics of the Generation of 1898

The authors of the generation, especially Azorín and Valle-Inclán, exhibit intellectual refinement and concern for artistic expression that sometimes leads them to indifference or scorn for the vulgarity of a literature for mass consumption. At the same time, Azorín found aesthetic attraction in some popular traditions, and Machado used a traditional art form, the *romance* (*romancero). The authors of 1898 also related literature to other arts. Baroja's interest and knowledge of art is evidenced in *Way to Perfection*, perhaps inspired by the fact that his brother was a famous painter and by his friendship with Zuloaga and Regoyos. Valle-Inclán's extensive allusions to art in the *Sonata de primavera* (1904; "Spring Sonata" in *The Pleasant Memoirs of the Marqués de Bradomín: Four Sonatas*, 1924) and articles on painters and painting come from a solid preparation in art, his experience as professor of aesthetics at the School of Fine Arts in Madrid and director of the Spanish Academy of Fine Arts in Rome, and friendship with Zuloaga and Julio Romero de Torres. Unamuno, who on occasion also sketched, found inspiration in Velázquez's painting of Christ, and wrote essays about art and about the painters Zuloaga, Carreño, Darío de Regoyos, among others. Manuel *Machado, brother of Antonio, wrote several poems about paintings and painters. Azorín wrote a series of articles about the fine arts and the painters Regoyos, Sorolla, Velázquez and El Greco. In fact, the Generation of 1898 is largely credited with the "discovery" of El Greco for the Spanish public. The generation was generally less involved in music, although Azorín calls Amadeo Vives the "musician of the generation," and in the 1930s Pío Baroja collaborated with the composer Pablo Zorozabal, also Basque, in a *zarzuela*, *Adiós a la bohemia* (Goodbye to Bohemia). Valle-Inclán's modernistic sensitivity to music is reflected in the title of his *Sonatas*.

Aesthetic concern also manifested itself in innovations pertaining to literary genre and in the attention accorded to prose style. Azorín shows a fondness for rare, archaic terms to achieve precision of expression as well as to evoke the past. With the arrival of Rubén Darío in Madrid precisely in the year 1898, the modernistic influence enriched Spanish letters with its sonority, musical quality and exoticism. Valle-Inclán was particularly influenced by modernism in his pursuit of verbal resonance and use of rich, exotic and archaic vocabulary to enhance mood or sensuality. Machado, who was attracted by modernism for a while, maintained that poetry was for him "essential word in time." Unamuno, as professor of Spanish and classical philology, often refers to the etymology and suggestive meaning of words and subjects language to maximum flexibility with his neologisms. His defense of certain novels criticized for being unconventional was to call them "nivolas," following the example of Manuel Machado's "sonite." Baroja introduced the "amorphous" rambling novel, defined the genre as "a sack anything fits into," and seemed to cultivate a deliberately direct and abrupt style. Valle-Inclán wrote plays of grotesque deformed reality he called "*esperpentos*," while Benavente revolutionized the exaggerated theater that preceded him and introduced structural innovations.

## Will and Apathy

The excess or lack of will is a major theme of the authors of 1898, inspired by their notions of Nietzsche. It is related to the "problem of Spain" in that apathy is seen as one of the Spanish defects that led to the tragedy of 1898 as the country, introverted and weak, allowed itself to deteriorate. At the same time, it seemed to reflect their own inability to translate their meditations and ideas into action to influence the national reality. Azorín named one of his novels *Voluntad* (1902; Will), pointing to the problem of his protagonist and alter ego Antonio Azorín, who suffers from lack of will, the "*no*lition" that became a major concern of the generation. Apathy is a common trait in Baroja's protagonists, who are usually uncommitted. Most wander about with no direction, like Andrés Hurtado in *El árbol de la ciencia* (1911; The Tree of Life) and Fernando Ossorio in *Way to Perfection*, but on the other hand, the hero of *Zalacaín el aventurero* (1909; Zalacaín the Adventurer) is a man of action. In Unamuno, Augusto Pérez of *Niebla* (1914; Mist) is the best example of the apathetic protagonist, who, despite leading an uneventful life excited only by his own illusions of a great love, confronts the author to plead for his survival. Perhaps Valle-Inclán's most apathetic character is Max Estrella of *Luces de Bohemia* (1920; Lights of Bohemia), a Bohemian poet who wanders aimlessly about Madrid. In Machado the theme is represented by poems like "La noria "(The Water Wheel), "Hastío" (Boredom) and "Las moscas" (Flies) about endless repetition and boredom.

In response to the problem of weakness of will and lack of direction, some writers resort to the classical Spanish example of the other extreme, *Don Juan, providing new versions of the old myth in extremely apathetic Don Juans like that of Azorín in his *Don Juan* (1922) and Unamuno's *El hermano Juan* (1934;

Brother Juan), where he is a religious brother. Valle-Inclán, on the other hand, develops the theme with more self-willed and stylized Don Juans, such as the Marqués de Bradomín of his *Sonatas*—"ugly, Catholic, and sentimental"—or Don Juan Manuel Montenegro of the *Comedias bárbaras* (1907, 1909, 1922; Barbaric Comedies).

Excessive will is related to another major theme, that of the conflict of wills leading to fratricide and fratricidal wars. This is especially prominent in Unamuno's *Tres novelas ejemplares y un prólogo* (1920; Three Exemplary Novels and a Prologue, 1956) and *Abel Sánchez* (1917), and in Machado's *La tierra de Alvargonzález* (1912; The Land of Alvargonzález). Many of Unamuno's willful protagonists are women, as are Benavente's creations Señora Ama (1908; The Lady of the House) and Imperia (*La noche del sábado* [1903; *Saturday Night*, 1923]) and Acacia (*La malquerida* [1913; *The Passion Flower*, 1920]). War appears in Valle-Inclán's novels set during the Carlist War, and in Unamuno's paradoxical *Paz en la guerra* (1897; Peace in War).

Also related to apathy in the absence of an active life is the subject of dreams, which bring about an ideal world that the inactive dreamer is incapable of otherwise achieving. The question has to do with the national destiny and the question that preoccupied the Generation of 1898, of whether Spain was asleep or dreaming. In Unamuno and Machado, dreams convey metaphorical philosophical significance. For Unamuno individual dreaming is vital to survival; both authors ponder the difficulty of distinguishing between dream and reality, which involves also Quixotic idealism. In Azorín dream takes the form of daydreaming and conjuring the past while Valle-Inclán's "Comedia de ensueño" (1914; "The Dream Comedy," 1961) and "Tragedia de ensueño" (1914; The Dream Tragedy) tend toward the exotic and the mysterious.

**Travel and Landscape**

Azorín says the Generation of 1898 loved and described landscape; Laín Entralgo calls them inventors and discoverers of the Spanish landscape that they observed in their travels through the country, and most especially, Castile. It became a labor of love to rediscover the old cities and monuments, the remnants of the historical and literary past, forgotten towns and villas. Azorín devoted several books to the description of landscape, such as *El paisaje de España visto por los españoles* (1917; Spanish Landscape Seen by Spaniards), and impressions of his travels, as did Unamuno (*Andanzas y visiones españolas* [1922; Spanish Wanderings and Visions], *Por tierras de Portugal y España* [1911; Through Lands of Portugal and Spain]), who, rather than fill his novels with landscape, reserved it mainly for his poetry and these books. Regoyos and later Solana also wrote travel impressions. Each author of the generation seems to prefer a specific region, often reflecting nostalgia for his place of birth or of particular suffering, as in the case of Machado and Soria. Valle-Inclán imparted lyrical qualities to the exuberant Galician landscape. The writers of the generation who came to Madrid from their native provinces around 1896 found the desolate Castilian landscape conducive to meditation and evocative of Spain's past. Some of them, like Baroja and Azorín, describe provincial life as backward and unbearable. Machado describes Soria and Castilian lands, according symbolic significance to many trees. For Azorín, the generation added the aesthetic enjoyment of color and smell to the description of Spanish landscapes. Generally the coloration of their Castilian descriptions is somber, reflecting not only reality but the mood of the times and circumstances.

A favorite place that appears in their works is the cemetery, which seems an appropriate place to reflect upon the sad destiny of Spain. Azorín describes the tribute offered by a group of authors at the tomb of Larra. Cemetery scenes appear, in Baroja's *Way to Perfection*, Valle-Inclán's *Lights of Bohemia* and Regoyos's *Black Spain*.

### Historicity

"The Generation of '98 is a historicist generation," affirms Azorín; "History captivated us." It was only natural that in seeking remedies for the ills of Spain they examine the past, as Ganivet had done, to find elements that had contributed to the waning of a once great culture or others capable of revitalizing the country. Each member of the generation had his own way of dealing with history. Unamuno conceptualizes in essays his ideas about history and its relation to what he called "intrahistory," the small, day-to-day events that are forgotten by the history books; for Azorín history served as a "trampoline" to the abstract question of time, as it did also for Machado. Azorín sought to recapture what he called "subhistorical" events that he saw as part of an eternal recurrence with some variation that made things the same and yet different. In books like *Una hora de España (entre 1560 y 1570)* (1924; An Hour of Spain [between 1560 and 1570]), he delved into a critical point of Spanish history. Baroja began writing in 1913 a twenty-two volume series of historical novels set in the immediate past of the nineteenth c. (*Memorias de un hombre de acción* [Memories of a Man of Action]), which Laín Entralgo calls novels of "intrahistory." Valle-Inclán uses allusions to conquistadors and heroes and wrote historical novels in his trilogy on the Carlist Wars, and includes copious allusions to Spanish conquistadors and heroes in his *Sonatas*.

In their revisionist examination of Spain's historical past as well as its literary and artistic heritage, the authors of 1898 find affinities with several figures from diverse historical periods. They admire the "primitives," *Berceo, *Santillana, Juan Ruiz, *Arcipreste de Hita, and also *Cervantes, *Góngora and Larra. Azorín studies Spain's classics in *Al margen de los clásicos* (1915; In the Margin of the Classics) and several other books; both he and Machado admire Berceo; Unamuno gives his subjective interpretations of Cervantes in *Vida de don Quijote y Sancho* (1905; *The Life of Don Quixote and Sancho*, 1927); Baroja evokes El Greco in *Way to Perfection*, and Maeztu studies the figures of Don Quixote, Don Juan, and the *Celestina.

In addition to delving into Spanish history, the members of the generation examined their personal histories in memories, autobiographical writings and fictionalized accounts of their childhood.

## Critical Attitude

In their desire to renovate and regenerate a stagnant and decadent culture, the authors of the generation maintained a general critical attitude toward "this and that" as the Unamuno title *Contra esto y aquello* (1912) states. Baroja, like his protagonist Andrés Hurtado, seems to feel "a profound irritation against everything" (*The Tree of Life*). His attitudes often approach nihilism, misogyny, xenophobia and anarchy, and his particular targets are the Spanish university, the clergy, the bullfight, moneylenders, pornography, the exploitation of women, and the lack of charitable spirit and collective instinct. Valle-Inclán sees the "aesthetics of the grotesque" as the only way to portray Spain; his *Lights of Bohemia* is filled with implicit criticism of Madrid in 1920, marked by prostitution, strikes, bad government, injustice, and an inquisitorial atmosphere. In other works he satirizes the Castilian tradition of "honor." Azorín, Baroja and Machado show the defects of education in Spain. Unamuno's criticisms are directed more to intellectual themes, against lazy thinking, passive erudition and systematization. Machado decries the sentiments of envy, malice, hypocrisy, and fratricide, and describes a Castile bogged down by boredom and filled with a decrepit aristocracy, old women in mourning, pilgrims and beggars, but still expresses hope for the Spaniard who fights to live between "one Spain that is dying and another that yawns." Regoyos's *Black Spain* and Solana's, with their terrible or sad descriptions, constitute implicit criticism of multiple aspects of Spanish customs and attitudes. Benavente largely focuses on social criticism of aristocratic and upper middle-class life. The revisionism of the generation expressed in their criticism was not intended to bring about real change but rather to express sadness and pain that gradually evolved into more of an acceptance of Spain's reality and destiny.

## Distinguishing Features from the Next Generation

Already in 1910 Azorín lamented the "new" pornographic novel and the lack of any dedication to art, and in 1914 the absence of the spirit of rebellion and independence that marked the Generation of 1898. The generation that follows is decidedly more scientific, guided by methods and systems; it is a generation of critics, historians, philosophers, scholars and professors rather than artists. The real heirs of the writers of 1898 seem to be the poets of the *Generation of 1927 and the rebellious authors of the *Generation of 1936.

BIBLIOGRAPHY

Primary Text

Azorín. *La generación del 98*. Madrid: Anaya, 1969.

English Translation

Ganivet, Ángel. *Spain: An Interpretation (Idearium español)*. Tr. J. R. Carey. London: Eyre and Spottiswood, 1964.

Criticism

Blanco Aguinaga, Carlos. *Juventud del 98*. Barcelona: Crítica, 1978.
Díaz Plaja, Guillermo. *Modernismo frente a 98*. Madrid: Espasa-Calpe, 1979.
Fernández Molina, Antonio. *La generación del 98*. Barcelona: Labor, 1968.
Granjel, Luis. *La generación literaria del noventa y ocho*. Salamanca: Anaya, 1966.
Gullón, Ricardo. *La invención del 98 y otros ensayos*. Madrid: Gredos, 1969.
Laín Entralgo, Pedro. *La generación del noventa y ocho*. 4th ed. Madrid: Espasa-Calpe, 1959.
López Morillas, Juan. *Hacia el 98. Literatura, sociedad e ideología*. Esplugas de Llobregat: Ariel, 1972.
Salinas, Pedro. "El concepto de generación literaria aplicada a la del 98." In *Literatura española Siglo XX*. 2nd ed. Mexico: Robredo (Porrúa), 1948. 26–33.

Estelle Irizarry

**GENERATION OF 1914.** Named either for the onset of World War I, which permanently changed European consciousness, or for the seminal lecture "Vieja y nueva política" (Old and New Politics) given by José *Ortega y Gasset at the Teatro de la Comedia in that year. The ambiguity in rationale for the 1914 designation—the dual reference to international and national events— marks one of the salient characteristics of this generation of writers and thinkers, which usually includes the following members born between 1879 and 1888 and who began to write in the first decade of the twentieth c.: José Ortega y Gasset, the generation's intellectual leader (philosopher, essayist and professor), Juan Ramón *Jiménez (poet and essayist), Ramón *Pérez de Ayala (novelist, essayist, poet and diplomat), Eugenio d'*Ors (essayist, novelist and dramatist), Gabriel *Miró (novelist), Ramón *Gómez de la Serna (novelist, journalist and essayist), and Benjamín *Jarnés (novelist, biographer, essayist, editor and teacher). The Generation of 1914 was the first truly international Spanish cultural phenomenon (in terms of travels, studies, influences and impact abroad) since the *Siglo de Oro, and yet was as profoundly preoccupied with Spanish culture and problems as was its predecesor, the *Generation of 1898, especially in its first phase from approximately 1907 to 1914.

Coming as it did between two powerful generations—the 1898 and the 1927, which have received more critical attention as groups—the Generation of 1914 tends to be ignored. Its older writers—Ortega, Jiménez, Miró, d'Ors and Pérez de Ayala—are often assigned to the Generation of 1898, and the younger writers—Gómez de la Serna and Jarnés— to the 1927. But such an arrangement of Spanish intellectual and literary history inaccurately diminishes the distinctive characteristics of the 1914 group, especially its cosmopolitan and international nature and the powerful, magnetic presence of José Ortega y Gasset. Ortega's possible influence on the art of some individual writers may be misconstrued, but he certainly set the tone for Spanish intellectual life between 1914 and 1925 or so. Having studied philosophy in Germany in 1906–8 and in 1911, he first introduced neo-Kantianism and then phenomenology into the peninsula through

his university chair and the journals he founded. All the writers (except Gabriel
Miró) collaborated on Ortega's journals and cultural and political projects.

It is perhaps helpful to see the generation's development in two phases, which
achieve continuity through Ortega's powerful leadership. The early phase from
about 1907 to 1914 displays many of the characteristics of the Generation of
1898 and *modernismo*, especially a preoccupation with the ills of Spain and a
cultivation of *modernista* stylistic techniques. Pérez de Ayala's first series of
novels, the tetralogy *Tinieblas en las cumbres* (1907; Darkness at the Top),
*AMDG* (1910), *La pata de la raposa* (1912; The Vixen's Paw), and *Troteras y
danzaderas* (1913; Mummers and Dancers) follows in the 1898 tradition of
depicting the problems of contemporary Spanish society through the fortunes of
a will-less protagonist in a series of loosely connected scenes. Gabriel Miró
achieved recognition in Madrid's literary circles when he received the Cuento
Semanal Prize for *Nómada* (1908), a harsh criticism of puritanical, heartless
orthodox Christianity. Also in 1908 Ramón Gómez de la Serna founded the
journal *Prometeo* for the dissemination of new cultural ideas and published
*Morbideces* (Morbidities), which borrowed the 1898's critical spirit to satirize
the Generation of 1898 itself. Juan Ramón Jiménez, who like Ramón Pérez de
Ayala had begun in full *modernista* dress early in the first decade, initiated (as
did the 1898 generationist poet Antonio *Machado in 1907) a "purification" of
his poetic style and themes during the latter part of the first decade and the first
part of the second to achieve the metaphysical lyricism of his mature years. In
1910 the Residencia de Estudiantes was founded, a continuation of *Giner de
los Ríos's Institución Libre de Enseñanza, which provided (until the mid-thirties)
a focal point for Madrid's intellectual activity. In 1913 Juan Ramón Jiménez
took charge of its publications.

What distinguishes the Generation of 1914's concern for Spain and her problems from the Generation of 1898's preoccupation with the country's ills is that
the 1914 writers returned to specific political solutions and to a need to Euro-
peanize Spain that the Generation of 1898 writers had abandoned early in the
first decade. In 1913 Ortega and Pérez de Ayala along with several others founded
the Liga de Educación Política Española (League for Spanish Political Education)
with the express purpose of enlightening the Spanish public about political matters, and Ortega's 1914 address at the Teatro de la Comedia was in this vein.
Ortega had carved out his new path five years earlier in a published letter to
*Unamuno, refuting the rector of Salamanca's emphasis on things Spanish over
the modernity represented by northern Europe. A young Ortega, fresh from his
studies at Freiberg, eagerly set himself apart from such "backward-looking"
policy. Ortega here was a precursor to the general international quality that
Western civilization would inevitably acquire after World War I, and his pointing
Spanish thought and letters in an international direction was successful until the
Civil War (1936–39) brought it to an abrupt halt. The Liga de Educación Política
Española and Ortega's *Revista de España*, founded in 1915 (including regular
critiques of the government of Alphonse XIII), provided concrete platforms that

gave the Generation of 1914 a more cohesive and programmatic nature than the Generation of 1898 had had. But, of course, the break with the previous generation was not absolute; all the members of the previous generation were still publishing vigorously during the period that the new outlook was taking shape, and some began associating themselves with Ortega's projects. The influence was necessarily mutual, but the overt stance of the 1914 group vis-à-vis the older generation remained ambiguous—respect and admiration combined with frequent rejection and pungent criticism.

The year 1914 not only provides a symbolic political watershed for the development of generational interests in Spain (it is important to note that in neutral Spain most of the forward-looking intellectuals of the 1914 group sided with the Allies in the war, while some of the 1898 group were Germanophiles), but also it marks an important moment in Spanish intellectual development. Ortega's first major philosophical work, *Meditaciones del Quijote* (Meditations on the Quijote), was published in that year, as was the Spanish translation of Eugenio d'Ors's *El hombre que trabaja y que juega* (The Man Who Works and Who Plays, originally published in Catalan). Ortega's essay, perhaps the first philosophical treatise fully within the modern European secular tradition ever to appear in Spain, established a Spanish philosophical movement that continues to bear fruit even today through Ortega's numerous disciples. The *Meditaciones* is Ortega's first full statement of his phenomenological approach to knowledge (frequently capsulized in the epigrammatic phrases "yo soy yo y mi circunstancia" [I am I and my circumstances] and "perspectivismo" [perspectivism]) developed after his 1911 studies in Marburg, Germany.

Ortega's philosophical and aesthetic ideas made their way (either by direct influence or simply through mutual interests) into the writings of the literary authors of his circle in a variety of ways, and like the previous Generation of 1898, the literature of the Generation of 1914 has a strong philosophical component, though in most cases the authors concentrate on questions of epistemology (especially perception) rather than on problems of metaphysics, ontology and ethics that preoccupied their predecessors. And it is this characteristic that marks the second phase of the Generation of 1914—an enhanced interest in philosophical and aesthetic matters—that will gradually supplant the earlier interest in national political and social reform. Pérez de Ayala's *Troteras y danzaderas* (Mummers and Dancers) and *Belarmino y Apolonio* (1925; Belarmino and Apolonio) employ a perspectival method that presents the narration from the points of view of a variety of characters, and both works are replete with philosophical discussions. Juan Ramón Jiménez's *Platero y yo* (1914; Platero and I) explores the relationship of human consciousness to the cosmos, and the novels of Benjamín Jarnés contain numerous scenes in which a character describes the contents of his perceptual consciousness. The later work of Gabriel Miró (especially *El humo dormido* [1918–19; Slumbering Smoke] and *Años y leguas* [1922–23; The Years and the Leagues]) attempts to employ language to capture the elusive nature of time and consciousness.

In fact, emphasis on language as a means of revealing the perceived world and states of consciousness is a common characteristic of this generation and is one of the major legacies it bequeathed to the stellar generation of poets (*Generation of 1927) that succeeded it. Juan Ramón Jiménez searched incessantly for the "exact name" of things, and Ramón Gómez de la Serna's *greguerías*—an innovative epigram combining humor and metaphor—attempts to reach the essence of objects. Miró appealed to archaic and regional vocabulary as well as difficult syntactical structures to evoke the perceptual experience of the physical world, and Pérez de Ayala endowed his eccentric characters Belarmino and Apolonio with singular linguistic traits. All these manifestations attest to this generation's faith in the power of language to produce reality, and, of course, links it to the many vanguardist movements in Europe and Latin America, whose aesthetics rested on the same faith.

The relationship between the Generation of 1914 and vanguardism is a difficult one to assess, because some of the 1914 group (especially the younger writers) were more involved with the "isms" (futurism, surrealism, ultraism, creationism, etc.) than others. In 1909 Gómez de la Serna published Marinetti's "Futurist Manifesto" in his journal *Prometeo*, and in 1914 he founded the *tertulia* (café literary circle) Pombo, which became an important vehicle for disseminating vanguardist ideas and trends. The aesthetics of the period between 1914 and about 1923 are confused and varied. Some writers defended a "realist" literature of social commitment, while others preferred the "art for art's sake" approach that Ortega elucidated in his 1925 essay *La deshumanización del arte* (The Dehumanization of Art). And most of the writers demonstrated aspects of each approach either consecutively or simultaneously in their work. Pérez de Ayala's early tetralogy is fairly straight-forward and realistic in its approach, but his *Tres novelas poemáticas de la vida española* (1916; Three Poematic Novels of Spanish Life), as the title suggests, conveys his view of Spanish life in much more experimental language and forms. Miró's *El abuelo del rey* (1912; The Grandfather of the King) is an incisive look at the decay of the old Spanish landed class and the materialism and opportunism of the new merchant and industrial classes, but couched in the highly elliptical and poetic style of his mature period. Juan Ramón Jiménez's *Platero y yo*, in the most lyrical and sensitive prose style of the generation's production, portrays the evils of the lives of Andalusian peasants and the problems of achieving certainty through sensual knowledge.

One of the marks of the generation is its tendency to theorize on aesthetic matters, which are often seen as an adjunct to the problem of perception and language. Ortega initiated the concern with aesthetic theory as early as 1910 in his essay "Adán en el Paraíso" (Adam in Paradise), in which he proclaimed art more appropriate than science for capturing particular human reality. Gómez de la Serna promoted new theories of art through his journal and *tertulia*, and Ramón Pérez de Ayala wrote numerous essays on different theoretical aspects of the novel and drama. Miró expressed his aesthetic ideas indirectly in the works mentioned above and was dragged out into an open declaration of his position in "Sigüenza y el mirador azul," an answer to Ortega's hostile criticism of his novel *El obispo leproso* (1925; The Leprous Bishop). A polemic between Pío *Baroja, a member of the Generation of 1898, and Ortega on the nature of the novel, which had been brewing since about 1915, erupted into open warfare in 1925. Ortega's seminal *La deshumanización del arte e Ideas sobre la novela*, published in that year, was an indirect critique of Baroja's open-ended, porous novels that wove elements from recognizable everyday Spanish political and social life into the fictional characters' story. Baroja immediately rallied in defense of his open, eclectic version of the novel in the introduction to his *La nave de los locos* (1925; Ship of Lunatics). For Ortega there should be a complete divorce between art and life (a strong reaction against Ruskin and Morris's utilitarian ideas of art), and the novel should create a tightly sealed, purely imaginative world that encapsulates the reader and does not allow him or her to think about the world beyond the fiction. Ortega's essay in a way marks the end of the Generation of 1914 and the coming of age of the next generation, whose interests were of a definitively aesthetic nature.

Presaging the end of the age of political consciousness and the dawning of a new aesthetic sensibility was Ortega's replacement in 1923 of the politically oriented journal *España* by *Revista de Occidente*, which turned its back on futile politics (in 1923 Primo de Rivera overwhelmed Alphonse XIII's weak monarchy and imposed a military dicatorship) and redirected the focus of Ortega's intellectual circle to cultural and sociological matters. Benjamín Jarnés, who began to collaborate with Ortega on the *Revista* in 1926, followed in the new orientation of a literature devoid of political content, but the older writers Pérez de Ayala, Miró and Juan Ramón continued to cultivate that aspect of their intellectual lives in one way or another—the first two in acerbic novelistic depictions of the traditional forces of Spanish society, Juan Ramón in his cultural and political activity during the twenties and thirties.

The heterogeneous directions of the new literature of the twenties were marked not only by local sensitivities and interests, but by the arrival of the work of the major European modernist writers—Proust, Joyce, and Eliot—and by the impact of the cinema. Influence of cinematographic techniques and themes is especially evident in the work of Jarnés and Gómez de la Serna. The more playful, less grotesque humor (in comparison to that of the 98ers), characteristic of the writing of Pérez de Ayala, Gómez de la Serna, and Jarnés, can be directly related to their contact with silent film, especially Charlie Chaplin. One of the aspects of the new art that Ortega took pains to elaborate in *La deshumanización* was that it did not take itself seriously, that it treated itself as a great joke. It is, however, more a characteristic that marks the second phase of the 1914 Generation rather than its early phase, which continued the introspective soul-searching of the 1898 group.

Other writers sometimes associated with the Generation of 1914, aside from those mentioned above, are Luis Araquistaín, Manuel *Azaña, Antonio *Espina, Julio *Camba, Enrique de *Mesa, León *Felipe, Jacinto *Grau, Ricardo *León,

Salvador de *Madariaga, Gregorio *Marañón, Gregorio *Martínez Sierra, and José *Moreno Villa. *See also* Essay.

BIBLIOGRAPHY

Criticism

Díaz-Plaja, Guillermo. *Estructura y sentido del Novecentismo español*. Madrid: Alianza, 1975.

Fernández Cifuentes, Luis. *Teoría y mercado de la novela en España: del 98 a la República*. Madrid: Gredos, 1982.

G. de la Concha, Víctor, ed. *Época contemporánea 1914–1939*. In *Historia y crítica de la literatura española*. Ed. Francisco Rico. Vol. 7. Barcelona: Crítica, 1984.

Livingstone, Leon. "Ortega y Gasset's Philosophy of Art." *PMLA* 67 (1952): 609–54.

Mainer, José-Carlos. *La edad de plata (1902–1939)*. Madrid: Cátedra, 1981.

Roberta Johnson

**GENERATION OF 1925.** Also called the "Generation of Ortega," "Generation of the Dictatorship [of Primo de Rivera]" and "generación escindida" (divided generation) because the Civil War and exile scattered its members. This term is applied to a group of mostly minor novelists (the most important being Benjamín *Jarnés) who developed under the influence of "dehumanized art" and the intellectual aegis of *Ortega y Gasset; it does not include the more important coetaneous poets of the so-called *Generation of 1927. Typical of their fiction is an emphasis upon psychological probing, Proustian exploration of memory, experimentation with interior monologue, somewhat alienated characters, and minimal action.

**GENERATION OF 1927.** An extraordinary group of poets and dramatists, led by Rafael *Alberti, Federico *García Lorca and Vicente *Aleixandre, but also including many other first-rate poets: Luis *Cernuda, Pedro *Salinas, Jorge *Guillén, Gerardo *Diego, Dámaso *Alonso, Miguel *Hernández and Manuel *Altolaguirre. The label is derived from the first joint public function undertaken by a majority of the group members, a homage to the Baroque poet Luis *Góngora on the occasion of the third centenary of his death. Most of these poets begin either as vaguely neo-Romantic or following the lead of Juan Ramón *Jiménez in works published before 1927; immediately afterward, the influence of Góngora is discernible in the cult of metaphor and hermeticism by almost all of the group. Following their neo-Góngorism comes a period of vanguardism and experimentalism, with surrealism being the most important: Aleixandre, Alberti, Lorca and Cernuda produced surrealist works. Futurism and ultraism left traces in the works of others, along with the "pure poetry" movement, but with the Civil War most began to write a more socially committed and politically oriented poetry. By the war's end, most of the group were dead or in exile, with the survivors ceasing to constitute a "generation."

**GENERATION OF 1936.** A term applied by some critics to a group of writers just beginning to publish at the outbreak of the Civil War (other critics reject the label as meaningless since the group was scattered almost before it was formed). Chronologically, it denotes a group from ten to fifteen years younger, on the average, than the *Generation of 1927, most of whom had completed only one or two works by the war's outbreak. However, some commentators include the novelists Ramón *Sender and Francisco *Ayala (both rather well-known before the war). Unlike the earlier "generation" labels, this one does not refer to any specific dominant genre. If there is a discernible literary common denominator, it is the movement away from vanguardism toward *engagement*, from experimentalism or "dehumanized" works to a neo-realist, socially committed literature. Other novelists sometimes assigned to this group include Camilo José *Cela, Juan A. de *Zunzunegui, Ignacio *Agustí and *Torrente Ballester. Enrique *Azcoaga, Carmen *Conde, Juan *Gil-Albert, José Antonio *Muñoz Rojas, Dionisio *Ridruejo, and Arturo *Serrano Plaja cultivate both poetry and fiction; other poets ascribed to this group are Germán *Bleiberg, José Luis *Cano, Gabriel *Celaya, Ildefonso Manuel *Gil, Federico Muelas, Juan *Panero, Leopoldo *Panero, Francisco Pino, Carlos *Rodríguez Spiteri, Félix *Ros, Luis *Rosales, Rafael *Santos Torroella and Luis Felipe *Vivanco. Essayists such as Aurora de *Albornoz and Guillermo *Díaz Plaja are likewise assigned to this "generation" which is too large and diffuse to represent a literary unit.

*GÉNERO CHICO*, a one-act, theatrical piece. The term *género chico* (literally, "little genre") is used principally to identify a lyric theater movement which developed in Madrid during the latter part of the nineteenth c. and continued to flourish well into the twentieth. In its broadest sense, the term *género chico* describes any theatrical piece in one act. Marciano Zurita has defined it in the following manner: "We may consider the *género chico* to be any theatrical work, with or without music, in one act, which is performed as an independent piece." By his definition Zurita contrasts the independent identity of a *género chico* work with the older traditions of the *entremés and the *sainete—short, comic works which were performed as interludes between the acts of full-length plays. This contrast notwithstanding, the *género chico* is closely linked to the long-standing traditions of the *Siglo de Oro *entremeses* of Lope de *Rueda, *Cervantes and *Quiñones de Benavente, and the eighteenth-c. *sainetes* of Francisco de Castro, Ramón de la *Cruz and *González del Castillo, through its comic and satiric tonality and its depiction of the characters and customs of everyday life. A further influence on the *género chico* can be seen in the development of the *tonadilla* during the late eighteenth and early nineteenth centuries. Although both the *entremés* and the *sainete* would often include music in connection with a special song or dance sequence, the *tonadilla* was conceived as musical entertainment, alternating solo and duo singing with ensemble and dance numbers into an integrated whole. The association of the *género chico* with another genre of lyric theater, the *zarzuela*, further complicates the former's parentage. The *género chico* shares with the *zarzuela* a similar structure wherein set musical numbers, often of considerable complexity and length, are woven into the overall drama of spoken dialogue. Through this similarity the *género chico* works have generally been characterized as a subgenre of the *zarzuela*. In reality this "little genre" arose largely as a reaction against the longer musical theater form. The *zarzuela* was given renewed life in the mid-nineteenth c. by Francisco *Asenjo Barbieri, Joaquín Gaztambide y Barbayo and Emilio Arrieta y Correa, among others. Whereas their two- and three-act *zarzuelas* were influenced both musically and thematically by Parisian and Viennese operetta, the *género chico* was an innately Spanish, and more specifically, Madrilenian phenomenon. The enormously successful premiere in 1870 of Tomás *Luceño's *sainete Cuadros al fresco* (Portraits in the Fresh Air) established the essential characteristics of the *género chico* and encouraged most of the librettists and composers of the day to produce works in a similar vein. Among the principal authors of the *género chico* were: Ricardo de la *Vega, Javier de *Burgos, Carlos *Arniches, Ramos Carrión, *López Silva, *Fernández Shaw, *Pérez y González, Miguel *Echegaray and Jackson Veyán; its composers included Tomás Bretón, Ruperto Chapí, Federico Chueca, Joaquín Valverde, Amadeo Vives, José Serrano and Pablo Sorozábal. The *género chico* also established its own circuit of theaters in Madrid which were dedicated almost exclusively to performances of these one-act pieces; the Felipe and Apolo theaters were the most important centers for the *género chico*. The success of their productions is confirmed by the lengthy performance runs enjoyed by many of the works: for example, *La Gran Vía* (1886; Broadway [performed in a modified English version as "Castles in Spain" in London, 1906]), with book by Ricardo de la Vega and music by Chueca and Valverde, ran for four straight years at the Felipe Theater. The *género chico*'s popularity in Madrid can be explained in large part by its contemporary and often satirical depiction of that city's social life and customs. The settings are invariably well-known promenades, parks and streets in Madrid, they normally take place in the summer and, consequently, the traditional festivals of the city, particularly those of San Lorenzo and of the Virgin of the Dove, figure prominently. The plots of these works are inconsequential fluff for the most part, as the principal interest lies in the parade of character types which populated the streets of Madrid. The types range from middle-class merchants and their families, through various working-class figures to myriad "low-lifes." Typical situations presented in the *género chico* are lovers' quarrels, disputes between neighbors, the actions of street rabble and similar pretexts for interaction. A representative work is *La verbena de la Paloma* (1894; The Festival of the Dove), with book by Ricardo de la Vega and music by Tomás Bretón. The action takes place in the section of the city known as La Latina, on the day and evening of the festival in honor of the Virgin of the Dove, patron saint of Madrid's working-class neighborhoods. The work's two subtitles reflect the two interwoven plots: the first, "El boticario y las chulapas" (The Pharmacist and the Coquettes), concerns the elderly Don Hilarión and his attempts to recapture his youth through Casta and Susana, two young sisters who string him along for fun and for his attentive gifts; the second, ''Los celos mal reprimidos'' (Jealousy Unrepressed), depicts Julián's jealous nature and its effect on his relationship with Susana, whom he loves. Over the course of the action we are introduced to a tavern-keeper, the night watchman, a folksinger and numerous other neighborhood residents. Bretón's music brings this festive atmosphere to life with typically Spanish song and dance forms: *seguidillas, soleares, habaneras* and even an ''up-to-date'' *mazurka*. Another important characteristic of the *género chico* is its topicality, especially its satiric barbs at the city government. A particularly fine example of this is *La Gran Vía*. In 1886 Madrid's city council developed an urban renewal plan to create a broad avenue which would cut through the center of downtown Madrid. Pérez, Chueca and Valverde created a satirical allegory of the project in which the chorus members are representations of the various streets, squares and neighborhoods in and around the affected area. The work is unified by two principal characters: a visitor to Madrid, and his guide, the Caballero de Gracia—an amalgam of the various dandies and social gadflies who stroll along such avenues. Although the City Fathers are roundly criticized for their ''folly,'' the final scene presents a preview of the new ''Broadway'' as a symbol of progress and modernization for Madrid. The topical nature of the *género chico* also extended into the language itself. Colloquial expressions abound, and some authors, notably Carlos Arniches, created neologisms which subsequently entered into the popular vocabulary. The combination of music and lyrics led to an expansion of the verse forms utilized. Rubén Darío, in the preface to his *Cantos de vida y esperanza* (1905; Songs of Life and Hope), regarded the *género chico* librettists as an important influence on Hispanic verse: ''When considering modern free verse, it is truly unique that, in this land of Quevedos and Góngoras, the only innovators of lyric techniques, the only liberators of rhythm, have been the poets of *Madrid Cómico* [the magazine Comical Madrid] and the librettists of the *género chico*.'' These authors looked to unusual or neglected verse forms, freely combining lines of different syllabic length and metric pattern, in large part because of the rhythmic and melodic requirements of the music. Although the musical language of the *género chico* composers has been criticized as impoverished in its creativity and development, it is generally recognized that, as a manifestation of a popular, lyric theater, these composers were gifted in producing a wealth of charming and expressive melodies perfectly suited to the requirements of the genre—that is, to create a popular musical idiom which evoked the festive, jocular atmosphere inherent to the *género chico*. And, considering the hundreds of pieces turned out by the librettists and composers, it is a tribute to their success that many of their works are still performed in the theaters and heard on recordings. *See also* Theater in Spain.

BIBLIOGRAPHY

Primary Text

*El género chico (antología de textos completos)*. Ed. Antonio Valencia. Madrid: Taurus, 1962.

Criticism

Deleito y Pinuela. *Origen y apogeo del género chico*. Madrid: RO, 1949.
Zurita, Marciano. *Historia del género chico*. Madrid: Prensa Popular, 1920.

Donald C. Buck

**GERARD HISPANO.** Pseudonym of *Céspedes y Meneses, Gonzalo.

**GERUNDIO, Fray.** *See* Lafuente, Modesto

*GESTA, Cantar de. See Cantar de Gesta*

**GETINO, Luis G. Alonso** (1877, Lugueros, León–1947, Madrid), literary scholar, editor. A member of the Dominican order, he founded the Biblioteca Clásica Dominicana and edited many texts of authors belonging to his order, accompanying the texts with critical studies and notes. A Thomist in his own thought, he wrote *El averroísmo de Santo Tomás* (The Influence of Averroes in St. Thomas) and *Vida de Santo Domingo de Guzmán* (1939; Life of St. Dominic de Guzmán). He was one of the major propagandists of the work of Fr. *Victoria as a founder of international law, with works such as *Francisco de Vitoria y el renacimiento filosófico teológico del siglo XVI en Salamanca* (1913; Francisco de Vitoria and the 16th-c. Theological Renaissance in Salamanca). He is best known literarily for his studies of Fray Luis de *León and his school, which he studied especially in *La lírica salmantina* (1929; Poetry in Salamanca).

BIBLIOGRAPHY

Primary Texts

*El maestro Fray Francisco de Vitoria y*. . . . Madrid: RABM, 1914.
. . . *Sto. Domingo de Guzmán*. Madrid: Biblioteca Nueva, 1939.
. . . *Nueva contribución al estudio de la lírica salmantina del siglo XVI*. . . . Salamanca: Calatrava, 1929.

English Translation

*A New Life of St. Dominic*. Tr. E. Ceslas McEniry. Columbus, OH: Aquinas College, 1926.

**GIL, Ildefonso Manuel** (1912, Paniza, Zaragoza– ), poet, novelist, short story writer, literary critic, lawyer and emeritus professor of Spanish literature at the City U of New York. His first published work of lyric poetry, *Borradores* (1931; Rough Drafts), was followed by *La voz cálida* (1934; The Warm Voice) and through the years by twenty-three other books of poetry, the latest being *En Venecia y otros poemas* (1984; In Venice and Other Poems). Writing before and after the Spanish Civil War, Gil allows his themes and his tone to evidence a reaction to events in his external world, while his sentimental outlook on life remains a constant in his poetry.

In 1950 the first of his three novels, *La moneda en el suelo* (The Coin on the

Ground), merited the Premio Internacional de Primera Novela (International Award for a First Novel) granted by the Barcelona publisher, Janés. Between the years 1957 and 1980 he published four collections of short stories, including *Amor y muerte y otras historias* (Love, Death, and Other Stories) published in Philadelphia in 1971. His work in literary criticism and biography covers the period 1943 to 1982 and includes essays on Portuguese poetry, *Ensayos sobre poesía portuguesa* (Essays on Portuguese Poetry), as well as biographical works on Goya, *Don Francisco de Goya*; and on *García Lorca, Federico García Lorca, el escritor y la crítica* (Federico García Lorca, the Writer and His Literary Critics), and most recently, *Francisco Ayala*.

BIBLIOGRAPHY

Primary Texts

*El corazón en los labios*. Valladolid: Halcón, 1974.
*El tiempo recobrado*. Madrid: *Insula*, 1950.
*La muerte hizo su agosto*. Zaragoza: Guara, 1980.
*Valle-Inclán, "Azorín" y Baroja*. Madrid: Hora H., 1975.
*Pueblonuevo*. Madrid: Aguilar, 1960.

English Translation

"The Generation of 1936: One Writer's Plea for Remembering." Tr. C. A. Sullivan. In *Spanish Writers of 1936*. Ed. J. Ferrán and D. P. Testa. London: Tamesis, 1973.

Criticism

Doménech, Ricardo. "Circunstancia y literatura actuales de Ildefonso Manuel Gil." *CH* 261 (n.d.): 591–602.
Miró, Emilio. "Poesía: Ildefonso Manuel Gil, Elena Andrés." *Insula* (Nov.-Dec. 1971): 24.

Elisa Fernández Cambria

**GIL, Ricardo** (1855, Murcia–1907, Murcia), poet. After completing law studies, he moved to Madrid, never practicing as an attorney. Aside from translating into Spanish various works by Alfred de Musset, he published two poetry collections: *De los quince a los treinta* (1885; From Fifteen to Thirty), and *La caja de música* (1898; The Music Box). *El último libro* (The Last Book), a posthumous collection of poems published in various magazines and periodicals, appeared in 1909. Gil was a forerunner of *modernism; his delicacy of expression and sensitivity to the musical value of words combine with melancholy and spiritual unrest in his verse. The influence of French poets and of *Zorrilla and *Bécquer are also apparent.

BIBLIOGRAPHY

Primary Texts

*Obras completas*. 3 vols. Murcia: San Francisco, 1931.
*La caja de música*. Ed., notes R. A. Cardwell. Exeter: U of Exeter, 1972. Intro. in English.

**GIL, Rodolfo** (1872, Puente Genil, Córdoba–1938, Valencia), journalist, politician, historian, poet. Andalusian culture served as the inspiration or focus of much of his writing. His works include the poetry collection *Mitos* (1919; Myths), *Romancero judeo-español* (Judeo-Spanish Ballad Book), and *Córdoba contemporánea* (1892; Contemporary Cordoba).

BIBLIOGRAPHY
*Córdoba contemporánea.* Cordoba: Jaime Costas, 1892.
*Romancero judeo-español.* Madrid: Alemana, 1911.

Isabel McSpadden

**GIL-ALBERT, Juan** (1906, Alcoy– ), Valencian poet and prose writer. He has achieved critical recognition during the past ten years for his extensive works. In 1984 there was an homage dedicated to him in Spain. His complete poetic works are published in the three-volume *Obra poética completa.* His complete works in prose are being published in the edition *Obra completa en prosa,* of which six volumes have appeared. Gil-Albert combines immense cultural knowledge with elegant style, and is an important link between pre–and post–Civil War Spanish poetry. A constant concern in all his works is to achieve a synthesis between the Greco-Roman and the Judeo-Christian cultural currents in Western civilization. His obvious preference for the former current, while acknowledging the undeniable impact of the latter on his own personal history and that of his country, often produces tension, especially in his poetic works. Outstanding among his poetic works are *Las ilusiones, con los poemas del convaleciente* (1944; The Illusions, with the Poems of the Convalescent), and *Homenajes e inpromptus* (1976; Homages and Impromptus). Among his prose works, *Concierto en «mi» menor* (1964; Concerto in E Minor) is of special biographical and historical interest.

BIBLIOGRAPHY
Primary Texts
*Obra completa en prosa.* Valencia: Alfonso el Magnánino, 1982- .
*Obra poética completa.* 3 vols. Valencia: Alfonso el Magnánimo, 1981.
Criticism
Bradford, C. A. "The Personal and the Universal Visions in the *Homenajes e inpromptus* of Juan Gil-Albert." *Hispanic Journal* 6.1 (1984): 101–9.
*Calle del aire* (Seville) 1977. Entire issue of this journal devoted to Gil-Albert, with numerous fine articles.

Carole Bradford

*GIL BLAS DE SANTILLANA* (*Gil Blas*), *picaresque narrative. This French work by Alain René Le Sage, first published in 1715, with continuations in 1724 and 1735, was rapidly translated into Spanish by Father *Isla, who angrily wrote in his prologue that the book's adventures had been "robadas a España y adoptadas en Francia por Le Sage . . . [y] restituidas a su patria y a su lengua nativa por un español celoso que no sufre se burlen de su nación'' (robbed from Spain and adopted in France by Lesage . . . [and] returned to its native country and language by a Spaniard zealous that his nation not be duped). Set in Spain between 1588 and 1649, the first-person account follows Gil and his ups and downs, repentance, service as secretary to Count Duke Olivares, and eventual retirement. Although Le Sage's borrowings from *Espinel's *Marcos de Obregón*, *Estebanillo González*, Castillo Solórzano's *Más puede amor que la sangre,* and other works are quite obvious, his hero is not a *pícaro*—he is handsome, engaging, he moves toward virtue, and finally is successful inside society. His life is exemplary rather than deplorable. After the success of *Gil Blas,* Le Sage adapted *Estebanillo González* and Mateo *Alemán's *Guzmán de Alfarache* for French tastes.

BIBLIOGRAPHY

Primary Text

*Historia de Gil Blas.* Tr. Father Isla. Buenos Aires: Sopena, 1945.

English Translation

*Gil Blas.* Tr. Smollet. Intro. J. B. Priestly. Oxford: Oxford UP, 1937.

Maureen Ihrie

**GIL DE BIEDMA, Jaime** (1929, Barcelona– ), poet, essayist, lawyer. His poetry, generally characterized by natural discourse and prosaic settings, treats social concerns, love, friendship, illusions, and passing time. Books of poetry include the early *Según sentencia del tiempo* (1953; According to the Verdict of Time), *Compañeros de viaje* (1959; Traveling Companions), *Moralidades, 1959–1964* (1966; Moralities), and *Poemas póstumos* (1968, 1970; Posthumous Poems). *Las personas del verbo* (1975, 1982; The Persons of the Verb) collects most of the poems from these books. His prose includes a volume of critical essays, *El pie de la letra* (1980; To the Letter), and a journal, *Diario del artista seriamente enfermo* (1974; Diary of the Seriously Ill Artist).

BIBLIOGRAPHY

Primary Texts

*Diario del artista seriamente enfermo.* Barcelona: Lumen, 1974.
*Las personas del verbo.* Barcelona: Seix Barral, 1982.
*El pie de la letra: Ensayos 1955–1979.* Barcelona: Crítica, 1980.

Criticism

Carnero, Guillermo. ''Jaime Gil de Biedma o la superación del realismo.'' *Insula* 351 (1976): 1, 3.
Debicki, Andrew P. ''Jaime Gil de Biedma: The Theme of Illusion.'' In *Poetry of Discovery: The Spanish Generation of 1956–1971.* Lexington: UP of Kentucky, 1982. 123–41.
González Muela, Joaquín. ''Imágenes de Gil de Biedma.'' In his *La nueva poesía española.* Madrid: Alcalá, 1973. 81–108.

Jiménez, José Olivio. *Diez años de poesía española (1960–1970)*. Madrid: Insula, 1972. 205–21.

Mangini González, Shirley. *Jaime Gil de Biedma*. Madrid: Júcar, 1980.

Martha Miller

**GIL Y CARRASCO, Enrique** (1815, Villafranca del Bierza–1846, Berlin), Romantic novelist and poet. Gil's most enduring work—and the only one published in book form during his short lifetime—is the Romantic novel *El señor de Bembibre* (1844; The Man from Bembibre), a historical adventure story in the tradition of Sir Walter Scott, *López Soler, Mariano José de *Larra, and *Espronceda. It is a tale of medieval daring, melancholy, tragic love, and war, narrated with grace and style. The dialogues are lively, the action swift-moving, and Gil's brilliant description abounds with the local color of his native region (near León).

Gil studied in Ponferrada, the seminary in Astorga, and the U of Valladolid (where he met Miguel de los Santos *Álvarez and José *Zorrilla) before moving to Madrid in 1836, where he befriended Espronceda, Larra and *Rivas. His first public success was the reading of his poem "Una gota de rocío" (1837; A Drop of Dew) at the Liceo, a cultural and literary center for Romantic authors. Many of Gil's poems were first introduced at readings there. He began to write for newspapers such as *El Español* (The Spaniard), *Mesonero Romanos's *Semanario Pintoresco Español* (Spanish Picturesque Weekly), *El Pensamiento* (Thought), and *El Laberinto* (The Labyrinth), and his fame as a poet and essayist grew quickly.

A serious illness struck Gil down in late 1839, but by the following spring he seemed to be recovered. He spent some time with his mother in Ponferrada, and he traveled around the favorite sights of his youth before returning to Madrid. The observations he recorded on his trip were rewoven into a short narrative tale, *El lago del Carucedo* (1840; Carucedo Lake), which he published in Mesonero's *Semanario*. For the same journal he produced a review of Espronceda's *Poesías* of 1840. In November of that year he was given a job at the *Biblioteca Nacional.

Espronceda's untimely death in 1842 deeply affected Gil. They had been intimate friends since Gil's arrival in Madrid, and Espronceda had served as Gil's patron, introducing him into intellectual circles and helping to shape his career as a poet. The elegy "A Espronceda" (To Espronceda), which he read at Espronceda's funeral, reportedly elicited "abundant tears" from those present. It was the last poem he ever wrote. Gil returned to his native region for solace, once again recording his observations of that beautiful countryside. The observations, which were published in the newspaper *El Sol* (The Sun) under the title "Bosquejo de un viaje por una provincia interior" (Outline of a Trip through an Interior Province), became background material for *El señor de Bembibre*. *Bembibre* appeared in poorly printed and irregular installments in *El Sol* in 1843. Gil worked as a theater critic for *El Laberinto* until early 1844. In February of that year he was appointed by the government to represent Isabel II's interests in Prussia, and in order to prepare for the post he studied that nation's language and political system. He arrived in Berlin in September 1844, and soon became a close friend of Baron Humboldt, a cultured aristocrat with an interest in Spanish who introduced Gil into the highest circles of Prussian society.

*El señor de Bembibre*, written perhaps as early as 1841, was finally published in book form in Madrid in 1844, but the book's reception there was tepid; its popularity grew slowly. Gil did receive a gold medal from the king of Prussia in 1845, but by then his old illness—pulmonary tuberculosis—had flared up again, this time fatally. He died in February 1846 and remains buried in what was East Berlin.

Gil wrote thirty-three poems, the best of which are "Una gota de rocío," "La violeta" (The Violet), "Un ensueño" (An Illusion), "A Espronceda," and "El ruiseñor y la rosa" (The Nightingale and the Rose). They reveal his Romantic interests in medieval topics, patriotism, dreams, death, sadness, and the world's indifference to human suffering. Similar themes reappear in *El señor de Bembibre*, which critics are recognizing as "a great novel from a great writer." *See also* Romanticism.

BIBLIOGRAPHY

Primary Texts

*Obras completas*. Ed. Jorge Campos. Madrid: Atlas, 1954.
*El señor de Bembibre*. Ed. Jean-Louis Picoche. Madrid: Castalia, 1986.
*El señor de Bembibre*. Ed. Enrique Rubio. Madrid: Cátedra, 1986.
*El señor de Bembibre*. Ed. Idlefonso M. Gil. Zaragoza: Ebro, 1975.

English Translation

*The Mystery of Bierzo Valley: A Tale of the Knights Templars*. Tr. G. W. Gethen and L. Veaho. London: Sydenham, 1938.

Criticism

Gullón, Ricardo. *Cisne sin lago*. Madrid: Insula, 1951.
Montes Huidobro, Matías. "Variedad formal y unidad interna en *El señor de Bembibre*." *Papeles de Son Armadans* 53 (1969): 233–55.
Picoche, Jean-Louis. *Un romántico español: Enrique Gil y Carrasco (1815–1846)*. Madrid: Gredos, 1978.
Samuel, D. G. *Enrique Gil y Carrasco: A Study in Spanish Romanticism*. New York: Instituto de las Españas, 1939.

David Thatcher Gies

**GIL Y ZÁRATE, Antonio** (1793, El Escorial–1861, Madrid), dramatist. Son of the singer Bernardo Gil and the actress Antonia Zárate, he was educated in France, where he studied physics. His professional plans in the sciences were cut short by the closing of the universities, and he pursued a career in governmental services, occupying several different positions. He joined the liberal militia in Cádiz in 1823 and as a result was prohibited from returning to Madrid until 1826. He was a member of the Academies of the Spanish Language and of Fine Arts, and frequented the *tertulia* known as *El Parnasillo* (Little Parnassus).

Gil y Zárate began his literary career as a neo-classicist, reflecting his educational background. His first dramatic works were of two styles: drawing-room comedies, influenced by Leandro Fernández de \*Moratín, such as ¡*Cuidado con las novias!* (1826; Careful with Girlfriends!), and *Un año después de la boda* (1826; One Year after the Wedding); and historical tragedies in the French mold, as with *Rodrigo, último rey de los godos* (1828; Roderick, Last King of the Goths) and *Blanca de Borbón* (1829; Blanca of the House of Bourbon). Neither of the tragedies was immediately produced due to the apparently vindictive persecution of Gil y Zárate by the censors. *Blanca de Borbón* was finally staged in 1835, after the first wave of \*romanticism had hit Spanish theater. Gil y Zárate responded to the new dramatic aesthetic with *Carlos II el Hechizado* (1837; Charles the Second, the Bewitched). Its melodramatic tone and occasionally sordid depictions of the final decadence of the Hapsburg line provoked a major scandal among his contemporaries. In subsequent plays he returned to a modified neo-classic style, freely combining classic and romantic elements. Most notable of these are *Rosamunda* (1839), a love drama produced for the literary society El Liceo, and historical plays such as *Don Alvaro de Luna* (1840), *Guillermo Tell* (1843) and *Guzmán el Bueno* (1842; Guzmán the Good). This latter play has been called the best dramatization of the Guzmán legend, superseding versions from the Golden Age and the eighteenth c.

Gil y Zárate also wrote essays on dramatic theory and literary history. Of the former, two articles stand out: *Sobre la poesía dramática* (1839; On Drama in Verse) and *Teatro antiguo y moderno* (1841; Classic and Modern Theater). In these essays Gil y Zárate proposed an eclectic combination of the poetic brillance of Golden Age drama, the regularity in form and style of neo-classic drama, and the emotional energy of romantic theater. His more ambitious *Manual de literatura* (2 vols., 1842–44; Literary Manual) adopts a basically conservative, neo-classic attitude toward literature in general and drama in particular. *See also* Siglo de Oro; Theater in Spain.

BIBLIOGRAPHY

Primary Text

Gil y Zárate, Antonio. *Guzmán el Bueno.* In *Nineteenth Century Spanish Plays.* Ed. Lewis E. Brett. New York: Appleton-Century, 1935.

Criticism

Caldera, Ermanno. *Il dramma romàntico in Spagna.* Pisa: Università di Pisa, 1974.
Cook, John A. *Neo-classic Drama in Spain.* Dallas: Southern Methodist U P, 1959.
Stoudemire, S. A. "Don Antonio Gil y Zárate's Birth Date." *MLN* 46 (1931): 171–72.
———. "Gil y Zárate's Translation of French Plays." *MLN* 48 (1933): 321–25.

Donald C. Buck

**GILI GAYA, Samuel** (1892, Lérida–1976, Madrid), Spanish literary historian, philologist and grammarian. A professor of literature and disciple of Ramón \*Menéndez Pidal, he collaborated with him at the Centro de Estudios Históricos.

Gili Gaya authored many works of literary scholarship, including critical editions of such writers of the Spanish Golden Age as *Alemán, *Espinel, *Moncada, Diego de *San Pedro and others. Among his best-known achievements are *Curso superior de sintaxis española* (1943; Advanced Course in Spanish Syntax) and *Tesoro lexicográfico (1492–1627)* (1947; Treasury of Lexicography, 1492–1627), which is an indispensable tool for the philologist.

BIBLIOGRAPHY

Primary Texts

*Curso superior de sintaxis española*. 8th ed. Barcelona: Specs, 1961.
*Nociones de gramática histórica española*. 7th ed. Barcelona: Bibliograf, 1979.
*Tesoro lexicográfico (1492–1726)*. 4 fascicles. Madrid: CSIC, 1947–56. Covers letters A-E.

**GIMÉNEZ-ARNAU, José Antonio** (1912, Laredo, Santander– ), novelist and playwright. Educated in Zaragoza, his early novels include *La colmena* (1945; The Beehive), *La hija de Jano* (1947; Janus's Daughter), *El puente* (1941; The Bridge), and *De pantalón largo* (1952; In Long Pants)—which won the National Literature Prize in 1952. In 1953 he published *Luna llena* (Full Moon), a psychological analysis of marital crises, written with restraint and profundity. His next work of fiction, *El canto del gallo* (1954; The Cock's Crow), presents the spiritual anguish of an apostate priest. *La tierra prometida* (1958; The Promised Land) treats the theme of exile, expatriates tormented by thoughts of home. *Este-Oeste* (1961; East-West) obliquely treats the problems of Spain's allegiances in the cold war in relation to the threat of atomic annihilation, and attempts to express the problem in terms of the individual and collective conscience. *La mecedora* (1964; The Rocking Chair) is a novel of political intrigue set in an imaginary Latin American Republic. *El distinguido delegado* (1970; The Distinguished Delegate) treats an international railway conference under UN auspices, wracked by internal politics.

As a playwright, Giménez-Arnau has written, among other titles, *Murió hace quince años* (1953; He Died Fifteen Years Ago) and *El rey ha muerto* (1960; The King Is Dead).

BIBLIOGRAPHY

Primary Texts

*El canto del gallo*. 4th ed. Barcelona: Destino, 1966.
*De pantalón largo*. 3rd ed. Barcelona: Destino, 1963.
*El distinguido delegado*. Barcelona: Destino, 1970.
*Este-Oeste*. Barcelona: Destino, 1961.
*Luna Llena*. 2nd ed. Barcelona: Destino, 1967.

*La mecedora.* Barcelona: Destino, 1964.
*La tierra prometida.* Barcelona: Destino, 1958.

Janet Pérez

**GIMÉNEZ CABALLERO, Ernesto** (1899, Madrid–1988, Madrid), Spanish journalist and essayist; he also taught at Madrid's Instituto del Cardenal Cisneros (high-school level). He became known with *Notas marruecas de un soldado* (1923; Moroccan Notes by a Soldier), and later contributed to the major Madrid daily, *El Sol.* He founded *La Gaceta Literaria* (1927), which was important in propagating literary novelties during the vanguard years. He used the pseudonyms Gecé (GC) and El Robinsón literario de España. Principal works include *Carteles* (1927; Posters); *Los toros, las castañuelas y la Virgen* (1927; Bulls, Castanets and the Virgin); *Yo, inspector de alcantarillas* (1928; I, the Sewer Inspector); *En torno al casticismo de España* (1929; On the Purity of Spain); *Circuito imperial* (1929; Imperial Circuit); *Cataluña ante España* (1930; Catalunya vis-à-vis Spain); and *Genio de España* (4th ed., 1937; Genius of Spain).

BIBLIOGRAPHY

Primary Texts

*Carteles.* Madrid: Espasa-Calpe, 1927.
*Circuito imperial.* Madrid: Gaceta, 1929.
*Genio de España.* 4th ed. Zaragoza?: Jerarquía, 1939.
*Los toros, las castañuelas y la Virgen.* Madrid: Raggio, 1927.
*Yo, inspector de alcantarillas.* Madrid: Biblioteca Nueva, 1928.

**GIMENO DE FLAQUER, Concepción** (1860, Alcañiz, Teruel–1919, Madrid), Spanish editor, novelist and feminist. Gimeno traveled extensively, living several years in Mexico, and edited a number of women's magazines both in Mexico and in Spain, beginning with *La Ilustración de la Mujer* in Madrid in 1872. She authored more than a dozen volumes on women, and lectured widely. She defended women's right to education, but not to vote; a Catholic conservative, Gimeno conceptualized woman's place as the home, despite her moderate feminism. She is the author of four postromantic novels: *Victorina, o heroísmo del corazón* (1873; 2nd ed., 2 vols; Victorina, or Heroism of the Heart); *El doctor alemán* (1880; The German Doctor); *Suplicio de una coqueta* (1885; The Suffering of a Coquette), and an amplified version of the latter with a debate-style postscript, *¿Culpa o expiación?* (1890; Guilt or Expiation?). The two interrelated novels have to do with the responsibility of a flirt for her impact upon men (in an extreme case, flirtation provokes a suicide), and in the extended version, the question of expiation of the coquette's destructive power through her early death and her possible salvation via repentance.

BIBLIOGRAPHY

Primary Texts

*¿Culpa o expiación?* 4th ed. Mexico: Secretaria de Fomento, 1890.
*El doctor alemán.* Zaragoza: Ariño, 1880.

*Madres de hombres célebres*. Madrid: Alfredo Alonso, 1895.
*La mujer ante el hombre*. Zaragoza: Ariño, 1882.
*La mujer española*. Madrid: n.p., 1877.
*La mujer intelectual*. Madrid: Asilo de huérfanos del Sagrado Corazón de Jesús, 1901.

Criticism

Ferreras, J. Ignacio. *Catálogo de novelas y novelistas españolas del s. XIX*. Madrid: Cátedra, 1979.
*Women Writers of Spain. An Annotated Bio-Bibliographical Guide*. Ed. Carolyn Galerstein and Kathleen McNerney. Westport, CT: Greenwood, 1987.

Cristina Enríquez

**GIMFERRER, Pedro** (or Pere) (1945, Barcelona– ), Spanish and Catalan poet and critic. A precocious newcomer to literature, Gimferrer won the National Poetry Prize in 1966. His books in Castilian include *Mensaje del Tetrarca* (1963; Message from the Tetrarch); *Arde el mar* (1966; The Sea Is Burning); and *La muerte en Beverly Hills* (1968; Death in Beverly Hills). Subsequently he was associated with the *Nueve novísimos poetas españoles* (1970; Nine Ultra-New Spanish Poets) anthology by J. M. *Castellet. Characteristic of his poetry of these years is a "camp" or "kitsch" tendency which reflects Spain's nascent consumerism, the invasion by various foreign cultures (especially the American), and a fascination with Hollywood. Other poems are vaguely surrealistic. Since the death of Franco, Gimferrer has become more politically oriented.

BIBLIOGRAPHY

Primary Texts

*Poemas, 1963–1969*. Madrid: Visor, 1979.
*Poesía 1970–1977*. Prol. J. M. Castellet. Madrid: Visor, 1978. Bilingual ed. in Catalan and Spanish.
*Segundo dietario, 1980–82*. Tr. to Spanish B. Losada. Barcelona: Seix Barral, 1985. Articles collected from a Barcelona daily.

Janet Pérez

**GINER DE LOS RÍOS, Francisco** (1839, Ronda–1915, Madrid), Krausist educator and essayist. He began his university studies in Barcelona, where the pedagogical excellence of the renowned professor Javier Lloréns left an indelible mark on the young Giner. He continued his studies in Granada, and in 1863 moved to Madrid, where he worked for a time in the Ministry of State before obtaining in 1866 the professorship of philosophy of law and international law at the U of Madrid. His first book, *Estudios literarios* (1866; Literary Studies), was published the same year. It was in the capital that he met and became a fervent disciple of Julián *Sanz del Río, Spain's leading proponent of Krausist thought. Early in 1868 Giner was suspended from the university due to his stand in support of three other professors (Sanz del Río, Fernando de *Castro, and Nicolás Salmerón) whose goal was the modernization of Spanish higher education and its removal from governmental and religious domination.

The September 1868 revolution lifted Giner's suspension and the prevailing liberal atmosphere offered the possibility of reorganizing university education along Krausist lines. However, the deteriorating political situation of the early 1870s eventually led to the Bourbon Restoration and with it strict controls on education and a purge of Krausist influence. For four months in 1875 Giner was exiled in Cádiz, during which time his correspondence indicates that the idea of establishing an independent center for learning was taking shape in his mind.

The idea became reality in the autumn of 1876 when the Institución Libre de Enseñanza (Free Pedagogical Institute) was founded by Giner along with Salmerón, Gumersindo de *Azcárate, and others. The institute attempted to implement the pedagogical theories of its founders. Central to these theories was the development of all aspects of human personality, and to that end the institute incorporated programs in such diverse areas as art, physical exercise, excursions, and practical aspects of education. Giner insisted on a closer relationship between teacher and student than had existed previously in Spain, and he encouraged an active dialogue in the classroom which forced the student to doubt, to question, and to defend his ideas. Besides the influence of Krause, this intuitive method obviously owed a great deal to Socrates and to more contemporary educators and philosophers, including Pestalozzi, Froebel, and Rousseau. Giner summarized his hopes for the institute when he wrote that its function was not to be limited to instruction, but that it aspired to form useful men in service to humanity and homeland.

In 1881 the government restored Giner's position as professor at the U of Madrid. During the next four years he devoted a great deal of time to foreign travel in England, France, and the Low Countries, where he participated in several pedagogical conferences. Throughout this period he was studying and writing constantly. Some of his most important essays include *Estudios de literatura y arte* (1876; Studies on Literature and Art), *Estudios filosóficos y religiosos* (1876; Philosophical and Religious Studies), *Estudios sobre educación* (1886; Studies on Education), and *Educación y enseñanza* (1889; Education and Teaching). Giner de los Ríos died in Madrid on February 18, 1915. He remains today one of the foremost figures of nineteenth-c. Spanish intellectual life, and one whose influence on contemporary Spain has been enormous. *See also* Krausism.

BIBLIOGRAPHY

Primary Texts

*Educación y enseñanza.* 2nd ed. Madrid: Espasa-Calpe, 1933.
*Estudios de literatura y arte.* Madrid: La Lectura, 1919.
*Estudios filosóficos y religiosos.* Madrid: Espasa-Calpe, 1922.
*Estudios sobre educación.* 3rd ed. Madrid: Espasa-Calpe, 1935.
*Pedagogía universitaria; Problemas y noticias.* Madrid: Impr. de Julio Cosano, 1924.

English Translation

"Some Account of the Technical Education in the 'Institución Libre de Enseñanza' at Madrid." Tr. S. H. Capper. In *Proceedings of International Conference on Education.* vol. 2. London: n.p., 1884.

Criticism

"Francisco Giner de los Ríos." *Cuadernos Americanos* 139 (March-April 1965): 61–160. Issue devoted to Giner.

Landa, Rubén. "D. Francisco Giner como educador." *Cuadernos Americanos* 129 (July-Aug. 1963): 88–110.

López-Morillas, Juan. Prologue to *Ensayos*. Ed. Juan López-Morillas. 2nd ed. Madrid: Alianza, 1973.

———. "Francisco Giner and the Redemption of Spain." In *The Analysis of Literary Texts: Current Trends in Methodology*. Randolph D. Pope. 3rd and 4th York College Colloquia. Ypsilanti: Bilingual Press, n.d.

Navarro, Martín. *Vida y obra de don Francisco Giner de los Ríos*. México: Orión, 1945.

Porter Conerly

**GINER DE LOS RÍOS, Francisco** (1917, Madrid– ), Spanish poet, exiled following the Civil War. His work has appeared in Mexico, and includes *La rama viva* (1940; The Living Branch); *Pasión primera y otros poemas* (1941; First Passion and Other Poems); *Los Laureles de Oaxaca* (1948; The Laurels of Oaxaca); *Poemas mexicanos* (1958; Mexican Poems); and *Llanto con Emilio Prados* (1962; Weeping with Emilio Prados). He has also published an anthology, *Las cien mejores poesías del destierro* (1945; The Hundred Best Poems of Exile).

BIBLIOGRAPHY

Primary Texts

*Jornada hecha; poesía 1934–1952*. Mexico: Tezontle, 1953.
*Poemas mexicanos*. Mexico: Universidad Nacional Autónoma, 1958.
*La rama viva*. Mexico: Tezontle, 1940.

**GINER DE LOS RÍOS, Hermenegildo** (1847, Cádiz–1923, Granada), Andalusian professor, politician and writer brother of Francisco, sharing with him a dedication to the pedagogical ideals of Spanish *Krausism. He wrote different kinds of plays and fiction, and on general aesthetics. His contributions to literary studies include *Curso de literatura* (1889; Literature Course), *Arte literario. Retórica y poética* (1891; Literary Art. Rhetoric and Poetics), *Principios de literatura* (1892; Basics of Literature), *Historia abreviada de literatura nacional y extranjera, antigua y moderna* (1910–12; Brief History of Spanish and Foreign Literature, Ancient and Modern).

BIBLIOGRAPHY

Primary Texts

*Curso de literatura*. Madrid: Jubera, 1889.
*Milton*. Rpt. Louisville, KY: Falls City Microcards, 1960. One-act play.
*Principios de literatura*. 2nd ed. Madrid: Hernando, 1892.

Stephen Miller

**GIRÓN, Diego** (1530?, Seville–1590, ?), rhetorician, translator, minor poet. A member of the *escuela sevillana*, his extant writings are scattered in various works, including *Herrera's annotations to Garcilaso's works, and a treatise on bloodletting by Fernando de Valdés. Girón is most remembered for continuing the literary academy (*academia) founded by Juan de *Mal Lara. Juan de la *Cueva composed an elegy to Girón after Girón's death.

BIBLIOGRAPHY

Primary Texts

*Obras de Garci Lasso de la Vega con Anotaciones de. . . .* By F. de Herrera. Ed. A. Gallego Morell. Madrid: CSIC, 1973. Facs.
*Tratado de la utilidad de las sangrías.* By F. de Valdés. Seville: Díaz, 1584.

**GIRONELLA, José María** (1917, Darnius–1983, Gerona), Spanish novelist. Inclined to the priesthood in his youth, Gironella worked as a day laborer, factory apprentice and bank clerk. He volunteered in the Nationalist (Franco) army, and later became a newspaper reporter in Gerona. After desultory attempts at poetry, he published his first novel, *Un hombre* (1946; A Man), winner of the Nadal Prize. He married and with his wife left Spain illegally in 1947, spending the next five years in France, Italy, Austria and Sweden. He published *La marea* (1949; The Tide), on World War II, and suffered a nervous breakdown in Paris in 1951. While seeking cures at clinics in Vienna and Helsinki (1951–53), he completed *Los cipreses creen en Dios* (1951; The Cypresses Believe in God), first volume of his Civil War trilogy. An international best-seller and Spain's most popular novel in the post-war period, *Los cipreses* relates events of the pre-war decade in Gerona, studying the conflict's causes through characters representing the contending factions. *El novelista ante el mundo* (1954; The Novelist Faces the World) is a brief essay on the narrative art, while a second non-fiction volume, *Los fantasmas de mi cerebro* (1958; The Phantoms of My Brain) documents the author's nervous breakdown. After a trip to Cuba and Mexico (1959–60), Gironella published the second volume of his trilogy, *Un millón de muertos* (1961; *One Million Dead*, 1963), which treats the Civil War itself. In 1962 appeared *Mujer, levántate y anda* (Woman, Rise Up and Walk), a short novel of biblical motif, followed by the travel books: *Personas, ideas y mares* (1964; People, Ideas and Seas) and *El Japón y su duende* (1964; Japan and Its Demon), and *China, lágrima innumerable* (1965; China, Innumerable Tears). The third volume of the trilogy, *Ha estallado la paz* (1966; *Peace After War*, 1969), which treats the post-war era, was anxiously awaited but proved somewhat disappointing. Basically a journalist who struck it rich with an international best-seller, Gironella was neither an innovator nor a truly great literary craftsman, but he is interesting as a narrator whose base is documentary writing.

BIBLIOGRAPHY

Primary Texts

*Gritos del mar.* Barcelona: Planeta, 1967.
*Todos somos fugitivos.* Barcelona: Planeta, 1961.

English Translations

*The Cypresses Believe in God*. Tr. Harriet de Onís. New York: Knopf, 1955.
*One Million Dead*. Tr. Joan MacLean. New York: Doubleday, 1963.
*Peace after War*. Tr. J. MacLean. New York: Knopf, 1969.
*Phantoms and Fugitives: Journeys to The Improbable*. Tr. T. Brock Fontseré. New York: Sheed & Ward, 1964.
*Where the Soil Was Shallow*. Tr. Anthony Kerrigan. Chicago: Henry Regnery, 1957.

Criticism

Grupp, William J. "J. M. Gironella, Spanish Novelist." *Kentucky Foreign Language Quarterly* 4.3 (1957): 129–35.
Klibbe, Lawrence H. "Gironella's *Where the Soil Was Shallow*." *Catholic World* 188 (Feb. 1959): 399–402.
Schwartz, Ronald. *José María Gironella*. TWAS 164. New York: Twayne, 1972. In English.
Urbanski, Edmund S. "Revolutionary Novels of Gironella and Pasternak." *Hispania* 43 (May 1960): 191–97.

Janet Pérez

**GLOSA** (gloss), indigenous type of verse. Introduced by late fourteenth- and early fifteenth-c. court poets, the *glosa* is a poem built around several lines taken from an existing poem. The gloss is quoted in the opening stanza, and then repeated, wholly or partially, in each subsequent stanza. All types of poetry were employed in *glosas*: verses from *romances* (*romancero), courtly love poems, religious or philosophical poems, etc., all inspired new creations in *glosas*, which remained a popular style of verse throughout the *Siglo de Oro.

BIBLIOGRAPHY

Primary Text

*La glosa en el siglo de oro*. By H. Janner. Madrid: Collantes and Rubio, 1946. Contains representative *glosas* and critical explanation.

**GODÍNEZ, Felipe** (c. 1585, ?–1659, Madrid), priest, playwright. Born to a well-connected *converso family, his childhood was spent in Moguer. In 1605 he moved to Seville, attending the Colegio de Sta. María de Jesús and graduating in 1610. In 1624, the Seville *Inquisition found him guilty of heresy (in part for two Old Testament plays he had written). As punishment he was forced to repent publicly in an *Auto de fe*, his property was confiscated, he was stripped of his priesthood, and sentenced to one year of seclusion in a convent or hospital and six years of exile from Seville. By 1626, he had moved to Madrid, remaining there until his death.

Godínez's earliest extant work is a poem written in 1609. Although *Cervantes praised Godínez in the *Viaje del Parnaso* (1614), most of his plays were written after 1624, and follow Lope de *Vega's precepts. Despite his known Judeo-*converso* past, he managed to become an active, successful member of the circle of Madrid playwrights. He wrote some sixteen plays of various types, four *autos* *sacramentales* (*autos), two colloquies, and poetry. After his death, Godínez's work was quickly neglected; this unjustifiable neglect has persisted down to the twentieth c. Piedad Bolaños has made major progress in rectifying the dearth of critical attention and lack of information regarding Godínez. She argues that his Judeo-*converso* heritage decisively determined his selection and presentation of subjects and themes. Godínez's most successful works include *Aún de noche alumbra el sol* (1630–33; Even at Night the Sun Illuminates), *O el fraile ha de ser ladrón o el ladrón ha de ser fraile* (after 1640; Either the Friar Must Be a Thief, or the Thief Must Be a Friar), *Las lágrimas de David* (n.d.; The Tears of David), and *La traición contra su dueño* (1615–20?; Betrayal of One's Master).

BIBLIOGRAPHY

Primary Texts

*Aún de noche alumbra el sol.* In BAE 45.

*Las lágrimas de David.* Ed., study, E. Coughlin and J. Valencia. Valencia: Albatrós Hispanófila, 1986.

*La traición contra su dueño.* Ed., intro., T. C. Turner. Chapel Hill: Hispanófila; Madrid: Castalia, 1975.

Criticism

Bolaños Donoso, P. *La obra dramática de Felipe Godínez.* Seville: Diputación Provincial de Sevilla, 1983.

Glaser, E. "Estudio sobre la comedia de Felipe Gódinez. *O el fraile ha de ser ladrón o el ladrón ha de ser fraile." Revista de Literatura* 12 (1957): 91–107.

Maureen Ihrie

**GOLDEN AGE.** *See* Siglo de Oro

*GOLIARDO* (Goliard). The final evolution of the *juglar*, or jester, the goliard was a late-medieval cleric or student who traveled from place to place and composed satiric, licentious verse. The type existed throughout Europe; in Spain, one of the finest writers of this period, the *Arcipreste de Hita, certainly falls within the category of goliard.

**GOMES, Soeiro Pereira** (1909, Ribatejo?–1949), Portuguese poet and prose writer. Considered one of the pioneers of neo-realism, Gomes produced the first noteworthy title of that school with *Esteiros* (1945; Forced Labor), a vigorous painting of the sufferings of two adolescents employed in the factories along the Tagus. Among his posthumous works are *Refúgio Perdido* (1950; Lost Refuge), *Contos Vermelhos* (1951; Vermillion Tales), and *Engrenagem* (1951; Cogs in the Wheel; 2 ed. 1961), the outline of a realistic novel of the industrial environment (a genre uncultivated in Portugal).

**GOMES LEAL, António Duarte,** occasional pseudonym João Ninguem = "Joe Nobody" (1848, Lisbon–1921, Lisbon), Portuguese poet and pamphleteer. He is probably the most enigmatic figure of late nineteenth- and early twentieth-

c. Portuguese literature whose career ran the gamut from loudly proclaimed atheism to an equally loudly stated belief, and from opulence to the gutter, and whose writing shows the same variation in content and quality. One is tempted to draw a comparison with Verlaine, for there are moments when Gomes Leal's career resembles that of the paradigmatic "poète maudit." He combined seriousness with scurrility and respectability with episodes of quite bizarre self-advertisement, high principled republicanism with praise of aristocracy, unintelligent anti-clericalism with equally unthinking belief. He was the natural son of moderately well-off parents. In contrast to the majority of his contemporaries in literature, he received little formal education, being largely self-taught. Never a man for sustained effort or social conformity, Gomes Leal lived hand to mouth with moments of prosperity interspersing long periods of penury. He spent his last years quite literally in the gutters of Lisbon.

He began to publish very young, starting with two short poems, "Aquela Morta" (1866; The Dead Woman) and "A Gondoleira" (1867; The Girl Gondolier), both of which appeared in *A Gazeta de Portugal*. Critical reaction, however, remained generally positive throughout his life. At the start he was rapidly seen as one of the up-and-coming talents with, for instance, Luciano Cordeiro. An article in *A Revolução de Setembro* included his name in a list of potentially great poets that also contained the names of Teófilo Braga, Antero de Quental, Guilherme Braga and Guerra Junqueiro.

During the sixties and seventies of the nineteenth c. Gomes Leal was active in literary journalism, helping to found *O Espectro de Juvenal* (a satiric periodical) in 1872 and contributing to *A Revolução de Setembro*, *O Diário de Notícias*, *A Órgia* and, later still, to *O Mundo*, *O Século* and *A Águia*. Here, too, he rang the changes on all points of view from iconoclastic socialism to emotional, conservative catholicism. He remained, however, known to, and appreciated by, each successive generation of writers in Portugal.

His own writing consists mainly of collections of poems of which the most notable are *Claridades do Sul* (1875; Southern Lights); *A Fome de Camões* (1880; The Hunger of Camões); *A Traição* (1881; Treason); *O Herege* (1881; The Heretic); *O AntiCristo* (two versions, 1884 and 1908; The Anti-Christ); *A Mulher de Luto* (1902; The Woman in Mourning); *Mefistófeles em Lisboa* (1907; Mephistopheles in Lisbon) and *Memórias de uma Epoca Maldita* (1912; Memoirs of a Cursed Time).

These poems, taken together with the following works will suffice to signpost his shifting attitudes: *Fim do Mundo* (1899; The End of the World), subtitled "sátiras modernas" or modern satires; *Pátria e Deus* (1914; For God and Country); *História de Jesus* (1924; The Story of Jesus) and his translation of Leo Taxil's (G. A. Jogand-Pages) *Les Mystères de l'Église* (1889; The Mysteries of the Church) and his own "open letter" to the Bishop of Porto (1901), "O Jesuita e o Mestre de Escola" (The Jesuit and the Schoolmaster).

BIBLIOGRAPHY

A compendious bibliography of Gomes Leal's work, journalism and other ephemera appears in Alvaro Neves and H. Marques Júnior, *Gomes Leal, a sua vida e a sua obra.*

Lisbon: Editorial Enciclopedia, 1948. None of his work is currently in print or readily available.

Peter Fothergill-Payne

**GÓMEZ, Valentín** (1843, Pedrola, Zaragoza–1907, Madrid), journalist and playwright. A journalist of conservative and Catholic ideas, he wrote historical dramas such as *La flor del espino* (1882; The Flower of the Hawthorn), based on an episode in the War of Succession, and *El soldado de San Marcial* (1885; The Soldier of Saint Martial), which deals with the War of Independence. His comedies include *Un alma de hielo* (1881; An Icy Soul), *El desheredado* (1884; The Disinherited), and *¡Por un hermano!* (c. 1870; For a Brother!). Because of his thematic eclecticism, he resembles *Tamayo y Baus and Adelardo *López de Ayala. He also wrote literary, historical, social and religious studies. In 1905 he was elected to the Royal Spanish Academy (\*Academia Española) to succeed Father Luis *Coloma.

BIBLIOGRAPHY

Primary Texts

*El celoso de sí mismo; drama trágico en tres actos, en verso.* Madrid: Montoya, 1882.
*La dama del rey; drama histórico.* Madrid: Pérez Dubrull, 1877.
*La flor del espino; drama en un acto y en verso.* Madrid: Pérez Dubrull, 1882.
*La novela del amor; comedia en tres actos, en prosa.* Madrid: Pérez Dubrull, 1879.
*Teatro.* 1 vol. of 8 pamphlets. Madrid: n.p., 1877–89.

Phoebe Porter Medina

**GÓMEZ DE AVELLANEDA, Gertrudis** (1814, Puerto Príncipe [now Camagüey], Cuba–1873, Madrid), poet, novelist and playwright. When she was twenty-two years old, she moved with her family to La Coruña, Spain. Later in 1838 she set up residence with her brother in Seville where she met her lifelong love, Ignacio de Cepeda. In 1840 her first play, *Leoncia*, was produced. That same year she moved to Madrid and met most of the important writers of Romantic Spain. In 1841 she published her first collection of poetry, *Poesías*, and her first novel, *Sab*. Her tragedy *Munio Alfonso* was produced in 1844, and her novel *Espatolino* (of the same name) about the Italian bandit appeared in serial form. During the following year she won both prizes in a poetry contest sponsored by the Liceo of Madrid. In this same year her tragedy *El príncipe de Viana* (The Prince of Viana) was produced, and she gave birth to an illegitimate daughter by the poet Gabriel *García Tassara, who refused to recognize his daughter. The child, named Brenhilde, died in infancy. In 1846, she married Pedro Sabater, who died within four months of the marriage. During this same year, her novel, *Guatimozín, último emperador de México* (*Cuauhtemoc, The Last Aztec Emperor,* 1898) appeared in serial form, and her tragedy *Egilona* was produced. Throughout the next decade she wrote numerous plays including the biblical tragedy *Saúl* (1849), *La verdad vence apariencias* (1852; Truth Conquers Appearances), *Errores del corazón* (1852; Errors of the Heart), *El* *donativo del diablo* (1852; The Devil's Donation), *La hija de las flores* (1852; The Daughter of the Flowers), *La aventurera* (1853; The Adventuress), *Hortensia* (1853), *Simpatía y Antipatía* (1855; Amity and Aversion), *Oráculos de Talia o los duendes en el palacio* (1855; Oracles of Thalia or the Ghosts in the Palace) and the biblical tragedy *Baltasar* (1858). She also published a second volume of poetry, *Poesías* (1850), a novel, *Dolores* (1851) and a number of legends during this period. In 1853 she was refused entry into the Royal Spanish Academy (*Academia Española) because she was a woman, and in 1855 she married Colonel Domingo Verdugo y Massieu. In 1859 her husband was named to the staff of the new governor-general of Cuba, and they moved to Cuba where Gómez de Avellaneda was crowned as poet laureate in Havana (1860). There she founded the literary magazine *Album cubano* (1860) and wrote the novel *El artista barquero o los cuatro cinco de junio* (1861; The Artist Boatman or the Four Fifths of June). In 1863 Verdugo died, and during the following year she traveled to the United States, London and Paris before she returned to Spain. In 1869 she began to publish her complete works which she edited and chose herself. She died of diabetes in 1873. An expanded edition of her complete works was published in Havana in 1914.

Gómez de Avellaneda was one of the most outstanding figures of Romantic Spain. She is best remembered for her poetry, which she began to write at the age of nine. She used a wide variety of metrical possibilities and rhyme schemes. The themes of her poetry include Cuba (''Al partir'' [1836, On Leaving] and ''La vuelta a la patria'' [1859; Return to the Homeland]), love (''A él'' [To Him] and ''Mi mal'' [My Torment]), poetry (''A la poesía'' [To Poetry] and ''El poeta'' [The Poet]) and religion (''La cruz'' [The Cross], ''A la Virgen, plegaria'' [Supplication to the Virgin]). She also began writing drama as a child. She has sixteen full-length dramas to her name, twelve of them written in verse. Some of these are classical tragedies; others are lively comedies and romantic dramas set in the Middle Ages. She used a wide variety of verse forms and dealt with the themes of love, religion, the beauty of nature, the family, filial duty and the emotions of jealousy, egotism and pride in her drama. Many of her dramatic works were triumphant successes in Madrid. In addition to her drama and poetry, she wrote six full-length novels of varied themes and settings (Cuba, Spain, France, Italy and Mexico). The themes of her novels include slavery in Cuba, romantic love, the brutality of the conquistadors in Mexico, power, justice and the enslavement of social systems in general. Her vast literary production was received with great critical acclaim and public enthusiasm in her day. *See also* Romanticism.

BIBLIOGRAPHY

Primary Texts

*Autobiografía y cartas de la ilustre poetisa hasta ahora inéditas.* Intro. D. Lorenzo Cruz de Fuentes. Huelva: Miguel Mora, 1907.

*Cartas inéditas y documentos relativos a su vida en Cuba de 1859 a 1864.* Matanzas: La Pluma de Oro, 1912.

*Diario de amor.* Intro. Alberto Ghiraldo. Madrid: Aguilar, 1928.

*Obras literarias*. 6 vols. Madrid: Rivadeneyra, 1869–71.
*Obras de la Avellaneda*. Havana: A. Miranda, 1914.

English Translations

*Belshazzar*. Tr. William Freeman Burbank. London: B. F. Stevens and Brown, 1914.
*Cuauhtemoc, The Last Aztec Emperor*. Tr. Mrs. Wilson W. Blake. Mexico: F. P. Hoeck, 1898.
*The Love Letters*. Tr. Dorrey Malcolm. Intro. José Antonio Portuondo. Havana: Juan Fernández Burgos, 1956.

Criticism

Ballesteros, Mercedes. *Vida de la Avellaneda*. Madrid: Cultura Hispánica, 1949.
Bravo Villasante, Carmen. *Sab*. Salamanca: Anaya, 1970.
————. *Una vida romántica, La Avellaneda*. Barcelona: Enrique Granados, 1967.
Cotarelo y Mori, Emilio. *La Avellaneda y sus obras: ensayo biográfico y crítico*. Madrid: Tipografía de Archivos, 1930.
Harter, Hugh A. *Gertrudis Gómez de Avellaneda*. TWAS 599. Boston: Twayne, 1981.
Kirkpatrick, Susan. "Gertrudis Gómez de Avellaneda, Carolina Coronado y Rosalía de Castro: Estudios recientes." *Insula* 44.516 (Dec. 1989): 12–13.
Lazo, Raimundo. *Gertrudis Gómez de Avellaneda. La mujer y la poetisa lírica*. Mexico: Porrúa, 1972.
Marquina, Rafael. *Gertrudis Gómez de Avellaneda. La Peregrina*. Havana: Trópico, 1939.

                                                                    Phoebe Porter Medina

**GÓMEZ DE BAQUERO, Eduardo.** *See* Andrenio

**GÓMEZ DE CIBDARREAL, El Bachiller Fernán,** pseudonym used for a literary hoax. The author of the *Centón epistolario* used this name; the work carries a publication date of 1499 but in fact was published shortly before 1650. The falsification was perpetrated for genealogical purposes. The true identity of the perpetrator is unknown, but possible candidates include *Pellicer de Ossau, Gil González Dávila, and Pedro Mantuano. *See also Centón*.

**GÓMEZ DE LA SERNA, Gaspar** (1918, Barcelona–1974, Madrid), lawyer, journalist, and critic. He was secretary of the review *Clavileño*, in which he published noteworthy studies on *Pérez Galdós and *Valle-Inclán. His books include *Después del desenlace* (1945; After the Denouement), which contains letters and lyric prose; and *Libro de Madrid* (1949; Book of Madrid), illustrated by Esplandiú, which won a municipal prize. Other books inspired by or related to Madrid include *Madrid y su gente* (1963; Madrid and Its People) and *Gracias y desgracias del Teatro Real* (1967; Charms and Misfortunes of the Royal Theater). Gómez de la Serna also published several books of travel impressions and a volume of critical essays, *España en sus episodios nacionales* (1954; Spain in Her National Episodes). His anthology *Cartas a mi hijo* (1961; Letters to My Son), containing a selection of texts on Spain, was awarded a prize by the Franco regime. *Goya y su España* (1969; Goya and His Spain) treats art and history.

The author also published a biography of his cousin, Ramón *Gómez de la Serna, together with a study of his work.

BIBLIOGRAPHY

Primary Texts

*Cartas a mi hijo*. 7th ed. Madrid: Doncel, 1967.
*Después del desenlace*. Madrid: RO, 1945.
*España en sus episodios nacionales*. Madrid: Movimiento, 1954.
*Goya y su España*. Madrid: Alianza, 1969.
*Ramón; obra y vida*. Madrid: Taurus, 1963.

**GÓMEZ DE LA SERNA, Ramón** (1888, Madrid–1963, Buenos Aires), writer. Although many sources list his birthdate as 1891, Ramón was born three years before. A writer by nature and inclination, he wrote his first book— *Entrando en fuego* (1904; Entering the Fray)—at the age of sixteen, and subsequently published some eighty novels, biographies, art books, works of humor, collections of journalistic articles, volumes of short stories, drama and pantomimes, and the almost unclassifiable *greguerías* (literally ''pig-squeals'')—daring, original metaphors, for which he is best known. His most enduring impact to date has been as popularizer of literary vanguard movements in Spain, especially ultraism, cubism, and surrealism. His own overpowering interest in the artistic innovations of the years between the wars was enhanced by his picturesque persona and striking, colorful eccentricities: he lectured on avant-garde movements from a trapeze, from the back of an elephant, and many similarly outrageous and imaginative postures. In 1915 he founded a *tertulia* (periodic literary gathering) at Café Pombo, which endured until his self-exile to Argentina in 1936; the internationally famous writers who gathered there and their amusing, iconoclastic sessions are chronicled in *Pombo* (1918) and *La sagrada cripta de Pombo* (1924; The Sacred Crypt at Pombo's). He made of himself and his lifestyle a living legend, with his home transformed to an ''ivory tower'' overflowing with objects of every imaginable kind and the ceiling plastered with photographs. Almost single-handedly, via his radio talks and much-publicized lectures, Ramón tried to create an avant-garde atmosphere in Madrid, becoming famed as a humorist in the process (as well as the only Spaniard ever invited to membership in the French Academy of Humor). During the 1920s and 1930s when Gómez de la Serna's fortune and fame were at their peak, he was known simply as Ramón throughout Europe and Latin America.

Many of his works are set in other cities of Europe; *La quinta de Palmyra* (1923; Palmyra's Country Villa) in Estoril, Portugal (where he planned to build his dream home); *La viuda blanca y negra* (1918; The Black-and-White Widow) in Paris (where he spent two years in a political post); and *La mujer de ámbar* (1927; The Amber Woman) in Naples (where he fled at a moment of financial crisis), but his lasting love was Madrid and its night life, which he re-created in many novels and essays, including *El Rastro* (1915; The Flea Market), *Toda la historia de la Puerta del Sol* (1920; The Whole Story of the Plaza Puerta del

Sol), *El Prado* (1931; The Prado Museum), *Elucidario de Madrid* (1931; Guide to Madrid), *La Nardo* (1930; The Lily, subtitled *Novel of Madrid*), and *Nostalgia de Madrid* (1956; Nostalgia for Madrid).

Many of Ramón's biographies and literary portraits were written later in life when he was in serious financial straits, but he actually first attempted the genre much earlier. Biographies— always imaginative and creatively literary as well as factual—include *Edgar Poe* (1920), *Oscar Wilde* (1921), *Azorín* (1923), *Goya* (1928), *El Greco* (1935), *Mi tía Carolina Coronado* (1942; My Aunt, Carolina Coronado), *Velázquez* (1943), *Don Ramón María del Valle-Inclán* (1942), *José Gutiérrez Solana* (1944), *Lope de Vega* (1945), and *Quevedo* (1953). Especially noteworthy is the number of painters among the biographical subjects. Shorter sketches or caricatures, far more numerous, portrayed dozens of literary and artistic figures: Pirandello, Manuel and Antonio *Machado, Ibsen, *Benavente, Vicente *Blasco Ibáñez, Emilia *Pardo Bazán, *Pérez Galdós, Darío de Regoyos, Marc Chagall, Kafka, Bernard Shaw, Pablo Neruda, Manuel de Falla, Toulouse-Lautrec, Apollinaire, Jean Cocteau, Charlie Chaplin, Picasso, Diego Rivera, Juan Gris, Salvador Dalí, Maruja Mallo, Vicente *Aleixandre, Juan Ramón *Jiménez, Eugenio d'*Ors, Pío *Baroja, *Unamuno, Colette, and many more.

Short story collections include *Morbideces* (1908; Morbidities), *La malicia de las acacias* (1924; The Malice of the Acacias, novelettes); *El dueño del átomo* (1928; The Lord of the Atom), and *El cólera azul* (1937; The Blue Cholera). Other short fiction collections are *Seis falsas novelas* (1927; Six False Novels), *La hiperestésica* (1934; The Hypersensitive Woman), *Doña Juana la loca: Novelas superhistóricas* (1944; Princess Juana the Mad: Superhistorical Novellas), and *Cuentos de fin de año* (1947; Year-End Tales). *Cuento de Calleja* (1909; Tale of Calleja) is actually a drama. *Ex-votos* (1910) contains eight plays: ''Los sonámbulos'' (Sleepwalkers), ''Siempreviva'' (Forget-Me-Not), ''La casa nueva'' (The New House), ''Los unánimes'' (The Unanimous Ones), ''Tránsito,'' ''Fiesta de Dolores'' and two others which reappear in *El drama del palacio deshabitado* (1926; The Drama of the Uninhabited Palace), which contains five theatrical works, the title piece and ''La utopía'' (Utopia), ''Beatriz,'' ''La corona de hierro'' (The Iron Crown), and ''El lunático'' (The Lunatic).

Gómez de la Serna's full-length novels tend to favor atmosphere or locale over plot and characterization, often personifying the ambient while dehumanizing the characters. The protagonist is often an allegorical spirit of the locale, or a particular landmark may become symbolic of the whole area (e.g., the ''Rastro'' Flea Market becomes the soul of Madrid). *El secreto del acueducto* (1922; The Secret of the Aqueduct) is a chronicle-portrait of Segovia, with a love-triangle plot of minimal importance: the protagonist's one claim to fame is as an expert on local history, which he recounts incessantly. *El torero Caracho* (1927; The Bullfighter Caracho), the rags-to-riches story of a Madrid toreador, ends with the death of the protagonist and his rival, and a macabre wake in which widow and mistress clash over the body. In *La Nardo* (1930; The Lily), the beautiful young heroine, Aurelia, initially pure and innocent, is seduced, exploited and prostituted, eventually becoming addicted to drugs. A relatively successful courtesan who wins a beauty contest, she ends up committing suicide, together with the elderly judge who had fallen in love with her. *Las tres gracias* (1949; The Three Graces) again employs a slim plot as a pretext for writing about Madrid's atmosphere and the nature of its residents. The three young ladies for which the novel is named explore the plazas and parks, nooks and crannies, streets and landmarks of Madrid, provoking lengthy descriptions. The same man falls in love with all three, for all represent Madrid in his mind. *Piso bajo* (1961; Basement Apartment), still another novel of Madrid, is described by the author as a "prose poem," typifying its relative lack of character development and sustained action, its nostalgic, penetrating *costumbrismo* (portrayal of local color and customs). Other novels are nebulous or anecdotal; Ramón was essentially a stylist, and it is on the level of style that his most original contributions were made.

BIBLIOGRAPHY

Primary Texts

*Automoribundia*. Buenos Aires: Sudamericana, 1948. Autobiography.

*El caballero del hongo gris*. Paris, Madrid, Lisbon: Agencia Mundial de Librería, 1928. Novel.

*Diario póstumo*. Ed. Luisa Sofovich. Barcelona: Plaza y Janés, 1972.

*Greguerías completas*. Barcelona: Lauro, 1947.

*Ismos*. Madrid: Biblioteca Nueva, 1931; Buenos Aires: Losada, 1948.

English Translations

*Movieland*. Tr. A. Flores. New York: Macaulay, 1930.

For short story translations, see *The Literature of Spain in English Translation*. Ed. R.S. Rudder. New York: Ungar, 1975. 443–46.

Criticism

Cardona, Rodolfo. *Ramón. A Study of Gómez de la Serna and His Works*. New York: Eliseo Torres and Sons, 1957.

Gardiol, Rita Mazzetti. *Ramón Gómez de la Serna*. TWAS 338. New York: Twayne, 1974.

Gómez de la Serna, Gaspar. *Ramón*. Madrid: Taurus, 1963.

Granjel, Luis. *Retrato de Ramón*. Madrid: Guadarrama, 1963.

Jackson, Richard Lawson. "The Greguería of Ramón Gómez de la Serna: A Study of the Genesis, Composition, and Significance of a New Literary Genre." Diss., Ohio State U, 1963.

*Studies on Ramón Gómez de la Serna*. Ed. N. Dennis. Ottawa: Dovehouse, 1988.

Janet Pérez

**GÓMEZ HERMOSILLA, José Mamerto** (1771, Madrid–1837, Madrid), professor of Greek and rhetoric, critic, grammarian. His dogmatic, rigid neoclassical tastes informed and distorted his critical evaluations, as seen in the posthumously published *Juicio crítico de los principales poetas españoles de la última era* (1840; Critical Evaluation of the Principal Spanish Poets of the Most

Recent Age). An *afrancesado* (supporter of the French in the Napoleonic invasion) like Leandro Fernández de \*Moratín, he records his years in exile in Paris (1814–20) in *El jacobinismo y los jacobinos* (1823; Jacobinism and the Jacobins). Most important is his *Arte de hablar en prosa y verso* (1826; Art of Speaking in Prose and Verse), which explains at length his literary views. It was republished many times.

BIBLIOGRAPHY

Primary Texts

*Arte de hablar en prosa y verso.* Buenos Aires: Glem, 1943.
*El jacobinismo y los jacobinos.* Madrid: Esperanza, 1866–67.
*Juicio crítico. . . .* Paris: Garnier, 1855.

**GÓMEZ MORENO, Manuel** (1870, Granada–1970, Madrid), eminent Granadine art historian. The son of an artist and archaeologist, he began his studies and teaching career in Granada before moving to Castile in 1900. There he started the *Catálogo Monumental de España* (Catalog of the Monuments of Spain), which surveys the great works of art in the various Spanish provinces. Gómez Moreno's distinguished publication career began when he was only seventeen and spanned more than three-quarters of a century. Although he was especially interested in the language and culture of the ancient Iberians, Mozarabic architecture, and Spanish sculpture, his was a multifaceted personality.

Founder and director of the Centro de Estudios Hispánicos (Center of Hispanic Studies), Gómez Moreno also held the chair of Arabic archaeology at the U of Madrid for many years. He was a member of the Royal Spanish Academy (\*Academia Española) as well as the Academies of History and Fine Arts. His death in Madrid in 1970 came three months after his 100th birthday.

BIBLIOGRAPHY

Primary Texts

*La escultura del Renacimiento en España.* Firenze: Pantheon, 1931.
*La novela de España.* Madrid: Marzo, 1928.
*Provincia de León (1906–1908).* Madrid: Ministerio de Instrucción Pública y Bellas Artes, 1925–26.
*Provincia de Salamanca.* Madrid: Ministerio de Educación y Ciencia, 1967.
*Provincia de Zamora (1903–1905).* Madrid: Ministerio de Instrucción Pública y Bellas Artes, 1927.

English Translation

*The Golden Age of Spanish Sculpture.* London: Thames and Hudson, 1964.

Criticism

Gaya Nuño, J. A. ''Ante el centenario de Gómez Moreno: Historia de sus libros.'' *Archivo Español de Arte* 42.165 (Jan.-March 1969): 1–12.

James F. Brown

**GÓMEZ OJEA, Carmen** (1945, Gijón– ), poet and prose author. She studied at the U of Oviedo, where she obtained her licenciate in Romance philology. After writing eight novels, a book of poems, and some fifty short stories—most of which remained unpublished— she won the Nadal Prize in 1981 with *Cantiga de agüero* (Canticle of Omens), a curious novel with a blend of magic and witchcraft, mystery and folkloric elements which presents the environment of rural Galicia. Also in 1981, Gómez Ojea won the Tigre Juan Prize for fiction with her short story collection *Otras mujeres y Fabia* (Other Women and Fabia). Proximity to Galicia has influenced her writing in this collection as well, where the local superstitions and ancient folkloric substrata of the area are frequently in evidence. Subsequently, Gómez Ojea published *Los perros de Hécate* (1985; Hecate's Hounds), her third novel, in which she presents another, irrational world which exists just beyond the sheltering walls and lighted windows of "normal" houses. Tarsiana, the protagonist, and her wise maid, Regalina, are mediums who can perceive events in both worlds, the quotidian and visible and the shadow world of night. Gómez Ojea has also written an *auto sacramental* (*auto), and avoids specialization in a single genre.

BIBLIOGRAPHY

Primary Texts

*Cantiga de agüero*. Barcelona: Destino, 1981.
*La novela que Marien no terminó*. Barcelona: Lasal, 1988.
*Otras mujeres y Fabia*. Barcelona: Argos Vergara, 1982.
*Los perros de Hécate*. Barcelona: Grijalbo, 1985.

Janet Pérez

**GÓMEZ PEREIRA, Antonio** (1500, Medina del Campo?–after 1558?, ?), philosopher and physician. He studied at the U of Salamanca, graduating from the School of Medicine. Gómez Pereira's fame as a physician prompted Philip II to summon him to treat his sickly son Carlos. In 1555, his *Antoniana Margarita* appeared. Named after his parents Antonio and Margarita, the work discusses, among other things, the differences between man and animals, asking whether they think and feel as man does (he rejects this hypothesis), and considers what motivates them. At the outset, he rejects established authority—except with regard to religion—and examines and draws conclusions on the basis of experience and reason alone. Despite various sorts of defects, some of the observations are quite original and advanced for their day. *Menéndez y Pelayo considers him a precursor of Descartes, and Marcial Solana concurs. Gómez Pereira also wrote a medical work which rejects the erroneous Arabic theory regarding the cause and role of fever, again using experience and reason as his criteria for judging. *See also* Humanism; Renaissance.

BIBLIOGRAPHY

Primary Texts

*Antoniana margarita*. Medina del Campo: Millis, 1555.
*Novae Veraeque Medicinae*. Medina del Campo: n.p., 1558.

Criticism

Bullón, E. *De los orígenes de la filosofía moderna. Los precursores españoles de Bacon y Descartes.* Salamanca: Calatrava, 1905.
Menéndez y Pelayo, M. "De los orígenes del criticismo y del escepticismo y especialmente los precursores españoles de Kant." *Ensayos de crítica filosófica.* Ed. E. Sánchez Reyes. Santander: Artes Gráficas, 1948.
Solana, M. *Historia de la filosofía española. Época del Renacimiento (siglo XVI).* Madrid: Asociación para el progreso de las ciencias, 1941.

Maureen Ihrie

**GOMIS, Lorenzo** (1924, Barcelona– ), poet, prose author. He received the Premio Correo Literario for poetry, and for many years was director of the magazine *El ciervo*, one of the most representative publications of neo-Catholic tendencies among Catalan youth. He also has contributed to the magazine *Destino*. His poetry book *El caballo* (1952; The Horse) merited the Adonais Prize. Gomis has also published prose works, including *La ciudad a medio hacer* (1956; The Halfway Finished City), *El sermón del laico* (1959; The Layman's Sermon), and *El hombre de la aguja en un pajar* (1966; The Man with a Needle in a Haystack).

BIBLIOGRAPHY

Primary Texts

*Poesía, 1950–1975.* Esplugas de Llobregat: Plaza & Janés, 1978.

Isabel McSpadden

**GONÇALVES, Egito** (1922, Lisbon– ), Portuguese poet. One of the most important imagists and surrealists, associated with Alexandre *O'Neill and compared with certain contemporary Spanish poets. *A Evasão Possível* (1952; The Evasion Possible), *O Vagabundo Decepado* (1957; The Deceived Vagabond), *Viagem com o teu rostro* (1958; Voyages Like Your Countenance) and other collections are thoroughly surrealistic, with a wealth of humor, together with heavy doses of the subconscious and frequent metaphysical implications. Gonçalves frequently combines such opposites as life and death, the real and the imaginary, or positive and negative, to denounce life's absurdities. *Os Arquivos do Silêncio* (1963; Archives of Silence) is closer to certain neorealist "social" poetry of the epoch, with a notable satiric content and a certain deliberate tendency to the prosaic.

BIBLIOGRAPHY

Primary Texts

*Os Arquivos do Silêncio.* Lisbon: Portugália, 1963.
*O fosforo na palha, seguido de O sistema interrogativo e outros poemas.* Lisbon: Dom Quixote, 1970.
*A viagem com o teu rostro.* Lisbon: Europa-América, 1958.

**GÓNGORA Y ARGOTE, Luis de** (1561, Córdoba–1627, Córdoba), poet. He is one of the major poets of Spain's Baroque period and perhaps the most controversial figure in Spanish literature. His erudite intensification and witty exploration of the poetic conventions he inherited have been for some the brilliant culmination of the Golden Age of Spanish literature and for others an obscure, pointless, and insidious aberration. Although the vast majority of his contemporaries acknowledged Góngora's talent, his style, particularly in the longer, mature poems, was the object of vilification and ridicule. Much of Góngora's poetry was considered incomprehensible until a sympathetic and systematic reevaluation was undertaken by a generation of critics in this c. who were influenced by modernist poetic theory. Although this difficult poetry still has its detractors, Góngora's eccentric genius is now generally recognized.

What his detractors have found so scandalous in Góngora's poetry can be summarized thus: inordinate use of neologism, excessive use of hyperbaton and other imitations of classical syntax, and the use of far-fetched or obscure metaphors. But all these tendencies are evident in the poetry of *Garcilaso de la Vega and Fernando de *Herrera and other poets who preceded Góngora. In part it was simply the relentless exaggeration of established conventions that offended, but some of the early criticism seems patently *ad hominem*.

Some of those who resisted the "new poetry" did so with the vehemence normally reserved for the rejection of heresy. The word *culterano*, referring to the highly Latinate style of Góngora and others, may even have been coined by association with *luterano* (Lutheran). Many of the harshest criticisms of Góngora's poetry refer, often insultingly, to him as a new Christian, something that two official investigations failed to prove. It is evident that Góngora's pride in his erudition and his insistence on his novelty were, in Counter-Reformation Spain, extremely suspect.

Part of the controversy surrounding Góngora seems to have been related to his uncompromising personality and his intransigence in the face of criticism. Góngora was arrogant in defense of his work, claiming that he had raised Spanish to the perfection and nobility of Latin and suggesting that any obscurity was in the minds of his readers. He believed strongly in a poetry for a minority well versed in classical language and literature. In a letter he went so far as to write of casting pearls before swine. Making no effort to endear himself to his critics, he had few friends and a great many enemies. With the chief of the latter, Francisco de *Quevedo, he sustained a vitriolic literary and personal feud ennobled only by the wit of some of the scurrilous verse it produced.

Góngora's life is known to us only in its broadest outlines. His letters are full of financial worries, and he seems to have lived all his life disillusioned by the lack of what he considered appropriate patronage or preferment. He was born in Córdoba in 1561. With the financial aid of his uncle, he studied there with the Jesuits and enrolled in 1576 at the U of Salamanca. Having established his reputation as a poet, he returned to Córdoba, apparently without a degree, to assume his uncle's cathedral prebend and spent the next years traveling throughout Spain representing the cathedral chapter. Having spent two periods at court, in 1603 and again in 1609, he moved there definitively in 1619 when he accepted a royal chaplaincy. He returned to Córdoba in ill health and died there in 1627.

Góngora's works were known and admired in ms. from his student days and were early anthologized in the *romanceros and other collections. The important *Flores de poetas ilustres* (Bouquets from Illustrious Poets) of 1605 contains more poems by Góngora than by any other single poet. Góngora intended to publish his works but the earliest printed edition appeared in the year of his death, followed by another in 1633. Leaving aside the three *comedias* which have never been taken seriously, his extant work consists of more than two hundred *letrillas* and *romances*, about a hundred sonnets and other short poems in Italian meters, and several longer poems which have been the focus of much of the controversy. Thanks to the publication in 1931 of the Chacón manuscript, annotated by the author and dating the compositions, we have a good idea of the development of Góngora's style.

Gongóra's poetic language is much influenced by his knowledge of Latin and Greek. In his desire to raise Spanish to the level of the classical languages, the poet tends to use a long sentence in which the word order imitates that of Latin. He uses words in their original, Latin, sense (*cándido* meaning "white"), modified normal prose word-order ("Pasos de un peregrino son errante / cuantos me dictó versos dulce musa..."), suppresses articles ("vulgo lascivo erraba"), the Greek accusative of respect ("desnuda el pecho anda ella"), and Latin absolute constructions ("—El sueño de sus miembros sacudido—gallardo el joven la persona ostenta"). He follows classical writers in his abundant use of elliptical allusions to classical mythology. Góngora's poetry is also full of striking metaphors, some classical, some Italian, some original. Many of these metaphors are surprising in their visual ingenuity as, for example, these lines in which the poet evokes a swift stream splashing around the trunk of a tree:

> Ella, pues, sierpe, y sierpe al fin pisada,
> —aljófar vomitando fugitivo
> en lugar de veneno—

> (Snake-like, and like a trodden snake it glides,
> But transient pearls of spray it vomits forth
> Instead of venomed rheum;)

But perhaps the most characteristic aspect of Góngora's poetry, whatever the form or theme, is what *Gracián y Morales most admired in Góngora, his *agudeza*, his ingenuity or wit. Góngora's fascination with language itself seems to give him a kind of ironic distance from his writing, giving at times an incongruous impression of playfulness in the most serious contexts. But it is wordplay of an enormously sophisticated kind.

Góngora inherited two poetic languages; on the one hand the highly ornate and conventional Petrarchan tradition of love poetry, and on the other the traditional Spanish meters, the *romances* and *letrillas* of popular tradition. Part of the novelty of Góngora's poetry is the mixture of genres. He wrote in eight syllables on traditional themes and in simpler language, but he was also capable of writing in the same forms with the complexity and erudition associated with Italian poetry. And he could write sonnets full of the kind of low language and obscenity normally found in traditional verse forms. Góngora's irreverent wit led him to compose burlesque versions of themes traditionally treated in a serious manner. The long *romances* on the story of Hero and Leander, where the conventions of courtly love and of Ovidian mythology are turned upside down, are typical.

The compositions in traditional Spanish meters cover an enormous variety of themes and styles. Many of the *letrillas* are sharply critical of the shallowness and preoccupation with money of court life, like the well known "Dineros son calidad" (Money is quality). But there are *romances* and *letrillas* on religious, amorous, patriotic, mythological and social subjects, both serious and burlesque, in lofty style and in slang. The ballad that Góngora is said to have liked most, a version of the Pyramus and Thisbe story, is as enigmatic a mixture of the sublime and ridiculous as anything he wrote. A distinction used to be made between the confusing complexity of the longer poems and the "simpler" language of the works in *arte menor*. But it is clear that the language of a good many of the compositions in Spanish meters is as learned and complex as anything in the *Solitudes*. The classic example of this is the ballad based on the Ariosto story of Angelica and Medoro. These lines evoke the moment in which Angelica falls in love with the wounded Medoro:

> Límpiale el rostro, y la mano
> siente al Amor que se esconde
> tras las rosas, que la muerte
> va violando sus colores.
>
> Escondióse tras las rosas
> porque labren sus arpones
> el diamante del Catay
> con aquella sangre noble.

(She bathes his face and her hand perceives Love hiding behind the roses [of his cheeks] for death is violating [making violet] their colors. Love hid behind the roses so that his arrows might work the diamond of Cathay [Angelica's heart] with that noble blood.)

Góngora's sonnets are among the finest in Spanish. The poet's intensity of imagery and fondness for correlation seem exactly suited to the strict form of the sonnet. Particularly fine is the version of Garcilaso's treatment of the Latin carpe diem theme, "Mientras por competir con tu cabello . . . " (While to compete with your hair . . . ) in which elements of nature vie in vain with the beauty of the beloved. The traits of her beauty (hair, forehead, lips, neck) and the elements of nature (gold, lily, carnation, crystal) are intricately correlated and lead inexorably toward the dramatic final lines which warn that earthly beauty will turn "en tierra, en humo, en polvo, en sombro, en nada (to earth, to smoke, to dust, to shadow, to nothing). Impressive also is "Menos solicitó veloz saeta . . . " (Less sought swift arrow . . . ), on the theme of the fugacity of human life, with its highly Latinate syntax, its compelling images of speed and its swiftly changing verb tenses. The epigraph to El Greco is a masterpiece of subtlety and conciseness and a fitting tribute to a contemporary whose art was also of a brilliant and surprising beauty.

The longer poems written around 1613 are usually considered the quintessence of Góngora's art. The "Fábula de Polifemo" (Fable of Polyphemus) narrates in sixty-three octaves the story of Polyphemus's love for Galatea, her rejection of him, his anger and eventual murder of Acis. The breadth of classical learning that informs this poem has been studied in detail by Antonio Vilanova. There is in the poem an underlying sympathy for the giant with whom, it has been suggested, the poet perhaps identifies.

The *Soledades* (*Solitudes*) is an ambitious work, consisting of two parts, each of about a thousand lines (the second is apparently incomplete) of *silva*. This very free form allows Góngora great freedom in length and structure of his sentences and suits the rather loose narrative. The poem begins with the arrival of a young courtier, shipwrecked as he flees an unhappy love at court, on a rocky shore. He is taken in by a group of goatherds and later by fishermen and witnesses hunting, fishing, banqueting, a wedding, a sports competition and other scenes of rustic innocence. These scenes illustrate the theme of the poem, disillusionment with the vanity, commercialism, and ambition of courtly life as contrasted with the simple innocence of country life. The individual scenes are presented in great detail, with enormous complexity of allusion. The opening lines of the poem give an impression of the kind of language Góngora uses. They are an evocation of spring, the time when the constellation Taurus rises in the sky.

> Era del año la estación florida
> en que el mentido robador de Europa
> —media luna las armas de su frente,
> y el sol todos los rayos de su pelo—,
>         luciente honor del cielo,
> en campos de zafiro pace estrellas.

> (In the sweet season decked with vernal flowers, / When the feigned bull
> that stole Europa's love / —Armed with the crescent moon upon his brow, /
> His hide resplendent in the solar beams—, / The pride of heaven, seems /
> Upon the stars in sapphire fields to graze;)

"Polyphemus" and "Solitudes" have both been translated by Gilbert F. Cunningham carefully and elegantly into English versions that respect the verse forms and rhyme schemes of the original works. The Spanish texts have all been edited, thanks in large measure to Dámaso *Alonso, whose *La lengua poética de Góngora* inspired much later criticism. *See also culteranismo*; Italian literary influences; Siglo de Oro.

BIBLIOGRAPHY

Primary Texts

*Obras completas.* Ed. Juan and Isabel Millé y Jiménez. 6th ed. Madrid: Aguilar, 1967.
*Las soledades.* Ed. Dámaso Alonso. 3rd ed. Madrid: RO, 1956.
*Sonetos completos.* Ed. Biruté Ciplijauskaite. Clásicos Castalia 1. Madrid: Castalia, 1969.

English Translation

*Polyphemus and Galatea: A Study in the Interpretation of a Baroque Poem.* Tr. Gilbert F. Cunningham. Edinburgh: Edinburgh UP, 1977.

Criticism

Alonso, Dámaso. *Estudios y ensayos gongorinos.* Madrid: Gredos, 1970.
———. *Góngora y el "Polifemo."* Madrid: Gredos, 1967.
———. *La lengua poética de Góngora.* 3rd ed. Madrid: Gredos, 1961.
Collard, Andrée. *Nueva poesía. Conceptismo y culturanismo en la crítica española.* 2nd ed. Madrid: Castalia, 1968.
Foster, D. W., and V. R. Foster. *Luis de Góngora.* TWAS 266, New York: Twayne, 1973.
Gates, E. J. *Documentos gongorinos.* Mexico: Colegio de México, 1960.
Jammes, R. *Etudes sur l'oeuvre poétique de Don Luis de Góngora y Argote.* Bordeaux: n.p., 1967.
Orozco Díaz, E. *Lope y Góngora frente a frente.* Madrid: Gredos, 1973.
Vilanova, Antonio. *Las fuentes y los temas del Polifemo de Góngora.* RFE Anejo 66. Madrid: CSIC, 1957.

John Turner

**GONZÁLEZ, Ángel** (1925, Oviedo– ), Spanish poet of the so-called mid-century generation, a group deeply scarred by their childhood experiences in the Civil War of 1936–39 and the difficult years of the Franco regime. This group is characterized by cultivation of "social" poetry of essentially political intent, a protest against political injustice and an expression of striving toward a more humane and just society. The ideological content of much of the group's writing led to deliberate neglect or rejection of many literary devices, resulting in prosaic and limited poetry whose primary aim was to be accessible to the majority of readers. González uses a Spanish approximation of free verse, usually with regular rhythmic patterns. His compositions are brief, and controlled in tone, melancholy or meditative by turns, occasionally ironic. The poet is visualized as simply another man in society, and his personal history is but another link in the collective chain of experience. His first book, *Áspero mundo* (1956; Harsh World), reflects the subdued, indirect criticism of Spanish society characteristic of much poetry of the "social" poets. *Sin esperanza con convencimiento* (1961; Hopelessly with Conviction), which treats the theme of the Spanish Civil War, is followed a year later by *Grado elemental* (1962; Elementary Grade). *Palabra* *sobre palabra* (1972; Word upon Word) repeats the title of a 1965 book but is actually a collection of González's poems to that date, including the foregoing as well as *Tratado de urbanismo* (1967; Treatise upon Urbanity) and *Breves acotaciones para una biografía* (1969; Brief Directions for a Biography) and *Procedimientos narrativos* (1972; Narrative Procedures). It is thus an almost complete poetic works. *Muestra, corregida y aumentada, de algunos procedimientos narrativos y de las actitudes sentimentales que habitualmente comportan* (1977; Sample, Revised and Expanded, of Certain Narrative Procedures and the Sentimental Attitudes That They Generally Accompany) expresses the poet's frustration and that of his generation, having devoted themselves somewhat fruitlessly over the years to opposing Franco without dislodging him until, with his death, their opposition was rendered moot.

BIBLIOGRAPHY

Primary Text

*Palabra sobre palabra.* Barcelona: Barral, 1972.

English Translation

*"Harsh World" and Other Poems.* Tr. Donald D. Walsh. Princeton: Princeton UP, 1977.

Criticism

Alarcos Llorach, E. *Angel González, poeta.* Oviedo: Universidad de Oviedo, 1969.
Brower, Gary. "Angel González: A Portrait, Introduction and Poems." *Mundus Artium: A Journal of International Literature and the Arts* 7.1 (1974): 144–51.
Debicki, Andrew P. "Transformation and Perspective: Angel González." *Poetry of Discovery: The Generation of 1956–1971.* Lexington: U of Kentucky P, 1981.
Palley, Julian. "Angel González and the Anxiety of Influence." *Anales de la Literatura Española Contemporánea* 9.1–3 (1984): n.p.
Villanueva, Tino. "Angel González: De la contemplación lírica a la poesía subversiva." In *Tres poetas de posguerra: Celaya, González y Caballero Bonald.* London: Tamesis, 1988. 117–86.

Janet Pérez

**GONZÁLEZ, Assumpta** (?–?), playwright. To date, there is no information available on her, or her work.

BIBLIOGRAPHY

Primary Texts

*Arribaré a les set . . . Mort!* Barcelona: Millà, 1972.
*El crit del cel.* Barcelona: Millà, 1973.
*De mes verdes en maduren.* Barcelona: Millà, 1970.
*Dos embolics i una recomanació.* Barcelona: Millà, 1961.
*Especialitat en homes.* Barcelona: Millà, 1979.
*La mare . . . Quina nit!* Barcelona: Millà, 1983.
*Les masies de la pau.* Barcelona: Millà, 1972.
*Necessito una infermera* Barcelona: Millà, 1976.
*El Passadís de la mort.* Barcelona: Millà, 1978.

*La Pepeta no és morta.* Barcelona: Millà, 1980.
*El polític supersticiós.* Barcelona: Millà, 1981.
*El preu d'una veritat.* Barcelona: Millà, 1971.
*Quan aparegui l'Estrella o El somni del Rabadà.* Barcelona: Millà, 1976.
*La rateta es vol casar.* Barcelona: Millà, 1962.

Kathleen McNerney

**GONZÁLEZ, Diego Tadeo** (1732, Ciudad Rodrigo, Salamanca–1794, Madrid), poet. González joined the Augustinian order at the age of eighteen and held many important posts within the order, including adjutant general in Andalusia; prior for the Augustinian monasteries in Salamanca, Pamplona and Madrid; secretary for the order in Castile; and rector for the School of Doña María de Aragón in Madrid. Although he dedicated himself to his religious vocation, González also maintained a lifelong interest in poetry which brought him in contact with many of the writers who would dominate Spanish letters in the latter part of the eighteenth c. The presence of José *Cadalso in Salamanca during the early 1770s provided the creative catalyst for the crystallization of a group of aspiring young poets. Cadalso's dominant personality and his stature as a writer were instrumental in developing a coherency of aesthetic principles within the group; Cadalso furnished the model which oriented them toward the lighter, *pastoral verse forms, particularly in the use of anacreontics. The group which formed around Cadalso included university students, such as Juan *Meléndez Valdés, Juan Pablo *Forner and José *Iglesias de la Casa, as well as two Augustinian friars, Juan *Fernández de Rojas and Andrés del Corral. González was introduced into the group by his Augustinian brothers, and after Cadalso left Salamanca in 1774, González assumed the role of adviser for the younger poets, becoming a father figure for them. Under his guidance the group continued to flourish in Salamanca until the end of the decade. Although Cadalso was their literary mentor, González also introduced his younger companions to the works of his close friend Gaspar Melchor de *Jovellanos, whose influence can be seen in their poetry which shows a moral-philosophical orientation.

As a poet himself, González displayed an early affinity for Horace and the classic poets of Spain's sixteenth c., especially *Garcilaso de la Vega and Fray Luis de *León. His mastery of the latter's style was such that he successfully expanded and completed Fray Luis's unfinished *Exposición del Libro de Job* (Exposition on the Book of Job). And, in imitation of Fray Luis, González translated into Spanish several Latin hymns and canticles, among them ''Veni, Creator Spiritus,'' ''Te Deum, Laudamus'' and the ''Magníficat,'' as well as Psalms 9 and 10 from the Old Testament. The majority of González's poetry was of an amorous, even erotic nature. Using the literary appelation Delio, he wrote highly sensuous love poems to ladies identified by the names Mirta, Melisa, Filis and Lisi. It has been intimated that his poetic lovers represented women whom he had known during his travels in Andalusia; certainly the natural sincerity and ardency of his poetic language belie mere repetition of literary conventions and suggests that González was an admirer, if only a spiritual one, of feminine beauty. One of González's most popular poems, the invective "El murciélago alevoso" (The Treacherous Bat), identifies Mirta as a lady from Cádiz who, while writing to her beloved Delio, is frightened by a bat which has flown into her room; the animated quality of the verse is indicative of González's expressive abilities. Resulting from Jovellanos's exhortations to abandon frivolous love poetry in favor of more significant themes, González wrote a very few poems in a more elevated, solemn style: the elegy "Llanto de Delio y profecía de Manzanares" (Delio's Lament and Prophesy of the Manzanares) and the ode "A las Nobles Artes" (To the Noble Arts) are two of his more successful attempts. However, González was unable to sustain the didactic style espoused by his friend. His more ambitious project, suggested by Jovellanos, on "Las edades" (The Ages of Man), was left unfinished at his death; only the first section, "La niñez" (Childhood), was completed. Just before his death González requested that his friend and fellow Augustinian, Fernández de Rojas, burn the manuscripts of his poems—perhaps due to his self-consciousness regarding the amorous nature of his poetry and his desire to leave a more serious-toned poetic legacy. Instead, Fernández saved the mss. and, two years after González's death, published his friend's works. Two further editions of the volume (1805 and 1812) are indications of the success which González achieved in his writings.

BIBLIOGRAPHY

Primary Texts

*Obras.* In *Poetas líricos del siglo XVIII. BAE* 61.
"El murciélago alevoso." Ed. León Verger. In *Revue Hispanique* 39 (1917): 294–301.

Criticism

Cossío, José María. "Naturalismo, convencionalismo. Fray Diego González." In *Notas y estudios de crítica literaria. Poesía española.* Madrid: Espasa-Calpe, 1936. 245–49.
Demerson, G. "Para una biografía de Fray Diego González." *BRAE* 53 (1973): 377–90.
Monguió, Luis. "Fray Diego Tadeo González and Spanish Taste in Poetry in the Eighteenth Century." *RR* 52 (1961): 241–60.
Rodríguez de la Flor, Fernando. "Diez poemas olvidados de Fray Diego González en el *Semanario Erudito y Curioso de Salamanca.*" *Dieciocho* 4.2 (1981): 105–33.

Donald C. Buck

**GONZÁLEZ, Fernando** (1901, Las Palmas, Canary Islands–1972, Valencia), poet. Within the Canary Islands, González's poetry serves as a bridge between Modernist poets and those belonging to later poetic groups. His poetry is intimate and simply structured. In Valladolid he founded Halcón, a publishing house for poetry. His own books include *Las canciones del alba* (1918; Dawn Songs), *Manantiales en la ruta* (1923; Springs along the Way), *Hogueras en la montaña* (1924; Bonfires on the Mountain), *El reloj sin horas* (1929; Hourless Clock), *Piedras blancas* (1934; White Stones) and *Ofrendas de la nada* (1949; Offering Out of Nothingness). *See also* Modernism.

BIBLIOGRAPHY
Primary Texts
*Hogueras en la montaña; poesías 1917–1923*. Madrid: Clásica Española, 1924.
*Piedras blancas*. Madrid: Sáez, 1934.
*El reloj sin horas*. Madrid: Ciudad Lineal, 1929.

Isabel McSpadden

**GONZÁLEZ ANAYA, Salvador** (1879, Málaga–1955, Málaga), novelist, poet. In 1899 he published a collection of poems, *Cantos sin eco* (Songs without Echo), and in 1900, *Medallones* (Medalions). His verse follows the regional trend initiated by *Estébanez Calderón, but through his regional touch one can perceive a romantic, poetic personality. His novels include *Rebelión* (1905; Rebellion), *Sangre de Abel* (1915; Abel's Blood), *El castillo de irás y no volverás* (1921; The Castle of No Return), *Las brujas de la ilusión* (1923; The Witches of Illusion), *La oración de la tarde* (1929; Evening Prayer), and *Nido real de gavilanes* (1931; Royal Nest of Hawks). In 1948 he became a member of the *Academia Española.

BIBLIOGRAPHY
Primary Text
*Obras completas*. Madrid: Biblioteca Nueva, 1948.

Isabel McSpadden

**GONZÁLEZ BLANCO, Andrés** (1888, Cuenca–1924, Madrid), poet, novelist, literary critic and scholar. His first book, *Los contemporáneos* (1907; The Contemporaries), was followed by *Historia de la novela en España* 1909; (History of the Novel in Spain). He published a biography of Ramón de *Campoamor and an annotated selection of his poetry, and directed an edition of Rubén Darío's complete works. Other publications by González Blanco include *Armando Palacio Valdés: Juicio crítico de sus obras* (Armando Palacio Valdés: A Critical Study of His Works), *Escritores representativos de América* (1917; Representative South American Writers), *Los dramaturgos españoles contemporáneos* (1917; Contemporary Spanish Playwrights). He has also contributed to awareness of Portuguese literature in Spain through articles and translations.

BIBLIOGRAPHY
Primary Texts
*Los contemporáneos*. 2 vols. Paris: Garnier, 1907–10.
*Escritores representativos de América*. Madrid: América, 1917.
*Los dramaturgos españoles contemporáneos*. Valencia: Cervantes, 1917.

Isabel McSpadden

**GONZÁLEZ BLANCO, Pedro** (1880, Llanes, Oviedo–1961, Villaseca de la Sagra, Toledo), journalist. Brother of Andrés and Eduardo Blanco, he was a prolific journalist, living in America and participating in the Mexican Revolution with Pancho Villa. He published numerous articles in American journals on the history of Spanish dominance in the Indies and attempted to combat the Spanish *Black Legend—the vision of Spain as a murderous exploiter of virgin lands and peoples.

BIBLIOGRAPHY

Primary Texts

*Conquista y colonización de América por la calumniada España.* Mexico: Rex, 1945.
*Trujillo; o La restauración de un pueblo.* Mexico: Rex, 1946.

English Translation

*Trujillo; the Rebirth of a Nation.* No tr. Trujillo: Caribe, 1953.

Isabel McSpadden

**GONZÁLEZ DE CANDAMO, Bernardo** (1881, Paris–1967, Madrid), journalist. He joined the literary group *Generation of 1898, who valued his knowledge of contemporary French culture. A friend also of Rubén Darío, he served as his guide during Darío's stay in Spain. He used the pseudonym Ivan d'Artedo in the Madrid paper *Hoja de lunes.*

Isabel McSpadden

**GONZÁLEZ DE CLAVIJO, Ruy.** *See* Clavijo, Ruy Gonzalo de

**GONZÁLEZ DE SALAS, José Antonio** (1588, Madrid–1654, Madrid), humanist, erudite scholar. One of the last humanists of *Siglo de Oro Spain, he wrote commentaries on many classical works, but his most lasting piece is the *Nueva idea de la tragedia antigua e ilustración última al libro singular de "Poética" de Aristóteles Stagirita* (1633; New Idea of Ancient Tragedy, and Latest Explanation of the Singular Poetics Book by Aristotle of Stagira). The first Spanish translation of Aristotle's *Poetics* had appeared only seven years earlier. González de Salas generally approved of the *Poetics,* but did defend Spanish theater against the Aristotelian dramatic unities. *See also* Humanism.

BIBLIOGRAPHY

Primary Text

*Nueva idea de la . . . de Aristóteles. . . .* Ed. Cerdá y Rico. 2 vols. Madrid: Sancha, 1778.

English Translation

*The "Satyricon" of Petronius Arbiter Complete . . . Tr. and the readings introduced into the text by De Salas.* Il. J. N. Lindsay. New York: Boni and Liveright, 1922.

**GONZÁLEZ DEL CASTILLO, Juan Ignacio** (1763, Cádiz–1800, Cádiz), dramatist. His work was well received in Cádiz but never found acceptance in Madrid. His *sainetes* boast much local color of Cádiz, and recall those of Ramón de la *Cruz. Representative titles are *El día de toros en Cádiz* (The Bullfight in Cadiz), *El soldado fanfarrón* (The Braggart Soldier), *La maja resuelta* (The Determined Beauty) and *El café de Cádiz* (Cadiz's Café).

BIBLIOGRAPHY

Primary Text

*Obras completas*. 3 vols. Madrid: Hernando, 1914–15.

**GONZÁLEZ LÓPEZ, Emilio** (1903, La Coruña– ), professor emeritus and founding executive officer of the doctoral program in Spanish at the City U of New York, lawyer, diplomat, representative to the Spanish Cortes, literary critic and specialist in Galician studies. His contributions to the fields of Spanish and Galician culture have been recognized through awards such as the Orden de Isabel la Católica (Order of Queen Isabel), the President of the U of the City of New York's medal and, most recently, the Medalla Castelao (Castelao Medal) from the Xunta de Galicia (Galician Autonomous Government).

The first three of his thirty-six books are titles relating to law, while others include monographic studies of Spanish authors such as Pío *Baroja, *Benavente, Emilia *Pardo Bazán and *Valle-Inclán. Twenty-one of his works examine various periods and aspects of Galician history and culture. One of these, *Galicia, su alma y su cultura* (1954; Galicia, Its Soul and Its Culture), was awarded first prize in the annual literary contest of the Centro Gallego de Buenos Aires (Galician Center of Buenos Aires).

A prolific writer, his opus also includes *Historia de la literatura española* (1962–1965; A History of Spanish Literature) in two volumes, and hundreds of articles in journals such as *Cuadernos Hispanoamericanos*, *Insula*, *Revista de La Coruña* and *Grial* on a wide range of topics covering all periods of Spanish and *Galician literature and history.

BIBLIOGRAPHY

Primary Texts

*Historia de la civilización española*. 3rd ed. New York: Las Américas, 1970.
*El arte dramático de Valle-Inclán*. New York: Las Américas, 1967.
*El arte narrativo de Pío Baroja: Las Trilogías*. Madrid: Las Américas, 1971.
*La Galicia de los Austrias*. 2 vols. La Coruña: Fundación Barrio de la Maza, 1981.
*El reinado de Isabel II en Galicia; La Regencia de María Cristina: moderados, pro-gresistas, y carlistas*. La Coruña: Castro, 1984.

Elisa Fernández Cambria

**GONZÁLEZ MARTÍN, Jerónimo P.** (1936, Salamanca– ), poet and founder of a magazine dedicated to Hispanic poetry, *Si la píldora bien supiera no la dorarían por defuera*. He writes protest and non-conformist poetry, in volumes such as *Canto a la desposada y otros versos* (1963; Song to the Married Woman and Other Poems), *Andar a grillos* (1966; Hunting Crickets), *Sinceramente decidido* (1966; Sincerely Decided), *Nuevos heraldos negros; o, Manual del hambriento* (1969; The New Black Heralds or Manual for the Hungry). Also his is the *Ensayo sobre la poesía gallega contemporánea*. (1972; Essay on Contemporary Galician Poetry). *See also* Galician Literature.

BIBLIOGRAPHY

Primary Texts

*Andar a grillos.* Barcelona: n.p., 1966.
*Canto a la desposada, y otros versos.* Zaragoza: Aragonés, 1963.
*Ensayo sobre la poesía gallega contemporánea.* La Coruña: Castro, 1972.
*Nuevos heraldos negros; o, Manual del hambriento.* Barcelona: Bardo, 1969.

Isabel McSpadden

**GONZÁLEZ RUANO, César** (1903, Madrid–1965, Madrid), poet, playwright, novelist, prolific journalist. A part of the *ultraísta* movement in 1920, he contributed to several magazines and was a correspondent in Europe and North Africa. In 1934 his poetic comedy *La luna en las manos* (The Moon in Your Hands) was first performed. His published poems are compiled in two anthologies: *Aún* (Still), writings from 1920 to 1934, and *Poesía* (Poetry), writings from 1934 to 1944. Aside from a biography of Baudelaire, other publications include *Diario íntimo* (1951; Intimate Diary), *A todo el mundo no le gusta el amarillo* (1961; Not Everybody Likes Yellow), *Nuevo descubrimiento del Mediterráneo* (1959; Rediscovering the Mediterranean), *Caliente Madrid* (1961; Hot Madrid), and *Pequeña ciudad* (1963; Small Town).

BIBLIOGRAPHY

Primary Texts

*Diario íntimo.* Barcelona: Noguer, 1952.
*Baudelaire.* Madrid: Hernando, 1931.
*Memorias.* Madrid: Tebas, 1979.
*Pequeña ciudad.* Madrid: Bullón, 1963.

English Translation

*Madrid.* Tr. J. Forrester. 2nd. ed. Barcelona: Noguer, 1955.

Isabel McSpadden

**GONZÁLEZ-RUIZ, Nicolás** (1897, Mataró, Barcelona–1965, Madrid), journalist, translator, biographer. He is author of *Antología de la literatura periodística* (1934; Anthology of Journalism Articles), *La literatura contemporánea* (1943; Contemporary Literature), and a two-volume selection of *Piezas maestras del teatro teológico español* (1946; Masterpieces of Spain's Theological Drama). Also his is a biography series titled "Vidas paralelas" (Parallel Lives), including such titles as *Dos cardenales que gobernaron: Cisneros, Richelieu* (1944; Two Cardinals Who Ruled: Cisneros, Richelieu), *Dos conquistadores: Hernán Cortés, Francisco Pizarro* (1952; Two Conquistadors: Hernán Cortés, Francisco Pizarro), and *Dos favoritos: Potemkin, Godoy* (1944; Two Favorites: Potemkin, Godoy).

BIBLIOGRAPHY

Primary Texts

*Antología de la literatura periodística.* Madrid: n.p., 1934.
*Dos cardenales.* . . . Barcelona: Cervantes, 1944.
*Dos conquistadores.* . . . Barcelona: Cervantes, 1952.
*Dos favoritos.* . . . Barcelona: Cervantes, 1944.

                                                     Isabel McSpadden

**GOY DE SILVA, Ramón** (1883, El Ferrol–1962, Madrid), poet, dramatist, prose author. Almost as forgotten now as he was little known in his lifetime, Goy de Silva nevertheless seems to have been a remarkable figure whose main downfall was writing in an age of literary giants, and never repudiating an art that was already outmoded when he first espoused it. His dramas *La reina silencio* (1911; The Queen of Silence) and *La corte del cuervo blanco* (1914; The Reign of the White Cormorant) as well as several other volumes of short stories and individual poems make up a sizable production of over twenty small volumes. The tired aesthetics of his models, Maurice Maeterlinck, Gabriel D'Annunzio and Edmund Rostand, however, plagued all of Goy's works, limiting his public, his fame, and ultimately his literary worth.

BIBLIOGRAPHY

Primary Texts

*La corte del cuervo blanco.* Madrid: Velasco, 1914.
*La reina silencio.* Madrid: Atenea, 1918.

Criticism

Cejador, J. *Historia de la lengua y literatura castellanas.* Madrid: RABM, 1920. 13: 126–32.
Sáinz de Robles, F. C. *Diccionario de la literatura.* Madrid: Aguilar, 1953. 2: 639.

                                                     Ricardo Landeira

**GOYTISOLO, José Agustín** (1928, Barcelona– ), Catalan poet and anthologist. His early poetry, which includes *El retorno* (1955; The Return), *Salmos al viento* (1956; Psalms to the Wind), *Claridad* (1961; Clarity), *Años decisivos* (1961; Decisive Years) and *Algo sucede* (1968; Something's Happening), established Goytisolo's affinity with the testimonial poets of the second post-war generation. With *Bajo tolerancia* (1973; With Tolerance), his poetry became more experimental. In 1980 he published *Los pazos de cazador* (The Steps of the Hunter), reminiscent of the 1920's imitations of traditional verse forms. He has translated several Italian and Catalan writers and published two anthologies of poetry, *Poetas catalanes contemporáneos* (1968; Contemporary Catalan Poets) and *Nueva poesía cubana* (1969; New Cuban Poetry).

BIBLIOGRAPHY

Primary Texts

*Algo sucede*. Madrid: El Bardo, 1968.
*Años decisivos: poesía 1954–1960*. Barcelona: Colliure, 1961.
*Bajo tolerancia*. Barcelona: Ocnos, 1973.
*Los pazos del cazador*. Barcelona: Lumen, 1980.
*Salmos al viento*. Prologue by José María Castellet. 5th ed. Barcelona: Lumen, 1980.

English Translations

"Silence only." Tr. L. Lowenfels and N. Braymer. In *Literary Review* 7 (1964): 633–34.
Three poems. Tr. T. Hoeksema. In *Dragonfly* 3 (1969): 26–33.
Two poems. Tr. anon. In *Arena* 23 (1965): 68.

Criticism

Castellet, José Maria. "La poesía de José Agustín Goytisolo." *Papeles de Son Armadans* 68 (1971): 302–35.
Miró, Emilio. "Poesía de José Luis Gallego y José Agustín Goytisolo. 2nd ed. Barcelona: Laia, 1980. 7–10.
Vilumara, Martín. "José Agustín Goytisolo: *"Bajo tolerancia."* *Camp de l'Arpa* 14 (1974): 30.

Kay Pritchett

**GOYTISOLO, Juan** (1931, Barcelona– ), novelist and essayist of Basque and Catalonian ancestry. His father, a chemical factory executive, was imprisoned by the Republicans during the Spanish Civil War, and his mother was killed by a Nationalist bombardment in 1938. Goytisolo has lived in France since 1956. *Juegos de manos* (1954; *The Young Assassins*, 1959), his first novel, a very conventional work, is basically a psychological study of a group of angry young men employing the social realism then in vogue. The literal translation of the title "sleight of hand," refers to the gang's tricking David to carry out the execution of a political figure.

*Duelo en el Paraíso* (1955; *Children of Chaos*, 1958) narrates the regression to a primitive state by a group of orphan children during the Spanish Civil War. The "paradise" in the title is ironic: bombs and destruction reign and children become cruel and destructive. Goytisolo experiments with time and space, and the point of view is complex, but progressions from one viewpoint to another lack smoothness. Social criticism appears along with motifs of escapism, executioner-victim, betrayal, loss of innocence, homosexuality, Protean changes (masks) and a mother figure. This novel foretells the type of works Goytisolo will write in his mature period.

With the trilogy *El mañana efímero* (The Ephemeral Tomorrow), Goytisolo both progresses and regresses. *El circo* (1957; The Circus) is probably his weakest novel. In *Fiestas* (1958; *Fiestas*, 1960), a superior work, Goytisolo uses motifs as building blocks; time and space are handled skillfully and viewpoint flows more smoothly. As in *El circo*, the epigraph has a direct relationship to the story.

The novel denounces the ossified social structure of Spanish society and the Catholic church, narrating the interwoven stories of four characters: Pipo, Gorilla, Pira and Professor Rafael Ortega. The background, a religious festival, moves the action to a crescendo at the end. Major motifs are loss of innocence, betrayal, executioner-victim, social criticism, escapism, and homosexuality. *Fiestas* may be considered the best novel of Goytisolo's conventional period.

With *La resaca* (1961; The Undertow), the third part of the trilogy, political preoccupation is more evident, but concern with construction overcomes the novel's documentary aspect. *La resaca* denounces mistreatment of the *murcianos*, shifting its viewpoint to achieve an interesting collage effect. Social criticism, loss of innocence, betrayal, escapism, executioner-victim, homosexuality, and criticism of the United States are among important motifs present.

A transitional period comprising *La isla* (1961; *Island of Women*, 1962) and two travelogues, *Campos de Níjar* (1960; Fields of Nijar) and *La Chanca* (1962; The Chanca), precedes the second trilogy. A definite connection emerges between awareness of the precarious social conditions of the *murcianos* in *Fiestas* and, particularly, *La resaca* and the novelist's subsequent travels throughout southern Spain, recorded in his travelogues. These travels inspire an admiration for Arab culture. Motifs from the travelogues which appear in *The Mendiola Trilogy* are use of cannabis, language itself, Arab culture, and criticism of Spain's past sins.

With *The Mendiola Trilogy* Goytisolo moves away from social criticism; protest is not so important as literature itself, the Spanish language, the sexual taboos of Western civilization, and the identity of man. In *Señas de identidad* (1966; *Marks of Identity*, 1969) Goytisolo begins his experimental phase, the most noticeable aspect being the variation of narrative viewpoints. The story is succinctly given in the epigraph: the life of a Spanish exile, Alvaro Mendiola, residing in France and his voyage back in time as he remembers his family and friends. Goytisolo criticizes the Franco regime by denouncing outrages committed by the Nationalists. Because of the complexity of its plot, *Señas de identidad* has myriad motifs: homosexuality, an overpowering mother figure, sexual phobias, social criticism, loss of innocence, executioner-victim, betrayal, and escapism. Two motifs are used to a greater extent than in earlier novels: a linguistic one which involves a great deal of experimentation and frequent allusions to Arab culture. The techniques of laying bare, de-familiarization, and retardation found throughout *Señas* constitute the first definite instance of the Russian formalists' influence upon Goytisolo.

*Reivindicación del Conde don Julián* (1970; *Count Julian*, 1974), second part of the trilogy, offers a totally new approach to fiction writing in peninsular literature. The plot is extremely complex, with prominent themes and motifs including sexual phobia, the deleterious influence of the United States, social criticism, and language itself. Betrayal, homosexuality, Protean changes (masks), escapism, executioner-victim, and loss of innocence appear in different guises throughout the work. The novel, set in Tangiers, occurs within twenty-four hours, as Alvaro Mendiola mentally assumes the ability to turn himself into the hated Julian to lead the Arabs in a second invasion of Spain, thereby sub-limating his frustration and hate for his mother country. Devices of interest include the utilization of a self-aware narrator, literary borrowing (and intertexts), retardation and de-familiarization. The use of intertexts is perhaps the most important device, endowing the work with a collage texture. Many critics, including Goytisolo himself, have commented on the musical construction of *Don Julián*, in addition to its collage aspect.

With *Juan sin tierra* (1975; *Juan the Landless*, 1977) Goytisolo enters the realm of poetry—oral poetry in prose. The work is basically a new genre, as with Joyce's *Finnegans Wake*, and will not be readily accepted or understood by most readers. There is no unity of time, place, action, characterization, point of view, story or plot (in the conventional sense), and only in the chapters and subdivisions is there evidence of a particular pattern. Certain themes and motifs, however, run throughout the work giving it unity. Epigraphs facilitate a general perspective of two major themes: destruction of language and of Western civilization. Alvaro Mendiola appears again in many guises as well as the author, Goytisolo, by name. The use of literary texts, as in *Don Julián*, serves to criticize as well as praise. Language per se, a creative medium and the primary one of which the work is composed, becomes paradoxically the most destructive tool available.

*Makbara* (1980; Makbara), a coda to the trilogy, continues in the same vein observed in *Juan sin tierra*. And the consensus of the critics is that it is not an improvement on *The Mendiola Trilogy*.

With *Paisajes después de la batalla* (1982; Landscapes after the Battle), however, Goytisolo has entered another stage in his writing. His social criticism is now universal rather than limited to Spanish culture. Furthermore, there is a sense of humor which was not previously noticeable. Further experimentation results in a continuous questioning of literature as an art and of the authority of the narrator. Intertextuality, the self-aware narrator, parody and satire are very important, requiring an active reader. The novel's setting is Paris, in a district called Sentier where many Arabs reside. The narrator-author-protagonist undergoes transformations, becoming several distinct characters, and motifs observed previously are important here as well. *Paisajes* is perhaps Goytisolo's best novel after *Juan sin tierra*.

## BIBLIOGRAPHY

### Primary Texts

*Coto vedado*. Barcelona: Seix Barral, 1985.
*Disidencias*. Barcelona: Seix Barral, 1977.
*En los reinos de taifa*. Barcelona: Seix Barral, 1986.
*Fin de fiesta*. Barcelona: Seix Barral, 1962.
*El furgón de cola*. Paris: Ruedo Ibérico, 1967; Barcelona: Seix Barral, 1976.
*Libertad, libertad, libertad*. Barcelona: Anagrama, 1978.
*Problemas de la novela*. Barcelona: Seix Barral, 1959.

*Pueblo en marcha*. Paris: Librería Española, 1963.
*Las virtudes del pájaro solitario*. Seix Barral, 1988.

English Translations

*Children of Chaos*. Tr. Christine Brooke-Rose. London: McGibbon and Kee, 1958.
*Count Julian*. Tr. Helen R. Lane. New York: Viking, 1974.
*Fiestas*. Tr. Herbert Weinstock. New York: Knopf, 1960.
*Juan the Landless*. Tr. Helen R. Lane. New York: Viking, 1977.
*Marks of Identity*. Tr. Gregory Rabassa. New York: Grove Press, 1969.
*The Young Assassins*. Tr. John Rust. New York: Knopf, 1960.

Criticism

Pérez, Genaro. "Form in Goytisolo's *Juan sin tierra*." *Journal of Spanish Studies: Twentieth Century* 5.2 (Fall 1977): 137–60.
———. *Formalist Elements in the Novels of Juan Goytisolo*. Madrid: Porrúa, 1979.
Schwartz, Kessel. *Juan Goytisolo*. TWAS 104. New York: Twayne, 1970.
Ugarte, Michael. *Trilogy of Treason: An Intertextual Study of Juan Goytisolo*. Columbia: U of Missouri P, 1982.
*The Review of Contemporary Fiction* 4.2 (Summer 1984). Special number on Goytisolo.

Genaro J. Pérez

**GOYTISOLO, Luis** (1937, Barcelona– ), Spanish novelist and short story writer. The youngest of the trio of literary brothers, he studied law and worked in several publishing houses. Early literary recognition came in 1956 when, at the age of nineteen, he won the Sésamo Prize for his short story "Niño mal" (The Sick Child). He was awarded the Biblioteca Breve Prize in 1958 for his novel *Las afueras* (1959; The Outskirts), a work written under the aegis of objectivist "critical realism." Not a novel in the traditional sense, it contains several short stories or novellas, whose characters all have the same set of names, thereby stressing the reiteration of certain similar themes and problems across generations. A definite Marxist substratum is in evidence. The writer's second novel, *Las mismas palabras* (1963; The Same Words), is much more traditional in form, with a straightforward, linear chronology covering only a few days in which the Catalan bourgeoisie is chronicled and dissected, and its underlying anguish revealed. Given the multiplicity of characters, a collective protagonist may be posited. Goytisolo returned to more experimental structures in *Ojos, círculos, buhos* (1970; Eyes, Circles, Owls) and *Devoraciones* (1976; Devourings). Meanwhile, he began his most ambitious and probably most significant novelistic undertaking, a tetralogy entitled *Antagonía*, initiated in 1973 with *Recuento* (Recounting), a complex and massive novel of more than 600 pages which focuses attention upon language and style in a conscious attempt to develop a formalist and structuralist poetics. A definite autobiographical substratum in the early, neo-realistic chapters is integrated with what initially appears to be an objective chronicle of Barcelona in the epoch stretching from the closing months of the civil conflict through the endless post-war years, but which soon proves to contain moral reflections, satire, metaphysical exploration, sexuality and political analysis as well as quantities of literary speculation. The three remaining novels of the cycle include *Los verdes de mayo hasta el mar* (1976; The Green of May as Far as the Sea), *La cólera de Aquiles* (1979; The Rage of Achilles) and *Teoría del conocimiento* (1981; Theory of Knowledge). Although complementary, they are not linked by strict continuity of plot and thus can be read independently. *Los verdes de mayo* is set primarily in Rosas, scene of the denouement of *Recuento*, but connections between the two works are oblique and tangential. Mythic concepts emerge, which are alluded to in the title of the third novel of the cycle. The characters, emblematic and allegorical, serve largely as vehicles for a critique of the writing process, while the narrative is transformed into a Neptunian universe of epically erotic characters. To some extent, the relationship between the first two works of the tetralogy is one of destruction and creation, destruction of "old" (Francoist) myths, and the creation of "new" vital and liberating ones.

In *Antagonía* as a whole, Luis Goytisolo is revealed as a consummate practitioner of the art of metafiction, exploring the nature and limits of the self-conscious novel or fiction within fiction. The creative act per se, the power of language, and the creativity in author and reader are raised to new heights within a series of theoretical pronouncements and speculations which question and explore underlying relationships between life and literature, the world and the written word. *Estela de fuego que se aleja* (1984; Wake of Fire Fading Away) is in some ways an extension of experiments begun in the tetralogy, a blending of fiction with theoretical fictional commentary which obliges the reader to examine the novel's nature and reasons for being. The concept of the writer's dependence upon his fiction for his own being (already implicit in so early a work as *Niebla* of \*Unamuno) is developed extensively in an exploration of the intricate labyrinth of mirrors and multiple levels of meaning which constitutes the text. The nature of the narrative and creative identity, of individual identity, and of the self or the character's relationship to others, to text and context, are additional preoccupations.

## BIBLIOGRAPHY

### Primary Texts

*Estela de fuego que se aleja*. Barcelona: Anagrama, 1984.
*Los verdes de mayo hasta el mar*. Barcelona: Seix Barral, 1976.
*Recuento*. Barcelona: Seix Barral, 1973.

### Criticism

Herzberger, David. "Luis Goytisolo's *Recuento*: Towards a Reconciliation of the Word/World Dialectic." *Anales de la novela de posguerra* 3 (1978): 39–56.
Navajas, Gonzalo. "Internalización e ideología en *La cólera de Aquiles* de Luis Goytisolo." *Hispania* 69.1 (March 1986): 23–33.
Nolens, Ludovico. "Haciendo recuento: Entrevista con Luis Goytisolo." *Quimera* 2 (December 1980): 26–30.
Ortega, José. "Asedio a *Recuento* de Luis Goytisolo." 317 (1976): 488–94.

Riccio, Alessandra. "De las ruinas al taller en la obra de Luis Goytisolo." *Anales de la novela de posguerra* 2 (1977): 31–42.
Suñén, Luis. "Luis Goytisolo o la vida es un libro." *Insula* 39.450 (May 1984): 5–6.

Janet Pérez

*GOZO* (Joy), a religious lyric composition. Popular in Middle Ages verse, the *gozo* praises the virtues, life or deeds of the Virgin Mary or the Saints.

**GRACIÁN, Jerónimo** (1545, Valladolid–1614, Brussels), Carmelite ascetic and mystic writer. Fourth of fifteen children born to *Gracián de Alderete, he became a priest after theological studies at the U of Alcalá. By chance, he became familiar with the Carmelites; quickly he became a follower and close collaborator of Sta. *Teresa and her reform efforts. After her death, he was expelled from the order; Gracián then traveled to Rome seeking reinstatement. In 1593, en route from Sicily to Naples in an *Inquisition ship, he was captured by the Moors and held captive for two years. Freed in 1595, he was reinstated in the order. The rest of his life, he wrote, published and pursued missionary activities in Italy, Spain, and Flanders, where he moved in 1607. His experiences and observations as a captive are contained in the *Tratado de la redención de cautivos* (1596; Treatise on the Redemption of Captives) and in *La peregrinación de Anastasio* (completed 1613; Anastasio's Pilgrimage). The latter also includes autobiographical information concerning years before and after his captivity; it remained unpublished until 1905. Other works include *La lámpara encendida* (1586; The Lighted Lamp), which discusses spiritual responsibilities, and the *Dilucidario del verdadero espíritu* (1604; Explanation of the True Spirit), which outlines the thought of Sta. Teresa. *See also* Asceticism; Mysticism.

BIBLIOGRAPHY

Primary Texts

*Diez lamentaciones del miserable*. Ed., study, O. Steggink. Madrid: Instituto de Estudios Políticos, 1959.
*Jerónimo Gracián, crónica de cautiverio y de misión*. Ed. L. Rosales. Madrid: Fe, 1942.
*Luz de perfección*. . . . Ed., prol. E. Juliá Martínez. Madrid: Suárez, 1927.
*Obras*. Ed., intro. Father Silverio de Sta. Teresa. 3 vols. Burgos: El Monte Carmelo, 1932–33.

Maureen Ihrie

**GRACIÁN DANTISCO, Lucas** (1543, Valladolid–1587, Madrid), erudite scholar, notary, censor, author. Son of *Gracián de Alderete, as censor he granted approval to *Cervantes's *Galatea*. He also worked in the Escorial Library. Two books by him have survived: the *Arte de escribir cartas familiares* (1589; Art of Writing Personal Letters) and the very popular *El Galateo español* (before 1586; *The Spanish Gallant*, 1640). It is an adaptation, not translation, of Giovanni della Casa's *Galateo* (1558). Following Casa's topics closely, but with numerous interpolations and other alterations, the *Galateo español* offers norms of proper conduct and manners to contemporary Spaniards. It underwent numerous editions and translations throughout the seventeenth and eighteenth centuries. M. Morrale provides a detailed comparison of the *Galateo español* with its model in her edition, and also includes new biographical information about Gracián Dantisco. *See also* Censorship.

BIBLIOGRAPHY

Primary Text

*Galateo español.* Ed. study, notes M. Morreale. Madrid: CSIC, 1968.

English Translations

*Galateo espagnol, or the Spanish gallant.* . . . Tr. W.S. London: E. Griffin, 1640.
*Narcissus; or The young man's entertaining mirror.* . . . *Taken from the Spanish and adapted to the manners of the British nation.* By C. Wiseman. London: Bew, 1778.

Maureen Ihrie

**GRACIÁN DE ALDERETE, Diego** (1510?, Valladolid–1600?, ?), secretary and interpreter for Charles V, erudite scholar. He studied with Joan Lluís *Vives in Louvain, and later translated Plutarch and Xenophon, among others. An original work is his *De re militari* (1566; On Warfare).

BIBLIOGRAPHY

Primary Text

*De re militari.* Barcelona: Bornat, 1566.

**GRACIÁN Y MORALES, Baltasar** (1601, Belmonte de Calatayud, Aragon–1657, Tarazona), prose writer. Not a great deal is known of the life of the troublesome Jesuit who, with *Calderón, is the principal literary figure of the denouement of the Golden Age. Possessed of a difficult personality, he was frequently at odds with his order, and of all his secular works, he submitted only one—the *Arte de ingenio, tratado de la agudeza* (1642; *The Mind's Wit and Art,* 1962)—for the company's requisite approval, publishing the rest under transparent pseudonyms. He played an important role in Spanish literature and in the literary circles of Aragon, in particular in that surrounding the famous collector and patron of the arts, Vincencio Juan de Lastanosa. His works distribute themselves into four groups: (1) the politico-moral treatises, *El héroe* (1637; *The Heroe,* 1652); *El político* (1640; The Statesman); and the *Oráculo manual (The Art of Worldly Wisdom,* 1967); (2) two versions of a literary treatise, the *Arte de ingenio* (1642; Art of Genius) and the *Agudeza y arte de ingenio* (1648; Wit and the Art of Genius, tr. *The Mind's Wit and Art,* 1962); (3) the three-part allegorical novel the *Criticón* (1651, 1653, 1657; *The Critick,* 1681); and (4) the religious work *El comulgatorio* (1655; The Communion Book). Of these, it is the first three that interest the student of literature.

## The Politico-Moral Treatises

*El héroe*, partly inspired by Pliny's *Panegyricus Traiano Augustus dictus,* is comprised of twenty sections denominating "qualities," each describing a characteristic technique necessary for the hero's perfection. The four essential abilities are virtue (given primacy of importance but presented last), intellect, valor, and good fortune, with fame the hero's motivating and defining quality. Military and gambling terminology is used to describe the various abilities necessary to avoid opposition and make oneself more powerful in the constant competitive psychological contest that defines interpersonal relationships for Gracián. *El político*, devoid of overt internal division (though some critics perceive a complex triple quintuple arrangement), develops certain particular aspects of the hero, while adding others, substituting prudence for valor, and focusing on the hero's special application to statecraft. The prime example is King Ferdinand the Catholic of Aragon, and the work constitutes a virtual panegyric of this monarch of Gracián's home province. As in *El héroe*, there is appreciation for the need to manipulate others and of the tactical skills to do so. The result in both works is the advocacy of procedures and attitudes that for the modern reader suggest a cynical Machiavellian pragmatism despite Gracián's clear rejection of the Italian's teachings. For Gracián, the essential distinction between the hero-statesman and Machiavelli's Prince is the former's ostensible dedication to virtue and the latter's amoral dedication to success.

*El discreto*, composed of twenty-five "highlights," adopts a different form for each, constituting a sampler of literary forms as well as a thematic continuation of the previous two works, but concentrating on the courtly attributes necessary for the individual to function discreetly and successfully among equals rather than on the uniquely pre-eminent individual. Temperament and intellect constitute discretion's fundaments. The work recommends a "cultural division" of life into three stages of reading, traveling (experiencing), and meditating. The problem of appearance and reality underlies the individual's social situation, which is seen as a constant interplay of the individual's identity, his projection of that identity to others, and his perspicacious penetration of others' projections. The influence of Antonio *Pérez, St. *Ignacio de Loyola, Tacitus and Seneca (*Senequism) is perceptible in parts.

The *Oráculo manual* is a compendium of 300 aphorisms and explications of the previous treatises' thought. It expands rather than adds to what has already been said, and carries to an extreme the laconic, elliptical style present in the previous works.

### The *Agudeza y arte de ingenio*

It is often considered the poetics of *conceptismo*. The work analyzes, documents and advocates the particular literary taste of its age, effectively combining in a conception of complexity, difficulty and tension, the common aesthetic underlying both *conceptismo* and *culteranismo*, regarded by many of Gracián's contemporaries as literary antitheses, though not recognized in the *Agudeza* as

independent or different. The work focuses on the conceit (*concepto), defined
as a concordance or harmonious correlation between two or more recognizable
extremes, expressed by an act of the intellect, as the means by which the desirable
wit is achieved. While metaphor is recognized as a rhetorical device and is one
of the types of conceits considered, it is not, despite its basis in a comparison
of terms, the essence of the conceit, which entails an undefined special tension,
complication, or difficulty in the relationship. In this preference for difficulty,
Gracián appears to follow Aristotle's *Rhetoric* (esp. 3.10), an important element
in the Jesuit *Ratio Studiorum* influencing his literary taste, and as well reflects
the literary preferences of the baroque. In its sixty-five sections or discourses
the work catalogs and exemplifies the various ways in which wit is achieved,
concentrating on literature and verbal wit, but extending the notion to such
combined pictorial-literary forms as the emblem books, and as well to actions
and deeds. The work is notable both for the Baroque aesthetic it embodies and
for its attempt at a national literary criticism that recognizes a unique sharp-
witted Spanish literary style particularly related to the Spanish character and
traceable from Seneca and Martial to *Góngora, *Quevedo, *Paravicino, Mateo
*Alemán, Lope de *Vega, Antonio Pérez, and Fray Luis de *León, chosen (though
not exclusively) in preference to writers of other nationalities, to exemplify the
various techniques under consideration. The definitive version published as the
*Agudeza y Arte de ingenio* is a reworking of the *Arte de ingenio* published several
years later.

### The *Criticón*

Gracián's major work is a three-part allegorical novel in which two protagonists, father and son, Critilo and Andrenio, are involved in a journey-quest
from the isle of St. Helena through seventeenth-c. Spain and Europe to Rome
in search of Felisinda, their wife and mother respectively. Simultaneously they
journey through life from birth to death and the afterlife in search of happiness.
The work is designed as an epic with elements of the Byzantine and *picaresque
particularly evident in its structure. The title, inspired by John Barclay's *Satyricon*
(1603), suggests both the penetrating criticism of seventeenth-c. Baroque society,
and the individual's precarious, vitally critical situation in that society; together
these are the work's constant preoccupations. These concerns are reflected as
well in the designation as *crises* of the thirty-eight individual chapters, and in
the name given to the senior protagonist, Critilo, who personifies judgment and
critical insight and with Andrenio, personifying instinctive inclination, embodies
part of the human spirit split into two contradictory but complementary aspects.
Although Virtelia, virtue, sits at the work's center as an important goal for the
individual, the work is wholly secular in its orientation. In the course of their
pilgrimage the protagonists pass through the major European courts, allegorized
to represent important way stations on life's journey, as well as numerous wholly
allegorical locales. The individual's goal is the successful completion of his life's
course while maintaining his status as a *person,* that is, without succumbing to
the numerous pitfalls of deceit, deception, and immorality that seek to entrap

him. Completion of life's course without falling prey to its dangers in a symbolic moral death is really to have lived, to have lived virtuously, and the individual who successfully completes this task deserves the hero's reward of fame. If he imitates the protagonists' pretended historical example, he will have accomplished a heroic feat and will thus himself be a hero, a worthy model for imitation. In this notion of the hero as a model, in the work's use of allegory, and in its consciousness of the period's emblem books, the *Criticón* forms part of the general emblematic pictorial tendency of the age. Although fundamentally pessimistic in its view of life as a vital struggle to escape entrapment, the work is guardedly optimistic in holding out *desengaño*, the judicious disillusionment and penetration of appearance to reach the reality underlying it, as a tactic for achieving success in that struggle. Within the encompassing form of the allegorical epic journey, the work's three parts correspond to the three stages of youth, maturity, and wise old age, and are loosely oriented in their thematic content, dealing respectively with the individual's formation, his rise to a position of prominence, and his achievement of a sage perspicacity. The thirty-eight *crises* expound the particular themes in a total of some sixty-five individual allegories in which the protagonists are generally either participants or observers. Each *crisis*, while organized around a central allegory that usually gives its name to the chapter, is thus composed of a variety of individual allegories that make masterful and varied use of dialogue, narration, description, satire, and social and psychological insight, and combine erudition, topical references, and satire of types in frequently animated allegorical images that are both aesthetically and intellectually noteworthy. The following *crises* or allegories are particularly successful: the "Fountain of Deceit" (1.7); the "Hermitage of Hipocrinda (Hypocrisy)" (2.7); "Virtelia (Virtue) Enchanted" (2.10); "Honors and Horrors of Vejecia (Old Age)" (3.1); and the jovial rejection of death in the "Mother-in-law of Life" (3.11). In their inspiration the various allegories spring from the author's imagination, classical mythology, medieval allegory, various other literary sources, and emblem literature, in particular that of Alciatus. Combining elements of the novel, historical theory, the epoch's various emblematic forms and medieval allegory, the *Criticón* is related to all but identifiable with none. It is an aggressively eclectic work, hybrid and encyclopedic, that resists categorization.

Gracián was one of the great stylists of his age, successfully employing both the complex oratorical style, and the concise laconic style discussed in the *Agudeza*. He is best known for the latter style, epitomized in the *Oráculo Manual*, and a constant tendency in the *Criticón*. His works show great perception and are modern in their psychological penetration. His writings were popular in Spain and throughout Europe in his own age and later, and his influence may be perceived in La Rouchefoucauld, Mme. de Sablé, Nietzsche, and especially Schopenhauer. Recently Gracián's works have undergone an appreciative reevaluation after having been underestimated for some time. *See also* Siglo de Oro.

BIBLIOGRAPHY

Primary Texts

*Agudeza y arte de ingenio.* Ed., intro, notes, E. Correa Calderón. Clásicos Castalia 14, 15. 2 vols. Madrid: Castalia, 1969.

*El comulgatorio.* Ed. E. Correa Calderón. Clásicos Castellanos 216. Madrid: Espasa-Calpe, 1977.

*El criticón.* Ed., study, J. M. Blecua. 5th ed. Zaragoza: Ebro, 1971.

*El criticón.* Ed. A. Prieto. 2 vols. Madrid: Iter, 1970.

*El discreto.* Ed. M. Romera-Navarro and J. M. Furt. Buenos Aires: Academia Argentina de Letras, 1960.

*El héroe.* Ed. A. Coster. Chartres: Lester, 1911. Facs. of 1639 ed. with unedited Madrid codex.

*Obras completas.* Ed. M. Batllori and C. Peralta. In BAE 229.

*Obras completas.* Ed. Arturo del Hoyo. 2nd ed. Madrid: Aguilar, 1960.

*Oráculo manual y arte de prudencia.* Ed. E. Correa Calderón. Salamanca: Anaya, 1968.

*El político.* Intro. E. Tierno Galván. Ed. E. Correa Calderón. Salamanca: Anaya, 1961.

*Tratados políticos.* Ed. G. Juliá Andreu. Barcelona: Miracle, 1941.

English Translations

*The Art of Prudence.* 3rd ed. London: n.p., 1714.

*The Art of Worldly Wisdom.* Tr. J. Jacobs. New York: Ungar, 1967. (*Oráculo manual*)

*The compleat gentleman.* . . . Tr. T. Saldheld. Dublin: For Whitestone, 1776.

*The critick.* Tr. P. Rycaut. London: Brome, 1681.

*The heroe.* Tr. J. Skeffington. London: Martin/Allestrye, 1652.

*The Mind's Wit and Art.* Tr. L. H. Chambers. Diss., U of Michigan, 1962.

*Sanctuary Meditations for Priests and Frequent Communicants.* Tr. M. Monteiro. London: Washbourne, 1900.

Criticism

Alonso, Santos. *Tensión semántica: lenguaje y estilo de Gracián.* Zaragoza: Institución "Fernando el Católico," 1981.

Borghini, V. *Baldassar Gracián, scritore morale e teorico del concettismo.* Milan: Ancora, 1947.

Bouillier, V. "Baltasar Gracian et Nietzsche." *Revue de Littérature Comparée* 6 (1926): 381–401.

Coster, A. *Baltasar Gracián, 1601–1658.* Zaragoza: Fernando el Católico, 1947.

Forcione, Alban K. "El desposeimiento del ser en la literatura renacentista: Cervantes, Gracián y los desafíos de *Nemo.*" NRFH 34.2 (1985–86): 654–90.

*Gracián y su época. Actas, ponencias y comunicaciones.* Zaragoza: Institución "Fernando el Católico," 1986.

Hartmann, Susanne. *Baltasar Gracián: Sehnsucht nacht dem verlorenen Paradies: Concepto und Weltanschauung.* Hamburg: Romanisches Seminar des Univ. Hamburg, 1986.

Heger, K. *Baltasar Gracián.* . . . Zaragoza: Fernando el Católico, 1960.

Hernández, María Teresa. "La teoría literaria del conceptismo en Baltasar Gracián." *Estudios de Lingüística* 3 (1985–86): 7–46.

Jansen, H. *Die Grundbegriffe des Baltasar Gracián.* Geneva: Droz, 1958.

Kassier, T. L. *The Truth Disguised: Allegorical Structure and Technique in Gracián's "Criticón."* London: Tamesis, 1976.

Lacoste, M. "Les Sources de l'*Oráculo manual* dans l'oeuvre de Baltasar Gracián." *BH* 31 (1929): 93–101.

Livosky, Isabel C. "Función de los personajes en la estructura narrativa de *El criticón* de Baltasar Gracián. *Hispanic Journal* 7.1 (Fall 1985): 29–39.

May, T. E. "An Interpretation of Gracián's *Agudeza y arte de ingenio.*" *HR* 16 (1948): 275–300.

――――. "Gracián's Idea of the 'Concept'." *HR* 18 (1950): 15–41.

Morel-Fatio, A. "Gracián interpreté par Schopenhauer." *BH* 12 (1910): 377–407.

Parker, Alexander A. " 'Concept and 'Conceit': An Aspect of Comparative Literary History." *MLR* 77.4 (Oct. 1982): xxi-xxxv.

Pelegrin, Benito. "Antithèse, métaphore, synecdoque et métonymie: Stratégie de la figure dans l'*Oráculo Manual* de Baltasar Gracián." *Revue de Littérature Comparée* 56.3 (July-Sept. 1982): 339–50.

――――. *Le Fil perdu du* Criticón *de Baltasar Gracián: Objectif Port-Royal: Allégorie et composition "conceptiste."* Aix-en-Provence: Univ. de Provence, 1984.

Pring-Mill, D. F. "Some Techniques of Representation in the *Sueños* and the *Criticón.*" *BHS* 45 (1968): 270–84.

Sarmiento, E. "Gracián's *Agudeza y arte de ingenio.*" *MLR* 27 (1932): 280–92, 420–29.

――――. "On Two Criticisms of Gracián's *Agudeza.*" *HR* 3 (1935): 23–35.

Schroder, G. *Baltasar Gracián's "Criticón."* Munich: Fink, 1966.

Sobejano, Gonzalo. "Prosa poética en *El Criticón*: Variaciones sobre el tiempo mortal." Ed. Hans Dieter Bork, Artur Greive, and Dieter Woll. *Romanica Europae et Americana.* Festschrift für Harri Meier, 8 Jan. 1980. Bonn: Bouvier, 1980. 602–14.

Stinglehamber, L. "Baltasar Gracián et la Compagnie de Jesus." *HR* 22 (1954): 195–207.

Strolle, Jon M. "*Engaño* and Art in the *Criticón.*" *Hispanófila* 58 (1976): 5–17.

Walton, L. B. "Two Allegorical Journeys: A Comparison between Bunyan's *Pilgrim's Progress* and Gracián's *El Criticón.*" *BHS* 36 (1959): 28–36.

Welles, M. L. *Style and Structure in Gracián's "El Criticón."* UNCSRLL Essays 7. Chapel Hill: U of North Carolina P., 1976.

Theodore L. Kassier

**GRACIOSO**, indigenous character type of *Siglo de Oro Spanish drama, a singular voice of realism who, through wit, contrast, and humor, defines and energizes the themes, characters and action of the theater. Also called the *figura del donaire* (character of grace, or charm), antecedents of the *gracioso* are the Greco-Roman slave characters of comedies by Plautus, Terence, and Menander. In Spain, closer forerunners include Calixto's servants in the *Celestina, Ribaldo of the *Libro del Caballero* *Cifar, and the *Arcipreste de Hita's *Libro de buen amor*. Lope de *Vega claimed to have invented the *gracioso;* although he did formalize the essential qualities of the character, the *gracioso* is found earlier in *Torres Naharro's work. Individual personalities of the *gracioso*, who appeared in virtually all Golden Age plays, vary from work to work, but share basic attributes. As C.D. Ley has noted, the *gracioso* was usually a servant or squire of the hero, and functioned as a counterpoint note of realism to his master in personality, deeds, and plot twists. He might satirize the hero's perfection, or balance his master's spiritual or amatory preoccupations and insensibility to time with his own temporal concerns for purely carnal delights and desire for food, drink, or sleep. To underscore the hero's bravery, he was often a coward. Always loyal to his master, frequently his confidant, he sometimes expressed facts or truths others dared not voice. A constant fount of humor, his shrewd, witty observations and repartee could glitter; in other cases, laughter stemmed from his foolishness. The function of the *gracioso* is particularly vivid in tragic works, where he could brilliantly, starkly accent the action and add intense, immediate realism to bridge the relation between hero and audience.

If Lope formulated the essential features of the *gracioso*, the character reached its apogee in *Moreto. *Rojas Zorrilla, *Tirso, *Calderón, and others employed him to great advantage. *Graciosos* continued to appear in eighteenth-c. theater, but by then they had deteriorated into cardboard figures. *See also* Theater in Spain.

BIBLIOGRAPHY

Criticism

Ley, C. D. *El gracioso en el teatro de la península: Siglos XVI-XVII.* Madrid: RO, 1954.
Montesinos, J. F. "Algunas observaciones sobre la figura del donaire en el teatro de Lope de Vega." In *Estudios sobre Lope.* Salamanca: Anaya, 1969.

                                                                                Maureen Ihrie

**GRANADA, Luis de,** religious name of Luis de Sarría (1504, Granada–1588, Lisbon), Dominican monk, preacher-orator and writer of ascetical, devotional literature. Luis de Granada spent many years in Lisbon and preached before Phillip II there. Although his works abound with references to St. Thomas Aquinas and to St. Augustine, Granada demonstrates a propensity to adhere to St. Francis's religious world view. This Franciscanism can be observed in his descriptions of nature as well as in his preference for an affective rather than speculative mode of prayer, meditation and contemplation; he imbues his Thomistic-Scholasticism with a love for all Creation that will ultimately lead him to love God. Granada also expounds an inner or interior religiosity in his methods of praying. His ascetical writings combine classical techniques of rhetoric (Cicero) with a profound knowledge of biblical and patristic sources and the writings of medieval Christian writers.

Luis de Granada is also noted for his strong defense of the use of the vernacular tongue in religious writing, to which his Dominican training was opposed. His most extensive ascetical work, *Introducción del símbolo de la fe* (Salamanca, 1583: *God Cares for You*, 1944), is a defense of the Christian (Catholic) faith divided into four books. Book 1 contains many beautiful descriptions of nature as Granada proposes to lead his reader to the knowledge of God through a detailed observation of all Creation.

In his most ascetical work, called *Guía de pecadores* (Lisbon, 1556; *The Sinner's Guyde*, 1598), he attempts to convince the sinner to abandon the sinful life by offering the necessary rules (reglas) to teach him how to live well (*bien vivir*). The book contains vividly horrid descriptions of eternal damnation in hell followed by discussion of the delights of paradise. In the *Memorial de la vida cristiana* (Salamanca, 1570; *A Memoriall of a Christian Life*, 1586), Granada comes closer to a mystical expression wherein he differentiates between ''la oración mental'' (mental prayer) and ''la oración vocal'' (oral prayer). He shows preference for mental prayer since it is by praying in this manner that the individual will hold God in his heart. The prologue to the *Memorial* outlines the essential differences between speculative or intellectual doctrines (catecismos) and a more practical one which can move the will to exercise the Christian virtues.

Granada wrote a meditative work called *Libro de la oración y meditación* (Salamanca, 1554; *Of Prayer and Meditation*, 1582 [not to be confused with a book of the same title by San Pedro of *Alcántara]). It guides the individual meditating with a series of daily meditations. His instructions on the manner in which one is to pray once more place emphasis on an inner lifting up of the soul to God. In Part 1, Ch. 10, Granada advises *quietud y recogimiento de corazón* (quietude and gathering in of the heart) in his instructions on how to pray and meditate. This method of prayer is common to religious reformers such as Francisco de *Osuna, Tomás de *Villanueva and St. *Teresa. Granada's influence is manifest not only in his religious writings, but also in his contribution to Castilian prose through his mixture of Ciceronian rhetorical devices with popular Castilian modes of expression that is so characteristic of Spain's *Renaissance. *See also* Asceticism; Catechetical Literature; Mysticism.

BIBLIOGRAPHY

Primary Texts

*Guía de pecadores*. Clásicos Castellanos 97. Madrid: Espasa-Calpe, 1953.
*Memorial de la vida cristiana*. Rev. ed. Madrid: G. Rodríguez, 1622.
*Obras. BAE*. Vols. 6, 8 and 11.

English Translations

*God Cares for You*. Tr. Edmond C. McEniry. Columbus, Ohio: College Book, 1944.
*A Memoriall of a Christian Life*. Tr. Richard Hopkins. St. Omer, France: John Heigham, 1625.
*Of Prayer and Meditation*. Tr. Richard Hopkins. Douai: n.p., 1612.
*The Sacred Passion*. Tr. Edward J. Schuster. St. Louis: Herder, 1960. (Taken from *Guía de pecadores, Libro de oración y meditación* and the *Adiciones al memorial*.)
*The Sinner's Guyde*. Tr. Francis Meres. Dublin: n.p., 1803.

Criticism

Cuervo, Fray Justo. *Biografía de Fray Luis de Granada*. 4 vols. Salamanca: Gel. del Amo, 1896.
Laín Entralgo, Pedro. *La antropología de Fray Luis de Granada*. Madrid: CSIC, 1947.

Llaneza, Maximino. *Bibliografía de Fray Luis de Granada*. 4 vols. Salamanca: Calatrava, 1926–28.

Angelo DiSalvo

**GRANDE, Félix** (1937, Mérida, Badajoz– ), poet, critic and fiction writer. His early poems recall the simple but original expression of Neruda; anguish and harsh images often mark his later compositions. His major collections include *Las piedras* (1964; Stones), *Música amenazada* (1966; Menaced Music), *Blanco spirituals* (1967; White Spiritual), *Taranto* (1971; Taranto), his collected poetry, *Biografía* (1971; Biography), and *Las rubáiyátas de Horacio Martín* (1978; The Rubaiyats of Horacio Martín). His collections of short fiction, essays and impressions include *Por ejemplo, dos cientos* (1968; For Example, Two Hundred), *Occidente, ficciones y yo* (1968; The West, Fictions and I) and *Elogio de la libertad* (1984; In Praise of Liberty). He has received important awards, such as the Adonais in 1963 and the National Prize for Literature in 1978. Currently he directs *Cuadernos Hispanoamericanos*.

BIBLIOGRAPHY

Primary Texts

*Años (Antología)*. Madrid: Nacional, 1975.
*Biografía (1964–1971)*. Barcelona: Seix Barral, 1971.
*Blanco spirituals*. Barcelona: El Bardo, 1969.
*Las piedras*. Madrid: Rialp, 1964.
*Las rubáiyátas de Horacio Martín*. Barcelona: Lumen, 1978.

English Translation

Poems in *Recent Poetry of Spain*. Tr. Louis Hammer and Sara Schyfter. Old Chatham, NY: Sachem, 1983. 252–65.

Criticism

Brotherston, G. "The Speaking Voice in Félix Grande's Poetry." In *Studies in Modern Spanish Literature and Art Presented to Helen F. Grant*. Ed. Nigel Glendinning. London: Tamesis, 1972. 1–12.
Carreño, Antonio. *La dialéctica de la identidad en la poesía contemporánea. La persona. La máscara*. Madrid: Gredos, 1984. 211–21.
García Martín, J. L. "Poesía social y creatividad lingüística." *CH* 129 (1982): 157–65.
Miró, Emilio. "Félix Grande y su heterónimo Horacio Martín." *Ínsula* 385 (1978):6.
Ortega, J. "Tanatos y Eros en la poesía de Félix Grande." *CH* 127 (1982): 141–51.

Kay Pritchett

**GRANDMONTAGNE, Francisco** (1866, Barbadillo de los Herreros, Burgos–1936, Barcelona), prose writer. Even after Grandmontagne emigrated to Argentina, he maintained contact with his native Spain and spent his final years in that country. His works deal with the difficulties encountered by immigrants and with life on the Argentinian pampa. A collaborator of Argentinian journals, Grandmontagne was himself the subject of articles by Ramiro de *Maeztu. Also esteemed by *Unamuno, he shared interests and ideas with the Spanish *Generation of 1898.

BIBLIOGRAPHY

Primary Texts

*Una gran potencia en esbozo.* Madrid: Diana, 1928.
*Los inmigrantes prósperos.* Madrid: Aguilar, 1933.
*La Maldonada (costumbres criollas).* Buenos Aires: Artística, 1898.
*Paisajes de España: Galicia y Navarra.* Buenos Aires: Montmasson, 1922.
*Teodoro Foronda (evoluciones de la sociedad argentina).* Buenos Aires: La Vasconia, 1896.
*Vivos, tilingos y locos lindos.* N.p.: n.p., n.d.

Kathleen March

**GRANELL, Eugenio Fernández** (1912, La Coruña– ), novelist and painter. Granell's early studies included music at the Conservatory of Madrid and painting with his mother and brother in his native Galicia. In 1939 he left Spain and lived in France, Santo Domingo, Guatemala, Puerto Rico and, in 1957, New York. He received his doctorate from the New School for Social Research and taught at Brooklyn College of the City U of New York until his retirement in 1983. He currently resides in Madrid.

After meeting André Breton in Santo Domingo in 1941, Granell joined the surrealist movement and participated in its international expositions, and in 1960, the "Phases" movement of Paris. His writing career began first as a journalist and in 1949 he published his first book, *Arte y artistas en Guatemala* (1949; Art and Artists in Guatemala), a literary collage of highly creative humorous notes and comments on a wide range of international artists and writers connected in some way with Guatemala. *Isla, cofre mítico* (1951; Island, Mythical Coffer) is a combination of poetry, essay, biography and criticism inspired by André Breton's visit to Martinique with a group of surrealists. Granell's *La novela del Indio Tupinamba* (1959; The Novel of the Indian Tupinamba) is his most outstanding achievement in fiction and has the distinction of being the only humoristic and surrealistic satire of the Spanish Civil War, covering its prelude, open hostilities and exile. The short novel *El clavo* (1967; The Nail) is a rare Spanish example of science fiction, satirizing a society that has supposedly reached perfection when it is suddenly menaced by the ominous reappearance of a relic of earlier violent times, a nail. *Lo que sucedió* (1968; What Happened), which won the International Don Quixote Prize, is a surrealist novel of loosely related episodes and satire of Spain set in Galicia and Europe during World War II. Granell published in 1970 *Federica no era tonta y otros cuentos* (Federica Wasn't Dumb and Other Stories), an extraordinary collection of ten stories that includes oneiric terror, poetic absurdity, and gratuitous humor, unified by the surrealist opposition to conformity. Federica, who manages to give birth in a totally new way, is one of Granell's most extraordinary creations.

Granell has written several books of essays on literature and painting. *"La leyenda"* *de Lorca y otros escritos* (1913; "The Legend" by Lorca and Other Writings) contains studies of *García Lorca, Pío *Baroja, *Valle-Inclán, *Garcilaso de la Vega, and Goya, as well as some unusual themes such as the motifs of the flying woman and the barking dog in literature and art. *Picasso's "Guernica"; the End of a Spanish Era* (1981) considers *Guernica* an epitaph for Republic Spain that depicts the demise of ancient Spanish myths and interprets its symbolic meaning. In 1981 Granell published a small volume of surrealist poetry, *Estela de presagios* (Trail of Presages).

Granell's commitment to surrealism is more than that of a stylist; it represents a total aesthetic commitment to the ideals of artistic nonconformity and creative freedom. Even within the surrealist movement his literary and pictorial works are considered highly original, characterized by uncontainable, spontaneous humor and extraordinary inventiveness.

BIBLIOGRAPHY

Primary Texts

*El clavo.* Madrid: Alfaguara, 1967.
*Federica no era tonta y otros cuentos.* Mexico: Costa-Amic, 1970.
*Lo que sucedió.* Mexico: España Errante, 1968. Illustrated by the author.
*La novela del Indio Tupinamba.* Madrid: Fundamentos, 1982.
*Picasso's "Guernica": The End of a Spanish Era.* Ann Arbor: UMI Research P, 1981.

Criticism

Baeza Flores, Alberto. "La odisea española del 'Guernica': Un libro de Fernández Granell." *Hoy* (Santo Domingo) Dec. 12, 1981: 16.
Galán Lores, Carlos. "El surrealista Tupinamba." *Alerta* (Santander) Oct. 20, 1982: 9.
Irizarry, Estelle. *La inventiva de E. F. Granell.* Madrid: Ínsula, 1976.
Sobejano, Gonzalo. *Novela española de nuestro tiempo.* 2nd ed. Madrid: Prensa española, 1975. 75–6.

Estelle Irizarry

**GRANELL, Manuel** (1906, ?– ), poet, prose writer. Under the pen name Manuel Cristóbal he published a book of sonnets, *Umbral* (1941; Threshold). He has written a book about *Azorín, and *Cartas filosóficas a una mujer* (1946; Philosophical Letters to a Woman), as well as *Lógica* (1948; Logic), *Ortega y su filosofía* (1960; Ortega and His Philosophy), *El hombre, un falsificador* (1968; Man, the Falsifier), and *La vecindad humana* (1970; Human Neighborhood).

BIBLIOGRAPHY

Primary Texts

*Etnología y existencia.* Caracas: Equinoccio, 1977.
*Estética de Azorín.* Madrid: Biblioteca Nueva, 1949.

*El hombre, un falsificador*. Madrid: RO, 1968.
*Ortega y su filosofía*. Madrid: RO, 1960.

Isabel McSpadden

**GRANJEL, Luis G.** (1920, Vigo?– ). The holder of a chair of the history of medicine at the U of Salamanca, he published several works related to his professional specialization, including *Gregorio Marañón, su vida y su obra* (1960; Gregorio Marañón's Life and Work), *Humanismo y medicina* (1968; Humanism and Medicine), etc. He has also contributed many biographies and critical studies of members of the *Generation of 1898 and of the group as a whole, and has written critical essays on some of the succeeding generation. Among his more significant titles are *Retrato de Pío Baroja* (1953; Portrait of Pío Baroja), *Retrato de Unamuno* (1957; Portrait of Unamuno), and *Retrato de Azorín* (1958; Portrait of Azorín). His overviews of this literary movement include *Panorama de la generación del 98* (1959; Panorama of the Generation of 1898) and *La generación literaria del 98* (1966; The Literary Generation of 1898).

BIBLIOGRAPHY

Primary Texts

*La generación literaria del noventa y ocho*. Salamanca: Anaya, 1966.
*Humanismo y medicina*. Salamanca: Universidad, 1968.
*Maestros y amigos de la Generación del noventa y ocho*. Salamanca: Universidad, 1981.
*La medicina española renacentista*. Salamanca: U of Salamanca, 1980.
*Retrato de Azorín*. Madrid: Guadarrama, 1958.

Janet Pérez

**GRASSI DE CUENCA, Angelina** (1823, Cremá, Italy–1883, Madrid), novelist, journalist, poet. The daughter of an Italian musician who moved to Barcelona in 1826, and later to Madrid, Angelina spoke French and Italian, but wrote in Spanish. Her brother, a distinguished musician and member of a national orchestra in Madrid, also owned the magazine *El correo de la moda*. For many years, Angelina managed this publication, collaborating with many authors and on other magazines. A member of various literary groups, she contributed to such poetry magazines as *El libro de la caridad* (1879), *Album calderoniano* (1881), *El novísimo romancero español* (1880), and, especially, *La violeta*, a feminist publication managed by her friend and colleague Faustina *Sáez de Melgar.

From 1842 to 1878, she published many novels, a book of poems, plays, and *Palmas y laureles* (1884; Palms and Laurels)—a collection of readings for schoolchildren which was awarded a prize in a contest in Caracas, Venezuela, declared an official textbook, and published posthumously. Her novel *La gota de agua* (1875; The Drop of Water) won a prize in Madrid (1875), and *Las riquezas del alma* (1866; The Riches of the Soul) was honored by the *Academia Española. Grassi de Cuenca's fiction possesses a moral tone and a focus on female characters and preoccupations; it often searches to define women's role in society. Her poetry tends toward *Romanticism.

BIBLIOGRAPHY

Primary Texts

*El copo de nieve. Novela moral y de costumbres.* Madrid: Estrada, 1876.
*La dicha en la tierra. Novela histórica original.* N.p.: n.p., n.d.
*La gota de agua. Novela moral.* Madrid: Estrada, 1875.
*Marina. Narración histórica.* Manila: Ramírez y Giraudier, 1878.
*Los que no siembran no cogen.* Madrid: Galiano, 1868.
*Palmas y laureles.* Barcelona: Bastinos, 1884.
*Poesías de la señorita.* . . . Madrid: Trujillo, 1851.
*Las riquezas del alma.* Madrid: El Cascabel, 1866.

Criticism

Cejador y Frauca, Julio. *Historia de la lengua y literatura castellana.* 14 vols. Madrid: Archivos, 1915–22. Vol. 7.
*Women Writers of Spain. An Annotated Bio-Bibliographical Guide.* Ed. C. Galerstein and K. McNerney. Westport, CT: Greenwood, 1986. 133–36.

Cristina Enríquez

**GRAU, Jacinto** (1877, Barcelona–1958, Buenos Aires), playwright and novelist, since 1939 exiled in Argentina. Among his major works are *Entre llamas* (1905; Amid Flames), *El conde Alarcos* (1907; Count Alarcos), *Don Juan de Carillana* (1913), *El hijo pródigo* (1917; The Prodigal Son, 192?), *En Ildaria* (1917), *El señor de Pigmalión* (1921; Mr. Pygmalion), *El caballero Varona* (1929; Varona, the Gentleman), *El burlador que no se burla* (1930; The Seducer Who Does Not Seduce), *Tres Locos del Mundo* (1930; The Three Madmen of the World), *La casa del diablo* (1942; The Devil's House), *Las gafas de don Telesforo* (1949; Don Telesforo's Glasses), *Bibí Carabé* (1954) and *En el infierno se están mudando* (1958; Moving Day in Hell). Grau is an important twentieth-c. Spanish dramatist who became embittered in light of the little recognition his theater attracted. His most famous play, *El señor de Pigmalión*, is an intensely dramatic work combining tragic and farcical elements in a successful manner. Throughout his career, Grau rejected the realistic bourgeois theater of his times as he found that commercial considerations, more often than not, were given greater importance than the artistic characteristics of plays. Beside experimenting with tragedy and farce, Grau devoted his attention to Spanish myths.

BIBLIOGRAPHY

Primary Texts

*El señor de Pigmalión. El burlador que no se burla.* Madrid: Espasa-Calpe, 1976.
*Teatro.* 2 vols. Buenos Aires: Losada, 1954 and 1959.

English Translation

*The Prodigal Son: Parable in Three Acts.* Tr. J. Garret Underhill. New York: Rosenfeld, 1920s.

Criticism

Díaz, Janet W. "Jacinto Grau and His Concept of the Theater." *REH* 5 (1971): 203–21.
García Lorenzo, Luciano. *El tema del Conde Alarcos. Del Romancero a Jacinto Grau.* Madrid: CSIC, 1972.
González-del-Valle, Luis T. "Farsa y tragedia en *El señor de Pigmalión.*" In *El teatro de Federico García Lorca y otros ensayos sobre literatura española e hispanoamericana.* Lincoln: Society of Spanish and Spanish American Studies, 1980. 197–212.
Kronik, John W. "Art and Ideology in the Theater of Jacinto Grau." *KRQ* 16 (1969): 261–76.
Navascués, Miguel. *El teatro de Jacinto Grau.* Madrid: Playor, 1975.

Luis T. González-del-Valle

**GRIEN, Raúl** (1924, La Coruña– ), journalist and novelist. His novel *A fuego lento* (Slow Fire) was a finalist for the Premio Planeta in 1956. He also writes novelettes: *Tronos de miseria* (Misery's Thrones) and *Diario hablado* (News Bulletin). His book of short stories *Haciéndome a la mar* (Going to Sea) has a foreword by Pío *Baroja.

BIBLIOGRAPHY

Primary Texts

*A fuego lento.* Barcelona: Mateu, 1957.
*Cuatro esquinas.* Montevideo: Alfa, 1968.

Isabel McSpadden

**GRIMALDI, Juan de** (1796, Avignon–1872, Paris), impresario, stage director, dramatist and journalist. Grimaldi wrote the most popular play performed in Spain in the first half of the nineteenth c.: *La pata de cabra* (1829; The Goat's Foot). It earned enormous sums of money when staged during the years preceding the apogee of *Romanticism—people flocked to Madrid from all over Spain to see this farcical, entertaining *comedia de magia (play with spectacular stage effects).* José *Zorrilla wrote that more than 72,000 provincial passports were stamped with approval for their bearers to come to Madrid to see it. It remained popular throughout the nineteenth c. and was only eclipsed after 1850 by the growing success of Zorrilla's *Don Juan Tenorio.* Grimaldi was a native Frenchman who served as impresario and stage director of the Cruz and Príncipe theaters in Madrid from 1823 to 1836. He was one of the most influential members of the *tertulia* "el Parnasillo" and a friend and patron of *Bretón de los Herreros, Ventura de la *Vega, Mariano José de *Larra, and *García Gutiérrez. He trained the best actors of the Romantic period—José García Luna, Antonio Guzmán, Julián Romea, Matilde Díez and Concepción Rodríguez (whom he married in 1825)—and staged the most famous Romantic plays, including *Martínez de la Rosa's *La conjuración de Venecia,* Larra's *Macías,* *Rivas's *Don Álvaro,* and García Gutiérrez's *El trovador.* As an editor of *La Revista Española* (Spanish

Review), he published articles on education, the Carlist War and Juan Alvarez
*Mendizábal.

He translated two plays from the French, the successful melodrama *La huér-
fana de Bruselas* (1825; The Orphan from Brussels) and the less popular *Lord
Dadvenant* (1826). In 1835, he collaborated with Bretón and Vega on a play
written to support the Queen Regent's cause against the rebel Carlists, titled
*1835 y 1836, o lo que es y lo que será* (1835 and 1836, or What Is and What
Will Be).

Following the Sargeant's Revolt at La Granja in 1836, Grimaldi left Spain
for Paris, where he served as a confidant and, ultimately, a diplomat and agent
for María Cristina and the Prime Minister Ramón de Narváez. His enormous
wealth and prestige made him one of the prime minister's most important contacts
abroad and one of the most trusted liaisons between the Spanish government
and the government of Napoleon III. *See also* Theater in Spain.

BIBLIOGRAPHY

Primary Text

*La pata de cabra.* 2nd ed. Madrid: Repullés, 1836.

Criticism

Duffey, F. M. "Juan de Grimaldi and the Madrid Stage." *HR* 10 (1942): 147–56.
Gies, D. T. "Juan de Grimaldi y el año teatral madrileño, 1823–24." In *Actas del VIII
       Congreso Internacional de Hispanistas.* Madrid: Istmo, 1986.
———. "Juan de Grimaldi y la máscara romántica." *Romanticismo 2: Atti del III-
       Congresso sul Romanticismo.* Genoa: Biblioteca di Lett., 1984. 133–40.
———. "Larra, Grimaldi and the Actors of Madrid." *Studies in Eighteenth-Century
       Spanish Literature and Romanticism.* Newark: Juan de la Cuesta, 1985. 113–22.
———. *Theatre and Politics in Nineteenth-Century Spain: Juan de Grimaldi as impre-
       sario and Government Agent.* Cambridge: Cambridge UP, 1988.

David Thatcher Gies

**GROSSO, Alfonso** (1928, Seville– ), novelist. A versatile writer, Grosso has
shown an ability to assimilate or anticipate new trends in the novel. He initiated
his career in the critical or social-realistic mode with novels like *La zanja* (1961;
The Ditch) and *El capirote* (1966; The Hood), set in Seville during Holy Week.
These provide a penetrating, yet somewhat tendentious, view of life in his native
Andalusia. The varied, complex narrative technique and baroque style which
characterize much of his later work are present even in these earlier novels, but
are confirmed in *Inés Just Coming* (1973), whose setting is the Cuban revolution.
The narration at several levels by different narrators, a technique continued in
*Guarnición de silla* (1970; Cavalry Troop) and *Florido Mayo* (1973; May in
Bloom), blends past and present through flashback and interior monologue. *Los
invitados* (1978; The Invited), which reconstructs the events that led to the
multiple murders on a farm in Paradas, and *El correo de Estambul* (1980; The
Istanbul Run), a story of international intrigue, are best-sellers. His most recently
published novel, *Con flores a María* (1981; With Flowers to Mary), was actually

written in 1962 and explores the corrupt values of an Andalusian aristocrat against the background of the annual pilgrimage to the Virgin of the Rocío.

BIBLIOGRAPHY

Primary Texts

*La buena muerte*. Barcelona: Planeta, 1976.
*El capirote*. Barcelona: Seix Barral, 1974.
*Un cielo difícilmente azul*. Barcelona: Seix Barral, 1972.
*Con flores a María*. Madrid: Cátedra, 1981.
*El correo de Estambul*. Barcelona: Planeta, 1980.
*Florido mayo*. Madrid: Alfaguara, 1973.
*Germinal y otros relatos*. Barcelona: Seix Barral, 1971.
*Guarnición de silla*. Barcelona: Seix Barral, 1971.
*Inés Just Coming*. Barcelona: Planeta, 1977.
*Los invitados*. Barcelona: Planeta, 1978.
*Por el río abajo*. Paris: Librairie du Globe, 1966.
*Testa de copo*. Barcelona: Seix Barral, 1971.
*La zanja*. Barcelona: Destino, 1961.

Criticism

Bosch, Rafael. *La novela española del siglo XX*. 2 vols. New York: Las Américas, 1970.
Domingo, José. *La novela española del siglo XX*. 2 vols. Barcelona: Labor, 1973.
————. "Del realismo crítico a la nueva novela." *Ínsula* 290 (1971): 5.
————. "Del hermetismo al barroco: Benet y Grosso." *Ínsula* 320–21 (1973): 30.
Gil Casado, Pablo. *La novela social española*. 2nd ed. Barcelona: Seix Barral, 1973.

Porter Conerly

**GUARNER, Luis** (1902, Valencia– ), Spanish poet and philologist, he spent most of his life as a teacher of literature. Among his poetic collections are *Breviario sentimental* (1921; Sentimental Breviary), *Realidad inefable* (1924; Ineffable Reality), and *Al aire de Tu vuelo* (1946; To the Air of Your Flight). He did a dual paleographic and modernized edition of the twelfth-c. *Cantar de mio Cid* and also translated various French poets including Hugo, Musset, Rodenbach and Verlaine, as well as translating works of Heine from German and *Verdaguer i Santaló from Catalan. He is the author of an extensive general bibliography on the latter, published by the *Academia Española.

BIBLIOGRAPHY

Primary Texts

*Al aire de Tu vuelo*. Madrid: EPESA, 1946.
*El amor en la poesía; breviario universal*. . . . Madrid: Aguayo, 1950.

**GUELBENZU, José María** (1944, Madrid– ), Spanish novelist whose early novels belong to the experimentalist phase which began at the end of the 1960s and beginning of the 1970s. His first novel, *El mercurio* (1968; Mercury), fits fully within the neo-vanguardist experimental mold, as does *Antifaz* (1970; Mask), which presents a number of parallel or alternative outcomes. Both are fragmented narratives with unconventional syntax and punctuation. Like the new poets emerging at the same time, many novelists of this period turned increasingly to linguistic and lexical innovation, incorporated a broad range of intellectual and cultural motifs and literary allusions, and returned to the subjectivity eschewed by their predecessors. A modified surrealism and neo-vanguardism are sometimes combined with startlingly Baroque elements, reality and verisimilitude cease their dominance, and clarity and facility of the text are no longer goals. Guelbenzu's literary apprenticeship produced a volume of poems, *Espectros, La casa antigua* (1967; Specters, the Ancient House). *El pasajero de Ultramar* (1976; The Passenger from Across the Sea) initiates the return to a more traditional form of punctuation and syntax, and is to a large extent a work of character analysis.

*La noche en casa* (1977; A Night at Home) presents a one-night sexual encounter between two former classmates who meet by chance in the train station while both are en route to other adventures. They apparently have known each other too long to be lovers or to expect too much of a "cosmic experience" from sexual union, and the resulting disillusionment spoils their friendship. *El río de la luna* (1981; Moon River) also revolves around an erotic liaison, in this case an overwhelmingly powerful sexual attraction which sweeps everything in its path, despite a lack of real love or communication between the partners. So powerful is the urge which overcomes them as they drive upon a narrow, dangerous road, that they are in imminent peril of death. The man's instinct for self-preservation, which recalls him to reality in the nick of time, is seen by the woman as an unforgivable shortcoming in love. *El esperado* (1984), by contrast with its two immediate predecessors, belongs to the general body of literature of apprenticeship, rites of passage and initiation. This novel presents the world of Spanish adolescents in the late 1950s via the fifteen-year-old protagonist's first stay away from home. His discovery of abnormal psychology and adult sexuality plus the strong erotic presence in the novel constitute links to the writer's preceding titles. All three share a more straightforward narrative style and technique, the interest in psychological problems and character development, and many of the same rhetorical figures.

BIBLIOGRAPHY

Primary Texts

*Antifaz*. Barcelona: Seix Barral, 1970.
*El esperado*. Madrid: Alianza, 1984.
*El Mercurio*. Barcelona: Seix Barral, 1968.
*La noche en casa*. Madrid: Alianza, 1977.
*El pasajero de Ultramar*. Barcelona: Galba, 1976.
*El río de la luna*. Madrid: Alianza, 1981.

Criticism

Herzberger, David. "Experimentation and Alienation in the Novels of José María Guelbenzu." *Hispania* 64 (September 1981): 367–75.
———. "The 'New' Characterization in José María Guelbenzu's *El río de la luna*." In

*Nuevos y novísimos: Algunas perspectivas críticas sobre la narrativa española desde la década de los 60*. Eds. R. Landeira and L.T. González-del-Valle. Boulder: Society of Spanish and Spanish American Studies, 1987. 83–95.

Pérez, Janet. "Rhetorical Structures and Narrative Techniques in Recent Fiction of José María Guelbenzu." In *Nuevos y novísimos*. . . . 131–49.

Roberts, Gemma. "Amor sexual y frustración existencial en dos novelas de Guelbenzu." In *Nuevos y novísimos*. . . . 151–68.

Román, Isabel. "La coherencia de *El río de la luna*, de José María Guelbenzu." *Anales de la literatura española contemporánea* 10 (1985): 111–22.

Janet Pérez

**GUERRA DA CAL, Ernesto,** pseudonym of Ernesto Pérez Guerra, (1911, Ferrol– ), Galician poet and essayist. His youth, spent in Quiroga, Lugo, is reflected in his work. After moving to Madrid, Guerra Da Cal participated in *García Lorca's La Barraca. During the Civil War, he collaborated in *Nova Galiza* (New Galicia), published in Barcelona, until in 1939 he was exiled to the United States. In that country he served on the faculty of the City U of New York and obtained a doctorate at Columbia U, where he subsequently founded the doctoral program in Portuguese studies. His thesis, *Lengua y estilo de Eça de Queiroz*, was published in Coimbra in 1954. Martínez López observes that Guerra Da Cal opted for a career in Portuguese studies because of the difficulties being experienced by Galician language and culture. In effect, the orthography he employs for his Galician writings is an approximation to Portuguese. However, Guerra Da Cal has always maintained contact with Galician letters and has cultivated that interest in others. He has been a collaborator for Galician and Portuguese themes for the *Columbia Dictionary of Contemporary European Literature, Collier's Encyclopedia*, J. Prado Coelho's *Dicionário* of Portuguese, Galician and Brazilian literatures, and others.

The author of two books of Galician verse, Guerra Da Cal is seen by Méndez Ferrín as distant from the Galician social context, as evidenced by echoes of pre–Civil War aesthetics and neo-troubadourism. Simultaneously, the sentimentality and sense of indefinition in these works are seen as coupled with Surrealist characteristics and a humanism of the sort prevalent during the decade of 1950. In effect, the nostalgic state of mind provoked by exile leaves a strong mark on Guerra Da Cal's poetry and is the common thread of compositions which deal with motifs of nature, children, and the passing of time. Never far from popular tradition, most of the poems, even when metaphysical or mystical in tone, leave the reader with the clear understanding of the author's intention. A thematic preference is the concept of a space in which the poet resides or which is located within him; this spatial construct allows him a site from which to observe himself. In a number of poems, the solitude he attributes to New York recalls, perhaps deliberately, the difficult experience of García Lorca, although in Guerra Da Cal the geographical distance strengthens the ties to Galicia and Portugal with their language, culture, and people. Only in *Futuro Imemorial* (*Manual de Velhice para Principiantes*) (1985; Future Immemorial. Old Age Manual for Beginners), written in Portuguese, does a sense of humor about the human condition make itself truly evident. Guerra Da Cal's dedication to bridging gaps between Galician and Portuguese is reinforced not only in its prologue, but also by his edition in 1985 of an anthology of Rosalía de *Castro's poetry, with Galician selections adapted to Portuguese orthography and those in Spanish accompanied by a Portuguese translation. In the same volume are poems dedicated to the writer in several languages, those not in Galician being accompanied by Portuguese translations. *See also* Galician Literature.

BIBLIOGRAPHY

Primary Texts

*Futuro Imemorial (Manual de velhice para Principiantes).* Lisboa: Sá da Costa, 1985.
*Lúa de Alén-Mar.* (1939–1958) Vigo: Galaxia, 1969.
*Motivos do Eu.* Madrid–Palma de Mallorca: Papeles de Son Armadans, 1966.
*Poemas.* Madrid–Palma de Mallorca: Papeles de Son Armadans, 1961.
*Rio de Sonho e Tempo.* (1959–1962) Vigo: Galaxia, 1963.

Criticism

Coelho, Jacinto do Prado. "Bibliografia. Artes e Letras. Ernesto Guerra da Cal—*Rio de Sonho e Tempo.*" *Colóquio* (Feb. 27, 1964): 55–56.
Fole, Anxel. "Leva Saudades o *Rio.*" *Grial* 2 (1963): 218–20.
Júlio, Maria Joaquina Nobre. "Ernesto Guerra Da Cal, um trovador galaico-português do século XX." *Perspectivas* 12 (1963): 270–74.
Lima Filho, Luís da Costa. "*Lua de Alén-Mar,* de Guerra Da Cal." *CH* 47.39 (1961): 163–68.
Méndez Ferrín, Xosé Luis. *De Pondal a Novoneyra.* Vigo: Xerais, 1984.
Martínez López, Ramón. "Literatura gallega en el exilio." In *El exilio español de 1939.* Ed. José Luis Abellán. Madrid: Taurus, 1978. 6: 287–323.

Kathleen March

**GUERRA GARRIDO, Raúl** (1935, Madrid– ), novelist, journalist. A doctor in pharmacy, Guerra Garrido has lived primarily in the Basque country. He is also a journalist and the author of several novels, including *Ni héroe ni nada* (1969: Not a Hero or Anything Else), *Cacereño* (1970; The Man from Cáceres), *Ay!* (1972), *La fuga de un cerebro* (1974; Brain Flight), and *Hipótesis* (1976; Hypothesis). In this last title, Guerra Garrido presents a satiric critique of mechanization and the worship of technology, of the sway of self-complacent materialism, and launches a transparent attack upon the blossoming consumerism of Spain in the 1970s. Utilizing an unusual viewpoint (the novel is supposedly written by a computer), he satirizes the values of the day. His first work to attract significant critical attention was *Lectura insólita de "El Capital"* (1977; Uncommon Reading of *Das Kapital*), based upon the topics of terrorism, political kidnapping and extortion. The protagonist—a hostage of terrorists—reads Marx's masterpiece as a counterpoint to a series of interviews intended to reconstruct his life and personality. Character and situation are an allegory of industrialization of the Basque country. The author's next work, *La pluma de* *pavo real, tambor de piel de perro* (1977; Peacock Feather, Dogskin Drum), seems to have disconcerted reviewers and public alike.

*Copenhague no existe* (1979; Copenhagen Doesn't Exist) returns to the theme of Spain's long-overdue industrial revolution, to reflect upon its relationship to individual liberty in the post-Franco era. Guerra Garrido presents the national problem on an individual level via the dilemma of a middle-aged citizen who for the first time confronts the options presented by elections, a less-restricted life-style, the free-wheeling economy, newly "liberated" sexuality, travel, arms trafficking—a series of moral and political choices which are frequently camouflaged as more elementary options. One of the author's most successful works, *Escrito en un dólar* (1982: Written on a Dollar), describes the American cultural invasion and economic-cultural domination by means of the symbolic confrontation between a Spanish advertising specialist and the assembled might of Madison Avenue experts. The unequal struggle for control of national markets is complicated by murders and inexplicable intrigue. *El año del Wolfram* (1984; The Wolfram Year) recreates a short-lived period during World War II when Spain's deposits of wolfram were vital to the war effort of both Hitler and the Allies, with resulting intriguing by both sides as well as individual scrambles for self-enrichment, as several self-made millionaires amassed their fortunes through means ranging from sheer good luck to violent foul play.

BIBLIOGRAPHY

Primary Texts

*El año del Wolfram*. Barcelona: Planeta, 1984.
*Escrito en un dólar*. Barcelona: Planeta, 1982.
*Lectura insólita de "El Capital."* Barcelona: Destino, 1977.
*La mar es mala mujer*. Madrid: Mondadori, 1987.
*Pluma de pavo real, tambor de piel de perro*. Barcelona: Grijalbo, 1977.

Criticism

Lezcano, Margarita M. "Las novelas ganadoras del premio Nadal 1970–1979." Diss., Florida State U.
Meneses, Carlos. "Raúl Guerra Garrido o la lucha del antihéroe." *Diario de Mallorca* March 27, 1977: 15.
Suñen, Luis y César Antonio Molina. "Premio Nadal 1977, Raúl Guerra Garrido." *Reseña* 103 (May 1977); 13.

Margarita Lezcano

**GUERRERO RUIZ, Juan** (1893, Murcia–1955, Madrid), attorney, translator, publisher. *García Lorca dubbed him "General Consul of Spanish Poetry." He studied law in Granada, obtaining his doctorate in Madrid. In 1913 he began what was to be a lifelong friendship with Juan Ramón *Jiménez, and seven years later became the secretary of the magazine *Indice*, founded by the latter. Guerrero Ruiz befriended several poets from the so-called Generation of the Dictatorship, including Lorca, Dámaso *Alonso, Jorge *Guillén, Pedro *Salinas, *Alberti, and *Cernuda. In Murcia, in 1922, he became director of the literary supplement to the daily newspaper *La Verdad*. Here, he published his translations of some of the best known foreign writers of the day, including James Joyce, D. H. Lawrence, and Valery Larbaud. Still in Murcia, he founded the magazine *Verso y Prosa* in collaboration with Jorge Guillén; they published twelve issues (1927–28). In 1940 Guerrero Ruiz founded in Madrid the publishing house Editorial Hispánica, which gave birth to the Adonais series, the most important collection for poetry in Spain after the Civil War. After his death, a collection of his conversations with Juan Ramón Jiménez was published.

BIBLIOGRAPHY

Primary Text

*Juan Ramón de viva voz*. Madrid: Insula, 1961.

Criticism

Roberts, William H. "Juan Guerrero Ruiz." *RHM* 22.2 (April 1956): 191–94.

Isabel McSpadden

**GUERRERO ZAMORA, Juan** (1927, Melilla– ), poet, playwright, novelist, theater director. His poetry books include *Alma desnuda* (1947; Naked Soul) and *Danza macabra, danza milagrosa* (n.d.; Macabre Dance, Miraculous Dance). He has written two books on Miguel *Hernández (1951 and 1955). Among his plays one especially worth mentioning is *Unos de nosotros* (1957; Some of Us), and among his novels, *Enterrar a los muertos* (1957; Burying the Dead). He also wrote short stories, as in *Un poco de ceniza* (1953; A Few Ashes).

BIBLIOGRAPHY

Primary Texts

*Alma desnuda*. Madrid: Soler, 1947.
*Danza macabra, danza milagrosa*. San Sebastián: Norte, 1951?
*Enterrar a los muertos*. Barcelona: Janés, 1957.
*Historia del teatro contemporáneo*. 4 vols. Barcelona: Flors, 1961–67.
*Unos de nosotros*. Barcelona: Flors, 1957.

Isabel McSpadden

**GUEVARA, Antonio de** (c. 1480, Santander–1545, Mondoñedo), Franciscan monk, preacher, chronicler, Bishop of Guadix and Mondoñedo, counselor to Charles V, writer of *ascetical literature and a guide for princes. He was one of the most universally read of Spanish *Siglo de Oro writers who was also popular outside of the Iberian Peninsula. His *Reloj de príncipes y Libro de Marco Aurelio* (Valladolid, 1529; *Diall of Princes*, 1557) influenced a work by the English writer John Lyly called *Euphues* or *Anatomy of Wit* (1579) which was replete with conceits and verbal antitheses. The affectation of speech called euphuism was later ridiculed by writers such as Ben Jonson. Guevara's *Reloj de príncipes* is a "mirror of princes" or a guide for those destined to rule. In his dedication to the English translation, Sir Thomas North sums up the ascetical contents of Guevara's religious works with these words: "There is no author (the sacred letters apart) that more effectively setteth out the omnipotency of God, the frailty of men, the inconstancy of fortune, the vanity of this world. . . . " In the England of Henry VIII the *Diall of Princes* was accepted as one of the significant achievements of the day.

Sir Thomas North's quote more specifically describes the contents of a religious work, *Menosprecio de corte y alabanza de aldea* (Valladolid, 1539; *A Dispraise of the Life of the Court and a Commentation of the Life of a Country Man*, 1584). As the title suggests, Guevara extols the virtues of rustic life as these contrast with the vanities and temptations of city life. Guevara's *Epístolas familiares* (Valladolid, 1553; *Familiar Epistles*, 1584) reveals a modern writer who maintains reader interest through a plethora of anecdotes and tales, a few of which became popular. *Cervantes immortalized Guevara in the prologue to *Quijote I* as Bishop of Mondoñedo where he referred to the writer's indiscriminate and blatant inclusion of incorrect references and inaccurate information within his literary creations. Nonetheless, Guevara's importance to Spanish prose rests on his literary style rather than his scholarly abilities.

## BIBLIOGRAPHY

### Primary Texts

*Menosprecio de corte y alabanza de aldea*. Clásicos Castellanos 29. Madrid: Espasa-Calpe, 1928.
*La primera parte del libro llamado Monte Calvario*. Valladolid: n.p., 1545.
*Reloj de príncipes y Libro de Marco Aurelio*. Madrid: Signo, 1936.

### English Translations

*The Diall of Princes*. Tr. Sir Thomas North. London: Allan, 1919.
*A Dispraise of the Life of a Courtier and a Commentation of the Life of a Labouring Man*. Tr. F. Bryan. London: Grafton, 1584.
*Spanish Letters: Historical, Satyrical and Moral. Letters of Wit, Politicks and Morality*. London: Hartley, 1701.

### Criticism

*Estudios acerca de Fr. Antonio de Guevara en el IV centenario de su muerte*. Madrid: Archivo Iberoamericano, 1946. 1: 178–607.
Gibbs, J. *Vida de Fr. Antonio de Guevara (1481–1545)*. Valladolid: Miñón, 1961.
Grey, Ernest. *Guevara, A Forgotten Renaissance Author*. The Hague: Nijhoff, 1973.
Lida, María Rosa. "Fray Antonio de Guevara. Edad Media y Siglo de Oro Español." *RFH* 7 (1945): 346–88.
Rallo, Asunción. *Antonio de Guevara en su contexto renascentista*. Madrid: Planeta, 1979.

                                                        Angelo DiSalvo

**GUEVARA, Miguel de** (1585?, ?–1640, ?), Augustinian priest. Author of a ms. dated 1638 and titled *Arte para aprender la lengua matlaltzinga* (Art of Learning the Matlaltzin Language), which included the masterful, inspired *"Soneto a Cristo crucificado.'' Thus, for a time, Guevara was assumed to be the author; later investigation and discovery disproved this theory.

## BIBLIOGRAPHY

Criticism

Adib, V. "Fray Miguel de Guevara y el soneto 'A Cristo crucificado.' " *Ábside* 13 (1949): 311–26.

Huff, M. C. *The sonnet 'No me mueve, mi Dios': Its Theme in Spanish Tradition.* Washington: Catholic U of America, 1948.

**GUILLÉN, Jorge** (1893, Valladolid–1986, Málaga), Spanish poet. A member of the *Generation of 1927, Guillén was a friend of Pedro *Salinas and *García Lorca and, like the former, taught Spanish literature at a number of foreign universities, supported the Republic, and was exiled at the close of the Spanish Civil War. Guillén studied in Switzerland and Germany and lived for several years in Paris before receiving his doctorate from the U of Madrid (1924). From 1926 to 1929, he taught at the U of Murcia, was a lecturer at Oxford from 1929 to 1931, and a professor at the U of Seville from 1931 to 1938. During these years, he published the first edition of *Cántico* (1928; Canticle), containing 75 poems; it was republished four more times before 1957, being augmented each time. Arrested and imprisoned for political reasons following the death of Lorca, Guillén went into voluntary exile in 1938, settling in the United States, where he taught at Middlebury College, Wellesley College, Yale U, the U of California at Berkeley, Ohio State U, and from 1957 onward at Harvard.

The second edition of *Cántico* (1936) contained 125 poems; the third (1945), with an added subtitle, *Fe de vida* (Canticle: Testimony of Life), 270 poems; and the similarly titled fourth edition (1950), the first complete edition, 334 poems. In 1957, Guillén published his first poetry with a different title, *Maremágnum* (Sea of Confusion), the first volume of another poetic cycle with the collective title of *Clamor: Tiempo de historia* (Clamor: Time of History); the second volume, *Que van a dar en la mar* (Emptying into the Sea), appeared in 1960, and the third and final volume, *A la altura de las circunstancias* (Rising to the Occasion), in 1963. A separate poetic entity, *Homenaje. Reunión de vidas* (Homage: A Gathering of Lives), published in 1967, was gathered together with the composite volumes of *Cántico* and *Clamor* in *Aire nuestro* (Our Air), Guillén's complete poetic works to that date, in 1968.

From the 1950s onward, Guillén was the recipient of scholarly grants and awards, literary prizes, and other critical and cultural accolades, although until the close of the Franco era, they came from countries other than Spain. Recognitions include the Award of Merit of the American Academy of Arts and Letters (1955), his being named Charles Eliot Norton Professor of Poetry at Harvard (1957–58), the Etna-Taormina Poetry Prize (Sicily, 1959), the International Grand Prize of Poetry (Belgium, 1961), the San Luca Prize (Florence, 1964), and numerous symposia in his honor. Finally, the year after the death of Franco, he was awarded the Miguel de Cervantes Prize of the *Academia Esñola (1976), the same year in which he ieceived the Bennett Prize for Poetry of the *Hudson Review*. In 1977, he was the recipient of the Fetrinelli Prize of the Lincei Academy (Rome) and the Alfonso Reyes Prize (Mexico). In 1978, he returned to Spain permanently, making his home in Málaga.

Guillén wrote his doctoral dissertation on *Góngora, so perhaps it is not surprising that his early poetry exhibits some of the same striving for formal perfection, the same cult of the image, typifying the revival of Góngorism by the Generation of 1927. Guillén's work is characterized by extreme condensation, a fondness for symmetry, and a desire for precision. His poetry has been termed "intellectual," perhaps because of the avoidance of sentiment (although Guillén is no different from the rest of the Generation of 1927 in rejection of sentimentality). The emphasis on art and form led to his being grouped with such French poets as Paul Valéry and Stephen Mallarmé, but Guillén is by no means nihilistic or cold: his poetry is a poetry of fulfillment and plenitude, aptly summarized by the subtitle of *Cántico: fe de vida* (Testimony of and Faith in Life), an affirmation of life, an acclamation of the universe as "well-made," a generalized song of praise to human existence. However, Guillén's poetry is not simply static and contemplative; he does not limit himself to the passive perception and enjoyment of the best of all possible worlds: there is active interaction and communication between the poetic "I" and the world around it, and there is an ethical or moral tension which requires striving toward perfection. An essential optimism throughout *Cántico* is reflected by the frequency of mention of dawn (new day, new life), which also stresses the sense of discovery, awareness, and plenitude of perception. Love is expressed for many elements of nature (flora and fauna), somewhat reminiscent of the poet's discovery of the universe in Vicente *Aleixandre's early books. And like the works of Aleixandre before the 1950s, *Cántico* exists apart from social protest and political concerns, in a world where art, language and sensation are supreme, a world of forms, metaphors, structural perfection, poetic and vital essence.

The major difference between *Clamor*, Guillén's "second stage" trilogy, and the preceding serial editions of *Cántico* is that there is a shift from the essential but sometimes solitary poetic ego to a more collective focus, an emphasis upon the community of men, the nation (and especially upon the fate of Spain in relation to its particular socio-political circumstances in the late 1950s and early 1960s), that is, the period of the "social" poets, of poets of social protest in Spain. There is more negativity, and as a consequence, more pessimism, less of an apprehension of the world as well-made and less emphasis upon art and form per se. The need for communication with one's fellow man and a certain human solidarity becomes a theme, and an existential preoccupation with time appears. Guillén's language becomes more epigrammatic and prosaic, with some compositions resembling rhythmic prose paragraphs more than poems. The poet's awareness of mortality, aging and death, come to the fore, and with them, an increase in irony, but Guillén never rejects or decries his human condition, nor does he lose his joy of life.

*Homenaje* may be differentiated from the two preceding major collections, *Cántico* and *Clamor*, by means of its more "literary" inspiration, for themes are often drawn from sources other than life and the poet's immediate surroundings, particularly from his readings (from the Bible to contemporary literature), his contacts with the world of art (paintings, artist, authors), and the realm of emotions (the central section is in effect a paean to love). *Clamor*, with its insistence on the here and now, tends to emphasize the ephemeral and fleeting, while *Homenaje* stresses the idea of permanence and continuity within flux and change, a perseverance of essential values, ideals and goals. Guillén's attention turns again to art in *Y otros poemas*, which fuses the concrete and abstract, the specific and universal, the fleeting moment of contemporary history with eternal themes. Several poems in this collection are retrospective, looking backward to the poet's youth or adolescence, reaffirming his vital open stance, and offering a fragmented autobiographical synthesis, moments of eternity in which much of the intellectual curiosity and rapt attention of *Cántico* are proclaimed anew. The poet's affirmative, disciplined attitude and his faith in art and life infuse his poetry with dynamism and prevent excessive abstraction. His outbursts of joy, his surprise and gratitude before the universe and plenitude of existence, and unceasing search for fulfillment are the most memorable characteristics.

BIBLIOGRAPHY

Primary Texts

*Language and Poetry: Some Poets of Spain*. Cambridge: Harvard UP, 1961.
*Final*. Barcelona: Barral, 1988(?).

English Translations

*Affirmation: A Bilingual Anthology, 1919–1966*. Tr. Julian Palley. Norman: U of Oklahoma P, 1968.
*Cántico: A Selection*. Ed. Norman Thomas di Giovanni. Boston: Little, Brown, 1965 (translations by several collaborators).
*Guillén on Guillén*. Tr. Reginald Gibbons and Anthony L. Geist. Princeton: Princeton UP, 1979.

Criticism

Caro Romero, Joaquín. *Jorge Guillén*. Madrid: Epesa, 1974.
Casalduero, Joaquín. *"Cántico" de Jorge Guillén y "Aire nuestro."* Madrid: Gredos, 1974.
Ciplijauskaite, Biruté. *Deber de plenitud: La poesía de Jorge Guillén*. Mexico City: SepSetentas, 1973.
Debicki, Andrew P. *La poesía de Jorge Guillén*. Madrid: Gredos, 1968.
MacCurdy, G. Grant. *Jorge Guillén*. Boston: Hall, 1982.

Janet Pérez

**GUILLÉN, Rafael** (1933, Granada– ), self-taught poet. With a fellow Granadinian poet, José Ladrón de Guevara, he founded and directed the poetic collection Veleta al Sur. Guillén has received numerous literary awards: Círculo de Escritores Iberoamericanos de Nueva York (1963); Internacional de Centroamérica (1965); Leopoldo Panero (1966); Boscán y Guipuzcua (1968); Ciudad de Barcelona (1969), etc. Thematically Guillén's poetry falls into three categories: (1) existentialist: *Antes de la esperanza* (1956; Before Hope); *Río de Dios* (1957; God's River); *Hombre en paz* (1966; Man in Peace); *Tercer gesto* (1967; Third Gesture); and *Límites* (1971; Limits); (2) love poems: *Pronuncio amor* (1960; I Pronounce Love); *Amor, acaso nada* (1968; Love, Perhaps Nothing), and *Moheda* (1979); and (3) social: *Gesto segundo* (1972; Second Gesture) and *Vasto poema de resistencia* (1981; Vast Poem of Resistance). Guillén is also author of two collections of circumstantial poetry: *Apuntes de la corrida* (1967; Notes on Bullfighting) and *Cancionero-guía para andar por el aire de Granada* (1970; Song-Book Guide to Walking in the Granadinian Mood).

In Guillén's poetry there is an evolution from an early preoccupation with form to a moral commitment to the transcendental problems of time, death, and nothingness. *Moheda* is a good example of the fusion of ethics and aesthetics. Guillén's poetry is clear, rich and precise. He skillfully uses classic meter and free verse.

BIBLIOGRAPHY

Primary Texts

*Amor, acaso nada.* Las Palmas: Exmo. Cabildo Insular de la Gran Canaria, 1968.
*Gesto segundo.* Barcelona: Instituto de Estudios Hispánicos, 1972.
*Límites.* Barcelona: El Bardo, 1971.
*Moheda.* Málaga: Revista Litoral, 1979.
*Tercer gesto.* Madrid: Cultura Hispánica, 1967.
*Los vientos.* Madrid: RO, 1970.

Criticism

Díaz Plaja, G. *Al pie de la poesía.* Madrid: Nacional, 1974. 120–24.
Muñiz Romero, Carlos. "Rafael Guillén, misterio y límites." In *Moheda.* 7–23.
Muñoz, Luis. "Rafael Guillén, evocación y esperanza." *CH* 171 (March 1964): 576–87.

José Ortega

**GUILLÉN DE SEGOVIA, Pero** (1413, Seville–1474?, Segovia?), poet. Although originally from Seville, this author spent almost his entire life in Segovia, whence his name. As a favorite of Don Álvaro de Luna, Guillén lived in a state of extreme poverty and had to earn a living as a scribe after his patron fell into disgrace. On the verge of committing suicide, he was recommended to Carrillo, Archbishop of Toledo, who became Guillén's new benefactor. His writings include *Decir sobre el amor* (Comment on Love) in which he imitates Dante; compositions with a political or moral theme, such as *Decires contra la pobreza* (Poems against Poverty), *Del día del Juicio* (About Judgment Day), and *Siete Pecados Mortales* (The Seven Deadly Sins)—which he based on Juan de *Mena; and *Querella de la gobernación* (Dispute about Government), a reply to Gómez *Manrique, who wrote a work with the same title. Guillén's social satire *Discursos de los doce estados del mundo* (On the Twelve Estates of the World) was inspired by the medieval theme of the "dance of death" and criticizes the clergy, businessmen, knights, etc. His best poetic work, *Los siete salmos penitenciales trovados* (The Seven Penitential Psalms), was censored by the \*Inquisition, and removed from the Cancionero general. According to Marcelino \*Menéndez y Pelayo, these psalms are almost the only effort at biblical poetry in Spanish medieval literature. Guillén also imitated Jaime March's *Libro de Concordances* (Book of Rhymes) and composed *La Gaya de Segovia* or *Silva copiosísima de consonantes para alivio de trovadores* (Miscellaneous Guide to Consonantal Rhyme for Poets), the ms. of which is in the National Library (\*Biblioteca Nacional) in Madrid. In its prologue the author tells the story of the Archbishop of Toledo, his protector. This work is the first known rhyming dictionary in Castilian.

BIBLIOGRAPHY

Primary Texts

*La gaya ciencia*. Transcription by O. J. Tulio. Intro., vocab. and indexes by J. M. Casas Homs. Madrid: CSIC, 1962.

*Obra de Pedro Guillén demandando consejo a un amigo sobre su vida*. Ed. M. D'Arrigo Bona. Turin: Giappichelli, 1974. Reprod. of orig. ms., notes, glossary.

Criticism

Cummins, J. G. "Pero Guillén de Segovia y el Ms. 4.114." *HR* 41 (1973): 6–32.

Lang, H. R. "The So-Called *Cancionero* de Pero Guillén de Segovia." *RH* 19 (1908): 51–81.

Marino, Nancy F. "The *Cancionero* de Pero Guillén de Segovia and Ms. 617 of the Royal Palace Library." *Corónica* 7 (n.d.): 20–23.

                                                                                        Lucy Sponsler

**GUILLÓ, Magdalena** (1940, Barcelona– ), Spanish and Catalan novelist. Guilló holds a degree in mathematics and since 1972 has resided and taught in Salamanca. *En una vall florida al peu de les espases* (1978; In a Flowery Vale at Sword-point), her first book, written in Catalan, was followed by two novels in Castilian, both treating Judaic themes: *Entre el ayer y el mañana* (1984; Between Yesterday and Tomorrow) is inspired by the life of Theodore Herzl and the foundation of Zionism; and *Un sambenito para el señor Santiago* (1986; Penitent's Garb for Santiago) is set in Seville in the atmosphere of the \*Inquisition, but emphasizes the vigor and importance of the heterodox tradition.

BIBLIOGRAPHY

Primary Texts

*En una vall florida al peu de les espases*. Barcelona: Destino, 1978.

*Un sambenito para el señor Santiago*. Barcelona: Muchnik, 1986.

                                                                                        Janet Pérez

**GUIMERÀ, Àngel** (1845, Santa Cruz de Tenerife–1924, Barcelona), playwright and poet. He was the son of a Catalan wine merchant established in the Canary Islands. When he was ten years old, he moved with his parents to Catalonia and learned Catalan. At a very early age he became interested in the theater; in 1871 he was one of the founders of the magazine *Renaixença* (Renaissance) and after 1874 was its director. During his long life he became world famous as a playwright; he is less well known as a poet and passionate orator on behalf of Catalan nationalism. His patriotic speeches were collected in the volume *Cants a la pàtria* (Songs to the Fatherland), and his poetry in *Poesies* (1877; Poems). Guimerà's plays were enormously successful all over the world and were staged in translation in the major European countries, the United States and even Japan. *Terra baixa* (1894; Lowlands), for example, was even the basis of the librettos of two operas in Germany and Belgium and of five films in five different countries. *Maria Rosa* was produced in a film by Cecil B. de Mille. But at the end of his life many of the younger generation of Catalan playwrights rejected, often with great disrespect, Guimerà's works, dismissing them *in toto* and somewhat unfairly. The truth is that before Guimerà a Catalan National Theater did not exist; after his death this was no longer true. Like Narcís *Oller in prose and *Verdaguer in poetry, Guimerà created from practically nothing the modern Catalan theater. In some instances he went to the romantics, the naturalists, the modernists or Castilian tradition, but his most deep influences came from Victor Hugo and Shakespeare. Unlike his rather "primitive" predecessors—Serafí Pitarra (1839–95) or Victor *Balaguer (1824–1901)—Guimerà's theater reflected all the European trends of his time. He started with historical dramas, the most outstanding being *Mar i cel* (Sea and Sky), a violent and passionate story of love and heroism of a Moslem pirate; *Galla Placídia* (1882) and *Rei i monjo* (1890; King and Monk). Then he moved into the realistic theater in which he achieved his greatest successes. *Terra baixa* shows his prodigious dramatic ability blended with believable and strong characters; Manelic is a man of primitive yet tender grandeur who is tricked into marrying the mistress of the town's "cacic" (political boss). When, after the marriage, he discovers the deceit, in a brutal act of self-justice he kills his tormentor in an electrifying last scene: "Fora tothom! Aparteu-se! He mort al llop! He mort al llop!" (Everyone out! Move aside! I've killed the wolf! I've killed the wolf!). *Maria Rosa* (1894) is another impressive drama that also builds up an intense situation, which results in a bloody denouement. Strongly influenced by the symbolists during the last years of his life, he ironically returns to the historical themes of his youth: *Indibil i Mandoni* (1917), *Joan Dalla* (1921) and *Alta banca* (1921). *See also* Catalan Literature.

## BIBLIOGRAPHY

### Primary Texts

*Obres completes.* 2 vols. Barcelona: Selecta, 1975–78.
*Obres selectes.* Barcelona: Biblioteca Perenne, 1948.
*Tierra baja.* Tr. to Spanish by José Echegaray. Madrid: Sucesores de Rodríguez y Ordiózola, 1896.

English Translations

*Marta of the lowlands (Terra baixa)*. Tr. Wallace Gilpatrick. Garden City, NY: Doubleday, 1915.
*La pecadora*. In *Masterpieces of Modern Spanish Drama*. Tr. Barrett H. Clark. Cincinnati: Stewart Kidd, 1922.

Criticism

Fàbregas, Xavier. *Angel Guimerà, les dimensions d'un mite*. Barcelona: Edicions 62, 1971.
Miracle, Josep. *Guimerà*. Barcelona: Aedos, 1958.
Poblet, Josep M. *Angel Guimerà*. Barcelona: Bruguera, 1967.
Yxart, Josep. *Ángel Guimerà*. Barcelona: n.p., 1975.

Joan Gilabert

**GUTIÉRREZ, José** (1955, Nigüelas, Granada– ), poet and literary critic. He is the coordinator of the Press Office at the U. of Granada and has been co-director of two poetry collections: Ánade and Silene. As a literary critic he has contributed to *Insula, Caballo griego para la poesía, Hora de Poesía, Nueva Estafeta, Cuadernos del Norte*, etc.

Gutiérrez published the following books of verse: *Ofrenda en la memoria* (1976; Offering in the Memory); *Espejo y laberinto* (1978; Mirror and Labyrinth); El *cerco de luz* (1978; The Circle of Light); *La armadura de sal* (1980; The Salt Armour), and *El don de la derrota* (1981; The Gift of Defeat).

*Espejo y laberinto*, perhaps Gutiérrez's best book, revolves around the theme of the irreversibility of time. His verses represent a way of searching for a meaning to the world, especially the inner world of the poet.

BIBLIOGRAPHY

Primary Texts

*La armadura de sal*. Madrid: Hiperión, 1980.
*El cerco de luz*. Granada: Ánade, 1978.
*El don de la derrota*. Rota: Cuaderno de cera, 1981.
*Espejo y laberinto*. Málaga: Cuadernos de María Isabel, A. Caffarena Editor, 1978.
*Ofrenda en la memoria*. Granada: Silene, 1976.

Criticism

Molina Campos, E. "La poesía última de José Gutiérrez." *Nueva Estafeta* 38 (Jan. 1982): 77–80.
Prat, Ignacio. "Sobre *Espejo y laberinto*." *Insula* 394 (Sept. 1979): 7–8.

José Ortega

**GUTIÉRREZ GAMERO, Emilio** (1844, Madrid–1935, Madrid), Spanish politician and novelist, who in his long life witnessed most of the important political and literary events of Spain in the past c. Because he voted in favor of the First Republic, he was exiled to Paris after the Restoration. He became a member of the *Academia Española in 1919. In works such as *El conde Perico* (1906; Count Parakeet) and *La olla grande* (1909; Big Stewpot) he reflected the political and business life of the epoch. Of special interest are his memoirs, *Mis primeros ochenta años* (1926; My First Eighty Years), which evoke national politics, narrate curious anecdotes and events of literary significance, portray well-known figures, and paint some writers such as *Campoamor and *Clarín. Strangely lacking in his memoirs is the sort of autobiographical data which usually typify the genre.

BIBLIOGRAPHY

Primary Texts

*Mis primereos ochenta años.* Madrid: Aguilar, 1948.

*La olla grande.* Barcelona: Edita, 1930.

*El conde Perico.* Madrid: Hernando, 1906.

**GUTIÉRREZ ORDÓÑEZ DE MONTALVO.** *See* Montalvo, Garci Ordóñez [or Rodríguez] de

**GUTIÉRREZ SOLANA, José** (1886, Madrid–1945, Madrid), extraordinary painter, engraver, and writer. He was one of nine children who grew up in a family disturbed by several cases of madness. After his father's death, he abandoned his studies of *bachillerato* at age fourteen to study painting at the Real Academia de San Fernando. He followed his family when they moved to Santander and remained in that city until 1917, when he returned to Madrid. While in Santander he wrote and published two series of literary sketches dealing with Madrid: *Madrid: escenas y costumbres* (1913 and 1918; Madrid: Scenes and Customs). Although in 1920 he published one of his best books, *España negra* (Black Spain), and a novel in 1926, *Fernando Cornejo*, his fame as a painter soon began to surpass his fame as a writer. In 1922 he won the first of several medals by taking first place in the Exposición Nacional de Pintura. Back in Madrid, Solana joined the *tertulias Candelas and Pombo, where he became closely associated with Ramón *Gómez de la Serna and his group, several of whose members he painted alone and as a group. With the outbreak of the Civil War (1936) Solana moved to Paris (where he wrote *París*); he remained there until his return to Madrid in 1942. The following year he won the Gold Medal of the Círculo de Bellas Artes; posthumously he won Medalla de Honor in the Exposición de Barcelona (1945).

Solana's first paintings have been compared to Zuloaga's because of his popular themes based on Madrid's scenes and characters. Nevertheless, his eccentric nature led him to develop a very personal brand of expressionism. His somber paintings emphasize a carnival atmosphere in which wax figures, masks, mannequins, and stiff human figures freely interact. Many of his paintings (including his self-portrait) reproduce the doll-like figures and the many other odd and anachronistic objects he picked up at the Rastro, Madrid's flea market. Solana's writings deal with identical themes and motifs. His words paint the same somber, bitter atmosphere that seems taken out of a sordidly *picaresque world, composed of absurdly grotesque scenes; violent skies; weird, doll-like figures; and dark, acrid colors. In his paintings the result is an extremely baroque and dramatic vision; in his literature the directness of his extreme realism is overpowering.

BIBLIOGRAPHY

Primary Text

*Obra literaria*. Prologue by Camilo José Cela. Madrid: Taurus, 1961.

Criticism

Barrio-Garay, José L. *José Gutiérrez-Solana: Painting and Writings*. Lewisburg, PA: Bucknell UP, 1978.

Flint, Weston. *Solana, escritor*. Madrid: RO, 1967.

———. "Wax Figures and Mannequins in Solana." *Hispania* 46 (1963): 740–47.

Kerrigan, Anthony. "Black Knight of Spanish Painting." *Arts Magazine*, May-June 1962: 16–20.

María A. Salgado

**GUTIÉRREZ TORRERO, Concepción.** *See* Lagos, Concha

# H

HAGIOGRAPHY, at its simplest, the biography of saints. Two principal types are (a) those that arise spontaneously to record the life of a particular saint for devotional reasons and (b) those concerned with the scientific study of the lives of saints. In Spain, hagiographical writings take a variety of literary forms depending on historical period and interest of the author. The majority, however, pertain to the first group and assume a literary approach.

In the Middle Ages (*Edad Media) the earliest examples appear in the thirteenth c. in the form of poetry of the *cuaderna vía tradition. While the majority of authors present Spanish-born saints, this is not exclusively the case. First among these is the Libre dels tres Reis [*Reys] d'Orient, which is less a life of the three kings than that of the Infant Christ. Another notable exception is the anonymous Vida de Santa *María Egipciaca, which presents a notorious sinner converted to a life of penance. It is a work that enjoyed widespread popularity not only in Spain but also throughout Europe, even though the veracity of the tale was questioned by ecclesiatical authority.

By far the best known hagiographical works of the period are those of Gonzalo de *Berceo who, in four poems, recounted the stories of Santo Domingo de Silos, San Millán de la Cogolla, Santa Oria, and the martyrdom of San Lorenzo. This last is fragmentary and only briefly treats the life of St. Lawrence before describing his martyrdom. In the other poems, however, Berceo follows a fairly set pattern with three divisions detailing the earthly life, following with the miracles performed during the saint's life, and concluding with the death and subsequent miracles associated with the saint. In the lives of Santo Domingo, San Millán, and Santa Oria, the poet draws on earlier Latin sources written by Grimaldo, San Braulio, and Munnio for details of these early, Spanish-born saints. The poems served a dual function of promoting the fame of saints associated with the monastery where Berceo lived as a monk and, concomitantly, of encouraging pilgrimage to the site. In addition to these literary sources, the Latin Flos sanctorum also circulated in medieval Spain. It provided spiritual reading in the monasteries and was certainly known by later writers.

The *Siglo de Oro* witnessed a new literary approach to hagiography in Spain in the form of the *comedia de santo*. Like Berceo's earlier poems, these plays tended to formulaic dramatizing of the lives of saints both foreign and domestic. Lope de *Vega is the greatest purveyor of the genre and utilizes some of his dramatic principles in writing a three-act play that presents the saint's early life in the first act; his dedication to a vocation of sanctity in the second; and his death and subsequent miracles in the third. Unfortunately, these do not rank among his best works in part because of his tendency to clutter them with too many extraneous characters and theological points only partly relevant to the life of the saint in question. Popular works depicting San Isidro, San Ginés, Santa *Teresa, San Francisco, and San Agustín were more concerned with dramatic possibilities than with historical accuracy. Other dramatists contributed to the genre as well, although with far fewer works than Lope. Among these are *Tirso de Molina (*Santo y Sastre* and *Santa Juana*), *Mira de Amescua (*El esclavo del demonio* and *Vida de San Pablo, Apóstol*), and *Calderón de la Barca (*El purgatorio de San Patricio*).

Prose examples of hagiography also appear in this period. *Malón de Chaide's *La conversión de la Magdalena* continues the appeal to popular taste in the story of a sinner turned saint in the person of Mary Magdalene. The Jesuit, Pedro de *Ribadeneyra, relies on his personal acquaintance with the founders of his order to write the *Vida de San Ignacio* (de Loyola) and the *Vida de San Francisco de Borja*. In addition, he also published a new *Flos Sanctorum o Libro de las vidas de los Santos*, which enjoyed great popularity in his time. The Hieronymite, José de *Sigüenza, produced a *Vida de San Jerónimo* and an *Historia de la Orden de San Jerónimo*, which include much biographical material on the order's patron. In the works of both priests, a shift from strictly popular devotion to more historical concerns is evident, as both become apologists and promoters of their respective orders' saints and histories.

After the *Siglo de Oro*, the focus of hagiography in Spain shifts from the popular mode to a more scientific approach when historical accuracy replaces the quasi-fictional accounts found in the poems and *comedias* of earlier periods. Such is certainly the case with Enrique *Flórez, whose *España sagrada* is a monumental work covering both history and hagiography in Spain. Exceptions to this scientific trend do occur as some Romantic writers partly revert to the popular recounting of saints' legends in the nineteenth c. Their works thus imitate the medieval models of hagiography. Similarly, José María *Pemán's *El divino impaciente*, detailing the life of San Francisco Javier, owes something to the *comedias de santo*. Nevertheless, in modern times, the genre has constituted a part of historiography much more than literature.

BIBLIOGRAPHY

Primary Texts

*La conversión de la Magdalena*. By Malón de Chaide. Ed. P. Félix García. 3 vols. Madrid: Espasa-Calpe, 1947.

*El divino impaciente.* By José María Pemán. 12th ed. Madrid: Sucesores de Rivadeneyra, 1933. Dramatic poem, including prologue, three acts, and epilogue.
*España sagrada.* Vols. 1–29 by Enrique Flórez. Madrid: Antonio Sancha, 1747–75. Ecclesiastical history in Spain.
*Historia de la Orden de San Jerónimo.* By José de Sigüenza. NBAE 7 and 9, 1907 and 1909.
*Milagros de nuestra Señora, Vida de Santo Domingo de Silos, Vida de San Millán de la Cogolla, Vida de Santa Oria, Martirio de San Lorenzo.* By Gonzalo de Berceo. Ed. Amancio Bolano e Isla. Mexico: Porrúa, 1965.
*Obras. Comedias de vidas de santos.* By Lope de Vega y Carpio. BAE 9–12.
*Obras completas.* By Pedro de Ribadeneyra. Madrid: Católica, 1945.
*La "Vida de San Millán de la Cogolla" de Gonzalo de Berceo.* Ed. Brian Dutton. London: Tamesis, 1967. 2nd ed. rev., 1984. (Vol. I of Dutton's four-volume ed. of the *Obras completas.)*

Elizabeth T. Howe

**HALCÓN, Manuel** (1902, Seville– ), Spanish novelist, whose first work, *El hombre que espera* (1922; The Man Who Waits), won a prize awarded by the *Ateneo of Seville. *Fin de raza* (1927; The End of a Race) is a short-story collection. Halcón, who was related to Villalón, published a memoir entitled *Recuerdos de Fernando Villalón* (1941; Recollections of Fernando Villalon), his memories of this Andalusian noble, bullfighter and poet. In 1939, Halcón won the Mariano de Cavia Prize (usually given for journalism). Further narrative works include *Aventuras de Juan Lucas* (1944; Adventures of John Lucas), *Cuentos* (1948; Tales), *La gran borrachera* (1953; The Big Binge), *Las Dueñas* (1956; Palace of the Dueñas), *Desnudo pudor* (1964; Naked Modesty), *Ir a más* (1967; To Get Somewhere), and *Manuela* (1970). His *Monólogo de una mujer fría* (1960; Monologue of a Frigid Woman) won for him the Miguel de Cervantes National Literary Prize and propelled him into the Royal Spanish Academy (*Academia Española).

BIBLIOGRAPHY

Primary Texts

*La condesa de la banda (teatro).* Madrid: Rivadeneyra, 1951.
*Narraciones.* Madrid: Rivadeneyra, 1957.
*Salto al cielo (teatro).* Buenos Aires: Estampa, 1946.
*La vuelta al Barrio de Salamanca.* Madrid: Rivadeneyra, 1950. Articles and lectures.

Janet Pérez

**HALEVI, Judah** (1075?, Toledo/Tudela–1141, Fustat/Jerusalem), Jewish poet, philosopher, and royal physician in Toledo. He is thought to have died in Egypt, on his way to Israel, the emigration reflecting an aspiration for personal redemption and a conviction about the centrality of Zion in Judaism. Well versed in Hebrew and Arabic literary cultures, the "divine poet" wrote over 800 poems which treat secular, religious, and nationalistic themes with artistic perfection and exhibit the content and form found in Arabic-Hebrew poetry, including the *jarcha*

(\*Kharja). He praised love, wine, and friendship in verses rich in imagery, lyricism, and genuine emotion and gave brilliant descriptions of nature while enriching the liturgy with hundreds of songs of prayer and penitence, of a humble and quiet tone. His *Poems of Zion* or *Zionides*, original in topic and beauty, immortalize the longing for Zion. The *Kuzari* is a classic and vigorous defense of ''the Despised Faith,'' written in Arabic, translated into Hebrew by the mid-twelfth c., and first printed in Fano in 1506. A dialogue, primarily between a Jewish teacher and the pagan Khazar king, whose conversion to Judaism provides the literary framework of the book, it debates Aristotelian, Islamic, Christian, and Jewish philosophies, in an effort to discredit rationalism, a theme used by later European writers. Demonstrating the superiority of Judaism, the *Kuzari* was influential in Cabbalistic circles (thirteenth c.), among the anti-Aristotelians, (fourteenth-fifteenth c.), and with Hasidism. *See also* Aristotelianism in Spain, Hispano-Judaic Literature.

BIBLIOGRAPHY

English Translations

*Jehuda Halevy: Kuzari. The Book of Proof and Argument.* Ed. and tr. Isaak Heinemann. Abr. ed., 1947. Rpt. in *Three Jewish Philosophers.* New York: Harper Torchbooks, 1965.

*Judah Halevi's Kitab al Khazari.* Tr. Hartwig Hirschfeld. 1905. Rpt. with intro. by Joshua Bloch. New York: Pardes, 1946.

*Selected Poems of Yehudah Halevi.* Ed. Heinrich Brody. Tr. Nina Salaman. New York: Arno, 1973.

Criticism

Burstein, Abraham. *Judah Halevi in Granada. A Story of His Boyhood.* New York: Bloch, 1941.

Druck, David. *Yehudah Halevy, His Life and Works.* Tr. by M.Z.R. Frank. New York: Bloch, 1941.

Efros, Israel I. *Judah Halevi as Poet and Thinker.* New York: Histadrut Ivrit of America, 1941.

Kayser, Rudolf. *Life and Time of Yehudah Halevi.* Tr. Frank Gaynor. New York: Philosophical Library, 1949.

Roth, Norman. ''The Lyric Tradition in Hebrew Secular Poetry of Medieval Spain.'' *Hispanic Journal* 2.2 (Spring, 1981): 7–26.

Wolfson, Harry A. ''The Platonic, Aristotelian and Stoic Theories of Creation in Hallevi and Maimonides.'' In *Essays in Honour of the Very Rev. Dr. J. H. Hertz.* Ed. I. Epstein, E. Levine and G. Roth. London: Edward Goldston, 1943. 427–42.

———. ''Hallevi and Maimonides on Design, Chance and Necessity.'' *Proceedings of the American Academy for Jewish Research* 11 (1941): 105–63.

———. ''Maimonides and Halevi.'' *Jewish Quarterly Review*, new series, 2.3 (1911–12): 297–337.

Reginetta Haboucha

**HALEVI, Selemoh.** *See* Santa María, Pablo de

**HARTZENBUSCH, Juan Eugenio** (1806, Madrid–1880, Madrid), Romantic dramatist, scholar, and poet. Hartzenbusch's German father was widowed in 1808. The son studied languages, read plays, worked in his father's carpentry shop, attended classes in philosophy at San Isidro, and was so impressed with his first trip to the theater in 1821 that he began to translate and adapt plays for private and public performance. He married in 1830 (widowed in 1836) and was swept into the Romantic world of Madrid in that decade, producing articles, speeches, and the play that brought him immediate attention and lasting fame, *Los amantes de Teruel* (1837; *The Lovers of Teruel*, 1950). When he married again in 1838 it was to a widow who brought with her a ready-made family— five children—to which Juan Eugenio added a sixth in 1840.

Hartzenbusch secured a position in the *Biblioteca Nacional and rose to become its director upon the death of Agustín *Durán in 1862. Throughout the 1840s and 1850s, Hartzenbusch wrote plays, poems, and essays, "reworked" Spanish classical dramas, and published important editions of *Siglo de Oro playwrights (*Tirso, *Calderón, Lope de *Vega, *Ruiz de Alarcón). He was elected to the Spanish Royal Academy (*Academia Española) in 1847 and named director of the Normal School for Elementary Education in 1855. Frail, sensitive, and kindly, he retired from the library in 1875, and died five years later.

Hartzenbush spent considerable energies on *refundiciones* (rewrites and/or free translations of other authors' efforts). These included *Floresinda* (written 1827, published 1844), reworked from Voltaire; *El amo criado* (staged 1829; published 1841; The Master Servant), taken from *Rojas Zorrilla; *Ernesto* (1837), based on a Dumas play; *Primero yo* (1842; The First), inspired by a German novel by Enrique Zschokke; *La abadía de Penmarch* (1844; Penmarch Abbey), translated from a play by Tournemine; and *La estrella de Sevilla o Sancho Ortiz de las Roelas* (staged in 1852; The Star of Seville or Sancho Ortiz de las Roelas), adapted from Lope's famous and disputed drama. He also wrote numerous original—and mediocre—plays: *La redoma encantada* (1839; The Enchanted Flask); *La visionaria* (1840; The Visionary); *Un sí y un no* (1854; A Yes and a No), and several plays in collaboration with friends. The Romantic attraction to Spain's historical and legendary past inspired Hartzenbusch's most interesting efforts. *Doña Mencía* (1838), *Alfonso el Casto* (1841; King Alphonse the Chaste), and *La jura de Santa Gadea* (1844; The Swearing at Saint Gadea) developed themes on historical figures, and were received with moderate applause in Madrid's theaters.

His scholarship was idiosyncratic, passionate, often imprecise, and incomplete, but it is impossible to fault his intentions. His *Romancero pintoresco* (1848; Illustrated Ballads) followed Durán's lead into the rediscovery of popular poetry, and his editions (with introductory studies) of Golden Age playwrights, published in Rivadeneyra's monumental collection called *Biblioteca de Autores Españoles, helped disseminate these plays for popular consumption. In addition, he produced a four-volume edition of *Don Quijote* (1863), complete with more than 1,600 notes (many of them speculative and unreliable); it was revised— though not much improved—in 1874.

But the all-too-numerous failures penned by Hartzenbusch during his lifetime have been largely forgotten due to the extraordinary success of one play. *Los amantes de Teruel*, when first staged in Madrid on January 19, 1837, and through its several different printed editions, captured the public's interest with its theme of doomed loved, its solid grounding in one of Spain's most cherished historical legends, and its agile execution in prose and verse. The theme of Diego Marsilla and Isabel, the tragic lovers of Teruel, has been dealt with frequently in Spanish literature (there are over one hundred treatments), but it is Hartzenbusch's version which is generally considered to be the best.

His constant imitation of others when combined with the incessant revision of his own works makes Juan Eugenio Hartzenbusch's career somewhat difficult to follow. There is no definitive collection of his works, although the *Obras escogidas* and *Obras* offer an initial sampling of his style and substance. *See also* Amantes de Teruel, Leyenda de los; Romanticism.

BIBLIOGRAPHY

Primary Texts

*Los amantes de Teruel*. Ed. Jean-Louis Picoche. Madrid: Alhambra, 1980.
*Los amantes de Teruel*. Ed. Salvador García Castañeda. Madrid: Castalia, 1971.
*Obras*. Leipzig: Brockhaus, 1887.
*Obras escogidas*. Paris: Baudry, 1850.

English Translation

*The Lovers of Teruel [Los amantes de Teruel]*. Tr. Luis Soto-Ruiz and Georgia Pappan-astos. In *Three Spanish Romantic Plays*. Intro. A. Pasero. Milwaukee: Marquette UP, 1990.
*The Lovers of Teruel*. Tr. Henry Thomas. Walton, Wales: Greynog, 1938.

Criticism

Curry, Richard A. "Dramatic Tension and Emotional Control in *Los amantes de Teruel*." *West Virginia U Philological Papers* 21 (1974): 36–47.
Engler, Kay. "Amor, muerte y destino: La psicología de *eros* en *Los amantes de Teruel*." *Hispanófila* 70 (1980): 1–15.
Hobbs, Gloria L. "Odyssey of *Los amantes de Teruel*." *South Central Bulletin* 26 (1966): 4–9.
Iranzo, Carmen. *Juan Eugenio Hartzenbusch*. TWAS 501. Boston: Twayne, 1978.
Picoche, Jean-Louis. "*Los amantes de Teruel* avant et après." *Recherches sur le monde hispanique au dix-neuvième siècle*. Lille: Université de Lille 3, 1973. 97–126.

David Thatcher Gies

**HATHERLY, Ana** (1929, Porto– ), Portuguese poet, essayist, literary critic, translator, writer of prose fiction. Hatherly studied music in Portugal, France and Germany. She earned a master's degree in Germanic philology from the U of Lisbon. A graduate in cinematographic arts from the London Film School, she teaches at the National School of Cinema and the Center for Visual Art and Communication (ARCO) in Lisbon. She is a member of the International Association of Literary Critics and on the directory of the Association of Portuguese Writers and a secretary of PEN of Portugal. She resides in Lisbon.

Very active in the visual arts connected to the "Poesia Experimental" movement, especially the concretist section, Hatherly, influenced by Oriental philosophy, combined with the occult, is preoccupied with the illusory character of reality that eludes and frustrates the desire for totality and neutral truths. She continues the thematic line of the disintegration of the relationship between "eu/I" and the cosmos, especially from the symbolist Camilo *Pessanha (1867–1926), with her Buddhistic and ascetic dream of reintegrating the poetically purified self with the world of things, a line evident in works such as *Um ritmo perdido* (1958; A Lost Rhythm); *As aparências* (1959; Appearances); and *A dama e o cavaleiro* (1960; The Damsel and the Knight). In 1963 her novella *O Mestre* (The Master) reflects her poetic preoccupations with its Promethean, labyrinthian struggles. With *Sigma* (1965) she joins the concretist movement, which she enriches with her cinematic and painterly games with the semiotic ambiguities of language and proceeds to develop in *Estruturas poéticas — Operação 2* (1967; Poetic Structures—Operation 2) and *Eros frenético* (1968; Frenetic Eros). With *39 Tisanas* (1969; 39 Decoctions), Hatherly refines her experiment with the ironic meaning and character of language, while in *Anagramático* (1970) she turns her concretism into tight poemagrams. In her *Poesia 1958–1978* (1980), Hatherly adds to her itinerary an odyssey lost between the this-sidedness and the other-sidedness of existence. With *O Cisne intacto* (1983; The Swan Intact), Hatherly returns to materialistic eros, complete with Medusan-phallic imagery and various erotic iconoclasms against official morality.

Hatherly produced critical essays on Portuguese *Simbolismo*, one of her favorite subjects, as well as a theoretical anthology of historical Portuguese visual texts and their magico-religious uses. With E. M. de Melo e Castro, she furnished an important resource book of documents of the experimental, *concretista* poetry movement of the 1960s. She is much anthologized and translated. She edits journals and contributes to journals in Europe, Brazil and the United States.

## BIBLIOGRAPHY

### Primary Texts

*O Cisne intacto*. Porto: Limiar, 1983. Poetry.
*O Espaço crítico; Do Simbolismo à vanguarda*. Lisbon: Caminho, 1979. Criticism.
*A Experiência do Prodígio: bases teóricas e antologia de textos visuais portugueses dos séculos XVII e XVIII*. Lisbon: Nacional—Casa da Moeda, 1983. Criticism.
*O Mestre*. 2nd ed. Lisbon: Moraes, 1976. Novella.
*Poesia, 1958–1978*. Lisbon: Moraes, 1980.
*PO-EX: textos básicos e documentos da poesia experimental portuguesa*. Lisbon: Moraes, 1981. Criticism.

### English Translations

Four poems. In *Contemporary Portuguese Poetry: An Anthology in English*. Sel. Helder Macedo and E. M. de Melo e Castro. Manchester: Carcaneti, 1978.

Criticism

Vasconcelos, Maria E. G. de. *"O Mestre*—o mito de Prometeu e o tema do labirinto."
   *Ocidente* 80 (n.d.): 182–95.

Robert R. Krueger

**HEBRAISMS,** Hebrew idioms occurring in another language as well as the
study of Hebrew and Hebraic texts. It flourished in Spain during the Golden
Age of Hispano-Judaic letters (tenth-thirteenth c.), with the interest in Hebrew
Scriptures (sixteenth and seventeenth c.), and in the nineteenth c., recognizing
Jewish contributions to Hispanic culture. Translating Arabic and Hebrew for
*Alphonse X, Jews helped establish Castilian as a literary language. Some He-
braisms were absorbed into Spanish: *sábado* (Saturday), *aleluya, hosanna, des-
mazalado* (weak; from *mazal* or fate), *malsín* (talebearer), *mancer* (son of a
prostitute), *rey de reyes* (King of Kings), *cantar de los cantares* (Song of Songs),
etc., and proper names in the Calendar of Saints.

Reginetta Haboucha

**HEBREO, León,** pseudonym of Judas Abravanel, or Abarbanel (1460?, Lisbon–
1521, Naples), Jewish philosopher and writer. Though of Portuguese origin, he
spent most of his life in Spain, where his father Isaac was physician for and
adviser to Alphonse V and later to Ferdinand. Hebreo followed suit, but the
family was forced to leave Spain in 1492 in spite of his father's pleas to the
king. Hebreo went to Italy, protected by the Aragonese court of Naples, and
died there. Hebreo fits roughly into the middle of a long series of neo-Platonists
who wrote about love, as he did in his best-known work, *Dialoghi d'amore*
(1535; Dialogues of Love). Some of his predecessors in this genre were Maimonides, Ben-Gabirol, Ficino, Pico della Mirandola, Avicebron and Plotinus.
His book was extremely popular and influential in Western Europe and especially
in Spain, in spite of having been placed on the Index (*\*Indice de libros prohibidos*). Traces of his Dialogues can be seen in *Castiglione, Bembo, Aldana,
Calvi, *Boscán, *Garcilaso, el Conde de *Rebolledo, *Nieremberg, and Fray Luis
de *León; Book 4 of *Montemayor's *Diana* and of *Cervantes's *La Galatea* are
particularly interesting examples of his widespread impact. The Dialogues, probably written around 1502, first appeared in Italian, but some believe there was
an earlier Castilian version. In any case they were quickly translated into Castilian, the best-known translation having been done by *Garcilaso de la Vega,
El Inca. It was also translated into Latin and French in the sixteenth c. The three
dialogues are between Sophía and Philón, abstract characters representing knowledge or science, and love. Sophía is a Socratic kind of student-teacher, asking
provocative questions of Philón, who answers explaining the philosophy of love.
The first dialogue deals with the nature and essence of love; the second, its
universality; the third and most successful, its origin. For Hebreo, beauty is the
essence, a grace which delights and moves the person who understands it to
love. A sublimation of form and matter leads to an idealistic aesthetic where the

world is an objectivization of harmonious love. Just as Hebreo forms a sort of transition between the earlier Medieval thinkers and the great writers of the *Siglo de Oro, in his characteristic syncretism he also bridges cultural gaps, as his knowledge of the Judeo-Christian and Arabic traditions attests. *See also* Humanism; Platonism; Renaissance.

BIBLIOGRAPHY

Primary Text

*Diálogos de amor.* Tr. Garcilaso de la Vega, El Inca. Ed. Eduardo Juliá. Madrid: V. Suárez, 1949. See also vol. 21 of the NBAE.

Criticism

Bellinotto, Elena Ofelia. "Un nuevo documento sobre los *Dialoghi d'amore* de Leone Ebreo." *Arquivos do centro cultural Português* 7 (1973): 399–409.
Carvalho, Joaquím. *Leão Hebreu, filósofo.* Coimbra: Imprensa da Universidade, 1918.
Cobos, Jean. "Léon l'Hébreu et ses *Dialogues d'Amour.*" In *Penseurs hétérodoxes du monde hispanique.* Toulouse: U of Toulouse, 1974. 11–35.
Damiens, Suzanne. *Amour et Intellect chez Léon l'Hébreu.* Toulouse: Edouard Privat, 1971.
González-Marcos, Florián-Máximo. "La necesidad en el *Quijote* frente a *Diálogos de amor.*" Diss., New York U, 1972.
Moreau, Joseph. "Penseurs Portugais dans l'Europe des Nations." *Arquivos do centro cultural Português* 7 (1973): 101–15.
Pflaum, Heinz. *Die Idee der Liebe. Leone Ebreo.* Tübingen: J. C. B. Mohr, 1926.
Vallese, Guilio. "La filosofia dell'Amore, dal Ficino al Bembo, da Leone Ebreo ai Minori." In *Studi di umanesimo.* Naples: Ferraro, 1971. 44–89.

Kathleen McNerney

**HEINZE, Úrsula** (1941, Cologne, Germany– ), prose writer. After studying Germanic philology, Heinze began to teach English and German at the high school level. In 1962, she met Ramón Lorenzo, whom she later married, moving to Galicia in 1968. From 1973 to 1977 she taught German at the U of Valladolid. Her early literary avocation (expressed in poems and stories published in German periodicals) led to publications in Gallego beginning in the early 1980s. These include *O soño perdido de Elvira M* (1982; The Lost Dream of Elvira M), a novel about the lives of two women, told from varying viewpoints which privilege their relationships with male characters; *Remuíños en coiro* (1984; Surprise and Confusion), a collection of short stories; and the children's novel *O buzón dos nenos* (1985; The Children's Mailbox). *Sempre Cristina* (1986; Always Cristina) is another novel for children. Heinze has also translated several works from Gallego to German and vice versa. *Arredor da muller en 18 mundos* (1985) is a collection of interviews with women from all parts of Galicia. *See also* Galician Literature.

BIBLIOGRAPHY

Primary Texts

*Remuíños en coiro.* Vigo: Xerais, 1984.
*O soño perdido de Elvira M.* Vigo: Xerais, 1982.

Janet Pérez

**HELDER DE OLIVEIRA, Herberto** (1930, Funchal [Madeira]– ), Portuguese poet and story writer. After publishing his first slim collection of poems, *O Amor em Visita* (1958; Love on a Visit), he abandoned his study at the U of Coimbra and went to work for a Lisbon publishing house. He treats eternal poetic themes—love and death, solitude and life's mysteries—but he is also interested in language per se, and his experiments are not only linguistic but visual, as he has become known as Portugal's leading exponent of "concrete" poetry. His volumes of poetry include *A Colher na Boca* (1961; Spoon in Mouth), *Poemacto* (1961; Poem-act), and *Lugar* (1962; Place). *Poesia Toda I* (1973; Complete Poems I) contains all his poetical works to the date of publication. Among Helder's short fiction are the story collections *Os Passos em Volta* (1963; Footsteps around Us) and *Apresentação do Rosto* (1963; Introduction of the Face). His narratives are usually first-person, surrealistic, hallucinatory or nightmarish, juggling chronological sequence and mixing dream, reality and memory, so that the "real" is nearly impossible to determine. Other works—mostly poems or collections of poetic essays—include *Electronicolírica* (1964; Electronic-Lyric), *Húmus* (1967, *Ofício Cantante* (1967; Singing Profession), *Retrato em Movimiento* (1967; Portrait in Motion) and *Vocação Animal* (1971; Animal Vocation).

BIBLIOGRAPHY

Primary Texts

*Poesia toda 1.* Lisbon: Plátano, 1973.
*Poesia Toda 1953–1980.* Lisbon: Assírio e Alvim, 1981.
*Vocação Animal.* Lisbon: Dom Quixote, 1971.

Janet Pérez

**HERBARIO** (*herbal*). It is a collection of descriptions of plants and herbs giving particular attention to the curative properties or virtues of each. The herbal, which frequently formed part of larger works, pervades the medico-literary tradition of the Middle Ages and the *Renaissance beginning with the *Etymologiae* of Isidore of Seville. The twelfth-c. *Macer Floridus de Viribus Herbarum* of Odo de Meung, which essentially popularizes Dioscorides's *De Materia Medica* and Pliny's *Natural History*, enjoyed a wide currency in Latin and the vernacular, including several versions in Catalan and Castilian. The unedited *Erbolaryo de Maçer* at the Colombine Library in Seville follows an alphabetical arrangement. A monument of Renaissance learning was Andrés de *Laguna's translation and commentary of Dioscorides's *De Materia Medica*. *See also* Edad Media, Literatura de la.

BIBLIOGRAPHY

Primary Texts

La *"Materia Medica" de Dioscórides, transmisión medieval y renacentista*. Ed. César
    Dubler. 6 vols. Barcelona: Tipografía Emporium, 1953–59.
*"Una versió catalana del Libre de les herbes de Macer."* By Lluis Faraudo de Saint
    Germain. *Estudis Románics* 5 (1959): 1–54.

Criticism

Arber, Agnes. *Herbals, Their Origin and Evolution; A Chapter in the History of Botany,
    1470–1670*. Cambridge: Cambridge UP, 1953.
See also Dubler and Faraudo de Saint Germain, Primary Texts.

Porter Conerly

**HERNÁNDEZ, Alonso** (between the fifteenth and sixteenth c., Seville–?) author. Very little is known of Hernández since the only indications about his life are found in his own *Historia Parthenopea* (History of Naples), published in Rome in 1516. According to this, he was an apostolic protonotary, born in Seville, who had lived a very long time in Rome. Apparently, his friend and mentor, Cardinal Bernardino de Carvajal, urged him to write the *Historia* as well as a few other works that are apparently now lost: *Vita Christi* (Life of Christ), *La educación del príncipe* (A Prince's Education), *Siete triumphos de las siete virtudes* (The Seven Victories of the Seven Virtues), and so on. The *Historia* takes the form of a narrative poem praising the heroic deeds of the Great Captain (Gonzalo Fernández de Córdoba) in the Spanish domination of Naples. Although of little literary merit, the *Historia* is an early indication of the learned epic in sixteenth-c. Spain. It still employs the long Castilian meters since the Italianate ones had not yet been introduced in Spain; he relies on Virgil, Dante and above all *Santillana and *Mena as literary models. Since Hernández was himself a witness to the events he describes, he succeeds in providing a reliable account of them. For the sake of style and elegance, he develops mythological and allegorical motifs to embellish the poem.

BIBLIOGRAPHY

Primary Text

*Historia Parthenopea*. Rome: n.p., 1516.

Criticism

Menéndez y Pelayo, M. *Obras completas*. Vol. 6. Vol. 3 of the *Historia de la poesía
    castellana de la Edad Media*. Madrid: Suárez, 1911–36. 118–22.
Pierce, F. *La poesía épica del Siglo de Oro*. 2nd ed. Madrid: Gredos, 1968.

María Teresa Pajares

**HERNÁNDEZ, Miguel** (1910, Orihuela–1942, Alicante), poet and dramatist. Son of a poor herdsman, Hernández left school at fifteen to tend goats. He began to read on his own, borrowing books wherever he could find them. He was drawn to the classics, whose traces are clear in all of his work: *Cervantes, Lope

de *Vega, *Góngora, *Garcilaso de la Vega, San *Juan de la Cruz, and Virgil
(Fray Luis de *León's tr.). He also read modern writers: Gabriel *Miró; the poets
Jorge *Guillén, A. *Machado, J. R. *Jiménez, R. Darío, Valéry, Verlaine.

Hernández began to write when he was sixteen, and at eighteen joined a
literary discussion group where he allowed others to read his work. During the
following years he was greatly influenced by his friend Ramón Sijé, who encouraged him to write religious poetry and drama in the Baroque (Counter-
Reformation) style. In 1930, Hernández began publishing poems and prose
poems—reminiscent of Miró and J. R. Jiménez—in regional newspapers; he
came to be known as the "shepherd poet." Over thirty prose poems have been
collected; they are similar in diction, syntax, and subject matter to his contemporaneous poetry. Hernández decided to move to Madrid in 1931, sure that his
talent would be recognized in the capital. He had to return to Orihuela in defeat
six months later. During the next two years Hernández met and fell in love with
his future wife, Josefina Manresa; he wrote assiduously, encouraged by Sijé,
producing an *auto sacramental* (*auto*) and a book of poetry, *Perito en lunas*
(1933; Expert in Moons). The *octavas reales* (eight hendecasyllabic verses) of
this book are fine examples of neo-Gongorine virtuosity: without titles, they are
so hermetic they have generated numerous misreadings. The *auto, Quien te ha
visto y quien te ve y Sombra de lo que eras* (1934; How You've Changed! and
A Shadow of Your Former Self), clearly reflects Sijé's neo-Catholic influence.
Like a Calderonian *auto* (except for its excessive length), it is a didactic religious
allegory characterized by parallelistic structuring and Baroque language and
figures. It served to open important doors for him when he returned to Madrid
in 1934; José *Bergamín, another neo-Catholic, published it in his prestigious
journal *Cruz y raya*.

Installed permanently in Madrid after 1934, Hernández quickly began expanding his artistic and political horizons. Unpretentious and direct, the "shepherd poet" was warmly received by fellow writers such as Pablo Neruda, Rafael
*Alberti, and Vicente *Aleixandre. He finished writing the poems of *El rayo que
no cesa* (1936; The Unending Thunderbolt), suffused with his longing for the
absent and resolutely chaste Josefina, and with a sense of his own impending
doom, the inevitable destruction he foresaw for a man so passionately involved
in life. This book—twenty-seven "classical" or hendecasyllabic sonnets and
three longer poems—identified him as one of the great poetic voices in pre–
Civil War Spain, so full of brilliant poets. The often-quoted poems of this book
combine an uncommon mastery of classical poetic forms, diction, and technique
with the expression of almost primal emotion. The three longer poems reflect
the influence of Neruda and Aleixandre, whom Hernández increasingly saw as
models for his own poetic development. He published a number of free verse,
surrealist and uninhibited poems during 1935, precipitating his break with Sijé,
with religion and the political right.

In 1936 he wrote two peasant plays, modern versions of Lope's *Fuenteovejuna*
and *Peribáñez*: *Los hijos de la piedra* (Sons of Stone) and *El labrador de más*

*aire* (The Comeliest Peasant). He uses a basic *comedia* theme—the peasants' honor vs. the nobles' depravity—to produce works to "exalt labor and condemn the bourgeoisie." During the war, he wrote the four one-act propaganda plays of *Teatro en la guerra* (1937; Wartime Theater), and *El pastor de la muerte* (1938; Shepherd of Death), combining elements of the peasant play with overt propaganda. Critics almost unanimously dismiss Hernández's drama as inferior to his poetry, but read together they yield interesting insights into this largely autodidactic, idealistic and politically committed man; both genres reflect his profound internalization of *Siglo de Oro models and his uncanny gift for mimesis.

He enlisted in the Republican army in August 1936; he married Josefina in January 1937, and their first son was born a year later, while he was on the front at Teruel. Assigned to a propaganda unit, Hernández traveled incessantly in this capacity, giving readings, organizing cultural activities, publishing newsletters. He represented the Republic in Russia in 1938; his proletarian origins made him an especially effective spokesperson for the Republic. He also served in the trenches when he was needed, wrote numerous hortatory essays and two books of poetry: *Viento del pueblo* (1937; Wind of the People) and *El hombre acecha* (Man the Spy; printed in 1939 but never bound). His health failing, he was sent home for a brief period in 1938. Those months spent with his wife, newly pregnant, and their small child—who died of malnutrition a few months later— would inspire many of the poignant poems of his last collection, *Cancionero y romancero de ausencias* (Songs and Ballads of Absence). Josefina was able to preserve these poems from confiscation by the Francoist authorities, and they were finally published in Buenos Aires in his *Obras completas* (1960; Complete Works).

The two poetry books written during the war are uneven in quality and show marked differences with respect to *El rayo que no cesa*. Longer verses prevail, chiefly alexandrines, and not the free verse of his Neruda-inspired poems of 1935. There are only two sonnets, both alexandrines. This "prophetic" poetry— as he called it, written to "spread emotions and inflame lives"—was often directed to illiterate listeners, so he eliminated from it all traces of Baroque wittiness, language and syntax. The diction becomes almost conversational; clichés, vulgarisms, and apostrophe abound. At its best, it is very powerful poetry, but there are many poems which fail on aesthetic grounds.

Hernández ignored advice to flee Spain before the fall of the Republic, and he was captured quickly. He was imprisoned for six months, during which time he wrote the poems of the *Cancionero*. Released on a fluke in September 1939, he again ignored friends' advice to flee. Reapprehended, he spent three years in various prisons and died in the prison hospital of Alicante of tuberculosis in 1942.

The poetry of his last years—the ninety-eight poems of the *Cancionero* and another group of twenty-five poems printed in the *Obras completas* as "Last Poems"—differ greatly from his earlier work. The *Cancionero* is principally *poesía de tipo tradicional* (poetry in the traditional mode), hepta- or octosyllabic assonant compositions with parallelistic structures. Like most traditional verse, it is enigmatic because of its brevity. Antithesis is pervasive, and the figurative language reflects his perception that life is polymorphous and always open to tragedy. The "Last Poems" are heterogeneous, generally *arte mayor (verses longer than octosyllables) with traditional fixed stanzas. Cosmogonic images are frequent; a high level of abstraction characterizes many of the very last compositions, where he pondered the nature of a world which could condemn so many innocent people.

Hernández's influence on post-war poetry is difficult to gauge; his works were banned in Spain until 1952, when a selection of his poetry—omitting almost everything written after *El rayo que no cesa*—was published. He became something of a political cult figure among those who opposed Franco, and after the *caudillo*'s death in 1975, he was lionized.

BIBLIOGRAPHY

Primary Texts

*Obras completas.* Ed. Elvio Romero and Andrés Ramón Vázquez. Buenos Aires: Losada, 1960.
*Obra poética completa.* Ed. Leopold de Luis and Jorge Urrutia. Bilbao: Zero, 1976.
*Poesía y prosa de guerra.* Ed. Juan Cano Ballesta and Robert Marrast. Madrid: Ayuso, 1977.

English Translations

*Selected Poems: Miguel Hernández and Blas de Otero.* Ed., tr. Timothy Baland and Hardie St. Martin. Boston: Beacon, 1972.
*The Sixties* 9 (Spring 1967). Nine poems, and writings about Hernández by Neruda, Alberti, Lorca, Aleixandre, Celaya.

Criticism

Berns, Gabriel. "Violence and Poetic Expression: A Study of the Poetry of Miguel Hernández." Diss., Ohio State, 1968.
Cano Ballesta, Juan. *La poesía de Miguel Hernández.* 2nd ed. Madrid: Gredos, 1971.
Chevallier, Marie. *La escritura poética de Miguel Hernández.* Madrid: Siglo XXI de España, 1977.
———. *Los temas poéticos de Miguel Hernández.* Madrid: Siglo XXI de España, 1978.
Ifach, María de Gracia. *Miguel Hernández, rayo que no cesa.* Barcelona: Plaza & Janés, 1975.
Manresa, Josefina. *Recuerdos de la viuda de Miguel Hernández.* Madrid: Torre, 1981.
Nichols, Geraldine Cleary. *Miguel Hernández.* TWAS 464. Boston: Twayne, 1978.
Puccini, Dario. *Miguel Hernández: Vida y poesía.* Buenos Aires: Losada, 1967.
Ramos, Vicente. *Miguel Hernández.* Madrid: Gredos, 1973.
Zardoya, Concha. *Miguel Hernández, Vida y obra—Bibliografía—Antología.* New York: Hispanic Institute, 1955.

                                                                                    Geraldine Nichols

**HERNÁNDEZ, Ramón** (1935, Madrid– ), novelist, short story writer, essayist and poet. Since 1966 he has written eleven important and, at times, experimental novels: *Presentimiento de lobos* (1966; Presentiment of Wolves), *Palabras en* *el muro* (1969; Words on the Wall; finalist of the Biblioteca Breve prize), *La ira de la noche* (1970; The Anger of Night; winner of the Aguilas prize), *El tirano inmóvil* (1970; The Unmoved Tyrant), *Invitado a morir* (1972; Invited to Die), *Eterna memoria* (1975; The Eternal Memory; winner of the Hispanoamericano de Novela prize), *Algo está ocurriendo aquí* (1976; *Something Is Happening Here*, 1983), *Fábula de la ciudad* (1979; Fable of the City), *Pido la muerte al rey* (1979; I Ask the King for Death), *Bajo palio* (1983; Under the Pallium), and *Los amantes del sol poniente* (1983; The Lovers of the Setting Sun; Casino de Mieres prize). Even though Spanish reality is detectable in Hernández's novels, more often than not his works are concerned with mankind in a transcendental sense and with its struggle and disorientation in light of the absurdities which prevail in contemporary society. In his works, Hernández demonstrates his mastery of interior monologue and stream of consciousness. Undoubtedly, he is among Spain's best twentieth-c. novelists.

BIBLIOGRAPHY

Primary Texts

*Eterna memoria.* 2nd ed. Barcelona: Argos Vergara, 1982.
*Invitado a morir.* Barcelona: Planeta, 1972.
*Palabras en el muro.* 2nd ed. Barcelona: Seix Barral, 1984.
*Pido la muerte al rey.* Barcelona: Argos Vergara, 1979.
*Presentimiento de lobos.* 2nd ed. Madrid: Espasa-Calpe, 1979.

English Translation

*Something Is Happening Here.* Tr. Margaret E. Beeson and María Castellanos Collins. Lincoln, NE: Society of Spanish and Spanish-American Studies, 1983.

Criticism

Cabrera, Vicente, and Luis T. González-del-Valle. "La intercomunicación narrativa multidimensional y *Algo está ocurriendo aquí*" and "Hacia una interpretación de *Fábula de la ciudad.*" In *El teatro de Federico Gárcia Lorca y otros ensayos sobre literatura española e hispanoamericana.* Lincoln, NE: Society of Spanish and Spanish-American Studies, 1980. 229–38, 239–47.
González-del-Valle, Luis T. "Lo interpersonal en *Presentimiento de lobos:* un estudio de los modos de transmisión." In *Estudios en honor a Ricardo Gullón.* Ed. L. T. González-del-Valle and Darío Villanueva. Lincoln, NE: Society of Spanish and Spanish-American Studies, 1984.
———. "El hombre: fluctuante realidad e inmutable fin. *Los amantes del sol poniente.*" *Los Cuadernos del norte* 30 (1985): 91–93.

Luis T. González-del-Valle

**HERRERA, Antonio de** (1549, Cuéllar, Segovia–1625, Madrid), historian. He studied in Spain and Italy and was secretary to the viceroy in Naples and an official chronicler of the Indies and Castile for three Kings (Phillip II, III, IV). His writing is extremely detailed and often verbose; this flaw is somewhat offset by his diligent use of many original documents. The voluminous *Décadas o Historia General de los hechos de los castellanos* (1601; Decades, or General History of Deeds of the Castilians) reports events from the discovery of the New World in 1492 up to 1554; it was widely translated and excerpted. The *Historia general del mundo en tiempo del rey Don Felipe II* (1601 and 1612; General History of the World in the Time of King Philip II) covers European history in a highly nationalistic fashion, with Spain at the center of all events. Interesting also is his history of Mary Stuart, the *Historia de lo sucedido en Escosia e Inglaterra en cuarenta y cuatro años que vivió María Estuardo* (1589; History of Events in Scotland and England during the Forty-four Years Mary Stuart Lived).

BIBLIOGRAPHY

Primary Texts

*Historia general de los hechos.* . . . 17 vols. Madrid: Archivos, 1934–58.
*Historia general del mundo en tiempo.* . . . Madrid: Sánchez, 1601–12.

English Translations

*Expeditions into the Valley of the Amazons, 1539–40, 1639.* Tr., ed., notes C. R. Markham. London: Hakluyt, 1859. Rpt. New York: Franklin, 1963.
*Landa's* Relación de las cosas de Yucatán, *a translation.* Ed., notes A. Tozzer. Millwood, NY: Kraus, 1975. From the *Historia general.*
*The general history of America.* Tr. J. Stevens. London: Longmans, 1740–43. Abridged and inaccurate.

Criticism

Alonso Cortés, N. "Datos sobre el cronista Antonio de Herrera." *Estudios sevillanos* 1 (1955): n.p.
Pérez Bustamante, C. *El cronista Antonio de Herrera y la historia de Alejandro Farnesio.* Madrid: Conde de Cartagena, 1933.

                                                                    Maureen Ihrie

**HERRERA, Fernando de** (1534, Seville–1597, Seville), poet, literary commentarist and historian, called "El divino" for the ideal of technical perfection set by his poetic and editorial achievements. He served as a minor lay functionary in the church of San Andrés in Seville after about 1565, and devoted himself primarily to literary pursuits. The little that is known of his austere scholarly existence is found mainly in his editor Francisco *Pacheco's *Libro de Descripción de los verdaderos retratos* (1599; Book of Description of True Portraits, a series of biographical sketches accompanied by portraits). Pacheco is better known as the father-in-law of Diego de Velázquez; he belonged to a circle of Sevillian writers and artists that met at the palace of Herrera's patron, the Count of Gelves, and included, in addition to Herrera, Juan de la *Cueva, Juan de *Mal Lara, and the historian *Argote de Molina. Herrera shared with his Andalusian colleagues a strong interest in classical and Italian Renaissance erudition, and sought in his poetry and prose to elevate vernacular literature to the elegance, expressive energy and clarity of classical models. Herrera's edition of and commentary on the works of *Garcilaso de la Vega, the *Anotaciones* (1580; Annotations), also constitute a coherent *Renaissance poetic that directed peninsular poetry toward the aristocratic exaltation of erudite and polished, or "culto," literary language brought to its limit in the seventeenth c. by the Andalusian Luis de *Góngora. While his commentary demonstrates a genuine admiration for Garcilaso's poetry, Herrera took the liberty of changing some of Garcilaso's vocabulary to avoid images or words he considered unpoetic, vulgar or archaic, and modifying an occasional line to achieve purer poetic expression. Herrera's sensitivity to the typographical presence of poetic and critical texts led him to orthographic reforms that, among other changes, obliged the printer to add to his fonts an undotted "i" and diacritical marks to indicate hiatus. The Castilian Juan Fernández de Velasco, under the pseudonym Prete Jacopín, attacked Herrera's "purification" of Garcilaso's poetic diction, but Herrera's reply only reconfirmed his dedication to polished and elegant style.

   In his own poetry, Herrera made multiple revisions to intensify musical or visual effects. Unusual though it was for the work of a sixteenth-c. poet to appear during his lifetime, he supervised the printing of *Algunas obras* (1582; Selected Works) with meticulous precision. His heroic poetry, resonating with biblical diction and solemn phrases echoing the Psalms, commemorates important battles, such as the Spanish victory at Lepanto (1571) and the Portuguese defeat and tragic loss of the young King Sebastian at Alcazarquivir (1578). Herrera's love poetry was inspired by his patron's wife, Doña Leonor de Milán, the Countess of Gelves. Her poetic name of "Luz" (Light) permitted a Neoplatonic play on the imagery associated with this term and attached a celestial value to her beauty. Herrera's finely crafted sonnets, elegies, sestinas and odes present the courtly dynamic of perpetual frustration of desire using the vivid imagery of classical mythology, Petrarchan moths and flames, fire and ice, hope and despair. His *Algunas obras* were published in the year following Leonor's death, and show the influence not only of *Castiglione, Bembo, Petrarch and Garcilaso but also of León *Hebreo, Ausiàs *March and the courtly aesthetic of the *cancionero* poets. Like Petrarch in his *Canzoniere*, Herrera organized his poems by form throughout this edition: a group of sonnets is followed by an ode or an elegy. After Herrera's death, Pacheco published his *Versos* (1619), and in 1948 José Manuel Blecua published as *Rimas inéditas* (Unpublished Verse) the poems found in a manuscript in the National Library (*Biblioteca Nacional) in Madrid. The meticulous work of Adolphe Coster, Blecua and Oreste Macrí has revealed numerous variants and some duplications of sonnets in Pacheco's edition, whose authenticity is controversial. Blecua agrees with Macrí that Pacheco had Herrera's final versions of the poems he published in the 1619 edition, but, unlike the Italian Hispanist, he believes that Pacheco made substantial changes in some of the poems, and that it was the editor, and not the poet himself, who organized the poems in the order in which they appear in the *Versos*. In any case, the corpus of Herrera's poems available to twentieth-c. readers presents a study in poetic perfectionism with the numerous subtle modifications made by the poet from one version to another.

   Herrera's historical prose includes his *Relación de la guerra de Chipre y batalla naval de Lepanto* (1572; Account of the War of Cyprus and the Naval

Battle of Lepanto) and *Tomás Moro* (1592; Thomas More). Among his lost works are a *Gigantomaquia* (a verse account of the revolt of the Titans) and a history of the world. In the absence of his projected *Arte poética* (Poetics), his commentary on Garcilaso furnishes a clear presentation of his poetic theory. Herrera's creative relationship with the poetry of his predecessors, ancient and modern, is manifested in the *Anotaciones* and in his own carefully polished texts. It defines the possibilities and limits of poetic language in the sixteenth c. and points the way for peninsular poetry in the seventeenth c. *See also* Escuela sevillana; Humanism; Italian literary influences.

BIBLIOGRAPHY

Primary Texts

*Controversia sobre sus Anotaciones a las Obras de Garcilaso de la Vega. Poesías inéditas.* Ed. José María Asensio. Seville: Sociedad de Bibliófilos Andaluces, 1870.

*Obra poética.* Ed. José Manuel Blecua. Anejo del BRAE, 32. 2 vols. Madrid: RAE, 1975. (Includes *Algunas obras* [1582], *Versos* [1619], and *Poemas sueltos* including *Rimas inéditas* [1948].)

*Obras de Garci Lasso de la Vega con Anotaciones de Fernando de Herrera.* Seville: Alonso de la Barrera, 1580. Published in Garcilaso de la Vega. *Obras completas del Poeta Garcilaso acompañadas de los textos íntegros de los comentarios. . . .* Ed. Antonio Gallego Morell. Granada: Universidad de Granada, 1966.

*Relación de la Guerra de Chipre, y sucesso de la batalla Naval de Lepanto.* Seville: Alonso Picardo, 1572.

*Tomás Moro.* Seville, 1592. Critical ed. Francisco López Estrada. *Archivo Hispalense* (Seville), 2nd series. (1950): 39–41.

Criticism

Alatorre, Antonio. "Garcilaso, Prete Jacopín y Don Tomás Tamayo de Vargas." *MLN* 78.2 (1963): 126–51.

Blecua, José Manuel. "De nuevo sobre los textos poéticos de Herrera." *BRAE* 38 (1958): 155.

Coster, Adolphe. *Fernando de Herrera, "El Divino."* Paris: Champion, 1908.

Ferguson, William. *La versificación imitativa en Fernando de Herrera.* London: Tamesis, 1980.

Guillén, Jorge. "The Poetical Life of Herrera." *Boston Public Library Quarterly* 3 (1951): 91–98.

Kossoff, David. *Vocabulario de la obra poética de Herrera.* Madrid: RAE, 1966.

Macrí, Oreste. *Fernando de Herrera.* Madrid: Gredos, 1972.

Pring-Mill, R.D.F. "Escalígero y Herrera: citas y plagios de los *Poeticas Libri Septem* en las *Anotaciones.*" *Actas del Segundo Congreso Internacional de Hispanistas.* Ed. J. Sánchez Romeralo and N. Poulssen. Nijmegen: Instituto Español de la Universidad de Nijmegen, 1967. 289–98.

Randel, Mary Gaylord. *The Historical Prose of Fernando de Herrera.* London: Tamesis, 1971.

                                                                      Emilie Bergmann

**HERRERA, Gabriel Alonso de** (1470, Talavera de la Reina–1540?, ?), agronomist and humanist. A beneficiary of the church school of Talavera, he attended the U of Granada and completed his education through travel to Spain, France,

Germany and Italy. Herrera later dedicated himself to the practice of agriculture with zeal and intelligence, probably having studied both Latin and Arabic sources. He was also a chaplain for Cardenal Jiménez de *Cisneros, a prime mover of the *Renaissance in Spain and founder of the U at Alcalá de Henares. Cisneros commissioned him to write *La Agricultura General* (1513; The Art of Agriculture), published the work in Alcalá, and distributed it free to local landowners. In the prologue, Herrera states that he is the first to write a treatise on agriculture in Castilian. The text is a model of the harmonious, Latinized prose so admired by Renaissance humanists. Herrera is also readable for his sound advice on farming, scientific acumen, and conviction that a bucolic life is both saintly and salutary. *See also* Humanism.

BIBLIOGRAPHY

Primary Text

*Agricultura General.* Ed. A. de Burgos. Madrid: A. Santa Coloma y Nieto y Cía, 1858.

Criticism

Bonilla y San Martín, Adolfo. "Hernando Alonso de Herrera." *Revue Hispanique* 50 (1920): 61–196. (See pp. 73–75; 130–41.)

Dubler C. E. "Posibles fuentes árabes de la 'Agricultura general' de Gabriel Alonso de Herrera." *Al Andaluz* 6 (1941): 135–56.

Vindel, Francisco. "Alonso de Herrera y su Libro de Agricultura." *Artículos bibliológicos.* Madrid, n.p 1948. 131–45.

Helen H. Reed

**HERRERA GARRIDO, Francisca** (1869, La Coruña–1950, La Coruña), Galician poet and novelist. Born into a wealthy family, Herrera Garrido lived in La Coruña and Madrid, returning to Oleiros at the outset of the Civil War. Self-taught, her first influence was that of Rosalía de *Castro, and she was a friend of the Murguía family after Rosalía's death. In 1915 she published the book of poetry *Almas de muller . . . ¡Volallas na luz!* (Woman's Souls . . . Flutterings in the Light!), with a prologue by Manuel Murguía. In 1925 she herself wrote the prologue to an edition of *Cantares Gallegos* (Galician Ballads). She was familiar with the writing of Noriega Varela, Cabanillas, *Curros, *Pérez Lugín, and *Valle-Inclán. Very conservative, Herrera Garrido attacked feminists working to obtain suffrage for women, and held a clear idea of class rights and obligations, including the fact that peasants inevitably were subject to emigration.

With Rosalía de Castro as model, and understanding her precursor as a romantic writer, Herrera Garrido composed lamentations and praises of the Galician land and people. Her preferred language for verse was Galician, while some of the novels are in Spanish. *Almas de muller* has long poems telling the story of peasant women who are miserable, and resigned to their fate, but who can only complain. *Flores do noso paxareco* (1919; Flowers from our Garden) represents a return to light rhythm and short compositions. At times Herrera Garrido's poetry becomes exaggeratedly sentimental, but her use of Galician for prose, both because she was a woman and because few novels were written in that language, is significant for the analysis of the rebirth of Galician literary creation. The three basic elements in her novels are ruralism, the woman as mother, and the sacrificing woman. The fundamental technique is of the nineteenth-c.; she believes in love and the goodness of women as the seat of all virtue, although they are victims of many human relationships. Although little known, her work has excellent linguistic quality in spite of an anachronistic style and content.

Herrera Garrido was the only woman elected to the Galician Royal Academy, but the unexplained long delay before she was inducted resulted in her dying before assuming the chair. *See also* Galician Literature.

BIBLIOGRAPHY

Primary Texts

*Almas de muller . . . ¡Volallas na luz!* La Coruña: Roel, 1915.
*Martes d'antroido.* La Coruña: Lar, 1925.
*Néveda.* La Coruña: Roel, 1920.
*Sorrisas e bágoas.* Madrid: Imprenta científica y artística de Alrededor del Mundo, 1913.
*A y-alma de Mingos.* El Ferrol: Céltiga, 1922.

Criticism

Naya, J. "Francisca Herrera Garrido." *Boletín de la Real Academia Gallega* 25 (1953): 160–61.
Noia, María del Camino. "Limiar." In *Néveda.* 2nd ed. Sada–La Coruña: Xerais, 1981. 9–29.
Ríos Panisse, M. "*Néveda,* Primeiro acerto." *Festa da palabra silenciada* (Vigo.) 3 (Jan. 1986): 6–9.
Romaní, A., and María Xosé Canitrot. "*Almas de muller . . . ¡Volallas na luz!*" *Festa da palabra silenciada* 3 (Jan. 1986): 17–19.

Kathleen March

**HERRERA PETERE, José** (1910, Guadalajara–1977, Geneva, Switzerland), Spanish poet and novelist. Exiled following the Spanish Civil War, he lived in France, Switzerland and Mexico. During the Republic, he published a novel, *Acero de Madrid* (1938; Steel of Madrid), apparently war propaganda, which won the National Literary Prize for that year. However, most of his work appeared in exile. *Niebla de cuernos (Entreacto en Europa)* (1940; Fog of Horns [Intermission in Europe]) presents the ironic reaction of a Spanish refugee from the fallen Republic in the face of the frivolity of life in France. Although the tone is humorous, the author's bitterness at French indifference for Spain's suffering shows through. *Cumbres de Extremadura* (1945; Peaks of Extremadura) is a collection of semi-journalistic narratives, apparently treating the theme of the Loyalist heroism during the Civil War. He also wrote three dramatic pieces: *Carpio de Tajo* (1954), *Plomo y mercurio* (1965; Lead and Mercury), and *Segunda semana* (1968; Second Week). His poetry was published in a bilingual (French-Spanish) edition entitled *Dimanche, vers le Sud . . .* (1956; Sunday, Toward the South . . . ). His last poetry book was *El incendio* (The Fire).

## BIBLIOGRAPHY

Primary Texts

*Acero de Madrid*. Madrid: Nuestro Pueblo, 1938.
*Cumbres de Extremadura*. Prol. M. Zambrano. Barcelona: Anthropos Editorial del Hombre, 1986.
*Dimanche, vers le Sud*. . . . Paris: Pierre Seghers, 1956.
*Niebla de cuernos (Entreacto en Europa)*. Mexico: Séneca, 1940.

Criticism

Marra-López, José R. *Narrativa española fuera de España (1939–1961)*. Madrid: Guadarrama, 1963. 510–11.

Janet Pérez

**HERRERA Y RIBERA, Rodrigo de** (1592, Madrid–1657, ?), dramatist. Part of the Lope de *Vega school, he was praised both by Lope and *Cervantes. His best works include *El primer templo de España* (The First Temple of Spain), *La fe no ha menester armas* (Faith Needs No Weapons), *Del cielo viene el buen rey* (The Good King Is from Heaven) and *Castigar por defender* (To Chastise in Order to Defend).

## BIBLIOGRAPHY

Primary Text

*Del cielo viene el buen rey*. In BAE 45.

Criticism

Bergamín, J. *Mangas y capirotes*. Madrid: Plutarco, 1933. Contains a study of *Del cielo viene el buen rey.*

**HERVÁS, José Gerardo de,** pseudonym Jorge Pitillas (?, ?–1742, Salamanca), cleric and satirist. Hervás is remembered primarily for his biting *Sátira contra los malos escritores de este siglo* (1742; Satire against the Bad Writers of This Century), which appeared in the seventh and final volume of the *Diario de los literatos* (Journal for Learned Men). His poem, composed in linking tercets, was heavily indebted to Boileau, and to some extent influenced by the Latin satirists. The true identity of Jorge Pitillas was not discovered until the nineteenth c., when the Marquis of Valmar established that the satire was the product of José Gerardo de Hervás y Cobo de la Torre, a priest and professor of law at the U of Salamanca. Hervás also published, under the anagrammatic pseudonym Don Hugo Herrera de Jaspedós, a few critical articles for the *Diario de los literatos,* and wrote the poem *El rasgo épico verídico epifonema* (The Veridical Epic Feature of Epiphonema).

## BIBLIOGRAPHY

Primary Texts

Works under pseud. Jorge Pitillas. In *Poetas líricos del siglo XVIII*. Ed. Marqués de Valmar. Vol. 1. *BAE 61.*

**HERVÁS Y PANDURO, Lorenzo** (1735, Horcajo de Santiago, Cuenca–1809, Rome), philologist. Hervás began his academic career as a teacher of humanities and philosophy in various Jesuit schools in Spain, and was for a time the rector of the Seminary for Nobles. As with many other Jesuit educators Hervás relocated in Italy after the expulsion from Spain of the Society of Jesus in 1767. He spent the greater part of his life in Italy, principally in Cesena, where he resided under the protection of the Marquis of Ghini, and later in Rome. He returned to Spain between 1798 and 1801, during the temporary relaxation of the ban on the Jesuit Society by Charles IV. He lived the remainder of his life as librarian of the papal residence of Quirinal in Rome.

During his long exile Hervás pursued his studies in mathematics, astronomy, natural sciences and linguistics with such fervor and thoroughness that he became recognized as one of the most erudite men of his times. He put his encyclopedic knowledge to use in an ambitious and massive twenty-two volume project, titled *Idea dell'Universo* (1778–92; Concept of the Universe). The first sixteen volumes (1778–84) encompass anthropological, cosmological and historical studies of man and his universe. Volumes 17–21, published between 1784 and 1787 under the title *Catalogo delle lingue* (Catalog of Languages), constitute the first serious study of comparative linguistics. A final volume, *Analisi filosofico-teologico della carità, ossia dell'amor di Dio* (1792; Philosophical-Theological Analysis of Charity, or, On the Love of God), attempts to reconcile humanistic philosophy and Catholic thought. From 1789 to 1805 Hervás revised and translated his works into Spanish, giving separate titles to each section: *Historia de la vida del hombre* (7 vols.; History of Man), *El hombre físico* (2 vols.; Physical Man), *Viaje estático al mundo planetario* (4 vols.; Ecstatic Voyage to the Planets), and *Catálogo de las lenguas de las naciones conocidas, y enumeración, división y clases de éstas según la diversidad de sus idiomas y dialectos* (6 vols., 1800–1805; Catalog of the Languages of the Known Nations, and Enumeration, Division and Classification of These According to the Diversity of Their Tongues and Dialects).

It is on the basis of his Catalog that Hervás is considered to be the father of comparative philology. Hervás amassed an impressive library of reference materials, including every grammar and dictionary available to him, as well as extensive notes and correspondence from Jesuit missionaries in the Americas, Asia and the Pacific. The scope of his research was such that Hervás himself compiled grammars for over forty languages, in addition to numerous vocabularies. The Catalog itself contains information on some 300 languages, categorized by language groups. His work is divided into four major sections: vol. 1, *Principios generales y lenguas de América* (General Principles and the Languages of the Americas); vol. 2, *Islas del Pacífico, del Índico y Asia continental* (Languages of the Pacific and Indian Ocean Isles and of the Asian Continent); vol. 3, *Lenguas de las naciones advenedizas de Europa* (Languages of the Nomadic Nations of Europe); vols. 4–5, *Naciones europeas primitivas* (Primitive European Nations [Celtic, Iberian and Basque]). In the preliminary chapters of his first volume Hervás assesses the various criteria upon which the study of man and his socio-cultural organization should be based: recorded history, customs and ethnography. And he considers the study of language to be the best source of information regarding the origins of and relationships among the peoples of the world. He establishes three interrelated categories for linguistic studies: the lexicon, the grammatical structure and the pronunciation of the language in question. Hervás cautions against the superficial comparison of lexical similarities between languages as a basis for comparative study. He recognized the deceptiveness of such similarities as a product of the intermingling of language groups rather than as evidence of a common root language. Thus he rejected the theory of Hebrew as being the universal root language, a theory commonly accepted during the eighteenth c. Hervás refuted the theories of his contemporary Antoine Court de Gebelin, who, on the basis of lexical comparison, tried to establish the Celtic language as a source for Basque, and Hebrew as the basis for Armenian, Egyptian and Malay. Hervás argued for the diverse origins of languages; as a religious man he accepted the theological explanation for language diversity from the Tower of Babel story, but he also found no scientific basis in his research to support belief in a universal root language. Hervás was one of the first linguists to consider grammatical structure as one of the distinctive features in language groups. He was also among the first to place phonetics alongside grammatical and lexical studies as an integral part of linguistic research. His works profoundly influenced such theorists as Max Müller and Wilhelm von Humbolt, who met Hervás and consulted with him in Rome. While these later philologists found fault with some of Hervás's theories and his methodology, they recognized the tremendous value of his research materials to linguistic studies. Although Hervás had compiled enough information for several additional volumes of his Catalog, he died before he could finish preparations for their publication. Other works left incomplete at his death include a treatise, *Historia del arte de escribir* (History of the Art of Writing), and a *Paleografía universal* (Universal Paleography). Hervás's interest in languages led him to investigate instructional techniques for the deaf. His two books, *Escuela española de sordomudos o arte para enseñarles a escribir y hablar el idioma español* (1795; Instruction of Deaf-mutes, or, the Art of Teaching Them to Write and Speak the Spanish Language) and *Catecismo para instrucción de los sordomudos* (1796; Catechism for the Instruction of Deaf-mutes), are pioneering works in the field. Considering the tremendous scope of Hervás's knowledge and his important contributions to language studies, Navarro Ledesma justly characterized Hervás as "el último humanista y primer filólogo del mundo" (the last humanist and first philologist in the world).

BIBLIOGRAPHY

Criticism

Batllori, Miguel. "El archivo lingüístico de Hervás en Roma y su reflejo en Wilhelm von Humbolt." *Archivum Historicum Societatis Iesu* 20 (1951): 59–116.
González Palencia, Angel. "Nuevas noticias bibliográficas del abate Hervás y Panduro."

*Revista de la Biblioteca, Archivo y Museo del Ayuntamiento de Madrid* 5 (1928): 345–59. Revised version in *Eruditos y libreros del siglo XVIII.* Madrid: CSIC, 1948. 195–279.

Niehaus, Thomas. "Two Studies on Lorenzo Hervás y Panduro, S.J. (1735–1809): I. As Newtonian Popularizer. II. As Anthropologist." *Archivum Historicum Societatis Iesu* 44 (1975): 105–30.

Portillo, E. del. "Lorenzo Hervás: su vida y sus escritos (1735–1809)." *Razón y Fé* 25 (1909): 34–50 and 277–292; 26 (1910): 307–24; 27 (1911): 176–85; 28 (1912): 59–72 and 463–75.

Rodríguez de Mora, Carlos. *Lorenzo Hervás y Panduro; su aportación a la filología española.* Madrid: Partenon, 1971.

Zarco Cuevas, Julián. *Estudios sobre Lorenzo Hervás y Panduro. I. Vida y escritos.* Madrid: Prieto, 1936.

Donald C. Buck

**HIDALGO, José Luis** (1919, Torres, Santander–1947, Madrid), Cantabrian poet and painter. Best known for his profound, meditative lyricism, he published three books of verse before his early death from tuberculosis. *Raíz* (1944; Root), heavily influenced by poets of the *García Lorca–*Guillén generation, was followed by eleven sketches titled *Los animales* (1945; Animals). His most significant work *Los muertos* (1947; The Dead), though conceived as a memorial to Spain's Civil War dead and largely written before he knew he was dying, seems to foreshadow his passing, which occurred shortly after its publication. His *Obra poética completa* (1976; Complete Poetic Works), includes, besides these books, his *Canciones para niños* (Songs for Children), first published in 1951, and numerous other poems unpublished during his lifetime.

BIBLIOGRAPHY

Primary Texts

*Obra poética completa.* Ed. María de Gracia Ifach. Santander: Institución Cultural de Cantabria, Diputación Provincial, 1976.

English Translations

"Estoy maduro" and "Muerte." In *The Penguin Book of Spanish Verse.* Ed. and tr. J. M. Cohen. Baltimore: Penguin, 1960.
"No." Tr. S. Berg. *Greenfield Reviews* 3 (1974): 26.

Criticism

Campos, Jorge. Introduction to *Los muertos.* Madrid: Taurus, 1966. 7–16.
DeTorre, Emilio E. "José Luis Hidalgo: Poeta vital." *HR* 49.4 (Autumn 1981): 469–82.
Fernández, Lidio Jesús. "Esthéthique et expression surréalistes chez José Luis Hidalgo." *Iris* 3 (1982): 15–45.
García Cantalapiedra, Aurelio. *Tiempo y vida de José Luis Hidalgo.* Madrid: Taurus, 1975.

Romano Colangeli, María. *José Luis Hidalgo, Poeta della morte.* Bologna: Patron, 1962.

Martha Miller

**HIERRO, José** (1922, Madrid– ), poet and art critic. One of Spain's most important post–Civil War poets, Hierro was a founder in 1944 of the Santander magazine *Proel*, the literary organ of a group of young artists who sought to express their social and ethical concerns within a new aesthetic framework. Hierro believes that historical circumstance determines the artistic choices of the individual writer and that the destiny of his own generation was to give testimony to contemporary problems.

Although the persistent commitment to social poetry is evident throughout his work, particularly in *Tierra sin nosotros* (1947; Earth without Us), *Alegría* (1947; Joy) and *Quinta del 42* (1953; The Draftees of 42), there is often a dynamic tension in Hierro's verse between the collective and the intimate, the historical and the personally irrational or, in his words, the "report" and the "hallucination." These elements are integrated in his major thematic preoccupation: time in its personal, existential and historical dimensions. Although Hierro rejects what he sees as the detachment of "pure" poetry and although he has a stated preference for direct and commonplace words, in his own work there is an interplay of rhythm and sound and a complexity of meaning in the use of poetic language.

The 1974 anthology *Cuanto sé de mí* (All That I Know of Me) brings together selections from his major works, including the *Libro de las alucinaciones* (1964; Book of Hallucinations) and previously unpublished poems.

BIBLIOGRAPHY

Primary Texts

*Antología.* Sel. and intro. Aurora de Albornoz. Madrid: Visor, 1980.
*Cuanto sé de mí.* Barcelona: Seix Barral, 1974.
*Libro de las alucinaciones.* Madrid: Nacional, 1964.
*Poesías completas (1944–1962).* Madrid: Giner, 1962.

English Translations

Selected poems. In *Translations from the Spanish.* Ed., Tr. Clayton Eshleman and Cid Corman. Reno: R. Morris, 1967.
6 poems. Tr. H. W. Patterson. In *Antología Bilingüe.* . . . Madrid: Cultura Hispánica, 1965.

Criticism

Albornoz, Aurora de. "Aproximación a la poética de José Hierro." *CH* 341 (n.d.): 273–90.
Jiménez, José Olivio. "La poesía de José Hierro." *Cinco poetas del tiempo.* Madrid: Insula, 1972. 177–326.
Otero, Isaac A. "La poética de José Hierro y análisis de 'Para un esteta.' " *CH* 303 (n.d.): 719–29.

Peña, Pedro J. de la. *Individuo y colectividad: El caso de José Hierro*. Valencia: U of Valencia, 1978.

Victoria Wolff Unruh

*HIJA DEL CONDE DON JULIÁN Y LA PÉRDIDA DE ESPAÑA*, **Cantar de la** (Song of Count Julian's Daughter and the Losing of Spain), a *cantar de gesta*. The oldest known *cantar de gesta*, it narrates the Mozarabic legend of how the Iberian Peninsula fell to the Arabs in 711. Rodrigo, a powerful king in Spain, raped the daughter of Count Julian, also a powerful leader. Enraged, Julian exacted revenge by assisting the Moors in their attack on Rodrigo, allowing them to sweep the entire peninsula. There are several variants to the basic story. As with similar folk material, this legend has undergone countless elaborations and inspired many literary works over the centuries.

BIBLIOGRAPHY

Primary Texts

*Floresta de leyendas heroicas españolas*. Ed. R. Menéndez Pidal. Clásicos Castellanos 62, 71, and 84. 3 vols. Madrid: Espasa-Calpe, 1925–27.
*Reliquias de la poesía épica española*. Ed. R. Menéndez Pidal. Madrid: Espasa-Calpe, 1951. 1–19. Historical sources.

*HIJOS DEL REY SANCHO DE NAVARRA*, **Cantar de los** (Song of the Children of King Sancho of Navarre), a *cantar de gesta*. Doña Urraca, wife of Sancho el Mayor, is defamed and insulted by her oldest child, García, but Ramiro, the illegitimate son of Sancho, comes to her defense. Urraca subsequently adopts Ramiro, and spurns her two legitimate sons.

BIBLIOGRAPHY

Primary Text

In BAE 16: 202–5.

**HISPANO-JUDAIC LITERATURE.** The Golden Age of Jewish letters in Moorish Spain lasted from the tenth to the twelfth centuries. In Córdoba, under Umayyad rule, scholarship prospered and was influenced by Arabic culture, particularly in poetry. With Abdel Rahman III, Caliph of Córdoba in 929, Jews achieved high posts in medicine, finances, agriculture, commerce, and crafts, and flourished in philosophy, astronomy, mathematics, natural sciences, and letters. His physician, Hasdai ibn Shaprut, was chief of customs and foreign trade and *Nasi* (prince) over the Jews. Hasdai helped revive Hebrew as a literary language and communicated with Talmudic academies in Bagdad and Kairuan. Hebrew philologists, Dunash b. Labrat and Menahem ben Saruq, whose rivalry motivated work on Hebrew poetry, grammar, and lexicography, benefited from his support. B. Labrat introduced Arabic metric rules and rhyme to secular Hebrew verse. Their successor, Meruan b. Hanai (eleventh c.) systematized the Hebrew language. Babylonian scholars corresponded about religious matters with rabbis in Lucena, Barcelona, Granada, and Tarragona, often called Jews' cities. Reliance on the Babylonian academies decreased when Córdoba flourished and Isaac b. Jacob Alfasi (eleventh c.) created an academy in Lucena. The first prominent Talmudic scholar, he wrote responsa in Arabic and stressed practical observance. Other dynamic centers included Seville, Saragossa, Denia, Tudela, Almeria, and Huesca.

When the Eastern academies were suppressed (eleventh c.), the center for literary activity shifted to Spain. Religious and secular poetry, philosophy, philology, exegesis, and codification thrived in Hebrew and Arabic. This period was characterized by bilingualism and interest in philosophical debates, with religious interpretations and responsa penned in Arabic, often with Hebrew characters, and legal compilations in Hebrew or hebraized Aramaic. Maimonides wrote mostly in Arabic to be understood by all. Moses ibn Ezra (eleventh-twelfth c.) studied biblical poetry in *adab*, a popular Arabic genre allowing digressions. Grammarians Judah b. David Hayyuj, Jonah ibn Janah, and Moses ibn Gikatilla of Saragossa wrote in both languages. Abraham ibn Ezra (twelfth c.) and others produced grammatical treatises and biblical exegeses in Hebrew. The *maqāma*, an Arabic verse form, appeared in Hebrew poetry with *Tahkemoni* (Wise Instructor) of Judah Al-Harizi (twelfth-thirteenth c.).

Religious philosophy and theology were more actively cultivated in Muslim Spain than in the East. Solomon ibn Gabirol (or Avicebron; eleventh c.) accepted the Aristotelian principles of matter and form and exhibited no particular Jewish character. *Mekor Hayim* (The Well of Life), a Neoplatonic dialogue in Arabic, explains the universality of matter, man's purpose in life, and his soul's communication with its spiritual source. The medieval Latin translation, *Fons Vitae*, greatly influenced Christian thought. Abraham ibn Ezra wrote a semiphilosophical study discussing God's attributes, man's psychology, and the metaphor in the Bible. Judah *Halevi (eleventh-twelfth c.), while critical of philosophy, rejected metaphysics because it could not attain the ultimate truth. His *Kuzari* is a vigorous apology of Judaism. Abraham ibn David (twelfth c.) was the first in Spain to attempt to fuse Jewish doctrines with Aristotelian philosophy while Moses ben Maimon (or Maimonides, Rambam; twelfth c.), the greatest representative of philosophical trends, formulated a classic definition of the dogma of Judaism and stimulated Talmudic studies. *Mishneh Torah* or *Yad ha-Hazakah* (Strong Hand), in Hebrew, is a codification of the law. *Moreh Nevukim* (Guide of the Perplexed), an analysis in Arabic of Jewish law and theology, according to the Aristotelian doctrine, created a heated controversy. It reconciled reason and faith for many while it made others wary of the intrusion of rationalism on religion. To them, Maimonides's ideas were a danger to faith. The *Zohar* (Brightness), compiled in large part by Moses b. Shem Tob de León (thirteenth c.), is a mystical commentary of the Pentateuch which gave a powerful impulse to the Cabbalistic trend. Jacob ben Asher (fourteenth c.) produced a partial codification of the law, which avoided cabbalistic speculations but remains the archetype of the rabbinic code, influencing Joseph Caro's *Shulkhan Arukh* (sixteenth c.; Prepared Table). Hasdai Crescas of Saragossa (fourteenth c.) and Joseph Albo (fifteenth c.) also produced philosophical works.

The earliest Spanish literary monuments are the *jarchas* (*Kharja*), short poetic endings to longer compositions in classical Arabic or Hebrew. In colloquial Arabic and Romance, they were borrowed from popular oral tradition and transcribed into Arabic or Hebrew characters. The earliest appeared in a panegyric by Joseph the Scribe for Samuel ibn Nagrela ha-Nagid (tenth-eleventh c.; vizir and military commander of Granada). Written before 1042, it is the oldest known lyric poetry in any language of Western Europe. One third of the known *jarchas* appear in the poems of the great Hebrew poets. Judah Halevi, the divine poet, sang to Zion; celebrated poet Moses ibn Ezra wrote beautiful spiritual verses; ibn Gabirol produced great ethical and philosophical ones. Together they enriched the liturgy with hymns and songs, covering many secular subjects as well: love and friendship, wisdom and eulogy, wine and nature. Rabbi Shem Tov (*Tob) b. Isaac Ardutiel (Don Santob of Carrión, or Don Santo), an early composer of Spanish verse, borrowed from rabbinic poetry. His *Proverbios Morales* (fourteenth c.; Moral Proverbs) was the first example of aphoristic verse in Spanish. Jews also produced a *literatura aljamiada*, works in Spanish with Arabic and Hebrew characters, such as *Coplas de *Yoçef.*

With the demise of the Umayyads in the 1030s, Córdoba lost its former prominence. By mid-twelfth c., the fanatic Almohads ended the Jewish communities of Andalusia. Abraham ibn Ezra composed a moving elegy on their demise. Many Jews emigrated to Christian Spain, and the continuous shift of population caused the gradual abandonment of Arabic. Knowledge of Arabic, however, remained essential for the translation of Oriental texts into Hebrew, Latin, and Spanish. From the time of Archbishop don *Raimundo (twelfth c.), who founded the School of Translation in Toledo (*Escuela de Traductores de Toledo), there had existed the practice of cooperative translation from the Arabic and Hebrew into Latin, to make Oriental works accessible to Western readers. The multilingual Jews, such as John Hispanus, were invaluable collaborators. Petrus Alfonsi (*Alfonso, Pero) a *converso, translated a series of Oriental tales and fables of didactic nature in *Disciplina Clericalis* (twelfth c.), first introducing the Oriental apologue to Latin literature in Spain. A century later, after Castile conquered most of Andalusia, Arabic was eliminated from Jewish life in favor of Romance in daily intercourse and of Hebrew in writing.

The active influence of Jews in Christian Spain occurred in Toledo, when *Alphonse X (thirteenth c.) revived the famous academies by surrounding himself with Jews and Arabs seeking shelter from the vanquished caliphate. To make the spoken language that of government and culture and to enrich Spanish culture, he turned into Castilian the great works of the Orient. Hebrew became important as a transmittal language, and Jews formed an indispensable bridge between Oriental knowledge and Spain. Among the translators were Yehuda b. Mosca, personal physician of Alphonse, and Rabbi Zag b. Zayut (Rabbiçag) of Toledo, compiler of *Las Tablas alfonsíes* (Tables of Astronomy). In Christian Spain, anti-Judaic apology had been a constant genre since Saint Isidore. To justify their conversion, Petrus Alfonsi and Alphonse of Valladolid wrote anti-Judaic works. Talmudist Moses ben Nahman (or Nahmanides, Ramban; thirteenth c.) reported on his disputation with convert Paul Christianus.

In the fourteenth c., polemics in writing between Christians and Jews became more intense. The famous disputation of Tortosa (fifteenth c.), initiated by Pope Benedict XIII, sought to reach religious peace by unification of faith. In the fifteenth c. and after the expulsion, New Christians made up a large part of the Spanish intellectual elite: poets, satirists, literary polemists, innovative prose writers. Possible converts (sixteenth and seventeenth c.) include Juan *Alvarez Gato, Juan de *Mena, Antón de *Montoro, Diego de *San Pedro, Fernando de *Rojas, Jorge de *Montemayor, the anonymous author of the *Lazarillo de Tormes*, Mateo *Alemán, and others. See also Aristotelianism in Spain; Platonism.

BIBLIOGRAPHY

English Translations

*The Guide for the Perplexed, by Moses Maimonides.* Tr. Michael Friedländer. New York: Pardes, 1946.
*Judah Halevi's Kitab al-Khazari.* Tr. Hartwig Hirschfeld. 1905. Rpt. with intro. by Joshua Bloch. New York: Pardes, 1946.
*Selected Poems by Yehudah Halevi.* Ed. H. Brody. Tr. Nina Salaman. New York: Arno, 1973.
*Selected Religious Poems of Solomon Ibn Gabirol.* Ed. Israel Davidson. Philadelphia: Jewish Publication Society of America, 1923.
*The Wisdom of the Zohar.* Ed. I. Tishbi and F. Lachsurer. Jerusalem: n.p., 1971.

Criticism

Ashtor, Eliyahu. *The Jews of Moslem Spain.* Tr. Aaron Klein and Jenny Machlowitz Klein. Philadelphia: Jewish Publication Society of America, c. 1973–84.
Baer, Yitzhak. *A History of the Jews in Christian Spain.* 2 vols. Philadelphia: Jewish Publication Society of America, 1966–71.
Cantera Burgos, Francisco. "Versos españoles en las muwassahas hispano-hebreas." *Sefarad* 9 (1949): n.p.
Davidson, Israel. *Fascinating Researches in Medieaval Hebrew Poetry.* Philadelphia: Dropsie College, 1935.
Deyermond, A. D. *A Literary History of Spain. The Middle Ages.* London: Ernest Benn; New York: Barnes and Nobles, 1971.
García Gómez, E. "Las jaryas mozárabes y los judíos de Al-Andalus." *BRAE* 37 (1957): 337–394.
García Iglesias, L. *Los judíos en la España antigua.* Madrid: Cristiandad, 1978.
Hirschfeld, Hartwig. *Literary History of Hebrew Grammarians and Lexicographers.* London: Oxford UP–Humphrey Milford, 1926.
Husik, Isaac. *A History of Medieval Jewish Philosophy.* New York: Macmillan, 1916.
Leibowitz, Joshua O. "Maimonides: The Man and His Work: Different Kinds of Wisdom." *Ariel* 40 (n.d.): 73–88.
Lewy, Hans, Alexander Altman, and Isaak Heinemann. *Three Jewish Philosophers.* New York: Harper Torchbooks, 1965.
Newman, A. *The Jews in Spain.* Philadelphia: n.p., 1944.

Pacio López, A. *La Disputa de Tortosa*. Madrid-Barcelona: n.p. 1957.
Roth, Norman. "The Lyric Tradition in Hebrew Secular Poetry in Spain." *Hispanic Journal* 2.2 (Spring 1981): 7–26.
Sholem, Gershom. *Major Trends in Jewish Mysticism*. New York: Shocken, 1965.
Slotki, Israel W. *Moses Maimonides: His Life and Times*. London: Jewish Religious Education Publications, 1952.
Valle Rodríguez, Carlos del. *La escuela hebrea de Córdoba: los orígenes de la escuela filológica hebrea de Córdoba*. Madrid: Nacional, c. 1981.
Wolfson, Harry A. *Contributions to Jewish Philosophy*. Philadelphia: n.p., 1912–25.
Yanover, Héctor. "La poesía hebráico-española." *CH* 342 (n.d.): 491–528.
Zinberg, Israel. *A History of Jewish Literature, I: The Arabic-Spanish Period*. Tr. Bernard Martin. Cleveland: Case Western Reserve UP, 1972.

Reginetta Haboucha

**HOJEDA, Diego de** (1570?, Seville–1615, Huánuco de los Caballeros, Peru), poet. He left Spain for Peru in about 1590, joining the Dominican order and rising to become vicar of all monasteries in the province, and then prior of the Lima House. Because of disagreements with superiors, he was replaced in 1612, then demoted and exiled, first to Cuzco, and finally to the primitive village of Huánuco.

Hojeda left one important work, a lengthy mystical epic poem titled *La Cristíada* (1611; Christiad). Divided into twelve books, it details Christ's suffering between the Last Supper and the Crucifixion. Although critics have considered the poem's characterizations weak, it does possess a sincere, dignified intensity and eloquent, baroque diction.

BIBLIOGRAPHY

Primary Texts

*La Cristíada*. In BAE 35.
*La Cristíada*. Ed., study M. H. Patricia Corcoran. Washington, DC: Catholic U of America, 1935.

Criticism

Meyer, M. E. *The Sources of Hojeda's "La Cristíada."* Ann Arbor: U of Michigan P, 1953.
Montoto, S. "Fray Diego de Hojeda." In *Ingenios sevillanos. . . .* Madrid: Ibero-americana, n.d. 81–100.

**HOMILIES D'ORGANYÀ** (Homilies from Organyà), fragment of a book of sermons from the end of the twelfth or beginning of the thirteenth c., originating in Organyà, Catalonia. The sermons explain and comment on the Scriptures or the Epistle of the main festivals of the liturgical year. It is considered the first document of Catalan prose and might have been adapted from the Provençal *Book of Sermons* by Saint Marçal de Llemotges which it parallels. The homilies show a change from the rhetorical rules of the *Ars Predicandi*. *See also* Catalan Literature.

## BIBLIOGRAPHY

### Primary Text

*Antics documents de llengua catalana; i, Reimpressió de les homilies d'Organyà*. Ed. J.
     Miret y Sans. Barcelona: Casa Provincial de Caritat, 1915.

### Criticism

Coromines, Joan. *Entre dos llenguatges, I*. Barcelona: Curial, 1976.
Molho, M. "Les Homélies d'Organyà." *BH* 63 (1961): 186–210.

                                                              Joan Gilabert

**HOROZCO, Juan.** *See* Orozco, Juan de

**HOROZCO, Sebastián de** (1510?, Toledo–1580, Toledo), poet, dramatist,
proverb collector. Probably of *converso* lineage, he graduated from the U of
Salamanca with a master's in canon law. Horozco's literary efforts are varied:
he amassed an important proverb collection, *Teatro universal de proverbios*
(Universal Theater of Proverbs); he composed a variety of reports, or *Relaciones*,
which are historical accounts of people and happenings in Toledo; and he wrote
a *Cancionero* (Songbook), comprising 383 items, many of which also revolve
around the people, problems and events of his birthplace. His poetry holds no
special literary merit, but the reflection of popular culture is quite vivid. The
Songbook includes several short dramatic pieces. Horozco's son was the famous
Sebastián de *Covarrubias.

## BIBLIOGRAPHY

### Primary Texts

*Algunas relaciones y noticias toledanas*. . . . Sel., Conde de Cedillo. Madrid: Sales, 1905.
*El Cancionero de Sebastián de Horozco*. Ed., intro., notes, biblio., J. Weiner. Frankfurt:
     Lang, 1975.
*Relaciones Históricas de los siglos XVI y XVII*. Ed. F. R. de Uhagón y Guardamino. In
     *Bibliófilos Españoles* 32 (1896): n.p.
*Refranes glosados*. Ed. E. Cotarelo y Mori. *BRAE* 2 (1914) and following vols.
"Un nuevo refranero inédito glosado por Sebastián de Horozco." Ed H. Serís. *BH* 60
     (1958): 364–66. Part of the *Teatro*.

### Criticism

See Weiner, above.

**HOYO, Arturo del** (1917, Madrid– ), prose author. He has published collections of stories: *Primera caza y otros cuentos* (1965; First Prey and Other Tales),
*El pequeñuelo y otros cuentos* (1967; The Little One and Other Stories), and,
most recently, *En la glorieta, y en otros sitios* (1972; At the Glorieta, and Other
Places). Hoyo also has composed many critical essays, often to precede editions
of the works of authors such as *García Lorca, Baltasar *Gracián, *Aub, Miguel
*Hernández, etc.

BIBLIOGRAPHY

Primary Texts

*En la glorieta, y en otros sitios.* Madrid: Aguilar, 1972.
*El pequeñuelo y otros cuentos.* Madrid: Aguilar, 1967.
*Primera caza y otros cuentos.* Madrid: Aguilar, 1965.

Isabel McSpadden

**HOZ Y MOTA, Juan de la** (1622, Madrid–1714, ?), alderman of Burgos, censor, dramatist. A talented member of the *Calderón school, he wrote (1) religious plays, such as *Morir en la cruz con Cristo, San Dimas* (To Die on the Cross With Christ, St. Dimas); (2) historical dramas, like *El montañés Juan Pascual, Primer asistente de Sevilla* (The Highlander Juan Pascual, First Syndic of Seville); (3) novelesque plays such as *El castigo de la miseria* (The Punishment of Stinginess)—which was inspired by María de *Zayas y Sotomayor's novel of the same name, and later was used by Scarron for his *Le châtiment de l'avarice*— and *El villano del Danubio* (The Peasant from the Danube), which elaborates an anecdote of Antonio de *Guevara. His two *entremeses, *Los toros de Alcalá* (The Bulls from Alcala) and *El invisible* (The Invisible One), are sprightly and well-wrought.

BIBLIOGRAPHY

Primary Texts

*El castigo de la miseria* and *El montañés.* . . . In BAE 49.
*Los toros de Alcalá* and *El invisible.* In NBAE 17.

**HUARTE DE SAN JUAN, Juan** (1530?, San Juan de Pie del Puerto [then Spanish Navarre, now part of France]–after 1588?, Linares, France), physician and humanist. Biographical information about Dr. Huarte is scanty. He studied at the U of Baeza, and then the U of Alcalá, receiving the degree of M.D. from Alcalá in 1559. He married, and later moved to Linares, where he practiced medicine.

Huarte's fame rests on his *Examen de ingenios para las ciencias* (1575; *Examination of Men's Wits*, 1594). This treatise, a new application of the medieval doctrine of the four humors, explores the variety and unreliability of capacities and talents, especially sense perceptions, among humans. It reverberated throughout Europe without delay—was translated into French in 1580, to Italian two years later, and to English in 1594—and influenced especially thinkers such as Pierre Charron and Montaigne. Within Spain, the first edition was placed on the 1583 Spanish *Index* (*Indice). After Huarte's death, his son revised the work in accord with with censor's wishes, but with substantial flaws. *Cervantes's use of the *Examen de ingenios* has been well documented.

Using direct observation and personal experience, Huarte presents a systematic analysis of different personalities, as determined by various physical make-ups, and also includes practical suggestions for coping with and/or compensating for the strengths and weaknesses of each type. The work displays an accomplished, wide-ranging erudition, and also betrays a skeptical spirit.

BIBLIOGRAPHY

Primary Text

*Examen de ingenios.* Ed. Esteban Torre. Madrid: Nacional, 1976.

English Translation

*The Examination of Men's Wits.* Tr. Richard Carew. 1594 rpt. ed. by Carmen Rogers. Gainesville, FL: Scholars Facsimiles and Reprints, 1959.

Criticism

Green. O. H. "El ingenioso hidalgo." *HR* 25 (1957): 175–93.
Iriarte, M. de. *El doctor Juan Huarte y su "Examen de ingenios."* 3rd rev. ed. Madrid: CSIC, 1948.
Noreña, Carlos. "Juan Huarte's Naturalistic Philosophy of Man." In his *Studies in Spanish Renaissance Thought.* The Hague: Nijhoff, 1975.
Read, Malcom K. *Juan Huarte de San Juan.* TWAS 619. Boston: Twayne, 1981.

Maureen Ihrie

**HUMANISM,** an ideological movement. Conventional wisdom holds that the *Renaissance and accompanying humanism were not deep-rooted phenomena in Spain, counteracted as they were by a persistent medievalism and vehement Counter-Reformation. The Catholic monarchs' policy of religious intolerance restricted the resonance of and heterodoxy in Spanish humanism. Yet, at the same time, imperialist expansion vitalized Spain intellectually and influenced the direction in which some interests of the humanists would evolve.

Humanism as the resurgence of the study of the classics is a major innovation during the reign of the Catholic kings, especially encouraged by Isabel, although already established in some noble families through contact with Italy much earlier. One of the chief patrons of this intellectual regeneration was Cardenal Jiménez de *Cisneros, who devoted himself, within the limits of orthodoxy, to both religious and educational reform. He founded the new university at Alcalá de Henares in 1498 with specialties in philosophy, theology, and classical literature. The major undertaking at Alcalá was the creation of the *Biblia Poliglota Complutense* (1514–17; The Polyglot *Bible of Alcalá) with its restoration of authentic original texts (Hebrew, Latin, Greek, and Chaldean), a labor later continued by Arias *Montano in Antwerp with the *Poliglota de Amberes* (1569–72; The Polyglot of Antwerp).

During the Renaissance, humanists shared a set of intellectual and literary interests encompassed by the study of liberal arts. In Spain, philosophical inquiry was curtailed and ideas derivative, in part due to the religious persecution enforced by the *Inquisition. Therefore, some important *converso* and/or heterodox Spanish humanists, Lluis *Vives, Arias Montano, and the brothers Juan and Alfonso de *Valdés, lived most of their lives outside Spain. Within Spain, humanism manifested itself in educational, linguistic, and stylistic changes brought about by a scholarly minority. A humanistic education was based on the reading and imitation of classical literature. Grammatically correct usage, concision, and clarity of thought were admired, and the corrupted Latin, sophism, and pedantic quibbling associated with medieval dialectics abhorred. Many humanists devoted themselves to philological study—the revival of learning of ancient languages and the production of dictionaries, grammars, and faithful versions of ancient texts. Probably the most erudite scholar of Greco-Roman culture was Antonio de *Nebrija. Other philologists of note were Arias Barbosa, Juan Ginés de *Sepúlveda, Pedro Simón *Abril, Cristóbal de *Villalón, and el Brocense (*see* Sánchez de las Brozas, F.).

Nebrija and Lluis Vives were profoundly affected by the ideas of the Italian Lorenzo Valla, an adversary of decadent scholasticism and impure Latin. Renaissance Spanish poets, *Boscán, *Garcilaso de la Vega, Fernando de *Herrera, Fray Luis de *León, and those following, were also influenced by humanists residing in Italy—such as Bembo, *Castiglione, and León *Hebreo—and their Neoplatonic philosophy. Spanish humanists translated and imitated the texts of Erasmus of Rotterdam (*Erasmism), especially between 1520 and 1538. His writings on ecclesiastical reform and a genuine, interior, or spiritual Christianity were well-received until suspected of an affinity to Protestantism. His use of the form of the dialogue, the ideal of universal peace, and the linking of madness and insight also left their mark in Spanish letters.

Some values and educational innovations introduced by the humanists had wide repercussions. They related the dignity of man to the study of the humanities and associated wisdom with eloquence. The study of classical languages led to a cultivation of the vernacular and fomented an interest in diverse aspects of language and related topics. These included proverbs (Juan de *Mal Lara), linguistic questions (Juan de Valdés), the poetic imagination (*Huarte de San Juan), humanistic dialectic (Lluis Vives), and Castilian as an imperial language (Nebrija). Manuals of rhetoric and imitations of classical literary forms, such as dialogues (the Valdés brothers, León Hebreo, Pero *Mexía, *Pérez de Oliva), abounded. The writing of prose was stylistically refined in virtually all disciplines, for example, theology (*Vitoria, Melchor *Cano, Luis de *Molina, and Francisco *Suárez) and medicine (Huarte de San Juan and Oliva *Sabuco de Nantes). Because of the discovery of America, Spanish humanists described the geography, *florae, faunae*, and peoples of the New World (noble savages to las *Casas and Antonio de *Guevara, barbarians to Ginés de Sepúlveda), and sought moral and legal justifications on which to base governing an empire (Francisco de Vitoria, Sepúlveda). Eventually, however, the stylistic revolution implanted was countered by the reassertion of scholasticism during the Counter-Reformation.

## BIBLIOGRAPHY

### Primary Texts

Mexía, Pero. *Silva de Varia Lección*. Ed. Justo García Soriano. 2 vols. Madrid: Sociedad de Bibliófilos Españoles, 1933–34.

Nebrija, Elio Antonio de. *Vocabulario de Romance en Latín.* Ed. Gerald J. Macdonald. Madrid: Editorial Castalia, 1973.

Sánchez Escribano, F. *Juan de Mal Lara. Su vida y sus obras.* New York: Hispanic Institute, 1941.

Valdés, Alfonso de. *Diálogo de las cosas ocurridas en Roma.* Ed. José F. Montesinos. Clásicos Castellanos 89. Madrid: La Lectura, 1928.

Valdés, Juan de. *Diálogo de la lengua.* Ed. José F. Montesinos. Clásicos Castellanos, 86. Madrid: La Lectura, 1928.

English Translations

Guerlac, Rita, tr., intro., and notes. *Juan Luis Vives against the Pseudodialecticians.* Dordrecth, Holland: D. Reidel, 1979.

Valdés, Alfonso de. *Alfonso de Valdés and the Sack of Rome.* Tr. John E. Longhurst with Raymond R. MacCurdy. Albuquerque: U of New Mexico P, 1952.

Vives, Juan Luis. *In Pseudodialecticos.* Tr., intro., and notes Charles Fantazzi. Studies in Medieval and Reformation Thought, vol 27. Leiden: E. J. Brill, 1979.

Criticism

Bataillon, Marcel. *Erasmo y España.* Tr. Antonio Latorre. 2 vols. Mexico: Fondo de Cultura Económica, 1966.

García Villoslada, Ricardo. "Humanismo y Renacimiento." *Historia General de las literaturas hispánicas.* Ed. Guillermo Díaz Plaja. Barcelona: Editorial Barna, 1951. 2: 319–433.

López Estrada, Francisco, ed. *Siglos de Oro: Renacimiento. Historia y Crítica de la Literatura española.* Ed. Francisco Rico. Barcelona: Editorial Crítica, 1980. 2: 1–271.

Parker, Alexander A. "An Age of Gold: Expansion and Scholarship in Spain." *The Age of the Renaissance.* Ed. Denis Hay. New York: McGraw Hill, 1967. 221–48.

Redondo, A., ed. *L'Humanisme dans les lettres espagnoles. XIXe Colloque international d'Etudes humanistes, Tours, 5–17 juillet 1976.* Paris: J. Vrin, 1979.

Rico, Francisco. *Nebrija frente a los Bárbaros.* Salamanca: Universidad de Salamanca, 1978.

Helen H. Reed

**HURTADO, Antonio** (1825, Cáceres–1878, Madrid), politician, dramatist. He served as civil governor of Albacete, Jaén, Valladolid, Cádiz, Valencia and Barcelona. Some of his works initially appeared first in newspapers and magazines. Hurtado was rather a late Romantic in many ways. His *costumbrista* novels were never well received, but his plays were very popular, especially historical dramas such as *Sueños y realidades* (1866; Dreams and Realities)—which treats Queen Isabella the Catholic's marriage, and *Herir en la sombra* (1866; To Wound in the Shade)—which deals with Antonio *Pérez. The latter was written in collaboration with *Núñez de Arce. Hurtado also composed legends in verse, in the manner of the Duque de *Rivas. *El romancero de Hernán Cortés* (1847; Ballad Book of Hernán Cortés) contains twenty-nine ballads on Cortés's life, journeys and battles. *El romancero de la princesa* (1852; The Princess's Ballad Book) is dedicated to Queen Isabella II, and was provoked by her attempted assassination by a priest, Martín Merino—it recounts moments of her life, including the attempt, and the subsequent reaction of the Spanish people. *Madrid dramático* (1876; Dramatic Madrid) vividly conjures real and imaginary encounters with *Siglo de Oro figures such as Lope de *Vega, *Quevedo, *Cervantes, etc. The first four lines quickly set the tone, and perhaps reveal some of the author's personality:

> De tantos recuerdos llena,
> lector, la cabeza tengo,
> que a pensar me doy a veces
> que he vivido en otro tiempo.

(Filled with so many memories / is my head, reader, / that at times I start to think / that I lived in another age.)

*See also* Romanticism.

BIBLIOGRAPHY

Primary Texts

*Herir en la sombra*. 2nd ed. Madrid: Rodríguez, 1868.
*Madrid dramático*. Ed. A. González Palencia. Madrid: Saeta, 1942.
*Romancero de Hernán Cortés*. Barcelona: Espasa, 1905?
*Romancero de la princesa*. Madrid: Sta. Coloma y San Martín, 1852.

**HURTADO DE LA VERA, Pedro,** pseudonym of Pedro Faria (fl. 1572, Plasencia–?,?), poet, writer. He composed an allegorical, satirical play, *Comedia intitulada Doleria, del sueño del mundo* (1572; Play of Doleria, the World Asleep), in which the characters symbolize virtues and vices. Clearly conceived in plot, it suffers from a ponderous style. He also wrote *Historia del Príncipe Erasto* (1573; History of Prince Erastus).

BIBLIGRAPHY

Primary Text

*Doleria*. In NBAE 14.

**HURTADO DE MENDOZA, Antonio** (1586, Castro-Urdiales–1644, Santander-Madrid), playwright and poet. As a member of an influential Biscayan family, he served at the royal court of Philip IV holding many important positions: assistant to the king, a *protégé* of the Count-Duke of Olivares, and secretaryships with the royal household and with the Holy Office. He was also accorded membership in the military Order of Calatrava. Hurtado, the poet, succeeded at blending his literary skills with the realities of political life; in fact, many of his plays were performed at court with notable success. Also his ties to leading literary circles led to friendship with Lope de *Vega and to occasional association with *Quevedo. While his dramatic talents surpassed his abilities as a poet, the *Obras líricas y cómicas, humanas y divinas* (1690; Lyrical and Comical, Human and Spiritual Works) shows a consistent knowledge of the literary traditions of the times, especially the *culterano* poem *Vida de Nuestra Señora* (1666; Life of Our Lady). But he displays more talent in plays such as *Cada loco con su tema* (Everyone Riding His Own Hobby Horse), *El marido hace mujer* (The Husband Makes the Wife), which shaped Molière's *L'école des maris*, and *Querer por sólo querer* (To Love for Love's Sake), where his dramatic instinct, the vivid portraits and often satirical rendering of society achieve their clearest expression. Hurtado also wrote a few less successful theatrical interludes (*entremeses*), the best known of which is *El examinador Miser Palomo* (1618; The Examiner Miser Palomo).

## BIBLIOGRAPHY

### Primary Texts

*El marido hace mujer y el trato muda costumbre, Los empeños del mentir, Cada loco con su tema*. Ed. Ramón de Mesonero Romanos. BAE 45.
*Obras poéticas*. Ed. Rafael Benítez Claros. 3 vols. Madrid: Gráficas Ultra, 1947–48.

### Criticism

Davies, Gareth A. *A Poet at Court: Antonio Hurtado de Mendoza (1586–1644)*. Oxford: Dolphin, 1971.
García Camino, Víctor. *Vida y obras de Antonio Hurtado de Mendoza. Aportación para su estudio*. Cáceres, Spain: Salamanca, 1977.
Kennedy, Ruth Lee. *Tirso, Antonio Hurtado de Mendoza, Lope and the Junta de Reformación*. Chapel Hill: U of North Carolina P, 1974.

María Teresa Pajares

**HURTADO DE MENDOZA, Diego** (1503, Granada–1575, Madrid), soldier, poet, historian, diplomat, and humanist. The direct descendant of the Marquis of *Santillana, Íñigo López de Mendoza, he was son of the Count of Tendilla, who was made governor of Granada after the fall of the Moors in 1492. The first Marquis of Mondéjar, he studied in Italy with Montesdoca and Nifo, as well as in Granada and Salamanca, mastering Arabic, Greek, Hebrew, and Latin. Destined by his family for service in the church, Mendoza served instead in the Spanish armies at Pavia (1525) and Tunis (1535), distinguishing himself in both campaigns. Indeed, he is the quintessential model of the aristocratic figure of the sixteenth c. dedicated to arms and letters.

As ambassador to England (1537–38), Mendoza was entrusted with arranging the marriage of Henry VIII to the Duchess of Milan (niece of Charles V) and of Mary Tudor to Don Luis of Portugal; both enterprises were unsuccessful. Thereafter, he was ambassador in Venice (1539–47), representing Charles V at the Council of Trent. While in Venice, he commissioned numerous searches for mss. in Greece and elsewhere, building one of the world's great private libraries. While governor of Siena (1547), he was sent to Rome to issue a public rebuke to Pope Julius III, after which he was regarded as a sort of viceroy of Italy. Charged with financial irregularities at this time, he demanded an investigation to clear his name—which would not be demonstrated, however, until three years after his death (1578). Recalled to Spain in 1554, his freedom of action was greatly curtailed with the accession to the throne of Philip II. After a violent dispute in the palace with one Diego de Leiva, just when the young Prince Charles lay dying (July 1568), Mendoza was exiled to Medina del Campo, where he was placed in the service of his nephew, the Marquis of Mondéjar, to combat Moorish uprisings. Thereafter, he joined the king's army in quelling the *morisco revolt in Alpujarras (1568–71), an experience described in his *La Guerra de Granada* (1610 [1730, 1970]; The War in Granada). He remained in Granada until 1574, at which time he returned to Madrid, but without access to the palace. In partial compensation to Philip II, Mendoza bequeathed his superb collection of mss. and books to the newly established Monastery Library at San Lorenzo de El Escorial, the transfer taking place the year after his death (1576); unhappily, many of the Arabic, Greek, and other codices would be destroyed by the fire that ravaged that library on June 7, 1671.

Born in the same year (1503) as *Garcilaso de la Vega, Mendoza helped to make popular the Italianate meters favored by Garcilaso and their mutual friend, Juan *Boscán. Notable are Mendoza's "Epístola a Boscán" (c. 1539; Epistle to Boscán), his Petrarchan sonnets, and, in *octavas reales* (see Octavas), the mythological "Fábula de Hipomenes y Atalanta" (Fable of Hippomenes and Atalanta), taken from Ovid. Mendoza's *redondillas* were praised, moreover, by Lope de *Vega, who says in the prologue to his *Isidro*: "¿Qué cosa iguala a una redondilla de Garci Sánchez o don Diego de Mendoza?" (What can equal a *redondilla* of Garci Sánchez or Sir Diego de Mendoza?) Many of his most famous lyrics are indecent, however, which reflects yet another facet of this individual, whose works also include a translation to Spanish of Aristotle's *Mechanica*.

Mendoza's *Guerra de Granada* has great historical value. In four books, its model is Sallust rather than Tacitus, and Mendoza's impartiality and candor recall that of *The Cataline Conspiracy* in sparing no figures of power—not even the king. The first reasonably faithful edition of this text was published by Luis Tribaldos of Toledo (1627). Recently, there have been attempts to show that Mendoza's work was a simplified prosification of Juan *Rufo's *La Austriada*; in fact, it appears that Rufo's work is a versification of Mendoza's *Guerra*.

There has been much debate, moreover, on the issue of Mendoza's authorship of the famous *picaresque novel *Lazarillo de Tormes*, but no definitive conclusions can be reached on the basis of available evidence (see R. L. Fiore, *Lazarillo de Tormes* [Boston; Twayne, 1984], pp. 22 and 108, n. 7). However, he does seem to be the Erasmian satirist who wrote the *Diálogo entre Caronte y el ánima de Pedro Luis Farnesio, hijo del Papa Paulo III* (1547; Dialogue between Caronte [Charon] and the Soul of Peter Louis Farnesio, Son of Pope Paul III). *See also* Erasmism; Italian Literary Influences; Siglo de Oro.

## BIBLIOGRAPHY

Primary Texts

*Algunas cartas... escritas 1538–1552*. Eds. Alberto Vázquez and Robert Selden Rose. New Haven: Yale UP; London: Humphrey Milford/Oxford UP, 1935.

*Carta de Diego de Mendoza al Capitán Salazar* and *Diálogo entre Caronte y el ánima de Pedro Luis Farnesio, hijo del Papa Paulo III.* In *Curiosidades bibliográficas.* Ed. Adolfo de Castro. BAE 36.

*Guerra de Granada.* Ed. Bernardo Blanco-González. Madrid: Castalia, 1970.

*Obras del insigne cavallero don Diego de Mendoza. . . . Recopiladas por Frey Juan Díaz Hidalgo.* Madrid: Juan de la Cuesta, 1610. [This edition of the *Guerras de Granada,* an incomplete text, was again so published (lacking Book 3) in Lisbon, 1627, by Luis Tribaldos. It was again published, with misprints, in 1730; a fifth edition appeared in Valencia, 1776.]

*Obras poéticas.* Ed. William I. Knapp. Madrid: Ginesta, 1877.

*Poesías satíricas y burlescas de Diego Hurtado de Mendoza.* Madrid: Ginesta, 1876.

English Translations

"Epistle to Boscán." Excerpts tr. by David H. Darst in *Juan Boscán.* TWAS 475. Boston: Twayne, 1978. 100–102.

*The War in Granada.* Tr. Martin Shuttleworth. London: Folio Society, 1982.

Criticism

Darst, David H. *Diego Hurtado de Mendoza.* TWAS 794. Boston: Twayne, 1987.

————. "El pensamiento histórico del granadino Diego Hurtado de Mendoza." *Hispania: Revista española de historia* 43 (1983): 281–94.

González Palencia, Angel, and Eugenio Mele. *Vida y obras de don Diego Hurtado de Mendoza.* 3 vols. Madrid: Instituto de Valencia de Don Juan, 1941–43.

Nader, Helen. *The Mendoza Family in the Spanish Renaissance: 1350–1550.* New Brunswick: Rutgers UP, 1979.

Simón Díaz, José. "Hurtado de Mendoza (Diego)." *Manual de bibliografía de la literatura española.* 3rd ed. Madrid: Gredos, 1980. 373–74; nos. 9726–50.

Spivakovsky, Erika. *Son of the Alhambra: Don Diego Hurtado de Mendoza.* Austin and London: U of Texas P, 1970.

Dennis P. Seniff

**HURTADO DE TOLEDO, Luis** (c. 1523, Toledo–c. 1590, Toledo), poet, dramatist, and priest. Though he may well have been a *converso, Hurtado de Toledo served as rector of the Church of San Vicente in his native city. He is best remembered not as a cleric or as the author of numerous compositions of his own, but as the editor and publisher of several works left unfinished by others, most notably Micael de *Carvajal's *Cortes de la muerte* (1557; The Court of Death). This he published with his own allegorical piece, *Cortes de casto amor* (1553; The Court of Pure Love), an unusual mingling of forms and subject matter. He had already composed the *Egloga sobre el galardón y premio de amor* (1553; Eclogue on the Reward of Love), a *pastoral work in four acts. Hurtado de Toledo edited and added approximately 200 lines to Perálvarez de Ayllón's pastoral *Comedia de Preteo y Tibaldo, llamada disputa y remedio de amor* (1553; Play Concerning Preteo and Tibaldo, Known as the Debate and Remedy of Love) and also translated Ovid's *Metamorphoses* in 1578. *See also* Humanism.

BIBLIOGRAPHY

Primary Text

*Cortes de casto amor* and *Cortes de la muerte*. Facs. of 1557 Toledo ed. Valencia: Andrés
    Ortega del Alamo, 1963.

Criticism

Crawford, J. P. Wickersham. *Spanish Drama before Lope de Vega*. Rev. ed. Philadelphia:
    U of Pennsylvania P, 1967.
Dale, George Irving. "*Las cortes de la muerte*." *MLN* 40 (1925): 276–81.
Rodríguez Moñino, Antonio. "El poeta Luis Hurtado de Toledo (1510-c. 1598)." In his
    *Relieves de erudición*. Madrid: Castalia 1959. 143–203.

                                                        C. Maurice Cherry

**HURTADO DE VELARDE, Alfonso** (?, Guadalajara–?,?), dramatist of the
cycle of Lope de *Vega. Originally from Guadalajara, he is sometimes called
Hurtado de Guadalajara Fajardo. He wrote several plays on heroic themes, but
most have been lost (*El Cid, Doña Sol y doña Elvira* and *El conde de las manos
blancas* [The Count of the White Hands]. Only one play of importance, *La
tragedia de los infantes de Lara* (The Tragedy of the Princes of Lara) has
survived. The play was published in the *Flor de las comedias de España, . . .
quinta parte* (Flower of Spanish Plays, fifth part), a collection of plays composed
by several authors and compiled by Francisco de Ávila, but once mistakenly
attributed in its entirety to Lope. Hurtado's play, written between 1612 and 1615
and inspired by Lope's *Bastardo Mudarra* (The Bastard Mudarra), has also been
attributed to Lope himself. The play conforms to the historical records and its
language imitates ancient speech. It also served as an inspiration to *Matos
Fragoso for his plays on the same theme and, through him, to the Duke of *Rivas
as well. *See also Infantes de Lara, Leyenda de los*; Theater in Spain.

BIBLIOGRAPHY

Primary Text

*Flor de las comedias de España. Quinta parte*. Ed. Francisco de Avila. Barcelona: S.
    de Comellas, 1616. Microfilm of orig. in National Library of Madrid.

                                                        Catherine Larson

# I

IBÁÑEZ DE SEGOVIA, Gaspar (1628, Madrid–1708, Mondéjar), historian. By marriage, he became Marquis of Mondéjar. His various historical publications—many of which focus on chronology—include *Noticia y juicio de los principales historiadores de España* (Notice and Evaluation of the Principal Historians of Spain), *Examen chronológico del año en que entraron los Moros en España* (Chronological Study of the Year in Which the Moors Entered Spain), and *Memorias históricas de la vida y acciones del rey D. Alonso el Noble* (Historical Memoirs of the Life and Deeds of King Alphonse the Noble), which was published posthumously.

BIBLIOGRAPHY

Primary Texts

*Advertencias a la historia del padre Mariana.* Madrid: Imprenta Real, 1795.
*Examen chronológico del año en que entraron los Moros en España.* Madrid: n.p., 1687.
*Memorias históricas de la vida y acciones del rey D. Alonso el Noble.* Madrid: Ibarra, 1777.
*Noticia y juicio del los principales historiadores de España.* Madrid: Pantaleón Aznar, 1784.

ICAZA, Carmen de (1899, Madrid– ), novelist. Daughter of well known writer Francisco A. de *Icaza, Carmen studied in Spain, France, and Germany, and traveled extensively because of her father's diplomatic career. She published her first novel, *La boda* (1916; The Wedding), at age seventeen. Her commercial success began with *Cristina de Guzmán* (1936) which was first published serially in *Blanco y negro* and quickly translated into French, appearing serially in the Parisian daily *Le Temps*. It has been translated into Italian, Czech, Portuguese, Norwegian, and Dutch (a student edition at the U of Utrecht), and edited as a reader for language students (1958). In the following decade, she published several more novels: *¿Quién sabe?* (1940; Who Knows?); *Vestido de tul* (1942; Dressed in Tulle), set in Madrid in the 1910s; *Soñar la vida* (1944; To Dream Life); *El tiempo vuelve* (1945; Time Returns); and *La fuente enterrada* (1947;

The Buried Fountain). These novels were followed by *Las horas contadas* (1951; Counted Hours), *Yo, la reina* (1955; I the Queen), *Irene* (1958), and *La casa de enfrente* (1960; The House in Front). In 1957, Colleción Summun issued Icaza's *Obras selectas* (Selected Works) which contained five previously published novels. All of these works have been translated into several languages and enjoyed widespread popularity. For the stage, Icaza wrote *Cristina de Guzmán* (opening in Madrid in 1939), *Frente a frente* (1941; Face to Face) and *Vestido de tul* (1944). In the post-war years, Icaza led a newspaper campaign to draw attention to destitute women and children. She helped found the Auxilio Social (Social Aid Society), receiving the Cruz de beneficiencia (Beneficience Cross) for this work. She also held key positions in the Spanish Red Cross. Icaza's works present detailed portraits of Madrid's aristocratic, diplomatic society. Her characters are well drawn, although lacking depth, and her dialogue is agile. Icaza's novels are labeled by most critics as "novelas rosas" (romances) for their love interests, emotionalism, and sentimentality.

BIBLIOGRAPHY

Primary Texts

*Obras selectas.* Barcelona: AHR, 1957. Five novels. 2nd ed., 1971, contains some different works.

*¿Quién sabe?* Madrid: Afrodisio Aguado, 1951.

*Yo, la reina.* 8th ed. Madrid: Clemanes, 1958.

*El tiempo vuelve.* 8th ed. Madrid: Afrodisio Aguado, 1945.

Frieda H. Blackwell

**ICAZA, Francisco de** (1863, Mexico–1925, Madrid), poet, critic. A Mexican diplomat, he spent most of his life in Madrid, enriching the peninsular literary world with critical works such as *Las novelas ejemplares de Cervantes* (1901; Cervantes's Exemplary Novels), *Supercherías y errores cervantinos* (1917; Cervantine Errors and Excesses), and *Conquistadores y pobladores de la Nueva España* (1923; Conquerors and Colonizers of New Spain). His poetry is characterized by its sensitivity; some of his poetry books are *Efímeras* (1892; The Ephemeral), *Lejanías* (1899; Distances), *Canciones de la vida honda y de la emoción fugitiva* (1922; Songs of Profound Life and Fugitive Emotion).

BIBLIOGRAPHY

Primary Texts

*Conquistadores y pobladores de la Nueva España.* Madrid: Adelantado de Segovia, 1923.

*Efímeras y Lejanías.* Sel. and ed. R.A. Cardwell. Exeter: U of Exeter, 1984.

*Las novelas ejemplares de Cervantes.* Madrid: Adelantado de Segovia, 1928.

*Obras.* Ed., study R. Castillo. 2 vols. Mexico: Fondo de Cultura Económica, 1980.

Isabel McSpadden

**IGLESIAS DE LA CASA, José** (1748, Salamanca–1791, Salamanca), poet. He studied humanities and theology at the U of Salamanca and in 1783 became a priest serving various parishes surrounding the city. Iglesias is associated with the *Escuela Salmantina of poets and distinguished himself in lyric poetry in a pastoral style, as well as in satirical and epigrammatical forms. During most of his life Iglesias's poetry circulated in ms. form only, but he was eventually persuaded to publish three poems: the elegy *El Llanto de Zaragoza* (1779; The Lament of Zaragoza), *La niñez laureada* (1785; Childhood Laureled) and *La teología* (1790; Theology). Not until two years after his death were Iglesias's works collected and published, in two volumes. Iglesias is remembered mostly for his light-hearted, satiric verse. In his *Letrillas satíricas* (Satirical Poems) he demonstrates his debt to both *Góngora and *Quevedo, in style and theme. His numerous *Epigramas* (Epigrams) display a similar mordant sense of humor, and his piquant wit shows the influence of Martial and Alcázar. Later in life Iglesias turned increasingly to pastoral verse forms as a means of finding a more serious mode of expression. His eclogues, idylls and *letrillas, which are grouped under the title *La esposa aldeana* (The Country Wife), exhibit a graceful, limpid style which recalls the pastoral verse of Luis de *León and Antonio de Villegas, and from an earlier age, the poetry of Horace and Anacreon. In general, Iglesias's major contribution to eighteenth-c. poetry was his extraordinary ability to use classic and *Siglo de Oro masters as models to create a vital and natural verse wholly within the spirit of Spanish neo-classicism.

BIBLIOGRAPHY

Primary Texts

Works. In *Poetas líricos del siglo XVIII*. Vol. 1. Ed. Marqués de Valmar. BAE 61. 407–86.

Criticism

Mazzei, A. "José Iglesias de la Casa." *Boletín de la Academia Argentina de Letras* 19 (1950): 237–44.
Sebold, Russell P. "Dieciochismo, estilo místico y contemplación en 'La esposa aldeana' de Iglesias de la Casa." *Papeles de Son Armadans* 49 (1968): 117–44.

Donald C. Buck

**IGLÉSIES, Ignasi** (1871, San Andres de Palomar–1928, Barcelona), Catalan dramatist known for introducing themes of individual materialism to the Catalan theater. His works were considered innovative early in this c., but perhaps were simply a novelty. Iglésies came from a laboring family, suffered hardships as a child, and idealized the working class in his writings to such an extent that he was known as "the poet of the humble." His most frequent plots treat the economic straits of workers and their resultant plights, traits in evidence in *Fructidor* (1897; The Fruit Seller), *L'escorço* (1902; The Scorpion), *Lari* (1902) and *La mare eterna* (The Eternal Mother) of the same year. *Els vells* (1903; The Old Ones) enjoyed a tremendous success in Barcelona and later in Paris in French translation. Probably his best work, it was followed by the social drama *Les Garces* (1905; The Herons). *La resclosa* (The Canal Lock) criticizes conventional morality, while *Girasol* (Sunflower) is a comedy of manners. Other works include

*El cor del poble* (1897; The Heart of Humble People), *Foc nou* (New Fire), *L'encis de la gloria* (The Attraction of Glory), and *La llar apagada* (The Extinguished Hearth).

BIBLIOGRAPHY

Primary Texts

*La madre eterna.* Spanish tr. J. Jerique and R Roca. Buenos Aires: Fuego, 1900's.
*Els vells. El cor del poble.* Barcelona: Selecta, 1963.

Janet Pérez

**IGNACIO ALDECOA.** *See* Aldecoa, José Ignacio

**IGNACIO DE LOYOLA, San** (1491, Loyola–1556, Rome), religious leader and writer, mystic. Founder of the Society of Jesus (Jesuits) in 1540, he is one of the most important instruments of the Counter-Reformation (Catholic reform), and one of the most influential religious leaders of his time in Europe. Born to a Basque family of minor nobility but with a deep sense of order and loyalty, he became a soldier in 1517, thus reflecting the family sense of duty and practical and realistic grasp of problems. In May 1521 Ignacio recived severe leg wounds in the skirmish with the French at Pamplona. An avid fan of chivalric romances (*libros de *caballerías*), he requested such reading during his convalescence. Instead, he was given a *Life of Christ* and a collection of saints' lives, as the requested escape reading was not readily available. This reading led to his conversion and subsequent pilgrimage to the monastery of Montserrat where he accepted the religious life. Loyola's spiritual transformation was truly a conversion since he had been an active participant in court life, with all its trappings and pleasures. Later at Manresa, from March 1522 to February 1523, after many hours in meditation, he formulated his *Ejercicios espirituales* (Rome, 1548; *Spiritual Exercises,* 1964). These were to become the cornerstone of his spiritual and apostolic life as well as that of his order.

In the subsequent years, Loyola traveled throughout Europe, studying grammar, humanities, philosophy, Latin and theology at various institutions, and giving the *Ejercicios*. Like other mystics, he experienced difficulties with the *Inquisition, especially around the year 1527. Only in March of 1539 did he deliberate seriously the formation of a new religious order. In September of 1540, the Society of Jesus was officially approved; by 1556, its members almost numbered one thousand. In July of 1556, after lifelong bouts of ill health, Ignacio de Loyola died.

The *Spiritual Exercises* are a guide to daily spiritual meditations for a period of four weeks. Each exercise is comprised by the purpose of the exercise, preparatory prayers, preludes (two or three), principal points and the colloquy. One feature of the preludes is a mental image of place (seeing of the place) where the object of the exercitant's meditation is present in the mind. The four weeks (in reality quite flexible) are also similarly divided: Week 1, the purification of the soul and the ordering of one's life; Week 2 and Week 3, meditations on the events of Christ's public life and passion; Week 4, Christ's risen life. The exercises clearly require the active participation of the exercitant under the direction of a spiritual director.

Loyola also left a voluminous correspondence, and a short autobiography, dictated to friends at their strong behest between 1553 and 1555. It spread in mss. form, but was not made public until the eighteenth c., in Latin, and the twentieth c., in the original Spanish and Italian. The Jesuit Order continued to grow, and for centuries exercised a profound influence on the intellectual development of the Western world. *See also* Mysticism.

BIBLIOGRAPHY

Primary Text

*Obras completas de San Ignacio de Loyola.* Ed. I. Iparraguirre and C. de Dalmases. 2nd ed. Madrid: Biblioteca de Autores Cristianos, 1977.

English Translations

*Constitutions of the Society of Jesus. Part 4.* Tr. G. E. Ganss. In *Saint Ignatius' Idea of a Jesuit University.* Milwaukee, WI: Marquette UP, 1954.
*Letters of St. Ignatius of Loyola.* Tr. W. J. Young. Chicago: Loyola UP, 1959.
*The Spiritual Exercises of St. Ignatius.* Tr. L. J. Puhl. Chicago: Loyola UP, 1968.
*The Spiritual Exercises of St. Ignatius.* Tr. A. Mottola. Garden City, NY: Doubleday, 1964.
*St. Ignatius' Own Story.* Tr. W. J. Young. Chicago: Loyola UP, 1956.

Criticism

Begheny, P. "A Bibliography on St. Ignatius' Spiritual Exercises." In *Studies in the Spirituality of the Jesuits.* St. Louis: American Assistancy Seminar on Jesuit Spirituality, 1981.
De Nicolás, A. *Powers of Imagining.* Albany: SUNY P, 1986. Includes translations, bibliography.
Iparraguirre, I. *Historia de los Ejercicios de San Ignacio.* 2 vols. Bilbao: Mensajero del Corazón de Jesús, 1946–55.
Juambelz, J. *Bibliografía sobre la vida, obras y escritos de San Ignacio de Loyola, 1900.* Madrid: Razón y Fe, 1956.
Larrañaga, V. *San Ignacio de Loyola. Estudios sobre su vida, sus obras, su espiritualidad.* Zaragoza: Hechos y Dichos, 1956.
Leturia, P. de. *Estudios ignacianos.* Rome: Institutum Societatis Jesu, 1957.
Maruga, D. *Instruments in the Hand of God. A Study of the Spirituality of San Ignacio de Loyola.* Rome: n.p., 1963.

*ILDEFONSO, Vida de San. See Vida de San Ildefonso.*

**ILDEFONSO DE TOLEDO, San** (607, Toledo–667, Toledo), bishop, ecclesiastical writer. Named Archbishop of Toledo in 657, he wrote hymns, biographies of fourteen illustrious men—all but one of whom lived in Spain, tracts on baptism, on how to reach heaven, etc., and a part of the Mozarabic liturgy. Also

his is the *Libellus de virginitate beatae Mariae,* an impassioned defense of the
Virgin Mary. Alfonso Martínez de Toledo (*see* Arcipreste de Talavera) translated
it into Spanish in 1444. *See also Mozárabe; Vida de San Ildefonso.*

BIBLIOGRAPHY

Primary Text

*Libellus de virginitate beatae Mariae.* . . . Ed., study V. Blanco García. Madrid: Rivadeneyra, 1937.

English Translation

*Liber de cognitione baptismi.* Tr. and notes, M. C. Billy. Washington, DC: Catholic U
of America P, 1951.

Criticism

Braegelmann, A. *The Life and Writings of St. Ildefonsus.* Washington, DC: Catholic U
of America P, 1942.

**ILLUMINISM.** *See* Alumbrados

**ILUMINADOS.** *See* Alumbrados

**IMPERIAL, Micer Francisco** (mid-fourteenth c., Genoa–early fifteenth c.,
Seville?), poet. Vice-admiral of Castile in 1403 when the admiral was Diego
*Hurtado de Mendoza, father of Iñigo López, Marqués de *Santillana. Diego
Hurtado died in July 1404, and if Imperial entertained any hopes of succeeding
him as admiral of Castile, he must have been bitterly disappointed when King
Henry III named Alonso Enríquez to the position on April 4, 1405. Many of
Imperial's poems, including the famous "Dezir a las syete virtudes" (Poem on
The Seven Virtues) and the "Dezir al nascimiento del Rey Don Juan II" (Poem
on The Birth of King John II), seem to have been written after Alonso Enríquez
was named admiral of Castile, which would explain in part why the theme of
Fortune is so predominant in them. All eighteen of Imperial's poems as anthologized in the *Cancionero de *Baena* were written in response to specific
historical events: for example, the downfall of Ruy López Dávalos, the arrival
in Spain of Angelina de Grecia, the birth of John II, the regency of Ferdinand
of Antequera, the literary challenges of Fray Alonso de la Monja and Ferrán
Sánchez de Talavera, etc. But these historical truths were subtly veiled by
Imperial under literary and theological artistic adornments, according to the
theories contained in the *Leys d'Amors.* The reader is enticed to unveil the full
meaning of these polysemous texts by means of devices such as "mozdobre,"
"rims equivocz," "collatio aperta et oculta," and hyperbaton. Dante's *Divine
Comedy* is the work most frequently referred to by Imperial, but one cannot
fully appreciate Imperial's poems by comparing them with Dante's major work
alone without taking into account as well his use of the Bible (especially the
Apocalyptic books), the *AntiClaudianus* of Alain de Lille, and the *Roman de la
Rose* of Jean de Meun, to name only a few of the books to which Imperial refers.

Imperial was aware that his allegorical styles of composition were a novelty in Castile. His poems seem to be aimed at introducing Castile to contemporary literary trends in the rest of Europe. Imperial's efforts in this regard can be said to be successful insofar as his styles of composition were continued by writers as important as Santillana and Juan de *Mena. *See also* Edad Media, Literatura de la; Italian Literary Influences.

BIBLIOGRAPHY

Primary Texts

"*El dezir a las syete virtudes*" *y otros poemas*. Ed. Colbert Nepaulsingh. Clásicos Castellanos 221. Madrid: Espasa-Calpe, 1977.

Criticism

Lapesa, Rafael. "Notas Sobre Micer Francisco Imperial." *NRFH* 7 (1953): 337–51.

Morreale, Margherita. "El Dezir a las siete virtudes' de Francisco Imperial, Lectura e imitación prerrenacentista de la *Divina Comedia*." In *Lengua, Literatura, folklore; estudios dedicados a Rodolfo Oroz*. Ed. Gaston Carrillo Herrera. Santiago: Universidad de Chile, 1967. 307–77.

Colbert Nepaulsingh

**INARCO CELENIO.** *See* Moratín, Leandro

*ÍNDICE DE LIBROS PROHIBIDOS* (Index of Forbidden Books), censorial tool of the Catholic church. In recognition of the power of the written word, the Catholic church has, since the second c. AD, passed judgment on written works. In 170 AD the Muratorian Canon separated authentic New Testament mss. from spurious accounts. Pope Innocent I compiled such a list in 405; Gelasius published one in 496. In the sixteenth c., England, the Low Countries, France, etc., all preceded Spain in publishing Indexes. In Spain, the most important Index was published in 1559, as part of the work of the Council of Trent (1545–63). In addition to many works in Greek and Latin, the 1559 *Indice* forbade 172 books in Spanish, including translations of Erasmus, *Lazarillo de Tormes*, and works by *Torres Naharro, Juan and Alfonso de *Valdés, Fray Luis de *Granada, Gil *Vicente, etc. The list sharply delimited critical inquiry, and was extremely sensitive to any hint of heresy. Although the harsh threat of the *Indice* and the spector of *censorship undeniably weighed heavily on writers and their readers, it must be remembered that many works did continue to circulate in ms. form, and that these most active years of censorship do coincide with a brilliant flowering in Spanish letters. *See also* Inquisition.

BIBLIOGRAPHY

Primary Text

*Tres índices expurgatorios de la Inquisición española en el siglo XVI*. Madrid: Castalia, 1952. Facs. of 1551 Toledo, 1551 Valladolid, and 1559 Valladolid Lists.

Maureen Ihrie

**INÉS DE CASTRO, Leyenda de.** The tragic tale of Inés de Castro and her affair with Prince Peter of Portugal is but another facet of political strife and violence on the Iberian Peninsula in the late Middle Ages. The story, however, inspired numerous writers and poets. It is a recurring theme in Spanish literature and stands as the Portuguese symbol for tragic love.

The first references to the story come from Pero *López de Ayala in his *Crónica de don Pedro I* (Chronicle of King Peter of Castile) and from the Portuguese historian Fernão Lopes in his *Crónica de D. Pedro I* (Chronicle of King Peter of Portugal). The beautiful Inés, traditionally known as "cuello de garza" (heron-necked), went to Portugal in 1335 as a lady-in-waiting to her cousin doña Constanza, who was the daughter of don Juan Manuel and betrothed to Prince Peter, son of Alphonse IV. The scandalous love affair which ensued between Inés and Peter, despite the objections of Alphonse, was not without its ironies: while she was to bear Peter three children, she was also the godmother of Constanza's firstborn. The liaison gained more enemies when Inés's brothers, who had fled Peter the Cruel, appeared to enjoy a great deal of influence in the Portuguese court as protégés of Prince Peter. At the advice of his counselors, Alphonse finally permitted the murder of Inés even though, according to legend, he had previously relented after being overcome by her pleas for mercy. The murder took place, according to a ballad, when Peter was hunting. Peter immediately revolted against his father, but was temporarily pacified. He sought his revenge in 1357 upon his father's death by seizing two of the three assassins in an exchange of prisoners with Peter the Cruel and having their hearts ripped out before him while he ate. In 1361 he assembled his court at Castanheda and declared before all that he had secretly married Inés some years earlier. Her body was disinterred and removed to the royal abbey at Alcobaça, the pantheon of Portuguese kings.

The Portuguese poet García de *Resende (d. 1536), the compiler of the vast *Cancioneiro Geral* (1516), captured the pathos of her death in his *Trovas à morte de D. Inés*. *Camões reviews the legend in the third canto of *Os Lusiadas* and cautions against the dangers of passionate love. Antonio Ferreira's *A Castro* (1557) is the first dramatization of the legend and conforms to the *Renaissance mold of classical tragedy. This inspired the Spanish dominican, Jerónimo *Bermúdez, to write his five-act *Nise lastimosa* (1577; Pitiful Ines) and a sequel celebrating her posthumous glory, *Nise laureada* (Ines Crowned). Mejía de la Cerda's *Tragedia famosa de Inés de Castro* (1611) closely follows *Nise lastimosa*, but introduces a new character, Rodrigo, a rejected admirer of Inés, who is the main force behind the murder. Luis *Vélez de Guevara infused new life into the theme with his famous *Reinar después de morir* (To Reign after Death). *Ver y creer* (See and Believe) by Juan de *Matos Fragoso is supposed to be a continuation of *Reinar después de morir*. Luciano *Comella wrote a one-act play (1799) with musical background. *Bretón de los Herreros translated the French dramatist Houdart de la Motte's tragedy on the theme. Manuel Amor Meilán wrote a long historical novel, *Reinar después de morir*. Juan José Cadenas adapted the theme to the *zarzuela in 1907. *See also* Edad Media, Literatura de la.

BIBLIOGRAPHY

Primary Texts

*Crónica de don Pedro I.* By Pero López de Ayala. In BAE 66. 393–614.

*Crónica do senhor rei dom Pedro.* By Fernão Lopes. Ed. Damião Peres. Porto: Livraria Civilizaçao, 1979.

*Nise lastimosa* and *Nise laureada.* By Jerónimo Bermúdez. In *Tesoro del teatro español* vol. 1. Ed. Eugenio de Ochoa. Paris: n.p., 1838.

*Reinar después de morir* and *El diablo está en Cantillana.* By Luis Vélez de Guevara. Ed. Manuel Muñoz Cortés. Madrid: Espasa-Calpe, 1959.

*La Tragédie "Castro" d'António Ferreira.* By António Ferreira. Ed. Adrien Roig. Paris: Centro Cultural Português, 1971.

"Trovas a morte de D. Inés de Castro." By García de Resende. In *The Oxford Book of Portuguese Verse.* Ed. Aubrey F. G. Bell. Oxford: Clarendon, 1925.

Criticism

Dugdale, B.E.C. "Inés de Castro and Pedro of Portugal." *Quarterly Review* 224 (1915): 356–78.

Hauer, Mary G. *Luis Vélez de Guevara: A Critical Bibliography.* UNCSRLL 5. Chapel Hill: U of North Carolina P, 1975.

Nozick, Martin. "The Inez de Castro Theme in European Literature." *Comparative Literature* 3 (1951): 330–41.

Sena, Jorge de. "Inês de Castro ou literatura portuguesa desde Fernão Lopes a Camões e história político social de D. Alfonso IV a D. Sebastião e compreendo especialmente a analise estrutural de *Castro* de Ferreira e do episodio camoniano de Inês." In *Estudos de História e Cultura* (la serie). Lisbon: Ediçao da Revista Occidente, 1963 [i.e., 1967]. 123–618.

Triwedi, Mitchell D. "Inés de Castro, 'cuello de garza': Una nota sobre el *Reinar después de morir* de Luis Vélez de Guevara." *Hispanófila* 5 (1962): 1–7.

Porter Conerly

***INFANTE DON GARCÍA, Cantar del*** (Song of the Infante D. García), lost *cantar de gesta.* In this historically based epic, García, the last Count of Castile, is assassinated by the Vela family just before he is to marry Sancha, sister to Bermudo III.

BIBLIOGRAPHY

Criticism

Menéndez Pidal, R. "El Romanz del Infant García y Sancho de Navarra antiemperador." In *Historia y epopeya.* Madrid: Hernando, 1934. 33–98.

***INFANTES DE LARA, Leyenda de los*** (Legend of the Seven Infantes of Lara), a legend belonging to the epic cycle of the Counts of Castile. Although this *cantar de gesta* does not survive in a poetic text, its preservation in the chronicles with frequent instances of assonance and paragogic E would indicate several earlier versions. *Menéndez Pidal, whose masterful study of the legend is still the most complete, considered there to be two distinct *cantares*. Thomas Lathrop has suggested that the later *cantar* represents just one variant in the continuous evolution of the *cantar*. The scene is set in the reign (970–95) of Garci Fernández, son of Fernán González. The events of the legend are entirely fictitious (beginning with the number of infantes), yet historians have recognized a strong, and more than fortuitous, resemblance between the political background portrayed in the legend and Spain's political and social history during the final years of the tenth c. Thus, despite the lack of mention of the infantes in such likely chronicles as the *Crónica de Nájera*, or \*Ximénez de Rada's *De rebus Hispaniae*, most scholars accept the idea that an epic on the infantes did exist around the millennium.

The principal chronicle sources of the legend are \*Alphonse X's *Crónica general*, the *Crónica de 1344*, and the so-called *Refundición toledana*, a reworking of the *Crónica de 1344*. To these may be added some six *romances viejos* (old ballads), authentic survivors of the epic tradition.

Like some other legendary accounts from the cycle of the Counts of Castile (*La \*Condesa traidora*, and the *Cantar del \*Infante don García*), the *Siete Infantes* is noted for its violence, where an affront or act of betrayal sets off a chain reaction of fatalistic and bloody vengeance. The events and their sequence as they appear in the several variants of the *Siete Infantes* are rather involved. The main points of the legend are as follows:

A family feud is incited when the seven infantes with their parents, Gonzalo Gustios and doña Sancha, and their governor, Nuño Salido, attend the wedding of their uncle, Ruy Veláquez, and doña Lambra. During the festivities a *tablado* (a mock castle made of boards) is erected which competing knights try to knock down by throwing short lances. A confrontation ensues between Alvar Sánchez, the cousin of doña Lambra, and the youngest of the infantes, Gonzalo González. Due to the persistence and ill will of doña Lambra, a series of affronts and counter-affronts between the two families is unleashed: Gonzalo kills Alvar Sánchez; Gonzalo smashes a hawk into his uncle's face after twice being attacked; a blood-filled cucumber is thrown at Gonzalo while he is preparing to bathe. (John Burt has recently studied the sexual overtones in the character of doña Lambra and the affronts.) When peace is ostensibly made, Ruy Velázquez, at his wife's insistence, devises a plan of revenge in which he delivers Gonzalo Gustios to Almanzor in Córdoba and betrays the seven infantes and Nuño Salido on the battlefield. Gonzalo Gustios is not killed, but imprisoned. The seven infantes are, along with their governor, decapitated and their heads sent to Almanzor in Córdoba, where in a poignant scene, their father pronounces a eulogy over each of their heads. Almanzor offers him a Moorish noblewoman to console him. She bears him a son, Mudarra González, to whom it falls to avenge the deaths of his half-brothers. The later version of the *cantar* reports the most gruesome vengeance: Mudarra wounds and delivers Ruy Velázquez to his sister, doña Sánchez, who kneels to drink the blood flowing from his wound. To exact vengeance she orders another *tablado* to be erected upon which her brother is to meet the cruelest of deaths. Later, Gonzalo Gustios subjects doña Lambra to an equally cruel death.

Juan de la \*Cueva was the first to bring the legend to the stage in 1579, followed by an anonymous *Famosos hechos de Mudarra* (1583; Famous Deeds of Mudarra). In 1617 Lope de *Vega's *El bastardo Mudarra* was presented in Madrid, giving the legend its most complete dramatic treatment. There are later renditions by *Hurtado de Velarde and *Matos Fragoso. Jerónimo *Cáncer and Juan *Vélez de Guevara brought out a burlesque treatment of the legend in 1650. The theme flourished during the Romantic period: *Rivas, *Trueba y Cossío, and later *Fernández y González.

BIBLIOGRAPHY

Primary Texts

Lathrop, T. A. *The Legend of the Siete Infantes de Lara. (Refundición toledana de la Crónica de 1344 version).* UNCSRLL 122. Chapel Hill: U of North Carolina P, 1971.

Menéndez Pidal, Ramón. *La leyenda de los Infantes de Lara.* 3rd ed. Madrid: Espasa-Calpe, 1971.

————. *Reliquias de la poesía épica española.* Madrid: Espasa-Calpe, 1951.

Criticism

Burt, J. R. "The Bloody Cucumber and Related Matters in the *Siete Infantes de Lara.*" *HR* 50 (1982): 345–52.

Chalon, L. *L'Histoire et l'épopée castillane du moyen âge.* Paris: Champion, 1976.

Deyermond, A. D. *A Literary History of Spain. The Middle Ages.* New York: Barnes and Noble; London: Benn, 1971.

Lapesa, R. "El cohombro arrojado como afrenta." In *De la edad media a nuestros días: Estudios de historia literaria.* Madrid: Gredos, 1962.

Lathrop, T. A. "The Singer of Tales and the *Siete Infantes de Lara.*" In *Studies in Honor of John Esten Keller.* Ed. J. R. Jones. Newark, DE: Juan de la Cuesta, 1980.

————. See Primary Texts, *The Legend.* . . .

Menéndez Pidal, R. See Primary Texts, *La Leyenda de.* . . .

                                                                    Porter Conerly


**INGENIO DE ESTA CORTE, Un** (A Wit Of This Court), pseudonym. Many seventeenth-c. plays were published under this cover. Philip IV was once thought to have employed the pseudonym, but this theory has been discarded. A c. later, the pen name was used by don Tomás Erauso y Zabaleta for the *Discurso crítico sobre el origen, calidad y estado presente de las comedias en España* (1750; Critical Discourse on the Origin, Quality and Present State of Plays in Spain). Eugenio d'*Ors also employed it for a section in *Blanco y Negro.*


**INQUISITION,** a religious institution. While the Inquisition in other parts of Europe served primarily to combat heresies such as that of the Cathars (the medieval Inquisition) and Protestantism (the Roman Inquisition), the Spanish Inquisition focused on the combat against apostate former Jews and Muslims, as well as witchcraft and sorcery. Its often obsessive concern was that of the purity of the blood and the establishment of a totalitarian and state religion in Catholicism. While the medieval Inquisition goes back to the thirteenth and fourteenth centuries in southern France and northern Italy, the Spanish Inquisition may be dated to 1478, when Sixtus IV authorized the establishment of a tribunal requested by the Catholic kings.

In 1483 Sixtus authorized the naming of an inquisitor general or grand inquisitor. As the first grand inquisitor, the Dominican Tomás de Torquemada became a notorious symbol of the horrors of the Inquisition itself, although the case can be made that he was no more terrible than the climate and processes over which he reigned.

The Spanish Inquisition spread to other Spanish territories: Mexico and Peru had particularly notorious tribunals; it was introduced into Sicily in 1517; the effort in the Netherlands starting in 1522 to have it eradicate Protestantism was a failure. In Spain, there were many cases of individuals of note who suffered at the hands of the Inquisition: St. *Ignacio de Loyola was twice arrested, Bartolomé de Carranza, Archbishop of Toledo, was incarcerated for seventeen years, and Fray Luis de *León was imprisoned for four years and tried. After March of 1492, Jews were by statute required either to convert or go into exile; the same proscription was established in 1502 for Muslims. The enforcement of these edicts, the monitoring of forced conversions and discovery of false converts of both religions gave the Spanish Inquisition its major focus for many years. The end of the Spanish Inquisition seemed to come with its suppression in 1808 by Joseph Bonaparte, but it was restored by Ferdinand VII in 1814 and endured to the end of his reign in 1832, with an interruption during the liberal uprising and regime of 1820–23.

The origins and effects of the special brand of Inquisition in and on Hispanic society has been the subject of much discussion, much of it of either an acrimonious or apologetic nature, making it difficult or impossible to establish any views that are generally accepted by a majority of historians. Condemnatory histories have been written by Spaniards (Llorente, for example) and non-Spaniards (H. C. Lea, for example) alike; their work is often regarded as based on anti-Catholic, anti-Spanish sentiments from the outset. Defenses of the Inquisition have come primarily from the Catholic camp; the two best-known examples are the works of Father Bernardino Llorca and Father La Pinta. The latter justifies the existence and actions of the Inquisition as being necessary and effective in the process of religious unification of the Spanish nation. The peculiarly anti-Semitic nature of the Spanish Inquisition, rooted in the equally peculiar tri-religious nature of Spanish society and culture in the Middle Ages, is a complex sociological phenomenon, with manifold literary manifestations, a subject which has been most explicitly explored by Américo *Castro.

Because of the sensitive racial and religious issues involved in any discussion of this historical phenomenon, issues which most would recognize have not lost their importance with the passing of time, and because of the recognition of many that these issues and occurrences have at least partially shaped the vicissitudes of Spanish history and the structure of Spanish society and its character, no definitive view or history of the Spanish Inquisition is likely to emerge in the near future. *See also* Censorship; Converso.

BIBLIOGRAPHY

Criticism

Castro, Américo. *The Structure of Spanish History.* Tr. E. King. Princeton: Princeton UP, 1954.

———. *An Idea of History.* Tr. E. King and S. Gilman. Columbia: Ohio State UP, 1976.

Lea, H. C. *A History of the Inquisition of Spain.* New York: AMS, 1966.

Llorca, B. *La inquisición en España.* Barcelona: Labor, 1954.

María Rosa Menocal


**INSTITUCIÓN LIBRE DE ENSEÑANZA.** *See* Giner de los Ríos, Francisco (1839–1915)


**IRANZO, Miguel Lucas de.** *See* Escavias, Pedro de


**IRIARTE, Juan de** (1702, Puerto de la Cruz de Orotava, Canary Islands–1771, Madrid), linguist and critic. The oldest of the literary Iriartes, Juan de Iriarte was educated in Paris, where he was a student of Voltaire. He completed his studies in England and, upon his return to Madrid, joined the staff of the Royal Library. In 1725 he was appointed tutor for the children of the Dukes of Béjar and of Alba. Iriarte was renowned for his knowledge of Latin, which he displayed as a member of both the Academy of San Fernando and the *Academia Española. His initiation speech to the latter was titled "Sobre la imperfección de los Diccionarios" (1747; On the Imperfection of Dictionaries). His fanaticism for Latin led him to translate into Latin numerous treatises on such diverse topics as the kings of Spain and France, a Latin grammar, and Spanish proverbs; he even composed a long poem, *Taurimaquia matritensis, sive taurorum ludi* (1725; The Art of Bullfighting in Madrid, or the Games of the Bulls). Iriarte compiled a catalog of mss. housed in the Royal Library, and published the first volume in 1769. He is best known for his participation as critic for the *Diario de los literatos* (Journal for Learned Men). His most important article for the *Diario* (4: 1–113) was a lengthy review of *Luzán's *Poética* (1737; Poetics). In it Iriarte lauds the attempt to compile a comprehensive poetics in Spanish. Moreover, according to *Menéndez y Pelayo, Iriarte refutes the anti-nationalistic stance of Luzán's work. Specifically, Iriarte defends Spain's national theater and especially Lope de *Vega's *Arte nuevo de hacer comedias* (1609; New Art of Writing Plays), calling it rather the "Arte nuevo de criticar comedias" (The New Art of Criticizing Plays). Iriarte opposes Luzán's rigid adherence to the classic unities, prefering to let the dramatist rely on his sense of decorum and propriety. Luzán published a friendly response in which he attributed his criticism of Lope to overzealousness. On the whole, Juan de Iriarte's influence on Hispanic letters will probably be remembered most in his role as uncle of the more famous *Tomás de Iriarte, whom he helped to enter Madrid's erudite society.

BIBLIOGRAPHY

Primary Texts

*Gramática latina, escrita con nuevo método y nuevas observaciones en verso castellano, con su explicación en prosa.* Paris: Librería de Rosa, 1841.

*Obras sueltas de D. Juan de Yriarte, publicadas en obsequio de la literatura, a expensas de varios caballeros.* . . . Madrid: Menal, 1774.

Donald C. Buck

**IRIARTE, Tomás de** (1750, Tenerife–1791, Madrid), neo-classical poet, dramatist, and theoretician. Iriarte traveled from his birthplace in the Canary Islands to Madrid when he was fourteen years old in order to live and study with his renowned uncle, Juan de *Iriarte. The elder Iriarte, the king's librarian and a noted Latin scholar and poet, saw to it that his nephew's education contained a solid foundation of classical instruction. Tomás, who had studied Latin in the Canary Islands, flourished under Juan's tutelege, and embarked on a career which would make him one of the Spanish eighteenth c.'s most gifted and active authors. His first endeavors were translations of foreign dramas for the Count of Aranda's Royal Theaters (1768–72), but during this time he also penned an original verse comedy, *Hacer que hacemos* (1770; The Busybody), which failed to reach the stage. Iriarte quit writing for the theater for a number of years, and only returned to it with *El señorito mimado* (1787; The Pampered Youth) and *La señorita mal criada* (1788; The Ill-Bred Miss), both of which were well written, full of acute observations on Spanish society, and very popular. Two other plays, *El don de gentes* (1790; Winning Ways) and *Donde menos se piensa salta la liebre* (1790; Things Happen Where Least Expected), were less successful. The short musical melologue, *Guzmán el Bueno* (1790; Guzmán the Brave), based on the same popular subject that *Moratín had developed in 1777, was immediately successful, and a humorously moralizing short play, *La librería* (The Bookstore), was staged several times in the 1780s.

Juan died in 1771, and Tomás succeeded him as official translator of the First Secretariat of State. He assiduously attended Nicolás Fernández de Moratín's *tertulia* at the San Sebastián Inn, discussing current literary trends with his fellow neo-classicists. Perhaps inspired by the popularity of *Cadalso' *Eruditos a la violeta* (1772; The Pseudo-Intellectuals), Iriarte wrote the satirical *Los literatos en cuaresma* (1773; Writers in Lent), in which he deplored the sorry state of Spanish letters. The attack was aimed mainly at Ramón de la *Cruz and other foes of neo-classicism. In order to help clarify the precepts that he upheld as a writer, he published a translation of Horace's *Arte poética* (1777; Poetics), but the translation prompted a negative response from Juan *López de Sedano; Iriarte answered him with *Donde las dan las toman* (1778; Give and Take).

In 1779 he finished his long didactic poem, *La música* (1779; *Music*, 1807), the initial drafts of which he had first read in the early 1770s at the San Sebastián Inn. For the *Academia Española's poetry competition of 1779 Iriarte handed in an eclogue, *La felicidad de la vida del campo* (1780; The Happiness of Country

Life), but he lost to Juan *Meléndez Valdés (known poetically as Batilo). The loss bothered him, and he could not resist publishing some observations on the matter, *Reflexiones sobre la égloga de Batilo* (1781; Reflections on Batilo's Eclogue), a publication which initiated one of the most bitter polemics of the eighteenth c. between Iriarte and Juan Pablo *Forner, who defended Meléndez and then later launched a series of vicious attacks against Iriarte and his most famous work, *Fábulas literarias* (1782; *Literary Fables*, 1855).

Iriarte's lasting fame was secured by the *Fábulas literarias*. These brief, witty, and charming fables encompass Iriarte's (and the neo-classicists') precepts for quality writing. Iriarte's claim that his collection was the first collection of "entirely original" fables produced in Spain angered Félix María *Samaniego, author of some *Fábulas morales* (1781; Moral Fables), and touched off yet another lengthy controversy. But Iriarte was in essence justified in his view— his fables were the first original collection, since no one had ever attempted to encompass the rules of literature in this popular literary form. Iriarte displayed a dazzling variety of Spanish verse forms and combined this technical accomplishment with skilled rhyming patterns, clever observations, and a rich sense of humor. He also infused the fables with allusions to contemporary figures, a ploy which whetted the public's appetite for gossip, and made the *Fábulas* an immediate success. Iriarte criticized literary vices, suggested examples of good writing, served up the rules of art, and provided a type of primer for the precise use of language. Forner, of course, thought them vapid, and produced two libelous pieces, *El asno erudito* (1782; The Erudite Ass) and *Los gramáticos: historia chinesca* (1782; The Grammarians: A Chinese Story), to express his views. Iriarte, however, has enjoyed the last word: his fables have been printed repeatedly, translated into many languages, and read with pleasure by generations of students and scholars. They obviously met his goal, taken from Horace's concept of *utile dulci*, which was to please and to teach at the same time.

The first edition of Iriarte's collected works appeared in 1787 (Madrid: Benito Cano), four years before Iriarte's death in 1791. The definitive edition was published posthumously (Madrid: Imprenta Real, 1805).

BIBLIOGRAPHY
Primary Texts
*Colección de obras en verso y prosa.* Madrid: Cano, 1787.
*Colección de obras en verso y prosa.* Madrid: Real, 1805.
*El mal hombre.* Ed. Patrizia Garelli. Albano Terme: Piovan, 1988.
*Poesías.* Ed. Alberto Navarro González. Madrid: Espasa-Calpe, 1953.
*El señorito mimado. La señorita mal criada.* Ed. Russell P. Sebold. Madrid: Castalia, 1978.

English Translation
*Literary Fables.* Tr. George Devereaux. Boston: Ticknor and Fields, 1855.

Criticism
Allué y Morer, F. "Un precursor de las formas modernistas: Don Tomás de Iriarte." *Poesía española* 210 (1970): 5–9.

Clarke, Dorothy C. "On Iriarte's Versification." *PMLA* 67 (1952): 411–19.
Cotarelo y Mori, Emilio. *Iriarte y su época*. Madrid: Rivadeneyra, 1897.
Cox, R. Merritt. *Tomás de Iriarte*. TWAS 228. New York: Twayne, 1972.
Queipo Rodríguez, Mario M. *Ideas ilustradas en las fábulas de Iriarte y Samaniego*.
    Oviedo: Universidad de Oviedo, 1986.
Sebold, Russell P. *El rapto de la mente. Poética y poesía dieciochescas*. Madrid: Prensa
    Española, 1970.

David Thatcher Gies

**IRIBARREN, José María** (1906, Tudela, Navarre–1971, Pamplona), essayist, philologist, folklorist, prose author. His publications include *El porqué de los dichos: Sentido, origen y anécdota de los dichos, modismos y frases proverbiales de España* (1955; The Reason for Sayings: Meanings and Origin of Sayings, Idioms and Proverbial Phrases in Spain), *Espoz y Mina, El guerrillero* (1965; Espoz y Mina, the Guerrilla Fighter), *El general Mola* (General Mola), etc.

BIBLIOGRAPHY

Primary Texts

*Espoz y Mina*. Madrid: Aguilar, 1965.
*El general Mola*. 3rd ed. Madrid: Bullón, 1963.
*El porqué de los dichos*. 2nd ed. Madrid: Aguilar, 1956.

Isabel McSpadden

**IRVING, Washington** (1783, New York–1859, Sleepy Hollow), diplomat, novelist and essayist. He was born to a large family of Scottish immigrants. At the age of nineteen, after leaving school, he started writing for several newspapers in New York, and soon became known as a person of literary talent.

In 1809 he wrote *A History of New York from the beginning of the World to the End of the Dutch Dynasty*, a book that was praised by the *Athenaeum* of London as an honest attempt to found an American literature. In the *Sketch Book of Geoffrey Crayon* (1819–20) he creates various images of America symbolized through his characters.

In his different trips to Spain, as a translator first (1826), and diplomat later (1842), he collected stories that would form the bulk of his books about Spain: *A History of the Life and Voyages of Christopher Columbus* (1828), and *Chronicle of the Conquest of Granada*, based on Ginés *Pérez de Hita's narration. His most famous series of stories and essays were published under the title of *The Alhambra* (1832), from which he earned a reputation for having an eye for the picturesque. His *Diary: Spain 1828–1829* was edited in 1920. His last important book on Spain is *Legend of the Conquest of Spain* (1835), well after his fame as a writer was established. Irving is well known as a romantic historian, impressionist biographer, and an exotic and local colorist writer with a subtle sense of humor. *See also* Romanticism.

BIBLIOGRAPHY

Primary Texts

*The Alhambra*. New York: Macmillan, 1967.
*Castles of Spain*. Ed. Jane W. Watson. Champaign, IL: Garrard, 1971.
*The Complete Works of Washington Irving*. 29 vols. Boston: Twayne, 1969–87.
*The Conquest of Granada*. New York: Dent, 1930.
*The Conquest of Spain*. New York: U.S. Book Co., 1890.
*Letters From Sunnyside and Spain by Washington Irving*. Ed. Stanley T. Williams. Norwood, PA: Norwood, 1976.
*The Life and Voyages of Christopher Columbus to Which are added those of his Companions*. New York: AMS, 1973.
*Life and Voyages of Columbus*. London: Bell, 1910.
*Washington Irving's Madrid Journal 1827–28 and Related Letters*. Ed. Andrew B. Myers. New York: Bulletin of the New York Public Library, 1958.

Spanish Translations

*Cuentos de la Alhambra*. Barcelona: Bruguera, 1972.
*Cuentos de la Alhambra*. Madrid: Espasa-Calpe, 1964.
*Leyendas de la Alhambra y de la conquista árabe de España*. Barcelona: Iberia, 1959.
*Leyendas españolas*. London: Appleton, 1919.

Criticism

Bowden, Mary W. *Washington Irving*. Boston: Twayne, 1981.
Bowers, Claude G. *The Spanish Adventures of Washington Irving*. Boston: Houghton Mifflin, 1940.
Hazlett, John D. "Literary Nationalism and Ambivalence in Washington Irving's *The Life and Voyages of Christopher Columbus*." *American Literature* 55.4 (1983): 560–75.
Johnson, Johanna. *The Heart That Would Not Hold. A Biography of Washington Irving*. New York: M. Evans, 1971.
McElroy, John. "The Integrity of Irving's *Columbus*." *American Literature*. 50.1 (1978): 1–16.

Fernando Operé

**ISABEL DE JESÚS, Sor** (1586, ?–1648, Avila), spiritual autobiographer. An illiterate shepherdess and visionary, María Isabel absorbed the hagiographic language and oral tradition of the Cloistered Augustinian convent in Arenas where she lived as a lay sister. Married against her will at fourteen to an old man, she bore three children, all of whom died in infancy or early childhood. After twenty-four years of marriage, nursing her infirm husband and working outside the home to support them both, she suffered three years of persecution and accusations of being a false prophet before she was able to realize her lifelong dream of becoming a nun. Nineteen years after entering the convent and three years before her death, Sor Isabel was assigned a secretary to whom she was asked to dictate her exemplary life for the benefit of nuns to come. Her work's title is *Vida de la Venerable Madre Isabel de Jesús, recoleta Augustina en el convento de San Juan Bautista de la villa de Arenas. Dictada por ella* *misma y añadido lo que faltó de su dichosa muerte* (1675; Life of the Venerable Mother Isabel de Jesús, Cloistered Augustinian of the Convent of St. John the Baptist in the Village of Arenas. Dictated by Her, with an Addition Telling of Her Blessed Death). This 470-page tome reveals, practically uncensored, the fantasy life of this obsessively religious woman. Although committed to paper, it remains essentially an oral history. Her proverbs and popular wisdom, her faith in the reality of her imaginings, and her portrayal of the various points of view of her family, her neighbors and ecclesiastics in disagreement with each other suggest a breadth of vision that is astonishing, in view of the limitations of Isabel de Jesús's life experience. *See also* mysticism.

BIBLIOGRAPHY

Primary Text

*Vida de la Venerable Madre Isabel de Jesús.* . . . Madrid: Nieto, 1675.

Criticism

Arenal, E. "The Convent as Catalyst for Autonomy: Two Hispanic Nuns of the Seventeenth Century." *Women in Hispanic Literature: Icons and Fallen Idols.* Ed. B. Miller. Berkeley: U of California P, 1983.

Arenal, E., and S. Schlau. "The Poor Pray More: A Peasant Nun." *Untold Sisters: Hispanic Nuns in Their Own Works.* Albuquerque: U of New Mexico P, 1989. Contains selections with English translations.

Stacey Schlau

**ISLA, José Francisco, El Padre** (1703, Vidanes, León–1781, Bologna, Italy), famed preacher, prose satirist. Trained with the Jesuits, in 1727 he was named a professor of theology. He taught theology, philosophy, and preached until 1767, when the order was expelled from Spain. With many other colleagues, he moved to Italy for the remainder of his life.

Padre Isla's writing throughout his life ridiculed the baroque decadence, excesses and lack of substance prevalent in public discourse of the day. Ironically, some pieces were mistaken for sincere praise. *Triunfo del amor y de la lealtad* (1746; Triumph of Love and Loyalty)—written with his Jesuit mentor, Luis de Losada—ridicules the excessive public spectacle produced upon the canonization of two saints. Throughout his life, he translated various works into Spanish (*Gil Blas*, for example) and penned many satirical pieces. His most important and most successful endeavor was the *Historia del famoso predicador Fray Gerundio de Campazas, alias Zotes* (*The history of the famous preacher, Friar Gerund de Campazas: otherwise Gerund Zotes*, 1772). Part 1, published not under Isla's name, but rather one Francisco *Lobón de Salazar, appeared in 1757, and the 1,500 copies of that printing sold out in three days. In 1760, after a two-year investigation by the *Inquisition, it was banned. A part 2 circulated in ms. form for many years, finally seeing print in 1768, the year following the expulsion of the Jesuits. A third part was never realized. Fray Gerundio is a stinging critique of pompous preachers, with their rhetorical excesses, their inaccurate use of mythology, the Bible, and other sources, their lax morals, and the dearth of spiritual content in their messages. Criticism has judged it the most important novel of the eighteenth c.

Father Isla devoted his final years to *El Cicerón*, a 12,000-line poem on Cicero's life, which also parodies excesses, decadence and superficiality in contemporary Spanish society. He left an interesting body of correspondence, which has been edited. Only recently, another ms. of Isla was published for the first time by Conrado Pérez Picón; written in Italy, it is a detailed refutation of charges composed by Pedro *Campomanes for Charles III in defense of the expulsion of the Jesuit order. The head of the exiled order directed it to be burned, but one copy was saved.

BIBLIOGRAPHY

Primary Texts

*Anatomía del informe de Campomanes*. Intro., notes P. Conrado Pérez Picón. Leon: CSIC, 1979.
*El Cicerón*. Intro., ed. Giuseppe de Gennaro. BRAE Anejo 12. Madrid: RAE, 1965.
*Descripción de la máscara o.* . . . Madrid: Espinosa, 1787.
*Fray Gerundio de Campazas*. Ed., intro., notes Russell P. Sebold. Clásicos Castellanos 148–51. 4 vols. Madrid: Espasa-Calpe, 1960–64.
*Obras escogidas*. In BAE 15 and 19.

English Translation

*The history of the famous preacher, Friar Gerund de Campazas: otherwise Gerund Zotes*. Tr. T. Nugent. London: Davies, 1772.

Criticism

Jurado, José. "Ediciones tempranas del Fray Gerundio de Campaza." *BH* 87 (1985): 137–65. Publishing history

**ITALIAN LITERARY INFLUENCES IN SPAIN.** The influence of Italian literature in Spain corresponds in great measure to the emergence in the fourteenth c. of Italy's three greatest writers: Dante (1265–1321), Petrarch (1304–74), and Boccaccio (1313–75). Italo-Spanish relations were strengthened during the reign of Alphonse V of Naples (1396–1458), at whose court resided such renowned humanists as Lorenzo Valla, Aeneas Sylvius, and George of Trebizond. The Neapolitan court remained an important point of contact throughout the sixteenth c., as Spanish authors such as Alfonso (1490?–1532) and Juan (1491–1541) de *Valdés and *Garcilaso de la Vega (1501?–36) met with Giulio Cesare Caracciolo, Luigi Tansillo and Bernardo Tasso, among others. Both before and after the Alphonsine court in Naples, Alonso de *Cartagena (1384–1456), Antonio de *Nebrija (1442–1522), Andrés *Laguna (1499–1560), Juan de *Lucena (d. 1506?), and Juan Ginés de *Sepúlveda (1490?–1573) were among the Spanish humanists who resided and studied in Italy. Italian humanists who lived at various times in Spain include Guiniforte Barzizza, Manual Crisolara, Angelo Decembrio, Pedro *Mártir, Marineo Sículo, Baldassare *Castiglione, and Andrea *Navaggiero.

Owing to Catalonia's proximity to the Italian peninsula and to their commercial and political relations, contact between Italian literature and the literatures of the Spanish peninsula is first evidenced in the Catalan region in the fourteenth c. The influence of Dante, Petrarch, and Boccaccio, therefore, is a significant factor in the development of *Catalan literature.

## Dante's Influence in Catalan Literature

An important source of Bernat *Metge's *Lo somni* (1399; The Dream), Dante's *Divina Commedia* was translated in its entirety in *tercia rima* by Andreu Febrer (1429). The great Catalan poet, Ausiàs *March (1397?–1459), reveals a knowledge of Dante's *Vita Nuova* and the *Convivium* in his *Cants d'amor* (1420–59; Songs of Love). The *Divina Commedia* inspired Fra Rocaberti's allegorical poem *Gloria de amor* (1446; Love's Glory). Joanot *Martorell (c. 1420–70), Ferrant Valenti, and the author of *Curial y Güelfa* were familiar with Dante's works, while Jaume Ferrer de Blanes's *Sentencia católicas y conclusions principals del preclarissim theolech y divi poeta Dante* (1545; Catholic Maxims and Principal Conclusions of the Illustrious Theologist and Divine Poet Dante) points to the Tuscan poet's continuing impact on Catalan literature.

## Catalan Petrarchism

Petrarch's influence in medieval *Catalan literature can be traced to Metge's *Valter e Griselda* (1388); his *Lo somni* alludes to the *Secretum*, the *De rebus familiaribus*, and the *De remediis*. Metge's contemporary, Antoni Canals (1352–1419), borrows from Petrarch's Latin epic *Africa* in his *Rahonament fet entre Scipió Africá e Annibal* (c. 1500; Reasoning between Scipius Africanus and Hannibal). Petrarch's *Canzoniere* influenced Jordi de *Sant Jordi (c. 1385-c. 1424), especially his "Cançió d'oposits" (1416–24; Song of Opposites). However, it is not until Ausiàs March's tormented love poetry, in particular his *Cant espiritual* (1420–59; Spiritual Song) written in free *estrams*, that the paradoxical nature of Petrarch's lyric poetry is finally understood and imitated.

## Dante's Influence in Castilian Literature

In 1428, Enrique de *Villena finished a prose translation into Castilian of the *Divina Commedia* commissioned by Iñigo López de Mendoza, Marqués de *Santillana (1398–1458). Santillana's library held Italian editions of Dante's *Divina Commedia*, the *Convivium*, and the *Vita Nuova*, as well as Petrarch's *Canzoniere*. Of his own works, the *Coronación de Mossén Jordi de San Jordi* (c. 1430; Coronation of the Poet Jordi de San Jordi), *El infierno de los enamorados* (c. 1430; Lover's Inferno), *La comedieta de Ponça* (c. 1444; Comedy on the Victory at Ponza), and his attack against Alvaro de Luna, *El diálogo de Bías contra Fortuna* (1448; Dialogue of Bias Against Fortune), were influenced most heavily by Santillana's readings of Dante. Francisco *Imperial (late fourteenth c.-fifteenth c.) was the first to introduce Dante's hendecasyllable line into Spain. Although Imperial's authorship of *Dezir a las syete virtudes* (c. 1405; Poem on the Seven Virtues) has come into question, the allegorical poem does imitate the *Commedia's* dream vision format, and includes Dante as one of the poem's protagonists. Juan de *Mena's *Laberinto de Fortuna* (1444; Labyrinth of Fortune) is an allegory wholly original in style yet influenced considerably by Dante.

Despite Juan de *Padilla's allegory in *arte mayor*, *Los doze triumphos de los doze apóstoles* (1521; The Twelve Triumphs of the Twelve Apostles), and Francisco de *Quevedo's *Los sueños* (1626; *Visions*), Dante's influence in Spanish *Siglo de Oro literature is almost entirely eclipsed by his contemporaries Petrarch and Boccaccio.

## Petrarch and Petrarchism in Castilian Literature

Petrarch's influence as a moral philosopher predates his impact as a lyric poet; the number of medieval Castilian translations of his *exempla* and *sententiae*, along with the popularity of his *De remediis utriusque fortunae* and his *Vita solitaria*, attests to the immediate reception of his humanistic works. Petrarch's Latin works influenced Enrique de Aragón, Marqués de Villena's (1384–1434) *Tratado de consolación* (1423; Treatise on Consolation) and the *Tratado del aojamiento* (1425; Treatise on the Evil Eye), while the *De remediis* is one of the important sources of Fernando de *Rojas' La *Celestina. The *De remediis* was translated by Francisco de *Madrid in 1510 as *De los remedios contra próspera fortuna* (Remedies against Good Fortune).

Petrarch's vernacular poetry was well known to Santillana, whose *Planto de la Reina Margarida* (c. 1430; Queen Margaret's Lament) and *Triumfete de Amor* (1440?; Minor Triumph on Love) are influenced by the allegorical *Trionfi*. Although characterized by elegance of expression and a renewed interest in classical mythology, Santillana's poetry nevertheless remains on the threshold of the *Renaissance as represented by Petrarch. While his forty-two *sonetos fechos al itálico modo* (1438–58; Sonnets Written in the Italian Style) imitate the *Canzoniere*, and employ the sonnet form with hendecasyllabic rhyme for the first time in Castilian, they did not occasion further imitations. The poems adhere to the form, but the sonnets lack the harmony and rhythm of the Italian model and the self-referential intensity of Petrarch's poetic persona as unrequited lover. Petrarch's poetic influence is strongest in the sixteenth c. The extremely popular *cancionero translations of the *Trionfi* were carried out by Antonio de *Obregón (1512), who translated the entire poem; and by Alvar Gómez de Ciudad Real, whose translation of the *Triumphus Cupidinis* appeared in the *Cancionero de Ixar* (1470–1556; Juan Fernández de Ixar Songbook) and the *Cancionero de Gallardo* (c. 1550; Bartolomé José Gallardo Songbook) as well as in a number of editions of Jorge de *Montemayor's *Los siete libros de la Diana* (1559?; *Diana, A Pastoral Romance*) throughout the sixteenth and early seventeenth c. Hernando de Hozes's Italianate version, *Los Triumphos de Francisco Petrarcha, ahora nuevamente traduzidos* (1554; Petrarch's Triumphs, now newly translated), remains the best translation of the *Trionfi* into Castilian. Petrarch's allegorical poem had also been a distant source for such religious poetry as Juan de los *Angeles's *Triunfos del amor* (1598; Triumphs of Love) and Francisco de Guzmán's *Triunfos morales* (1587; Moral Triumphs). In an example of *a lo *divino* poetry, Lope de *Vega Carpio (1562–1635) relies most heavily on the *Trionfi* for his *Triunfos divinos* (1625; Divine Triumphs).

A literary phenomenon of immense import, Petrarchism, as the imitation of Petrarch's *Canzoniere* came to be called, flourished throughout Europe, giving impetus to the revolutionary poetics of the Renaissance and to modern poetry. The *Canzoniere* represents the first attempt by a poet to express subjectively in stylized and elegant poetic language his profound emotional and spiritual conflicts, subsumed in the figure of the elusive Laura. Although many minor poets abused such Petrarchan conventions as the codified descriptions of the lady's beauty and the fire/ice paradox, Petrarchism did encourage poets to achieve excellence in the vernacular, to attempt the new Italianate meters and rhyme schemes, and to reinterpret classical authors. The *Canzoniere* provided poets with the formal models of the sonnet, *canzone*, and madrigal, as well as with the novel concept of the *imitatio vitae*—the introspective narration, through a series of lyric poems, of a lover's fictive autobiography. In Spain, Petrarchism also took into account Ausiàs March's earlier interpretation of the *Canzoniere*.

While there are recognizable traces of the *Canzoniere* in the *cancionero* poetry of the fifteenth and early sixteenth centuries, the first Castilian imitations of the *Canzoniere* in the Italianate style were made by Juan *Boscán (1487?–1542) who, inspired by Andrea Navaggiero (1483–1529), attempted such Italian meters and forms as the sonnet and the *canzone*, as well as the *terza rima*, the *ottava rima*, and blank verse. Boscán in turn encouraged his protégé Garcilaso de la Vega to imitate the novel lyric forms. Lacking Garcilaso's eclectic imitative approach, Boscán's Italianate poetry in the second of his four books, *Las obras de Boscán y algunas de Garcilasso de la Vega* (1543, posthumously; Works by Boscán, Including Some by Garcilaso de la Vega) is written in the form of an *imitatio vitae*, imitating the *Canzoniere* through the classical Petrarchist *Rime* of Pietro Bembo (1470–1547). Bembo, who rejected the excesses of *Quattrocentisti* Petrarchists such as Antonio Tebaldeo and Serafino Ciminelli dall'Aquila, advocated a return to Petrarch's *Canzoniere* as the model for Petrarchist poetry in his *Prose della volgar lingua* (1525; Discussions of the Italian Language), the manifesto of Italian Petrarchism, which influenced Juan de Valdés's *Diálogo de la lengua* (1535–36; Dialogue on Language). Despite Boscán's excellent translation of Castiglione's *Il Cortegiano* as *El cortesano*, printed in thirteen editions in the sixteenth c., and his familiarity with other Neoplatonist treatises such as León *Hebreo's *Dialoghi d'amore* (c. 1502; Dialogues on Love) and Bembo's *Gli Asolani*, his poetry's overtly Christian stance discloses his strong attachment to medieval scholasticism. The resultant conflictive poetic attitudes of Neoplatonic love and Christian repentance exemplify Boscán's inability to delimit fully the historical and philosophical differences between the medieval Spanish convention and Renaissance poetics. In this, he again approximates Bembo, whose poetic reform serves as transition between the Italian *Quattrocento* and the *Cinquecento*.

Marsilio Ficino's (1433–99) Neoplatonist treatise, the *Theologia Platonica*, was of major influence to sixteenth-c. Petrarchist poetry and the *trattati d'amore* by León Hebreo, Castiglione, Bembo, and Torquato Tasso. These treatises were well known in Spain both in the original and through translations, as in Boscán's translation of the *Cortesano*, and *Garcilaso de la Vega, el Inca's version of León Hebreo's *Dialoghi d'Amore* (1590). Neoplatonist thought was well represented by the Spanish humanists Joan Lluís *Vives (1492–1540), who strove to replace medieval scholasticism with classical humanism; and Sebastián *Fox Morcillo (1528?–60?), whose *De naturae philosophia seu de Platonis et Aristotelis consensione libri V* (1554; Five Books on the Philosophy of Nature or the Accord between Plato and Aristotle) attempted to reconcile *Platonism with Aristotelian form; and by the poet Francisco de *Aldana (1537–78), whose *Carta para Arias Montano sobre la contemplación de Dios y los requisitos della* (1577; Letter to Arias Montano on Divine Contemplation and Its Requirements), according to Alexander A. Parker, represents Spanish Christian Platonism at its finest.

Traditionalist defenses against the novel Italianate style, associated mainly with Cristóbal de *Castillejo (1491–1550), proved ultimately unsuccessful. Boscán's Italianate poetry, and in particular Garcilaso's more subtle Petrarchist stance in his sonnets and eclogues, became the primary model for classical Petrarchism in Spain. Salomon Usque (Salusque Lusitano) translated the *in vita* poems of the *Canzoniere* in 1567, but even before then, the many available Italian editions of the collection had assured its influence on the majority of sixteenth-c. poets. These included Diego de *Hurtado y Mendoza (1503–75), who with Boscán helped popularize the *ottava rima*; Gutierre de *Cetina (1520–57?); Hernando de *Acuña (1520–80), translator of the first four books of Boiardo's *Orlando Innamorato*; Francisco de Aldana; and Francisco de *Figueroa (1536–1617), who acclimatized the *rime sciolti* and was an accomplished poet in the Italian vernacular; Luis *Barahona de Soto (1548–95), and the brothers Lupercio (1559–1613) and Leonardo (1562–1631) de *Argensola.

Influenced by Girolamo Malipiero's *Il Petrarcha spirituale*, Sebastián de *Córdoba (1545?–1604?) reworked Boscán's and Garcilaso's poetry *a lo divino* in his *Las obras de Boscán y Garcilaso trasladadas en materias christianas* (1575; Boscán's and Garcilaso's Works Translated into Christian Themes). This work influenced San *Juan de la Cruz's (1542–91) incommensurately superior mystical poetry, and became the model for the religious *contrafacta* poetry written by Lope de Vega, Santa *Teresa de Ávila (1515–82), and Luisa de *Carvajal y Mendoza (1566–1614), among others.

Petrarchism was a decisive influence in the so-called poetic schools of both Seville and Salamanca. The Salmantine school (*Escuela Salmantina), emphasizing content over form in a limpid, restrained style, was typified by the Neoplatonist poetry of Luis de *León (1527–91), who, together with San Juan de la Cruz, brought Garcilaso's *lira* to its full potential. Unpublished in his lifetime, Fray Luis's poetry, along with the Petrarchist poetry attributed to a Francisco de la *Torre (b. 1534?), was issued by Quevedo in 1631 as a counterattack on *gongorismo*. Fernando de *Herrera (1534–97) headed the contrasting Sevillan school (Escuela Sevillana), which was concerned with exaggerated sentiment and style. Herrera's *Rimas inéditas* (1578; Unpublished Poems) expands upon the traditional Petrarchist paradoxes, prefiguring Luis de *Góngora's (1561–1627) poetic extravagance in their hyperbole and imagery.

The *Canzoniere* was not translated in its entirety until 1591 by the Portuguese translator Enrique Garcés. The late sixteenth and early seventeenth c. manifested Petrarchism through the interrelated movements of *culteranismo* and *conceptismo*. Góngora, Quevedo, and, to a lesser extent, Lope de Vega and Miguel de *Cervantes Saavedra (1547–1616), among others, emulated traditional Petrarchist conceits in order to surpass earlier poetic endeavors with their complex metaphors, extreme syntax, and inventive neologisms intended to cause *admiratio*. With Pellegrini's *Acutezze* as his model, Baltasar *Gracián y Morales drew from these poets to illustrate *conceptismo* in his important *Arte de ingenio* (1648; The Art of Wit). Spanish Petrarchism was exported to the New World by writers like Gutierre de Cetina, Eugenio de Salazar (1530?–1612?), Juan de la *Cueva (1543–1610), and Diego Dávalos y Figueroa, who traveled to Peru as a youth and remained there for the rest of his life. Dávalos's secular poetry, included in his *Miscelánea austral* (1603; Austral Miscellany) is, according to Alicia de Colombí-Monguió, the richest example of Petrarchism in colonial Peru.

Besides Petrarch's *Canzoniere* and Bembo's *Rime*, the Petrarchist poetry of Ariosto, Luigi Tansillo (whose *Lagrime di San Pietro* was translated by Luis *Gálvez de Montalvo in 1587), Annibale Caro, Bernardo and Torquato Tasso, Benedetto Varchi, and Giambattista Amalteo was circulated and read by most Spanish poets in the sixteenth c. The later *culterano* poets owe much besides to Giambattista Marino, author of a large collection of lyric verse, *La lira* (1602, 1608–14), and a long mythological poem, *Adone* (1623). Like *gongorismo*, *marinismo* is characterized by ingenious conceits, sensuality, and great technical skill.

### Castilian Prose

The prose works of the Italian *Cinquecento* that most influenced Spanish Renaissance writers were Machiavelli's *Il principe* (1513), Castiglione's *Il cortegiano* (1513–18), and Giovanni Della Casa's *Galateo* (1550–55). Machiavelli's treatise remained a model for European absolutism, and inspired Quevedo's *La política de Dios* (1625–55; The Politics of God); Baltasar Gracián's *El héroe* (1647; The Hero); and Diego de Saavedra Fajardo's Christian reply, *Idea de un príncipe político cristiano* (1640; The Concept of a Christian Prince); and through Saavedra's version, reworked *a lo divino* by Franciso Núñez de Cepeda as the *Idea del buen pastor representada en empresas sacras* (1682; The Concept of the Good Shepherd Illustrated in Sacred Concerns). Boscán's translation of the *Cortegiano* served as a model for Luis Milán's *Cortesano* (The Courtier), and the *Scolástico* (The Scholastic), attributed to Cristóbal de *Villalón (1505–58). The popularity of Della Casa's treatise on manners, the *Galateo*, was reflected in the six widely circulated editions of L. *Gracián Dantisco's *El Galateo español* (1593; The Spanish Galateo).

## Castilian Epic

The chivalric epic gained importance in Italy through Boiardo's *Orlando Innamorato* (1476), translated into Castilian by Francisco Garrido de Villena in 1555. Ludovico Ariosto's continuation, *Orlando Furioso* (1507–32), was translated by Jerónimo de *Urrea (1549), Hernando de Alcocer (1550) and Diego Vásquez de Contreras (1585). Ariosto's expressive influence can readily be discerned throughout Garcilaso's poetry. Spanish epics such as Alonso de *Ercilla's *La Araucana* (1589) were heavily influenced by Ariosto. Luis Barahona de Soto wrote the *Primera parte de la Angélica*, known as *Las lágrimas de Angélica* (1586; The Tears of Angelica), one of the best continuations of Ariosto's epic, and derived in part also from Aretino's *Lagrime di Angelica*. Ballads emphasizing a single episode from the *Orlando furioso* were popular from 1550 through the 1580s; these, and his desire to outdo Lope de Vega's *Hermosura de Angélica* (1602; Angelica's Beauty), inspired Góngora's *Romance de Angélica y Medoro* (Ballad of Angelica and Medoro) that same year. Quevedo burlesqued the *Orlando* epics both in ballad form and in his burlesque heroic *Poema heroico de las necedades y locuras de Orlando el Enamorado* (pub. 1670; Heroic Poem on the Foolishness and Madness of the Lover Orlando). In Jamaica, Bernardo de *Balbuena (1562?–1627) wrote his Baroque imitation of the *Orlando* epic, *El Bernardo, o Victoria de Roncesvalles* (1624; The Bernardo, or Victory at Roncesvalles).

The *Orlando Furioso* was also influential in a number of plays, such as Cervantes's *La casa de los celos* (1615; The House of Jealousy) and *El laberinto de amor* (1615; Love's Labyrinth); Cristóbal de *Virués's *La infelice Marcela* (1609; The Unfortunate Marcela); Lope de Vega's *Los celos de Radamonte* (bef. 1603; Radamontes's Jealousy), *Angélica en el Catay* (1599–1603; Angelica at Cathay) and *Un pastoral albergue* (A Pastoral Refuge), considered by some critics of doubtful authorship; Guillén de *Castro's *El desengaño dichoso* (The Fortunate Disillusionment); and Francisco de *Bances Candamo's (1662–1704) *Cómo se curan los celos* (late seventeenth c.; How to Cure Jealousy).

As Bernard Weinberg has observed, Ariosto's *Orlando Furioso* came under attack as early as 1549 by Aristotelian theorists who criticized the *romanzo*'s aesthetic independence from the classical epic. Giangiorgio Trissino's *Italia liberata dai Goti* (1547–48) and Bernardo Tasso's *Amadigi* (1560)—based on the Spanish novel of chivalry *Amadís de Gaula*—attempted to revive the classicism of the earlier Italian epics. Torquato Tasso's creative efforts, from the *Rinaldo* (1562) to his *Mondo creato* (1607), and his *Gerusalemme liberata* (1575) and *Gerusalemme conquistata* (1593) in particular, give evidence of the poet's conflictive desire to reconcile the positive qualities of romance with the neoclassical principles of the epic—the "legitimation of the marvelous and the matter of unity," as Alban K. Forcione has pointed out.

Tasso's re-creations of the classical epic were much imitated in Spain. His

*Gerusalemme liberata* was translated by Cayrasco (1585), Sedeño (1587) and Sarmiento de Mendoza (1636). The poem influenced Virués's *El Monserrate* (1587), which was saved in the book-burning scene in *Don Quixote*; Juan de la Cueva's tedious *La conquista de Bética, poema heroico* (1603; Heroic Poem on the Conquest of Andalusia); and Juan Rufo y Gutiérrez's *La Austríada* on Don Juan de Austria. Other epic poets influenced by Tasso were Cristóbal de *Mesa (1561–1633); Francisco de Borja y Aragón, Prince of *Esquilache (1581–1658); and Francisco López de Zárate (1580–1658). The most important poem deriving from Tasso's was Lope de Vega's *La Jerusalén conquistada* (1609; Jerusalem Conquered), which, however, placed Spain at the center of the battle between Christians and Saracens. Lope's *Dragontea* (1589) on Sir Francis Drake, and his *Corona trágica* (1627; The Tragic Crown) on Mary Stuart, demonstrate the taste for historical epic poems; Alonso de *Acevedo's (1550–1620) *Creación del mundo* (Creation of the World) derives in part from Tasso's *Il mondo creato*. As the Italian epics had been influenced in part by the chivalric tradition, so the Spanish epic poems conserved the adventurous character of the romances of chivalry while expounding heroic and even amorous and religious themes.

Spanish classicism was concerned more with the novels of chivalry than with verse romance. Alonso *López Pinciano's work of literary criticism, *Philosophia antigua poética* (1596; Ancient Poetic Philosophy), represents the Aristotelian position in its view of Heliodorus's recently discovered *Aethiopica* as an excellent example of prose fiction. As Forcione has demonstrated, Cervantes's *Los trabajos de Persiles y Sigismunda* (1617; The Labors of Persiles and Sigismunda) and his *Don Quixote* cannot be fully understood without taking into account the complex theoretical background of the romance and the chivalric epic during the sixteenth and seventeenth centuries which Cervantes shared with Ariosto and Tasso.

### The Pastoral

Incorporating both an idealized nature and the Petrarchan lyric convention, the *pastoral genre explores the realm of the emotions, and includes diverse forms such as the elegy, the romance, and the drama. In Italy, the genre was anticipated by Boccaccio's *Ninfale d'Ameto* (1342), and represented by Jacopo Sannazaro's *L'Arcadia* (1504), a pastoral romance consisting of a long prose narrative interspersed with lyric poetry, with love-struck shepherds as protagonists. The first pastoral romance in Spain, Montemayor's *Diana*, can be traced to these two works. Sannazaro's *Arcadia* was a source for Garcilaso's three eclogues, and was translated into Castilian in 1547. In 1564, Gaspar Gil *Polo wrote his *Los cinco libros de la Diana enamorada* (The Five Books of Diana in Love) as a rejoinder to Montemayor. Luis Gálvez de Montalvo left an unfinished translation of Torquato Tasso's *Gerusalemme liberata*, and wrote the well-received *El pastor de Phílida* (1582; Philida's Shepherd), probably influenced also by Tasso's *Aminta* (1573), the greatest example of Italian pastoral drama. Tasso's *Aminta* was translated by the anti-Gongorist Juan de *Jáuregui y Hurtado de Sal (in 1607 and again in 1618); and influenced the *Constante Amarilis* (1609;

The Faithful Amarilis) of Cristóbal *Suárez de Figueroa (1571?–1644) who, in 1602, had translated the second most important Italian tragicomedy, Giovanni Batista Guarini's *Il Pastor Fido*. Lope de Vega's pastoral novel *Arcadia* (1598) follows both Sannazaro and Tasso; his *Los pastores de Belén* (1612; The Shepherds of Bethlehem), described as an *Arcadia a lo divino*, includes popular metrical forms and characterizations. Written in Mexico in 1585–90, Bernardo de Balbuena's *Siglo de Oro en las selvas de Erifile* (The Golden Age in the Forests of Erifile) derives from Sannazaro's *Arcadia*, as does Cervantes's pastoral novel *La Galatea*, published in 1585 but composed earlier. Like the Italian epic, the pastoral novel is also parodied in several episodes of Cervantes's *Don Quixote*.

## Boccaccio in Spain

Boccaccio's influence in Spain begins with his *Decameron*, anonymously translated into Catalan in 1429, into Castilian about the middle of the fifteenth c. and first printed in Seville in 1496. Enrique de Villena cites Boccaccio's *De casibus virorum illustrium*, of which the first eight books were translated by Pedro *López de Ayala as *Cayda de príncipes* (1495; Fall of Princes); the last two books were translated by Alfonso de Cartagena. Its *Ubi sunt* topos was utilized often by Spanish writers. Boccaccio's *De claris mulieribus*, with its inversion of the *Ubi sunt* theme, was translated anonymously during John II's reign, and also enjoyed a wide reading. It inspired Alvaro de Luna's imitation, *Libro de las claras y virtuosas mugeres* (1446; Book of Illustrious and Virtuous Women). The library of the Marquis of Santillana included manuscripts by Boccaccio. He figures as a protagonist in Santillana's *Comedieta de Ponça* (Comedy on the Victory at Ponza), which also avails itself of the theme from the *De casibus*, as does his *Diálogo de Bías contra Fortuna* (Dialogue of Bias against Fortune). Santillana's *Prohemio é carta . . . al condestable de Portugal* (1449; Preface and Letter to the Constable of Portugal) shows evidence of the author's acquaintance with Boccaccio's encyclopedic *De genealogia deorum gentilium*.

Derived from medieval romances, Boccaccio's vernacular novel, the *Elegia di Madonna Fiammetta* (1343–44), was translated into Catalan and Castilian at the beginning of the fifteenth c., and had at least three printings: 1497, 1523, and 1541. This novel demonstrated considerable psychological penetration, and, together with Aeneas Sylvius Piccolomini's *Historia de duobus amantibus Eurialo et Lucretia* (1442), contributed greatly to the development of the Spanish sentimental novel, among whose examples are Juan *Rodríguez de la Cámara's *El siervo libre de amor* (1439–40; Love's Unfettered Slave), a mainly autobiographical novel which includes a tale of star-crossed lovers, and Diego de *San Pedro's *Tractado de amores de Arnalte e Lucenda* (1491; The Loves of Arnalt and Lucenda) and his superior *Cárcel de amor* (1492; Love's Prison). Juan de *Flores's (1470–1525) *Breve tractado de Grimalte y Gradissa* (Tale of Grimalte and Gradissa) is a continuation of Boccaccio's *Fiammetta*, and his *Historia de Grisel y Mirabella* (Story of Grisel and Mirabella) demonstrates its influence, as well as that of the *Filostroto*, a short poem in *ottava rima* relating the story of Troilus and Criseida.

Together with Matteo Bandello's *Novelle* (1554–73), and Giambattista Giraldi Cinthio's *Hecatommithi ouero Cento Novelle* (1565), both of which were modeled on the *Decameron*, Boccaccio's collection of novels had enormous impact on the development of narrative in Spain. While brevity, action, and spareness of detail were pertinent characteristics of the genre, the *novella* eventually evolved to include disparate features such as social and philosophical concerns, sentimental expressiveness, and the exploration of psychological motives. In Spain, the genre was of import to such works as Antonio de *Torquemada's Lucianesque *Coloquios satíricos* (1553; Satirical Colloquies), and Juan de *Timoneda's collection of stories, *El sobremesa y alivio de caminantes* (1563; The After-dinner Talk and Relief for Travelers), and *El patrañuelo* (1565; The Hoax), which were also influenced by Ariosto and Masuccio Salernitano's *Novellino*. Timoneda in particular was aware of the Italian term *novella*, which he remarked was translated as *maraña* in Castilian and *rondalles* in his native Valencian. Although technically not the first to *novelar*, Cervantes was called the "Spanish Boccaccio" by *Tirso de Molina, as his *Novelas ejemplares* (1613; Exemplary Novels) are perhaps the best example of the new genre's flexibility, attesting to its ability to adapt to a variety of themes. Lope de Vega's collection of four novels, *Novelas a Marcia Leonarda* (1621–24), was apparently an attempt by Lope to compete with Cervantes's success. The Italian *novella* influenced several episodes of *picaresque novels, such as the vendor of Papal bulls in the *Lazarillo de Tormes* (1554), a possible imitation of the *Novellino*, as were the interpolated tales of Dorido y Clorinia, Bonifacio y Dorotea, and don Luis de Castro in Mateo *Alemán's *Guzmán de Alfarache* (1599).

Francisco *López de Ubeda's *La pícara Justina* (1605; The Rogue Justina) may have been influenced by Aretino's realistic dialogues, the *Ragionamenti* (1534), which in turn are acknowledged to owe their salacious nature in part to *La lozana andaluza* (1527; The Vivacious Andalusian), Francisco *Delicado's novel in dialogue form dealing with the adventures of an Andalusian prostitute in Rome. Despite their anti-Spanish stance, Traiano Boccalini's satires, *Ragguagli di Parnasio* (1612–13) and *Pietra del paragone politico* (1615) were widely known; their influence is evident in Luis *Vélez de Guevara's *El diablo cojuelo* (1641; The Lame Devil) and in Quevedo's *La hora de todos* (1645; The Hour for Everyone).

The framework of the Italian *novella* became exceedingly popular in the seventeenth c., and was appropriated by such writers as Alonso Jerónimo de *Salas Barbadillo (1581–1635), in his *Casa del placer* (House of Pleasure) and *Corrección de vicios* (Reform of Vices); and Alonso de *Castillo Solórzano (1584–1648?), in his several collections, among them the *Tardes entretenidas* (Amusing Afternoons), *Jornadas alegres* (Cheerful Days), and *Huerta de Valencia* (Valencian Field). In the *Quinta de Laura* (Laura's Villa), Castillo describes this activity as "exercicio muy usado en Italia; díganlo los Vandelos,

Sansovinos y Bocacios . . . y aora en España los han exedido con grandes ventajas." Peter N. Dunn has explained that when Spanish novelists wished to publish a collection of *novelas*, they either reverted to the Decameronesque framework, wove stories to form a full-length novel, or combined the two. Example of the latter is Tirso de Molina's miscellany, the *Cigarrales de Toledo* (1621; Toledan Country Houses). Gonzalo de *Céspedes y Meneses (1585?– 1638) is one of the few who avoids direct imitation of the Italian model in his *Historias peregrinas* (Extraordinary Stories), each of which is associated with a different city of Spain; while María de *Zayas y Sotomayor (1590–1660?) presents a feminist perspective in her collections, *Novelas amorosas y exemplares* (1637; Exemplary Love Novels) and *Parte segunda del sarao, y entretenimientos honestos* (1647; Second Part of the Afternoon Party, and Modest Diversions).

The Italian *novella* contributed considerably to Spanish theater. The legend of the *Amantes de Teruel*, adapted by Tirso de Molina, by Juan *Pérez de Montalbán (1602–38), and also by Andrés *Rey de Artieda (1549–1613) as *Los amantes* (The Lovers) is based on Boccaccio's novella of Girolamo and Silvestra, (*Decameron* 4.8). The best-known version, however, is Juan Eugenio *Hartzenbush's play of the same name (1837). Lope de Vega's *La quinta de Florencia* (bef. 1604; Florencia's Villa) is a reworking of Bandello's *novella* 15, which the playwright continues to elaborate in three of his most famous plays: *Peribáñez* (c. 1610; *Peribáñez and the Knight Commander of Ocaña*), *Fuente Ovejuna* (c. 1612; *The Sheep Well*), and *El mejor alcalde el Rey* (1620–23; *The King, the Greatest Alcalde*).

Forming part of a broad movement extending throughout Europe, Italian humanist theater first comes into contact with Spanish drama in Fernando de Rojas's *Tragicomedia de Calisto y Melibea* (1500), whose main character, the old bawd Celestina, is similar to the procuress Tharatantara of the *Poliscena*, attributed to Leonardo Bruni (d. 1444), although the prototype of the go-between first appears in the *Disciplina clericalis*, a collection of medieval exemplary tales by Pero *Alfonso (1062–1110). Juan del *Encina (1468?–1530?), considered the progenitor of Spanish Renaissance drama, resided in Rome for over ten years, and his later plays imitate Italian models and techniques. Like the *Scornetta* (1497), a verse comedy published in Bologna by the Hollander Knuyt von Slyterhoven, Encina's plays combine realistic depictions of shepherds with Virgilian reminiscences. His *Egloga de Fileno, Zambardo y Cardonio* (1509; Eclogue of Fileno, Zambardo, and Cardonio) is an adaptation of Antonio Tebaldeo's "Second Eclogue." The most ambitious of Encina's Italianate eclogues, the *Egloga de Plácida y Vitoriano* (1509; Eclogue of Placida and Vitoriano) includes a scene derived from the *Celestina*, and imitates Italian pastoral drama in the intervention by the goddess Venus. Bartolomé de *Torres Naharro (1485?–1524?) wrote all his plays in Italy, learning stage techniques and employing novelistic devices. Several scenes of his *Calamita* are derived from Bernardo Dovizi da Bibbiena's *Calandria*, staged in 1513 with a prologue written by Castiglione describing the canon of Italian comedy—in particular, praising the play's use of the vernacular. Perhaps owing to Castiglione's prologue, the *Prohemio* to Torres Naharro's *Propalladia* (1517) includes the first statement of dramatic theory in Renaissance Europe.

Lope de *Rueda (1509–65?), the most notable Spanish playwright before Lope de Vega, was an *italianizante*, well-read in the Italian *novelle*. His play, *Los engañados* (1567; The Deceived), is taken from the anonymous *Gl'Ingannati*, and the *Medora* is devised from Giancarli's *La Cingana*. The *Comedia llamada Eufemia* (1567; Play Called Eufemia) is based on the ninth story of the second day of the *Decameron*, and the *Comedia llamada Armelina* (1567; Play Called Armelina) borrows from Cecchi's *Il servigiale* and Rainieri's *L'Altilia*. Juan de Timoneda's *Comedia llamada Cornelia* (1559; Play Called Cornelia) takes various passages from Ariosto's *Negromante*, while his *Farsa Trapacera* (1565; Malicious Farce) borrows from Ariosto's *Lena*, but eliminates the character of the braggart. For his *Comedia del degollado* (1583; The Beheaded Man), Juan de la Cueva draws on Giraldi Cinthio, whose influence on Golden Age drama has been insufficiently studied.

The narrative mode of the *novelle* is easily adapted by Lope de Vega in his *Arte nuevo de hacer comedias* (1609; *The New Art of Writing Plays*), which breaks with classical dramatic precepts. Possibly influenced by the success of Guarini's *Il pastor fido*, Lope appears to use Guarini's defense of the mixture of tragicomedy, *Compendio della poesia tragicomica* (1602), in his own treatise to justify his use of the *gracioso*, and the abundant characters, scenes, and subplots. According to Joaquín Arce, Lope takes at least fourteen plots from Bandello; adapts eight of his comedies from Boccaccio; and incorporates five novels of Giraldi Cinthio into his plays. These numbers are based on Lope's extant plays, and are therefore conservative.

Italian influence diminishes considerably as Spanish literature declines after the Renaissance and Baroque periods. During the early nineteenth c., the Italian poets Vittorio Alfieri and Metastasio contributed to the beginnings of Spanish *Romanticism. Giacomo Leopardi's philosophical influence is evident in the Romantic poet José de *Espronceda (1808–42), the Catalan poet Joaquín *Bartrina (1850–80), Leopoldo Alas (*Clarín; 1852–1901), and especially, Miguel de *Unamuno (1846–1936). Alessandro Manzoni's *I promessi sposi* was translated in 1833, while his *Cinque Maggio* were known in twenty-six different translations. Franco Meregalli has judged Pedro Antonio de *Alarcón's *El sombrero de tres picos* (1874; *The Three-Cornered Hat*) the most Manzonian work in Spanish. The poems of Eugenio Montale (1896–1981) and Jorge *Guillén (1891–1984), contemporaries who translated each other's works, exemplify in their reciprocity the present state of literary relations between Spain and Italy.

BIBLIOGRAPHY

Criticism

Arce, Joaquín. "Boccaccio nella letteratura castigliana: panorama generale e rassegna bibliografico-critica." *Il Boccaccio nelle culture e letterature nazionali*. Firenze: Olschki, 1978. 63–105.

————. *Literaturas italiana y española frente a frente.* Madrid: Espasa-Calpe, 1982.

Bocchetta, Vittore. *Sannazaro en Garcilaso.* Madrid: Gredos, 1976.

Bourland, Caroline. "Boccaccio and the 'Decameron' in Castilian and Catalán Literature." *Revue Hispanique* 12 (1905): 1–232.

Colombí-Monguió, Alicia de. *Petrarquismo peruano: Diego Dávalos y Figueroa y la poesía de la "Miscelánea austral."* London: Tamesis, 1985.

Cruz, Anne J. *Imitación y transformación: El petrarquismo en la poesía de Boscán y Garcilaso de la Vega.* Purdue U Monographs in the Romance Languages. Amsterdam: John Benjamins, 1987–1989.

D'Antuono, Nancy L. *Boccaccio's "Novelle" in the Theater of Lope de Vega.* Studia Humanitatis. Madrid: Porrúa Turanzas, 1983.

Deyermond, A. D. *The Petrarchan Sources of "La Celestina."* Oxford: Oxford UP, 1961.

Dunn, Peter N. *Castillo Solórzano and the Decline of the Spanish Novel.* Oxford: Basil Blackwell, 1952.

Farinelli, Arturo. *Italia e Spagna.* 2 vols. Torino: Fratelli Bocca, 1929.

Forcione, Alban K. *Cervantes, Aristotle, and the "Persiles."* Princeton: Princeton UP, 1970.

————. *Cervantes and the Humanist Vision.* Princeton: Princeton UP, 1982.

Fucilla, Joseph G. *Estudios sobre el petrarquismo en España.* Madrid: CSIC, 1960.

————. *Relaciones hispanoitalianas.* Madrid: CSIC, 1953.

González Martín, Vicente. *La cultura italiana en Miguel de Unamuno.* Salamanca: Ediciones Univ. de Salamanca, 1978.

Hart, Thomas R. *Cervantes and Ariosto: Renewing Fiction.* Princeton: Princeton UP, 1989.

Helí Hernández, Jesús. *Antecedentes italianos de la novela picaresca española.* Studia Humanitatis. Madrid: Porrúa Turanzas, 1982.

Lapesa, Rafael. *Garcilaso: estudios completos.* Madrid: Istmo, 1985.

Macrí, Oreste. *Varia fortuna del Manzoni in terre iberiche.* Ravenna: Longo, 1976.

Manero Sorolla, María Pilar. *Introducción al estudio del petrarquismo en España.* Barcelona: Promociones y Publicaciones Universitarias, 1987.

Menéndez y Pelayo, Marcelino. *Orígenes de la novela.* Vol. 2. Madrid: Nacional, 1927.

Meregalli, Franco. "Manzoni in Spagna." *Annali Manzoniani* 7 (1977): 199–214.

————. *Storia delle relazioni letterarie tra Italia e Spagna.* Venice: Librería Universitaria, 1962.

Morreale, Margherita. *Castiglione y Boscán: El ideal cortesano en el Renacimiento español.* Madrid: BRAE, 1949.

Parker, Alexander A. *The Philosophy of Love in Spanish Literature, 1480–1680.* Edinburgh: Edinburgh UP, 1985.

Reyes Cano, Rogelio. *La Arcadia de Sannazaro en España.* Seville: U of Sevilla, 1973.

Silió y Cortés, César. *Maquiavelo y su tiempo.* Madrid: Espasa-Calpe, 1946.

Siracusa, Joseph, and Joseph L. Laurenti. *Relaciones literarias entre España e Italia: Ensayo de una bibliografía de literatura comparada.* Boston: Hall, 1972.

Weinberg, Bernard. *A History of Literary Criticism in the Italian Renaissance.* 2 vols. Chicago: U of Chicago P, 1963.

Anne Cruz

**IZA ZAMÁCOLA, Juan Antonio de** (1756, Dima, Biscay–1826, Madrid), historian, musicologist, satirist. He used various pseudonyms, such as Don Extravagantísimo, Don Preciso, etc.; he published other works using only his mother's surname, Zamácola. From 1812 to 1822 he lived in France in exile. Zamácola wrote a three-volume *Historia de las naciones vascas* (1818; History of the Basque Nations), and also published a collection of folksongs, *Colección de las mejores coplas, seguidillas . . .* (1799; Collection of the Best Songs, Seguidillas . . . ). He is most remembered for burlesque social satire, as in *Elementos de la ciencia contradanzaria* (1796; Elements of the Cotillionese Science).

BIBLIOGRAPHY

Primary Texts

*Colección de las mejores coplas, seguidillas. . . .* 7th ed. Madrid: Repullés, 1869.
*Elementos de la ciencia contradanzaria.* Madrid: García, 1796.
*Historia de las naciones vascas.* 3 vols. Bilbao: Astuy, 1898–1900.

Criticism

Cossío, J. M. "Una biografía de 'Don Preciso.' " *Revista de Bibliografía Nacional* 5 (1944): 385–406.

# J

*JÁCARA*, theatrical term. It may refer either to (1) a humorous ballad which celebrates the low life; (2) a song used to entertain the public for ten to fifteen minutes between acts of a play—an alternate to the *entremés*; or (3) a short musical play. *Calderón, *Quevedo and *Quiñones de Benavente composed some of this type.

BIBLIOGRAPHY

Primary Texts

*Entremeses, loas, bailes, jácaras y mojigangas desde fines del siglo XVI a mediados del XVIII.* Ed. E. Cotarelo y Mori. In NBAE 17 and 18.

**JANÉS, Clara** (1940, Barcelona– ), novelist, poet, translator, essayist and biographer. Although born and raised in Barcelona, Janés has written most of her work in Castilian rather than Catalan. She has studied comparative literature at the Sorbonne and is an especially well-informed writer. Her poetic works include *Las estrellas vencidas* (1964; Conquered Stars); *Límite humano* (1973; Human Limitations); *En busca de Cordelia* and *Poemas rumanos* (1975; Searching for Cordelia, and Rumanian Poems); *Antología personal (1959–1979)* (1979; Personal Anthology); *Obra poética* (1981; Poetic Works); *Vivir* (1983; Living), and *Antología poética* (1984; Poetic Anthology). Among her narrative works are *La noche de Abel Micheli* (1965; The Night of Abel Micheli), a novelette, and *Desintegración* (1969; Disintegration), a longer novel. Janés's biography *La vida callada de Federico Mompou* (1975; The Quiet Life of Frederic Mompou) won the City of Barcelona Prize the year of its publication; her *Pureza Canelo* (1981) is a life-and-works study.

BIBLIOGRAPHY

Primary Texts

*Antología personal (1959–1979).* Madrid: Rialp, 1979.

*Eros.* Madrid: n.p., 1981.

*Libro de alienaciones.* Madrid: n.p., 1980.
*Sendas de Rumania.* Barcelona: Plaza y Janés, 1981.

Janet Pérez

**JARCHA.** *See* KHARJA

**JARDIEL PONCELA, Enrique** (1901, Madrid–1952, Madrid), Spanish play-wright, novelist and author of movie scripts, known for his original, bizarre and absurd humor. An innovative experimenter, somewhat influenced by the example and personality of Ramón *Gómez de la Serna, Jardiel was a forerunner of European absurdists such as Ionesco in his audacity, his disregard for logic, and original comic imagination. *Una noche de primavera sin sueño* (1927; A Sleep-less Spring Night) appeared the same year as his first book, a collection of short stories, *Pirulís de la Habana* (Pirulis of Havana). Although normally associated with the theater, for which he wrote sixty-four plays, Jardiel was equally original and perhaps still more extravagant in his fiction. Four full-length, published novels and some thirty short ones evince similar inventive humor, often intel-lectualized to a point beyond the comprehension of the average Spaniard, but equally often facile or frivolous and superficial. Although he wrote rapidly, Jardiel was by no means unexacting as a creator, and close to half his work was repudiated and remained unpublished. *Amor se escribe sin hache* (1929; Love Is Spelled Without an ''H''), his first major novel, alludes to a common error of Spanish orthography, but in fact parodies erotic pulp fiction (B novels). It was followed by *¡Espérame en Siberia, vida mía!* (1930; Await Me in Siberia, Darling!), a parody of adventure, intrigue and murder stories; *Pero . . . ¿hubo alguna vez once mil vírgenes?* (1931; Were There Ever Really Eleven Thousand Virgins?), a travesty of the *Don Juan myth; and *La ''tournée'' de Dios* (1932; The ''Tour'' of God), a bitter, satirical mockery of human folly with a cast of thousands ranging from the pope to perverts and featuring a world tour by the Almighty, complete with press conferences and riots (in which he has to be rescued by the Guardia Civil, an episode ending with the slaughter of multitudes).

For most of his literary life, Jardiel carried on a vituperative running battle with hostile and unforgiving critics. Some of his works saw considerable financial success while others failed at the box office, but nearly all were attacked with aggressive derision by a hostile press which seldom hesitated to censure works not fully understood. His most celebrated play, *Eloísa está debajo de un almendro* (1940; Heloise Lies [Buried] under an Almond Tree), a comedy displaying sophisticated techniques, hilarious dialogue and situations of bizarre humor, enjoyed a success which enabled him to become the director of his own theatrical troupe. *Blanca por fuera y Rosa por dentro* (1943; Blanca on the Outside and Rosa Inside) is another of his best-constructed works with typically side-splitting repartee. His one significant critical success, *El sexo débil ha hecho gimnasia* (1946; The Weaker Sex Has Been Doing Exercises), a tragicomedy dealing with women's liberation, was one of his final plays. His final years, of prolonged and lingering illness, were plagued as well by paranoia and severe depression, in stark contrast to the burlesque and ludic spirit for which he is known.

BIBLIOGRAPHY

Primary Texts

*Agua, aceite y gasolina y otras dos mezclas explosivas.* Madrid: Biblioteca Nueva, 1946.
*Cuarenta y nueve personajes que encontraron a su autor.* Madrid: Biblioteca Nueva, 1936.
*Dos farsas y una opereta.* Madrid: Biblioteca Nueva, 1939.
*Obras completas.* 4 vols. Barcelona: Editorial AHR, 1965.
*Obra inédita.* Barcelona: Editorial AHR, 1967.
*Obras teatrales escogidas.* Madrid: Aguilar, 1964.
*Tres comedias con un solo ensayo.* Madrid: Biblioteca Nueva, 1933.
*Una letra protestada y dos letras a la vista.* Madrid: Biblioteca Nueva, 1942.

Criticism

McKay, Douglas R. *Enrique Jardiel Poncela.* New York: Twayne, 1974.
Rof Carballo, J. et al. *El teatro de humor en España.* Madrid: Editora Nacional, 1966. 31–44; 45–61; 63–81; 83–104.
*TEATRO: Revista Internacional de la Escena* 4 (February 1953): 27–44. Commemorative issue.

Douglas McKay

**JARNÉS, Benjamín** (1888, Codo, Zaragoza–1949, Madrid), novelist, journalist, biographer, editor and teacher. Born into a large family, Jarnés suffered neglect and privation as a child, leaving him a lifelong legacy of humility and self-effacement. He studied philosophy and theology at the Pontifical U in Zaragoza and the San Carlos Seminary, but he was never ordained for lack of vocation. The negative experiences of the seminary found their way into his novels in the form of a trenchant anti-clericalism (see especially *El convidado de papel* [1929; The Paper Guest]). In 1910 Jarnés joined the army as an administrator and also studied for a teaching career, which he did not exercise until his exile in Mexico after the Civil War (1939). Between 1917 and 1925 he contributed articles to several journals and helped found the magazine *Plural*.

When a fragment of his novel *El profesor inútil* (1926; The Useless Professor) published in a journal brought him to the attention of José *Ortega y Gasset, indisputable Spanish intellectual leader of the twenties, Jarnés was invited to collaborate on Ortega's prestigious *Revista de Occidente*. Jarnés's aesthetics, as developed in his novels and essays, coincide with those expressed by Ortega in *La deshumanización de la novela e Ideas sobre la novela* —namely, that art should be divorced from life. Art need not and indeed should not be a vehicle for faithfully reproducing "real life" or for engaging in political or social criticism. Style thus takes precedence over thematics, and cultivation of the non-transcendental aspects of art leads to a concern with itself as a self-contained form. Jarnés has often been seen as a disciple of Ortega, but his aesthetics were already well formed before he moved into the Ortegean intellectual orbit. However, his association with Ortega and his editorial enterprises from the mid-twenties until the Civil War surely strengthened his proclivity for the innovative spirit of vanguardism that dominated Spanish and European literature of the 1920s and early thirties.

In Jarnés's most important long novels, he eschews traditional plots for series of loosely connected vignettes, he frequently describes characters in geometrical terms reminiscent of the futurist paintings of Fernand Légèr, and his angles of vision often recall cinematographic techniques. In fact, other elements of his fictional style owe their inspiration to film, especially to the comic vision of Walt Disney and Charlie Chaplin, on whom Jarnés wrote journal articles. He had the rare gift of combining humor and lyrical grace that one associates with the tone of Chaplin's films. Jarnés was also fascinated with classical and medieval myth, which sometimes provides the humorous and ironic counterpoint to the dilemmas of his modern anti-heroes. He even rewrote Arthurian legend in *Viviana y Merlín: leyenda* (1930; Vivien and Merlin: Legend). And his novels are replete with digressions on art, a sort of running self-commentary so typical of the self-consciousness of all modern painting and literature.

Jarnés's protagonists are pre-existential, unheroic types, and he portrays them with an objective geometry that underscores their lack of transcendent being. In two of the novels, *El convidado de papel* and *Lo rojo y lo azul* (1932; The Red and the Blue), the main character, Julio, modeled on Stendhal's Julian Sorel, aspires to raise his low-born station in life. But unlike Sorel's character, Jarnés's does not have the will and single-mindedness to carry out his desires. Juan Sánchez of *Locura y muerte de nadie* (1929; Madness and Death of Nobody) comes even closer to the existential struggle to achieve identity in modern, alienating society. But despite the coincidence of Jarnés's thematics with those of existentialism, his novels have none of the psychological passion we associate with the existential drama in the novels of *Unamuno or Sartre, for example. Jarnés's novels perhaps have more in common with the French *nouveau roman*, not only for their poetics of the mundane, but for their emphasis on objective, perceptual observation and refusal to call on depth psychology in presenting characters.

In 1936 Jarnés re-entered the army to fight on the Republican side during the Civil War. His subsequent exile in Mexico had grave consequences for his rising literary career. The need to make a living in his new home forced him to limit his fiction writing and devote himself primarily to editing, translating, biographies and teaching. He had already written several biographies while still in Spain (among them one on a nineteenth-c. Spanish nun and another on Zumalacárregui, a military and political leader of the Romantic period), and in Mexico he produced accounts of lives of other prominent Spaniards, notably *Castelar, *Bécquer, and *Cervantes. In 1948 Jarnés returned to Spain and died a year later.

BIBLIOGRAPHY

Primary Texts

*El convidado de papel.* 2nd ed. Madrid: Espasa-Calpe, 1935.
*Locura y muerte de nadie.* 2nd ed. In *Las mejores novelas contemporáneas.* Ed. J. Entrambasaguas. Vol. 7. Barcelona: Planeta, 1961. 1379–1564.
*Lo rojo y lo azul.* Madrid: Espasa-Calpe, 1932.
*El profesor inútil.* 2nd ed. Madrid: Espasa-Calpe, 1934.
*Teoría del zumbel.* Madrid: Espasa-Calpe, 1930.

Criticism

Bernstein, J. S. *Benajamín Jarnés.* TWAS 128. New York: Twayne, 1972.
Ilie, Paul. "Benjamín Jarnés: Aspects of the Dehumanized Novel." *PMLA* 76 (1961): 247–53.
Martínez Latre, María Pilar. *La novela intelectual de Benjamín Jarnés.* Zaragoza: Fernando El Católico, 1979.
Pérez Firmat, Gustavo. *Idle Fictions: The Hispanic Vanguard Novel 1926–1934.* Durham, NC: Duke UP, 1982.
Zuleta, Emilia de. *Arte y vida en la obra de Benjamín Jarnés.* Madrid: Gredos, 1977.

Roberta Johnson

**JÁUREGUI Y HURTADO DE SAL, Juan de** (1583, Seville–1641, Madrid), poet, intellectual, translator, critic, painter, and enemy of *Quevedo and *Góngora. A friend of Lope de *Vega and of *Cervantes, whose portrait he presumably painted, Jáuregui studied art in Rome. He married Mariana Loaísa after overcoming a series of obstacles, including spending time in prison (1611). In 1639 he became a member of the Order of Calatrava. Jáuregui could be termed a true genius. He is known, above all, as a theorist in his analyses of Gongorism; his principal works attacking the *culteranos* are the *Antídoto contra las Soledades* (1624; Antidote against the *Soledades*) and *Discurso poético* (1624; Poetic Discourse). The *Antídoto*'s caustic attack on the *Soledades* was countered by a number of rebuttals by Góngora's defenders, including Francisco *Fernández de Córdoba's *Examen del antídoto* and *Apología de las soledades.*

Nevertheless, Jáuregui, who exhibited an early interest in Italianate poetry, later became a Gongorist in his own poetic style. His *Orfeo* (1624; Orpheus), in imitation of Ovid, and his translation of Lucan's *Pharsalia* or *Bellum Civile* (1684) show him to have cultivated typically cultist stylistic techniques, such as linguistic excesses and the use of neologisms. Jáuregui's translation of Lucan is perhaps the best extant verse translation of the work; it is characterized by expressive pomp and stylized language. He also successfully translated Tasso's *Aminta* (1607, 1906); Cervantes cited Jáuregui as a famous translator. Finally, this same critic of *culteranismo* also wrote in support of the movement with *Apología por la verdad* (1625; Apology for Truth), a defense of the *culterano* preacher, Fray Hortensio *Paravicino. Jáuregui's poetry achieves poetic dignity without unwanted exaggeration. His *Rimas* (1618; Poems), sacred and profane, reveal him to be a competent versifier of exquisite taste and verbal refinement and a master of *terza rima*, but with limited poetic scope. He is also the author of an unstaged dramatic satire, *El Retraído* (The Unsociable Man). *See also* Italian literary influences.

BIBLIOGRAPHY

Primary Texts

*Aminta.* Ed. J. Arce. Madrid: Clásicos Castalia, 1970.
*El Antídoto.* In *Documentos gongorinos.* Ed., intro. Eunice J. Gates. Mexico: El Colegio de México, 1960.
*Discurso poético.* Valencia: " . . . la fonte que mana y corre . . . ," 1960s.
*La farsalia* and *Orfeo.* Ed. P. Estala. Madrid: Imprenta real, 1819.
*Obras.* Ed. I. Ferrer de Alba. 2 vols. Madrid: Espasa Calpe, 1973. (*Orfeo, Aminta,* and *Rimas*)
"Poesías." In BAE 42.

Criticism

Jordán de Urríes, José. *Biografía y estudio crítico de Jáuregui.* Madrid: Rivadeneyra, 1899.
See Gates, in Primary Texts.

Catherine Larson

**JEREZ, Francisco de** (1499, Jerez–?, Seville?), soldier, historian. At age fifteen (1514), he left for the New World, leading an unknown existence until he was enlisted by Pizarro in 1524. He accompanied Pizarro on three trips involving the discovery and conquest of Peru, serving as secretary in the final incursion. As secretary, he wrote the *Verdadera relación de la conquista del Perú y provincia del Cuzco . . .* (1534; *The Conquest of Peru and Cuzco . . .*, 1625), a clear, objective, detailed account of his observations. In 1534 Jerez returned to Spain wealthy from his share of the spoils, married, and lived a life of luxury.

BIBLIOGRAPHY

Primary Text

*Conquista del Perú, y viaje de Hernando Pizarro.* Ed. A. Rodríguez Moñino. Badajoz: Arqueros, 1929.

English Translation

*Reports on the discovery of Peru.* Tr. and ed., intro., C. R. Markham. London: Hakluyt, 1872.

**JIMÉNEZ, Alberto** (?, ?–1964, ?), educator. In 1910, together with the Junta para ampliación de estudios (Council for the Expansion of Studies), Jiménez founded the Residencia de Estudiantes de Madrid (Student Residence of Madrid), which he directed until 1936. The Residencia was characterized by a singular intellectual orientation and atmosphere, and left a lasting impression on Spanish culture of the first third of this c. Typical speakers who addressed the students there include *Ortega y Gasset, *Unamuno, *Azorín, Juan Ramón *Jiménez, and other authors, both Spanish and foreign. In 1936, Jiménez became a professor at Cambridge and Oxford universities. His publications include *La ciudad del* *estudio* (1944; City of Studies), *Selección y reforma* (1944; Selection and Reform), and *Ocaso y restauración* (1948; Decline and Restoration); all discuss the history of Spanish education in this c.

BIBLIOGRAPHY

Primary Texts

*La ciudad del estudio.* Mexico: Colegio de México, 1944.
*Juan Valera y la generación del 1868.* Madrid: Taurus, 1973.
*La Residencia de Estudiantes. Visita a Maquiavelo.* Intro. L. G. Valdeavellano. Barcelona: Ariel, 1972.
*Selección y reforma.* Mexico: Colegio de México, 1944.

Isabel McSpadden

**JIMÉNEZ, Juan Ramón** (1881, Moguer–1958, San Juan, Puerto Rico), Andalusian poet. Known as Juan Ramón, he was born—at midnight on December 23—in the southern Spanish town of Moguer, where he spent his early life. He once represented himself as a "christ-child" ("niñodiós"), whose idyllic years had been spent in a "white marvel" ("blanca maravilla") of an Andalusian village. Against such implicit idealization of self and world must be set the solid reality of the poet's "Work" (*Obra*) to which he devoted himself daily, to which he dedicated his life in its entirety, and for which in 1956 he was awarded the Nobel Prize for Literature.

The poet's life, studied by his biographer Graciela Palau de Nemes, falls into three parts. His early years were lived mainly in Moguer; his middle years were spent in Madrid; his final twenty years were passed in North America and the Caribbean.

As a child in Moguer, Juan Ramón was withdrawn; he seemed to prefer his house and garden to people and streets. At age eleven, he went to the nearby Jesuit school in Puerto de Santa María. From there, he went to the U of Seville, where painting and poetry took all his time. A crucial change in his fortunes ("destino," he would call it) occurred in 1900: he was called to Madrid to meet Rubén Darío—the greatest Hispanic poet of the age—who was immensely impressed by the moonstruck ephebe's first poems and began to see him as his heir. As a result, Juan Ramón's first books of poetry were published: *Ninfeas* (1900; Water-Lilies) and *Almas de violeta* (1900; *Souls of Violet*). Darío himself provided the title for the first collection, which was printed in green ink; Ramón del *Valle-Inclán chose the second, which was printed in violet. The early-modernist ("modernista") preciousness of these first books of poetry so infuriated Juan Ramón in later life that he destroyed every copy he could lay his hands on.

Although little is known of Juan Ramón's relationship with his father, the latter's sudden death in 1901 affected him profoundly, and the poet spent the first few years of the c. in sanatoria in and around Bordeaux and Madrid. (See Ignacio Prat, *El muchacho despatriado*.) During this time he published *Rimas* (1902; Rhymes), *Arias tristes* (1903; Sad Airs), and *Jardines lejanos* (1904; Distant Gardens).

When he left the care of his doctors, Juan Ramón returned to his family in Moguer, where he enjoyed the peace of the village, the "casa de campo" (country house), and the company of Platero, his donkey. During this time—1905 to 1912—Juan Ramón devoted himself to his work and wrote *Pastorales* (1905, pub. 1911; Pastorals); *Olvidanzas: Las hojas verdes* (1909; Forgotten Memories: Green Leaves); *Baladas de primavera* (1907, pub. 1910; Spring Ballads); *Elegías puras*, *Elegías intermedias*, and *Elegías lamentables* (1908, 1909, 1910; Pure, Intermediate, and Sorrowful Elegies); *La soledad sonora* (1908, pub. 1911; The Sounding Silence); *Poemas mágicos y dolientes* (1906, pub. 1911; Painful and Magical Poems); *Laberinto* (1910–11, pub. 1913; Labyrinth); *Melancolía* (1910–11, pub. 1912; Melancholy). In addition, Juan Ramón's lyrical novel, the much loved *Platero and I*, was written at this time, though published in 1916. In exquisite prose it reflects the poet's sensitivity and symbolizes his yearnings.

In general, the poetry of this period—with the exception of some of the *Baladas*—betrays the poet's dissatisfaction with the present moment, which is unfulfilling. He mitigates the sadness, nostalgia, and lethargy of his life by cultivating sensual pleasures (touch, sound, smell), and by swearing his allegiance to an art that is mournful.

At the end of December 1912, Juan Ramón established his home in the Residencia de Estudiantes—the famous college that housed Spain's artists and intellectuals. In 1913 there occurred a further twist in the poet's destiny, when he met the woman who would eventually agree to marry him. Their stormy courtship is reflected in two books of poetry: *Estío* (1915, pub. 1916; Summer) and *Sonetos espirituales* (1914–15, pub. 1917; Spiritual Sonnets)—works in which the pervasive depression of the first period is cast aside, like an ornate garment "fastuosa de tesoros" (replete with treasures). Juan Ramón and Zenobia—the member of a wealthy Spanish family and fluent in English from her North American education—married in New York City in February 1916. As a result of this visit, the Hispanic Society of America commissioned the first "Poetic Anthology" of Juan Ramón's work: *Poesías escogidas: 1899–1917* (1917; Selected Poems). After their honeymoon in the United States, the couple returned to Madrid, where they resided until August 1936.

The mottoes Juan Ramón selected for these years of his life and work are significant: "Amor y Poesía / Cada Día" (Love and Poetry / Each Day), and "Wie das Gestirn, / Ohne Hast, / Aber ohne last . . . " (Like the stars, / Without haste, / But without rest . . . ). The first motto appeared as the preface to *Eternidades* (1918; Eternities). The second he took from Goethe, where it forms part of a stanza that ends "each man must circle round his own task." The latter first appeared in *Poesía* (1923; Poetry), and preceded Juan Ramón's dedication to his worldwide readership—"The Immense Minority" ("A La Inmensa Minoría").

During the Madrid years Juan Ramón worked indefatigably—on poetry, prose, journals, reviews, prefaces, introductions—and fastidiously subjected all he wrote to constant revision. Though he lived a quiet and dedicated life—it is said that he had the walls of his study lined with cork—he kept abreast of literary movements in Spain and Spanish America, and assiduously broadened his knowledge of world poetry. This discipline enabled him both to concentrate on "la realidad invisible" (the invisible reality), which he articulated in the "Obra," and to refine his style, to "strip" or "divest" it of its adornments, to distill ("depurar") rather than to "purify" in the manner of a Paul Valéry or a Jorge *Guillén; Juan Ramón's goal was to achieve a "poesía desnuda" (naked poetry) rather than a "poésie pure." (Juan Ramón's phonetic spelling—e.g., "je" for "ge"—stems from these years.)

The "naked poetry" includes *Diario de un poeta recién casado* (1916, pub. 1917; Diary of a Newly Married Poet); *Eternidades* (1916–17, pub. 1918; Eternities); *Piedra y cielo* (1919; Stone and Sky). After this Juan Ramón began to be selective and published only some of the vast quantity of work he produced: *Segunda antolojía poética* (1922; Second Poetic Anthology) contains rewritten—or re-created—poetry from 1898 to 1918; the two volumes *Poesía (en verso)* (1923; Poetry [In Verse]) and *Belleza (en verso)* (1923; Beauty [In Verse]) comprise selections from more than a dozen books he planned to issue between 1917 and 1923. (A. Sánchez Romeralo reconstituted one of these: *La realidad invisible* [London: Tamesis, 1983].) A final anthology, *Canción* (1936; Song), was the last book Juan Ramón published in Spain in his lifetime.

The poetry of this middle period is indeed a "song" to the beauty of the beloved and to the perfection of art. The work affirms the glory that is life, but also expresses the anguish of one who, alert to the inadequacy of traditional religions, would like to articulate a faith that is an authentic expression of the spirit today (see Leo R. Cole, *The Religious Instinct in the Poetry of Juan Ramón Jiménez*).

With the outbreak of the Civil War in 1936, the Jiménezes left the Spanish Peninsula for the United States where, until the fall of the Republic in 1939, Juan Ramón was a cultural attaché at the Spanish embassy in Washington, D.C. The rest of the couple's peripatetic years were spent teaching and writing in the Caribbean and the United States. They lived in Cuba (1937–38), resided on the East Coast (1939–51, Maryland, Florida), and thereafter settled in Puerto Rico, where Zenobia died in 1956 (just after hearing of her husband's Nobel Prize) and Juan Ramón in 1958 (see Ricardo Gullón, *El último Juan Ramón Jiménez*).

The poems of these years are complex; they reach heights of ecstasy, in which all is affirmed to have been brought to fruition, and they express depths of despair. Only a selection of this poetry was ever published in Juan Ramón's lifetime: *La estación total con las canciones de la nueva luz* (1923–36, pub. 1946; The Total Season with Songs of New Light); *Romances de Coral Gables* (1939–42, pub. 1948; Coral Gables Ballads); *Animal de fondo* (1949; Animal of Depth); and *Tercera antolojía poética* (1957; Third Poetic Anthology). Juan Ramón's final period is actually more extensive, and today a reader can consult, in addition to *Libros de poesía: En el otro costado* (ed. A. de Albornoz), *Dios deseado y deseante* (ed. A. Sánchez-Barbudo), *Tiempo y Espacio* (ed. A. de Vilar), and *Leyenda* (ed. A. Sánchez Romeralo).

## Poetic Trajectory

Juan Ramón's 1,900 poems (*Ninfeas, Almas*...)—studied by Richard A. Cardwell—reflect a polarity found in decadent literature: that "reality" is corrupt and subject to untimely death, whereas "dream" offers both pleasure and fulfillment. Between 1902 and 1904 (*Arias*..., *Jardines*...), a minor symbolic mode is introduced into the *Obra*, as the sensitive and impressionistic poet chooses those aspects of the landscape that best reflect his lovesick feelings: "Tarde en gris y en plata, tarde / violentamente nostálgica" (Evening in grey and silver, evening / violently nostalgic). Between 1905 and 1908 (*Pastorales, Olvidanzas, Baladas*..., *La soledad*...), landscape gains importance in the work, as the poet pursues a pantheistic mode of communion with nature. The poetry experiments with impressionism ("Granados en cielo azul!" [Pomegranates in blue sky!], and it symbolizes a languid, lovelorn state which is occasionally assuaged by joy (*Baladas*...) and meditative peace (*La soledad*...). Between 1908 and 1912 (*Elegías*..., *Poemas mágicos*..., *Laberinto, Melancolía*), the work oscillates between bitter disillusionment and languid nostalgia, as the poet reflects on all he misses and has lost. This condition is ameliorated by intensely sensual memories: "Oh! en el hondo crepúsculo, Francina y las estrellas! / Desnudez de cristal y desnudez de tierra!" (In the depths of twilight, Francina and the stars! / Crystal nakedness with the nakedness of earth!).

Between 1913 and 1916 (*Sonetos*..., *Estío, Diario*...), Juan Ramón underwent a change of style and mind. In their self-discipline, his *Sonetos* are an ascetic reaction to a decade of morbid and sensual languor. *Estío*, in which he initiates his experimentation with freer verse forms, is assertive in its newfound determinaton to succeed—in love, life, and art. The *Diario*, a blend of modern poetry and prose, revolutionized the Hispanic poem with its exploration of the perils—doubt, nihilism—encountered by a modern questor who desires to find meaning, and discover love and beauty in the modern world.

Juan Ramón's "naked" style crystallizes between 1916 and 1923. The "naked" *Obra* in its entirety is a ceaseless and complex meditation on love, poetry, and death ("la mujer, la obra, la muerte"). The restlessness of the poet's mind and spirit is contained within a series of formally perfect lyrics. *Eternidades* expresses the wish that "intelligence" guide the poet ("Inteligencia, dame / el nombre exacto de las cosas!" [Intelligence, give me / The exact name of things]); it also represents aesthetic evolution as a stripping away of excessive "garments" ("Vino, primero, pura, / vestida de inocencia." [She came, first, pure, / Dressed in innocence.]). *Piedra y cielo* selects the rose to symbolize the essence of lyrical beauty ("No le toques ya más, / que así es la rosa!" [Don't touch it again, / For that's just how the rose is!]); it also selects the butterfly to symbolize Juan Ramón's desire to capture the essence from a moment of beauty in time (see Paul R. Olson, *Circle of Paradox*). *Poesía* and *Belleza* stress the immortal beauty of the *Obra* itself ("ascua pura inmortal" [pure, immortal coal]), compared with which the poet's life itself seems unimportant (see Mervyn Coke-Enguídanos, *Word and Work In The Poetry of Juan Ramón Jiménez*).

The final phase of Juan Ramón's work, written after his move to "The Other Shore" of the Atlantic Ocean, synthesizes the *Obra*'s resplendent vision. *La estación total*, parts of which appeared in *Canción* in 1936, displays a sense of aesthetic mastery and life-enhancing fulfillment, a state in which "La armonía recóndita / de nuestro estar coincide con la vida" (The hidden harmony / of our being coincides with life). *En el otro costado*, a book of several sections, contains the intensely lyrical, long prose-poem "Espacio," which reflects euphoria and depression (and which can now be read alongside the more anecdotic "Tiempo"), as well as *Romances de Coral Gables*, a sober meditation on love and life. *Dios deseado y deseante* falls into two sections: "Animal de fondo" (Animal of depth) and "Dios deseado y deseante" (Desired and Desiring god—with a lowercase g), which are separated by the poet's "Notes." These poems, some of Juan Ramón's most stunning and profound, represent a heightened awareness, or mystical experience, which the poet underwent during a sea voyage between North and South America in 1949: "Dios del venir, te siento entre mis manos, / aquí estás enredado conmigo, en lucha hermosa / de amor, lo mismo / que un fuego con su aire." (God of becoming, I feel you between my hands, / here you are entwined with me, in a beautiful tryst / of love, the same / as a flame with its air.) *Ríos que se van (1951–54)* are poems of mature, human love, intended as Juan Ramón's eulogy to Zenobia. *Leyenda*—which contains an estimated 200 new poems—is Juan Ramón's final selection and distillation, from all phases of the *Obra*, of 1,303 poems, most of which have been "re-created" in free verse or poetic prose. In this, the final phase of the *Obra*, jubilance is curtailed by doubt: words do indeed express the vision of a twentieth-c. mystic (*Dios deseado y deseante*), but in addition they uncover profound depths of existential anguish and despair as the poet confronts—in "Espacio"—his imminent extinction (see John C. Wilcox, *Self and Image in Juan Ramón Jiménez*).

Juan Ramón's lyrical purity, as well as his poetic integrity, have proved to be unique models for Hispanic poets, who still react to his influence. For the Spanish reading public, which for almost forty years knew little of Juan Ramón except the *Segunda antolojía poética*, the breadth and depth of the poet's work are proving to be an inspiration. The wider his audience, the more Juan Ramón grows in stature. *See also* Modernism.

BIBLIOGRAPHY

Primary Texts

Poetry 1900–1913:
*Libros inéditos de poesía I y II*. Madrid: Aguilar, 1964 and 1967.
*Primeros libros de poesía*. Madrid: Aguilar, 1959.
Poetry 1914–1958:
*En el otro costado*. Madrid: Júcar, 1974.
*Leyenda*. Madrid: Cupsa, 1978.
*Libros de poesía*. Madrid: Aguilar, 1957.
*La realidad invisible*. Reconstituted by A. Sánchez Romeralo. London: Tamesis, 1983.
*Tiempo y Espacio*. Madrid: Edaf, 1986.

Published prose:

*La colina de los chopos.* Madrid: Taurus, 1966.

*Con el carbón del sol.* Madrid: Magisterio Español, 1973.

*Cuadernos.* Madrid: Taurus, 1960.

*Españoles de tres mundos.* Madrid: Aguilar, 1969.

*Olvidos de Granada.* Madrid: Padre Suárez, 1969.

*Platero y yo.* Barcelona: Plaza y Janés, 1986.

*Platero y yo.* Ed. R. Gullón. Madrid: Taurus, 1978.

*Por el cristal amarillo.* Madrid: Aguilar, 1961.

*Primeras prosas.* Madrid: Aguilar, 1962.

Lectures:

*Alerta.* Salamanca: Studia Philologica, 1983.

*Guerra en España.* Barcelona: Seix Barral, 1985.

*Política poética.* Madrid: Alianza, 1982.

*El trabajo gustoso.* Mexico: Aguilar, 1961.

Criticism and aphorisms:

*El andarín en su órbita.* Madrid: Magisterio Español, 1974.

*La corriente infinita.* Madrid: Aguilar, 1961.

*Crítica paralela.* Madrid: Narcea, 1975.

*Estética y ética estética.* Madrid: Aguilar, 1967.

*El modernismo: Notas de un curso.* Mexico: Aguilar, 1962.

Letters:

*Cartas literarias (1937–54).* Barcelona: Bruguera, 1977.

*Cartas (Primera selección).* Madrid: Aguilar, 1962.

*Selección de cartas (1899–1958).* Barcelona: Picazo, 1973.

Diaries of conversations with Juan Ramón:

Guerrero Ruiz, Juan. *Juan Ramón de viva voz.* Madrid: Ínsula, 1960.

Gullón, Ricardo. *Conversaciones con Juan Ramón Jiménez.* Madrid: Taurus, 1958.

English Translations

*Fifty Spanish Poems.* Ed. J. B. Trend. Oxford: Dolphin, 1950.

*God desired and desiring.* Tr. Antonio de Nicolás. Intro. L. Simpson. New York: Paragon, 1987. English and Spanish.

*Invisible reality: 1917–1920, 1924.* Tr. A. de Nicolás. Intro. L. Simpson. New York: Paragon, 1987. English and Spanish.

*Platero and I.* Tr. Eloise Roach. Austin: U of Texas P, 1967.

*Selected Poems by Juan Ramón Jiménez.* Tr. Robert Bly. New York: Seventies, 1970.

*The Selected Writings of Juan Ramón Jiménez.* Tr. H. R. Hayes. Ed. E. Florit. New York: Farrar, Strauss and Cudahy, 1957.

*Three Hundred Poems: 1903–1953.* Tr. E. Roach. Austin: U of Texas P, 1962.

*Time; and Space: a poetic autobiography.* Ed. and Tr. A. T. de Nicolás. Pref. L. Simpson. New York: Paragon, 1988. English and Spanish.

Criticism

Campoamor González, Antonio. *Bibliografía general de Juan Ramón Jiménez.* Madrid: Taurus, 1982.

Cardwell, Richard A. *Juan Ramón Jiménez: The Modernist Apprenticeship.* Berlin: Colloquium, 1978.

Coke-Enguídanos, Mervyn. *Word and Work in The Poetry of Juan Ramón Jiménez*. London: Tamesis, 1982.

Cole, Leo R. *The Religious Instinct In the Poetry of Juan Ramón Jiménez*. Oxford: Dolphin, 1969.

Fogelquist, Donald F. *Juan Ramón Jiménez*. Boston: Twayne, 1976.

Gullón, Ricardo. *El último Juan Ramón Jiménez*. Madrid: Alfaguara, 1963.

Olson, Paul R. *Circle of Paradox*. Baltimore: Johns Hopkins UP, 1967.

Palau de Nemes, Graciela. *Vida y obra de Juan Ramón Jiménez*. 2 vols. Madrid: Gredos, 1974.

Prat, Ignacio. *El muchacho despatriado*. Madrid: Taurus, 1987.

Predmore, Michael. *La obra en prosa de Juan Ramón Jiménez*. Madrid: Gredos, 1966.

Wilcox, John R. *Self and Image in Juan Ramón Jiménez*. Urbana: U of Illinois P, 1987.

Young, Howard T. *The Line in the Margin: Juan Ramón Jiménez and His Readings in Blake, Shelley, and Yeats*. Wisconsin: U of Wisconsin P, 1980.

———. *The Victorious Expression*. Madison: U of Wisconsin P, 1964.

John Wilcox

**JIMÉNEZ DE CISNEROS, Francisco.** *See* Cisneros, Francisco Jímenez de

**JIMÉNEZ DE ENCISO, Diego** (1585, Seville–1634, ?), dramatist, knight of the Order of St. James, city councilor in Seville, treasurer of the Bureau of Commerce. He lived on several occasions in Madrid, where his plays enjoyed wide acceptance. His *Júpiter vengado* (Jupiter Avenged) was performed in the palace in 1632 on the occasion of Prince Baltasar Carlos's oath before the Cortes. National history provided him many themes: *El encubierto* (The Concealed) dramatizes the famous episode of the Valencian "germanías," or brotherhoods; *La mayor hazaña de Carlos V* (The Greatest Feat of Charles V) alludes to the retirement of Charles at the Monastery at Yuste. Enciso's greatest creation, *El príncipe don Carlos* (Prince Charles), is considered the first treatment of Philip II's son in dramatic literature. A play of acute psychological analysis, it illustrates the Aristotelian idea that poetic truth is superior to historical truth. Enciso's best known play in his own day was *Los Médicis de Florencia* (The Medicis of Florence). He also wrote some dramas of saints' lives. Enciso's theater is polished and well versified. *See also* Theater in Spain.

BIBLIOGRAPHY

Primary Texts

*Dramáticos contemporáneos a Lope de Vega*. Madrid: Rivadeneyra, 1881.

*"El encubierto" y "Juan Latino."* Ed. Juliá Martínez. Madrid: RAE, 1951.

*El príncipe don Carlos: comedia famosa*. Valencia: J. y T. de Orga, 1773.

Criticism

Ivory, Annette. "*Juan Latino*: The Struggles of Blacks, Jews and Moors in Golden Age Spain." *Hispania* 62 (1979): 613–18.

Williamsen, Vern G. "Women and Blacks Have Brains Too: A Play by Diego Ximénez de Enciso." *Studies in Honor of Everett W. Hesse*. Ed. W. C. McCrary, J. A.

Madrigal, J. E. Keller. Lincoln, NE: Society of Spanish and Spanish-American Studies, 1981.

Andrea Warren Hamos

**JIMÉNEZ DE PATÓN, Bartolomé** (1569, Almedina, Ciudad Real–1640, Villanueva de los Infantes, Ciudad Real), humanist scholar and rhetorician. He was a learned man and a prestigious scholar, widely esteemed by the writers of his time, a friend to *Quevedo and above all to Lope de *Vega, whom he admired and praised enthusiastically. He studied with the Jesuits in Madrid, Baeza (Jaén) and Salamanca. He was a preceptor to the Count of Villamediana, an editor of note, and taught humanities all his life. Jiménez de Patón wrote abundantly on history, grammar, oratory and rhetoric. Precisely because of his knowledge of and writings in the latter field, he has been recognized as the first rhetorician of the Baroque period in Spain. The *Elocuencia española en arte* (1604; Spanish Eloquence in Art) was at the time the only rhetorical treatise that contained no adaptations from Greek or Latin, and was fully devoted to Spanish writers. It illustrated the use of rhetorical and literary devices through examples chosen exclusively from Spanish literary texts. The *Elocuencia* was re-edited in 1621 as a part of the *Mercurius Trimegistus* which also contained, written in Latin, the *Elocuencia sacra* (Holy Eloquence), the *Elocuencia romana* (Roman Eloquence) and the *Instituciones de la gramática española* (Rules of Spanish Grammar), a book that follows closely the observations of Francisco *Sánchez *el Brocense* and brings an unusual awareness to the importance of usage in the rules of grammar. *See also* Humanism; Siglo de Oro.

BIBLIOGRAPHY

Primary Texts

*Epítome de la ortografía latina y castellana. Instituciones de la gramática española.* Ed. Antonio Quilis and Juan Manuel Rozas. Madrid: CSIC, 1965.
*Elocuencia española en arte. La retórica en España.* Ed. Elena Casas. Madrid: Nacional, 1980.

Criticism

Terry, Arthur. "The Continuity of Renaissance Criticism. Poetic Theory in Spain between 1535 and 1650." *BHS* 31 (1954): 27–36.
Vilanova, Antonio. "Preceptistas de los siglos XVI y XVII." *Historia General de las literaturas hispánicas.* Ed. Guillermo Díaz-Plaja. 6 vols. Barcelona: Barna, 1953. 3: 565–692.

María Teresa Pajares

**JIMÉNEZ DE QUESADA, Gonzalo** (1503?, Granada–1579, Mariquita, Spain), soldier, New World explorer, chronicler. Arriving in the New World in 1536, he founded the city of Bogota (1538), and explored the region of what is now Colombia. Most of his writings have been lost. One, the *Historiarum sui temporis libri 45*, popularly titled *El antijovio* (The Anti-Giovio), was written to refute Italian Paulo Giovio's *Historias de su tiempo*, which contained a negative portrayal of the Spanish military in Italy. His *Compendio historial* (Historical Compendium) survives only in part. Jiménez de Quesada died in poverty, from leprosy.

BIBLIOGRAPHY

Primary Texts

*El antijovio.* Ed. R. Torres Quintero. Study M. Ballesteros Gaibrois. Bogota: Caro y
    Cuervo, 1952.
*Archivo de Gonzalo de Quesada: Epistolario.* Havana: Siglo XX, 1948–51.

Criticism

Frankl, V. *"El Antijovio" de Gonzalo Jímenez de Quesada y las concepciones de realidad
    y verdad en la época de la contrarreforma y del manierismo.* Madrid: Cultura
    Hispánica, 1963.

**JIMÉNEZ DE URREA, Jerónimo.** *See* Urrea, Jerónimo Jiménez de

**JIMÉNEZ FARO, Luzmaría** (1937, Madrid– ), Spanish poet and editor-publisher. Jiménez Faro and her husband, the poet Antonio Porpetta, are instances of singular and intense devotion to poetry, not only producing their own poems, but assisting other poets in finding outlets for their works, and through critical and editorial endeavors, preserving some poetic texts of the past from oblivion. She is the founder and director of Ediciones Torremozas in Madrid, a publishing house specializing in the works of women poets. Jiménez Faro began publishing her own poems in 1978, with the collection *Por un cálido sendero* (Along a Warm Path), followed by *Cuarto de estar* (1980; Sitting Room) and *Sé que vivo* (1984; I Know That I Live). The first of several books of criticism, in collaboration with Antonio Porpetta, was *Carolina Coronado: Apunte biográfico y Antología* (1983; Carolina Coronado: Biographical Notes and Anthology), a contribution to the scholarly re-evaluation of the nineteenth-c. woman poet. In the same year, she published *Poemas*, a selection of works by new women poets, and in 1984, *Veinte poetisas* (Twenty Women Poets), a second anthological selection of new or relatively little-known women lyricists. Several similar anthologies have been published, more or less annually, as well as a number of specialized anthologies, including her *Panorama Antológico de Poetisas Españolas (Siglos XV al XX)* (1987; Panoramic Anthology of Spanish Women Poets from the Fifteenth to the Twentieth Centuries), *Ernestina de Champourcín: Antología poética* (1988; Anthology of Poems of Ernestina de Champourcín), and *Breviario del deseo (Poesía erótica escrita por mujeres)* (1989; Prayer Book of Desire: Erotic Poetry by Women). *Letanía doméstica para mujeres enamoradas* (1986; Domestic Litany for Women in Love) is her most recent collection of original poems, and typical of her intimate, passionate dialogue with a beloved interlocutor, poetry of communication whose persona is unfailingly feminine, but whose images frequently evoke the biblical Song of Songs and recall the erotic metaphors of the mystics.

Janet Pérez

**JIMÉNEZ LOZANO, José** (1930, Luaga, Avila– ), historian, prose writer. After obtaining degrees in law and in philosophy and literature at the Universities of Valladolid and Salamanca, he worked as a journalist in Madrid, then as editor of the veteran daily *El Norte de Castilla* in Valladolid. As a specialist in ecclesiastical history (which colors most of his fictional writings), he covered the Vatican II deliberations for the Spanish press, and later published *Meditación española sobre la libertad religiosa* (Spanish Meditation on Religious Freedom). He researched anti-clerical sentiment in Spain, publishing a series of relevant articles in the Barcelona magazine *Destino*, and developed the religious drama of eighteenth-c. Jansenists in his novel *Historia de un otoño* (1971; History of Autumn), treating the crisis of church authority, the conflict between church and state, the decline of faith, the erotic obsessions of the Court of Versailles, and satanic celebrations of the Black Mass. In *El sambenito* (1972; The Saffron Tunic), another historical novel, he concentrates upon the final years of the *Inquisition, and the doubts aroused by the trial of Pablo de *Olavide in 1778. The guilty sentence is seen from the viewpoint of the wife of the accused, his friends and even the Grand Inquisitor, none of whom are fully convinced of his guilt, but all of whom are afraid of facing the Inquisition themselves. In *La salamandra* (1973; The Salamander), a dialogue between two aged village men, characters brought together in an asylum, recalls their lives. The reader thus witnesses not only several decades of Spanish history from the perspective of two who were participants and spectators, but also the psychological disintegration of the protagonist (who nonetheless believes that he has reached a superior truth in his madness). *La ronquera de Fray Luis y otras inquisiciones* (1973; The Hoarseness of Friar Luis and Other Investigations) is a selection of Jiménez Lozano's articles on religious problems, while *El santo de mayo* (1976; May's Saint) is a collection of short stories of widely varied themes and techniques, usually nightmarish or dreamlike in atmosphere, often set in remote times because of the parallel established between long-ago lives and present-day problems to which they are directly or symbolically related.

BIBLIOGRAPHY

Primary Texts

*Historia de un otoño*. Barcelona: Destino, 1971.
*La salamandra*. Barcelona: Destino, 1973.
*El sambenito*. Barcelona: Destino, 1972.
*El santo de mayo*. Barcelona: Destino, 1976. Short stories.
*La ronquera*. Barcelona: Destino, 1973.

Janet Pérez

**JIMÉNEZ MARTOS, Luis** (1926, Córdoba– ), poet and narrator. He is also director of the well-known poetry collection *Adonais*. He has published several books of poems, such as *Encuentros con Ulises* (1969; Encounters with Ulysses), which won the Premio Nacional de Poesía; *Con los ojos distantes* (1970; With Distant Eyes); and *Molino de Martos* (1985; Windmill of Martos). He is also a literary critic and anthologist.

BIBLIOGRAPHY

Primary Texts

*Con los ojos distantes 1952–1970*. Avila: Institución Gran Duque de Alba, 1970.
*Encuentros con Ulises*. Madrid: Rialp, 1969.
*Molino de Martos*. Madrid: Asociación de Escritores y Artistas Españoles, 1985.

Isabel McSpadden

**JORNADA** (one day), theatrical term. In sixteenth-c. Spain, it meant "act," as the action of any act of a play was to be confined to a single day, no matter how much time might intervene between each *jornada*.

**JOVELLANOS, Gaspar Melchor de**, pseudonym Jovino (1744, Gijón–1811, Puerto de Vega), Enlightenment essayist and neo-classical dramatist and poet. Jovellanos was one of the most encyclopedic talents of the Spanish Enlightenment. In an endless stream of essays, reports, memoirs, and studies he discussed the problems of agriculture, the economy, public celebrations, political organization, education, police protection, law, natural science, industry, and literature, and offered suggestions on areas of improvement. He was an active member of numerous intellectual groups—Royal Economic Society, Royal Academy of History, Royal Academy of the Language (\*Academia Española), Royal Academy of Fine Arts, Academy of Public Law—and, during the years he spent in the government's favor, a close adviser to the kings. His enormous activity in the service of his country earned him great prestige and respect as a liberal, progressive thinker.

Asturias nurtured Jovellanos: born in Gijón, he was educated at the U of Oviedo, and he spent much of his life working to improve conditions in his native province. At first he wished to be church canon, and in 1764 he ventured from Oviedo to study canon law in Avila, but the intellectual ferment of the mid eighteenth century (represented in the works of \*Feijoo, \*Clavijo y Fajardo, Voltaire, Rousseau, Diderot) redirected him toward civil matters. He was elected to the School of San Ildefonso at the U of Alcalá in 1764 and there he met José \*Cadalso. Jovellanos, while not yet committed to literary pursuits, encouraged his friend to follow his inclinations, and the two embarked on a deep friendship which remained spiritually close even when they were separated, as they often were, by circumstances. In fact, Jovellanos was to become one of the major sources of encouragement to the best poets of his day. Although he dismissed love poetry as frivolous (he exhorted his friends to dedicate their skills to more weighty matters), he was frequently consulted by the young neo-classical poets, especially those known in the mid–1770s as the Salamancan School (\*Escuela Salmantina). Jovellanos's ideas on poetry are advanced in his "Carta de Jovino a sus amigos salmantinos" (1776; Letter from Jovino to his Salamancan Friends).

Much of his own poetry remained unpublished during his lifetime, and it tended toward reflection, sobriety, and social satire, since he regarded poetry to be an undignified pastime for serious minds.

When he was just twenty-four years old, in 1768, he was named criminal magistrate of Seville. There he read Montesquieu and Beccaria, learned English in order to study Milton, Young, Richardson and, later, Adam Smith, and befriended Pablo de *Olavide, an Enlightened thinker who would later suffer persecution by the *Inquisition. Jovellanos's interest in the penal system stimulated him to write a sentimental drama in 1773, *El delincuente honrado* (performed in 1774; The Honorable Delinquent), which dealt with the problems of criminal justice, and which achieved instant popularity. Jovellanos was frequently consulted on matters concerning law, civil liberties, and the economy, and he received promotion to the magistrature of Seville in 1774. Four years later he was appointed to the magistrature of Madrid.

For the next twelve years Jovellanos produced thoughtful essays on a wide variety of topics: *Discurso sobre los medios de promover la felicidad de Asturias* (1781; An Address on the Means of Promoting the Prosperity of Asturias), *Elogio de Bellas Artes* (1781; In Praise of Fine Arts), *Sobre el estudio de Ciencias Naturales en Asturias* (1782; On the Study of Natural Science in Asturias), *Causa de la decadencia de las Sociedades Económicas* (1786; Causes for the Decline of the Economic Societies), *Elogio de Carlos III* (1788; In Praise of Charles III), etc. In 1786 and 1787 he published two verse satires in the enlightened newspaper *El Censor*, in which he brilliantly satirized the decline of feminine morals and the poor education of the nobles (a subject also addressed by Cadalso in the *Cartas marruecas*). He gained entry into the capital's most distinguished intellectual circles; was befriended by politicians, writers, and members of the aristocracy; and achieved a large forum for his progressive ideas.

When a friend, Francisco de Cabarrús, was accused by the government of financial mismanagement in 1790, Jovellanos, whose sense of loyalty and friendship were deeply ingrained, came to his defense. But Cabarrús fell from power, and his accusers, including the powerful member of Council of Castile, the Count of Campomanes, resented Jovellanos's interference in the case and had him banished to Asturias (ostensibly to study road conditions and the mining industry). In a seven-year exile, 1790–97, Jovellanos turned his apparent defeat into triumph, for he worked arduously on behalf of both Asturias and Spain: he wrote two of his most important studies, *Memoria para el arreglo de la policía de los espectáculos y diversiones públicas y sobre su origen en España* (1790; Memoir on the Regulation of Spectacles and Public Entertainments and on Their Origins in Spain) and *Informe en el expediente de ley agraria* (1794; Report on the Agrarian Law), and he created a center for provincial studies, the Royal Asturian Institute. His exile ended when Cabarrús was freed in 1797, and Manuel Godoy, the handsome young prime minister to King Charles IV, named Jovellanos minister of justice. He returned to Madrid.

Political turmoil in the capital enmeshed Jovellanos, and in 1798 he was sent back to Asturias. He had powerful enemies, especially in those institutions which he sought to reform. When a translation of Rousseau's *Social Contract* (a book considered subversive by the Inquisition) mentioned Jovellanos approvingly in a footnote, suspicions and accusations began to swirl around him. In 1801 he was arrested, taken to far-off Palma de Majorca and imprisoned, first in a monastery at Valldermossa, and later in the castle of Bellver. For seven years he suffered deprivation, ill health, and humiliation, but he managed to write, producing studies on Majorcan botany, historical and artistic descriptions of Bellver, lyrical descriptions of his surroundings, and even a treatise on education.

The tumultous events of 1808 had an enormous impact on Jovellanos. In April he was freed from prison and made his way back to Madrid, but he could not accept an appointment to serve in the government of the Napoleonic invaders (to his disappointment, his old friend Cabarrús did serve). Jovellanos joined the patriotic Junta Central, the ruling council of the Spanish government-in-exile. As the War of Independence progressed, the Junta was forced to flee Madrid, and Jovellanos traveled with it to Seville and finally to Cádiz in 1810. His *Memoria en defensa de la Junta Central* (1811; Memoir in Defense of the Junta Central) is a stirring political document of unabashed patriotism. In 1811 Jovellanos returned to his hometown, Gijón, but a French attack forced him to leave once more. He was old, ill, and tired. On November 27, he died in Puerto de Vega, away from his birthplace, but still in his beloved Asturias.

Jovellanos loved patriotism, sincerity, justice, reason, progress, and hard work. He dedicated his life and his intellect to these qualities, and in his writings, from his first play—the patriotic *Pelayo* (1769)—to his last essays on public instruction, he never strayed from them. His important *Diario* (Diary) records his private thoughts on a wide range of subjects. No definitive collection of his complete works exists, but a good sampling of his thought and expression can be found in the five-volume *Obras publicadas e inéditas* (Published and Unpublished Works) by Cándido Nocedal (vols. 1–2, Madrid: Rivadeneyra, 1858–1898) and by Miguel Artola (vols. 3–5, Madrid: Atlas, 1956), and in the *Obras en prosa* (Works in Prose), edited by José Caso González. *See also* Essay.

## BIBLIOGRAPHY

### Primary Texts

*Diarios*. Ed. J. Somoza. Oviedo: Instituto de Estudios Asturianos, 1953–55.
*Escritos literarios*. Ed. José Miguel Caso González. Madrid: Espasa-Calpe, 1987.
*Espectáculos y diversiones públicas. Informe sobre ley agraria*. Ed. J. Lage. Madrid: Cátedra, 1982.
*Obras*. 8 vols. Ed. Linares Pacheco. Barcelona: Oliva, 1839–40.
*Obras completas*. Ed. José Miguel Caso González. 5 vols. Oviedo: Centro de Estudios del Siglo XVIII, 1984–90.
*Obras en prosa*. Ed. J. Caso González. Madrid: Castalia, 1969.
*Obras publicadas e inéditas*. Ed. M. Artola. 3 vols. BAE 85–87.

*Obras publicadas e inéditas.* Ed. C. Nocedal. 2 vols. BAE 49–50.

*Poesías.* Ed. J. Caso González. Oviedo: Instituto de Estudios Asturianos, 1961.

English Translation

"Paper on the Games, Exhibitions and Public Diversions of Spain." Tr. Lord Holland. In *Some Accounts of the Life and Writings of Lope Felix de Vega.* London: Longman, 1806.

Criticism

Arce, J. "Jovellanos y la sensibilidad prerromántica." *BBMP* 36 (1960): 139–77.

Beverly, J. "The Dramatic Logic of *El delincuente honrado. RHM* 37 (1972): 155–61.

Cabezas, Juan Antonio. *Jovellanos: El Fracaso de la Ilustración.* Madrid: Silex, 1985.

Caso González, J. *La poética de Jovellanos.* Madrid: Prensa Española, 1972.

———. *"El delincuente honrado:* drama sentimental." *Archivum* 14 (1964): 103–33.

Helman, E. *Jovellanos y Goya.* Madrid: Aturus, 1970.

Polt, John H. R. *Gaspar Melchor de Jovellanos.* New York: Twayne, 1971.

———. *Jovellanos and His English Sources.* Philadelphia: American Philosophical Society, 1964.

Rick, L. *Bibliografía crítica de Jovellanos.* Oviedo: Cátedra Feijoo, 1977.

Sebold, Russell P. "Jovellanos, dramaturgo romántico." *Anales de Literatura Española* 4 (1985): 415–37.

Zavala, I. M. "Jovellanos y la poesía burguesa." *NRFH* 18 (1956): 47–64.

David Thatcher Gies

**JUAN.** *See* Don Juan, The Myth of

**JUAN II, Crónica de** (1455–60; Chronicle of John II), very important medieval Spanish chronicle (\*Crónica). Once attributed to \*Pérez de Guzmán, it was probably composed by \*converso Alvar García de Sta. María, brother to Pablo de \*Sta. María. The compilation exhibits historical rigor and contains many interesting details concerning John II (1398–1479), key members of his court, and leading political figures of the day.

BIBLIOGRAPHY

Primary Text

*Crónica del señor rey don Juan.* Ed. Galíndez de Carvajal. Valencia: Montfort, 1779.

Criticism

Cantera Burgos, F. *Alvar García de Santa María: historia de la judería de Burgos y de sus conversos más egregios.* Madrid: Arias Montano, 1952.

**JUAN DE LA CRUZ, San** (1542, Fontiveros, Avila–1591, Úbeda, Jaén), poet, mystic, religious writer, reformer, commonly known in English as Saint John of the Cross. Born Juan de Yepes to a poor family in Fontiveros, he moved soon after to the commercial center of Medina del Campo. As a boy he studied briefly with the Jesuits but entered the Carmelites in Medina del Campo in 1563. During his studies in theology at the U of Salamanca he probably came into contact with Fray Luis de \*León. Anxious to enter a stricter order, he was on the point of joining the Carthusians in 1568 when he met Santa *Teresa who urged him instead to join in the reform of the Carmelites. With another priest he established the first house of the reform for men in Duruelo. From 1572 to 1576 he was chaplain of the Carmelite nuns at La Encarnación in Avila where Santa Teresa served as prioress (1572–74). In December of 1576, Carmelite friars opposed to the reform kidnapped Juan and held him prisoner in Toledo until August of 1577 when he managed to escape. With the help of nuns sympathetic to the reform, he made his way to Andalusia, where he began writing the commentaries to the poems he had composed as a prisoner. While there he also helped found a monastery of the reform in Baeza and, after the division of the order, held a number of posts among the Discalced. He died in Ubeda in the province of Jaén in December of 1591. His remains were taken to Segovia in 1593 where they are interred. He was beatified in 1675 and canonized in 1726. In 1926 Pope Pius XI declared him a Doctor of the Church. In 1952 he was named the patron of Spanish poets.

His works include both poetry and prose. The latter principally consists of commentaries on his major poems, interpreting them in light of their mystical content. The *Subida del monte Carmelo* (1578–85; *Ascent of Mt. Carmel, 1979*), the *Noche oscura* (1582–85; *Dark Night of the Soul*, 1979), and the *Llama de amor viva* (1585–87, 1586–91; *The Living Flame of Love*, 1979) consider the poems by the same names in terms of their mystical message. Some other minor prose works also exist, mainly in the form of spiritual aphorisms. Only a handful of his letters survive. None of his correspondence with Santa Teresa remains, since he chose to destroy her letters to him.

In contrast to those of Santa Teresa, San Juan's prose commentaries reveal an author well versed in theological terminology and reasoning. Where she is colloquial, episodic, and personal in her explanations of mystical states, he is exacting in his terminology, logical in his structured presentation, and objective in his examples. In each case, the commentaries were written in order to accommodate those who had difficulty culling the mystical message he claimed to present in his poems. The *Ascent of Mount Carmel* and the *Dark Night* consider the mystical implications of the poem the "Noche oscura" by developing the image of night. Although Juan is undoubtedly familiar with earlier mystical writers, he does not cite many directly. While some medieval mystics had written of the divine darkness, nevertheless, none developed the symbol of night as extensively as did Juan de la Cruz. His detailed analysis of the "dark nights" experienced by the soul as it moves toward union is recognized as one of his most important contributions to mystical theology. In both commentaries on this poem, Juan's debt to St. Augustine is also evident in his detailed consideration of the three powers of the soul and their role in prayer.

In the *Ascent* he focuses on the first two stanzas of the poem and then touches only tangentially on the lines of the poetic source. In this first commentary, he describes what he terms the active nights of the senses (both those of the body and those of the soul), which are essential ascetic and purgative stages in prayer.

The *Dark Night* also draws on the verses of the poem by the same name but carries the analysis further by describing the passive nights of the spirit as preludes to illumination. This second commentary follows the poem more closely in citing specific verses, but, unfortunately, the ms. ends abruptly after explicating only the first two stanzas of the poem.

The *Spiritual Canticle* is the most thorough commentary on its poetic source, offering the reader a detailed analysis of each line of the poem. Two mss. of the work exist, although neither is an autograph by San Juan. *Cántico A*, found in Sanlúcar de Barrameda, contains a thirty-nine-stanza poem with accompanying commentary, while *Cántico B* of Jaén has an additional stanza and a different ordering of the remaining stanzas. The commentaries differ only slightly in content. Drawing heavily on Scripture, especially the Song of Songs, for further elucidation, the author delineates a complete schema of the stages of mystical progress from purgation through illumination to union.

Two versions of the commentary on the *Living Flame of Love* also exist although the poem that they explain remains unchanged. Both commentaries continue the line-by-line analysis characteristic of the *Spiritual Canticle* and, again, give an overview of the entire mystical experience, although they dwell in greater detail on the final stage of union.

The poetry of San Juan may be divided into those works which utilize traditional Spanish meters, such as *romances*, *\*coplas*, and other octosyllabic forms, and those which employ the Italian meters, principally the *lira*. The three major poems use the latter. Among those in traditional meters, the *romances* are probably the earliest works by the poet, written when he was a student. Like Teresa, Juan also glossed a number of popular verses *\*a lo divino*, using traditional lines, such as "Vivo sin vivir en mí" (I live without living in myself) and "Tras de un amoroso lance" (After an amorous encounter), as sources for religious statements. The *romances* are essentially theological in their themes and rarely evidence the lyrical flights characteristic of his other poems.

Consideration of mystical union first appears in poems such as *El pastorcico* (The Little Shepherd), which glosses a popular love poem to present a poignant picture of Christ pining for love of souls. The poet begins to approach the principal concerns of his later works in the famous *Cantar del alma que se huelga de conoscer a Dios* (Song of the soul longing to know God), whose title indicates the theme of the poem. Although evocative of traditional forms, it effectively uses repetition of the *estribillo* "Aunque es de noche" and the undiphthongized *fonte* (rather than *fuente* [fountain]) to build a crescendo of emotion. The use of parallel structure and paradox also emphasizes the theme of faith.

In his major poems, however, Juan chooses to use the newer poetic forms introduced in the *\*Renaissance and mastered by such poets as *\*Garcilaso de la Vega and Fray Luis de León. Although these works have been interpreted in a variety of ways from erotic love lyrics to the quintessential poetic rendering of mystical union, the poet himself chose to interpret them in his commentaries as songs celebrating the soul's union with God. The three poems written in *liras*, the "Noche oscura," the "Cántico espiritual," and the "Llama de amor viva," resemble each other not only in their metrical form but also in the intensity of their feeling and imagery. Together they delineate the path of the soul drawn through the stages of mystical prayer to ultimate union with the *Amado* (Lover).

The "Noche oscura" describes a woman slipping from a darkened house by night, drawn inexorably to an amorous rendezvous with her waiting lover. The mystery of the encounter is enhanced by the dominant image of night and the secrecy with which she moves through the deserted streets. The climax of the poem occurs in the fifth stanza where a series of exclamatory phrases captures the moment of union in both sight and sound. The remaining stanzas suggest the languor of the recumbent lovers in language evocative of the Song of Songs.

In the "Cántico espiritual" the poet draws heavily on the imagery of the biblical Song of Songs in order to create a poem suggesting the loss, search, and eventual union of two lovers. Structured in part as a dialogue, the poem opens with queries by the abandoned bride who goes in search of her missing lover. Their reunion at the "cristalina fuente" (crystal well) concludes the search and initiates those stanzas describing their intimacy and enjoyment of each other. Oxymorons such as "la música callada" (the silent music), "la soledad sonora" (the solitude of cries) and "la llama que consume y no da pena" (the flames that embrace without pain) emphasize the paradoxical nature of the experience of union. A wealth of imagery rich in sensuous detail characterizes this poem in contrast to the dominant use of night in the "Noche oscura."

The "Llama de amor viva" is the shortest and most lyrical of the major poems, consisting of a bare four stanzas replete with exclamatory phrases addressing the flame as a personification of the soul's lover. The poet develops a concatenation of images, beginning with the flame and evolving through cautery, wound, hand, touch, and finally, lamps of fire. As the complete title indicates, the poem presents the "Songs of the soul in its intimate communion of union with God's love."

The sources cited by Juan in his commentaries are principally those of Scripture, the Fathers of the Church, and the *Flos Sanctorum*. Apparent in his poems are other influences such as traditional Spanish poetry, classical literature, the Renaissance poems of such predecessors as Garcilaso, and other mystical writers. Perhaps his greatest influence is that of nature itself, especially evident in the detail of the "Cántico espiritual."

San Juan de la Cruz is unique not only for the mystical message he presents in his works but also and most especially for the intensity of feeling expressed in his poems. Few poets before or since have conveyed the compelling nature of the quest for union with the object of one's love with equal skill and intimacy. Modern poets have been especially drawn to his work and have contributed significantly to critical appreciation of his poetry "desde esta ladera" (from this side), as Dámaso *Alonso has put it. With the four-hundredth anniversary celebration of San Juan's birth in 1942, a number of Spanish poets renewed interest in his contributions to Spanish lyric poetry and to his stature as a "pure poet."

Jorge *Guillén puts that contribution most succinctly when he says of the three major poems of Juan de la Cruz that they "form a series which is perhaps the highest culmination of Spanish poetry." *See also* Mysticism.

## BIBLIOGRAPHY

### Primary Texts

*Cántico espiritual.* Ed. Eulogio Pacho. Madrid: Fundación Universitaria Española, 1981.
*Cántico espiritual Poesías.* Ed. Cristóbal Cuevas García. Madrid: Alhambra, 1979.
*Obras completas de San Juan de la Cruz.* Ed. Lucinio Ruano de la Iglesia. 11th ed. Madrid: Católica, 1982.
*Poesias.* Ed. Domingo Yndurain. Madrid: Cátedra, 1983.

### English Translations

*The Collected Works of St. John of the Cross.* Tr. Kieran Kavanaugh and Otilio Rodríguez. 2nd ed. Washington, DC: Institute of Carmelite Studies Publications, 1979.
*The Complete Works of St. John of the Cross.* Ed. E. Allison Peers. 3 vols. Rpt. 1978. Wheathampstead-Herfordshire: Anthony Clarke, 1953.
*The Poems of St. John of the Cross.* Tr. John Frederick Nims. 3rd ed. Chicago and London: U of Chicago P, 1979.

### Criticism

Alonso, Dámaso. *La poesía de San Juan de la Cruz (Desde esta ladera).* 6th ed. Madrid: Aguilar, 1966.
Brenan, Gerald. *St. John of the Cross. His Life and Poetry.* Cambridge: Cambridge UP, 1973.
Crisógono de Jesús Sacramentado. *Vida de San Juan de la Cruz.* Ed. Matías del Niño Jesús, O.C.D. 11th ed. Madrid: Católica, 1982.
Peers, E. Allison. *Spirit of Flame: A Study of St. John of the Cross.* Wilton, CT: Morehouse-Barlow, 1946.
Thompson, Colin P. *The Poet and the Mystic. A Study of the Cántico Espiritual of San Juan de la Cruz.* Oxford: Oxford UP, 1977.

Elizabeth T. Howe

**JUAN MANUEL, Don** (1282, Escalona–1348, Murcia), prose writer. Nephew of *Alphonse X the Wise and proud grandson of Ferdinand the Saint. Although he was constantly involved in political intrigue and warfare, Juan Manuel devoted much time to reading and writing. He took special interest in the works of his uncle, Alphonse the Wise, and one of his early literary efforts, the *Crónica abreviada* (Abridged Chronicle), consists of a summary chapter by chapter of a version of Alphonse's *Primera crónica* (the so-called *Crónica manuelina,* or Chronicle of Manuel) now believed to be lost. Although Juan Manuel admired Alphonse the Wise and used him as a model, he was not afraid to chart new literary directions on his own; thus his *Libro de la caza* (Hunting Book) is an updating of Aphonse's *Libro de la montería.* Juan Manuel took extreme care to leave a ms. (which he himself had corrected) of all his works in the Dominican monastery which he founded at Peñafiel. Unfortunately this ms. has been lost, as have been at least five or six of the works which don Manuel said he wrote.

Of the seven works that have survived, two have already been mentioned; the remaining five are the *Libro del cavallero et del escudero* (Book of the Gentleman and Squire), a work about chivalry inspired by Ramón *Llull's *Llibre del orde de la cavaylería*; the *Libro de los estados* (Book of Estates), a narrative in dialogue whose main purpose is to show that only Christianity can explain satisfactorily what happens after death to people of all social classes; the *Libro infinido* (The Unfinished Book), a book of instructions to Juan Manuel's son, Fernando, written in the tradition of the *De regimine principum;* the *Libro de las armas* (Book of Arms), a work of heraldry and genealogy which explains the author's lineage; and the *Conde Lucanor* (*Count Lucanor*, 1977), Juan Manuel's masterpiece. The *Conde Lucanor* consists of two prologues and five main parts. The first prologue states the author's purpose in composing the work and enters into a fascinating discussion, from the point of view of the history of textual criticism, of the problems of the transmission of mss. The second prologue consists of a short invocation in one sentence, and a discussion of human individuality and variety as a justification for the contents of the book. Since the book is intended to be an instrument for saving the human soul, this prologue, like many other medieval prologues, makes mention of the three parts of the soul: *voluntad* (will), *entendimiento* (understanding), and *memoria* (memory), except that for *memoria* is substituted *aprender* (learning). The first of the five main parts of the book is also the longest; in it the Count Lucanor poses a problem to his adviser Patronio who replies with a solution in the form of an *exemplum*. Each of the fifty-one *exempla* in part 1 is followed by a moral in two or four lines of poetry. María Rosa Lida de Malkiel listed the Dominican and Oriental sources for these *exempla*, and Reinaldo Ayerbe-Chaux has recently studied them in this context. The next three sections of the book consist of lists of learned *setentiae* (100, 51, and 29 respectively) which become progressively more recondite. The fifth and final section of the book explains how man can save his soul by obeying the sacraments of the Roman Catholic church. There is in this fifth section one more *exemplum*, making a total of fifty-two *exempla* in the entire work. The importance of Juan Manuel to Spanish and world literature will continue to be defined by scholars. *See also* Edad Media, Literatura de la.

BIBLIOGRAPHY

Primary Texts

*El Conde Lucanor*. Ed. R. Ayerbe-Chaux. Madrid: Porrúa, 1975.
*El Conde Lucanor*. Ed. J. M. Blecua. Clásicos Castalia 9. Madrid: Castalia, 1969.
*El libro de la caza*. Ed. G. Baist. Halle: Niemeyer, 1880. Rpt. New York: Hildesheim; Zurich: Olms, 1984.
*Obras completas*. Ed., prol., and notes, J. M. Blecua. 2 vols. Madrid: Gredos, 1982–83.

English Translations

*The Book of Count Lucanor and Patronio*. Tr. J. E. Keller and L. Clark Keating. Lexington, KY: UP of Kentucky, 1977.

*Count Lucanor or the Fifty Pleasant Stories of Patronio.* Tr. J. York. Westminster:
  Pickering, 1868. Rpt. London: Routledge; New York: Dutton, 1924.

Criticism

Devoto, D. *Introducción al estudio de don Juan Manuel.* Madrid: Clásicos Castalia,
  1972.
Lida de Malkiel, M. R. "Tres notas sobre don Juan Manuel." *RPH* 4 (1950–51): 155–
  94.
Macpherson, I, ed. *Juan Manuel Studies.* London: Tamesis, 1977.

Colbert Nepaulsingh

**JUARROS, César** (1879, Madrid–1942, Madrid), novelist, a psychiatrist by
profession. His novels include *El niño que no tuvo infancia* (1927; The Boy
without a Childhood) and *Sor Alegría* (1930; Sister Alegría). Juarros also wrote
essays on medical topics such as *El momento de la muerte* (1924; The Moment
of Death), and *Los senderos de la locura* (1927; The Pathways of Insanity).

BIBLIOGRAPHY

Primary Texts

*El amor en España.* Madrid: Sucesores de Rivadeneyra, 1927.
*Los senderos de la locura.* Madrid: Mundo latino, 1927.
*El momento de la muerte.* Madrid: Mundo latino, 1924.
*El niño que no tuvo infancia.* Madrid: Mundo latino, 1927.
*Sor Alegría.* Madrid: Mundo latino, 1930.

Isabel McSpadden

*JUEGOS* (Medieval one-act plays). The ancient Greeks and Romans already
had public presentations which they called *juegos*, for example, Apollonian,
Augustan, Capitoline, Olympian, Neronian plays, etc. Poetry was very much
present in these works, and poets sang the praises of gods, heroes and athletic
champions. In the Middle Ages (*Edad Media, Literatura de la) three types of
*juegos* developed: the *escolares* (scholarly or clerical plays), those *de escarnio*
(farcical plays), and the *florales* (poetry competitions). The first two types date
from the origins of medieval theater at the end of the eleventh or beginning of
the twelfth c.

### Juegos escolares

It is generally believed that medieval religious drama or mystery plays originated in the abundant dramatic elements present in Catholic liturgy. In churches
themselves, as part of religious ceremonies, actual dramatic presentations du-
plicated the Divine Offices. There were three specific periods in the evolution
of this theatrical genre: liturgical drama, scholarly or clerical plays (*juegos
escolares*) and the one-act plays (*autos or *piezas*) already written in the vernacular. The first was closely tied to liturgical ceremony and dramatized details
of Christmas and the Crucifixion. Although there are no such plays extant, there
is proof of their existence and even vestiges in the liturgy. The *juegos escolares*

were plays written and acted out by clergymen, and they evolved in imitation of the liturgical drama. The same themes were used and presentations took place in the same churches. During this period the lives and miracles of the saints were added as themes. Audiences were so large, it became necessary to use cloisters and other church annexes for performances; this permitted the inclusion of further profane elements. The liturgical drama and the *juegos escolares* were both written in Latin. However, as *universities were created, dispersing alumni far and wide, and as the Romance languages became more widely used, Latin slowly was forgotten by the audience that came to these plays. This finally ended the *juegos escolares,* and then only the one-act plays (*autos*) in the vernacular were presented. The only one of the latter which still survives is the *Auto de los Reyes Magos.*

### Juegos de escarnio

While primitive religious theater dramatized the Divine Offices, secular theater satirized customs of the period. In these farces, minstrels blended sacred and profane elements with an often sacrilegious result. Religious observances were mocked in vulgar or obscene language and action. At the behest of *Alphonse the Wise, in about 1255 the clergy were forbidden to attend or participate in the *juegos de escarnio* (*Siete Partidas* 1, 6, 34), and these plays could not be staged in churches as could the mystery or miracle plays. Although there are no early examples of the *juegos de escarnio* extant, the farsas of Diego *Sánchez de Badajoz (early sixteenth c.) are a later example of this secular type of drama.

### Juegos florales

These constitute the brilliant expression of Provençal troubadour poetry in which competing poets displayed their genius in debates (*tensones*), ballads, *albas (poems related to the dawn), and other poems. The poet to win received a flower to symbolize his poetic talent. This type of play was introduced into Spain by Don Juan I of Aragón, and the first *juegos florales* were celebrated in Catalonia, spreading subsequently to the entire peninsula. In many parts of Spain this type of festival is still celebrated, and forms part of local celebrations in particular cities or provinces. Often it is presented to commemorate a national historic or literary event (literary competition).

BIBLIOGRAPHY

Primary Texts

*As Cantigas d'Escarnho e de Maldizer.* By M. Rodrigues Lapa. Vigo: Galaxia, 1965.
*Auto de los Reyes Magos.* Ed. Mary Borelli. Valencia: López Mezquida, 1968.

English Translation

*Auto de los Reyes Magos.* Tr. Willis Knapp-Jones. Boston: Poet Lore, 1928.

Criticism

Rodríguez Puértolas, J. *Poesía de protesta en la Edad Media castellana.* Madrid: Gredos, 1968.

Romas, Epifanio. *Las cantigas de escarnio y maldizer de Alfonso X.* Lugo: n.p., 1973.
Scholberg, Kenneth R. *Sátira e invectiva en la España medieval.* Madrid: Gredos, 1971.

Lucy Sponsler

*JUGUETE,* theatrical term. It refers to a short, lighthearted skit, often with intercalated music. In modern times, two- or three-act comic *juguetes* have also been written.

# K

KARR I ALFONSETTI, Carme, pseudonym L. Escardot (1865, Barcelona–1943, Barcelona), short story writer, playwright and early feminist. A musician and a writer like her uncle the French novelist Alphonse Karr, Carme Karr first published songs in her native Catalan. Using her pseudonym L. Escardot, she collaborated in the weekly literary magazine, *Joventut*, contributing sketches and short fiction which later formed the basis of two collections of short pieces: *Bolves, quadrets* (1906; Specks of Dust: Sketches) and *Clixès, estudis en prosa* (1906; Photographic Negatives: Prose Studies). In 1907 when the literary and cultural review *Ilustració Catalana* founded *Feminal*, a monthly supplement devoted to women, Karr became editor; she continued to edit the magazine until 1918. One of the first women to have a play performed in Barcelona, Karr produced at least three works for the theater: *Els idols* (1911; The Idols), a one-act play; *Raig de sol* (Sunbeam); and *Caritat* (1918; Charity). In 1912 Karr's short novel, *La vida d'en Joan Franch* (The Life of John Franch), won the silver cup at the *Juegos Florales literary competition in Barcelona. Part of the *modernism movement in Barcelona, Karr also brought a female voice and perspective to her fiction. She became a staunch advocate of the educational and cultural advancement of women, emerging as a leading figure of the early women's movement in Catalonia. In literature as well as social reform she was one of the new generation of women writers and polemicists who sought a wider audience for women's social concerns and literary creations. In 1913 Karr founded La Llar (The Home), a residential school for women teachers and students, the first of its kind in Spain; she also served as its director. After a long hiatus, Karr published a collection of short stories, *Garba de contes* (1935; A Sheaf of Stories). In later years she also wrote children's stories in Spanish, published as *Cuentos a mis nietos* (1932; Stories for My Grandchildren).

BIBLIOGRAPHY

Primary Texts

*Bolves, quadrets.* Biblioteca Popular de "L'Avenç," no. 52. Barcelona: Llibrería "L'Avenç," 1906.

*Caritat*. Barcelona: n.p., 1918.

*Clixès, estudis en prosa*. Barcelona: Publicació "Joventut," 1906.

*Els idols, comedia en un acte i en prosa*. Biblioteca De tots colors. Barcelona: B. Baxarias, 1911.

*Garba de contes*. Gerona: Dalmau Carles Plá, 1935.

Maryellen Bieder

**KHARJA** (in Spanish often transcribed as Jarcha), name given to the last strophe or refrain of an Arabic muwashshaḥ. The muwashshaḥ is a specific genre of Arabic popular poetry that was created in Spain and flourished by the eleventh century. It is characterized by its strophic form, unlike classical Arabic poetry, which is generally not strophic and is monorhyme. The term *kharja* comes from the Arabic root *KRJ* ("to go out"), indicating the "leave-taking" function of the kharja. While the main body of a muwashshaḥ was written in the classical language (Arabic or Hebrew), the poem "embodied the symbiotic culture of al-Andalus rather than its classical Arabic heritage, and it vaunted its uniqueness with something revolutionary: a final verse in Mozarabic, the Romance vernacular of this world" (Menocal, *The Arabic Role*, 30).

The *kharjas* in Romance (Mozarabic) were first identified by Samuel M. Stern in 1948. Although the muwashshaḥāt (plural form of muwashshaḥ) in both Arabic and Hebrew had been known for some time before, the final verses of these poems remained unidentified and unstudied for reasons that continue, to a lesser extent, to make their study difficult: they are written in a Romance dialect about which comparatively little is known, and in Arabic or Hebrew script (thus making them *\*aljamiado* texts), which are, of course, not vocalized. For the Semiticist, the Mozarabic in the Arabic or Hebrew scripts looked like gibberish; Romance scholars, on the other hand, would not have had occasion to read such texts in Arabic and Hebrew and would have been unable, most likely, to read the Arabic or Hebrew alphabets needed to decipher the texts. In any case, the texts were (and are) especially difficult because of the lack of vocalization; a lack which does not affect the reading of classical Arabic or Hebrew, where it is standard practice, but which substantially obscures the decipherment of a text in Romance.

The vast and widespread interest generated by Stern's breakthrough has continued to this day, and indeed, various issues raised with regard to "*kharja* scholarship" are currently being actively debated. Some critics affirm that the tendency to consider the *kharjas* as separate entities, independent of the muwashshaḥāt they conclude, has hampered proper appreciation of their worth. María Rosa Menocal has argued that these final strophes are intimately related to the main bodies of muwashshaḥāt, for while the main body presents traditional formal laments and language via a male speaker, the concluding *kharjas* employ informal, nontraditional laments and language, often through a female speaker. Both the main body and concluding refrain of the muwashshaḥ are structurally united by music, metrics, and rhyme (Menocal, *The Arabic Role*, 99–101). The focus on *kharjas* independent of their context has also, according to the same scholars, contributed to the failure to address larger issues, such as the origins of lyric poetry in the vernacular. To quote María Menocal, "What we have, in al-Andalus' polycultural, bilingual poetry is the opportunity to be critically involved with the major intellectual issues of the day: we have at hand poems that clearly challenge the most basic notions of what constitutes Western culture and its canon in the medieval period and thus the chance, as part of the new historicism, to reevaluate and redefine what the canon, our cultural heritage, was and is and, perhaps, to substantially enrich it" (Menocal, "Bottom of the Ninth," 38). As texts become more accessible to non-Arabists, an increasing number of scholars continue to be attracted to the study of these earliest Romance lyrics.

BIBLIOGRAPHY

Primary Texts

*Die Bisher veröffentlichten Harğas und ihre Deutungen*. Ed. Klaus Heger. Tübingen: Niemeyer, 1960.
*Las jarchas romances de la serie árabe en su marco*. Ed. E. García Gómez. Barcelona: Seix Barral, 1975.

English Translations

*Hispano-Arabic Poetry: A Student Anthology*. Ed. and tr. James T. Monroe. Berkeley: U of California P, 1974.
*Ten Hispano-Arabic Strophic Songs in the Modern Oral Tradition: Music and Texts*. Ed. Benjamin M. Liu and James T. Monroe. Berkeley: U of California P, 1989.

Criticism

Armistead, Samuel G. "A Brief History of Kharja Studies." *Hispania* 70 (1987): 8–15.
———. "Some Recent Developments in *Kharja* Scholarship." *La Corónica* 8 (1980): 199–203.
Hitchcock, R. *The Kharjas: A Critical Bibliography*. London: Grant and Cutler, 1977.
Menocal, María Rosa. "Bottom of the Ninth: Bases Loaded." *La Corónica* 17.1 (1988–89): 32–40.
———. *The Arabic Role in Medieval Literary History*. Philadelphia: U of Pennsylvania P, 1987. Ch. 4.
Monroe, James T. "Poetic Quotation in the Muwaššaḥa and Its Implications." *La Corónica* 14 (1986): 230–50.
Stern, S. M. "Les vers finaux en espagnol dans les muwaššaḥs hispano-hebraiques: une contribution a l'histoire du muwaššaḥ et à l'étude du vieux dialecte espagnole 'mozárabe'." *Al Andalus* 13 (1948): 299–346.

**KRAUSISM,** a Spanish philosophical movement with origins in the work of the German idealist philosopher Karl Christian Friedrich Krause (1781–1832), and whose formation and propagation from the 1850s until the mid–1870s in Spain was chiefly effected by Julián *Sanz del Río (1814–69).

In 1843, during a time of great prestige for German culture as a result of that country's role in the fomenting of Spanish nationalistic *Romanticism, Sanz del Río, a professor of canonical law at the U of Granada, was sent by the government to study and bring back to Spain contemporary German philosophy. Until that time philosophy was not a field of university study because of the state-supported domination of theology. Through a series of personal relations and chance, Sanz fixed on the work of Krause, as taught by two of his disciples at the U of Heidelberg. On return to his country at the end of 1844, Krause chose not to assume the university chair waiting for him in the new Central U in Madrid. Instead he went into a ten-year-long retreat of study before re-emerging to exercise his professorship in philosophy. While his writing requires more study than it has received heretofore, it is certain that Sanz's chief importance derives from the group of professors he formed around himself and from the students they taught and influenced during the two decades Krausism flourished.

Benito *Pérez Galdós, Manuel de la *Revilla, Urbano González Serrano and Leopoldo Alas (*Clarín) are the most famous of those students formed by Sanz's group: Nicolás Salmerón (1838–1908), Gumersindo de *Azcárate (1840–1917) and Francisco *Giner de los Ríos (1839–1915). In political articles and novels by Pérez Galdós such as La familia de León Roch (León Roch, tr. 1888) and El amigo Manso (Our Friend Manso, tr. 1987), and in articles and shorter narrations by Alas such as ''Don Ermeguncio o la vocación'' (Don Ermeguncio or the Vocation), ''Doctor Angelicus'' and the novella Zurita, Krausism and earnest Krausists are portrayed critically, but sympathetically. The movement fostered a high degree of metaphysical, epistemological and ethical idealism that lent itself to good-intentioned exaggeration on one hand and self-interested opportunism on the other. Some of the most poignant characters in Pérez Galdós and Clarín are those who take seriously learning and upright conduct without understanding that the ways of the world are inimicable to both. As a result they fail to understand the situations in which they find themselves and lead lives of unhappiness and frustration. Galdós and Alas in all likelihood portray in the above-mentioned fictions a version of the process by which they and many of their fellows came to understand the shortcomings of Krausism as a guide to personal, social and political action.

The liberal Revolution of 1868 incarnated many ideals of Galdós, Alas and the Krausists, but its failure and substitution by the Restoration of the Bourbon monarchy in 1875 signaled the distance between Krausism and a workable public praxis. Nonetheless, in 1876 Giner de los Ríos was the leading spirit in the founding of the Institución Libre de Enseñanza (Free Institute of Teaching). This was Krausism's answer to reactionary government interference in university curricula and teaching. And with more of a mind to adapting itself to the real conditions of Spanish life, the Institución dedicated itself to the project of forming, in Gerald Brenan's words, ''men with a sense of vocation in life, who would feel a real responsibility for the state of their country.'' This project was continued, by the *Generations of 1898, 1914 and 1927, but came to an end in the post–Civil War Spain of Franco.

Sanz del Río's principal writings are Lecciones para el Sistema de Filosofía analítica de Krause (1850; Readings in Krause's System of Analytic Philosophy), Ideal de la humanidad para la vida (1860; The Human Ideal for Life), and Análisis del pensamiento racional (1877; Analysis of Rational Thought). See also Universities.

Criticism

Díaz, Elías. *La filosofía social del krausismo español.* Madrid: Cuadernos para el diálogo, 1973.
Jongh Rossel, Elena de. *El krausismo y la generación de 1898.* Valencia/Chapel Hill: Albatrós Hispanófila, 1985.
López-Morillas, Juan. *Krausismo: estética y literatura.* Barcelona: Labor, 1973. Anthology.
———. *The Krausist Movement and Ideological Change in Spain.* Tr. F. M. López-Morillas. 2nd ed. Cambridge, England and New York: Cambridge UP, 1981.
Martín Buezas, Fernando. *El krausismo español desde dentro: Sanz del Río, autobiografía de intimidad.* Madrid: Tecnos, 1978.
Oria, Tomás G. *Martí y el krausismo.* Boulder, CO: Society of Spanish and Spanish-American Studies, 1987.

Stephen Miller

**KRUCKENBERG SANJURJO, María del Carmen** (1926, Vigo– ), Galician poet, prose author. From an early age, María del Carmen Kruckenberg wrote and read poetry, attending a writers' *tertulia* in her native Vigo. During her residence of several years in Buenos Aires, she maintained contact with Spaniards living in that city, many of them exiled, such as *Alberti, Lorenzo *Varela, Luis Seoane, and *Castelao. Back in Spain, she came to know *Aleixandre and Gerardo *Diego. By profession a representative of a pharmaceutical company, she has written numerous books of poetry, both in Galician and Spanish.

Kruckenberg's early books have love as their theme, and one—*Farol de aire* (1958; Streetlight of Air)—is children's verse. In 1960, *Poemas inevitables* (Inevitable Poems) appeared; the author considers it her most important book in Spanish. *Tauromaquia en línea y verso* (1964; Bullfighting in Line and Verse) was praised highly by Aleixandre. *Cantigas de amigo a Ramón González Sierra do Pampillón* (1972) is an example of the Galician neo-troubador lyrical tendency which since Fermín Bouza Brey has attempted to emulate medieval compositions. The author considers *A sombra ergueita* (1976; The Firm Shadow) her best book in Galician, and in it she reveals her concept of life as difficult while not admitting defeat.

Kruckenberg has also translated Rilke and other works into Spanish, has written short stories and journalistic articles. Her prose writing has generally been in Spanish.

BIBLIOGRAPHY

Primary Texts

*Cantares de mi silencio.* Vigo: Acebo 1980.
*Cantigas de amigo a Ramón González Sierra do Pampillón.* Vigo: Author's ed., 1972.
*Farol de aire.* Vigo: Author's ed., 1958.
*Poemas y canciones de aquí y de allí.* Bilbao: Alrededor de la mesa, 1962.
*Poemas inevitables.* Vigo: Author's ed., 1960.
*A sombra ergueita.* Vigo: Author's ed., 1976.
*Tauromaquia en línea y verso.* Vigo: Author's ed., 1964.

Criticism

Alonso Montero, Xesús. Kruckenberg Sanjurjo, María del Carmen. "María del Carmen Kruckenberg Sanjurjo." *Gran Enciclopedia Gallega.* Santiago-Gijón: Silverio Caneda, 1974 ff.

Cunqueiro, Alvaro. "Nin os muros da pedra do camino." *Faro de Vigo* 1977.

Quijano, Adolfo. "María del Carmen Kruckenberg." *La Noche* (Santiago) Dec. 5, 1960.

Trabazo, Luis. "Cantigas do vento." *Poesía española* (May 1956): n.p.

Kathleen March

**KURTZ, Carmen,** pseudonym of Carmen de Rafael Marés de Kurz (1911, Barcelona– ), Catalonian writer of adult and juvenile narrative fiction in Spanish. Though from Barcelona, this award-winning author writes exclusively in Spanish. Her works have an international perspective: her paternal great-grandfather and her maternal grandfather were Catalan emigrants who married women from the United States. Her father was born in Cuba and her mother in Baltimore, Maryland. After her mother's death when Carmen was only five years old, she and her three brothers and one sister were reared solely by their strict father.

Carmen studied in the Sacred Heart and Our Lady of Loreto schools in Barcelona. In 1929, she, like the protagonist in her first novel, *Duermen bajo las aguas* (1955; They Sleep Underwater), spent a year studying English at the Sacred Heart School in West-Hill, England, receiving a first class certificate from the National Union of Teachers. In addition to English and Spanish, she also speaks Catalan and French.

She married a Frenchman, Pierre Kurz Klein, in 1935 in Barcelona. Their daughter, Odile, was born in 1936, during their eight-year sojourn in France (1935–43). Odile Kurz is a frequent illustrator of her mother's stories for children. Carmen Kurtz has been a widow since 1962, the same year her only grandchild, Carolina, was born.

Kurtz began her literary career rather late, publishing her first novel at the age of forty-four. Perhaps because she belongs chronologically to the generation of 1910–20, her novels are more personal than those of her literary contemporaries of the Generation of 1954. She explores the effects of war on individuals, the relationships between men and women, and the importance of one's family heritage. The Spanish Civil War is not an important topic in her works, for she was living in France during the conflict. She has said that her purpose in writing is to criticize the hypocrisy and self-righteousness of the Spanish middle class, thus awakening it to its responsibilities to the poor and to the nation.

Kurtz's previously mentioned first novel (which won the 1954 Ciudad de Barcelona Prize) is a largely autobiographical account of her childhood, marriage, and life in France. The Planeta Prize followed in 1956 for her *El desconocido* (The Stranger), which explores the psycho-social crises of a couple reunited after the husband's return from a twelve-year captivity in Russia. *La vieja ley* (1956; The Old Law) treats a young woman's stifling provincial life in the 1920s to 1940s and the search for happiness and love; *Detrás de la piedra* (1958; Behind the Rock), which chronicles small-town hypocrisy and ideological repression, is based on a true story; *Al lado del hombre* (1961; Beside the Man) explores the themes of search for self and of sexual awakening. *El becerro de oro* (1964; The Golden Calf) shows bourgeois obsession with money; *Las algas* (1966; Seaweed) contrasts country/city and authenticity/artificiality; *En la punta de los dedos* (1968; At Your Fingertips) repeats the themes of hypocrisy and old age; and in *Entre dos oscuridades* (1969; Between Two Darknesses) a dying executioner remembers his "innocent" victims. The lighter novel *Cándidas palomas* (1975; Innocent Doves) depicts pre-adolescents in the 1970s. The trilogy *Sic transit* (So Goes Glory) is the history of three generations of Catalonian immigrants: *Al otro lado del mar* (1973; To the Other Side of the Sea), *El viaje* (1975; The Voyage), and *El regreso* (1976; The Return).

Kurtz's shorter works are *En la oscuridad* (1963; In the Dark), a finalist for the Café Gijón Prize; two collections of short stories, *El último camino* (1961; The Last Road) and *Siete tiempos* (1964; Seven Epochs); and at least twenty-seven books for young readers.

Most popular of the latter are fifteen novels about the adventures of a twelve-year-old boy named Oscar and his pet goose Kina. Among these are *Oscar Cosmonauta* (1962), translated into German, finalist for the Lazarillo Prize, and Honorable Mention for the international Hans Christian Andersen Prize; *Oscar espía atómico* (1963; Oscar Atomic Spy), winner of the CCEI Prize for children's literature; *Oscar espeleólogo* (1966; Oscar the Spelunker), winner of the CCEI Prize; *Oscar y los OVNI* (1967; Oscar and the UFOs); *Oscar, agente secreto* (1968; Oscar, Secret Agent); *Oscar en el Polo Sur* (1969; Oscar at the South Pole); *Oscar en el laboratorio* (1970; Oscar in the Laboratory), translated into Polish; *Oscar en los juegos olímpicos* (1971; Oscar in the Olympics), Polish translation; *Oscar en Africa* (1974), winner of two Spanish prizes for children's literature; *Oscar, Kina y el laser* (1979), winner of the Ministry of Culture's prize for children's literature. The movie of the latter won both the Gold Medal at the Children's Film Festival of Gijón in 1978 and a film award from the Ministry of Culture. These novels both entertain and teach.

Other children's novels include *Color de fuego* (1964; The Color of Fire), winner of the Lazarillo Prize and translated into German; *Chepita* (1975); *Veva* (1980), which won the 1981 CCEI Prize; *Veva y el mar* (1981; Veva and the Sea); *Fanfamús* (1982); and *Querido Tim* (1983; Dear Tim). Juvenile short story collections are *Piedras y trompetas* (1981; Rocks and Trumpets), *La paloma y el cuervo* (1981; The Dove and the Crow), *La ballena y el cordero* (1981; The Whale and the Lamb), *Pepe y Dudú* (1983), and *Pitos y flautas* (1983; Whistles and Flutes).

The author has also collaborated with Arturo Kaps and Herta Frankel on five movies using marionettes. One of these, *Violeta en el oeste* (Violet in the West), won the Gold Medal in the Children's Film Festival of Gijón in 1971.

BIBLIOGRAPHY

Primary Texts

Selected Works

*El becerro de oro*. Barcelona: Plaza y Janés, 1979.
*Detrás de la piedra*. Colección Libros Reno. Barcelona: Plaza y Janés, 1975.
*Duermen bajo las aguas*. Barcelona: Plaza y Janés, 1976.
*El desconocido*. In *Premios Planeta, 1955–1958*. Ed. Carlos Pujol. Intro. José María
    Gironella. Barcelona: Planeta, 1979.
*Sic Transit*. 3 vols. Barcelona: Planeta, 1973, 1975, 1976.

Criticism

Díaz-Plaja, Guillermo. *"Entre dos oscuridades de Carmen Kurtz." Cien libros españoles*.
    Salamanca: Anaya, 1971. 317–20.
Iglesias Laguna, Antonio. *Treinta años de novela española (1938–1968)*. 2 vols. Madrid:
    Prensa Española, 1969. 1:241–46, 347–51.
Kurtz, Carmen. *El autor enjuicia su obra*. Madrid: Nacional, 1966. 111–22.
Myers, Eunice. "Four Female Novelists and Spanish Children's Fiction." *Letras fe-
    meninas* 10.2 (Fall 1984): 40–49.
Myers, Eunice D. "Autotextuality and Intertextuality in *El desconocido* by Carmen
    Kurtz." *Hispania* 71.1 (March 1988): 43–49.

Eunice D. Myers